D1034440

GREAT BOOKS
OF THE WESTERN WORLD

ROBERT MAYNARD HUTCHINS, *EDITOR IN CHIEF*

26.

SHAKESPEARE: I

❧ The Plays and Sonnets of William Shakespeare

Volume One

Edited by William George Clarke *and* William Aldis Wright

WILLIAM BENTON, *Publisher*

ENCYCLOPÆDIA BRITANNICA, INC.

CHICAGO · LONDON · TORONTO · GENEVA

THE UNIVERSITY OF CHICAGO

The Great Books
is published with the editorial advice of the faculties
of The University of Chicago

BIOGRAPHICAL NOTE

WILLIAM SHAKESPEARE, 1564–1616

SHAKESPEARE was baptized in the parish church of Stratford-on-Avon in Warwickshire on April 26, 1564. His father, John Shakespeare, was a burgess of the recently constituted corporation of Stratford, and filled certain municipal offices, including that of high bailiff. By occupation he was a glover, although he appears to have dealt from time to time in various kinds of agricultural produce and may have combined a certain amount of farming with the practice of his trade. His wife, and the mother of the dramatist, Mary Arden, came of a distinguished Catholic family, and had brought her husband a farm of about fifty or sixty acres, known as the Asbies. There were at least eight children, William being the third child and eldest son.

Stratford possessed a free grammar-school, and Shakespeare presumably obtained his education there. When he was about thirteen, his father's fortunes took a turn for the worse, and it seems likely that Shakespeare was apprenticed to some local trade. According to one story, he killed calves for his father, and "would do it in a high style, and make a speech." In November, 1582, he married Anne Hathaway, a woman eight years his senior, and their first child Susanna, was baptized on May 26, 1583, followed by twins, Hamnet and Judith, in 1585. Before the birth of the twins Shakespeare's career in Stratford seems to have come to a tempestuous close. One tradition, coming from two different sources, asserts that he got into trouble through poaching on the estates of a considerable Warwickshire magnate, Sir Thomas Lucy, and found it necessary to leave town. But from this event until he emerges as an actor and rising playwright in 1592, his history is unknown. His entry into the theatrical world, according to the stage tradition, was in a menial capacity, perhaps even as a holder of horses at the doors.

By 1592, when he was twenty-eight, Shakespeare had begun to emerge as a playwright and had evoked the jealousy of at least one of the group of scholar poets who claimed a monopoly of the stage. Robert Greene, in an invective against the play-actors in his *Groats-worth of Wit*, parodies a line from *Henry VI* and speaks of an "upstart crow" who is "in his own conceit the only Shake-scene in the country." While the theatres were closed from 1592 to 1594 because of riot and the plague, Shakespeare further enhanced his literary reputation by the publication of *Venus and Adonis* and *Lucrece*. It is also probable that the first of his sonnets then began to circulate privately, although they were not published as a whole until 1609.

After the reopening of the theatres in 1594, Shakespeare is listed among the "servauntes of the Lord Chamberlayne," the company for which he wrote and acted throughout his life. His acting seems to have been limited to such roles as the Ghost in *Hamlet* and Adam in *As You Like It*, but as a dramatist he was the mainstay of the company for some fifteen years. As early as 1598 the *Palladis Tamia*, a kind of literary handbook published by Francis Meres, extols Shakespeare as "the most excellent in both kinds (*i.e.* comedy and tragedy) for the state," and one of "the most passionate among us to bewaile and bemoane the perplexities of love"; it also provides a list of twelve plays already written, which serves as a starting point for modern attempts at a chronological arrangement of his work. Shakespeare seems to have written more rapidly during these early years than later, but on an average he wrote for his company about two plays a year. His fellow-dramatists writing for the Chamberlain's men included Ben Jonson, Dekker, Beaumont and Fletcher, and Tourneur. He seems to have been particularly intimate with Jonson; there are stories of their jests and drinking bouts, and Jonson later declared, "I lov'd the man and do honour his memory (on this side idolatry) as much as any."

In addition to being both actor and playwright, Shakespeare was also a shareholder in the company, and his prosperity was joined with that of his theatre. They were frequently asked to play at court, and *The Merry Wives of Windsor* is said to owe its origin to Elizabeth's desire to see Falstaff in love. James I on his accession took the company under his patronage, and during the remainder of Shakespeare's connection with the stage they were "the King's men." The records of performances at court show that they were by far the most favored of the companies. Shakespeare was particularly popular; Jonson refers to his flights "that so did take Eliza and our James," and he is said to have received an autograph letter from King James. He appears also to have been on cordial terms with his fellows of the stage; one of them left him a small legacy, and in his own will he paid a similar compliment to three of his theatrical associates.

Shakespeare's increasing prosperity is reflected in the restored fortunes of his family at Stratford. The prosecutions of John Shakespeare for debt ceased, and in 1596 his application for a coat-of-arms, made at the time he was bailiff, was at length granted. In 1597 the playwright purchased New Place, one of the largest houses in Stratford. Here he established his wife and two daughters, his son having died the year before. Until 1610 he apparently lived and worked in London, making only occasional visits to Stratford, but in that year he seems to have returned to his birthplace. He lived as a retired gentleman on friendly terms with the richest of his neighbors and showed interest in local affairs which might affect his income or his comfort, such as a bill for the improvement of the highways in 1611, or a proposed enclosure of the open fields in 1614. His retirement did not imply a complete break with London life; his plays were still being produced, and he was providing new ones, although the last few may have been written at Stratford. As late as 1613 he is known to have bought a house in London at the Blackfriars, perhaps for purposes of investment rather than residence. It is likely that his connection with the king's company ended when the Globe theatre was burnt down during a performance of *Henry VIII* in 1613.

In March of 1616 Shakespeare made his will, leaving to his daughter Susanna the bulk of his estate and to his wife "the second best bed with the furniture," although she also legally enjoyed until her death a third of his lands and houses. A month after his will was signed, on April 23, 1616, Shakespeare died and as a tithe-owner was buried in the chancel of the parish church.

Contents, Volume One

❧ The First Part of
KING HENRY THE SIXTH

DRAMATIS PERSONÆ

KING HENRY THE SIXTH
DUKE OF GLOUCESTER, *uncle to the King and Lord Protector*
DUKE OF BEDFORD, *uncle to the King and Regent of France*
HENRY BEAUFORT, BISHOP OF WINCHESTER, *great-uncle to the King, afterwards* CARDINAL
THOMAS BEAUFORT, DUKE OF EXETER, *great-uncle to the King*
JOHN BEAUFORT, EARL OF SOMERSET, *afterwards* DUKE
RICHARD PLANTAGENET, *son of Richard late Earl of Cambridge, afterwards* DUKE OF YORK
EARL OF WARWICK
EARL OF SALISBURY
WILLIAM DE LA POLE, EARL OF SUFFOLK
LORD TALBOT, *afterwards Earl of Shrewsbury*
JOHN TALBOT, *his son*
EDMUND MORTIMER, *Earl of March*
SIR JOHN FASTOLFE
SIR WILLIAM LUCY
SIR WILLIAM GLANSDALE
SIR THOMAS GARGRAVE
MAYOR OF LONDON
OFFICER *of the Mayor of London*
WOODVILE, *Lieutenant of the Tower*
VERNON, *of the White Rose or York faction*
BASSET, *of the Red Rose or Lancaster faction*
LAWYER
GAOLER
SIX MESSENGERS
TWO WARDERS
THREE SERVANTS *to Gloucester*
SERVANT *to Talbot*

ENGLISH CAPTAIN
CAPTAIN *of Talbot's Army*
ENGLISH SOLDIER

CHARLES, *Dauphin, and afterwards King, of France*
REIGNIER, *Duke of Anjou and Maine, and titular King of Naples and Jerusalem*
DUKE OF BURGUNDY
DUKE OF ALENÇON
BASTARD OF ORLEANS
GOVERNOR OF PARIS
MASTER-GUNNER *of Orleans*
BOY *of Master-Gunner*
GENERAL *of the French Forces in Bourdeaux*
FRENCH SERGEANT
FRENCH SENTINEL
PORTER
SHEPHERD, *father to Joan La Pucelle*
FRENCH SOLDIER
WATCHMAN *of Rouen*
FRENCH SCOUT
PAPAL LEGATE

MARGARET, *daughter to Reignier, afterwards married to King Henry*
COUNTESS OF AUVERGNE
JOAN LA PUCELLE, *commonly called Joan of Arc*

NON-SPEAKING: *French Herald, Ambassadors, Soldiers, Gaolers, Servingmen, Attendants, and Fiends appearing to Joan La Pucelle*

SCENE: *Partly in England, and partly in France*

ACT I

SCENE I. *Westminster Abbey*

Dead March. Enter the Funeral of King Henry the Fifth, attended on by the DUKE OF BEDFORD, *Regent of France; the* DUKE OF GLOUCESTER, *Protector; the* DUKE OF EXETER, *the* EARL OF WARWICK, *the* BISHOP OF WINCHESTER, *the* DUKE OF SOMERSET, Heralds, &c.

Bed. Hung be the heavens with black, yield day
    to night!
Comets, importing change of times and states,
Brandish your crystal tresses in the sky,
And with them scourge the bad revolting stars
That have consented unto Henry's death!
King Henry the Fifth, too famous to live long!
England ne'er lost a king of so much worth.

Glou. England ne'er had a king until his time.
Virtue he had, deserving to command:
His brandish'd sword did blind men with his
    beams: 10
His arms spread wider than a dragon's wings;
His sparkling eyes, replete with wrathful fire,
More dazzled and drove back his enemies
Than mid-day sun fierce bent against their faces.
What should I say? his deeds exceed all speech:
He ne'er lift up his hand but conquered.

Exe. We mourn in black: why mourn we not in
    blood?
Henry is dead and never shall revive:
Upon a wooden coffin we attend,
And death's dishonourable victory   20
We with our stately presence glorify,
Like captives bound to a triumphant car.

1

What! shall we curse the planets of mishap
That plotted thus our glory's overthrow?
Or shall we think the subtle-witted French
Conjurers and sorcerers, that, afraid of him,
By magic verses have contrived his end?

Win. He was a king bless'd of the King of
 Kings.
Unto the French the dreadful judgement-day
So dreadful will not be as was his sight. 30
The battles of the Lord of hosts he fought:
The church's prayers made him so prosperous.

Glou. The church! where is it? Had not church-
men pray'd,
His thread of life had not so soon decay'd.
None do you like but an effeminate prince,
Whom, like a school-boy, you may over-awe.

Win. Gloucester, whate'er we like, thou art
 protector
And lookest to command the prince and realm.
Thy wife is proud; she holdeth thee in awe,
More than God or religious churchmen may. 40

Glou. Name not religion, for thou lovest the
 flesh,
And ne'er throughout the year to church thou
 go'st
Except it be to pray against thy foes.

Bed. Cease, cease these jars and rest your minds
 in peace:
Let's to the altar: heralds, wait on us:
Instead of gold, we'll offer up our arms;
Since arms avail not now that Henry's dead.
Posterity, await for wretched years,
When at their mothers' moist eyes babes shall
 suck,
Our isle be made a nourish of salt tears, 50
And none but women left to wail the dead.
Henry the Fifth, thy ghost I invocate:
Prosper this realm, keep it from civil broils,
Combat with adverse planets in the heavens!
A far more glorious star thy soul will make
Than Julius Cæsar or bright——

Enter a MESSENGER.

Mess. My honourable lords, health to you all!
Sad tidings bring I to you out of France,
Of loss, of slaughter and discomfiture:
Guienne, Champagne, Rheims, Orleans, 60
Paris, Guysors, Poictiers, are all quite lost.

Bed. What say'st thou, man, before dead
 Henry's corse?
Speak softly, or the loss of those great towns
Will make him burst his lead and rise from death.

Glou. Is Paris lost? is Rouen yielded up?
If Henry were recall'd to life again,
These news would cause him once more yield
 the ghost.

Exe. How were they lost? what treachery was
 used?

Mess. No treachery; but want of men and
 money.
Amongst the soldiers this is muttered, 70
That here you maintain several factions,
And whilst a field should be dispatch'd and
 fought,
You are disputing of your generals:
One would have lingering wars with little cost;
Another would fly swift, but wanteth wings;
A third thinks, without expense at all,
By guileful fair words peace may be obtain'd.
Awake, awake, English nobility!
Let not sloth dim your honours new-begot:
Cropp'd are the flower-de-luces in your arms; 80
Of England's coat one half is cut away.

Exe. Were our tears wanting to this funeral,
These tidings would call forth their flowing tides.

Bed. Me they concern; Regent I am of France.
Give me my steeled coat. I'll fight for France.
Away with these disgraceful wailing robes!
Wounds will I lend the French instead of eyes,
To weep their intermissive miseries.

Enter to them a SECOND MESSENGER.

2nd Mess. Lords, view these letters full of bad
 mischance.
France is revolted from the English quite, 90
Except some petty towns of no import:
The Dauphin Charles is crowned king in Rheims;
The Bastard of Orleans with him is join'd;
Reignier, Duke of Anjou, doth take his part,
The Duke of Alençon flieth to his side.

Exe. The Dauphin crowned king! all fly to him!
O, whither shall we fly from this reproach?

Glou. We will not fly, but to our enemies'
 throats.
Bedford, if thou be slack, I'll fight it out.

Bed. Gloucester, why doubt'st thou of my for-
 wardness? 100
An army have I muster'd in my thoughts,
Wherewith already France is overrun.

Enter a THIRD MESSENGER.

3rd Mess. My gracious lords, to add to your
 laments,
Wherewith you now bedew King Henry's
 hearse,
I must inform you of a dismal fight
Betwixt the stout Lord Talbot and the French.

Win. What! wherein Talbot overcame? is't so?

3rd Mess. O, no; wherein Lord Talbot was o'er-
 thrown:
The circumstance I'll tell you more at large.
The tenth of August last this dreadful lord, 110

Retiring from the siege of Orleans,
Having full scarce six thousand in his troop,
By three-and-twenty thousand of the French
Was round encompassed and set upon.
No leisure had he to enrank his men;
He wanted pikes to set before his archers;
Instead whereof sharp stakes pluck'd out of
     hedges
They pitched in the ground confusedly,
To keep the horsemen off from breaking in.
More than three hours the fight continued;   120
Where valiant Talbot above human thought
Enacted wonders with his sword and lance:
Hundreds he sent to hell, and none durst stand
     him;
Here, there, and everywhere, enraged he flew:
The French exclaim'd, the devil was in arms;
All the whole army stood agazed on him:
His soldiers spying his undaunted spirit,
"A Talbot! a Talbot!" cried out amain
And rush'd into the bowels of the battle.
Here had the conquest fully been seal'd up,   130
If Sir John Fastolfe had not play'd the coward:
He, being in the vaward, placed behind
With purpose to relieve and follow them,
Cowardly fled, not having struck one stroke.
Hence grew the general wreck and massacre;
Enclosed were they with their enemies:
A base Walloon, to win the Dauphin's grace,
Thrust Talbot with a spear into the back,
Whom all France with their chief assembled
     strength
Durst not presume to look once in the face.   140
  Bed. Is Talbot slain? then I will slay myself,
For living idly here in pomp and ease,
Whilst such a worthy leader, wanting aid,
Unto his dastard foemen is betray'd.
  3rd Mess. O no, he lives; but is took prisoner,
And Lord Scales with him and Lord Hungerford:
Most of the rest slaughter'd or took likewise.
  Bed. His ransom there is none but I shall pay:
I'll hale the Dauphin headlong from his throne:
His crown shall be the ransom of my friend;   150
Four of their lords I'll change for one of ours.
Farewell, my masters; to my task will I;
Bonfires in France forthwith I am to make,
To keep our great Saint George's feast withal:
Ten thousand soldiers with me I will take,
Whose bloody deeds shall make all Europe
     quake.
  3rd Mess. So you had need; for Orleans is
     besieged;
The English army is grown weak and faint:
The Earl of Salisbury craveth supply,
And hardly keeps his men from mutiny,   160
Since they, so few, watch such a multitude.

  Exe. Remember, lords, your oaths to Henry
     sworn,
Either to quell the Dauphin utterly,
Or bring him in obedience to your yoke.
  Bed. I do remember it; and here take my leave,
To go about my preparation.   [*Exit.*
  Glou. I'll to the Tower with all the haste I can,
To view the artillery and munition;
And then I will proclaim young Henry king.
                                   [*Exit.*
  Exe. To Eltham will I, where the young king is,
Being ordain'd his special governor,   171
And for his safety there I'll best devise.   [*Exit.*
  Win. Each hath his place and function to
     attend:
I am left out; for me nothing remains.
But long I will not be Jack out of office:
The king from Eltham I intend to steal
And sit at chiefest stern of public weal.   [*Exeunt.*

SCENE II. *France: Before Orleans*

Sound a flourish. Enter CHARLES, ALENÇON, *and*
     REIGNIER, *marching with drum and Soldiers.*

  Char. Mars his true moving, even as in the
     heavens
So in the earth, to this day is not known:
Late did he shine upon the English side;
Now we are victors; upon us he smiles.
What towns of any moment but we have?
At pleasure here we lie near Orleans;
Otherwhiles the famish'd English, like pale
     ghosts,
Faintly besiege us one hour in a month.
  Alen. They want their porridge and their fat
     bull-beeves:
Either they must be dieted like mules   10
And have their provender tied to their mouths,
Or piteous they will look, like drowned mice.
  Reig. Let's raise the siege: why live we idly here?
Talbot is taken, whom we wont to fear:
Remaineth none but mad-brain'd Salisbury;
And he may well in fretting spend his gall,
Nor men nor money hath he to make war.
  Char. Sound, sound alarum! we will rush on
     them.
Now for the honour of the forlorn French!
Him I forgive my death that killeth me   20
When he sees me go back one foot or fly.[*Exeunt.*
*Here alarum; they are beaten back by the English
     with great loss. Re-enter* CHARLES, ALENÇON,
     and REIGNIER.
  Char. Who ever saw the like? what men have I!
Dogs! cowards! dastards! I would ne'er have fled,
But that they left me 'midst my enemies.
  Reig. Salisbury is a desperate homicide;
He fighteth as one weary of his life.

The other lords, like lions wanting food,
Do rush upon us as their hungry prey.
  Alen. Froissart, a countryman of ours, records,
England all Olivers and Rowlands bred   30
During the time Edward the Third did reign.
More truly now may this be verified;
For none but Samsons and Goliases
It sendeth forth to skirmish. One to ten!
Lean raw-boned rascals! who would e'er suppose
They had such courage and audacity?
  Char. Let's leave this town; for they are hare-
    brain'd slaves,
And hunger will enforce them to be more eager:
Of old I know them; rather with their teeth   39
The walls they'll tear down than forsake the
    siege.
  Reig. I think, by some odd gimmors or device
Their arms are set like clocks, still to strike on;
Else ne'er could they hold out so as they do.
By my consent, we'll even let them alone.
  Alen. Be it so.

     Enter the BASTARD OF ORLEANS.

  Bast. Where's the Prince Dauphin? I have news
    for him.
  Char. Bastard of Orleans, thrice welcome to us.
  Bast. Methinks your looks are sad, your cheer
    appall'd:
Hath the late overthrow wrought this offence?
Be not dismay'd, for succour is at hand: 50
A holy maid hither with me I bring,
Which by a vision sent to her from heaven
Ordained is to raise this tedious siege
And drive the English forth the bounds of France.
The spirit of deep prophecy she hath,
Exceeding the nine Sibyls of old Rome:
What's past and what's to come she can descry.
Speak, shall I call her in? Believe my words,
For they are certain and unfallible.
  Char. Go, call her in. [*Exit Bastard.*] But first,
    to try her skill,   60
Reignier, stand thou as Dauphin in my place;
Question her proudly; let thy looks be stern:
By this means shall we sound what skill she
    hath.

  Re-enter the BASTARD OF ORLEANS, *with* JOAN
            LA PUCELLE.

  Reig. Fair maid, is't thou wilt do these
    wondrous feats?
  Puc. Reignier, is't thou that thinkest to beguile
    me?
Where is the Dauphin? Come, come from
    behind;
I know thee well, though never seen before.
Be not amazed, there's nothing hid from me:

In private will I talk with thee apart.   69
Stand back, you lords, and give us leave awhile.
  Reig. She takes upon her bravely at first dash.
  Puc. Dauphin, I am by birth a shepherd's
    daughter,
My wit untrain'd in any kind of art.
Heaven and our Lady gracious hath it pleased
To shine on my contemptible estate:
Lo, whilst I waited on my tender lambs,
And to sun's parching heat display'd my cheeks,
God's mother deigned to appear to me
And in a vision full of majesty
Will'd me to leave my base vocation   80
And free my country from calamity:
Her aid she promised and assured success:
In complete glory she reveal'd herself;
And, whereas I was black and swart before,
With those clear rays which she infused on me
That beauty am I bless'd with which you see.
Ask me what question thou canst possible,
And I will answer unpremeditated:
My courage try by combat, if thou darest,
And thou shalt find that I exceed my sex.   90
Resolve on this, thou shalt be fortunate,
If thou receive me for thy warlike mate.
  Char. Thou hast astonish'd me with thy high
    terms:
Only this proof I'll of thy valour make,
In single combat thou shalt buckle with me,
And if thou vanquishest, thy words are true;
Otherwise I renounce all confidence.
  Puc. I am prepared: here is my keen-edged
    sword,
Deck'd with five flower-de-luces on each side;
The which at Touraine, in Saint Katharine's
    churchyard,   100
Out of a great deal of old iron I chose forth.
  Char. Then come, o' God's name; I fear no
    woman.
  Puc. And while I live, I'll ne'er fly from a man.
  Here they fight, and JOAN LA PUCELLE *overcomes.*
  Char. Stay, stay thy hands! thou art an Amazon
And fightest with the sword of Deborah.
  Puc. Christ's mother helps me, else I were too
    weak.
  Char. Whoe'er helps thee, 'tis thou that must
    help me:
Impatiently I burn with thy desire:
My heart and hands thou hast at once subdued.
Excellent Pucelle, if thy name be so,   110
Let me thy servant and not sovereign be:
'Tis the French Dauphin sueth to thee thus.
  Puc. I must not yield to any rites of love,
For my profession's sacred from above:
When I have chased all thy foes from hence,
Then will I think upon a recompense.

Char. Meantime look gracious on thy prostrate
    thrall.
Reig. My lord, methinks, is very long in talk.
Alen. Doubtless he shrives this woman to her
    smock;
Else ne'er could he so long protract his speech.
Reig. Shall we disturb him, since he keeps no
    mean?   121
Alen. He may mean more than we poor men do
    know:
These women are shrewd tempters with their
    tongues.
Reig. My lord, where are you? what devise you
    on?
Shall we give over Orleans, or no?
Puc. Why, no, I say, distrustful recreants!
Fight till the last gasp; I will be your guard.
Char. What she says, I'll confirm: we'll fight it
    out.
Puc. Assign'd am I to be the English scourge.
This night the siege assuredly I'll raise: 130
Expect Saint Martin's summer, halcyon days,
Since I have entered into these wars.
Glory is like a circle in the water,
Which never ceaseth to enlarge itself
Till by broad spreading it disperse to nought.
With Henry's death the English circle ends;
Dispersed are the glories it included.
Now am I like that proud insulting ship
Which Cæsar and his fortune bare at once.
Char. Was Mahomet inspired with a dove?
Thou with an eagle art inspired then.   141
Helen, the mother of great Constantine,
Nor yet Saint Philip's daughters, were like thee.
Bright star of Venus, fall'n down on the earth,
How may I reverently worship thee enough?
Alen. Leave off delays, and let us raise the siege.
Reig. Woman, do what thou canst to save our
    honours;
Drive them from Orleans and be immortalized.
Char. Presently we'll try: come, let's away
    about it:
No prophet will I trust, if she proves false.   150
                      [*Exeunt.*

SCENE III. *London: Before the Tower*

Enter the DUKE OF GLOUCESTER, *with his Servingmen in blue coats.*

Glou. I am come to survey the Tower this day:
Since Henry's death, I fear, there is conveyance.
Where be these warders, that they wait not
    here?
Open the gates; 'tis Gloucester that calls.
                  [*Servingmen knock.*
1st Warder. [*Within*] Who's there that knocks
    so imperiously?

1st Serv. It is the noble Duke of Gloucester.
2nd Warder. [*Within*] Whoe'er he be, you may
    not be let in.
1st Serv. Villains, answer you so the lord
    protector?
1st Warder. [*Within*] The Lord protect him! so
    we answer him:
We do no otherwise than we are will'd.   10
Glou. Who willed you? or whose will stands
    but mine?
There's none protector of the realm but I.
Break up the gates, I'll be your warrantize:
Shall I be flouted thus by dunghill grooms?
    Gloucester's men rush at the Tower Gates, and
      WOODVILE, *the Lieutenant, speaks within.*
Wood. What noise is this? what traitors have
    we here?
Glou. Lieutenant, is it you whose voice I hear?
Open the gates: here's Gloucester that would
    enter.
Wood. Have patience, noble duke; I may not
    open:
The Cardinal of Winchester forbids;
From him I have express commandment   20
That thou nor none of thine shall be let in.
Glou. Faint-hearted Woodvile, prizest him
    'fore me?
Arrogant Winchester, that haughty prelate,
Whom Henry, our late sovereign, ne'er could
    brook?
Thou art no friend to God or to the king:
Open the gates, or I'll shut thee out shortly.
Servingmen. Open the gates unto the lord
    protector,
Or we'll burst them open, if that you come not
    quickly.

    Enter to the Lord Protector at the Tower Gates
    WINCHESTER, *and his men in tawny coats.*

Win. How now, ambitious Humphrey! what
    means this?
Glou. Peel'd priest, dost thou command me to
    be shut out?   30
Win. I do, thou most usurping proditor,
And not protector, of the king or realm.
Glou. Stand back, thou manifest conspirator,
Thou that contrivedst to murder our dead lord;
Thou that givest whores indulgences to sin:
I'll canvass thee in thy broad cardinal's hat,
If thou proceed in this thy insolence.
Win. Nay, stand thou back; I will not budge a
    foot:
This be Damascus, be thou cursed Cain,
To slay thy brother Abel, if thou wilt.   40
Glou. I will not slay thee, but I'll drive thee
    back:

Thy scarlet robes as a child's bearing-cloth
I'll use to carry thee out of this place.
Win. Do what thou darest; I beard thee to thy
    face.
Glou. What! am I dared and bearded to my
    face?
Draw, men, for all this privileged place;
Blue coats to tawny coats. Priest, beware your
    beard;
I mean to tug it and to cuff you soundly:
Under my feet I stamp thy cardinal's hat:
In spite of Pope or dignities of church,   50
Here by the cheeks I'll drag thee up and down.
Win. Gloucester, thou wilt answer this before
    the Pope.
Glou. Winchester goose, I cry, a rope! a rope!
Now beat them hence; why do you let them
    stay?
Thee I'll chase hence, thou wolf in sheep's array.
Out, tawny coats! out, scarlet hypocrite!

*Here Gloucester's men beat out the Cardinal's men,
    and enter in the hurly-burly the* MAYOR OF LON-
    DON *and his* OFFICERS.

May. Fie, lords! that you, being supreme
    magistrates,
Thus contumeliously should break the peace!
Glou. Peace, mayor! thou know'st little of my
    wrongs:
Here's Beaufort, that regards nor God nor
    king,
Hath here distrain'd the Tower to his use.   61
Win. Here's Gloucester, a foe to citizens,
One that still motions war and never peace,
O'ercharging your free purses with large fines,
That seeks to overthrow religion,
Because he is protector of the realm,
And would have armour here out of the Tower,
To crown himself king and suppress the prince.
Glou. I will not answer thee with words, but
    blows.   [*Here they skirmish again.*
May. Nought rests for me in this tumultuous
    strife   70
But to make open proclamation:
Come, officer; as loud as e'er thou canst
Cry.
Off. All manner of men assembled here in arms
this day against God's peace and the King's, we
charge and command you, in his Highness' name,
to repair to your several dwelling-places; and not
to wear, handle, or use any sword, weapon or
dagger, henceforward, upon pain of death.
Glou. Cardinal, I'll be no breaker of the law:
But we shall meet, and break our minds at large.
Win. Gloucester, we will meet; to thy cost, be
    sure:

Thy heart-blood I will have for this day's work.
    May. I'll call for clubs, if you will not away.
This cardinal's more haughty than the devil.
    Glou. Mayor, farewell: thou dost but what thou
    mayst.
    Win. Abominable Gloucester, guard thy head;
For I intend to have it ere long.
    [*Exeunt, severally,* GLOUCESTER *and* WIN-
        CHESTER *with their Servingmen.*
    May. See the coast clear'd, and then we will
    depart.
Good God, these nobles should such stomachs
    bear!   90
I myself fight not once in forty year. [*Exeunt.*

SCENE IV. *Before Orleans*

Enter, on the walls, a MASTER GUNNER *and his* BOY.

    Gun. Sirrah, thou know'st how Orleans is
    besieged,
And how the English have the suburbs won.
    Boy. Father, I know; and oft have shot at them,
Howe'er unfortunate I miss'd my aim.
    Gun. But now thou shalt not. Be thou ruled by
    me:
Chief master-gunner am I of this town;
Something I must do to procure me grace.
The prince's espials have informed me
How the English, in the suburbs close intrench'd,
Wont through a secret grate of iron bars   10
In yonder tower to overpeer the city
And thence discover how with most advantage
They may vex us with shot or with assault.
To intercept this inconvenience,
A piece of ordnance 'gainst it I have placed;
And even these three days have I watch'd,
If I could see them.
Now do thou watch, for I can stay no longer.
If thou spy'st any, run and bring me word;
And thou shalt find me at the governor's. [*Exit.*
    Boy. Father, I warrant you; take you no care;
I'll never trouble you, if I may spy them. [*Exit.*

Enter, on the turrets, the LORDS SALISBURY *and* TAL-
    BOT, SIR WILLIAM GLANSDALE, SIR THOMAS GAR-
    GRAVE, *and others.*

    Sal. Talbot, my life, my joy, again return'd!
How wert thou handled being prisoner?
Or by what means got'st thou to be released?
Discourse, I prithee, on this turret's top.
    Tal. The Duke of Bedford had a prisoner
Call'd the brave Lord Ponton de Santrailles;
For him was I exchanged and ransomed.
But with a baser man of arms by far   30
Once in contempt they would have barter'd me;
Which I disdaining scorn'd and craved death
Rather than I would be so vile-esteem'd.

In fine, redeem'd I was as I desired.
But, O! the treacherous Fastolfe wounds my heart,
Whom with my bare fists I would execute
If I now had him brought into my power.
  Sal. Yet tell'st thou not how thou wert en-
    tertain'd.
  Tal. With scoffs and scorns and contumelious
    taunts.
In open market-place produced they me,   *40*
To be a public spectacle to all:
Here, said they, is the terror of the French,
The scarecrow that affrights our children so.
Then broke I from the officers that led me,
And with my nails digg'd stones out of the ground,
To hurl at the beholders of my shame:
My grisly countenance made others fly;
None durst come near for fear of sudden death.
In iron walls they deem'd me not secure;
So great fear of my name 'mongst them was
    spread
That they supposed I could rend bars of steel *51*
And spurn in pieces posts of adamant:
Wherefore a guard of chosen shot I had
That walk'd about me every minute while;
And if I did but stir out of my bed,
Ready they were to shoot me to the heart.

      Enter the BOY *with a linstock.*

  Sal. I grieve to hear what torments you en-
    dured,
But we will be revenged sufficiently.
Now it is supper-time in Orleans:
Here, through this grate, I count each one   *60*
And view the Frenchmen how they fortify:
Let us look in; the sight will much delight thee.
Sir Thomas Gargrave, and Sir William Glans-
    dale,
Let me have your express opinions
Where is best place to make our battery next.
  Gar. I think, at the north gate; for there stand
    lords.
  Glan. And I, here, at the bulwark of the bridge.
  Tal. For aught I see, this city must be famish'd,
Or with light skirmishes enfeebled.
Here they shoot. SALISBURY *and* GARGRAVE *fall.*
  Sal. O Lord, have mercy on us, wretched
    sinners!   *70*
  Gar. O Lord, have mercy on me, woful man!
  Tal. What chance is this that suddenly hath
    cross'd us?
Speak, Salisbury; at least, if thou canst speak:
How farest thou, mirror of all martial men?
One of thy eyes and thy cheek's side struck off!
Accursed tower! accursed fatal hand
That hath contrived this woful tragedy!
In thirteen battles Salisbury o'ercame;

Henry the Fifth he first train'd to the wars;
Whilst any trump did sound, or drum struck up,
His sword did ne'er leave striking in the field. *81*
Yet livest thou, Salisbury? though thy speech
    doth fail,
One eye thou hast, to look to heaven for grace:
The sun with one eye vieweth all the world.
Heaven, be thou gracious to none alive,
If Salisbury wants mercy at thy hands!
Bear hence his body; I will help to burn it.
Sir Thomas Gargrave, hast thou any life?
Speak unto Talbot; nay, look up to him.
Salisbury, cheer thy spirit with this comfort; *90*
Thou shalt not die whiles—
He beckons with his hand and smiles on me,
As who should say "When I am dead and gone,
Remember to avenge me on the French."
Plantagenet, I will; and like thee, Nero,
Play on the lute, beholding the towns burn:
Wretched shall France be only in my name.
Here an alarum, and it thunders and lightens.
What stir is this? what tumult's in the heavens?
Whence cometh this alarum and the noise?

      Enter a MESSENGER.

  Mess. My lord, my lord, the French have
    gather'd head: *100*
The Dauphin, with one Joan la Pucelle join'd,
A holy prophetess new risen up,
Is come with a great power to raise the siege.
Here SALISBURY *lifteth himself up and groans.*
  Tal. Hear, hear how dying Salisbury doth
    groan!
It irks his heart he cannot be revenged.
Frenchmen, I'll be a Salisbury to you:
Pucelle or puzzel, dolphin or dogfish,
Your hearts I'll stamp out with my horse's heels,
And make a quagmire of your mingled brains.
Convey me Salisbury into his tent,   *110*
And then we'll try what these dastard French-
    men dare.   [*Alarum. Exeunt.*

      SCENE V. *The same*

Here an alarum again: and TALBOT *pursueth the*
DAUPHIN, *and driveth him: then enter* JOAN LA
PUCELLE, *driving Englishmen before her, and
exit after them: then re-enter* TALBOT.

  Tal. Where is my strength, my valour, and my
    force?
Our English troops retire, I cannot stay them;
A woman clad in armour chaseth them.

      Re-enter LA PUCELLE.

Here, here she comes. I'll have a bout with thee;
Devil or devil's dam, I'll conjure thee:
Blood will I draw on thee, thou art a witch,

And straightway give thy soul to him thou
    servest.
Puc. Come, come, 'tis only I that must disgrace
    thee.   [*Here they fight.*
Tal. Heavens, can you suffer hell so to pre-
    vail?   9
My breast I'll burst with straining of my courage
And from my shoulders crack my arms asunder,
But I will chastise this high-minded strumpet.
    They fight again.
Puc. Talbot, farewell; thy hour is not yet come:
I must go victual Orleans forthwith.
    A short alarum: then enter the town with soldiers.
O'ertake me, if thou canst; I scorn thy strength.
Go, go, cheer up thy hungry-starved men;
Help Salisbury to make his testament:
This day is ours, as many more shall be. [*Exit.*
    Tal. My thoughts are whirled like a potter's
    wheel;
I know not where I am, nor what I do: 20
A witch, by fear, not force, like Hannibal,
Drives back our troops and conquers as she lists:
So bees with smoke and doves with noisome stench
Are from their hives and houses driven away.
They call'd us for our fierceness English dogs;
Now, like to whelps, we crying run away.
    A short alarum.
Hark, countrymen! either renew the fight,
Or tear the lions out of England's coat;
Renounce your soil, give sheep in lions' stead:
Sheep run not half so treacherous from the wolf,
Or horse or oxen from the leopard,   *31*
As you fly from your oft-subdued slaves.

    Alarum. Here another skirmish.

It will not be: retire into your trenches:
You all consented unto Salisbury's death,
For none would strike a stroke in his revenge.
Pucelle is enter'd into Orleans,
In spite of us or aught that we could do.
O, would I were to die with Salisbury!
The shame hereof will make me hide my head.
    [*Exit* TALBOT. *Alarum; retreat; flourish.*

       SCENE VI. *The same*

Enter, *on the walls,* LA PUCELLE, CHARLES, REIG-
    NIER, ALENÇON, *and Soldiers.*

Puc. Advance our waving colours on the walls;
Rescued is Orleans from the English:
Thus Joan la Pucelle hath perform'd her word.
    Char. Divinest creature, Astræa's daughter,
How shall I honour thee for this success?
Thy promises are like Adonis' gardens
That one day bloom'd and fruitful were the next.
France, triumph in thy glorious prophetess!
Recover'd is the town of Orleans:

More blessed hap did ne'er befall our state.   10
    Reig. Why ring not out the bells aloud through-
    out the town?
Dauphin, command the citizens make bonfires
And feast and banquet in the open streets,
To celebrate the joy that God hath given us.
    Alen. All France will be replete with mirth and
    joy,
When they shall hear how we have play'd the
    men.
    Char. 'Tis Joan, not we, by whom the day is
    won;
For which I will divide my crown with her,
And all the priests and friars in my realm
Shall in procession sing her endless praise.   20
A statelier pyramis to her I'll rear
Than Rhodope's or Memphis' ever was:
In memory of her when she is dead,
Her ashes, in an urn more precious
Than the rich-jewel'd coffer of Darius,
Transported shall be at high festivals
Before the kings and queens of France.
No longer on Saint Denis will we cry,
But Joan la Pucelle shall be France's saint.
Come in, and let us banquet royally,   30
After this golden day of victory.
                [*Flourish. Exeunt.*

          # ACT II
      SCENE I. *Before Orleans*

Enter a SERGEANT *of a band, with two* SENTINELS.

    Serg. Sirs, take your places and be vigilant:
If any noise or soldier you perceive
Near to the walls, by some apparent sign
Let us have knowledge at the court of guard.
    1st Sent. Sergeant, you shall.   [*Exit Sergeant.*
Thus are poor servitors,
When others sleep upon their quiet beds,
Constrain'd to watch in darkness, rain and cold.

Enter TALBOT, BEDFORD, BURGUNDY, *and forces,*
    with scaling-ladders, their drums beating a dead
    march.

    Tal. Lord Regent, and redoubted Burgundy,
By whose approach the regions of Artois,
Wallon and Picardy are friends to us,   10
This happy night the Frenchmen are secure,
Having all day caroused and banqueted:
Embrace we then this opportunity
As fitting best to quittance their deceit,
Contrived by art and baleful sorcery.
    Bed. Coward of France! how much he wrongs
    his fame,
Despairing of his own arm's fortitude,
To join with witches and the help of hell!

Bur. Traitors have never other company.
But what's that Pucelle whom they term so
    pure?   20
Tal. A maid, they say.
Bed.   A maid! and be so martial!
Bur. Pray God she prove not masculine ere
    'long,
If underneath the standard of the French
She carry armour as she hath begun.
Tal. Well, let them practise and converse with
    spirits:
God is our fortress, in whose conquering name
Let us resolve to scale their flinty bulwarks.
Bed. Ascend, brave Talbot; we will follow
    thee.
Tal. Not all together: better far, I guess,
That we do make our entrance several ways;   *30*
That, if it chance the one of us do fail,
The other yet may rise against their force.
Bed. Agreed: I'll to yond corner.
Bur.   And I to this.
Tal. And here will Talbot mount, or make his
    grave.
Now, Salisbury, for thee, and for the right
Of English Henry, shall this night appear
How much in duty I am bound to both.
1st Sent. Arm! arm! the enemy doth make
    assault!
    Cry: "St. George," "A Talbot." *The English*
    scale the walls.

The French leap over the walls in their shirts. Enter,
    several ways, the BASTARD OF ORLEANS, ALEN-
    ÇON, *and* REIGNIER, *half ready, and half unready.*

Alen. How now, my lords! what, all unready
    so?
Bast. Unready! ay, and glad we 'scaped so
    well.   40
Reig. 'Twas time, I trow, to wake and leave
    our beds,
Hearing alarums at our chamber-doors.
Alen. Of all exploits since first I follow'd arms,
Ne'er heard I of a warlike enterprise
More venturous or desperate than this.
Bast. I think this Talbot be a fiend of hell.
Reig. If not of hell, the heavens, sure, favour
    him.
Alen. Here cometh Charles: I marvel how he
    sped.
Bast. Tut, holy Joan was his defensive guard.

      Enter CHARLES *and* LA PUCELLE.

Char. Is this thy cunning, thou deceitful dame?
                      50
Didst thou at first, to flatter us withal,
Make us partakers of a little gain,

That now our loss might be ten times so much?
Puc. Wherefore is Charles impatient with his
    friend?
At all times will you have my power alike?
Sleeping or waking must I still prevail,
Or will you blame and lay the fault on me?
Improvident soldiers! had your watch been good,
This sudden mischief never could have fall'n.
Char. Duke of Alençon, this was your
    default,   60
That, being captain of the watch to-night,
Did look no better to that weighty charge.
Alen. Had all your quarters been as safely kept
As that whereof I had the government,
We had not been thus shamefully surprised.
Bast. Mine was secure.
Reig.   And so was mine, my lord.
Char. And, for myself, most part of all this
    night,
Within her quarter and mine own precinct
I was employ'd in passing to and fro,
About relieving of the sentinels: 70
Then how or which way should they first
    break in?
Puc. Question, my lords, no further of the case,
How or which way: 'tis sure they found some
    place
But weakly guarded, where the breach was made.
And now there rests no other shift but this;
To gather our soldiers, scatter'd and dispersed,
And lay new platforms to endamage them.

Alarum. Enter an ENGLISH SOLDIER, *crying* "A
    Talbot! a Talbot!" *They fly, leaving their*
    clothes behind.

Sold. I'll be so bold to take what they have left.
The cry of Talbot serves me for a sword;
For I have loaden me with many spoils,   80
Using no other weapon but his name.   [*Exit.*

    SCENE II. *Orleans: Within the town*

Enter TALBOT, BEDFORD, BURGUNDY, *a* CAPTAIN,
    and others.

Bed. The day begins to break, and night is fled,
Whose pitchy mantle over-veil'd the earth.
Here sound retreat, and cease our hot pursuit.
                [*Retreat sounded.*
Tal. Bring forth the body of old Salisbury,
And here advance it in the market-place,
The middle centre of this cursed town.
Now have I paid my vow unto his soul;
For every drop of blood was drawn from him
There hath at least five Frenchmen died to-night.
And that hereafter ages may behold   10
What ruin happen'd in revenge of him,
Within their chiefest temple I'll erect

A tomb, wherein his corpse shall be interr'd:
Upon the which, that every one may read,
Shall be engraved the sack of Orleans,
The treacherous manner of his mournful death,
And what a terror he had been to France.
But, lords, in all our bloody massacre,
I muse we met not with the Dauphin's grace,
His new-come champion, virtuous Joan of Arc,
Nor any of his false confederates.   21
  Bed. 'Tis thought, Lord Talbot, when the fight
    began,
Roused on the sudden from their drowsy beds,
They did amongst the troops of armed men
Leap o'er the walls for refuge in the field.
  Bur. Myself, as far as I could well discern
For smoke and dusky vapours of the night,
Am sure I scared the Dauphin and his trull,
When arm in arm they both came swiftly
    running,
Like to a pair of loving turtle-doves   30
That could not live asunder day or night.
After that things are set in order here,
We'll follow them with all the power we have.

Enter a MESSENGER

  Mess. All hail, my lords! Which of this
    princely train
Call ye the warlike Talbot, for his acts
So much applauded through the realm of France?
  Tal. Here is the Talbot: who would speak with
    him?
  Mess. The virtuous lady, Countess of Auvergne,
With modesty admiring thy renown,
By me entreats, great lord, thou wouldst vouch-
    safe   40
To visit her poor castle where she lies,
That she may boast she hath beheld the man
Whose glory fills the world with loud report.
  Bur. Is it even so? Nay, then, I see our wars
Will turn unto a peaceful comic sport,
When ladies crave to be encounter'd with.
You may not, my lord, despise her gentle suit.
  Tal Ne'er trust me then; for when a world of
    men
Could not prevail with all their oratory,
Yet hath a woman's kindness over-ruled: 50
And therefore tell her I return great thanks,
And in submission will attend on her.
Will not your honours bear me company?
  Bed. No truly; it is more than manners will:
And I have heard it said, unbidden guests
Are often welcomest when they are gone.
  Tal. Well then, alone, since there's no remedy,
I mean to prove this lady's courtesy.
Come hither, captain. [*Whispers.*] You perceive
    my mind?

  Capt. I do, my lord, and mean accordingly.
                              [*Exeunt.* 60

SCENE III. *Auvergne: The Countess's castle*
Enter the COUNTESS *and her* PORTER.

  Count. Porter, remember what I gave in charge;
And when you have done so, bring the keys to me.
  Port. Madam, I will.   [*Exit.*
  Count. The plot is laid: if all things fall out
    right,
I shall as famous be by this exploit
As Scythian Tomyris by Cyrus' death.
Great is the rumour of this dreadful knight,
And his achievements of no less account:
Fain would mine eyes be witness with mine ears,
To give their censure of these rare reports. 10

Enter MESSENGER *and* TALBOT.

  Mess. Madam,
According as your ladyship desired,
By message craved, so is Lord Talbot come.
  Count. And he is welcome. What! is this the
    man?
  Mess. Madam, it is.
  Count.   Is this the scourge of France?
Is this the Talbot, so much fear'd abroad
That with his name the mothers still their babes?
I see report is fabulous and false:
I thought I should have seen some Hercules,
A second Hector, for his grim aspect,   20
And large proportion of his strong-knit limbs.
Alas, this is a child, a silly dwarf!
It cannot be this weak and writhled shrimp
Should strike such terror to his enemies.
  Tal. Madam, I have been bold to trouble you;
But since your ladyship is not at leisure,
I'll sort some other time to visit you.
  Count. What means he now? Go ask him
    whither he goes.
  Mess. Stay, my Lord Talbot; for my lady
    craves
To know the cause of your abrupt departure. 30
  Tal. Marry, for that she's in a wrong belief,
I go to certify her Talbot's here.

Re-enter PORTER *with keys.*

  Count. If thou be he, then art thou prisoner.
  Tal. Prisoner! to whom?
  Count.   To me, blood-thirsty lord;
And for that cause I train'd thee to my house.
Long time thy shadow hath been thrall to me,
For in my gallery thy picture hangs:
But now the substance shall endure the like,
And I will chain these legs and arms of thine,
That hast by tyranny these many years   40
Wasted our country, slain our citizens

And sent our sons and husbands captivate.

Tal. Ha, ha, ha!

Count. Laughest thou, wretch? thy mirth shall
turn to moan.

Tal. I laugh to see your ladyship so fond
To think that you have aught but Talbot's
shadow
Whereon to practise your severity.

Count. Why, art not thou the man?

Tal.   I am indeed.

Count. Then have I substance too.

Tal. No, no, I am but shadow of myself: 50
You are deceived, my substance is not here;
For what you see is but the smallest part
And least proportion of humanity:
I tell you, madam, were the whole frame here,
It is of such a spacious lofty pitch,
Your roof were not sufficient to contain 't.

Count. This is a riddling merchant for the
nonce;
He will be here, and yet he is not here:
How can these contrarieties agree?

Tal. That will I show you presently.   60
*Winds his horn. Drums strike up: a peal of ord-
nance. Enter Soldiers.*
How say you, madam? are you now persuaded
That Talbot is but shadow of himself?
These are his substance, sinews, arms and
strength,
With which he yoketh your rebellious necks,
Razeth your cities, and subverts your towns
And in a moment makes them desolate.

Count. Victorious Talbot! pardon my abuse:
I find thou art no less than fame hath bruited
And more than may be gather'd by thy shape.
Let my presumption not provoke thy wrath;   70
For I am sorry that with reverence
I did not entertain thee as thou art.

Tal. Be not dismay'd, fair lady; nor misconstrue
The mind of Talbot, as you did mistake
The outward composition of his body.
What you have done hath not offended me;
Nor other satisfaction do I crave,
But only, with your patience, that we may
Taste of your wine and see what cates you have;
For soldiers' stomachs always serve them well. *80*

Count. With all my heart, and think me
honoured
To feast so great a warrior in my house. [*Exeunt.*

SCENE IV. *London: The Temple-garden*

Enter the EARLS OF SOMERSET, SUFFOLK, *and* WAR-
WICK; RICHARD PLANTAGENET, VERNON, *and
another* LAWYER.

Plan. Great lords and gentlemen, what means
this silence?

Dare no man answer in a case of truth?

Suf. Within the Temple-hall we were too loud;
The garden here is more convenient.

Plan. Then say at once if I maintain'd the truth;
Or else was wrangling Somerset in the error?

Suf. Faith, I have been a truant in the law,
And never yet could frame my will to it;
And therefore frame the law unto my will.

Som. Judge you, my Lord of Warwick, then,
between us.   10

War. Between two hawks, which flies the
higher pitch;
Between two dogs, which hath the deeper mouth;
Between two blades, which bears the better
temper;
Between two horses, which doth bear him best;
Between two girls, which hath the merriest eye;
I have perhaps some shallow spirit of judgement;
But in these nice sharp quillets of the law,
Good faith, I am no wiser than a daw.

Plan. Tut, tut, here is a mannerly forbearance:
The truth appears so naked on my side   20
That any purblind eye may find it out.

Som. And on my side it is so well apparell'd,
So clear, so shining and so evident
That it will glimmer through a blind man's eye.

Plan. Since you are tongue-tied and so loath to
speak,
In dumb significants proclaim your thoughts:
Let him that is a true-born gentleman
And stands upon the honour of his birth,
If he suppose that I have pleaded truth,
From off this brier pluck a white rose with
me.   30

Som. Let him that is no coward nor no flatterer,
But dare maintain the party of the truth,
Pluck a red rose from off this thorn with me.

War. I love no colours, and without all colour
Of base insinuating flattery
I pluck this white rose with Plantagenet.

Suf. I pluck this red rose with young Somerset
And say withal I think he held the right.

Ver. Stay, lords and gentlemen, and pluck no
more,
Till you conclude that he upon whose side   40
The fewest roses are cropp'd from the tree
Shall yield the other in the right opinion.

Som. Good Master Vernon, it is well objected:
If I have fewest, I subscribe in silence.

Plan. And I.

Ver. Then for the truth and plainness of the
case,
I pluck this pale and maiden blossom here,
Giving my verdict on the white rose side.

Som. Prick not your finger as you pluck it off,
Lest bleeding you do paint the white rose red   50

And fall on my side so, against your will.
  Ver. If I, my lord, for my opinion bleed,
Opinion shall be surgeon to my hurt
And keep me on the side where still I am.
  Som. Well, well, come on: who else?
  Law. Unless my study and my books be false,
The argument you held was wrong in you;
  To SOMERSET.
In sign whereof I pluck a white rose too.
  Plan. Now, Somerset, where is your argument?
  Som. Here in my scabbard, meditating that
Shall dye your white rose in a bloody red.   61
  Plan. Meantime your cheeks do counterfeit our
    roses;
For pale they look with fear, as witnessing
The truth on our side.
  Som.   No, Plantagenet,
'Tis not for fear but anger that thy cheeks
Blush for pure shame to counterfeit our roses,
And yet thy tongue will not confess thy error.
  Plan. Hath not thy rose a canker, Somerset?
  Som. Hath not thy rose a thorn, Plantagenet?
  Plan. Ay, sharp and piercing, to maintain his
    truth;   70
Whiles thy consuming canker eats his falsehood.
  Som. Well, I'll find friends to wear my bleeding
    roses,
That shall maintain what I have said is true
Where false Plantagenet dare not be seen.
  Plan. Now, by this maiden blossom in my hand,
I scorn thee and thy fashion, peevish boy.
  Suf. Turn not thy scorns this way, Plantagenet.
  Plan. Proud Pole, I will, and scorn both him
    and thee.
  Suf. I'll turn my part thereof into thy throat.
  Som. Away, away, good William de la Pole!
We grace the yeoman by conversing with him. 81
  War. Now, by God's will, thou wrong'st him,
    Somerset;
His grandfather was Lionel Duke of Clarence,
Third son to the third Edward King of England:
Spring crestless yeomen from so deep a root?
  Plan. He bears him on the place's privilege,
Or durst not, for his craven heart, say thus.
  Som. By him that made me, I'll maintain my
    words
On any plot of ground in Christendom.
Was not thy father, Richard Earl of Cambridge,
For treason executed in our late king's days?   91
And, by his treason, stand'st not thou attainted,
Corrupted, and exempt from ancient gentry?
His trespass yet lives guilty in thy blood;
And, till thou be restored, thou art a yeoman.
  Plan. My father was attached, not attainted,
Condemn'd to die for treason, but no traitor;
And that I'll prove on better men than Somerset,

Were growing time once ripen'd to my will.
For your partaker Pole, and you yourself,   100
I'll note you in my book of memory,
To scourge you for this apprehension:
Look to it well and say you are well warn'd.
  Som. Ah, thou shalt find us ready for thee still;
And know us by these colours for thy foes,
For these my friends in spite of thee shall wear.
  Plan. And, by my soul, this pale and angry rose,
As cognizance of my blood-drinking hate,
Will I for ever and my faction wear, .
Until it wither with me to my grave   110
Or flourish to the height of my degree.
  Suf. Go forward and be choked with thy
    ambition!
And so farewell until I meet thee next.   [*Exit.*
  Som. Have with thee, Pole. Farewell, ambitious
    Richard.   [*Exit.*
  Plan. How I am braved and must perforce
    endure it!
  War. This blot that they object against your
    house
Shall be wiped out in the next parliament
Call'd for the truce of Winchester and
    Gloucester;
And if thou be not then created York,
I will not live to be accounted Warwick.   120
Meantime, in signal of my love to thee,
Against proud Somerset and William Pole,
Will I upon thy party wear this rose:
And here I prophesy: this brawl to-day,
Grown to this faction in the Temple-garden,
Shall send between the red rose and the white
A thousand souls to death and deadly night.
  Plan. Good Master Vernon, I am bound to you,
That you on my behalf would pluck a flower.
  Ver. In your behalf still will I wear the same.
  Law. And so will I.   131
  Plan. Thanks, gentle sir.
Come, let us four to dinner: I dare say
This quarrel will drink blood another day.
                                      [*Exeunt.*

SCENE V. *The Tower of London.*
Enter MORTIMER, *brought in a chair, and*
                  GAOLERS.

  Mor. Kind keepers of my weak decaying age,
Let dying Mortimer here rest himself.
Even like a man new haled from the rack,
So fare my limbs with long imprisonment;
And these grey locks, the pursuivants of death,
Nestor-like aged in an age of care,
Argue the end of Edmund Mortimer.
These eyes, like lamps whose wasting oil is
    spent,
Wax dim, as drawing to their exigent;

Weak shoulders, overborne with burthening
 grief,
And pithless arms, like to a wither'd vine *11*
That droops his sapless branches to the ground:
Yet are these feet, whose strengthless stay is
 numb,
Unable to support this lump of clay,
Swift-winged with desire to get a grave,
As witting I no other comfort have.
But tell me, keeper, will my nephew come?
 1st Gaol. Richard Plantagenet, my lord, will
 come:
We sent unto the Temple, unto his chamber;
And answer was return'd that he will come. *20*
 Mor. Enough: my soul shall then be satisfied.
Poor gentleman! his wrong doth equal mine.
Since Henry Monmouth first began to reign,
Before whose glory I was great in arms,
This loathsome sequestration have I had;
And even since then hath Richard been obscured,
Deprived of honour and inheritance.
But now the arbitrator of despairs,
Just death, kind umpire of men's miseries,
With sweet enlargement doth dismiss me hence:
I would his troubles likewise were expired, *31*
That so he might recover what was lost.

   Enter RICHARD PLANTAGENET.

 1st Gaol. My lord, your loving nephew now is
 come.
 Mor. Richard Plantagenet, my friend, is he
 come?
 Plan. Ay, noble uncle, thus ignobly used,
Your nephew, late despised Richard, comes.
 Mor. Direct mine arms I may embrace his neck,
And in his bosom spend my latter gasp:
O, tell me when my lips do touch his cheeks,
That I may kindly give one fainting kiss. *40*
And now declare, sweet stem from York's
 great stock,
Why didst thou say, of late thou wert despised?
 Plan. First, lean thine aged back against mine
 arm;
And, in that ease, I'll tell thee my disease.
This day, in argument upon a case,
Some words there grew 'twixt Somerset and me;
Among which terms he used his lavish tongue
And did upbraid me with my father's death:
Which obloquy set bars before my tongue,
Else with the like I had requited him. *50*
Therefore, good uncle, for my father's sake,
In honour of a true Plantagenet
And for alliance sake, declare the cause
My father, Earl of Cambridge, lost his head.
 Mor. That cause, fair nephew, that imprison'd
 me

And hath detain'd me all my flowering youth
Within a loathsome dungeon, there to pine,
Was cursed instrument of his decease.
 Plan. Discover more at large what cause that
 was,
For I am ignorant and cannot guess. *60*
 Mor. I will, if that my fading breath permit
And death approach not ere my tale be done.
Henry the Fourth, grandfather to this king,
Deposed his nephew Richard, Edward's son,
The first-begotten and the lawful heir
Of Edward king, the third of that descent:
During whose reign the Percies of the north,
Finding his usurpation most unjust,
Endeavour'd my advancement to the throne:
The reason moved these warlike lords to this *70*
Was for that—young King Richard thus
 removed,
Leaving no heir begotten of his body—
I was the next by birth and parentage;
For by my mother I derived am
From Lionel Duke of Clarence, the third son
To King Edward the Third; whereas he
From John of Gaunt doth bring his pedigree,
Being but fourth of that heroic line.
But mark: as in this haughty great attempt
They laboured to plant the rightful heir, *80*
I lost my liberty and they their lives.
Long after this, when Henry the Fifth,
Succeeding his father Bolingbroke, did reign,
Thy father, Earl of Cambridge, then derived
From famous Edmund Langley, Duke of York,
Marrying my sister that thy mother was,
Again in pity of my hard distress
Levied an army, weening to redeem
And have install'd me in the diadem:
But, as the rest, so fell that noble earl *90*
And was beheaded. Thus the Mortimers,
In whom the title rested, were suppress'd.
 Plan. Of which, my lord, your honour is the last.
 Mor. True; and thou seest that I no issue have
And that my fainting words do warrant death:
Thou art my heir; the rest I wish thee gather:
But yet be wary in thy studious care.
 Plan. Thy grave admonishments prevail with
 me:
But yet, methinks, my father's execution
Was nothing less than bloody tyranny. *100*
 Mor. With silence, nephew, be thou politic:
String-fixed is the house of Lancaster
And like a mountain, not to be removed.
But now thy uncle is removing hence;
As princes do their courts, when they are cloy'd
With long continuance in a settled place.
 Plan. O, uncle, would some part of my young
 years

Might but redeem the passage of your age!
Mor. Thou dost then wrong me, as that
    slaughterer doth   *109*
Which giveth many wounds when one will kill.
Mourn not, except thou sorrow for my good;
Only give order for my funeral:
And so farewell, and fair be all thy hopes
And prosperous be thy life in peace and war![*Dies.*
Plan. And peace, no war, befall thy parting soul!
In prison hast thou spent a pilgrimage
And like a hermit overpass'd thy days.
Well, I will lock his counsel in my breast;
And what I do imagine, let that rest.
Keepers, convey him hence, and I myself   *120*
Will see his burial better than his life.
    [*Exeunt* GAOLERS, *bearing out the body*
                            of MORTIMER.
Here dies the dusky torch of Mortimer,
Choked with ambition of the meaner sort:
And for those wrongs, those bitter injuries,
Which Somerset hath offer'd to my house,
I doubt not but with honour to redress;
And therefore haste I to the parliament,
Either to be restored to my blood,
Or make my ill the advantage of my good. [*Exit.*

ACT III

SCENE I. *London: The Parliament-house*

Flourish. Enter KING, EXETER, GLOUCESTER, WAR-
WICK, SOMERSET, *and* SUFFOLK; *the* BISHOP OF
WINCHESTER, RICHARD PLANTAGENET, *and
others.* GLOUCESTER *offers to put up a bill;* WIN-
CHESTER *snatches it, and tears it.*

Win. Comest thou with deep premeditated
    lines,
With written pamphlets studiously devised,
Humphrey of Gloucester? If thou canst accuse,
Or aught intend'st to lay unto my charge,
Do it without invention, suddenly;
As I with sudden and extemporal speech
Purpose to answer what thou canst object.
Glou. Presumptuous priest! this place commands
    my patience,
Or thou shouldst find thou hast dishonour'd me.
Think not, although in writing I preferr'd   *10*
The manner of thy vile outrageous crimes,
That therefore I have forged, or am not able
Verbatim to rehearse the method of my pen:
No, prelate: such is thy audacious wickedness,
Thy lewd, pestiferous and dissentious pranks,
As very infants prattle of thy pride.
Thou art a most pernicious usurer,
Froward by nature, enemy to peace:
Lascivious, wanton, more than well beseems
A man of thy profession and degree;   *20*

And for thy treachery, what's more manifest?
In that thou laid'st a trap to take my life,
As well at London bridge as at the Tower.
Beside, I fear me, if thy thoughts were sifted,
The king, thy sovereign, is not quite exempt
From envious malice of thy swelling heart.
Win. Gloucester, I do defy thee. Lords,
    vouchsafe
To give me hearing what I shall reply.
If I were covetous, ambitious or perverse,
As he will have me, how am I so poor?   *30*
Or how haps it I seek not to advance
Or raise myself, but keep my wonted calling?
And for dissension, who preferreth peace
More than I do?—except I be provoked.
No, my good lords, it is not that offends;
It is not that that hath incensed the duke:
It is, because no one should sway but he;
No one but he should be about the king:
And that engenders thunder in his breast
And makes him roar these accusations forth.   *40*
But he shall know I am as good—
Glou.   As good!
Thou bastard of my grandfather!
Win. Ay, lordly sir; for what are you, I pray,
But one imperious in another's throne?
Glou. Am I not protector, saucy priest?
Win. And am not I a prelate of the church?
Glou. Yes, as an outlaw in a castle keeps
And useth it to patronage his theft.
Win. Unreverent Gloucester!
Glou.   Thou art reverent
Touching thy spiritual function, not thy life. *50*
Win. Rome shall remedy this.
War.   Roam thither, then.
Som. My lord, it were your duty to forbear.
War. Ay, see the bishop be not overborne.
Som. Methinks my lord should be religious
And know the office that belongs to such.
War. Methinks his lordship should be humbler;
It fitteth not a prelate so to plead.
Som. Yes, when his holy state is touch'd so
    near.
War. State holy or unhallow'd, what of that?
Is not his grace protector to the king?   *60*
Plan. [*Aside*] Plantagenet, I see, must hold his
    tongue,
Lest it be said "Speak, sirrah, when you should;
Must your bold verdict enter talk with lords?"
Else would I have a fling at Winchester.
King. Uncles of Gloucester and of Winchester,
The special watchmen of our English weal,
I would prevail, if prayers might prevail,
To join your hearts in love and amity.
O, what a scandal is it to our crown
That two such noble peers as ye should jar!   *70*

Believe me, lords, my tender years can tell
Civil dissension is a viperous worm
That gnaws the bowels of the commonwealth.
  [*A noise within,* "Down with the tawny-
    coats!"]
What tumult's this?
  War.   An uproar, I dare warrant,
Begun through malice of the bishop's men.
  [*A noise again,* "Stones! stones!"]

      Enter MAYOR.

  May. O, my good lords, and virtuous Henry,
Pity the city of London, pity us!
The bishop and the Duke of Gloucester's men,
Forbidden late to carry any weapon,
Have fill'd their pockets full of pebble stones *80*
And banding themselves in contrary parts
Do pelt so fast at one another's pate
That many have their giddy brains knock'd out:
Our windows are broke down in every street
And we for fear compell'd to shut our shops.

    Enter SERVING-MEN, *in skirmish, with bloody
        pates.*

  King. We charge you, on allegiance to ourself,
To hold your slaughtering hands and keep the
    peace.
Pray, uncle Gloucester, mitigate this strife.
  1st Serv. Nay, if we be forbidden stones, we'll
fall to it with our teeth.   *90*
  2nd Serv. Do what ye dare, we are as resolute.
                            [*Skirmish again.*
  Glou. You of my household, leave this peevish
    broil
And set this unaccustom'd fight aside.
  3rd Serv. My lord, we know your grace to be a
    man
Just and upright; and, for your royal birth,
Inferior to none but to his majesty:
And ere that we will suffer such a prince,
So kind a father of the commonweal,
To be disgraced by an inkhorn mate,
We and our wives and children all will fight *100*
And have our bodies slaughter'd by thy foes.
  1st Serv. Ay, and the very parings of our nails
Shall pitch a field when we are dead.
  Begin again.
  Glou.   Stay, stay, I say!
And if you love me, as you say you do,
Let me persuade you to forbear awhile.
  King. O, how this discord doth afflict my soul!
Can you, my Lord of Winchester, behold
My sighs and tears and will not once relent?
Who should be pitiful, if you be not?
Or who should study to prefer a peace,   *110*
If holy churchmen take delight in broils?

  War. Yield, my lord protector; yield, Win-
    chester;
Except you mean with obstinate repulse
To slay your sovereign and destroy the realm.
You see what mischief and what murder too
Hath been enacted through your enmity;
Then be at peace, except ye thirst for blood.
  Win. He shall submit, or I will never yield.
  Glou. Compassion on the king commands me
    stoop;
Or I would see his heart out, ere the priest   *120*
Should ever get that privilege of me.
  War. Behold, my Lord of Winchester, the duke
Hath banish'd moody discontented fury,
As by his smoothed brows it doth appear:
Why look you still so stern and tragical?
  Glou. Here, Winchester, I offer thee my hand.
  King. Fie, uncle Beaufort! I have heard you
    preach
That malice was a great and grievous sin;
And will not you maintain the thing you teach,
But prove a chief offender in the same?   *130*
  War. Sweet king! the bishop hath a kindly gird.
For shame, my lord of Winchester, relent!
What, shall a child instruct you what to do?
  Win. Well, Duke of Gloucester, I will yield to
    thee;
Love for thy love and hand for hand I give.
  Glou. [*Aside*] Ay, but, I fear me, with a hollow
    heart.—
See here, my friends and loving countrymen,
This token serveth for a flag of truce
Betwixt ourselves and all our followers:
So help me God, as I dissemble not!   *140*
  Win. [*Aside*] So help me God, as I intend it not!
  King. O loving uncle, kind Duke of Gloucester,
How joyful am I made by this contract!
Away, my masters! trouble us no more;
But join in friendship, as your lords have done.
  1st Serv. Content: I'll to the surgeon's.
  2nd Serv.   And so will I.
  3rd Serv. And I will see what physic the tavern
    affords.
                [*Exeunt* SERVING-MEN, MAYOR, &c.
  War. Accept this scroll, most gracious
    sovereign,
Which in the right of Richard Plantagenet   *150*
We do exhibit to your majesty.
  Glou. Well urged, my Lord of Warwick: for
    sweet prince,
An if your grace mark every circumstance,
You have great reason to do Richard right;
Especially for those occasions
At Eltham Place I told your majesty.
  King. And those occasions, uncle, were of force:
Therefore, my loving lords, our pleasure is

That Richard be restored to his blood.

War. Let Richard be restored to his blood;
So shall his father's wrongs be recompensed. *161*

Win. As will the rest, so willeth Winchester.

King. If Richard will be true, not that alone
But all the whole inheritance I give
That doth belong unto the house of York,
From whence you spring by lineal descent.

Plan. Thy humble servant vows obedience
And humble service till the point of death.

King. Stoop then and set your knee against
my foot;
And, in reguerdon of that duty done, *170*
I gird thee with the valiant sword of York:
Rise, Richard, like a true Plantagenet,
And rise created princely Duke of York.

Plan. And so thrive Richard as thy foes may
fall!
And as my duty springs, so perish they
That grudge one thought against your majesty!

All. Welcome, high prince, the mighty Duke
of York!

Som. [*Aside*] Perish, base prince, ignoble
Duke of York!

Glou. Now will it best avail your majesty
To cross the seas and to be crown'd in France:
The presence of a king engenders love *181*
Amongst his subjects and his loyal friends,
As it disanimates his enemies.

King. When Gloucester says the word, King
Henry goes;
For friendly counsel cuts off many foes.

Glou. Your ships already are in readiness.
[*Sennet. Flourish. Exeunt all but* EXETER.

Exe. Ay, we may march in England or in France,
Not seeing what is likely to ensue.
This late dissension grown betwixt the peers
Burns under feigned ashes of forged love *190*
And will at last break out into a flame:
As fester'd members rot but by degree,
Till bones and flesh and sinews fall away,
So will this base and envious discord breed.
And now I fear that fatal prophecy
Which in the time of Henry named the Fifth
Was in the mouth of every sucking babe;
That Henry born at Monmouth should win all
And Henry born at Windsor lose all:
Which is so plain that Exeter doth wish *200*
His days may finish ere that hapless time. [*Exit.*

SCENE II. *France: Before Rouen*

Enter LA PUCELLE *disguised, with four* SOLDIERS
with sacks upon their backs.

Puc. These are the city gates, the gates of
Rouen,
Through which our policy must make a breach:

Take heed, be wary how you place your words;
Talk like the vulgar sort of market men
That come to gather money for their corn.
If we have entrance, as I hope we shall,
And that we find the slothful watch but weak,
I'll by a sign give notice to our friends,
That Charles the Dauphin may encounter them.

1st Sol. Our sacks shall be a mean to sack the
city, *10*
And we be lords and rulers over Rouen;
Therefore we'll knock. [*Knocks.*

Watch. [*Within*] *Qui est là?*

Puc. Paysans, pauvres gens de France;
Poor market folks that come to sell their corn.

Watch. Enter, go in; the market bell is rung.

Puc. Now, Rouen, I'll shake thy bulwarks to
the ground. [*Exeunt.*

Enter CHARLES, *the* BASTARD OF ORLEANS,
ALENÇON, REIGNIER, *and forces.*

Char. Saint Denis bless this happy stratagem!
And once again we'll sleep secure in Rouen.

Bast. Here enter'd Pucelle and her practisants;
Now she is there, how will she specify *21*
Where is the best and safest passage in?

Reign. By thrusting out a torch from yonder
tower;
Which, once discern'd, shows that her meaning
is,
No way to that, for weakness, which she
enter'd.

Enter LA PUCELLE *on the top, thrusting out a
torch burning.*

Puc. Behold, this is the happy wedding torch
That joineth Rouen unto her countrymen,
But burning fatal to the Talbotites! [*Exit.*

Bast. See, noble Charles, the beacon of our
friend;
The burning torch in yonder turret stands. *30*

Char. Now shine it like a comet of revenge,
A prophet to the fall of all our foes!

Reign. Defer no time, delays have dangerous
ends:
Enter, and cry "The Dauphin!" presently,
And then do execution on the watch.
[*Alarum. Exeunt.*

An alarum. Enter TALBOT *in an excursion.*

Tal. France, thou shalt rue this treason with
thy tears,
If Talbot but survive thy treachery.
Pucelle, that witch, that damned sorceress,
Hath wrought this hellish mischief unawares,
That hardly we escaped the pride of France. *40*
[*Exit.*

An alarum: excursions. BEDFORD, *brought in sick in*
a chair. Enter TALBOT *and* BURGUNDY *without:*
within LA PUCELLE, CHARLES, BASTARD, ALEN-
ÇON, *and* REIGNIER, *on the walls.*

Puc. Good morrow, gallants! want ye corn for
   bread?
I think the Duke of Burgundy will fast
Before he'll buy again at such a rate:
'Twas full of darnel; do you like the taste?
Bur. Scoff on, vile fiend and shameless
   courtezan!
I trust ere long to choke thee with thine own
And make thee curse the harvest of that corn.
Char. Your grace may starve perhaps before
   that time.
Bed. O, let no words, but deeds, revenge this
   treason!
Puc. What will you do, good grey-beard?
   break a lance,   50
And run a tilt at death within a chair?
Tal. Foul fiend of France, and hag of all despite,
Encompass'd with thy lustful paramours!
Becomes it thee to taunt his valiant age
And twit with cowardice a man half dead?
Damsel, I'll have a bout with you again,
Or else let Talbot perish with this shame.
Puc. Are ye so hot, sir? yet, Pucelle, hold thy
   peace;
If Talbot do but thunder, rain will follow.
   The English whisper together in council
God speed the parliament! who shall be the
   speaker?   60
Tal. Dare ye come forth and meet us in the
   field?
Puc. Belike your lordship takes us then for fools,
To try if that our own be ours or no.
Tal. I speak not to that railing Hecate,
But unto thee, Alençon, and the rest;
Will ye, like soldiers, come and fight it out?
Alen. Signior, no.
Tal. Signior, hang! base muleters of France!
Like peasant foot-boys do they keep the walls
And dare not take up arms like gentlemen.   70
Puc. Away, captains! let's get us from the walls;
For Talbot means no goodness by his looks.
God be wi' you, my lord! we came but to tell
   you
That we are here.   [*Exeunt from the walls.*
Tal. And there will we be too, ere it be long,
Or else reproach be Talbot's greatest fame!
Vow, Burgundy, by honour of thy house,
Prick'd on by public wrongs sustain'd in France,
Either to get the town again or die:
And I, as sure as English Henry lives   80
And as his father here was conqueror,

As sure as in this late-betrayed town
Great Cœur-de-lion's heart was buried,
So sure I swear to get the town or die.
Bur. My vows are equal partners with thy
   vows.
Tal. But, ere we go, regard this dying prince,
The valiant Duke of Bedford. Come, my lord,
We will bestow you in some better place,
Fitter for sickness and for crazy age.
Bed. Lord Talbot, do not so dishonour me:
Here will I sit before the walls of Rouen   91
And will be partner of your weal or woe.
But. Courageous Bedford, let us now persuade
   you.
Bed. Not to be gone from hence; for once I read
That stout Pendragon in his litter sick
Came to the field and vanquished his foes:
Methinks I should revive the soldiers' hearts,
Because I ever found them as myself.
Tal. Undaunted spirit in a dying breast!
Then be it so: heavens keep old Bedford safe!
And now no more ado, brave Burgundy,   101
But gather we our forces out of hand
And set upon our boasting enemy.
      [*Exeunt all but* BEDFORD *and Attendants.*

   An alarum: excursions. Enter SIR JOHN
         FASTOLFE *and a* CAPTAIN.

Cap. Whither away, Sir John Fastolfe, in such
   haste?
Fast. Whither away! to save myself by flight:
We are like to have the overthrow again.
Cap. What! will you fly, and leave Lord
   Talbot?
Fast.   Ay,
All the Talbots in the world, to save my life.
                                             [*Exit.*
Cap. Cowardly knight! ill fortune follow thee!
                                             [*Exit.*

   Retreat: excursions. LA PUCELLE, ALENÇON, *and*
   CHARLES, *enter from the town and fly.*

Bed. Now, quiet soul, depart when heaven
   please,   110
For I have seen our enemies' overthrow.
What is the trust or strength of foolish man?
They that of late were daring with their scoffs
Are glad and fain by flight to save themselves.
      [*Bedford dies, and is carried in by two in his*
                                              chair.

   An alarum. Re-enter TALBOT, BURGUNDY,
            and the rest.

Tal. Lost, and recover'd in a day again!
This is a double honour, Burgundy:
Yet heavens have glory for this victory!

Bur. Warlike and martial Talbot, Burgundy
Enshrines thee in his heart and there erects
Thy noble deeds as valour's monuments.   *120*
    Tal. Thanks, gentle Duke. But where is Pucelle
    now?
I think her old familiar is asleep:
Now where's the Bastard's braves, and Charles
    his gleeks?
What, all amort? Rouen hangs her head for grief
That such a valiant company are fled.
Now will we take some order in the town,
Placing therein some expert officers,
And then depart to Paris to the king,
For there young Henry with his nobles lie.
    Bur. What wills Lord Talbot pleaseth
    Burgundy.   *130*
    Tal. But yet, before we go, let's not forget
The noble Duke of Bedford, late deceased,
But see his exequies fulfill'd in Rouen:
A braver soldier never couched lance,
A gentler heart did never sway in court;
But kings and mightiest potentates must die,
For that's the end of human misery.   [*Exeunt.*

SCENE III. *The plains near Rouen*

Enter CHARLES, *the* BASTARD OF ORLEANS,
ALENÇON, LA PUCELLE, *and forces.*

    Puc. Dismay not, princes, at this accident,
Nor grieve that Rouen is so recovered:
Care is no cure, but rather corrosive,
For things that are not to be remedied.
Let frantic Talbot triumph for a while
And like a peacock sweep along his tail:
We'll pull his plumes and take away his train,
If Dauphin and the rest will be but ruled.
    Char. We have been guided by thee hitherto
And of thy cunning had no diffidence: *10*
One sudden foil shall never breed distrust.
    Bast. Search out thy wit for secret policies,
And we will make thee famous through the world.
    Alen. We'll set thy statue in some holy place,
And have thee reverenced like a blessed saint:
Employ thee then, sweet virgin, for our good.
    Puc. Then thus it must be; this doth Joan devise:
By fair persuasions mix'd with sugar'd words
We will entice the Duke of Burgundy
To leave the Talbot and to follow us.   *20*
    Char. Ay, marry, sweeting, if we could do that,
France were no place for Henry's warriors;
Nor should that nation boast it so with us,
But be extirped from our provinces.
    Alen. For ever should they be expulsed from
    France
And not have title of an earldom here.
    Puc. Your honours shall perceive how I will
    work

To bring this matter to the wished end.
    Drum sounds afar off.
Hark! by the sound of drum you may perceive
Their powers are marching unto Paris-ward.   *30*
*Here sound an English march. Enter, and pass over
    at a distance,* TALBOT *and his forces.*
There goes the Talbot, with his colours spread,
And all the troops of English after him.

French march. Enter the DUKE OF BURGUNDY
    and forces.

Now in the rearward comes the duke and his:
Fortune in favour makes him lag behind.
Summon a parley; we will talk with him.
    Trumpets sound a parley.
    Char. A parley with the Duke of Burgundy!
    Bur. Who craves a parley with the Burgundy?
    Puc. The princely Charles of France thy
    countryman.
    Bur. What say'st thou, Charles? for I am
    marching hence.
    Char. Speak, Pucelle, and enchant him with thy
    words.   *40*
    Puc. Brave Burgundy, undoubted hope of
    France!
Stay, let thy humble handmaid speak to thee.
    Bur. Speak on; but be not over-tedious.
    Puc. Look on thy country, look on fertile
    France,
And see the cities and the towns defaced
By wasting ruin of the cruel foe.
As looks the mother on her lowly babe
When death doth close his tender dying eyes,
See, see the pining malady of France: *49*
Behold the wounds, the most unnatural wounds,
Which thou thyself hast given her woful breast.
O, turn thy edged sword another way;
Strike those that hurt, and hurt not those that
    help.
One drop of blood drawn from thy country's
    bosom
Should grieve thee more than streams of foreign
    gore:
Return thee therefore with a flood of tears,
And wash away thy country's stained spots.
    Bur. Either she hath bewitch'd me with her
    words,
Or nature makes me suddenly relent.
    Puc. Besides, all French and France exclaims
    on thee,   *60*
Doubting thy birth and lawful progeny.
Who join'st thou with but with a lordly nation
That will not trust thee but for profit's sake?
When Talbot hath set footing once in France
And fashion'd thee that instrument of ill,
Who then but English Henry will be lord

And thou be thrust out like a fugitive?
Call we to mind, and mark but this for proof,
Was not the Duke of Orleans thy foe?
And was he not in England prisoner?   70
But when they heard he was thine enemy,
They set him free without his ransom paid,
In spite of Burgundy and all his friends.
See, then, thou fight'st against thy countrymen
And join'st with them will be thy slaughter-men.
Come, come, return; return, thou wandering lord
Charles and the rest will take thee in their arms.
  Bur. I am vanquished; these haughty words
    of hers
Have batter'd me like roaring cannon-shot,
And made me almost yield upon my knees.   80
Forgive me, country, and sweet countrymen,
And, lords, accept this hearty kind embrace:
My forces and my power of men are yours:
So farewell, Talbot; I'll no longer trust thee.
  Puc. [*Aside*] Done like a Frenchman: turn, and
    turn again!
  Char. Welcome, brave duke! thy friendship
    makes us fresh.
  Bast. And doth beget new courage in our breasts.
  Alen. Pucelle hath bravely play'd her part in this,
And doth deserve a coronet of gold.
  Char. Now let us on, my lords, and join our
    powers,   90
And seek how we may prejudice the foe.
                           [*Exeunt.*

Scene IV. *Paris: The palace*

Enter the KING, GLOUCESTER, BISHOP OF WIN-
CHESTER, YORK [RICHARD PLANTAGENET], SUF-
FOLK, SOMERSET, WARWICK, EXETER: VERNON,
BASSET, *and others. To them with his* Soldiers,
TALBOT.

  Tal. My gracious prince, and honourable peers,
Hearing of your arrival in this realm,
I have awhile given truce unto my wars,
To do my duty to my sovereign:
In sign whereof, this arm, that hath reclaim'd
To your obedience fifty fortresses,
Twelve cities and seven walled towns of strength,
Beside five hundred prisoners of esteem,
Lets fall his sword before your highness' feet,
And with submissive loyalty of heart   10
Ascribes the glory of his conquest got
First to my God and next unto your Grace.
                           [*Kneels.*
  King. Is this the Lord Talbot, uncle Gloucester,
That hath so long been resident in France?
  Glou. Yes, if it please your majesty, my liege.
  King. Welcome, brave captain and victorious
    lord!
When I was young, as yet I am not old,

I do remember how my father said
A stouter champion never handled sword.
Long since we were resolved of your truth,   20
Your faithful service, and your toil in war;
Yet never have you tasted our reward,
Or been reguerdon'd with so much as thanks,
Because till now we never saw your face:
Therefore, stand up; and, for these good deserts,
We here create you Earl of Shrewsbury;
And in our coronation take your place.
   [*Sennet. Flourish. Exeunt all but* VERNON *and*
    BASSET.
  Ver. Now, sir, to you, that were so hot at sea,
Disgracing of these colours that I wear
In honour of my noble Lord of York: 30
Darest thou maintain the former words thou
    spakest?
  Bas. Yes, sir; as well as you dare patronage
The envious barking of your saucy tongue
Against my lord the Duke of Somerset.
  Ver. Sirrah, thy lord I honour as he is.
  Bas. Why, what is he? as good a man as York.
  Ver. Hark ye; not so: in witness, take ye
    that. [*Strikes him.*]
  Bas. Villain, thou know'st the law of arms is
    such
That whoso draws a sword, 'tis present death,
Or else this blow should broach thy dearest
    blood.   40
But I'll unto his majesty, and crave
I may have liberty to venge this wrong;
When thou shalt see I'll meet thee to thy cost.
  Ver. Well, miscreant, I'll be there as soon as
    you;
And, after, meet you sooner than you would.
                          [*Exeunt.*

ACT IV

Scene I. *Paris: A hall of state*

Enter the KING, GLOUCESTER, BISHOP OF WIN-
CHESTER, YORK, SUFFOLK, SOMERSET, WAR-
WICK, TALBOT, EXETER, *the* GOVERNOR OF PARIS,
and others.

  Glou. Lord Bishop, set the crown upon his
    head.
  Win. God save King Henry, of that name the
    Sixth!
  Glou. Now, Governor of Paris, take your oath,
   [GOVERNOR *kneels.*]
That you elect no other king but him;
Esteem none friends but such as are his friends,
And none your foes but such as shall pretend
Malicious practices against his state:
This shall ye do, so help you righteous God!
        [*Exeunt* GOVERNOR *and train.*]

Enter SIR JOHN FASTOLFE.

Fast. My gracious sovereign, as I rode from
  Calais,
To haste unto your coronation,   10
A letter was deliver'd to my hands,
Writ to your grace from the Duke of Burgundy.
  Tal. Shame to the Duke of Burgundy and thee!
I vow'd, base knight, when I did meet thee next,
To tear the Garter from thy craven's leg,
  Plucking it off.
Which I have done, because unworthily
Thou wast installed in that high degree.
Pardon me, princely Henry, and the rest:
This dastard, at the battle of Patay,
When but in all I was six thousand strong   20
And that the French were almost ten to one,
Before we met or that a stroke was given,
Like to a trusty squire did run away:
In which assault we lost twelve hundred men;
Myself and divers gentlemen beside
Were there surprised and taken prisoners.
Then judge, great lords, if I have done amiss;
Or whether that such cowards ought to wear
This ornament of knighthood, yea or no.
  Glou. To say the truth, this fact was infamous
And ill beseeming any common man,   31
Much more a knight, a captain and a leader.
  Tal. When first this order was ordain'd, my
  lords,
Knights of the Garter were of noble birth,
Valiant and virtuous, full of haughty courage,
Such as were grown to credit by the wars;
Not fearing death, nor shrinking for distress,
But always resolute in most extremes.
He then that is not furnish'd in this sort
Doth but usurp the sacred name of knight,   40
Profaning this most honourable order,
And should, if I were worthy to be judge,
Be quite degraded, like a hedge-born swain
That doth presume to boast of gentle blood.
  King. Stain to thy countrymen, thou hear'st
  thy doom!
Be packing, therefore, thou that wast a knight:
Henceforth we banish thee, on pain of death.
                    [*Exit* FASTOLFE.
And now, my lord protector, view the letter
Sent from our uncle Duke of Burgundy.
  Glou. What means his grace, that he hath
  changed his style?   50
No more but, plain and bluntly, "To the king!"
Hath he forgot he is his sovereign?
Or doth this churlish superscription
Pretend some alteration in good will?
What's here? [*Reads*] "I have, upon especial
  cause,

Moved with compassion of my country's wreck,
Together with the pitiful complaints
Of such as your oppression feeds upon,
Forsaken your pernicious faction
And join'd with Charles, the rightful King of
  France."   60
O monstrous treachery! can this be so,
That in alliance, amity and oaths,
There should be found such false dissembling
  guile?
  King. What! doth my uncle Burgundy revolt?
  Glou. He doth, my lord, and is become your foe.
  King. Is that the worst this letter doth contain?
  Glou. It is the worst, and all, my lord, he
  writes.
  King. Why, then, Lord Talbot there shall talk
  with him
And give him chastisement for this abuse.
How say you, my lord? are you not content?   70
  Tal. Content, my liege! yes, but that I am
  prevented,
I should have begg'd I might have been employ'd.
  King. Then gather strength and march unto him
  straight:
Let him perceive how ill we brook his treason
And what offence it is to flout his friends.
  Tal. I go, my lord, in heart desiring still
You may behold confusion of your foes.   [*Exit.*

Enter VERNON *and* BASSET.

  Ver. Grant me the combat, gracious sovereign.
  Bas. And me, my lord, grant me the combat too.
  York. This is my servant: hear him, noble
  prince.   80
  Som. And this is mine: sweet Henry, favour
  him.
  King.   Be patient, lords; and give them
  leave to speak.
Say, gentlemen, what makes you thus exclaim?
And wherefore crave you combat? or with
  whom?
  Ver. With him, my lord; for he hath done me
  wrong.
  Bas. And I with him; for he hath done me
  wrong.
  King.   What is that wrong whereof you
  both complain?
First let me know, and then I'll answer you.
  Bas. Crossing the sea from England into France,
This fellow here, with envious carping tongue,
Upbraided me about the rose I wear;   91
Saying, the sanguine colour of the leaves
Did represent my master's blushing cheeks,
When stubbornly he did repugn the truth
About a certain question in the law
Argued betwixt the Duke of York and him;

With other vile and ignominious terms:
In confutation of which rude reproach
And in defence of my lord's worthiness,
I crave the benefit of law of arms. *100*
  Ver. And that is my petition, noble lord:
For though he seem with forged quaint conceit
To set a gloss upon his bold intent,
Yet know, my lord, I was provoked by him;
And he first took exceptions at this badge,
Pronouncing that the paleness of this flower
Bewray'd the faintness of my master's heart.
  York. Will not this malice, Somerset, be left?
  Som. Your private grudge, my Lord of York,
    will out,
Though ne'er so cunningly you smother it. *110*
  King.   Good Lord, what madness rules in
    brainsick men,
When for so slight and frivolous a cause
Such factious emulations shall arise!
Good cousins both, of York and Somerset,
Quiet yourselves, I pray, and be at peace.
  York. Let this dissension first be tried by fight,
And then your highness shall command a peace.
  Som. The quarrel toucheth none but us alone;
Betwixt ourselves let us decide it then. *119*
  York. There is my pledge: accept it, Somerset.
  Ver. Nay, let it rest where it began at first.
  Bas. Confirm it so, mine honourable lord.
  Glou. Confirm it so! Confounded be your strife!
And perish ye, with your audacious prate!
Presumptuous vassals, are you not ashamed
With this immodest clamorous outrage
To trouble and disturb the king and us?
And you, my lords, methinks you do not well
To bear with their perverse objections;
Much less to take occasion from their mouths *130*
To raise a mutiny betwixt yourselves:
Let me persuade you take a better course.
  Exe. It grieves his Highness: good my lords,
    be friends.
  King.   Come hither, you that would be
    combatants:
Henceforth I charge you, as you love our favour,
Quite to forget this quarrel and the cause.
And you, my lords, remember where we are;
In France, amongst a fickle wavering nation:
If they perceive dissension in our looks
And that within ourselves we disagree, *140*
How will their grudging stomachs be provoked
To wilful disobedience, and rebel!
Beside, what infamy will there arise,
When foreign princes shall be certified
That for a toy, a thing of no regard,
King Henry's peers and chief nobility
Destroy'd themselves, and lost the realm of
    France!

O, think upon the conquest of my father,
My tender years, and let us not forego
That for a trifle that was bought with blood! *150*
Let me be umpire in this doubtful strife.
I see no reason, if I wear this rose,
    Putting on a red rose.
That any one should therefore be suspicious
I more incline to Somerset than York:
Both are my kinsmen, and I love them both:
As well they may upbraid me with my crown,
Because, forsooth, the King of Scots is crown'd.
But your discretions better can persuade
Than I am able to instruct or teach:
And therefore, as we hither came in peace, *160*
So let us still continue peace and love.
Cousin of York, we institute your Grace
To be our Regent in these parts of France:
And, good my Lord of Somerset, unite
Your troops of horsemen with his bands of foot;
And, like true subjects, sons of your progenitors,
Go cheerfully together and digest
Your angry choler on your enemies.
Ourself, my Lord Protector and the rest
After some respite will return to Calais; *170*
From thence to England; where I hope ere long
To be presented, by your victories,
With Charles, Alençon and that traitorous rout.
    [*Flourish. Exeunt all but* YORK, WARWICK, EXE-
        TER *and* VERNON.
  War. My Lord of York, I promise you, the king
Prettily, methought, did play the orator.
  York. And so he did: but yet I like it not,
In that he wears the badge of Somerset.
  War. Tush, that was but his fancy, blame
    him not;
I dare presume, sweet prince, he thought no
    harm.
  York. An if I wist he did—but let it rest; *180*
Other affairs must now be managed.
        [*Exeunt all but Exeter.*
  Exe. Well didst thou, Richard, to suppress thy
    voice;
For, had the passions of thy heart burst out,
I fear we should have seen decipher'd there
More rancorous spite, more furious raging
    broils,
Than yet can be imagined or supposed.
But howsoe'er, no simple man that sees
This jarring discord of nobility,
This shouldering of each other in the court,
This factious bandying of their favourites, *190*
But that it doth presage some ill event.
'Tis much when sceptres are in children's hands;
But more when envy breeds unkind division;
There comes the ruin, there begins confusion.
        [*Exit.*

Scene II. *Before Bourdeaux*

Enter TALBOT, *with trump and drum.*

Tal. Go to the gates of Bourdeaux, trumpeter;
Summon their general unto the wall.

Trumpet sounds. Enter GENERAL *and others, aloft.*

English John Talbot, Captains, calls you forth,
Servant in arms to Harry King of England;
And thus he would: Open your city gates;
Be humble to us; call my sovereign yours,
And do him homage as obedient subjects;
And I'll withdraw me and my bloody power:
But, if you frown upon this proffer'd peace,
You tempt the fury of my three attendants,   *10*
Lean famine, quartering steel, and climbing fire;
Who in a moment even with the earth
Shall lay your stately and air-braving towers,
If you forsake the offer of their love.
  Gen. Thou ominous and fearful owl of death,
Our nation's terror and their bloody scourge!
The period of thy tyranny approacheth.
On us thou canst not enter but by death;
For, I protest, we are well fortified
And strong enough to issue out and fight: *20*
If thou retire, the Dauphin, well appointed,
Stands with the snares of war to tangle thee:
On either hand thee there are squadrons pitch'd,
To wall thee from the liberty of flight;
And no way canst thou turn thee for redress,
But death doth front thee with apparent spoil
And pale destruction meets thee in the face.
Ten thousand French have ta'en the sacrament
To rive their dangerous artillery
Upon no Christian soul but English Talbot.   *30*
Lo, there thou stand'st, a breathing valiant man,
Of an invincible unconquer'd spirit!
This is the latest glory of thy praise
That I, thy enemy, due thee withal;
For ere the glass, that now begins to run,
Finish the process of his sandy hour,
These eyes, that see thee now well coloured,
Shall see thee wither'd, bloody, pale and dead.
  Drum afar off.
Hark! hark! the Dauphin's drum, a warning bell,
Sings heavy music to thy timorous soul;   *40*
And mine shall ring thy dire departure out.
                [Exeunt GENERAL, *&c.*
  Tal. He fables not; I hear the enemy:
Out, some light horsemen, and peruse their wings.
O, negligent and heedless discipline!
How are we park'd and bounded in a pale,
A little herd of England's timorous deer,
Mazed with a yelping kennel of French curs!
If we be English deer, be then in blood;
Not rascal-like, to fall down with a pinch,

But rather, moody-mad and desperate stags,   *50*
Turn on the bloody hounds with heads of steel
And make the cowards stand aloof at bay:
Sell every man his life as dear as mine,
And they shall find dear deer of us, my friends.
God and Saint George, Talbot and England's
    right,
Prosper our colours in this dangerous fight!
                      [Exeunt.

Scene III. *Plains in Gascony*

Enter a MESSENGER *that meets* YORK. *Enter* YORK *with trumpet and many Soldiers.*

York. Are not the speedy scouts return'd again,
That dogg'd the mighty army of the Dauphin?
  Mess. They are return'd, my lord, and give it
    out
That he is march'd to Bourdeaux with his power,
To fight with Talbot: as he march'd along,
By your espials were discovered
Two mightier troops than that the Dauphin led,
Which join'd with him and made their march for
    Bourdeaux.
  York. A plague upon that villain Somerset,
That thus delays my promised supply   *10*
Of horsemen, that were levied for this siege!
Renowned Talbot doth expect my aid,
And I am lowted by a traitor villain
And cannot help the noble chevalier:
God comfort him in this necessity!
If he miscarry, farewell wars in France.

Enter SIR WILLIAM LUCY.

  Lucy. Thou princely leader of our English
    strength,
Never so needful on the earth of France,
Spur to the rescue of the noble Talbot,
Who now is girdled with a waist of iron   *20*
And hemm'd about with grim destruction:
To Bourdeaux, warlike duke! to Bourdeaux,
    York!
Else, farewell Talbot, France, and England's
    honour.
  York. O God, that Somerset, who in proud
    heart
Doth stop my cornets, were in Talbot's place!
So should we save a valiant gentleman
By forfeiting a traitor and a coward.
Mad ire and wrathful fury makes me weep,
That thus we die, while remiss traitors sleep.
  Lucy. O, send some succour to the distress'd
    lord!   *30*
  York. He dies, we lose; I break my warlike
    word;
We mourn, France smiles; we lose, they daily
    get;

All 'long of this vile traitor Somerset.
 Lucy. Then God take mercy on brave Talbot's
  soul;
And on his son young John, who two hours since
I met in travel toward his warlike father!
This seven years did not Talbot see his son;
And now they meet where both their lives are
  done.
 York. Alas, what joy shall noble Talbot have
To bid his young son welcome to his grave? 40
Away! vexation almost stops my breath,
That sunder'd friends greet in the hour of death.
Lucy, farewell: no more my fortune can,
But curse the cause I cannot aid the man.
Maine, Blois, Poictiers, and Tours, are won away,
'Long all of Somerset and his delay.
       [Exit, with his soldiers.
 Lucy. Thus, while the vulture of sedition
Feeds in the bosom of such great commanders,
Sleeping neglection doth betray to loss
The conquest of our scarce cold conqueror, 50
That ever living man of memory,
Henry the Fifth: whiles they each other cross,
Lives, honours, lands and all hurry to loss. *[Exit.*

  SCENE IV. *Other plains in Gascony*

Enter SOMERSET, *with his army; a* CAPTAIN *of*
    TALBOT'S *with him.*

 Som. It is too late; I cannot send them now:
This expedition was by York and Talbot
Too rashly plotted: all our general force
Might with a sally of the very town
Be buckled with: the over-daring Talbot
Hath sullied all his gloss of former honour
By this unheedful, desperate, wild adventure:
York set him on to fight and die in shame,
That, Talbot dead, great York might bear the
  name.
 Cap. Here is Sir William Lucy, who with me
Set from our o'ermatch'd forces forth for aid. 11

  Enter SIR WILLIAM LUCY.

 Som. How now, Sir William! whither were
  you sent?
 Lucy. Whither, my lord? from bought and
  sold Lord Talbot;
Who, ring'd about with bold adversity,
Cries out for noble York and Somerset,
To beat assailing death from his weak legions:
And whiles the honourable captain there
Drops bloody sweat from his war-wearied limbs,
And, in advantage lingering, looks for rescue,
You, his false hopes, the trust of England's
  honour, 20
Keep off aloof with worthless emulation.
Let not your private discord keep away

The levied succours that should lend him aid,
While he, renowned noble gentleman,
Yields up his life unto a world of odds:
Orleans the Bastard, Charles, Burgundy,
Alençon, Reignier, compass him about,
And Talbot perisheth by your default.
 Som. York set him on; York should have sent
  him aid.
 Lucy. And York as fast upon your grace
  exclaims; 30
Swearing that you withhold his levied host,
Collected for this expedition.
 Som. York lies; he might have sent and had
  the horse;
I owe him little duty, and less love;
And take foul scorn to fawn on him by sending.
 Lucy. The fraud of England, not the force of
  France,
Hath now entrapp'd the noble-minded Talbot:
Never to England shall he bear his life;
But dies, betray'd to fortune by your strife.
 Som. Come, go; I will dispatch the horsemen
  straight: 40
Within six hours they will be at his aid.
 Lucy. Too late comes rescue: he is ta'en or
  slain;
For fly he could not, if he would have fled;
And fly would Talbot never, though he might.
 Som. If he be dead, brave Talbot, then adieu!
 Lucy. His fame lives in the world, his shame in
  you.   *[Exeunt.*

  SCENE V. *The English camp near Bourdeaux*
   Enter TALBOT *and* JOHN *his son.*

 Tal. O young John Talbot! I did send for thee
To tutor thee in stratagems of war,
That Talbot's name might be in thee revived
When sapless age and weak unable limbs
Should bring thy father to his drooping chair.
But, O malignant and ill-boding stars!
Now thou art come unto a feast of death,
A terrible and unavoided danger:
Therefore, dear boy, mount on my swiftest horse;
And I'll direct thee how thou shalt escape 10
By sudden flight: come, dally not, be gone.
 John. Is my name Talbot? and am I your son?
And shall I fly? O, if you love my mother,
Dishonour not her honourable name,
To make a bastard and a slave of me!
The world will say he is not Talbot's blood
That basely fled when noble Talbot stood.
 Tal. Fly, to revenge my death, if I be slain.
 John. He that flies so will ne'er return again.
 Tal. If we both stay, we both are sure to die. *20*
 John. Then let me stay; and, father, do you fly:
Your loss is great, so your regard should be;

My worth unknown, no loss is known in me.
Upon my death the French can little boast;
In yours they will, in you all hopes are lost.
Flight cannot stain the honour you have won;
But mine it will, that no exploit have done:
You fled for vantage, every one will swear;
But, if I bow, they'll say it was for fear.
There is no hope that ever I will stay,   30
If the first hour I shrink and run away.
Here on my knee I beg mortality,
Rather than life preserved with infamy.
    Tal. Shall all thy mother's hopes lie in one
        tomb?
    John. Ay, rather than I'll shame my mother's
        womb.
    Tal. Upon my blessing, I command thee go.
    John. To fight I will, but not to fly the foe.
    Tal. Part of thy father may be saved in thee.
    John. No part of him but will be shame in me.
    Tal. Thou never hadst renown, nor canst not
        lose it.   40
    John. Yes, your renowned name: shall flight
        abuse it?
    Tal. Thy father's charge shall clear thee from
        that stain.
    John. You cannot witness for me, being slain.
If death be so apparent, then both fly.
    Tal. And leave my followers here to fight and
        die?
My age was never tainted with such shame.
    John. And shall my youth be guilty of such
        blame?
No more can I be sever'd from your side,
Than can yourself yourself in twain divide:
Stay, go, do what you will, the like do I;   50
For live I will not, if my father die.
    Tal. Then here I take my leave of thee, fair
        son,
Born to eclipse thy life this afternoon.
Come, side by side together live and die;
And soul with soul from France to heaven fly.
                                        [*Exeunt.*

SCENE VI. *A field of battle*

Alarum: excursions, wherein JOHN TALBOT *is
hemmed about, and* TALBOT *rescues him.*

    Tal. Saint George and victory! fight, soldiers,
        fight:
The Regent hath with Talbot broke his word
And left us to the rage of France his sword.
Where is John Talbot? Pause, and take thy
        breath;
I gave thee life and rescued thee from death.
    John. O, twice my father, twice am I thy son!
The life thou gavest me first was lost and done,
Till with thy warlike sword, despite of fate,

To my determined time thou gavest new date.
    Tal. When from the Dauphin's crest thy sword
        struck fire,   10
It warm'd thy father's heart with proud desire
Of bold-faced victory. Then leaden age,
Quicken'd with youthful spleen and warlike
        rage,
Beat down Alençon, Orleans, Burgundy,
And from the pride of Gallia rescued thee.
The ireful Bastard Orleans, that drew blood
From thee, my boy, and had the maidenhood
Of thy first fight, I soon encountered,
And interchanging blows, I quickly shed
Some of his bastard blood; and in disgrace   20
Bespoke him thus: "Contaminated, base,
And misbegotten blood I spill of thine,
Mean and right poor, for that pure blood of
        mine
Which thou didst force from Talbot, my brave
        boy":
Here, purposing the Bastard to destroy,
Came in strong rescue. Speak, thy father's care,
Art thou not weary, John? how dost thou fare?
Wilt thou yet leave the battle, boy, and fly,
Now thou art seal'd the son of chivalry?
Fly, to revenge my death when I am dead: 30
The help of one stands me in little stead.
O, too much folly is it, well I wot,
To hazard all our lives in one small boat!
If I to-day die not with Frenchmen's rage,
To-morrow I shall die with mickle age:
By me they nothing gain an if I stay;
'Tis but the shortening of my life one day:
In thee thy mother dies, our household's name,
My death's revenge, thy youth, and England's
        fame:
All these and more we hazard by thy stay;   40
All these are saved if thou wilt fly away.
    John. The sword of Orleans hath not made me
        smart;
These words of yours draw life-blood from my
        heart:
On that advantage, bought with such a shame,
To save a paltry life and slay bright fame,
Before young Talbot from old Talbot fly,
The coward horse that bears me fall and die!
And like me to the peasant boys of France,
To be shame's scorn and subject of mischance!
Surely, by all the glory you have won,   50
An if I fly, I am not Talbot's son:
Then talk no more of flight, it is no boot;
If son to Talbot, die at Talbot's foot.
    Tal. Then follow thou thy desperate sire of
        Crete,
Thou Icarus; thy life to me is sweet:
If thou wilt fight, fight by thy father's side;

And, commendable proved, let's die in pride.

                                   [*Exeunt.*

SCENE VII. *Another part of the field*
Alarum: excursions. Enter old TALBOT
led by a SERVANT.

Tal. Where is my other life? mine own is gone;
O, where's young Talbot? where is valiant John?
Triumphant death, smear'd with captivity,
Young Talbot's valour makes me smile at thee:
When he perceived me shrink and on my knee,
His bloody sword he brandish'd over me,
And, like a hungry lion, did commence
Rough deeds of rage and stern impatience;
But when my angry guardant stood alone,
Tendering my ruin and assail'd of none,   *10*
Dizzy-eyed fury and great rage of heart
Suddenly made him from my side to start
Into the clustering battle of the French;
And in that sea of blood my boy did drench
His over-mounting spirit, and there died,
My Icarus, my blossom, in his pride.
  Serv. O my dear lord, lo, where your son is
    borne!

Enter Soldiers, with the body of JOHN TALBOT.

Tal. Thou antic death, which laugh'st us here
    to scorn,
Anon, from thy insulting tyranny,
Coupled in bonds of perpetuity,   *20*
Two Talbots, winged through the lither sky,
In thy despite shall 'scape mortality.
O thou, whose wounds become hard-favour'd
    death,
Speak to thy father ere thou yield thy breath!
Brave death by speaking, whether he will or no;
Imagine him a Frenchman and thy foe.
Poor boy! he smiles, methinks, as who should say,
Had death been French, then death had died
    to-day.
Come, come and lay him in his father's arms:
My spirit can no longer bear these harms.   *30*
Soldiers, adieu! I have what I would have,
Now my old arms are young John Talbot's grave.
                                   [*Dies.*

Enter CHARLES, ALENÇON, BURGUNDY, BASTARD,
    LA PUCELLE, *and forces.*

  Char. Had York and Somerset brought rescue in,
We should have found a bloody day of this.
  Bast. How the young whelp of Talbot's, raging-
    wood,
Did flesh his puny sword in Frenchmen's blood!
  Puc. Once I encounter'd him, and thus I said:
"Thou maiden youth, be vanquish'd by a maid":
But, with proud majestical high scorn,

He answer'd thus: "Young Talbot was not born
To be the pillage of a giglot wench":   *41*
So, rushing in the bowels of the French,
He left me proudly, as unworthy fight.
  Bur. Doubtless he would have made a noble
    knight:
See, where he lies inhearsed in the arms
Of the most bloody nurser of his harms!
  Bast. Hew them to pieces, hack their bones
    asunder,
Whose life was England's glory, Gallia's wonder.
  Char. O, no, forbear! for that which we have
    fled
During the life, let us not wrong it dead.   *50*

Enter SIR WILLIAM LUCY, *attended; Herald of the*
French preceding.

  Lucy. Herald, conduct me to the Dauphin's tent.
To know who hath obtained the glory of the day,
  Char. On what submissive message art thou
    sent?
  Lucy. Submission, Dauphin! 'tis a mere French
    word;
We English warriors wot not what it means.
I come to know what prisoners thou hast ta'en
And to survey the bodies of the dead.
  Char. For prisoners ask'st thou? hell our
    prison is.
But tell me whom thou seek'st.
  Lucy. But where's the great Alcides of the
    field,   *60*
Valiant Lord Talbot, Earl of Shrewsbury,
Created, for his rare success in arms,
Great Earl of Washford, Waterford and Valence;
Lord Talbot of Goodrig and Urchinfield,
Lord Strange of Blackmere, Lord Verdun of
    Alton,
Lord Cromwell of Wingfield, Lord Furnival of
    Sheffield,
The thrice-victorious Lord of Falconbridge;
Knight of the noble order of Saint George,
Worthy Saint Michael and the Golden Fleece;
Great marshal to Henry the Sixth   *70*
Of all his wars within the realm of France?
  Puc. Here is a silly stately style indeed!
The Turk, that two and fifty kingdoms hath,
Writes not so tedious a style as this.
Him that thou magnifiest with all these titles
Stinking and fly-blown lies here at our feet.
  Lucy. Is Talbot slain, the Frenchmen's only
    scourge,
Your kingdom's terror and black Nemesis?
O, were mine eye-balls into bullets turn'd,
That I in rage might shoot them at your faces! *80*
O, that I could but call these dead to life!
It were enough to fright the realm of France:

Were but his picture left amongst you here,
It would amaze the proudest of you all.
Give me their bodies, that I may bear them hence
And give them burial as beseems their worth.
  Puc. I think this upstart is old Talbot's ghost,
He speaks with such a proud commanding spirit.
For God's sake, let him have 'em; to keep them
  here,
They would but stink, and putrefy the air.   *90*
  Char. Go, take their bodies hence.
  Lucy. I'll bear them hence; but from their ashes
  shall be rear'd
A phœnix that shall make all France afeard.
  Char. So we be rid of them, do with 'em what
  thou wilt.
And now to Paris, in this conquering vein:
All will be ours, now bloody Talbot's slain.
                                     [*Exeunt.*

ACT V

SCENE I. *London: The palace*

Sennet. Enter KING, GLOUCESTER, *and* EXETER.

  King. Have you perused the letters from the
  Pope,
The Emperor and the Earl of Armagnac?
  Glou. I have, my lord: and their intent is this:
They humbly sue unto your Excellence
To have a godly peace concluded of
Between the realms of England and of France.
  King. How doth your Grace affect their motion?
  Glou. Well, my good lord; and as the only means
To stop effusion of our Christian blood
And stablish quietness on every side.   *10*
  King. Ay, marry, uncle; for I always thought
It was both impious and unnatural
That such immanity and bloody strife
Should reign among professors of one faith.
  Glou. Beside, my lord, the sooner to effect
And surer bind this knot of amity,
The Earl of Armagnac, near knit to Charles,
A man of great authority in France,
Proffers his only daughter to your grace   *19*
In marriage, with a large and sumptuous dowry.
  King. Marriage, uncle! alas, my years are
  young!
And fitter is my study and my books
Than wanton dalliance with a paramour.
Yet call the ambassadors; and, as you please,
So let them have their answers every one:
I shall be well content with any choice
Tends to God's glory and my country's weal.

Enter WINCHESTER *in Cardinal's habit, a* PAPAL
  LEGATE *and two Ambassadors.*

  Exe. What! is my Lord of Winchester install'd,

And call'd unto a cardinal's degree?
Then I perceive that will be verified   *30*
Henry the Fifth did sometime prophesy,
"If once he come to be a cardinal,
He'll make his cap co-equal with the crown."
  King. My Lords Ambassadors, your several
  suits
Have been consider'd and debated on.
Your purpose is both good and reasonable;
And therefore are we certainly resolved
To draw conditions of a friendly peace;
Which by my Lord of Winchester we mean
Shall be transported presently to France.   *40*
  Glou. And for the proffer of my lord your
  master,
I have inform'd his highness so at large
As liking of the lady's virtuous gifts,
Her beauty, and the value of her dower,
He doth intend she shall be England's Queen.
  King. In argument and proof of which contract,
Bear her this jewel, pledge of my affection.
And so, my Lord Protector, see them guarded
And safely brought to Dover; where inshipp'd
Commit them to the fortune of the sea.   *50*
       [*Exeunt all but* WINCHESTER *and* LEGATE.
  Win. Stay, my Lord Legate: you shall first re-
  ceive
The sum of money which I promised
Should be deliver'd to his Holiness
For clothing me in these grave ornaments.
  Leg. I will attend upon your lordship's leisure.
  Win. [*Aside*] Now Winchester will not submit,
  I trow,
Or be inferior to the proudest peer.
Humphrey of Gloucester, thou shalt well perceive
That, neither in birth or for authority,
The bishop will be overborne by thee: *60*
I'll either make thee stoop and bend thy knee,
Or sack this country with a mutiny.   [*Exeunt.*

SCENE II. *France: Plains in Anjou*

Enter CHARLES, BURGUNDY, ALENÇON, BASTARD,
  REIGNIER, LA PUCELLE, *and forces.*

  Char. These news, my lords, may cheer our
  drooping spirits:
'Tis said the stout Parisians do revolt
And turn again unto the warlike French.
  Alen. Then march to Paris, royal Charles of
  France,
And keep not back your powers in dalliance.
  Puc. Peace be amongst them, if they turn to us;
Else, ruin combat with their palaces!

Enter SCOUT

  Scout. Success unto our valiant general,
And happiness to his accomplices!

Char. What tidings send our scouts? I prithee,
  speak.   10
Scout. The English army, that divided was
Into two parties, is now conjoin'd in one,
And means to give you battle presently.
  Char. Somewhat too sudden, sirs, the warning
    is:
But we will presently provide for them.
  Bur. I trust the ghost of Talbot is not there:
Now he is gone, my lord, you need not fear.
  Puc. Of all base passions, fear is most accursed.
Command the conquest, Charles, it shall be
  thine,
Let Henry fret and all the world repine.   20
  Char. Then on, my lords; and France be fortu-
    nate!   [*Exeunt.*

SCENE III. *Before Angiers*

Alarum. Excursions. Enter LA PUCELLE.

Puc. The Regent conquers, and the Frenchmen
  fly.
Now help, ye charming spells and periapts;
And ye choice spirits that admonish me
And give me signs of future accidents. [*Thunder.*
You speedy helpers, that are substitutes
Under the lordly monarch of the north,
Appear and aid me in this enterprise.

Enter Fiends.

This speedy and quick appearance argues proof
Of your accustom'd diligence to me.
Now, ye familiar spirits, that are cull'd   10
Out of the powerful regions under earth,
Help me this once, that France may get the field.
  They walk, and speak not.
O, hold me not with silence over-long!
Where I was wont to feed you with my blood,
I'll lop a member off and give it you
In earnest of a further benefit,
So you do condescend to help me now.
  They hang their heads.
No hope to have redress? My body shall
Pay recompense, if you will grant my suit.
  They shake their heads.
Cannot my body nor blood-sacrifice   20
Entreat you to your wonted furtherance?
Then take my soul, my body, soul and all,
Before that England give the French the foil.
  They depart.
See, they forsake me! Now the time is come
That France must vail her lofty-plumed crest
And let her head fall into England's lap.
My ancient incantations are too weak,
And hell too strong for me to buckle with:
Now, France, thy glory droopeth to the dust.
                                         [*Exit.*

Excursions. Enter BURGUNDY *and* YORK *fighting
  hand to hand. The French fly.* LA PUCELLE *is
  brought in captive.*

York. Damsel of France, I think I have you
  fast: 30
Unchain your spirits now with spelling charms
And try if they can gain your liberty.
A goodly prize, fit for the devil's grace!
See, how the ugly witch doth bend her brows,
As if with Circe she would change my shape!
  Puc. Changed to a worser shape thou canst not
    be.
  York. O, Charles the Dauphin is a proper man;
No shape but his can please your dainty eye.
  Puc. A plaguing mischief light on Charles and
    thee!
And may ye both be suddenly surprised   40
By bloody hands, in sleeping on your beds!
  York. Fell banning hag, enchantress, hold thy
    tongue!
  Puc. I prithee, give me leave to curse awhile.
  York. Curse, miscreant, when thou comest to
    the stake.   [*Exeunt.*

Alarum. Enter SUFFOLK, *with* MARGARET *in his
  hand.*

Suf. Be what thou wilt, thou art my prisoner.
                                    [*Gazes on her.*
O fairest beauty, do not fear nor fly!
For I will touch thee but with reverent hands;
I kiss these fingers for eternal peace,
And lay them gently on thy tender side.
Who art thou? say, that I may honour thee.   50
  Mar. Margaret my name, and daughter to a
    king,
The King of Naples, whosoe'er thou art.
  Suf. An earl I am, and Suffolk am I call'd.
Be not offended, nature's miracle,
Thou art allotted to be ta'en by me:
So doth the swan her downy cygnets save,
Keeping them prisoner underneath her wings.
Yet, if this servile usage once offend,
Go and be free again as Suffolk's friend.
                                   [*She is going.*
O, stay! [*Aside*] I have no power to let her pass; 60
My hand would free her, but my heart says no.
As plays the sun upon the glassy streams,
Twinkling another counterfeited beam,
So seems this gorgeous beauty to mine eyes.
Fain would I woo her, yet I dare not speak:
I'll call for pen and ink, and write my mind.
Fie, de la Pole! disable not thyself;
Hast not a tongue? is she not here?
Wilt thou be daunted at a woman's sight?
Ay, beauty's princely majesty is such,   70

Confounds the tongue and makes the senses rough.
  Mar. Say, Earl of Suffolk—if thy name be so—
What ransom must I pay before I pass?
For I perceive I am thy prisoner.
  Suf. [*Aside*] How canst thou tell she will deny
    thy suit,
Before thou make a trial of her love?
  Mar. Why speak'st thou not? what ransom
    must I pay?
  Suf. [*Aside*] She's beautiful and therefore to be
    woo'd;
She is a woman, therefore to be won.
  Mar. Wilt thou accept of ransom? yea, or no. *80*
  Suf. [*Aside*] Fond man, remember that thou hast
    a wife;
Then how can Margaret be thy paramour?
  Mar. I were best to leave him, for he will not
    hear.
  Suf. [*Aside*] There all is marr'd; there lies a
    cooling card.
  Mar. He talks at random; sure, the man is mad.
  Suf. [*Aside*] And yet a dispensation may be
    had.
  Mar. And yet I would that you would answer
    me.
  Suf. [*Aside*] I'll win this Lady Margaret. For
    whom?
Why, for my king: tush, that's a wooden thing!
  Mar. He talks of wood: it is some carpenter.
  Suf. [*Aside*] Yet so my fancy may be satisfied, *91*
And peace established between these realms.
But there remains a scruple in that too;
For though her father be the King of Naples,
Duke of Anjou and Maine, yet is he poor,
And our nobility will scorn the match.
  Mar. Hear ye, captain, are you not at leisure?
  Suf. [*Aside*] It shall be so, disdain they ne'er so
    much:
Henry is youthful and will quickly yield.
Madam, I have a secret to reveal. *100*
  Mar. [*Aside*] What though I be enthrall'd? he
    seems a knight,
And will not any way dishonour me.
  Suf. Lady, vouchsafe to listen what I say.
  Mar. [*Aside*] Perhaps I shall be rescued by the
    French;
And then I need not crave his courtesy.
  Suf. Sweet madam, give me hearing in a cause—
  Mar. [*Aside*] Tush, women have been captivate
    ere now.
  Suf. Lady, wherefore talk you so?
  Mar. I cry you mercy, 'tis but Quid for Quo.
  Suf. Say, gentle princess, would you not sup-
    pose   *110*
Your bondage happy, to be made a queen?
  Mar. To be a queen in bondage is more vile

Than is a slave in base servility;
For princes should be free.
  Suf.   And so shall you,
If happy England's royal king be free.
  Mar. Why, what concerns his freedom unto me?
  Suf. I'll undertake to make thee Henry's queen,
To put a golden sceptre in thy hand
And set a precious crown upon thy head,
If thou wilt condescend to be my—
  Mar.   What? *120*
  Suf. His love.
  Mar. I am unworthy to be Henry's wife.
  Suf. No, gentle madam; I unworthy am
To woo so fair a dame to be his wife
And have no portion in the choice myself.
How say you, madam, are ye so content?
  Mar. An if my father please, I am content.
  Suf. Then call our captains and our colours
    forth.
And, madam, at your father's castle walls
We'll crave a parley, to confer with him. *130*

A parley sounded. Enter REIGNIER *on the walls.*

See, Reignier, see, thy daughter prisoner!
  Reig. To whom?
  Suf.   To me.
  Reig.   Suffolk, what remedy?
I am a soldier and unapt to weep
Or to exclaim on fortune's fickleness.
  Suf. Yes, there is remedy enough, my lord:
Consent, and for thy honour give consent,
Thy daughter shall be wedded to my king;
Whom I with pain have woo'd and won thereto;
And this her easy-held imprisonment
Hath gain'd thy daughter princely liberty. *140*
  Reig. Speaks Suffolk as he thinks?
  Suf.   Fair Margaret knows
That Suffolk doth not flatter, face, or feign.
  Reig. Upon thy princely warrant, I descend
To give thee answer of thy just demand.
                    [*Exit from the walls.*
  Suf. And here I will expect thy coming.

Trumpets sound. Enter REIGNIER, *below.*

  Reig. Welcome, brave Earl, into our territories:
Command in Anjou what your Honour pleases.
  Suf. Thanks, Reignier, happy for so sweet a
    child,
Fit to be made companion with a king: *149*
What answer makes your Grace unto my suit?
  Reig. Since thou dost deign to woo her little
    worth
To be the princely bride of such a lord;
Upon condition I may quietly
Enjoy mine own, the country Maine and Anjou,
Free from oppression or the stroke of war,

My daughter shall be Henry's, if he please.
  Suf. That is her ransom; I deliver her;
And those two counties I will undertake
Your grace shall well and quietly enjoy.
  Reig. And I again, in Henry's royal name,
As deputy unto that gracious king,   *161*
Give thee her hand, for sign of plighted faith.
  Suf. Reignier of France, I give thee kingly
    thanks,
Because this is in traffic of a king.
[*Aside*] And yet, methinks, I could be well con-
    tent
To be mine own attorney in this case.
I'll over then to England with this news,
And make this marriage to be solemnized.
So farewell, Reignier: set this diamond safe
In golden palaces, as it becomes.   *170*
  Reig. I do embrace thee, as I would embrace
The Christian prince, King Henry, were he here.
  Mar. Farewell, my lord: good wishes, praise
    and prayers
Shall Suffolk ever have of Margaret.   [*Going.*
  Suf. Farewell, sweet madam: but hark you,
    Margaret;
No princely commendations to my king?
  Mar. Such commendations as becomes a maid,
A virgin, and his servant, say to him.
  Suf. Words sweetly placed and modestly di-
    rected.
But, madam, I must trouble you again;   *180*
No loving token to his majesty?
  Mar. Yes, my good lord, a pure unspotted
    heart,
Never yet taint with love, I send the King.
  Suf. And this withal.   [*Kisses her.*
  Mar. That for thyself: I will not so presume
To send such peevish tokens to a king.
               [*Exeunt* REIGNIER *and* MARGARET.
  Suf. O, wert thou for myself! But, Suffolk,
    stay;
Thou mayst not wander in that labyrinth;
There Minotaurs and ugly treasons lurk.
Solicit Henry with her wondrous praise: *190*
Bethink thee on her virtues that surmount,
And natural graces that extinguish art;
Repeat their semblance often on the seas,
That, when thou comest to kneel at Henry's
    feet,
Thou mayst bereave him of his wits with wonder.
                                              [*Exit.*

SCENE IV. *Camp of the* DUKE OF YORK
in Anjou

Enter YORK, WARWICK, *and others.*

  York. Bring forth that sorceress condemn'd
    to burn.

Enter LA PUCELLE, *guarded, and a* SHEPHERD.

  Shep. Ah, Joan, this kills thy father's heart
    outright!
Have I sought every country far and near,
And, now it is my chance to find thee out,
Must I behold thy timeless cruel death?
Ah, Joan, sweet daughter Joan, I'll die with
    thee!
  Puc. Decrepit miser! base ignoble wretch!
I am descended of a gentler blood:
Thou art no father nor no friend of mine.
  Shep. Out, out! My lords, an please you,
    'tis not so;   *10*
I did beget her, all the parish knows:
Her mother liveth yet, can testify
She was the first fruit of my bachelorship.
  War. Graceless! wilt thou deny thy parentage?
  York. This argues what her kind of life hath
    been,
Wicked and vile; and so her death concludes.
  Shep. Fie, Joan, that thou wilt be so obstacle!
God knows thou art a collop of my flesh;
And for thy sake have I shed many a tear:
Deny me not, I prithee, gentle Joan.   *20*
  Puc. Peasant, avaunt! You have suborn'd
    this man,
Of purpose to obscure my noble birth.
  Shep. 'Tis true, I gave a noble to the priest
The morn that I was wedded to her mother.
Kneel down and take my blessing, good my girl.
Wilt thou not stoop? Now cursed be the time
Of thy nativity! I would the milk
Thy mother gave thee when thou suck'dst her
    breast,
Had been a little ratsbane for thy sake!
Or else, when thou didst keep my lambs a-field,
I wish some ravenous wolf had eaten thee!   *31*
Dost thou deny thy father, cursed drab?
O, burn her, burn her! hanging is too good.
                                              [*Exit.*
  York. Take her away; for she hath lived too
    long,
To fill the world with vicious qualities.
  Puc. First, let me tell you whom you have
    condemn'd:
Not me begotten of a shepherd swain,
But issued from the progeny of kings;
Virtuous and holy; chosen from above,
By inspiration of celestial grace,   *40*
To work exceeding miracles on earth.
I never had to do with wicked spirits:
But you, that are polluted with your lusts,
Stain'd with the guiltless blood of innocents,
Corrupt and tainted with a thousand vices,
Because you want the grace that others have,

You judge it straight a thing impossible
To compass wonders but by help of devils.
No, misconceived! Joan of Arc hath been
A virgin from her tender infancy,   50
Chaste and immaculate in very thought;
Whose maiden blood, thus rigorously effused,
Will cry for vengeance at the gates of heaven.
    York. Ay, ay: away with her to execution!
    War. And hark ye, sirs; because she is a
        maid,
Spare for no faggots, let there be enow:
Place barrels of pitch upon the fatal stake,
That so her torture may be shortened.
    Puc. Will nothing turn your unrelenting
        hearts?
Then, Joan, discover thine infirmity,   60
That warranteth by law to be thy privilege.
I am with child, ye bloody homicides:
Murder not then the fruit within my womb,
Although ye hale me to a violent death.
    York. Now heaven forfend! the holy maid
        with child!
    War. The greatest miracle that e'er ye
        wrought:
Is all your strict preciseness come to this?
    York. She and the Dauphin have been jug-
        gling:
I did imagine what would be her refuge.
    War. Well, go to; we'll have no bastards
        live;   70
Expecially since Charles must father it.
    Puc. You are deceived; my child is none of
        his:
It was Alençon that enjoy'd my love.
    York. Alençon! that notorious Machiavel!
It dies, an if it had a thousand lives.
    Puc. O, give me leave, I have deluded you:
'Twas neither Charles nor yet the duke I named,
But Reignier, King of Naples, that prevail'd.
    War. A married man! that's most intolerable.
    York. Why, here's a girl! I think she knows
        not well,   80
There were so many, whom she may accuse.
    War. It's sign she hath been liberal and free.
    York. And yet, forsooth, she is a virgin pure.
Strumpet, thy words condemn thy brat and
        thee:
Use no entreaty, for it is in vain.
    Puc. Then lead me hence; with whom I leave
        my curse.
May never glorious sun reflex his beams
Upon the country where you make abode;
But darkness and the gloomy shade of death
Environ you, till mischief and despair   90
Drive you to break your necks or hang your-
        selves!   [*Exit, guarded.*

    York. Break thou in pieces and consume to
        ashes,
Thou foul accursed minister of hell!

Enter CARDINAL BEAUFORT [WINCHESTER],
        attended.

    Car. Lord Regent, I do greet your Excellence
With letters of commission from the King.
For know, my lords, the states of Christendom,
Moved with remorse of these outrageous broils,
Have earnestly implored a general peace
Betwixt our nation and the aspiring French;
And here at hand the Dauphin and his train   100
Approacheth, to confer about some matter.
    York. Is all our travail turn'd to this effect?
After the slaughter of so many peers,
So many captains, gentlemen and soldiers,
That in this quarrel have been overthrown
And sold their bodies for their country's benefit,
Shall we at last conclude effeminate peace?
Have we not lost most part of all the towns,
By treason, falsehood and by treachery,
Our great progenitors had conquered?   110
O, Warwick, Warwick! I foresee with grief
The utter loss of all the realm of France.
    War. Be patient, York: if we conclude a
        peace,
It shall be with such strict and severe covenants
As little shall the Frenchmen gain thereby.

Enter CHARLES, ALENÇON, BASTARD, REIGNIER,
        and others.

    Char. Since, lords of England, it is thus
        agreed
That peaceful truce shall be proclaim'd in France,
We come to be informed by yourselves
What the conditions of that league must be.
    York. Speak, Winchester; for boiling choler
        chokes   120
The hollow passage of my poison'd voice,
By sight of these our baleful enemies.
    Car. Charles, and the rest, it is enacted thus:
That, in regard King Henry gives consent,
Of mere compassion and of lenity,
To ease your country of distressful war,
And suffer you to breathe in fruitful peace,
You shall become true liegemen to his crown:
And, Charles, upon condition thou wilt swear
To pay him tribute, and submit thyself,   130
Thou shalt be placed as viceroy under him,
And still enjoy thy regal dignity.
    Alen. Must he be then as shadow of himself?
Adorn his temples with a coronet,
And yet, in substance and authority,
Retain but privilege of a private man?
This proffer is absurd and reasonless.

Char. 'Tis known already that I am possess'd
With more than half the Gallian territories,
And therein reverenced for their lawful king: *140*
Shall I, for lucre of the rest unvanquish'd,
Detract so much from that prerogative,
As to be call'd but viceroy of the whole?
No, Lord Ambassador, I'll rather keep
That which I have than, coveting for more,
Be cast from possibility of all.

   York. Insulting Charles! hast thou by secret
      means
Used intercession to obtain a league,
And, now the matter grows to compromise,
Stand'st thou aloof upon comparison? *150*
Either accept the title thou usurp'st,
Of benefit proceeding from our king
And not of any challenge of desert,
Or we will plague thee with incessant wars.

   Reig. My lord, you do not well in obstinacy
To cavil in the course of this contract:
If once it be neglected, ten to one
We shall not find like opportunity.

   Alen. To say the truth, it is your policy
To save your subjects from such massacre *160*
And ruthless slaughters as are daily seen
By our proceeding in hostility;
And therefore take this compact of a truce,
Although you break it when your pleasure serves.

   War. How say'st thou, Charles? shall our
      condition stand?

   Char. It shall;
Only reserved, you claim no interest
In any of our towns of garrison.

   York. Then swear allegiance to his majesty,
As thou art knight, never to disobey *170*
Nor be rebellious to the crown of England,
Thou, nor thy nobles, to the crown of England.
So, now dismiss your army when ye please;
Hang up your ensigns, let your drums be still,
For here we entertain a solemn peace.   [*Exeunt*.

SCENE V. London: The palace
Enter SUFFOLK in conference with the KING,
GLOUCESTER and EXETER.

   King. Your wondrous rare description, noble
      earl,
Of beauteous Margaret hath astonish'd me:
Her virtues graced with external gifts
Do breed love's settled passions in my heart:
And like as rigour of tempestuous gusts
Provokes the mightiest hulk against the tide,
So am I driven by breath of her renown
Either to suffer shipwreck or arrive
Where I may have fruition of her love.

   Suf. Tush, my good lord, this superficial tale
Is but a preface of her worthy praise;   *11*

The chief perfections of that lovely dame,
Had I sufficient skill to utter them,
Would make a volume of enticing lines,
Able to ravish any dull conceit:
And, which is more, she is not so divine,
So full-replete with choice of all delights,
But with as humble lowliness of mind
She is content to be at your command;
Command, I mean, of virtuous chaste intents, *20*
To love and honour Henry as her lord.

   King. And otherwise will Henry ne'er pre-
      sume.
Therefore, my Lord Protector, give consent
That Margaret may be England's royal Queen.

   Glou. So should I give consent to flatter sin.
You know, my lord, your highness is betroth'd
Unto another lady of esteem:
How shall we then dispense with that contract,
And not deface your honour with reproach?

   Suf. As doth a ruler with unlawful oaths; *30*
Or one that, at a triumph having vow'd
To try his strength, forsaketh yet the lists
By reason of his adversary's odds:
A poor earl's daughter is unequal odds,
And therefore may be broke without offence.

   Glou. Why, what, I pray, is Margaret more
      than that?
Her father is no better than an earl,
Although in glorious titles he excel.

   Suf. Yes, my lord, her father is a king,
The King of Naples and Jerusalem; *40*
And of such great authority in France
As his alliance will confirm our peace
And keep the Frenchmen in allegiance.

   Glou. And so the Earl of Armagnac may do,
Because he is near kinsman unto Charles.

   Exe. Beside, his wealth doth warrant a liberal
      dower,
Where Reignier sooner will receive than give.

   Suf. A dower, my lords! disgrace not so your
      king,
That he should be so abject, base and poor,
To choose for wealth and not for perfect love. *50*
Henry is able to enrich his queen
And not to seek a queen to make him rich:
So worthless peasants bargain for their wives,
As market-men for oxen, sheep, or horse.
Marriage is a matter of more worth
Than to be dealt in by attorneyship;
Not whom we will, but whom his Grace affects,
Must be companion of his nuptial bed:
And therefore, lords, since he affects her most,
It most of all these reasons bindeth us, *60*
In our opinions she should be preferr'd.
For what is wedlock forced but a hell,
An age of discord and continual strife?

Whereas the contrary bringeth bliss,
And is a pattern of celestial peace.
Whom should we match with Henry, being a
    king,
But Margaret, that is daughter to a king?
Her peerless feature, joined with her birth,
Approves her fit for none but for a king:
Her valiant courage and undaunted spirit,   70
More than in women commonly is seen,
Will answer our hope in issue of a king;
For Henry, son unto a conqueror,
Is likely to beget more conquerors,
If with a lady of so high resolve
As is fair Margaret he be link'd in love.
Then yield, my lords; and here conclude with me
That Margaret shall be queen, and none but she.
  King. Whether it be through force of your
    report,
My noble Lord of Suffolk, or for that   80
My tender youth was never yet attaint
With any passion of inflaming love,
I cannot tell; but this I am assured,
I feel such sharp dissension in my breast,
Such fierce alarums both of hope and fear,
As I am sick with working of my thoughts.

Take, therefore, shipping; post, my lord, to
    France;
Agree to any covenants, and procure
That Lady Margaret do vouchsafe to come
To cross the seas to England and be crown'd   90
King Henry's faithful and anointed queen;
For your expenses and sufficient charge,
Among the people gather up a tenth.
Be gone, I say; for, till you do return,
I rest perplexed with a thousand cares.
And you, good uncle, banish all offence:
If you do censure me by what you were,
Not what you are, I know it will excuse
This sudden execution of my will.
And so, conduct me where, from company,   100
I may revolve and ruminate my grief.   [*Exit.*
  Glou. Ay, grief, I fear me, both at first and last.
                    [*Exeunt* GLOUCESTER *and* EXETER.
  Suf. Thus Suffolk hath prevail'd; and thus he
    goes,
As did the youthful Paris once to Greece,
With hope to find the like event in love,
But prosper better than the Trojan did.
Margaret shall now be queen, and rule the king;
But I will rule both her, the king, and realm.
                                         [*Exit.*

❧ The Second Part of
KING HENRY THE SIXTH

DRAMATIS PERSONÆ

KING HENRY THE SIXTH
HUMPHREY, DUKE OF GLOUCESTER, *his uncle*
CARDINAL BEAUFORT, BISHOP OF WINCHESTER,
  great-uncle to the King
RICHARD PLANTAGENET, DUKE OF YORK
EDWARD ⎱ *sons of the Duke of York*
RICHARD ⎰
DUKE OF SOMERSET
WILLIAM DE LA POLE, DUKE OF SUFFOLK ⎱ *King's*
DUKE OF BUCKINGHAM   *Party*
LORD CLIFFORD
YOUNG CLIFFORD, *his son*
EARL OF SALISBURY ⎱ *York Faction*
EARL OF WARWICK   ⎰
LORD SCALES
LORD SAY
SIR HUMPHREY STAFFORD
WILLIAM STAFFORD, *his brother*
SIR JOHN STANLEY
VAUX
SEA-CAPTAIN
MASTER
MASTER'S MATE
WALTER WHITMORE
TWO GENTLEMEN, *prisoners with Suffolk*
JOHN HUME   ⎱ *priests*
JOHN SOUTHWELL ⎰
BOLINGBROKE, *a conjurer*
THOMAS HORNER, *an armourer*
PETER THUMP, *his man*
CLERK *of Chatham*
MAYOR *of Saint Alban's*

SIMPCOX, *an imposter*
ALEXANDER IDEN, *a Kentish gentleman*
JACK CADE, *a rebel*
GEORGE BEVIS
JOHN HOLLAND
DICK, *the butcher*   ⎱ *followers of Cade*
SMITH, *the weaver*   ⎰
MICHAEL
TWO MURDERERS
FIVE MESSENGERS
TWO PETITIONERS
SPIRIT
BEADLE
TWO 'PRENTICES
THREE NEIGHBORS TO HORNER
SERVANT *to Gloucester*
SHERIFF
HERALD
A POST
COMMONS
A CITIZEN
A SOLDIER

MARGARET, *Queen to King Henry*
ELEANOR, *Duchess of Gloucester*
MARGARET JOURDAIN, *a witch*
WIFE *to Simpcox*

NON-SPEAKING: *Mathew Goffe, Petitioners, Guards,
Servants, Attendants, Citizens, 'Prentices, Officers of
the Sheriff, Lords, Ladies, and Soldiers*

SCENE: *England*

❧

ACT I

SCENE I. *London: The palace*

Flourish of trumpets: then hautboys. Enter the KING,
DUKE OF GLOUCESTER, SALISBURY, WARWICK,
and CARDINAL BEAUFORT, *on the one side; the*
QUEEN, SUFFOLK, YORK, SOMERSET, *and* BUCK-
INGHAM, *on the other.*

Suf. As by your high imperial majesty
I had in charge at my depart for France,
As procurator to your Excellence,
To marry Princess Margaret for your Grace,
So, in the famous ancient city Tours,
In presence of the Kings of France and Sicil,
The Dukes of Orleans, Calaber, Bretagne and
    Alençon,
Seven earls, twelve barons and twenty reverend
    bishops,

I have perform'd my task and was espoused:
And humbly now upon my bended knee,   *10*
In sight of England and her lordly peers,
Deliver up my title in the Queen
To your most gracious hands, that are the sub-
    stance
Of that great shadow I did represent;
The happiest gift that ever marquess gave,
The fairest queen that ever king received.
  King. Suffolk, arise. Welcome, Queen Mar-
    garet:
I can express no kinder sign of love
Than this kind kiss. O Lord, that lends me
    life,
Lend me a heart replete with thankfulness!   *20*
For thou hast given me in this beauteous face
A world of earthly blessings to my soul,
If sympathy of love unite our thoughts.

33

Queen. Great King of England and my gracious
      lord,
The mutual conference that my mind hath had,
By day, by night, waking and in my dreams,
In courtly company or at my beads,
With you, mine alder-liefest sovereign,
Makes me the bolder to salute my king
With ruder terms, such as my wit affords   30
And over-joy of heart doth minister.
   King. Her sight did ravish; but her grace in
      speech,
Her words y-clad with wisdom's majesty,
Makes me from wondering fall to weeping joys;
Such is the fulness of my heart's content.
Lords, with one cheerful voice welcome my love.
   All [*kneeling*]. Long live Queen Margaret, Eng-
      land's happiness!
   Queen. We thank you all.   [*Flourish*.
   Suf. My Lord Protector, so it please your
      Grace,
Here are the articles of contracted peace   40
Between our soveriegn and the French King
      Charles,
For eighteen months concluded by consent.
   Glou. [*Reads*] "*Imprimis*, It is agreed between
the French king Charles, and William de la Pole,
Marquess of Suffolk, ambassador for Henry King
of England, that the said Henry shall espouse the
Lady Margaret, daughter unto Reignier King of
Naples, Sicilia and Jerusalem, and crown her
Queen of England ere the thirtieth of May next
ensuing. *Item*, that the duchy of Anjou and the
county of Maine shall be released and delivered
to the king her father"—[*Lets the paper fall*.
   King. Uncle, how now!
   Glou.   Pardon me, gracious lord;
Some sudden qualm hath struck me at the heart
And dimm'd mine eyes, that I can read no fur-
      ther.
   King. Uncle of Winchester, I pray, read on.
   Car. [*Reads*] "*Item*, It is further agreed between
them, that the duchies of Anjou and Maine shall
be released and delivered over to the king her
father, and she sent over of the King of England's
own proper cost and charges, without having any
dowry."
   King. They please us well. Lord Marquess,
      kneel down:
We here create thee the first Duke of Suffolk,
And gird thee with the sword. Cousin of York,
We here discharge your Grace from being regent
I' the parts of France, till term of eighteen
      months
Be full expired. Thanks, uncle Winchester,
Gloucester, York, Buckingham, Somerset,
Salisbury, and Warwick;   70

We thank you all for this great favour done,
In entertainment to my princely queen.
Come, let us in, and with all speed provide
To see her coronation be perform'd.
          [*Exeunt* KING, QUEEN, *and* SUFFOLK.
   Glou. Brave peers of England, pillars of the
      state,
To you Duke Humphrey must unload his grief,
Your grief, the common grief of all the land.
What! did my brother Henry spend his youth,
His valour, coin and people, in the wars?
Did he so often lodge in open field,   80
In winter's cold and summer's parching heat,
To conquer France, his true inheritance?
And did my brother Bedford toil his wits,
To keep by policy what Henry got?
Have you yourselves, Somerset, Buckingham,
Brave York, Salisbury, and victorious Warwick,
Received deep scars in France and Normandy?
Or hath mine uncle Beaufort and myself,
With all the learned council of the realm,
Studied so long, sat in the council-house   90
Early and late, debating to and fro
How France and Frenchmen might be kept in
      awe,
And had his highness in his infancy
Crowned in Paris in despite of foes?
And shall these labours and these honours die?
Shall Henry's conquest, Bedford's vigilance,
Your deeds of war and all our counsel die?
O peers of England, shameful is this league!
Fatal this marriage, cancelling your fame,
Blotting your names from books of memory,   100
Razing the characters of your renown,
Defacing monuments of conquer'd France,
Undoing all, as all had never been!
   Car. Nephew, what means this passionate dis-
      course,
This peroration with such circumstance?
For France, 'tis ours; and we will keep it still.
   Glou. Ay, uncle, we will keep it, if we can;
But now it is impossible we should:
Suffolk, the new-made duke that rules the roast,
Hath given the duchy of Anjou and Maine   110
Unto the poor King Reignier, whose large style
Agrees not with the leanness of his purse.
   Sal. Now, by the death of Him that died for all,
These counties were the keys of Normandy.
But wherefore weeps Warwick, my valiant son?
   War. For grief that they are past recovery:
For, were there hope to conquer them again,
My sword should shed hot blood, mine eyes no
      tears.
Anjou and Maine! myself did win them both;
Those provinces these arms of mine did conquer:
And are the cities, that I got with wounds,   121

Deliver'd up again with peaceful words?
Mort Dieu!

York. For Suffolk's duke, may he be suffocate,
That dims the honour of this warlike isle!
France should have torn and rent my very heart,
Before I would have yielded to this league.
I never read but England's kings have had
Large sums of gold and dowries with their wives;
And our King Henry gives away his own,   *130*
To match with her that brings no vantages.

Glou. A proper jest, and never heard before,
That Suffolk should demand a whole fifteenth
For costs and charges in transporting her!
She should have stay'd in France and starved in
     France,
Before—

Car. My Lord of Gloucester, now ye grow too
     hot:
It was the pleasure of my lord the King.

Glou. My Lord of Winchester, I know your
     mind;
'Tis not my speeches that you do mislike,   *140*
But 'tis my presence that doth trouble ye.
Rancour will out: proud prelate, in thy face
I see thy fury: if I longer stay,
We shall begin our ancient bickerings.
Lordings, farewell; and say, when I am gone,
I prophesied France will be lost ere long.   [*Exit.*

Car. So, there goes our Protector in a rage.
'Tis known to you he is mine enemy,
Nay, more, an enemy unto you all,
And no great friend, I fear me, to the King.   *150*
Consider, lords, he is the next of blood,
And heir apparent to the English crown:
Had Henry got an empire by his marriage,
And all the wealthy kingdoms of the west,
There's reason he should be displeased at it.
Look to it, lords; let not his smoothing words
Bewitch your hearts; be wise and circumspect.
What though the common people favour him,
Calling him "Humphrey, the good Duke of
     Gloucester,"   *159*
Clapping their hands, and crying with loud voice,
"Jesu maintain your royal Excellence!"
With "God preserve the good Duke Humphrey!"
I fear me, lords, for all this flattering gloss,
He will be found a dangerous protector.

Buck. Why should he, then, protect our sover-
     eign,
He being of age to govern of himself?
Cousin of Somerset, join you with me,
And all together, with the Duke of Suffolk,
We'll quickly hoise Duke Humphrey from his
     seat.

Car. This weighty business will not brook de-
     lay;   *170*

I'll to the Duke of Suffolk presently.   [*Exit.*

Som. Cousin of Buckingham, though Hum-
     phrey's pride
And greatness of his place be grief to us,
Yet let us watch the haughty cardinal:
His insolence is more intolerable
Than all the princes in the land beside:
If Gloucester be displaced, he'll be Protector.

Buck. Or thou or I, Somerset, will be Protector,
Despite Duke Humphrey or the Cardinal.   *179*
          [*Exeunt* BUCKINGHAM *and* SOMERSET.

Sal. Pride went before, ambition follows him.
While these do labour for their own preferment,
Behoves it us to labour for the realm.
I never saw but Humphrey Duke of Gloucester
Did bear him like a noble gentleman.
Oft have I seen the haughty Cardinal,
More like a soldier than a man o' the church,
As stout and proud as he were lord of all,
Swear like a ruffian and demean himself
Unlike the ruler of a commonweal.
Warwick, my son, the comfort of my age,   *190*
Thy deeds, thy plainness, and thy housekeeping,
Hath won the greatest favour of the commons,
Excepting none but good Duke Humphrey:
And, brother York, thy acts in Ireland,
In bringing them to civil discipline,
Thy late exploits done in the heart of France,
When thou wert regent for out sovereign,
Have made thee fear'd and honour'd of the
     people:
Join we together, for the public good,
In what we can, to bridle and suppress   *200*
The pride of Suffolk and the Cardinal,
With Somerset's and Buckingham's ambition;
And, as we may, cherish Duke Humphrey's
     deeds,
While they do tend the profit of the land.

War. So God help Warwick, as he loves the
     land,
And common profit of his country!

York. [*Aside*] And so says York, for he hath
     greatest cause.

Sal. Then let's make haste away, and look unto
     the main.

War. Unto the main! O father, Maine is lost;
That Maine which by main force Warwick did
     win,   *210*
And would have kept so long as breath did last!
Main chance, father, you meant; but I meant
     Maine,
Which I will win from France, or else be slain.
          [*Exeunt* WARWICK *and* SALISBURY.

York. Anjou and Maine are given to the French;
Paris is lost; the state of Normandy
Stands on a tickle point, now they are gone:

Suffolk concluded on the articles,
The peers agreed, and Henry was well pleased
To change two dukedoms for a duke's fair daugh-
    ter.
I cannot blame them all: what is't to them?   220
'Tis thine they give away, and not their own.
Pirates may make cheap pennyworths of their
    pillage
And purchase friends and give to courtezans,
Still revelling like lords till all be gone;
While as the silly owner of the goods
Weeps over them and wrings his hapless hands
And shakes his head and trembling stands aloof,
While all is shared and all is borne away,
Ready to starve and dare not touch his own:
So York must sit and fret and bite his tongue,   230
While his own lands are bargain'd for and sold.
Methinks the realms of England, France and Ire-
    land
Bear that proportion to my flesh and blood
As did the fatal brand Althæa burn'd
Unto the Prince's heart of Calydon.
Anjou and Maine both given unto the French!
Cold news for me, for I had hope of France,
Even as I have of fertile England's soil.
A day will come when York shall claim his own;
And therefore I will take the Nevils' parts   240
And make a show of love to proud Duke Hum-
    phrey,
And, when I spy advantage, claim the crown,
For that's the golden mark I seek to hit:
Nor shall proud Lancaster usurp my right,
Nor hold the sceptre in his childish fist,
Nor wear the diadem upon his head,
Whose church-like humours fits not for a crown.
Then, York, be still awhile, till time do serve:
Watch thou and wake when others be asleep,
To pry into the secrets of the state;   250
Till Henry, surfeiting in joys of love,
With his new bride and England's dear-bought
    queen,
And Humphrey with the peers be fall'n at jars:
Then will I raise aloft the milk-white rose,
With whose sweet smell the air shall be per-
    fumed;
And in my standard bear the arms of York,
To grapple with the house of Lancaster;
And, force perforce, I'll make him yield the
    crown,
Whose bookish rule hath pull'd fair England
    down.   [Exit.

SCENE II. *The Duke of Gloucester's house*

Enter DUKE HUMPHREY *and his wife* ELEANOR.

    Duch. Why droops my lord, like over-ripen'd
        corn,

Hanging the head at Ceres' plenteous load?
Why doth the great Duke Humphrey knit his
    brows,
As frowning at the favours of the world?
Why are thine eyes fix'd to the sullen earth,
Gazing on that which seems to dim thy sight?
What seest thou there? King Henry's diadem,
Enchased with all the honours of the world?
If so, gaze on, and grovel on thy face,
Until thy head be circled with the same.   10
Put forth thy hand, reach at the glorious gold.
What, is't too short? I'll lengthen it with mine;
And, having both together heaved it up,
We'll both together lift our heads to heaven,
And never more abase our sight so low
As to vouchsafe one glance unto the ground.
    Glou. O Nell, sweet Nell, if thou dost love thy
        lord,
Banish the canker of ambitious thoughts.
And may that thought, when I imagine ill
Against my king and nephew, virtuous Henry,   20
Be my last breathing in this mortal world!
My troublous dream this night doth make me
    sad.
    Duch. What dream'd my lord? tell me, and I'll
        requite it
With sweet rehearsal of my morning's dream.
    Glou. Methought this staff, mine office-badge in
        court,
Was broke in twain; by whom I have forgot,
But, as I think, it was by the Cardinal;
And on the pieces of the broken wand
Were placed the heads of Edmund Duke of
    Somerset,
And William de la Pole, first Duke of Suffolk.   30
This was my dream: what it doth bode, God
    knows.
    Duch. Tut, this was nothing but an argument
That he that breaks a stick of Gloucester's grove
Shall lose his head for his presumption.
But list to me, my Humphrey, my sweet duke:
Methought I sat in seat of majesty
In the cathedral church of Westminster,
And in that chair where kings and queens are
    crown'd;
Where Henry and dame Margaret kneel'd to me
And on my head did set the diadem.   40
    Glou. Nay, Eleanor, then must I chide outright:
Presumptuous dame, ill-nurtured Eleanor,
Art thou not second woman in the realm,
And the Protector's wife, beloved of him?
Hast thou not worldly pleasure at command,
Above the reach or compass of thy thought?
And wilt thou still be hammering treachery,
To tumble down thy husband and thyself
From top of honour to disgrace's feet?

Away from me, and let me hear no more!   50
  Duch. What, what, my lord! are you so choleric
With Eleanor, for telling but her dream?
Next time I'll keep my dreams unto myself,
And not be check'd.
  Glou. Nay, be not angry; I am pleased again.

Enter MESSENGER.

  Mess. My Lord Protector, 'tis his Highness'
    pleasure
You do prepare to ride unto Saint Alban's,
Where as the King and Queen do mean to hawk.
  Glou. I go. Come, Nell, thou wilt ride with us?
  Duch. Yes, my good lord, I'll follow presently.
        [*Exeunt* GLOUCESTER *and* MESSENGER.
Follow I must; I cannot go before,   61
While Gloucester bears this base and humble
    mind.
Were I a man, a duke, and next of blood,
I would remove these tedious stumbling-blocks
And smooth my way upon their headless necks;
And, being a woman, I will not be slack
To play my part in Fortune's pageant.
Where are you there? Sir John! nay, fear not,
    man,
We are alone; here's none but thee and I.

Enter HUME.

  Hume. Jesus preserve your royal majesty!   70
  Duch. What say'st thou? majesty! I am but
    Grace.
  Hume. But, by the grace of God, and Hume's
    advice,
Your Grace's title shall be multiplied.
  Duch. What say'st thou, man? hast thou as yet
    conferr'd
With Margery Jourdain, the cunning witch,
With Roger Bolingbroke, the conjurer?
And will they undertake to do me good?
  Hume. This they have promised, to show your
    highness
A spirit raised from depth of under-ground,
That shall make answer to such questions   80
As by your Grace shall be propounded him.
  Duch. It is enough; I'll think upon the questions:
When from Saint Alban's we do make return,
We'll see these things effected to the full.
Here, Hume, take this reward; make merry,
    man,
With thy confederates in this weighty cause.
                    [*Exit.*
  Hume. Hume must make merry with the Duch-
    ess' gold;
Marry, and shall. But, how now, Sir John Hume!
Seal up your lips, and give no words but mum:
The business asketh silent secrecy.   90

Dame Eleanor gives gold to bring the witch:
Gold cannot come amiss, were she a devil.
Yet have I gold flies from another coast;
I dare not say from the rich Cardinal
And from the great and new-made Duke of Suf-
    folk,
Yet I do find it so; for, to be plain,
They, knowing Dame Eleanor's aspiring humour,
Have hired me to undermine the Duchess
And buz these conjurations in her brain.
They say, "A crafty knave does need no broker";
Yet am I Suffolk and the Cardinal's broker.   101
Hume, if you take not heed, you shall go near
To call them both a pair of crafty knaves.
Well, so it stands; and thus, I fear, at last
Hume's knavery will be the Duchess' wreck,
And her attainture will be Humphrey's fall:
Sort how it will, I shall have gold for all.   [*Exit.*

SCENE III. *The palace*

Enter three or four PETITIONERS, PETER, *the*
Armourer's man, being one.

  1st Petit. My masters, let's stand close: my Lord
Protector will come this way by and by, and then
we may deliver our supplications in the quill.
  2nd Petit. Marry, the Lord protect him, for he's
a good man! Jesu bless him!

Enter SUFFOLK *and* QUEEN.

  Peter. Here a'comes, methinks, and the Queen
with him. I'll be the first, sure.
  2nd Petit. Come back, fool; this is the Duke of
Suffolk, and not my Lord Protector.   10
  Suf. How now, fellow! wouldst any thing with
me?
  1st Petit. I pray, my lord, pardon me; I took ye
for my Lord Protector.
  Queen. [*Reading*] "To my Lord Protector!" Are
your supplications to his lordship? Let me see
them: what is thine?
  1st Petit. Mine is, an't please your Grace, against
John Goodman, my Lord Cardinal's man, for
keeping my house, and lands, and wife, and all,
from me.   21
  Suf. Thy wife too! that's some wrong, indeed.
What's yours? What's here! [*Reads*] "Against
the Duke of Suffolk, for enclosing the commons
of Melford." How now, sir knave!
  2nd Petit. Alas, sir, I am but a poor petitioner of
our whole township.
  Peter. [*Giving his petition*] Against my master,
Thomas Horner, for saying that the Duke of
York was rightful heir to the crown.   30
  Queen. What say'st thou? did the Duke of York
say he was rightful heir to the crown?
  Peter. That my master was? no, forsooth: my

master said that he was, and that the King was an
usurper.

Suf. Who is there? [*Enter Servant.*] Take this
fellow in, and send for his master with a pursuivant presently: we'll hear more of your matter
before the King.   [*Exit Servant with* PETER.

Queen. And as for you, that love to be protected
Under the wings of our Protector's grace,   41
Begin your suits anew, and sue to him. [*Tears the
supplications.*]
Away, base cullions! Suffolk, let them go.

All. Come, let's be gone.   [*Exeunt.*

Queen. My Lord of Suffolk, say, is this the guise,
Is this the fashion in the court of England?
Is this the government of Britain's isle,
And this the royalty of Albion's king?
What, shall King Henry be a pupil still
Under the surly Gloucester's governance?   50
Am I a queen in title and in style,
And must be made a subject to a duke?
I tell thee, Pole, when in the city Tours
Thou ran'st a tilt in honour of my love
And stolest away the ladies' hearts of France,
I thought King Henry had resembled thee
In courage, courtship and proportion:
But all his mind is bent to holiness,
To number Ave-Maries on his beads;
His champions are the prophets and apostles,   60
His weapons holy saws of sacred writ,
His study is his tilt-yard, and his loves
Are brazen images of canonized saints.
I would the college of the cardinals
Would choose him Pope and carry him to Rome,
And set the triple crown upon his head:
That were a state fit for his holiness.

Suf. Madam, be patient: as I was cause
Your Highness came to England, so will I
In England work your Grace's full content.   70

Queen. Beside the haughty Protector, have we
Beaufort
The imperious churchman, Somerset, Bucking-
ham,
And grumbling York; and not the least of these
But can do more in England than the king.

Suf. And he of these that can do most of all
Cannot do more in England than the Nevils:
Salisbury and Warwick are no simple peers.

Queen. Not all these lords do vex me half so
much
As that proud dame, the Lord Protector's wife.
She sweeps it through the court with troops of
ladies,   80
More like an empress than Duke Humphrey's
wife:
Strangers in court do take her for the Queen:
She bears a duke's revenues on her back,

And in her heart she scorns our poverty:
Shall I not live to be avenged on her?
Contemptuous base-born callet as she is,
She vaunted 'mongst her minions t'other day,
The very train of her worst wearing gown
Was better worth than all my father's lands,   89
Till Suffolk gave two dukedoms for his daughter.

Suf. Madam, myself have limed a bush for her,
And placed a quire of such enticing birds
That she will light to listen to the lays,
And never mount to trouble you again.
So, let her rest: and, madam, list to me;
For I am bold to counsel you in this.
Although we fancy not the Cardinal,
Yet must we join with him and with the lords,
Till we have brought Duke Humphrey in dis-
grace.
As for the Duke of York, this late complaint   100
Will make but little for his benefit.
So, one by one, we'll weed them all at last,
And you yourself shall steer the happy helm.

Sound a sennet. Enter the KING, DUKE HUMPHREY
OF GLOUCESTER, CARDINAL BEAUFORT, BUCKING-
INGHAM, YORK, SOMERSET, SALISBURY, WAR-
WICK, *and the* DUCHESS OF GLOUCESTER.

King. For my part, noble lords, I care not which;
Or Somerset or York, all's one to me.

York. If York have ill demean'd himself in
France,
Then let him be denay'd the regentship.

Som. If Somerset be unworthy of the place,
Let York be regent; I will yield to him.   109

War. Whether your Grace be worthy, yea or
no,
Dispute not that: York is the worthier.

Car. Ambitious Warwick, let thy betters speak.

War. The Cardinal's not my better in the field.

Buck. All in this presence are thy betters, Warwick.

War. Warwick may live to be the best of all.

Sal. Peace, son! and show some reason, Buckingham,
Why Somerset should be preferr'd in this.

Queen. Because the King, forsooth, will have it
so.

Glou. Madam, the King is old enough himself
To give his censure: these are no women's matters.

Queen. If he be old enough, what needs your
Grace   121
To be Protector of his Excellence?

Glou. Madam, I am Protector of the realm;
And, at his pleasure, will resign my place.

Suf. Resign it then and leave thine insolence.
Since thou wert king—as who is king but thou?—
The commonwealth hath daily run to wreck;

The Dauphin hath prevail'd beyond the seas;
And all the peers and nobles of the realm
Have been as bondmen to thy sovereignty.   *130*
  Car. The commons hast thou rack'd; the cler-
    gy's bags
Are lank and lean with thy extortions.
  Som. Thy sumptuous buildings and thy wife's
    attire
Have cost a mass of public treasury.
  Buck. Thy cruelty in execution
Upon offenders hath exceeded law
And left thee to the mercy of the law.
  Queen. Thy sale of offices and towns in France,
If they were known, as the suspect is great,
Would make thee quickly hop without thy head.
        [*Exit* GLOUCESTER. *The* QUEEN *drops her fan.*
Give me my fan: what, minion! can ye not?   *141*
  She gives the DUCHESS *a box on the ear.*
I cry you mercy, madam; was it you?
  Duch. Was't I! yea, I it was, proud French-
    woman:
Could I come near your beauty with my nails,
I'ld set my ten commandments in your face.
  King. Sweet aunt, be quiet; 'twas against her
    will.
  Duch. Against her will! good King, look to't in
    time;
She'll hamper thee, and dandle thee like a baby:
Though in this place most master wear no
    breeches,
She shall not strike Dame Eleanor unrevenged.
                                    [*Exit.*
  Buck. Lord Cardinal, I will follow Eleanor,
And listen after Humphrey, how he proceeds:
She's tickled now; her fume needs no spurs,
She'll gallop far enough to her destruction. [*Exit.*

Re-enter GLOUCESTER.

  Glou. Now, lords, my choler being over-blown
With walking once about the quadrangle,
I come to talk of commonwealth affairs.
As for your spiteful false objections,
Prove them, and I lie open to the law;
But God in mercy so deal with my soul   *160*
As I in duty love my king and country!
But, to the matter that we have in hand:
I say, my sovereign, York is meetest man
To be your regent in the realm of France.
  Suf. Before we make election, give me leave
To show some reason, of no little force,
That York is most unmeet of any man.
  York. I'll tell thee, Suffolk, why I am unmeet:
First, for I cannot flatter thee in pride;
Next, if I be appointed for the place,   *170*
My Lord of Somerset will keep me here,
Without discharge, money, or furniture,

Till France be won into the Dauphin's hands:
Last time, I danced attendance on his will
Till Paris was besieged, famish'd, and lost.
  War. That can I witness; and a fouler fact
Did never traitor in the land commit.
  Suf. Peace, headstrong Warwick!
  War. Image of pride, why should I hold my
    peace?

Enter HORNER, *the Armourer, and his man* PETER, *guarded.*

  Suf. Because here is a man accused of treason:
Pray God the Duke of York excuse himself!   *181*
  York. Doth any one accuse York for a traitor?
  King. What mean'st thou, Suffolk; tell me,
    what are these?
  Suf. Please it your Majesty, this is the man
That doth accuse his master of high treason:
His words were these: that Richard Duke of
    York
Was rightful heir unto the English crown
And that your majesty was an usurper.
  King. Say, man, were these thy words?
  Hor. An't shall please your Majesty, I never
said nor thought any such matter: God is my wit-
ness, I am falsely accused by the villain.
  Pet. By these ten bones, my lords, he did speak
them to me in the garret one night, as we were
scouring my Lord of York's armour.
  York. Base dunghill villain and mechanical,
I'll have thy head for this thy traitor's speech.
I do beseech your royal Majesty,
Let him have all the rigour of the law.   *199*
  Hor. Alas, my lord, hang me, if ever I spake the
words. My accuser is my 'prentice; and when I
did correct him for his fault the other day, he did
vow upon his knees he would be even with me: I
have good witness of this: therefore I beseech
your Majesty, do not cast away an honest man
for a villain's accusation.
  King. Uncle, what shall we say to this in law?
  Glou. This doom, my lord, if I may judge:
Let Somerset be regent o'er the French,
Because in York this breeds suspicion: *210*
And let these have a day appointed them
For single combat in convenient place,
For he hath witness of his servant's malice:
This is the law, and this Duke Humphrey's doom.
  Som. I humbly thank your royal Majesty.
  Hor. And I accept the combat willingly.
  Pet. Alas, my lord, I cannot fight; for God's
sake, pity my case. The spite of man prevaileth
against me. O Lord, have mercy upon me! I shall
never be able to fight a blow. O Lord, my heart!
  Glou. Sirrah, or you must fight, or else be
    hang'd.

King. Away with them to prison; and the day
of combat shall be the last of the next month.
Come, Somerset, we'll see thee sent away.

[*Flourish. Exeunt.*

SCENE IV. *Gloucester's garden*

Enter MARGERY JOURDAIN, HUME, SOUTH-
WELL, *and* BOLINGBROKE.

Hume. Come, my masters; the Duchess, I tell
you, expects performance of your promises.

Boling. Master Hume, we are therefore provided: will her ladyship behold and hear our exor-
cisms?

Hume. Ay, what else? fear you not her courage.

Boling. I have heard her reported to be a woman
of an invincible spirit: but it shall be convenient,
Master Hume, that you be by her aloft, while we
be busy below; and so, I pray you, go, in God's
name, and leave us. [*Exit* HUME.] Mother Jourdain, be you prostrate and grovel on the earth;
John Southwell, read you; and let us to our work.

Enter DUCHESS *aloft*, HUME *following*.

Duch. Well said, my masters; and welcome all.
To this gear, the sooner the better.

Boling. Patience, good lady; wizards know their
times:
Deep night, dark night, the silent of the night,
The time of night when Troy was set on fire;   20
The time when screech-owls cry and ban-dogs
howl
And spirits walk and ghosts break up their graves,
That time best fits the work we have in hand.
Madam, sit you and fear not: whom we raise,
We will make fast within a hallow'd verge.

*Here they do the ceremonies belonging, and make
the circle;* BOLINGBROKE *or* SOUTHWELL *reads,*
"Conjuro te," &c. *It thunders and lightens
terribly; then the Spirit riseth.*

Spir. Adsum.

M. Jourd. Asmath,
By the eternal God, whose name and power
Thou tremblest at, answer that I shall ask;
For, till thou speak, thou shalt not pass from
hence.   30

Spir. Ask what thou wilt. That I had said and
done!

Boling. [*Reading out of a paper*]. "First of the
king: what shall of him become?"

Spir. The duke yet lives that Henry shall depose;
But him outlive, and die a violent death.

As the Spirit speaks, SOUTHWELL *writes the answer.*

Boling. "What fates await the Duke of Suffolk?"

Spir. By water shall he die, and take his end.

Boling. "What shall befall the Duke of Somerset?"

Spir. Let him shun castles;
Safer shall he be upon the sandy plains
Than where castles mounted stand.   40
Have done, for more I hardly can endure.

Boling. Descend to darkness and the burning
lake!
False fiend, avoid!

[*Thunder and lightning. Exit* SPIRIT.

Enter the DUKE OF YORK *and the* DUKE OF
BUCKINGHAM *with their guard and break in.*

York. Lay hands upon these traitors and their
trash.
Beldam, I think we watch'd you at an inch.
What, madam, are you there? the King and com-
monweal
Are deeply indebted for this piece of pains:
My Lord Protector will, I doubt it not,
See you well guerdon'd for these good deserts.

Duch. Not half so bad as thine to England's
king,   50
Injurious duke, that threatest where's no cause.

Buck. True, madam, none at all: what call you
this?
Away with them! let them be clapp'd up close,
And kept asunder. You, madam, shall with us.
Stafford, take her to thee.

[*Exeunt above* DUCHESS *and* HUME, *guarded.*

We'll see your trinkets here all forthcoming.
All, away!

[*Exeunt guard with* JOURDAIN, SOUTHWELL, &c.

York. Lord Buckingham, methinks, you watch'd
her well:
A pretty plot, well chosen to build upon!
Now, pray, my lord, let's see the devil's writ.   60
What have we here? [*Reads.*]
"The duke yet lives, that Henry shall depose;
But him outlive, and die a violent death."
Why, this is just
"*Aio te, Æacida, Romanos vincere posse.*"
Well, to the rest:
"Tell me what fate awaits the Duke of Suffolk?
By water shall he die, and take his end.
What shall betide the Duke of Somerset?
Let him shun castles;   70
Safer shall he be upon the sandy plains
Than where castles mounted stand."
Come, come, my lords;
These oracles are hardly attain'd,
And hardly understood.
The King is now in progress towards Saint
Alban's,
With him the husband of this lovely lady:

Thither go these news, as fast as horse can carry
them:
A sorry breakfast for my Lord Protector.
Buck. Your grace shall give me leave, my Lord
of York,   *80*
To be the post, in hope of his reward.
York. At your pleasure, my good lord. Who's
within there, ho!

Enter a Servingman.

Invite my Lords of Salisbury and Warwick
To sup with me to-morrow night. Away!
                [*Exeunt.*

ACT II

Scene i. *Saint Alban's*

Enter the KING, QUEEN, GLOUCESTER, CARDINAL,
and SUFFOLK, *with* FALCONERS *halloing.*

Queen. Believe me, lords, for flying at the
brook,
I saw not better sport these seven years' day:
Yet, by your leave, the wind was very high;
And, ten to one, old Joan had not gone out.
King. But what a point, my lord, your falcon
made,
And what a pitch she flew above the rest!
To see how God in all his creatures works!
Yea, man and birds are fain of climbing high.
Suf. No marvel, an it like your Majesty,
My Lord Protector's hawks do tower so well; *10*
They know their master loves to be aloft
And bears his thoughts above his falcon's pitch.
Glou. My lord, 'tis but a base ignoble mind
That mounts no higher than a bird can soar.
Car. I thought as much; he would be above the
clouds.
Glou. Ay, my Lord Cardinal? how think you by
that?
Were it not good your Grace could fly to heaven?
King. The treasury of everlasting joy.
Car. Thy heaven is on earth; thine eyes and
thoughts
Beat on a crown, the treasure of thy heart: *20*
Pernicious Protector, dangerous peer,
That smooth'st it so with king and commonweal!
Glou. What, Cardinal, is your priesthood grown
peremptory?
Tantæne animis cœlestibus iræ?
Churchmen so hot? good uncle, hide such malice;
With such holiness can you do it?
Suf. No malice, sir; no more than well becomes
So good a quarrel and so bad a peer.
Glou. As who, my lord?
Suf.   Why, as you, my lord,
An't like your lordly Lord-protectorship.   *30*

Glou. Why, Suffolk, England knows thine inso-
lence.
Queen. And thy ambition, Gloucester.
King. I prithee, peace, good queen,
And whet not on these furious peers;
For blessed are the peacemakers on earth.
Car. Let me be blessed for the peace I make,
Against this proud Protector, with my sword!
Glou. [*Aside to* CARDINAL] Faith, holy uncle,
would 'twere come to that!
Car. [*Aside to* GLOUCESTER] Marry, when thou
darest.
Glou. [*Aside to* CARDINAL] Make up no factious
numbers for the matter;   *40*
In thine own person answer thy abuse.
Car. [*Aside to* GLOUCESTER] Ay, where thou dar-
est not peep: an if thou darest,
This evening, on the east side of the grove.
King. How now, my lords!
Car.   Believe me, cousin Gloucester,
Had not your man put up the fowl so suddenly,
We had had more sport. [*Aside to* GLOUCESTER]
Come with thy two-hand sword.
Glou. True, uncle.
Car. [*Aside to* GLOUCESTER] Are ye advised? the
east side of the grove?
Glou. [*Aside to* CARDINAL] Cardinal, I am with
you.
King.   Why, how now, uncle Gloucester!
Glou. Talking of hawking; nothing else, my
lord.   *50*
[*Aside to* CARDINAL] Now, by God's mother,
priest, I'll shave your crown for this,
Or all my fence shall fail.
Car. [*Aside to* GLOUCESTER] *Medice, teipsum*—
Protector, see to't well, protect yourself.
King. The winds grow high; so do your stom-
achs, lords.
How irksome is this music to my heart!
When such strings jar, what hope of harmony?
I pray, my lords, let me compound this strife.

Enter a TOWNSMAN *of Saint Alban's, crying*
"A miracle!"

Glou. What means this noise?
Fellow, what miracle dost thou proclaim?   *60*
Towns. A miracle! a miracle!
Suf. Come to the King and tell him what
miracle.
Towns. Forsooth, a blind man at Saint Alban's
shrine,
Within this half-hour, hath received his sight;
A man that ne'er saw in his life before.
King. Now, God be praised, that to believing
souls
Gives light in darkness, comfort in despair!

Enter the MAYOR *of Saint Alban's and his brethren, bearing* SIMPCOX, *between two in a chair,* SIMP- COX'S WIFE *following.*

Car. Here comes the townsmen on procession,
To present your highness with the man.
King. Great is his comfort in this earthly
vale,
Although by his sight his sin be multiplied.   71
Glou. Stand by, my masters: bring him near the
king;
His highness' pleasure is to talk with him.
King. Good fellow, tell us here the circum-
stance,
That we for thee may glorify the Lord.
What, hast thou been long blind and now re-
stored?
Simp. Born blind, an't please your Grace.
Wife. Ay, indeed, was he.
Suf. What woman is this?
Wife. His wife, an't like your worship.   80
Glou. Hadst thou been his mother, thou couldst
have better told.
King. Where wert thou born?
Simp. At Berwick in the north, an't like your
Grace.
King. Poor soul, God's goodness hath been
great to thee:
Let never day nor night unhallow'd pass,
But still remember what the Lord hath done.
Queen. Tell me, good fellow, camest thou here
by chance,
Or of devotion, to this holy shrine?
Simp. God knows, of pure devotion; being
call'd
A hundred times and oftener, in my sleep,   90
By good Saint Alban; who said, "Simpcox,
come,
Come, offer at my shrine, and I will help thee."
Wife. Most true, forsooth; and many time and
oft
Myself have heard a voice to call him so.
Car. What, art thou lame?
Simp.   Ay, God Almighty help me!
Suf. How camest thou so?
Simp.   A fall off of a tree.
Wife. A plum-tree, master.
Glou.   How long hast thou been blind?
Simp. O, born so, master.
Glou.   What, and wouldst climb a tree?
Simp. But that in all my life, when I was a
youth.
Wife. Too true; and bought his climbing very
dear.   100
Glou. Mass, thou lovedst plums well, that
wouldst venture so.

Simp. Alas, good master, my wife desired some
damsons,
And made me climb, with danger of my life.
Glou. A subtle knave! but yet it shall not serve.
Let me see thine eyes: wink now: now open
them:
In my opinion yet thou see'st not well.
Simp. Yes, master, clear as day, I thank God
and Saint Alban.
Glou. Say'st thou me so? What colour is this
cloak of?
Simp. Red, master; red as blood.   110
Glou. Why, that's well said. What colour is my
gown of?
Simp. Black, forsooth: coal-black as jet.
King. Why, then, thou know'st what colour
jet is of?
Suf. And yet, I think, jet did he never see.
Glou. But cloaks and gowns, before this day,
a many.
Wife. Never, before this day, in all his life.
Glou. Tell me, sirrah, what's my name?
Simp. Alas, master, I know not.
Glou. What's his name?
Simp. I know not.   120
Glou. Nor his?
Simp. No, indeed, master.
Glou. What's thine own name?
Simp. Saunder Simpcox, and if it please you,
master.
Glou. Then Saunder, sit there, the lyingest
knave in Christendom. If thou hadst been born
blind, thou mightst as well have known all our
names as thus to name the several colours we do
wear. Sight may distinguish of colours, but sud-
denly to nominate them all, it is impossible. My
lords, Saint Alban here hath done a miracle; and
would ye not think his cunning to be great, that
could restore this cripple to his legs again?
Simp. O master, that you could!
Glou. My masters of Saint Alban's, have you
not beadles in your own, and things called
whips?
May. Yes, my lord, if it please your Grace.
Glou. Then send for one presently.
May. Sirrah, to fetch the beadle hither straight.
[*Exit an Attendant.* 141
Glou. Now fetch me a stool hither by and by.
Now, sirrah, if you mean to save yourself from
whipping, leap me over this stool and run away.
Simp. Alas, master, I am not able to stand
alone:
You go about to torture me in vain.

Enter a BEADLE *with whips.*

Glou. Well, sir, we must have you find your

legs. Sirrah, beadle whip him till he leap over
that same stool.

Bead. I will, my lord. Come on, sirrah; off with
your doublet quickly.

Simp. Alas, master, what shall I do? I am not
able to stand.

After the BEADLE *hath hit him once, he leaps over
the stool and runs away; and they follow and
cry, "A miracle!"*

King. O God, seest Thou this, and bearest so
long?

Queen. It made me laugh to see the villain run.

Glou. Follow the knave; and take this drab
away.

Wife. Alas, sir, we did it for pure need.

Glou. Let them be whipped through every
market-town, till they come to Berwick, from
whence they came.   *160*

[*Exeunt* WIFE, BEADLE, MAYOR, *&c.*

Car. Duke Humphrey has done a miracle to-day.

Suf. True; made the lame to leap and fly away.

Glou. But you have done more miracles than I;
You made in a day, my lord, whole towns to fly.

Enter BUCKINGHAM.

King. What tidings with our cousin Buckingham?

Buck. Such as my heart doth tremble to unfold.
A sort of naughty persons, lewdly bent,
Under the countenance and confederacy
Of Lady Eleanor, the Protector's wife,
The ringleader and head of all this rout,   *170*
Have practised dangerously against your state,
Dealing with witches and with conjurers:
Whom we have apprehended in the fact;
Raising up wicked spirits from under ground,
Demanding of King Henry's life and death,
And other of your Highness' privy-council;
As more at large your Grace shall understand.

Car. [*Aside to* GLOUCESTER] And so, my Lord
Protector, by this means
Your lady is forthcoming yet at London.
This news, I think, hath turn'd your weapon's
edge;   *180*
'Tis like, my lord, you will not keep your hour.

Glou. Ambitious churchman, leave to afflict my
heart:
Sorrow and grief have vanquish'd all my powers;
And, vanquish'd as I am, I yield to thee,
Or to the meanest groom.

King. O God, what mischiefs work the wicked
ones,
Heaping confusion on their own heads thereby!

Queen. Gloucester, see here the tainture of thy
nest,
And look thyself be faultless, thou wert best.

Glou. Madam, for myself, to heaven I do
appeal,   *190*
How I have loved my king and commonweal:
And, for my wife, I know not how it stands;
Sorry I am to hear what I have heard:
Noble she is, but if she have forgot
Honour and virtue and conversed with such
As, like to pitch, defile nobility,
I banish her my bed and company
And give her as a prey to law and shame,
That hath dishonour'd Gloucester's honest name.

King. Well, for this night we will repose us
here: *200*
To-morrow toward London back again,
To look into this business thoroughly
And call these foul offenders to their answers
And poise the cause in justice' equal scales,
Whose beam stands sure, whose rightful cause
prevails.   [*Flourish. Exeunt.*

SCENE II. *London: The Duke of York's
garden*

Enter YORK, SALISBURY, *and* WARWICK.

York. Now, my good Lords of Salisbury and
Warwick,
Our simple supper ended, give me leave
In this close walk to satisfy myself,
In craving your opinion of my title,
Which is infallible, to England's crown.

Sal. My Lord, I long to hear it at full.

War. Sweet York, begin: and if thy claim be
good,
The Nevils are thy subjects to command.

York. Then thus:
Edward the Third, my lords, had seven sons: *10*
The first, Edward the Black Prince, Prince of
Wales;
The second, William of Hatfield, and the third,
Lionel Duke of Clarence; next to whom
Was John of Gaunt, the Duke of Lancaster;
The fifth was Edmund Langley, Duke of York;
The sixth was Thomas of Woodstock, Duke of
Gloucester;
William of Windsor was the seventh and last.
Edward the Black Prince died before his father
And left behind him Richard, his only son,
Who after Edward the Third's death reign'd as
king;   *20*
Till Henry Bolingbroke, Duke of Lancaster,
The eldest son and heir of John of Gaunt,
Crown'd by the name of Henry the Fourth,
Seized on the realm, deposed the rightful king,
Sent his poor queen to France, from whence she
came,
And him to Pomfret; where, as all you know,
Harmless Richard was murder'd traitorously.

War. Father, the Duke hath told the truth;
Thus got the house of Lancaster the crown.
York. Which now they hold by force and not by
right; 30
For Richard, the first son's heir, being dead,
The issue of the next son should have reign'd.
Sal. But William of Hatfield died without an
heir.
York. The third son, Duke of Clarence, from
whose line
I claim the crown, had issue, Philippe, a daughter,
Who married Edmund Mortimer, Earl of March:
Edmund had issue, Roger Earl of March;
Roger had issue, Edmund, Anne and Eleanor.
Sal. This Edmund, in the reign of Bolingbroke,
As I have read, laid claim unto the crown; 40
And, but for Owen Glendower, had been king,
Who kept him in captivity till he died.
But to the rest.
York. His eldest sister, Anne,
My mother, being heir unto the crown,
Married Richard Earl of Cambridge, who was
son
To Edmund Langley, Edward the Third's fifth
son.
By her I claim the kingdom: she was heir
To Roger Earl of March, who was the son
Of Edmund Mortimer, who married Philippe,
Sole daughter unto Lionel Duke of Clarence: 50
So, if the issue of the elder son
Succeed before the younger, I am king.
War. What plain proceeding is more plain than
this?
Henry doth claim the crown from John of Gaunt,
The fourth son; York claims it from the third.
Till Lionel's issue fails, his should not reign:
It fails not yet, but flourishes in thee
And in thy sons, fair slips of such a stock.
Then, father Salisbury, kneel we together;
And in this private plot be we the first 60
That shall salute our rightful sovereign
With honour of his birthright to the crown.
Both. Long life our sovereign Richard, Eng-
land's king!
York. We thank you, lords. But I am not your
king
Till I be crown'd and that my sword be stain'd
With heart-blood of the house of Lancaster;
And that's not suddenly to be perform'd,
But with advice and silent secrecy.
Do you as I do in these dangerous days:
Wink at the Duke of Suffolk's insolence, 70
At Beaufort's pride, at Somerset's ambition,
At Buckingham and all the crew of them,
Till they have snared the shepherd of the flock,
That virtuous prince, the good Duke Humphrey;

'Tis that they seek, and they in seeking that
Shall find their deaths, if York can prophesy.
Sal. My lord, break we off; we know your
mind at full.
War. My heart assures me that the Earl of
Warwick
Shall one day make the Duke of York a king.
York. And, Nevil, this I do assure myself:
Richard shall live to make the Earl of Warwick
The greatest man in England but the king.
[*Exeunt.*

SCENE III. *A hall of justice*

Sound trumpets. Enter the KING, *the* QUEEN, GLOU-
CESTER, YORK, SUFFOLK, *and* SALISBURY; *the*
DUCHESS OF GLOUCESTER, MARGERY JOURDAIN,
SOUTHWELL, HUME, *and* BOLINGBROKE, *under
guard.*

King. Stand forth, Dame Eleanor Cobham,
Gloucester's wife:
In sight of God and us, your guilt is great:
Receive the sentence of the law for sins
Such as by God's book are adjudged to death.
You four, from hence to prison back again;
From thence unto the place of execution:
The witch in Smithfield shall be burn'd to ashes,
And you three shall be strangled on the gallows.
You, madam, for you are more nobly born,
Despoiled of your honour in your life, 10
Shall, after three days' open penance done,
Live in your country here in banishment,
With Sir John Stanley, in the Isle of Man.
Duch. Welcome is banishment; welcome were
my death.
Glou. Eleanor, the law, thou see'st, hath
judged thee:
I cannot justify whom the law condemns.
[*Exeunt* DUCHESS *and other prisoners, guarded.*
Mine eyes are full of tears, my heart of grief.
Ah, Humphrey, this dishonour in thine age
Will bring thy head with sorrow to the ground!
I beseech your Majesty, give me leave to go; 20
Sorrow would solace and mine age would ease.
King. Stay, Humphrey Duke of Gloucester:
ere thou go,
Give up thy staff; Henry will to himself
Protector be; and God shall be my hope,
My stay, my guide and lantern to my feet:
And go in peace, Humphrey, no less beloved
Than when thou wert Protector to thy king.
Queen. I see no reason why a king of years
Should be to be protected like a child.
God and King Henry govern England's realm. 30
Give up your staff, sir, and the King his realm.
Glou. My staff? here, noble Henry, is my staff:
As willingly do I the same resign

As e'er thy father Henry made it mine;
And even as willingly at thy feet I leave it
As others would ambitiously receive it.
Farewell, good king: when I am dead and gone,
May honourable peace attend thy throne! [*Exit.*
  Queen. Why, now is Henry king, and Margaret
    queen;
And Humphrey Duke of Gloucester scarce him-
    self,　　40
That bears so shrewd a maim; two pulls at once;
His lady banish'd, and a limb lopp'd off.
This staff of honour raught, there let it stand
Where it best fits to be, in Henry's hand.
  Suf. Thus droops this lofty pine and hangs his
    sprays;
Thus Eleanor's pride dies in her youngest days.
  York. Lords, let him go. Please it your majesty,
This is the day appointed for the combat;
And ready are the appellant and defendant,
The armourer and his man, to enter the lists,　　50
So please your Highness to behold the fight.
  Queen. Ay, good my lord; for purposely there-
    fore
Left I the court, to see this quarrel tried.
  King. O' God's name, see the lists and all things
    fit:
Here let them end it; and God defend the right!
  York. I never saw a fellow worse bested,
Or more afraid to fight, than is the appellant,
The servant of this armourer, my lords.

Enter at one door, HORNER, *the Armourer, and his*
NEIGHBOURS, *drinking to him so much that he is*
drunk; and he enters with a drum before him and
his staff with a sand-bag fastened to it; and at the
other door PETER, *his man, with a drum and sand-*
bag, and 'PRENTICES *drinking to him.*

  1st Neigh. Here, neighbour Horner, I drink to
you in a cup of sack: and fear not, neighbour, you
shall do well enough.　　61
  2nd Neigh. And here, neighbour, here's a cup
of charneco.
  3rd Neigh. And here's a pot of good double
beer, neighbour: drink, and fear not your man.
  Hor. Let it come, i' faith, and I'll pledge you all;
and a fig for Peter!
  1st 'Pren. Here, Peter, I drink to thee: and be
not afraid.
  2nd 'Pren. Be merry, Peter, and fear not thy
master: fight for credit of the 'prentices.　　71
  Peter. I thank you all: drink, and pray for me,
I pray you; for I think I have taken my last
draught in this world. Here, Robin, an if I die, I
give thee my apron: and, Will, thou shall have
my hammer: and here, Tom, take all the money
that I have. O Lord bless me! I pray God! for

I am never able to deal with my master, he hath
learnt so much fence already.
  Sal. Come, leave your drinking, and fall to
blows. Sirrah, what's thy name?　　81
  Peter. Peter, forsooth.
  Sal. Peter! what more?
  Peter. Thump.
  Sal. Thump! then see thou thump thy master
well.
  Hor. Masters, I am come hither, as it were, up-
on my man's instigation, to prove him a knave
and myself an honest man: and touching the
Duke of York, I will take my death, I never
meant him any ill, nor the King, nor the Queen:
and therefore, Peter, have at thee with a down-
right blow!
  York. Dispatch: this knave's tongue begins to
    double.
Sound, trumpets, alarum to the combatants!
  Alarum. They fight, and PETER *strikes him down.*
  Hor. Hold, Peter, hold! I confess, I confess
treason.　　　　　　　　　　　　　　　　[*Dies.*
  York. Take away his weapon. Fellow, thank
God, and the good wine in thy master's way.　　99
  Peter. O God, have I overcome mine enemy in
this presence? O Peter, thou hast prevailed in
right!
  King. Go, take hence that traitor from our
    sight;
For by his death we do perceive his guilt:
And God in justice hath reveal'd to us
The truth and innocence of this poor fellow,
Which he had thought to have murder'd wrong-
    fully.
Come, fellow, follow us for thy reward.
          [*Sound a flourish. Exeunt.*

SCENE IV. *A street*

Enter GLOUCESTER *and his* SERVINGMEN, *in*
mourning cloaks.

  Glou. Thus sometimes hath the brightest day
    a cloud;
And after summer evermore succeeds
Barren winter, with his wrathful nipping cold:
So cares and joys abound, as seasons fleet.
Sirs, what's o'clock?
  Serv.　　　　　　　　Ten, my lord.
  Glou. Ten is the hour that was appointed me
To watch the coming of my punish'd duchess:
Uneath may she endure the flinty streets,
To tread them with her tender-feeling feet.
Sweet Nell, ill can thy noble mind abrook　　10
The abject people gazing on thy face,
With envious looks, laughing at thy shame,
That erst did follow thy proud chariot-wheels

When thou didst ride in triumph through the
    streets.
But, soft! I think she comes; and I'll prepare
My tear-stain'd eyes to see her miseries.

Enter the DUCHESS OF GLOUCESTER *in a white sheet,
and a taper burning in her hand; with* SIR JOHN
STANLEY, *the* SHERIFF, *and Officers.*

Serv. So please your Grace, we'll take her from
    the sheriff.
Glou. No, stir not, for your lives; let her pass by.
Duch. Come you, my lord, to see my open shame?
Now thou dost penance too. Look how they gaze!
See how the giddy multitude do point,   21
And nod their heads, and throw their eyes on
    thee!
Ah, Gloucester, hide thee from their hateful
    looks,
And, in thy closet pent up, rue my shame,
And ban thine enemies, both mine and thine!
Glou. Be patient, gentle Nell; forget this grief.
Duch. Ah, Gloucester, teach me to forget my-
    self!
For whilst I think I am thy married wife
And thou a prince, Protector of this land,
Methinks I should not thus be led along,   30
Mail'd up in shame, with papers on my back,
And follow'd with a rabble that rejoice
To see my tears and hear my deep-fet groans.
The ruthless flint doth cut my tender feet,
And when I start, the envious people laugh
And bid me be advised how I tread.
Ah, Humphrey, can I bear this shameful yoke?
Trow'st thou that e'er I'll look upon the world,
Or count them happy that enjoy the sun?
No; dark shall be my light and night my day;   40
To think upon my pomp shall be my hell.
Sometime I'll say I am Duke Humphrey's wife,
And he a prince and ruler of the land:
Yet so he ruled and such a prince he was
As he stood by whilst I, his forlorn duchess,
Was made a wonder and a pointing-stock
To every idle rascal follower.
But be thou mild and blush not at my shame,
Nor stir at nothing till the axe of death
Hang over thee, as, sure, it shortly will;   50
For Suffolk, he that can do all in all
With her that hateth thee and hates us all,
And York and impious Beaufort, that false priest,
Have all limed bushes to betray thy wings,
And, fly thou how thou canst, they'll tangle thee:
But fear not thou, until thy foot be snared,
Nor never seek prevention of thy foes.
Glou. Ah, Nell, forbear! thou aimest all awry;
I must offend before I be attainted;

And had I twenty times so many foes,   60
And each of them had twenty times their power,
All these could not procure me any scathe,
So long as I am loyal, true and crimeless.
Wouldst have me rescue thee from this reproach?
Why, yet thy scandal were not wiped away,
But I in danger for the breach of law.
Thy greatest help is quiet, gentle Nell:
I pray thee, sort thy heart to patience;
These few days' wonder will be quickly worn.

Enter a HERALD.

Her. I summon your Grace to his Majesty's
    parliament,   70
Holden at Bury the first of this next month.
Glou. And my consent ne'er ask'd herein be-
    fore!
This is close dealing. Well, I will be there.
                                        [*Exit* HERALD
My Nell, I take my leave: and, master sheriff,
Let not her penance exceed the King's commis-
    sion.
Sher. An't please your Grace, here my commis-
    sion stays,
And Sir John Stanley is appointed now
To take her with him to the Isle of Man.
Glou. Must you, Sir John, protect my lady here?
Stan. So am I given in charge, may't please your
    Grace.   80
Glou. Entreat her not the worse in that I pray
You use her well: the world may laugh again;
And I may live to do you kindness if
You do it her: and so, Sir John, farewell!
Duch. What, gone, my lord, and bid me not
    farewell!
Glou. Witness my tears, I cannot stay to speak.
            [*Exeunt* GLOUCESTER *and* SERVINGMEN.
Duch. Art thou gone too? all comfort go with
    thee!
For none abides with me: my joy is death;
Death, at whose name I oft have been afear'd,
Because I wish'd this world's eternity.   90
Stanley, I prithee, go, and take me hence;
I care not whither, for I beg no favour,
Only convey me where thou art commanded.
Stan. Why, madam, that is to the Isle of Man;
There to be used according to your state.
Duch. That's bad enough, for I am but re-
    proach:
And shall I then be used reproachfully?
Stan. Like to a duchess, and Duke Hum-
    phrey's lady.
According to that state you shall be used.   99
Duch. Sheriff, farewell, and better than I fare,
Although thou hast been conduct of my shame.
Sher. It is my office; and, madam, pardon me.

Duch. Ay, ay, farewell; thy office is discharged.
Come, Stanley, shall we go?
  Stan. Madam, your penance done, throw off
    this sheet,
And go we to attire you for our journey.
  Duch. My shame will not be shifted with my
    sheet:
No, it will hang upon my richest robes
And show itself, attire me how I can.
Go, lead the way; I long to see my prison.   *110*
                                 [Exeunt.

ACT III

SCENE I. *The Abbey at Bury St. Edmund's*

Sound a sennet. Enter the KING, *the* QUEEN, CAR-
DINAL BEAUFORT, SUFFOLK, YORK, BUCKING-
HAM, SALISBURY *and* WARWICK *to the Parlia-
ment.*

King. I muse my Lord of Gloucester is not
  come:
'Tis not his wont to be the hindmost man,
Whate'er occasion keeps him from us now.
  Queen. Can you not see? or will ye not observe
The strangeness of his alter'd countenance?
With what a majesty he bears himself,
How insolent of late he is become,
How proud, how peremptory, and unlike him-
  self?
We know the time since he was mild and affable,
And if we did but glance a far-off look,   *10*
Immediately he was upon his knee,
That all the court admired him for submission:
But meet him now, and, be it in the morn,
When every one will give the time of day,
He knits his brow and shows an angry eye
And passeth by with stiff unbowed knee,
Disdaining duty that to us belongs.
Small curs are not regarded when they grin;
But great men tremble when the lion roars;
And Humphrey is no little man in England.   *20*
First note that he is near you in descent,
And should you fall, he is the next will mount.
Me seemeth then it is no policy,
Respecting what a rancorous mind he bears
And his advantage following your decease,
That he should come about your royal person
Or be admitted to your Highness' council.
By flattery hath he won the commons' hearts,
And when he please to make commotion,
'Tis to be fear'd they all will follow him.   *30*
Now 'tis the spring, and weeds are shallow-
  rooted;
Suffer them now, and they'll o'ergrow the garden
And choke the herbs for want of husbandry.
The reverent care I bear unto my lord

Made me collect these dangers in the Duke.
If it be fond, call it a woman's fear;
Which fear if better reasons can supplant,
I will subscribe and say I wrong'd the Duke.
My Lord of Suffolk, Buckingham, and York,
Reprove my allegation, if you can;   *40*
Or else conclude my words effectual.
  Suf. Well hath your Highness seen into this
    duke;
And, had I first been put to speak my mind,
I think I should have told your Grace's tale.
The Duchess by his subornation,
Upon my life, began her devilish practices:
Or, if he were not privy to those faults,
Yet, by reputing of his high descent,
As next the King he was successive heir,
And such high vaunts of his nobility,   *50*
Did instigate the bedlam brain-sick Duchess
By wicked means to frame our sovereign's fall.
Smooth runs the water where the brook is deep;
And in his simple show he harbours treason.
The fox barks not when he would steal the lamb.
No, no, my sovereign; Gloucester is a man
Unsounded yet and full of deep deceit.
  Car. Did he not, contrary to form of law,
Devise strange deaths for small offences done?
  York. And did he not, in his protectorship,   *60*
Levy great sums of money through the realm
For soldiers' pay in France, and never sent it?
By means whereof the towns each day revolted.
  Buck. Tut, these are petty faults to faults
    unknown,
Which time will bring to light in smooth Duke
  Humphrey.
  King. My lords, at once: the care you have of
    us,
To mow down thorns that would annoy our foot,
Is worthy praise: but, shall I speak my con-
  science,
Our kinsman Gloucester is as innocent
From meaning treason to our royal person   *70*
As is the sucking lamb or harmless dove:
The Duke is virtuous, mild and too well given
To dream on evil or to work my downfall.
  Queen. Ah, what's more dangerous than this
    fond affiance!
Seems he a dove? his feathers are but borrow'd,
For he's disposed as the hateful raven:
Is he a lamb? his skin is surely lent him,
For he's inclined as is the ravenous wolf.
Who cannot steal a shape that means deceit?
Take heed, my lord; the welfare of us all   *80*
Hangs on the cutting short that fraudful man.

Enter SOMERSET.

  Som. All health unto my gracious sovereign!

King. Welcome, Lord Somerset. What news
  from France?

Som. That all your interest in those territories
Is utterly bereft you; all is lost.

King. Cold news, Lord Somerset: but God's
  will be done!

York. [*Aside*] Cold news for me; for I had hope
  of France
As firmly as I hope for fertile England.
Thus are my blossoms blasted in the bud
And caterpillars eat my leaves away;   90
But I will remedy this gear ere long,
Or sell my title for a glorious grave.

        Enter GLOUCESTER.

Glou. All happiness unto my lord the king!
Pardon, my liege, that I have stay'd so long.

Suf. Nay, Gloucester, know that thou art
  come too soon,
Unless thou wert more loyal than thou art.
I do arrest thee of high treason here.

Glou.Well, Suffolk, thou shalt not see me
  blush
Nor change my countenance for this arrest:
A heart unspotted is not easily daunted.   100
The purest spring is not so free from mud
As I am clear from treason to my sovereign:
Who can accuse me? wherein am I guilty?

York. 'Tis thought, my lord, that you took
  bribes of France,
And, being Protector, stay'd the soldiers' pay;
By means whereof his Highness hath lost France.

Glou. Is it but thought so? what are they that
  think it?
I never robb'd the soldiers of their pay,
Nor ever had one penny bribe from France.
So help me God, as I have watch'd the night,   110
Ay, night by night, in studying good for Eng-
  land,
That doit that e'er I wrested from the king,
Or any groat I hoarded to my use,
Be brought against me at my trial-day!
No; many a pound of mine own proper store,
Because I would not tax the needy commons,
Have I dispursed to the garrisons,
And never ask'd for restitution.

Car. It serves you well, my lord, to say so
  much.

Glou. I say no more than truth, so help me
  God!   120

York. In your protectorship you did devise
Strange tortures for offenders never heard of,
That England was defamed by tyranny.

Glou. Why, 'tis well known that, whiles I was
  Protector,
Pity was all the fault that was in me;
For I should melt at an offender's tears,

And lowly words were ransom for their fault.
Unless it were a bloody murderer,
Or foul felonious thief that fleeced poor passen-
  gers,
I never gave them condign punishment: 130
Murder indeed, that bloody sin, I tortured
Above the felon or what trespass else.

Suf. My lord, these faults are easy, quickly
  answer'd:
But mightier crimes are laid unto your charge,
Whereof you cannot easily purge yourself.
I do arrest you in his Highness' name;
And here commit you to my Lord Cardinal
To keep, until your further time of trial.

King. My Lord of Gloucester, 'tis my special
  hope
That you will clear yourself from all suspect: 140
My conscience tells me you are innocent.

Glou. Ah, gracious lord, these days are dan-
  gerous:
Virtue is choked with foul ambition
And charity chased hence by rancour's hand;
Foul subornation is predominant
And equity exiled your Highness' land.
I know their complot is to have my life,
And if my death might make this island happy
And prove the period of their tyranny,
I would expend it with all willingness: 150
But mine is made the prologue to their play;
For thousands more, that yet suspect no peril,
Will not conclude their plotted tragedy.
Beaufort's red sparkling eyes blab his heart's
  malice,
And Suffolk's cloudy brow his stormy hate;
Sharp Buckingham unburthens with his tongue
The envious load that lies upon his heart;
And dogged York, that reaches at the moon,
Whose overweening arm I have pluck'd back,
By false accuse doth level at my life: 160
And you, my sovereign lady, with the rest,
Causeless have laid disgraces on my head
And with your best endeavour have stirr'd up
My liefest liege to be mine enemy:
Ay, all of you have laid your heads together—
Myself had notice of your conventicles—
And all to make away my guiltless life.
I shall not want false witness to condemn me,
Nor store of treasons to augment my guilt;
The ancient proverb will be well effected: 170
"A staff is quickly found to beat a dog."

Car. My liege, his railing is intolerable:
If those that care to keep your royal person
From treason's secret knife and traitors' rage
Be thus upbraided, chid, and rated at,
And the offender granted scope of speech,
'Twill make them cool in zeal unto your Grace.

Suf. Hath he not twit our sovereign lady here
With ignominious words, though clerkly
   couch'd,
As if she had suborned some to swear   180
False allegations to o'erthrow his state?
  Queen. But I can give the loser leave to chide.
  Glou. Far truer spoke than meant: I lose,
   indeed;
Beshrew the winners, for they play'd me false!
And well such losers may have leave to speak.
  Buck. He'll wrest the sense and hold us here all
   day:
Lord Cardinal, he is your prisoner.
  Car. Sirs, take away the Duke, and guard him
   sure.
  Glou. Ah! thus King Henry throws away his
   crutch
Before his legs be firm to bear his body.   190
Thus is the shepherd beaten from thy side
And wolves are gnarling who shall gnaw thee first.
Ah, that my fear were false! ah, that it were!
For, good King Henry, thy decay I fear.
               [Exit guarded.
  King. My lords, what to your wisdoms seem-
   eth best,
Do or undo, as if ourself were here.
  Queen. What, will your Highness leave the par-
   liament?
  King. Ay, Margaret; my heart is drown'd with
   grief,
Whose flood begins to flow within mine eyes,
My body round engirt with misery,   200
For what's more miserable than discontent?
Ah, uncle Humphrey! in thy face I see
The map of honour, truth and loyalty:
And yet, good Humphrey, is the hour to come
That e'er I proved thee false or fear'd thy faith.
What louring star now envies thy estate,
That these great lords and Margaret our queen
Do seek subversion of thy harmless life?
Thou never didst them wrong nor no man wrong;
And as the butcher takes away the calf   210
And binds the wretch and beats it when it strays,
Bearing it to the bloody slaughter-house,
Even so remorseless have they borne him hence;
And as the dam runs lowing up and down,
Looking the way her harmless young one went,
And can do nought but wail her darling's loss,
Even so myself bewails good Gloucester's case
With sad unhelpful tears, and with dimm'd eyes
Look after him and cannot do him good,
So mighty are his vowed enemies.   220
His fortunes I will weep and 'twixt each groan
Say, "Who's a traitor? Gloucester he is none."
  [Exeunt all but QUEEN, CARDINAL BEAUFORT,
SUFFOLK, *and* YORK; SOMERSET *remains apart.*

  Queen. Free lords, cold snow melts with the
   sun's hot beams.
Henry my lord is cold in great affairs,
Too full of foolish pity, and Gloucester's show
Beguiles him as the mournful crocodile
With sorrow snares relenting passengers,
Or as the snake roll'd in a flowering bank,
With shining checker'd slough, doth sting a
   child
That for the beauty thinks it excellent.   230
Believe me, lords, were none more wise than I—
And yet herein I judge mine own wit good—
This Gloucester should be quickly rid the world,
To rid us from the fear we have of him.
  Car. That he should die is worthy policy;
But yet we want a colour for his death:
'Tis meet he be condemn'd by course of law.
  Suf. But, in my mind, that were no policy:
The King will labour still to save his life,
The commons haply rise, to save his life;   240
And yet we have but trivial argument,
More than mistrust, that shows him worthy
   death.
  York. So that, by this, you would not have him
   die.
  Suf. Ah, York, no man alive so fain as I!
  York. 'Tis York that hath more reason for his
   death.
But, my Lord Cardinal, and you, my Lord of
   Suffolk,
Say as you think, and speak it from your souls,
Were't not all one, an empty eagle were set
To guard the chicken from a hungry kite,
As place Duke Humphrey for the King's Pro-
   tector?   250
  Queen. So the poor chicken should be sure of
   death.
  Suf. Madam, 'tis true; and were't not madness,
   then,
To make the fox surveyor of the fold?
Who being accused a crafty murderer,
His guilt should be but idly posted over,
Because his purpose is not executed.
No; let him die, in that he is a fox,
By nature proved an enemy to the flock,
Before his chaps be stain'd with crimson blood,
As Humphrey, proved by reasons, to my liege.
And do not stand on quillets how to slay him: 261
Be it by gins, by snares, by subtlety,
Sleeping or waking, 'tis no matter how,
So he be dead; for that is good deceit
Which mates him first that first intends deceit.
  Queen. Thrice-noble Suffolk, 'tis resolutely
   spoke.
  Suf. Not resolute, except so much were done;
For things are often spoke and seldom meant:

But that my heart accordeth with my tongue,
Seeing the deed is meritorious,   *270*
And to preserve my sovereign from his foe,
Say but the word, and I will be his priest.

Car. But I would have him dead, my Lord of
    Suffolk,
Ere you can take due orders for a priest:
Say you consent and censure well the deed,
And I'll provide his executioner,
I tender so the safety of my liege.

Suf. Here is my hand, the deed is worthy
    doing.

Queen. And so say I.

York. And I: and now we three have spoke
    it,   *280*
It skills not greatly who impugns our doom.

Enter a POST.

Post. Great lords, from Ireland am I come
    amain,
To signify that rebels there are up
And put the Englishmen unto the sword:
Send succours, lords, and stop the rage betime,
Before the wound do grow uncurable;
For, being green, there is great hope of help.

Car. A breach that craves a quick expedient
    stop!
What counsel give you in this weighty cause?

York. That Somerset be sent as regent thither:
'Tis meet that lucky ruler be employ'd;   *291*
Witness the fortune he hath had in France.

Som. If York, with all his far-fet policy,
Had been the regent there instead of me,
He never would have stay'd in France so long.

York. No, not to lose it all, as thou hast done:
I rather would have lost my life betimes
Than bring a burthen of dishonour home
By staying there so long till all were lost.
Show me one scar character'd on thy skin: *300*
Men's flesh preserved so whole do seldom win.

Queen. Nay, then, this spark will prove a raging
    fire,
If wind and fuel be brought to feed it with:
No more, good York; sweet Somerset, be still:
Thy fortune, York, hadst thou been regent there,
Might happily have proved far worse than his.

York. What, worse than nought? nay, then, a
    shame take all!

Som. And, in the number, thee that wishest
    shame!

Car. My Lord of York, try what your fortune is.
The uncivil kerns of Ireland are in arms   *310*
And temper clay with blood of Englishmen:
To Ireland will you lead a band of men,
Collected choicely, from each county some,
And try your hap against the Irishmen?

York. I will, my lord, so please his Majesty.

Suf. Why, our authority is his consent,
And what we do establish he confirms:
Then, noble York, take thou this task in hand.

York. I am content: provide me soldiers, lords,
Whiles I take order for mine own affairs.   *320*

Suf. A charge, Lord York, that I will see per-
    form'd.
But now return we to the false Duke Humphrey.

Car. No more of him, for I will deal with him
That henceforth he shall trouble us no more.
And so break off; the day is almost spent:
Lord Suffolk, you and I must talk of that event.

York. My Lord of Suffolk, within fourteen days
At Bristol I expect my soldiers;
For there I'll ship them all for Ireland.

Suf. I'll see it truly done, my Lord of York.
    [*Exeunt all but* YORK.

York. Now, York, or never, steel thy fearful
    thoughts,   *331*
And change misdoubt to resolution:
Be that thou hopest to be, or what thou art
Resign to death; it is not worth the enjoying:
Let pale-faced fear keep with the mean-born man,
And find no harbour in a royal heart.
Faster than spring-time showers comes thought
    on thought,
And not a thought but thinks on dignity.
My brain more busy than the labouring spider
Weaves tedious snares to trap mine enemies. *340*
Well, nobles, well, 'tis politicly done,
To send me packing with an host of men:
I fear me you but warm the starved snake,
Who, cherish'd in your breasts, will sting your
    hearts.
'Twas men I lack'd and you will give them me
I take it kindly; yet be well assured
You put sharp weapons in a madman's hands.
Whiles I in Ireland nourish a mighty band,
I will stir up in England some black storm
Shall blow ten thousand souls to heaven or hell;
And this fell tempest shall not cease to rage   *351*
Until the golden circuit on my head,
Like to the glorious sun's transparent beams,
Do calm the fury of this mad-bred flaw.
And, for a minister of my intent,
I have seduced a headstrong Kentishman,
John Cade of Ashford,
To make commotion, as full well he can,
Under the title of John Mortimer.
In Ireland have I seen this stubborn Cade   *360*
Oppose himself against a troop of kerns,
And fought so long, till that his thighs with darts
Were almost like a sharp-quill'd porpentine;
And, in the end being rescued, I have seen
Him caper upright like a wild Morisco,

Shaking the bloody darts as he his bells.
Full often, like a shag-hair'd crafty kern,
Hath he conversed with the enemy,
And undiscover'd come to me again
And given me notice of their villainies.   370
This devil here shall be my substitute;
For that John Mortimer, which now is dead,
In face, in gait, in speech, he doth resemble:
By this I shall perceive the commons' mind,
How they affect the house and claim of York.
Say he be taken, rack'd and tortured,
I know no pain they can inflict upon him
Will make him say I moved him to those arms.
Say that he thrive, as 'tis great like he will,
Why, then from Ireland come I with my strength
And reap the harvest which that rascal sow'd; 381
For Humphrey being dead, as he shall be,
And Henry put apart, the next for me.   [*Exit.*

SCENE II. *Bury St Edmund's: A room of state*
Enter certain MURDERERS, *hastily.*

1st Mur. Run to my Lord of Suffolk; let him
    know
We have dispatch'd the Duke, as he commanded.
2nd Mur. O that it were to do! What have we
    done?
Didst ever hear a man so penitent?

Enter SUFFOLK.

1st Mur. Here comes my lord.
Suf. Now, sirs, have you dispatch'd this thing?
1st Mur. Ay, my good lord, he's dead.
Suf. Why, that's well said. Go, get you to my
    house;
I will reward you for this venturous deed.
The King and all the peers are here at hand.   10
Have you laid fair the bed? Is all things well,
According as I gave directions?
1st Mur. 'Tis, my good lord.
Suf. Away! be gone.   [*Exeunt* MURDERERS.

Sound trumpets. Enter the KING, *the* QUEEN, CARDI-
NAL BEAUFORT, SOMERSET, *with Attendants.*

King. Go, call our uncle to our presence
    straight;
Say we intend to try his Grace to-day,
If he be guilty, as 'tis published.
Suf. I'll call him presently, my noble lord.
          [*Exit.*
King. Lords, take your places; and, I pray you
    all,
Proceed no straiter 'gainst our uncle Gloucester
Than from true evidence of good esteem   21
He be approved in practice culpable.
Queen. God forbid any malice should prevail,
That faultless may condemn a nobleman!

Pray God he may acquit him of suspicion!
King. I thank thee, Meg; these words content
    me much.

Re-enter SUFFOLK.

How now! why look'st thou pale? why tremblest
    thou?
Where is our uncle? what's the matter, Suffolk?
Suf. Dead in his bed, my lord; Gloucester is
    dead.
Queen. Marry, God forfend!   30
Car. God's secret judgement: I did dream to-
    night
The Duke was dumb and could not speak a word.
          The KING *swoons.*
Queen. How fares my lord? Help, lords! the
    King is dead.
Som. Rear up his body; wring him by the nose.
Queen. Run, go, help, help! O Henry, ope thine
    eyes!
Suf. He doth revive again: madam, be patient.
King. O heavenly God!
Queen.   How fares my gracious lord?
Suf. Comfort, my sovereign! gracious Henry,
    comfort!
King. What, doth my Lord of Suffolk comfort
    me?
Came he right now to sing a raven's note,   40
Whose dismal tune bereft my vital powers;
And thinks he that the chirping of a wren,
By crying comfort from a hollow breast,
Can chase away the first-conceived sound?
Hide not thy poison with such sugar'd words:
Lay not thy hands on me; forbear, I say;
Their touch affrights me as a serpent's sting.
Thou baleful messenger, out of my sight!
Upon thy eye-balls murderous tyranny
Sits in grim majesty, to fright the world.   50
Look not upon me, for thine eyes are wounding:
Yet do not go away: come, basilisk,
And kill the innocent gazer with thy sight;
For in the shade of death I shall find joy:
In life but double death, now Gloucester's dead.
  Queen. Why do you rate my Lord of Suffolk
    thus?
Although the Duke was enemy to him,
Yet he most Christian-like laments his death:
And for myself, foe as he was to me,
Might liquid tears or heart-offending groans   60
Or blood-consuming sighs recall his life,
I would be blind with weeping, sick with groans,
Look pale as primrose with blood-drinking sighs,
And all to have the noble Duke alive.
What know I how the world may deem of me?
For it is known we were but hollow friends:
It may be judged I made the Duke away;

So shall my name with slander's tongue be
  wounded,
And princes' courts be fill'd with my reproach.
This get I by his death: ay me, unhappy!   70
To be a queen, and crown'd with infamy!
  King. Ah, woe is me for Gloucester, wretched
  man!
  Queen. Be woe for me, more wretched than he
  is.
What, dost thou turn away and hide thy face?
I am no loathsome leper; look on me.
What! art thou, like the adder, waxen deaf?
Be poisonous too and kill thy forlorn queen.
Is all thy comfort shut in Gloucester's tomb?
Why, then, Dame Margaret was ne'er thy joy.
Erect his statua and worship it,   80
And make my image but an alehouse sign.
Was I for this nigh wreck'd upon the sea
And twice by awkward wind from England's
  bank
Drove back again unto my native clime?
What boded this, but well forewarning wind
Did seem to say, "Seek not a scorpion's nest,
Nor set no footing on this unkind shore"?
What did I then, but cursed the gentle gusts
And he that loosed them forth their brazen caves:
And bid them blow towards England's blessed
  shore,   90
Or turn our stern upon a dreadful rock?
Yet Æolus would not be a murderer,
But left that hateful office unto thee:
The pretty-vaulting sea refused to drown me,
Knowing that thou wouldst have me drown'd on
  shore
With tears as salt as sea, through thy unkindness:
The splitting rocks cower'd in the sinking sands
And would not dask me with their ragged sides,
Because thy flinty heart, more hard than they,
Might in thy palace perish Margaret.   100
As far as I could ken thy chalky cliffs,
When from thy shore the tempest beat us back,
I stood upon the hatches in the storm,
And when the dusky sky began to rob
My earnest-gaping sight of thy land's view,
I took a costly jewel from my neck,
A heart it was, bound in with diamonds,
And threw it towards thy land: the sea received
  it,
And so I wish'd thy body might my heart:
And even with this I lost fair England's view   110
And bid mine eyes be packing with my heart
And call'd them blind and dusky spectacles,
For losing ken of Albion's wished coast.
How often have I tempted Suffolk's tongue,
The agent of thy foul inconstancy,
To sit and witch me, as Ascanius did

When he to madding Dido would unfold
His father's acts commenced in burning Troy!
Am I not witch'd like her? or thou not false like
  him?
Ay me, I can no more! die, Margaret!   120
For Henry weeps that thou dost live so long.

Noise within. Enter WARWICK, SALISBURY,
and many COMMONS.

  War. It is reported, mighty sovereign,
That good Duke Humphrey traitorously is mur-
  der'd
By Suffolk and the Cardinal Beaufort's means.
The commons, like an angry hive of bees
That want their leader, scatter up and down
And care not who they sting in his revenge.
Myself have calm'd their spleenful mutiny,
Until they hear the order of his death.
  King. That he is dead, good Warwick, 'tis too
  true;   130
But how he died God knows, not Henry:
Enter his chamber, view his breathless corpse,
And comment then upon his sudden death.
  War. That shall I do, my liege. Stay, Salis-
  bury,
With the rude multitude till I return.   [*Exit.*
  King. O Thou that judgest all things, stay my
  thoughts,
My thoughts, that labour to persuade my soul
Some violent hands were laid on Humphrey's
  life!
If my suspect be false, forgive me, God,
For judgement only doth belong to thee.   140
Fain would I go to chafe his paly lips
With twenty thousand kisses and to drain
Upon his face an ocean of salt tears,
To tell my love unto his dumb deaf trunk
And with my fingers feel his hand unfeeling:
But all in vain are these mean obsequies;
And to survey his dead and earthly image,
What were it but to make my sorrow greater?

Re-enter WARWICK *and others, bearing Gloucester's
body on a bed.*

  War. Come hither, gracious sovereign, view
  this body.
  King. That is to see how deep my grave is
  made;   150
For with his soul fled all my worldly solace,
For seeing him I see my life in death.
  War. As surely as my soul intends to live
With that dread King that took our state upon
  him
To free us from his father's wrathful curse,
I do believe that violent hands were laid
Upon the life of this thrice-famed duke.

Suf. A dreadful oath, sworn with a solemn
   tongue!
What instance gives Lord Warwick for his vow?
   War. See how the blood is settled in his face.
Oft have I seen a timely-parted ghost,   *161*
Of ashy semblance, meagre, pale and bloodless,
Being all descended to the labouring heart;
Who, in the conflict that it holds with death,
Attracts the same for aidance 'gainst the enemy;
Which with the heart there cools and ne'er re-
   turneth
To blush and beautify the cheek again.
But see, his face is black and full of blood,
His eye-balls further out than when he lived,
Staring full ghastly like a strangled man;   *170*
His hair uprear'd, his nostrils stretched with
   struggling;
His hands abroad display'd, as one that grasp'd
And tugg'd for life and was by strength subdued:
Look, on the sheets his hair, you see, is sticking;
His well-proportion'd beard made rough and
   rugged,
Like to the summer's corn by tempest lodged.
It cannot be but he was murder'd here;
The least of all these signs were probable.
   Suf. Why, Warwick, who should do the Duke
   to death?
Myself and Beaufort had him in protection;   *180*
And we, I hope, sir, are no murderers.
   War. But both of you were vow'd Duke Hum-
   phrey's foes,
And you, forsooth, had the good Duke to keep:
'Tis like you would not feast him like a friend;
And 'tis well seen he found an enemy.
   Queen. Then you, belike, suspect these noble-
   men
As guilty of Duke Humphrey's timeless death.
   War. Who finds the heifer dead and bleeding
   fresh
And sees fast by a butcher with an axe,
But will suspect 'twas he that made the slaughter?
Who finds the partridge in the puttock's nest,   *191*
But may imagine how the bird was dead,
Although the kite soar with unbloodied beak?
Even so suspicious is this tragedy.
   Queen. Are you the butcher, Suffolk? Where's
   your knife?
Is Beaufort term'd a kite? Where are his talons?
   Suf. I wear no knife to slaughter sleeping men;
But here's a vengeful sword, rusted with ease,
That shall be scoured in his rancorous heart   *199*
That slanders me with murder's crimson badge.
Say, if thou darest, proud Lord of Warwick-
   shire,
That I am faulty in Duke Humphrey's death.
        [*Exeunt* CARDINAL, SOMERSET, *and others*.

War. What dares not Warwick, if false Suffolk
   dare him?
   Queen. He dares not calm his contumelious spirit
Nor cease to be an arrogant controller,
Though Suffolk dare him twenty thousand times.
   War. Madam, be still; with reverence may I
   say;
For every word you speak in his behalf
Is slander to your royal dignity.
   Suf. Blunt-witted lord, ignoble in demeanour!
If ever lady wrong'd her lord so much,   *211*
Thy mother took into her blameful bed
Some stern untutor'd churl, and noble stock
Was graft with crab-tree slip; whose fruit thou
   art
And never of the Nevils' noble race.
   War. But that the guilt of murder bucklers thee
And I should rob the deathsman of his fee,
Quitting thee thereby of ten thousand shames,
And that my sovereign's presence makes me
   mild,   *219*
I would, false murderous coward, on thy knee
Make thee beg pardon for thy passed speech
And say it was thy mother that thou meant'st,
That thou thyself wast born in bastardy;
And after all this fearful homage done,
Give thee thy hire and send thy soul to hell,
Pernicious blood-sucker of sleeping men!
   Suf. Thou shalt be waking while I shed thy
   blood,
If from this presence thou darest go with me.
   War. Away even now, or I will drag thee hence:
Unworthy though thou art, I'll cope with thee *230*
And do some service to Duke Humphrey's ghost.
        [*Exeunt* SUFFOLK *and* WARWICK.
   King. What stronger breastplate than a heart
   untainted!
Thrice is he arm'd that hath his quarrel just,
And he but naked, though lock'd up in steel,
Whose conscience with injustice is corrupted.
   A noise within.
   Queen. What noise is this?

   Re-enter SUFFOLK *and* WARWICK, *with their
      weapons drawn*.

King. Why, how now, lords! your wrathful
   weapons drawn
Here in our presence! dare you be so bold?
Why, what tumultous clamour have we here?
   Suf. The traitorous Warwick with the men of
   Bury   *240*
Set all upon me, mighty sovereign.
   Sal. [*To the* COMMONS, *entering*] Sirs, stand apart;
   the King shall know your mind.
Dread lord, the commons send you word by me,
Unless Lord Suffolk straight be done to death,

Or banished fair England's territories,
They will by violence tear him from your palace
And torture him with grievous lingering death.
They say, by him the good Duke Humphrey
   died;
They say, in him they fear your Highness' death;
And mere instinct of love and loyalty,   *250*
Free from a stubborn opposite intent,
As being thought to contradict your liking,
Makes them thus forward in his banishment.
They say, in care of your most royal person,
That if your Highness should intend to sleep
And charge that no man should disturb your rest
In pain of your dislike or pain of death,
Yet, notwithstanding such a strait edict,
Were there a serpent seen, with forked tongue,
That slily glided towards your Majesty,   *260*
It were but necessary you were waked,
Lest, being suffer'd in that harmful slumber,
The mortal worm might make the sleep eternal;
And therefore do they cry, though you forbid,
That they will guard you, whether you will or
   no,
From such fell serpents as false Suffolk is,
With whose envenomed and fatal sting,
Your loving uncle, twenty times his worth,
They say, is shamefully bereft of life.
  Commons. [*Within*] An answer from the King,
   my Lord of Salisbury!   *270*
  Suf. 'Tis like the commons, rude unpolish'd
   hinds,
Could send such message to their sovereign:
But you, my lord, were glad to be employ'd,
To show how quaint an orator you are:
But all the honour Salisbury hath won
Is, that he was the lord ambassador
Sent from a sort of tinkers to the King.
  Commons. [*Within*] An answer from the King,
   or we will all break in!
  King. Go, Salisbury, and tell them all from me,
I thank them for their tender loving care;   *280*
And had I not been cited so by them,
Yet did I purpose as they do entreat;
For, sure, my thoughts do hourly prophesy
Mischance unto my state by Suffolk's means:
And therefore, by His majesty I swear,
Whose far unworthy deputy I am,
He shall not breathe infection in this air
But three days longer, on the pain of death.
              [*Exit* SALISBURY.
  Queen. O Henry, let me plead for gentle Suffolk!
  King. Ungentle queen, to call him gentle Suf-
   folk!   *290*
No more, I say: if thou dost plead for him,
Thou wilt but add increase unto my wrath.
Had I but said, I would have kept my word,

But when I swear, it is irrevocable.
If, after three days' space, thou here be'st found
On any ground that I am ruler of,
The world shall not be ransom for thy life.
Come, Warwick, come, good Warwick, go with
  me;
I have great matters to impart to thee.
        [*Exeunt all but* QUEEN *and* SUFFOLK.
  Queen. Mischance and sorrow go along with
   you!   *300*
Heart's discontent and sour affliction
Be playfellows to keep you company!
There's two of you; the devil make a third!
And threefold vengeance tend upon your steps!
  Suf. Cease, gentle queen, these execrations
And let thy Suffolk take his heavy leave.
  Queen. Fie, coward woman and soft-hearted
   wretch!
Hast thou not spirit to curse thine enemy?
  Suf. A plague upon them! wherefore should I
   curse them?
Would curses kill, as doth the mandrake's groan,
I would invent as bitter-searching terms,   *311*
As curst, as harsh and horrible to hear,
Deliver'd strongly through my fixed teeth,
With full as many signs of deadly hate,
As lean-faced Envy in her loathsome cave:
My tongue should stumble in mine earnest words;
Mine eyes should sparkle like the beaten flint;
Mine hair be fix'd on end, as one distract;
Ay, every joint should seem to curse and ban:
And even now my burthen'd heart would break,
Should I not curse them. Poison be their
   drink!   *321*
Gall, worse than gall, the daintiest that they
   taste!
Their sweetest shade a grove of cypress trees!
Their chiefest prospect murdering basilisks!
Their softest touch as smart as lizards' stings!
Their music frightful as the serpent's hiss,
And boding screech-owls make the concert full!
All the foul terrors in dark-seated hell—
  Queen. Enough, sweet Suffolk; thou torment'st
   thyself;
And these dread curses, like the sun 'gainst glass,
Or like an overcharged gun, recoil,   *331*
And turn the force of them upon thyself.
  Suf. You bade me ban, and will you bid me
   leave?
Now, by the ground that I am banish'd from,
Well could I curse away a winter's night,
Though standing naked on a mountain top,
Where biting cold would never let grass grow,
And think it but a minute spent in sport.
  Queen. O, let me entreat thee cease. Give me
   thy hand,

That I may dew it with my mournful tears;   *340*
Nor let the rain of heaven wet this place,
To wash away my woful monuments.
O, could this kiss be printed in thy hand,
That thou mightst think upon these by the seal,
Through whom a thousand sighs are breathed
      for thee!
So, get thee gone, that I may know my grief;
'Tis but surmised whiles thou art standing by,
As one that surfeits thinking on a want.
I will repeal thee, or, be well assured,
Adventure to be banished myself: *350*
And banished I am, if but from thee.
Go; speak not to me; even now be gone.
O, go not yet! Even thus two friends condemn'd
Embrace and kiss and take ten thousand leaves,
Loather a hundred times to part than die.
Yet now farewell; and farewell life with thee!
Suf. Thus is poor Suffolk ten times banished;
Once by the king, and three times thrice by thee.
'Tis not the land I care for, wert thou thence;
A wilderness is populous enough,   *360*
So Suffolk had thy heavenly company:
For where thou art, there is the world itself,
With every several pleasure in the world,
And where thou art not, desolation.
I can no more: live thou to joy thy life;
Myself no joy in nought but that thou livest.

Enter VAUX.

Queen. Whither goes Vaux so fast? what news,
      I prithee?
Vaux. To signify unto his Majesty
That Cardinal Beaufort is at point of death;
For suddenly a grievous sickness took him,   *370*
That makes him gasp and stare and catch the air,
Blaspheming God and cursing men on earth.
Sometime he talks as if Duke Humphrey's ghost
Were by his side; sometime he calls the King
And whispers to his pillow as to him
The secrets of his overcharged soul:
And I am sent to tell his Majesty
That even now he cries aloud for him.
Queen. Go tell this heavy message to the King.
                              [*Exit* VAUX.
Ay me! what is this world! what news are these!
But wherefore grieve I at an hour's poor loss,   *381*
Omitting Suffolk's exile, my soul's treasure?
Why only, Suffolk, mourn I not for thee,
And with the southern clouds contend in tears,
Theirs for the earth's increase, mine for my
      sorrows?
Now get thee hence: the King, thou know'st, is
      coming;
If thou be found by me, thou art but dead.
Suf. If I depart from thee, I cannot live;

And in thy sight to die, what were it else
But like a pleasant slumber in thy lap?   *390*
Here could I breathe my soul into the air,
As mild and gentle as the cradle-babe
Dying with mother's dug between its lips:
Where, from thy sight, I should be raging mad
And cry out for thee to close up mine eyes,
To have thee with thy lips to stop my mouth;
So shouldst thou either turn my flying soul,
Or I should breathe it so into thy body,
And then it lived in sweet Elysium.
To die by thee were but to die in jest;   *400*
From thee to die were torture more than death:
O, let me stay, befall what may befall!
   Queen. Away! though parting be a fretful corro-
      sive,
It is applied to a deathful wound.
To France, sweet Suffolk: let me hear from thee;
For wheresoe'er thou art in this world's globe,
I'll have an Iris that shall find thee out.
   Suf. I go.
   Queen.   And take my heart with thee.
   Suf. A jewel, lock'd into the wofull'st cask
That ever did contain a thing of worth.   *410*
Even as a splitted bark, so sunder we:
This way fall I to death.
   Queen.   This way for me.
                              [*Exeunt severally.*

SCENE III. *A bedchamber*

Enter the KING, SALISBURY, WARWICK, *to the*
      CARDINAL *in bed.*

King. How fares my lord? speak, Beaufort, to
      thy sovereign.
Car. If thou be'st death, I'll give thee England's
      treasure,
Enough to purchase such another island,
So thou wilt let me live, and feel no pain.
   King. Ah, what a sign it is of evil life,
Where death's approach is seen so terrible!
   War. Beaufort, it is thy sovereign speaks to thee.
   Car. Bring me unto my trial when you will.
Died he not in his bed? where should he die?
Can I make men live, whether they will or no? *10*
O, torture me no more! I will confess.
Alive again? then show me where he is:
I'll give a thousand pound to look upon him.
He hath no eyes, the dust hath blinded them.
Comb down his hair; look, look! it stands up-
      right,
Like lime-twigs set to catch my winged soul.
Give me some drink; and bid the apothecary
Bring the strong poison that I bought of him.
   King. O thou eternal Mover of the heavens,
Look with a gentle eye upon this wretch!   *20*
O, beat away the busy meddling fiend

That lays strong siege unto this wretch's soul
And from his bosom purge this black despair!
War. See, how the pangs of death do make him
grin!
Sal. Disturb him not; let him pass peaceably.
King. Peace to his soul, if God's good pleasure
be!
Lord Cardinal, if thou think'st on heaven's bliss,
Hold up thy hand, make signal of thy hope.
He dies, and makes no sign. O God, forgive
him!   29
War. So bad a death argues a monstrous life.
King. Forbear to judge, for we are sinners all.
Close up his eyes and draw the curtain close;
And let us all to meditation.   [*Exeunt*.

ACT IV

Scene 1. *The coast of Kent*

Alarum. Fight at sea. Ordnance goes off. Enter a
CAPTAIN, *a* MASTER, *a* MASTER'S-MATE, WALTER
WHITMORE, *and others; with them* SUFFOLK, *dis-*
guised, and other gentlemen, prisoners.

Cap. The gaudy, blabbing and remorseful day
Is crept into the bosom of the sea;
And now loud-howling wolves arouse the jades
That drag the tragic melancholy night;
Who, with their drowsy, slow, and flagging
wings,
Clip dead men's graves and from their misty
jaws
Breathe foul contagious darkness in the air.
Therefore bring forth the soldiers of our prize;
For, whilst out pinnace anchors in the Downs,
Here shall they make their ransom on the sand, 10
Or with their blood stain this discolour'd shore.
Master, this prisoner freely give I thee;
And thou that art his mate, make boot of this;
The other, Walter Whitmore, is thy share.
1st Gent. What is my ransom, master? let me
know.
Mast. A thousand crowns, or else lay down your
head.
Mate. And so much shall you give, or off goes
yours.
Cap. What, think you much to pay two thou-
sand crowns,
And bear the name and port of gentlemen?
Cut both the villains' throats; for die you shall:
The lives of those which we have lost in fight   21
Be counterpoised with such a petty sum!
1st Gent. I'll give it, sir; and therefore spare my
life.
2nd Gent. And so will I and write home for it
straight.
Whit. I lost mine eye in laying the prize aboard,

And therefore to revenge it, shalt thou die;
                                        [*To* SUFFOLK.
And so should these, if I might have my will.
Cap. Be not so rash; take ransom, let him live.
Suf. Look on my George; I am a gentleman:
Rate me at what thou wilt, thou shalt be paid.   30
Whit. And so am I; my name is Walter Whit-
more.
How now! why start'st thou? what, doth death
affright?
Suf. Thy name affrights me, in whose sound is
death.
A cunning man did calculate my birth
And told me that by water I should die:
Yet let not this make thee be bloody-minded;
Thy name is Gaultier, being rightly sounded.
Whit. Gaultier or Walter, which it is, I care
not:
Never yet did base dishonour blur our name,
But with our sword we wiped away the blot;   40
Therefore, when merchant-like I sell revenge,
Broke be my sword, my arms torn and defaced,
And I proclaim'd a coward through the world!
Suf. Stay, Whitmore; for thy prisoner is a
prince,
The Duke of Suffolk, William de la Pole.
Whit. The Duke of Suffolk muffled up in
rags!
Suf. Ay, but these rags are no part of the
duke:
Jove sometime went disguised, and why not I?
Cap. But Jove was never slain, as thou shalt be.
Suf. Obscure and lowly swain, King Henry's
blood,   50
The honourable blood of Lancaster,
Must not be shed by such a jaded groom.
Hast thou not kiss'd thy hand and held my stir-
rup?
Bare-headed plodded by my foot-cloth mule
And thought thee happy when I shook my head?
How often hast thou waited at my cup,
Fed from my trencher, kneel'd down at the
board,
When I have feasted with Queen Margaret?
Remember it and let it make thee crest-fall'n,
Ay, and allay this thy abortive pride;   60
How in our voiding lobby hast thou stood
And duly waited for my coming forth?
This hand of mine hath writ in thy behalf
And therefore shall it charm thy riotous tongue.
Whit. Speak, captain, shall I stab the forlorn
swain?
Cap. First let my words stab him, as he hath
me.
Suf. Base slave, thy words are blunt and so art
thou.

Cap. Convey him hence and on our long-boat's
    side

Strike off his head.

Suf.   Thou darest not, for thy own.

Cap. Yes, Pole.

Suf.   Pole!

Cap.   Pool! Sir Pool! lord! 70

Ay, kennel, puddle, sink; whose filth and dirt
Troubles the silver spring where England drinks.
Now will I dam up this thy yawning mouth
For swallowing the treasure of the realm:
Thy lips that kiss'd the queen shall sweep the
    ground;
And thou that smiled at good Duke Humphrey's
    death
Against the senseless winds shalt grin in vain,
Who in contempt shall hiss at thee again:
And wedded be thou to the hags of hell,
For daring to affy a mighty lord   80
Unto the daughter of a worthless king,
Having neither subject, wealth, nor diadem.
By devilish policy art thou grown great
And, like ambitious Sylla, overgorged
With gobbets of thy mother's bleeding heart.
By thee Anjou and Maine were sold to France,
The false revolting Normans thorough thee
Disdain to call us lord, and Picardy
Hath slain their governors, surprised our forts
And sent the ragged soldiers wounded home. 90
The princely Warwick, and the Nevils all,
Whose dreadful swords were never drawn in
    vain,
As hating thee, are rising up in arms:
And now the house of York, thrust from the
    crown
By shameful murder of a guiltless king
And lofty proud encroaching tyranny,
Burns with revenging fire; whose hopeful colours
Advance our half-faced sun, striving to shine,
Under the which is writ "*Invitis nubibus*."
The commons here in Kent are up in arms: 100
And, to conclude, reproach and beggary
Is crept into the palace of our king,
And all by thee. Away! convey him hence.

Suf. O that I were a god, to shoot forth
    thunder
Upon these paltry, servile, abject drudges!
Small things make base men proud: this villain
    here,
Being captain of a pinnace, threatens more
Than Bargulus the strong Illyrian pirate.
Drones suck not eagles' blood but rob bee-hives:
It is impossible that I should die   110
By such a lowly vassal as thyself.
Thy words move rage and not remorse in me:
I go of message from the Queen to France;

I charge thee waft me safely cross the Channel.

Capt. Walter,—

Whit. Come, Suffolk, I must waft thee to thy
    death.

Suf. Gelidus timor occupat artus, it is thee I fear.

Whit. Thou shalt have cause to fear before I
    leave thee.

What, are ye daunted now? now will ye stoop?

1st Gent. My gracious lord, entreat him, speak
    him fair.   120

Suf. Suffolk's imperial tongue is stern and rough,
Used to command, untaught to plead for favour.
Far be it we should honour such as these
With humble suit: no, rather let my head
Stoop to the block than these knees bow to any
Save to the God of heaven and to my king;
And sooner dance upon a bloody pole
Than stand uncover'd to the vulgar groom.
True nobility is exempt from fear:
More can I bear than you dare execute.   130

Cap. Hale him away, and let him talk no more.

Suf. Come, soldiers, show what cruelty ye can,
That this my death may never be forgot!
Great men oft die by vile bezonians:
A Roman sworder and banditto slave
Murder'd sweet Tully; Brutus' bastard hand
Stabb'd Julius Cæsar; savage islanders
Pompey the Great; and Suffolk dies by pirates.

    [*Exeunt* WHITMORE *and others with* SUFFOLK.

Cap. And as for these whose ransom we have
    set,
It is our pleasure one of them depart: 140
Therefore come you with us and let him go.

    [*Exeunt all but the* FIRST GENTLEMAN.

Re-enter WHITMORE *with* SUFFOLK's *body.*

Whit. There let his head and lifeless body lie,
Until the queen his mistress bury it.   [*Exit.*

1st Gent. O barbarous and bloody spectacle!
His body will I bear unto the King:
If he revenge it not, yet will his friends;
So will the Queen, that living held him dear.

    [*Exit with the body.*

SCENE II. *Blackheath*

Enter GEORGE BEVIS *and* JOHN HOLLAND.

Bevis. Come, and get thee a sword, though made
of a lath: they have been up these two days.

Holl. They have the more need to sleep now,
then.

Bevis. I tell thee, Jack Cade the clothier means
to dress the commonwealth, and turn it, and set a
new nap upon it.

Holl. So he had need, for 'tis threadbare. Well, I
say it was never merry world in England since
gentlemen came up.   10

Bevis. O miserable age! virtue is not regarded in handicrafts-men.

Holl. The nobility think scorn to go in leather aprons.

Bevis. Nay, more, the King's council are no good workmen.

Holl. True; and yet it is said, "Labour in thy vocation"; which is as much to say as, "Let the magistrates be labouring men; and therefore should we be magistrates."   20

Bevis. Thou hast hit it; for there's no better sign of a brave mind than a hard hand.

Holl. I see them! I see them! There's Best's son, the tanner of Wingham—

Bevis. He shall have the skins of our enemies, to make dog's-leather of.

Holl. And Dick the Butcher—

Bevis. Then is sin struck down like an ox, and iniquity's throat cut like a calf.

Holl. And Smith the weaver—   30

Bevis. Argo, their thread of life is spun.

Holl. Come, come, let's fall in with them.

Drum. Enter CADE, DICK *the Butcher*, SMITH *the Weaver, and a Sawyer, with infinite numbers.*

Cade. We John Cade, so termed of our supposed father—

Dick. [*Aside*] Or rather, of stealing a cade of herrings.

Cade. For our enemies shall fall before us, inspired with the spirit of putting down kings and princes—Command silence.

Dick. Silence!   40

Cade. My father was a Mortimer—

Dick. [*Aside*] He was an honest man, and a good bricklayer.

Cade. My mother a Plantagenet—

Dick. [*Aside*] I knew her well; she was a midwife.

Cade. My wife descended of the Lacies—

Dick. [*Aside*] She was, indeed, a pedler's daughter, and sold many laces.   49

Smith. [*Aside*] But now of late, not able to travel with her furred pack, she washes bucks here at home.

Cade. Therefore am I of an honourable house.

Dick. [*Aside*] Ay, by my faith, the field is honourable; and there was he born, under a hedge, for his father had never a house but the cage.

Cade. Valiant I am.

Smith. [*Aside*] A' must needs; for beggary is valiant.

Cade. I am able to endure much.   60

Dick. [*Aside*] No question of that: for I have seen him whipped three market-days together.

Cade. I fear neither sword nor fire.

Smith. [*Aside*] He need not fear the sword; for his coat is of proof.

Dick. [*Aside*] But methinks he should stand in fear of fire, being burnt i' the hand for stealing of sheep.

Cade. Be brave, then; for your captain is brave, and vows reformation. There shall be in England seven halfpenny loaves sold for a penny: the three-hooped pot shall have ten hoops; and I will make it felony to drink small beer: all the realm shall be in common; and in Cheapside shall my palfry go to grass: and when I am king, as king I will be—

All. God save your majesty!

Cade. I thank you, good people: there shall be no money; all shall eat and drink on my score; and I will apparel them all in one livery, that they may agree like brothers and worship me their lord.

Dick. The first thing we do, let's kill all the lawyers.

Cade. Nay, that I mean to do. Is not this a lamentable thing, that of the skin of an innocent lamb should be made parchment? that parchment, being scribbled o'er, should undo a man? Some say the bee stings: but I say, 'tis the bee's wax; for I did but seal once to a thing, and I was never mine own man since. How now! who's there?   91

Enter some, bringing forward the CLERK OF
CHATHAM.

Smith. The clerk of Chatham: he can write and read and cast accompt.

Cade. O monstrous!

Smith. We took him setting of boys' copies.

Cade. Here's a villain!

Smith. Has a book in his pocket with red letters in't.

Cade. Nay, then, he is a conjurer.

Dick. Nay, he can make obligations, and write court-hand.   101

Cade. I am sorry for't: the man is a proper man, of mine honour; unless I find him guilty, he shall not die. Come hither, sirrah, I must examine thee: what is thy name?

Clerk. Emmanuel.

Dick. They use to write it on the top of letters: 'twill go hard with you.

Cade. Let me alone. Dost thou use to write thy name? or hast thou a mark to thyself, like an honest plain-dealing man?   111

Clerk. Sir, I thank God, I have been so well brought up that I can write my name.

All. He hath confessed: away with him! he's a villain and a traitor.

Cade. Away with him, I say! hang him with his

pen and ink-horn about his neck.

[*Exit one with the* CLERK.

Enter MICHAEL.

Mich. Where's our general?

Cade. Here I am, thou particular fellow.   *119*

Mich. Fly, fly, fly! Sir Humphrey Stafford and his brother are hard by, with the King's forces.

Cade. Stand, villain, stand, or I'll fell thee down. He shall be encountered with a man as good as himself: he is but a knight, is a'?

Mich. No.

Cade. To equal him, I will make myself a knight presently. [*Kneels*] Rise up Sir John Mortimer. [*Rises*] Now have at him!

Enter SIR HUMPHREY STAFFORD *and* WILLIAM STAFFORD, *his Brother, with drum and soldiers.*

H. Staf. Rebellious hinds, the filth and scum of Kent,   *130*
Mark'd for the gallows, lay your weapons down;
Home to your cottages, forsake this groom:
The King is merciful, if you revolt.

W. Staf. But angry, wrathful, and inclined to blood,
If you go forward; therefore yield, or die.

Cade. As for these silken-coated slaves, I pass not:
It is to you, good people, that I speak,
Over whom, in time to come, I hope to reign;
For I am rightful heir unto the crown.

H. Staf. Villain, thy father was a plasterer;   *140*
And thou thyself a shearman, art thou not?

Cade. And Adam was a gardener.

W. Staf. And what of that?

Cade. Marry this: Edmund Mortimer, Earl of March,
Married the Duke of Clarence' daughter, did he not?

H. Staf. Ay, sir.

Cade. By her he had two children at one birth.

W. Staf. That's false.

Cade. Ay, there's the question; but I say, 'tis true:
The elder of them, being put to nurse,   *150*
Was by a beggar-woman stolen away;
And, ignorant of his birth and parentage,
Became a bricklayer when he came to age:
His son am I; deny it, if you can.

Dick. Nay, 'tis too true; therefore he shall be king.

Smith. Sir, he made a chimney in my father's house, and the bricks are alive at this day to testify it; therefore deny it not.

H. Staf. And will you credit this base drudge's words,

That speaks he knows not what?   *160*

All. Ay, marry, will we; therefore get ye gone.

W. Staf. Jack Cade, the Duke of York hath taught you this.

Cade. [*Aside*] He lies, for I invented it myself.
Go to, sirrah, tell the King from me, that, for his father's sake, Henry the Fifth, in whose time boys went to span-counter for French crowns, I am content he shall reign; but I'll be Protector over him.

Dick. And furthermore, we'll have the Lord Say's head for selling the dukedom of Maine. *170*

Cade. And good reason; for thereby is England mained, and fain to go with a staff, but that my puissance holds it up. Fellow kings, I tell you that that Lord Say hath gelded the commonwealth, and made it an eunuch: and more than that, he can speak French; and therefore he is a traitor.

H. Staf. O gross and miserable ignorance!

Cade. Nay, answer, if you can: the Frenchmen are our enemies; go to, then, I ask but this: can he that speaks with the tongue of an enemy be a good counsellor, or no?

All. No, no; and therefore we'll have his head.

W. Staf. Well, seeing gentle words will not prevail,
Assail them with the army of the King.

H. Staf. Herald, away; and throughout every town
Proclaim them traitors that are up with Cade;
That those which fly before the battle ends
May, even in their wives' and children's sight,
Be hang'd up for example at their doors: *190*
And you that be the King's friends, follow me.

[*Exeunt the* TWO STAFFORDS, *and soldiers.*

Cade. And you that love the commons, follow me.
Now show yourselves men; 'tis for liberty.
We will not leave one lord, one gentleman:
Spare none but such as go in clouted shoon;
For they are thrifty honest men and such
As would, but that they dare not, take our parts.

Dick. They are all in order and march toward us.

Cade. But then are we in order when we are most out of order. Come, march forward.   *200*

[*Exeunt.*

SCENE III. *Another part of Blackheath*

Alarums to the fight, wherein both the STAFFORDS *are slain. Enter* CADE *and the rest.*

Cade. Where's Dick, the butcher of Ashford?

Dick. Here, sir.

Cade. They fell before thee like sheep and oxen, and thou behavedst thyself as if thou hadst been in thine own slaughter-house: therefore thus will

I reward thee, the Lent shall be as long again as
it is; and thou shalt have a license to kill for a
hundred lacking one.

Dick. I desire no more.   *10*

Cade. And, to speak truth, thou deservest no
less. This monument of the victory will I bear
[*putting on Sir Humphrey's brigandine*]; and the
bodies shall be dragged at my horse heels till I do
come to London, where we will have the mayor's
sword borne before us.

Dick. If we mean to thrive and do good, break
open the gaols and let out the prisoners.

Cade. Fear not that, I warrant thee. Come, let's
march towards London.   [*Exeunt.* *20*

SCENE IV. *London: The palace*

Enter the KING *with a supplication, and the* QUEEN
with Suffolk's head, the DUKE OF BUCKINGHAM
and the LORD SAY.

Queen. Oft have I heard that grief softens the
    mind
And makes it fearful and degenerate;
Think therefore on revenge and cease to weep.
But who can cease to weep and look on this?
Here may his head lie on my throbbing breast:
But where's the body that I should embrace?

Buck. What answer makes your grace to the
rebel's supplication?

King. I'll send some holy bishop to entreat;
For God forbid so many simple souls   *10*
Should perish by the sword! And I myself,
Rather than bloody war shall cut them short,
Will parley with Jack Cade their general:
But stay, I'll read it over once again.

Queen. Ah, barbarous villains! hath this lovely
    face
Ruled, like a wandering planet, over me,
And could it not enforce them to relent,
That were unworthy to behold the same?

King. Lord Say, Jack Cade hath sworn to have
    thy head.

Say. Ay, but I hope your Highness shall have
    his.   *20*

King. How now, madam!
Still lamenting and mourning for Suffolk's death?
I fear me, love, if that I had been dead,
Thou wouldest not have mourn'd so much for me.

Queen. No, my love, I should not mourn, but
    die for thee.

Enter a MESSENGER.

King. How now! what news? why comest thou
    in such haste?

Mess. The rebels are in Southwark; fly, my lord!
Jack Cade proclaims himself Lord Mortimer,
Descended from the Duke of Clarence' house,

And calls your Grace usurper openly   *30*
And vows to crown himself in Westminster.
His army is a ragged multitude
Of hinds and peasants, rude and merciless:
Sir Humphrey Stafford and his brother's death
Hath given them heart and courage to proceed:
All scholars, lawyers, courtiers, gentlemen,
They call false caterpillars and intend their death.

King. O graceless men! they know not what
    they do.

Buck. My gracious lord, retire to Killingworth,
Until a power be raised to put them down.   *40*

Queen. Ah, were the Duke of Suffolk now alive,
These Kentish rebels would be soon appeased!

King. Lord Say, the traitors hate thee;
Therefore away with us to Killingworth.

Say. So might your Grace's person be in danger.
The sight of me is odious in their eyes;
And therefore in this city will I stay
And live alone as secret as I may.

Enter another MESSENGER.

Mess. Jack Cade hath gotten London bridge:
The citizens fly and forsake their houses: *50*
The rascal people, thirsting after prey,
Join with the traitor, and they jointly swear
To spoil the city and your royal court.

Buck. Then linger not, my lord; away, take
    horse.

King. Come, Margaret; God, our hope, will
    succour us.

Queen. My hope is gone, now Suffolk is de-
    ceased.

King. Farewell, my lord: trust not the Kentish
    rebels.

Buck. Trust nobody, for fear you be betray'd.

Say. The trust I have is in mine innocence,
And therefore am I bold and resolute.   *60*
    [*Exeunt.*

SCENE V. *London: The Tower*

Enter LORD SCALES *upon the Tower, walking.*
Then enter two or three CITIZENS *below.*

Scales. How now! is Jack Cade slain?

1st Cit. No, my lord, nor likely to be slain; for
they have won the bridge, killing all those that
withstand them: the Lord Mayor craves aid of
your honour from the Tower to defend the city
from the rebels.

Scales. Such aid as I can spare you shall com-
    mand;
But I am troubled here with them myself;
The rebels have assay'd to win the Tower.
But get you to Smithfield and gather head,   *10*
And thither I will send you Matthew Goffe;
Fight for your King, your country and your lives;

And so, farewell, for I must hence again.

[Exeunt.

SCENE VI. London: Cannon Street

Enter JACK CADE and the rest, and strikes his staff on London-stone.

Cade. Now is Mortimer lord of this city. And here, sitting upon London-stone, I charge and command that, of the city's cost, the pissing-conduit run nothing but claret wine this first year of our reign. And now henceforward it shall be treason for any that calls me other than Lord Mortimer.

Enter a SOLDIER, running.

Sold. Jack Cade! Jack Cade!

Cade. Knock him down there. [They kill him.]

Smith. If this fellow be wise, he'll never call ye Jack Cade more: I think he hath a very fair warning.

Dick. My lord, there's an army gathered together in Smithfield.

Cade. Come, then, let's go fight with them: but first, go and set London bridge on fire: and, if you can, burn down the Tower too. Come, let's away.

[Exeunt.

SCENE VII. London: Smithfield

Alarums. MATTHEW GOFFE is slain, and all the rest. Then enter JACK CADE, with his company.

Cade. So, sirs: now go some and pull down the Savoy; others to the inns of court; down with them all.

Dick. I have a suit unto your lordship.

Cade. Be it a lordship, thou shalt have it for that word.

Dick. Only that the laws of England may come out of your mouth.

Holl. [Aside] Mass, 'twill be sore law, then; for he was thrust in the mouth with a spear, and 'tis not whole yet.　　11

Smith. [Aside] Nay, John, it will be stinking law; for his breath stinks with eating toasted cheese.

Cade. I have thought upon it, it shall be so. Away, burn all the records of the realm: my mouth shall be the parliament of England.

Holl. [Aside] Then we are like to have biting statutes, unless his teeth be pulled out.

Cade. And henceforward all things shall be in common.　　21

Enter a MESSENGER.

Mess. My lord, a prize, a prize! here's the Lord Say, which sold the towns in France; he that made us pay one and twenty fifteens, and one shilling to the pound, the last subsidy.

Enter GEORGE BEVIS, with the LORD SAY.

Cade.Well, he shall be beheaded for it ten times. Ah, thou say, thou serge, nay thou buckram lord! now art thou within point-blank of our jurisdiction regal. What canst thou answer to my Majesty for giving up of Normandy unto Mounsieur Basimecu, the dauphin of France? Be it known unto thee by these presence, even the presence of Lord Mortimer, that I am the besom that must sweep the court clean of such filth as thou art. Thou hast most traitorously corrupted the youth of the realm in erecting a grammar school: and whereas, before, our forefathers had no other books but the score and the tally, thou hast caused printing to be used, and, contrary to the King, his crown and dignity, thou hast built a paper-mill. It will be proved to thy face that thou hast men about thee that usually talk of a noun and a verb, and such abominable words as no Christian ear can endure to hear. Thou hast appointed justices of peace, to call poor men before them about matters they were not able to answer. Moreover, thou hast put them in prison; and, because they could not read, thou hast hanged them; when, indeed, only for that cause they have been most worthy to live. Thou dost ride in a foot-cloth, dost thou not?

Say.What of that?

Cade. Marry, thou oughtest not to let thy horse wear a cloak, when honester men than thou go in their hose and doublets.

Dick. And work in their shirt too; as myself, for example, that am a butcher.

Say. You men of Kent—

Dick.What say you of Kent?　　60

Say. Nothing but this; 'tis "bona terra, mala gens."

Cade. Away with him, away with him! he speaks Latin.

Say. Hear me but speak, and bear me where you will.

Kent, in the Commentaries Cæsar writ,

Is term'd the civil'st place of all this isle:

Sweet is the country, because full riches;

The people liberal, valiant, active, wealthy;

Which makes me hope you are not void of pity.

I sold not Maine, I lost not Normandy,　　70

Yet, to recover them, would lose my life.

Justice with favour have I always done;

Prayers and tears have moved me, gifts could never.

When have I aught exacted at your hands,

But to maintain the King, the realm and you?

Large gifts have I bestow'd on learned clerks,

Because my book preferr'd me to the King,

And seeing ignorance is the curse of God,
Knowledge the wing wherewith we fly to heaven,
Unless you be possess'd with devilish spirits,   80
You cannot but forbear to murder me:
This tongue hath parley'd unto foreign kings
For your behoof—
  Cade. Tut, when struck'st thou one blow in the
field?
  Say. Great men have reaching hands: oft have I
    struck
Those that I never saw and struck them dead.
  Geo. O monstrous coward! what, to come be-
hind folks?
  Say. These cheeks are pale for watching for
    your good.   90
  Cade. Give him a box o' the ear and that will
make 'em red again.
  Say. Long sitting to determine poor men's
    causes
Hath made me full of sickness and diseases.
  Cade. Ye shall have a hempen caudle then and
the help of hatchet.
  Dick. Why dost thou quiver, man?
  Say. The palsy, and not fear, provokes me.
  Cade. Nay, he nods at us, as who should say,
"I'll be even with you": I'll see if his head will
stand steadier on a pole, or no. Take him away,
and behead him.
  Say. Tell me wherein have I offended most?
Have I affected wealth or honour? speak.
Are my chests fill'd up with extorted gold?
Is my apparel sumptuous to behold?
Whom have I injured, that ye seek my death?
These hands are free from guiltless blood-shed-
    ding,
This breast from harbouring foul deceitful
    thoughts.
O, let me live!   110
  Cade. [*Aside*] I feel remorse in myself with his
words; but I'll bridle it: he shall die, an it be but
for pleading so well for his life. Away with him!
he has a familiar under his tongue; he speaks not
o' God's name. Go, take him away, I say, and
strike off his head presently; and then break into
his son-in-law's house, Sir James Cromer, and
strike off his head, and bring them both upon two
poles hither.
  All. It shall be done.   120
  Say. Ah, countrymen! if when you make your
    prayers,
God should be so obdurate as yourselves,
How would it fare with your departed souls?
And therefore yet relent, and save my life.
  Cade. Away with him! and do as I command ye.
                    [*Exeunt some with* LORD SAY.
The proudest peer in the realm shall not wear a

head on his shoulders, unless he pay me tribute;
there shall not a maid be married, but she shall
pay to me her maidenhead ere they have it: men
shall hold of me *in capite;* and we charge and command that their wives be as free as heart can wish
or tongue can tell.
  Dick. My lord, when shall we go to Cheapside
and take up commodities upon our bills?
  Cade. Marry, presently.
  All. O, brave!

Re-enter one with the heads.

  Cade. But is not this braver? Let them kiss one
another, for they loved well when they were
alive. Now part them again, lest they consult
about the giving up of some more towns in
France. Soldiers, defer the spoil of the city until
night: for with these borne before us, instead of
of maces, will we ride through the streets; and
at every corner have them kiss. Away! [*Exeunt.*

SCENE VIII. *Southwark*

Alarum and retreat. Enter CADE *and all
his rabblement.*

  Cade. Up Fish Street! down Saint Magnus'
Corner! kill and knock down! throw them into
Thames! [*Sound a parley.*] What noise is this I
hear? Dare any be so bold to sound retreat or
parley, when I command them kill?

Enter BUCKINGHAM *and old* CLIFFORD, *attended.*

  Buck. Ay, here they be that dare and will disturb
    thee:
Know, Cade, we come ambassadors from the
    King
Unto the commons whom thou hast misled;
And here pronounce free pardon to them all
That will forsake thee and go home in peace.   10
  Clif. What say ye, countrymen? will ye relent,
And yield to mercy whilst 'tis offer'd you;
Or let a rebel lead you to your deaths?
Who loves the King and will embrace his pardon,
Fling up his cap, and say "God save his Ma-
    jesty!"
Who hateth him and honours not his father,
Henry the Fifth, that made all France to quake,
Shake he his weapon at us and pass by.
  All. God save the King! God save the King!
  Cade. What, Buckingham and Clifford, are ye
so brave? And you, base peasants, do ye believe
him? will you needs be hanged with your pardons
about your necks? Hath my sword therefore
broke through London gates, that you should
leave me at the White Hart in Southwark? I
thought ye would never have given out these
arms till you had recovered your ancient free-

dom: but you are all recreants and dastards, and
delight to live in slavery to the nobility. Let them
break your backs with burthens, take your houses
over your heads, ravish your wives and daughters before your faces: for me, I will make shift
for one; and so, God's curse light upon you all!

All. We'll follow Cade, we'll follow Cade!

Clif. Is Cade the son of Henry the Fifth,
That thus you do exclaim you'll go with him?
Will he conduct you through the heart of France,
And make the meanest of you earls and dukes?
Alas, he hath no home, no place to fly to;   40
Nor knows he how to live but by the spoil,
Unless by robbing of your friends and us.
Were't not a shame, that whilst you live at jar,
The fearful French, whom you late vanquished,
Should make a start o'er seas and vanquish you?
Methinks already in this civil broil
I see them lording it in London streets,
Crying "*Villiago!*" unto all they meet.
Better ten thousand base-born Cades miscarry   49
Than you should stoop unto a Frenchman's
    mercy.
To France, to France, and get what you have
    lost;
Spare England, for it is your native coast:
Henry hath money, you are strong and manly;
God on our side, doubt not of victory.

All. A Clifford! a Clifford! we'll follow the
King and Clifford.

Cade. Was ever feather so lightly blown to and
fro as this multitude? The name of Henry the
Fifth hales them to an hundred mischiefs and
makes them leave me desolate. I see them lay
their heads together to surprise me. My sword
make way for me, for here is no staying. In despite of the devils and hell, through the very
middest of you! and heavens and honour be witness that no want of resolution in me, but only
my followers' base and ignominious treasons,
makes me betake me to my heels.   [*Exit.*

Buck. What, is he fled? Go some, and follow
him;
And he that brings his head unto the King
Shall have a thousand crowns for his reward.   70
              [*Exeunt some of them.*
Follow me, soldiers: we'll devise a mean
To reconcile you all unto the King.   [*Exeunt.*

SCENE IX. *Kenilworth Castle*

Sound trumpets. Enter KING, QUEEN, *and*
SOMERSET, *on the terrace.*

King. Was ever king that joy'd an earthly
    throne,
And could command no more content than I?
No sooner was I crept out of my cradle

But I was made a king, at nine months old.
Was never subject long'd to be a king
As I do long and wishsto be a subject.

Enter BUCKINGHAM *and old* CLIFFORD.

Buck. Health and glad tidings to your Majesty!
King. Why, Buckingham, is the traitor Cade
    surprised?
Or is he but retired to make him strong?

*Enter, below, multitudes, with halters about
their necks.*

Clif. He is fled, my lord, and all his powers do
    yield;   10
And humbly thus, with halters on their necks,
Expect your Highness' doom, of life or death.

King. Then, heaven, set ope thy everlasting
    gates,
To entertain my vows of thanks and praise!
Soldiers, this day have you redeem'd your lives
And show'd how well you love your prince and
    country:
Continue still in this so good a mind,
And Henry, though he be infortunate,
Assure yourselves, will never be unkind:
And so, with thanks and pardon to you all,   20
I do dismiss you to your several countries.

All. God save the King! God save the King!

Enter a MESSENGER.

Mess. Please it your grace to be advertised
The Duke of York is newly come from Ireland,
And with a puissant and a mighty power
Of gallowglasses and stout kerns
Is marching hitherward in proud array,
And still proclaimeth, as he comes along,
His arms are only to remove from thee
The Duke of Somerset, whom he terms a traitor.

King. Thus stands my state, 'twixt Cade and
    York distress'd;   31
Like to a ship that, having 'scaped a tempest,
Is straightway calm'd and boarded with a pirate:
But now is Cade driven back, his men dispersed;
And now is York in arms to second him.
I pray thee, Buckingham, go and meet him,
And ask him what's the reason of these arms.
Tell him I'll send Duke Edmund to the Tower;
And, Somerset, we will commit thee thither,
Until his army be dismiss'd from him.   40

Som. My lord,
I'll yield myself to prison willingly,
Or unto death, to do my country good.

King. In any case, be not too rough in terms;
For he is fierce and cannot brook hard language.

Buck. I will, my lord; and doubt not so to deal
As all things shall redound unto your good.

King. Come, wife, let's in, and learn to govern
better;
For yet may England curse my wretched reign.
[*Flourish. Exeunt.*

SCENE X. *Kent: Iden's garden*

Enter CADE.

Cade. Fie on ambition! fie on myself, that have a
sword, and yet am ready to famish! These five
days have I hid me in these woods and durst not
peep out, for all the country is laid for me; but
now am I so hungry that if I might have a lease
of my life for a thousand years I could stay
no longer. Wherefore, on a brick wall have I
climbed into this garden, to see if I can eat grass,
or pick a sallet another while, which is not amiss
to cool a man's stomach this hot weather. And I
think this word "sallet" was born to do me good:
for many a time, but for a sallet, my brain-pan
had been cleft with a brown bill; and many a
time, when I have been dry and bravely marching, it hath served me instead of a quart pot to
drink in; and now the word "sallet" must serve
me to feed on.

Enter IDEN.

Iden. Lord, who would live turmoiled in the
court,
And may enjoy such quiet walks as these?
This small inheritance my father left me   20
Contenteth me, and worth a monarchy.
I seek not to wax great by others' waning,
Or gather wealth, I care not, with what envy:
Sufficeth that I have maintains my state
And sends the poor well pleased from my gate.
Cade. Here's the lord of the soil come to seize
me for a stray, for entering his fee-simple with-
out leave. Ah, villain, thou wilt betray me, and
get a thousand crowns of the King by carrying
my head to him: but I'll make thee eat iron like
an ostrich, and swallow my sword like a great
pin, ere thou and I part.
Iden. Why, rude companion, whatsoe'er thou be,
I know thee not; why, then should I betray thee?
Is't not enough to break into my garden,
And, like a thief, to come to rob my grounds,
Climbing my walls in spite of me the owner,
But thou wilt brave me with these saucy terms?
Cade. Brave thee! ay, by the best blood that ever
was broached, and beard thee too. Look on me
well: I have eat no meat these five days; yet,
come thou and thy five men, and if I do not leave
you all as dead as a door-nail, I pray God I may
never eat grass more.
Iden. Nay, it shall ne'er be said, while England
stands,

That Alexander Iden, an esquire of Kent,
Took odds to combat a poor famish'd man.
Oppose thy steadfast-gazing eyes to mine,
See if thou canst outface me with thy looks:
Set limb to limb, and thou art far the lesser;   50
Thy hand is but a finger to my fist,
Thy leg a stick compared with this truncheon;
My foot shall fight with all the strength thou hast;
And if mine arm be heaved in the air,
Thy grave is digg'd already in the earth.
As for words, whose greatness answers words,
Let this my sword report what speech forbears.
Cade. By my valour, the most complete cham-
pion that ever I heard! Steel, if thou turn the
edge, or cut not out the burly-boned clown in
chines of beef ere thou sleep in thy sheath, I beseech God on my knees thou mayst be turned to
hobnails. [*Here they fight.* CADE *falls.*]
    O, I am slain! famine and no other hath slain
me: let ten thousand devils come against me, and
give me but the ten meals I have lost, and I'ld
defy them all. Wither, garden; and be henceforth
a burying-place to all that do dwell in this house,
because the unconquered soul of Cade is fled.   70
Iden. Is't Cade that I have slain, that monstrous
traitor?
Sword, I will hallow thee for this thy deed,
And hang thee o'er my tomb when I am dead:
Ne'er shall this blood be wiped from thy point;
But thou shalt wear it as a herald's coat,
To emblaze the honour that thy master got.
Cade. Iden, farewell, and be proud of thy vic-
tory. Tell Kent from me she hath lost her best
man, and exhort all the world to be cowards; for
I, that never feared any, am vanquished by fam-
ine, not by valour.   [*Dies.* 81
Iden. How much thou wrong'st me, heaven be
my judge.
Die, damned wretch, the curse of her that bare
thee;
And as I thrust thy body in with my sword,
So wish I, I might thrust thy soul to hell.
Hence will I drag thee headlong by the heels
Unto a dunghill which shall be thy grave,
And there cut off thy most ungracious head;
Which I will bear in triumph to the King,   89
Leaving thy trunk for crows to feed upon. [*Exit.*

ACT V

SCENE I. *Fields between Dartford and Blackheath*

Enter YORK, *and his army of Irish, with drum and colours.*

York. From Ireland thus comes York to claim
his right,

And pluck the crown from feeble Henry's head:
Ring, bells, aloud; burn, bonfires, clear and
    bright,
To entertain great England's lawful king.
Ah! *sancta majestas*, who would not buy thee
    dear?
Let them obey that know not how to rule;
This hand was made to handle nought but gold.
I cannot give due action to my words,
Except a sword or sceptre balance it:
A sceptre shall it have, have I a soul,   10
On which I'll toss the flower-de-luce of France.

Enter BUCKINGHAM.

Whom have we here? Buckingham, to disturb
    me?
The King hath sent him, sure: I must dissemble.
  Buck. York, if thou meanest well, I greet thee
    well.
  York. Humphrey of Buckingham, I accept thy
    greeting.
Art thou a messenger, or come of pleasure?
  Buck. A messenger from Henry, our dread liege,
To know the reason of these arms in peace;
Or why thou, being a subject as I am,
Against thy oath and true allegiance sworn,   20
Should raise so great a power without his leave,
Or dare to bring thy force so near the court.
  York. [*Aside*] Scarce can I speak, my choler is
    so great:
O, I could hew up rocks and fight with flint,
I am so angry at these abject terms;
And now, like Ajax Telamonius,
On sheep or oxen could I spend my fury.
I am far better born than is the King,
More like a king, more kingly in my thoughts:
But I must make fair weather yet a while,   30
Till Henry be more weak and I more strong.—
Buckingham, I prithee, pardon me,
That I have given no answer all this while;
My mind was troubled with deep melancholy.
The cause why I have brought this army hither
Is to remove proud Somerset from the King,
Seditious to his Grace and to the state.
  Buck. That is too much presumption on thy
    part:
But if thy arms be to no other end,
The King hath yielded unto thy demand: 40
The Duke of Somerset is in the Tower.
  York. Upon thine honour, is he prisoner?
  Buck. Upon mine honour, he is prisoner.
  York. Then, Buckingham, I do dismiss my
    powers.
Soldiers, I thank you all; disperse yourselves;
Meet me to-morrow in Saint George's field,
You shall have pay and everything you wish.

And let my sovereign, virtuous Henry,
Command my eldest son, nay, all my sons,
As pledges of my fealty and love;   50
I'll send them all as willing as I live:
Lands, goods, horse, armour, any thing I have,
Is his to use, so Somerset may die.
  Buck. York, I commend this kind submission:
We twain will go into his Highness' tent.

Enter KING and Attendants.

  King. Buckingham, doth York intend no harm
    to us,
That thus he marcheth with thee arm in arm?
  York. In all submission and humility
York doth present himself unto your Highness.
  King. Then what intends these forces thou dost
    bring?   60
  York. To heave the traitor Somerset from hence,
And fight against that monstrous rebel Cade,
Who since I heard to be discomfited.

Enter IDEN, with Cade's head.

  Iden. If one so rude and of so mean condition
May pass into the presence of a king,
Lo, I present your Grace a traitor's head,
The head of Cade, whom I in combat slew.
  King. The head of Cade! Great God, how just
    art Thou!
O, let me view his visage, being dead,
That living wrought me such exceeding trouble.
Tell me, my friend, art thou the man that slew
    him?   71
  Iden. I was, an't like your Majesty.
  King. How art thou call'd? and what is thy de-
    gree?
  Iden. Alexander Iden, that's my name;
A poor esquire of Kent, that loves his king.
  Buck. So please it you, my lord, 'twere not amiss
He were created knight for his good service.
  King. Iden, kneel down. [*He kneels.*] Rise up a
    knight.
We give thee for reward a thousand marks,
And will that thou henceforth attend on us.   80
  Iden. May Iden live to merit such a bounty,
And never live but true unto his liege! [*Rises.*]

Enter QUEEN and SOMERSET.

  King. See, Buckingham, Somerset comes with
    the queen:
Go, bid her hide him quickly from the Duke.
  Queen. For thousand Yorks he shall not hide his
    head,
But boldly stand and front him to his face.
  York. How now! is Somerset at liberty?
Then, York, unloose thy long-imprison'd
    thoughts,

And let thy tongue be equal with thy heart.
Shall I endure the sight of Somerset?   90
False King! why hast thou broken faith with
      me,
Knowing how hardly I can brook abuse?
King did I call thee? no, thou art not King,
Not fit to govern and rule multitudes,
Which darest not, no, nor canst not rule a traitor.
That head of thine doth not become a crown;
Thy hand is made to grasp a palmer's staff,
And not to grace an awful princely sceptre.
That gold must round engirt these brows of mine,
Whose smile and frown, like to Achilles' spear,
Is able with the change to kill and cure.   101
Here is a hand to hold a sceptre up
And with the same to act controlling laws.
Give place: by heaven, thou shalt rule no more
O'er him whom heaven created for thy ruler.
  Som. O monstrous traitor! I arrest thee, York,
Of capital treason 'gainst the King and crown:
Obey, audacious traitor; kneel for grace.
  York. Wouldst have me kneel? first let me ask
      of these,
If they can brook I bow a knee to man.   110
Sirrah, call in my sons to be my bail:
                                        [*Exit Attendant.*
I know, ere they will have me go to ward,
They'll pawn their swords for my enfranchise-
      ment.
  Queen. Call hither Clifford; bid him come amain,
To say if that the bastard boys of York
Shall be the surety for their traitor father.
                                        [*Exit* BUCKINGHAM.
  York. O blood-bespotted Neapolitan,
Outcast of Naples, England's bloody scourge!
The sons of York, thy betters in their birth,
Shall be their father's bail; and bane to those   120
That for my surety will refuse the boys!

          Enter EDWARD *and* RICHARD.

See where they come: I'll warrant they'll make
      it good.

          Enter old CLIFFORD *and his* SON.

  Queen. And here comes Clifford to deny their
      bail.
  Clif. Health and all happiness to my lord the
      King! [*Kneels.*]
  York. I thank thee, Clifford: say, what news
      with thee?
Nay, do not fright us with an angry look:
We are thy sovereign, Clifford, kneel again;
For thy mistaking so, we pardon thee.
  Clif. This is my king, York, I do not mistake;
But thou mistakest me much to think I do: 130
To Bedlam with him! is the man grown mad?

  King. Ay, Clifford; a bedlam and ambitious
      humour
Makes him oppose himself against his king.
  Clif. He is a traitor; let him to the Tower,
And chop away that factious pate of his.
  Queen. He is arrested, but will not obey;
His sons, he says, shall give their words for him.
  York. Will you not, sons?
  Edw. Ay, noble father, if our words will serve.
  Rich. And if words will not, then our weapons
      shall.   140
  Clif. Why, what a brood of traitors have we
      here!
  York. Look in a glass, and call thy image so:
I am thy king, and thou a false-heart traitor.
Call hither to the stake my two brave bears,
That with the very shaking of their chains
They may astonish these fell-lurking curs:
Bid Salisbury and Warwick come to me.

      Enter the EARLS OF WARWICK *and* SALISBURY.

  Clif. Are these thy bears? we'll bait thy bears
      to death,
And manacle the bear-ward in their chains,
If thou darest bring them to the baiting place.   150
  Rich. Oft have I seen a hot o'erweening cur
Run back and bite, because he was withheld;
Who, being suffer'd with the bear's fell paw,
Hath clapp'd his tail between his legs and cried:
And such a piece of service will you do,
If you oppose yourselves to match Lord War-
      wick.
  Clif. Hence, heap of wrath, foul indigested
      lump,
As crooked in thy manners as thy shape!
  York. Nay, we shall heat you thoroughly anon.
  Clif. Take heed, lest by your heat you burn
      yourselves.   160
  King. Why, Warwick, hath thy knee forgot to
      bow?
Old Salisbury, shame to thy silver hair,
Thou mad misleader of thy brain-sick son!
What, wilt thou on thy death-bed play the ruffian,
And seek for sorrow with thy spectacles?
O, where is faith? O, where is loyalty?
If it be banish'd from the frosty head,
Where shall it find a harbour in the earth?
Wilt thou go dig a grave to find out war,
And shame thine honourable age with blood?   170
Why art thou old, and want'st experience?
Or wherefore dost abuse it, if thou hast it?
For shame! in duty bend thy knee to me
That bows unto the grave with mickle age.
  Sal. My lord, I have consider'd with myself
The title of this most renowned duke;
And in my conscience do repute his Grace

The rightful heir to England's royal seat.
King. Hast thou not sworn allegiance unto me?
Sal. I have.   *180*
King. Canst thou dispense with heaven for such
   an oath?
Sal. It is great sin to swear unto a sin,
But greater sin to keep a sinful oath.
Who can be bound by any solemn vow
To do a murderous deed, to rob a man,
To force a spotless virgin's chastity,
To reave the orphan of his patrimony,
To wring the widow from her custom'd right,
And have no other reason for this wrong
But that he was bound by a solemn oath?   *190*
   Queen. A subtle traitor needs no sophister.
   King. Call Buckingham, and bid him arm him-
   self.
   York. Call Buckingham, and all the friends thou
   hast,
I am resolved for death or dignity.
   Clif. The first I warrant thee, if dreams prove
   true.
   War. You were best to go to bed and dream
   again,
To keep thee from the tempest of the field.
   Clif. I am resolved to bear a greater storm
Than any thou canst conjure up to-day;
And that I'll write upon thy burgonet,   *200*
Might I but know thee by thy household badge.
   War. Now, by my father's badge, old Nevil's
   crest,
The rampant bear chain'd to the ragged staff,
This day I'll wear aloft my burgonet,
As on a mountain top the cedar shows
That keeps his leaves in spite of any storm,
Even to affright thee with the view thereof.
   Clif. And from thy burgonet I'll rend thy bear
And tread it under foot with all contempt,
Despite the bear-ward that protects the bear. *210*
   Y. Clif. And so to arms, victorious father,
To quell the rebels and their complices.
   Rich. Fie! charity, for shame! speak not in spite,
For you shall sup with Jesu Christ to-night.
   Y. Clif. Foul stigmatic, that's more than thou
   canst tell.
   Rich. If not in heaven, you'll surely sup in hell.
                                          [*Exeunt severally.*

Scene ii. *Saint Alban's*

Alarums to the battle. Enter WARWICK.

War. Clifford of Cumberland, 'tis Warwick
   calls:
And if thou dost not hide thee from the bear,
Now, when the angry trumpet sounds alarum
And dead men's cries do fill the empty air,
Clifford, I say, come forth and fight with me:

Proud northern lord, Clifford of Cumberland,
Warwick is hoarse with calling thee to arms.

Enter YORK.

How now, my noble lord! what, all afoot?
   York. The deadly-handed Clifford slew my
   steed,
But match to match I have encounter'd him   *10*
And made a prey for carrion kites and crows
Even of the bonny beast he loved so well.

Enter old CLIFFORD.

War. Of one or both of us the time is come.
York. Hold, Warwick, seek thee out some other
   chase,
For I myself must hunt this deer to death.
War. Then, nobly, York; 'tis for a crown thou
   fight'st.
As I intend, Clifford, to thrive to-day,
It grieves my soul to leave thee unassail'd. [*Exit.*
   Clif. What seest thou in me, York? why dost
   thou pause?
   York. With thy brave bearing should I be in
   love,   *20*
But that thou art so fast mine enemy.
   Clif. Nor should thy prowess want praise and
   esteem,
But that 'tis shown ignobly and in treason.
   York. So let it help me now against thy sword
As I in justice and true right express it.
   Clif. My soul and body on the action both!
   York. A dreadful lay! Address thee instantly.
      They fight, and CLIFFORD *falls.*
   Clif. La fin couronne les œuvres.   [*Dies.*
   York. Thus war hath given thee peace, for thou
   art still.
Peace with his soul, Heaven, if it be thy will! *30*
                                          [*Exit.*

Enter YOUNG CLIFFORD.

   Y. Clif. Shame and confusion! all is on the rout;
Fear frames disorder, and disorder wounds
Where it should guard. O war, thou son of hell,
Whom angry heavens do make their minister,
Throw in the frozen bosoms of our part
Hot coals of vengeance! Let no soldier fly.
He that is truly dedicate to war
Hath no self-love, nor he that loves himself
Hath not essentially but by circumstance
The name of valour. [*Seeing his dead father*]
      O, let the vile world end,   *40*
And the premised flames of the last day
Knit earth and heaven together!
Now let the general trumpet blow his blast,
Particularities and petty sounds
To cease! Wast thou ordain'd, dear father,

To lose thy youth in peace, and to achieve
The silver livery of advised age,
And, in thy reverence thy chair-days, thus
To die in ruffian battle? Even at this sight   49
My heart is turn'd to stone: and while 'tis
    mine,
It shall be stony. York not our old men spares;
No more will I their babes: tears virginal
Shall be to me even as the dew to fire,
And beauty that the tyrant oft reclaims
Shall to my flaming wrath be oil and flax.
Henceforth I will not have to do with pity:
Meet I an infant of the house of York,
Into as many gobbets will I cut it
As wild Medea young Absyrtus did:
In cruelty will I seek out my fame.   60
Come, thou new ruin of old Clifford's house:
As did Æneas old Anchises bear,
So bear I thee upon my manly shoulders;
But then Æneas bare a living load,
Nothing so heavy as these woes of mine.
       [*Exit, bearing off his father.*

Enter RICHARD *and* SOMERSET *to fight.*
     SOMERSET *is killed.*

Rich. So, lie thou there;
For underneath an alehouse' paltry sign,
The Castle in Saint Alban's, Somerset
Hath made the wizard famous in his death.   69
Sword, hold thy temper; heart, be wrathful
    still:
Priests pray for enemies, but princes kill.   [*Exit.*

Fight: excursions. Enter KING, QUEEN, *and
others.*

Queen. Away, my lord! you are slow; for shame,
    away!
King. Can we outrun the heavens? good Mar-
    garet, stay.
Queen. What are you made of? you'll nor fight
    nor fly:
Now is it manhood, wisdom, and defence,
To give the enemy way, and to secure us
By what we can, which can no more but fly.
    Alarum afar off.
If you be ta'en, we then should see the bottom
Of all our fortunes: but if we haply scape,
As well we may, if not through your neglect,   80
We shall to London get, where you are loved
And where this breach now in our fortunes
    made
May readily be stopp'd.

Re-enter YOUNG CLIFFORD.

Y. Clif. But that my heart's on future mischief
    set,
I would speak blasphemy ere bid you fly:
But fly you must; uncurable discomfit
Reigns in the hearts of all our present parts.
Away, for your relief! and we will live
To see their day and them our fortune give:
Away, my lord, away!   [*Exeunt.*

SCENE III. *Fields near St Alban's*

Alarum. Retreat. Enter YORK, RICHARD, WARWICK,
    and Soldiers, with drum and colours.

York. Of Salisbury, who can report of him,
That winter lion, who in rage forgets
Aged contusions and all brush of time,
And, like a gallant in the brow of youth,
Repairs him with occasion? This happy day
Is not itself, nor have we won one foot,
If Salisbury be lost.
Rich.   My noble father,
Three times to-day I holp him to his horse,
Three times bestrid him; thrice I led him off,
Persuaded him from any further act: 10
But still, where danger was, still there I met him;
And like rich hangings in a homely house,
So was his will in his old feeble body.
But, noble as he is, look where he comes.

Enter SALISBURY.

Sal. Now, by my sword, well hast thou fought
    to-day;
By the mass, so did we all. I thank you, Richard:
God knows how long it is I have to live;
And it hath pleased him that three times to-day
You have defended me from imminent death.
Well, lords, we have not got that which we have:
'Tis not enough our foes are this time fled,   21
Being opposites of such repairing nature.
York. I know our safety is to follow them;
For, as I hear, the King is fled to London,
To call a present court of parliament.
Let us pursue him ere the writs go forth.
What says Lord Warwick? shall we after them?
War. After them! nay, before them, if we can.
Now, by my faith, lords, 'twas a glorious day:
Saint Alban's battle won by famous York   30
Shall be eternized in all age to come.
Sound drums and trumpets, and to London all:
And more such days as these to us befall!
       [*Exeunt.*

The Third Part of
KING HENRY THE SIXTH

DRAMATIS PERSONÆ

KING HENRY THE SIXTH
EDWARD, PRINCE OF WALES, *his son*
LEWIS XI, *King of France*
DUKE OF SOMERSET
DUKE OF EXETER
EARL OF OXFORD
EARL OF NORTHUMBERLAND
EARL OF WESTMORELAND
LORD CLIFFORD
RICHARD PLANTAGENET, DUKE OF YORK
EDWARD, *Earl of March, afterwards* KING
  EDWARD IV
EDMUND, *Earl of Rutland*
GEORGE, *afterwards* DUKE OF CLARENCE
RICHARD, *afterwards* DUKE OF GLOUCESTER
DUKE OF NORFOLK
MARQUESS OF MONTAGUE
EARL OF WARWICK
EARL OF PEMBROKE
LORD HASTINGS
LORD STAFFORD
SIR JOHN MORTIMER } *uncles to the Duke of York*
SIR HUGH MORTIMER
LORD RIVERS, *brother to Lady Grey*
SIR WILLIAM STANLEY

his sons

SIR JOHN MONTGOMERY
SIR JOHN SOMERVILLE
TUTOR TO RUTLAND
MAYOR OF YORK
LIEUTENANT OF THE TOWER
NOBLEMAN
TWO KEEPERS
HUNTSMAN
SON *that has killed his father*
FATHER *that has killed his son*
SEVEN MESSENGERS
POST
SOLDIER

QUEEN MARGARET
ELIZABETH WOODVILLE, LADY GREY, *afterwards*
  QUEEN *to Edward IV*
BONA, *sister to the French Queen*

NON-SPEAKING: *Henry, Earl of Richmond; Mayor of*
  Coventry; Admiral called Bourbon; Nurse; Alder-
  men; Soldiers; Attendants

SCENE: *England and France*

ACT I

SCENE I. *London: The Parliament-house*

Alarum. Enter the DUKE OF YORK, EDWARD, RICH-
ARD, NORFOLK, MONTAGUE, WARWICK, *and Sol-*
diers.

War. I wonder how the King escaped our hands.
York. While we pursued the horsemen of the
  north,
He slily stole away and left his men:
Whereat the great Lord of Northumberland,
Whose warlike ears could never brook retreat,
Cheer'd up the drooping army; and himself,
Lord Clifford, and Lord Stafford, all abreast,
Charged our main battle's front, and breaking in
Were by the swords of common soldiers slain.
  Edw. Lord Stafford's father, Duke of Bucking-
  ham,   10
Is either slain or wounded dangerously;
I cleft his beaver with a downright blow:
That this is true, father, behold his blood.
  Mont. And, brother, here's the Earl of Wilt-
  shire's blood,

Whom I encounter'd as the battles join'd.
  Rich. Speak thou for me and tell them what I
  did. [*Throwing down the Duke of Somerset's*
  head.]
  York. Richard hath best deserved of all my sons.
But is your Grace dead, my Lord of Somerset?
  Norf. Such hope have all the line of John of
  Gaunt!
  Rich. Thus do I hope to shake King Henry's
  head.   20
  War. And so do I. Victorious Prince of York,
Before I see thee seated in that throne
Which now the house of Lancaster usurps,
I vow by heaven these eyes shall never close.
This is the palace of the fearful king,
And this the regal seat: possess it, York;
For this is thine and not King Henry's heirs'.
  York. Assist me, then, sweet Warwick, and I
  will;
For hither we have broken in by force.   29
  Norf. We'll all assist you; he that flies shall die.
  York. Thanks, gentle Norfolk: stay by me, my
  lords;

And, soldiers, stay and lodge by me this night.
[*They go up.*

War. And when the King comes, offer him no
violence,
Unless he seek to thrust you out perforce.
York. The Queen this day here holds her parlia-
ment,
But little thinks we shall be of her council:
By words or blows here let us win our right.
Rich. Arm'd as we are, let's stay within this
house.
War. The bloody parliament shall this be call'd,
Unless Plantagenet, Duke of York, be king,   *40*
And bashful Henry deposed, whose cowardice
Hath made us by-words to our enemies.
York. Then leave me not, my lords; be reso-
lute;
I mean to take possession of my right.
War. Neither the King, nor he that loves him
best,
The proudest he that holds up Lancaster,
Dares stir a wing, if Warwick shake his bells.
I'll plant Plantagenet, root him up who dares;
Resolve thee, Richard; claim the English crown.

Flourish. Enter KING HENRY, CLIFFORD, NORTH-
UMBERLAND, WESTMORELAND, EXETER, *and the
rest, wearing red roses.*

K. Hen. My lords, look where the sturdy rebel
sits,   *50*
Even in the chair of state: belike he means,
Back'd by the power of Warwick, that false
peer,
To aspire unto the crown and reign as king.
Earl of Northumberland, he slew thy father,
And thine, Lord Clifford; and you both have
vow'd revenge
On him, his sons, his favourites and his friends.
North. If I be not, heavens be revenged on me!
Clif. The hope thereof makes Clifford mourn in
steel.
West. What, shall we suffer this? let's pluck
him down.
My heart for anger burns; I cannot brook it.   *60*
K. Hen. Be patient, gentle Earl of Westmore-
land.
Clif. Patience is for poltroons, such as he:
He durst not sit there, had your father lived.
My gracious lord, here in the parliament
Let us assail the family of York.
North. Well hast thou spoken, cousin: be it so.
K. Hen. Ah, know you not the city favours
them,
And they have troops of soldiers at their beck?
Exe. But when the Duke is slain, they'll quickly
fly.

K. Hen. Far be the thought of this from Henry's
heart,   *70*
To make a shambles of the parliament-house!
Cousin of Exeter, frowns, words, and threats
Shall be the war that Henry means to use.
Thou factious Duke of York, descend my throne,
And kneel for grace and mercy at my feet;
I am thy sovereign.
York.   I am thine.
Exe. For shame, come down: he made thee
Duke of York.
York. 'Twas my inheritance, as the earldom
was.
Exe. Thy father was a traitor to the crown.
War. Exeter, thou art a traitor to the crown
In following this usurping Henry.   *81*
Clif. Whom should he follow but his natural
king?
War. True, Clifford; and that's Richard Duke
of York.
K. Hen. And shall I stand, and thou sit in my
throne?
York. It must and shall be so: content thyself.
War. Be Duke of Lancaster; let him be King.
West. He is both King and Duke of Lancaster;
And that the Lord of Westmoreland shall main-
tain.
War. And Warwick shall disprove it. You for-
get   *89*
That we are those which chased you from the
field
And slew your fathers, and with colours spread
March'd through the city to the palace gates.
North. Yes, Warwick, I remember it to my
grief;
And, by his soul, thou and thy house shall rue it.
West. Plantagenet, of thee and these thy sons,
Thy kinsmen and thy friends, I'll have more
lives
Than drops of blood were in my father's veins.
Clif. Urge it no more; lest that, instead of
words,
I send thee, Warwick, such a messenger
As shall revenge his death before I stir.   *100*
War. Poor Clifford! how I scorn his worthless
threats!
York. Will you we show our title to the crown?
If not, our swords shall plead it in the field.
K. Hen. What title hast thou, traitor, to the
crown?
Thy father was, as thou art, Duke of York;
Thy grandfather, Roger Mortimer, Earl of
March:
I am the son of Henry the Fifth,
Who made the Dauphin and the French to stoop
And seized upon their towns and provinces.

War. Talk not of France, sith thou hast lost it
   all.   *110*
K. Hen. The Lord Protector lost it, and not I:
When I was crown'd I was but nine months old.
Rich. You are old enough now, and yet, me-
   thinks, you lose.
Father, tear the crown from the usurper's head.
Edw. Sweet father, do so; set it on your head.
Mont. Good brother, as thou lovest and honour-
   est arms,
Let's fight it out and not stand cavilling thus.
Rich. Sound drums and trumpets, and the King
   will fly.
York. Sons, peace!
K. Hen. Peace, thou! and give King Henry leave
   to speak.   *120*
War. Plantagenet shall speak first: hear him,
   lords;
And be you silent and attentive too,
For he that interrupts him shall not live.
K. Hen. Think'st thou that I will leave my
   kingly throne,
Wherein my grandsire and my father sat?
No: first shall war unpeople this my realm;
Ay, and their colours, often borne in France,
And now in England to our heart's great sorrow,
Shall be my winding-sheet. Why faint you, lords?
My title's good, and better far than his.   *130*
War. Prove it, Henry, and thou shalt be King.
K. Hen. Henry the Fourth by conquest got the
   crown.
York. 'Twas by rebellion against his king.
K. Hen. [*Aside*] I know not what to say; my
   title's weak.—
Tell me, may not a king adopt an heir?
York. What then?
K. Hen. An if he may, then am I lawful king;
For Richard, in the view of many lords,
Resign'd the crown to Henry the Fourth,
Whose heir my father was, and I am his.   *140*
York. He rose against him, being his sovereign,
And made him to resign his crown perforce.
War. Suppose, my lords, he did it unconstrain'd,
Think you 'twere prejudicial to his crown?
Exe. No; for he could not so resign his crown
But that the next heir should succeed and reign.
K. Hen. Art thou against us, Duke of Exeter?
Exe. His is the right, and therefore pardon me.
York. Why whisper you, my lords, and answer
   not?
Exe. My conscience tells me he is lawful king.
K. Hen. [*Aside*] All will revolt from me, and
   turn to him.   *151*
North. Plantagenet, for all the claim thou lay'st,
Think not that Henry shall be so deposed.
War. Deposed he shall be, in despite of all.

North. Thou art deceived: 'tis not thy southern
   power,
Of Essex, Norfolk, Suffolk, nor of Kent,
Which makes thee thus presumptuous and proud,
Can set the Duke up in despite of me.
Clif. King Henry, be thy title right or wrong,
Lord Clifford vows to fight in thy defence: *160*
May that ground gape and swallow me alive,
Where I shall kneel to him that slew my father!
K. Hen. O Clifford, how thy words revive my
   heart!
York. Henry of Lancaster, resign thy crown.
What mutter you, or what conspire you, lords?
War. Do right unto this princely Duke of York,
Or I will fill the house with armed men,
And over the chair of state, where now he sits,
Write up his title with usurping blood.
   [*He stamps with his foot, and the Soldiers show
     themselves.*
K. Hen. My Lord of Warwick, hear me but one
   word: *170*
Let me for this my life-time reign as king.
York. Confirm the crown to me and to mine
   heirs,
And thou shalt reign in quiet while thou livest.
King. I am content: Richard Plantagenet,
Enjoy the kingdom after my decease.
Clif. What wrong is this unto the Prince your
   son!
War. What good is this to England and himself!
West. Base, fearful and despairing Henry!
Clif. How hast thou injured both thyself and us!
West. I cannot stay to hear these articles.
North. Nor I.   *181*
Clif. Come, cousin, let us tell the Queen these
   news.
West. Farewell, faint-hearted and degenerate
   king,
In whose cold blood no spark of honour bides.
North. Be thou a prey unto the house of York,
And die in bands for this unmanly deed!
Clif. In dreadful war mayst thou be overcome,
Or live in peace abandon'd and despised!
   [*Exeunt* NORTHUMBERLAND, CLIFFORD,
     and WESTMORELAND.
War. Turn this way, Henry, and regard them
   not.
Exe. They seek revenge and therefore will not
   yield.   *190*
K. Hen. Ah, Exeter!
War.   Why should you sigh, my lord?
K. Hen. Not for myself, Lord Warwick, but
   my son,
Whom I unnaturally shall disinherit.
But be it as it may: I here entail
The crown to thee and to thine heirs for ever;

Conditionally, that here thou take an oath
To cease this civil war, and, whilst I live
To honour me as thy king and sovereign,
And neither by treason nor hostility
To seek to put me down and reign thyself.   200
  York. This oath I willingly take and will per-
    form.
  War. Long live King Henry! Plantagenet, em-
    brace him.
  K. Hen. And long live thou and these thy for-
    ward sons!
  York. Now York and Lancaster are reconciled.
  Exe. Accursed be he that seeks to make them
    foes!
  Sennet. Here they come down.
  York. Farewell, my gracious lord; I'll to my
    castle.
  War. And I'll keep London with my soldiers.
  Norf. And I to Norfolk with my followers.
  Mont. And I unto the sea from whence I came.
              [*Exeunt* YORK *and his Sons,* WARWICK,
                    NORFOLK, MONTAGUE, *their Sol-
                    diers, and Attendants.*
  K. Hen. And I, with grief and sorrow, to the
    court.   210

      Enter QUEEN MARGARET *and the* PRINCE OF
                        WALES.

  Exe. Here comes the Queen, whose looks be-
    wray her anger:
I'll steal away.
  K. Hen. Exeter, so will I.
  Q. Mar. Nay, go not from me; I will follow
    thee.
  K. Hen. Be patient, gentle queen, and I will stay.
  Q. Mar. Who can be patient in such extremes?
Ah, wretched man! would I had died a maid,
And never seen thee, never borne thee son,
Seeing thou hast proved so unnatural a father!
Hath he deserved to lose his birthright thus?
Hadst thou but loved him half so well as I,   220
Or felt that pain which I did for him once,
Or nourish'd him as I did with my blood,
Thou wouldst have left thy dearest heart-blood
    there,
Rather than have made that savage duke thine
    heir
And disinherited thine only son.
  Prince. Father, you cannot disinherit me:
If you be King, why should not I succeed?
  K. Hen. Pardon me, Margaret; pardon me,
    sweet son:
The Earl of Warwick and the Duke enforced me.
  Q. Mar. Enforced thee! art thou King, and wilt
    be forced?   230
I shame to hear thee speak. Ah, timorous wretch!

Thou hast undone thyself, thy son, and me;
And given unto the house of York such head
As thou shalt reign but by their sufferance.
To entail him and his heirs unto the crown,
What is it, but to make thy sepulchre
And creep into it far before thy time?
Warwick is chancellor and the lord of Calais;
Stern Falconbridge commands the narrow seas;
The Duke is made Protector of the realm;   240
And yet shalt thou be safe? such safety finds
The trembling lamb environed with wolves.
Had I been there, which am a silly woman,
The soldiers should have toss'd me on their pikes
Before I would have granted to that act.
But thou preferr'st thy life before thine honour:
And seeing thou dost, I here divorce myself
Both from thy table, Henry, and thy bed,
Until that act of parliament be repeal'd
Whereby my son is disinherited.   250
The northern lords that have forsworn thy col-
    ours
Will follow mine, if once they see them spread;
And spread they shall be, to thy foul disgrace
And utter ruin of the house of York.
Thus do I leave thee. Come, son, let's away;
Our army is ready; come, we'll after them.
  K. Hen. Stay, gentle Margaret, and hear me
    speak.
  Q. Mar. Thou hast spoke too much already:
    get thee gone.
  K. Hen. Gentle son, Edward, thou wilt stay
    with me?
  Q. Mar. Ay, to be murder'd by his enemies.
  Prince. When I return with victory from the
    field   261
I'll see your Grace: till then I'll follow her.
  Q. Mar. Come, son, away; we may not linger
    thus.
              [*Exeunt* QUEEN MARGARET *and the* PRINCE.
  K. Hen. Poor queen! how love to me and to her
    son
Hath made her break out into terms of rage!
Revenged may she be on that hateful duke,
Whose haughty spirit, winged with desire,
Will cost my crown, and like an empty eagle
Tire on the flesh of me and of my son!
The loss of those three lords torments my heart:
I'll write unto them and entreat them fair.   271
Come, cousin, you shall be the messenger.
  Exe. And I, I hope, shall reconcile them all.
                                          [*Exeunt.*

              SCENE II. *Sandal Castle*
    Enter RICHARD, EDWARD, *and* MONTAGUE.
  Rich. Brother, though I be youngest, give me
    leave.

Edw. No, I can better play the orator.
Mont. But I have reasons strong and forcible.

Enter the DUKE OF YORK.

York. Why, how now, sons and brother! at a
    strife?
What is your quarrel? how began it first?
Edw. No quarrel, but a slight contention.
York. About what?
Rich. About that which concerns your Grace
    and us;
The crown of England, father, which is yours. 9
York. Mine, boy? not till King Henry be dead.
Rich. Your right depends not on his life or
    death.
Edw. Now you are heir, therefore enjoy it
    now:
By giving the house of Lancaster leave to breathe,
It will outrun you, father, in the end.
York. I took an oath that he should quietly reign.
Edw. But for a kingdom any oath may be
    broken:
I would break a thousand oaths to reign one year.
Rich. No; God forbid your Grace should be
    forsworn.
York. I shall be, if I claim by open war.
Rich. I'll prove the contrary, if you'll hear me
    speak. 20
York. Thou canst not, son; it is impossible.
Rich. An oath is of no moment, being not took
Before a true and lawful magistrate,
That hath authority over him that swears:
Henry had none, but did usurp the place;
Then, seeing 'twas he that made you to depose,
Your oath, my lord, is vain and frivolous.
Therefore, to arms! And, father, do but think
How sweet a thing it is to wear a crown;
Within whose circuit is Elysium 30
And all that poets feign of bliss and joy.
Why do we linger thus? I cannot rest
Until the white rose that I wear be dyed
Even in the lukewarm blood of Henry's heart.
  York. Richard, enough; I will be King, or die.
Brother, thou shalt to London presently,
And whet on Warwick to this enterprise.
Thou, Richard, shalt to the Duke of Norfolk,
And tell him privily of our intent.
You, Edward, shall unto my Lord Cobham, 40
With whom the Kentishmen will willingly rise:
In them I trust; for they are soldiers,
Witty, courteous, liberal, full of spirit.
While you are thus employ'd, what resteth
    more,
But that I seek occasion how to rise,
And yet the King not privy to my drift,
Nor any of the house of Lancaster?

Enter a MESSENGER.

But, stay: what news? Why comest thou in such
    post?
Mess. The Queen with all the northern earls
    and lords
Intend here to besiege you in your castle: 50
She is hard by with twenty thousand men;
And therefore fortify your hold, my lord.
  York. Ay, with my sword. What! think'st thou
    that we fear them?
Edward and Richard, you shall stay with me;
My brother Montague shall post to London:
Let noble Warwick, Cobham, and the rest,
Whom we have left protectors of the King,
With powerful policy strengthen themselves,
And trust not simple Henry nor his oaths. 59
  Mont. Brother, I go; I'll win them, fear it not:
And thus most humbly I do take my leave. [*Exit.*

Enter SIR JOHN MORTIMER *and* SIR HUGH MORTIMER.

York. Sir John and Sir Hugh Mortimer, mine
    uncles,
You are come to Sandal in a happy hour;
The army of the Queen mean to besiege us.
Sir John. She shall not need; we'll meet her in
    the field.
York. What, with five thousand men?
Rich. Ay, with five hundred, father, for a need:
A woman's general; what should we fear?
    A march afar off.
Edw. I hear their drums: let's set our men in
    order,
And issue forth and bid them battle straight. 70
  York. Five men to twenty! though the odds be
    great,
I doubt not, uncle, of our victory.
Many a battle have I won in France,
When as the enemy hath been ten to one:
Why should I not now have the like success?
    [*Alarum. Exeunt.*

SCENE III. *Field of battle betwixt Sandal Castle and Wakefield*

Alarums. Enter RUTLAND *and his* TUTOR.

Rut. Ah, whither shall I fly to 'scape their
    hands?
Ah, tutor, look where bloody Clifford comes!

Enter CLIFFORD *and Soldiers.*

Clif. Chaplain, away! thy priesthood saves thy
    life.
As for the brat of this accursed duke,
Whose father slew my father, he shall die.
Tut. And I, my lord, will bear him company.

Clif. Soldiers, away with him!

Tut. Ah, Clifford, murder not this innocent
    child,
Lest thou be hated both of God and man!
           [Exit, dragged off by Soldiers.

Clif. How now! is he dead already? or is it
    fear   10
That makes him close his eyes? I'll open them.

Rut. So looks the pent-up lion o'er the wretch
That trembles under his devouring paws;
And so he walks, insulting o'er his prey,
And so he comes, to rend his limbs asunder.
Ah, gentle Clifford, kill me with thy sword,
And not with such a cruel threatening look.
Sweet Clifford, hear me speak before I die.
I am too mean a subject for thy wrath:
Be thou revenged on men, and let me live. 20

Clif. In vain thou speak'st, poor boy; my
    father's blood
Hath stopp'd the passage where thy words
    should enter.

Rut. Then let my father's blood open it again:
He is a man, and, Clifford, cope with him.

Clif. Had I thy brethren here, their lives and
    thine
Were not revenge sufficient for me;
No, if I digg'd up thy forefathers' graves
And hung their rotten coffins up in chains,
It could not slake mine ire, nor ease my heart.
The sight of any of the house of York 30
Is as a fury to torment my soul;
And till I root out their accursed line
And leave not one alive, I live in hell.
Therefore— *[Lifting his hand.]*

Rut. O, let me pray before I take my death!
To thee I pray; sweet Clifford, pity me!

Clif. Such pity as my rapier's point affords.

Rut. I never did thee harm: why wilt thou slay
    me?

Clif. Thy father hath.

Rut.   But 'twas ere I was born.
Thou hast one son; for his sake pity me, 40
Lest in revenge thereof, sith God is just,
He be as miserably slain as I.
Ah, let me live in prison all my days;
And when I give occasion of offence,
Then let me die, for now thou hast no cause.

Clif. No cause!
Thy father slew my father; therefore, die. *[Stabs
    him.]*

Rut. Di faciant laudis summa sit ista tuæ!   *[Dies.*

Clif. Plantagenet! I come, Plantagenet!
And this thy son's blood cleaving to my blade 50
Shall rust upon my weapon, till thy blood,
Congeal'd with this, do make me wipe off both.
                   [Exit.

SCENE IV. *Another part of the field*

Alarum. Enter RICHARD, DUKE OF YORK.

York. The army of the Queen hath got the field:
My uncles both are slain in rescuing me;
And all my followers to the eager foe
Turn back and fly, like ships before the wind
Or lambs pursued by hunger-starved wolves.
My sons, God knows what hath bechanced them:
But this I know, they have demean'd themselves
Like men born to renown by life or death.
Three times did Richard make a lane to me,
And thrice cried, "Courage, father! fight it out!"
And full as oft came Edward to my side, 11
With purple falchion, painted to the hilt
In blood of those that had encounter'd him:
And when the hardiest warriors did retire,
Richard cried, "Charge! and give no foot of
    ground!"
And cried, "A crown, or else a glorious tomb!
A sceptre, or an earthly sepulchre!"
With this, we charged again: but, out, alas!
We bodged again; as I have seen a swan
With bootless labour swim against the tide 20
And spend her strength with over-matching
    waves. *[A short alarum within.]*
Ah, hark! the fatal followers do pursue;
And I am faint and cannot fly their fury:
And were I strong, I would not shun their fury:
The sands are number'd that make up my life;
Here must I stay, and here my life must end.

Enter QUEEN MARGARET, CLIFFORD, NORTHUM-
BERLAND, *the* PRINCE OF WALES, *and* Soldiers.

Come, bloody Clifford, rough Northumberland,
I dare your quenchless fury to more rage:
I am your butt, and I abide your shot. 29

North. Yield to our mercy, proud Plantagenet.

Clif. Ay, to such mercy as his ruthless arm,
With downright payment, show'd unto my fa-
    ther.
Now Phaëthon hath tumbled from his car,
And made an evening at the noontide prick.

York. My ashes, as the phœnix, may bring forth
A bird that will revenge upon you all:
And in that hope I throw mine eyes to heaven,
Scorning whate'er you can afflict me with.
Why come you not? what! multitudes, and fear?

Clif. So cowards fight when they can fly no fur-
    ther; 40
So doves do peck the falcon's piercing talons;
So desperate thieves, all hopeless of their lives,
Breathe out invectives 'gainst the officers.

York. O Clifford, but bethink thee once again,
And in thy thought o'er-run my former time;
And, if thou canst for blushing, view this face,

And bite thy tongue, that slanders him with
    cowardice
Whose frown hath made thee faint and fly ere
    this!
  Clif. I will not bandy with thee word for word,
But buckle with thee blows, twice two for one. 50
  Q. Mar. Hold, valiant Clifford! for a thousand
    causes
I would prolong awhile the traitor's life.
Wrath makes him deaf: speak thou, Northum-
    berland.
  North. Hold, Clifford! do not honour him so
    much
To prick thy finger, though to wound his heart:
What valour were it, when a cur doth grin,
For one to thrust his hand between his teeth,
When he might spurn him with his foot away?
It is war's prize to take all vantages;
And ten to one is no impeach of valour.   60
  They lay hands on YORK, *who struggles.*
  Clif. Ay, ay, so strives the woodcock with the
    gin.
  North. So doth the cony struggle in the net.
  York. So triumph thieves upon their conquer'd
    booty;
So true men yield, with robbers so o'ermatch'd.
  North. What would your grace have done unto
    him now?
  Q. Mar. Brave warriors, Clifford and Northum-
    berland,
Come, make him stand upon this molehill here,
That raught at mountains with outstretched arms,
Yet parted but the shadow with his hand.
What! was it you that would be England's king?
Was't you that revell'd in our parliament,   71
And made a preachment of your high descent?
Where are your mess of sons to back you now?
The wanton Edward, and the lusty George?
And where's that valiant crook-back prodigy,
Dicky your boy, that with his grumbling voice
Was wont to cheer his dad in mutinies?
Or, with the rest, where is your darling Rutland?
Look, York: I stain'd this napkin with the blood
That valiant Clifford, with his rapier's point, 80
Made issue from the bosom of the boy;
And if thine eyes can water for his death,
I give thee this to dry thy cheeks withal.
Alas, poor York! but that I hate thee deadly,
I should lament thy miserable state.
I prithee, grieve, to make me merry, York.
What, hath thy fiery heart so parch'd thine en-
    trails
That not a tear can fall for Rutland's death?
Why art thou patient, man? thou shouldst be
    mad;
And I, to make thee mad, do mock thee thus. 90

Stamp, rave, and fret, that I may sing and dance.
Thou wouldst be fee'd, I see, to make me sport:
York cannot speak, unless he wear a crown.
A crown for York! and, lords, bow low to him:
Hold you his hands, whilst I do set it on.
  Putting a paper crown on his head.
Ay, marry, sir, now looks he like a king!
Ay, this is he that took King Henry's chair,
And this is he was his adopted heir.
But how is it that great Plantagenet
Is crown'd so soon, and broke his solemn oath?
As I bethink me, you should not be King   101
Till our King Henry had shook hands with death.
And will you pale your head in Henry's glory,
And rob his temples of the diadem,
Now in his life, against your holy oath?
O, 'tis a fault too too unpardonable!
Off with the crown; and, with the crown, his
    head;
And, whilst we breathe, take time to do him dead.
  Clif. That is my office, for my father's sake.
  Q. Mar. Nay, stay; let's hear the orisons he
    makes.   110
  York. She-wolf of France, but worse than wolves
    of France,
Whose tongue more poisons than the adder's
    tooth!
How ill-beseeming is it in thy sex
To triumph, like an Amazonian trull,
Upon their woes whom fortune captivates!
But that thy face is, visard-like, unchanging,
Made impudent with use of evil deeds,
I would assay, proud queen, to make thee blush.
To tell thee whence thou camest, of whom de-
    rived,
Were shame enough to shame thee, wert thou
    not shameless.   120
Thy father bears the type of King of Naples,
Of both the Sicils and Jerusalem,
Yet not so wealthy as an English yeoman.
Hath that poor monarch taught thee to insult?
It needs not, nor it boots thee not, proud queen,
Unless the adage must be verified,
That beggars mounted run their horse to death.
'Tis beauty that doth oft make women proud;
But, God he knows, thy share thereof is small:
'Tis virtue that doth make them most admired;
The contrary doth make thee wonder'd at: 131
'Tis government that makes them seem divine;
The want thereof makes thee abominable:
Thou art as opposite to every good
As the Antipodes are unto us,
Or as the south to the septentrion.
O tiger's heart wrapt in a woman's hide!
How couldst thou drain the life-blood of the
    child,

To bid the father wipe his eyes withal,
And yet be seen to bear a woman's face?   *140*
Women are soft, mild, pitiful, and flexible;
Thou stern, obdurate, flinty, rough, remorseless.
Bid'st thou me rage? why, now thou hast thy
    wish:
Wouldst have me weep? why, now thou hast thy
    will:
For raging wind blows up incessant showers,
And when the rage allays, the rain begins.
These tears are my sweet Rutland's obsequies:
And every drop cries vengeance for his death,
'Gainst thee, fell Clifford, and thee, false French-
    woman.
    North. Beshrew me, but his passion moves me
        so   *150*
That hardly can I check my eyes from tears.
    York. That face of his the hungry cannibals
Would not have touch'd, would not have stain'd
    with blood:
But you are more inhuman, more inexorable,
O, ten times more, than tigers of Hyrcania.
See, ruthless queen, a hapless father's tears:
This cloth thou dip'dst in blood of my sweet boy,
And I with tears do wash the blood away.
Keep thou the napkin, and go boast of this:
And if thou tell'st the heavy story right,   *160*
Upon my soul, the hearers will shed tears;
Yea even my foes will shed fast-falling tears,
And say, "Alas, it was a piteous deed!"
There, take the crown, and, with the crown, my
    curse;
And in thy need such comfort come to thee
As now I reap at thy too cruel hand!
Hard-hearted Clifford, take me from the world:
My soul to heaven, my blood upon your heads!
    North. Had he been slaughter-man to all my
        kin,
I should not for my life but weep with him,   *170*
To see how inly sorrow gripes his soul.
    Q. Mar. What, weeping-ripe, my Lord North-
    umberland?
Think but upon the wrong he did us all,
And that will quickly dry thy melting tears.
    Clif. Here's for my oath, here's for my father's
    death. [*Stabbing him.*]
    Q. Mar. And here's to right our gentle-hearted
    king. [*Stabbing him.*]
    York. Open Thy gate of mercy, gracious
    God!
My soul flies through these wounds to seek out
    Thee.   [*Dies.*
    Q. Mar. Off with his head, and set it on York
    gates;
So York may overlook the town of York.   *180*
                    [*Flourish. Exeunt.*

ACT II

SCENE I. *A plain near Mortimer's Cross in Herefordshire*

A march. Enter EDWARD, RICHARD, *and their power.*

    Edw. I wonder how our princely father 'scaped,
Or whether he be 'scaped away or no
From Clifford's and Northumberland's pursuit:
Had he been ta'en, we should have heard the
    news;
Had he been slain, we should have heard the
    news;
Or had he 'scaped, methinks we should have
    heard
The happy tidings of his good escape.
How fares my brother? why is he so sad?
    Rich. I cannot joy, until I be resolved
Where our right valiant father is become.   *10*
I saw him in the battle range about;
And watch'd him how he singled Clifford
    forth.
Methought he bore him in the thickest troop
As doth a lion in a herd of neat;
Or as a bear, encompass'd round with dogs,
Who having pinch'd a few and made them cry,
The rest stand all aloof, and bark at him.
So fared our father with his enemies;
So fled his enemies my warlike father:
Methinks, 'tis prize enough to be his son.   *20*
See how the morning opes her golden gates,
And takes her farewell of the glorious sun!
How well resembles it the prime of youth,
Trimm'd like a younker prancing to his love!
    Edw. Dazzle mine eyes, or do I see three
    suns?
    Rich. Three glorious suns, each one a perfect
    sun;
Not separated with the racking clouds,
But sever'd in a pale clear-shining sky.
See, see! they join, embrace, and seem to kiss,
As if they vow'd some league inviolable: *30*
Now are they but one lamp, one light, one sun.
In this the heaven figures some event.
    Edw. 'Tis wondrous strange, the like yet never
    heard of.
I think it cites us, brother, to the field,
That we, the sons of brave Plantagenet,
Each one already blazing by our meeds,
Should notwithstanding join our lights together
And over-shine the earth as this the world.
Whate'er it bodes, henceforward will I bear
Upon my target three fair-shining suns.   *40*
    Rich. Nay, bear three daughters: by your leave
    I speak it,
You love the breeder better than the male.

Enter a MESSENGER.

But what art thou, whose heavy looks foretell
Some dreadful story hanging on thy tongue?
　Mess. Ah, one that was a woeful looker-on
When as the noble Duke of York was slain,
Your princely father and my loving lord!
　Edw. O, speak no more, for I have heard too
　　much.
　Rich. Say how he died, for I will hear it all.
　Mess. Environed he was with many foes,　　50
And stood against them, as the hope of Troy
Against the Greeks that would have enter'd
　　Troy.
But Hercules himself must yield to odds;
And many strokes, though with a little axe,
Hew down and fell the hardest-timber'd oak.
By many hands your father was subdued;
But only slaughter'd by the ireful arm
Of unrelenting Clifford and the Queen,
Who crown'd the gracious Duke in high despite,
Laugh'd in his face; and when with grief he
　　wept,
The ruthless Queen gave him to dry his cheeks 61
A napkin steeped in the harmless blood
Of sweet young Rutland, by rough Clifford slain:
And after many scorns, many foul taunts,
They took his head, and on the gates of York
They set the same; and there it doth remain,
The saddest spectacle that e'er I view'd.
　Edw. Sweet Duke of York, our prop to lean
　　upon,
Now thou art gone, we have no staff, no stay.
O Clifford, boisterous Clifford! thou hast slain
The flower of Europe for his chivalry;　　71
And treacherously hast thou vanquish'd him,
For hand to hand he would have vanquish'd thee.
Now my soul's palace is become a prison:
Ah, would she break from hence, that this my
　　body
Might in the ground be closed up in rest!
For never henceforth shall I joy again,
Never, O never, shall I see more joy!
　Rich. I cannot weep; for all my body's moisture
Scarce serves to quench my furnace-burning
　　heart:
Nor can my tongue unload my heart's great
　　burthen;　　81
For selfsame wind that I should speak withal
Is kindling coals that fires all my breast,
And burns me up with flames that tears would
　　quench.
To weep is to make less the depth of grief:
Tears then for babes; blows and revenge for me.
Richard, I bear thy name; I'll venge thy death,
Or die renowned by attempting it.

　Edw. His name that valiant duke hath left with
　　thee;
His dukedom and his chair with me is left.　　90
　Rich. Nay, if thou be that princely eagle's bird,
Show thy descent by gazing 'gainst the sun:
For chair and dukedom, throne and kingdom say;
Either that is thine, or else thou wert not his.

　March. Enter WARWICK, MARQUESS OF
　　MONTAGUE, *and their army.*

　War. How now, fair lords! What fare? what
　　news abroad?
　Rich. Great Lord of Warwick, if we should re-
　　count
Our baleful news, and at each word's deliverance
Stab poniards in our flesh till all were told,
The words would add more anguish than the
　　wounds.
O valiant lord, the Duke of York is slain!　　100
　Edw. O Warwick, Warwick! that Plantagenet,
Which held thee dearly as his soul's redemption,
Is by the stern Lord Clifford done to death.
　War. Ten days ago I drown'd these news in
　　tears;
And now, to add more measure to your woes,
I come to tell you things sith then befall'n.
After the bloody fray at Wakefield fought,
Where your brave father breathed his latest gasp,
Tidings, as swiftly as the posts could run,
Were brought me of your loss and his depart.　*110*
I, then in London, keeper of the King,
Muster'd my soldiers, gather'd flocks of friends,
And very well appointed, as I thought,
March'd toward Saint Alban's to intercept the
　　Queen,
Bearing the King in my behalf along;
For by my scouts I was advertised
That she was coming with a full intent
To dash our late decree in parliament
Touching King Henry's oath and your succes-
　　sion.
Short tale to make, we at Saint Alban's met,　*120*
Our battles join'd, and both sides fiercely fought:
But whether 'twas the coldness of the King,
Who look'd full gently on his warlike Queen,
That robb'd my soldiers of their heated spleen;
Or whether 'twas report of her success;
Or more than common fear of Clifford's rigour,
Who thunders to his captives blood and death,
I cannot judge: but, to conclude with truth,
Their weapons like to lightning came and went;
Our soldiers', like the night-owl's lazy flight, *130*
Or like an idle thresher with a flail,
Fell gently down, as if they struck their friends.
I cheer'd them up with justice of our cause,
With promise of high pay and great rewards:

But all in vain; they had no heart to fight,
And we in them no hope to win the day;
So that we fled; the King unto the Queen;
Lord George your brother, Norfolk, and myself,
In haste, post-haste, are come to join with you;
For in the marches here we heard you were, *140*
Making another head to fight again.
  Edw. Where is the Duke of Norfolk, gentle
    Warwick?
And when came George from Burgundy to Eng-
    land?
  War. Some six miles off the Duke is with the
    soldiers;
And for your brother, he was lately sent
From your kind aunt, Duchess of Burgundy,
With aid of soldiers to this needful war.
  Rich. 'Twas odds, belike, when valiant War-
    wick fled:
Oft have I heard his praises in pursuit,
But ne'er till now his scandal of retire. *150*
  War. Nor now my scandal, Richard, dost thou
    hear;
For thou shalt know this strong right hand of
    mine
Can pluck the diadem from faint Henry's head,
And wring the awful sceptre from his fist,
Were he as famous and as bold in war
As he is famed for mildness, peace, and prayer.
  Rich. I know it well, Lord Warwick; blame me
    not:
'Tis love I bear thy glories makes me speak.
But in this troublous time what's to be done?
Shall we go throw away our coats of steel, *160*
And wrap our bodies in black mourning gowns,
Numbering our Ave-Maries with our beads?
Or shall we on the helmets of our foes
Tell our devotion with revengeful arms?
If for the last, say ay, and to it, lords.
  War. Why, therefore Warwick came to seek
    you out;
And therefore comes my brother Montague.
Attend me, lords. The proud insulting Queen,
With Clifford and the haught Northumberland,
And of their feather many moe proud birds, *170*
Have wrought the easy-melting King like wax.
He swore consent to your succession,
His oath enrolled in the parliament;
And now to London all the crew are gone,
To frustrate both his oath and what beside
May make against the house of Lancaster.
Their power, I think, is thirty thousand strong:
Now, if the help of Norfolk and myself,
With all the friends that thou, brave Earl of
    March,
Amongst the loving Welshmen canst procure,*180*
Will but amount to five and twenty thousand,

Why, Via! to London will we march amain,
And once again bestride our foaming steeds,
And once again cry, "Charge upon our foes!"
But never once again turn back and fly.
  Rich. Ay, now methinks I hear great Warwick
    speak:
Ne'er may he live to see a sunshine day,
That cries "Retire," if Warwick bid him stay.
  Edw. Lord Warwick, on thy shoulder will I
    lean; *189*
And when thou fail'st—as God forbid the
    hour—
Must Edward fall, which peril heaven forfend!
  War. No longer Earl of March, but Duke of
    York:
The next degree is England's royal throne;
For King of England shalt thou be proclaim'd
In every borough as we pass along;
And he that throws not up his cap for joy
Shall for the fault make forfeit of his head.
King Edward, valiant Richard, Montague,
Stay we no longer, dreaming of renown,
But sound the trumpets, and about our task. *200*
  Rich. Then, Clifford, were thy heart as hard as
    steel,
As thou hast shown it flinty by thy deeds,
I come to pierce it, or to give thee mine.
  Edw. Then strike up drums: God and Saint
    George for us!

Enter a SECOND MESSENGER.

  War. How now! what news?
  2nd Mess. The Duke of Norfolk sends you word
    by me,
The Queen is coming with a puissant host;
And craves your company for speedy counsel.
  War. Why then it sorts, brave warriors, let's
    away. [*Exeunt.*

SCENE II. *Before York*

Flourish. Enter KING HENRY, QUEEN MARGARET,
the PRINCE OF WALES, CLIFFORD, *and* NORTH-
UMBERLAND, *with drum and trumpets.*

  Q. Mar. Welcome, my lord, to this brave town
    of York.
Yonder's the head of that arch-enemy
That sought to be encompass'd with your crown:
Doth not the object cheer your heart, my lord?
  K. Hen. Ay, as the rocks cheer them that fear
    their wreck:
To see this sight, it irks my very soul.
Withhold revenge, dear God! 'tis not my fault,
Nor wittingly have I infringed my vow.
  Clif. My gracious liege, this too much lenity
And harmful pity must be laid aside. *10*
To whom do lions cast their gentle looks?

Not to the beast that would usurp their den.
Whose hand is that the forest bear doth lick?
Not his that spoils her young before her face.
Who 'scapes the lurking serpent's mortal sting?
Not he that sets his foot upon her back.
The smallest worm will turn being trodden on,
And doves will peck in safeguard of their brood.
Ambitious York did level at thy crown,
Thou smiling while he knit his angry brows: 20
He, but a duke, would have his son a king,
And raise his issue, like a loving sire;
Thou, being a king, blest with a goodly son,
Didst yield consent to disinherit him,
Which argued thee a most unloving father.
Unreasonable creatures feed their young;
And though man's face be fearful to their eyes,
Yet, in protection of their tender ones,
Who hath not seen them, even with those wings
Which sometime they have used with fearful
    flight,   30
Make war with him that climb'd unto their nest,
Offering their own lives in their young's de-
    fence?
For shame, my liege, make them your precedent!
Were it not pity that this goodly boy
Should lose his birthright by his father's fault,
And long hereafter say unto his child,
"What my great-grandfather and grandsire got
My careless father fondly gave away"?
Ah, what a shame were this! Look on the boy;
And let his manly face, which promiseth   40
Successful fortune, steel thy melting heart
To hold thine own and leave thine own with him.
    K. Hen. Full well hath Clifford play'd the ora-
    tor,
Inferring arguments of mighty force.
But, Clifford, tell me, didst thou never hear
That things ill-got had ever bad success?
And happy always was it for that son
Whose father for his hoarding went to hell?
I'll leave my son my virtuous deeds behind;
And would my father had left me no more!   50
For all the rest is held at such a rate
As brings a thousand-fold more care to keep
Than in possession any jot of pleasure.
Ah, cousin York! would thy best friends did
    know
How it doth grieve me that thy head is here!
    Q. Mar. My lord, cheer up your spirits: our
    foes are nigh,
And this soft courage makes your followers faint.
You promised knighthood to our forward son:
Unsheathe your sword, and dub him presently.
Edward, kneel down.   60
    K. Hen. Edward Plantagenet, arise a knight;
And learn this lesson, draw thy sword in right.

    Prince. My gracious father, by your kingly
    leave,
I'll draw it as apparent to the crown,
And in that quarrel use it to the death.
    Clif. Why, that is spoken like a toward prince.

Enter a MESSENGER.

    Mess. Royal commanders, be in readiness:
For with a band of thirty thousand men
Comes Warwick, backing of the Duke of
    York;
And in the towns, as they do march along,   70
Proclaims him king, and many fly to him:
Darraign your battle, for they are at hand.
    Clif. I would your Highness would depart the
    field:
The Queen hath best success when you are ab-
    sent.
    Q. Mar. Ay, good my lord, and leave us to our
    fortune.
    K. Hen. Why, that's my fortune too; therefore
    I'll stay.
    North. Be it with resolution then to fight.
    Prince. My royal father, cheer these noble lords
And hearten those that fight in your defence:
Unsheathe your sword, good father; cry "Saint
    George!"   80

March. Enter EDWARD, GEORGE, RICHARD, WAR-
    WICK, NORFOLK, MONTAGUE, *and Soldiers.*

    Edw. Now, perjured Henry! wilt thou kneel for
    grace,
And set thy diadem upon my head;
Or bide the mortal fortune of the field?
    Q. Mar. Go, rate thy minions, proud insulting
    boy!
Becomes it thee to be thus bold in terms
Before thy sovereign and thy lawful king?
    Edw. I am his king, and he should bow his knee;
I was adopted heir by his consent:
Since when, his oath is broke; for, as I hear,
You, that are king, though he do wear the crown,
Have caused him, by new act of parliament,   91
To blot out me, and put his own son in.
    Clif. And reason too:
Who should succeed the father but the son?
    Rich. Are you there, butcher? O, I cannot
    speak!
    Clif. Ay, crook-back, here I stand to answer
    thee,
Or any he the proudest of thy sort.
    Rich. 'Twas you that kill'd young Rutland,
    was it not?
    Clif. Ay, and old York, and yet not satisfied.
    Rich. For God's sake, lords, give signal to the
    fight.   100

War. What say'st thou, Henry, wilt thou yield
  the crown?
Q. Mar. Why, how now, long-tongued War-
  wick! dare you speak?
When you and I met at Saint Alban's last,
Your legs did better service than your hands.
  War. Then 'twas my turn to fly, and now 'tis
  thine.
  Clif. You said so much before, and yet you fled.
  War. 'Twas not your valour, Clifford, drove me
  thence.
  North. No, nor your manhood that durst make
  you stay.
  Rich. Northumberland, I hold thee reverently.
Break off the parley; for scarce I can refrain   110
The execution of my big-swoln heart
Upon that Clifford, that cruel child-killer.
  Clif. I slew thy father, call'st thou him a child?
  Rich. Ay, like a dastard and a treacherous
  coward,
As thou didst kill our tender brother Rutland;
But ere sunset I'll make thee curse the deed.
  K. Hen. Have done with words, my lords, and
  hear me speak.
  Q. Mar. Defy them then, or else hold close thy
  lips.
  K. Hen. I prithee, give no limits to my tongue:
I am a king, and privileged to speak.   120
  Clif. My liege, the wound that bred this meet-
  ing here
Cannot be cured by words; therefore be still.
  Rich. Then, executioner, unsheathe thy sword:
By him that made us all, I am resolved
That Clifford's manhood lies upon his tongue.
  Edw. Say, Henry, shall I have my right, or no?
A thousand men have broke their fasts to-day,
That ne'er shall dine unless thou yield the crown.
  War. If thou deny, their blood upon thy head;
For York in justice puts his armour on.   130
  Prince. If that be right which Warwick says is
  right,
There is no wrong, but every thing is right.
  Rich. Whoever got thee, there thy mother
  stands;
For, well I wot, thou hast thy mother's tongue.
  Q. Mar. But thou art neither like thy sire nor
  dam;
But like a foul mis-shapen stigmatic,
Mark'd by the destinies to be avoided,
As venom toads, or lizards' dreadful stings.
  Rich. Iron of Naples hid with English gilt,
Whose father bears the title of a king—   140
As if a channel should be call'd the sea—
Shamest thou not, knowing whence thou art ex-
  traught,
To let thy tongue detect thy base-born heart?

Edw. A wisp of straw were worth a thousand
  crowns,
To make this shameless callet know herself.
Helen of Greece was fairer far than thou,
Although thy husband may be Menelaus;
And ne'er was Agamemnon's brother wrong'd
By that false woman, as this King by thee.
His father revell'd in the heart of France,   150
And tamed the King, and made the Dauphin
  stoop;
And had he match'd according to his state,
He might have kept that glory to this day;
But when he took a beggar to his bed,
And graced thy poor sire with his bridal-day,
Even then that sunshine brew'd a shower for him,
That wash'd his father's fortunes forth of France
And heap'd sedition on his crown at home.
For what hath broach'd this tumult but thy pride?
Hadst thou been meek, our title still had slept;
And we, in pity of the gentle king,   161
Had slipp'd our claim until another age.
  Geo. But when we saw our sunshine made thy
  spring,
And that thy summer bred us no increase,
We set the axe to thy usurping root;
And though the edge hath something hit our-
  selves,
Yet, know thou, since we have begun to strike,
We'll never leave till we have hewn thee down,
Or bathed thy growing with our heated bloods.
  Edw. And, in this resolution, I defy thee;   170
Not willing any longer conference,
Since thou deniest the gentle king to speak.
Sound trumpets! let our bloody colours wave!
And either victory, or else a grave.
  Q. Mar. Stay, Edward.
  Edw. No, wrangling woman, we'll no longer
  stay:
These words will cost ten thousand lives this day.
                                    [*Exeunt.*

SCENE III. *A field of battle between Towton
and Saxton, in Yorkshire*

Alarum. Excursions. Enter WARWICK.

War. Forspent with toil, as runners with a race,
I lay me down a little while to breathe;
For strokes received, and many blows repaid,
Have robb'd my strong-knit sinews of their
  strength,
And spite of spite needs must I rest awhile.

Enter EDWARD, *running.*

Edw. Smile, gentle heaven! or strike, ungentle
  death!
For this world frowns, and Edward's sun is
  clouded.

War. How now, my lord! what hap? what hope
of good?

Enter GEORGE.

Geo. Our hap is loss, our hope but sad despair;
Our ranks are broke, and ruin follows us: 10
What counsel give you? whither we fly?
  Edw. Bootless is flight, they follow us with
wings;
And weak we are and cannot shun pursuit.

Enter RICHARD.

Rich. Ah, Warwick, why hast thou withdrawn
thyself?
Thy brother's blood the thirsty earth hath drunk,
Broach'd with the steely point of Clifford's lance;
And in the very pangs of death he cried,
Like to a dismal clangor heard from far,
"Warwick, revenge! brother, revenge my
death!"
So, underneath the belly of their steeds,   20
That stain'd their fetlocks in his smoking
blood,
The noble gentleman gave up the ghost.
  War. Then let the earth be drunken with our
blood:
I'll kill my horse, because I will not fly.
Why stand we like soft-hearted women here,
Wailing our losses, whiles the foe doth rage;
And look upon, as if the tragedy
Were play'd in jest by counterfeiting actors?
Here on my knee I vow to God above,
I'll never pause again, never stand still,   30
Till either death hath closed these eyes of mine
Or fortune given me measure of revenge.
  Edw. O Warwick, I do bend my knee with
thine;
And in this vow do chain my soul to thine!
And, ere my knee rise from the earth's cold face,
I throw my hands, mine eyes, my heart to thee,
Thou setter up and plucker down of kings,
Beseeching thee, if with thy will it stands
That to my foes this body must be prey,
Yet that thy brazen gates of heaven may ope,   40
And give sweet passage to my sinful soul!
Now, lords, take leave until we meet again,
Where'er it be, in heaven or in earth.
  Rich. Brother, give me thy hand; and, gentle
Warwick,
Let me embrace thee in my weary arms:
I, that did never weep, now melt with woe
That winter should cut off our spring-time so.
  War. Away, away! Once more, sweet lords,
farewell.
  Geo. Yet let us all together to our troops,
And give them leave to fly that will not stay;   50

And call them pillars that will stand to us;
And, if we thrive, promise them such rewards
As victors at the Olympian games:
This may plant courage in their quailing breasts;
For yet is hope of life and victory.
Forslow no longer, make we hence amain.
                                        [*Exeunt.*

SCENE IV. *Another part of the field*

Excursions. Enter RICHARD *and* CLIFFORD.

  Rich. Now, Clifford, I have singled thee alone:
Suppose this arm is for the Duke of York,
And this for Rutland; both bound to revenge,
Wert thou environ'd with a brazen wall.
  Clif. Now, Richard, I am with thee here alone:
This is the hand that stabb'd thy father York;
And this the hand that slew thy brother Rutland;
And here's the heart that triumphs in their death
And cheers these hands that slew thy sire and
brother
To execute the like upon thyself;   10
And so, have at thee!
                They fight. WARWICK *comes;* CLIFFORD *flies.*
  Rich. Nay, Warwick, single out some other
chase;
For I myself will hunt this wolf to death.
                                        [*Exeunt.*

SCENE V. *Another part of the field*

Alarum. Enter KING HENRY *alone.*

  King. This battle fares like to the morning's
war,
When dying clouds contend with growing light,
What time the shepherd, blowing of his nails,
Can neither call it perfect day nor night.
Now sways it this way, like a mighty sea
Forced by the tide to combat with the wind;
Now sways it that way, like the selfsame sea
Forced to retire by fury of the wind:
Sometime the flood prevails, and then the wind;
Now one the better, then another best;   10
Both tugging to be victors, breast to breast,
Yet neither conqueror nor conquered:
So is the equal poise of this fell war.
Here on this molehill will I sit me down.
To whom God will, there be the victory!
For Margaret my queen, and Clifford too,
Have chid me from the battle; swearing both
They prosper best of all when I am thence.
Would I were dead! if God's good will were so;
For what is in this world but grief and woe?   20
O God! methinks it were a happy life,
To be no better than a homely swain;
To sit upon a hill, as I do now,
To carve out dials quaintly, point by point,
Thereby to see the minutes how they run,

How many make the hour full complete;
How many hours bring about the day;
How many days will finish up the year;
How many years a mortal man may live.
When this is known, then to divide the times: 30
So many hours must I tend my flock;
So many hours must I take my rest;
So many hours must I contemplate;
So many hours must I sport myself;
So many days my ewes have been with young;
So many weeks ere the poor fools will ean;
So many years ere I shall shear the fleece:
So minutes, hours, days, months, and years,
Pass'd over to the end they were created,
Would bring white hairs unto a quiet grave. 40
Ah, what a life were this! how sweet! how lovely!
Gives not the hawthorn-bush a sweeter shade
To shepherds looking on their silly sheep
Than doth a rich embroider'd canopy
To kings that fear their subjects' treachery?
O, yes it doth; a thousand-fold it doth.
And to conclude, the shepherd's homely curds,
His cold thin drink out of his leather bottle,
His wonted sleep under a fresh tree's shade,
All which secure and sweetly he enjoys, 50
Is far beyond a prince's delicates,
His viands sparkling in a golden cup,
His body couched in a curious bed,
When care, mistrust, and treason waits on him.

Alarum. Enter a son *that has killed his father,*
dragging in the dead body.

Son. Ill blows the wind that profits nobody.
This man, whom hand to hand I slew in fight,
May be possessed with some store of crowns;
And I, that haply take them from him now,
May yet ere night yield both my life and them
To some man else, as this dead man doth me. 60
Who's this? O God, it is my father's face,
Whom in this conflict I unawares have kill'd.
O heavy times, begetting such events!
From London by the King was I press'd forth;
My father, being the Earl of Warwick's man,
Came on the part of York, press'd by his master;
And I, who at his hands received my life,
Have by my hands of life bereaved him.
Pardon me, God, I knew not what I did!
And pardon, father, for I knew not thee! 70
My tears shall wipe away these bloody marks;
And no more words till they have flow'd their
fill.
K. Hen. O piteous spectacle! O bloody times!
Whiles lions war and battle for their dens,
Poor harmless lambs abide their enmity.
Weep, wretched man, I'll aid thee tear for tear;
And let out hearts and eyes, like civil war,

Be blind with tears, and break o'ercharged with
grief.

Enter a FATHER *that has killed his son, bringing*
in the body.

Fath. Thou that so stoutly hast resisted me,
Give me thy gold, if thou hast any gold; 80
For I have bought it with an hundred blows.
But let me see: is this our foeman's face?
Ah, no, no, no, it is mine only son!
Ah, boy, if any life be left in thee,
Throw up thine eye! see, see what showers arise,
Blown with the windy tempest of my heart,
Upon thy wounds, that kill mine eye and heart!
O, pity, God, this miserable age!
What stratagems, how fell, how butcherly,
Erroneous, mutinous and unnatural, 90
This deadly quarrel daily doth beget!
O boy, thy father gave thee life too soon,
And hath bereft thee of thy life too late!
K. Hen. Woe above woe! grief more than
common grief!
O that my death would stay these ruthful deeds!
O, pity, pity, gentle heaven, pity!
The red rose and the white are on his face,
The fatal colours of our striving houses:
The one his purple blood right well resembles;
The other his pale cheeks, methinks, presenteth:
Wither one rose, and let the other flourish; 101
If you contend, a thousand lives must wither.
Son. How will my mother for a father's death
Take on with me and ne'er be satisfied!
Fath. How will my wife for slaughter of my
son
Shed seas of tears and ne'er be satisfied!
K. Hen. How will the country for these woful
chances
Misthink the King and not be satisfied!
Son. Was ever son so rued a father's death?
Fath. Was ever father so bemoan'd his son?
K. Hen. Was ever king so grieved for subjects'
woe? 111
Much is your sorrow; mine ten times so much.
Son. I'll bear thee hence, where I may weep my
fill.   [*Exit with the body.*
Fath. These arms of mine shall be thy winding-
sheet;
My heart, sweet boy, shall be thy sepulchre,
For from my heart thine image ne'er shall go;
My sighing breast shall be thy funeral bell;
And so obsequious will thy father be,
Even for the loss of thee, having no more,
As Priam was for all his valiant sons. 120
I'll bear thee hence; and let them fight that will,
For I have murdered where I should not kill.
[*Exit with the body.*

K. Hen. Sad-hearted men, much overgone with care,
Here sits a king more woeful than you are.

Alarums: excursions. Enter QUEEN MARGARET,
the PRINCE OF WALES, *and* EXETER.

Prince. Fly, father, fly! for all your friends are fled,
And Warwick rages like a chafed bull:
Away! for death doth hold us in pursuit.
    Q. Mar. Mount you, my lord: towards Berwick post amain:
Edward and Richard, like a brace of greyhounds
Having the fearful flying hare in sight,   *130*
With fiery eyes sparkling for very wrath,
And bloody steel grasp'd in their ireful hands,
Are at our backs; and therefore hence amain.
    Exe. Away! for vengeance comes along with them:
Nay, stay not to expostulate, make speed;
Or else come after: I'll away before.
    K. Hen. Nay, take me with thee, good sweet Exeter:
Not that I fear to stay, but love to go
Whither the Queen intends. Forward; away!
               [*Exeunt.*

SCENE VI. *Another part of the field*
A loud alarum. Enter CLIFFORD, *wounded.*

Clif. Here burns my candle out; ay, here it dies,
Which, whiles it lasted, gave King Henry light.
O Lancaster, I fear thy overthrow
More than my body's parting with my soul!
My love and fear glued many friends to thee;
And, now I fall, thy tough commixture melts.
Impairing Henry, strengthening misproud York,
The common people swarm like summer flies;
And whither fly the gnats but to the sun?
And who shines now but Henry's enemies?   *10*
O Phœbus, hadst thou never given consent
That Phaëthon should check thy fiery steeds,
Thy burning car never had scorch'd the earth!
And, Henry, hadst thou sway'd as kings should do,
Or as thy father and his father did,
Giving no ground unto the house of York,
They never then had sprung like summer flies;
I and ten thousand in this luckless realm
Had left no mourning widows for our death;
And thou this day hadst kept thy chair in peace.
For what doth cherish weeds but gentle air?   *21*
And what makes robbers bold but too much lenity?
Bootless are plaints, and cureless are my wounds;
No way to fly, nor strength to hold out flight:
The foe is merciless, and will not pity;

For at their hands I have deserved no pity.
The air hath got into my deadly wounds,
And much effuse of blood doth make me faint.
Come, York and Richard, Warwick and the rest;
I stabb'd your fathers' bosoms, split my breast.
               [*He faints.*]

Alarum and retreat. Enter EDWARD, GEORGE,
RICHARD, MONTAGUE, WARWICK, *and Soldiers.*

Edw. Now breathe we, lords: good fortune bids us pause,   *31*
And smooth the frowns of war with peaceful looks.
Some troops pursue the bloody-minded Queen,
That led calm Henry, though he were a king,
As doth a sail, fill'd with a fretting gust,
Command an argosy to stem the waves.
But think you, lords, that Clifford fled with them?
    War. No, 'tis impossible he should escape;
For, though before his face I speak the words,
Your brother Richard mark'd him for the grave:
And wheresoe'er he is, he's surely dead.   *41*
          [CLIFFORD *groans, and dies.*
    Edw. Whose soul is that which takes her heavy leave?
    Rich. A deadly groan, like life and death's departing.
    Edw. See who it is: and, now the battle's ended,
If friend or foe, let him be gently used.
    Rich. Revoke that doom of mercy, for 'tis Clifford;
Who not contented that he lopp'd the branch
In hewing Rutland when his leaves put forth,
But set his murdering knife unto the root
From whence that tender spray did sweetly spring,
I mean our princely father, Duke of York.   *51*
    War. From off the gates of York fetch down the head,
Your father's head, which Clifford placed there;
Instead whereof let this supply the room:
Measure for measure must be answered.
    Edw. Bring forth that fatal screech-owl to our house,
That nothing sung but death to us and ours:
Now death shall stop his dismal threatening sound,
And his ill-boding tongue no more shall speak.
    War. I think his understanding is bereft.   *60*
Speak, Clifford, dost thou know who speaks to thee?
Dark cloudy death o'ershades his beams of life,
And he nor sees nor hears us what we say.
    Rich. O, would he did! and so perhaps he doth:
'Tis but his policy to counterfeit,

Because he would avoid such bitter taunts
Which in the time of death he gave our father.
Geo. If so thou think'st, vex him with eager
    words.
Rich. Clifford, ask mercy and obtain no grace.
Edw. Clifford, repent in bootless penitence.70
War. Clifford, devise excuses for thy faults.
Geo. While we devise fell tortures for thy faults.
Rich. Thou didst love York, and I am son to
    York.
Edw. Thou pitied'st Rutland; I will pity thee.
Geo. Where's Captain Margaret, to fence you
    now?
War. They mock thee, Clifford: swear as thou
    wast wont.
Rich. What, not an oath? nay, then the world
    goes hard
When Clifford cannot spare his friends an oath.
I know by that he's dead; and, by my soul,
If this right hand would buy two hours' life,   80
That I in all despite might rail at him,
This hand should chop it off, and with the issuing
    blood
Stifle the villain whose unstanched thirst
York and young Rutland could not satisfy.
War. Ay, but he's dead: off with the traitor's
    head,
And rear it in the place your father's stands.
And now to London with triumphant march,
There to be crowned England's royal king:
From whence shall Warwick cut the sea to
    France,
And ask the Lady Bona for thy queen: 90
So shalt thou sinew both these lands together;
And, having France thy friend, thou shalt not
    dread
The scatter'd foe that hopes to rise again;
For though they cannot greatly sting to hurt,
Yet look to have them buzz to offend thine ears.
First will I see the coronation;
And then to Brittany I'll cross the sea,
To effect this marriage, so it please my lord.
Edw. Even as thou wilt, sweet Warwick, let it
    be;
For in thy shoulder do I build my seat,   100
And never will I undertake the thing
Wherein thy counsel and consent is wanting.
Richard, I will create thee Duke of Gloucester,
And George, of Clarence: Warwick, as ourself,
Shall do and undo as him pleaseth best.
Rich. Let me be Duke of Clarence, George of
    Gloucester;
For Gloucester's dukedom is too ominous.
War. Tut, that's a foolish observation:
Richard, be Duke of Gloucester. Now to Lon-
    don,

To see these honours in possession.   *110*
    [*Exeunt.*

ACT III

SCENE I. *A forest in the north of England*

Enter TWO KEEPERS, *with cross-bows in their
hands.*

1st Keep. Under this thick-grown brake we'll
    shroud ourselves;
For through this laund anon the deer will come;
And in this covert will we make our stand,
Culling the principal of all the deer.
2nd Keep. I'll stay above the hill, so both may
    shoot.
1st Keep. That cannot be; the noise of thy cross-
    bow
Will scare the herd, and so my shoot is lost.
Here stand we both, and aim we at the best:
And, for the time shall not seem tedious,
I'll tell thee what befel me on a day   *10*
In this self-place where now we mean to stand.
2nd Keep. Here comes a man; let's stay till he
    be past.

Enter KING HENRY, *disguised, with a
prayerbook.*

K. Hen. From Scotland am I stol'n, even of pure
    love,
To greet mine own land with my wishful sight.
No, Harry, Harry, 'tis no land of thine;
Thy place is fill'd, thy sceptre wrung from thee,
Thy balm wash'd off wherewith thou wast
    anointed:
No bending knee will call thee Cæsar now,
No humble suitors press to speak for right,
No, not a man comes for redress of thee;   *20*
For how can I help them, and not myself?
1st Keep. Ay, here's a deer whose skin's a
    keeper's fee:
This is the quondam king; let's seize upon him.
K. Hen. Let me embrace thee, sour adversity,
For wise men say it is the wisest course.
2nd Keep. Why linger we? let us lay hands upon
    him.
1st Keep. Forbear awhile; we'll hear a little
    more.
K. Hen. My queen and son are gone to France
    for aid;
And, as I hear, the great commanding Warwick
Is thither gone, to crave the French King's sister
To wife for Edward: if this news be true,   *31*
Poor queen and son, your labour is but lost;
For Warwick is a subtle orator,
And Lewis a prince soon won with moving
    words.

By this account then Margaret may win him;
For she's a woman to be pitied much:
Her sighs will make a battery in his breast;
Her tears will pierce into a marble heart;
The tiger will be mild whiles she doth mourn;
And Nero will be tainted with remorse,   40
To hear and see her plaints, her brinish tears.
Ay, but she's come to beg, Warwick, to give;
She, on his left side, craving aid for Henry,
He, on his right, asking a wife for Edward.
She weeps, and says her Henry is deposed;
He smiles, and says his Edward is install'd;
That she, poor wretch, for grief can speak no
   more;
Whiles Warwick tells his title, smooths the
   wrong,
Inferreth arguments of mighty strength,
And in conclusion wins the King from her,   50
With promise of his sister, and what else,
To strengthen and support King Edward's place.
O Margaret, thus 'twill be; and thou, poor soul,
Art then forsaken, as thou went'st forlorn!
    2nd Keep. Say, what art thou that talk'st of
     kings and queens?
    K. Hen. More than I seem, and less than I was
     born to:
A man at least, for less I should not be;
And men may talk of kings, and why not I?
    2nd Keep. Ay, but thou talk'st as if thou wert a
     king.
    K. Hen. Why, so I am, in mind; and that's
     enough.   60
    2nd Keep. But, if thou be a king, where is thy
     crown?
    K. Hen. My crown is in my heart, not on my
     head;
Not deck'd with diamonds and Indian stones,
Nor to be seen: my crown is called content:
A crown it is that seldom kings enjoy.
    2nd Keep. Well, if you be a king crown'd with
     content,
Your crown content and you must be contented
To go along with us; for, as we think,
You are the king King Edward hath deposed;
And we his subjects sworn in all allegiance   70
Will apprehend you as his enemy.
    K. Hen. But did you never swear, and break an
     oath?
    2nd Keep. No, never such an oath; nor will not
     now.
    K. Hen. Where did you dwell when I was King
     of England?
    2nd Keep. Here in this country, where we now
     remain.
    K. Hen. I was anointed king at nine months old;
My father and my grandfather were kings,

And you were sworn true subjects unto me:
And tell me, then, have you not broke your oaths?
    1st Keep. No;   80
For we were subjects but while you were king.
    K. Hen. Why, am I dead? do I not breathe a
     man?
Ah, simple men, you know not what you swear!
Look, as I blow this feather from my face,
And as the air blows it to me again,
Obeying with my wind when I do blow,
And yielding to another when it blows,
Commanded always by the greater gust;
Such is the lightness of you common men.
But do not break your oaths; for of that sin   90
My mild entreaty shall not make you guilty.
Go where you will, the king shall be command-
   ed;
And be you kings, command, and I'll obey.
    1st Keep. We are true subjects to the King, King
     Edward.
    K. Hen. So would you be again to Henry,
If he were seated as King Edward is.
    1st Keep. We charge you, in God's name, and
     the King's,
To go with us unto the officers.
    K. Hen. In God's name, lead; your king's name
     be obey'd:
And what God will, that let your king perform;
And what he will, I humbly yield unto.   101
               [*Exeunt.*

SCENE II. *London: The palace*

Enter KING EDWARD, GLOUCESTER, CLARENCE,
and LADY GREY.

    K. Edw. Brother of Gloucester, at Saint Alban's
     field
This lady's husband, Sir Richard Grey, was
   slain,
His lands then seized on by the conqueror:
Her suit is now to repossess those lands;
Which we in justice cannot well deny,
Because in quarrel of the house of York
Thy worthy gentleman did lose his life.
    Glou. Your highness shall do well to grant her
     suit;
It were dishonour to deny it her.
    K. Edw. It were no less; but yet I'll make a
     pause.   10
    Glou. [*Aside to* CLARENCE] Yea, is it so?
I see the lady hath a thing to grant,
Before the King will grant her humble suit.
    Clar. [*Aside to* GLOUCESTER] He knows the
     game: how true he keeps the wind!
    Glou. [*Aside to* CLARENCE] Silence!
    K. Edw. Widow, we will consider of your suit;
And come some other time to know our mind.

L. Grey. Right gracious lord, I cannot brook
   delay:
May it please your Highness to resolve me now;
And what your pleasure is, shall satisfy me.   20
  Glou. [*Aside to* CLARENCE] Ay, widow? then I'll
   warrant you all your lands,
An if what pleases him shall pleasure you.
Fight closer, or, good faith, you'll catch a blow.
  Clar. [*Aside to* GLOUCESTER] I fear her not, un-
   less she chance to fall.
  Glou. [*Aside to* CLARENCE] God forbid that! for
   he'll take vantages.
  K. Edw. How many children hast thou, widow?
   tell me.
  Clar. [*Aside to* GLOUCESTER] I think he means to
   beg a child of her.
  Glou. [*Aside to* CLARENCE] Nay, whip me then:
   he'll rather give her two.
  L. Grey. Three, my most gracious lord.
  Glou. [*Aside to* CLARENCE] You shall have four,
   if you'll be ruled by him.   30
  K. Edw. 'Twere pity they should lose their
   father's lands.
  L. Grey. Be pitiful, dread lord, and grant it then.
  K. Edw. Lords, give us leave: I'll try this
   widow's wit.
  Glou. [*Aside to* CLARENCE] Ay, good leave have
   you; for you will have leave,
Till youth take leave and leave you to the crutch.
          [GLOUCESTER *and* CLARENCE *retire.*
  K. Edw. Now tell me, madam, do you love
   your children?
  L. Grey. Ay, full as dearly as I love myself.
  K. Edw. And would you not do much to do
   them good?
  L. Grey. To do them good, I would sustain
   some harm.
  K. Edw. Then get your husband's lands, to do
   them good.   40
  L. Grey. Therefore I came unto your Majesty.
  K. Edw. I'll tell you how these lands are to be
   got.
  L. Grey. So shall you bind me to your Highness'
   service.
  K. Edw. What service wilt thou do me, if I give
   them?
  L. Grey. What you command, that rests in me
   to do.
  K. Edw. But you will take exceptions to my
   boon.
  L. Grey. No, gracious lord, except I cannot do
   it.
  K. Edw. Ay, but thou canst do what I mean to
   ask.
  L. Grey. Why, then I will do what your grace
   commands.

  Glou. [*Aside to* CLARENCE] He plies her hard; and
   much rain wears the marble.   50
  Clar. [*Aside to* GLOUCESTER] As red as fire! nay,
   then her wax must melt.
  L. Grey. Why stops my lord? shall I not hear
   my task?
  K. Edw. An easy task; 'tis but to love a king.
  L. Grey. That's soon perform'd, because I am a
   subject.
  K. Edw. Why, then, thy husband's lands I
   freely give thee.
  L. Grey. I take my leave with many thousand
   thanks.
  Glou. [*Aside to* CLARENCE] The match is made;
   she seals it with a curtsy.
  K. Edw. But stay thee, 'tis the fruits of love I
   mean.
  L. Grey. The fruits of love I mean, my loving
   liege.
  K. Edw. Ay, but, I fear me, in another sense.   60
What love, think'st thou, I sue so much to get?
  L. Grey. My love till death, my humble thanks,
   my prayers;
That love which virtue begs and virtue grants.
  K. Edw. No, by my troth, I did not mean such
   love.
  L. Grey. Why, then you mean not as I thought
   you did.
  K. Edw. But now you partly may perceive my
   mind.
  L. Grey. My mind will never grant what I per-
   ceive
Your Highness aims at, if I aim aright.
  K. Edw. To tell thee plain, I aim to lie with
   thee.
  L. Grey. To tell you plain, I had rather lie in
   prison.   70
  K. Edw. Why, then thou shalt not have thy
   husband's lands.
  L. Grey. Why, then mine honesty shall be my
   dower;
For by that loss I will not purchase them.
  K. Edw. Therein thou wrong'st thy children
   mightily.
  L. Grey. Herein your Highness wrongs both
   them and me.
But, mighty lord, this merry inclination
Accords not with the sadness of my suit:
Please you dismiss me, either with "ay" or "no."
  K. Edw. Ay, if thou wilt say "ay" to my re-
   quest;
No, if thou dost say "no" to my demand.   80
  L. Grey. Then, no, my lord. My suit is at an
   end.
  Glou. [*Aside to* CLARENCE] The widow likes him
   not, she knits her brows.

Clar. [*Aside to* GLOUCESTER] He is the bluntest
    wooer in Christendom.
K. Edw. [*Aside*] Her looks do argue her replete
    with modesty;
Her words do show her wit incomparable;
All her perfections challenge sovereignty:
One way or other, she is for a king;
And she shall be my love, or else my queen.—
Say that King Edward take thee for his queen?
L. Grey. 'Tis better said than done, my gra-
    cious lord: *90*
I am a subject fit to jest withal,
But far unfit to be a sovereign.
K. Edw. Sweet widow, by my state I swear to
    thee
I speak no more than what my soul intends;
And that is, to enjoy thee for my love.
L. Grey. And that is more than I will yield unto:
I know I am too mean to be your queen,
And yet too good to be your concubine.
K. Edw. You cavil, widow: I did mean, my
    queen.
L. Grey. 'Twill grieve your Grace my sons
    should call you father.   *100*
K. Edw. No more than when my daughters call
    thee mother.
Thou art a widow, and thou hast some children;
And, by God's mother, I, being but a bachelor,
Have other some: why, 'tis a happy thing
To be the father unto many sons.
Answer no more, for thou shalt be my queen.
Glou. [*Aside to* CLARENCE] The ghostly father
    now hath done his shrift.
Clar. [*Aside to* GLOUCESTER] When he was made
    a shriver, 'twas for shift.
K. Edw. Brothers, you muse what chat we two
    have had.
Glou. The widow likes it not, for she looks very
    sad.   *110*
K. Edw. You'ld think it strange if I should
    marry her.
Clar. To whom, my lord?
K. Edw.   Why, Clarence, to myself.
Glou. That would be ten days' wonder at the
    least.
Clar. That's a day longer than a wonder lasts.
Glou. By so much is the wonder in extremes.
K. Edw. Well, jest on, brothers: I can tell you
    both
Her suit is granted for her husband's lands.

Enter a NOBLEMAN.

Nob. My gracious lord, Henry your foe is taken,
And brought your prisoner to your palace gate.
K. Edw. See that he be convey'd unto the
    Tower: *120*

And go we, brothers, to the man that took him,
To question of his apprehension.
Widow, go you along. Lords, use her honour-
    ably.   [*Exeunt all but* GLOUCESTER.
Glou. Ay, Edward will use women honourably.
Would he were wasted, marrow, bones and all,
That from his loins no hopeful branch may spring,
To cross me from the golden time I look for!
And yet, between my soul's desire and me—
The lustful Edward's title buried—   *129*
Is Clarence, Henry, and his son young Edward,
And all the unlook'd for issue of their bodies
To take their rooms, ere I can place myself:
A cold premeditation for my purpose!
Why, then, I do but dream on sovereignty;
Like one that stands upon a promontory
And spies a far-off shore where he would tread,
Wishing his foot were equal with his eye,
And chides the sea that sunders him from thence,
Saying, he'll lade it dry to have his way:
So do I wish the crown, being so far off;   *140*
And so I chide the means that keeps me from it;
And so I say, I'll cut the causes off,
Flattering me with impossibilities.
My eye's too quick, my heart o'erweens too
    much,
Unless my hand and strength could equal them.
Well, say there is no kingdom then for Richard;
What other pleasure can the world afford?
I'll make my heaven in a lady's lap,
And deck my body in gay ornaments,
And witch sweet ladies with my words and looks.
O miserable thoughts! and more unlikely   *151*
Than to accomplish twenty golden crowns!
Why, love forswore me in my mother's womb:
And, for I should not deal in her soft laws,
She did corrupt frail nature with some bribe,
To shrink mine arm up like a wither'd shrub;
To make an envious mountain on my back,
Where sits deformity to mock my body;
To shape my legs of an unequal size;
To disproportion me in every part,   *160*
Like to a chaos, or an unlick'd bear-whelp
That carries no impression like the dam.
And am I then a man to be beloved?
O monstrous fault, to harbour such a thought!
Then, since this earth affords no joy to me,
But to command, to check, to o'erbear such
As are of better person than myself,
I'll make my heaven to dream upon the crown,
And, whiles I live, to account this world but hell,
Until my mis-shaped trunk that bears this head
Be round impaled with a glorious crown.   *171*
And yet I know not how to get the crown,
For many lives stand between me and home:
And I—like one lost in a thorny wood,

That rends the thorns and is rent with the thorns,
Seeking a way and straying from the way;
Not knowing how to find the open air,
But toiling desperately to find it out—
Torment myself to catch the English crown:
And from that torment I will free myself,   *180*
Or hew my way out with a bloody axe.
Why, I can smile, and murder whiles I smile,
And cry "Content" to that which grieves my
      heart,
And wet my cheeks with artificial tears,
And frame my face to all occasions.
I'll drown more sailors than the mermaid shall;
I'll slay more gazers than the basilisk;
I'll play the orator as well as Nestor,
Deceive more slily than Ulysses could,
And, like a Sinon, take another Troy.   *190*
I can add colours to the chameleon,
Change shapes with Proteus for advantages,
And set the murderous Machiavel to school.
Can I do this, and cannot get a crown?
Tut, were it farther off, I'll pluck it down. [*Exit.*

Scene iii. *France: The King's palace*

Flourish. Enter lewis *the French King, his sister*
bona, *his Admiral, called Bourbon:* prince edward, queen margaret, *and the* earl of oxford. lewis *sits, and riseth up again.*

  K. Lew. Fair Queen of England, worthy Mar-
      garet,
Sit down with us: it ill befits thy state
And birth, that thou shouldst stand while Lewis
      doth sit.
  Q. Mar. No, mighty King of France: now Mar-
      garet
Must strike her sail and learn awhile to serve
Where kings command. I was, I must confess,
Great Albion's queen in former golden days:
But now mischance hath trod my title down,
And with dishonour laid me on the ground;
Where I must take like seat unto my fortune,   *10*
And to my humble seat conform myself.
  K. Lew. Why, say, fair queen, whence springs
      this deep despair?
  Q. Mar. From such a cause as fills mine eyes
      with tears
And stops my tongue, while heart is drown'd in
      cares.
  K. Lew. Whate'er it be, be thou still like thy-
      self,
And sit thee by our side: [*Seats her by him*] yield
      not thy neck
To fortune's yoke, but let thy dauntless mind
Still ride in triumph over all mischance.
Be plain, Queen Margaret, and tell thy grief;
It shall be eased, if France can yield relief.   *20*

  Q. Mar. Those gracious words revive my
      drooping thoughts
And give my tongue-tied sorrows leave to speak.
Now, therefore, be it known to noble Lewis,
That Henry, sole possessor of my love,
Is of a king become a banish'd man,
And forced to live in Scotland a forlorn;
While proud ambitious Edward, Duke of York,
Usurps the regal title and the seat
Of England's true-anointed lawful king.
This is the cause that I, poor Margaret,   *30*
With this my son, Prince Edward, Henry's heir,
Am come to crave thy just and lawful aid;
And if thou fail us, all our hope is done:
Scotland hath will to help, but cannot help;
Our people and our peers are both misled,
Our treasure seized, our soldiers put to flight,
And, as thou seest, ourselves in heavy plight.
  K. Lew. Renowned queen, with patience calm
      the storm,
While we bethink a means to break it off.
  Q. Mar. The more we stay, the stronger grows
      our foe.
  K. Lew. The more I stay, the more I'll succour
      thee.
  Q. Mar. O, but impatience waiteth on true
      sorrow.
And see where comes the breeder of my sorrow!

Enter warwick.

  K. Lew. What's he approacheth boldly to our
      presence?
  Q. Mar. Our Earl of Warwick, Edward's great-
      est friend.
  K. Lew. Welcome, brave Warwick! What
      brings thee to France?
  He descends. She ariseth.
  Q. Mar. Ay, now begins a second storm to rise;
For this is he that moves both wind and tide.
  War. From worthy Edward, King of Albion,
My lord and sovereign, and thy vowed friend,   *50*
I come, in kindness and unfeigned love,
First, to do greetings to thy royal person;
And then to crave a league of amity;
And lastly, to confirm that amity
With nuptial knot, if thou vouchsafe to grant
That virtuous Lady Bona, thy fair sister,
To England's king in lawful marriage.
  Q. Mar. [*Aside*] If that go forward, Henry's
      hope is done.
  War. [*To* bona] And, gracious madam, in our
      king's behalf,
I am commanded, with your leave and favour,   *60*
Humbly to kiss your hand and with my tongue
To tell the passion of my sovereign's heart;
Where fame, late entering at his heedful ears,

Hath placed thy beauty's image and thy virtue.
  Q. Mar. King Lewis and Lady Bona, hear me
    speak
Before you answer Warwick. His demand
Springs not from Edward's well-meant honest
    love,
But from deceit bred by necessity;
For how can tyrants safely govern home,
Unless abroad they purchase great alliance?   70
To prove him tyrant this reason may suffice,
That Henry liveth still; but were he dead,
Yet here Prince Edward stands, King Henry's
    son.
Look, therefore, Lewis, that by this league and
    marriage
Thou draw not on thy danger and dishonour;
For though usurpers sway the rule awhile,
Yet heavens are just, and time suppresseth
    wrongs.
  War. Injurious Margaret!
  Prince.   And why not Queen?
  War. Because thy father Henry did usurp;
And thou no more art prince than she is queen.   80
  Oxf. Then Warwick disannuls great John of
    Gaunt,
Which did subdue the greatest part of Spain;
And, after John of Gaunt, Henry the Fourth,
Whose wisdom was a mirror to the wisest;
And, after that wise prince, Henry the Fifth,
Who by his prowess conquered all France:
From these our Henry lineally descends.
  War. Oxford, how haps it, in this smooth dis-
    course,
You told not how Henry the Sixth hath lost
All that which Henry the Fifth had gotten?   90
Methinks these peers of France should smile at
    that.
But for the rest, you tell a pedigree
Of threescore and two years; a silly time
To make prescription for a kingdom's worth.
  Oxf. Why, Warwick, canst thou speak against
    thy liege,
Whom thou obeyed'st thirty and six years,
And not bewray thy treason with a blush?
  War. Can Oxford, that did ever fence the right,
Now buckler falsehood with a pedigree?   99
For shame! leave Henry, and call Edward king.
  Oxf. Call him my king by whose injurious
    doom
My elder brother, the Lord Aubrey Vere,
Was done to death? and more than so, my father,
Even in the downfall of his mellow'd years,
When nature brought him to the door of death?
No, Warwick, no; while life upholds this arm,
This arm upholds the house of Lancaster.
  War. And I the house of York.

  K. Lew. Queen Margaret, Prince Edward, and
    Oxford,
Vouchsafe, at our request, to stand aside,   110
While I use further conference with Warwick.
    They stand aloof.
  Q. Mar. Heavens grant that Warwick's words
    bewitch him not!
  K. Lew. Now, Warwick, tell me, even upon
    thy conscience,
Is Edward your true king? for I were loath
To link with him that were not lawful chosen.
  War. Thereon I pawn my credit and mine hon-
    our.
  K. Lew. But is he gracious in the people's eye?
  War. The more that Henry was unfortunate.
  K. Lew. Then further, all dissembling set aside,
Tell me for truth the measure of his love   120
Unto our sister Bona.
  War.   Such it seems
As may beseem a monarch like himself.
Myself have often heard him say and swear
That this his love was an eternal plant,
Whereof the root was fix'd in virtue's ground,
The leaves and fruit maintain'd with beauty's sun,
Exempt from envy, but not from disdain,
Unless the Lady Bona quit his pain.
  K. Lew. Now, sister, let us hear your firm re-
    solve.   129
  Bona. Your grant, or your denial, shall be mine:
[*To* WARWICK] Yet I confess that often ere this
    day,
When I have heard your king's desert recounted,
Mine ear hath tempted judgment to desire.
  K. Lew. Then, Warwick, thus: our sister shall
    be Edward's;
And now forthwith shall articles be drawn
Touching the jointure that your king must make,
Which with her dowry shall be counterpoised.
Draw near, Queen Margaret, and be a witness
That Bona shall be wife to the English king.   139
  Prince. To Edward, but not to the English king.
  Q. Mar. Deceitful Warwick! it was thy device
By this alliance to make void my suit:
Before thy coming Lewis was Henry's friend.
  K. Lew. And still is friend to him and Margaret:
But if your title to the crown be weak,
As may appear by Edward's good success,
Then 'tis but reason that I be released
From giving aid which late I promised.
Yet shall you have all kindness at my hand
That your estate requires and mine can yield.   150
  War. Henry now lives in Scotland at his ease,
Where having nothing, nothing can he lose.
And as for you yourself, our quondam queen,
You have a father able to maintain you;
And better 'twere you troubled him than France.

Q. Mar. Peace, impudent and shameless War-
  wick, peace,
Proud setter up and puller down of kings!
I will not hence, till, with my talk and tears,
Both full of truth, I make King Lewis behold
Thy sly conveyance and thy lord's false love; *160*
For both of you are birds of selfsame feather.
  Post blows a horn within.
  K. Lew. Warwick, this is some post to us or
    thee.

  Enter a POST.

Post. [*To* WARWICK] My lord ambassador, these
  letters are for you,
Sent from your brother, Marquess Montague:
[*To Lewis*] These from our king unto your ma-
  jesty:
[*To* MARGARET] And, madam, these for you;
  from whom I know not.
  They all read their letters.
  Oxf. I like it well that our fair queen and mis-
    tress
Smiles at her news, while Warwick frowns at
  his.
  Prince. Nay, mark how Lewis stamps, as he
    were nettled:
I hope all's for the best.   *170*
  K. Lew. Warwick, what are thy news? and
    yours, fair queen?
  Q. Mar. Mine, such as fill my heart with un-
    hoped joys.
  War. Mine, full of sorrow and heart's discon-
    tent.
  K. Lew. What! has your king married the Lady
    Grey?
And now, to soothe your forgery and his,
Sends me a paper to persuade me patience?
Is this the alliance that he seeks with France?
Dare he presume to scorn us in this manner?
  Q. Mar. I told your Majesty as much before:
This proveth Edward's love and Warwick's hon-
  esty.   *180*
  War. King Lewis, I here protest, in sight of
    heaven,
And by the hope I have of heavenly bliss,
That I am clear from this misdeed of Edward's,
No more my king, for he dishonours me,
But most himself, if he could see his shame.
Did I forget that by the house of York
My father came untimely to his death?
Did I let pass the abuse done to my niece?
Did I impale him with the regal crown?
Did I put Henry from his native right?   *190*
And am I guerdon'd at the last with shame?
Shame on himself! for my desert is honour:
And to repair my honour lost for him,

I here renounce him and return to Henry.
My noble queen, let former grudges pass,
And henceforth I am thy true servitor:
I will revenge his wrong to Lady Bona
And replant Henry in his former state.
  Q. Mar. Warwick, these words have turn'd my
    hate to love;
And I forgive and quite forget old faults,   *200*
And joy that thou becomest King Henry's friend.
  War. So much his friend, ay, his unfeigned
    friend,
That, if King Lewis vouchsafe to furnish us
With some few bands of chosen soldiers,
I'll undertake to land them on our coast
And force the tyrant from his seat by war.
'Tis not his new-made bride shall succour him:
And as for Clarence, as my letters tell me,
He's very likely now to fall from him,   *209*
For matching more for wanton lust than honour,
Or than for strength and safety of our country.
  Bona. Dear brother, how shall Bona be revenged
But by thy help to this distressed queen?
  Q. Mar. Renowned prince, how shall poor
    Henry live,
Unless thou rescue him from foul despair?
  Bona. My quarrel and this English queen's are
    one.
  War. And mine, fair lady Bona, joins with yours.
  K. Lew. And mine with hers, and thine, and
    Margaret's.
Therefore at last I firmly am resolved
You shall have aid.   *220*
  Q. Mar. Let me give humble thanks for all at
    once.
  K. Lew. Then, England's messenger, return in
    post,
And tell false Edward, thy supposed king,
That Lewis of France is sending over masquers
To revel it with him and his new bride:
Thou seest what's past, go fear thy king withal.
  Bona. Tell him, in hope he'll prove a widower
    shortly,
I'll wear the willow garland for his sake.
  Q. Mar. Tell him, my mourning weeds are laid
    aside,
And I am ready to put armour on.   *230*
  War. Tell him from me that he hath done me
    wrong,
And therefore I'll uncrown him ere't be long.
There's thy reward: be gone.   [*Exit* POST.
  K. Lew.   But, Warwick,
Thou and Oxford, with five thousand men,
Shall cross the seas, and bid false Edward battle;
And, as occasion serves, this noble queen
And prince shall follow with a fresh supply.
Yet, ere thou go, but answer me one doubt,

What pledge have we of thy firm loyalty?   *239*
War. This shall assure my constant loyalty,
That if our queen and this young prince agree,
I'll join mine eldest daughter and my joy
To him forthwith in holy wedlock bands.
  Q. Mar. Yes, I agree, and thank you for your
    motion.
Son Edward, she is fair and virtuous,
Therefore delay not, give thy hand to Warwick;
And, with thy hand, thy faith irrevocable,
That only Warwick's daughter shall be thine.
  Prince. Yes, I accept her, for she well deserves
    it;
And here, to pledge my vow, I give my hand. *250*
  He gives his hand to WARWICK.
  K. Lew. Why stay we now? These soldiers
    shall be levied,
And thou, Lord Bourbon, our high admiral,
Shalt waft them over with our royal fleet.
I long till Edward fall by war's mischance,
For mocking marriage with a dame of France.
                    [*Exeunt all but* WARWICK.
War. I came from Edward as ambassador,
But I return his sworn and mortal foe:
Matter of marriage was the charge he gave me,
But dreadful war shall answer his demand.
Had he none else to make a stale but me?   *260*
Then none but I shall turn his jest to sorrow.
I was the chief that raised him to the crown,
And I'll be chief to bring him down again:
Not that I pity Henry's misery,
But seek revenge on Edward's mockery.   [*Exit.*

ACT IV

SCENE I. *London: The palace*

Enter GLOUCESTER, CLARENCE, SOMERSET,
and MONTAGUE.

  Glou. Now tell me, brother Clarence, what
    think you
Of this new marriage with the Lady Grey?
Hath not our brother made a worthy choice?
  Clar. Alas, you know, 'tis far from hence to
    France;
How could he stay till Warwick made return?
  Som. My lords, forbear this talk; here comes
    the king.
  Glou. And his well-chosen bride.
  Clar. I mind to tell him plainly what I think.

Flourish. Enter KING EDWARD, *attended;* LADY
GREY, *as Queen;* PEMBROKE, STAFFORD, HAST-
INGS, *and others. Four stand on one side, and four
on the other.*

  K. Edw. Now, brother of Clarence, how like
    you our choice,

That you stand pensive, as half malcontent?   *10*
  Clar. As well as Lewis of France, or the Earl of
    Warwick,
Which are so weak of courage and in judgement
That they'll take no offence at our abuse.
  K. Edw. Suppose they take offence without a
    cause,
They are but Lewis and Warwick: I am Edward,
Your king and Warwick's, and must have my
    will.
  Glou. And shall have your will, because our
    king:
Yet hasty marriage seldom proveth well.
  K. Edw. Yea, brother Richard, are you offend-
    ed too?
  Glou. Not I: *20*
No, God forbid that I should wish them sever'd
Whom God hath join'd together; ay, and 'twere
    pity
To sunder them that yoke so well together.
  K. Edw. Setting your scorns and your mislike
    aside,
Tell me some reason why the Lady Grey
Should not become my wife and England's
    queen.
And you too, Somerset and Montague,
Speak freely what you think.
  Clar. Then this is mine opinion: that King
    Lewis
Becomes your enemy, for mocking him   *30*
About the marriage of the Lady Bona.
  Glou. And Warwick, doing what you gave in
    charge,
Is now dishonoured by this new marriage.
  K. Edw. What if both Lewis and Warwick be
    appeased
By such invention as I can devise?
  Mont. Yet, to have join'd with France in such
    alliance
Would more have strengthen'd this our common-
    wealth
'Gainst foreign storms than any home-bred mar-
    riage.
  Hast. Why, knows not Montague that of itself
England is safe, if true within itself?   *40*
  Mont. But the safer when 'tis back'd with
    France.
  Hast. 'Tis better using France than trusting
    France:
Let us be back'd with God and with the seas
Which He hath given for fence impregnable,
And with their helps only defend ourselves;
In them and in ourselves our safety lies.
  Clar. For this one speech Lord Hastings well
    deserves
To have the heir of the Lord Hungerford.

K. Edw. Ay, what of that? it was my will and
grant;
And for this once my will shall stand for law. 50
  Glou. And yet methinks your Grace hath not
done well,
To give the heir and daughter of Lord Scales
Unto the brother of your loving bride;
She better would have fitted me or Clarence:
But in your bride you bury brotherhood.
  Clar. Or else you would not have bestow'd the
heir
Of the Lord Bonville on your new wife's son,
And leave your brothers to go speed elsewhere.
  K. Edw. Alas, poor Clarence! is it for a wife
That thou art malcontent? I will provide thee. 60
  Clar. In choosing for yourself, you show'd your
judgement,
Which being shallow, you shall give me leave
To play the broker in mine own behalf;
And to that end I shortly mind to leave you.
  K. Edw. Leave me, or tarry, Edward will be
king,
And not be tied unto his brother's will.
  Q. Eliz. My lords, before it pleased his Majesty
To raise my state to title of a queen,
Do me but right, and you must all confess
That I was not ignoble of descent; 70
And meaner than myself have had like fortune.
But as this title honours me and mine,
So your dislike, to whom I would be pleasing,
Doth cloud my joys with danger and with sor-
row.
  K. Edw. My love, forbear to fawn upon their
frowns:
What danger or what sorrow can befall thee,
So long as Edward is thy constant friend
And their true sovereign, whom they must obey?
Nay, whom they shall obey, and love thee too,
Unless they seek for hatred at my hands; 80
Which if they do, yet will I keep thee safe,
And they shall feel the vengeance of my wrath.
  Glou. [*Aside*] I hear, yet say not much, but think
the more.

Enter a POST.

K. Edw. Now, messenger, what letters or what
news
From France?
  Post. My sovereign liege, no letters; and few
words,
But such as I, without your special pardon.
Dare not relate.
  K. Edw. Go to, we pardon thee: therefore, in
brief,
Tell me their words as near as thou canst guess
them. 90

What answer makes King Lewis unto our letters?
  Post. At my depart, these were his very words:
"Go tell false Edward, thy supposed king,
That Lewis of France is sending over masquers
To revel it with him and his new bride."
  K. Edw. Is Lewis so brave? belike he thinks me
Henry.
But what said Lady Bona to my marriage?
  Post. These were her words, utter'd with mild
disdain:
"Tell him, in hope he'll prove a widower shortly,
I'll wear the willow garland for his sake." 100
  K. Edw. I blame not her, she could say little
less;
She had the wrong. But what said Henry's
queen?
For I have heard that she was there in place.
  Post. "Tell him," quoth she, "my mourning
weeds are done,
And I am ready to put armour on."
  K. Edw. Belike she minds to play the Amazon.
But what said Warwick to these injuries?
  Post. He, more incensed against your Majesty
Than all the rest, discharged me with these
words:
"Tell him from me that he hath done me
wrong, 110
And therefore I'll uncrown him ere't be long."
  K. Edw. Ha! durst the traitor breathe out so
proud words?
Well, I will arm me, being thus forewarn'd:
They shall have wars and pay for their presump-
tion.
But say, is Warwick friends with Margaret?
  Post. Ay, gracious sovereign; they are so link'd
in friendship,
That young Prince Edward marries Warwick's
daughter.
  Clar. Belike the elder; Clarence will have the
younger.
Now, brother king, farewell, and sit you fast, 119
For I will hence to Warwick's other daughter;
That, though I want a kingdom, yet in marriage
I may not prove inferior to yourself.
You that love me and Warwick, follow me.
          [*Exit* CLARENCE, *and* SOMERSET *follows.*
  Glou. [*Aside*] Not I:
My thoughts aim at a further matter: I
Stay not for the love of Edward, but the crown.
  K. Edw. Clarence and Somerset both gone to
Warwick!
Yet am I arm'd against the worst can happen;
And haste is needful in this desperate case.
Pembroke and Stafford, you in our behalf 130
Go levy men, and make prepare for war;
They are already, or quickly will be landed:

Myself in person will straight follow you.

[*Exeunt* PEMBROKE *and* STAFFORD.

But, ere I go, Hastings and Montague,
Resolve my doubt. You twain, of all the rest,
Are near to Warwick by blood and by alliance:
Tell me if you love Warwick more than me?
If it be so, then both depart to him;
I rather wish you foes than hollow friends:
But if you mind to hold your true obedience, *140*
Give me assurance with some friendly vow,
That I may never have you in suspect.

Mont. So God help Montague as he proves true!

Hast. And Hastings as he favours Edward's cause!

K. Edw. Now, brother Richard, will you stand by us?

Glou. Ay, in despite of all that shall withstand you.

K. Edw. Why, so! then am I sure of victory.
Now therefore let us hence; and lose no hour,
Till we meet Warwick with his foreign power.

[*Exeunt.*

SCENE II. *A plain in Warwickshire*

Enter WARWICK *and* OXFORD, *with French soldiers.*

War. Trust me, my lord, all hitherto goes well;
The common people by numbers swarm to us.

Enter CLARENCE *and* SOMERSET.

But see where Somerset and Clarence comes!
Speak suddenly, my lords, are we all friends?

Clar. Fear not that, my lord.

War. Then, gentle Clarence, welcome unto Warwick;
And welcome, Somerset: I hold it cowardice
To rest mistrustful where a noble heart
Hath pawn'd an open hand in sign of love;
Else might I think that Clarence, Edward's brother, *10*
Were but a feigned friend to our proceedings:
But welcome, sweet Clarence; my daughter shall be thine.
And now what rests but, in night's coverture,
Thy brother being carelessly encamp'd,
His soldiers lurking in the towns about,
And but attended by a simple guard,
We may surprise and take him at our pleasure?
Our scouts have found the adventure very easy:
That as Ulysses and stout Diomede *19*
With sleight and manhood stole to Rhesus' tents,
And brought from thence the Thracian fatal steeds,
So we, well cover'd with the night's black mantle,

At unawares may beat down Edward's guard
And seize himself; I say not, slaughter him,
For I intend but only to surprise him.
You that will follow me to this attempt,
Applaud the name of Henry with your leader.

They all cry, "Henry!"

Why, then, let's on our way in silent sort:
For Warwick and his friends, God and Saint George! [*Exeunt.*

SCENE III. *Edward's camp, near Warwick*

Enter THREE WATCHMEN, *to guard the King's tent.*

1st Watch. Come on, my masters, each man take his stand:
The King by this is set him down to sleep.

2nd Watch. What, will he not to bed?

1st Watch. Why, no; for he hath made a solemn vow
Never to lie and take his natural rest
Till Warwick or himself be quite suppress'd.

2nd Watch. To-morrow then belike shall be the day,
If Warwick be so near as men report.

3rd Watch. But say, I pray, what nobleman is that
That with the King here resteth in his tent? *10*

1st Watch. 'Tis the Lord Hastings, the King's chiefest friend.

3rd Watch. O, is it so? But why commands the King
That his chief followers lodge in towns about him,
While he himself keeps in the cold field?

2nd Watch. 'Tis the more honour, because more dangerous.

3rd Watch. Ay, but give me worship and quietness;
I like it better than a dangerous honour.
If Warwick knew in what estate he stands,
'Tis to be doubted he would waken him.

1st Watch. Unless our halberds did shut up his passage. *20*

2nd Watch. Ay, wherefore else guard we his royal tent,
But to defend his person from night-foes?

Enter WARWICK, CLARENCE, OXFORD, SOMER-
SET, *and French soldiers, silent all.*

War. This is his tent; and see where stand his guard.
Courage, my masters! honour now or never!
But follow me, and Edward shall be ours.

1st Watch. Who goes there?

2nd Watch. Stay, or thou diest!

Warwick and the rest cry all, "Warwick!

Warwick!" *and set upon the Guard, who fly,
crying,* "Arm! arm!" *Warwick and the rest following them.*

The drum playing and trumpet sounding, re-enter
WARWICK, SOMERSET, *and the rest, bringing the*
KING *out in his gown, sitting in a chair.* RICHARD
and HASTINGS *fly over the stage.*

Som. What are they that fly there?

War. Richard and Hastings: let them go; here is
The Duke.

K. Edw. The Duke! Why, Warwick, when we
parted, 30
Thou call'dst me king.

War. Ay, but the case is alter'd:
When you disgraced me in my embassade,
Then I degraded you from being king,
And come now to create you Duke of York.
Alas! how should you govern any kingdom,
That know not how to use ambassadors,
Nor how to be contented with one wife,
Nor how to use your brothers brotherly,
Nor how to study for the people's welfare,
Nor how to shroud yourself from enemies? 40

K. Edw. Yea, brother of Clarence, art thou here
too?
Nay, then I see that Edward needs must down.
Yet, Warwick, in despite of all mischance,
Of thee thyself and all thy complices,
Edward will always bear himself as king:
Though fortune's malice overthrow my state,
My mind exceeds the compass of her wheel.

War. Then, for his mind, be Edward England's
king: [*Takes off his crown.*
But Henry now shall wear the English crown,
And be true king indeed, thou but the shadow. 50
My Lord of Somerset, at my request,
See that forthwith Duke Edward be convey'd
Unto my brother, Archbishop of York.
When I have fought with Pembroke and his
fellows,
I'll follow you, and tell what answer
Lewis and the Lady Bona send to him.
Now, for a while farewell, good Duke of York.
[*They lead him out forcibly.*

K. Edw. What fates impose, that men must
needs abide;
It boots not to resist both wind and tide.
[*Exit, guarded*

Oxf. What now remains, my lords, for us to
do 60
But march to London with our soldiers?

War. Ay, that's the first thing that we have to
do;
To free King Henry from imprisonment
And see him seated in the regal throne. [*Exeunt.*

SCENE IV. *London: The palace*

Enter QUEEN ELIZABETH *and* RIVERS.

Riv. Madam, what makes you in this sudden
change?

Q. Eliz. Why, brother Rivers, are you yet to
learn
What late misfortune is befall'n King Edward?

Riv. What! loss of some pitch'd battle against
Warwick?

Q. Eliz. No, but the loss of his own royal person

Riv. Then is my sovereign slain?

Q. Eliz. Ay, almost slain, for he is taken prison-
er,
Either betray'd by falsehood of his guard
Or by his foe surprised at unawares:
And, as I further have to understand, 10
Is new committed to the Bishop of York,
Fell Warwick's brother and by that our foe.

Riv. These news I must confess are full of grief;
Yet, gracious madam, bear it as you may:
Warwick may lose, that now hath won the day.

Q. Eliz. Till then fair hope must hinder life's
decay.
And I the rather wean me from despair
For love of Edward's offspring in my womb:
This is it that makes me bridle passion
And bear with mildness my misfortune's cross;
Ay, ay, for this I draw in many a tear 20
And stop the rising of blood-sucking sighs,
Lest with my sighs or tears I blast or drown
King Edward's fruit, true heir to the English
crown.

Riv. But, madam, where is Warwick then become?

Q. Eliz. I am inform'd that he comes towards
London,
To set the crown once more on Henry's head:
Guess thou the rest; King Edward's friends must
down,
But, to prevent the tyrant's violence—
For trust not him that hath once broken faith—
I'll hence forthwith unto the sanctuary, 31
To save at least the heir of Edward's right:
There shall I rest secure from force and fraud.
Come, therefore, let us fly while we may fly:
If Warwick take us we are sure to die. [*Exeunt.*

SCENE V. *A park near Middleham Castle in*
Yorkshire

Enter GLOUCESTER, LORD HASTINGS, *and* SIR
WILLIAM STANLEY.

Glou. Now, my Lord Hastings and Sir William
Stanley,
Leave off to wonder why I drew you hither,
Into the chiefest thicket of the park.

Thus stands the case: you know our king, my
   brother,
Is prisoner to the Bishop here, at whose hands
He hath good usage and great liberty,
And, often but attended with weak guard,
Comes hunting this way to disport himself.
I have advertised him by secret means
That if about this hour he make this way   *10*
Under the colour of his usual game,
He shall here find his friends with horse and men
To set him free from his captivity.

Enter KING EDWARD *and a* HUNTSMAN *with him.*

Hunt. This way, my lord; for this way lies the
   game.
K. Edw. Nay, this way, man: see where the
   huntsmen stand.
Now, brother of Gloucester, Lord Hastings, and
   the rest,
Stand you thus close, to steal the Bishop's deer?
Glou. Brother, the time and case requireth haste:
Your horse stands ready at the park-corner.
K. Edw. But whither shall we then?
Hast.   To Lynn, my lord,   *20*
And ship from thence to Flanders.
Glou. Well guess'd, believe me; for that was
   my meaning.
K. Edw. Stanley, I will requite thy forward-
   ness.
Glou. But wherefore stay we? 'tis no time to
   talk.
K. Edw. Huntsman, what say'st thou? wilt thou
   go along?
Hunt. Better do so than tarry and be hang'd.
Glou. Come then, away; let's ha' no more ado.
K. Edw. Bishop, farewell: shield thee from
   Warwick's frown;
And pray that I may repossess the crown.
                             [Exeunt.

SCENE VI. *London: The Tower*

Flourish. Enter KING HENRY, CLARENCE, WARWICK,
   SOMERSET, *young* RICHMOND, OXFORD, MON-
   TAGUE, *and* LIEUTENANT OF THE TOWER.

K. Hen. Master lieutenant, now that God and
   friends
Have shaken Edward from the regal seat,
And turn'd my captive state to liberty,
My fear to hope, my sorrows unto joys,
At our enlargement what are thy due fees?
Lieu. Subjects may challenge nothing of their
   sovereigns;
But if an humble prayer may prevail,
I then crave pardon of your Majesty.
K. Hen. For what, lieutenant? for well using
   me?

Nay, be thou sure I'll well requite thy kindness,
For that it made my imprisonment a pleasure;
Ay, such a pleasure as incaged birds,
Conceive when after many moody thoughts
At last by notes of household harmony
They quite forget their loss of liberty.
But, Warwick, after God, thou set'st me free,
And chiefly therefore I thank God and thee;
He was the author, thou the instrument.
Therefore, that I may conquer Fortune's spite
By living low, where Fortune cannot hurt me, *20*
And that the people of this blessed land
May not be punish'd with my thwarting stars,
Warwick, although my head still wear the
   crown,
I here resign my government to thee,
For thou art fortunate in all thy deeds.
War. Your Grace hath still been famed for vir-
   tuous;
And now may seem as wise as virtuous,
By spying and avoiding Fortune's malice,
For few men rightly temper with the stars:
Yet in this one thing let me blame your Grace, *30*
For choosing me when Clarence is in place.
Clar. No, Warwick, thou art worthy of the
   sway,
To whom the heavens in thy nativity
Adjudged an olive branch and laurel crown,
As likely to be blest in peace and war;
And therefore I yield thee my free consent.
War. And I choose Clarence only for Protector.
K. Hen. Warwick and Clarence, give me both
   your hands:
Now join your hands, and with your hands your
   hearts,
That no dissension hinder government: *40*
I make you both Protectors of this land,
While I myself will lead a private life
And in devotion spend my latter days,
To sin's rebuke and my Creator's praise.
War. What answers Clarence to his sovereign's
   will?
Clar. That he consents, if Warwick yield con-
   sent;
For on thy fortune I repose myself.
War. Why, then, though loath, yet must I be
   content:
We'll yoke together, like a double shadow
To Henry's body, and supply his place;   *50*
I mean, in bearing weight of government,
While he enjoys the honour and his ease.
And, Clarence, now then it is more than needful
Forthwith that Edward be pronounced a traitor,
And all his lands and goods be confiscate.
Clar. What else? and that succession be deter-
   mined.

War. Ay, therein Clarence shall not want his
  part.
K. Hen. But, with the first of all your chief
  affairs,
Let me entreat, for I command no more,   59
That Margaret your queen and my son Edward
Be sent for, to return from France with speed;
For, till I see them here, by doubtful fear
My joy of liberty is half eclipsed.
Clar. It shall be done, my sovereign, with all
  speed.
K. Hen. My Lord of Somerset, what youth is
  that,
Of whom you seem to have so tender care?
Som. My liege, it is young Henry, Earl of Rich-
  mond.
K. Hen. Come hither, England's hope. [*Lays his
  hand on his head.*] If secret powers
Suggest but truth to my divining thoughts,
This pretty lad will prove our country's bliss. 70
His looks are full of peaceful majesty,
His head by nature framed to wear a crown,
His hand to wield a sceptre, and himself
Likely in time to bless a regal throne.
Make much of him, my lords, for this is he
Must help you more than you are hurt by me.
          Enter a POST.

War. What news, my friend?
Post. That Edward is escaped from your brother,
And fled, as he hears since, to Burgundy.
War. Unsavoury news! but how made he es-
  cape?   80
Post. He was convey'd by Richard Duke of
  Gloucester
And the Lord Hastings, who attended him
In secret ambush on the forest side
And from the Bishop's huntsmen rescued him;
For hunting was his daily exercise.
War. My brother was too careless of his charge.
But let us hence, my sovereign, to provide
A salve for any sore that may betide.
          [*Exeunt all but* SOMERSET, RICHMOND,
                              and OXFORD.

Som. My lord, I like not of this flight of Ed-
  ward's;
For doubtless Burgundy will yield him help, 90
And we shall have more wars before 't be long.
As Henry's late presaging prophecy
Did glad my heart with hope of this young Rich-
  mond,
So doth my heart misgive me, in these conflicts
What may befall him, to his harm and ours:
Therefore, Lord Oxford, to prevent the worst,
Forthwith we'll send him hence to Brittany,
Till storms be past of civil enmity.
Oxf. Ay, for if Edward repossess the crown,

'Tis like that Richmond with the rest shall down.
Som. It shall be so; he shall to Brittany.   101
Come, therefore, let's about it speedily. [*Exeunt.*

          SCENE VII. *Before York*
Flourish. Enter KING EDWARD, GLOUCESTER,
          HASTINGS, *and soldiers.*

K. Edw. Now, brother Richard, Lord Hastings,
  and the rest,
Yet thus far Fortune maketh us amends,
And says that once more I shall interchange
My waned state for Henry's regal crown.
Well have we pass'd and now repass'd the seas
And brought desired help from Burgundy:
What then remains, we being thus arrived
From Ravenspurgh haven before the gates of
  York,
But that we enter as into our dukedom?
Glou. The gates made fast! Brother, I like not
  this;   10
For many men that stumble at the threshold
Are well foretold that danger lurks within.
K. Edw. Tush, man, abodements must not now
  affright us:
By fair or foul means we must enter in,
For hither will our friends repair to us.
Hast. My liege, I'll knock once more to sum-
  mon them.

Enter, on the walls, the MAYOR OF YORK, *and
          his Brethren.*

May. My lords, we were forewarned of your
  coming,
And shut the gates for safety of ourselves;
For now we owe allegiance unto Henry.
K. Edw. But, master mayor, if Henry be your
  king,   20
Yet Edward at the least is Duke of York.
May. True, my good lord; I know you for no
  less.
K. Edw. Why, and I challenge nothing but my
  dukedom,
As being well content with that alone.
Glou. [*Aside*] But when the fox hath once got in
  his nose,
He'll soon find means to make the body follow.
Hast. Why, master mayor, why stand you in a
  doubt?
Open the gates; we are King Henry's friends.
May. Ay, say you so? the gates shall then be
  open'd.   [*They descend.*
Glou. A wise stout captain, and soon persuaded!
Hast. The good old man would fain that all were
  well,   31
So 'twere not 'long of him; but being enter'd,
I doubt not, I, but we shall soon persuade

Both him and all his brothers unto reason.

Enter the MAYOR *and two Aldermen, below.*

K. Edw. So, master mayor: these gates must
   not be shut
But in the night or in the time of war.
What! fear not, man, but yield me up the keys;
   [*Takes his keys.*]
For Edward will defend the town and thee,
And all those friends that deign to follow me.

March. Enter MONTGOMERY, *with drum and*
   soldiers.

Glou. Brother, this is Sir John Montgomery,
Our trusty friend, unless I be deceived.   *41*
K. Edw. Welcome, Sir John! But why come
   you in arms?
Mont. To help King Edward in his time of
   storm,
As every loyal subject ought to do.
K. Edw. Thanks, good Montgomery; but we
   now forget
Our title to the crown and only claim
Our dukedom till God please to send the rest.
Mont. Then fare you well, for I will hence
   again:
I came to serve a king and not a duke.
Drummer, strike up, and let us march away.   *50*
The drum begins to march.
K. Edw. Nay, stay, Sir John, awhile, and we'll
   debate
By what safe means the crown may be recover'd.
Mont. What talk you of debating? in few words,
If you'll not here proclaim yourself our king,
I'll leave you to your fortune and be gone
To keep them back that come to succour you:
Why shall we fight, if you pretend no title?
Glou. Why, brother, wherefore stand you on
   nice points?
K. Edw. When we grow stronger, then we'll
   make our claim:
Till then, 'tis wisdom to conceal our meaning.   *60*
Hast. Away with scrupulous wit! now arms
   must rule.
Glou. And fearless minds climb soonest unto
   crowns.
Brother, we will proclaim you out of hand:
The bruit thereof will bring you many friends.
K. Edw. Then be it as you will; for 'tis my
   right,
And Henry but usurps the diadem.
Mont. Ay, now my sovereign speaketh like
   himself;
And now will I be Edward's champion.
Hast. Sound trumpet; Edward shall be here pro-
   claim'd:

Come, fellow-soldier, make thou proclamation.
   Giving him a paper. Flourish.   *70*
Sold. [*Reads.*] "Edward the Fourth, by the grace
of God, king of England and France, and lord of
Ireland," &c.
Mont. And whosoe'er gainsays King Edward's
   right,
By this I challenge him to single fight.
   Throws down his gauntlet.
All. Long live Edward the Fourth!
K. Edw. Thanks, brave Montgomery; and
   thanks unto you all:
If fortune serve me, I'll requite this kindness.
Now, for this night, let's harbour here in York;
And when the morning sun shall raise his car   *80*
Above the border of this horizon,
We'll forward towards Warwick and his mates;
For well I wot that Henry is no soldier.
Ah, froward Clarence! how evil it beseems thee,
To flatter Henry and forsake thy brother!
Yet, as we may, we'll meet both thee and War-
   wick.
Come on, brave soldiers: doubt not of the day,
And, that once gotten, doubt not of large pay.
   [*Exeunt.*

SCENE VIII. *London: The palace*

Flourish. Enter KING HENRY, WARWICK, MON-
   TAGUE, CLARENCE, EXETER, *and* OXFORD.

War. What counsel, lords? Edward from Belgia,
With hasty Germans and blunt Hollanders,
Hath pass'd in safety through the narrow seas,
And with his troops doth march amain to Lon-
   don;
And many giddy people flock to him.
K. Hen. Let's levy men, and beat him back
   again.
Clar. A little fire is quickly trodden out;
Which, being suffer'd, rivers cannot quench.
War. In Warwickshire I have true-hearted
   friends,
Not mutinous in peace, yet bold in war;   *10*
Those will I muster up: and thou, son Clarence,
Shalt stir up in Suffolk, Norfolk, and in Kent,
The knights and gentlemen to come with thee:
Thou, brother Montague, in Buckingham,
Northampton, and in Leicestershire, shalt find
Men well inclined to hear what thou command'st:
And thou, brave Oxford, wondrous well beloved,
In Oxfordshire shalt muster up thy friends.
My sovereign, with the loving citizens,
Like to his island girt in with the ocean,   *20*
Or modest Dian circled with her nymphs,
Shall rest in London till we come to him.
Fair lords, take leave and stand not to reply.
Farewell, my sovereign.

K. Hen. Farewell, my Hector, and my Troy's true hope.

Clar. In sign of truth, I kiss your Highness' hand.

K. Hen. Well-minded Clarence, be thou fortunate!

Mont. Comfort, my lord; and so I take my leave.

Oxf. And thus I seal my truth, and bid adieu.

K. Hen. Sweet Oxford, and my loving Montague, 30
And all at once, once more a happy farewell.

War. Farewell, sweet lords: let's meet at Coventry.

    [*Exeunt all but* KING HENRY *and* EXETER.

K. Hen. Here at the palace will I rest awhile.
Cousin of Exeter, what thinks your lordship?
Methinks the power that Edward hath in field
Should not be able to encounter mine.

Exe. The doubt is that he will seduce the rest.

K. Hen. That's not my fear; my meed hath got me fame:
I have not stopp'd mine ears to their demands,
Nor posted off their suits with slow delays; 40
My pity hath been balm to heal their wounds,
My mildness hath allay'd their swelling griefs,
My mercy dried their water-flowing tears;
I have not been desirous of their wealth,
Nor much oppress'd them with great subsidies,
Nor forward of revenge, though they much err'd:
Then why should they love Edward more than me?
No, Exeter, these graces challenge grace:
And when the lion fawns upon the lamb,
The lamb will never cease to follow him. 50

  Shout within, "A Lancaster! A Lancaster!"

Exe. Hark, hark, my lord! what shouts are these?

  Enter KING EDWARD, GLOUCESTER, *and soldiers.*

K. Edw. Seize on the shame-faced Henry, bear him hence;
And once again proclaim us King of England.
You are the fount that makes small brooks to flow:
Now stops thy spring; my sea shall suck them dry,
And swell so much the higher by their ebb.
Hence with him to the Tower; let him not speak.

    [*Exeunt some with* KING HENRY.

And, lords, towards Coventry bend we our course,
Where peremptory Warwick now remains:
The sun shines hot; and, if we use delay, 60
Cold biting winter mars our hoped-for hay.

Glou. Away betimes, before his forces join,
And take the great-grown traitor unawares:
Brave warriors, march amain towards Coventry.

    [*Exeunt.*

ACT V

SCENE I. *Coventry*

Enter WARWICK, *the Mayor of Coventry, two* MESSENGERS, *and others upon the walls.*

War. Where is the post that came from valiant Oxford?
How far hence is thy lord, mine honest fellow?

1st Mess. By this at Dunsmore, marching hitherward.

War. How far off is our brother Montague?
Where is the post that came from Montague?

2nd Mess. By this at Daintry, with a puissant troop.

    Enter SIR JOHN SOMERVILLE.

War. Say, Somerville, what says my loving son?
And, by thy guess, how nigh is Clarence now?

Som. At Southam I did leave him with his forces,
And do expect him here some two hours hence.

  Drum heard.

War. Then Clarence is at hand; I hear his drum.

Som. It is not his, my lord; here Southam lies:
The drum your honour hears marcheth from Warwick.

War. Who should that be? belike, unlook'd-for friends.

Som. They are at hand, and you shall quickly know.

  March: flourish. Enter KING EDWARD, GLOUCESTER, *and soldiers.*

K. Edw. Go, trumpet, to the walls, and sound a parle.

Glou. See how the surly Warwick mans the wall!

War. O unbid spite! is sportful Edward come?
Where slept our scouts, or how are they seduced,
That we could hear no news of his repair? 20

K. Edw. Now, Warwick, wilt thou ope the city gates,
Speak gentle words and humbly bend thy knee,
Call Edward king and at his hands beg mercy?
And he shall pardon thee these outrages.

War. Nay, rather, wilt thou draw thy forces hence,
Confess who set thee up and pluck'd thee down,
Call Warwick patron and be penitent?
And thou shalt still remain the Duke of York.

Glou. I thought, at least, he would have said the King;

Or did he make the jest against his will?   *30*
  War. Is not a dukedom, sir, a goodly gift?
  Glou. Ay, by my faith, for a poor earl to give:
I'll do thee service for so good a gift.
  War. 'Twas I that gave the kingdom to thy
    brother.
  K. Edw. Why then 'tis mine, if but by War-
    wick's gift.
  War. Thou art no Atlas for so great a weight:
And, weakling, Warwick takes his gift again;
And Henry is my king, Warwick his subject.
  K. Edw. But Warwick's king is Edward's pris-
    oner:
And, gallant Warwick, do but answer this: *40*
What is the body when the head is off?
  Glou. Alas, that Warwick had no more fore-
    cast,
But, whiles he thought to steal the single ten,
The king was slily finger'd from the deck!
You left poor Henry at the Bishop's palace,
And, ten to one, you'll meet him in the Tower.
  K. Edw. 'Tis even so; yet you are Warwick
    still.
  Glou. Come, Warwick, take the time; kneel
    down, kneel down:
Nay, when? strike now, or else the iron cools.
  War. I had rather chop this hand off at a blow *50*
And with the other fling it at thy face
Than bear so low a sail to strike to thee.
  K. Edw. Sail how thou canst, have wind and
    tide thy friend,
This hand, fast wound about thy coal-black hair,
Shall, whiles thy head is warm and new cut off,
Write in the dust this sentence with thy blood,
"Wind-changing Warwick now can change no
    more."

    Enter OXFORD, *with drum and colours.*

  War. O cheerful colours! see where Oxford
    comes!
  Oxf. Oxford, Oxford, for Lancaster!
    He and his forces enter the city.
  Glou. The gates are open, let us enter too.   *60*
  K. Edw. So other foes may set upon our backs.
Stand we in good array; for they no doubt
Will issue out again and bid us battle:
If not, the city being but of small defence,
We'll quickly rouse the traitors in the same.
  War. O, welcome, Oxford! for we want thy
    help.

    Enter MONTAGUE, *with drum and colours.*

  Mont. Montague, Montague, for Lancaster!
    He and his forces enter the city.
  Glou. Thou and thy brother both shall buy this
    treason

Even with the dearest blood your bodies bear.
  K. Edw. The harder match'd, the greater vic-
    tory: *70*
My mind presageth happy gain and conquest.

    Enter SOMERSET, *with drum and colours.*

  Som. Somerset, Somerset, for Lancaster!
    He and his forces enter the city.
  Glou. Two of thy name, both Dukes of Somer-
    set,
Have sold their lives unto the house of York;
And thou shalt be the third, if this sword hold.

    Enter CLARENCE, *with drum and colours.*

  War. And lo, where George of Clarence sweeps
    along,
Of force enough to bid his brother battle;
With whom an upright zeal to right prevails
More than the nature of a brother's love!
Come, Clarence, come; thou wilt, if Warwick
    call.   *80*
  Clar. Father of Warwick, know you what this
    means?
    Taking his red rose out of his hat.
Look here, I throw my infancy at thee:
I will not ruinate my father's house,
Who gave his blood to line the stones together,
And set up Lancaster. Why, trow'st thou, War-
    wick,
That Clarence is so harsh, so blunt, unnatural,
To bend the fatal instruments of war
Against his brother and his lawful king?
Perhaps thou wilt object my holy oath:
To keep that oath were more impiety   *90*
Than Jephthah's, when he sacrificed his daughter.
I am so sorry for my trespass made
That, to deserve well at my brother's hands,
I here proclaim myself thy mortal foe,
With resolution, wheresoe'er I meet thee—
As I will meet thee, if thou stir abroad—
To plague thee for thy foul misleading me.
And so, proud-hearted Warwick, I defy thee,
And to my brother turn my blushing cheeks.
Pardon me, Edward, I will make amends: *100*
And, Richard, do not frown upon my faults,
For I will henceforth be no more unconstant.
  K. Edw. Now welcome more, and ten times
    more beloved,
Than if thou never hadst deserved our hate.
  Glou. Welcome, good Clarence; this is brother-
    like.
  War. O passing traitor, perjured and unjust!
  K. Edw. What, Warwick, wilt thou leave the
    town and fight?
Or shall we beat the stones about thine ears?
  War. Alas, I am not coop'd here for defence!

I will away towards Barnet presently,   *110*
And bid thee battle, Edward, if thou darest.
  K. Edw. Yes, Warwick, Edward dares, and
    leads the way.
Lords, to the field; Saint George and victory!
    [*Exeunt* KING EDWARD *and his company.
    March.* WARWICK *and his company
    follow.*

SCENE II. *A field of battle near Barnet*

Alarum and excursions. Enter KING EDWARD,
  bringing forth WARWICK *wounded.*

  K. Edw. So, lie thou there: die thou, and die our
    fear;
For Warwick was a bug that fear'd us all.
Now, Montague, sit fast; I seek for thee,
That Warwick's bones may keep thine company.
    [*Exit.*
  War. Ah, who is nigh? come to me, friend or
    foe,
And tell me who is victor, York or Warwick?
Why ask I that? my mangled body shows,
My blood, my want of strength, my sick heart
    shows
That I must yield my body to the earth
And, by my fall, the conquest to my foe.   *10*
Thus yields the cedar to the axe's edge,
Whose arms gave shelter to the princely eagle,
Under whose shade the ramping lion slept,
Whose top-branch overpeer'd Jove's spreading
    tree
And kept low shrubs from winter's powerful
    wind.
These eyes, that now are dimm'd with death's
    black veil,
Have been as piercing as the mid-day sun,
To search the secret treasons of the world:
The wrinkles in my brows, now fill'd with blood,
Were liken'd oft to kingly sepulchres;   *20*
For who lived king, but I could dig his grave?
And who durst smile when Warwick bent his
    brow?
Lo, now my glory smear'd in dust and blood!
My parks, my walks, my manors that I had,
Even now forsake me, and of all my lands
Is nothing left me but my body's length.
Why, what is pomp, rule, reign, but earth and
    dust?
And, live we how we can, yet die we must.

    Enter OXFORD *and* SOMERSET.

  Som. Ah, Warwick, Warwick! wert thou as we
    are,
We might recover all our loss again: *30*
The Queen from France hath brought a puissant
    power:

Even now we heard the news: ah, couldst thou
    fly!
  War. Why, then I would not fly. Ah, Montague,
If thou be there, sweet brother, take my hand,
And with thy lips keep in my soul awhile!
Thou lovest me not; for, brother, if thou didst,
Thy tears would wash this cold congealed blood
That glues my lips and will not let me speak.
Come quickly, Montague, or I am dead.
  Som. Ah, Warwick! Montague hath breathed
    his last;   *40*
And to the latest gasp cried out for Warwick
And said, "Commend me to my valiant brother."
And more he would have said, and more he spoke,
Which sounded like a clamour in a vault,
That mought not be distinguish'd; but at last
I well might hear, deliver'd with a groan,
"O, farewell, Warwick!"
  War. Sweet rest his soul! Fly, lords, and save
    yourselves;
For Warwick bids you all farewell, to meet in
    heaven.   [*Dies.*
  Oxf. Away, away, to meet the Queen's great
    power!   [*Here they bear away his body.
    Exeunt.*

SCENE III. *Another part of the field*

Flourish. Enter KING EDWARD *in triumph; with*
  GLOUCESTER, CLARENCE, *and the rest.*

  K. Edw. Thus far our fortune keeps an upward
    course,
And we are graced with wreaths of victory.
But, in the midst of this bright-shining day,
I spy a black, suspicious, threatening cloud,
That will encounter with our glorious sun,
Ere he attain his easeful western bed:
I mean, my lords, those powers that the Queen
Hath raised in Gallia have arrived our coast
And, as we hear, march on to fight with us.   *9*
  Clar. A little gale will soon disperse that cloud
And blow it to the source from whence it came:
Thy very beams will dry those vapours up,
For every cloud engenders not a storm.
  Glou. The Queen is valued thirty thousand
    strong,
And Somerset, with Oxford, fled to her:
If she have time to breathe, be well assured
Her faction will be full as strong as ours.
  K. Edw. We are advertised by our loving
    friends
That they do hold their course toward Tewks-
    bury:
We, having now the best at Barnet field,   *20*
Will thither straight, for willingness rids way;
And, as we march, our strength will be aug-
    mented

In every county as we go along.
Strike up the drum; cry "Courage!" and away.
                                    [*Exeunt.*

SCENE IV. *Plains near Tewksbury*

March. Enter QUEEN MARGARET, PRINCE
EDWARD, SOMERSET, OXFORD, *and soldiers.*

Q. Mar. Great lords, wise men ne'er sit and
    wail their loss,
But cheerly seek how to redress their harms.
What though the mast be now blown overboard,
The cable broke, the holding-anchor lost,
And half our sailors swallow'd in the flood?
Yet lives our pilot still. Is't meet that he
Should leave the helm and like a fearful lad
With tearful eyes add water to the sea
And give more strength to that which hath too
    much,   9
Whiles, in his moan, the ship splits on the rock,
Which industry and courage might have saved?
Ah, what a shame! ah, what a fault were this!
Say Warwick was our anchor; what of that?
And Montague our topmast; what of him?
Our slaughter'd friends the tackles; what of
    these?
Why, is not Oxford here another anchor?
And Somerset another goodly mast?
The friends of France our shrouds and tacklings?
And, though unskilful, why not Ned and I
For once allow'd the skilful pilot's charge?   20
We will not from the helm to sit and weep,
But keep our course, though the rough wind say
    no,
From shelves and rocks that threaten us with
    wreck.
As good to chide the waves as speak them fair.
And what is Edward but a ruthless sea?
What Clarence but a quicksand of deceit?
And Richard but a ragged fatal rock?
All these the enemies to our poor bark.
Say you can swim; alas, 'tis but a while!
Tread on the sand; why, there you quickly sink:
Bestride the rock; the tide will wash you off,   31
Or else you famish; that's a threefold death.
This speak I, lords, to let you understand,
If case some one of you would fly from us,
That there's no hoped-for mercy with the broth-
    ers
More than with ruthless waves, with sands, and
    rocks.
Why, courage then! what cannot be avoided
'Twere childish weakness to lament or fear.
Prince. Methinks a woman of this valiant spirit
Should, if a coward heard her speak these words,
Infuse his breast with magnanimity   41
And make him, naked, foil a man at arms.

I speak not this as doubting any here;
For did I but suspect a fearful man,
He should have leave to go away betimes,
Lest in our need he might infect another
And make him of like spirit to himself.
If any such be here—as God forbid!—
Let him depart before we need his help.   49
  Oxf. Women and children of so high a courage,
And warriors faint! why, 'twere perpetual shame.
O brave young prince! thy famous grandfather
Doth live again in thee: long mayst thou live
To bear his image and renew his glories!
  Som. And he that will not fight for such a
    hope,
Go home to bed, and like the owl by day,
If he arise, be mock'd and wonder'd at.
  Q. Mar. Thanks, gentle Somerset; sweet Ox-
    ford, thanks.
  Prince. And take his thanks that yet hath nothing
    else.

Enter a MESSENGER.

Mess. Prepare you, lords, for Edward is at
    hand,   60
Ready to fight; therefore be resolute.
  Oxf. I thought no less: it is his policy
To haste thus fast, to find us unprovided.
  Som. But he's deceived; we are in readiness.
  Q. Mar. This cheers my heart, to see your for-
    wardness.
  Oxf. Here pitch our battle; hence we will not
    budge.

Flourish and march. Enter KING EDWARD,
GLOUCESTER, CLARENCE, *and soldiers.*

K. Edw. Brave followers, yonder stands the
    thorny wood,
Which, by the heavens' assistance and your
    strength,
Must by the roots be hewn up yet ere night.
I need not add more fuel to your fire,   70
For well I wot ye blaze to burn them out:
Give signal to the fight, and to it, lords!
  Q. Mar. Lords, knights, and gentlemen, what
    I should say
My tears gainsay; for every word I speak,
Ye see, I drink the water of mine eyes.
Therefore, no more but this: Henry, your sover-
    eign,
Is prisoner to the foe; his state usurp'd,
His realm a slaughter-house, his subjects slain,
His statutes cancell'd, and his treasure spent;
And yonder is the wolf that makes this spoil.   80
You fight in justice: then, in God's name, lords,
Be valiant and give signal to the fight.
            [*Alarum: Retreat: Excursions. Exeunt.*

SCENE V. *Another part of the field*

Flourish. Enter KING EDWARD, GLOUCESTER, CLAR-
ENCE, *and soldiers; with* QUEEN MARGARET, OX-
FORD, *and* SOMERSET, *prisoners.*

K. Edw. Now here a period of tumultuous
broils.
Away with Oxford to Hames Castle straight:
For Somerset, off with his guilty head.
Go, bear them hence; I will not hear them speak.
Oxf. For my part, I'll not trouble thee with
words.
Som. Nor I, but stoop with patience to my for-
tune.

        [*Exeunt* OXFORD *and* SOMERSET, *guarded.*

Q. Mar. So part we sadly in this troublous
world,
To meet with joy in sweet Jerusalem.
K. Edw. Is proclamation made, that who finds
Edward
Shall have a high reward, and he his life?   10
Glou. It is: and lo, where youthful Edward
comes!

    Enter soldiers, with PRINCE EDWARD.

K. Edw. Bring forth the gallant, let us hear him
speak.
What! can so young a thorn begin to prick?
Edward, what satisfaction canst thou make
For bearing arms, for stirring up my subjects,
And all the trouble thou hast turn'd me to?
Prince. Speak like a subject, proud ambitious
York!
Suppose that I am now my father's mouth;
Resign thy chair, and where I stand kneel thou,
Whilst I propose the selfsame words to thee, 20
Which, traitor, thou wouldst have me answer to.
Q. Mar. Ah, that thy father had been so re-
solved!
Glou. That you might still have worn the petti-
coat
And ne'er have stol'n the breech from Lancaster.
Prince. Let Æsop fable in a winter's night;
His currish riddles sort not with this place.
Glou. By heaven, brat, I'll plague ye for that
word.
Q. Mar. Ay, thou wast born to be a plague to
men.
Glou. For God's sake, take away this captive
scold.
Prince. Nay, take away this scolding crook-
back rather.   30
K. Edw. Peace, wilful boy, or I will charm your
tongue.
Clar. Untutor'd lad, thou art too malapert.
Prince. I know my duty; you are all undutiful:

Lascivious Edward, and thou perjured George,
And thou mis-shapen Dick, I tell ye all
I am your better, traitors as ye are:
And thou usurp'st my father's right and mine.
K. Edw. Take that, thou likeness of this railer
here. [*Stabs him.*]
Glou. Sprawl'st thou? take that, to end thy
agony. [*Stabs him.*]
Clar. And there's for twitting me with perjury.
[*Stabs him.*]   40
Q. Mar. O, kill me too!
Glou. Marry, and shall. [*Offers to kill her.*]
K. Edw. Hold, Richard, hold; for we have done
too much.
Glou. Why should she live, to fill the world with
words?
K. Edw. What, doth she swoon? use means for
her recovery.
Glou. Clarence, excuse me to the King my
brother;
I'll hence to London on a serious matter:
Ere ye come there, be sure to hear some news.
Clar. What? what?
Glou. The Tower, the Tower.   [*Exit.* 50
Q. Mar. O Ned, sweet Ned! speak to thy
mother, boy!
Canst thou not speak? O traitors! murderers!
They that stabb'd Cæsar shed no blood at all,
Did not offend, nor were not worthy blame,
If this foul deed were by to equal it:
He was a man; this, in respect, a child:
And men ne'er spend their fury on a child.
What's worse than murderer, that I may name
it?
No, no, my heart will burst, an if I speak:
And I will speak, that so my heart may burst. 60
Butchers and villains! bloody cannibals!
How sweet a plant have you untimely cropp'd!
You have no children, butchers! if you had,
The thought of them would have stirr'd up re-
morse:
But if you ever chance to have a child,
Look in his youth to have him cut off
As, deathsmen, you have rid this sweet young
prince!
K. Edw. Away with her; go, bear her hence
perforce.
Q. Mar. Nay, never bear me hence, dispatch me
here;
Here sheathe thy sword, I'll pardon thee my
death:
What, wilt thou not? then, Clarence, do it thou.
Clar. By heaven, I will not do thee so much
ease.
Q. Mar. Good Clarence, do; sweet Clarence,
do thou do it.

Clar. Didst thou not hear me swear I would not
    do it?

Q. Mar. Ay, but thou usest to forswear thyself:
'Twas sin before, but now 'tis charity.
What, wilt thou not? Where is that devil's
    butcher,
Hard-favour'd Richard? Richard, where art
    thou?
Thou art not here: murder is thy alms-deed;
Petitioners for blood thou ne'er put'st back.   80

K. Edw. Away, I say; I charge ye, bear her
    hence.

Q. Mar. So come to you and yours, as to this
    prince!   *[Exit, led out forcibly.*

K. Edw. Where's Richard gone?

Clar. To London, all in post; and, as I guess,
To make a bloody supper in the Tower.

K. Edw. He's sudden, if a thing comes in his
    head.
Now march we hence: discharge the common
    sort
With pay and thanks, and let's away to London
And see our gentle queen how well she fares:
By this, I hope, she hath a son for me.   90
                                          [Exeunt.

SCENE VI. *London: The Tower*

Enter KING HENRY *and* GLOUCESTER, *with the*
LIEUTENANT, *on the walls.*

Glou. Good day, my lord. What, at your book
    so hard?

K. Hen. Ay, my good lord:—my lord, I should
    say rather;
'Tis sin to flatter; "good" was little better:
"Good Gloucester" and "good devil" were alike,
And both preposterous; therefore, not "good
    lord."

Glou. Sirrah, leave us to ourselves: we must
    confer.   *[Exit* LIEUTENANT.

K. Hen. So flies the reckless shepherd from the
    wolf;
So first the harmless sheep doth yield his fleece
And next his throat unto the butcher's knife.
What scene of death hath Roscius now to act?   10

Glou. Suspicion always haunts the guilty mind;
The thief doth fear each bush an officer.

K. Hen. The bird that hath been limed in a bush,
With trembling wings misdoubteth every bush;
And I, the hapless male to one sweet bird,
Have now the fatal object in my eye
Where my poor young was limed, was caught,
    and kill'd.

Glou. Why, what a peevish fool was that of
    Crete,
That taught his son the office of a fowl!   19
And yet, for all his wings, the fool was drown'd.

K. Hen. I, Dædalus; my poor boy, Icarus;
Thy father, Minos, that denied our course;
The sun that sear'd the wings of my sweet boy
Thy brother Edward, and thyself the sea
Whose envious gulf did swallow up his life.
Ah, kill me with thy weapon, not with words!
My breast can better brook thy dagger's point
Than can my ears that tragic history.
But wherefore dost thou come? is't for my life?

Glou. Think'st thou I am an executioner?   30

K. Hen. A persecutor, I am sure, thou art:
If murdering innocents be executing,
Why, then thou art an executioner.

Glou. Thy son I kill'd for his presumption.

K. Hen. Hadst thou been kill'd when first thou
    didst presume,
Thou hadst not lived to kill a son of mine.
And thus I prophesy, that many a thousand,
Which now mistrust no parcel of my fear,
And many an old man's sigh and many a widow's,
And many an orphan's water-standing eye—   40
Men for their sons, wives for their husbands,
And orphans for their parents' timeless death—
Shall rue the hour that ever thou wast born.
The owl shriek'd at thy birth, an evil sign;
The night-crow cried, aboding luckless time;
Dogs howl'd, and hideous tempest shook down
    trees;
The raven rook'd her on the chimney's top,
And chattering pies in dismal discords sung.
Thy mother felt more than a mother's pain,
And yet brought forth less than a mother's hope,
To wit, an indigested and deformed lump,   51
Not like the fruit of such a goodly tree.
Teeth hadst thou in thy head when thou wast
    born,
To signify thou camest to bite the world:
And, if the rest be true which I have heard,
Thou camest—

Glou. I'll hear no more: die, prophet, in thy
    speech: *[Stabs him.]*
For this, amongst the rest, was I ordain'd.

K. Hen. Ay, and for much more slaughter after
    this.
O, God forgive my sins, and pardon thee!   *[Dies.*

Glou. What, will the aspiring blood of Lan-
    caster   61
Sink in the ground? I thought it would have
    mounted.
See how my sword weeps for the poor king's
    death!
O, may such purple tears be alway shed
From those that wish the downfall of our house!
If any spark of life be yet remaining,
Down, down to hell; and say I sent thee thither:
    [Stabs him again.]

I, that have neither pity, love, nor fear.
Indeed, 'tis true that Henry told me of;
For I have often heard my mother say   70
I came into the world with my legs forward:
Had I not reason, think ye, to make haste,
And seek their ruin that usurp'd our right?
The midwife wonder'd and the women cried,
"O Jesus bless us, he is born with teeth!"
And so I was; which plainly signified
That I should snarl and bite and play the dog.
Then, since the heavens have shaped my body so,
Let hell make crook'd my mind to answer it.
I have no brother, I am like no brother;   80
And this word "love," which greybeards call
    divine,
Be resident in men like one another
And not in me: I am myself alone.
Clarence, beware; thou keep'st me from the
    light:
But I will sort a pitchy day for thee;
For I will buz abroad such prophecies
That Edward shall be fearful of his life,
And then, to purge his fear, I'll be thy death.
King Henry and the Prince his son are gone:
Clarence, thy turn is next, and then the rest,   90
Counting myself but bad till I be best.
I'll throw thy body in another room
And triumph, Henry, in thy day of doom.
                              [Exit, with the body.

SCENE VII. London: The palace

Flourish. Enter KING EDWARD, QUEEN ELIZABETH,
    CLARENCE, GLOUCESTER, HASTINGS, a Nurse
    with the young Prince Edward, and Attendants.

  K. Edw. Once more we sit in England's royal
      throne,
Re-purchased with the blood of enemies.
What valiant foemen, like to autumn's corn,
Have we mow'd down in tops of all their pride!
Three Dukes of Somerset, threefold renown'd
For hardy and undoubted champions;
Two Cliffords, as the father and the son,
And two Northumberlands; two braver men
Ne'er spurr'd their coursers at the trumpet's
    sound;
With them, the two brave bears, Warwick and
    Montague,   10

That in their chains fetter'd the kingly lion
And made the forest tremble when they roar'd.
Thus have we swept suspicion from our seat
And made our footstool of security.
Come hither, Bess, and let me kiss my boy.
Young Ned, for thee, thine uncles and myself
Have in our armours watch'd the winter's night,
Went all afoot in summer's scalding heat,
That thou mightst repossess the crown in
    peace;
And of our labours thou shalt reap the gain.   20
  Glou. [Aside] I'll blast his harvest, if your head
      were laid;
For yet I am not look'd on in the world.
This shoulder was ordain'd so thick to heave;
And heave it shall some weight, or break my
    back:
Work thou the way,—and thou shalt execute.
  K. Edw. Clarence and Gloucester, love my
      lovely queen;
And kiss your princely nephew, brothers both.
  Clar. The duty that I owe unto your Majesty
I seal upon the lips of this sweet babe.
  Q. Eliz. Thanks, noble Clarence; worthy broth-
      er, thanks.   30
  Glou. And, that I love the tree from whence
      thou sprang'st,
Witness the loving kiss I give the fruit.
[Aside] To say the truth, so Judas kiss'd his
    master,
And cried "All hail!" when as he meant all
    harm.
  K. Edw. Now am I seated as my soul delights,
Having my country's peace and brothers' loves.
  Clar. What will your Grace have done with
      Margaret?
Reignier, her father, to the King of France
Hath pawn'd the Sicils and Jerusalem,
And hither have they sent it for her ransom.
  K. Edw. Away with her, and waft her hence to
      France.
And now what rests but that we spend the time
With stately triumphs, mirthful comic shows,
Such as befits the pleasure of the court?
Sound drums and trumpets! farewell sour annoy!
For here, I hope, begins our lasting joy.
                              [Exeunt.

❧ The Tragedy of
KING RICHARD THE THIRD

DRAMATIS PERSONÆ

KING EDWARD THE FOURTH
EDWARD, PRINCE OF WALES, *afterwards* KING EDWARD V, *later as a* GHOST | *sons to the King*
RICHARD, DUKE OF YORK, *later as a* GHOST |
GEORGE, DUKE OF CLARENCE, *later as a* GHOST | *brothers to the King*
RICHARD, DUKE OF GLOUCESTER, *afterwards* KING RICHARD III |
EDWARD, EARL OF WARWICK, *son of Clarence*
HENRY, EARL OF RICHMOND, *afterwards* KING HENRY VII
CARDINAL BOURCHIER, ARCHBISHOP OF CANTERBURY
THOMAS ROTHERHAM, ARCHBISHOP OF YORK
JOHN MORTON, BISHOP OF ELY
DUKE OF BUCKINGHAM, *later as a* GHOST
DUKE OF NORFOLK
EARL OF SURREY, *his son*
EARL RIVERS, *brother to Elizabeth, later as a* GHOST
MARQUIS OF DORSET | *sons to Elizabeth*
LORD GREY, *later as a* GHOST |
EARL OF OXFORD
LORD HASTINGS, *later as a* GHOST
LORD STANLEY, *later* EARL OF DERBY
LORD LOVEL
SIR THOMAS VAUGHAN, *later as a* GHOST
SIR RICHARD RATCLIFF
SIR WILLIAM CATESBY
SIR JAMES TYRREL

SIR JAMES BLUNT
SIR WALTER HERBERT
SIR ROBERT BRAKENBURY, *Lieutenant of the Tower*
CHRISTOPHER URSWICK, *a priest*
LORD MAYOR OF LONDON
SHERIFF OF WILTSHIRE
GENTLEMAN MOURNER
TWO MURDERERS
THREE CITIZENS
SIX MESSENGERS
PURSUIVANT
PRIEST
SCRIVENER
PAGE *to Richard III*
GHOSTS OF KING HENRY VI
LORDS

ELIZABETH, *queen to King Edward IV*
MARGARET, *widow of King Henry VI*
DUCHESS OF YORK, *mother to King Edward IV*
LADY ANNE, *widow of Edward Prince of Wales, son to King Henry VI, afterwards married to Richard, later as a* GHOST
MARGARET PLANTAGENET, *daughter of Clarence*

NON-SPEAKING: *Lords and other attendants,* TWO *Bishops, Sir William Brandon, Citizens, Soldiers*

SCENE: *England*

❧

ACT I

SCENE I. *London: a street*

Enter RICHARD, DUKE OF GLOUCESTER, *solus.*

Glou. Now is the winter of our discontent
Made glorious summer by this sun of York;
And all the clouds that lour'd upon our house
In the deep bosom of the ocean buried.
Now are our brows bound with victorious wreaths;
Our bruised arms hung up for monuments;
Our stern alarums changed to merry meetings,
Our dreadful marches to delightful measures.
Grim-visaged War hath smooth'd his wrinkled front;
And now, instead of mounting barbed steeds   10
To fright the souls of fearful adversaries,
He capers nimbly in a lady's chamber
To the lascivious pleasing of a lute.

But I, that am not shaped for sportive tricks,
Nor made to court an amorous looking-glass;
I, that am rudely stamp'd, and want love's majesty
To strut before a wanton ambling nymph;
I, that am curtail'd of this fair proportion,
Cheated of feature by dissembling nature,
Deform'd, unfinish'd, sent before my time   20
Into this breathing world, scarce half made up,
And that so lamely and unfashionable
That dogs bark at me as I halt by them;
Why, I, in this weak piping time of peace,
Have no delight to pass away the time,
Unless to spy my shadow in the sun
And descant on mine own deformity:
And therefore, since I cannot prove a lover,
To entertain these fair well-spoken days,
I am determined to prove a villian   30
And hate the idle pleasures of these days.
Plots have I laid, inductions dangerous,

By drunken prophecies, libels, and dreams,
To set my brother Clarence and the King
In deadly hate the one against the other:
And if King Edward be as true and just
As I am subtle, false, and treacherous,
This day should Clarence closely be mew'd up,
About a prophecy, which says that G
Of Edward's heirs the murderer shall be.   40
Dive, thoughts, down to my soul: here Clarence
    comes.

Enter CLARENCE, *guarded, and* BRAKENBURY.

Brother, good day: what means this armed guard
That waits upon your Grace?
  Clar.   His majesty,
Tendering my person's safety, hath appointed
This conduct to convey me to the Tower.
  Glou. Upon what cause?
  Clar.   Because my name is George.
  Glou. Alack, my lord, that fault is none of
    yours;
He should, for that, commit your godfathers:
O, belike his Majesty hath some intent   49
That you shall be new-christen'd in the Tower.
But what's the matter, Clarence? may I know?
  Clar. Yea, Richard, when I know; for I protest
As yet I do not: but, as I can learn,
He hearkens after prophecies and dreams;
And from the cross-row plucks the letter G,
And says a wizard told him that by G
His issue disinherited should be;
And, for my name of George begins with G,
It follows in his thought that I am he.
These, as I learn, and such like toys as these   60
Have moved his Highness to commit me now.
  Glou. Why, this it is, when men are ruled by
    women:
'Tis not the King that sends you to the Tower;
My Lady Grey his wife, Clarence, 'tis she
That tempers him to this extremity.
Was it not she and that good man of worship,
AnthonyWoodville, her brother there,
That made him send Lord Hastings to the Tower,
From whence this present day he is deliver'd?
We are not safe, Clarence; we are not safe.   70
  Clar. By heaven, I think there's no man is secure
But the Queen's kindred and night-walking
    heralds
That trudge betwixt the King and Mistress Shore.
Heard ye not what an humble suppliant
Lord Hastings was to her for his delivery?
  Glou. Humbly complaining to her deity
Got my Lord Chamberlain his liberty.
I'll tell you what; I think it is our way,
If we will keep in favour with the King,
To be her men and wear her livery: 80

The jealous o'erworn widow and herself,
Since that our brother dubb'd them gentlewomen,
Are mighty gossips in this monarchy.
  Brak. I beseech your Graces both to pardon
    me;
His Majesty hath straitly given in charge
That no man shall have private conference,
Of what degree soever, with his brother.
  Glou. Even so; an't please your worship,
    Brakenbury,
You may partake of any thing we say:
We speak no treason, man: we say the King   90
Is wise and virtuous, and his noble queen
Well struck in years, fair, and not jealous;
We say that Shore's wife hath a pretty foot,
A cherry lip, a bonny eye, a passing pleasing
    tongue;
And that the Queen's kindred are made gentle-
    folks:
How say you, sir? can you deny all this?
  Brak. With this, my lord, myself have nought
    to do.
  Glou. Naught to do with Mistress Shore! I
    tell thee, fellow,
He that doth naught with her, excepting one,
Were best he do it secretly, alone.   100
  Brak. What one, my lord?
  Glou. Her husband, knave: wouldst thou
    betray me?
  Brak. I beseech your Grace to pardon me,
    and withal
Forbear your conference with the noble Duke.
  Clar. We know thy charge, Brakenbury, and
    will obey.
  Glou. We are the Queen's abjects, and must
    obey.
Brother, farewell: I will unto the King;
And whatsoever you will employ me in,
Were it to call King Edward's widow sister,
I will perform it to enfranchise you.   110
Meantime, this deep disgrace in brotherhood
Touches me deeper than you can imagine.
  Clar. I know it pleaseth neither of us well.
  Glou. Well, your imprisonment shall not be
    long;
I will deliver you, or else lie for you:
Meantime, have patience.
  Clar.   I must perforce.   Farewell.
    [*Exeunt* CLARENCE, BRAKENBURY, *and Guard.*
  Glou. Go, tread the path that thou shalt ne'er
    return,
Simple, plain Clarence! I do love thee so,
That I will shortly send thy soul to heaven,
If heaven will take the present at our hands.   120
But who comes here? the new-deliver'd Hast-
    ings?

Enter LORD HASTINGS.

Hast. Good time of day unto my gracious lord!
Glou. As much unto my good Lord Chamberlain!
Well are you welcome to the open air.
How hath your lordship brook'd imprisonment?
Hast. With patience, noble lord, as prisoners
    must:
But I shall live, my lord, to give them thanks
That were the cause of my imprisonment.
Glou. No doubt, no doubt; and so shall
    Clarence too;
For they that were your enemies are his,   *130*
And have prevail'd as much on him as you.
Hast. More pity that the eagle should be
    mew'd,
While kites and buzzards prey at liberty.
Glou. What news abroad?
Hast. No news so bad abroad as this at
    home;
The King is sickly, weak, and melancholy,
And his physicians fear him mightily.
Glou. Now, by Saint Paul, this news is bad
    indeed.
O, he hath kept an evil diet long,
And overmuch consumed his royal person: *140*
'Tis very grievous to be thought upon.
What, is he in his bed?
 Hast, He is.
Glou. Go you before, and I will follow you.
                    [*Exit* HASTINGS.
He cannot live, I hope; and must not die
Till George be pack'd with post-horse up to
    heaven.
I'll in, to urge his hatred more to Clarence,
With lies well steel'd with weighty argu-
    ments;
And, if I fail not in my deep intent,
Clarence hath not another day to live: *150*
Which done, God take King Edward to his
    mercy,
And leave the world for me to bustle in!
For then I'll marry Warwick's youngest daugh-
    ter.
What though I kill'd her husband and her
    father?
The readiest way to make the wench amends
Is to become her husband and her father:
The which will I; not all so much for love
As for another secret close intent,
By marrying her which I must reach unto.
But yet I run before my horse to market: *160*
Clarence still breathes; Edward still lives and
    reigns:
When they are gone, then must I count my gains.
                        [*Exit.*

SCENE II. *The same: another street*

Enter the corpse of King Henry the Sixth,
GENTLEMEN *with halberds to guard it, among
them* TRESSEL *and* BERKELEY; LADY ANNE *being
the mourner.*

Anne. Set down, set down your honourable
    load,
If honour may be shrouded in a hearse,
Whilst I awhile obsequiously lament
The untimely fall of virtuous Lancaster.
          The coffin is set down.
Poor key-cold figure of a holy king!
Pale ashes of the house of Lancaster!
Thou bloodless remnant of that royal blood!
Be it lawful that I invocate thy ghost,
To hear the lamentations of poor Anne,
Wife to thy Edward, to thy slaughter'd son,   *10*
Stabb'd by the selfsame hand that made these
    wounds!
Lo, in these windows that let forth thy life,
I pour the helpless balm of my poor eyes.
Cursed be the hand that made these fatal holes!
Cursed be the heart that had the heart to do it!
Cursed the blood that let this blood from hence!
More direful hap betide that hated wretch
That makes us wretched by the death of thee
Than I can wish to adders, spiders, toads,
Or any creeping venom'd thing that lives!   *20*
If ever he have child, abortive be it,
Prodigious, and untimely brought to light,
Whose ugly and unnatural aspect
May fright the hopeful mother at the view;
And that be heir to his unhappiness!
If ever he have wife, let her be made
As miserable by the death of him
As I am made by my poor lord and thee!
Come, now towards Chertsey with your holy
    load,
Taken from Paul's to be interred there;   *30*
And still, as you are weary of the weight,
Rest you, whiles I lament King Henry's corse.

Enter GLOUCESTER.

Glou. Stay, you that bear the corse, and set
    it down.
Anne. What black magician conjures up this
    fiend,
To stop devoted charitable deeds?
Glou. Villains, set down the corse; or, by
    Saint Paul,
I'll make a corse of him that disobeys.
Gent. My lord, stand back, and let the coffin
    pass.
Glou. Unmanner'd dog! stand thou, when I
    command:

Advance thy halberd higher than my breast,   40
Or, by Saint Paul, I'll strike thee to my foot,
And spurn upon thee, beggar, for thy boldness.
  Anne. What, do you tremble? are you all
    afraid?
Alas, I blame you not; for you are mortal,
And mortal eyes cannot endure the devil.
Avaunt, thou dreadful minister of hell!
Thou hadst but power over his mortal body,
His soul thou canst not have; therefore, be gone.
  Glou. Sweet saint, for charity, be not so curst.
  Anne. Foul devil, for God's sake, hence, and
    trouble us not;   50
For thou hast made the happy earth thy hell,
Fill'd it with cursing cries and deep exclaims.
If thou delight to view thy heinous deeds,
Behold this pattern of thy butcheries.
O, gentlemen, see, see! dead Henry's wounds
Open their congeal'd mouths and bleed afresh!
Blush, blush, thou lump of foul deformity;
For 'tis thy presence that exhales this blood
From cold and empty veins, where no blood
    dwells;
Thy deed, inhuman and unnatural,   60
Provokes this deluge most unnatural.
O God, which this blood madest, revenge his
    death!
O earth, which this blood drink'st, revenge his
    death!
Either heaven with lightning strike the murderer
    dead,
Or earth, gape open wide and eat him quick,
As thou dost swallow up this good king's blood,
Which his hell-govern'd arm hath butchered!
  Glou. Lady, you know no rules of charity,
Which renders good for bad, blessings for curses.
  Anne. Villain, thou know'st no law of God
    nor man: 70
No beast so fierce but knows some touch of pity.
  Glou. But I know none, and therefore am no
    beast.
  Anne. O wonderful, when devils tell the truth!
  Glou. More wonderful, when angels are so
    angry.
Vouchsafe, divine perfection of a woman,
Of these supposed evils to give me leave
By circumstance but to acquit myself.
  Anne. Vouchsafe, defused infection of a man,
For these known evils but to give me leave
By circumstance to curse thy cursed self.   80
  Glou. Fairer than tongue can name thee, let
    me have
Some patient leisure to excuse myself.
  Anne. Fouler than heart can think thee, thou
    canst make
No excuse current, but to hang thyself.

  Glou. By such despair, I should accuse myself.
  Anne. And, by despairing, shouldst thou stand
    excused;
For doing worthy vengeance on thyself,
Which didst unworthy slaughter upon others.
  Glou. Say that I slew them not?
  Anne.   Why, then they are not dead:
But dead they are, and, devilish slave, by thee.
  Glou. I did not kill your husband.   91
  Anne.   Why, then he is alive.
  Glou. Nay, he is dead; and slain by Edward's
    hand.
  Anne. In thy foul throat thou liest: Queen
    Margaret saw
Thy murderous falchion smoking in his blood;
The which thou once didst bend against her
    breast,
But that thy brothers beat aside the point.
  Glou. I was provoked by her slanderous tongue,
Which laid their guilt upon my guiltless
    shoulders.
  Anne. Thou wast provoked by thy bloody mind
Which never dreamt on aught but butcheries :100
Didst thou not kill this king?
  Glou.   I grant ye.
  Anne. Dost grant me, hedgehog? then, God
    grant me too
Thou mayst be damned for that wicked deed!
O, he was gentle, mild, and virtuous!
  Glou. The fitter for the King of heaven, that
    hath him.
  Anne. He is in heaven, where thou shalt
    never come.
  Glou. Let him thank me, that holp to send
    him thither;
For he was fitter for that place than earth.
  Anne. And thou unfit for any place but hell.
  Glou. Yes, one place else, if you will hear me
    name it.   110
  Anne. Some dungeon.
  Glou.   Your bed-chamber.
  Anne. Ill rest betide the chamber where thou
    liest!
  Glou. So will it, madam, till I lie with you.
  Anne. I hope so.
  Glou.   I know so. But, gentle Lady Anne,
To leave this keen encounter of our wits,
And fall somewhat into a slower method,
Is not the causer of the timeless deaths
Of these Plantagenets, Henry and Edward,
As blameful as the executioner?
  Anne. Thou art the cause, and most accursed
    effect.   120
  Glou. Your beauty was the cause of that effect;
Your beauty, which did haunt me in my sleep
To undertake the death of all the world,

So I might live one hour in your sweet bosom.
  Anne. If I thought that, I tell thee, homicide,
These nails should rend that beauty from my
    cheeks.
  Glou. These eyes could never endure sweet
    beauty's wreck;
You should not blemish it, if I stood by:
As all the world is cheered by the sun,
So I by that; it is my day, my life.   *130*
  Anne. Black night o'ershade thy day, and
    death thy life!
  Glou. Curse not thyself, fair creature; thou
    art both.
  Anne. I would I were, to be revenged on thee.
  Glou. It is a quarrel most unnatural,
To be revenged on him that loveth you.
  Anne. It is a quarrel just and reasonable,
To be revenged on him that slew my husband.
  Glou. He that bereft thee, lady, of thy husband,
Did it to help thee to a better husband.
  Anne. His better doth not breathe upon the
    earth.   *140*
  Glou. He lives that loves thee better than he
    could.
  Anne. Name him.
  Glou.   Plantagenet.
  Anne.   Why, that was he.
  Glou. The salfsame name, but one of better
    nature.
  Anne. Where is he?
  Glou.   Here. [*She spitteth at him.*]
Why dost thou spit at me?
  Anne. Would it were mortal poison, for thy
    sake!
  Glou. Never came poison from so sweet a place.
  Anne. Never hung poison on a fouler toad.
Out of my sight! thou dost infect my eyes.
  Glou. Thine eyes, sweet lady, have infected
    mine.   *150*
  Anne. Would they were basilisks, to strike
    thee dead!
  Glou. I would they were, that I might die at
    once;
For now they kill me with a living death.
Those eyes of thine from mine have drawn salt
    tears,
Shamed their aspect with store of childish drops:
These eyes, which never shed remorseful tear,
No, when my father York and Edward wept,
To hear the piteous moan that Rutland made
When black-faced Clifford shook his sword at
    him;
Nor when thy warlike father, like a child,   *160*
Told the sad story of my father's death,
And twenty times made pause to sob and weep,
That all the standers-by had wet their cheeks,

Like trees bedash'd with rain: in that sad time
My manly eyes did scorn an humble tear;
And what these sorrows could not thence exhale,
Thy beauty hath, and made them blind with
    weeping.
I never sued to friend nor enemy;
My tongue could never learn sweet smoothing
    words;
But, now thy beauty is proposed my fee,   *170*
My proud heart sues and prompts my tongue to
    speak. [*She looks scornfully at him.*]
Teach not thy lips such scorn, for they were made
For kissing, lady, not for such contempt.
If thy revengeful heart cannot forgive,
Lo, here I lend thee this sharp-pointed sword;
Which if thou please to hide in this true bosom,
And let the soul forth that adoreth thee,
I lay it naked to the deadly stroke,
And humbly beg the death upon my knee.
    *He lays his breast open: she offers at it with his
    sword.*
Nay, do not pause; for I did kill King Henry,
But 'twas thy beauty that provoked me.   *181*
Nay, now dispatch; 'twas I that stabb'd young
    Edward,
But 'twas thy heavenly face that set me on.
    Here she lets fall the sword.
Take up the sword again, or take up me.
  Anne. Arise, dissembler: though I wish thy
    death,
I will not be the executioner.
  Glou. Then bid me kill myself, and I will do it.
  Anne. I have already.
  Glou.   Tush, that was in thy rage:
Speak it again, and even with the word,
That hand, which, for thy love, did kill thy love,
Shall, for thy love, kill a far truer love;   *191*
To both their deaths thou shalt be accessary.
  Anne. I would I knew thy heart.
  Glou. 'Tis figured in my tongue.
  Anne. I fear me both are false.
  Glou. Then never man was true.
  Anne. Well, well, put up your sword.
  Glou. Say, then, my peace is made.
  Anne. That shall you know hereafter.
  Glou. But shall I live in hope?   *200*
  Anne. All men, I hope, live so.
  Glou. Vouchsafe to wear this ring.
  Anne. To take is not to give.
  Glou. Look, how this ring encompasseth thy
    finger,
Even so thy breast encloseth my poor heart;
Wear both of them, for both of them are thine.
And if thy poor devoted suppliant may
But beg one favour at thy gracious hand,
Thou dost confirm his happiness for ever.

Anne. What is it?   210

Glou. That it would please thee leave these
    sad designs
To him that hath more cause to be a mourner,
And presently repair to Crosby Place;
Where, after I have solemnly interr'd
At Chertsey monastery this noble king,
And wet his grave with my repentant tears,
I will with all expedient duty see you:
For divers unknown reasons, I beseech you,
Grant me this boon.

  Anne. With all my heart; and much it joys
    me too,   220
To see you are become so penitent.
Tressel and Berkeley, go along with me.

Glou. Bid me farewell.

Anne.   'Tis more than you deserve;
But since you teach me how to flatter you,
Imagine I have said farewell already.

    [*Exeunt* LADY ANNE, TRESSEL, *and* BERKELEY.

Glou. Sirs, take up the corse.

Gent.   Towards Chertsey, noble lord?

Glou. No, to White-Friars; there attend my
    coming.   [*Exeunt all but* GLOUCESTER.
Was ever woman in this humour woo'd?
Was ever woman in this humour won?
I'll have her; but I will not keep her long.   230
What! I, that kill'd her husband and his father,
To take her in her heart's extremest hate,
With curses in her mouth, tears in her eyes,
The bleeding witness of her hatred by;
Having God, her conscience, and these bars
    against me,
And I nothing to back my suit at all
But the plain devil and dissembling looks,
And yet to win her, all the world to nothing!
Ha!
Hath she forgot already that brave prince,   240
Edward, her lord, whom I, some three months
    since,
Stabb'd in my angry mood at Tewksbury?
A sweeter and a lovelier gentleman,
Framed in the prodigality of nature,
Young, valiant, wise, and, no doubt, right royal,
The spacious world cannot again afford:
And will she yet debase her eyes on me,
That cropp'd the golden prime of this sweet
    prince
And made her widow to a woeful bed?
On me, whose all not equals Edward's moiety?
On me, that halt and am unshapen thus?   251
My dukedom to a beggarly denier,
I do mistake my person all this while:
Upon my life, she finds, although I cannot,
Myself to be a marvellous proper man.
I'll be at charges for a looking-glass,

And entertain some score or two of tailors
To study fashions to adorn my body:
Since I am crept in favour with myself,
I will maintain it with some little cost.   260
But first I'll turn yon fellow in his grave;
And then return lamenting to my love.
Shine out, fair sun, till I have bought a glass,
That I may see my shadow as I pass.   [*Exit.*

SCENE III. *The palace*

Enter QUEEN ELIZABETH, LORD RIVERS, *and*
LORD GREY.

Riv. Have patience, madam: there's no
    doubt his Majesty
Will soon recover his accustom'd health.

Grey. In that you brook it ill, it makes him
    worse:
Therefore, for God's sake, entertain good
    comfort,
And cheer his Grace with quick and merry words.

Q. Eliz. If he were dead, what would betide
    of me?

Riv. No other harm but loss of such a lord.

Q. Eliz. The loss of such a lord includes all
    harm.

Grey. The heavens have bless'd you with a
    goodly son,
To be your comforter when he is gone.   10

Q. Eliz. Oh, he is young, and his minority
Is put unto the trust of Richard Gloucester,
A man that loves not me, nor none of you.

Riv. Is it concluded he shall be Protector?

Q. Eliz. It is determined, not concluded yet:
But so it must be, if the King miscarry.

Enter BUCKINGHAM *and* LORD STANLEY,
EARL OF DERBY.

Grey. Here come the lords of Buckingham
    and Derby.

Buck. Good time of day unto your royal Grace!

Stan. God make your Majesty joyful as you
    have been!

Q. Eliz. The Countess Richmond, good my
    Lord of Derby,   20
To your good prayers will scarcely say amen.
Yet, Derby, notwithstanding she's your wife,
And loves not me, be you, good lord, assured
I hate not you for her proud arrogance.

Stan. I do beseech you, either not believe
The envious slanders of her false accusers;
Or, if she be accused in true report,
Bear with her weakness, which, I think, proceeds
From wayward sickness and no grounded malice.

Riv. Saw you the King to-day, my Lord of
    Derby?   30

Stan. But now the Duke of Buckingham and I

Are come from visiting his majesty.

Q. Eliz. What likelihood of his amendment,
lords?

Buck. Madam, good hope; his Grace speaks
cheerfully.

Q. Eliz. God grant him health! Did you
confer with him?

Buck. Madam, we did: he desires to make
atonement
Betwixt the Duke of Gloucester and your
brothers,
And betwixt them and my Lord Chamberlain;
And sent to warn them to his royal presence.

Q. Eliz. Would all were well! but that will
never be: 40
I fear our happiness is at the highest.

Enter GLOUCESTER, HASTINGS, *and* DORSET.

Glou. They do me wrong, and I will not en-
dure it:
Who are they that complain unto the King
That I, forsooth, am stern and love them not?
By holy Paul, they love his Grace but lightly
That fill his ears with such dissentious rumours.
Because I cannot flatter and speak fair,
Smile in men's faces, smooth, deceive and cog,
Duck with French nods and apish courtesy,
I must be held a rancorous enemy.   50
Cannot a plain man live and think no harm,
But thus his simple truth must be abused
By silken, sly, insinuating Jacks?

Riv. To whom in all this presence speaks
your Grace?

Glou. To thee, that hast nor honesty nor grace.
When have I injured thee? when done thee
wrong?
Or thee? or thee? or any of your faction?
A plague upon you all! His royal person—
Whom God preserve better than you would
wish!—
Cannot be quiet scarce a breathing-while   60
But you must trouble him with lewd complaints.

Q. Eliz. Brother of Gloucester, you mistake
the matter.
The King, of his own royal disposition,
And not provoked by any suitor else,
Aiming, belike, at your interior hatred,
Which in your outward actions shows itself
Against my kindred, brothers, and myself,
Makes him to send that thereby he may gather
The ground of your ill-will and so remove it.

Glou. I cannot tell: the world is grown so
bad   70
That wrens make prey where eagles dare not
perch:
Since every Jack became a gentleman,

There's many a gentle person made a Jack.

Q. Eliz. Come, come, we know your meaning,
brother Gloucester;
You envy my advancement and my friends':
God grant we never have need of you!

Glou. Meantime, God grants that we have
need of you:
Our brother is imprison'd by your means,
Myself disgraced, and the nobility
Held in contempt; whilst many fair promotions
Are daily given to ennoble those   81
That scarce, some two days since, were worth a
noble.

Q. Eliz. By Him that raised me to this care-
ful height
From that contented hap which I enjoy'd,
I never did incense his Majesty
Against the Duke of Clarence, but have been
An earnest advocate to plead for him.
My lord, you do me shameful injury,
Falsely to draw me in these vile suspects.

Glou. You may deny that you were not the
cause   90
Of my Lord Hastings' late imprisonment.

Riv. She may, my lord, for—

Glou. She may, Lord Rivers! why, who
knows not so?
She may do more, sir, than denying that:
She may help you to many fair preferments
And then deny her aiding hand therein,
And lay those honours on your high deserts.
What may she not? She may, yea, marry, may
she—

Riv. What, marry, may she?

Glou. What, marry, may she! marry with a
king,   100
A bachelor, a handsome stripling too:
I wis your grandam had a worser match.

Q. Eliz. My Lord of Gloucester, I have too
long borne
Your blunt upbraidings and your bitter scoffs:
By heaven, I will acquaint his Majesty
With those gross taunts I often have endured.
I had rather be a country servant-maid
Than a great queen, with this condition,
To be thus taunted, scorn'd, and baited at:

Enter QUEEN MARGARET, *behind.*

Small joy have I in being England's queen.   110

Q. Mar. And lessen'd be that small, God, I
beseech thee!
Thy honour, state, and seat is due to me.

Glou. What! threat you me with telling of
the King?
Tell him, and spare not: look, what I have said
I will avouch in presence of the King:

I dare adventure to be sent to the Tower.
'Tis time to speak; my pains are quite forgot.
  Q. Mar. Out, devil! I remember them too
    well:
Thou slewest my husband Henry in the Tower,
And Edward, my poor son, at Tewksbury.   *120*
  Glou. Ere you were queen, yea, or your
    husband king,
I was a pack-horse in his great affairs;
A weeder-out of his proud adversaries,
A liberal rewarder of his friends:
To royalise his blood I spilt mine own.
  Q. Mar. Yea, and much better blood than his
    or thine.
  Glou. In all which time you and your husband
    Grey
Were factious for the house of Lancaster;
And, Rivers, so were you. Was not your husband
In Margaret's battle at Saint Alban's slain?   *130*
Let me put in your minds, if you forget,
What you have been ere now and what you are;
Withal, what I have been and what I am.
  Q. Mar. A murderous villain, and so still
    thou art.
  Glou. Poor Clarence did forsake his father,
    Warwick;
Yea, and forswore himself—which Jesu
    pardon!—
  Q. Mar. Which God revenge!
  Glou. To fight on Edward's party for the
    crown;
And for his meed, poor lord, he is mew'd up.
I would to God my heart were flint, like
    Edward's;   *140*
Or Edward's soft and pitiful, like mine:
I am too childish-foolish for this world.
  Q. Mar. Hie thee to hell for shame, and leave
    the world,
Thou cacodemon! there thy kingdom is.
  Riv. My Lord of Gloucester, in those busy
    days
Which here you urge to prove us enemies,
We follow'd then our lord, our lawful king:
So should we you, if you should be our king.
  Glou. If I should be! I had rather be a pedlar:
Far be it from my heart, the thought of it!   *150*
  Q. Eliz. As little joy, my lord, as you suppose
You should enjoy, were you this country's king,
As little joy may you suppose in me,
That I enjoy, being the queen thereof.
  Q. Mar. A little joy enjoys the queen thereof;
For I am she, and altogether joyless.
I can no longer hold me patient. [*Advancing.*]
Hear me, you wrangling pirates, that fall out
In sharing that which you have pill'd from me!
Which of you trembles not that looks on me?   *160*

If not that, I being queen, you bow like subjects,
Yet that, by you deposed, you quake like rebels?
O gentle villain, do not turn away!
  Glou. Foul wrinkled witch, what makest thou
    in my sight?
  Q. Mar. But repetition of what thou hast
    marr'd;
That will I make before I let thee go.
  Glou. Wert thou not banished on pain of death?
  Q. Mar. I was; but I do find more pain in
    banishment
Than death can yield me here by my abode.
A husband and a son thou owest to me;   *170*
And thou a kingdom; all of you allegiance:
The sorrow that I have by right is yours,
And all the pleasures you usurp are mine.
  Glou. The curse my noble father laid on thee,
When thou didst crown his warlike brows with
    paper
And with thy scorns drew'st rivers from his eyes,
And then, to dry them, gavest the Duke a clout
Steep'd in the faultless blood of pretty Rutland—
His curses, then from bitterness of soul   *179*
Denounced against thee, are all fall'n upon thee;
And God, not we, hath plagued thy bloody deed.
  Q. Eliz. So just is God, to right the innocent.
  Hast. O, 'twas the foulest deed to slay that
    babe,
And the most merciless that e'er was heard of!
  Riv. Tyrants themselves wept when it was
    reported.
  Dor. No man but prophesied revenge for it.
  Buck. Northumberland, then present, wept
    to see it.
  Q. Mar. What! were you snarling all before I
    came,
Ready to catch each other by the throat,
And turn you all your hatred now on me?   *190*
Did York's dread curse prevail so much with
    heaven
That Henry's death, my lovely Edward's death,
Their kingdom's loss, my woeful banishment,
Could all but answer for that peevish brat?
Can curses pierce the clouds and enter heaven?
Why, then, give way, dull clouds, to my quick
    curses!
If not by war, by surfeit die your king,
As ours by murder, to make him a king!
Edward thy son, which now is Prince of Wales,
For Edward my son, which was Prince of Wales,
Die in his youth by like untimely violence!   *201*
Thyself a queen, for me that was a queen,
Outlive thy glory, like my wretched self!
Long mayst thou live to wail thy children's loss;
And see another, as I see thee now,
Deck'd in thy rights, as thou art stall'd in mine!

Long die thy happy days before thy death;
And, after many lengthen'd hours of grief,
Die neither mother, wife, nor England's Queen!
Rivers and Dorset, you were standers by,   210
And so wast thou, Lord Hastings, when my son
Was stabb'd with bloody daggers: God, I pray
    him,
That none of you may live your natural age,
But by some unlook'd accident cut off!
  Glou. Have done thy charm, thou hateful
    wither'd hag!
  Q. Mar. And leave out thee? stay, dog, for
    thou shalt hear me.
If heaven have any grievous plague in store
Exceeding those that I can wish upon thee,
O, let them keep it till thy sins be ripe,
And then hurl down their indignation   220
On thee, the troubler of the poor world's peace!
The worm of conscience still begnaw thy soul!
Thy friends suspect for traitors while thou livest,
And take deep traitors for thy dearest friends!
No sleep close up that deadly eye of thine,
Unless it be whilst some tormenting dream
Affrights thee with a hell of ugly devils!
Thou elvish-mark'd, abortive, rooting hog!
Thou that wast seal'd in thy nativity
The slave of nature and the son of hell!   230
Thou slander of thy mother's heavy womb!
Thou loathed issue of thy father's loins!
Thou rag of honour! thou detested—
  Glou. Margaret.
  Q. Mar.   Richard!
  Glou.   Ha!
  Q. Mar.   I call thee not.
  Glou. I cry thee mercy then, for I had
    thought
That thou hadst call'd me all these bitter names.
  Q. Mar. Why, so I did; but look'd for no
    reply.
O, let me make the period to my curse!
  Glou. 'Tis done by me, and ends in "Margaret."
  Q. Eliz. Thus have you breathed your curse
    against yourself.   240
  Q. Mar. Poor painted queen, vain flourish of
    my fortune!
Why strew'st thou sugar on that bottled spider,
Whose deadly web ensnareth thee about?
Fool, fool! thou whet'st a knife to kill thyself.
The time will come when thou shalt wish for me
To help thee curse that poisonous bunch-back'd
    toad.
  Hast. False-boding woman, end thy frantic
    curse,
Lest to thy harm thou move our patience.
  Q. Mar. Foul shame upon you! you have
    all moved mine.

  Riv. Were you well served, you would be
    taught your duty.   250
  Q. Mar. To serve me well, you all should do
    me duty,
Teach me to be your queen, and you my subjects:
O, serve me well, and teach yourselves that
    duty!
  Dor. Dispute not with her; she is lunatic.
  Q. Mar. Peace, master marquess, you are
    malapert:
Your fire-new stamp of honour is scarce current.
O, that your young nobility could judge
What 'twere to lose it, and be miserable!
They that stand high have many blasts to shake
    them;   259
And if they fall, they dash themselves to pieces.
  Glou. Good counsel, marry: learn it, learn it,
    marquess.
  Dor. It toucheth you, my lord, as much as me.
  Glou. Yea, and much more: but I was born
    so high,
Our aery buildeth in the cedar's top,
And dallies with the wind and scorns the sun.
  Q. Mar. And turns the sun to shade; alas!
    alas!
Witness my son, now in the shade of death;
Whose bright out-shining beams thy cloudy
    wrath
Hath in eternal darkness folded up.
Your aery buildeth in our aery's nest.   270
O God, that seest it, do not suffer it;
As it was won with blood, lost be it so!
  Buck. Have done! for shame, if not for charity.
  Q. Mar. Urge neither charity nor shame to me:
Uncharitably with me have you dealt,
And shamefully by you my hopes are butcher'd.
My charity is outrage, life my shame;
And in that shame still live my sorrow's rage!
  Buck. Have done, have done.
  Q. Mar. O princely Buckingham, I'll kiss
    thy hand,   280
In sign of league and amity with thee:
Now fair befal thee and thy noble house!
Thy garments are not spotted with our blood,
Nor thou within the compass of my curse.
  Buck. Nor no one here; for curses never pass
The lips of those that breathe them in the air.
  Q. Mar. I'll not believe but they ascend the sky,
And there awake God's gentle-sleeping peace.
[*Aside to* BUCKINGHAM.]
O Buckingham, take heed of yonder dog!
Look, when he fawns, he bites; and when he
    bites,   290
His venom tooth will rankle to the death:
Have not to do with him, beware of him;
Sin, death, and hell have set their marks on him,

And all their ministers attend on him.
  Glou. What doth she say, my Lord of
    Buckingham?
  Buck. Nothing that I respect, my gracious lord.
  Q. Mar. What, dost thou scorn me for my
    gentle counsel?
And soothe the devil that I warn thee from?
O, but remember this another day,
When he shall split thy very heart with sorrow,
And say poor Margaret was a prophetess!   *301*
Live each of you the subjects to his hate,
And he to yours, and all of you to God's!   [*Exit.*
  Hast. My hair doth stand on end to hear her
    curses.
  Riv. And so doth mine: I muse why she's at
    liberty.
  Glou. I cannot blame her: by God's holy
    mother,
She hath had too much wrong; and I repent
My part thereof that I have done to her.
  Q. Eliz. I never did her any, to my knowledge.
  Glou. But you have all the vantage of her
    wrong.   *310*
I was too hot to do somebody good
That is too cold in thinking of it now.
Marry, as for Clarence, he is well repaid;
He is frank'd up to fatting for his pains:
God pardon them that are the cause of it!
  Riv. A virtuous and a Christian-like conclusion,
To pray for them that have done scathe to us.
  Glou. So do I ever: [*Aside*] being well advised.
For had I cursed now, I had cursed myself.

Enter CATESBY.

  Cates. Madam, his Majesty doth call for you;   *320*
And for your Grace; and you, my noble lords.
  Q. Eliz. Catesby, we come. Lords, will
    you go with us?
  Riv. Madam, we will attend your Grace.
              [*Exeunt all but* GLOUCESTER
  Glou. I do the wrong, and first begin to brawl.
The secret mischiefs that I set abroach
I lay unto the grievous charge of others.
Clarence, whom I, indeed, have laid in dark-
    ness,
I do beweep to many simple gulls;
Namely, to Hastings, Derby, Buckingham;
And say it is the Queen and her allies   *330*
That stir the King against the Duke my brother.
Now, they believe it; and withal whet me
To be revenged on Rivers, Vaughan, Grey:
But then I sigh, and, with a piece of scripture,
Tell them that God bids us do good for evil:
And thus I clothe my naked villainy
With old odd ends stolen out of holy writ,
And seem a saint, when most I play the devil.

Enter TWO MURDERERS.

But, soft! here come my executioners.
How now, my hardy, stout, resolved mates!   *340*
Are you now going to dispatch this deed?
  1st Murd. We are, my lord; and come to
    have the warrant,
That we may be admitted where he is.
  Glou. Well thought upon; I have it here about
    me. [*Gives the warrant.*
When you have done, repair to Crosby Place.
But, sirs, be sudden in the execution,
Withal obdurate, do not hear him plead;
For Clarence is well-spoken, and perhaps
May move your hearts to pity, if you mark him.
  1st Murd. Tush!   *350*
Fear not, my lord, we will not stand to prate;
Talkers are no good doers: be assured
We come to use our hands and not our tongues.
  Glou. Your eyes drop millstones, when fools'
    eyes drop tears:
I like you, lads; about your business straight;
Go, go, dispatch.
  1st Murd. We will, my noble lord. [*Exeunt.*

SCENE IV. *London: the Tower.*

Enter CLARENCE *and* BRAKENBURY.

  Brak. Why looks your Grace so heavily to-day?
  Clar. O, I have pass'd a miserable night,
So full of ugly sights, of ghastly dreams,
That, as I am a Christian faithful man,
I would not spend another such a night,
Though 'twere to buy a world of happy days,
So full of dismal terror was the time!
  Brak. What was your dream? I long to hear
    you tell it.
  Clar. Methoughts that I had broken from the
    Tower,
And was embark'd to cross to Burgundy;   *10*
And, in my company, my brother Gloucester,
Who from my cabin tempted me to walk
Upon the hatches: thence we look'd toward
    England,
And cited up a thousand fearful times,
During the wars of York and Lancaster
That had befall'n us. As we paced along
Upon the giddy footing of the hatches,
Methought that Gloucester stumbled; and, in
    falling,
Struck me, that thought to stay him, overboard,
Into the tumbling billows of the main.   *20*
Lord, Lord! methought what pain it was to
    drown!
What dreadful noise of waters in mine ears!
What ugly sights of death within mine eyes!
Methought I saw a thousand fearful wrecks;

Ten thousand men that fishes gnaw'd upon;
Wedges of gold, great anchors, heaps of pearl,
Inestimable stones, unvalued jewels,
All scatter'd in the bottom of the sea:
Some lay in dead men's skulls; and, in those holes
Where eyes did once inhabit, there were crept,
As 'twere in scorn of eyes, reflecting gems,   *31*
Which woo'd the slimy bottom of the deep
And mock'd the dead bones that lay scatter'd by.
Brak. Had you such leisure in the time of
    death
To gaze upon the secrets of the deep?
Clar. Methought I had; and often did I strive
To yield the ghost: but still the envious flood
Kept in my soul and would not let it forth
To seek the empty, vast, and wandering air;
But smother'd it within my panting bulk,   *40*
Which almost burst to belch it in the sea.
Brak. Awaked you not with this sore agony?
Clar. O, no, my dream was lengthen'd after life;
O, then began the tempest to my soul,
Who pass'd, methought, the melancholy flood,
With that grim ferryman which poets write of,
Unto the kingdom of perpetual night.
The first that there did greet my stranger soul
Was my great father-in-law, renowned
    Warwick,
Who cried aloud, "What scourge for perjury   *50*
Can this dark monarchy afford false Clarence?"
And so he vanish'd: then came wandering by
A shadow like an angel, with bright hair
Dabbled in blood; and he squeak'd out aloud,
'Clarence is come; false, fleeting, perjured
    Clarence,
That stabb'd me in the field by Tewksbury;
Seize on him, Furies, take him to your torments!"
With that, methoughts, a legion of foul fiends
Environ'd me about, and howled in mine ears
Such hideous cries that with the very noise   *60*
I trembling waked, and for a season after
Could not believe but that I was in hell,
Such terrible impression made the dream.
Brak. No marvel, my lord, though it affrighted
    you;
I promise you, I am afraid to hear you tell it.
Clar. O Brakenbury, I have done those things,
Which now bear evidence against my soul,
For Edward's sake; and see how he requites me!
O God! if my deep prayers cannot appease thee,
But thou wilt be avenged on my misdeeds,   *70*
Yet execute thy wrath in me alone,
O, spare my guiltless wife and my poor children!
I pray thee, gentle keeper, stay by me;
My soul is heavy, and I fain would sleep.
Brak. I will, my lord: God give your Grace
good rest! [*Clarence sleeps.*]

Sorrow breaks seasons and reposing hours,
Makes the night morning, and the noon-tide
    night.
Princes have but their titles for their glories,
An outward honour for an inward toil;
And, for unfelt imagination,   *80*
They often feel a world of restless cares:
So that, betwixt their titles and low names,
There's nothing differs but the outward fame.

Enter the TWO MURDERERS.

1st Murd. Ho! who's here?
Brak. In God's name what are you, and how
    came you hither?
1st Murd. I would speak with Clarence,
and I came hither on my legs.
Brak. Yea, are you so brief?
2nd Murd. O sir, it is better to be brief than
tedious. Shew him our commission; talk no
more.
    [*Brakenbury reads it.*
Brak. I am, in this, commanded to deliver
The noble Duke of Clarence to your hands:
I will not reason what is meant hereby,
Because I will be guiltless of the meaning.
Here are the keys, there sits the Duke asleep:
I'll to the King; and signify to him
That thus I have resign'd my charge to you
1st Murd. Do so, it is a point of wisdom:
fare you well.   [*Exit* BRAKENBURY   *100*
2nd Murd. What, shall we stab him as he
sleeps?
1st Murd. No; then he will say 'twas done
cowardly, when he wakes.
2nd Murd. When he wakes! why, fool, he
shall never wake till the judgement-day.
1st Murd. Why, then he will say we stabbed
him sleeping.
2nd Murd. The urging of that word "judgement" hath bred a kind of remorse in me.   *110*
1st Murd. What, art thou afraid?
2nd Murd. Not to kill him, having a warrant
for it; but to be damned for killing him, from
which no warrant can defend us.
1st Murd. I thought thou hadst been resolute.
2nd Murd. So I am to let him live.
1st Murd. Back to the Duke of Gloucester,
tell him so.   *119*
2nd Murd. I pray thee, stay a while: I hope my
holy humour will change; 'twas wont to hold me
but while one would tell twenty.
1st Murd. How dost thou feel thyself now?
2nd Murd. 'Faith, some certain dregs of
conscience are yet within me.
1st Murd. Remember our reward, when the
deed is done.

2nd Murd. 'Zounds, he dies: I had forgot the reward.   *129*

1st Murd. Where is thy conscience now?

2nd Murd. In the Duke of Gloucester's purse.

1st Murd. So when he opens his purse to give us our reward, thy conscience flies out.

2nd Murd. Let it go; there's few or none will entertain it.

1st Murd. How if it come to thee again?

2nd Murd. I'll not meddle with it: it is a dangerous thing: it makes a man a coward: a man cannot steal, but it accuseth him; he cannot swear, but it checks him; he cannot lie with his neighbour's wife, but it detects him: 'tis a blushing shamefast spirit that mutinies in a man's bosom; it fills one full of obstacles: it made me once restore a purse of gold that I found; it beggars any man that keeps it: it is turned out of all towns and cities for a dangerous thing; and every man that means to live well endeavours to trust himself and to live without it.

1st Murd. 'Zounds, it is even now at my elbow, persuading me not to kill the Duke.   *150*

2nd Murd. Take the devil in thy mind, and believe him not: he would insinuate with thee but to make thee sigh.

1st Murd. Tut, I am strong-framed, he cannot prevail with me, I warrant thee.

2nd Murd. Spoke like a tall fellow that respects his reputation. Come, shall we to this gear?

1st Murd. Take him over the costard with the hilts of thy sword, and then we will chop him in the malmsey-butt in the next room.   *161*

2nd Murd. O excellent device! make a sop of him.

1st Murd. Hark! he stirs: shall I strike?

2nd Murd. No, first let's reason with him.

Clar. Where art thou, keeper? give me a cup of wine.

2nd Murd. You shall have wine enough, my lord, anon.

Clar. In God's name, what art thou?

2nd Murd. A man, as you are.   *170*

Clar. But not, as I am, royal.

2nd Murd. Nor you, as we are, loyal.

Clar. Thy voice is thunder, but thy looks are humble.

2nd Murd. My voice is now the King's, my looks mine own.

Clar. How darkly and how deadly dost thou speak!

Your eyes do menace me: why look you pale?

Who sent you hither? Wherefore do you come?

Both. To, to, to—

Clar. To murder me?

Both. Ay, ay.

Clar. You scarcely have the hearts to tell me so,   *180*

And therefore cannot have the hearts to do it.

Wherein, my friends, have I offended you?

1st Murd. Offended us you have not, but the King.

Clar. I shall be reconciled to him again.

2nd Murd. Never, my lord; therefore prepare to die.

Clar. Are you call'd forth from out a world of men

To slay the innocent? What is my offence?

Where are the evidence that do accuse me?

What lawful quest have given their verdict up

Unto the frowning judge? or who pronounced *190*

The bitter sentence of poor Clarence' death?

Before I be convict by course of law,

To threaten me with death is most unlawful.

I charge you, as you hope to have redemption

By Christ's dear blood shed for our grievous sins,

That you depart and lay no hands on me:

The deed you undertake is damnable.

1st Murd. What we will do, we do upon command.

2nd Murd. And he that hath commanded is the King.

Clar. Erroneous vassal! the great King of kings   *200*

Hath in the tables of his law commanded

That thou shalt do no murder: and wilt thou, then,

Spurn at his edict and fulfil a man's?

Take heed; for he holds vengeance in his hands,

To hurl upon their heads that break his law.

2nd Murd. And that same vengeance doth he hurl on thee,

For false forswearing and for murder too:

Thou didst receive the holy sacrament,

To fight in quarrel of the house of Lancaster.

1st Murd. And, like a traitor to the name of God,   *210*

Didst break that vow; and with thy treacherous blade

Unrip'dst the bowels of thy sovereign's son.

2nd Murd. Whom thou wert sworn to cherish and defend.

1st Murd. How canst thou urge God's dreadful law to us,

When thou hast broke it in so dear degree?

Clar. Alas! for whose sake did I that ill deed?

For Edward, for my brother, for his sake:

Why, sirs,

He sends ye not to murder me for this;

For in this sin he is as deep as I.   *220*

If God will be revenged for this deed,

O, know you yet he doth it publicly:

Take not the quarrel from his powerful arm;
He needs no indirect nor lawless course
To cut off those that have offended him.
1st Murd. Who made thee, then, a bloody
minister,
When gallant-springing brave Plantagenet,
That princely novice, was struck dead by thee?
Clar. My brother's love, the devil, and my rage.
1st Murd. Thy brother's love, our duty,
and thy fault, 230
Provoke us hither now to slaughter thee.
Clar. Oh, if you love my brother, hate not me;
I am his brother, and I love him well.
If you be hired for meed, go back again,
And I will send you to my brother Gloucester,
Who shall reward you better for my life
Than Edward will for tidings of my death.
2nd Murd. You are deceived, your brother
Gloucester hates you.
Clat. O, no, he loves me, and he holds me dear:
Go you to him from me.
Both.   Ay, so we will. 240
Clar. Tell him, when that our princely father
York
Bless'd his three sons with his victorious arm,
And charged us from his soul to love each other,
He little thought of this divided friendship:
Bid Gloucester think of this, and he will weep.
1st Murd. Ay, millstones; as he lesson'd us to
weep.
Clar. O, do not slander him, for he is kind.
1st Murd. Right,
As snow in harvest. Thou deceivest thyself:
'Tis he that sent us hither now to slaughter thee.
Clar. It cannot be; for when I parted with him,
He hugg'd me in his arms, and swore, with sobs,
That he would labour my delivery.
2nd Murd. Why, so he doth, now he delivers
thee
From this world's thraldom to the joys of heaven.
1st Murd. Make peace with God, for you must
die, my lord.
Clar. Hast thou that holy feeling in thy soul,
To counsel me to make my peace with God,
And art thou yet to thy own soul so blind,
That thou wilt war with God by murdering me?
Ah, sirs, consider, he that set you on 261
To do this deed will hate you for the deed.
2nd Murd. What shall we do?
Clar.   Relent, and save your souls.
1st Murd. Relent! 'tis cowardly and womanish.
Clar. Not to relent is beastly, savage, devilish.
Which of you, if you were a prince's son,
Being pent from liberty, as I am now,
If two such murderers as yourselves came to you,
Would not entreat for life?

My friend, I spy some pity in thy looks; 270
O, if thine eye be not a flatterer,
Come thou on my side, and entreat for me,
As you would beg, were you in my distress:
A begging prince what beggar pities not?
2nd Murd. Look behind you, my lord.
1st Murd. Take that, and that: if all this will not
do, [*Stabs him.*]
I'll drown you in the malmsey-butt within.
                    [*Exit, with the body.*
2nd Murd. A bloody deed, and desperately
dispatch'd!
How fain, like Pilate, would I wash my hands
Of this most grievous guilty murder done! 280

Re-enter FIRST MURDERER.

1st Murd. How now! what mean'st thou, that
thou help'st me not?
By heavens, the Duke shall know how slack thou
art!
2nd Murd. I would he knew that I had saved his
brother!
Take thou the fee, and tell him what I say;
For I repent me that the Duke is slain. [*Exit.*
1st Murd. So do not I: go, coward as thou art.
Now must I hide his body in some hole,
Until the Duke take order for his burial:
And when I have my meed, I must away;
For this will out, and here I must not stay. 290

ACT II

SCENE I. *London: the palace*

Flourish. Enter KING EDWARD *sick,* QUEEN ELIZA-
BETH, DORSET, RIVERS, HASTINGS, BUCKINGHAM,
GREY, *and others.*

K. Edw. Why, so: now have I done a good
day's work:
You peers, continue this united league:
I every day expect an embassage
From my Redeemer to redeem me hence;
And now in peace my soul shall part to heaven,
Since I have set my friends at peace on earth.
Rivers and Hastings, take each other's hand;
Dissemble not your hatred, swear your love.
Riv. By heaven, my heart is purged from grudg-
ing hate;
And with my hand I seal my true heart's love. 10
Hast. So thrive I, as I truly swear the like!
K. Edw. Take heed you dally not before your
king;
Lest he that is the supreme King of kings
Confound your hidden falsehood and award
Either of you to be the other's end.
Hast. So prosper I, as I swear perfect love!
Riv. And I, as I love Hastings with my heart!

K. Edw. Madam, yourself are not exempt in this,
Nor your son Dorset, Buckingham, nor you;
You have been factious one against the other. *20*
Wife, love Lord Hastings, let him kiss your hand;
And what you do, do it unfeignedly.
  Q. Eliz. Here, Hastings; I will never more remember
Our former hatred, so thrive I and mine!
  K. Edw. Dorset, embrace him; Hastings, love lord marquess.
  Dor. This interchange of love, I here protest,
Upon my part shall be unviolable.
  Hast. And so swear I, my lord.
    They embrace.
  K. Edw. Now, princely Buckingham, seal thou this league
With thy embracements to my wife's allies, *30*
And make me happy in your unity.
  Buck. Whenever Buckingham doth turn his hate
On you or yours [*to the* QUEEN], but with all duteous love
Doth cherish you and yours, God punish me
With hate in those where I expect most love!
When I have most need to employ a friend,
And most assured that he is a friend,
Deep, hollow, treacherous, and full of guile,
Be he unto me! this do I beg of God,
When I am cold in zeal to you or yours. *40*
    They embrace.
  K. Edw. A pleasing cordial, princely Buckingham,
Is this thy vow unto my sickly heart.
There wanteth now our brother Gloucester here,
To make the perfect period of this peace.
  Buck. And, in good time, here comes the noble Duke.

Enter GLOUCESTER.

  Glou. Good morrow to my sovereign king and queen;
And, princely peers, a happy time of day!
  K. Edw. Happy, indeed, as we have spent the day.
Brother, we have done deeds of charity;
Made peace of enmity, fair love of hate, *50*
Between these swelling wrong-incensed peers.
  Glou. A blessed labour, my most sovereign liege:
Amongst this princely heap, if any here,
By false intelligence, or wrong surmise,
Hold me a foe;
If I unwittingly, or in my rage,
Have aught committed that is hardly borne
By any in this presence, I desire

To reconcile me to his friendly peace:
'Tis death to me to be at enmity; *60*
I hate it and desire all good men's love.
First, madam, I entreat true peace of you,
Which I will purchase with my duteous service;
Of you, my noble cousin Buckingham,
If ever any grudge were lodged between us;
Of you, Lord Rivers, and, Lord Grey, of you;
That all without desert have frown'd on me;
Dukes, earls, lords, gentlemen; indeed, of all.
I do not know that Englishman alive
With whom my soul is any jot at odds *70*
More than the infant that is born to-night:
I thank my God for my humility.
  Q. Eliz. A holy day shall this be kept hereafter:
I would to God all strifes were well compounded.
My sovereign liege, I do beseech your Majesty
To take our brother Clarence to your grace.
  Glou. Why, madam, have I offer'd love for this,
To be so flouted in this royal presence?
Who knows not that the noble Duke is dead?
    They all start.
You do him injury to scorn his corse. *80*
  Riv. Who knows not he is dead! who knows he is?
  Q. Eliz. All-seeing heaven, what a world is this!
  Buck. Look I so pale, Lord Dorset, as the rest?
  Dor. Ay, my good lord; and no one in this presence
But his red colour hath forsook his cheeks.
  K. Edw. Is Clarence dead? the order was reversed.
  Glou. But he, poor soul, by your first order died,
And that a winged Mercury did bear;
Some tardy cripple bore the countermand,
That came too lag to see him buried. *90*
God grant that some, less noble and less loyal,
Nearer in bloody thoughts, but not in blood,
Deserve not worse than wretched Clarence did,
And yet go current from suspicion!

Enter STANLEY.

  Stan. A boon, my sovereign, for my service done!
  K. Edw. I pray thee, peace: my soul is full of sorrow.
  Stan. I will not rise, unless your Highness grant.
  K. Edw. Then speak at once what is it thou demand'st.
  Stan. The forfeit, sovereign, of my servant's life;
Who slew to-day a riotous gentleman *100*
Lately attendant on the Duke of Norfolk.
  K. Edw. Have I a tongue to doom my brother's death,
And shall the same give pardon to a slave?

My brother slew no man; his fault was thought,
And yet his punishment was cruel death.
Who sued to me for him? who, in my rage,
Kneel'd at my feet, and bade me be advised?
Who spake of brotherhood? who spake of love?
Who told me how the poor soul did forsake
The mighty Warwick and did fight for me? *110*
Who told me, in the field by Tewksbury,
When Oxford had me down, he rescued me,
And said, "Dear brother, live, and be a king"?
Who told me, when we both lay in the field
Frozen almost to death, how he did lap me
Even in his own garments, and gave himself,
All thin and naked, to the numb cold night?
All this from my remembrance brutish wrath
Sinfully pluck'd, and not a man of you
Had so much grace to put it in my mind.   *120*
But when your carters or your waiting-vassals
Have done a drunken slaughter and defaced
The precious image of our dear Redeemer,
You straight are on your knees for pardon,
    pardon;
And I, unjustly too, must grant it you:
But for my brother not a man would speak,
Nor I, ungracious, speak unto myself
For him, poor soul. The proudest of you all
Have been beholding to him in his life;
Yet none of you would once plead for his life. *130*
O God, I fear thy justice will take hold
On me, and you, and mine, and yours for this!
Come, Hastings, help me to my closet. Oh, poor
    Clarence!
            [*Exeunt some with* KING *and* QUEEN.
Glou. This is the fruit of rashness! Mark'd
you not
How that the guilty kindred of the Queen
Look'd pale when they did hear of Clarence'
    death?
O, they did urge it still unto the King!
God will revenge it. But come, let us in,
To comfort Edward with our company.
Buck. We wait upon your grace.   [*Exeunt.*

Scene ii. *The palace*

Enter the DUCHESS OF YORK, *with the two children
of* CLARENCE, EDWARD EARL OF WARWICK *and*
MARGARET PLANTAGENET.

War. Tell me, good grandam, is our father
    dead?
Duch. No, boy.
War. Why do you wring your hands, and beat
    your breast,
And cry, "O Clarence, my unhappy son!"
Mar. Why do you look on us, and shake your
    head,
And call us wretches, orphans, castaways,

If that our noble father be alive?
    Duch. My pretty cousins, you mistake me
        much;
I do lament the sickness of the King,
As loath to lose him, not your father's death;   *10*
It were lost sorrow to wail one that's lost.
    War. Then, grandam, you conclude that he is
        dead.
The King my uncle is to blame for this:
God will revenge it; whom I will importune
With daily prayers all to that effect.
    Mar. And so will I.
    Duch. Peace, children, peace! the King doth
        love you well:
Incapable and shallow innocents,
You cannot guess who caused your father's death.
    War. Grandam, we can; for my good uncle
        Gloucester   *20*
Told me, the King, provoked by the Queen,
Devised impeachments to imprison him:
And when my uncle told me so, he wept,
And hugg'd me in his arm, and kindly kiss'd my
        cheek;
Bade me rely on him as on my father,
And he would love me dearly as his child.
    Duch. Oh, that deceit should steal such gentle
        shapes,
And with a virtuous vizard hide foul guile!
He is my son; yea, and therein my shame;
Yet from my dugs he drew not this deceit.   *30*
    War. Think you my uncle did dissemble,
        grandam?
    Duch. Ay, boy.
    War. I cannot think it. Hark! what noise is this?

Enter QUEEN ELIZABETH, *with her hair about her
    ears;* RIVERS *and* DORSET *after her.*

    Q. Eliz. Oh, who shall hinder me to wail and
        weep,
To chide my fortune, and torment myself?
I'll join with black despair against my soul,
And to myself become an enemy.
    Duch. What means this scene of rude
        impatience?
    Q. Eliz. To make an act of tragic violence:
Edward, my lord, your son, our king, is dead. *40*
Why grow the branches now the root is
    wither'd?
Why wither not the leaves the sap being gone?
If you will live, lament; if die, be brief,
That our swift-winged souls may catch the
    King's;
Or, like obedient subjects, follow him
To his new kingdom of perpetual rest.
    Duch. Ah, so much interest have I in thy
        sorrow

As I had title in thy noble husband!
I have bewept a worthy husband's death,
And lived by looking on his images: 50
But now two mirrors of his princely semblance
Are crack'd in pieces by malignant death,
And I for comfort have but one false glass,
Which grieves me when I see my shame in him.
Thou art a widow; yet thou art a mother,
And hast the comfort of thy children left thee:
But death hath snatch'd my husband from mine
     arms,
And pluck'd two crutches from my feeble limbs,
Edward and Clarence. O, what cause have I,
Thine being but a moiety of my grief,   60
To overgo thy plaints and drown thy cries!
  War. Good aunt, you wept not for our father's
     death;
How can we aid you with our kindred tears?
  Mar. Our fatherless distress was left unmoan'd;
Your widow-dolour likewise be unwept!
  Q. Eliz. Give me no help in lamentation;
I am not barren to bring forth complaints:
All springs reduce their currents to mine eyes,
That I, being govern'd by the watery moon,
May send forth plenteous tears to drown the
     world!   70
Oh for my husband, for my dear lord Edward!
  War. and Mar. Oh for our father, for our dear
     lord Clarence!
  Duch. Alas for both, both mine, Edward and
     Clarence!
  Q. Eliz. What stay had I but Edward? and he's
     gone.
  War. and Mar. What stay had we but Clarence?
     and he's gone.
  Duch. What stays had I but they? and they are
     gone.
  Q. Eliz. Was never widow had so dear a loss!
  War. and Mar. Were never orphans had so dear
     a loss!
  Duch. Was never mother had so dear a loss!
Alas, I am the mother of these moans!   80
Their woes are parcell'd, mine are general.
She for an Edward weeps, and so do I;
I for a Clarence weep, so doth not she:
These babes for Clarence weep and so do I;
I for an Edward weep, so do not they:
Alas, you three, on me, threefold distress'd,
Pour all your tears! I am your sorrow's nurse,
And I will pamper it with lamentations.
  Dor. Comfort, dear mother: God is much
     displeased
That you take with unthankfulness his doing: 90
In common worldly things, 'tis call'd ungrateful
With dull unwillingness to repay a debt
Which with a bounteous hand was kindly lent;

Much more to be thus opposite with heaven,
For it requires the royal debt it lent you.
  Riv. Madam, bethink you, like a careful
     mother,
Of the young prince your son: send straight for
     him;
Let him be crown'd; in him your comfort lives:
Drown desperate sorrow in dead Edward's grave,
And plant your joys in living Edward's
     throne.   100

    Enter GLOUCESTER, BUCKINGHAM, DERBY,
         HASTINGS, *and* RATCLIFF.

  Glou. Madam, have comfort: all of us have
     cause
To wail the dimming of our shining star;
But none can cure their harms by wailing them.
Madam, my mother, I do cry you mercy;
I did not see your Grace: humbly on my knee
I crave your blessing.
  Duch. God bless thee; and put meekness in thy
     mind,
Love, charity, obedience, and true duty!
  Glou. [*Aside*] Amen; and make me die a good
     old man!
That is the butt-end of a mother's blessing: 110
I marvel why her Grace did leave it out.
  Buck. You cloudy princes and heart-sorrowing
     peers
That bear this mutual heavy load of moan,
Now cheer each other in each other's love:
Though we have spent our harvest of this king,
We are to reap the harvest of his son.
The broken rancour of your high-swoln hearts,
But lately splinter'd, knit, and join'd together,
Must gently be preserved, cherish'd, and kept:
Me seemeth good, that, with some little train,
Forthwith from Ludlow the young prince
     be fetch'd   121
Hither to London, to be crown'd our king.
  Riv. Why with some little train, my Lord of
     Buckingham?
  Buck. Marry, my lord, lest, by a multitude,
The new-heal'd wound of malice should break
     out;
Which would be so much the more dangerous,
By how much the estate is green and yet
     ungovern'd:
Where every horse bears his commanding rein,
And may direct his course as please himself,
As well the fear of harm, as harm apparent,   130
In my opinion, ought to be prevented.
  Glou. I hope the King made peace with all of us;
And the compact is firm and true in me.
  Riv. And so in me; and so, I think, in all:
Yet, since it is but green, it should be put

To no apparent likelihood of breach,
Which haply by much company might be urged:
Therefore I say with noble Buckingham
That it is meet so few should fetch the Prince.
  Hast. And so say I. 140
  Glou. Then be it so; and go we to determine
Who they shall be that straight shall post to
    Ludlow.
Madam, and you, my mother, will you go
To give your censures in this weighty business?
  Q. Eliz. } With all our hearts.
  Duch. }
    [*Exeunt all but* BUCKINGHAM *and* GLOUCESTER.
  Buck. My Lord, whoever journeys to the
    Prince,
For God's sake, let not us two be behind;
For, by the way, I'll sort occasion,
As index to the story we late talk'd of,
To part the Queen's proud kindred from the
    King. 150
  Glou. My other self, my counsel's consistory,
My oracle, my prophet! My dear cousin,
I, like a child, will go by thy direction.
Towards Ludlow then, for we'll not stay
    behind. [*Exeunt.*

SCENE III. *London: a street*

Enter TWO CITIZENS, *meeting.*

  1st Cit. Neighbour, well met: whither away so
    fast?
  2nd Cit. I promise you, I scarcely know myself:
Hear you the news abroad?
  1st Cit.   Ay, that the King is dead.
  2nd Cit. Bad news, by'r lady; seldom comes
    the better:
I fear, I fear 'twill prove a troublous world.

Enter THIRD CITIZEN.

  3rd Cit. Neighbours, God speed!
  1st Cit.   Give you good morrow, sir.
  3rd Cit. Doth this news hold of good King
    Edward's death?
  2nd Cit. Ay, sir, it is too true; God help the
    while!
  3rd Cit. Then, masters, look to see a troublous
    world.
  1st Cit. No, no; by God's good grace his son
    shall reign. 10
  3rd Cit. Woe to that land that's govern'd by a
    child!
  2nd Cit. In him there is a hope of government,
That in his nonage council under him,
And in his full and ripen'd years himself,
No doubt, shall then and till then govern well.
  1st Cit. So stood the state when Henry the Sixth
Was crown'd in Paris but at nine months old.

  3rd Cit. Stood the state so? No, no, good
    friends, God wot;
For then this land was famously enrich'd
With politic grave counsel; then the King 20
Had virtuous uncles to protect his grace.
  1st Cit. Why, so hath this, both by the father and
    mother.
  3rd Cit. Better it were they all came by the
    father,
Or by the father there were none at all;
For emulation now, who shall be nearest,
Will touch us all too near, if God prevent not.
O, full of danger is the Duke of Gloucester!
And the Queen's sons and brothers haught and
    proud:
And were they to be ruled, and not to rule,
This sickly land might solace as before. 30
  1st Cit. Come, come, we fear the worst; all shall
    be well.
  3rd Cit. When clouds appear, wise men put on
    their cloaks;
When great leaves fall, the winter is at hand;
When the sun sets, who doth not look for night?
Untimely storms make men expect a dearth.
All may be well; but, if God sort it so,
'Tis more than we deserve, or I expect.
  2nd Cit. Truly, the souls of men are full of
    dread:
Ye cannot reason almost with a man
That looks not heavily and full of fear. 40
  3rd Cit. Before the times of change, still is it so:
By a divine instinct men's minds mistrust
Ensuing dangers; as, by proof, we see
The waters swell before a boisterous storm.
But leave it all to God. Whither away?
  2nd Cit. Marry, we were sent for to the justices.
  3rd Cit. And so was I: I'll bear you company.
    [*Exeunt.*

SCENE IV. *London: the palace*

Enter the ARCHBISHOP OF YORK, *the young* DUKE OF
YORK, QUEEN ELIZABETH, *and the* DUCHESS OF
YORK.

  Arch. Last night, I hear, they lay at North-
    ampton;
At Stony-Stratford will they be to-night:
To-morrow, or next day, they will be here.
  Duch. I long with all my heart to see the Prince:
I hope he is much grown since last I saw him.
  Q. Eliz. But I hear, no; they say my son of York
Hath almost overta'en him in his growth.
  York. Ay, mother; but I would not have it so.
  Duch. Why, my young cousin, it is good to
    grow.
  York. Grandam, one night, as we did sit at
    supper, 10

My uncle Rivers talk'd how I did grow
More than my brother: "Ay," quoth my uncle
    Gloucester,
"Small herbs have grace, great weeds do grow
    apace":
And since, methinks, I would not grow so fast,
Because sweet flowers are slow and weeds
    make haste.
Duch. Good faith, good faith, the saying did
    not hold
In him that did object the same to thee:
He was the wretched'st thing when he was young,
So long a-growing and so leisurely
That, if this rule were true, he should be gracious.
    Arch. Why, madam, so, no doubt, he is.   21
    Duch. I hope he is; but yet let mothers doubt.
    York.   Now, by my troth, if I had been
        remember'd,
I could have given my uncle's Grace a flout,
To touch his growth nearer than he touch'd
    mine.
    Duch. How, my pretty York? I pray thee, let
        me hear it.
    York. Marry, they say my uncle grew so fast
That he could gnaw a crust at two hours old:
'Twas full two years ere I could get a tooth.
Grandam, this would have been a biting jest.   30
    Duch. I pray thee, pretty York, who told thee
this?
    York. Grandam, his nurse.
    Duch. His nurse! why, she was dead ere thou
        wert born.
    York. If 'twere not she, I cannot tell who told
        me.
    Q. Eliz. A parlous boy: go to, you are too
        shrewd.
    Arch. Good madam, be not angry with the child.
    Q. Eliz. Pitchers have ears.

        Enter a MESSENGER.

    Arch. Here comes a messenger. What news?
    Mess. Such news, my lord, as grieves me to
        unfold.
    Q. Eliz. How fares the Prince?
    Mess.   Well, madam, and in health.   40
    Duch. What is thy news then?
    Mess. Lord Rivers and Lord Grey are sent to
        Pomfret,
With them Sir Thomas Vaughan, prisoners.
    Duch. Who hath committed them?
    Mess.   The mighty dukes
Gloucester and Buckingham.
    Q. Eliz.   For what offence?
    Mess. The sum of all I can, I have disclosed;
Why or for what these nobles were committed
Is all unknown to me, my gracious lady.

    Q. Eliz. Ay me, I see the downfall of our
        house!
The tiger now hath seized the gentle hind;   50
Insulting tyranny begins to jet
Upon the innocent and aweless throne:
Welcome, destruction, death, and massacre!
I see, as in a map, the end of all.
    Duch. Accursed and unquiet wrangling days,
How many of you have mine eyes beheld!
My husband lost his life to get the crown;
And often up and down my sons were toss'd,
For me to joy and weep their gain and loss:
And being seated, and domestic broils   60
Clean over-blown, themselves, the conquerors
Make war upon themselves; blood against blood,
Self against self: O, preposterous
And frantic outrage, end thy damned spleen;
Or let me die, to look on death no more!
    Q. Eliz. Come, come, my boy; we will to
        sanctuary.
Madam, farewell.
    Duch.   I'll go along with you.
    Q. Eliz. You have no cause.
    Arch.   My gracious lady, go;
And thither bear your treasure and your goods.
For my part, I'll resign unto your Grace   70
The seal I keep: and so betide to me
As well I tender you and all of yours!
Come, I'll conduct you to the sanctuary.
                                        [*Exeunt.*

ACT III

SCENE I. *London: a street*

The trumpets sound. Enter the young PRINCE, *the
    Dukes of* GLOUCESTER *and* BUCKINGHAM, CAR-
    DINAL BOURCHIER, CATESBY, *and others.*

    Buck. Welcome, sweet prince, to London to
        your chamber.
    Glou. Welcome, dear cousin, my thoughts'
        sovereign:
The weary way hath made you melancholy.
    Prince. No, uncle; but our crosses on the way
Have made it tedious, wearisome, and heavy:
I want more uncles here to welcome me.
    Glou. Sweet prince, the untainted virtue of
        your years
Hath not yet dived into the world's deceit:
Nor more can you distinguish of a man
Than of his outward show; which, God he knows,
Seldom or never jumpeth with the heart.   11
Those uncles which you want were dangerous;
Your Grace attended to their sugar'd words,
But look'd not on the poison of their hearts:
God keep you from them, and from such false
        friends!

Prince. God keep me from false friends! but
they were none.
Glou. My lord, the Mayor of London comes to
greet you.

Enter the LORD MAYOR, *and his train.*

May. God bless your Grace with health and
happy days!
Prince. I thank you, good my lord; and thank
you all.
I thought my mother, and my brother York,   20
Would long ere this have met us on the way:
Fie, what a slug is Hastings, that he comes not
To tell us whether they will come or no!

Enter LORD HASTINGS.

Buck. And, in good time, here comes the
sweating lord.
*Prince.*Welcome, my lord: what, will our
mother come?
Hast. On what occasion, God he knows, not I,
The Queen your mother, and your brother York,
Have taken sanctuary: the tender prince
Would fain have come with me to meet your
Grace,
But by his mother was perforce withheld.   30
Buck. Fie, what an indirect and peevish course
Is this of hers! Lord Cardinal, will your Grace
Persuade the Queen to send the Duke of York
Unto his princely brother presently?
If she deny, Lord Hastings, go with him,
And from her jealous arms pluck him perforce.
Card. My Lord of Buckingham, if my weak
oratory
Can from his mother win the Duke of York,
Anon expect him here; but if she be obdurate
To mild entreaties, God in heaven forbid   40
We should infringe the holy privilege
Of blessed sanctuary! not for all this land
Would I be guilty of so deep a sin.
Buck. You are too senseless-obstinate, my
lord,
Too ceremonious and traditional:
Weigh it but with the grossness of his age,
You break not sanctuary in seizing him.
The benefit thereof is always granted
To those whose dealings have deserved the place,
And those who have the wit to claim the place:
This prince hath neither claim'd it nor deserved it;
And therefore, in mine opinion, cannot have it:
Then, taking him from thence that is not there,
You break no privilege nor charter there.
Oft have I heard of sanctuary men;
But sanctuary children ne'er till now.
Card. My lord, you shall o'er-rule my mind
for once.

Come on, Lord Hastings, will you go with me?
Hast. I go, my lord.
Prince. Good lords, make all the speedy haste
you may.   60
[*Exeunt* CARDINAL *and* HASTINGS.
Say, uncle Gloucester, if our brother come,
Where shall we sojourn till our coronation?
*Glou.*Where it seems best unto your royal self.
If I may counsel you, some day or two
Your highness shall repose you at the Tower:
Then where you please, and shall be thought
most fit
For your best health and recreation.
Prince. I do not like the Tower, of any place.
Did Julius Cæsar build that place, my lord?
Buck. He did, my gracious lord, begin that
place;   70
Which, since, succeeding ages have re-edified.
Prince. Is it upon record, or else reported
Successively from age to age, he built it?
Buck. Upon record, my gracious lord.
Prince. But say, my lord, it were not register'd,
Methinks the truth should live from age to age,
As 'twere retail'd to all posterity,
Even to the general all-ending day.
Glou. [*Aside*] So wise so young, they say, do
never live long.
*Prince.*What say you, uncle?   80
Glou. I say, without characters, fame lives long.
[*Aside*] Thus, like the formal vice, Iniquity,
I moralize two meanings in one word.
Prince. That Julius Cæsar was a famous man;
With what his valour did enrich his wit,
His wit set down to make his valour live:
Death makes no conquest of this conqueror;
For now he lives in fame, though not in life.
I'll tell you what, my cousin Buckingham—
*Buck.*What, my gracious lord?   90
Prince. An if I live until I be a man,
I'll win our ancient right in France again,
Or die a soldier, as I lived a king.
Glou. [*Aside*] Short summers lightly have a
forward spring.

Enter young YORK, HASTINGS, *and the* CARDINAL.

Buck. Now, in good time, here comes the
Duke of York.
Prince. Richard of York! how fares our loving
brother?
*York.*Well, my dread lord; so must I call you
now.
Prince. Ay, brother, to our grief, as it is yours:
Too late he died that might have kept that title
Which by his death hath lost much majesty.   100
Glou. How fares our cousin, noble Lord of
York?

York. I thank you, gentle uncle. O, my lord,
You said that idle weeds are fast in growth:
The prince my brother hath outgrown me far.
  Glou. He hath, my lord.
  York.   And therefore is he idle?
  Glou. O, my fair cousin, I must not say so.
  York. Then he is more beholding to you than I.
  Glou. He may command me as my sovereign;
But you have power in me as in a kinsman.
  York. I pray you, uncle, give me this dagger.
  Glou. My dagger, little cousin? with all my
    heart.   111
  Prince. A beggar, brother?
  York. Of my kind uncle, that I know will give;
And being but a toy, which is no grief to give.
  Glou. A greater gift than that I'll give my
    cousin.
  York. A greater gift! O, that's the sword to it.
  Glou. Ay, gentle cousin, were it light enough.
  York. O, then, I see, you will part but with
    light gifts;
In weightier things you'll say a beggar nay.
  Glou. It is too heavy for your Grace to wear.
  York. I weigh it lightly, were it heavier.   121
  Glou. What, would you have my weapon,
    little lord?
  York. I would, that I might thank you as you
    call me.
  Glou. How?
  York. Little.
  Prince. My Lord of York will still be cross in
    talk:
Uncle, your Grace knows how to bear with him.
  York. You mean, to bear me, not to bear with
    me:
Uncle, my brother mocks both you and me;
Because that I am little, like an ape,   130
He thinks that you should bear me on your
    shoulders.
  Buck. [*Aside to* HASTINGS] With what a sharp-
    provided wit he reasons!
To mitigate the scorn he gives his uncle,
He prettily and aptly taunts himself:
So cunning and so young is wonderful.
  Glou. My lord, will't please you pass along?
Myself and my good cousin Buckingham
Will to your mother, to entreat of her
To meet you at the Tower and welcome you.
  York.What, will you go unto the Tower, my
    lord?   140
  Prince. My Lord Protector needs will have it so.
  York. I shall not sleep in quiet at the Tower.
  Glou. Why, what should you fear?
  York. Marry, my uncle Clarence' angry ghost:
My grandam told me he was murder'd there.
  Prince. I fear no uncles dead.

  Glou. Nor none that live, I hope.
  Prince. An if they live, I hope I need not fear.
But come, my lord; and with a heavy heart,
Thinking on them, go I unto the Tower.   150
      [*A Sennet. Exeunt all but* GLOUCESTER,
                         BUCKINGHAM *and* CATESBY.
  Buck. Think you, my lord, this little prating
    York
Was not incensed by his subtle mother
To taunt and scorn you thus opprobriously?
  Glou. No doubt, no doubt: O, 'tis a parlous boy;
Bold, quick, ingenious, forward, capable:
He is all the mother's, from the top to toe.
  Buck. Well, let them rest.Come hither,Catesby.
Thou art sworn as deeply to effect what we
    intend
As closely to conceal what we impart:
Thou know'st our reasons urged upon the way;
What think'st thou? is it not an easy matter 161
To make William Lord Hastings of our mind
For the instalment of this noble duke
In the seat royal of this famous isle?
  Cate. He for his father's sake so loves the
    Prince
That he will not be won to aught against him.
  Buck. What think'st thou, then, of Stanley?
    what will he?
  Cate. He will do all in all as Hastings doth.
  Buck.Well, then, no more but this: go, gentle
    Catesby,
And, as it were far off, sound thou Lord Hastings,
How he doth stand affected to our purpose;   171
And summon him to-morrow to the Tower,
To sit about the coronation.
If thou dost find him tractable to us,
Encourage him and show him all our reasons:
If he be leaden, icy-cold, unwilling,
Be thou so too; and so break off your talk,
And give us notice of his inclination:
For we to-morrow hold divided councils,
Wherein thyself shalt highly be employ'd.   180
  Glou. Commend me to Lord William: tell him,
    Catesby,
His ancient knot of dangerous adversaries
To-morrow are let blood at Pomfret-castle;
And bid my friend, for joy of this good news,
Give Mistress Shore one gentle kiss the more.
  Buck. Good Catesby, go, effect this business
    soundly.
  Cate. My good lords both, with all the heed I
    may.
  Glou. Shall we hear from you, Catesby, ere
    we sleep?
  Cate. You shall, my lord.
  Glou. At Crosby Place, there shall you find us
    both.   [*Exit* CATESBY. 190

Buck. Now, my lord, what shall we do, if we perceive

Lord Hastings will not yield to our complots?

Glou. Chop off his head, man; somewhat we will do:

And, look, when I am king, claim thou of me

The earldom of Hereford, and the moveables

Whereof the King my brother stood possess'd.

Buck. I'll claim that promise at your Grace's hands.

Glou. And look to have it yielded with all willingness.

Come, let us sup betimes, that afterwards

We may digest our complots in some form.   *200*

                     [*Exeunt.*

SCENE II. *Before Lord Hastings' house*

Enter a MESSENGER.

Mess. What, ho! my lord!

Hast. [*Within*] Who knocks at the door?

Mess. A messenger from the Lord Stanley.

Enter LORD HASTINGS.

Hast. What is't o'clock?

Mess. Upon the stroke of four.

Hast. Cannot thy master sleep these tedious nights?

Mess. So it should seem by that I have to say.

First, he commends him to your noble lordship.

Hast. And then?

Mess. And then he sends you word   *10*

He dreamt to-night the boar had razed his helm:

Besides, he says there are two councils held;

And that may be determined at the one

Which may make you and him to rue at the other.

Therefore he sends to know your lordship's pleasure,

If presently you will take horse with him,

And with all speed post with him toward the north

To shun the danger that his soul divines.

Hast. Go, fellow, go, return unto thy lord;

Bid him not fear the separated councils: *20*

His honour and myself are at the one,

And at the other is my servant Catesby;

Where nothing can proceed that toucheth us

Whereof I shall not have intelligence.

Tell him his fears are shallow, wanting instance:

And for his dreams, I wonder he is so fond

To trust the mockery of unquiet slumbers:

To fly the boar before the boar pursues

Were to incense the boar to follow us

And make pursuit where he did mean no chase.

Go, bid thy master rise and come to me;   *31*

And we will both together to the Tower,

Where, he shall see, the boar will use us kindly.

Mess. My gracious lord, I'll tell him what you say.   [*Exit.*

Enter CATESBY.

Cate. Many good morrows to my noble lord!

Hast. Good morrow, Catesby; you are early stirring:

What news, what news, in this our tottering state?

Cate. It is a reeling world, indeed, my lord;

And I believe 'twill never stand upright

Till Richard wear the garland of the realm.   *40*

Hast. How! wear the garland! dost thou mean the crown?

Cate. Ay, my good lord.

Hast. I'll have this crown of mine cut from my shoulders

Ere I will see the crown so foul misplaced.

But canst thou guess that he doth aim at it?

Cate. Ay, on my life; and hopes to find you forward

Upon his party for the gain thereof:

And thereupon he sends you this good news,

That this same very day your enemies,   *49*

The kindred of the Queen, must die at Pomfret.

Hast. Indeed, I am no mourner for that news,

Because they have been still mine enemies:

But, that I'll give my voice on Richard's side,

To bar my master's heirs in true descent,

God knows I will not do it, to the death.

Cate. God keep your lordship in that gracious mind!

Hast. But I shall laugh at this a twelve-month hence,

That they who brought me in my master's **hate**,

I live to look upon their tragedy.

I tell thee, Catesby—   *60*

Cate. What, my lord?

Hast. Ere a fortnight make me elder,

I'll send some packing that yet think not on **it**.

Cate. 'Tis a vile thing to die, my gracious lord,

When men are unprepared and look not for it.

Hast.   O monstrous, monstrous! and so falls it out

With Rivers, Vaughan, Grey: and so 'twill do

With some men else, who think themselves as safe

As thou and I; who, as thou know'st, are dear

To princely Richard and to Buckingham.   *70*

Cate. The Princes both make high account of you;

[*Aside*] For they account his head upon the bridge.

Hast. I know they do; and I have well **deserved**

It.

Enter LORD STANLEY.

Come on, come on; where is your boar-spear,
    man?
Fear you the boar, and go so unprovided?
  Stan. My lord, good morrow; good morrow,
    Catesby:
You may jest on, but, by the holy rood,
I do not like these several councils, I.
  Hast. My lord,
I hold my life as dear as you do yours;   80
And never in my life, I do protest,
Was it more precious to me than 'tis now:
Think you, but that I know our state secure,
I would be so triumphant as I am?
  Stan. The lords at Pomfret, when they rode
    from London,
Were jocund, and supposed their state was
    sure,
And they indeed had no cause to mistrust;
But yet, you see, how soon the day o'ercast.
This sudden stab of rancour I misdoubt:
Pray God, I say, I prove a needless coward!   90
What, shall we toward the Tower? the day is
    spent.
  Hast. Come, come, have with you. Wot you
    what, my lord?
To-day the lords you talk of are beheaded.
  Stan. They, for their truth, might better wear
    their heads
Than some that have accused them wear their
    hats.
But, come, my lord, let us away.

Enter a PURSUIVANT.

  Hast. Go on before; I'll talk with this good
    fellow.   [*Exeunt* STANLEY *and* CATESBY.
How now, sirrah! how goes the world with thee?
  Purs. The better that your lordship please
    to ask.   99
  Hast. I tell thee, man, 'tis better with me now
Than when I met thee last where now we meet:
Then was I going prisoner to the Tower,
By the suggestion of the Queen's allies;
But now, I tell thee—keep it to thyself—
This day those enemies are put to death,
And I in better state than e'er I was.
  Purs. God hold it, to your honour's good
    content!
  Hast. Gramercy, fellow: there, drink that for
    me. [*Throws him his purse.*]
  Purs. God save your lordship!   [*Exit.*

Enter a PRIEST.

  Priest. Well met, my lord; I am glad to see
    your honour.   110

  Hast. I thank thee, good Sir John, with all my
    heart.
I am in your debt for your last exercise;
Come the next Sabbath, and I will content you.
  He whispers in his ear.

Enter BUCKINGHAM.

  Buck. What, talking with a priest, Lord
    Chamberlain?
Your friends at Pomfret, they do need the
    priest;
Your honour hath no shriving work in hand.
  Hast. Good faith, and when I met this holy man,
Those men you talk of came into my mind.
What, go you toward the Tower?
  Buck. I do, my lord; but long I shall not stay:
I shall return before your lordship thence.   121
  Hast. 'Tis like enough, for I stay dinner there.
  Buck. [*Aside*] And supper too, although thou
    know'st it not.
Come, will you go?
  Hast. I'll wait upon your lordship.   [*Exeunt.*

SCENE III. *Pomfret Castle*

Enter SIR RICHARD RATCLIFF, *with halberds, carrying* RIVERS, GREY, *and* VAUGHAN *to death.*

  Rat. Come, bring forth the prisoners.
  Riv. Sir Richard Ratcliff, let me tell thee this:
To-day shalt thou behold a subject die
For truth, for duty, and for loyalty.
  Grey. God keep the Prince from all the pack
    of you!
A knot you are of damned blood-suckers.
  Vaug. You live that shall cry woe for this
    hereafter.
  Rat. Dispatch; the limit of your lives is out.
  Riv. O Pomfret, Pomfret! O thou bloody
    prison,
Fatal and ominous to noble peers!   10
Within the guilty closure of thy walls
Richard the Second here was hack'd to death;
And, for more slander to thy dismal seat,
We give thee up our guiltless blood to drink.
  Grey. Now Margaret's curse is fall'n upon our
    heads,
For standing by when Richard stabb'd her son.
  Riv. Then cursed she Hastings, then cursed
    she Buckingham,
Then cursed she Richard. O, remember, God,
To hear her prayers for them, as now for us!
And for my sister and her princely sons,   20
Be satisfied, dear God, with our true blood,
Which, as thou know'st, unjustly must be spilt.
  Rat. Make haste; the hour of death is expiate.
  Riv. Come, Grey, come, Vaughan, let us all
    embrace;

And take our leave, until we meet in heaven.
                       [*Exeunt.*

SCENE IV. *The Tower of London*

Enter BUCKINGHAM, STANLEY, HASTINGS, *the* BISH-
OP OF ELY, RATCLIFF, LOVEL, *with others, and
take their seats at a table.*

Hast. My lords, at once: the cause why we are
     met
Is to determine of the coronation.
In God's name, speak: when is the royal day?
  Buck. Are all things fitting for that royal time?
  Stan. It is, and wants but nomination.
  Ely. To-morrow, then, I judge a happy day.
  Buck. Who knows the Lord Protector's mind
     herein?
Who is most inward with the noble Duke?
  Ely. Your Grace, we think, should soonest
     know his mind.
  Buck. Who, I, my lord! we know each other's
     faces,   10
But for our hearts, he knows no more of mine,
Than I of yours;
Nor I no more of his, than you of mine.
Lord Hastings, you and he are near in love.
  Hast. I thank his Grace, I know he loves me
     well;
But, for his purpose in the coronation,
I have not sounded him, nor he deliver'd
His gracious pleasure any way therein:
But you, my noble lords, may name the time;
And in the Duke's behalf I'll give my voice,   20
Which, I presume, he'll take in gentle part.

Enter GLOUCESTER.

  Ely. Now in good time, here comes the Duke
     himself.
  Glou. My noble lords and cousins all, good
     morrow.
I have been long a sleeper; but, I hope,
My absence doth neglect no great designs
Which by my presence might have been
     concluded.
  Buck. Had not you come upon your cue, my
     lord,
William Lord Hastings had pronounced your
     part—
I mean, your voice—for crowning of the King.
  Glou. Than my Lord Hastings no man might
     be bolder;   30
His lordship knows me well, and loves me well.
  Hast. I thank your Grace.
  Glou.   My lord of Ely!
  Ely.   My lord?
  Glou. When I was last in Holborn,
I saw good strawberries in your garden there:

I do beseech you send for some of them.
  Ely. Marry, and will, my lord, with all my
     heart.   [*Exit.*
  Glou. Cousin of Buckingham, a word with you.
  Drawing him aside.
Catesby hath sounded Hastings in our business,
And finds the testy gentleman so hot,
As he will lose his head ere give consent   40
His master's son, as worshipful he terms it,
Shall lose the royalty of England's throne.
  Buck. Withdraw you hence, my lord, I'll
     follow you.
         [*Exit* GLOUCESTER, BUCKINGHAM *following*.
  Stan. We have not yet set down this day of
     triumph.
To-morrow, in mine opinion, is too sudden;
For I myself am not so well provided
As else I would be, were the day prolong'd.

Re-enter BISHOP OF ELY.

  Ely. Where is my Lord Protector? I have sent
     for these strawberries.
  Hast. His Grace looks cheerfully and smooth
     to-day;   50
There's some conceit or other likes him well,
When he doth bid good morrow with such a
     spirit.
I think there's never a man in Christendom
That can less hide his love or hate than he;
For by his face straight shall you know his heart.
  Stan. What of his heart perceive you in his face
By any likelihood he show'd to-day?
  Hast. Marry, that with no man here he is
     offended;
For, were he, he had shown it in his looks.
  Stan. I pray God he be not, I say.   60

Re-enter GLOUCESTER *and* BUCKINGHAM.

  Glou. I pray you all, tell me what they deserve
That do conspire my death with devilish plots
Of damned witchcraft, and that have prevail'd
Upon my body with their hellish charms?
  Hast. The tender love I bear your Grace, my
     lord,
Makes me most forward in this noble presence
To doom the offenders, whatsoever they be:
I say, my lord, they have deserved death.
  Glou. Then be your eyes the witness of this ill:
See how I am bewitch'd; behold mine arm   70
Is, like a blasted sapling, wither'd up:
And this is Edward's wife, that monstrous
     witch,
Consorted with that harlot strumpet Shore,
That by their witchcraft thus have marked me.
  Hast. If they have done this thing, my gracious
     lord—

Glou. If! thou protector of this damned
    strumpet,
Tellest thou me of "ifs"? Thou art a traitor:
Off with his head! Now, by Saint Paul I swear,
I will not dine until I see the same.
Lovel and Ratcliff, look that it be done: 80
The rest, that love me, rise and follow me.
    [*Exeunt all but* HASTINGS, RATCLIFF, *and* LOVEL.
  Hast. Woe, woe for England! not a whit for me;
For I, too fond, might have prevented this.
Stanley did dream the boar did raze his helm;
But I disdain'd it, and did scorn to fly:
Three times to-day my foot-cloth horse did
    stumble,
And startled when he look'd upon the Tower,
As loath to bear me to the slaughter-house.
O, now I want the priest that spake to me:
I now repent I told the pursuivant,   90
As 'twere triumphing at mine enemies,
How they at Pomfret bloodily were butcher'd,
And I myself secure in grace and favour.
O Margaret, Margaret, now thy heavy curse
Is lighted on poor Hastings' wretched head!
  Rat. Dispatch, my lord; the Duke would be at
    dinner:
Make a short shrift; he longs to see your head.
  Hast. O momentary grace of mortal men,
Which we more hunt for than the grace of God!
Who builds his hopes in air of your good looks,
Lives like a drunken sailor on a mast,   101
Ready, with every nod, to tumble down
Into the fatal bowels of the deep.
  Lov. Come, come, dispatch; 'tis bootless to
    exclaim.
  Hast. O bloody Richard! miserable England!
I prophesy the fearfull'st time to thee
That ever wretched age hath look'd upon.
Come, lead me to the block; bear him my head:
They smile at me that shortly shall be dead.
    [*Exeunt.*

SCENE V. *The Tower-walls*

Enter GLOUCESTER *and* BUCKINGHAM, *in rotten
armour, marvellous ill-favoured.*

  Glou. Come, cousin, canst thou quake, and
    change thy colour,
Murder thy breath in middle of a word,
And then begin again, and stop again,
As if thou wert distraught and mad with terror?
  Buck. Tut, I can counterfeit the deep tragedian;
Speak and look back, and pry on every side,
Tremble and start at wagging of a straw,
Intending deep suspicion: ghastly looks
Are at my service, like enforced smiles;
And both are ready in their offices,   10
At any time, to grace my stratagems.

But what, is Catesby gone?
  Glou. He is; and, see, he brings the Mayor
    along.

Enter the MAYOR *and* CATESBY.

  Buck. Lord mayor—
  Glou. Look to the drawbridge there!
  Buck. Hark! a drum.
  Glou. Catesby, o'erlook the walls.
  Buck. Lord Mayor, the reason we have sent—
  Glou. Look back, defend thee, here are enemies.
  Buck. God and our innocency defend and
    guard us!   20
  Glou. Be patient, they are friends, Ratcliff and
    Lovel.

Enter LOVEL *and* RATCLIFF, *with* HASTINGS' *head.*

  Lov. Here is the head of that ignoble traitor,
The dangerous and unsuspected Hastings.
  Glou. So dear I loved the man, that I must
    weep.
I took him for the plainest harmless creature
That breathed upon this earth a Christian;
Made him my book, wherein my soul recorded
The history of all her secret thoughts:
So smooth he daub'd his vice with show of virtue
That, his apparent open guilt omitted,   30
I mean, his conversation with Shore's wife,
He lived from all attainder of suspect.
  Buck. Well, well, he was the covert'st shelter'd
    traitor
That ever lived.
Would you imagine, or almost believe,
Were't not that, by great preservation,
We live to tell it you, the subtle traitor
This day had plotted, in the council-house
To murder me and my good Lord of Gloucester?
  May. What, had he so?   40
  Glou. What, think you we are Turks or infidels?
Or that we would, against the form of law,
Proceed thus rashly to the villain's death,
But that the extreme peril of the case,
The peace of England and our persons' safety,
Enforced us to this execution?
  May. Now, fair befall you! he deserved his
    death;
And you my good lords, both have well proceeded
To warn false traitors from the like attempts.
I never look'd for better at his hands   50
After he once fell in with Mistress Shore.
  Glou. Yet had not we determined he should die,
Until your lordship came to see his death;
Which now the loving haste of these our friends,
Somewhat against our meaning, have prevented:
Because, my lord, we would have had you heard
The traitor speak, and timorously confess

The manner and the purpose of his treason;
That you might well have signified the same
Unto the citizens, who haply may   60
Misconstrue us in him and wail his death.
  May. But, my good lord, your Grace's word
        shall serve
As well as I had seen and heard him speak:
And doubt you not, right noble princes both,
But I'll acquaint our duteous citizens
With all your just proceedings in this cause.
  Glou. And to that end we wish'd your lordship
        here,
To avoid the carping censures of the world.
  Buck. But since you come too late of our intents,
Yet witness what you hear we did intend: 70
And so, my good Lord Mayor, we bid farewell.
                              [*Exit* MAYOR.
  Glou. Go, after, after, cousin Buckingham.
The Mayor towards Guildhall hies him in all
        post:
There, at your meet'st advantage of the time,
Infer the bastardy of Edward's children:
Tell them how Edward put to death a citizen
Only for saying he would make his son
Heir to the crown; meaning indeed his house,
Which, by the sign thereof, was termed so.
Moreover, urge his hateful luxury,   80
And bestial appetite in change of lust;
Which stretched to their servants, daughters,
        wives,
Even where his lustful eye or savage heart,
Without control, listed to make his prey.
Nay, for a need, thus far come near my person:
Tell them, when that my mother went with child
Of that unsatiate Edward, noble York
My princely father then had wars in France;
And, by just computation of the time,
Found that the issue was not his begot;   90
Which well appeared in his lineaments,
Being nothing like the noble Duke my father:
But touch this sparingly, as 'twere far off;
Because you know, my lord, my mother lives.
  Buck. Fear not, my lord, I'll play the orator
As if the golden fee for which I plead
Were for myself: and so, my lord, adieu.
  Glou. If you thrive well, bring them to
        Baynard's Castle;
Where you shall find me well accompanied   99
With reverend fathers and well-learned bishops.
  Buck. I go; and towards three or four o'clock
Look for the news that the Guildhall affords.
                              [*Exit.*
  Glou. Go, Lovel, with all speed to Doctor
        Shaw;
[*To* CATESBY.] Go thou to Friar Penker; bid
        them both

Meet me within this hour at Baynard's Castle.
                    [*Exeunt all but* GLOUCESTER.
Now will I in, to take some privy order,
To draw the brats of Clarence out of sight;
And to give notice that no manner of person
At any time have recourse unto the princes. [*Exit.*

SCENE VI. *The same: a street*

Enter a SCRIVENER, *with a paper in his hand.*

  Scriv. This is the indictment of the good Lord
        Hastings;
Which in a set hand fairly is engross'd
That it may be this day read o'er in Paul's.
And mark how well the sequel hangs together:
Eleven hours I spent to write it over,
For yesternight by Catesby was it brought me;
The precedent was full as long a-doing:
And yet within these five hours lived Lord
        Hastings,
Untainted, unexamined, free, at liberty.
Here's a good world the while! Why who's so
        gross   10
That seeth not this palpable device?
Yet who's so blind, but says he sees it not?
Bad is the world; and all will come to nought
When such bad dealing must be seen in thought.
                              [*Exit.*

SCENE VII. *Baynard's Castle*

Enter GLOUCESTER *and* BUCKINGHAM, *at
several doors.*

  Glou. How now, my lord, what say the citizens?
  Buck. Now, by the holy mother of our Lord,
The citizens are mum and speak not a word.
  Glou. Touch'd you the bastardy of Edward's
        children?
  Buck. I did; with his contract with Lady
        Lucy,
And his contract by deputy in France;
The insatiate greediness of his desires,
And his enforcement of the city wives;
His tyranny for trifles; his own bastardy,
As being got, your father then in France,   10
And his resemblance, being not like the duke:
Withal I did infer your lineaments,
Being the right idea of your father,
Both in your form and nobleness of mind;
Laid open all your victories in Scotland,
Your discipline in war, wisdom in peace,
Your bounty, virtue, fair humility;
Indeed, left nothing fitting for the purpose
Untouch'd or slightly handled in discourse:
And when mine oratory grew to an end,   20
I bid them that did love their country's good
Cry "God save Richard, England's royal king!"
  Glou. Ah! and did they so?

Buck. No, so God help me, they spake not a
    word;
But, like dumb statuas or breathing stones,
Gazed each on other and look'd deadly pale.
Which when I saw, I reprehended them;
And ask'd the Mayor what meant this wilful
    silence:
His answer was, the people were not wont
To be spoke to but by the Recorder.   30
Then he was urged to tell my tale again,
"Thus saith the Duke, thus hath the Duke
    inferr'd";
But nothing spake in warrant from himself.
When he had done, some followers of mine own,
At the lower end of the hall, hurl'd up their caps,
And some ten voices cried "God save King
    Richard!"
And thus I took the vantage of those few,
"Thanks, gentle citizens and friends," quoth I;
"This general applause and loving shout   39
Argues your wisdoms and your love to Richard":
And even here brake off, and came away.
  Glou. What tongueless blocks were they!
    would they not speak?
  Buck. No, by my troth, my lord.
  Glou. Will not the Mayor then and his
    brethren come?
  Buck. The Mayor is here at hand: intend
    some fear;
Be not you spoke with but by mighty suit:
And look you get a prayer-book in your hand
And stand betwixt two churchmen, good my lord;
For on that ground I'll build a holy descant:
And be not easily won to our request: 50
Play the maid's part, still answer nay and take it.
  Glou. I go; and if you plead as well for them
As I can say nay to thee for myself,
No doubt we'll bring it to a happy issue.
  Buck. Go, go, up to the leads; the lord Mayor
    knocks.   [*Exit* GLOUCESTER.
      Enter the MAYOR *and Citizens.*
Welcome, my lord: I dance attendance here;
I think the Duke will not be spoke withal.

      Enter CATESBY.

Here comes his servant: how now, Catesby,
What says he?
  Cate. My lord, he doth entreat your Grace
To visit him to-morrow or next day: 60
He is within, with two right reverend fathers,
Divinely bent to meditation;
And in no worldly suit would he be moved
To draw him from his holy exercise.
  Buck. Return, good Catesby, to thy lord again;
Tell him, myself, the Mayor and citizens,
In deep designs and matters of great moment,

No less importing than our general good,
Are come to have some conference with his
    Grace.
  Cate. I'll tell him what you say, my lord.   70
                          [*Exit.*
  Buck. Ah, ha, my lord, this prince is not an
    Edward!
He is not lolling on a lewd day-bed,
But on his knees at meditation;
Not dallying with a brace of courtezans,
But meditating with two deep divines;
Not sleeping, to engross his idle body,
But praying, to enrich his watchful soul:
Happy were England, would this gracious prince
Take on himself the sovereignty thereof:
But, sure, I fear, we shall ne'er win him to it.   80
  May. Marry, God forbid his Grace should say
    us nay!
  Buck. I fear he will.

      Re-enter CATESBY.

How now, Catesby, what says your lord?
  Cate.   My lord,
He wonders to what end you have assembled
Such troops of citizens to speak with him,
His Grace not being warn'd thereof before:
My lord, he fears you mean no good to him.
  Buck. Sorry I am my noble cousin should
Suspect me, that I mean no good to him:
By heaven, I come in perfect love to him;   90
And so once more return and tell his Grace.
                  [*Exit* CATESBY.
When holy and devout religious men
Are at their beads, 'tis hard to draw them thence,
So sweet is zealous contemplation.

    Enter GLOUCESTER *aloft, between two* BISHOPS.
           CATESBY *returns.*

  May. See, where he stands between two
    clergymen!
  Buck. Two props of virtue for a Christian
    prince,
To stay him from the fall of vanity:
And, see, a book of prayer in his hand,
True ornaments to know a holy man.
Famous Plantagenet, most gracious prince,   *100*
Lend favourable ears to our request;
And pardon us the interruption
Of thy devotion and right Christian zeal.
  Glou. My lord, there needs no such apology:
I rather do beseech you pardon me,
Who, earnest in the service of my God,
Neglect the visitation of my friends.
But, leaving this, what is your Grace's pleasure?
  Buck Even that, I hope, which pleaseth God
    above,

And all good men of this ungovern'd isle.   110
  Glou. I do suspect I have done some offence
That seems disgracious in the city's eyes,
And that you come to reprehend my ignorance.
  Buck. You have, my lord: would it might
    please your Grace,
At our entreaties, to amend that fault!
  Glou. Else wherefore breathe I in a Christian
    land?
  Buck. Then know, it is your fault that you
    resign
The supreme seat, the throne majestical,
The scepter'd office of your ancestors,
Your state of fortune and your due of birth,   120
The lineal glory of your royal house,
To the corruption of a blemish'd stock:
Whilst, in the mildness of your sleepy thoughts,
Which here we waken to our country's good,
This noble isle doth want her proper limbs;
Her face defaced with scars of infamy,
Her royal stock graft with ignoble plants,
And almost shoulder'd in the swallowing gulf
Of blind forgetfulness and dark oblivion.
Which to recure, we heartily solicit   130
Your gracious self to take on you the charge
And kingly government of this your land,
Not as protector, steward, substitute,
Or lowly factor for another's gain;
But as successively from blood to blood,
Your right of birth, your empery, your own.
For this, consorted with the citizens,
Your very worshipful and loving friends,
And by their vehement instigation,
In this just suit come I to move your Grace.   140
  Glou. I know not whether to depart in silence,
Or bitterly to speak in your reproof,
Best fitteth my degree or your condition:
If not to answer, you might haply think
Tongue-tied ambition, not replying, yielded
To bear the golden yoke of sovereignty,
Which fondly you would here impose on me;
If to reprove you for this suit of yours,
So season'd with your faithful love to me,
Then, on the other side, I check'd my friends.
Therefore, to speak, and to avoid the first,   151
And then, in speaking, not to incur the last,
Definitively thus I answer you.
Your love deserves my thanks; but my desert
Unmeritable shuns your high request.
First, if all obstacles were cut away,
And that my path were even to the crown,
As my ripe revenue and due by birth;
Yet so much is my poverty of spirit,
So mighty and so many my defects,   160
As I had rather hide me from my greatness,
Being a bark to brook no mighty sea,

Than in my greatness covet to be hid,
And in the vapour of my glory smother'd.
But, God be thanked, there's no need of me,
And much I need to help you, if need were;
The royal tree hath left us royal fruit,
Which, mellow'd by the stealing hours of time,
Will well become the seat of majesty,
And make, no doubt, us happy by his reign.   170
On him I lay what you would lay on me,
The right and fortune of his happy stars,
Which God defend that I should wring from him!
  Buck. My lord, this argues conscience in your
    Grace;
But the respects thereof are nice and trivial,
All circumstances well considered.
You say that Edward is your brother's son:
So say we too, but not by Edward's wife;
For first he was contract to Lady Lucy—
Your mother lives a witness to that vow—   180
And afterward by substitute betroth'd
To Bona, sister to the King of France.
These both put by, a poor petitioner,
A care-crazed mother of a many children,
A beauty-waning and distressed widow,
Even in the afternoon of her best days,
Made prize and purchase of his lustful eye,
Seduced the pitch and height of all his thoughts
To base declension and loathed bigamy:
By her, in his unlawful bed, he got   190
This Edward, whom our manners term the
    Prince.
More bitterly could I expostulate
Save that, for reverence to some alive,
I give a sparing limit to my tongue.
Then, good my lord, take to your royal self
This proffer'd benefit of dignity;
If not to bless us and the land withal,
Yet to draw forth your noble ancestry
From the corruption of abusing times
Unto a lineal true-derived course.   200
  May. Do, good my lord, your citizens entreat
    you.
  Buck. Refuse not, mighty lord, this proffer'd
    love.
  Cate. O, make them joyful, grant their lawful
    suit!
  Glou. Alas, why would you heap these cares
    on me?
I am unfit for state and majesty:
I do beseech you, take it not amiss;
I cannot nor I will not yield to you.
  Buck. If you refuse it—as, in love and zeal,
Loath to depose the child, your brother's son;
As well we know your tenderness of heart   210
And gentle, kind, effeminate remorse,
Which we have noted in you to your kin,

And egally indeed to all estates—
Yet whether you accept our suit or no,
Your brother's son shall never reign our king;
But we will plant some other in the throne,
To the disgrace and downfall of your house:
And in this resolution here we leave you.
Come, citizens: 'zounds! I'll entreat no more.
Glou. O, do not swear, my lord of Buckingham.
                    [*Exit* BUCKINGHAM *with the Citizens.*
Cate. Call them again, my lord, and accept
    their suit.   221
Another. Do, good my lord, lest all the land
    do rue it.
Glou. Would you enforce me to a world of
    care?
Well, call them again. I am not made of stones,
But penetrable to your kind entreats,
Albeit against my conscience and my soul.

Re-enter BUCKINGHAM and the rest.

Cousin of Buckingham, and you sage, grave
    men,
Since you will buckle fortune on my back
To bear her burthen whether I will or no,
I must have patience to endure the load: 230
But if black scandal or foul-faced reproach
Attend the sequel of your imposition,
Your mere enforcement shall acquittance me
From all the impure blots and stains thereof;
For God he knows, and you may partly see,
How far I am from the desire thereof.
May. God bless your Grace! we see it and will
    say it.
Glou. In saying so, you shall but say the truth.
Buck. Then I salute you with this kingly title:
Long live Richard, England's royal king!   240
May. and Cit. Amen.
Buck. To-morrow will it please you to be
    crown'd?
Glou. Even when you please, since you will
    have it so.
Buck. To-morrow, then, we will attend your
    Grace:
And so most joyfully we take our leave.
Glou. Come, let us to our holy task again.
Farewell, good cousin; farewell, gentle friends.
                                        [*Exeunt.*

ACT IV

Scene i. *Before the Tower*

Enter, on one side, QUEEN ELIZABETH, DUCHESS OF
    YORK, *and* MARQUESS OF DORSET; *on the other,*
    ANNE, DUCHESS OF GLOUCESTER, *leading* LADY
    MARGARET PLANTAGENET, *Clarence's young*
    Daughter.

Duch. Who meets us here? my niece Plantagenet
Led in the hand of her kind aunt of Gloucester?
Now, for my life, she's wandering to the Tower
On pure heart's love to greet the tender princes.
Daughter, well met.
Anne.   God give your Graces both
A happy and a joyful time of day!
Q. Eliz. As much to you, good sister! Whither
    away?
Anne. No farther than the Tower; and, as I
    guess,
Upon the like devotion as yourselves,
To gratulate the gentle princes there.   10
Q. Eliz. Kind sister, thanks: we'll enter all
    together.

Enter BRAKENBURY.

And, in good time, here the lieutenant comes.
Master lieutenant, pray you, by your leave,
How doth the Prince, and my young son of York?
Brak. Right well, dear madam. By your
    patience,
I may not suffer you to visit them;
The King hath straitly charged the contrary.
Q. Eliz. The King! why, who's that?
Brak. I cry you mercy: I mean the Lord
    Protector.
Q. Eliz. The Lord protect him from that kingly
    title!   20
Hath he set bounds betwixt their love and me?
I am their mother; who should keep me from
    them?
Duch. I am their father's mother; I will see
    them.
Anne. Their aunt I am in law, in love their
    mother:
Then bring me to their sights; I'll bear thy
    blame
And take thy office from thee, on my peril.
Brak. No, madam, no; I may not leave it so:
I am bound by oath, and therefore pardon me.
                                        [*Exit.*

Enter LORD STANLEY.

Stan. Let me but meet you, ladies, one hour
    hence,
And I'll salute your Grace of York as mother, 30
And reverend looker on, of two fair queens.
[*To Anne*] Come, madam, you must straight to
    Westminster,
There to be crowned Richard's royal queen.
Q. Eliz. O, cut my lace in sunder, that my pent
    heart
May have some scope to beat, or else I swoon
With this dead-killing news!
Anne. Despiteful tidings! O unpleasing news!

Dor. Be of good cheer: mother, how fares your
Grace?

Q. Eliz. O Dorset, speak not to me, get thee
hence!

Death and destruction dog thee at the heels;   40
Thy mother's name is ominous to children.
If thou wilt outstrip death, go cross the seas,
And live with Richmond, from the reach of hell:
Go, hie thee, hie thee from this slaughter-house,
Lest thou increase the number of the dead;
And make me die the thrall of Margaret's curse,
Nor mother, wife, nor England's counted queen.

Stan. Full of wise care is this your counsel,
madam.

Take all the swift advantage of the hours;
You shall have letters from me to my son   50
To meet you on the way and welcome you.
Be not ta'en tardy by unwise delay.

Duch. O ill-dispersing wind of misery!
O my accursed womb, the bed of death!
A cockatrice hast thou hatch'd to the world,
Whose unavoided eye is murderous.

Stan. Come, madam, come; I in all haste was
sent.

Anne. And I in all unwillingness will go.
I would to God that the inclusive verge
Of golden metal that must round my brow   60
Were red-hot steel, to sear me to the brain!
Anointed let me be with deadly venom,
And die ere men can say, "God save the Queen!"

Q. Eliz. Go, go, poor soul, I envy not thy glory;
To feed my humour, wish thyself no harm.

Anne. No! why? When he that is my husband
now
Came to me, as I follow'd Henry's corse,
When scarce the blood was well wash'd from his
hands
Which issued from my other angel husband
And that dead saint which then I weeping
follow'd;
O, when, I say, I look'd on Richard's face,   71
This was my wish: "Be thou," quoth I,
"accursed,
For making me, so young, so old a widow!
And, when thou wed'st, let sorrow haunt thy bed;
And be thy wife—if any be so mad—
As miserable by the life of thee
As thou hast made me by my dear lord's death!"
Lo, ere I can repeat this curse again,
Even in so short a space, my woman's heart
Grossly grew captive to his honey words   80
And proved the subject of my own soul's curse,
Which ever since hath kept my eyes from rest;
For never yet one hour in his bed
Have I enjoy'd the golden dew of sleep,
But have been waked by his timorous dreams.

Besides, he hates me for my father Warwick,
And will, no doubt, shortly be rid of me.

Q. Eliz. Poor heart, adieu! I pity thy complaining.

Anne. No more than from my soul I mourn for
yours.

Q. Eliz. Farewell, thou woeful welcomer of
glory!   90

Anne. Adieu, poor soul, that takest thy leave
of it!

Duch. [*To* DORSET] Go thou to Richmond, and
good fortune guide thee!

[*To* ANNE] Go thou to Richard, and good angels
guard thee!

[*To* QUEEN ELIZABETH] Go thou to sanctuary,
and good thoughts possess thee!
I to my grave, where peace and rest lie with me!
Eighty odd years of sorrow have I seen,
And each hour's joy wreck'd with a week of teen.

Q. Eliz. Stay, yet look back with me unto the
Tower.
Pity, you ancient stones, those tender babes
Whom envy hath immured within your walls!
Rough cradle for such little pretty ones!   101
Rude ragged nurse, old sullen playfellow
For tender princes, use my babies well!
So foolish sorrow bids your stones farewell.
[*Exeunt.*

SCENE II. *London: the palace*

Sennet. Enter RICHARD, *in pomp, crowned;*
BUCKINGHAM, CATESBY, *a* PAGE, *and others.*

K. Rich. Stand all apart. Cousin of Buckingham!

Buck. My gracious sovereign?

K. Rich. Give me thy hand. [*Here he ascendeth
his throne.*] Thus high, by thy advice
And thy assistance, is King Richard seated:
But shall we wear these honours for a day?
Or shall they last, and we rejoice in them?

Buck. Still live they and for ever may they last!

K. Rich. O Buckingham, now do I play the
touch
To try if thou be current gold indeed:
Young Edward lives: think now what I would
say.   10

Buck. Say on, my loving lord.

K. Rich. Why, Buckingham, I say, I would be
king.

Buck. Why, so you are, my thrice renowned
liege.

K. Rich. Ha! am I king? 'tis so: but Edward
lives.

Buck. True, noble prince.

K. Rich.   O bitter consequence,
That Edward still should live! "True, noble
prince!"

Cousin, thou wert not wont to be so dull:
Shall I be plain? I wish the bastards dead;
And I would have it suddenly perform'd.
What sayest thou? speak suddenly; be brief.   20
  Buck. Your Grace may do your pleasure.
  K. Rich. Tut, tut, thou art all ice, thy kindness
    freezeth:
Say, have I thy consent that they shall die?
  Buck. Give me some breath, some little pause,
    my lord,
Before I positively speak herein:
I will resolve your Grace immediately.   [*Exit.*
  Cate. [*Aside to a stander by*] The King is angry:
    see, he bites the lip.
  K. Rich. I will converse with iron-witted fools
And unrespective boys: none are for me
That look into me with considerate eyes: 30
High-reaching Buckingham grows circumspect.
Boy!
  Page. My lord?
  K. Rich. Know'st thou not any whom
    corrupting gold
Would tempt unto a close exploit of death?
  Page. My lord, I know a discontented gentleman,
Whose humble means match not his haughty
    mind:
Gold were as good as twenty orators,
And will, no doubt, tempt him to anything.
  K. Rich. What is his name?   40
  Page.   His name, my lord, is Tyrrel.
  K. Rich. I partly know the man: go, call him
    hither.   [*Exit* PAGE.
The deep-revolving witty Buckingham
No more shall be the neighbour to my counsel:
Hath he so long held out with me untired,
And stops he now for breath?

                Enter STANLEY.

                How now! what news with you?
  Stan. My lord, I hear the Marquis Dorset's fled
To Richmond, in those parts beyond the sea
Where he abides.   [*Stands apart.*
  K. Rich. Catesby!
  Cate. My lord?   50
  K. Rich. Rumour it abroad
That Anne, my wife, is sick and like to die:
I will take order for her keeping close.
Inquire me out some mean-born gentleman,
Whom I will marry straight to Clarence'
    daughter:
The boy is foolish, and I fear not him.
Look, how thou dream'st! I say again, give out
That Anne my wife is sick and like to die:
About it; for it stands me much upon   59
To stop all hopes whose growth may damage me.
                            [*Exit* CATESBY.

I must be married to my brother's daughter,
Or else my kingdom stands on brittle glass.
Murder her brothers and then marry her!
Uncertain way of gain! But I am in
So far in blood that sin will pluck on sin:
Tear-falling pity dwells not in this eye.

            Re-enter PAGE *with* TYRREL.

Is thy name Tyrrel?
  Tyr. James Tyrrel, and your most obedient
    subject.
  K. Rich. Art thou, indeed?
  Tyr.   Prove me, my gracious sovereign.
  K. Rich. Darest thou resolve to kill a friend
    of mine?   70
  Tyr. Ay, my lord;
But I had rather kill two enemies.
  K. Rich. Why, there thou hast it: two deep
    enemies,
Foes to my rest and my sweet sleep's disturbers
Are they that I would have thee deal upon
Tyrrel, I mean those bastards in the Tower.
  Tyr. Let me have open means to come to them,
And soon I'll rid you from the fear of them.
  K. Rich. Thou sing'st sweet music. Hark, come
    hither, Tyrrel:
Go, by this token: rise, and lend thine ear: 80
                            [*Whispers.*
There is no more but so: say it is done,
And I will love thee and prefer thee too.
  Tyr. 'Tis done, my gracious lord.
  K. Rich. Shall we hear from thee, Tyrrel, ere
    we sleep?
  Tyr. Ye shall, my lord.   [*Exit.*

            Re-enter BUCKINGHAM.

  Buck. My lord, I have consider'd in my mind
The late demand that you did sound me in.
  K. Rich. Well, let that pass. Dorset is fled to
    Richmond.
  Buck. I hear that news, my lord.
  K. Rich. Stanley, he is your wife's son: well,
    look to it.   90
  Buck. My lord, I claim your gift, my due by
    promise,
For which your honour and your faith is pawn'd;
The earldom of Hereford and the moveables
The which you promised I should possess.
  K. Rich. Stanley, look to your wife: if she
    convey
Letters to Richmond, you shall answer it.
  Buck. What says your Highness to my just
    demand?
  K. Rich. As I remember, Henry the Sixth
Did prophesy that Richmond should be king,
When Richmond was a little peevish boy.   100

A king, perhaps, perhaps—
Buck. My lord!
K. Rich. How chance the prophet could not at
    that time
Have told me, I being by, that I should kill him?
Buck. My lord, your promise for the earldom—
K. Rich. Richmond! When last I was at Exeter,
The mayor in courtesy show'd me the castle
And call'd it Rougemont: at which name I
    started,
Because a bard of Ireland told me once,
I should not live long after I saw Richmond.   *110*
Buck. My lord!
K. Rich. Ay, what's o'clock?
Buck. I am thus bold to put your Grace in mind
Of what you promised me.
K. Rich.   Well, but what's o'clock?
Buck. Upon the stroke of ten.
K. Rich.   Well, let it strike.
Buck. Why let it strike?
K. Rich. Because that, like a Jack, thou keep'st
    the stroke
Betwixt thy begging and my mediation.
I am not in the giving vein to-day.
Buck. Why, then resolve me whether you will
    or no.   *120*
K. Rich. Tut, tut,
Thou troublest me; I am not in the vein.
                    [*Exeunt all but* BUCKINGHAM.
Buck. Is it even so? rewards he my true service
With such deep contempt? made I him king for
    this?
O, let me think on Hastings, and be gone
To Brecknock while my fearful head is on!
                                        [*Exit.*

SCENE III. *The same*
Enter TYRREL.

Tyr. The tyrannous and bloody deed is done,
The most arch act of piteous massacre
That ever yet this land was guilty of.
Dighton and Forrest, whom I did suborn
To do this ruthless piece of butchery,
Although they were flesh'd villains, bloody dogs,
Melting with tenderness and kind compassion
Wept like two children in their deaths' sad
    stories.
"Lo, thus," quoth Dighton, "lay those tender
    babes":
"Thus, thus," quoth Forrest, "girdling one
    another
Within their innocent alabaster arms: *11*
Their lips were four red roses on a stalk,
Which in their summer beauty kiss'd each
    other.
A book of prayers on their pillow lay;

Which once," quoth Forrest, "almost changed
    my mind
But O! the devil"—there the villain stopp'd;
Whilst Dighton thus told on: "We smothered
The most replenished sweet work of nature
That from the prime creation e'er she framed."
Thus both are gone with conscience and remorse;
They could not speak; and so I left them both,
To bring this tidings to the bloody King.
And here he comes.

Enter KING RICHARD.

                    All hail, my sovereign liege!
K. Rich. Kind Tyrrel, am I happy in thy news?
Tyr. If to have done the thing you gave in
    charge
Beget your happiness, be happy then,
For it is done, my lord.
K. Rich.   But didst thou see them dead?
Tyr. I did, my lord.
K. Rich.   And buried, gentle Tyrrel?
Tyr. The chaplain of the Tower hath buried
    them;
But how or in what place I do not know.   *30*
K. Rich. Come to me, Tyrrel, soon at after
    supper,
And thou shalt tell the process of their death.
Meantime, but think how I may do thee good,
And be inheritor of thy desire.
Farewell till soon.   [*Exit* TYRREL.
The son of Clarence have I pent up close;
His daughter meanly have I match'd in marriage;
The sons of Edward sleep in Abraham's bosom,
And Anne my wife hath bid the world good
    night.
Now, for I know the Breton Richmond aims   *40*
At young Elizabeth, my brother's daughter,
And, by that knot, looks proudly o'er the crown,
To her I go, a jolly thriving wooer.

Enter RATCLIFF.

Rat. My lord!
K. Rich. Good news or bad, that thou comest
    in so bluntly?
Rat. Bad news, my lord: Ely is fled to Richmond;
And Buckingham, back'd with the hardy Welsh-
    men,
Is in the field, and still his power increaseth.
K. Rich. Ely with Richmond troubles me
    more near
Than Buckingham and his rash-levied army.   *50*
Come, I have heard that fearful commenting
Is leaden servitor to dull delay;
Delay leads impotent and snail-paced beggary:
Then fiery expedition be my wing,
Jove's Mercury, and herald for a king!

Come, muster men: my counsel is my shield;
We must be brief when traitors brave the field.
                                        [*Exeunt.*

SCENE IV. *Before the palace*
Enter QUEEN MARGARET.

Q. Mar. So, now prosperity begins to mellow
And drop into the rotten mouth of death.
Here in these confines slily have I lurk'd,
To watch the waning of mine adversaries.
A dire induction am I witness to,
And will to France, hoping the consequence
Will prove as bitter, black, and tragical.
Withdraw thee, wretched Margaret: who comes
        here?

Enter QUEEN ELIZABETH *and the* DUCHESS OF YORK.

Q. Eliz. Ah, my young princes! ah, my tender
        babes!
My unblown flowers, new-appearing sweets! *10*
If yet your gentle souls fly in the air
And be not fix'd in doom perpetual,
Hover about me with your airy wings
And hear your mother's lamentation!
Q. Mar. Hover about her; say that right for
        right
Hath dimm'd your infant morn to aged night.
Duch. So many miseries have crazed my voice,
That my woe-wearied tongue is mute and dumb,
Edward Plantagenet, why art thou dead?
Q. Mar. Plantagenet doth quit Plantagenet.
Edward for Edward pays a dying debt. *21*
Q. Eliz. Wilt thou, O God, fly from such
        gentle lambs,
And throw them in the entrails of the wolf?
When didst thou sleep when such a deed was
        done?
Q. Mar. When holy Harry died, and my sweet
        son.
Duch. Blind sight, dead life, poor mortal
        living ghost,
Woe's scene, world's shame, grave's due by
        life usurp'd,
Brief abstract and record of tedious days,
Rest thy unrest on England's lawful earth,
        Sitting down.
Unlawfully made drunk with innocents' blood!
Q. Eliz. O, that thou wouldst as well afford a
        grave *31*
As thou canst yield a melancholy seat!
Then would I hide my bones, not rest them here.
O, who hath any cause to mourn but I?
        Sitting down by her.
Q. Mar. If ancient sorrow be most reverend,
Give mine the benefit of seniory,

And let my woes frown on the upper hand.
If sorrow can admit society,
        Sitting down with them.
Tell o'er your woes again by viewing mine:
I had an Edward, till a Richard kill'd him; *40*
I had a Harry, till a Richard kill'd him:
Thou hadst an Edward, till a Richard kill'd him;
Thou hadst a Richard, till a Richard kill'd him.
Duch. I had a Richard too, and thou didst
        kill him;
I had a Rutland too, thou holp'st to kill him.
Q. Mar. Thou hadst a Clarence too, and
        Richard kill'd him.
From forth the kennel of thy womb hath crept
A hell-hound that doth hunt us all to death:
That dog, that had his teeth before his eyes,
To worry lambs and lap their gentle blood, *50*
That foul defacer of God's handiwork,
That excellent grand tyrant of the earth
That reigns in galled eyes of weeping souls,
Thy womb let loose, to chase us to our graves.
O upright, just, and true-disposing God,
How do I thank thee that this carnal cur
Preys on the issue of his mother's body
And makes her pew-fellow with others' moan!
Duch. O Harry's wife, triumph not in my woes!
God witness with me, I have wept for thine. *60*
Q. Mar. Bear with me; I am hungry for revenge,
And now I cloy me with beholding it.
Thy Edward he is dead, that stabb'd my Edward;
Thy other Edward dead, to quit my Edward;
Young York he is but boot, because both
        they
Match not the high perfection of my loss:
Thy Clarence he is dead that kill'd my Edward;
And the beholders of this tragic play,
The adulterate Hastings, Rivers, Vaughan,
        Grey,
Untimely smother'd in their dusky graves. *70*
Richard yet lives, hell's black intelligencer,
Only reserved their factor, to buy souls
And send them thither: but at hand, at hand,
Ensues his piteous and unpitied end:
Earth gapes, hell burns, fiends roar, saints pray,
To have him suddenly convey'd away.
Cancel his bond of life, dear God, I pray,
That I may live to say, "The dog is dead!"
Q. Eliz. O, thou didst prophesy the time
        would come
That I should wish for thee to help me curse *80*
That bottled spider, that foul bunch-back'd toad!
Q. Mar. I call'd thee then vain flourish of my
        fortune;
I call'd thee then poor shadow, painted queen;
The presentation of but what I was;
The flattering index of a direful pageant;

One heaved a-high, to be hurl'd down below;
A mother only mock'd with two sweet babes;
A dream of what thou wert, a breath, a bubble,
A sign of dignity, a garish flag,
To be the aim of every dangerous shot;   90
A queen in jest, only to fill the scene.
Where is thy husband now? where be thy
    brothers?
Where are thy children? wherein dost thou joy?
Who sues to thee and cries "God save the
    Queen"?
Where be the bending peers that flatter'd thee?
Where be the thronging troops that follow'd thee?
Decline all this, and see what now thou art:
For happy wife, a most distressed widow;
For joyful mother, one that wails the name;
For queen, a very caitiff crown'd with care;   100
For one being sued to, one that humbly sues;
For one that scorn'd at me, now scorn'd of me;
For one being fear'd of all, now fearing one;
For one commanding all, obey'd of none.
Thus hath the course of justice wheel'd about,
And left thee but a very prey to time;
Having no more but thought of what thou wert,
To torture thee the more, being what thou art.
Thou didst usurp my place, and dost thou not
Usurp the just proportion of my sorrow?   110
Now thy proud neck bears half my burthen'd
    yoke;
From which even here I slip my weary neck,
And leave the burthen of it all on thee.
Farewell, York's wife, and queen of sad
    mischance:
These English woes will make me smile in
    France.
  Q. Eliz. O thou well skill'd in curses, stay
    awhile,
And teach me how to curse mine enemies!
  Q. Mar. Forbear to sleep the nights, and fast
    the days;
Compare dead happiness with living woe;
Think that thy babes were fairer than they were,
And he that slew them fouler than he is: 121
Bettering thy loss makes the bad causer worse:
Revolving this will teach thee how to curse.
  Q. Eliz. My words are dull; O, quicken them
    with thine!
  Q. Mar. Thy woes will make them sharp and
    pierce like mine.   [*Exit.*
  Duch. Why should calamity be full of words?
  Q. Eliz. Windy attorneys to their client woes,
Airy succeeders of intestate joys,
Poor breathing orators of miseries!
Let them have scope: though what they do
    impart   130
Help not at all, yet do they ease the heart.

  Duch. If so, then be not tongue-tied: go with me,
And in the breath of bitter words let's smother
My damned son, which thy two sweet sons
    smother'd.
I hear his drum: be copious in exclaims.

    Enter KING RICHARD, *marching, with drums
            and trumpets.*

  K. Rich. Who intercepts my expedition?
  Duch. O, she that might have intercepted thee,
By strangling thee in her accursed womb,
From all the slaughters, wretch, that thou hast
    done!
  Q. Eliz. Hidest thou that forehead with a
    golden crown,   140
Where should be graven, if that right were right,
The slaughter of the prince that owed that
    crown,
And the dire death of my two sons and brothers?
Tell me, thou villain slave, where are my
    children?
  Duch. Thou toad, thou toad, where is thy
    brother Clarence?
And little Ned Plantagenet, his son?
  Q. Eliz. Where is kind Hastings, Rivers,
    Vaughan, Grey?
  K. Rich. A flourish, trumpets! strike alarum,
    drums!
Let not the heavens hear these tell-tale women
Rail on the Lord's anointed: strike, I say!   150
    Flourish. Alarums.
Either be patient, and entreat me fair,
Or with the clamorous report of war
Thus will I drown your exclamations.
  Duch. Art thou my son?
  K. Rich. Ay, I thank God, my father, and
    yourself.
  Duch. Then patiently hear my impatience.
  K. Rich. Madam, I have a touch of your
    condition,
Which cannot brook the accent of reproof.
  Duch. O, let me speak!
  K. Rich.   Do then; but I'll not hear.   159
  Duch. I will be mild and gentle in my speech.
  K. Rich. And brief, good mother; for I am in
    haste.
  Duch. Art thou so hasty? I have stay'd for thee,
God knows, in anguish, pain, and agony.
  K. Rich. And came I not at last to comfort you?
  Duch. No, by the holy rood, thou know'st it
    well,
Thou camest on earth to make the earth my hell
A grievous burthen was thy birth to me;
Tetchy and wayward was thy infancy;
Thy school-days frightful, desperate, wild, and
    furious,

Thy prime of manhood daring, bold, and
  venturous,   *170*
Thy age confirm'd, proud, subtle, bloody,
  treacherous,
More mild, but yet more harmful, kind in hatred:
What comfortable hour canst thou name,
That ever graced me in thy company?
  K. Rich. Faith, none, but Humphrey Hour,
  that call'd your Grace
To breakfast once forth of my company.
If I be so disgracious in your sight,
Let me march on, and not offend your Grace.
Strike up the drum.
  Duch.   I prithee, hear me speak.
  K. Rich. You speak too bitterly.
  Duch.   Hear me a word;   *180*
For I shall never speak to thee again.
  K. Rich. So.
  Duch. Either thou wilt die, by God's just
  ordinance,
Ere from this war thou turn a conqueror,
Or I with grief and extreme age shall perish
And never look upon thy face again.
Therefore take with thee my most heavy curse;
Which in the day of battle tire thee more
Than all the complete armour that thou wear'st!
My prayers on the adverse party fight;   *190*
And there the little souls of Edward's children
Whisper the spirits of thine enemies
And promise them success and victory.
Bloody thou art, bloody will be thy end;
Shame serves thy life and doth thy death attend.
                              [*Exit.*
  Q. Eliz. Though far more cause, yet much less
  spirit to curse
Abides in me; I say amen to all.
  K. Rich. Stay, madam; I must speak a word
  with you.
  Q. Eliz. I have no more sons of the royal
  blood   *199*
For thee to murder: for my daughters, Richard,
They shall be praying nuns, not weeping queens;
And therefore level not to hit their lives.
  K. Rich. You have a daughter call'd Elizabeth,
Virtuous and fair, royal and gracious.
  Q. Eliz. And she must die for this? O, let her
  live,
And I'll corrupt her manners, stain her beauty;
Slander myself as false to Edward's bed;
Throw over her the veil of infamy:
So she may live unscarr'd of bleeding slaughter,
I will confess she was not Edward's daughter.
  K. Rich. Wrong not her birth, she is of royal
  blood.   *211*
  Q. Eliz. To save her life, I'll say she is not so.
  K. Rich. Her life is only safest in her birth.

  Q. Eliz. And only in that safety died her
  brothers.
  K. Rich. Lo, at their births good stars were
  opposite.
  Q. Eliz. No, to their lives bad friends were
  contrary.
  K. Rich. All unavoided is the doom of destiny.
  Q. Eliz. True, when avoided grace makes
  destiny:
My babes were destined to a fairer death,
If grace had bless'd thee with a fairer life.   *220*
  K. Rich. You speak as if that I had slain my
  cousins.
  Q. Eliz. Cousins, indeed; and by their uncle
  cozen'd
Of comfort, kingdom, kindred, freedom, life.
Whose hand soever lanced their tender hearts,
Thy head, all indirectly, gave direction:
No doubt the murderous knife was dull and blunt
Till it was whetted on thy stone-hard heart,
To revel in the entrails of my lambs.
But that still use of grief makes wild grief tame,
My tongue should to thy ears not name my boys
Till that my nails were anchor'd in thine eyes;
And I, in such a desperate bay of death,
Like a poor bark, of sails and tackling reft,
Rush all to pieces on thy rock bosom.
  K. Rich. Madam, so thrive I in my enterprise
And dangerous success of bloody wars,
As I intend more good to you and yours
Than ever you or yours were by me wrong'd!
  Q. Eliz. What good is cover'd with the face of
  heaven,
To be discover'd, that can do me good?   *240*
  K. Rich. The advancement of your children,
  gentle lady.
  Q. Eliz. Up to some scaffold, there to lose
  their heads?
  K. Rich. No, to the dignity and height of
  honour,
The high imperial type of this earth's glory.
  Q. Eliz. Flatter my sorrows with report of it;
Tell me what state, what dignity, what honour,
Canst thou demise to any child of mine?
  K. Rich. Even all I have; yea, and myself and
  all,
Will I withal endow a child of thine;
So in the Lethe of thy angry soul   *250*
Thou drown the sad remembrance of those
  wrongs
Which thou supposest I have done to thee.
  Q. Eliz. Be brief, lest that the process of thy
  kindness
Last longer telling than thy kindness' date.
  K. Rich. Then know, that from my soul I love
  thy daughter.

Q. Eliz. My daughter's mother thinks it with
   her soul.

K. Rich. What do you think?

Q. Eliz. That thou dost love my daughter from
   thy soul:
So from thy soul's love didst thou love her
   brothers;   *259*
And from my heart's love I do thank thee for it.

K. Rich. Be not so hasty to confound my
   meaning:
I mean, that with my soul I love thy daughter,
And mean to make her queen of England.

Q. Eliz. Say then, who dost thou mean shall
   be her king?

K. Rich. Even he that makes her queen: who
   should be else?

Q. Eliz. What, thou?

K. Rich. I, even I: what think you of it,
   madam?

Q. Eliz. How canst thou woo her?

K. Rich.   That would I learn of you,
As one that are best acquainted with her humour.

Q. Eliz. And wilt thou learn of me?

K. Rich.   Madam, with all my heart.   *270*

Q. Eliz. Send to her, by the man that slew her
   brothers,
A pair of bleeding hearts; thereon engrave
Edward and York; then haply she will weep:
Therefore present to her—as sometime Margaret
Did to thy father, steep'd in Rutland's blood—
A handkerchief; which, say to her, did drain
The purple sap from her sweet brother's body,
And bid her dry her weeping eyes therewith.
If this inducement force her not to love,
Send her a story of thy noble acts;   *280*
Tell her thou madest away her uncle Clarence,
Her uncle Rivers; yea, and, for her sake,
Madest quick conveyance with her good aunt
   Anne.

K. Rich. Come, come, you mock me; this is
   not the way
To win your daughter.

Q. Eliz.   There is no other way;
Unless thou couldst put on some other shape
And not be Richard that hath done all this.

K. Rich. Say that I did all this for love of her.

Q. Eliz. Nay, then indeed she cannot choose
   but hate thee,
Having bought love with such a bloody spoil.

K. Rich. Look, what is done cannot be now
   amended: *291*
Men shall deal unadvisedly sometimes,
Which after hours give leisure to repent.
If I did take the kingdom from your sons,
To make amends, I'll give it to your daughter.
If I have kill'd the issue of your womb,

To quicken your increase, I will beget
Mine issue of your blood upon your daughter:
A grandam's name is little less in love
Than is the doting title of a mother;   *300*
They are as children but one step below,
Even of your mettle, of your very blood;
Of all one pain, save for a night of groans
Endured of her, for whom you bid like sor-
   row,
Your children were vexation to your youth,
But mine shall be a comfort to your age.
The loss you have is but a son being king,
And by that loss your daughter is made queen.
I cannot make you what amends I would,
Therefore accept such kindness as I can.   *310*
Dorset your son, that with a fearful soul
Leads discontented steps in foreign soil,
This fair alliance quickly shall call home
To high promotions and great dignity:
The king, that calls your beauteous daughter
   wife,
Familiarly shall call thy Dorset brother;
Again shall you be mother to a king,
And all the ruins of distressful times
Repair'd with double riches of content.
What! we have many goodly days to see: *320*
The liquid drops of tears that you have shed
Shall come again, transform'd to orient pearl,
Advantaging their loan with interest
Of ten times double gain of happiness.
Go, then, my mother, to thy daughter go;
Make bold her bashful years with your
   experience;
Prepare her ears to hear a wooer's tale;
Put in her tender heart the aspiring flame
Of golden sovereignty; acquaint the princess
With the sweet silent hours of marriage joys:
And when this arm of mine hath chastised   *331*
The petty rebel, dull-brain'd Buckingham,
Bound with triumphant garlands will I come
And lead thy daughter to a conqueror's bed;
To whom I will retail my conquest won,
And she shall be sole victress, Cæsar's Cæsar.

Q. Eliz. What were I best to say? her father's
   brother
Would be her lord? or shall I say, her uncle?
Or, he that slew her brothers and her uncles?
Under what title shall I woo for thee,   *340*
That God, the law, my honour, and her love,
Can make seem pleasing to her tender years?

K. Rich. Infer fair England's peace by this
   alliance.

Q. Eliz. Which she shall purchase with still
   lasting war.

K. Rich. Say that the king, which may command,
   entreats.

Q. Eliz. That at her hands which the king's
 King forbids.
K. Rich. Say, she shall be a high and mighty
 queen.
Q. Eliz. To wail the title, as her mother doth.
K. Rich. Say, I will love her everlastingly.
Q. Eliz. But how long shall that title "ever"
 last?   *350*
K. Rich. Sweetly in force unto her fair life's end.
Q. Eliz. But how long fairly shall her sweet
 life last?
K. Rich. So long as heaven and nature lengthens
 it.
Q. Eliz. So long as hell and Richard likes of it.
K. Rich. Say, I, her sovereign, am her subject
 love.
Q. Eliz. But she, your subject, loathes such
 sovereignty.
K. Rich. Be eloquent in my behalf to her.
Q. Eliz. An honest tale speeds best being
 plainly told.
K. Rich. Then in plain terms tell her my
 loving tale.
Q. Eliz. Plain and not honest is too harsh a
 style.   *360*
K. Rich. Your reasons are too shallow and too
 quick.
Q. Eliz. O no, my reasons are too deep and
 dead;
Too deep and dead, poor infants, in their grave.
K. Rich. Harp not on that string, madam; that
 is past.
Q. Eliz. Harp on it still shall I till heartstrings
 break.
K. Rich. Now, by my George, my Garter, and
 my crown—
Q. Eliz. Profaned, dishonour'd, and the third
 usurp'd.
K. Rich. I swear—
Q. Eliz.   By nothing; for this is no oath:
The George, profaned, hath lost his holy honour;
The Garter, blemish'd, pawn'd his knightly
 virtue;   *370*
The crown, usurp'd, disgraced his kingly glory.
If something thou wilt swear to be believed,
Swear then by something that thou hast not
 wrong'd.
K. Rich. Now, by the world—
Q. Eliz.   'Tis full of thy foul wrongs.
K. Rich. My father's death—
Q. Eliz.   Thy life hath that dishonour'd.
K. Rich. Then, by myself—
Q. Eliz.   Thyself thyself misusest.
K. Rich. Why then, by God—
Q. Eliz.   God's wrong is most of all.
If thou hadst fear'd to break an oath by Him,

The unity the king thy brother made
Had not been broken, nor my brother slain: *380*
If thou hadst fear'd to break an oath by Him,
The imperial metal, circling now thy brow,
Had graced the tender temples of my child,
And both the princes had been breathing here,
Which now, two tender playfellows for dust,
Thy broken faith hath made a prey for worms.
What canst thou swear by now?
 K. Rich.   The time to come.
 Q. Eliz. That thou hast wronged in the time
 o'erpast;
For I myself have many tears to wash *389*
Hereafter time, for time past wrong'd by thee.
The children live, whose parents thou hast
 slaughter'd,
Ungovern'd youths, to wail it in their age;
The parents live, whose children thou hast
 butcher'd,
Old wither'd plants, to wail it with their age.
Swear not by time to come; for that thou hast
Misused ere used, by time misused o'erpast.
 K. Rich. As I intend to prosper and repent,
So thrive I in my dangerous attempt
Of hostile arms! myself myself confound!
Heaven and fortune bar me happy hours! *400*
Day, yield me not thy light; nor, night, thy rest!
Be opposite all planets of good luck
To my proceedings, if, with pure heart's love,
Immaculate devotion, holy thoughts,
I tender not thy beauteous princely daughter!
In her consists my happiness and thine;
Without her, follows to this land and me,
To thee, herself, and many a Christian soul,
Death, desolation, ruin and decay:
It cannot be avoided but by this;   *410*
It will not be avoided but by this.
Therefore, good mother—I must call you so—
Be the attorney of my love to her:
Plead what I will be, not what I have been;
Not my deserts, but what I will deserve:
Urge the necessity and state of times,
And be not peevish-fond in great designs.
 Q. Eliz. Shall I be tempted of the devil thus?
 K. Rich. Ay, if the devil tempt thee to do good.
 Q. Eliz. Shall I forget myself to be myself? *420*
 K. Rich. Ay, if yourself's remembrance wrong
 yourself.
 Q. Eliz. But thou didst kill my children.
 K. Rich. But in your daughter's womb I bury
 them:
Where in that nest of spicery they shall breed
Selves of themselves, to your recomforture.
 Q. Eliz. Shall I go win my daughter to thy will?
 K. Rich. And be a happy mother by the deed.
 Q. Eliz. I go. Write to me very shortly,

And you shall understand from me her mind.
  K. Rich. Bear her my true love's kiss; and so,
    farewell.   [*Exit* QUEEN ELIZABETH.   *430*
Relenting fool, and shallow, changing woman!

Enter RATCLIFF; CATESBY *following*.

How now! what news?
  Rat. My gracious sovereign, on the western
    coast
Rideth a puissant navy; to the shore
Throng many doubtful hollow-hearted friends,
Unarm'd, and unresolved to beat them back:
'Tis thought that Richmond is their admiral;
And there they hull, expecting but the aid
Of Buckingham to welcome them ashore.
  K. Rich. Some light-foot friend post to the
    Duke of Norfolk: *440*
Ratcliff, thyself, or Catesby; where is he?
  Cate. Here, my lord.
  K. Rich. Fly to the Duke: [*To* RATCLIFF] Post
    thou to Salisbury:
When thou comest thither—[*To* CATESBY] Dull,
    unmindful villain,
Why stand'st thou still, and go'st not to the
    Duke?
  Cate. First, mighty sovereign, let me know
    your mind,
What from your Grace I shall deliver to him.
  K. Rich. O, true, good Catesby: bid him levy
    straight
The greatest strength and power he can make,
And meet me presently at Salisbury.   *450*
  Cate. I go.   [*Exit.*
  Rat. What is't your Highness' pleasure I shall do
At Salisbury?
  K. Rich. Why, what wouldst thou do there
    before I go?
  Rat. Your Highness told me I should post
    before.
  K. Rich. My mind is changed, sir, my mind is
    changed.

Enter LORD STANLEY.

How now, what news with you?
  Stan. None good, my lord, to please you with
    the hearing;
Nor none so bad, but it may well be told.
  K. Rich. Hoyday, a riddle! neither good nor
    bad!   *460*
Why dost thou run so many mile about,
When thou mayst tell thy tale a nearer way?
Once more, what news?
  Stan.   Richmond is on the seas.
  K. Rich. There let him sink, and be the seas on
    him!
White-liver'd runagate, what doth he there?

  Stan. I know not, mighty sovereign, but by
    guess.
  K. Rich. Well, sir, as you guess, as you guess?
  Stan. Stirr'd up by Dorset, Buckingham, and
    Ely,
He makes for England, there to claim the crown.
  K. Rich. Is the chair empty? is the sword
    unsway'd?   *470*
Is the King dead? the empire unpossess'd?
What heir of York is there alive but we?
And who is England's king but great York's
    heir?
Then, tell me, what doth he upon the sea?
  Stan. Unless for that, my liege, I cannot guess.
  K. Rich. Unless for that he comes to be your
    liege,
You cannot guess wherefore the Welshman
    comes.
Thou wilt revolt, and fly to him, I fear.
  Stan. No, mighty liege, therefore mistrust me
    not.
  K. Rich. Where is thy power, then, to beat
    him back?   *480*
Where are thy tenants and thy followers?
Are they not now upon the western shore,
Safe-conducting the rebels from their ships?
  Stan. No, my good lord, my friends are in the
    north.
  K. Rich. Cold friends to Richard: what do they
    in the north,
When they should serve their sovereign in the
    west?
  Stan. They have not been commanded, mighty
    sovereign:
Please it your majesty to give me leave,
I'll muster up my friends, and meet your Grace
Where and what time your Majesty shall please.
  K. Rich. Ay, ay, thou wouldst be gone to join
    with Richmond:
I will not trust you, sir.
  Stan.   Most mighty sovereign,
You have no cause to hold my friendship doubtful:
I never was nor never will be false.
  K. Rich. Well,
Go muster men; but, hear you, leave behind
Your son, George Stanley: look your faith be
    firm,
Or else his head's assurance is but frail.
  Stan. So deal with him as I prove true to you.
    [*Exit.*

Enter a MESSENGER.

  Mess. My gracious sovereign, now in Devon-
    shire,   *500*
As I by friends am well advertised,
Sir Edward Courtney, and the haughty prelate

Bishop of Exeter, his brother there,
With many moe confederates, are in arms.

Enter SECOND MESSENGER.

2nd Mess. My liege, in Kent the Guildfords are
in arms;
And every hour more competitors
Flock to their aid, and still their power increaseth.

Enter THIRD MESSENGER.

3rd Mess. My lord, the army of the Duke of
Buckingham—
K. Rich. Out on you, owls! nothing but songs
of death? [He striketh him.]
Take that, until thou bring me better news.   *510*
3rd Mess. The news I have to tell your Majesty
Is that by sudden floods and fall of waters
Buckingham's army is dispersed and scatter'd;
And he himself wander'd away alone,
No man knows whither.
K. Rich.   I cry thee mercy:
There is my purse to cure that blow of thine.
Hath any well-advised friend proclaim'd
Reward to him that brings the traitor in?
3rd Mess. Such proclamation hath been made,
my liege.

Enter FOURTH MESSENGER.

4th Mess. Sir Thomas Lovel and Lord
Marquis Dorset,   *520*
'Tis said, my liege, in Yorkshire are in arms.
Yet this good comfort bring I to your Grace,
The Breton navy is dispersed by tempest:
Richmond, in Dorsetshire, sent out a boat
Unto the shore, to ask those on the banks
If they were his assistants, yea or no;
Who answer'd him, they came from Buckingham
Upon his party: he, mistrusting them,
Hoised sail and made away for Brittany.
K. Rich. March on, march on, since we are
up in arms;   *530*
If not to fight with foreign enemies,
Yet to beat down these rebels here at home.

Re-enter CATESBY.

Cate. My liege, the Duke of Buckingham is
taken;
That is the best news: that the Earl of Richmond
Is with a mighty power landed at Milford,
Is colder tidings, yet they must be told.
K. Rich. Away towards Salisbury! while we
reason here,
A royal battle might be won and lost:
Some one take order Buckingham be brought
To Salisbury; the rest march on with me.   *540*
                            [*Flourish. Exeunt.*

SCENE V. *Lord Stanley's house*

Enter STANLEY *and* SIR CHRISTOPHER URSWICK.
Stan. Sir Christopher, tell Richmond this from
me:
That in the sty of this most bloody boar
My son George Stanley is frank'd up in hold:
If I revolt, off goes young George's head;
The fear of that withholds my present aid.
But, tell me, where is princely Richmond now?
Chris. At Pembroke, or at Ha'rford-west, in
Wales.
Stan. What men of name resort to him?
Chris. Sir Walter Herbert, a renowned soldier;
Sir Gilbert Talbot, Sir William Stanley;   *10*
Oxford, redoubted Pembroke, Sir James Blunt,
And Rice ap Thomas, with a valiant crew;
And many moe of noble fame and worth:
And towards London they do bend their course,
If by the way they be not fought withal.
Stan. Return unto thy lord; commend me to him:
Tell him the Queen hath heartily consented
He shall espouse Elizabeth her daughter.
These letters will resolve him of my mind.
Farewell.   [*Exeunt.*   *20*

ACT V

SCENE I. *Salisbury: an open place*

Enter the SHERIFF, *and* BUCKINGHAM, *with
halberds, led to execution.*

Buck. Will not King Richard let me speak
with him?
Sher. No, my good lord; therefore be patient.
Buck. Hastings, and Edward's children, Rivers,
Grey,
Holy King Henry and thy fair son Edward,
Vaughan, and all that have miscarried
By underhand corrupted foul injustice,
If that your moody discontented souls
Do through the clouds behold this present hour,
Even for revenge mock my destruction!
This is All-Souls' day, fellows, is it not?   *10*
Sher. It is, my lord.
Buck. Why, then All-Souls' day is my body's
doomsday.
This is the day that, in King Edward's time,
I wish'd might fall on me, when I was found
False to his children or his wife's allies;
This is the day wherein I wish'd to fall
By the false faith of him I trusted most;
This, this All-Souls' day to my fearful soul
Is the determined respite of my wrongs:
That high All-Seer that I dallied with   *20*
Hath turn'd my feigned prayer on my head
And given in earnest what I begg'd in jest.

Thus doth he force the swords of wicked men
To turn their own points on their masters'
    bosoms:
Now Margaret's curse is fallen upon my head;
"When he," quoth she, "shall split thy heart
    with sorrow,
Remember Margaret was a prophetess."
Come, sirs, convey me to the block of shame;
Wrong hath but wrong, and blame the due of
    blame.   [*Exeunt.*

SCENE II. *The camp near Tamworth*

Enter RICHMOND, OXFORD, BLUNT, HERBERT,
    and others, with drum and colours.

Richm. Fellows in arms, and my most loving
    friends,
Bruised underneath the yoke of tyranny,
Thus far into the bowels of the land
Have we march'd on without impediment;
And here receive we from our father Stanley
Lines of fair comfort and encouragement.
The wretched, bloody, and usurping boar,
That spoil'd your summer fields and fruitful
    vines,
Swills your warm blood like wash, and makes his
    trough
In your embowell'd bosoms, this foul swine   *10*
Lies now even in the centre of this isle,
Near to the town of Leicester, as we learn:
From Tamworth thither is but one day's march.
In God's name, cheerly on, courageous friends,
To reap the harvest of perpetual peace
By this one bloody trial of sharp war.
Oxf. Every man's conscience is a thousand
    swords
To fight against that bloody homicide.
Herb. I doubt not but his friends will fly to us.
Blunt. He hath no friends but who are friends
    for fear,   *20*
Which in his greatest need will shrink from him.
Richm. All for our vantage. Then, in God's
    name, march:
True hope is swift and flies with swallow's
    wings;
Kings it makes gods and meaner creatures kings.
                            [*Exeunt.*

SCENE III. *Bosworth Field*

Enter KING RICHARD *in arms, with* NORFOLK,
    the EARL OF SURREY, *and others.*

K. Rich. Here pitch our tents, even here in
    Bosworth field.
My Lord of Surrey, why look you so sad?
Sur. My heart is ten times lighter than my looks.
K. Rich. My Lord of Norfolk—
Nor.   Here, most gracious liege.

K. Rich. Norfolk, we must have knocks; ha!
    must we not?
Nor. We must both give and take, my gracious
    lord.
K. Rich. Up with my tent there! here will I
    lie to-night;
But where to-morrow? Well, all's one for that.
Who hath descried the number of the foe?
Nor. Six or seven thousand is their utmost
    power.   *10*
K. Rich. Why, our battalion trebles that
    account:
Besides, the King's name is a tower of strength,
Which they upon the adverse party want.
Up with my tent there! Valiant gentlemen,
Let us survey the vantage of the field;
Call for some men of sound direction:
Let's want no discipline, make no delay;
For, lords, to-morrow is a busy day.   [*Exeunt.*

Enter, on the other side of the field, RICHMOND, *Sir*
    William Brandon, OXFORD, DORSET, BLUNT, *and*
    others. Some of the Soldiers pitch Richmond's
    tent.

Richm. The weary sun hath made a golden set,
And, by the bright track of his fiery car,   *20*
Gives signal of a goodly day to-morrow.
Sir William Brandon, you shall bear my standard.
Give me some ink and paper in my tent:
I'll draw the form and model of our battle,
Limit each leader to his several charge,
And part in just proportion our small strength.
My Lord of Oxford, you, Sir William Brandon,
And you, Sir Walter Herbert, stay with me.
The Earl of Pembroke keeps his regiment:
Good Captain Blunt, bear my good-night to him,
And by the second hour in the morning   *31*
Desire the Earl to see me in my tent:
Yet one thing more, good Blunt, before thou go'st,
Where is Lord Stanley quarter'd, dost thou
    know?
Blunt. Unless I have mista'en his colours
    much,
Which well I am assured I have not done,
His regiment lies half a mile at least
South from the mighty power of the King.
Richm. If without peril it be possible,   *39*
Good captain Blunt, bear my good-night to him,
And give him from me this most needful scroll.
Blunt. Upon my life, my lord, I'll undertake it;
And so, God give you quiet rest to-night!
Richm. Good night, good Captain Blunt.
    Come, gentlemen,
Let us consult upon to-morrow's business:
In to our tent; the air is raw and cold.
              [*They withdraw into the tent.*

Enter, to his tent, KING RICHARD, NORFOLK,
RATCLIFF, CATESBY, *and others.*

K. Rich. What is't o'clock?

Cate.   It's supper-time, my lord;
It's nine o'clock.

K. Rich.   I will not sup to-night.
Give me some ink and paper.
What, is my beaver easier than it was?   50
And all my armour laid into my tent?

Cate. It is, my liege; and all things are in
readiness.

K. Rich. Good Norfolk, hie thee to thy charge;
Use careful watch, choose trusty sentinels.

Nor. I go, my lord.

K. Rich. Stir with the lark to-morrow, gentle
Norfolk.

Nor. I warrant you, my lord.   [*Exit.*

K. Rich. Catesby!

Cate. My lord?

K. Rich.   Send out a pursuivant at arms
To Stanley's regiment; bid him bring his power
Before sunrising, lest his son George fall   61
Into the blind cave of eternal night.

[*Exit* CATESBY.

Fill me a bowl of wine. Give me a watch.
Saddle white Surrey for the field to-morrow.
Look that my staves be sound, and not too heavy.
Ratcliff!

Rat. My lord?

K. Rich. Saw'st thou the melancholy Lord
Northumberland?

Rat. Thomas the Earl of Surrey, and himself,
Much about cock-shut time, from troop to troop
Went through the army, cheering up the
soldiers.   71

K. Rich. So, I am satisfied. Give me a bowl of
wine:
I have not that alacrity of spirit
Nor cheer of mind that I was wont to have.
Set it down. Is ink and paper ready?

Rat. It is, my lord.

K. Rich.   Bid my guard watch; leave me.
Ratcliff, about the mid of night come to my tent
And help to arm me. Leave me, I say.

[*Exeunt* RATCLIFF *and other Attendants.*

Enter STANLEY *to* RICHMOND *in his tent, Lords
and others attending.*

Stan. Fortune and victory sit on thy helm!

Richm. All comfort that the dark night can
afford   80
Be to thy person, noble father-in-law!
Tell me, how fares our loving mother?

Stan. I, by attorney, bless thee from thy mother,
Who prays continually for Richmond's good:

So much for that. The silent hours steal on,
And flaky darkness breaks within the east.
In brief—for so the season bids us be—
Prepare thy battle early in the morning,
And put thy fortune to the arbitrement
Of bloody strokes and mortal-staring war.   90
I, as I may—that which I would I cannot—
With best advantage will deceive the time,
And aid thee in this doubtful shock of arms:
But on thy side I may not be too forward,
Lest, being seen, thy brother, tender George,
Be executed in his father's sight.
Farewell: the leisure and the fearful time
Cuts off the ceremonious vows of love
And ample interchange of sweet discourse,
Which so long sunder'd friends should dwell
upon:
God give us leisure for these rites of love!   101
Once more, adieu: be valiant, and speed well!

Richm. Good lords, conduct him to his regi-
ment:
I'll strive with troubled thoughts to take a nap,
Lest leaden slumber peise me down to-morrow,
When I should mount with wings of victory:
Once more, good night, kind lords and gentlemen.

[*Exeunt all but* RICHMOND.

O Thou, whose captain I account myself,
Look on my forces with a gracious eye;
Put in their hands thy bruising irons of wrath,   110
That they may crush down with a heavy fall
The usurping helmets of our adversaries!
Make us thy ministers of chastisement,
That we may praise thee in the victory!
To thee I do commend my watchful soul,
Ere I let fall the windows of mine eyes:
Sleeping and waking, O, defend me still!

[*Sleeps.*

Enter the GHOST OF PRINCE EDWARD, *son to*
HENRY THE SIXTH.

Ghost. [*To* RICHARD] Let me sit heavy on thy
soul to-morrow!
Think, how thou stab'dst me in my prime of
youth
At Tewksbury: despair, therefore, and die!   120
[*To* RICHMOND] Be cheerful, Richmond; for the
wronged souls
Of butcher'd princes fight in thy behalf:
King Henry's issue, Richmond, comforts thee.

Enter the GHOST OF HENRY THE SIXTH.

Ghost. [*To* RICHARD] When I was mortal, my
anointed body
By thee was punched full of deadly holes:
Think on the Tower and me: despair, and die!
Harry the Sixth bids thee despair and die!

[*To* RICHMOND] Virtuous and holy, be thou
    conqueror!
Harry, that prophesied thou shouldst be king,
Doth comfort thee in sleep: live, and flourish!

Enter the GHOST OF CLARENCE.

Ghost. [*To* RICHARD] Let me sit heavy on thy
    soul to-morrow!   *131*
I, that was wash'd to death with fulsome wine,
Poor Clarence, by thy guile betrayed to death!
To-morrow in the battle think on me
And fall thy edgeless sword: despair, and die!
[*To* RICHMOND] Thou offspring of the house of
    Lancaster,
The wronged heirs of York do pray for thee:
Good angels guard thy battle! live, and flourish!

Enter the GHOSTS OF RIVERS, GREY, *and*
    VAUGHAN.

Ghost of R. [*To* RICHARD] Let me sit heavy on
    thy soul to-morrow,
Rivers, that died at Pomfret! despair, and die!
Ghost of G. [*To* RICHARD] Think upon Grey,
    and let thy soul despair!   *141*
Ghost of V. [*To* RICHARD] Think upon
    Vaughan and with guilty fear
Let fall thy lance: despair, and die!
All. [*To* RICHMOND] Awake, and think our
    wrongs in Richard's bosom
Will conquer him! awake, and win the day!

Enter the GHOST OF HASTINGS.

Ghost. [*To* RICHARD] Bloody and guilty,
    guiltily awake,
And in a bloody battle end thy days!
Think on Lord Hastings: despair, and die!
[*To* RICHMOND] Quiet untroubled soul, awake,
    awake!
Arm, fight, and conquer, for fair England's sake!

Enter the GHOSTS OF THE TWO YOUNG PRINCES.

Ghosts. [*To* RICHARD] Dream on thy cousins
    smother'd in the Tower: *151*
Let us be lead within thy bosom, Richard,
And weigh thee down to ruin, shame, and death!
Thy nephews' souls bid thee despair and die!
[*To* RICHMOND] Sleep, Richmond, sleep in
    peace, and wake in joy;
Good angels guard thee from the boar's annoy!
Live, and beget a happy race of kings!
Edward's unhappy sons do bid thee flourish.

Enter the GHOST OF LADY ANNE.

Ghost. [*To* RICHARD] Richard, thy wife, that
    wretched Anne thy wife,
That never slept a quiet hour with thee,   *160*

Now fills thy sleep with perturbations:
To-morrow in the battle think on me,
And fall thy edgeless sword: despair, and die!
[*To* RICHMOND] Thou quiet soul, sleep thou a
    quiet sleep;
Dream of success and happy victory!
Thy adversary's wife doth pray for thee.

Enter the GHOST OF BUCKINGHAM.

Ghost. [*To* RICHARD] The first was I that
    help'd thee to the crown;
The last was I that felt thy tyranny:
O, in the battle think on Buckingham,
And die in terror of thy guiltiness!   *170*
Dream on, dream on, of bloody deeds and death:
Fainting, despair; despairing, yield thy breath!
[*To* RICHMOND] I died for hope ere I could lend
    thee aid:
But cheer thy heart, and be thou not dismay'd:
God and good angels fight on Richmond's side;
And Richard falls in height of all his pride.
    [*The* GHOSTS *vanish.* KING RICHARD *starts*
        out of his dream.
K. Rich. Give me another horse: bind up my
    wounds.
Have mercy, Jesu!—Soft! I did but dream.
O coward conscience, how dost thou afflict
    me!
The lights burn blue. It is now dead midnight.
Cold fearful drops stand on my trembling flesh.
What do I fear? myself? there's none else by:
Richard loves Richard; that is, I am I.
Is there a murderer here? No. Yes, I am.
Then fly. What, from myself? Great reason
    why:
Lest I revenge. What, myself upon myself?
Alack, I love myself. Wherefore? for any good
That I myself have done unto myself?
O, no! alas, I rather hate myself
For hateful deeds committed by myself!   *190*
I am a villain: yet I lie, I am not.
Fool, of thyself speak well: fool, do not flatter.
My conscience hath a thousand several tongues,
And every tongue brings in a several tale,
And every tale condemns me for a villain.
Perjury, perjury, in the high'st degree;
Murder, stern murder, in the direst degree;
All several sins, all used in each degree,
Throng to the bar, crying all, "Guilty! guilty!"
I shall despair. There is no creature loves me;
And if I die, no soul shall pity me: *201*
Nay, wherefore should they, since that I myself
Find in myself no pity to myself?
Methought the souls of all that I had murder'd
Came to my tent; and every one did threat
To-morrow's vengeance on the head of Richard.

Enter RATCLIFF.

Rat. My lord!

K. Rich. 'Zounds! who is there?

Rat. Ratcliff, my lord; 'tis I. The early village-cock

Hath twice done salutation to the morn;   210
Your friends are up, and buckle on their armour.

K. Rich. O Ratcliff, I have dream'd a fearful dream!

What thinkest thou, will our friends prove all true?

Rat. No doubt, my lord.

K. Rich.   O Ratcliff, I fear, I fear—

Rat. Nay, good my lord, be not afraid of shadows.

K. Rich. By the apostle Paul, shadows to-night
Have struck more terror to the soul of Richard
Than can the substance of ten thousand soldiers
Armed in proof and led by shallow Richmond.
It is not yet near day. Come, go with me;   220
Under our tents I'll play the eaves-dropper,
To see if any mean to shrink from me.   [*Exeunt.*

Enter the LORDS *to* RICHMOND, *sitting in his tent.*

Lords. Good morrow, Richmond!

Richm. Cry mercy, lords and watchful gentlemen,

That you have ta'en a tardy sluggard here.

Lords. How have you slept, my lord?

Richm. The sweetest sleep and fairest-boding dreams

That ever enter'd in a drowsy head
Have I since your departure had, my lords.
Methought their souls, whose bodies Richard murder'd,   230
Came to my tent, and cried on victory:
I promise you, my soul is very jocund
In the remembrance of so fair a dream.
How far into the morning is it, lords?

Lords. Upon the stroke of four.

Richm. Why, then 'tis time to arm and give direction.

HIS ORATION TO HIS SOLDIERS

More than I have said, loving countrymen,
The leisure and enforcement of the time
Forbids to dwell upon: yet remember this,
God and our good cause fight upon our side;   240
The prayers of holy saints and wronged souls,
Like high-rear'd bulwarks, stand before our faces;
Richard except, those whom we fight against
Had rather have us win than him they follow:
For what is he they follow? truly, gentlemen,
A bloody tyrant and a homicide;
One raised in blood, and one in blood establish'd;

One that made means to come by what he hath,
And slaughter'd those that were the means to help him;

A base foul stone, made precious by the foil   250
Of England's chair, where he is falsely set;
One that hath ever been God's enemy:
Then, if you fight against God's enemy,
God will in justice ward you as his soldiers;
If you do sweat to put a tyrant down,
You sleep in peace, the tyrant being slain;
If you do fight against your country's foes,
Your country's fat shall pay your pains the hire;

If you do fight in safeguard of your wives,
Your wives shall welcome home the conquerors;
If you do free your children from the sword,   261
Your children's children quit it in your age.
Then, in the name of God and all these rights,
Advance your standards, draw your willing swords.

For me, the ransom of my bold attempt
Shall be this cold corpse on the earth's cold face;

But if I thrive, the gain of my attempt
The least of you shall share his part thereof.
Sound drums and trumpets boldly and cheer-fully;

God and Saint George! Richmond and victory!

            [*Exeunt.* 270

Re-enter KING RICHARD, RATCLIFF, *Attendants and Forces.*

K. Rich. What said Northumberland as touching Richmond?

Rat. That he was never trained up in arms.

K. Rich. He said the truth: and what said Surrey then?

Rat. He smiled and said, "The better for our purpose."

K. Rich. He was in the right; and so indeed it is. [*Clock striketh.*]

Tell the clock there. Give me a calendar.
Who saw the sun to-day?

Rat.   Not I, my lord.

K. Rich. Then he disdains to shine; for by the book

He should have braved the east an hour ago:
A black day will it be to somebody.   280
Ratcliff!

Rat. My lord?

K. Rich.   The sun will not be seen to-day;
The sky doth frown and lour upon our army.
I would these dewy tears were from the ground.
Not shine to-day! Why, what is that to me
More than to Richmond? for the selfsame heaven
That frowns on me looks sadly upon him.

Enter NORFOLK.

Nor. Arm, arm, my lord; the foe vaunts in the
   field.

K. Rich. Come, bustle, bustle, caparison my
   horse.
Call up Lord Stanley, bid him bring his power:
I will lead forth my soldiers to the plain,   *291*
And thus my battle shall be ordered:
My foreward shall be drawn out all in length,
Consisting equally of horse and foot;
Our archers shall be placed in the midst:
John Duke of Norfolk, Thomas Earl of Surrey,
Shall have the leading of this foot and horse.
They thus directed, we will follow
In the main battle, whose puissance on either
   side
Shall be well winged with our chiefest horse. *300*
This, and Saint George to boot! What think'st
   thou, Norfolk?

Nor. A good direction, warlike sovereign.
This found I on my tent this morning.
   He sheweth him a paper.

K. Rich. [*Reads*] "Jockey of Norfolk, be not
   too bold,
For Dickon thy master is bought and sold."
A thing devised by the enemy.
Go, gentlemen, every man unto his charge:
Let not our babbling dreams affright our
   souls:
Conscience is but a word that cowards use,
Devised at first to keep the strong in awe: *310*
Our strong arms be our conscience, swords our
   law.
March on, join bravely, let us to't pell-mell;
If not to heaven, then hand in hand to hell.

His oration to his Army

What shall I say more than I have inferr'd?
Remember whom you are to cope withal;
A sort of vagabonds, rascals, and runaways,
A scum of Bretons, and base lackey peasants,
Whom their o'er-cloyed country vomits
   forth
To desperate ventures and assured destruc-
   tion.
You sleeping safe, they bring to you unrest;   *320*
You having lands, and blest with beauteous
   wives,
They would restrain the one, distain the other.
And who doth lead them but a paltry fellow,
Long kept in Bretagne at our mother's cost?
A milk-sop, one that never in his life
Felt so much cold as over shoes in snow?
Let's whip these stragglers o'er the seas
   again;

Lash hence these overweening rags of France,
These famish'd beggars weary of their lives;
Who, but for dreaming on this fond exploit,   *330*
For want of means, poor rats, had hang'd them-
   selves:
If we be conquer'd, let men conquer us,
And not these bastard Bretons; whom our
   fathers
Have in their own land beaten, bobb'd, and
   thump'd,
And in record, left them the heirs of shame.
Shall these enjoy our lands? lie with our wives?
Ravish our daughters? [*Drum afar off.*] Hark!
   I hear their drum.
Fight! gentlemen of England! fight, bold yeomen!
Draw, archers, draw your arrows to the head!
Spur your proud horses hard, and ride in blood;
Amaze the welkin with your broken staves!   *341*

Enter a MESSENGER.

What says Lord Stanley? will he bring his
   power?

Mess. My lord, he doth deny to come.

K. Rich. Off with his son George's head!

Nor. My lord, the enemy is past the marsh:
After the battle let George Stanley die.

K. Rich. A thousand hearts are great within
   my bosom:
Advance our standards, set upon our foes;
Our ancient word of courage, fair Saint George,
Inspire us with the spleen of fiery dragons!   *350*
Upon them! Victory sits on our helms.
                           [*Exeunt.*

SCENE IV. *Another part of the field*

Alarum: excursions. Enter NORFOLK *and
forces fighting; to him* CATESBY.

Cate. Rescue, my Lord of Norfolk, rescue,
   rescue!
The King enacts more wonders than a man,
Daring an opposite to every danger:
His horse is slain, and all on foot he fights,
Seeking for Richmond in the throat of death.
Rescue, fair lord, or else the day is lost!

Alarums. Enter KING RICHARD.

K. Rich. A horse! a horse! my kingdom for a
   horse!

Cate. Withdraw, my lord; I'll help you to a
   horse.

K. Rich. Slave, I have set my life upon a cast
And I will stand the hazard of the die: *10*
I think there be six Richmonds in the field;
Five have I slain to-day instead of him.
A horse! a horse! my kingdom for a horse!
                           [*Exeunt.*

SCENE V. *Another part of the field*

Alarum. Enter RICHARD *and* RICHMOND; *they fight.*
RICHARD *is slain. Retreat and flourish. Re-enter*
RICHMOND, STANLEY *bearing the crown, with*
divers other Lords.

 Richm. God and your arms be praised, victorious
  friends;
The day is ours, the bloody dog is dead.
 Stan. Courageous Richmond, well hast thou
  acquit thee.
Lo, here, this long-usurped royalty
From the dead temples of this bloody wretch
Have I pluck'd off, to grace thy brows withal:
Wear it, enjoy it, and make much of it.
 Richm. Great God of heaven, say Amen to all!
But, tell me, is young George Stanley living?
 Stan. He is, my lord, and safe in Leicester
  town;   *10*
Whither, if it please you, we may now with-
  draw us.
 Richm. What men of name are slain on either
  side?
 Stan. John Duke of Norfolk, Walter Lord
  Ferrers,
Sir Robert Brakenbury, and Sir William Brandon.
 Richm. Inter their bodies as becomes their
  births:
Proclaim a pardon to the soldiers fled

That in submission will return to us:
And then, as we have ta'en the sacrament,
We will unite the white rose and the red:
Smile heaven upon this fair conjunction, *20*
That long have frown'd upon their enmity!
What traitor hears me, and says not amen?
England hath long been mad, and scarr'd herself;
The brother blindly shed the brother's blood,
The father rashly slaughter'd his own son,
The son, compell'd, been butcher to the sire:
All this divided York and Lancaster,
Divided in their dire division,
O, now, let Richmond and Elizabeth,
The true succeeders of each royal house, *30*
By God's fair ordinance conjoin together!
And let their heirs, God, if thy will be so,
Enrich the time to come with smooth-faced
  peace,
With smiling plenty and fair prosperous days!
Abate the edge of traitors, gracious Lord,
That would reduce these bloody days again
And make poor England weep in streams of
  blood!
Let them not live to taste land's increase
That would with treason wound this fair land's
  peace!
Now civil wounds are stopp'd, peace lives again:
That she may long live here, God say amen! *40*
               [Exeunt.

THE COMEDY OF ERRORS

DRAMATIS PERSONÆ

SOLINUS, DUKE OF EPHESUS.
ÆGEON, *a merchant of Syracuse*
ANTIPHOLUS OF EPHESUS | *twin brothers, and sons*
ANTIPHOLUS OF SYRACUSE | *of Ægeon and Æmilia*
DROMIO OF EPHESUS | *twin brothers, and attend-*
DROMIO OF SYRACUSE | *ants on the two Antipholuses*
BALTHAZAR, *a merchant*
ANGELO, *a goldsmith*
FIRST MERCHANT, *friend to Antipholus of
   Syracuse*
SECOND MERCHANT, *to whom Angelo is a debtor*
PINCH, *a schoolmaster*

A SERVANT
A GAOLER
AN OFFICER

ÆMILIA, *wife to Ægeon, an abbess at Ephesus*
ADRIANA, *wife to Antipholus of Ephesus*
LUCIANA, *her sister*
LUCE, *servant to Adriana*
A COURTEZAN

NON-SPEAKING: *Officers and other Attendants*

SCENE: *Ephesus*

ACT I

SCENE I. *A hall in the Duke's palace*

Enter DUKE, ÆGEON, GAOLER, *Officers, and
other Attendants.*

Æge. Proceed, Solinus, to procure my fall
And by the doom of death end woes and all.
  Duke. Merchant of Syracusa, plead no more;
I am not partial to infringe our laws:
The enmity and discord which of late
Sprung from the rancorous outrage of your duke
To merchants, our well-dealing countrymen,
Who, wanting guilders to redeem their lives
Have seal'd his rigorous statutes with their
       bloods,
Excludes all pity from our threatening looks. 10
For, since the mortal and intestine jars
'Twixt thy seditious countrymen and us,
It hath in solemn synods been decreed,
Both by the Syracusians and ourselves,
To admit no traffic to our adverse towns:
Nay, more,
If any born at Ephesus be seen
At any Syracusian marts and fairs;
Again: if any Syracusian born
Come to the bay of Ephesus, he dies,   20
His goods confiscate to the Duke's dispose,
Unless a thousand marks be levied,
To quit the penalty and to ransom him.
Thy substance, valued at the highest rate,
Cannot amount unto a hundred marks;
Therefore by law thou art condemn'd to die.
  Æge. Yet this my comfort: when your words
       are done,
My woes end likewise with the evening sun.
  Duke. Well, Syracusian, say in brief the cause

Why thou departed'st from thy native home   30
And for what cause thou camest to Ephesus.
  Æge. A heavier task could not have been im-
       posed
Than I to speak my griefs unspeakable:
Yet, that the world may witness that my end
Was wrought by nature, not by vile offence,
I'll utter what my sorrow gives me leave.
In Syracusa was I born, and wed
Unto a woman, happy but for me,
And by me, had not our hap been bad.
With her I lived in joy; our wealth increased   40
By prosperous voyages I often made
To Epidamnum; till my factor's death
And the great care of goods at random left
Drew me from kind embracements of my spouse:
From whom my absence was not six months old
Before herself, almost at fainting under
The pleasing punishment that women bear,
Had made provision for her following me
And soon and safe arrived where I was.
There had she not been long but she became   50
A joyful mother of two goodly sons;
And, which was strange, the one so like the
       other
As could not be distinguish'd but by names.
That very hour and in the self-same inn
A meaner woman was delivered
Of such a burden, male twins, both alike:
Those, for their parents were exceeding poor,
I bought and brought up to attend my sons.
My wife, not meanly proud of two such boys,
Made daily motions for our home return: 60
Unwilling I agreed; alas! too soon
We came aboard.
A league from Epidamnum had we sail'd,

149

Before the always wind-obeying deep
Gave any tragic instance of our harm:
But longer did we not retain much hope;
For what obscured light the heavens did grant
Did but convey unto our fearful minds
A doubtful warrant of immediate death;
Which though myself would gladly have em-
    braced,
Yet the incessant weepings of my wife,   71
Weeping before for what she saw must come,
And piteous plainings of the pretty babes,
That mourn'd for fashion, ignorant what to fear,
Forced me to seek delays for them and me.
And this it was, for other means was none:
The sailors sought for safety by our boat,
And left the ship, then sinking-ripe, to us:
My wife, more careful for the latter-born,
Had fasten'd him unto a small spare mast,   80
Such as seafaring men provide for storms;
To him one of the other twins was bound,
Whilst I had been like heedful of the other:
The children thus disposed, my wife and I,
Fixing our eyes on whom our care was fix'd,
Fasten'd ourselves at either end the mast;
And floating straight, obedient to the stream,
Was carried towards Corinth, as we thought.
At length the sun, gazing upon the earth,
Dispersed those vapours that offended us;   90
And, by the benefit of his wished light,
The seas wax'd calm, and we discovered
Two ships from far making amain to us,
Of Corinth that, of Epidaurus this:
But ere they came—O, let me say no more!
Gather the sequel by that went before.
    Duke. Nay, forward, old man; do not break off
    so;
For we may pity, though not pardon thee.
    Æge. O, had the gods done so, I had not now
Worthily term'd them merciless to us!   100
For, ere the ships could meet by twice five leagues,
We were encounter'd by a mighty rock;
Which being violently borne upon,
Our helpful ship was splitted in the midst;
So that, in this unjust divorce of us,
Fortune had left to both of us alike
What to delight in, what to sorrow for.
Her part, poor soul! seeming as burdened
With lesser weight but not with lesser woe,
Was carried with more speed before the wind;
And in our sight they three were taken up   111
By fishermen of Corinth, as we thought.
At length, another ship had seized on us;
And, knowing whom it was their hap to save,
Gave healthful welcome to their shipwreck'd
    guests;
And would have reft the fishers of their prey,

Had not their bark been very slow of sail;
And therefore homeward did they bend their
    course.
Thus have you heard me sever'd from my bliss,
That by misfortunes was my life prolong'd   120
To tell sad stories of my own mishaps.
    Duke. And, for the sake of them thou sorrowest
    for,
Do me the favour to dilate at full
What hath befall'n of them and thee till now.
    Æge. My youngest boy, and yet my eldest care,
At eighteen years became inquisitive
After his brother: and importuned me
That his attendant—so his case was like,
Reft of his brother, but retain'd his name—
Might bear him company in the quest of him:
Whom whilst I labour'd of a love to see,   131
I hazarded the loss of whom I loved.
Five summers have I spent in furthest Greece,
Roaming clean through the bounds of Asia,
And, coasting homeward, came to Ephesus;
Hopeless to find, yet loath to leave unsought
Or that or any place that harbours men.
But here must end the story of my life;
And happy were I in my timely death,
Could all my travels warrant me they live.   140
    Duke. Hapless Ægeon, whom the fates have
    mark'd
To bear the extremity of dire mishap!
Now, trust me, were it not against our laws,
Against my crown, my oath, my dignity,
Which princes, would they, may not disannul,
My soul should sue as advocate for thee.
But, though thou art adjudged to the death
And passed sentence may not be recall'd
But to our honour's great disparagement,
Yet I will favour thee in what I can.   150
Therefore, merchant, I'll limit thee this day
To seek thy life by beneficial help:
Try all the friends thou hast in Ephesus;
Beg thou, or borrow, to make up the sum,
And live; if no, then thou art doom'd to die.
Gaoler, take him to thy custody.
    Gaol. I will, my lord.
    Æge. Hopeless and helpless doth Ægeon wend,
But to procrastinate his lifeless end.   [*Exeunt.*

SCENE II. *The Mart*

Enter ANTIPHOLUS OF SYRACUSE, DROMIO OF
SYRACUSE, *and* FIRST MERCHANT.

    1st Mer. Therefore give out you are of Epi-
    damnum,
Lest that your goods too soon be confiscate.
This very day a Syracusian merchant
Is apprehended for arrival here;
And not being able to buy out his life

According to the statute of the town
Dies ere the weary sun set in the west.
There is your money that I had to keep.
  Ant. S. Go bear it to the Centaur, where we
    host,
And stay there, Dromio, till I come to thee.   *10*
Within this hour it will be dinner-time:
Till that, I'll view the manners of the town,
Peruse the traders, gaze upon the buildings,
And then return and sleep within mine inn,
For with long travel I am stiff and weary.
Get thee away.
  Dro. S. Many a man would take you at your
    word,
And go indeed, having so good a mean,   [*Exit.*
  Ant. S. A trusty villain, sir, that very oft,
When I am dull with care and melancholy,   *20*
Lightens my humour with his merry jests.
What, will you walk with me about the town,
And then go to my inn and dine with me?
  1st Mer. I am invited, sir, to certain merchants,
Of whom I hope to make much benefit;
I crave your pardon. Soon at five o'clock,
Please you, I'll meet with you upon the mart
And afterward consort you till bed-time:
My present business calls me from you now.
  Ant. S. Farewell till then: I will go lose myself
And wander up and down to view the city.   *31*
  1st Mer. Sir, I commend you to your own con-
    tent.   [*Exit.*
  Ant. S. He that commends me to mine own con-
    tent
Commends me to the thing I cannot get.
I to the world am like a drop of water
That in the ocean seeks another drop,
Who, falling there to find his fellow forth,
Unseen, inquisitive, confounds himself:
So I, to find a mother and a brother,
In quest of them, unhappy, lose myself.   *40*

    Enter DROMIO OF EPHESUS.

Here comes the almanac of my true date.
What now? how chance thou art return'd so
    soon?
  Dro. E. Return'd so soon! rather approach'd too
    late:
The capon burns, the pig falls from the spit,
The clock hath strucken twelve upon the bell;
My mistress made it one upon my cheek:
She is so hot because the meat is cold;
The meat is cold because you come not home;
You come not home because you have no stom-
    ach;
You have no stomach having broke your fast;
But we that know what 'tis to fast and pray   *51*
Are penitent for your default to-day.

  Ant. S. Stop in your wind, sir: tell me this, I
    pray:
Where have you left the money that I gave you?
  Dro. E. O—sixpence, that I had o' Wednesday
    last
To pay the saddler for my mistress' crupper?
The saddler had it, sir; I kept it not.
  Ant. S. I am not in a sportive humour now:
Tell me, and dally not, where is the money?
We being strangers here, how darest thou trust
So great a charge from thine own custody?   *61*
  Dro. E. I pray you, jest, sir, as you sit at dinner:
I from my mistress come to you in post;
If I return, I shall be post indeed,
For she will score your fault upon my pate.
Methinks your maw, like mine, should be your
    clock
And strike you home without a messenger.
  Ant. S. Come, Dromio, come, these jests are
    out of season;
Reserve them till a merrier hour than this.
Where is the gold I gave in charge to thee?   *70*
  Dro. E. To me, sir? why, you gave no gold to
    me.
  Ant. S. Come on, sir knave, have done your
    foolishness
And tell me how thou hast disposed thy charge.
  Dro. E. My charge was but to fetch you from
    the mart
Home to your house, the Phœnix, sir, to dinner:
My mistress and her sister stays for you.
  Ant. S. Now, as I am a Christian, answer me
In what safe place you have bestow'd my money,
Or I shall break that merry sconce of yours
That stands on tricks when I am undisposed: *80*
Where is the thousand marks thou hadst of me?
  Dro. E. I have some marks of yours upon my
    pate,
Some of my mistress' marks upon my shoulders,
But not a thousand marks between you both.
If I should pay your worship those again,
Perchance you will not bear them patiently.
  Ant. S. Thy mistress' marks? what mistress,
    slave, hast thou?
  Dro. E. Your worship's wife, my mistress at the
    Phœnix;
She that doth fast till you come home to dinner
And prays that you will hie you home to dinner.
  Ant. S. What, wilt thou flout me thus unto my
    face,   *91*
Being forbid? There, take you that, sir knave.
  Dro. E. What mean you, sir? for God's sake,
    hold your hands!
Nay, an you will not, sir, I'll take my heels.
        [*Exit.*
  Ant. S. Upon my life, by some device or other

The villain is o'er-raught of all my money.
They say this town is full of cozenage,
As, nimble jugglers that deceive the eye,
Dark-working sorcerers that change the mind,
Soul-killing witches that deform the body,   100
Disguised cheaters, prating mountebanks,
And many such-like liberties of sin:
If it prove so, I will be gone the sooner.
I'll to the Centaur, to go seek this slave:
I greatly fear my money is not safe.   [*Exit.*

ACT II

SCENE I. *The house of Antipholus of Ephesus*
    Enter ADRIANA *and* LUCIANA.

  Adr. Neither my husband nor the slave re-
    turn'd,
That in such haste I sent to seek his master!
Sure, Luciana, it is two o'clock.
  Luc. Perhaps some merchant hath invited him
And from the mart he's somewhere gone to
    dinner.
Good sister, let us dine and never fret:
A man is master of his liberty:
Time is their master, and when they see time
They'll go or come: if so, be patient, sister.
  Adr. Why should their liberty than ours be
    more?   .   10
  Luc. Because their business still lies out o' door.
  Adr. Look, when I serve him so, he takes it ill.
  Luc. O, know he is the bridle of your will.
  Adr. There's none but asses will be bridled so.
  Luc. Why, headstrong liberty is lash'd with
    woe.
There's nothing situate under heaven's eye
But hath his bound, in earth, in sea, in sky:
The beasts, the fishes and the winged fowls
Are their males' subjects and at their controls:
Men, more divine, the masters of all these,   20
Lords of the wide world and wild watery seas,
Indued with intellectual sense and souls,
Of more pre-eminence than fish and fowls,
Are masters to their females, and their lords:
Then let your will attend on their accords.
  Adr. This servitude makes you to keep unwed.
  Luc. Not this, but troubles of the marriage-bed.
  Adr. But, were you wedded, you would hear
    some sway.
  Luc. Ere I learn love, I'll practise to obey.
  Adr. How if your husband start some other
    where?   30
  Luc. Till he come home again, I would forbear.
  Adr. Patience unmoved! no marvel though she
    pause;
They can be meek that have no other cause.
A wretched soul, bruised with adversity,

We bid be quiet when we hear it cry;
But were we burden'd with like weight of pain,
As much or more we should ourselves complain:
So thou, that hast no unkind mate to grieve thee,
With urging helpless patience wouldst relieve
    me;
But, if thou live to see like right bereft,   40
This fool-begg'd patience in thee will be left.
  Luc. Well, I will marry one day, but to try.
Here comes your man; now is your husband nigh.

       Enter DROMIO OF EPHESUS.

  Adr. Say, is your tardy master now at hand?
  Dro. E. Nay, he's at two hands with me, and
that my two ears can witness.
  Adr. Say, didst thou speak with him? know'st
    thou his mind?
  Dro. E. Ay, ay, he told his mind upon mine
    ear:
Beshrew his hand, I scarce could understand it.
  Luc. Spake he so doubtfully, thou couldst not
feel his meaning?
  Dro. E. Nay, he struck so plainly, I could too
well feel his blows; and withal so doubtfully that
I could scarce understand them.
  Adr. But say, I prithee, is he coming home?
It seems he hath great care to please his wife.
  Dro. E. Why, mistress, sure my master is horn-
mad.
  Adr. Horn-mad, thou villain!
  Dro. E.   I mean not cuckold-mad;
But, sure, he is stark mad.
When I desired him to come home to dinner,   60
He ask'd me for a thousand marks in gold:
"'Tis dinner-time," quoth I; "My gold!" quoth
    he:
"Your meat doth burn," quoth I; "My gold!"
    quoth he:
"Will you come home?" quoth I; "My gold!"
    quoth he,
"Where is the thousand marks I gave thee, vil-
    lain?"
"The pig," quoth I, "is burn'd"; "My gold!"
    quoth he:
"My mistress, sir," quoth I; "Hang up thy mis-
    tress!
I know not thy mistress; out on thy mistress!"
  Luc. Quoth who?
  Dro. E. Quoth my master: 70
"I know," quoth he, "no house, no wife, no mis-
    tress."
So that my errand, due unto my tongue,
I thank him, I bare home upon my shoulders;
For, in conclusion, he did beat me there.
  Adr. Go back again, thou slave, and fetch him
    home.

Dro. E. Go back again, and be new beaten
    home?
For God's sake, send some other messenger.
  Adr. Back, slave, or I will break thy pate
    across.
  Dro. E. And he will bless that cross with other
    beating:
Between you I shall have a holy head.   80
  Adr. Hence, prating peasant! fetch thy master
    home.
  Dro. E. Am I so round with you as you with me,
That like a football you do spurn me thus?
You spurn me hence, and he will spurn me hither:
If I last in this service, you must case me in
    leather.   [*Exit.*
  Luc. Fie, how impatience loureth in your face!
  Adr. His company must do his minions grace,
Whilst I at home starve for a merry look.
Hath homely age the alluring beauty took
From my poor cheek? then he hath wasted it: 90
Are my discourses dull? barren my wit?
If voluble and sharp discourse be marr'd,
Unkindness blunts it more than marble hard:
Do their gay vestments his affections bait?
That's not my fault: he's master of my state:
What ruins are in me that can be found,
By him not ruin'd? then is he the ground
Of my defeatures. My decayed fair
A sunny look of his would soon repair:
But, too unruly deer, he breaks the pale   100
And feeds from home; poor I am but his stale.
  Luc. Self-harming jealousy! fie, beat it hence!
  Adr. Unfeeling fools can with such wrongs dis-
    pense.
I know his eye doth homage otherwhere;
Or else what lets it but he would be here?
Sister, you know he promised me a chain;
Would that alone, alone he would detain,
So he would keep fair quarter with his bed!
I see the jewel best enamelled
Will lose his beauty; yet the gold bides still 110
That others touch, and often touching will
Wear gold: and no man that hath a name
By falsehood and corruption doth it shame.
Since that my beauty cannot please his eye,
I'll weep what's left away, and weeping die.
  Luc. How many fond fools serve mad jealousy!
                        [*Exeunt.*

SCENE II. *A public place*

Enter ANTIPHOLUS OF SYRACUSE.

  Ant. S. The gold I gave to Dromio is laid up
Safe at the Centaur; and the heedful slave
Is wander'd forth, in care to seek me out
By computation and mine host's report.
I could not speak with Dromio since at first

I sent him from the mart. See, here he comes.

Enter DROMIO OF SYRACUSE.

How now, sir! is your merry humour alter'd?
As you love strokes, so jest with me again.
You know no Centaur? you received no gold?
Your mistress sent to have me home to dinner? 10
My house was at the Phœnix? Wast thou mad
That thus so madly thou didst answer me?
  Dro. S. What answer, sir? when spake I such a
    word?
  Ant. S. Even now, even here, not half an hour
    since.
  Dro. S. I did not see you since you sent me
    hence,
Home to the Centaur, with the gold you gave
    me.
  Ant. S. Villain, thou didst deny the gold's re-
    ceipt
And told'st me of a mistress and a dinner;
For which, I hope, thou felt'st I was displeased.
  Dro. S. I am glad to see you in this merry vein:
What means this jest? I pray you, master, tell
    me.   21
  Ant. S. Yea, dost thou jeer and flout me in the .
    teeth?
Think'st thou I jest? Hold, take thou that, and
    that. [*Beating him.*]
  Dro. S. Hold, sir, for God's sake! now your jest
    is earnest:
Upon what bargain do you give it me?
  Ant. S. Because that I familiarly sometimes
Do use you for my fool and chat with you,
Your sauciness will jest upon my love
And make a common of my serious hours.   29
When the sun shines let foolish gnats make sport,
But creep in crannies when he hides his beams.
If you will jest with me, know my aspect
And fashion your demeanour to my looks,
Or I will beat this method in your sconce.
  Dro. S. Sconce call you it? so you would leave
battering, I had rather have it a head: an you use
these blows long, I must get a sconce for my
head and insconce it too; or else I shall seek my
wit in my shoulders. But, I pray, sir, why am I
beaten?   40
  Ant. S. Dost thou not know?
  Dro. S. Nothing, sir, but that I am beaten.
  Ant. S. Shall I tell you why?
  Dro. S. Ay, sir, and wherefore; for they say
every why hath a wherefore.
  Ant. S. Why, first, for flouting me; and then,
    wherefore,
For urging it the second time to me.
  Dro. S. Was there ever any man thus beaten out
    of season,

When in the why and the wherefore is neither
    rhyme nor reason?
Well, sir, I thank you.   50

Ant. S. Thank me, sir! for what?

Dro. S. Marry, sir, for this something that you
gave me for nothing.

Ant. S. I'll make you amends next, to give you
nothing for something. But say, sir, is it dinner-
time?

Dro. S. No, sir: I think the meat wants that I
have.

Ant. S. In good time, sir; what's that?

Dro. S. Basting.

Ant. S. Well, sir, then 'twill be dry.   60

Dro. S. If it be, sir, I pray you, eat none of it.

Ant. S. Your reason?

Dro. S. Lest it make you choleric and purchase
me another dry basting.

Ant. S. Well, sir, learn to jest in good time:
there's a time for all things.

Dro. S. I durst have denied that, before you
were so choleric.

Ant. S. By what rule, sir?

Dro. S. Marry, sir, by a rule as plain as the plain
bald pate of father Time himself.   71

Ant. S. Let's hear it.

Dro. S. There's no time for a man to recover his
hair that grows bald by nature.

Ant. S. May he not do it by fine and recovery?

Dro. S. Yes, to pay a fine for a periwig and recover the lost hair of another man.

Ant. S. Why is Time such a niggard of hair,
being, as it is, so plentiful an excrement?   79

Dro. S. Because it is a blessing that he bestows
on beasts; and what he hath scanted men in hair
he hath given them in wit.

Ant. S. Why, but there's many a man hath more
hair than wit.

Dro. S. Not a man of those but he hath the wit
to lose his hair.

Ant. S. Why, thou didst conclude hairy men
plain dealers without wit.

Dro. S. The plainer dealer, the sooner lost: yet
he loseth it in a kind of jollity.   90

Ant. S. For what reason?

Dro. S. For two; and sound ones too.

Ant. S. Nay, not sound, I pray you.

Dro. S. Sure ones then.

Ant. S. Nay, not sure, in a thing falsing.

Dro. S. Certain ones then.

Ant. S. Name them.

Dro. S. The one, to save the money that he
spends in tiring; the other that at dinner they
should not drop in his porridge.   100

Ant. S. You would all this time have proved
there is no time for all things.

Dro. S. Marry, and did, sir; namely, no time to
recover hair lost by nature.

Ant. S. But your reason was not substantial,
why there is no time to recover.

Dro. S. Thus I mend it: Time himself is bald
and therefore to the world's end will have bald
followers.

Ant. S. I knew 'twould be a bald conclusion:
But, soft! who wafts us yonder?   111

Enter ADRIANA *and* LUCIANA.

Adr. Ay, ay, Antipholus, look strange and
    frown;
Some other mistress hath thy sweet aspects;
I am not Adriana nor thy wife.
The time was once when thou unurged wouldst
    vow
That never words were music to thine ear,
That never object pleasing in thine eye,
That never touch well welcome to thy hand,
That never meat sweet-savour'd in thy taste,
Unless I spake, or look'd, or touch'd, or carved
    to thee.   120
How comes it now, my husband, O, how comes
    it
That thou art thus estranged from thyself?
Thyself I call it, being strange to me,
That, undividable, incorporate,
Am better than thy dear self's better part.
Ah, do not tear away thyself from me!
For know, my love, as easy mayst thou fall
A drop of water in the breaking gulf
And take unmingled thence that drop again,
Without addition or diminishing,   130
As take from me thyself and not me too.
How dearly would it touch thee to the quick
Shouldst thou but hear I were licentious
And that this body, consecrate to thee,
By ruffian lust should be contaminate!
Wouldst thou not spit at me and spurn at me
And hurl the name of husband in my face
And tear the stain'd skin off my harlot-brow
And from my false hand cut the wedding-ring
And break it with a deep-divorcing vow?   140
I know thou canst; and therefore see thou do it.
I am possess'd with an adulterate blot;
My blood is mingled with the crime of lust:
For if we two be one and thou play false,
I do digest the poison of thy flesh,
Being strumpeted by thy contagion.
Keep then fair league and truce with thy true
    bed;
I live unstain'd, thou undishonoured.

Ant. S. Plead you to me, fair dame? I know you
    not:
In Ephesus I am but two hours old,   150

As strange unto your town as to your talk;
Who, every word by all my wit being scann'd,
Want wit in all one word to understand.
    Luc. Fie, brother! how the world is changed
        with you!
When were you wont to use my sister thus?
She sent for you by Dromio home to dinner.
    Ant. S. By Dromio?
    Dro. S. By me?
    Adr. By thee; and this thou didst return from
        him,
That he did buffet thee and in his blows   160
Denied my house for his, me for his wife.
    Ant. S. Did you converse, sir, with this gentle-
        woman?
What is the course and drift of your compact?
    Dro. S. I, sir? I never saw her till this time.
    Ant. S. Villain, thou liest; for even her very
        words
Didst thou deliver to me on the mart.
    Dro. S. I never spake with her in all my life.
    Ant. S. How can she thus then call us by our
        names?
Unless it be by inspiration.
    Adr. How ill agrees it with your gravity   170
To counterfeit thus grossly with your slave,
Abetting him to thwart me in my mood!
Be it my wrong you are from me exempt,
But wrong not that wrong with a more contempt.
Come, I will fasten on this sleeve of thine:
Thou art an elm, my husband, I a vine,
Whose weakness married to thy stronger state
Makes me with thy strength to communicate:
If aught possess thee from me, it is dross,
Usurping ivy, brier, or idle moss;   180
Who, all for want of pruning, with intrusion
Infect thy sap and live on thy confusion.
    Ant. S. To me she speaks; she moves me for her
        theme:
What, was I married to her in my dream?
Or sleep I now and think I hear all this?
What error drives our eyes and ears amiss?
Until I know this sure uncertainty,
I'll entertain the offer'd fallacy.
    Luc. Dromio, go bid the servants spread for
        dinner.
    Dro. S. O, for my beads! I cross me for a sinner.
This is the fairy land: O spite of spites!   191
We talk with goblins, owls and sprites:
If we obey them not, this will ensue,
They'll suck our breath or pinch us black and
    blue.
    Luc. Why pratest thou to thyself and answer'st
        not?
Dromio, thou drone, thou snail, thou slug, thou
    sot!

    Dro. S. I am transformed, master, am I not?
    Ant. S. I think thou art in mind, and so am I.
    Dro. S. Nay, master, both in mind and in my
        shape.
    Ant. S. Thou hast thine own form.
    Dro. S.   No, I am an ape.   200
    Luc. If thou art changed to aught, 'tis to an ass.
    Dro. S. 'Tis true; she rides me and I long for
        grass.
'Tis so, I am an ass; else it could never be
But I should know her as well as she knows
    me.
    Adr. Come, come, no longer will I be a fool,
To put the finger in the eye and weep,
Whilst man and master laugh my woes to scorn.
Come, sir, to dinner. Dromio, keep the gate.
Husband, I'll dine above with you to-day
And shrive you of a thousand idle pranks.   210
Sirrah, if any ask you for your master,
Say he dines forth and let no creature enter.
Come, sister. Dromio, play the porter well.
    Ant. S. Am I in earth, in heaven, or in hell?
Sleeping or waking? mad or well-advised?
Known unto these, and to myself disguised!
I'll say as they say and persever so
And in this mist at all adventures go.
    Dro. S. Master, shall I be porter at the gate?
    Adr. Ay; and let none enter, lest I break your
        pate.   220
    Luc. Come, come, Antipholus, we dine too late.
                                        [*Exeunt.*

ACT III

Scene I. *Before the house of Antipholus of Ephesus.*

Enter ANTIPHOLUS OF EPHESUS, DROMIO OF
EPHESUS, ANGELO, *and* BALTHAZAR.

    Ant. E. Good Signior Angelo, you must excuse
        us all;
My wife is shrewish when I keep not hours:
Say that I linger'd with you at your shop
To see the making of her carcanet
And that to-morrow you will bring it home.
But here's a villain that would face me down
He met me on the mart and that I beat him
And charged him with a thousand marks in gold
And that I did deny my wife and house.
Thou drunkard, thou, what didst thou mean by
    this?   10
    Dro. E. Say what you will, sir, but I know what
        I know;
That you beat me at the mart, I have your hand
    to show:
If the skin were parchment and the blows you
    gave were ink,

Your own handwriting would tell you what I
      think.
      Ant. E. I think thou art an ass.
      Dro. E.   Marry, so it doth appear
By the wrongs I suffer and the blows I
      bear.
I should kick, being kick'd; and, being at that
      pass,
You would keep from my heels and beware of an
      ass.
      Ant. E. You're sad, Signior Balthazar: pray
      God our cheer
May answer my good will and your good wel-
      come here.   20
      Bal. I hold your dainties cheap, sir, and your
      welcome dear.
      Ant. E. O, Signior Balthazar, either at flesh or
      fish,
A table full of welcome makes scarce one dainty
      dish.
      Bal. Good meat, sir, is common; that every
      churl affords.
      Ant. E. And welcome more common; for that's
      nothing but words.
      Bal. Small cheer and great welcome makes a
      merry feast.
      Ant. E. Ay to a niggardly host and more spar-
      ing guest:
But though my cates be mean, take them in good
      part;
Better cheer may you have, but not with better
      heart.
But, soft! my door is lock'd. Go bid them let us
      in.   30
      Dro. E. Maud, Bridget, Marian, Cicely, Gil-
      lian, Ginn!
      Dro. S. [*Within*] Mome, malt-horse, capon,
      coxcomb, idiot, patch!
Either get thee from the door or sit down at the
      hatch.
Dost thou conjure for wenches, that thou call'st
      for such store,
When one is one too many? Go get thee from
      the door.
      Dro. E. What patch is made our porter? My
      master stays in the street.
      Dro. S. [*Within*] Let him walk from whence he
      came, lest he catch cold on's feet.
      Ant. E. Who talks within there? ho, open the
      door!
      Dro. S. [*Within*] Right, sir; I'll tell you when,
      an you'll tell me wherefore.
      Ant. E. Wherefore? for my dinner: I have not
      dined to-day.   40
      Dro. S. [*Within*] Nor to-day here you must not;
      come again when you may.

      Ant. E. What art thou that keepest me out from
      the house I owe?
      Dro. S. [*Within*] The porter for this time, sir,
      and my name is Dromio.
      Dro. E. O villain! thou hast stolen both mine
      office and my name.
The one ne'er got me credit, the other mickle
      blame.
If thou hadst been Dromio to-day in my
      place,
Thou wouldst have changed thy face for a name
      or thy name for an ass.
      Luce. [*Within*] What a coil is there, Dromio?
      who are those at the gate?
      Dro. E. Let my master in, Luce.
      Luce. [*Within*] Faith, no; he comes too late;
And so tell your master.
      Dro. E.   O Lord, I must laugh!
Have at you with a proverb: Shall I set in my
      staff?
      Luce. [*Within*] Have at you with another;
      that's: When? can you tell?
      Dro. S. [*Within*] If thy name be call'd Luce—
      Luce, thou hast answer'd him well.
      Ant. E. Do you hear, you minion? you'll let us
      in, I hope?
      Luce. [*Within*] I thought to have ask'd you.
      Dro. S.   [*Within*] And you said no.
      Dro. E. So, come, help: well struck! there was
      blow for blow.
      Ant. E. Thou baggage, let me in.
      Luce. [*Within*] Can you tell for whose sake?
      Dro. E. Master, knock the door hard.
      Luce.   [*Within*] Let him knock till it ache.
      Ant. E. You'll cry for this, minion, if I beat the
      door down.
      Luce. [*Within*] What needs all that, and a pair
      of stocks in the town?   60
      Adr. [*Within*] Who is that at the door that
      keeps all this noise?
      Dro. S. [*Within*] By my troth, your town is
      troubled with unruly boys.
      Ant. E. Are you there, wife? you might have
      come before.
      Adr. [*Within*] Your wife, sir knave! go get you
      from the door.
      Dro. E. If you went in pain, master, this "knave"
      would go sore.
      Ang. Here is neither cheer, sir, nor welcome:
      we would fain have either.
      Bal. In debating which was best, we shall part
      with neither.
      Dro. E. They stand at the door, master; bid
      them welcome hither.
      Ant. E. There is something in the wind, that we
      cannot get in.

Dro. E. You would say so, master, if your gar-
    ments were thin.   70
Your cake there is warm within; you stand here
    in the cold:
It would make a man mad as a buck, to be so
    bought and sold.
Ant. E. Go fetch me something: I'll break ope
    the gate.
Dro. S. [*Within*] Break any breaking here, and
    I'll break your knave's pate.
Dro. E. A man may break a word with you, sir,
    and words are but wind,
Ay, and break it in your face, so he break it not
    behind.
Dro. S. [*Within*] It seems thou want'st break-
    ing: out upon thee, hind!
Dro. E. Here's too much "out upon thee!" I
    pray thee, let me in.
Dro. S. [*Within*] Ay, when fowls have no
    feathers and fish have no fin.
Ant. E. Well, I'll break in: go borrow me a
    crow.   80
Dro. E. A crow without feather? Master, mean
    you so?
For a fish without a fin, there's a fowl without a
    feather:
If a crow help us in, sirrah, we'll pluck a crow
    together.
Ant. E. Go get thee gone; fetch me an iron
    crow.
Bal. Have patience, sir; O, let it not be so!
Herein you war against your reputation
And draw within the compass of suspect
The unviolated honour of your wife.
Once this—your long experience of her wisdom,
Her sober virtue, years and modesty,   90
Plead on her part some cause to you unknown;
And doubt not, sir, but she will well excuse
Why at this time the doors are made against
    you.
Be ruled by me: depart in patience,
And let us to the Tiger all to dinner,
And about evening come yourself alone
To know the reason of this strange restraint.
If by strong hand you offer to break in
Now in the stirring passage of the day,
A vulgar comment will be made of it,   100
And that supposed by the common rout
Against your yet ungalled estimation
That may with foul intrusion enter in
And dwell upon your grave when you are dead;
For slander lives upon succession,
For ever housed where it gets possession.
Ant. E. You have prevail'd: I will depart in
    quiet,
And, in despite of mirth, mean to be merry.

I know a wench of excellent discourse,
Pretty and witty, wild and yet, too, gentle: 110
There will we dine. This woman that I mean,
My wife—but, I protest, without desert—
Hath oftentimes upbraided me withal;
To her will we to dinner. [*To* ANGELO] Get you
    home
And fetch the chain; by this I know 'tis made:
Bring it, I pray you, to the Porpentine;
For there's the house: that chain will I bestow—
Be it for nothing but to spite my wife—
Upon mine hostess there: good sir, make haste.
Since mine own doors refuse to entertain me,   120
I'll knock elsewhere, to see if they'll disdain me.
Ang. I'll meet you at that place some hour
    hence.
Ant. E. Do so. This jest shall cost me some
    expense.   [*Exeunt.*

SCENE II. *The same*

Enter LUCIANA *and* ANTIPHOLUS OF SYRACUSE.

Luc. And may it be that you have quite forgot
    A husband's office? shall, Antipholus,
Even in the spring of love, thy love-springs rot?
    Shall love, in building, grow so ruinous?
If you did wed my sister for her wealth,
    Then for her wealth's sake use her with more
      kindness;
Or if you like elsewhere, do it by stealth;
    Muffle your false love with some show of
      blindness:
Let not my sister read it in your eye;
    Be not thy tongue thy own shame's orator;   10
Look sweet, speak fair, become disloyalty;
    Apparel vice like virtue's harbinger;
Bear a fair presence, though your heart be
      tainted;
    Teach sin the carriage of a holy saint;
Be secret-false: what need she be acquainted?
    What simple thief brags of his own attaint?
'Tis double wrong, to truant with your bed
    And let her read it in thy looks at board:
Shame hath a bastard fame, well managed;
    Ill deeds are doubled with an evil word.   20
Alas, poor women! make us but believe,
    Being compact of credit, that you love us;
Though others have the arm, show us the sleeve;
    We in your motion turn and you may move us.
Then, gentle brother, get you in again;
    Comfort my sister, cheer her, call her wife:
'Tis holy sport to be a little vain,
    When the sweet breath of flattery conquers
      strife.
Ant. S. Sweet mistress—what your name is
    else, I know not,
    Nor by what wonder you do hit of mine—   30

Less in your knowledge and your grace you
    show not
    Than our earth's wonder, more than earth di-
      vine.
Teach me, dear creature, how to think and speak;
    Lay open to my earthly-gross conceit,
Smother'd in errors, feeble, shallow, weak,
    The folded meaning of your words' deceit.
Against my soul's pure truth why labour you
    To make it wander in an unknown field?
Are you a god? would you create me new?
    Transform me then, and to your power I'll
      yield.   40
But if that I am I, then well I know
    Your weeping sister is no wife of mine,
    Nor to her bed no homage do I owe:
    Far more, far more to you do I decline.
O, train me not, sweet mermaid, with thy note,
    To drown me in thy sister's flood of tears:
Sing, siren, for thyself and I will dote:
    Spread o'er the silver waves thy golden hairs,
And as a bed I'll take them and there lie,
    And in that glorious supposition think   50
He gains by death that hath such means to die:
    Let Love, being light, be drowned if she sink!
Luc. What, are you mad, that you do reason so?
Ant. S. Not mad, but mated; how, I do not
    know.
Luc. It is a fault that springeth from your eye.
Ant. S. For gazing on your beams, fair sun,
    being by.
Luc. Gaze where you should, and that will clear
    your sight.
Ant. S. As good to wink, sweet love, as look on
    night.
Luc. Why call you me love? call my sister so.
Ant. S. Thy sister's sister.
Luc.   That's my sister.
Ant. S.   No;   60
It is thyself, mine own self's better part,
Mine eye's clear eye, my dear heart's dearer heart,
My food, my fortune and my sweet hope's aim,
My sole earth's heaven and my heaven's claim.
Luc. All this my sister is, or else should be.
Ant. S. Call thyself sister, sweet, for I am thee.
Thee will I love and with thee lead my life:
Thou hast no husband yet nor I no wife.
Give me thy hand.
Luc.   O, soft, sir! hold you still:
I'll fetch my sister, to get her good will. [*Exit.* 70

     Enter DROMIO OF SYRACUSE.

Ant. S. Why, how now, Dromio! where runn'st
thou so fast?
Dro. S. Do you know me, sir? am I Dromio?
am I your man? am I myself?

Ant. S. Thou art Dromio, thou art my man,
thou art thyself.
Dro. S. I am an ass, I am a woman's man and
besides myself.
Ant. S. What woman's man? and how besides
thyself?   80
Dro. S. Marry, sir, besides myself, I am due to
a woman; one that claims me, one that haunts
me, one that will have me.
Ant. S. What claim lays she to thee?
Dro. S. Marry, sir, such claim as you would
lay to your horse; and she would have me as a
beast: not that, I being a beast, she would have
me; but that she, being a very beastly creature,
lays claim to me.
Ant. S. What is she?   90
Dro. S. A very reverent body; ay, such a one
as a man may not speak of without he say "Sir-
reverence." I have but lean luck in the match,
and yet is she a wondrous fat marriage.
Ant. S. How dost thou mean a fat marriage?
Dro. S. Marry, sir, she's the kitchen wench and
all grease; and I know not what use to put her to
but to make a lamp of her and run from her by
her own light. I warrant, her rags and the tallow
in them will burn a Poland winter: if she lives
till doomsday, she'll burn a week longer than
the whole world.
Ant. S. What complexion is she of?
Dro. S. Swart, like my shoe, but her face nothing like so clean kept: for why, she sweats; a
man may go over shoes in the grime of it.
Ant. S. That's a fault that water will mend.
Dro. S. No, sir, 'tis in grain; Noah's flood could
not do it.
Ant. S. What's her name?   110
Dro. S. Nell, sir; but her name and three quar-
ters, that's an ell and three quarters, will not
measure her from hip to hip.
Ant. S. Then she bears some breadth?
Dro. S. No longer from head to foot than from
hip to hip: she is spherical, like a globe; I could
find out countries in her.
Ant. S. In what part of her body stands Ire-
land?
Dro. S. Marry, sir, in her buttocks: I found it
out by the bogs.   120
Ant. S. Where Scotland?
Dro. S. I found it by the barrenness; hard in the
palm of the hand.
Ant. S. Where France?
Dro. S. In her forehead; armed and reverted,
making war against her heir.
Ant. S. Where England?
Dro. S. I looked for the chalky cliffs, but I
could find no whiteness in them; but I guess it

stood in her chin, by the salt rheum that ran between France and it.

Ant. S. Where Spain?

Dro. S. Faith, I saw it not; but I felt it hot in
her breath.

Ant. S. Where America, the Indies?

Dro. S. Oh, sir, upon her nose, all o'er embell-
ished with rubies, carbuncles, sapphires, declining their rich aspect to the hot breath of Spain;
who sent whole armadoes of caracks to be bal-
last at her nose.   *141*

Ant. S. Where stood Belgia, the Netherlands?

Dro. S. Oh, sir, I did not look so low. To conclude, this drudge, or diviner, laid claim to me;
called me Dromio; swore I was assured to her;
told me what privy marks I had about me, as,
the mark of my shoulder, the mole in my neck,
the great wart on my left arm, that I amazed ran
from her as a witch:

And, I think, if my breast had not been made of
    faith and my heart of steel,   *150*
She had transform'd me to a curtal dog and made
    me turn i' the wheel.

Ant. S. Go hie thee presently, post to the road:
An if the wind blow any way from shore,
I will not harbour in this town to-night:
If any bark put forth, come to the mart,
Where I will walk till thou return to me.
If every one knows us and we know none,
'Tis time, I think, to trudge, pack, and be gone.

Dro. S. As from a bear a man would run for life,
So fly I from her that would be my wife.   [*Exit.*

Ant. S. There's none but witches do inhabit
    here;   *161*
And therefore 'tis high time that I were hence.
She that doth call me husband, even my soul
Doth for a wife abhor. But her fair sister,
Possess'd with such a gentle sovereign grace,
Of such enchanting presence and discourse,
Hath almost made me traitor to myself:
But, lest myself be guilty to self-wrong,
I'll stop mine ears against the mermaid's song.

Enter ANGELO *with the chain.*

Ang. Master Antipholus—

Ant. S.   Ay, that's my name.   *170*

Ang. I know it well, sir: lo, here is the chain.
I thought to have ta'en you at the Porpentine:
The chain unfinish'd made me stay thus long.

Ant. S. What is your will that I shall do with
    this?

Ang. What please yourself, sir: I have made it
    for you.

Ant. S. Made it for me, sir! I bespoke it not.

Ang. Not once, nor twice, but twenty times
    you have.

Go home with it and please your wife withal;
And soon at supper-time I'll visit you
And then receive my money for the chain.   *180*

Ant. S. I pray you, sir, receive the money now,
For fear you ne'er see chain nor money more.

Ang. You are a merry man, sir: fare you well.
                                              [*Exit.*

Ant. S. What I should think of this, I cannot
    tell:
But this I think, there's no man is so vain
That would refuse so fair an offer'd chain.
I see a man here needs not live by shifts
When in the streets he meets such golden gifts.
I'll to the mart and there for Dromio stay:
If any ship put out, then straight away.   [*Exit.*

ACT IV

SCENE I. *A public place*

Enter SECOND MERCHANT, ANGELO, *and an*
OFFICER.

2nd Mer. You know since Pentecost the sum is
    due,
And since I have not much importuned you;
Nor now I had not, but that I am bound
To Persia and want guilders for my voyage:
Therefore make present satisfaction,
Or I'll attach you by this officer.

Ang. Even just the sum that I do owe to you
Is growing to me by Antipholus,
And in the instant that I met with you
He had of me a chain: at five o'clock   *10*
I shall receive the money for the same.
Pleaseth you walk with me down to his house,
I will discharge my bond and thank you too.

Enter ANTIPHOLUS OF EPHESUS *and* DROMIO
OF EPHESUS *from the courtezan's.*

Off. That labour may you save: see where he
    comes.

Ant. E. While I go to the goldsmith's house, go
    thou
And buy a rope's end: that will I bestow
Among my wife and her confederates,
For locking me out of my doors by day.
But, soft! I see the goldsmith. Get thee gone;
Buy thou a rope and bring it home to me.   *20*

Dro. E. I buy a thousand pound a year: I buy a
    rope.   [*Exit.*

Ant. E. A man is well holp up that trusts to
    you:
I promised your presence and the chain;
But neither chain nor goldsmith came to me.
Belike you thought our love would last too long,
If it were chain'd together, and therefore came
    not.

Ang. Saving your merry humour, here's the
note
How much your chain weighs to the utmost
carat,
The fineness of the gold and chargeful fashion,
Which doth amount to three odd ducats more *30*
Than I stand debted to this gentleman:
I pray you, see him presently discharged,
For he is bound to sea and stays but for it.
Ant. E. I am not furnish'd with the present
money;
Besides, I have some business in the town.
Good signior, take the stranger to my house
And with you take the chain and bid my wife
Disburse the sum on the receipt thereof:
Perchance I will be there as soon as you.
Ang. Then you will bring the chain to her your-
self?
Ant. E. No; bear it with you, lest I come not
time enough.
Ang. Well, sir, I will. Have you the chain about
you?
Ant. E. An if I have not, sir, I hope you have;
Or else you may return without your money.
Ang. Nay, come, I pray you, sir, give me the
chain:
Both wind and tide stays for this gentleman,
And I, to blame, have held him here too long.
Ant. E. Good Lord! you use this dalliance to
excuse
Your breach of promise to the Porpentine.
I should have chid you for not bringing it, *50*
But, like a shrew, you first begin to brawl.
2nd Mer. The hour steals on; I pray you, sir,
dispatch.
Ang. You hear how he importunes me; the
chain!
Ant. E. Why, give it to my wife and fetch your
money.
Ang. Come, come, you know I gave it you even
now.
Either send the chain or send me by some token.
Ant. E. Fie, now you run this humour out of
breath,
Come, where's the chain? I pray you, let me see
it.
2nd Mer. My business cannot brook this dalli-
ance.
Good sir, say whether you'll answer me or no: *60*
If not, I'll leave him to the officer.
Ant. E. I answer you! what should I answer
you?
Ang. The money that you owe me for the
chain.
Ant. E. I owe you none till I receive the chain.
Ang. You know I gave it you half an hour since.

Ant. E. You gave me none: you wrong me
much to say so.
Ang. You wrong me more, sir, in denying it:
Consider how it stands upon my credit.
2nd Mer. Well, officer, arrest him at my suit.
Off. I do; and charge you in the Duke's name
to obey me. *70*
Ang. This touches me in reputation.
Either consent to pay this sum for me
Or I attach you by this officer.
Ant. E. Consent to pay thee that I never had!
Arrest me, foolish fellow, if thou darest.
Ang. Here is thy fee; arrest him, officer.
I would not spare my brother in this case,
If he should scorn me so apparently.
Off. I do arrest you, sir: you hear the suit.
Ant. E. I do obey thee till I give thee bail.
But, sirrah, you shall buy this sport as dear *81*
As all the metal in your shop will answer.
Ang. Sir, sir, I shall have law in Ephesus,
To your notorious shame; I doubt it not.

Enter DROMIO OF SYRACUSE, *from the bay.*

Dro. S. Master, there is a bark of Epidamnum
That stays but till her owner comes aboard
And then, sir, she bears away. Our fraught-
age, sir,
I have convey'd aboard and I have bought
The oil, the balsamum and aqua-vitæ.
The ship is in her trim; the merry wind *90*
Blows fair from land: they stay for nought at all
But for their owner, master, and yourself.
Ant. E. How now! a madman! Why, thou
peevish sheep,
What ship of Epidamnum stays for me?
Dro. S. A ship you sent me to, to hire waftage.
Ant. E. Thou drunken slave, I sent thee for a
rope
And told thee to what purpose and what end.
Dro. S. You sent me for a rope's end as soon:
You sent me to the bay, sir, for a bark.
Ant. E. I will debate this matter at more lei-
sure *100*
And teach your ears to list me with more heed.
To Adriana, villain, hie thee straight:
Give her this key, and tell her, in the desk
That's cover'd o'er with Turkish tapestry
There is a purse of ducats; let her send it:
Tell her I am arrested in the street
And that shall bail me: hie thee, slave, be gone!
On, officer, to prison till it come.
  [*Exeunt* SECOND MERCHANT, ANGELO,
    OFFICER *and* ANTIPHOLUS OF
      EPHESUS.
Dro. S. To Adriana! that is where we dined,
Where Dowsabel did claim me for her husband:

She is too big, I hope, for me to compass.   *111*
Thither I must, although against my will,
For servants must their masters' minds fulfil.
                                [*Exit.*

SCENE II. *The house of Antipholus of Ephesus*

Enter ADRIANA *and* LUCIANA.

Adr. Ah, Luciana, did he tempt thee so?
  Mightst thou perceive austerely in his eye
That he did plead in earnest? yea or no?
  Look'd he or red or pale, or sad or merrily?
What observation madest thou in this case
Of his heart's meteors tilting in his face?
Luc. First he denied you had in him no right.
Adr. He meant he did me none; the more my
  spite.
Luc. Then swore he that he was a stranger here.
Adr. And true he swore, though yet forsworn
  he were.   *10*
Luc. Then pleaded I for you.
Adr.   And what said he?
Luc. That love I begg'd for you he begg'd of me.
Adr. With what persuasion did he tempt thy
  love?
Luc. With words that in an honest suit might
  move.
First he did praise my beauty, then my speech.
Adr. Didst speak him fair?
Luc.   Have patience, I beseech.
Adr. I cannot, nor I will not, hold me still;
My tongue, though not my heart, shall have his
  will.
He is deformed, crooked, old and sere,
Ill-faced, worse bodied, shapeless everywhere;
Vicious, ungentle, foolish, blunt, unkind,   *21*
Stigmatical in making, worse in mind.
Luc. Who would be jealous then of such a one?
No evil lost is wail'd when it is gone.
Adr. Ah, but I think him better than I say,
And yet would herein others' eyes were worse.
Far from her nest the lapwing cries away:
My heart prays for him, though my tongue do
  curse.

Enter DROMIO OF SYRACUSE.

Dro. S. Here! go; the desk, the purse! sweet,
  now, make haste.
Luc. How hast thou lost thy breath?
Dro. S.   By running fast.   *30*
Adr. Where is thy master, Dromio? is he well?
Dro. S. No, he's in Tartar limbo, worse than hell.
A devil in an everlasting garment hath him;
One whose hard heart is button'd up with steel;
A fiend, a fury, pitiless and rough;
A wolf, nay, worse, a fellow all in buff;

A back-friend, a shoulder-clapper, one that coun-
  termands
The passages of alleys, creeks, and narrow lands;
A hound that runs counter and yet draws dry-
  foot well;
One that before the judgement carries poor souls
  to hell.   *40*
Adr. Why, man, what is the matter?
Dro. S. I do not know the matter: he is 'rested
  on the case.
Adr. What, is he arrested? Tell me at whose
  suit.
Dro. S. I know not at whose suit he is arrested
  well;
But he's in a suit of buff which 'rested him, that
  can I tell.
Will you send him, mistress, redemption, the
  money in his desk?
Adr. Go fetch it, sister. [*Exit* LUCIANA.] This I
  wonder at,
That he, unknown to me, should be in debt.
Tell me, was he arrested on a band?
Dro. S. Not on a band, but on a stronger thing;
A chain, a chain! Do you not hear it ring?   *51*
Adr. What, the chain?
Dro. S. No, no, the bell: 'tis time that I were
  gone:
It was two ere I left him, and now the clock
  strikes one.
Adr. The hours come back! that did I never
  hear.
Dro. S. O, yes; if any hour meet a sergeant, a'
  turns back for very fear.
Adr. As if Time were in debt! how fondly dost
  thou reason!
Dro. S. Time is a very bankrupt and owes more
  than he's worth to season.
Nay, he's a thief too: have you not heard men
  say,
That Time comes stealing on by night and day?
If Time be in debt and theft, and a sergeant in
  the way,   *61*
Hath he not reason to turn back an hour in a day?

Re-enter LUCIANA *with a purse.*

Adr. Go, Dromio; there's the money, bear it
  straight,
And bring thy master home immediately.
Come, sister: I am press'd down with conceit—
Conceit, my comfort and my injury.   [*Exeunt.*

SCENE III. *A public place*

Enter ANTIPHOLUS OF SYRACUSE.

Ant. S. There's not a man I meet but doth salute
  me
As if I were their well-acquainted friend;

And every one doth call me by my name.
Some tender money to me; some invite me;
Some other give me thanks for kindnesses;
Some offer me commodities to buy:
Even now a tailor call'd me in his shop
And show'd me silks that he had bought for me
And therewithal took measure of my body.
Sure, these are but imaginary wiles 10
And Lapland sorcerers inhabit here.

Enter DROMIO OF SYRACUSE.

Dro. S. Master, here's the gold you sent me for.
What, have you got the picture of old Adam
new-apparelled?
Ant. S. What gold is this? what Adam dost thou
mean?
Dro. S. Not that Adam that kept the Paradise,
but that Adam that keeps the prison: he that goes
in the calf's skin that was killed for the Prodigal;
he that came behind you, sir, like an evil angel,
and bid you forsake your liberty. 20
Ant. S. I understand thee not.
Dro. S. No? why, 'tis a plain case: he that went,
like a bass-viol, in a case of leather; the man, sir,
that, when gentlemen are tired, gives them a sob
and 'rests them; he, sir, that takes pity on decayed men and gives them suits of durance; he
that sets up his rest to do more exploits with his
mace than a morris-pike.
Ant. S. What, thou meanest an officer?
Dro. S. Ay, sir, the sergeant of the band; he that
brings any man to answer it that breaks his band;
one that thinks a man always going to bed and
says, "God give you good rest!"
Ant. S. Well, sir, there rest in your foolery. Is
there any ship puts forth to-night? may we be
gone?
Dro. S. Why, sir, I brought you word an hour
since that the bark Expedition put forth to-night;
and then were you hindered by the sergeant, to
tarry for the hoy Delay. Here are the angels that
you sent for to deliver you.
Ant. S. The fellow is distract, and so am I;
And here we wander in illusions:
Some blessed power deliver us from hence!

Enter a COURTEZAN.

Cour. Well met, well met, Master Antipholus.
I see, sir, you have found the goldsmith now:
Is that the chain you promised me to-day?
Ant. S. Satan, avoid! I charge thee, tempt me
not.
Dro. S. Master, is this Mistress Satan?
Ant. S. It is the devil. 50
Dro. S. Nay, she is worse, she is the devil's
dam; and here she comes in the habit of a light

wench: and thereof comes that the wenches say
"God damn me"; that's as much to say "God
make me a light wench." It is written, they appear to men like angels of light: light is an effect
of fire, and fire will burn; ergo, light wenches
will burn. Come not near her.
Cour. Your man and you are marvellous merry,
sir.
Will you go with me? We'll mend our dinner
here? 60
Dro. S. Master, if you do, expect spoon-meat;
or bespeak a long spoon.
Ant. S. Why, Dromio?
Dro. S. Marry, he must have a long spoon that
must eat with the devil.
Ant. S. Avoid then, fiend! what tell'st thou me
of supping?
Thou art, as you are all, a sorceress:
I conjure thee to leave me and be gone.
Cour. Give me the ring of mine you had at
dinner,
Or, for my diamond, the chain you promised, 70
And I'll be gone, sir, and not trouble you.
Dro. S. Some devils ask but the parings of one's
nail,
A rush, a hair, a drop of blood, a pin,
A nut, a cherry-stone;
But she, more covetous, would have a chain.
Master, be wise: an if you give it her,
The devil will shake her chain and fright us with
it.
Cour. I pray you, sir, my ring, or else the chain:
I hope you do not mean to cheat me so.
Ant. S. Avaunt, thou witch! Come, Dromio, let
us go. 80
Dro. S. "Fly pride," says the peacock: mistress,
that you know.

[*Exeunt* ANTIPHOLUS OF SYRACUSE *and*
DROMIO OF SYRACUSE.

Cour. Now, out of doubt Antipholus is mad,
Else would he never so demean himself.
A ring of mine he hath worth forty ducats,
And for the same he promised me a chain:
Both one and other he denies me now.
The reason that I gather he is mad,
Besides this present instance of his rage,
Is a mad tale he told to-day at dinner,
Of his own doors being shut against his en-
trance.
Belike his wife, acquainted with his fits, 91
On purpose shut the doors against his way.
My way is now to hie home to his house,
And tell his wife that, being lunatic,
He rush'd into my house and took perforce
My ring away. This course I fittest choose;
For forty ducats is too much to lose. [*Exit.*

SCENE IV. *A street*

Enter ANTIPHOLUS OF EPHESUS *and the* OFFICER.

Ant. E. Fear me not, man; I will not break
    away:
I'll give thee, ere I leave thee, so much money,
To warrant thee, as I am 'rested for.
My wife is in a wayward mood to-day,
And will not lightly trust the messenger.
That I should be attach'd in Ephesus,
I tell you, 'twill sound harshly in her ears.

Enter DROMIO OF EPHESUS *with a rope's-end.*

Here comes my man; I think he brings the
    money.
How now, sir! have you that I sent you for?
Dro. E. Here's that, I warrant you, will pay
    them all.   *10*
Ant. E. But where's the money?
Dro. E. Why, sir, I gave the money for the
    rope.
Ant. E. Five hundred ducats, villain, for a
    rope?
Dro. E. I'll serve you, sir, five hundred at the
    rate.
Ant. E. To what end did I bid thee hie thee
    home?
Dro. E. To a rope's-end, sir; and to that end am
I returned.
Ant. E. And to that end, sir, I will welcome
    you. [*Beating him.*]
Off. Good sir, be patient.
Dro. E. Nay, 'tis for me to be patient; I am in
adversity.   *21*
Off. Good now, hold thy tongue.
Dro. E. Nay, rather persuade him to hold his
hands.
Ant. E. Thou whoreson, senseless villain!
Dro. E. I would I were senseless, sir, that I
might not feel your blows.
Ant. E. Thou art sensible in nothing but blows,
and so is an ass.
Dro. E. I am an ass, indeed; you may prove it
by my long ears. I have served him from the hour
of my nativity to this instant, and have nothing
at his hands for my service but blows. When I
am cold, he heats me with beating; when I am
warm, he cools me with beating: I am waked
with it when I sleep; raised with it when I sit;
driven out of doors with it when I go from home;
welcomed home with it when I return: nay, I
bear it on my shoulders, as a beggar wont her
brat; and, I think, when he hath lamed me, I
shall beg with it from door to door.
Ant. E. Come, go along; my wife is coming
    yonder.

Enter ADRIANA, LUCIANA, *the* COURTEZAN,
    and PINCH.

Dro. E. Mistress, "*respice finem*," respect your
end; or rather, the prophecy like the parrot, "be-
ware the rope's-end."
Ant. E. Wilt thou still talk? [*Beating him.*]
Cour. How say you now? is not your husband
    mad?
Adr. His incivility confirms no less.
Good Doctor Pinch, you are a conjurer;   *50*
Establish him in his true sense again,
And I will please you what you will demand.
Luc. Alas, how fiery and how sharp he looks!
Cour. Mark how he trembles in his ecstasy!
Pinch. Give me your hand and let me feel your
    pulse.
Ant. E. There is my hand, and let it feel your
    ear. [*Striking him.*]
Pinch. I charge thee, Satan, housed within this
    man,
To yield possession to my holy prayers
And to thy state of darkness hie thee straight:
I conjure thee by all the saints in heaven!   *60*
Ant. E. Peace, doting wizard, peace! I am not
    mad.
Adr. O, that thou were not, poor distressed
    soul!
Ant. E. You minion, you, are these your cus-
    tomers?
Did this companion with the saffron face
Revel and feast it at my house to-day,
Whilst upon me the guilty doors were shut
And I denied to enter in my house?
Adr. O husband, God doth know you dined at
    home;
Where would you had remain'd until this time,
Free from these slanders and this open shame!
Ant. E. Dined at home! Thou villain, what say-
    est thou?   *71*
Dro. E. Sir, sooth to say, you did not dine at
    home.
Ant. E. Were not my doors lock'd up and I shut
    out?
Dro. E. Perdie, your doors were lock'd and you
    shut out.
Ant. E. And did not she herself revile me there?
Dro. E. Sans fable, she herself reviled you there.
Ant. E. Did not her kitchen-maid rail, taunt,
    and scorn me?
Dro. E. Certes, she did; the kitchen-vestal
    scorn'd you.
Ant. E. And did not I in rage depart from
    thence?
Dro. E. In verity you did; my bones bear wit-
    ness,   *80*

That since have felt the vigour of his rage.

Adr. Is't good to soothe him in these contraries?

Pinch. It is no shame: the fellow finds his vein
And yielding to him humours well his frenzy.

Ant. E. Thou hast suborn'd the goldsmith to
arrest me.

Adr. Alas, I sent you money to redeem you,
By Dromio here, who came in haste for it.

Dro. E. Money by me! heart and good-will you
might;
But, surely, master, not a rag of money.

Ant. E. Went'st not thou to her for a purse of
ducats?   90

Adr. He came to me and I deliver'd it.

Luc. And I am witness with her that she did.

Dro. E. God and the rope-maker bear me witness
That I was sent for nothing but a rope!

Pinch. Mistress, both man and master is pos-
sess'd;
I know it by their pale and deadly looks:
They must be bound and laid in some dark room.

Ant. E. Say, wherefore didst thou lock me forth
to-day?
And why dost thou deny the bag of gold?

Adr. I did not, gentle husband, lock thee forth. 100

Dro. E. And, gentle master, I received no gold;
But I confess, sir, that we were lock'd out.

Adr. Dissembling villain, thou speak'st false in
both.

Ant. E. Dissembling harlot, thou art false in all
And art confederate with a damned pack
To make a loathsome abject scorn of me:
But with these nails I'll pluck out these false eyes
That would behold in me this shameful sport.

*Enter three or four, and offer to bind him. He
strives.*

Adr. O, bind him, bind him! let him not come
near me.

Pinch. More company! The fiend is strong
within him.   110

Luc. Ay me, poor man, how pale and wan he
looks!

Ant. E. What, will you murder me? Thou
gaoler, thou,
I am thy prisoner: wilt thou suffer them
To make a rescue?

Off.   Masters, let him go:
He is my prisoner, and you shall not have him.

Pinch. Go bind this man, for he is frantic too.

They offer to bind DROMIO OF EPHESUS.

Adr. What wilt thou do, thou peevish officer?
Hast thou delight to see a wretched man
Do outrage and displeasure to himself?

Off. He is my prisoner: if I let him go,   120

The debt he owes will be required of me.

Adr. I will discharge thee ere I go from thee:
Bear me forthwith unto his creditor
And, knowing how the debt grows, I will pay it.
Good master doctor, see him safe convey'd
Home to my house. O most unhappy day!

Ant. E. O most unhappy strumpet!

Dro. E. Master, I am here enter'd in bond for
you.

Ant. E. Out on thee, villain! wherefore dost
thou mad me?

Dro. E. Will you be bound for nothing? be mad,
good master: cry "The devil!"   131

Luc. God help, poor souls, how idly do they
talk!

Adr. Go bear him hence. Sister, go you with
me.   [*Exeunt all but* ADRIANA, LUCIANA,
OFFICER *and* COURTEZAN.

Say now, whose suit is he arrested at?

Off. One Angelo, a goldsmith: do you know
him?

Adr. I know the man. What is the sum he owes?

Off. Two hundred ducats.

Adr.   Say, how grows it due?

Off. Due for a chain your husband had of him.

Adr. He did bespeak a chain for me, but had it
not.

Cour. When as your husband all in rage to-day
Came to my house and took away my ring— 141
The ring I saw upon his finger now—
Straight after did I meet him with a chain.

Adr. It may be so, but I did never see it.
Come, gaoler, bring me where the goldsmith is:
I long to know the truth hereof at large.

Enter ANTIPHOLUS OF SYRACUSE *with his rapier
drawn, and* DROMIO OF SYRACUSE.

Luc. God, for thy mercy! they are loose again.

Adr. And come with naked swords.
Let's call more help to have them bound again.

Off. Away! they'll kill us.   150
[*Exeunt all but* ANTIPHOLUS OF SYRACUSE
and DROMIO OF SYRACUSE.

Ant. S. I see these witches are afraid of swords.

Dro. S. She that would be your wife now ran
from you.

Ant. S. Come to the Centaur; fetch our stuff
from thence:
I long that we were safe and sound aboard.

Dro. S. Faith, stay here this night; they will
surely do us no harm: you saw they speak us fair,
give us gold: methinks they are such a gentle
nation that, but for the mountain of mad flesh
that claims marriage of me, I could find in my
heart to stay here still and turn witch.   160

Ant. S. I will not stay to-night for all the town;

Therefore away, to get our stuff aboard.

                [*Exeunt.*

ACT V

SCENE I. *A street before a Priory*

Enter SECOND MERCHANT *and* ANGELO.

Ang. I am sorry, sir, that I have hinder'd you;
But, I protest, he had the chain of me,
Though most dishonestly he doth deny it.

2nd Mer. How is the man esteem'd here in the
    city?

Ang. Of very reverend reputation, sir,
Of credit infinite, highly beloved,
Second to none that lives here in the city:
His word might bear my wealth at any time.

2nd Mer. Speak softly: yonder, as I think, he
    walks.   9

Enter ANTIPHOLUS OF SYRACUSE *and* DROMIO
OF SYRACUSE.

Ang. 'Tis so; and that self chain about his neck
Which he forswore most monstrously to have.
Good sir, draw near to me, I'll speak to him.
Signior Antipholus, I wonder much
That you would put me to this shame and trouble;
And, not without some scandal to yourself,
With circumstance and oaths so to deny
This chain which now you wear so openly:
Beside the charge, the shame, imprisonment,
You have done wrong to this my honest friend,
Who, but for staying on our controversy,   20
Had hoisted sail and put to sea to-day:
This chain you had of me; can you deny it?

Ant. S. I think I had; I never did deny it.

2nd Mer. Yes, that you did, sir, and forswore
    it too.

Ant. S. Who heard me to deny it or forswear
    it?

2nd Mer. These ears of mine, thou know'st, did
    hear thee.
Fie on thee, wretch! 'tis pity that thou livest
To walk where any honest men resort.

Ant. S. Thou art a villain to impeach me thus:
I'll prove mine honour and mine honesty   30
Against thee presently, if thou darest stand.

2nd Mer. I dare, and do defy thee for a villain.
    They draw.

Enter ADRIANA, LUCIANA, *the* COURTEZAN, *and
others.*

Adr. Hold, hurt him not, for God's sake! he is
    mad.
Some get within him, take his sword away:
Bind Dromio too, and bear them to my house.

Dro. S. Run, master, run; for God's sake, take
    a house!
This is some priory. In, or we are spoil'd!

       [*Exeunt* ANTIPHOLUS OF SYRACUSE *and*
         DROMIO OF SYRACUSE *to the Priory.*

Enter the LADY ABBESS.

Abb. Be quiet, people. Wherefore throng you
    hither?

Adr. To fetch my poor distracted husband
    hence.
Let us come in, that we may bind him fast   40
And bear him home for his recovery.

Ang. I knew he was not in his perfect wits.

2nd Mer. I am sorry now that I did draw on
    him.

Abb. How long hath this possession held the
    man?

Adr. This week he hath been heavy, sour, sad,
And much different from the man he was;
But till this afternoon his passion
Ne'er brake into extremity of rage.

Abb. Hath he not lost much wealth by wreck
    of sea?
Buried some dear friend? Hath not else his eye
Stray'd his affection in unlawful love?   51
A sin prevailing much in youthful men,
Who give their eyes the liberty of gazing.
Which of these sorrows is he subject to?

Adr. To none of these, except it be the last;
Namely, some love that drew him oft from home.

Abb. You should for that have reprehended him.

Adr. Why, so I did.

Abb.   Ay, but not rough enough.

Adr. As roughly as my modesty would let me.

Abb. Haply, in private.

Adr.   And in assemblies too.

Abb. Ay, but not enough.   61

Adr. It was the copy of our conference:
In bed he slept not for my urging it;
At board he fed not for my urging it;
Alone, it was the subject of my theme;
In company I often glanced it;
Still did I tell him it was vile and bad.

Abb. And thereof came it that the man was
    mad:
The venom clamours of a jealous woman
Poisons more deadly than a mad dog's tooth.   70
It seems his sleeps were hinder'd by thy railing,
And thereof comes it that his head is light.
Thou say'st his meat was sauced with thy up-
    braidings:
Unquiet meals make ill digestions;
Thereof the raging fire of fever bred;
And what's a fever but a fit of madness?

Thou say'st his sports were hinder'd by thy
    brawls:
Sweet recreation barr'd, what doth ensue
But moody and dull melancholy,
Kinsman to grim and comfortless despair,   80
And at her heels a huge infectious troop
Of pale distemperatures and foes to life?
In food, in sport, and life-preserving rest
To be disturb'd, would mad or man or beast:
The consequence is then thy jealous fits
Have scared thy husband from the use of wits.
  Luc. She never reprehended him but mildly,
When he demean'd himself rough, rude, and
    wildly.
Why bear you these rebukes and answer not?
  Adr. She did betray me to my own reproof. 90
Good people, enter and lay hold on him.
  Abb. No, not a creature enters in my house.
  Adr. Then let your servants bring my husband
    forth.
  Abb. Neither: he took this place for sanctuary,
And it shall privilege him from your hands
Till I have brought him to his wits again,
Or lose my labour in assaying it.
  Adr. I will attend my husband, be his nurse,
Diet his sickness, for it is my office,
And will have no attorney but myself;   100
And therefore let me have him home with me.
  Abb. Be patient; for I will not let him stir
Till I have used the approved means I have,
With wholesome syrups, drugs and holy prayers,
To make of him a formal man again:
It is a branch and parcel of mine oath,
A charitable duty of my order.
Therefore depart and leave him here with me.
  Adr. I will not hence and leave my husband
    here:
And ill it doth beseem your holiness   110
To separate the husband and the wife.
  Abb. Be quiet and depart: thou shalt not have
    him.   [*Exit.*
  Luc. Complain unto the Duke of this indignity.
  Adr. Come, go: I will fall prostrate at his feet
And never rise until my tears and prayers
Have won his Grace to come in person hither
And take perforce my husband from the abbess.
  2nd Mer. By this, I think, the dial points at five:
Anon, I'm sure, the Duke himself in person
Comes this way to the melancholy vale,   120
The place of death and sorry execution,
Behind the ditches of the abbey here.
  Ang. Upon what cause?
  2nd Mer. To see a reverend Syracusian mer-
    chant,
Who put unluckily into this bay
Against the laws and statutes of this town,

Beheaded publicly for his offence.
  Ang. See where they come: we will behold his
    death.
  Luc. Kneel to the Duke before he pass the
    abbey.

Enter DUKE, *attended;* ÆGEON *bareheaded;*
with the Headsman and other Officers.

  Duke. Yet once again proclaim it publicly,   130
If any friend will pay the sum for him,
He shall not die; so much we tender him.
  Adr. Justice, most sacred Duke, against the
    abbess!
  Duke. She is a virtuous and a reverend lady:
It cannot be that she hath done thee wrong.
  Adr. May it please your grace, Antipholus my
    husband,
Whom I made lord of me and all I had,
At your important letters—this ill day
A most outrageous fit of madness took him;
That desperately he hurried through the street—
With him his bondman, all as mad as he—   141
Doing displeasure to the citizens
By rushing in their houses, bearing thence
Rings, jewels, any thing his rage did like.
Once did I get him bound and sent him home,
Whilst to take order for the wrongs I went
That here and there his fury had committed.
Anon, I wot not by what strong escape,
He broke from those that had the guard of him;
And with his mad attendant and himself,   150
Each one with ireful passion, with drawn swords,
Met us again and madly bent on us
Chased us away, till raising of more aid
We came again to bind them. Then they fled
Into this abbey, whither we pursued them:
And here the abbess shuts the gates on us
And will not suffer us to fetch him out,
Nor send him forth that we may bear him hence.
Therefore, most gracious Duke, with thy com-
    mand
Let him be brought forth and borne hence for
    help.
  Duke. Long since thy husband served me in my
    wars,   161
And I to thee engaged a prince's word,
When thou didst make him master of thy bed,
To do him all the grace and good I could.
Go, some of you, knock at the abbey-gate
And bid the lady abbess come to me.
I will determine this before I stir.

Enter a SERVANT.

  Serv. O mistress, mistress, shift and save your-
    self!
My master and his man are both broke loose,

Beaten the maids a-row and bound the doctor, *170*
Whose beard they have singed off with brands
    of fire;
And ever, as it blazed, they threw on him
Great pails of puddled mire to quench the hair:
My master preaches patience to him and the
    while
His man with scissors nicks him like a fool,
And sure, unless you send some present help,
Between them they will kill the conjurer.
  Adr. Peace, fool! thy master and his man are
    here,
And that is false thou dost report to us.
  Serv. Mistress, upon my life, I tell you true;
I have not breathed almost since I did see it. *181*
He cries for you and vows, if he can take you,
To scorch your face and to disfigure you.
    Cry within.
Hark! hark! I hear him, mistress: fly, be gone!
  Duke. Come, stand by me; fear nothing. Guard
    with halberds!
  Adr. Ay me, it is my husband! Witness you,
That he is borne about invisible:
Even now we housed him in the abbey here;
And now he's there, past thought of human
    reason.

    Enter ANTIPHOLUS OF EPHESUS *and* DROMIO
            OF EPHESUS.

  Ant. E. Justice, most gracious Duke, O, grant
    me justice!   *190*
Even for the service that long since I did thee,
When I bestrid thee in the wars and took
Deep scars to save thy life; even for the blood
That then I lost for thee, now grant me justice.
  Æge. Unless the fear of death doth make me
    dote,
I see my son Antipholus and Dromio.
  Ant. E. Justice, sweet prince, against that
    woman there!
She whom thou gavest to me to be my wife,
That hath abused and dishonour'd me
Even in the strength and height of injury!   *200*
Beyond imagination is the wrong
That she this day hath shameless thrown on me.
  Duke. Discover how, and thou shalt find me
    just.
  Ant. E. This day, great Duke, she shut the
    doors upon me,
While she with harlots feasted in my house.
  Duke. A grievous fault! Say, woman, didst thou
    so?
  Adr. No, my good lord: myself, he and my
    sister
To-day did dine together. So befall my soul
As this is false he burdens me withal!

  Luc. Ne'er may I look on day, nor sleep on
    night,   *210*
But she tells to your Highness simple truth!
  Ang. O perjured woman! They are both for-
    sworn:
In this the madman justly chargeth them.
  Ant. E. My liege, I am advised what I say,
Neither disturbed with the effect of wine,
Nor heady-rash, provoked with raging ire,
Albeit my wrongs might make one wiser mad.
This woman lock'd me out this day from dinner:
That goldsmith there, were he not pack'd with
    her,
Could witness it, for he was with me then;   *220*
Who parted with me to go fetch a chain,
Promising to bring it to the Porpentine,
Where Balthazar and I did dine together.
Our dinner done, and he not coming thither,
I went to seek him: in the street I met him
And in his company that gentleman.
There did this perjured goldsmith swear me
    down
That I this day of him received the chain,
Which, God he knows, I saw not: for the which
He did arrest me with an officer.   *230*
I did obey, and sent my peasant home
For certain ducats: he with none return'd.
Then fairly I bespoke the officer
To go in person with me to my house.
By the way we met
My wife, her sister, and a rabble more
Of vile confederates. Along with them
They brought one Pinch, a hungry lean-faced
    villain,
A mere anatomy, a mountebank,
A threadbare juggler and a fortune-teller,
A needy, hollow-eyed, sharp-looking wretch,*240*
A living-dead man: this pernicious slave,
Forsooth, took on him as a conjurer,
And, gazing in mine eyes, feeling my pulse,
And with no face, as 'twere, outfacing me,
Cries out, I was possess'd. Then all together
They fell upon me, bound me, bore me thence
And in a dark and dankish vault at home
There left me and my man, both bound together;
Till, gnawing with my teeth my bonds in sunder,
I gain'd my freedom and immediately   *250*
Ran hither to your Grace; whom I beseech
To give me ample satisfaction
For these deep shames and great indignities.
  Ang. My lord, in truth, thus far I witness with
    him,
That he dined not at home, but was lock'd out.
  Duke. But had he such a chain of thee or no?
  Ang. He had, my lord: and when he ran in here,
These people saw the chain about his neck.

2nd Mer. Besides, I will be sworn these ears of
   mine
Heard you confess you had the chain of him   *260*
After you first forswore it on the mart:
And thereupon I drew my sword on you;
And then you fled into this abbey here,
From whence, I think, you are come by miracle.
  Ant. E. I never came within these abbey-walls,
Nor ever didst thou draw thy sword on me:
I never saw the chain, so help me Heaven!
And this is false you burden me withal.
  Duke. Why, what an intricate impeach is this!
I think you all have drunk of Circe's cup.   *270*
If here you housed him, here he would have been;
If he were mad, he would not plead so coldly:
You say he dined at home; the goldsmith here
Denies that saying. Sirrah, what say you?
  Dro. E. Sir, he dined with her there, at the Por-
  pentine.
  Cour. He did, and from my finger snatch'd that
  ring.
  Ant. E. 'Tis true, my liege; this ring I had of
  her.
  Duke. Saw'st thou him enter at the abbey here?
  Cour. As sure, my liege, as I do see your Grace.
  Duke. Why, this is strange. Go call the abbess
  hither.   *280*
I think you are all mated or stark mad.
                   [*Exit one to the Abbess.*
  Æge. Most mighty duke, vouchsafe me speak a
  word:
Haply I see a friend will save my life
And pay the sum that may deliver me.
  Duke. Speak freely, Syracusian, what thou wilt.
  Æge. Is not your name, sir, call'd Antipholus?
And is not that your bondman, Dromio?
  Dro. E. Within this hour I was his bondman,
  sir,
But he, I thank him, gnaw'd in two my cords:
Now am I Dromio and his man unbound.   *290*
  Æge. I am sure you both of you remember me.
  Dro. E. Ourselves we do remember, sir, by you;
For lately we were bound, as you are now.
You are not Pinch's patient, are you, sir?
  Æge. Why look you strange on me? you know
  me well.
  Ant. E. I never saw you in my life till now.
  Æge. O, grief hath changed me since you saw
  me last,
And careful hours with time's deformed hand
Have written strange defeatures in my face:
But tell me yet, dost thou not know my voice?
  Ant. E. Neither.   *301*
  Æge. Dromio, nor thou?
  Dro. E.   No, trust me, sir, nor I.
  Æge. I am sure thou dost.

  Dro. E. Ay, sir, but I am sure I do not; and
whatsoever a man denies, you are now bound to
believe him.
  Æge. Not know my voice! O time's extremity,
Hast thou so crack'd and splitted my poor tongue
In seven short years, that here my only son
Knows not my feeble key of untuned cares?   *310*
Though now this grained face of mine be hid
In sap-consuming winter's drizzled snow
And all the conduits of my blood froze up,
Yet hath my night of life some memory,
My wasting lamps some fading glimmer left,
My dull deaf ears a little use to hear:
All these old witnesses—I cannot err—
Tell me thou art my son Antipholus.
  Ant. E. I never saw my father in my life.   *319*
  Æge. But seven years since, in Syracusa, boy,
Thou know'st we parted: but perhaps, my son,
Thou shamest to acknowledge me in misery.
  Ant. E. The Duke and all that know me in the
  city
Can witness with me that it is not so:
I ne'er saw Syracusa in my life.
  Duke. I tell thee, Syracusian, twenty years
Have I been patron to Antipholus,
During which time he ne'er saw Syracusa:
I see thy age and dangers make thee dote.

  Re-enter ABBESS, *with* ANTIPHOLUS OF SYRACUSE
          and DROMIO OF SYRACUSE.

  Abb. Most mighty Duke, behold a man much
  wrong'd. [*All gather to see them.*]   *330*
  Adr. I see two husbands, or mine eyes deceive
  me.
  Duke. One of these men is Genius to the other;
And so of these. Which is the natural man,
And which the spirit? who deciphers them?
  Dro. S. I, sir, am Dromio: command him away.
  Dro. E. I, sir, am Dromio: pray, let me stay.
  Ant. S. Ægeon art thou not? or else his ghost?
  Dro. S. O, my old master! who hath bound him
  here?
  Abb. Whoever bound him, I will loose his
  bonds
And gain a husband by his liberty.   *340*
Speak, old Ægeon, if thou be'st the man
That hadst a wife once call'd Æmilia
That bore thee at a burden two fair sons:
O, if thou be'st the same Ægeon, speak,
And speak unto the same Æmilia!
  Æge. If I dream not, thou art Æmilia:
If thou art she, tell me where is that son
That floated with thee on the fatal raft?
  Abb. By men of Epidamnum he and I
And the twin Dromio all were taken up;   *350*
But by and by rude fishermen of Corinth

By force took Dromio and my son from them
And me they left with those of Epidamnum.
What then became of them I cannot tell;
I to this fortune that you see me in.

Duke. Why, here begins his morning story
    right:
These two Antipholuses, these two so like,
And these two Dromios, one in semblance—
Besides her urging of her wreck at sea—
These are the parents to these children,   *360*
Which accidentally are met together.
Antipholus, thou camest from Corinth first?

Ant. S. No, sir, not I; I came from Syracuse.

Duke. Stay, stand apart; I know not which is
    which.

Ant. E. I came from Corinth, my most gracious
    lord—

Dro. E. And I with him.

Ant. E. Brought to this town by that most fa-
    mous warrior,
Duke Menaphon, your most renowned uncle.

Adr. Which of you two did dine with me to-day?

Ant. S. I, gentle mistress.

Adr.   And are not you my husband?

Ant. E. No; I say nay to that.   *371*

Ant. S. And so do I; yet did she call me so;
And this fair gentlewoman, her sister here,
Did call me brother. [*To* LUCIANA] What I told
    you then,
I hope I shall have leisure to make good;
If this be not a dream I see and hear.

Ang. That is the chain, sir, which you had of
    me.

Ant. S. I think it be, sir; I deny it not.

Ant. E. And you, sir, for this chain arrested me.

Ang. I think I did, sir; I deny it not.   *380*

Adr. I sent you money, sir, to be your bail,
By Dromio; but I think he brought it not.

Dro. E. No, none by me.

Ant. S. This purse of ducats I received from
    you
And Dromio my man did bring them us.
I see we still did meet each other's man,
And I was ta'en for him, and he for me,
And thereupon these errors are arose.

Ant. E. These ducats pawn I for my father here.

Duke. It shall not need; thy father hath his
    life.   *390*

Cour. Sir, I must have that diamond from you.

Ant. E. There, take it; and much thanks for my
    good cheer.

Abb. Renowned Duke, vouchsafe to take the
    pains
To go with us into the abbey here
And hear at large discoursed all our fortunes:
And all that are assembled in this place,
That by this sympathized one day's error
Have suffer'd wrong, go keep us company,
And we shall make full satisfaction.
Thirty-three years have I but gone in travail   *400*
Of you, my sons; and till this present hour
My heavy burthen ne'er delivered.
The Duke, my husband and my children both,
And you the calendars of their nativity,
Go to a gossips' feast, and go with me;
After so long grief, such festivity!

Duke. With all my heart, I'll gossip at this feast.
    [*Exeunt all but* ANTIPHOLUS OF SYRACUSE,
        ANTIPHOLUS OF EPHESUS, DROMIO OF
        SYRACUSE, *and* DROMIO OF EPHESUS.

Dro. S. Master, shall I fetch your stuff from
    shipboard?

Ant. E. Dromio, what stuff of mine hast thou
    embark'd?

Dro. S. Your goods that lay at host, sir, in the
    Centaur.   *410*

Ant. S. He speaks to me. I am your master,
    Dromio:
Come, go with us; we'll look to that anon:
Embrace thy brother there; rejoice with him.
    [*Exeunt* ANTIPHOLUS OF SYRACUSE *and*
        ANTIPHOLUS OF EPHESUS.

Dro. S. There is a fat friend at your master's
    house,
That kitchen'd me for you to-day at dinner:
She now shall be my sister, not my wife.

Dro. E. Methinks you are my glass, and not my
    brother:
I see by you I am a sweet-faced youth.
Will you walk in to see their gossiping?

Dro. S. Not I, sir; you are my elder.   *420*

Dro. E. That's a question: how shall we try it?

Dro. S. We'll draw cuts for the senior: till then
    lead thou first.

Dro. E. Nay, then, thus:
We came into the world like brother and brother;
And now let's go hand in hand, not one before
    another.   [*Exeunt.*

🐦 TITUS ANDRONICUS

DRAMATIS PERSONÆ

SATURNINUS, *oldest son to the late Emperor of Rome, and afterwards declared* EMPEROR

BASSIANUS, *brother to Saturninus; in love with Lavinia*

TITUS ANDRONICUS, *a noble Roman, general against the Goths*

MARCUS ANDRONICUS, *tribune of the people and brother to Titus*

LUCIUS
QUINTUS
MARTIUS } *sons to Titus Andronicus*
MUTIUS

YOUNG LUCIUS, *a boy, son to Lucius*

PUBLIUS, *son to Marcus the tribune*

ÆMILIUS, *a noble Roman*

DEMETRIUS
CHIRON } *sons to Tamora*

AARON, *a Moor, beloved by Tamora*
A CAPTAIN
A TRIBUNE
A MESSENGER
A CLOWN
THREE GOTHS

TAMORA, *Queen of the Goths*
LAVINIA, *daughter to Titus Andronicus*
A NURSE

NON-SPEAKING: *Sempronius, Caius, and Valentine, kinsmen to Titus; Alarbus, oldest son to Tamora; Senators, Tribunes, Soldiers, Attendants, Romans, and Goths*

SCENE: *Rome, and the country near it*

🐦

ACT I

SCENE I. *Rome: before the Capitol*

The Tomb of the Andronici appearing; the TRIBUNES *and Senators aloft. Enter, below, from one side,* SATURNINUS *and his followers; and, from the other side,* BASSIANUS *and his followers; with drum and colours.*

Sat. Noble patricians, patrons of my right,
Defend the justice of my cause with arms,
And, countrymen, my loving followers,
Plead my successive title with your swords:
I am his first-born son, that was the last
That wore the imperial diadem of Rome;
Then let my father's honours live in me,
Nor wrong mine age with this indignity.

Bas. Romans, friends, followers, favourers of
    my right,
If ever Bassianus, Cæsar's son,   10
Were gracious in the eyes of royal Rome,
Keep then this passage to the Capitol
And suffer not dishonour to approach
The imperial seat, to virtue consecrate,
To justice, continence and nobility;
But let desert in pure election shine,
And, Romans, fight for freedom in your
    choice.

Enter MARCUS ANDRONICUS, *aloft, with the crown.*

Marc. Princes, that strive by factions and by
    friends
Ambitiously for rule and empery,
Know that the people of Rome, for whom we
    stand   20
A special party, have, by common voice,
In election for the Roman empery,
Chosen Andronicus, surnamed Pius
For many good and great deserts to Rome:
A nobler man, a braver warrior,
Lives not this day within the city walls:
He by the senate is accited home
From weary wars against the barbarous Goths;
That, with his sons, a terror to our foes,
Hath yoked a nation strong, train'd up in arms.
Ten years are spent since first he undertook   31
This cause of Rome and chastised with arms
Our enemies pride: five times he hath return'd
Bleeding to Rome, bearing his valiant sons
In coffins from the field;
And now at last, laden with honour's spoils,
Returns the good Andronicus to Rome,
Renowned Titus, flourishing in arms.
Let us entreat, by honour of his name,
Whom worthily you would have now succeed,
And in the Capitol and senate's right,   41
Whom you pretend to honour and adore,
That you withdraw you and abate your strength;
Dismiss your followers and, as suitors should,
Plead your deserts in peace and humbleness.

Sat. How fair the tribune speaks to calm my
    thoughts!

Bas. Marcus Andronicus, so I do affy
In thy uprightness and integrity,
And so I love and honour thee and thine,
Thy noble brother Titus and his sons,   50

170

And her to whom my thoughts are humbled all,
Gracious Lavinia, Rome's rich ornament,
That I will here dismiss my loving friends,
And to my fortunes and the people's favour
Commit my cause in balance to be weigh'd.

            [*Exeunt the followers of Bassianus.*
  Sat. Friends, that have been thus forward in
    my right,
I thank you all and here dismiss you all,
And to the love and favour of my country
Commit myself, my person, and the cause.

            [*Exeunt the followers of Saturninus.*
Rome, be as just and gracious unto me   60
As I am confident and kind to thee.
Open the gates, and let me in.

  Bas. Tribunes, and me, a poor competitor.

  [*Flourish.* SATURNINUS *and* BASSIANUS *go up
               into the Capitol.*

Enter a CAPTAIN.

  Cap. Romans, make way: the good Andronicus,
Patron of virtue, Rome's best champion,
Successful in the battles that he fights,
With honour and with fortune is return'd
From where he circumscribed with his sword
And brought to yoke the enemies of Rome.

Drums and trumpets sounded. Enter MARTIUS *and*
  MUTIUS; *after them, two men bearing a coffin
  covered with black; then* LUCIUS *and* QUINTUS.
  After them, TITUS ANDRONICUS; *and then* TA-
  MORA, *with Alarbus,* DEMETRIUS, CHIRON,
  AARON, *and other Goths, prisoners; Soldiers and
  People following. The bearers set down the coffin,
  and* TITUS *speaks.*

  Tit. Hail, Rome, victorious in thy mourning
    weeds!   70
Lo, as the bark that hath discharged her fraught
Returns with precious lading to the bay
From whence at first she weigh'd her anchorage,
Cometh Andronicus, bound with laurel boughs,
To re-salute his country with his tears,
Tears of true joy for his return to Rome.
Thou great defender of this Capitol,
Stand gracious to the rites that we intend!
Romans, of five and twenty valiant sons,
Half of the number that King Priam had,   80
Behold the poor remains, alive and dead!
These that survive let Rome reward with love;
These that I bring unto their latest home,
With burial amongst their ancestors:
Here Goths have given me leave to sheathe my
    sword.
Titus, unkind and careless of thine own,
Why suffer'st thou thy sons, unburied yet,
To hover on the dreadful shore of Styx?

Make way to lay them by their brethren.

    The tomb is opened.
There greet in silence, as the dead are wont,   90
And sleep in peace, slain in your country's wars!
O sacred receptacle of my joys,
Sweet cell of virtue and nobility,
How many sons of mine hast thou in store,
That thou wilt never render to me more!

  Luc. Give us the proudest prisoner of the Goths,
That we may hew his limbs and on a pile
Ad manes fratrum sacrifice his flesh
Before this earthy prison of their bones;
That so the shadows be not unappeased,   100
Nor we disturb'd with prodigies on earth.

  Tit. I give him you, the noblest that survives,
The eldest son of this distressed queen.

  Tam. Stay, Roman brethren! Gracious
    conqueror,
Victorious Titus, rue the tears I shed,
A mother's tears in passion for her son:
And if thy sons were ever dear to thee,
O, think my son to be as dear to me!
Sufficeth not that we are brought to Rome,
To beautify thy triumphs and return,   110
Captive to thee and to thy Roman yoke,
But must my sons be slaughter'd in the streets
For valiant doings in their country's cause?
O, if to fight for king and commonweal
Were piety in thine, it is in these.
Andronicus, stain not thy tomb with blood:
Wilt thou draw near the nature of the gods?
Draw near them then in being merciful:
Sweet mercy is nobility's true badge:
Thrice noble Titus, spare my first-born son.   120

  Tit. Patient yourself, madam, and pardon me.
These are their brethren, whom you Goths
    beheld
Alive and dead, and for their brethren slain
Religiously they ask a sacrifice:
To this your son is mark'd, and die he must,
To appease their groaning shadows that are gone.

  Luc. Away with him! and make a fire straight;
And with our swords, upon a pile of wood,
Let's hew his limbs till they be clean consumed.

       [*Exeunt* LUCIUS, QUINTUS, MARTIUS, *and*
            MUTIUS, *with Alarbus.*

  Tam. O cruel, irreligious piety!   130

  Chi. Was ever Scythia half so barbarous?

  Dem. Oppose not Scythia to ambitious Rome.
Alarbus goes to rest; and we survive
To tremble under Titus' threatening looks.
Then, madam, stand resolved, but hope withal
The self-same gods that arm'd the Queen of
    Troy
With opportunity of sharp revenge
Upon the Thracian tyrant in his tent,

May favour Tamora. the Queen of Goths—
When Goths were Goths and Tamora was
    queen—
To quit the bloody wrongs upon her foes. *141*

Re-enter LUCIUS, QUINTUS, MARTIUS, *and*
MUTIUS, *with their swords bloody.*

Luc. See, lord and father, how we have
    perform'd
Our Roman rites: Alarbus' limbs are lopp'd,
And entrails feed the sacrificing fire,
Whose smoke, like incense, doth perfume the
    sky.
Remaineth nought but to inter our brethren
And with loud 'larums welcome them to Rome.
Tit. Let it be so; and let Andronicus
Make this his latest farewell to their souls.
Trumpets sounded, and the coffin laid in the tomb.
In peace and honour rest you here, my sons; *150*
Rome's readiest champions, repose you here in
    rest,
Secure from worldly chances and mishaps!
Here lurks no treason, here no envy swells,
Here grow no damned grudges; here are no
    storms,
No noise, but silence and eternal sleep:
In peace and honour rest you here, my sons!

Enter LAVINIA.

Lav. In peace and honour live Lord Titus long;
My noble lord and father, live in fame!
Lo, at this tomb my tributary tears
I render, for my brethren's obsequies; *160*
And at thy feet I kneel, with tears of joy
Shed on the earth for thy return to Rome:
O, bless me here with thy victorious hand,
Whose fortunes Rome's best citizens applaud!
Tit. Kind Rome, that hast thus lovingly
    reserved
The cordial of mine age to glad my heart!
Lavinia, live; outlive thy father's days,
And fame's eternal date, for virtue's praise!

Enter, below, MARCUS ANDRONICUS *and* TRIBUNES;
re-enter SATURNINUS *and* BASSIANUS, *attended.*

Marc. Long live Lord Titus, my beloved
    brother,
Gracious triumpher in the eyes of Rome! *170*
Tit. Thanks, gentle tribune, noble brother
    Marcus.
Marc. And welcome, nephews, from successful
    wars.
You that survive, and you that sleep in fame!
Fair lords, your fortunes are alike in all,
That in your country's service drew your swords:
But safer triumph is this funeral pomp,

That hath aspired to Solon's happiness
And triumphs over chance in honour's bed.
Titus Andronicus, the people of Rome,
Whose friend in justice thou hast ever been, *180*
Send thee by me, their tribune and their trust,
This palliament of white and spotless hue;
And name thee in election for the empire,
With these our late-deceased emperor's sons:
Be *candidatus* then, and put it on,
And help to set a head on headless Rome.
Tit. A better head her glorious body fits
Than his that shakes for age and feebleness:
What should I don this robe and trouble you?
Be chosen with proclamations to-day, *190*
To-morrow yield up rule, resign my life,
And set abroad new business for you all?
Rome, I have been thy soldier forty years,
And led my country's strength successfully,
And buried one and twenty valiant sons,
Knighted in field, slain manfully in arms
In right and service of their noble country:
Give me a staff of honour for mine age,
But not a sceptre to control the world:
Upright he held it, lords, that held it last. *200*
Marc. Titus, thou shalt obtain and ask the
    empery.
Sat. Proud and ambitious tribune, canst thou
    tell?
Tit. Patience, Prince Saturninus.
Sat.   Romans, do me right:
Patricians, draw your swords, and sheathe them
    not
Till Saturninus be Rome's emperor.
Andronicus, would thou wert shipp'd to hell
Rather than rob me of the people's hearts!
Luc. Proud Saturnine, interrupter of the good
That noble-minded Titus means to thee!
Tit. Content thee, Prince; I will restore to
    thee *210*
The people's hearts, and wean them from them-
    selves.
Bas. Andronicus, I do not flatter thee,
But honour thee, and will do till I die:
My faction if thou strengthen with thy friends,
I will most thankful be; and thanks to men
Of noble minds is honourable meed.
Tit. People of Rome, and people's tribunes here,
I ask your voices and your suffrages:
Will you bestow them friendly on Andronicus?
Tribunes. To gratify the good Andronicus, *220*
And gratulate his safe return to Rome,
The people will accept whom he admits.
Tit. Tribunes, I thank you: and this suit I
    make,
That you create your Emperor's eldest son,
Lord Saturnine; whose virtues will, I hope,

Reflect on Rome as Titan's rays on earth,
And ripen justice in this commonweal:
Then, if you will elect by my advice,
Crown him, and say "Long live our Emperor!"
  Marc. With voices and applause of every sort,
Patricians and plebeians, we create 231
Lord Saturninus Rome's great Emperor,
And say "Long live our Emperor Saturnine!"
  A long flourish till they come down.
  Sat. Titus Andronicus, for thy favours done
To us in our election this day,
I give thee thanks in part of thy deserts,
And will with deeds requite thy gentleness:
And, for an onset, Titus, to advance
Thy name and honourable family,
Lavinia will I make my empress, 240
Rome's royal mistress of my heart,
And in the sacred Pantheon her espouse:
Tell me, Andronicus, doth this motion please
  thee?
  Tit. It doth, my worthy lord; and in this match
I hold me highly honour'd of your Grace:
And here in sight of Rome to Saturnine,
King and commander of our commonweal,
The wide world's Emperor, do I consecrate
My sword, my chariot, and my prisoners;
Presents well worthy Rome's imperial lord: 250
Receive them then, the tribute that I owe,
Mine honour's ensigns humbled at thy feet.
  Sat. Thanks, noble Titus, father of my life!
How proud I am of thee and of thy gifts
Rome shall record, and when I do forget
The least of these unspeakable deserts,
Romans, forget your fealty to me.
  Tit. [*To* TAMORA] Now, madam, are you
  prisoner to an emperor;
To him that, for your honour and your state,
Will use you nobly and your followers. 260
  Sat. A goodly lady, trust me; of the hue
That I would choose, were I to choose anew.
Clear up, fair queen, that cloudy countenance:
Though chance of war hath wrought this change
  of cheer,
Thou comest not to be made a scorn in Rome:
Princely shall be thy usage every way.
Rest on my word, and let not discontent
Daunt all your hopes: madam, he comforts you
Can make you greater than the Queen of
  Goths.
Lavinia, you are not displeased with this? 270
  Lav. Not I, my lord; sith true nobility
Warrants these words in princely courtesy.
  Sat. Thanks, sweet Lavinia. Romans, let us go:
Ransomless here we set our prisoners free:
Proclaim our honours, lords, with trump and
  drum.

Flourish. SATURNINUS *courts* TAMORA
  in dumb show.
  Bas. Lord Titus, by your leave, this maid is
  mine. [*Seizing Lavinia.*]
  Tit. How, sir! are you earnest then, my
  lord?
  Bas. Ay, noble Titus; and resolved withal
To do myself this reason and this right. 279
  Marc. "*Suum cuique*" is our Roman justice:
This prince in justice seizeth but his own.
  Luc. And that he will, and shall, if Lucius live.
  Tit. Traitors, avaunt! Where is the Emperor's
  guard?
Treason, my lord! Lavinia is surprised!
  Sat. Surprised! by whom?
  Bas.   By him that justly may
Bear his betroth'd from all the world away.
[*Exeunt* BASSIANUS *and* MARCUS *with* LAVINIA.
  Mut. Brothers, help to convey her hence away,
And with my sword I'll keep this door safe.
      [*Exeunt* LUCIUS, QUINTUS, *and* MARTIUS.
  Tit. Follow, my lord, and I'll soon bring her
  back.
  Mut. My lord, you pass not here.
  Tit.   What, villain boy! 290
Barr'st me my way in Rome? [*Stabbing* MUTIUS.
  Mut.   Help, Lucius, help! [*Dies.*
[*During the fray,* SATURNINUS, TAMORA, DEME-
  TRIUS, CHIRON *and* AARON *go out and re-enter,
  above.*

                 Re-enter LUCIUS.

  Luc. My lord, you are unjust, and, more than so,
In wrongful quarrel you have slain your son.
  Tit. Nor thou, nor he, are any sons of mine;
My sons would never so dishonour me:
Traitor, restore Lavinia to the Emperor.
  Luc. Dead, if you will; but not to be his wife,
That is another's lawful promised love.   [*Exit.*
  Sat. No, Titus, no; the Emperor needs her not,
Nor her, nor thee, nor any of thy stock: 300
I'll trust, by leisure, him that mocks me once;
Thee never, nor thy traitorous haughty sons,
Confederates all thus to dishonour me.
Was there none else in Rome to make a stale,
But Saturnine? Full well, Andronicus,
Agree these deeds with that proud brag of thine,
That said'st I begg'd the empire at thy hands.
  Tit. O monstrous! what reproachful words are
  these?
  Sat. But go thy ways; go, give that changing
  piece 309
To him that flourish'd for her with his sword:
A valiant son-in-law thou shalt enjoy;
One fit to bandy with thy lawless sons,
To ruffle in the commonwealth of Rome.

Tit. These words are razors to my wounded
   heart.
Sat. And therefore, lovely Tamora, queen of
   Goths,
That like the stately Phœbe 'mongst her nymphs
Dost overshine the gallant'st dames of Rome,
If thou be pleased with this my sudden choice,
Behold, I choose thee, Tamora, for my bride,
And will create thee Empress of Rome.   *320*
Speak, Queen of Goths, dost thou applaud my
   choice?
And here I swear by all the Roman gods,
Sith priest and holy water are so near
And tapers burn so bright and everything
In readiness for Hymenæus stand,
I will not re-salute the streets of Rome,
Or climb my palace, till from forth this place
I lead espoused my bride along with me.
  Tam. And here, in sight of heaven, to Rome I
   swear,
If Saturnine advance the Queen of Goths,   *330*
She will a handmaid be to his desires,
A loving nurse, a mother to his youth.
  Sat. Ascend, fair queen, Pantheon. Lords,
   accompany
Your noble emperor and his lovely bride,
Sent by the heavens for Prince Saturnine,
Whose wisdom hath her fortune conquered:
There shall we consummate our spousal rites.
                  [Exeunt all but TITUS.
  Tit. I am not bid to wait upon this bride.
Titus, when wert thou wont to walk alone,
Dishonour'd thus, and challenged of wrongs? *340*

Re-enter MARCUS, LUCIUS, QUINTUS, *and* MARTIUS.

  Marc. O Titus, see, O, see what thou hast done!
In a bad quarrel slain a virtuous son.
  Tit. No, foolish tribune, no; no son of mine,
Nor thou, nor these, confederates in the deed
That hath dishonour'd all our family;
Unworthy brother, and unworthy sons!
  Luc. But let us give him burial, as becomes;
Give Mutius burial with our brethren.
  Tit. Traitors, away! he rests not in this tomb:
This monument five hundred years hath stood,
Which I have sumptuously re-edified:
Here none but soldiers and Rome's servitors
Repose in fame; none basely slain in brawls:
Bury him where you can; he comes not here.
  Marc. My lord, this is impiety in you:
My nephew Mutius' deeds do plead for him;
He must be buried with his brethren.
  Quin. ⎫ And shall, or him we will accom-
  Mart. ⎭   pany.
  Tit. "And shall!" What villain was it spake
   that word?

  Quin. He that would vouch it in any place but
   here   *360*
  Tit. What, would you bury him in my
   despite?
  Marc. No, noble Titus, but entreat of thee
To pardon Mutius and to bury him.
  Tit. Marcus, even thou hast struck upon my
   crest,
And, with these boys, mine honour thou hast
   wounded:
My foes I do repute you every one:
So, trouble me no more, but get you gone.
  Mart. He is not with himself; let us withdraw.
  Quin. Not I, till Mutius' bones be buried.
      MARCUS *and the* SONS *of Titus kneel.*
  Marc. Brother, for in that name doth nature
   plead—   *370*
  Quin. Father, and in that name doth nature
   speak—
  Tit. Speak thou no more, if all the rest will
   speed.
  Marc. Renowned Titus, more than half my
   soul—
  Luc. Dear father, soul and substance of us
   all—
  Marc. Suffer thy brother Marcus to inter
His noble nephew here in virtue's nest,
That died in honour and Lavinia's cause.
Thou art a Roman; be not barbarous:
The Greeks upon advice did bury Ajax
That slew himself; and wise Laertes' son   *380*
Did graciously plead for his funerals:
Let not young Mutius, then, that was thy joy,
Be barr'd his entrance here.
  Tit.   Rise, Marcus, rise.
The dismall'st day is this that e'er I saw,
To be dishonour'd by my sons in Rome!
Well, bury him, and bury me the next.
              [Mutius is put into the tomb.
  Luc. There lie thy bones, sweet Mutius, with
   thy friends,
Till we with trophies do adorn thy tomb.
  All. [*Kneeling*] No man shed tears for noble
   Mutius;
He lives in fame that died in virtue's cause.   *390*
  Marc. My lord, to step out of these dreary
   dumps,
How comes it that the subtle Queen of Goths
Is of a sudden thus advanced in Rome?
  Tit. I know not, Marcus; but I know it is:
Whether by device or no, the heavens can
   tell:
Is she not then beholding to the man
That brought her for this high good turn so
   far?
Yes, and will nobly him remunerate.

Flourish. Re-enter, from one side, SATURNINUS
   attended, TAMORA, DEMETRIUS, CHIRON, *and*
   AARON; *from the other,* BASSIANUS, LAVINIA, *and*
   others.

Sat. So, Bassianus, you have play'd your prize:
God give you joy, sir, of your gallant bride!   *400*
Bas. And you of yours, my lord! I say no more,
Nor wish no less; and so, I take my leave.
  Sat. Traitor, if Rome have law or we have
    power,
Thou and thy faction shall repent this rape.
  Bas. Rape, call you it, my lord, to seize my own,
My true-betrothed love and now my wife?
But let the laws of Rome determine all;
Meanwhile I am possess'd of that is mine.
  Sat. 'Tis good, sir: you are very short with us;
But, if we live, we'll be as sharp with you.   *410*
  Bas. My lord, what I have done, as best I may,
Answer I must and shall do with my life.
Only thus much I give your Grace to know:
By all the duties that I owe to Rome,
This noble gentleman, Lord Titus here,
Is in opinion and in honour wrong'd;
That in the rescue of Lavinia
With his own hand did slay his youngest son,
In zeal to you and highly moved to wrath
To be controll'd in that he frankly gave: *420*
Receive him, then, to favour, Saturnine,
That hath express'd himself in all his deeds
A father and a friend to thee and Rome.
  Tit. Prince Bassianus, leave to plead my deeds:
'Tis thou and those that have dishonour'd me.
Rome and the righteous heavens be my judge,
How I have loved and honour'd Saturnine!
  Tam. My worthy lord, if ever Tamora
Were gracious in those princely eyes of thine,
Then hear me speak indifferently for all;   *430*
And at my suit, sweet, pardon what is past.
  Sat. What, madam! be dishonour'd openly
And basely put it up without revenge?
  Tam. Not so, my lord; the gods of Rome
    forfend
I should be author to dishonour you!
But on mine honour dare I undertake
For good Lord Titus' innocence in all;
Whose fury not dissembled speaks his griefs:
Then, at my suit, look graciously on him;
Lose not so noble a friend on vain suppose,   *440*
Nor with sour looks afflict his gentle heart.
[*Aside to* SATURNINUS] My lord, be ruled by me,
    be won at last;
Dissemble all your griefs and discontents:
You are but newly planted in your throne;
Lest, then, the people, and patricians too,
Upon a just survey, take Titus' part,

And so supplant you for ingratitude,
Which Rome reputes to be a heinous sin,
Yield at entreats; and then let me alone:
I'll find a day to massacre them all   *450*
And raze their faction and their family,
The cruel father and his traitorous sons,
To whom I sued for my dear son's life,
And make them know what 'tis to let a queen
Kneel in the streets and beg for grace in vain.
  Again speaking openly to SATURNINUS.
Come, come, sweet emperor; come, Andronicus;
Take up this good old man, and cheer the heart
That dies in tempest of thy angry frown.
  Sat. Rise, Titus, rise; my empress hath pre-
    vail'd.   *459*
  Tit. I thank your Majesty, and her, my lord:
These words, these looks, infuse new life in me.
  Tam. Titus, I am incorporate in Rome,
A Roman now adopted happily,
And must advise the Emperor for his good.
This day all quarrels die, Andronicus;
And let it be mine honour, good my lord,
That I have reconciled your friends and you.
For you, Prince Bassianus, I have pass'd
My word and promise to the Emperor,
That you will be more mild and tractable.   *470*
And fear not, lords, and you, Lavinia;
By my advice, all humbled on your knees,
You shall ask pardon of his Majesty.
  Luc. We do, and vow to heaven and to his
    Highness,
That what we did was mildly as we might,
Tendering our sister's honour and our own.
  Marc. That, on mine honour, here I do protest.
  Sat. Away, and talk not; trouble us no more.
  Tam. Nay, nay, sweet emperor, we must all
    be friends: *479*
The tribune and his nephews kneel for grace;
I will not be denied: sweet heart, look back.
  Sat. Marcus, for thy sake and thy brother's here,
And at my lovely Tamora's entreats,
I do remit these young men's heinous faults:
Stand up.
Lavinia, though you left me like a churl,
I found a friend, and sure as death I swore
I would not part a bachelor from the priest.
Come, if the Emperor's court can feast two
    brides,
You are my guest, Lavinia, and your friends. *490*
This day shall be a love-day, Tamora.
  Tit. To-morrow, an it please your Majesty
To hunt the panther and the hart with me,
With horn and hound we'll give your Grace
    bonjour.
  Sat. Be it so, Titus, and gramercy too.
                [*Flourish. Exeunt.*

ACT II

SCENE I. *Rome: before the palace*
Enter AARON.

Aar. Now climbeth Tamora Olympus' top,
Safe out of fortune's shot; and sits aloft,
Secure of thunder's crack or lightning flash;
Advanced above pale envy's threatening reach.
As when the golden sun salutes the morn,
And, having gilt the ocean with his beams,
Gallops the zodiac in his glistering coach,
And overlooks the highest-peering hills;
So Tamora:
Upon her wit doth earthly honour wait,   10
And virtue stoops and trembles at her frown.
Then, Aaron, arm thy heart and fit thy thoughts,
To mount aloft with thy imperial mistress,
And mount her pitch, whom thou in triumph
      long
Hast prisoner held, fetter'd in amorous chains
And faster bound to Aaron's charming eyes
Than is Prometheus tied to Caucasus.
Away with slavish weeds and servile thoughts!
I will be bright, and shine in pearl and gold,
To wait upon this new-made empress.   20
To wait, said I? to wanton with this queen,
This goddess, this Semiramis, this nymph,
This siren, that will charm Rome's Saturnine,
And see his shipwreck and his commonweal's.
Holloa! what storm is this?

Enter DEMETRIUS *and* CHIRON, *braving.*

Dem. Chiron, thy years want wit, thy wit
      wants edge,
And manners, to intrude where I am graced;
And may, for aught thou know'st, affected be.
Chi. Demetrius, thou dost over-ween in all;
And so in this, to bear me down with braves.   30
'Tis not the difference of a year or two
Makes me less gracious or thee more fortunate:
I am as able and as fit as thou
To serve, and to deserve my mistress' grace;
And that my sword upon thee shall approve,
And plead my passions for Lavinia's love.
Aar. [*Aside*] Clubs, clubs! these lovers will
      not keep the peace.
Dem. Why, boy, although our mother,
      unadvised,
Gave you a dancing-rapier by your side,
Are you so desperate grown, to threat your
      friends?   40
Go to; have your lath glued within your sheath
Till you know better how to handle it.
Chi. Meanwhile, sir, with the little skill I have,
Full well shalt thou perceive how much I dare.
Dem. Ay, boy, grow ye so brave? [*They draw.*]

Aar. [*Coming forward*] Why, how now, lords!
So near the Emperor's palace dare you draw,
And maintain such a quarrel openly?
Full well I wot the ground of all this grudge:
I would not for a million of gold
The cause were known to them it most con-
      cerns;
Nor would your noble mother for much more   51
Be so dishonour'd in the court of Rome.
For shame, put up.
Dem.   Not I, till I have sheathed
My rapier in his bosom and withal
Thrust these reproachful speeches down his
      throat
That he hath breathed in my dishonour here.
Chi. For that I am prepared and full resolved.
Foul-spoken coward, that thunder'st with thy
      tongue,
And with thy weapon nothing darest perform!
Aar. Away, I say!   60
Now, by the gods that warlike Goths adore,
This petty brabble will undo us all.
Why, lords, and think you not how dangerous
It is to jet upon a prince's right?
What, is Lavinia then become so loose,
Or Bassianus so degenerate,
That for her love such quarrels may be broach'd
Without controlment, justice, or revenge?
Young lords, beware! an should the Empress
      know
This discord's ground, the music would not
      please.   70
Chi. I care not, I, knew she and all the world:
I love Lavinia more than all the world.
Dem. Youngling, learn thou to make some
      meaner choice:
Lavinia is thine elder brother's hope.
Aar. Why, are ye mad? or know ye not, in
      Rome
How furious and impatient they be,
And cannot brook competitors in love?
I tell you, lords, you do but plot your deaths
By this device.
Chi.   Aaron, a thousand deaths
Would I propose to achieve her whom I love.   80
Aar. To achieve her! how?
Dem.   Why makest thou it so strange?
She is a woman, therefore may be woo'd;
She is a woman, therefore may be won;
She is Lavinia, therefore must be loved.
What, man! more water glideth by the mill
Than wots the miller of; and easy it is
Of a cut loaf to steal a shive, we know:
Though Bassianus be the Emperor's brother,
Better than he have worn Vulcan's badge.
Aar. [*Aside*] Ay, and as good as Saturninus may.

Dem. Then why should he despair that knows
  to court it   91
With words, fair looks, and liberality?
What, hast not thou full often struck a doe,
And borne her cleanly by the keeper's nose?
  Aar. Why, then, it seems, some certain snatch
  or so
Would serve your turns.
  Chi.   Ay, so the turn were served.
  Dem. Aaron, thou hast hit it.
  Aar.   Would you had hit it too!
Then should not we be tired with this ado.
Why, hark ye, hark ye! and are you such fools
To square for this? would it offend you, then,
That both should speed?   *101*
  Chi. Faith, not me.
  Dem.   Nor me, so I were one.
  Aar. For shame, be friends, and join for that
  you jar:
'Tis policy and stratagem must do
That you affect; and so must you resolve
That what you cannot as you would achieve
You must perforce accomplish as you may.
Take this of me: Lucrece was not more chaste
Than this Lavinia, Bassianus' love.
A speedier course than lingering languishment
Must we pursue, and I have found the path.   *111*
My lords, a solemn hunting is in hand;
There will the lovely Roman ladies troop:
The forest walks are wide and spacious;
And many unfrequented plots there are
Fitted by kind for rape and villany:
Single you thither then this dainty doe,
And strike her home by force, if not by
  words:
This way, or not at all, stand you in hope.
Come, come, our empress, with her sacred
  wit
To villainy and vengeance consecrate,   *121*
Will we acquaint with all that we intend;
And she shall file our engines with advice,
That will not suffer you to square yourselves,
But to your wishes' height advance you both.
The Emperor's court is like the house of Fame,
The palace full of tongues, of eyes, and ears:
The woods are ruthless, dreadful, deaf, and
  dull;
There speak, and strike, brave boys, and take
  your turns;
There serve your lusts, shadow'd from heaven's
  eye,   *130*
And revel in Lavinia's treasury.
  Chi. Thy counsel, lad, smells of no cowardice,
  Dem. *Sit fas aut nefas*, till I find the stream
To cool this heat, a charm to calm these fits,
Per Styga, per manes vehor.   [*Exeunt.*

SCENE II. *A forest near Rome: horns and
cry of hounds heard*

Enter TITUS ANDRONICUS, *with Hunters, &c.,*
MARCUS, LUCIUS, QUINTUS, *and* MARTIUS.

  Tit. The hunt is up, the morn is bright and grey,
The fields are fragrant and the woods are green:
Uncouple here and let us make a bay
And wake the Emperor and his lovely bride
And rouse the Prince and ring a hunter's peal,
That all the court may echo with the noise.
Sons, let it be your charge, as it is ours,
To attend the Emperor's person carefully:
I have been troubled in my sleep this night,
But dawning day new comfort hath inspired.   *10*

A cry of hounds, and horns winded in a peal. Enter
SATURNINUS, TAMORA, BASSIANUS, LAVINIA, DE-
METRIUS, CHIRON, *and Attendants.*

Many good morrows to your Majesty;
Madam, to you as many and as good:
I promised your Grace a hunter's peal.
  Sat. And you have rung it lustily, my lord;
Somewhat too early for new-married ladies.
  Bas. Lavinia, how say you?
  Lav.   I say, no;
I have been broad awake two hours and more.
  Sat. Come on, then; horse and chariots let us
  have,
And to our sport. [*To* TAMORA] Madam, now
  shall ye see
Our Roman hunting.
  Marc.   I have dogs, my lord,   *20*
Will rouse the proudest panther in the chase,
And climb the highest promontory top.
  Tit. And I have horse will follow where the
  game
Makes way, and run like swallows o'er the plain.
  Dem. Chiron, we hunt not, we, with horse
  nor hound,
But hope to pluck a dainty doe to ground.
                                [*Exeunt.*

SCENE III. *A lonely part of the forest*
Enter AARON, *with a bag of gold.*

  Aar. He that had wit would think that I had
  none,
To bury so much gold under a tree
And never after to inherit it.
Let him that thinks of me so abjectly
Know that this gold must coin a stratagem,
Which, cunningly effected, will beget
A very excellent piece of villainy:
And so repose, sweet gold, for their unrest
                             [*Hides the gold.*
That have their alms out of the Empress' chest.

Enter TAMORA.

Tam. My lovely Aaron, wherefore look'st
    thou sad, 10
When everything doth make a gleeful boast?
The birds chant melody on every bush,
The snake lies rolled in the cheerful sun,
The green leaves quiver with the cooling wind
And make a chequer'd shadow on the ground:
Under their sweet shade, Aaron, let us sit,
And, whilst the babbling echo mocks the hounds,
Replying shrilly to the well-tuned horns,
As if a double hunt were heard at once,
Let us sit down and mark their yelping noise; 20
And, after conflict such as was supposed
The wandering prince and Dido once enjoy'd,
When with a happy storm they were surprised
And curtain'd with a counsel-keeping cave,
We may, each wreathed in the other's arms,
Our pastimes done, possess a golden slumber;
Whiles hounds and horns and sweet melodious
    birds
Be unto us as is a nurse's song
Of lullaby to bring her babe asleep.
   Aar. Madam, though Venus govern your
    desires, 30
Saturn is dominator over mine:
What signifies my deadly-standing eye,
My silence and my cloudy melancholy,
My fleece of wooly hair that now uncurls
Even as an adder when she doth unroll
To do some fatal execution?
No, madam, these are no venereal signs:
Vengeance is in my heart, death in my hand,
Blood and revenge are hammering in my head.
Hark, Tamora, the empress of my soul, 40
Which never hopes more heaven than rests in
    thee,
This is the day of doom for Bassianus:
His Philomel must lose her tongue to-day,
Thy sons make pillage of her chastity
And wash their hands in Bassianus' blood.
Seest thou this letter? take it up, I pray thee,
And give the King this fatal-plotted scroll.
Now question me no more; we are espied;
Here comes a parcel of our hopeful booty,
Which dreads not yet their lives' destruction. 50
   Tam. Ah, my sweet Moor, sweeter to me than
    life!
   Aar. No more, great Empress; Bassianus comes:
Be cross with him; and I'll go fetch thy sons
To back thy quarrels, whatsoe'er they be. [*Exit.*

Enter BASSIANUS *and* LAVINIA.

Bas. Who have we here? Rome's royal Empress,
Unfurnish'd of her well-beseeming troop?

Or is it Dian, habited like her,
Who hath abandoned her holy groves
To see the general hunting in this forest?
   Tam. Saucy controller of our private steps!
Had I the power that some say Dian had, 61
Thy temples should be planted presently
With horns, as was Actæon's; and the hounds
Should drive upon thy new-transformed limbs,
Unmannerly intruder as thou art!
   Lav. Under your patience, gentle Empress,
'Tis thought you have a goodly gift in horning;
And to be doubted that your Moor and you
Are singled forth to try experiments:
Jove shield your husband from his hounds to-day!
'Tis pity they should take him for a stag. 71
   Bas. Believe me, Queen, your swarth Cimmerian
Doth make your honour of his body's hue,
Spotted, detested, and abominable.
Why are you sequester'd from all your train,
Dismounted from your snow-white goodly
    steed,
And wander'd hither to an obscure plot,
Accompanied but with a barbarous Moor,
If foul desire had not conducted you?
   Lav. And, being intercepted in your sport, 80
Great reason that my noble lord be rated
For sauciness. I pray you, let us hence,
And let her joy her raven-colour'd love:
This valley fits the purpose passing well.
   Bas. The King my brother shall have note of
    this.
   Lav. Ay, for these slips have made him noted
    long:
Good king, to be so mightily abused!
   Tam. Why have I patience to endure all this?

Enter DEMETRIUS *and* CHIRON.

   Dem. How now, dear sovereign, and our
    gracious mother!
Why doth your Highness look so pale and wan?
   Tam. Have I not reason, think you, to look
    pale? 91
These two have 'ticed me hither to this place:
A barren detested vale, you see it is;
The trees, though summer, yet forlorn and lean,
O'ercome with moss and baleful mistletoe:
Here never shines the sun; here nothing breeds,
Unless the nightly owl or fatal raven:
And when they show'd me this abhorred pit,
They told me, here, at dead time of the night,
A thousand fiends, a thousand hissing snakes, 100
Ten thousand swelling toads, as many urchins,
Would make such fearful and confused cries
As any mortal body hearing it
Should straight fall mad, or else die suddenly.
No sooner had they told this hellish tale,

But straight they told me they would bind me
　　here
Unto the body of a dismal yew,
And leave me to this miserable death:
And then they call'd me foul adulteress,
Lascivious Goth, and all the bitterest terms　　*110*
That ever ear did hear to such effect:
And, had you not by wondrous fortune come,
This vengeance on me had they executed.
Revenge it, as you love your mother's life,
Or be ye not henceforth call'd my children.
　Dem. This is a witness that I am thy son.
　　Stabs BASSIANUS.
　Chi. And this for me, struck home to show my
　　strength. [*Also stabs* BASSIANUS, *who dies.*]
　Lav. Ay, come, Semiramis, nay, barbarous
　　Tamora,
For no name fits thy nature but thy own!
　Tam. Give me thy poniard; you shall know,
　　my boys,　　　　　　　　　　　　　*120*
Your mother's hand shall right your mother's
　　wrong.
　Dem. Stay, madam; here is more belongs to her;
First thrash the corn, then after burn the straw:
This minion stood upon her chastity,
Upon her nuptial vow, her loyalty,
And with that painted hope braves your mighti-
　　ness:
And shall she carry this unto her grave?
　Chi. An if she do, I would I were an eunuch.
Drag hence her husband to some secret hole,
And make his dead trunk pillow to our lust.　*130*
　Tam. But when ye have the honey ye desire,
Let not this wasp outlive, us both to sting.
　Chi. I warrant you, madam, we will make that
　　sure.
Come, mistress, now perforce we will enjoy
That nice-preserved honesty of yours.
　Lav. O Tamora! thou bear'st a woman's face—
　Tam. I will not hear her speak; away with her!
　Lav. Sweet lords, entreat her hear me but a
　　word.
　Dem. Listen, fair madam: let it be your glory
To see her tears; but be your heart to them　　*140*
As unrelenting flint to drops of rain.
　Lav. When did the tiger's young ones teach
　　the dam?
O, do not learn her wrath; she taught it thee;
The milk thou suck'dst from her did turn to
　　marble;
Even at thy teat thou hadst thy tyranny.
Yet every mother breeds not sons alike:
[*To* CHIRON] Do thou entreat her show a woman
　　pity.
　Chi. What, wouldst thou have me prove myself
　　a bastard?

　Lav. 'Tis true; the raven doth not hatch a lark:
Yet have I heard—O, could I find it now!—　*150*
The lion moved with pity did endure
To have his princely paws pared all away:
Some say that ravens foster forlorn children,
The whilst their own birds famish in their nests:
O, be to me, though thy hard heart say no,
Nothing so kind, but something pitiful!
　Tam. I know not what it means; away with her!
　Lav. O, let me teach thee! for my father's sake,
That gave thee life, when well he might have
　　slain thee,
Be not obdurate, open thy deaf ears.　　　　*160*
　Tam. Hadst thou in person ne'er offended me,
Even for his sake am I pitiless.
Remember, boys, I pour'd forth tears in vain,
To save your brother from the sacrifice;
But fierce Andronicus would not relent:
Therefore, away with her, and use her as you
　　will,
The worse to her, the better loved of me.
　Lav. O Tamora, be call'd a gentle queen,
And with thine own hands kill me in this place!
For 'tis not life that I have begg'd so long;　*170*
Poor I was slain when Bassianus died.
　Tam. What begg'st thou, then? fond woman,
　　let me go.
　Lav. 'Tis present death I beg; and one thing
　　more
That womanhood denies my tongue to tell:
O, keep me from their worse than killing lust,
And tumble me into some loathsome pit,
Where never man's eye may behold my body:
Do this, and be a charitable murderer.
　Tam. So should I rob my sweet sons of their
　　fee:
No, let them satisfy their lust on thee.　　　*180*
　Dem. Away! for thou hast stay'd us here too
　　long.
　Lav. No grace? no womanhood? Ah, beastly
　　creature!
The blot and enemy to our general name!
Confusion fall—
　Chi. Nay, then I'll stop your mouth. Bring thou
　　her husband:
This is the hole where Aaron bid us hide him.
[*Demetrius throws the body of Bassianus into the
　　pit; then exeunt* DEMETRIUS *and* CHIRON, *dragging
　　off* LAVINIA.
　Tam. Farewell, my sons: see that you make
　　her sure.
Ne'er let my heart know merry cheer indeed,
Till all the Andronici be made away.
Now will I hence to seek my lovely Moor,　　*190*
And let my spleenful sons this trull deflow'r.
　　　　　　　　　　　　　　　　　　[*Exit.*

Re-enter AARON, *with* QUINTUS *and* MARTIUS.

Aar. Come on, my lords, the better foot before:
Straight will I bring you to the loathsome pit
Where I espied the panther fast asleep.
　Quin. My sight is very dull, whate'er it bodes.
　Mart. And mine, I promise you; were't not for
　　shame,
Well could I leave our sport to sleep awhile.
　Falls into the pit.
　Quin. What, art thou fall'n? What subtle hole
　　is this,
Whose mouth is cover'd with rude-growing
　　briers,
Upon whose leaves are drops of new-shed blood
As fresh as morning dew distill'd on flowers?
A very fatal place it seems to me.
Speak, brother, hast thou hurt thee with the fall?
　Mart. O brother, with the dismall'st object
　　hurt
That ever eye with sight made heart lament!
　Aar. [*Aside*] Now will I fetch the King to find
　　them here,
That he thereby may give a likely guess
How these were they that made away his
　　brother.   [*Exit.*
　Mart. Why dost not comfort me and help
　　me out   209
From this unhallowed and blood-stained hole?
　Quin. I am surprised with an uncouth fear:
A chilling sweat o'er-runs my trembling joints:
My heart suspects more than mine eye can see.
　Mart. To prove thou hast a true-divining heart,
Aaron and thou look down into this den,
And see a fearful sight of blood and death.
　Quin. Aaron is gone; and my compassionate
　　heart
Will not permit mine eyes once to behold
The thing whereat it trembles by surmise:
O, tell me how it is; for ne'er till now   220
Was I a child to fear I know not what.
　Mart. Lord Bassianus lies embrewed here,
All on a heap, like to a slaughter'd lamb,
In this detested, dark, blood-drinking pit.
　Quin. If it be dark, how dost thou know 'tis he?
　Mart. Upon his bloody finger he doth wear
A precious ring, that lightens all the hole,
Which, like a taper in some monument,
Doth shine upon the dead man's earthy cheeks
And shows the ragged entrails of the pit: 230
So pale did shine the moon on Pyramus
When he by night lay bathed in maiden blood.
O brother, help me with thy fainting hand—
If fear hath made thee faint, as me it hath—
Out of this fell devouring receptacle,
As hateful as Cocytus' misty mouth.

　Quin. Reach me thy hand, that I may help thee
　　out;
Or, wanting strength to do thee so much good,
I may be pluck'd into the swallowing womb
Of this deep pit, poor Bassianus' grave.   240
I have no strength to pluck thee to the brink.
　Mart. Nor I no strength to climb without thy
　　help.
　Quin. Thy hand once more; I will not loose
　　again,
Till thou art here aloft or I below:
Thou canst not come to me: I come to thee.
　Falls in.

Enter SATURNINUS *with* AARON.

　Sat. Along with me: I'll see what hole is here,
And what he is that now is leap'd into it.
Say, who art thou that lately didst descend
Into this gaping hollow of the earth?
　Mart. The unhappy son of old Andronicus;
Brought hither in a most unlucky hour,   251
To find thy brother Bassianus dead.
　Sat. My brother dead! I know thou dost but jest:
He and his lady both are at the lodge
Upon the north side of this pleasant chase;
'Tis not an hour since I left him there.
　Mart. We know not where you left him all alive;
But, out, alas! here have we found him dead.

Re-enter TAMORA, *with Attendants;* TITUS
ANDRONICUS, *and* LUCIUS.

　Tam. Where is my lord the King?
　Sat. Here, Tamora, though grieved with killing
　　grief.   260
　Tam. Where is thy brother Bassianus?
　Sat. Now to the bottom dost thou search my
　　wound:
Poor Bassianus here lies murdered.
　Tam. Then all too late I bring this fatal writ,
The complot of this timeless tragedy;
And wonder greatly that man's face can fold
In pleasing smiles such murderous tyranny.
　She giveth SATURNINUS *a letter.*
　Sat. [*Reads*] "An if we miss to meet him
　　handsomely—
Sweet huntsman, Bassianus 'tis we mean—
Do thou so much as dig the grave for him: 270
Thou know'st our meaning. Look for thy reward
Among the nettles at the elder-tree
Which overshades the mouth of that same pit
Where we decreed to bury Bassianus.
Do this, and purchase us thy lasting friends."
O Tamora! was ever heard the like?
This is the pit, and this the elder-tree.
Look, sirs, if you can find the huntsman out

That should have murder'd Bassianus here.

Aar. My gracious lord, here is the bag of
   gold.   280

Sat. [*To* TITUS] Two of thy whelps, fell curs of
   bloody kind,

Have here bereft my brother of his life.

Sirs, drag them from the pit unto the prison:

There let them bide until we have devised

Some never-heard-of torturing pain for them.

Tam. What, are they in this pit? O wondrous
   thing!

How easily murder is discovered!

Tit. High Emperor, upon my feeble knee

I beg this boon, with tears not lightly shed,

That this fell fault of my accursed sons,   290

Accursed, if the fault be proved in them—

Sat. If it be proved! you see it is apparent.

Who found this letter? Tamora, was it you?

Tam. Andronicus himself did take it up.

Tit. I did, my lord: yet let me be their bail;

For, by my father's reverend tomb, I vow

They shall be ready at your Highness' will

To answer their suspicion with their lives.

Sat. Thou shalt not bail them: see thou follow
   me.

Some bring the murder'd body, some the
   murderers: 300

Let them not speak a word; the guilt is plain;

For, by my soul, were there worse end than
   death,

That end upon them should be executed.

Tam. Andronicus, I will entreat the King:

Fear not thy sons; they shall do well enough.

Tit. Come, Lucius, come; stay not to talk with
   them.   [*Exeunt.*

SCENE IV. *Another part of the forest*

Enter DEMETRIUS *and* CHIRON, *with* LAVINIA,
*ravished; her hands cut off, and her tongue cut
out.*

Dem. So, now go tell, an if thy tongue can speak,

Who 'twas that cut thy tongue and ravish'd thee.

Chi. Write down thy mind, bewray thy
   meaning so,

An if thy stumps will let thee play the scribe.

Dem. See, how with signs and tokens she can
   scrowl.

Chi. Go home, call for sweet water, wash thy
   hands.

Dem. She hath no tongue to call, nor hands to
   wash;

And so let's leave her to her silent walks.

Chi. An 'twere my case, I should go hang
   myself.

Dem. If thou hadst hands to help thee knit the
   cord. [*Exeunt* DEMETRIUS *and* CHIRON.

Enter MARCUS.

Mar. Who is this? my niece, that flies away so
   fast!   11

Cousin, a word; where is your husband?

If I do dream, would all my wealth would wake
   me!

If I do wake, some planet strike me down,

That I may slumber in eternal sleep!

Speak, gentle niece, what stern ungentle hands

Have lopp'd and hew'd and made thy body bare

Of her two branches, those sweet ornaments

Whose circling shadows kings have sought to
   sleep in,

And might not gain so great a happiness   20

As have thy love? Why dost not speak to me?

Alas, a crimson river of warm blood,

Like to a bubbling fountain stirr'd with wind,

Doth rise and fall between thy rosed lips,

Coming and going with thy honey breath,

But, sure, some Tereus hath deflowered thee,

And, lest thou shouldst detect him, cut thy
   tongue.

Ah, now thou turn'st away thy face for shame!

And, notwithstanding all this loss of blood,

As from a conduit with three issuing spouts,   30

Yet do thy cheeks look red as Titan's face

Blushing to be encounter'd with a cloud.

Shall I speak for thee? shall I say 'tis so?

O, that I knew thy heart; and knew the beast,

That I might rail at him, to ease my mind!

Sorrow concealed, like an oven stopp'd,

Doth burn the heart to cinders where it is.

Fair Philomela, she but lost her tongue,

And in a tedious sampler sew'd her mind:

But, lovely niece, that mean is cut from thee;

A craftier Tereus, cousin, hast thou met,   41

And he hath cut those pretty fingers off

That could have better sew'd than Philomel.

O, had the monster seen those lily hands

Tremble, like aspen-leaves, upon a lute

And make the silken strings delight to kiss them,

He would not then have touch'd them for his
   life!

Or, had he heard the heavenly harmony

Which that sweet tongue hath made,

He would have dropp'd his knife, and fell asleep

As Cerberus at the Thracian poet's feet.   51

Come, let us go, and make thy father blind;

For such a sight will blind a father's eye:

One hour's storm will drown the fragrant meads;

What will whole months of tears thy father's
   eyes?

Do not draw back, for we will mourn with thee:

O, could our mourning ease thy misery!   [*Exeunt.*

ACT III

SCENE I. *Rome: a street*

Enter Judges, Senators and Tribunes, with MARTIUS
and QUINTUS, *bound, passing on to the place of
execution;* TITUS *going before, pleading.*

Tit. Hear me, grave fathers! noble tribunes,
    stay!
For pity of mine age, whose youth was spent
In dangerous wars, whilst you securely slept;
For all my blood in Rome's great quarrel shed;
For all the frosty nights that I have watch'd;
And for these bitter tears, which now you see
Filling the aged wrinkles in my cheeks;
Be pitiful to my condemned sons,
Whose souls are not corrupted as 'tis thought.
For two and twenty sons I never wept,   10
Because they died in honour's lofty bed.
         [*Lieth down; the Judges, &c. pass by
                 him, and Exeunt.*
For these, these, tribunes, in the dust I write
My heart's deep languor and my soul's sad
    tears:
Let my tears stanch the earth's dry appetite;
My sons' sweet blood will make it shame and
    blush.
O earth, I will befriend thee more with rain,
That shall distil from these two ancient urns,
Than youthful April shall with all his showers:
In summer's drought I'll drop upon thee still;
In winter with warm tears I'll melt the snow,   20
And keep eternal spring-time on thy face,
So thou refuse to drink my dear sons' blood.

Enter LUCIUS, *with his sword drawn.*

O reverend tribunes! O gentle, aged men!
Unbind my sons, reverse the doom of death;
And let me say, that never wept before,
My tears are now prevailing orators.
  Luc. O noble father, you lament in vain:
The tribunes hear you not; no man is by;
And you recount your sorrows to a stone.
  Tit. Ah, Lucius, for thy brothers let me plead.
Grave tribunes, once more I entreat of you—   31
  Luc. My gracious lord, no tribune hears you
    speak.
  Tit. Why, 'tis no matter, man: if they did hear,
They would not mark me, or if they did mark,
They would not pity me; yet plead I must,
And bootless unto them.
Therefore I tell my sorrows to the stones;
Who, though they cannot answer my distress,
Yet in some sort they are better than the
    tribunes,
For that they will not intercept my tale: 40
When I do weep, they humbly at my feet

Receive my tears and seem to weep with me;
And, were they but attired in grave weeds,
Rome could afford no tribune like to these.
A stone is soft as wax, tribunes more hard than
    stones;
A stone is silent, and offendeth not,
And tribunes with their tongues doom men to
    death. [*Rises.*]
But wherefore stand'st thou with thy weapon
    drawn?
  Luc. To rescue my two brothers from their
    death:
For which attempt the judges have pronounced
My everlasting doom of banishment.   51
  Tit. O happy man! they have befriended thee.
Why, foolish Lucius, dost thou not perceive
That Rome is but a wilderness of tigers?
Tigers must prey, and Rome affords no prey
But me and mine: how happy art thou, then,
From these devourers to be banished!
But who comes with our brother Marcus here?

Enter MARCUS *and* LAVINIA.

  Marc. Titus, prepare thy aged eyes to weep;
Or, if not so, thy noble heart to break: 60
I bring consuming sorrow to thine age.
  Tit. Will it consume me? let me see it, then.
  Marc. This was thy daughter.
  Tit.   Why, Marcus, so she is.
  Luc. Ay me, this object kills me!
  Tit. Faint-hearted boy, arise, and look upon her.
Speak, Lavinia, what accursed hand
Hath made thee handless in thy father's sight?
What fool hath added water to the sea,
Or brought a faggot to bright-burning Troy?
My grief was at the height before thou camest,
And now, like Nilus, it disdaineth bounds.   71
Give me a sword, I'll chop off my hands too;
For they have fought for Rome, and all in vain;
And they have nursed this woe, in feeding life;
In bootless prayer have they been held up,
And they have served me to effectless use:
Now all the service I require of them
Is that the one will help to cut the other.
'Tis well, Lavinia, that thou hast no hands;
For hands, to do Rome service, are but vain.   80
  Luc. Speak, gentle sister, who hath martyr'd
    thee?
  Marc. O, that delightful engine of her thoughts,
That blabb'd them with such pleasing eloquence,
Is torn from forth that pretty hollow cage,
Where, like a sweet melodious bird, it sung
Sweet varied notes, enchanting every ear!
  Luc. O, say thou for her, who hath done this
    deed?
  Marc. O, thus I found her, straying in the park,

Seeking to hide herself, as doth the deer
That hath received some unrecuring wound.   *90*
  Tit. It was my deer; and he that wounded her
Hath hurt me more than had he kill'd me dead:
For now I stand as one upon a rock
Environ'd with a wilderness of sea,
Who marks the waxing tide grow wave by
    wave,
Expecting ever when some envious surge
Will in his brinish bowels swallow him.
This way to death my wretched sons are gone;
Here stands my other son, a banish'd man,
And here my brother, weeping at my woes: *100*
But that which gives my soul the greatest spurn
Is dear Lavinia, dearer than my soul.
Had I but seen thy picture in this plight,
It would have madded me: what shall I do
Now I behold thy lively body so?
Thou hast no hands, to wipe away thy tears;
Nor tongue, to tell me who hath martyr'd thee:
Thy husband he is dead; and for his death
Thy brothers are condemn'd, and dead by this.
Look, Marcus! ah, son Lucius, look on her!   *110*
When I did name her brothers, then fresh tears
Stood on her cheeks, as doth the honey-dew
Upon a gather'd lily almost wither'd.
  Marc. Perchance she weeps because they kill'd
    her husband;
Perchance because she knows them innocent.
  Tit. If they did kill thy husband, then be joyful,
Because the law hath ta'en revenge on them.
No, no, they would not do so foul a deed;
Witness the sorrow that their sister makes.
Gentle Lavinia, let me kiss thy lips;   *120*
Or make some sign how I may do thee ease:
Shall thy good uncle, and thy brother Lucius,
And thou, and I, sit round about some fountain,
Looking all downwards, to behold our cheeks
How they are stain'd, as meadows yet not dry
With miry slime left on them by a flood?
And in the fountain shall we gaze so long
Till the fresh taste be taken from that clearness,
And made a brine-pit with our bitter tears?
Or shall we cut away our hands, like thine?   *130*
Or shall we bite our tongues, and in dumb shows
Pass the remainder of our hateful days?
What shall we do? let us, that have our tongues,
Plot some device of further misery,
To make us wonder'd at in time to come.
  Luc. Sweet father, cease your tears; for, at
    your grief,
See how my wretched sister sobs and weeps.
  Marc. Patience, dear niece. Good Titus, dry
    thine eyes.
  Tit. Ah, Marcus, Marcus! brother, well I wot
Thy napkin cannot drink a tear of mine,   *140*

For thou, poor man, hast drown'd it with thine
    own.
  Luc. Ah, my Lavinia, I will wipe thy cheeks.
  Tit. Mark, Marcus, mark! I understand her
    signs:
Had she a tongue to speak, now would she say
That to her brother which I said to thee:
His napkin, with his true tears all bewet,
Can do no service on her sorrowful cheeks.
O, what a sympathy of woe is this,
As far from help as Limbo is from bliss!   *149*

Enter AARON.

  Aar. Titus Andronicus, my lord the Emperor
Sends thee this word—that, if thou love thy
    sons,
Let Marcus, Lucius, or thyself, old Titus,
Or any one of you, chop off your hand,
And send it to the King: he for the same
Will send thee hither both thy sons alive;
And that shall be the ransom for their fault.
  Tit. O gracious Emperor! O gentle Aaron!
Did ever raven sing so like a lark
That gives sweet tidings of the sun's uprise?
With all my heart, I'll send the Emperor   *160*
My hand:
Good Aaron, wilt thou help to chop it off?
  Luc. Stay, father! for that noble hand of thine
That hath thrown down so many enemies
Shall not be sent: my hand will serve the turn:
My youth can better spare my blood than you;
And therefore mine shall save my brothers' lives.
  Marc. Which of your hands hath not defended
    Rome,
And rear'd aloft the bloody battle-axe,
Writing destruction on the enemy's castle?   *170*
O, none of both but are of high desert:
My hand hath been but idle; let it serve
To ransom my two nephews from their death;
Then have I kept it to a worthy end.
  Aar. Nay, come, agree whose hand shall go
    along,
For fear they die before their pardon come.
  Marc. My hand shall go.
  Luc.   By heaven, it shall not go!
  Tit. Sirs, strive no more: such wither'd herbs
    as these
Are meet for plucking up, and therefore mine.
  Luc. Sweet father, if I shall be thought thy
    son,   *·180*
Let me redeem my brothers both from death.
  Marc. And, for our father's sake and mother's
    care,
Now let me show a brother's love to thee.
  Tit. Agree between you; I will spare my hand.
  Luc. Then I'll go fetch an axe.

Marc. But I will use the axe.

> [*Exeunt* LUCIUS *and* MARCUS.

Tit. Come hither, Aaron; I'll deceive them both:
Lend me thy hand, and I will give thee mine.

Aar. [*Aside*] If that be call'd deceit, I will be
honest,
And never, whilst I live, deceive men so: 190
But I'll deceive you in another sort,
And that you'll say, ere half an hour pass.

> *Cuts off* TITUS's *hand.*

Re-enter LUCIUS *and* MARCUS.

Tit. Now stay your strife: what shall be is
dispatch'd.
Good Aaron, give his Majesty my hand:
Tell him it was a hand that warded him
From thousand dangers; bid him bury it;
More hath it merited; that let it have.
As for my sons, say I account of them
As jewels purchased at an easy price;   199
And yet dear too, because I bought mine own.

Aar. I go, Andronicus: and for thy hand
Look by and by to have thy sons with thee.
[*Aside*] Their heads, I mean. O, how this
villainy
Doth fat me with the very thoughts of it!
Let fools do good, and fair men call for grace,
Aaron will have his soul black like his face. [*Exit.*

Tit. O, here I lift this one hand up to heaven,
And bow this feeble ruin to the earth:
If any power pities wretched tears,
To that I call! [*To* LAVINIA] What, wilt thou
kneel with me?   210
Do, then, dear heart; for heaven shall hear our
prayers;
Or with our sighs we'll breathe the welkin dim,
And stain the sun with fog, as sometime clouds
When they do hug him in their melting bosoms.

Marc. O brother, speak with possibilities,
And do not break into these deep extremes.

Tit. Is not my sorrow deep, having no bottom?
Then be my passions bottomless with them.

Marc. But yet let reason govern thy lament.

Tit. If there were reason for these miseries,
Then into limits could I bind my woes: 221
When heaven doth weep, doth not the earth
o'erflow?
If the winds rage, doth not the sea wax mad,
Threatening the welkin with his big-swoln face?
And wilt thou have a reason for this coil?
I am the sea; hark, how her sighs do blow!
She is the weeping welkin, I the earth:
Then must my sea be moved with her sighs;
Then must my earth with her continual tears
Become a deluge, overflow'd and drown'd;   230
For why my bowels cannot hide her woes,

But like a drunkard must I vomit them.
Then give me leave, for losers will have leave
To ease their stomachs with their bitter tongues.

Enter a MESSENGER, *with two heads and a hand.*

Mess. Worthy Andronicus, ill art thou repaid
For that good hand thou sent'st the Emperor.
Here are the heads of thy two noble sons;
And here's thy hand, in scorn to thee sent back;
Thy griefs their sports, thy resolution mock'd;
That woe is me to think upon thy woes   240
More than remembrance of my father's death.

> [*Exit.*

Marc. Now let hot Ætna cool in Sicily,
And be my heart an ever-burning hell!
These miseries are more than may be borne.
To weep with them that weep doth ease some
deal;
But sorrow flouted at is double death.

Luc. Ah, that this sight should make so deep a
wound,
And yet detested life not shrink thereat!
That ever death should let life bear his name,   249
Where life hath no more interest but to breathe!

> LAVINIA *kisses* TITUS.

Marc. Alas, poor heart, that kiss is comfortless
As frozen water to a starved snake.

Tit. When will this fearful slumber have an
end?

Marc. Now, farewell, flattery: die, Andronicus;
Thou dost not slumber: see, thy two sons' heads,
Thy warlike hand, thy mangled daughter here;
Thy other banish'd son, with this dear sight
Struck pale and bloodless; and thy brother, I,
Even like a stony image, cold and numb.
Ah, now no more will I control thy griefs: 260
Rend off thy silver hair, thy other hand
Gnawing with thy teeth; and be this dismal sight
The closing up of our most wretched eyes:
Now is a time to storm; why art thou still?

Tit. Ha, ha, ha!

Marc. Why dost thou laugh? it fits not with
this hour.

Tit. Why, I have not another tear to shed:
Besides, this sorrow is an enemy,
And would usurp upon my watery eyes,
And make them blind with tributary tears: 270
Then which way shall I find Revenge's cave?
For these two heads do seem to speak to me
And threat me I shall never come to bliss
Till all these mischiefs be return'd again.
Even in their throats that have committed them.
Come, let me see what task I have to do.
You heavy people, circle me about,
That I may turn me to each one of you,
And swear unto my soul to right your wrongs.

The vow is made. Come, brother, take a head;
And in this hand the other will I bear.   281
Lavinia, thou shalt be employ'd: these arms!
Bear thou my hand, sweet wench, between thy
      teeth.
As for thee, boy, go get thee from my sight;
Thou art an exile, and thou must not stay:
Hie to the Goths, and raise an army there:
And, if you love me, as I think you do,
Let's kiss and part, for we have much to do.
            [*Exeunt* TITUS, MARCUS, *and* LAVINIA.
  Luc. Farewell, Andronicus, my noble father,
The woefull'st man that ever lived in Rome: 290
Farewell, proud Rome; till Lucius come again,
He leaves his pledges dearer than his life:
Farewell, Lavinia, my noble sister;
O, would thou wert as thou tofore hast been!
But now nor Lucius nor Lavinia lives
But in oblivion and hateful griefs.
If Lucius live, he will requite your wrongs;
And make proud Saturnine and his empress
Beg at the gates, like Tarquin and his queen.
Now will I to the Goths, and raise a power. 300
To be revenged on Rome and Saturnine.   [*Exit.*

SCENE II. *A room in Titus's house:*
a banquet set out.

Enter TITUS, MARCUS, LAVINIA, *and* YOUNG
LUCIUS, *a Boy.*

  Tit. So, so; now sit: and look you eat no more
Than will preserve just so much strength in us
As will revenge these bitter woes of ours.
Marcus, unknit that sorrow-wreathen knot:
Thy niece and I, poor creatures, want our hands,
And cannot passionate our tenfold grief
With folded arms, This poor right hand of mine
Is left to tyrannize upon my breast;
Who, when my heart, all mad with misery,
Beats in this hollow prison of my flesh,   10
Then thus I thump it down.
[*To* LAVINIA.] Thou map of woe, that thus dost
      talk in signs!
When thy poor heart beats with outrageous
      beating,
Thou canst not strike it thus to make it still.
Wound it with sighing, girl, kill it with groans;
Or get some little knife between thy teeth,
And just against thy heart make thou a hole;
That all the tears that thy poor eyes let fall
May run into that sink, and soaking in
Drown the lamenting fool in sea-salt tears.   20
  Marc. Fie, brother, fie! teach her not thus to lay
Such violent hands upon her tender life.
  Tit. How now! has sorrow made thee dote
      already?
Why, Marcus, no man should be mad but I.

What violent hands can she lay on her life?
Ah, wherefore dost thou urge the name of hands;
To bid Æneas tell the tale twice o'er,
How Troy was burnt and he made miserable?
O, handle not the theme, to talk of hands,
Lest we remember still that we have none.   30
Fie, fie, how frantically I square my talk,
As if we should forget we had no hands,
If Marcus did not name the word of hands!
Come, let's fall to; and, gentle girl, eat this:
Here is no drink! Hark, Marcus, what she says;
I can interpret all her martyr'd signs;
She says she drinks no other drink but tears,
Brew'd with her sorrow, mesh'd upon her cheeks:
Speechless complainer, I will learn thy thought;
In thy dumb action will I be as perfect   40
As begging hermits in their holy prayers:
Thou shalt not sigh, nor hold thy stumps to
      heaven,
Nor wink, nor nod, nor kneel, nor make a sign,
But I of these will wrest an alphabet
And by still practice learn to know thy meaning.
  Young Luc. Good grandsire, leave these bitter
      deep laments:
Make my aunt merry with some pleasing tale.
  Marc. Alas, the tender boy, in passion moved,
Doth weep to see his grandsire's heaviness.
  Tit. Peace, tender sapling; thou art made of
      tears,   50
And tears will quickly melt thy life away.
            MARCUS *strikes the dish with a knife.*
What dost thou strike at, Marcus, with thy
      knife?
  Marc. At that that I have kill'd, my lord; a fly.
  Tit. Out on thee, murderer! thou kill'st my
      heart;
Mine eyes are cloy'd with view of tyranny:
A deed of death done on the innocent
Becomes not Titus' brother: get thee gone;
I see thou art not for my company.
  Marc. Alas, my lord, I have but kill'd a fly.
  Tit. But how, if that fly had a father and
      mother?   60
How would he hang his slender gilded wings,
And buzz lamenting doings in the air!
Poor harmless fly,
That, with his pretty buzzing melody,
Came here to make us merry! and thou hast kill'd
      him.
  Marc. Pardon me, sir; it was a black ill-favour'd
      fly,
Like to the Empress' Moor; therefore I kill'd him.
  Tit. O, O, O,
Then pardon me for reprehending thee,
For thou hast done a charitable deed.   70
Give me thy knife, I will insult on him;

Flattering myself, as if it were the Moor
Come hither purposely to poison me.
There's for thyself, and that's for Tamora.
Ah, sirrah!
Yet, I think, we are not brought so low,
But that between us we can kill a fly
That comes in likeness of a coal-black Moor.
  Marc. Alas, poor man! grief has so wrought on
    him,
He takes false shadows for true substances.   80
  Tit. Come, take away. Lavinia, go with me:
I'll to thy closet; and go read with thee
Sad stories chanced in the times of old.
Come, boy, and go with me: thy sight is young,
And thou shalt read when mine began to dazzle.
                          [*Exeunt.*

ACT IV

Scene i. *Rome: Titus's garden*

Enter young lucius, *and* lavinia *running after
him, and the boy flies from her, with books under
his arm. Then enter* titus *and* marcus.

  Young Luc. Help, grandsire, help! my aunt
    Lavinia
Follows me everywhere, I know not why:
Good uncle Marcus, see how swift she comes.
Alas, sweet aunt, I know not what you mean.
  Marc. Stand by me, Lucius; do not fear thine
    aunt.
  Tit. She loves thee, boy, too well to do thee
    harm.
  Young Luc. Ay, when my father was in Rome
    she did.
  Marc. What means my niece Lavinia by these
    signs?
  Tit. Fear her not, Lucius: somewhat doth she
    mean:
See, Lucius, see how much she makes of thee: 10
Somewhither would she have thee go with
    her.
Ah, boy, Cornelia never with more care
Read to her sons than she hath read to thee
Sweet poetry and Tully's *Orator.*
  Marc. Canst thou not guess wherefore she plies
    thee thus?
  Young Luc. My lord, I know not, I, nor can I
    guess,
Unless some fit or frenzy do possess her:
For I have heard my grandsire say full oft,
Extremity of griefs would make men mad;
And I have read that Hecuba of Troy   20
Ran mad for sorrow: that made me to fear;
Although, my lord, I know my noble aunt
Loves me as dear as e'er my mother did,
And would not, but in fury, fright my youth:

Which made me down to throw my books,
    and fly—
Causeless, perhaps. But pardon me, sweet aunt:
And, madam, if my uncle Marcus go,
I will most willingly attend your ladyship.
  Marc. Lucius, I will.
    lavinia *turns over with her stumps the books
    which* lucius *has let fall.*
  Tit. How now, Lavinia! Marcus, what means
    this?   30
Some book there is that she desires to see.
Which is it, girl, of these? Open them, boy.
But thou art deeper read, and better skill'd:
Come, and take choice of all my library,
And so beguile thy sorrow, till the heavens
Reveal the damn'd contriver of this deed.
Why lifts she up her arms in sequence thus?
  Marc. I think she means that there was more
    than one
Confederate in the fact: ay, more there was;
Or else to heaven she heaves them for revenge.
  Tit. Lucius, what book is that she tosseth so? 41
  Young Luc. Grandsire, 'tis Ovid's *Metamor-
    phoses;*
My mother gave it me.
  Marc.   For love of her that's gone,
Perhaps she cull'd it from among the rest.
  Tit. Soft! see how busily she turns the leaves!
    [*Helping her.*]
What would she find? Lavinia, shall I read?
This is the tragic tale of Philomel,
And treats of Tereus' treason and his rape;
And rape, I fear, was root of thine annoy.
  Marc. See, brother, see; note how she quotes
    the leaves.   50
  Tit. Lavinia, wert thou thus surprised, sweet
    girl,
Ravish'd and wrong'd, as Philomela was,
Forced in the ruthless, vast, and gloomy woods?
See, see!
Ay, such a place there is, where we did hunt—
O, had we never, never hunted there!—
Pattern'd by that the poet here describes,
By nature made for murders and for rapes.
  Marc. O, why should nature build so foul a den,
Unless the gods delight in tragedies?   60
  Tit. Give signs, sweet girl, for here are none but
    friends,
What Roman lord it was durst do the deed:
Or slunk not Saturnine, as Tarquin erst,
That left the camp to sin in Lucrece' bed?
  Marc. Sit down, sweet niece: brother, sit
    down by me.
Apollo, Pallas, Jove, or Mercury,
Inspire me, that I may this treason find!
My lord, look here: look here, Lavinia:

This sandy plot is plain; guide if thou canst,
This after me, when I have writ my name   70
Without the help of any hand at all.

    *He writes his name with his staff, and guides it
    with feet and mouth.*

Cursed be that heart that forced us to this shift!
Write thou, good niece; and her display, at last,
What God will have discover'd for revenge:
Heaven guide thy pen to print thy sorrows plain,
That we may know the traitors and the truth!

    *She takes the staff in her mouth, and guides it with
    her stumps, and writes.*

    Tit. O, do ye read, my lord, what she hath writ?
"*Stuprum. Chiron. Demetrius.*"

    Marc. What, what! the lustful sons of Tamora
Performers of this heinous, bloody deed?   80

    Tit. Magni Dominator poli,
Tam lentus audis scelera? tam lentus vides?

    Marc. O, calm thee, gentle lord; although I
        know
There is enough written upon this earth
To stir a mutiny in the mildest thoughts
And arm the minds of infants to exclaims.
My lord, kneel down with me; Lavinia, kneel;
And kneel, sweet boy, the Roman Hector's
        hope;
And swear with me, as, with the woeful fere
And father of that chaste dishonour'd dame,   90
Lord Junius Brutus sware for Lucrece' rape,
That we will prosecute by good advice
Mortal revenge upon these traitorous Goths,
And see their blood, or die with this reproach.

    Tit. 'Tis sure enough, an you knew how.
But if you hunt these bear-whelps, then beware:
The dam will wake; and, if she wind you once,
She's with the lion deeply still in league,
And lulls him whilst she playeth on her back,
And when he sleeps will she do what she list.   100
You are a young huntsman, Marcus; let it alone;
And, come, I will go get a leaf of brass,
And with a gad of steel will write these words,
And lay it by: the angry northern wind
Will blow these sands, like Sibyl's leaves, abroad
And where's your lesson, then? Boy, what say
        you?

    Young Luc. I say, my lord, that if I were a man,
Their mother's bed-chamber should not be safe
For these bad bondmen to the yoke of Rome.

    Marc. Ay, that's my boy! thy father hath
        full oft   110
For his ungrateful country done the like.

    Young Luc. And, uncle, so will I, an if I live.

    Tit. Come, go with me into mine armoury;
Lucius, I'll fit thee; and withal, my boy,
Shalt carry from me to the Empress' sons
Presents that I intend to send them both:

Come, come; thou'lt do thy message, wilt thou
    not?

    Young Luc. Ay, with my dagger in their
        bosoms, grandsire.

    Tit. No, boy, not so; I'll teach thee another
        course.
Lavinia, come. Marcus, look to my house: 120
Lucius and I'll go brave it at the court:
Ay, marry, will we, sir; and we'll be waited on.

        [*Exeunt* TITUS, LAVINIA, *and* YOUNG LUC.

    Marc. O heavens, can you hear a good man
        groan
And not relent or not compassion him?
Marcus, attend him in his ecstasy,
That hath more scars of sorrow in his heart
Than foemen's marks upon his batter'd shield;
But yet so just that he will not revenge.
Revenge, ye heavens, for old Andronicus! [*Exit.*

SCENE II. *The same: a room in the palace*

Enter, from one side, AARON, DEMETRIUS, *and*
    CHIRON; *from the other side,* YOUNG LUCIUS, *and*
    an Attendant, with a bundle of weapons, and
    verses writ upon them.

    Chi. Demetrius, here's the son of Lucius;
He hath some message to deliver us.

    Aar. Ay, some mad message from his mad
        grandfather.

    Young Luc. My lords, with all the humbleness
        I may,
I greet your honours from Andronicus.
[*Aside*] And pray the Roman gods confound you
        both!

    Dem. Gramercy, lovely Lucius: what's the
        news?

    Young Luc. [*Aside*] That you are both
        decipher'd, that's the news,
For villains mark'd with rape.—May it please
        you,
My grandsire, well advised, hath sent by me   10
The goodliest weapons of his armoury
To gratify your honourable youth,
The hope of Rome; for so he bade me say;
And so I do, and with his gifts present
Your lordships, that, whenever you have need,
You may be armed and appointed well:
And so I leave you both: [*Aside*] like bloody
        villains.

        [*Exeunt* YOUNG LUCIUS *and Attendant.*

    Dem. What's here? A scroll; and written round
        about?
Let's see:
[*Reads*] *Integer vitæ, scelerisque purus,*   20
        Non eget Mauri jaculis, nec arcu.

    Chi. O, 'tis a verse in Horace; I know it well:
I read it in the grammar long ago.

Aar. Ay, just; a verse in Horace; right, you
have it.
[*Aside*] Now, what a thing it is to be an ass!
Here's no sound jest! the old man hath found
their guilt;
And sends them weapons wrapp'd about with
lines,
That wound, beyond their feeling, to the quick.
But were our witty empress well afoot,
She would applaud Andronicus' conceit: 30
But let her rest in her unrest awhile.—
And now, young lords, was't not a happy star
Led us to Rome, strangers, and more than so,
Captives, to be advanced to this height?
It did me good, before the palace gate
To brave the tribune in his brother's hearing.
Dem. But me more good, to see so great a lord
Basely insinuate and send us gifts.
Aar. Had he not reason, Lord Demetrius?
Did you not use his daughter very friendly? 40
Dem. I would we had a thousand Roman dames
At such a bay, by turn to serve our lust.
Chi. A charitable wish and full of love.
Aar. Here lacks but your mother for to say
amen.
Chi. And that would she for twenty thousand
more.
Dem. Come, let us go; and pray to all the gods
For our beloved mother in her pains.
Aar. [*Aside*] Pray to the devils; the gods have
given us over.
Trumpets sound within.
Dem. Why do the Emperor's trumpets flourish
thus?
Chi. Belike, for joy the Emperor hath a son. 50
Dem. Soft! who comes here?

Enter a NURSE, *with a blackamoor child in her arms.*

Nur.   Good morrow, lords:
O, tell me, did you see Aaron the Moor?
Aar. Well, more or less, or ne'er a whit at all,
Here Aaron is; and what with Aaron now?
Nur. O gentle Aaron, we are all undone!
Now help, or woe betide thee evermore!
Aar. Why, what a caterwauling dost thou keep!
What dost thou wrap and fumble in thine arms?
Nur. O, that which I would hide from heaven's
eye, 59
Our Empress' shame, and stately Rome's
disgrace!
She is deliver'd, lords; she is deliver'd.
Aar. To whom?
Nur.   I mean, she is brought a-bed.
Aar. Well, God give her good rest! What
hath he sent her?
Nur. A devil.

Aar. Why, then she is the devil's dam; a
joyful issue.
Nur. A joyless, dismal, black, and sorrowful
issue:
Here is the babe, as loathsome as a toad
Amongst the fairest breeders of our clime:
The Empress sends it thee, thy stamp, thy seal,
And bids thee christen it with thy dagger's point.
Aar. 'Zounds, ye whore! is black so base a hue?
Sweet blowse, you are a beauteous blossom, sure.
Dem. Villain, what hast thou done?
Aar. That which thou canst not undo.
Chi. Thou hast undone our mother.
Aar. Villain, I have done thy mother.
Dem. And therein, hellish dog, thou hast undone.
Woe to her chance, and damn'd her loathed
choice!
Accursed the offspring of so foul a fiend!
Chi. It shall not live.   80
Aar. It shall not die.
Nur. Aaron, it must; the mother wills it so.
Aar. What, must it, nurse? then let no man but I
Do execution on my flesh and blood.
Dem. I'll broach the tadpole on my rapier's
point:
Nurse, give it me; my sword shall soon dispatch
it.
Aar. Sooner this sword shall plough thy bowels
up.
Takes the child from the NURSE *and draws.*
Stay, murderous villains! will you kill your
brother?
Now, by the burning tapers of the sky,
That shone so brightly when this boy was got,
He dies upon my scimitar's sharp point   91
That touches this my first-born son and heir!
I tell you, younglings, not Enceladus,
With all his threatening band of Typhon's brood,
Nor great Alcides, nor the god of war,
Shall seize this prey out of his father's hands.
What, what, ye sanguine, shallow-hearted boys!
Ye white-limed walls! ye alehouse painted signs!
Coal-black is better than another hue,
In that it scorns to bear another hue;   100
For all the water in the ocean
Can never turn the swan's black legs to white,
Although she lave them hourly in the flood.
Tell the Empress from me, I am of age
To keep mine own, excuse it how she can.
Dem. Wilt thou betray thy noble mistress thus?
Aar. My mistress is my mistress; this myself,
The vigour and the picture of my youth:
This before all the world do I prefer;
This maugre all the world will I keep safe,   110
Or some of you shall smoke for it in Rome.
Dem. By this our mother is for ever shamed.

Chi. Rome will despise her for this foul escape.

Nur. The Emperor, in his rage, will doom her
   death.

Chi. I blush to think upon this ignomy.

Aar. Why, there's the privilege your beauty
   bears:

Fie, treacherous hue, that will betray with
   blushing

The close enacts and counsels of the heart!

Here's a young lad framed of another leer:

Look, how the black slave smiles upon the father,

As who should say, "Old lad, I am thine own." *121*

He is your brother, lords, sensibly fed

Of that self-blood that first gave life to you,

And from that womb where you imprison'd were

He is enfranchised and come to light:

Nay, he is your brother by the surer side,

Although my seal be stamped in his face.

Nur. Aaron, what shall I say unto the Empress?

Dem. Advise thee, Aaron, what is to be done,

And we will all subscribe to thy advice: *130*

Save thou the child, so we may all be safe.

Aar. Then sit we down, and let us all consult.

My son and I will have the wind of you:

Keep there: now talk at pleasure of your safety.
   They sit.

Dem. How many women saw this child of his?

Aar. Why, so, brave lords! when we join in
   league,

I am a lamb: but if you brave the Moor,

The chafed boar, the mountain lioness,

The ocean swells not so as Aaron storms.

But say, again, how many saw the child? *140*

Nur. Cornelia the midwife and myself;

And no one else but the deliver'd Empress.

Aar. The Empress the midwife, and yourself:

Two may keep counsel when the third's away:

Go to the Empress, tell her this I said.
   He kills the nurse.

Weke, weke! so cries a pig prepared to the spit.

Dem. What mean'st thou, Aaron? wherefore
   didst thou this?

Aar. O Lord, sir, 'tis a deed of policy:

Shall she live to betray this guilt of ours,

A long-tongued babbling gossip? no, lords, no:

And now be it known to you my full intent. *151*

Not far, one Muli lives, my countryman;

His wife but yesternight was brought to bed;

His child is like to her, fair as you are:

Go pack with him, and give the mother gold,

And tell them both the circumstance of all;

And how by this their child shall be advanced,

And be received for the Emperor's heir,

And substituted in the place of mine,

To calm this tempest whirling in the court; *160*

And let the Emperor dandle him for his own.

Hark ye, lords; ye see I have given her physic,
   Pointing to the nurse.

And you must needs bestow her funeral;

The fields are near, and you are gallant grooms:

This done, see that you take no longer days,

But send the midwife presently to me.

The midwife and the nurse well made away,

Then let the ladies tattle what they please.

Chi. Aaron, I see thou wilt not trust the air

With secrets.

Dem.   For this care of Tamora,   *170*

Herself and hers are highly bound to thee.
   [*Exeunt* DEMETRIUS *and* CHIRON *bearing off the*
               Nurse's body.

Aar. Now to the Goths, as swift as swallow
   flies;

There to dispose this treasure in mine arms,

And secretly to greet the Empress' friends.

Come on, you thick-lipp'd slave, I'll bear you
   hence;

For it is you that puts us to our shifts:

I'll make you feed on berries and on roots,

And feed on curds and whey, and suck the goat,

And cabin in a cave, and bring you up   *179*

To be a warrior, and command a camp.   [*Exit.*

SCENE III. *The same: a public place*

Enter TITUS, *bearing arrows with letters at the ends*
of them; with him, MARCUS, YOUNG LUCIUS,
PUBLIUS, *Sempronius, Caius, and other Gentle-*
men with bows.

Tit. Come, Marcus; come, kinsmen; this is
   the way.

Sir boy, now let me see your archery;

Look ye draw home enough, and 'tis there
   straight.

Terras Astræa reliquit:

Be you remember'd, Marcus, she's gone, she's
   fled.

Sirs, take you to your tools. You, cousins, shall

Go sound the ocean, and cast your nets;

Happily you may catch her in the sea;

Yet there's as little justice as at land:

No; Publius and Sempronius, you must do it;   *10*

'Tis you must dig with mattock and with spade,

And pierce the inmost centre of the earth:

Then when you come to Pluto's region,

I pray you, deliver him this petition;

Tell him, it is for Justice and for aid,

And that it comes from old Andronicus,

Shaken with sorrows in ungrateful Rome.

Ah, Rome! Well, well; I made thee miserable

What time I threw the people's suffrages

On him that thus doth tyrannize o'er me.   *20*

Go, get you gone; and pray be careful all,

And leave you not a man-of-war unsearch'd:

This wicked Emperor may have shipp'd her
    hence;
And, kinsmen, then we may go pipe for Justice.
  Marc. O Publius, is not this a heavy case,
To see thy noble uncle thus distract?
  Pub. Therefore, my lord, it highly us concerns
By day and night to attend him carefully,
And feed his humour kindly as we may,
Till time beget some careful remedy.   *30*
  Marc. Kinsmen, his sorrows are past remedy.
Join with the Goths; and with revengeful war
Take wreak on Rome for this ingratitude,
And vengeance on the traitor Saturnine.
  Tit. Publius, how now! how now, my masters!
What, have you met with her?
  Pub. No, my good lord; but Pluto sends you
    word,
If you will have Revenge from hell, you shall:
Marry, for Justice, she is so employ'd,
He thinks, with Jove in heaven, or somewhere
    else,   *40*
So that perforce you must needs stay a time.
  Tit. He doth me wrong to feed me with delays.
I'll dive into the burning lake below,
And pull her out of Acheron by the heels.
Marcus, we are but shrubs, no cedars we,
No big-boned men framed of the Cyclops' size;
But metal, Marcus, steel to the very back,
Yet wrung with wrongs more than our backs can
    bear:
And, sith there's no justice in earth nor hell,
We will solicit heaven and move the gods   *50*
To send down Justice for to wreak our wrongs.
Come, to this gear. You are a good archer,
    Marcus; [*He gives them the arrows.*]
"*Ad Jovem,*" that's for you: here, "*Ad Apolli-*
    nem":
"*Ad Martem,*" that's for myself:
Here, boy, to Pallas: here, to Mercury:
To Saturn, Caius, not to Saturnine;
You were as good to shoot against the wind.
To it, boy! Marcus, loose when I bid.
Of my word, I have written to effect;
There's not a god left unsolicited.   *60*
  Marc. Kinsmen, shoot all your shafts into the
    court:
We will afflict the Emperor in his pride.
  Tit. Now, masters, draw. [*They shoot.*] O,
    well said, Lucius!
Good boy, in Virgo's lap; give it Pallas.
  Marc. My lord, I aim a mile beyond the
    moon;
Your letter is with Jupiter by this.
  Tit. Ha, ha!
Publius, Publius, what hast thou done?
See, see, thou hast shot off one of Taurus' horns.

  Marc. This was the sport, my lord: when
    Publius shot,   *70*
The Bull, being gall'd, gave Aries such a knock
That down fell both the Ram's horns in the court;
And who should find them but the Empress'
    villain?
She laugh'd, and told the Moor he should not
    choose
But give them to his master for a present.
  Tit. Why, there it goes: God give his lordship
    joy!

Enter a CLOWN, *with a basket, and two pigeons in it.*

News, news from heaven! Marcus, the post is
    come.
Sirrah, what tidings? have you any letters?
Shall I have justice? what says Jupiter?   *79*
  Clo. O, the gibbet-maker! he says that he hath
taken them down again, for the man must not be
hanged till the next week.
  Tit. But what says Jupiter, I ask thee?
  Clo. Alas, sir, I know not Jupiter; I never drank
with him in all my life.
  Tit. Why, villain, art not thou the carrier?
  Clo. Ay, of my pigeons, sir; nothing else.
  Tit. Why, didst thou not come from heaven?
  Clo. From heaven! alas, sir, I never came there:
God forbid I should be so bold to press to heaven
in my young days. Why, I am going with my
pigeons to the tribunal plebs, to take up a matter
of brawl betwixt my uncle and one of the empe-
rial's men.
  Marc. Why, sir, that is as fit as can be to serve
for your oration; and let him deliver the pigeons
to the Emperor from you.
  Tit. Tell me, can you deliver an oration to the
Emperor with a grace?
  Clo. Nay, truly, sir, I could never say grace in
all my life.   *101*
  Tit. Sirrah, come hither: make no more ado,
But give your pigeons to the Emperor:
By me thou shalt have justice at his hands.
Hold, hold; meanwhile here's money for thy
    charges.
Give me pen and ink. Sirrah, can you with a
grace deliver a supplication?
  Clo. Ay, sir.
  Tit. Then here is a supplication for you. And
when you come to him, at the first approach you
must kneel, then kiss his foot, then deliver up
your pigeons, and then look for your reward. I'll
be at hand, sir; see you do it bravely.
  Clo. I warrant you, sir, let me alone.
  Tit. Sirrah, hast thou a knife? come, let me
    see it.
Here, Marcus, fold it in the oration;

For thou hast made it like an humble suppliant.
And when thou hast given it the Emperor,
Knock at my door and tell me what he says.
  Clo. God be with you, sir; I will.   *120*
  Tit. Come, Marcus, let us go. Publius, follow
  me.   [*Exeunt.*

SCENE IV. *The same: before the palace*

Enter SATURNINUS, TAMORA, DEMETRIUS, CHIRON,
  Lords, and others; SATURNINUS *with the arrows
  in his hand that* TITUS *shot.*

  Sat. Why, lords, what wrongs are these! was
    ever seen
An Emperor in Rome thus overborne,
Troubled, confronted thus; and, for the extent
Of egal justice, used in such contempt?
My lords, you know, as know the mightful gods,
However these disturbers of our peace
Buz in the people's ears, there nought hath pass'd,
But even with law, against the wilful sons
Of old Andronicus. And what an if
His sorrows have so overwhelm'd his wits,   *10*
Shall we be thus afflicted in his wreaks,
His fits, his frenzy, and his bitterness?
And now he writes to heaven for his redress:
See, here's to Jove, and this to Mercury;
This to Apollo; this to the god of war;
Sweet scrolls to fly about the streets of Rome!
What's this but libelling against the senate,
And blazoning our injustice every where?
A goodly humour, is it not, my lords?
As who would say, in Rome no justice were   *20*
But if I live, his feigned ecstasies
Shall be no shelter to these outrages:
But he and his shall know that justice lives
In Saturninus' health, whom, if she sleep,
He'll so awake as she in fury shall
Cut off the proud'st conspirator that lives.
  Tam. My gracious lord, my lovely Saturnine,
Lord of my life, commander of my thoughts,
Calm thee, and bear the faults of Titus' age,
The effects of sorrow for his valiant sons,   *30*
Whose loss hath pierced him deep and scarr'd his
    heart;
And rather comfort his distressed plight
Than prosecute the meanest or the best
For these contempts. [*Aside*] Why, thus it shall
    become
High-witted Tamora to gloze with all:
But, Titus, I have touch'd thee to the quick,
Thy life-blood out: if Aaron now be wise,
Then is all safe, the anchor's in the port.

Enter CLOWN.

How now, good fellow! wouldst thou speak
  with us?

  Clo. Yea, forsooth, an your mistership be
    emperial.   *40*
  Tam. Empress I am, but yonder sits the
    Emperor.
  Clo. 'Tis he. God and Saint Stephen give you
good den: I have brought you a letter and a
couple of pigeons here.
  Saturninus reads the letter.
  Sat. Go, take him away, and hang him presently.
  Clo. How much money must I have?
  Tam. Come, sirrah, you must be hanged.
  Clo. Hanged! by'r lady, then I have brought up
a neck to a fair end.   [*Exit, guarded.*
  Sat. Despiteful and intolerable wrongs!   *50*
Shall I endure this monstrous villainy?
I know from whence this same device proceeds:
May this be borne? As if his traitorous sons,
That died by law for murder of our brother,
Have by my means been butcher'd wrongfully!
Go, drag the villain hither by the hair;
Nor age nor honour shall shape privilege:
For this proud mock I'll be thy slaughter-man;
Sly frantic wretch, that holp'st to make me great,
In hope thyself should govern Rome and me.   *60*

Enter ÆMILIUS.

What news with thee, Æmilius?
  Æmil. Arm, arm, my lord; Rome never had
    more cause.
The Goths have gather'd head; and with a power
Of high-resolved men, bent to the spoil,
They hither march amain, under conduct
Of Lucius, son to old Andronicus;
Who threats, in course of this revenge, to do
As much as ever Coriolanus did.
  Sat. Is warlike Lucius general of the Goths?
These tidings nip me, and I hang the head   *70*
As flowers with frost or grass beat down with
    storms:
Ay, now begin our sorrows to approach:
'Tis he the common people love so much;
Myself hath often over-heard them say,
When I have walked like a private man,
That Lucius' banishment was wrongfully,
And they have wish'd that Lucius were their
    emperor.
  Tam. Why should you fear? is not your city
    strong?
  Sat. Ay, but the citizens favour Lucius,
And will revolt from me to succour him.   *80*
  Tam. King, be thy thoughts imperious, like thy
    name.
Is the sun dimm'd, that gnats do fly in it?
The eagle suffers little birds to sing,
And is not careful what they mean thereby,
Knowing that with the shadow of his wings

He can at pleasure stint their melody:
Even so mayst thou the giddy men of Rome.
Then cheer thy spirit: for know, thou emperor,
I will enchant the old Andronicus
With words more sweet, and yet more danger-
    ous,   90
Than baits to fish, or honey-stalks to sheep,
When as the one is wounded with the bait,
The other rotted with delicious feed.
  Sat. But he will not entreat his son for us.
  Tam. If Tamora entreat him, then he will:
For I can smooth and fill his aged ear
With golden promises; that, were his heart
Almost impregnable, his old ears deaf,
Yet should both ear and heart obey my tongue.
[*To* ÆMILIUS] Go thou before, be our ambassa-
    dor: 100
Say that the Emperor requests a parley
Of warlike Lucius, and appoint the meeting
Even at his father's house, the old Andronicus.
  Sat. Æmilius, do this message honourably:
And if he stand on hostage for his safety,
Bid him demand what pledge will please him best.
  Æmil. Your bidding shall I do effectually.
                                              [*Exit.*
  Tam. Now will I to that old Andronicus,
And temper him with all the art I have
To pluck proud Lucius from the warlike Goths.
And now, sweet emperor, be blithe again,   111
And bury thy fear in my devices.
  Sat. Then go successantly, and plead to him.
                                              [*Exeunt.*

ACT V

SCENE I. *Plains bear Rome*

Enter LUCIUS *with an army of* GOTHS, *with
drum and colours.*

  Luc. Approved warriors, and my faithful friends,
I have received letters from great Rome,
Which signify what hate they bear their Emperor
And how desirous of our sight they are.
Therefore, great lords, be, as your titles witness,
Imperious and impatient of your wrongs,
And wherein Rome hath done you any scath,
Let him make treble satisfaction.
  1st Goth. Brave slip, sprung from the great
    Andronicus,
Whose name was once our terror, now our
    comfort;   10
Whose high exploits and honourable deeds
Ingrateful Rome requites with foul contempt,
Be bold in us: we'll follow where thou lead'st,
Like stinging bees in hottest summer's day
Led by their master to the flowered fields,
And be avenged on cursed Tamora.

  All the Goths. And as he saith, so say we all
    with him.
  Luc. I humbly thank him, and I thank you all.
But who comes here, led by a lusty Goth?

Enter SECOND GOTH, *leading* AARON *with his child
in his arms.*

  2nd Goth. Renowned Lucius, from our troops I
    stray'd   20
To gaze upon a ruinous monastery;
And, as I earnestly did fix mine eye
Upon the wasted building, suddenly
I heard a child cry underneath a wall.
I made unto the noise; when soon I heard
The crying babe controll'd with this discourse:
"Peace, tawny slave, half me and half thy dam!
Did not thy hue bewray whose brat thou art,
Had nature lent thee but thy mother's look,
Villain, thou mightst have been an emperor: 30
But where the bull and cow are both milk-white,
They never do beget a coal-black calf.
Peace, villain, peace!"—even thus he rates the
    babe—
"For I must bear thee to a trusty Goth;
Who, when he knows thou art the Empress' babe,
Will hold thee dearly for thy mother's sake."
With this, my weapon drawn, I rush'd upon him,
Surprised him suddenly, and brought him hither
To use as you think needful of the man.
  Luc. O worthy Goth, this is the incarnate devil
That robb'd Andronicus of his good hand;   41
This is the pearl that pleased your Empress' eye,
And here's the base fruit of his burning lust.
Say, wall-eyed slave, whither wouldst thou
    convey
This growing image of thy fiend-like face?
Why dost not speak? what, deaf? not a word?
A halter, soldiers! hang him on this tree,
And by his side his fruit of bastardy.
  Aar. Touch not the boy; he is of royal blood.
  Luc. Too like the sire for ever being good.   50
First hang the child, that he may see it sprawl;
A sight to vex the father's soul withal.
Get me a ladder.
        A ladder brought, which AARON *is made to ascend.*
  Aar.   Lucius, save the child
And bear it from me to the Empress.
If thou do this, I'll show thee wondrous things,
That highly may advantage thee to hear:
If thou wilt not, befall what may befall,
I'll speak no more but "Vengeance rot you all!"
  Luc. Say on: an if it please me which thou
    speak'st,
Thy child shall live, and I will see it nourish'd.
  Aar. An if it please thee! why, assure thee,
    Lucius,   61

'Twill vex thy soul to hear what I shall speak;
For I must talk of murders, rapes and massacres,
Acts of black night, abominable deeds,
Complots of mischief, treason, villainies
Ruthful to hear, yet piteously perform'd:
And this shall all be buried by my death
Unless thou swear to me my child shall live.
   Luc. Tell on thy mind; I say thy child shall
     live.
   Aar. Swear that he shall, and then I will begin.
   Luc. Who should I swear by? thou believest
     no god: *71*
That granted, how canst thou believe an oath?
   Aar. What if I do not? as, indeed, I do not;
Yet, for I know thou art religious
And hast a thing within thee called conscience,
With twenty popish tricks and ceremonies
Which I have seen thee careful to observe,
Therefore I urge thy oath; for that I know
An idiot holds his bauble for a god   *79*
And keeps the oath which by that god he swears,
To that I'll urge him: therefore thou shalt vow
By that same god, what god soe'er it be,
That thou adorest and hast in reverence,
To save my boy, to nourish and bring him up;
Or else I will discover nought to thee.
   Luc. Even by my god I swear to thee I will.
   Aar. First know thou, I begot him on the
     Empress.
   Luc. O most insatiate and luxurious woman!
   Aar. Tut, Lucius, this was but a deed of charity
To that which thou shalt hear of me anon.   *90*
'Twas her two sons that murder'd Bassianus;
They cut thy sister's tongue and ravish'd her
And cut her hands and trimm'd her as thou saw'st.
   Luc. O detestable villain! call'st thou that
     trimming?
   Aar. Why, she was wash'd and cut and
     trimm'd, and 'twas
Trim sport for them that had the doing of it.
   Luc. O barbarous, beastly villains, like thyself!
   Aar. Indeed, I was their tutor to instruct them:
That codding spirit had they from their mother,
As sure a card as ever won the set;   *100*
That bloody mind, I think, they learn'd of me,
As true a dog as ever fought at head.
Well, let my deeds be witness of my worth.
I train'd thy brethren to that guileful hole
Where the dead corpse of Bassianus lay:
I wrote the letter that thy father found
And hid the gold within the letter mention'd,
Confederate with the Queen and her two sons:
And what not done, that thou hast cause to rue,
Wherein I had no stroke of mischief in it?   *110*
I play'd the cheater for thy father's hand,
And, when I had it, drew myself apart

And almost broke my heart with extreme laughter:
I pry'd me through the crevice of a wall
When, for his hand, he had his two sons' heads;
Beheld his tears, and laugh'd so heartily,
That both mine eyes were rainy like to his:
And when I told the Empress of this sport,
She swooned almost at my pleasing tale
And for my tidings gave me twenty kisses.   *120*
   1st Goth. What, canst thou say all this, and
     never blush?
   Aar. Ay, like a black dog, as the saying is.
   Luc. Art thou not sorry for these heinous deeds?
   Aar. Ay, that I had not done a thousand more.
Even now I curse the day—and yet, I think,
Few come within the compass of my curse—
Wherin I did not some notorious ill,
As kill a man, or else devise his death,
Ravish a maid, or plot the way to do it,
Accuse some innocent and forswear myself,   *130*
Set deadly enmity between two friends,
Make poor men's cattle break their necks;
Set fires on barns and hay-stacks in the night,
And bid the owners quench them with their tears.
Oft have I digg'd up dead men from their graves,
And set them upright at their dear friends' doors,
Even when their sorrows almost were forgot;
And on their skins, as on the bark of trees,
Have with my knife carved in Roman letters,
"Let not your sorrow die, though I am dead."
Tut, I have done a thousand dreadful things   *141*
As willingly as one would kill a fly,
And nothing grieves me heartily indeed
But that I cannot do ten thousand more.
   Luc. Bring down the devil; for he must not die
So sweet a death as hanging presently.
   Aar. If there be devils, would I were a devil,
To live and burn in everlasting fire,
So I might have your company in hell,
But to torment you with my bitter tongue!   *150*
   Luc. Sirs, stop his mouth, and let him speak
     no more.

               Enter THIRD GOTH.

   3rd Goth. My lord, there is a messenger from
     Rome
Desires to be admitted to your presence.
   Luc. Let him come near.

               Enter ÆMILIUS.

Welcome, Æmilius: what's the news from Rome?
   Æmil. Lord Lucius, and you princes of the
     Goths,
The Roman Emperor greets you all by me;
And, for he understands you are in arms,
He craves a parley at your father's house,
Willing you to demand your hostages,   *160*

And they shall be immediately deliver'd.
1st Goth. What says our general?
Luc. Æmilius, let the Emperor give his pledges
Unto my father and my uncle Marcus,
And we will come. March away.   [*Exeunt.*

SCENE II. *Rome: before Titus's house*

Enter TAMORA, DEMETRIUS, *and* CHIRON, *disguised·*

Tam. Thus, in this strange and sad habiliment,
I will encounter with Andronicus,
And say I am Revenge, sent from below
To join with him and right his heinous wrongs.
Knock at his study, where, they say, he keeps,
To ruminate strange plots of dire revenge;
Tell him Revenge is come to join with him,
And work confusion on his enemies.
          They knock.

Enter TITUS, *above.*

Tit. Who doth molest my contemplation?
Is it your trick to make me ope the door   10
That so my sad decrees may fly away
And all my study be to no effect?
You are deceived: for what I mean to do
See here in bloody lines I have set down;
And what is written shall be executed.
Tam. Titus, I am come to talk with thee.
Tit. No, not a word; how can I grace my talk,
Wanting a hand to give it action?
Thou hast the odds of me; therefore no more.
Tam. If thou didst know me, thou wouldest
          talk with me.   20
Tit. I am not mad; I know thee well enough:
Witness this wretched stump, witness these
          crimson lines;
Witness these trenches made by grief and care;
Witness the tiring day and heavy night;
Witness all sorrow, that I know thee well
For our proud empress, mighty Tamora:
Is not thy coming for my other hand?
Tam. Know, thou sad man, I am not Tamora;
She is thy enemy, and I thy friend:
I am Revenge: sent from the infernal kingdom 30
To ease the gnawing vulture of thy mind
By working wreakful vengeance on thy foes.
Come down and welcome me to this world's light;
Confer with me of murder and of death:
There's not a hollow cave or lurking-place,
No vast obscurity or misty vale,
Where bloody murder or detested rape
Can couch for fear, but I will find them out;
And in their ears tell them my dreadful name,
Revenge, which makes the foul offender quake.
Tit. Art thou Revenge? and art thou sent to
          me,   41
To be a torment to mine enemies?

Tam. I am; therefore come down and welcome
          me.
Tit. Do me some service, ere I come to thee.
Lo, by thy side where Rape and Murder stands;
Now give some surance that thou art Revenge,
Stab them, or tear them on thy chariot-wheels;
And then I'll come and be thy waggoner,
And whirl along with thee about the globe.
Provide thee two proper palfreys, black as jet, 50
To hale thy vengeful waggon swift away
And find our murderers in their guilty caves:
And when thy car is loaden with their heads,
I will dismount, and by the waggon-wheel
Trot, like a servile footman, all day long,
Even from Hyperion's rising in the east
Until his very downfall in the sea:
And day by day I'll do this heavy task,
So thou destroy Rapine and Murder there.
Tam. These are my ministers, and come with
          me.   60
Tit. Are these thy ministers? what are they
          call'd?
Tam. Rapine and Murder; therefore called so,
·Cause they take vengeance of such kind of men.
Tit. Good Lord, how like the Empress' sons
          they are!
And you, the Empress! but we worldly men
Have miserable, mad, mistaking eyes.
O sweet Revenge, now do I come to thee;
And, if one arm's embracement will content thee,
I will embrace thee in it by and by. [*Exit above.*
Tam. This closing with him fits his lunacy:
Whate'er I forge to feed his brain-sick fits,   71
Do you uphold and maintain in your speeches,
For now he firmly takes me for Revenge;
And, being credulous in this mad thought,
I'll make him send for Lucius his son;
And, whilst I at a banquet hold him sure,
I'll find some cunning practice out of hand
To scatter and disperse the giddy Goths,
Or, at the least, make them his enemies.
See, here he comes, and I must ply my theme.

Enter TITUS *below.*

Tit. Long have I been forlorn, and all for
          thee: 81
Welcome, dread Fury, to my woful house:
Rapine and Murder, you are welcome too.
How like the Empress and her sons you are!
Well are you fitted, had you but a Moor:
Could not all hell afford you such a devil?
For well I wot the Empress never wags
But in her company there is a Moor;
And, would you represent our Queen aright,
It were convenient you had such a devil: 90
But welcome, as you are. What shall we do?

Tam. What wouldst thou have us do,
   Andronicus?

Dem. Show me a murderer, I'll deal with him.

Chi. Show me a villain that hath done a rape,
And I am sent to be revenged on him.

Tam. Show me a thousand that have done thee
   wrong,
And I will be revenged on them all.

   Tit. Look round about the wicked streets of
   Rome;
And when thou find'st a man that's like thy-
   self,
Good Murder, stab him; he's a murderer.   *100*
Go thou with him; and when it is thy hap
To find another that is like to thee,
Good Rapine, stab him; he's a ravisher.
Go thou with them; and in the Emperor's court
There is a Queen, attended by a Moor:
Well mayst thou know her by thy own
   proportion,
For up and down she doth resemble thee:
I pray thee, do on them some violent death;
They have been violent to me and mine.

   Tam. Well hast thou lesson'd us; this shall
   we do.   *110*
But would it please thee, good Andronicus,
To send for Lucius, thy thrice-valiant son,
Who leads towards Rome a band of warlike
   Goths,
And bid him come and banquet at thy house;
When he is here, even at thy solemn feast,
I will bring in the Empress and her sons,
The Emperor himself and all thy foes;
And at thy mercy shall they stoop and kneel,
And on them shalt thou ease thy angry heart.
What says Andronicus to this device?   *120*

   Tit. Marcus, my brother! 'tis sad Titus calls.

Enter MARCUS.

Go, gentle Marcus, to thy nephew Lucius;
Thou shalt inquire him out among the Goths:
Bid him repair to me, and bring with him
Some of the chiefest princes of the Goths;
Bid him encamp his soldiers where they are:
Tell him the Emperor and the Empress too
Feast at my house, and he shall feast with them.
This do thou for my love; and so let him,
As he regards his aged father's life.   *130*

   Marc. This will I do, and soon return again.
                                [Exit.

   Tam. Now will I hence about thy business,
And take my ministers along with me.

   Tit. Nay, nay, let Rape and Murder stay
   with me;
Or else I'll call my brother back again,
And cleave to no revenge but Lucius.

   Tam. [*Aside to her sons*] What say you, boys?
   will you bide with him,
Whiles I go tell my lord the Emperor
How I have govern'd our determined jest?
Yield to his humour, smooth and speak him fair,
And tarry with him till I turn again.   *141*

   Tit. [*Aside*] I know them all, though they
   suppose me mad,
And will o'erreach them in their own devices:
A pair of cursed hell-hounds and their dam!

   Dem. Madam, depart at pleasure; leave us here.

   Tam. Farewell, Andronicus: Revenge now goes
To lay a complot to betray thy foes.

   Tit. I know thou dost; and, sweet Revenge,
   farewell.   *[Exit* TAMORA.

   Chi. Tell us, old man, how shall we be
   employ'd?

   Tit. Tut, I have work enough for you to do.
Publius, come hither, Caius, and Valentine!   *151*

Enter PUBLIUS *and others.*

   Pub. What is your will?

   Tit. Know you these two?

   Pub. The Empress' sons, I take them, Chiron
   and Demetrius.

   Tit. Fie, Publius, fie! thou art too much
   deceived;
The one is Murder, Rape is the other's name;
And therefore bind them, gentle Publius.
Caius and Valentine, lay hands on them.
Oft have you heard me wish for such an hour, *160*
And now I find it; therefore bind them sure,
And stop their mouths, if they begin to cry. [*Exit.*
   Publius, &c. lay hold on CHIRON *and*
   DEMETRIUS.

   Chi. Villains, forbear! we are the Empress' sons.

   Pub. And therefore do we what we are
   commanded.
Stop close their mouths, let them not speak a
   word.
Is he sure bound? look that you bind them fast.

Re-enter TITUS, *with* LAVINIA; *he bearing a
knife, and she a basin.*

   Tit. Come, come, Lavinia; look, thy foes are
   bound.
Sirs, stop their mouths, let them not speak to
   me;
But let them hear what fearful words I utter.
O villains, Chiron and Demetrius!   *170*
Here stands the spring whom you have stain'd
   with mud,
This goodly summer with your winter mix'd.
You kill'd her husband, and for that vile fault
Two of her brothers were condemn'd to death,
My hand cut off and made a merry jest;

Both her sweet hands, her tongue, and that more
    dear
Than hands or tongue, her spotless chastity,
Inhuman traitors, you constrain'd and forced.
What would you say, if I should let you speak?
Villains, for shame you could not beg for grace.
Hark, wretches! how I mean to martyr you.   *181*
This one hand yet is left to cut your throats,
Whilst that Lavinia 'tween her stumps doth hold
The basin that receives your guilty blood.
You know your mother means to feast with me,
And calls herself Revenge, and thinks me mad:
Hark, villains! I will grind your bones to dust
And with your blood and it I'll make a paste,
And of the paste a coffin I will rear
And make two pastries of your shameful heads,
And bid that strumpet, your unhallow'd dam, *191*
Like to the earth swallow her own increase.
This is the feast that I have bid her to,
And this the banquet she shall surfeit on;
For worse than Philomel you used my daughter,
And worse than Progne I will be revenged:
And now prepare your throats. Lavinia, come,
  He cuts their throats.
Receive the blood: and when that they are dead,
Let me go grind their bones to powder small
And with this hateful liquor temper it;   *200*
And in that paste let their vile heads be baked.
Come, come, be every one officious
To make this banquet, which I wish may prove
More stern and bloody then the Centaurs' feast.
So, now bring them in, for I'll play the cook,
And see them ready 'gainst their mother comes.
  [Exeunt, bearing the dead bodies.

SCENE III. *Court of Titus's house: a banquet
set out*

Enter LUCIUS, MARCUS, *and* GOTHS, *with*
AARON *prisoner.*

Luc. Uncle Marcus, since it is my father's mind
That I repair to Rome, I am content.
  1st Goth. And ours with thine, befall what
    fortune will.
  Luc. Good uncle, take you in this barbarous
    Moor,
This ravenous tiger, this accursed devil;
Let him receive no sustenance, fetter him,
Till he be brought unto the Empress' face,
For testimony of her foul proceedings:
And see the ambush of our friends be strong;
I fear the Emperor means no good to us.   *10*
  Aar. Some devil whisper curses in mine ear,
And prompt me, that my tongue may utter forth
The venomous malice of my swelling heart!
  Luc. Away, inhuman dog! unhallow'd slave!
Sirs, help our uncle to convey him in.

  [Exeunt GOTHS, *with* AARON. *Flourish within.*
The trumpets show the Emperor is at hand.

Enter SATURNINUS *and* TAMORA, *with* ÆMILIUS,
    Tribunes, Senators, and others.

  Sat. What, hath the firmament more suns than
    one?
  Luc. What boots it thee to call thyself a sun?
  Marc. Rome's Emperor, and nephew, break
    the parle;
These quarrels must be quietly debated.   *20*
The feast is ready, which the careful Titus
Hath ordain'd to an honourable end,
For peace, for love, for league, and good to Rome:
Please you, therefore, draw nigh, and take your
    places.
  Sat. Marcus, we will.
  *Hautboys sound. The Company sit down at
    table.*

Enter TITUS *dressed like a Cook,* LAVINIA *veiled,*
YOUNG LUCIUS, *and others.* TITUS *places the
dishes on the table.*

  Tit. Welcome, my gracious lord; welcome,
    dread Queen;
Welcome, ye warlike Goths; welcome, Lucius;
And welcome, all : although the cheer be poor,
'Twill fill your stomachs; please you eat of it. *29*
  Sat. Why art thou thus attired, Andronicus?
  Tit. Because I would be sure to have all well,
To entertain your Highness and your Empress.
  Tam. We are beholding to you, good
    Andronicus.
  Tit. An if your Highness knew my heart, you
    were.
My lord the Emperor, resolve me this:
Was it well done of rash Virginius
To slay his daughter with his own right hand,
Because she was enforced, stain'd, and
    deflower'd?
  Sat. It was, Andronicus.
  Tit. Your reason, mighty lord?   *40*
  Sat. Because the girl should not survive her
    shame,
And by her presence still renew sorrows.
  Tit. A reason mighty, strong, and effectual;
A pattern, precedent, and lively warrant,
For me, most wretched, to perform the like.
Die, die, Lavinia, and thy shame with thee;
  [Kills LAVINIA.
And, with thy shame, thy father's sorrow die!
  Sat. What hast thou done, unnatural and unkind?
  Tit. Kill'd her, for whom my tears have made
    me blind.
I am as woful as Virginius was,   *50*
And have a thousand times more cause than he

To do this outrage: and it now is done.

Sat. What, was she ravish'd? tell who did the
   deed.

Tit. Will't please you eat? will't please your
   Highness feed?

Tam. Why hast thou slain thine only daughter
   thus?

Tit. Not I; 'twas Chiron and Demetrius:
They ravish'd her, and cut away her tongue;
And they, 'twas they, that did her all this wrong.

Sat. Go fetch them hither to us presently.

Tit. Why, there they are both, baked in that pie;
Whereof their mother daintily hath fed,   61
Eating the flesh that she herself hath bred.
'Tis true, 'tis true; witness my knife's sharp
   point.
   [*Kills* TAMORA.

Sat. Die, frantic wretch, for this accursed deed!
   [*Kills* TITUS.

Luc. Can the son's eye behold his father bleed?
There's meed for meed, death for a deadly deed!
   [*Kills* SATURNINUS. *A great tumult.*
      LUCIUS, MARCUS, *and others go up into the*
                                       balcony.

Marc. You sad-faced men, people and sons of
   Rome,
By uproar sever'd, like a flight of fowl
Scatter'd by winds and high tempestuous
   gusts,
O, let me teach you how to knit again   70
This scatter'd corn into one mutual sheaf,
These broken limbs again into one body;
Lest Rome herself be bane unto herself,
And she whom mighty kingdoms court'sy to,
Like a forlorn and desperate castaway,
Do shameful execution on herself.
But if my frosty signs and chaps of age.
Grave witnesses of true experience,
Cannot induce you to attend my words,
[*To* LUCIUS] Speak, Rome's dear friend, as erst
   our ancestor,   80
When with his solemn tongue he did discourse
To love-sick Dido's sad attending ear
The story of that baleful burning night
When subtle Greeks surprised King Priam's
   Troy,
Tell us what Sinon hath bewitch'd our ears,
Or who hath brought the fatal engine in
That gives our Troy, our Rome, the civil wound.
My heart is not compact of flint nor steel;
Nor can I utter all our bitter grief,
But floods of tears will drown my oratory,   90
And break my utterance, even in the time
When it should move you to attend me most,
Lending your kind commiseration.
Here is a captain, let him tell the tale;

Your hearts will throb and weep to hear him
   speak.

Luc. Then, noble auditory, be it known to you,
That cursed Chiron and Demetrius
Were they that murdered our Emperor's brother;
And they it were that ravished our sister: 99
For their fell faults our brothers were beheaded;
Our father's tears despised, and basely cozen'd
Of that true hand that fought Rome's quarrel out,
And sent her enemies unto the grave.
Lastly, myself unkindly banished,
The gates shut on me, and turn'd weeping out
To beg relief among Rome's enemies;
Who drown'd their enmity in my true tears,
And oped their arms to embrace me as a friend.
I am the turned forth, be it known to you,
That have preserved her welfare in my blood;
And from her bosom took the enemy's point,   111
Sheathing the steel in my adventurous body.
Alas, you know I am no vaunter, I;
My scars can witness, dumb although they are,
That my report is just and full of truth.
But, soft! methinks I do disgress to much,
Citing my worthless praise: O, pardon me;
For when no friends are by, men praise them-
   selves.

Marc. Now is my turn to speak. Behold this
   child:
   [*Pointing to the child in the arms of an Attendant.*
Of this was Tamora delivered;   120
The issue of an irreligious Moor,
Chief architect and plotter of these woes:
The villain is alive in Titus' house,
And as he is, to witness this is true.
Now judge what cause had Titus to revenge
These wrongs, unspeakable, past patience,
Or more than any living man could bear.
Now you have heard the truth, what say you,
   Romans?
Have we done aught amiss? Show us wherein,
And, from the place where you behold us now,
The poor remainder of Andronici   131
Will, hand in hand, all headlong cast us down,
And on the ragged stones beat forth our brains,
And make a mutual closure of our house.
Speak, Romans, speak; and if you say we shall,
Lo, hand in hand, Lucius and I will fall.

Æmil. Come, come, thou reverend man of
   Rome,
And bring our Emperor gently in thy hand,
Lucius our Emperor; for well I know
The common voice do cry it shall be so.   140

All. Lucius, all hail, Rome's royal Emperor!

Marc. Go, go into old Titus' sorrowful house,
   To Attendants.
And hither hale that misbelieving Moor,

To be adjudged some direful slaughtering death,
As punishment for his most wicked life.
                    [*Exeunt Attendants.*

LUCIUS, MARCUS, *and the others descend.*

All. Lucius, all hail, Rome's gracious governor!
Luc. Thanks, gentle Romans: may I govern so,
To heal Rome's harms, and wipe away her woe!
But, gentle people, give me aim awhile,
For nature puts me to a heavy task: 150
Stand all aloof: but, uncle, draw you near,
To shed obsequious tears upon this trunk.
O, take this warm kiss on thy pale cold lips,
    Kissing Titus.
These sorrowful drops upon thy blood-stain'd
    face,
The last true duties of thy noble son!
Marc. Tear for tear, and loving kiss for kiss,
Thy brother Marcus tenders on thy lips:
O, were the sum of these that I should pay
Countless and infinite, yet would I pay them!
Luc. Come hither, boy; come, come, and learn
    of us   160
To melt in showers: thy grandsire loved thee
    well:
Many a time he danced thee on his knee,
Sung thee asleep, his loving breast thy pillow;
Many a matter hath he told to thee,
Meet and agreeing with thine infancy;
In that respect, then, like a loving child,
Shed yet some small drops from thy tender spring,
Because kind nature doth require it so:
Friends should associate friends in grief and woe:
Bid him farewell; commit him to the grave;   170
Do him that kindness, and take leave of him.
    Young Luc. O grandsire, grandsire! even with
    all my heart

Would I were dead, so you did live again!
O Lord, I cannot speak to him for weeping;
My tears will choke me, if I ope my mouth.

Re-enter Attendants with AARON.

Æm. You sad Andronici, have done with woes:
Give sentence on this execrable wretch,
That hath been breeder of these dire events.
    Luc. Set him breast-deep in earth, and famish
    him;   179
There let him stand, and rave, and cry for food:
If any one relieves or pities him,
For the offence he dies. This is our doom:
Some stay to see him fasten'd in the earth.
    Aar. O, why should wrath be mute and fury
    dumb?
I am no baby, I, that with base prayers
I should repent the evils I have done:
Ten thousand worse than ever yet I did
Would I perform, if I might have my will:
If one good deed in all my life I did,
I do repent it from my very soul.   190
    Luc. Some loving friends convey the Emperor
    hence,
And give him burial in his father's grave:
My father and Lavinia shall forthwith
Be closed in our household's monument.
As for that heinous tiger, Tamora,
No funeral rite, nor man in mourning weeds,
No mournful bell shall ring her burial;
But throw her forth to beasts and birds of prey:
Her life was beast-like and devoid of pity;
And, being so, shall have like want of pity.   200
See justice done on Aaron, that damn'd Moor,
By whom our heavy haps had their beginning:
Then, afterwards, to order well the state,
That like events may ne'er it ruinate.   [*Exeunt.*

❧ THE TAMING OF THE SHREW

DRAMATIS PERSONÆ

A Lord
Christopher Sly, *a tinker*
Two Huntsmen
Servingman
Page
Messenger   *Persons in the Induction*
Three Servants
Players
Hostess
Baptista Minola, *a rich gentleman of Padua*
Vincentio, *an old gentleman of Pisa*
Lucentio, *son to Vincentio, in love with Bianca*
Petruchio, *a gentleman of Verona, a suitor to Katharina*
Gremio | *suitors to Bianca*
Hortensio |
Tranio | *servants to Lucentio*
Biondello |

Grumio |
Curtis |
Peter |
Nathaniel | *servants to Petruchio*
Philip |
Joseph |
Nicholas |
A Pedant
A Tailor
A Haberdasher

Katharina, *the shrew* | *daughters to Baptista*
Bianca |
Widow

Non-Speaking: *Attendants and servants*

Scene: *Padua, and Petruchio's country house*

INDUCTION

SCENE I. *Before an alehouse on a heath*

Enter HOSTESS *and* SLY.

Sly. I'll pheeze you, in faith.

Host. A pair of stocks, you rogue!

Sly. Ye are a baggage: the Slys are no rogues;
look in the chronicles; we came in with Richard
Conqueror. Therefore *paucas pallabris*; let the
world slide: sessa!

Host. You will not pay for the glasses you have
burst?

Sly. No, not a denier. Go by, Jeronimy: go to
thy cold bed, and warm thee.   10

Host. I know my remedy; I must go fetch the
third-borough.   [*Exit.*

Sly. Third, or fourth, or fifth borough, I'll answer him by law: I'll not budge an inch, boy:
let him come, and kindly. [*Falls asleep.*]

Horns winded. Enter a LORD *from hunting,
with his train.*

Lord. Huntsman, I charge thee, tender well my
hounds:
Brach Merriman, the poor cur, is emboss'd;
And couple Clowder with the deep-mouth'd
brach.
Saw'st thou not, boy, how Silver made it good
At the hedge-corner, in the coldest fault?   20

I would not lose the dog for twenty pound.

1st. Hun. Why, Belman is as good as he, my lord;
He cried upon it at the merest loss
And twice to-day pick'd out the dullest scent:
Trust me, I take him for the better dog.

Lord. Thou art a fool: if Echo were as
fleet,
I would esteem him worth a dozen such.
But sup them well and look unto them all:
To-morrow I intend to hunt again.

1st Hun. I will, my lord.   30

Lord. What's here? one dead, or drunk? See,
doth he breathe?

2nd Hun. He breathes, my lord. Were he not
warm'd with ale,
This were a bed but cold to sleep so soundly.

Lord. O monstrous beast! how like a swine he
lies!
Grim death, how foul and loathsome is thine
image!
Sirs, I will practice on this drunken man.
What think you, if he were convey'd to bed,
Wrapp'd in sweet clothes, rings put upon his
fingers,
A most delicious banquet by his bed,
And brave attendants near him when he wakes,
Would not the beggar then forget himself?   41

1st Hun. Believe me, lord, I think he cannot
choose.

2nd Hun. It would seem strange unto him when
he waked.

Lord. Even as a flattering dream or worthless
fancy.
Then take him up and manage well the jest:
Carry him gently to my fairest chamber
And hang it round with all my wanton pictures:
Balm his foul head in warm distilled waters
And burn sweet wood to make the lodging sweet:
Procure me music ready when he wakes,   50
To make a dulcet and a heavenly sound;
And if he chance to speak, be ready straight
And with a low submissive reverence
Say, "What is it your honour will command?"
Let one attend him with a silver basin
Full of rose-water and bestrew'd with flowers;
Another bear the ewer, the third a diaper,
And say, "Will't please your lordship cool your
hands?"
Some one be ready with a costly suit
And ask him what apparel he will wear;   60
Another tell him of his hounds and horse,
And that his lady mourns at his disease:
Persuade him that he hath been lunatic;
And when he says he is, say that he dreams,
For he is nothing but a mighty lord.
This do and do it kindly, gentle sirs:
It will be pastime passing excellent,
If it be husbanded with modesty.

1st Hun. My lord, I warrant you we will play
our part,
As he shall think by our true diligence   70
He is no less than what we say he is.

Lord. Take him up gently and to bed with him;
And each one to his office when he wakes.
Some bear out SLY. *A trumpet sounds.*
Sirrah, go see what trumpet 'tis that sounds:
[*Exit* SERVINGMAN.
Belike, some noble gentleman that means,
Travelling some journey, to repose him here.

Re-enter SERVINGMAN.

How now! who is it?
Serv.   An't please your honour, players
That offer service to your lordship.
Lord. Bid them come near.

Enter PLAYERS.

Now, fellows, you are welcome.
Players. We thank your honour.   80
Lord. Do you intend to stay with me to-night?
A Player. So please your lordship to accept our
duty.
Lord. With all my heart. This fellow I remem-
ber,
Since once he play'd a farmer's eldest son:

'Twas where you woo'd the gentlewoman so
well:
I have forgot your name; but, sure, that part
Was aptly fitted and naturally perform'd.
A Player. I think 'twas Soto that your honour
means.
Lord. 'Tis very true: thou didst it excellent.
Well, you are come to me in happy time;   90
The rather for I have some sport in hand
Wherein your cunning can assist me much.
There is a lord will hear you play to-night:
But I am doubtful of your modesties;
Lest over-eyeing of his odd behaviour,—
For yet his honour never heard a play—
You break into some merry passion
And so offend him; for I tell you, sirs,
If you should smile he grows impatient.
A Player. Fear not, my lord: we can contain
ourselves
Were he the veriest antic in the world.
Lord. Go, sirrah, take them to the buttery,
And give them friendly welcome every one:
Let them want nothing that my house affords.
[*Exit one with the* PLAYERS.
Sirrah, go you to Barthol'mew my page,
And see him dress'd in all suits like a lady:
That done, conduct him to the drunkard's cham-
ber;
And call him "madam," do him obeisance.
Tell him from me, as he will win my love,
He bear himself with honourable action,   110
Such as he hath observed in noble ladies
Unto their lords, by them accomplished:
Such duty to the drunkard let him do
With soft low tongue and lowly courtesy,
And say "What is't your honour will command,
Wherein your lady and your humble wife
May show her duty and make known her love?"
And then with kind embracements, tempting
kisses,
And with declining head into his bosom,
Bid him shed tears, as being overjoy'd   120
To see her noble lord restored to health,
Who for this seven years hath esteemed him
No better than a poor and loathsome beggar:
And if the boy have not a woman's gift
To rain a shower of commanded tears,
An onion will do well for such a shift,
Which in a napkin being close convey'd
Shall in despite enforce a watery eye.
See this dispatch'd with all the haste thou canst:
Anon I'll give thee more instructions.   130
[*Exit a* SERVINGMAN.
I know the boy will well usurp the grace,
Voice, gait, and action of a gentlewoman:
I long to hear him call the drunkard husband,

And how my men will stay themselves from
    laughter
When they do homage to this simple peasant.
I'll in to counsel them; haply my presence
May well abate the over-merry spleen
Which otherwise would grow into extremes.

                               [Exeunt.

SCENE II. *A bedchamber in the Lord's house*

Enter aloft SLY, *with Attendants; some with apparel, others with basin and ewer and other appurtenances; and* LORD.

Sly. For God's sake, a pot of small ale.

1st Serv. Will't please your lordship drink a cup
    of sack?

2nd Serv. Will't please your honour taste of
    these conserves?

3rd Serv. What raiment will your honour wear
    to-day?

Sly. I am Christophero Sly; call not me "honour" nor "lordship": I ne'er drank sack in my
life; and if you give me any conserves, give me
conserves of beef: ne'er ask me what raiment I'll
wear; for I have no more doublets than backs,
no more stockings than legs, nor no more shoes
than feet; nay, sometime more feet than shoes, or
such shoes as my toes look through the over-leather.

Lord. Heaven cease this idle humour in your
    honour!
O, that a mighty man of such descent,
Of such possessions, and so high esteem,
Should be infused with so foul a spirit!

Sly. What, would you make me mad? Am not I
Christopher Sly, old Sly's son of Burtonheath, by
birth a pedlar, by education a cardmaker, by
transmutation a bear-herd, and now by present
profession a tinker? Ask Marian Hacket, the fat
ale-wife of Wincot, if she know me not: if she
say I am not fourteen pence on the score for sheer
ale, score me up for the lyingest knave in Christendom. What! I am not bestraught: here's—

3rd Serv. O, this it is that makes your lady
    mourn!

2nd Serv. O, this is it that makes your servants
    droop!

Lord. Hence comes it that your kindred shuns
    your house,   30
As beaten hence by your strange lunacy.
O noble lord, bethink thee of thy birth,
Call home thy ancient thoughts from banishment
And banish hence these abject lowly dreams.
Look how thy servants do attend on thee,
Each in his office ready at thy beck.
Wilt thou have music? hark! Apollo plays,
    Music.

And twenty caged nightingales do sing:
Or wilt thou sleep? we'll have thee to a couch
Softer and sweeter than the lustful bed   40
On purpose trimm'd up for Semiramis.
Say thou wilt walk; we will bestrew the ground:
Or wilt thou ride? thy horses shall be trapp'd,
Their harness studded all with gold and pearl.
Dost thou love hawking? thou hast hawks will soar
Above the morning lark: or wilt thou hunt?
Thy hounds shall make the welkin answer them
And fetch shrill echoes from the hollow earth.

1st Serv. Say thou wilt course; thy greyhounds
    are as swift
As breathed stags, ay, fleeter than the roe.   50

2nd Serv. Dost thou love pictures? we will fetch
    thee straight
Adonis painted by a running brook,
And Cytherea all in sedges hid,
Which seem to move and wanton with her breath,
Even as the waving sedges play with wind.

Lord. We'll show thee Io as she was a maid,
And how she was beguiled and surprised,
As lively painted as the deed was done.

3rd Serv. Or Daphne roaming through a thorny
    wood,
Scratching her legs that one shall swear she
    bleeds,   60
And at that sight shall sad Apollo weep,
So workmanly the blood and tears are drawn.

Lord. Thou art a lord and nothing but a lord:
Thou hast a lady far more beautiful
Than any woman in this waning age.

1st Serv. And till the tears that she hath shed for
    thee
Like envious floods o'er-run her lovely face,
She was the fairest creature in the world;
And yet she is inferior to none.

Sly. Am I a lord? and have I such a lady?   70
Or do I dream? or have I dream'd till now?
I do not sleep: I see, I hear, I speak;
I smell sweet savours and I feel soft things:
Upon my life, I am a lord indeed
And not a tinker nor Christophero Sly.
Well, bring our lady hither to our sight;
And once again, a pot o' the smallest ale.

2nd Serv. Will't please your mightiness to wash
    your hands?
O, how we joy to see your wit restored!   79
O, that once more you knew but what you are!
These fifteen years you have been in a dream;
Or when you waked, so waked as if you slept.

Sly. These fifteen years! by my fay, a goodly
    nap.
But did I never speak of all that time?

1st Serv. O, yes, my lord, but very idle words:
For though you lay here in this goodly chamber,

Yet would you say ye were beaten out of door;
And rail upon the hostess of the house;
And say you would present her at the leet,
Because she brought stone jugs and no seal'd
    quarts: 90
Sometimes you would call out for Cicely Hacket.
Sly. Ay, the woman's maid of the house.
3rd Serv. Why, sir, you know no house nor no
    such maid,
Nor no such men as you have reckon'd up,
As Stephen Sly, and old John Naps of Greece,
And Peter Turph, and Henry Pimpernell,
And twenty more such names and men as these
Which never were, nor no man ever saw.
Sly. Now Lord be thanked for my good amends!
All. Amen.   100
Sly. I thank thee: thou shalt not lose by it.

Enter the PAGE *as a lady, with attendants.*

Page. How fares my noble lord?
Sly. Marry, I fare well; for here is cheer enough.
Where is my wife?
Page. Here, noble lord: what is thy will with her?
Sly. Are you my wife and will not call me hus-
    band?
My men should call me "lord": I am your good-
    man.
Page. My husband and my lord, my lord and
    husband;
I am your wife in all obedience.
Sly. I know it well. What must I call her?
Lord. Madam.   111
Sly. Al'ce madam, or Joan madam?
Lord. "Madam," and nothing else: so lords call
    ladies.
Sly. Madam wife, they say that I have dream'd
And slept above some fifteen year or more.
Page. Ay, and the time seems thirty unto me,
Being all this time abandon'd from your bed.
Sly. 'Tis much. Servants, leave me and her alone.
Madam, undress you and come now to bed.
Page. Thrice-noble lord, let me entreat of you
To pardon me yet for a night or two,   121
Or, if not so, until the sun be set:
For your physicians have expressly charged,
In peril to incur your former malady,
That I should yet absent me from your bed:
I hope this reason stands for my excuse.
Sly. Ay, it stands so that I may hardly tarry so
long. But I would be loath to fall into my dreams
again: I will therefore tarry in despite of the
flesh and the blood.   130

Enter a MESSENGER.

Mess. Your honour's players, hearing your
    amendment,

Are come to play a pleasant comedy;
For so your doctors hold it very meet,
Seeing too much sadness hath congeal'd your
    blood,
And melancholy is the nurse of frenzy:
Therefore they thought it good you hear a play
And frame your mind to mirth and merriment,
Which bars a thousand harms and lengthens life.
Sly. Marry, I will, let them play it. Is not a
comonty a Christmas gambold or a tumbling-
trick?   141
Page. No, my good lord; it is more pleasing stuff.
Sly. What, household stuff?
Page. It is a kind of history.
Sly. Well, we'll see't. Come, madam wife, sit
by my side and let the world slip: we shall ne'er
be younger.

Flourish.

ACT I

SCENE I. *Padua: a public place*
Enter LUCENTIO *and his man* TRANIO.

Luc. Tranio, since for the great desire I had
To see fair Padua, nursery of arts,
I am arrived for fruitful Lombardy,
The pleasant garden of great Italy;
And by my father's love and leave am arm'd
With his good will and thy good company,
My trusty servant, well approved in all,
Here let us breathe and haply institute
A course of learning and ingenious studies.
Pisa renown'd for grave citizens   10
Gave me my being and my father first,
A merchant of great traffic through the world,
Vincentio, come of the Bentivolii.
Vincentio's son brought up in Florence
It shall become to serve all hopes conceived,
To deck his fortune with his virtuous deeds:
And therefore, Tranio, for the time I study,
Virtue and that part of philosophy
Will I apply that treats of happiness
By virtue specially to be achieved.   20
Tell me thy mind; for I have Pisa left
And am to Padua come, as he that leaves
A shallow plash to plunge him in the deep
And with satiety seeks to quench his thirst.
Tra. Mi perdonato, gentle master mine,
I am in all affected as yourself;
Glad that you thus continue your resolve
To suck the sweets of sweet philosophy.
Only, good master, while we do admire
This virtue and this moral discipline,   30
Let's be no stoics nor no stocks, I pray;
Or so devote to Aristotle's checks
As Ovid be an outcast quite abjured:

Balk logic with acquaintance that you have
And practise rhetoric in your common talk;
Music and poesy use to quicken you;
The mathematics and the metaphysics,
Fall to them as you find your stomach serves you;
No profit grows where is no pleasure ta'en:
In brief, sir, study what you most affect. 40

Luc. Gramercies, Tranio, well dost thou advise.
If, Biondello, thou wert come ashore,
We could at once put us in readiness,
And take a lodging fit to entertain
Such friends as time in Padua shall beget.
But stay a while: what company is this?

Tra. Master, some show to welcome us to town.

Enter BAPTISTA, KATHARINA, BIANCA, GREMIO, *a
pantaloon, and* HORTENSIO. LUCENTIO *and* TRA-
NIO *stand by.*

Bap. Gentlemen, importune me no farther,
For how I firmly am resolved you know;
That is, not to bestow my youngest daughter 50
Before I have a husband for the elder:
If either of you both love Katharina,
Because I know you well and love you well,
Leave shall you have to court her at your pleas-
ure.

Gre. [*Aside*] To cart her rather: she's too rough
for me.
There, there, Hortensio, will you any wife?

Kath. I pray you, sir, is it your will
To make a stale of me amongst these mates?

Hor. Mates, maid! how mean you that? no
mates for you,
Unless you were of gentler, milder mould. 60

Kath. I'faith, sir, you shall never need to fear:
I wis it is not half way to her heart;
But if it were, doubt not her care should be
To comb your noddle with a three-legg'd stool
And paint your face and use you like a fool.

Hor. From all such devils, good Lord deliver
us!

Gre. And me too, good Lord!

Tra. Hush, master! here's some good pastime
toward:
That wench is stark mad or wonderful froward.

Luc. But in the other's silence do I see 70
Maid's mild behaviour and sobriety.
Peace, Tranio!

Tra. Well said, master; mum! and gaze your
fill.

Bap. Gentlemen, that I may soon make good
What I have said, Bianca, get you in:
And let it not displease thee, good Bianca,
For I will love thee ne'er the less, my girl.

Kath. A pretty peat! it is best
Put finger in the eye, an she knew why.

Bian. Sister, content you in my discontent. 80
Sir, to your pleasure humbly I subscribe:
My books and instruments shall be my company,
On them to look and practise by myself.

Luc. Hark, Tranio! thou may'st hear Minerva
speak.

Hor. Signior Baptista, will you be so strange?
Sorry am I that our good will effects
Bianca's grief.

Gre. Why will you mew her up,
Signior Baptista, for this fiend of hell,
And make her bear the penance of her tongue?

Bap. Gentlemen, content ye; I am resolved: 90
Go in, Bianca: [*Exit* BIANCA.
And for I know she taketh most delight
In music, instruments, and poetry,
Schoolmasters will I keep within my house,
Fit to instruct her youth. If you, Hortensio,
Or Signior Gremio, you, know any such,
Prefer them hither; for to cunning men
I will be very kind, and liberal
To mine own children in good bringing up:
And so farewell. Katharina, you may stay; 100
For I have more to commune with Bianca. [*Exit.*

Kath. Why, and I trust I may go too, may I not?
What, shall I be appointed hours; as though, belike, I knew not what to take, and what to leave,
ha? [*Exit.*

Gre. You may go to the devil's dam: your gifts
are so good, here's none will hold you. Their love
is not so great, Hortensio, but we may blow our
nails together, and fast it fairly out: our cake's
dough on both sides. Farewell: yet, for the love I
bear my sweet Bianca, if I can by any means light
on a fit man to teach her that wherein she delights, I will wish him to her father.

Hor. So will I, Signior Gremio: but a word, I
pray. Though the nature of our quarrel yet never
brooked parle, know now, upon advice, it toucheth us both, that we may yet again have access
to our fair mistress and be happy rivals in
Bianca's love, to labour and effect one thing
specially. 121

Gre. What's that, I pray?

Hor. Marry, sir, to get a husband for her sister.

Gre. A husband! a devil.

Hor. I say, a husband.

Gre. I say, a devil. Thinkest thou, Hortensio,
though her father be very rich, any man is so
very a fool to be married to hell?

Hor. Tush, Gremio, though it pass your patience and mine to endure her loud alarums, why,
man, there be good fellows in the world, an a
man could light on them, would take her with all
faults, and money enough.

Gre. I cannot tell; but I had as lief take her

dowry with this condition, to be whipped at the high cross every morning.

Hor. Faith, as you say, there's small choice in rotten apples. But come; since this bar in law makes us friends, it shall be so far forth friendly maintained, till by helping Baptista's eldest daughter to a husband we set his youngest free for a husband, and then have to't afresh. Sweet Bianca! Happy man be his dole! He that runs fastest gets the ring. How say you, Signior Gremio?

Gre. I am agreed; and would I had given him the best horse in Padua to begin his wooing that would thoroughly woo her, wed her and bed her, and rid the house of her! Come on.   *150*

[*Exeunt* GREMIO *and* HORTENSIO.

Tra. I pray, sir, tell me, is it possible
That love should of a sudden take such hold?

Luc. O Tranio, till I found it to be true,
I never thought it possible or likely;
But see, while idly I stood looking on,
I found the effect of love in idleness:
And now in plainness do confess to thee,
That art to me as secret and as dear
As Anna to the queen of Carthage was,
Tranio, I burn, I pine, I perish, Tranio,   *160*
If I achieve not this young modest girl.
Counsel me, Tranio, for I know thou canst;
Assist me, Tranio, for I know thou wilt.

Tra. Master, it is no time to chide you now;
Affection is not rated from the heart:
If love have touch'd you, nought remains but so,
Redime te captum quam queas minimo.

Luc. Gramercies, lad, go forward; this contents:
The rest will comfort, for thy counsel's sound.

Tra. Master, you look'd so longly on the maid,
Perhaps you mark'd not what's the pith of all.

Luc. O yes, I saw sweet beauty in her face,
Such as the daughter of Agenor had,
That made great Jove to humble him to her hand,
When with his knees he kiss'd the Cretan strand.

Tra. Saw you no more? mark'd you not how her sister
Began to scold and raise up such a storm
That mortal ears might hardly endure the din?

Luc. Tranio, I saw her coral lips to move
And with her breath she did perfume the air: *180*
Sacred and sweet was all I saw in her.

Tra. Nay, then, 'tis time to stir him from his trance.
I pray, awake, sir: if you love the maid,
Bend thoughts and wits to achieve her. Thus it stands:
Her elder sister is so curst and shrewd
That till the father rid his hands of her,
Master, your love must live a maid at home;

And therefore has he closely mew'd her up,
Because she will not be annoy'd with suitors.

Luc. Ah, Tranio, what a cruel father's he!
But art thou not advised, he took some care   *191*
To get her cunning schoolmasters to instruct her?

Tra. Ay, marry, am I, sir; and now 'tis plotted.

Luc. I have it, Tranio.

Tra.   Master, for my hand,
Both our inventions meet and jump in one.

Luc. Tell me thine first.

Tra.   You will be schoolmaster
And undertake the teaching of the maid:
That's your device.

Luc.   It is: may it be done?

Tra. Not possible; for who shall bear your part,
And be in Padua here Vincentio's son,   *200*
Keep house and ply his book, welcome his friends,
Visit his countrymen and banquet them?

Luc. Basta; content thee, for I have it full.
We have not yet been seen in any house,
Nor can we be distinguish'd by our faces
For man or master; then it follows thus;
Thou shalt be master, Tranio, in my stead,
Keep house and port and servants, as I should:
I will some other be, some Florentine,
Some Neapolitan, or meaner man of Pisa.   *210*
'Tis hatch'd and shall be so: Tranio, at once
Uncase thee; take my colour'd hat and cloak:
When Biondello comes, he waits on thee;
But I will charm him first to keep his tongue.

Tra. So had you need.
In brief, sir, sith it your pleasure is,
And I am tied to be obedient;
For so your father charged me at our parting,
"Be serviceable to my son," quoth he,
Although I think 'twas in another sense;   *220*
I am content to be Lucentio,
Because so well I love Lucentio.

Luc. Tranio, be so, because Lucentio loves:
And let me be a slave, to achieve that maid
Whose sudden sight hath thrall'd my wounded eye.
Here comes the rogue.

Enter BIONDELLO.

Sirrah, where have you been?

Bion. Where have I been! Nay, how now! where are you? Master, has my fellow Tranio stolen your clothes? Or you stolen his? or both? pray, what's the news?   *230*

Luc. Sirrah, come hither: 'tis no time to jest,
And therefore frame your manners to the time.
Your fellow Tranio here, to save my life,
Puts my apparel and my countenance on,
And I for my escape have put on his;

For in a quarrel since I came ashore
I kill'd a man and fear I was descried:
Wait you on him, I charge you, as becomes,
While I make way from hence to save my life:
You understand me?
    Bion.   I, sir! ne'er a whit.   240
    Luc. And not a jot of Tranio in your mouth:
Tranio is changed into Lucentio.
    Bion. The better for him: would I were so too!
    Tra. So could I, faith, boy, to have the next wish
        after,
That Lucentio indeed had Baptista's youngest
        daughter.
But, sirrah, not for my sake, but your master's, I
        advise
You use your manners discreetly in all kind of
        companies:
When I am alone, why, then I am Tranio;
But in all places else your master Lucentio.   249
    Luc. Tranio, let's go: one thing more rests, that
thyself execute, to make one among these woo-
ers: if thou ask me why, sufficeth, my reasons
are both good and weighty.   [*Exeunt.*

    The presenters above speak.

    1st Serv. My lord, you nod; you do not mind
        the play.
    Sly. Yes, by Saint Anne, do I. A good matter,
surely: comes there any more of it?
    Page. My lord, 'tis but begun.
    Sly. 'Tis a very excellent piece of work, madam
lady: would 'twere done!   259
    They sit and mark.

    SCENE II. *Padua: before Hortensio's house*
    Enter PETRUCHIO *and his man* GRUMIO.

    Pet. Verona, for a while I take my leave,
To see my friends in Padua, but of all
My best beloved and approved friend,
Hortensio; and I trow this is his house.
Here, sirrah Grumio; knock, I say.
    Gru. Knock, sir! whom should I knock? is there
any man has rebused your worship?
    Pet. Villain, I say, knock me here soundly.
    Gru. Knock you here, sir! why, sir, what am I,
sir, that I should knock you here, sir?   10
    Pet. Villain, I say, knock me at this gate
And rap me well, or I'll knock your knave's pate.
    Gru. My master is grown quarrelsome. I should
        knock you first,
And then I know after who comes by the worst.
    Pet. Will it not be?
Faith, sirrah, an you'll not knock, I'll ring it;
I'll try how you can sol, fa, and sing it.
    He wrings him by the ears.
    Gru. Help, masters, help! my master is mad.

    Pet. Now, knock when I bid you, sirrah villain!

    Enter HORTENSIO.

    Hor. How now! what's the matter? My old
friend Grumio! and my good friend Petruchio!
How do you all at Verona?
    Pet. Signior Hortensio, come you to part the
        fray?
Con tutto il cuore, ben trovato, may I say.
    *Hor. Alla nostra casa ben venuto, molto honorato
signor mio Petruchio.*
Rise, Grumio, rise: we will compound this
        quarrel.
    Gru. Nay, 'tis no matter, sir, what he 'leges in
Latin. If this be not a lawful cause for me to leave
his service, look you, sir, he bid me knock him
and rap him soundly, sir: well, was it fit for a
servant to use his master so, being perhaps, for
aught I see, two and thirty, a pip out?
Whom would to God I had well knock'd at first,
Then had not Grumio come by the worst.
    Pet. A senseless villain! Good Hortensio,
I bade the rascal knock upon your gate
And could not get him for my heart to do it.
    Gru. Knock at the gate! O heavens! Spake you
not these words plain, "Sirrah, knock me here,
rap me here, knock me well, and knock me
soundly"? And come you now with, "knocking
at the gate"?
    Pet. Sirrah, be gone, or talk not, I advise you.
    Hor. Petruchio, patience; I am Grumio's pledge:
Why, this's a heavy chance 'twixt him and you,
Your ancient, trusty, pleasant servant Grumio.
And tell me now, sweet friend, what happy gale
Blows you to Padua here from old Verona?
    Pet. Such wind as scatters young men through
        the world   50
To seek their fortunes farther than at home
Where small experience grows. But in a few,
Signior Hortensio, thus it stands with me:
Antonio, my father, is deceased;
And I have thrust myself into this maze,
Haply to wive and thrive as best I may:
Crowns in my purse I have and goods at home,
And so am come abroad to see the world.
    Hor. Petruchio, shall I then come roundly to
        thee
And wish thee to a shrew ill-favour'd wife?   60
Thou'ldst thank me but a little for my counsel:
And yet I'll promise thee she shall be rich
And very rich: but thou'rt too much my friend,
And I'll not wish thee to her.
    Pet. Signior Hortensio, 'twixt such friends as we
Few words suffice: and therefore, if thou know
One rich enough to be Petruchio's wife,
As wealth is burden of my wooing dance,

Be she as foul as was Florentius' love,
As old as Sibyl, and as curst and shrewd   70
As Socrates' Xanthippe, or a worse,
She moves me not, or not removes, at least,
Affection's edge in me, were she as rough
As are the swelling Adriatic seas:
I come to wive it wealthily in Padua;
If wealthily, then happily in Padua.

  Gru. Nay, look you, sir, he tells you flatly what
his mind is: why, give him gold enough and
marry him to a puppet or an aglet-baby; or an
old trot with ne'er a tooth in her head, though she
have as many diseases as two and fifty horses:
why, nothing comes amiss, so money comes
withal.

  Hor. Petruchio, since we are stepp'd thus far in,
I will continue that I broach'd in jest.
I can, Petruchio, help thee to a wife
With wealth enough and young and beauteous,
Brought up as best becomes a gentlewoman:
Her only fault, and that is faults enough,
Is that she is intolerable curst
And shrewd and froward, so beyond all measure
That, were my state far worser than it is,   91
I would not wed her for a mine of gold.

  Pet. Hortensio, peace! thou know'st not gold's
    effect:
Tell me her father's name and 'tis enough:
For I will board her, though she chide as loud
As thunder when the clouds in autumn crack.

  Hor. Her father is Baptista Minola,
An affable and courteous gentleman:
Her name is Katharina Minola,
Renown'd in Padua for her scolding tongue.   100

  Pet. I know her father, though I know not her;
And he knew my deceased father well,
I will not sleep, Hortensio, till I see her;
And therefore let me be thus bold with you
To give you over at this first encounter,
Unless you will accompany me thither.

  Gru. I pray you, sir, let him go while the humour lasts. O' my word, an she knew him as
well as I do, she would think scolding would do
little good upon him: she may perhaps call him
half a score knaves or so: why, that's nothing;
an he begin once, he'll rail in his rope-tricks. I'll
tell you what, sir, an she stand him but a little,
he will throw a figure in her face and so disfigure
her with it that she shall have no more eyes to
see withal than a cat. You know him not, sir.

  Hor. Tarry, Petruchio, I must go with thee,
For in Baptista's keep my treasure is:
He hath the jewel of my life in hold,
His youngest daughter, beautiful Bianca,   120
And her withholds from me and other more,
Suitors to her and rivals in my love,

Supposing it a thing impossible,
For those defects I have before rehearsed,
That ever Katharina will be woo'd;
Therefore this order hath Baptista ta'en,
That none shall have access unto Bianca
Till Katharine the curst have got a husband.

  Gru. Katharine the curst!
A title for a maid of all titles the worst.   130

  Hor. Now shall my friend Petruchio do me
    grace,
And offer me disguised in sober robes
To old Baptista as a schoolmaster
Well seen in music, to instruct Bianca;
That so I may, by this device, at least
Have leave and leisure to make love to her
And unsuspected court her by herself.

  Gru. Here's no knavery! See, to beguile the old
folks, how the young folks lay their heads together!   140

    Enter GREMIO, *and* LUCENTIO *disguised.*

Master, master, look about you: who goes there,
    ha?

  Hor. Peace, Grumio! it is the rival of my love.
Petruchio, stand by a while.

  Gru. A proper stripling and an amorous!

  Gre. O, very well; I have perused the note.
Hark you, sir; I'll have them very fairly bound:
All books of love, see that at any hand;
And see you read no other lectures to her:
You understand me: over and beside
Signior Baptista's liberality,   150
I'll mend it with a largess. Take your paper too,
And let me have them very well perfumed:
For she is sweeter than perfume itself
To whom they go to. What will you read to her?

  Luc. Whate'er I read to her, I'll plead for you
As for my patron, stand you so assured,
As firmly as yourself were still in place:
Yea, and perhaps with more successful words
Than you, unless you were a scholar, sir.

  Gre. O this learning, what a thing it is!   160

  Gru. O this woodcock, what an ass it is!

  Pet. Peace, sirrah!

  Hor. Grumio, mum! God save you, Signior
    Gremio.

  Gre. And you are well met, Signior Hortensio.
Trow you whither I am going? To Baptista
    Minola.
I promised to inquire carefully
About a schoolmaster for the fair Bianca:
And by good fortune I have lighted well
On this young man, for learning and behaviour
Fit for her turn, well read in poetry   170
And other books, good ones, I warrant ye.

  Hor. 'Tis well; and I have met a gentleman

Hath promised me to help me to another,
A fine musician to instruct our mistress;
So shall I no whit be behind in duty
To fair Bianca, so beloved of me.
  Gre. Beloved of me; and that my deeds shall
    prove.
  Gru. And that his bags shall prove.
  Hor. Gremio, 'tis now no time to vent our love:
Listen to me, and if you speak me fair,   180
I'll tell you news indifferent good for either.
Here is a gentleman whom by chance I met,
Upon agreement from us to his liking,
Will undertake to woo curst Katharine,
Yea, and to marry her, if her dowry please.
  Gre. So said, so done, is well.
Hortensio, have you told him all her faults?
  Pet. I know she is an irksome brawling scold:
If that be all, masters, I hear no harm.
  Gre. No. say'st me so, friend? What country-
    man?   190
  Pet. Born in Verona, old Antonio's son:
My father dead, my fortune lives for me;
And I do hope good days and long to see.
  Gre. O sir, such a life, with such a wife, were
    strange!
But if you have a stomach, to't i' God's name:
You shall have me assisting you in all.
But will you woo this wild-cat?
  Pet.   Will I live?
  Gru. Will he woo her? ay, or I'll hang her.
  Pet. Why came I hither but to that intent?
Think you a little din can daunt mine ears?   200
Have I not in my time heard lions roar?
Have I not heard the sea puff'd up with winds
Rage like an angry boar chafed with sweat?
Have I not heard great ordnance in the field,
And heaven's artillery thunder in the skies?
Have I not in a pitched battle heard
Loud 'larums, neighing steeds, and trumpets'
    clang?
And do you tell me of a woman's tongue,
That gives not half so great a blow to hear
As will a chestnut in a farmer's fire?   210
Tush, tush! fear boys with bugs.
  Gru.   For he fears none.
  Gre. Hortensio, hark:
This gentleman is happily arrived,
My mind presumes, for his own good and ours.
  Hor. I promised we would be contributors
And bear his charge of wooing, whatsoe'er.
  Gre. And so we will, provided that he win her.
  Gru. I would I were as sure of a good dinner.

      Enter TRANIO *brave, and* BIONDELLO.

  Tra. Gentlemen, God save you. If I may be
  bold,

Tell me, I beseech you, which is the readiest way
To the house of Signior Baptista Minola?   221
  Bion. He that has the two fair daughters: is't he
you mean?
  Tra. Even he, Biondello.
  Gre. Hark you, sir; you mean not her to—
  Tra. Perhaps, him and her, sir: what have you
to do?
  Pet. Nor her that chides, sir, at any hand, I pray.
  Tra. I love no chiders, sir. Biondello, let's away.
  Luc. Well begun, Tranio.
  Hor.   Sir, a word ere you go;
Are you a suitor to the maid you talk of, yea or
  no?
  Tra. And if I be, sir, is it any offence?   231
  Gre. No; if without more words you will get
  you hence.
  Tra. Why, sir, I pray, are not the streets as free
For me as for you?
  Gre.   But so is not she.
  Tra. For what reason, I beseech you?
  Gre.   For this reason, if you'll know,
That she's the choice love of Signior Gremio.
  Hor. That she's the chosen of Signior Horten-
  sio.
  Tra. Softly, my masters! if you be gentlemen,
Do me this right; hear me with patience,
Baptista is a noble gentleman,   240
To whom my father is not all unknown;
And were his daughter fairer than she is,
She may more suitors have and me for one.
Fair Leda's daughter had a thousand wooers;
Then well one more may fair Bianca have:
And so she shall; Lucentio shall make one,
Though Paris came in hope to speed alone.
  Gre. What! this gentleman will out-talk us all.
  Luc. Sir, give him head; I know he'll prove a
    jade.   249
  Pet. Hortensio, to what end are all these words?
  Hor. Sir, let me be so bold as ask you,
Did you yet ever see Baptista's daughter?
  Tra. No, sir; but hear I do that he hath two,
The one as famous for a scolding tongue
As is the other for beauteous modesty.
  Pet. Sir, sir, the first's for me; let her go by.
  Gre. Yea, leave that labour to great Hercules;
And let it be more than Alcides' twelve.
  Pet. Sir, understand you this of me in sooth:
The youngest daughter whom you hearken for
Her father keeps from all access of suitors,   261
And will not promise her to any man
Until the elder sister first be wed:
The younger then is free and not before.
  Tra. If it be so, sir, that you are the man
Must stead us all and me amongst the rest,
And if you break the ice and do this feat,

Achieve the elder, set the younger free
For our access, whose hap shall be to have her
Will not so graceless be to be ingrate.   270
  Hor. Sir, you say well and well you do con-
    ceive;
And since you do profess to be a suitor,
You must, as we do, gratify this gentleman,
To whom we all rest generally beholding.
  Tra. Sir, I shall not be slack: in sign whereof,
Please ye we may contrive this afternoon,
And quaff carouses to our mistress' health,
And do as adversaries do in law,
Strive mightily, but eat and drink as friends.
  Gru. Bion. O excellent motion! Fellows, let's
    be gone.   280
  Hor. The motion's good indeed and be it so,
Petruchio, I shall be your *ben venuto*.   [*Exeunt.*

ACT II

Scene I. *Padua: a room in Baptista's house*
    Enter KATHARINA *and* BIANCA.

  Bian. Good sister, wrong me not, nor wrong
    yourself,
To make a bondmaid and a slave of me;
That I disdain: but for these other gawds,
Unbind my hands, I'll pull them off myself,
Yea, all my raiment, to my petticoat;
Or what you will command me will I do,
So well I know my duty to my elders.
  Kath. Of all thy suitors, here I charge thee, tell
Whom thou lovest best: see thou dissemble not.
  Bian. Believe me, sister, of all the men alive
I never yet beheld that special face   11
Which I could fancy more than any other.
  Kath. Minion, thou liest. Is't not Hortensio?
  Bian. If you affect him, sister, here I swear
I'll plead for you myself, but you shall have him.
  Kath. O then, belike, you fancy riches more:
You will have Gremio to keep you fair.
  Bian. Is it for him you do envy me so?
Nay then you jest, and now I well perceive
You have but jested with me all this while: 20
I prithee, sister Kate, untie my hands.
  Kath. If that be jest, then all the rest was so.
    Strikes her.

    Enter BAPTISTA.

  Bap.Why, how now, dame! whence grows this
    insolence?
Bianca, stand aside. Poor girl! she weeps.
Go ply thy needle; meddle not with her.
For shame, thou hilding of a devilish spirit,
Why dost thou wrong her that did ne'er wrong
    thee?
When did she cross thee with a bitter word?

  Kath. Her silence flouts me, and I'll be revenged.
    [*Flies after* BIANCA.
  Bap.What, in my sight? Bianca, get thee in.
    [*Exit* BIANCA.   30
  Kath. What, will you not suffer me? Nay, now
    I see
She is your treasure, she must have a husband;
I must dance barefoot on her wedding day
And for your love to her lead apes in hell.
Talk not to me: I will go sit and weep
Till I can find occasion of revenge.   [*Exit.*
  Bap. Was ever gentleman thus grieved as I?
But who comes here?

Enter GREMIO, LUCENTIO *in the habit of a mean
    man;* PETRUCHIO, *with* HORTENSIO *as a musician;
    and* TRANIO, *with* BIONDELLO *bearing a lute and
    books.*

  Gre. Good morrow, neighbour Baptista.
  Bap. Good morrow, neighbour Gremio. God
    save you, gentlemen!   41
  Pet. And you, good sir! Pray, have you not a
    daughter
Call'd Katharina, fair and virtuous?
  Bap. I have a daughter, sir, called Katharina.
  Gre. You are too blunt: go to it orderly.
  Pet. You wrong me, Signior Gremio: give me
    leave.
I am a gentleman of Verona, sir,
That, hearing of her beauty and her wit,
Her affability and bashful modesty,
Her wondrous qualities and mild behaviour,   50
Am bold to show myself a forward guest
Within your house, to make mine eye the witness
Of that report which I so oft have heard.
And, for an entrance to my entertainment,
I do present you with a man of mine,
    Presenting HORTENSIO.
Cunning in music and the mathematics,
To instruct her fully in those sciences,
Whereof I know she is not ignorant:
Accept of him, or else you do me wrong:
His name is Licio, born in Mantua.   60
  Bap. You're welcome, sir; and he, for your
    good sake.
But for my daughter Katharine, this I know,
She is not for your turn, the more my grief.
  Pet. I see you do not mean to part with her,
Or else you like not of my company.
  Bap. Mistake me not; I speak but as I find.
Whence are you, sir? what may I call your name?
  Pet. Petruchio is my name; Antonio's son,
A man well known throughout all Italy.
  Bap. I know him well: you are welcome for his
    sake.   70
  Gre. Saving your tale, Petruchio, I pray,

Let us, that are poor petitioners, speak too:
Baccare! you are marvellous forward.

Pet. O, pardon me, Signior Gremio; I would
    fain be doing.

Gre. I doubt it not, sir; but you will curse your
    wooing.
Neighbour, this is a gift very grateful, I am sure
of it. To express the like kindness, myself, that
have been more kindly beholding to you than
any, freely give unto you this young scholar [*presenting* LUCENTIO], that hath been long studying
at Rheims; as cunning in Greek, Latin, and
other languages, as the other in music and mathematics: his name is Cambio; pray, accept his
service.

Bap. A thousand thanks, Signior Gremio. Welcome, Cambio. [*To* TRANIO] But, gentle sir, methinks you walk like a stranger: may I be so
bold to know the cause of your coming?

Tra. Pardon me, sir, the boldness is mine own,
That, being a stranger in this city here,   *90*
Do make myself a suitor to your daughter,
Unto Bianca, fair and virtuous.
Nor is your firm resolve unknown to me,
In the preferment of the eldest sister.
This liberty is all that I request,
That, upon knowledge of my parentage,
I may have welcome 'mongst the rest that woo
And free access and favour as the rest:
And, toward the education of your daughters,
I here bestow a simple instrument,   *100*
And this small packet of Greek and Latin books:
If you accept them, then their worth is great.

Bap. Lucentio is your name; of whence, I pray?

Tra. Of Pisa, sir; son to Vincentio.

Bap. A mighty man of Pisa; by report
I know him well: you are very welcome, sir.
Take you the lute, and you the set of books;
You shall go see your pupils presently.
Holla, within!

Enter a Servant.

    Sirrah, lead these gentlemen
To my daughters; and tell them both,   *110*
These are their tutors: bid them use them well.

[*Exit Servant, with* LUCENTIO *and* HORTENSIO,
                BIONDELLO *following.*

We will go walk a little in the orchard,
And then to dinner. You are passing welcome,
And so I pray you all to think yourselves.

Pet. Signior Baptista, my business asketh haste,
And every day I cannot come to woo.
You knew my father well, and in him me,
Left solely heir to all his lands and goods,
Which I have better'd rather than decreased:
Then tell me, if I get your daughter's love,   *120*

What dowry shall I have with her to wife?

Bap. After my death the one half of my lands,
And in possession twenty thousand crowns.

Pet. And, for that dowry, I'll assure her of
Her widowhood, be it that she survive me,
In all my lands and leases whatsoever:
Let specialties be therefore drawn between us,
That covenants may be kept on either hand.

Bap. Ay, when the special thing is well ob-
    tain'd,
That is, her love; for that is all in all.   *130*

Pet. Why, that is nothing; for I tell you, father,
I am as peremptory as she proud-minded;
And where two raging fires meet together
They do consume the thing that feeds their fury:
Though little fire grows great with little wind,
Yet extreme gusts will blow out fire and all:
So I to her, and so she yields to me;
For I am rough and woo not like a babe.

Bap. Well mayst thou woo, and happy be thy
    speed!
But be thou arm'd for some unhappy words.   *140*

Pet. Ay, to the proof; as mountains are for
    winds,
That shake not, though they blow perpetually.

Re-enter HORTENSIO, *with his head broke.*

Bap. How now, my friend! why dost thou look
    so pale?

Hor. For fear, I promise you, if I look pale.

Bap. What, will my daughter prove a good mu-
    sician?

Hor. I think she'll sooner prove a soldier:
Iron may hold with her, but never lutes.

Bap. Why, then thou canst not break her to the
    lute?

Hor. Why, no; for she hath broke the lute to
    me.
I did but tell her she mistook her frets,   *150*
And bow'd her hand to teach her fingering;
When, with a most impatient devilish spirit,
"Frets, call you these?" quoth she; "I'll fume
    with them":
And, with that word, she struck me on the head,
And through the instrument my pate made way;
And there I stood amazed for a while,
As on a pillory, looking through the lute:
While she did call me rascal fiddler
And twangling Jack; with twenty such vile
    terms,
As had she studied to misuse me so.   *160*

Pet. Now, by the world, it is a lusty wench;
I love her ten times more than e'er I did:
O, how I long to have some chat with her!

Bap. Well, go with me and be not so discom-
    fited:
Proceed in practice with my younger daughter;

She's apt to learn and thankful for good turns.
Signior Petruchio, will you go with us,
Or shall I send my daughter Kate to you?
  Pet. I pray you do. [*Exeunt all but* PETRUCHIO.]
    I will attend her here,
And woo her with some spirit when she
    comes.
Say that she rail; why then I'll tell plain   *171*
She sings as sweetly as a nightingale:
Say that she frown; I'll say she looks as clear
As morning roses newly wash'd with dew:
Say she be mute and will not speak a word:
Then I'll commend her volubility,
And say she uttereth piercing eloquence:
If she do bid me pack, I'll give her thanks,
As though she bid me stay by her a week:
If she deny to wed, I'll crave the day   *180*
When I shall ask the banns and when be married.
But here she comes; and now, Petruchio, speak.

      Enter KATHARINA.

Good morrow, Kate; for that's your name, I hear.
  Kath. Well have you heard, but something hard
    of hearing:
They call me Katharine that do talk of me.
  Pet. You lie, in faith; for you are call'd plain
    Kate,
And bonny Kate and sometimes Kate the curst;
But Kate, the prettiest Kate in Christendom,
Kate of Kate Hall, my super-dainty Kate,   *189*
For dainties are all Kates, and therefore, Kate,
Take this of me, Kate of my consolation;
Hearing thy mildness praised in every town,
Thy virtues spoke of, and thy beauty sounded,
Yet not so deeply as to thee belongs,
Myself am moved to woo thee for my wife.
  Kath. Moved! in good time: let him that moved
    you hither
Remove you hence: I knew you at the first
You were a moveable.
  Pet.   Why, what's a moveable?
  Kath. A join'd-stool.
  Pet.   Thou hast hit it: come, sit on me.
  Kath. Asses are made to bear, and so are you.
  Pet. Women are made to bear, and so are you.
  Kath. No such jade as you, if me you mean.
  Pet. Alas! good Kate, I will not burden thee;
For, knowing thee to be but young and light—
  Kath. Too light for such a swain as you to
    catch;
And yet as heavy as my weight should be.
  Pet. Should be! should —buzz!
  Kath.   Well ta'en, and like a buzzard.
  Pet. O slow-wing'd turtle! shall a buzzard take
    thee?
  Kath. Ay, for a turtle, as he takes a buzzard.

  Pet. Come, come, you wasp; i' faith, you are
    too angry.   *210*
  Kath. If I be waspish, best beware my sting.
  Pet. My remedy is then, to pluck it out.
  Kath. Ay, if the fool could find it where it lies.
  Pet. Who knows not where a wasp does wear
    his sting? In his tail.
  Kath. In his tongue.
  Pet. Whose tongue?
  Kath. Yours, if you talk of tails: and so fare-
    well.
  Pet. What, with my tongue in your tail? nay,
    come again,
Good Kate; I am a gentleman.
  Kath. That I'll try. [*She strikes him.*]   *220*
  Pet. I swear I'll cuff you, if you strike again.
  Kath. So may you lose your arms;
If you strike me, you are no gentleman;
And if no gentleman, why then no arms.
  Pet. A herald, Kate? O, put me in thy books!
  Kath. What is your crest? a coxcomb?
  Pet. A combless cock, so Kate will be my hen.
  Kath. No cock of mine; you crow too like a
    craven.
  Pet. Nay, come, Kate, come; you must not
    look so sour.
  Kath. It is my fashion, when I see a crab.   *230*
  Pet. Why, here's no crab; and therefore look
    not sour.
  Kath. There is, there is.
  Pet. Then show it me.
  Kath. Had I a glass, I would.
  Pet. What, you mean my face?
  Kath. Well aim'd of such a young one.
  Pet. Now, by Saint George, I am too young for
    you.
  Kath. Yet you are wither'd.
  Pet. 'Tis with cares.   *240*
  Kath. I care not.
  Pet. Nay, hear you, Kate: in sooth you scape
    not so.
  Kath. I chafe you, if I tarry: let me go.
  Pet. No, not a whit: I find you passing gentle.
'Twas told me you were rough and coy and sul-
    len,
And not I find report a very liar;
For thou are pleasant, gamesome, passing cour-
    teous,
But slow in speech, yet sweet as spring-time
    flowers;
Thou canst not frown, thou canst not look askance,
Nor bite the lip, as angry wenches will,   *250*
Nor hast thou pleasure to be cross in talk,
But thou with mildness entertain'st thy wooers,
With gentle conference, soft and affable.
Why does the world report that Kate doth limp?

O slanderous world! Kate like the hazel-twig
Is straight and slender and as brown in hue
As hazel nuts and sweeter than the kernels.
O, let me see thee walk: thou dost not halt.
    Kath. Go, fool, and whom thou keep'st com-
        mand.
    Pet. Did ever Dian so become a grove   260
As Kate this chamber with her princely gait?
O, be thou Dian, and let her be Kate;
And then let Kate be chaste and Dian sportful!
    Kath. Where did you study all this goodly
        speech?
    Pet. It is extempore, from my mother-wit.
    Kath. A witty mother! witless else her son.
    Pet. Am I not wise?
    Kath. Yes; keep you warm.
    Pet. Marry, so I mean, sweet Katharine, in thy
        bed:
And therefore, setting all this chat aside,   270
Thus in plain terms: your father hath consented
That you shall be my wife; your dowry 'greed
        on;
And, will you, nill you, I will marry you.
Now, Kate, I am a husband for your turn;
For, by this light, whereby I see thy beauty,
Thy beauty, that doth make me like thee well,
Thou must be married to no man but me;
For I am he am born to tame you Kate,
And bring you from a wild Kate to a Kate
Conformable as other household Kates.   280
Here comes your father: never make denial;
I must and will have Katharine to my wife.

Re-enter BAPTISTA, GREMIO, *and* TRANIO.

    Bap. Now, Signior Petruchio, how speed you
        with my daughter?
    Pet. How but well, sir? how but well?
It were impossible I should speed amiss.
    Bap. Why, how now, daughter Katharine! in
        your dumps?
    Kath. Call you me daughter? now, I promise
        you
You have show'd a tender fatherly regard,
To wish me wed to one half lunatic;
A mad-cap ruffian and a swearing Jack,   290
That thinks with oaths to face the matter out.
    Pet. Father, 'tis thus: yourself and all the world,
That talk'd of her, have talk'd amiss of her:
If she be curst, it is for policy,
For she's not froward, but modest as the dove;
She is not hot, but temperate as the morn;
For patience she will prove a second Grissel,
And Roman Lucrece for her chastity:
And to conclude, we have 'greed so well together,
That upon Sunday is the wedding-day.   300
    Kath. I'll see thee hang'd on Sunday first.

    Gre. Hark, Petruchio; she says she'll see thee
        hang'd first.
    Tra. Is this your speeding? nay, then, good
        night our part!
    Pet. Be patient, gentlemen; I choose her for
        myself:
If she and I be pleased, what's that to you?
'Tis bargain'd twixt us twain, being alone,
That she shall still be curst in company.
I tell you, 'tis incredible to believe
How much she loves me: O, the kindest Kate!
She hung about my neck; and kiss on kiss   310
She vied so fast, protesting oath on oath,
That in a twink she won me to her love.
O, you are novices! 'tis a world to see,
How tame, when men and women are alone,
A meacock wretch can make the curstest shrew.
Give me thy hand, Kate: I will unto Venice,
To buy apparel 'gainst the wedding-day.
Provide the feast, father, and bid the guests;
I will be sure my Katharine shall be fine.
    Bap. I know not what to say: but give me your
        hands;   320
God send you joy, Petruchio! 'tis a match.
    Gre. Tra. Amen, say we: we will be witnesses.
    Pet. Father, and wife, and gentlemen, adieu:
I will to Venice; Sunday comes apace:
We will have rings and things and fine array;
And kiss me, Kate, we will be married o' Sunday.
    [*Exeunt* PETRUCHIO *and* KATHARINA *severally.*
    Gre. Was ever match clapp'd up so suddenly?
    Bap. Faith, gentlemen, now I play a merchant's
        part,
And venture madly on a desperate mart.
    Tra. 'Twas a commodity lay fretting by
        you:
'Twill bring you gain, or perish on the seas.   331
    Bap. The gain I seek is, quiet in the match.
    Gre. No doubt but he hath got a quiet catch.
But now, Baptista, to your younger daughter:
Now is the day we long have looked for:
I am your neighbour, and was suitor first.
    Tra. And I am one that love Bianca more
Than words can witness, or your thoughts can
        guess.
    Gre. Youngling, thou canst not love so dear as I.
    Tra. Greybeard, thy love doth freeze.
    Gre.   But thine doth fry.   340
Skipper, stand back: 'tis age that nourisheth.
    Tra. But youth in ladies' eyes that flourisheth.
    Bap. Content you, gentlemen: I will compound
        this strife:
'Tis deeds must win the prize; and he of both
That can assure my daughter greatest dower
Shall have my Bianca's love.
Say, Signior Gremio, what can you assure her?

Gre. First, as you know, my house within the
  city
Is richly furnished with plate and gold;
Basins and ewers to lave her dainty hands;   *350*
My hangings all of Tyrian tapestry;
In ivory coffers I have stuff'd my crowns;
In cypress chests my arras counterpoints,
Costly apparel, tents, and canopies,
Fine linen, Turkey cushions boss'd with pearl,
Valance of Venice gold in needlework,
Pewter and brass and all things that belong
To house or housekeeping: then, at my farm
I have a hundred milch-kine to the pail,
Sixscore fat oxen standing in my stalls,   *360*
And all things answerable to this portion.
Myself am struck in years, I must confess;
And if I die to-morrow, this is hers,
If whilst I live she will be only mine.
  Tra. That "only" came well in. Sir, list to me:
I am my father's heir and only son:
If I may have your daughter to my wife,
I'll leave her houses three or four as good,
Within rich Pisa walls, as any one
Old Signior Gremio has in Padua;   *370*
Besides two thousand ducats by the year
Of fruitful land, all which shall be her jointure.
What, have I pinch'd you, Signior Gremio?
  Gre. Two thousand ducats by the year of land!
My land amounts not to so much in all:
That she shall have; besides an argosy
That now is lying in Marseilles' road.
What, have I choked you with an argosy?
  Tra. Gremio, 'tis known my father hath no less
Than three great argosies; besides two galliases,
And twelve tight galleys: these I will assure her,
And twice as much, whate'er thou offer'st next.
  Gre. Nay, I have offer'd all, I have no more;
And she can have no more than all I have:
If you like me, she shall have me and mine.
  *Tra.*Why, then the maid is mine from all the
  world,
By your firm promise: Gremio is out-vied.
  Bap. I must confess your offer is the best;
And, let your father make her the assurance,
She is your own; else, you must pardon me,   *390*
If you should die before him, where's her dower?
  Tra. That's but a cavil: he is old, I young.
  Gre. And may not young men die, as well as
  old?
  Bap. Well, gentlemen,
I am thus resolved: on Sunday next you know
My daughter Katharine is to be married:
Now, on the Sunday following, shall Bianca
Be bride to you, if you make this assurance;
If not, to Signior Gremio:
And so, I take my leave, and thank you both.

  Gre. Adieu, good neighbour. [*Exit* BAPTISTA.
            Now I fear thee not: *401*
Sirrah young gamester, your father were a fool
To give thee all, and in his waning age
Set foot under thy table: tut, a toy!
An old Italian fox is not so kind, my boy. [*Exit.*
  Tra. A vengeance on your crafty wither'd hide!
Yet I have faced it with a card of ten.
'Tis in my head to do my master good:
I see no reason but supposed Lucentio
Must get a father, call'd "supposed Vincentio";
And that's a wonder: fathers commonly   *411*
Do get their children; but in this case of wooing,
A child shall get a sire, if I fail not of my cun-
  ning.   [*Exit.*

ACT III

SCENE I. *Padua: Baptista's house*

Enter LUCENTIO, HORTENSIO, *and* BIANCA.

  Luc. Fiddler, forbear; you grow too forward,
  sir:
Have you so soon forgot the entertainment
Her sister Katharine welcomed you withal?
  Hor. But, wrangling pedant, this is
The patroness of heavenly harmony:
Then give me leave to have prerogative;
And when in music we have spent an hour,
Your lecture shall have leisure for as much.
  Luc. Preposterous ass, that never read so far
To know the cause why music was ordain'd!   *10*
Was it not to refresh the mind of man
After his studies or his usual pain?
Then give me leave to read philosophy,
And while I pause, serve in your harmony.
  Hor. Sirrah, I will not bear these braves of
  thine.
  *Bian.*Why, gentlemen, you do me double
  wrong,
To strive for that which resteth in my choice:
I am no breeching scholar in the schools;
I'll not be tied to hours nor 'pointed times,
But learn my lessons as I please myself.   *20*
And, to cut off all strife, here sit we down:
Take you your instrument, play you the whiles;
His lecture will be done ere you have tuned.
  Hor. You'll leave his lecture when I am in
  tune?
  Luc. That will be never: tune your instrument.
  Bian. Where left we last?
  Luc. Here, madam:
    Hic ibat Simois; hic est Sigeia tellus;
    Hic steterat Priami regia celsa senis.
  Bian. Construe them.   *30*
  Luc. Hic ibat, as I told you before, *Simois,* I am
Lucentio, *hic est,* son unto Vincentio of Pisa,

Sigeia tellus, disguised thus to get your love; *Hic*
steterat, and that Lucentio that comes a-wooing,
Priami, is my man Tranio, *regia*, bearing my port,
celsa senis, that we might beguile the old pantaloon.

Hor. Madam, my instrument's in tune.

Bian. Let's hear. O fie! the treble jars.

Luc. Spit in the hold, man, and tune again.   40

Bian. Now let me see if I can construe it:
Hic ibat Simois, I know you not, *hic est Sigeia*
tellus, I trust you not; *His steterat Priami*, take
heed he hear us not, *regia*, presume not, *celsa senis*,
despair not.

Hor. Madam, 'tis now in tune.

Luc.   All but the base.

Hor. The base is right; 'tis the base knave that
jars.

[*Aside*] How fiery and forward our pendant is!
Now, for my life, the knave doth court my
love:
Pedascule, I'll watch you better yet.   50

Bian. In time I may believe, yet I mistrust.

Luc. Mistrust it not; for, sure, Æacides
Was Ajax, call'd so from his grandfather.

Bian. I must believe my master; else, I promise
you,
I should be arguing still upon that doubt:
But let it rest. Now, Licio, to you:
Good masters, take it not unkindly, pray,
That I have been thus pleasant with you both.

Hor. You may go walk, and give me leave a
while:
My lessons make no music in three parts.   60

Luc. Are you so formal, sir? well, I must wait,
[*Aside*] And watch withal; for, but I be
deceived,
Our fine musician groweth amorous.

Hor. Madam, before you touch the instrument,
To learn the order of my fingering,
I must begin with rudiments of art;
To teach you gamut in a briefer sort,
More pleasant, pithy, and effectual,
Than hath been taught by any of my trade:
And there it is in writing, fairly drawn.   70

Bian. Why, I am past my gamut long ago.

Hor. Yet read the gamut of Hortensio.

Bian. [*Reads*] " 'Gamut' I am, the ground of all
accord,
'A re,' to plead Hortensio's passion;
'B mi,' Bianca, take him for thy lord,
'C fa ut,' that loves with all affection:
'D sol re,' one clef, two notes have I:
'E la mi,' show pity, or I die."
Call you this gamut? tut, I like it not:
Old fashions please me best; I am not so nice,   80
To change true rules for old inventions.

Enter a SERVANT.

Serv. Mistress, your father prays you leave
your books
And help to dress your sister's chamber up:
You know to-morrow is the wedding-day.

Bian. Farewell, sweet masters both; I must be
gone.   [*Exeunt Bianca and Servant.*

Luc. Faith, mistress, then I have no cause to
stay.   [*Exit.*

Hor. But I have cause to pry into this pedant:
Methinks he looks as though he were in love:
Yet if thy thoughts, Bianca, be so humble
To cast thy wandering eyes on every stale,   90
Seize thee that list: if once I find thee ranging,
Hortensio will be quit with thee by changing.
          [*Exit.*

SCENE II. *Padua: before Baptista's house*

Enter BAPTISTA, GREMIO, TRANIO, KATHARINA,
BIANCA, LUCENTIO, *and others, attendants.*

Bap. [*To* TRANIO] Signior Lucentio, this is the
'pointed day.
That Katharine and Petruchio should be married,
And yet we hear not of our son-in-law.
What will be said? what mockery will it be,
To want the bridegroom when the priest attends
To speak the ceremonial rites of marriage!
What says Lucentio to this shame of ours?

Kath. No shame but mine: I must, forsooth, be
forced
To give my hand opposed against my heart
Unto a mad-brain rudesby full of spleen;   10
Who woo'd in haste and means to wed at leisure.
I told you, I, he was a frantic fool,
Hiding his bitter jests in blunt behaviour:
And, to be noted for a merry man,
He'll woo a thousand, 'point the day of marriage,
Make feasts, invite friends, and proclaim the
banns;
Yet never means to wed where he hath woo'd.
Now must the world point at poor Katharine,
And say, "Lo, there is mad Petruchio's wife,
If it would please him come and marry her!"   20

Tra. Patience, good Katharine, and Baptista too.
Upon my life, Petruchio means but well,
Whatever fortune stays him from his word:
Though he be blunt, I know him passing wise;
Though he be merry, yet withal he's honest.

Kath. Would Katharine had never seen him
though!
[*Exit weeping, followed by* BIANCA *and others.*

Bap. Go, girl; I cannot blame thee now to
weep;
For such an injury would vex a very saint,
Much more a shrew of thy impatient humour.

Enter BIONDELLO.

Bion. Master, master! news, old news, and such
news as you never heard of!　　　　*31*

Bap. Is it new and old too? how may that be?

Bion. Why, is it not news, to hear of Petruchio's
coming?　·

Bap. Is he come?

Bion. Why, no, sir.

Bap. What then?

Bion. He is coming.

Bap. When will he be here?

Bion. When he stands where I am and sees you
there.　　　　*41*

Tra. But say, what to thine old news?

Bion. Why, Petruchio is coming in a new hat
and an old jerkin, a pair of old breeches thrice
turned, a pair of boots that have been candle-
cases, one buckled, another laced, an old rusty
sword ta'en out of the town-armoury, with a
broken hilt, and chapeless; with two broken
points: his horse hipped with an old mothy saddle
and stirrups of no kindred; besides, possessed
with the glanders and like to mose in the chine;
troubled with the lampass, infected with the
fashions, full of windgalls, sped with spavins,
rayed with the yellows, past cure of the fives,
stark spoiled with the staggers, begnawn with the
bots, swayed in the back and shoulder-shotten;
near-legged before and with a half-checked bit
and a head-stall of sheep's leather which, being
restrained to keep him from stumbling, hath been
often burst and now repaired with knots; one
girth six times pieced and a woman's crupper of
velure, which hath two letters for her name fairly
set down in studs, and here and there pierced
with packthread.

Bap. Who comes with him?

Bion. O, sir, his lackey, for all the world caparisoned like the horse; with a linen stock on
one leg and a kersey boot-hose on the other,
gartered with a red and blue list; an old hat and
"the humour of forty fancies" pricked in't for a
feather: a monster, a very monster in apparel,
and not like a Christian footboy or a gentleman's lackey.

Tra. 'Tis some odd humour pricks him to this
fashion;
Yet oftentimes he goes but mean-apparell'd.

Bap. I am glad he's come, howsoe'er he comes.

Bion. Why, sir, he comes not.

Bap. Didst thou not say he comes?

Bion. Who? that Petruchio came?

Bap. Ay, that Petruchio came.　　　　*80*

Bion. No, sir; I say his horse comes, with him
on his back.

Bap. Why, that's all one.

Bion. Nay, by Saint Jamy,
　　I hold you a penny,
　　A horse and a man
　　Is more than one,
　　And yet not many.

Enter PETRUCHIO *and* GRUMIO.

Pet. Come, where be these gallants? who's at
　　home?

Bap. You are welcome, sir.

Pet.　　　　And yet I come not well.　　*90*

Bap. And yet you halt not.

Tra.　　　　Not so well apparell'd
As I wish you were.

Pet. Were it better, I should rush in thus.
But where is Kate? where is my lovely bride?
How does my father? Gentles, methinks you
　　frown:
And wherefore gaze this goodly company,
As if they saw some wondrous monument,
Some comet or unusual prodigy?

Bap. Why, sir, you know this is your wedding-
　　day:
First were we sad, fearing you would not come;
Now sadder, that you come so unprovided.　*101*
Fie, doff this habit, shame to your estate,
An eye-sore to our solemn festival!

Tra. And tell us, what occasion of import
Hath all so long detain'd you from your wife,
And sent you hither so unlike yourself?

Pet. Tedious it were to tell, and harsh to hear:
Sufficeth, I am come to keep my word,
Though in some part enforced to digress;
Which, at more leisure, I will so excuse　　*110*
As you shall well be satisfied withal.
But where is Kate? I stay too long from her:
The morning wears, 'tis time we were at church.

Tra. See not your bride in these unreverent
　　robes:
Go to my chamber; put on clothes of mine.

Pet. Not I, believe me: thus I'll visit her.

Bap. But thus, I trust, you will not marry her.

Pet. Good sooth, even thus; therefore ha' done
　　with words:
To me she's married, not unto my clothes:
Could I repair what she will wear in me,　　*120*
As I can change these poor accoutrements,
'Twere well for Kate and better for myself.
But what a fool am I to chat with you,
When I should bid good morrow to my bride,
And seal the title with a lovely kiss!

　　　　　　[*Exeunt* PETRUCHIO *and* GRUMIO.

Tra. He hath some meaning in his mad attire:
We will persuade him, be it possible,
To put on better ere he go to church.

Bap. I'll after him, and see the event of this.

   [*Exeunt* BAPTISTA, GREMIO, *and attendants.*

 Tra. But to her love concerneth us to add
Her father's liking: which to bring to pass, *131*
As I before imparted to your worship,
I am to get a man—whate'er he be,
It skills not much, we'll fit him to our turn—
And he shall be Vincentio of Pisa;
And make assurance here in Padua
Of greater sums than I have promised.
So shall you quietly enjoy your hope,
And marry sweet Bianca with consent.

 Luc. Were it not that my fellow-schoolmaster
Doth watch Bianca's steps so narrowly, *141*
'Twere good, methinks, to steal our marriage;
Which once perform'd, let all the world say no,
I'll keep mine own, despite of all the world.

 Tra. That by degrees we mean to look into,
And watch our vantage in this business:
We'll over-reach the greybeard, Gremio,
The narrow-prying father, Minola,
The quaint musician, amorous Licio;
All for my master's sake, Lucentio. *150*

Re-enter GREMIO.

Signior Gremio, came you from the church?

 Gre. As willingly as e'er I came from school.

 Tra. And is the bride and bridegroom coming
  home?

 Gre. A bridegroom say you? 'tis a groom indeed,
A grumbling groom, and that the girl shall find.

 Tra. Curster than she? why, 'tis impossible.

 Gre. Why, he's a devil, a devil, a very fiend.

 Tra. Why, she's a devil, a devil, the devil's dam.

 Gre. Tut, she's a lamb, a dove, a fool to him!
I'll tell you, Sir Lucentio: when the priest *160*
Should ask, if Katharine should be his wife,
"Ay, by gogs-wouns," quoth he; and swore so
  loud,
That, all-amazed, the priest let fall the book;
And, as he stoop'd again to take it up,
This mad-brain'd bridegroom took him such a
  cuff
That down fell priest and book and book and
  priest:
"Now take them up," quoth he, "if any list."

 Tra. What said the wench when he rose again?

 Gre. Trembled and shook; for why, he stamp'd
  and swore,
As if the vicar meant to cozen him. *170*
But after many ceremonies done,
He calls for wine: "A health!" quoth he, as if
He had been aboard, carousing to his mates
After a storm; quaff'd off the muscadel
And threw the sops all in the sexton's face;
Having no other reason

But that his beard grew thin and hungerly
And seem'd to ask him sops as he was drinking.
This done, he took the bride about the neck
And kiss'd her lips with such a clamorous smack
That at the parting all the church did echo: *181*
And I seeing this came thence for very shame;
And after me, I know, the rout is coming.
Such a mad marriage never was before:
Hark, hark! I hear the minstrels play. [*Music.*

Re-enter PETRUCHIO, KATHARINA, BIANCA,
 BAPTISTA, HORTENSIO, GRUMIO, *and train.*

 Pet. Gentlemen and friends, I thank you for
  your pains:
I know you think to dine with me to-day,
And have prepared great store of wedding cheer;
But so it is, my haste doth call me hence,
And therefore here I mean to take my leave. *190*

 Bap. Is't possible you will away to-night?

 Pet. I must away to-day, before night come:
Make it no wonder; if you knew my business,
You would entreat me rather go than stay.
And, honest company, I thank you all,
That have beheld me give away myself
To this most patient, sweet, and virtuous wife:
Dine with my father, drink a health to me;
For I must hence; and farewell to you all.

 Tra. Let us entreat you stay till after dinner.

 Pet. It may not be.

 Gre.   Let me entreat you. *201*

 Pet. It cannot be.

 Kath.   Let me entreat you.

 Pet. I am content.

 Kath.   Are you content to stay?

 Pet. I am content you shall entreat me stay;
But yet not stay, entreat me how you can.

 Kath. Now, if you love me, stay.

 Pet.   Grumio, my horse.

 Gru. Ay, sir, they be ready: the oats have eaten
the horses.

 Kath. Nay, then,
Do what thou canst, I will not go to-day; *210*
No, nor to-morrow, not till I please myself.
The door is open, sir; there lies your way;
You may be jogging whiles your boots are green;
For me, I'll not be gone till I please myself:
'Tis like you'll prove a jolly surly groom,
That take it on you at the first so roundly.

 Pet. O Kate, content thee; prithee, be not
  angry.

 Kath. I will be angry: what hast thou to do?
Father, be quiet: he shall stay my leisure. *219*

 Gre. Ay, marry, sir, now it begins to work.

 Kath. Gentlemen, forward to the bridal dinner:
I see a woman may be made a fool,
If she had not a spirit to resist.

Pet. They shall go forward, Kate, at thy com-
    mand.
Obey the bride, you that attend on her;
Go to the feast, revel and domineer,
Carouse full measure to her maidenhead,
Be mad and merry, or go hang yourselves;
But for my bonny Kate, she must with me.
Nay, look not big, nor stamp, nor stare, nor fret;
I will be master of what is mine own: 231
She is my goods, my chattels; she is my house,
My household stuff, my field, my barn,
My horse, my ox, my ass, my any thing;
And here she stands, touch her whoever dare;
I'll bring mine action on the proudest he
That stops my way in Padua. Grumio,
Draw forth thy weapon, we are beset with
    thieves;
Rescue thy mistress, if thou be a man.
Fear not, sweet wench, they shall not touch thee,
    Kate: 240
I'll buckler thee against a million.
    [*Exeunt* PETRUCHIO, KATHARINA, *and* GRUMIO.
Bap. Nay, let them go, a couple of quiet ones.
Gre. Went they not quickly, I should die with
    laughing.
Tra. Of all mad matches never was the like.
Luc. Mistress, what's your opinion of your
    sister?
Bian. That, being mad herself, she's madly
    mated.
Gre. I warrant him, Petruchio is Kated.
Bap. Neighbours and friends, though bride and
    bridegroom wants
For to supply the places at the table,   249
You know there wants no junkets at the
    feast.
Lucentio, you shall supply the bridegroom's
    place;
And let Bianca take her sister's room.
Tra. Shall sweet Bianca practise how to bride
    it?
Bap. She shall, Lucentio. Come, gentlemen,
    let's go.   [*Exeunt.*

ACT IV

SCENE I. *Petruchio's country house*
Enter GRUMIO.

Gru. Fie, fie on all tired jades, on all mad masters, and all foul ways! Was ever man so beaten?
was ever man so rayed? was ever man so weary?
I am sent before to make a fire, and they are
coming after to warm them. Now, were not I a
little pot and soon hot, my very lips might freeze
to my teeth, my tongue to the roof of my mouth,
my heart in my belly, ere I should come by a fire

to thaw me: but I, with blowing the fire, shall
warm myself; for, considering the weather, a
taller man than I will take cold. Holla, ho!
Curtis.

Enter CURTIS.

Curt. Who is that calls so coldly?
Gru. A piece of ice: if thou doubt it, thou mayst
slide from my shoulder to my heel with no great-
er a run but my head and my neck. A fire, good
Curtis.
Curt. Is my master and his wife coming, Grumio?
Gru. O, ay, Curtis, ay: and therefore fire, fire;
cast on no water.   21
Curt. Is she so hot a shrew as she's reported?
Gru. She was, good Curtis, before this frost:
but, thou knowest, winter tames man, woman,
and beast; for it hath tamed my old master and
my new mistress and myself, fellow Curtis.
Curt. Away, you three-inch fool! I am no beast.
Gru. Am I but three inches? why, thy horn is a
foot; and so long am I at the least. But wilt thou
make a fire, or shall I complain on thee to our
mistress, whose hand, she being now at hand,
thou shalt soon feel, to thy cold comfort, for
being slow in thy hot office?
Curt. I prithee, good Grumio, tell me, how goes
the world?
Gru. A cold world, Curtis, in every office but
thine; and therefore fire: do thy duty, and have
thy duty; for my master and mistress are almost
frozen to death.   40
Curt. There's fire ready; and therefore, good
Grumio, the news.
Gru. Why, "Jack, boy! ho! boy!" and as much
news as will thaw.
Curt. Come, you are so full of cony-catching!
Gru. Why, therefore fire; for I have caught
extreme cold. Where's the cook? is supper ready,
the house trimmed, rushes strewed, cobwebs
swept; the serving-men in their new fustian, their
white stockings, and every officer his wedding-
garment on? Be the jacks fair within, the jills fair
without, the carpets laid, and every thing in
order?
Curt. All ready; and therefore, I pray thee,
news.
Gru. First, know, my horse is tired; my master
and mistress fallen out.
Curt. How?
Gru. Out of their saddles into the dirt; and
thereby hangs a tale.   60
Curt. Let's ha't, good Grumio.
Gru. Lend thine ear.
Curt. Here.

Gru. There. [*Strikes him.*]

Curt. This is to feel a tale, not to hear a tale.

Gru. And therefore 'tis called a sensible tale: and this cuff was but to knock at your ear, and beseech listening. Now I begin: *Imprimis*, we came down a foul hill, my master riding behind my mistress—   70

Curt. Both of one horse?

Gru. What's that to thee?

Curt. Why, a horse.

Gru. Tell thou the tale: but hadst thou not crossed me, thou shouldst have heard how her horse fell and she under her horse; thou shouldst have heard in how miry a place, how she was bemoiled, how he left her with the horse upon her, how he beat me because her horse stumbled, how she waded through the dirt to pluck him off me, how he swore, how she prayed, that never prayed before, how I cried, how the horses ran away, how her bridle was burst, how I lost my crupper, with many things of worthy memory, which now shall die in oblivion and thou return unexperienced to thy grave.

Curt. By this reckoning he is more shrew than she.

Gru. Ay: and that thou and the proudest of you all shall find when he comes home. But what talk I of this? Call forth Nathaniel, Joseph, Nicholas, Philip, Walter, Sugarsop and the rest: let their heads be sleekly combed, their blue coats brushed and their garters of an indifferent knit: let them curtsy with their left legs and not presume to touch a hair of my master's horsetail till they kiss their hands. Are they all ready?

Curt. They are.

Gru. Call them forth.

Curt. Do you hear, ho? you must meet my master to countenance my mistress.   101

Gru. Why, she hath a face of her own.

Curt. Who knows not that?

Gru. Thou, it seems, that calls for company to countenance her.

Curt. I call them forth to credit her.

Gru. Why, she comes to borrow nothing of them.

Enter four or five SERVING-MEN.

Nath. Welcome home, Grumio!

Phil. How now, Grumio!   110

Jos. What, Grumio!

Nich. Fellow Grumio!

Nath. How now, old lad?

Gru. Welcome, you;—how now, you;—what, you;—fellow, you;—and thus much for greeting. Now, my spruce companions, is all ready, and all things neat?

Nath. All things is ready. How near is our master?   119

Gru. E'en at hand, alighted by this; and therefore be not—Cock's passion, silence! I hear my master.

Enter PETRUCHIO *and* KATHARINA.

Pet. Where be these knaves? What, no man at door
To hold my stirrup nor to take my horse!
Where is Nathaniel, Gregory, Philip?

All Serv. Here, here, sir; here, sir.

Pet. Here, sir! here, sir! here, sir! here, sir!
You logger-headed and unpolish'd grooms!
What, no attendance? no regard? no duty?
Where is the foolish knave I sent before?   130

Gru. Here, sir; as foolish as I was before.

Pet. You peasant swain! you whoreson malt-horse drudge!
Did I not bid thee meet me in the park,
And bring along these rascal knaves with thee?

Gru. Nathaniel's coat, sir, was not fully made,
And Gabriel's pumps were all unpink'd i' the heel;
There was no link to colour Peter's hat,
And Walter's dagger was not come from sheathing:
There were none fine but Adam, Ralph, and Gregory;
The rest were ragged, old, and beggarly;   140
Yet, as they are, here are they come to meet you.

Pet. Go, rascals, go, and fetch my supper in.
                                   [*Exeunt* SERVANTS.
[*Singing*] "Where is the life that late I led"—
Where are those—Sit down, Kate, and welcome.—
Soud, soud, soud, soud!

Re-enter SERVANTS *with supper.*

Why, when, I say? Nay, good sweet Kate, be merry.
Off with my boots, you rogues! you villains, when?
[*Sings*] "It was the friar of orders grey,
            As he forth walked on his way:"—
Out, you rogue! you pluck my foot awry: 150
Take that, and mend the plucking off the other.
            Strikes him.
Be merry, Kate. Some water, here; what, ho!
Where's my spaniel Troilus? Sirrah, get you hence,
And bid my cousin Ferdinand come hither:
One, Kate, that you must kiss, and be acquainted with.
Where are my slippers? Shall I have some water?

Enter one with water.

Come, Kate, and wash, and welcome heartily.
You whoreson villain! will you let it fall?
  Strikes him.
  Kath. Patience, I pray you; 'twas a fault un-
    willing.
  Pet. A whoreson beetle-headed, flap-ear'd
    knave!   160
Come, Kate, sit down; I know you have a
  stomach.
Will you give thanks, sweet Kate; or else shall I?
What's this? mutton?
  1st Serv.   Ay.
  Pet.   Who brought it?
  Peter.   I.
  Pet. 'Tis burnt; and so is all the meat.
What dogs are these! Where is the rascal cook?
How durst you, villains, bring it from the dresser,
And serve it thus to me that love it not?
There, take it to you, trenchers, cups, and all:
  Throws the meat, &c. about the stage.
You heedless joltheads and unmanner'd slaves!
What, do you grumble? I'll be with you straight.
  Kath. I pray you, husband, be not so disquiet:
The meat was well, if you were so contented. *171*
  Pet. I tell thee, Kate, 'twas burnt and dried
    away;
And I expressly am forbid to touch it,
For it engenders choler, planteth anger;
And better 'twere that both of us did fast,
Since, of ourselves, ourselves are choleric,
Than feed it with such over-roasted flesh.
Be patient; to-morrow 't shall be mended,
And, for this night, we'll fast for company: *180*
Come, I will bring thee to thy bridal chamber.
                [Exeunt.

Re-enter SERVANTS *severally.*

  Nath. Peter, didst ever see the like?
  Peter. He kills her in her own humour.

Re-enter CURTIS.

  Gru. Where is he?
  Curt. In her chamber, making a sermon of conti-
    nency to her;
And rails, and swears, and rates, that she, poor
  soul,
Knows not which way to stand, to look, to
  speak,
And sits as one new-risen from a dream. *189*
Away, away! for he is coming hither. *[Exeunt.*

Re-enter PETRUCHIO.

  Pet. Thus have I politicly begun my reign,
And 'tis my hope to end successfully.

My falcon now is sharp and passing empty;
And till she stoop she must not be full-gorged,
For then she never looks upon her lure.
Another way I have to man my haggard,
To make her come and know her keeper's call,
That is, to watch her, as we watch these kites
That bate and beat and will not be obedient.
She eat no meat to-day, nor none shall eat; 200
Last night she slept not, nor to-night she shall
  not;
As with the meat, some undeserved fault
I'll find about the making of the bed;
And here I'll fling the pillow, there the bolster,
This way the coverlet, another way the sheets:
Ay, and amid this hurly I intend
That all is done in reverend care of her;
And in conclusion she shall watch all night:
And if she chance to nod I'll rail and brawl
And with the clamour keep her still awake. 210
This is a way to kill a wife with kindness;
And thus I'll curb her mad and headstrong hum-
  our.
He that knows better how to tame a shrew.
Now let him speak: 'tis charity to show. *[Exit.*

SCENE II. *Padua: before Baptista's house*
Enter TRANIO *and* HORTENSIO.

  Tra. Is't possible, friend Licio, that Mistress
    Bianca
Doth fancy any other but Lucentio?
I tell you, sir, she bears me fair in hand.
  Hor. Sir, to satisfy you in what I have said,
Stand by and mark the manner of his teaching.

Enter BIANCA *and* LUCENTIO.

  Luc. Now, mistress, profit you in what you
    read?
  Bian. What, master, read you? first resolve me
    that.
  Luc. I read that I profess, *The Art to Love.*
  Bian. And may you prove, sir, master of your
    art!
  Luc. While you, sweet dear, prove mistress of
    my heart!   10
  Hor. Quick proceeders, marry! Now, tell me, I
    pray,
You that durst swear that your mistress Bianca
Loved none in the world so well as Lucentio.
  Tra. O despiteful love! unconstant womankind!
I tell thee, Licio, this is wonderful.
  Hor. Mistake no more: I am not Licio,
Nor a musician, as I seem to be;
But one that scorn to live in this disguise,
For such a one as leaves a gentleman,
And makes a god of such a cullion: 20
Know, sir, that I am call'd Hortensio.

Tra. Signior Hortensio, I have often heard
Of your entire affection to Bianca;
And since mine eyes are witness of her lightness,
I will with you, if you be so contented,
Forswear Bianca and her love for ever.

Hor. See, how they kiss and court! Signior
Lucentio,
Here is my hand, and here I firmly vow
Never to woo her more, but do forswear her,
As one unworthy all the former favours 30
That I have fondly flatter'd her withal.

Tra. And here I take the like unfeigned oath,
Never to marry with her though she would en-
treat:
Fie on her! see, how beastly she doth court him!

Hor. Would all the world but he had quite for-
sworn!
For me, that I may surely keep mine oath,
I will be married to a wealthy widow,
Ere three days pass, which hath as long loved me
As I have loved this proud disdainful haggard.
And so farewell, Signior Lucentio. 40
Kindness in women, not their beauteous looks,
Shall win my love: and so I take my leave,
In resolution as I swore before. [*Exit.*

Tra. Mistress Bianca, bless you with such grace
As 'longeth to a lover's blessed case!
Nay, I have ta'en you napping, gentle love,
And have forsworn you with Hortensio.

Bian. Tranio, you jest: but have you both forsworn me?

Tra. Mistress, we have.

Luc.   Then we are rid of Licio.

Tra. I' faith, he'll have a lusty widow now,
That shall be woo'd and wedded in a day. 51

Bian. God give him joy!

Tra. Ay, and he'll tame her.

Bian.   He says so, Tranio.

Tra. Faith, he is gone unto the taming-school.

Bian. The taming-school! what, is there such a
place?

Tra. Ay, mistress, and Petruchio is the master;
That teacheth tricks eleven and twenty long,
To tame a shrew and charm her chattering
tongue.

Enter BIONDELLO.

Bion. O master, master, I have watch'd so long
That I am dog-weary: but at last I spied 60
An ancient angel coming down the hill,
Will serve the turn.

Tra.   What is he, Biondello?

Bion. Master, a mercatante, or a pedant,
I know not what; but formal in apparel,
In gait and countenance surely like a father.

Luc. And what of him, Tranio?

Tra. If he be credulous and trust my tale,
I'll make him glad to seem Vincentio,
And give assurance to Baptista Minola,
As if he were the right Vincentio. 70
Take in your love, and then let me alone.
[*Exeunt* LUCENTIO *and* BIANCA.

Enter a PEDANT.

Ped. God save you, sir!

Tra.   And you, sir! you are welcome.
Travel you far on, or are you at the farthest?

Ped. Sir, at the farthest for a week or two:
But then up farther, and as far as Rome;
And so to Tripoli, if God lend me life.

Tra. What countryman, I pray?

Ped.   Of Mantua.

Tra. Of Mantua, sir? marry, God forbid!
And come to Padua, careless of your life?

Ped. My life, sir! how, I pray? for that goes
hard. 80

Tra. 'Tis death for any one in Mantua
To come to Padua. Know you not the cause?
Your ships are stay'd at Venice, and the Duke,
For private quarrel 'twixt your Duke and him,
Hath publish'd and proclaim'd it openly:
'Tis marvel, but that you are but newly come,
You might have heard it else proclaim'd about.

Ped. Alas! sir, it is worse for me than so;
For I have bills for money by exchange
From Florence and must here deliver them. 90

Tra. Well, sir, to do you courtesy,
This will I do, and this I will advise you:
First, tell me, have you ever been at Pisa?

Ped. Ay, sir, in Pisa have I often been,
Pisa renowned for grave citizens.

Tra. Among them know you one Vincentio?

Ped. I know him not, but I have heard of him;
A merchant of incomparable wealth.

Tra. He is my father, sir; and, sooth to say,
In countenance somewhat doth resemble you. *100*

Bion. [*Aside*] As much as an apple doth an
oyster, and all one.

Tra. To save your life in this extremity,
This favour will I do you for his sake;
And think it not the worst of all your fortunes
That you are like to Sir Vincentio.
His name and credit shall you undertake,
And in my house you shall be friendly lodged:
Look that you take upon you as you should;
You understand me, sir: so shall you stay
Till you have done your business in the city: *110*
If this be courtesy, sir, accept of it.

Ped. O sir, I do; and will repute you ever
The patron of my life and liberty.

Tra. Then go with me to make the matter good.
This, by the way, I let you understand;

My father is here look'd for every day,
To pass assurance of a dower in marriage
'Twixt me and one Baptista's daughter here:
In all these circumstances I'll instruct you:
Go with me to clothe you as becomes you.   120
                                    [*Exeunt.*

SCENE III. *A room in Petruchio's house*

Enter KATHARINA *and* GRUMIO.

Gru. No, no, forsooth; I dare not for my life.
Kath. The more my wrong, the more his spite
     appears:
What, did he marry me to famish me?
Beggars, that come unto my father's door,
Upon entreaty have a present alms;
If not, elsewhere they meet with charity:
But I, who never knew how to entreat,
Nor never needed that I should entreat,
Am starved for meat, giddy for lack of sleep,   9
With oaths kept waking and with brawling fed:
And that which spites me more than all these
     wants,
He does it under name of perfect love;
As who should say, if I should sleep or eat,
'Twere deadly sickness or else present death.
I prithee go and get me some repast;
I care not what, so it be wholesome food.
Gru. What say you to a neat's foot?
Kath. 'Tis passing good: I prithee let me have it.
Gru. I fear it is too choleric a meat.
How say you to a fat tripe finely broil'd?   20
Kath. I like it well: good Grumio, fetch it me.
Gru. I cannot tell; I fear 'tis choleric.
What say you to a piece of beef and mustard?
Kath. A dish that I do love to feed upon.
Gru. Ay, but the mustard is too hot a little.
Kath. Why then, the beef, and let the mustard
     rest.
Gru. Nay then, I will not: you shall have the
     mustard,
Or else you get no beef of Grumio.
Kath. Then both, or one, or anything thou wilt.
Gru. Why then, the mustard without the beef.
Kath. Go, get thee gone, thou false deluding
     slave,   [*Beats him.*
That feed'st me with the very name of meat:
Sorrow on thee and all the pack of you,
That triumph thus upon my misery!
Go, get thee gone, I say.

Enter PETRUCHIO *and* HORTENSIO *with meat.*

Pet. How fares my Kate? What, sweeting, all
     amort?
Hor. Mistress, what cheer?
Kath.   Faith, as cold as can be.

Pet. Pluck up thy spirits; look cheerfully upon
     me.
Here, love; thou see'st how diligent I am
To dress thy meat myself and bring it thee: 40
I am sure, sweet Kate, this kindness merits
     thanks.
What, not a word? Nay, then thou lovest it not;
And all my pains is sorted to no proof.
Here, take away this dish.
Kath.   I pray you, let it stand.
Pet. The poorest service is repaid with thanks;
And so shall mine, before you touch the meat.
Kath. I thank you, sir.
Hor. Signior Petruchio, fie! you are to blame.
Come, Mistress Kate, I'll bear you company.
Pet. [*Aside*] Eat it up all, Hortensio, if thou
     lovest me.   50
Much good do it unto thy gentle heart!
Kate, eat apace: and now, my honey love,
Will we return unto thy father's house
And revel it as bravely as the best,
With silken coats and caps and golden rings,
With ruffs and cuffs and fardingales and things;
With scarfs and fans and double change of
     bravery,
With amber bracelets, beads, and all this knav-
     ery.
What, hast thou dined? The tailor stays thy lei-
     sure,
To deck thy body with his ruffling treasure.   60

Enter TAILOR.

Come, tailor, let us see these ornaments;
Lay forth the gown.

Enter HABERDASHER.

                    What news with you, sir?
Hab. Here is the cap your worship did bespeak.
Pet. Why, this was moulded on a porringer;
A velvet dish: fie, fie! 'tis lewd and filthy:
Why, 'tis a cockle or a walnut-shell,
A knack, a toy, a trick, a baby's cap:
Away with it! come, let me have a bigger.
Kath. I'll have no bigger: this doth fit the time,
And gentlewomen wear such caps as these.   70
Pet. When you are gentle, you shall have one
     too,
And not till then.
Hor. [*Aside*] That will not be in haste.
Kath. Why, sir, I trust I may have leave to
     speak;
And speak I will; I am no child, no babe:
Your betters have endured me say my mind,
And if you cannot, best you stop your ears.
My tongue will tell the anger of my heart,
Or else my heart concealing it will break,

And rather than it shall, I will be free
Even to the uttermost, as I please, in words.   80
  Pet. Why, thou say'st true; it is a paltry cap,
A custard-coffin, a bauble, a silken pie:
I love thee well, in that thou likest it not.
  Kath. Love me or love me not, I like the cap;
And it I will have, or I will have none.
                        [*Exit* HABERDASHER.
  Pet. Thy gown? why, ay: come, tailor, let us
      see't.
O mercy, God! what masquing stuff is here?
What's this? a sleeve? 'tis like a demi-cannon:
What, up and down, carved like an apple-tart?
Here's snip and nip and cut and slish and slash,
Like to a censer in a barber's shop: 91
Why, what, i' devil's name, tailor, call'st thou
      this?
  Hor. [*Aside*] I see she's like to have neither cap
      nor gown.
  Tai. You bid me make it orderly and well,
According to the fashion and the time.
  Pet. Marry, and did; but if you be remember'd,
I did not bid you mar it to the time.
Go, hop me over every kennel home,
For you shall hop without my custom, sir:
I'll none of it: hence! make your best of it.   100
  Kath. I never saw a better-fashion'd gown,
More quaint, more pleasing, nor more commend-
      able:
Belike you mean to make a puppet of me.
  Pet. Why, true; he means to make a puppet of
      thee.
  Tai. She says your worship means to make a
puppet of her.
  Pet. O monstrous arrogance! Thou liest, thou
thread, thou thimble,
Thou yard, three-quarters, half-yard, quarter,
      nail!
Thou flea, thou nit, thou winter-cricket thou!
Braved in mine own house with a skein of thread?
Away, thou rag, thou quantity, thou remnant;
Or I shall so be-mete thee with thy yard
As thou shalt think on prating whilst thou livest!
I tell thee, I, that thou hast marr'd her gown.
  Tai. Your worship is deceived; the gown is
      made
Just as my master had direction:
Grumio gave order how it should be done.
  Gru. I gave him no order; I gave him the stuff.
  Tai. But how did you desire it should be made?
  Gru. Marry, sir, with needle and thread.   121
  Tai. But did you not request to have it cut?
  Gru. Thou hast faced many things.
  Tai. I have.
  Gru. Face not me: thou hast braved many men;
brave not me; I will neither be faced nor braved.

I say unto thee, I bid thy master cut out the
gown; but I did not bid him cut it to pieces: *ergo*,
thou liest.
  Tai. Why, here is the note of the fashion to
testify.   131
  Pet. Read it.
  Gru. The note lies in's throat, if he say I said so.
  Tai. [*Reads*] "Imprimis, a loose-bodied gown":
  Gru. Master, if ever I said loose-bodied gown,
sew me in the skirts of it, and beat me to death
with a bottom of brown thread: I said a gown.
  Pet. Proceed.
  Tai. [*Reads*] "With a small compassed cape":
  Gru. I confess the cape.   141
  Tai. [*Reads*] "With a trunk sleeve":
  Gru. I confess two sleeves.
  Tai. [*Reads*] "The sleeves curiously cut."
  Pet. Ay, there's the villainy.
  Gru. Error i' the bill, sir; error i' the bill. I
commanded the sleeves should be cut out and
sewed up again; and that I'll prove upon thee,
though thy little finger be armed in a thimble.
  Tai. This is true that I say: an I had thee in
place where, thou shouldst know it.   151
  Gru. I am for thee straight: take thou the bill,
give me thy mete-yard, and spare not me.
  Hor. God-a-mercy, Grumio! then he shall have
no odds.
  Pet. Well, sir, in brief, the gown is not for me.
  Gru. You are i' the right, sir: 'tis for my mis-
tress.
  Pet. Go, take it up unto thy master's use.
  Gru. Villain, not for thy life: take up my mis-
tress' gown for thy master's use!   161
  Pet. Why, sir, what's your conceit in that?
  Gru. O, sir, the conceit is deeper than you think
for:
Take up my mistress' gown to his master's use!
O, fie, fie, fie!
  Pet. [*Aside*] Hortensio, say thou wilt see the
tailor paid.
Go take it hence; be gone, and say no more.
  Hor. Tailor, I'll pay thee for thy gown to-
morrow:
Take no unkindness of his hasty words:
Away! I say; commend me to thy master.   170
                        [*Exit* TAILOR.
  Pet. Well, come, my Kate; we will unto your
father's
Even in these honest mean habiliments:
Our purses shall be proud, our garments poor;
For 'tis the mind that makes the body rich;
And as the sun breaks through the darkest clouds,
So honour peereth in the meanest habit.
What is the jay more precious than the lark,
Because his feathers are more beautiful?

Or is the adder better than the eel,
Because his painted skin contents the eye?   *180*
O, no, good Kate; neither art thou the worse
For this poor furniture and mean array.
If thou account'st it shame, lay it on me;
And therefore frolic: we will hence forthwith,
To feast and sport us at thy father's house.
Go, call my men, and let us straight to him;
And bring our horses unto Long-lane end;
There will we mount, and thither walk on foot.
Let's see; I think 'tis now some seven o'clock,
And well we may come there by dinner-time. *190*
    Kath. I dare assure you, sir, 'tis almost two;
And 'twill be supper-time ere you come there.
    Pet. It shall be seven ere I go to horse:
Look, what I speak, or do, or think to do,
You are still crossing it. Sirs, let 't alone:
I will not go to-day; and ere I do,
It shall be what o'clock I say it is.
    Hor. [*Aside*] Why, so this gallant will com-
        mand the sun.   [*Exeunt.*

SCENE IV. *Padua: before Baptista's house*
Enter TRANIO, *and the* PEDANT *dressed like*
VINCENTIO.

    Tra. Sir, this is the house: please it you that I
        call?
    Ped. Ay, what else? and but I be deceived
Signior Baptista may remember me,
Near twenty years ago, in Genoa,
Where we were lodgers at the Pegasus.
    Tra. 'Tis well; and hold your own, in any case,
With such austerity as 'longeth to a father.
    Ped. I warrant you.

Enter BIONDELLO.

                    But, sir, here comes your boy;
'Twere good he were school'd.
    Tra. Fear you not him. Sirrah Biondello,
Now do your duty throughly, I advise you: *11*
Imagine 'twere the right Vincentio.
    Bion. Tut, fear not me.
    Tra. But hast thou done thy errand to Baptista?
    Bion. I told him that your father was at Venice,
And that you look'd for him this day in Padua.
    Tra. Thou'rt a tall fellow: hold thee that to
        drink.
Here comes Baptista: set your countenance, sir.

Enter BAPTISTA *and* LUCENTIO.

Signior Baptista, you are happily met.
[*To the* PEDANT] Sir, this is the gentleman I told
        you of: *20*
I pray you, stand good father to me now,
Give me Bianca for my patrimony.
    Ped. Soft, son!

Sir, by your leave: having come to Padua
To gather in some debts, my son Lucentio
Made me acquainted with a weighty cause
Of love between your daughter and himself:
And, for the good report I hear of you
And for the love he beareth to your daughter
And she to him, to stay him not too long,   *30*
I am content, in a good father's care,
To have him match'd; and if you please to like
No worse than I, upon some agreement
Me shall you find ready and willing
With one consent to have her so bestow'd;
For curious I cannot be with you,
Signior Baptista, of whom I hear so well.
    Bap. Sir, pardon me in what I have to say:
Your plainness and your shortness please me well.
Right true it is, your son Lucentio here   *40*
Doth love my daughter and she loveth him,
Or both dissemble deeply their affections:
And therefore, if you say no more than this,
That like a father you will deal with him
And pass my daughter a sufficient dower,
The match is made, and all is done:
Your son shall have my daughter with consent.
    Tra. I thank you, sir. Where then do you know
        best
We be affied and such assurance ta'en
As shall with either part's agreement stand?   *50*
    Bap. Not in my house, Lucentio; for, you
        know,
Pitchers have ears, and I have many servants:
Besides, old Gremio is hearkening still;
And happily we might be interrupted.
    Tra. Then at my lodging, an it like you:
There doth my father lie; and there, this night,
We'll pass the business privately and well.
Send for your daughter by your servant here;
My boy shall fetch the scrivener presently.
The worst is this, that, at so slender warning, *60*
You are like to have a thin and slender pittance.
    Bap. It likes me well. Biondello, hie you home,
And bid Bianca make her ready straight;
And, if you will, tell what hath happened,
Lucentio's father is arrived in Padua,
And how she's like to be Lucentio's wife.
    Bion. I pray the gods she may with all my heart!
    Tra. Dally not with the gods, but get thee gone.
                                [*Exit* BIONDELLO.
Signior Baptista, shall I lead the way?
Welcome! one mess is like to be your cheer: *70*
Come, sir; we will better it in Pisa.
    Bap. I follow you.
            [*Exeunt* TRANIO, PEDANT, *and* BAPTISTA.

Re-enter BIONDELLO.

    Bion. Cambio!

Luc. What sayest thou, Biondello?

Bion. You saw my master wink and laugh upon you?

Luc. Biondello, what of that?

Bion. Faith, nothing; but has left me here behind, to expound the meaning or moral of his signs and tokens.   80

Luc. I pray thee, moralize them.

Bion. Then thus. Baptista is safe, talking with the deceiving father of a deceitful son.

Luc. And what of him?

Bion. His daughter is to be brought by you to the supper.

Luc. And then?

Bion. The old priest of Saint Luke's church is at your command at all hours.

Luc. And what of all this?   90

Bion. I cannot tell; expect they are busied about a counterfeit assurance: take you assurance of her, *"cum privilegio ad imprimendum solum"*: to the church; take the priest, clerk, and some sufficient honest witnesses:

If this be not that you look for, I have no more
      to say,
But bid Bianca farewell for ever and a day.

Luc. Hearest thou, Biondello?

Bion. I cannot tarry: I knew a wench married in an afternoon as she went to the garden for parsley to stuff a rabbit; and so may you, sir: and so, adieu, sir. My master hath appointed me to go to Saint Luke's, to bid the priest be ready to come against you come with your appendix.
                                                  [*Exit.*

Luc. I may, and will, if she be so contented:
She will be pleased; then wherefore should I
      doubt?
Hap what hap may, I'll roundly go about her:
It shall go hard if Cambio go without her. [*Exit.*

SCENE V. *A public road*

Enter PETRUCHIO, KATHARINA, HORTENSIO,
and Servants.

Pet. Come on, i' God's name; once more toward
      our father's.
Good Lord, how bright and goodly shines the
      moon!

Kath. The moon! the sun: it is not moonlight
      now.

Pet. I say it is the moon that shines so bright.

Kath. I know it is the sun that shines so
      bright.

Pet. Now, by my mother's son, and that's my-
      self,
It shall be moon, or star, or what I list,
Or ere I journey to your father's house.
Go on, and fetch our horses back again.

Evermore cross'd and cross'd; nothing but
      cross'd!

Hor. Say as he says, or we shall never go.   *11*

Kath. Forward, I pray, since we have come so
      far,
And be it moon, or sun, or what you please:
An if you please to call it a rush-candle,
Henceforth I vow it shall be so for me.

Pet. I say it is the moon.

Kath.   I know it is the moon.

Pet. Nay, then you lie; it is the blessed sun.

Kath. Then, God be bless'd, it is the blessed
      sun:
But sun it is not, when you say it is not;
And the moon changes even as your mind.   *20*
What you will have it named, even that it is;
And so it shall be so for Katharine.

Hor. Petruchio, go thy ways; the field is
      won.

Pet. Well, forward, forward! thus the bowl
      should run,
And not unluckily against the bias.
But, soft! company is coming here.

Enter VINCENTIO.

[*To* VINCENTIO] Good morrow, gentle mistress:
      where away?
Tell me, sweet Kate, and tell me truly too,
Hast thou beheld a fresher gentlewoman?
Such war of white and red within her cheeks! *30*
What stars do spangle heaven with such beauty,
As those two eyes become that heavenly face?
Fair lovely maid, once more good day to thee.
Sweet Kate, embrace her for her beauty's sake.

Hor. A' will make the man mad, to make a
      woman of him.

Kath. Young budding virgin, fair and fresh and
      sweet,
Whither away, or where is thy abode?
Happy the parents of so fair a child;
Happier the man, whom favourable stars   *40*
Allot thee for his lovely bed-fellow!

Pet. Why, how now, Kate! I hope thou art not
      mad:
This is a man, old, wrinkled, faded, wither'd,
And not a maiden, as thou say'st he is.

Kath. Pardon, old father, my mistaking eyes,
That have been so bedazzled with the sun
That everything I look on seemeth green:
Now I perceive thou art a reverend father;
Pardon, I pray thee, for my mad mistaking.

Pet. Do, good old grandsire; and withal make
      known   *50*
Which way thou travellest: if along with us,
We shall be joyful of thy company.

Vin. Fair sir, and you my merry mistress,

That with your strange encounter much amazed
　me,
My name is call'd Vincentio; my dwelling
　Pisa;
And bound I am to Padua; there to visit
A son of mine, which long I have not seen.
　Pet. What is his name?
　Vin.　　　　　　　　　　　Lucentio, gentle sir.
　Pet. Happily met; the happier for thy son.
And now by law, as well as reverend age,　　60
I may entitle thee my loving father:
The sister to my wife, this gentlewoman,
Thy son by this hath married. Wonder not,
Nor be not grieved: she is of good esteem,
Her dowry wealthy, and of worthy birth;
Beside, so qualified as may beseem
The spouse of any noble gentleman.
Let me embrace with old Vincentio,
And wander we to see thy honest son,
Who will of thy arrival be full joyous.　　70
　Vin. But is this true? or is it else your pleas-
　　ure,
Like pleasant travellers, to break a jest
Upon the company you overtake?
　Hor. I do assure thee, father, so it is.
　Pet. Come, go along, and see the truth hereof;
For our first merriment hath made thee jealous.
　　　　　　　　　[*Exeunt all but* HORTENSIO.
　Hor. Well, Petruchio, this has put me in
　　heart.
Have to my widow! and if she be froward,
Then hast thou taught Hortensio to be untoward.
　　　　　　　　　　　　　　　　　[*Exit.*

ACT V

Scene i. *Padua: before Lucentio's house*
GREMIO *discovered. Enter behind* BIONDELLO,
LUCENTIO, *and* BIANCA.

　Bion. Softly and swiftly, sir; for the priest is
ready.
　Luc. I fly, Biondello: but they may chance to
need thee at home; therefore leave us.
　Bion. Nay, faith, I'll see the church o' your
back; and then come back to my master's as soon
as I can.
　　　　　[*Exeunt* LUCENTIO, BIANCA, *and* BIONDELLO.
　Gre. I marvel Cambio comes not all this while.

Enter PETRUCHIO, KATHARINA, VINCENTIO,
GRUMIO, *with Attendants.*

　Pet. Sir, here's the door, this is Lucentio's
house:
My father's bears more toward the market-
place;
Thither must I, and here I leave you, sir.　　11

　Vin. You shall not choose but drink before you
　　go:
I think I shall command your welcome here,
And, by all likelihood, some cheer is toward.
　Knocks.
　Gre. They're busy within; you were best knock
louder.

PEDANT *looks out of the window.*
　Ped. What's he that knocks as he would beat
down the gate?
　Vin. Is Signior Lucentio within, sir?
　Ped. He's within, sir, but not to be spoken
withal.　　21
　Vin. What if a man bring him a hundred pound
or two, to make merry withal?
　Ped. Keep your hundred pounds to yourself: he
shall need none, so long as I live.
　Pet. Nay, I told you your son was well beloved
in Padua. Do you hear, sir? To leave frivolous
circumstances, I pray you, tell Signior Lucentio
that his father is come from Pisa and is here at
the door to speak with him.　　30
　Ped. Thou liest: his father is come from Padua
and here looking out at the window.
　Vin. Art thou his father?
　Ped. Ay, sir; so his mother says, if I may believe her.
　Pet. [*To* VINCENTIO] Why, how now, gentleman! why, this is flat knavery, to take upon you
another man's name.
　Ped. Lay hands on the villain: I believe a' means
to cozen somebody in this city under my countenance.　　41

Re-enter BIONDELLO.

　Bion. I have seen them in the church together:
God send 'em good shipping! But who is here?
mine old master Vincentio! now we are undone
and brought to nothing.
　Vin. [*Seeing* BIONDELLO] Come hither, crack-
hemp.
　Bion. I hope I may choose, sir.
　Vin. Come hither, you rogue. What, have you
forgot me?　　50
　Bion. Forgot you! no, sir: I could not forget
you, for I never saw you before in all my life.
　Vin. What, you notorious villain, didst thou
never see thy master's father, Vincentio?
　Bion. What, my old worshipful old master? yes,
marry, sir: see where he looks out of the win-
dow.
　Vin. Is't so, indeed? [*Beats* BIONDELLO.]
　Bion. Help, help, help! here's a madman will
murder me.　　　　　　　　　　[*Exit.* 61
　Ped. Help, son! help, Signior Baptista!
　　　　　　　　　　　　　　　[*Exit from above.*

Pet. Prithee, Kate, let's stand aside and see the end of this controversy.   [*They retire.*

Re-enter PEDANT *below;* TRANIO, BAPTISTA, *and Servants.*

Tra. Sir, what are you that offer to beat my servant?

Vin. What am I, sir! nay, what are you, sir? O immortal gods! O fine villain! A silken doublet! a velvet hose! a scarlet cloak! and a copatain hat! O, I am undone! I am undone! while I play the good husband at home, my son and my servant spend all at the university.

Tra. How now! what's the matter?

Bap. What, is the man lunatic?

Tra. Sir, you seem a sober ancient gentleman by your habit, but your words show you a madman. Why, sir, what 'cerns it you if I wear pearl and gold? I thank my good father, I am able to maintain it.   79

Vin. Thy father! O villain! he is a sail-maker in Bergamo.

Bap. You mistake, sir, you mistake, sir. Pray, what do you think is his name?

Vin. His name! as if I knew not his name: I have brought him up ever since he was three years old, and his name is Tranio.

Ped. Away, away, mad ass! his name is Lucentio; and he is mine only son, and heir to the lands of me, Signior Vincentio.   89

Vin. Lucentio! O, he hath murdered his master! Lay hold on him, I charge you, in the Duke's name. O, my son, my son! Tell me, thou villain, where is my son Lucentio?

Tra. Call forth an officer.

Enter one with an Officer.

Carry this mad knave to the gaol. Father Baptista, I charge you see that he be forthcoming.

Vin. Carry me to the gaol!

Gre. Stay, officer: he shall not go to prison.

Bap. Talk not, Signior Gremio: I say he shall go to prison.   100

Gre. Take heed, Signior Baptista, lest you be cony-catched in this business: I dare swear this is the right Vincentio.

Ped. Swear, if thou darest.

Gre. Nay, I dare not swear it.

Tra. Then thou wert best say that I am not Lucentio.

Gre. Yes, I know thee to be Signior Lucentio.

Bap. Away with the dotard! to the gaol with him!   110

Vin. Thus strangers may be haled and abused: O monstrous villain!

Re-enter BIONDELLO, *with* LUCENTIO *and* BIANCA.

Bion. O! we are spoiled and—yonder he is: deny him, forswear him, or else we are all undone.

Luc. [*Kneeling*] Pardon, sweet father.

Vin.   Lives my sweet son?
[*Exeunt* BIONDELLO, TRANIO, *and* PEDANT, *as fast as may be.*

Bian. Pardon, dear father.

Bap.   How hast thou offended? Where is Lucentio?

Luc.   Here's Lucentio, Right son to the right Vincentio; That have by marriage made thy daughter mine, While counterfeit supposes blear'd thine eyne.

Gre. Here's packing, with a witness, to deceive us all!

Vin. Where is that damned villain Tranio, That faced and braved me in this matter so?

Bap. Why, tell me, is not this my Cambio?

Bian. Cambio is changed into Lucentio.

Luc. Love wrought these miracles. Bianca's love Made me exchange my state with Tranio, While he did bear my countenance in the town; And happily I have arrived at the last   130 Unto the wished haven of my bliss. What Tranio did, myself enforced him to; Then pardon him, sweet father, for my sake.

Vin. I'll slit the villain's nose, that would have sent me to the gaol.

Bap. But do you hear, sir? have you married my daughter without asking my good will?

Vin. Fear not, Baptista: we will content you, go to: but I will in, to be revenged for this villainy.   [*Exit.* 140

Bap. And I, to sound the depth of this knavery.
[*Exit.*

Luc. Look not pale, Bianca; thy father will not frown.   [*Exeunt* LUCENTIO *and* BIANCA.

Gre. My cake is dough; but I'll in among the rest, Out of hope of all, but my share of the feast.
[*Exit.*

Kath. Husband, let's follow, to see the end of this ado.

Pet. First kiss me, Kate, and we will.

Kath. What, in the midst of the street?

Pet. What, are thou ashamed of me?   150

Kath. No, sir, God forbid; but ashamed to kiss.

Pet. Why, then let's home again. Come, sirrah, let's away.

Kath. Nay, I will give thee a kiss: now pray thee, love, stay.

Pet. Is not this well? Come, my sweet Kate:

Better once than never, for never too late.

[*Exeunt.*

SCENE II. *Padua: Lucentio's house*

Enter BAPTISTA, VINCENTIO, GREMIO, *the* PEDANT,
LUCENTIO, BIANCA, PETRUCHIO, KATHARINA,
HORTENSIO, *and* WIDOW, TRANIO, BIONDELLO,
and GRUMIO: *the* SERVINGMEN *with* TRANIO
bringing in a banquet.

Luc. At last, though long, our jarring notes
agree:
And time it is, when raging war is done,
To smile at scapes and perils overblown.
My fair Bianca, bid my father welcome,
While I with self-same kindness welcome thine.
Brother Petruchio, sister Katharina,
And thou, Hortensio, with thy loving widow,
Feast with the best, and welcome to my house:
My banquet is to close our stomachs up,
After our great good cheer. Pray you, sit
down;
For now we sit to chat as well as eat.   *11*
Pet. Nothing but sit and sit, and eat and eat!
Bap. Padua affords this kindness, son Petruchio.
Pet. Padua affords nothing but what is kind.
Hor. For both our sakes, I would that word
were true.
Pet. Now, for my life, Hortensio fears his
widow.
Wid. Then never trust me, if I be afeard.
Pet. You are very sensible, and yet you miss my
sense:
I mean, Hortensio is afeard of you.
Wid. He that is giddy thinks the world turns
round.   *20*
Pet. Roundly replied.
Kath.   Mistress, how mean you that?
Wid. Thus I conceive by him.
Pet. Conceives by me! How likes Hortensio
that?
Hor. My widow says, thus she conceives her
tale.
Pet. Very well mended. Kiss him for that, good
widow.
Kath. "He that is giddy thinks the world turns
round":
I pray you, tell me what you meant by that.
Wid. Your husband, being troubled with a
shrew,
Measures my husband's sorrow by his woe:
And now you know my meaning.   *30*
Kath. A very mean meaning.
Wid.   Right, I mean you.
Kath. And I am mean indeed, respecting you.
Pet. To her, Kate!
Hor. To her, widow!

Pet. A hundred marks, my Kate does put her
down.
Hor. That's my office.
Pet. Spoke like an officer: ha' to thee, lad!
Drinks to Hortensio.
Bap. How likes Gremio these quick-witted
folks?
Gre. Believe me, sir, they butt together well.
Bian. Head, and butt! an hasty-witted body
Would say your head and butt were head and
horn.
Vin. Ay, mistress bride, hath that awaken'd
you?
Bian. Ay, but not frighted me; therefore I'll
sleep again.
Pet. Nay, that you shall not: since you have be-
gun,
Have at you for a bitter jest or two!
Bian. Am I your bird? I mean to shift my
bush;
And then pursue me as you draw your bow.
You are welcome all.

[*Exeunt* BIANCA, KATHARINA, *and* WIDOW.

Pet. She hath prevented me. Here, Signior
Tranio,
This bird you aim'd at, though you hit her not;
Therefore a health to all that shot and miss'd.   *51*
Tra. O, sir, Lucentio slipp'd me like his grey-
hound,
Which runs himself and catches for his master.
Pet. A good swift simile, but something currish.
Tra. 'Tis well, sir, that you hunted for yourself:
'Tis thought your deer does hold you at a bay.
Bap. O ho, Petruchio! Tranio hits you now.
Luc. I thank thee for that gird, good Tranio.
Hor. Confess, confess, hath he not hit you here?
Pet. A' has a little gall'd me, I confess;   *60*
And, as the jest did glance away from me,
'Tis ten to one it maim'd you two outright.
Bap. Now, in good sadness, son Petruchio,
I think thou hast the veriest shrew of all.
Pet. Well, I say no: and therefore for assurance
Let's each one send unto his wife;
And he whose wife is most obedient
To come at first when he doth send for her,
Shall win the wager which we will propose.
Hor. Content. What is the wager?
Luc.   Twenty crowns.   *70*
Pet. Twenty crowns!
I'll venture so much of my hawk or hound,
But twenty times so much upon my wife.
Luc. A hundred then.
Hor.   Content.
Pet.   A match! 'tis done.
Hor. Who shall begin?
Luc.   That will I.

Go, Biondello, bid your mistress come to me.
Bion. I go.   [*Exit.*
Bap. Son, I'll be your half, Bianca comes.
Luc. I'll have no halves; I'll bear it all myself.

Re-enter BIONDELLO.

How now! what news?
Bion. Sir, my mistress sends you word   80
That she is busy and she cannot come.
Pet. How! she is busy and she cannot come!
Is that an answer?
Gre.   Ay, and a kind one too:
Pray God, sir, your wife send you not a worse.
Pet. I hope, better.
Hor. Sirrah Biondello, go and entreat my wife
To come to me forthwith.   [*Exit* BIONDELLO.
Pet.   O, ho! entreat her!
Nay, then she must needs come.
Hor.   I am afraid, sir,
Do what you can, yours will not be entreated.

Re-enter BIONDELLO.

Now, where's my wife?   90
Bion. She says you have some goodly jest in
hand:
She will not come; she bids you come to her.
Pet. Worse and worse; she will not come!
O vile,
Intolerable, not to be endured!
Sirrah Grumio, go to your mistress;
Say, I command her come to me. [*Exit* GRUMIO.
Hor. I know her answer.
Pet.   What?
Hor.   She will not.
Pet. The fouler fortune mine, and there an end.
Bap. Now, by my holidame, here comes
Katharina!

Re-enter KATHARINA.

Kath. What is your will, sir, that you send for
me?   100
Pet. Where is your sister, and Hortensio's wife?
Kath. They sit conferring by the parlour fire.
Pet. Go, fetch them hither: if they deny to come,
Swinge me them soundly forth unto their hus-
bands:
Away, I say, and bring them hither straight.
                            [*Exit* KATHARINA.
Luc. Here is a wonder, if you talk of a wonder.
Hor. And so it is: I wonder what it bodes.
Pet. Marry, peace it bodes, and love, and quiet
life,
And awful rule, and right supremacy;
And, to be short, what not, that's sweet and
happy?   110
Bap. Now, fair befal thee, good Petruchio!

The wager thou hast won; and I will add
Unto their losses twenty thousand crowns;
Another dowry to another daughter,
For she is changed, as she had never been.
Pet. Nay, I will win my wager better yet
And show more sign of her obedience,
Her new-built virtue and obedience.
See where she comes and brings your froward
wives
As prisoners to her womanly persuasion.   120

Re-enter KATHARINA, *with* BIANCA *and* WIDOW.

Katharine, that cap of yours becomes you not:
Off with that bauble, throw it under-foot.
Wid. Lord, let me never have a cause to sigh,
Till I be brought to such a silly pass!
Bian. Fie! what a foolish duty call you this?
Luc. I would your duty were as foolish too:
The wisdom of your duty, fair Bianca,
Hath cost me an hundred crowns since supper-
time.
Bian. The more fool you, for laying on my duty.
Pet. Katharine, I charge thee, tell these head-
strong women   130
What duty they do owe their lords and husbands.
Wid. Come, come, you're mocking: we will
have no telling.
Pet. Come on, I say; and first begin with her.
Wid. She shall not.
Pet. I say she shall: and first begin with her.
Kath. Fie, fie! unknit that threatening unkind
brow,
And dart not scornful glances from those eyes,
To wound thy lord, thy king, thy governor:
It blots thy beauty as frosts do bite the meads,
Confounds thy fame as whirlwinds shake fair
buds,   140
And in no sense is meet or amiable.
A woman moved is like a fountain troubled,
Muddy, ill-seeming, thick, bereft of beauty;
And while it is so, none so dry or thirsty
Will deign to sip or touch one drop of it.
Thy husband is thy lord, thy life, thy keeper,
Thy head, thy sovereign; one that cares for thee,
And for thy maintenance commits his body
To painful labour both by sea and land,
To watch the night in storms, the day in cold, *150*
Whilst thou liest warm at home, secure and safe;
And craves no other tribute at thy hands
But love, fair looks, and true obedience;
Too little payment for so great a debt.
Such duty as the subject owes the prince
Even such a woman oweth to her husband;
And when she is froward, peevish, sullen, sour,
And not obedient to his honest will,
What is she but a foul contending rebel

And graceless traitor to her loving lord?   *160*
I am ashamed that women are so simple
To offer war where they should kneel for peace,
Or seek for rule, supremacy and sway,
When they are bound to serve, love, and obey.
Why are our bodies soft and weak and smooth,
Unapt to toil and trouble in the world,
But that our soft conditions and our hearts
Should well agree with our external parts?
Come, come, you froward and unable worms!
My mind hath been as big as one of yours,   *170*
My heart as great, my reason haply more,
To bandy word for word and frown for frown;
But now I see our lances are but straws,
Our strength as weak, our weakness past compare,
That seeming to be most which we indeed least are.
Then vail your stomachs, for it is no boot,
And place your hands below your husband's foot:
In token of which duty, if he please,
My hand is ready; may it do him ease.

Pet. Why, there's a wench! Come on, and kiss me, Kate.   *180*

Luc. Well, go thy ways, old lad; for thou shalt ha't.

Vin. 'Tis a good hearing when children are toward.

Luc. But a harsh hearing when women are froward.

Pet. Come, Kate, we'll to bed.
We three are married, but you two are sped.
[*To* LUCENTIO] 'Twas I won the wager, though you hit the white;
And, being a winner, God give you good night!
                         [*Exeunt* PETRUCHIO *and* KATHARINA.

Hor. Now, go thy ways; thou hast tamed a curst shrew.

Luc. 'Tis a wonder, by your leave, she will be tamed so.   [*Exeunt.*

THE TWO GENTLEMEN OF VERONA

DRAMATIS PERSONÆ

DUKE OF MILAN, *Father to Silvia*
VALENTINE | *the two Gentlemen*
PROTEUS
ANTONIO, *Father to Proteus*
THURIO, *a foolish rival to Valentine*
EGLAMOUR, *Agent for Silvia in her escape*
HOST, *where Julia lodges*
THREE OUTLAWS, *with Valentine*
SPEED, *a clownish servant to Valentine*

LAUNCE, *the like to Proteus*
PANTHINO, *Servant to Antonio*

JULIA, *beloved of Proteus*
SILVIA, *beloved of Valentine*
LUCETTA, *waiting-woman to Julia*

NON-SPEAKING: *Servants and musicians*

SCENE: *Verona, Milan, and the frontiers of Mantua*

ACT I

SCENE I. *Verona: an open place*

Enter VALENTINE *and* PROTEUS.

Val. Cease to persuade, my loving Proteus:
Home-keeping youth have ever homely wits.
Were't not affection chains thy tender days
To the sweet glances of thy honour'd love,
I rather would entreat thy company
To see the wonders of the world abroad
Than, living dully sluggardized at home,
Wear out thy youth with shapeless idleness.
But since thou lovest, love still and thrive therein,
Even as I would when I to love begin.   10
Pro. Wilt thou be gone? Sweet Valentine, adieu!
Think on thy Proteus, when thou haply seest
Some rare note-worthy object in thy travel:
Wish me partaker in thy happiness
When thou dost meet good hap; and in thy danger,
If ever danger do environ thee,
Commend thy grievance to my holy prayers,
For I will be thy beadsman, Valentine.
Val. And on a love-book pray for my success?
Pro. Upon some book I love I'll pray for thee.
Val. That's on some shallow story of deep
love: 21
How young Leander cross'd the Hellespont.
Pro. That's a deep story of a deeper love;
For he was more than over shoes in love.
Val. 'Tis true; for you are over boots in love,
And yet you never swum the Hellespont.
Pro. Over the boots? nay, give me not the
boots.
Val. No, I will not, for it boots thee not.
Pro.   What?

Val. To be in love, where scorn is bought with
groans;
Coy looks with heart-sore sighs; one fading
moment's mirth   30
With twenty watchful, weary, tedious nights:
If haply won, perhaps a hapless gain;
If lost, why then a grievous labour won;
However, but a folly bought with wit,
Or else a wit by folly vanquished.
Pro. So, by your circumstance, you call me fool.
Val. So, by your circumstance, I fear you'll
prove.
Pro. 'Tis love you cavil at: I am not Love.
Val. Love is your master, for he masters you:
And he that is so yoked by a fool,   40
Methinks, should not be chronicled for wise.
Pro. Yet writers say, as in the sweetest bud
The eating canker dwells, so eating love
Inhabits in the finest wits of all.
Val. And writers say, as the most forward **bud**
Is eaten by the canker ere it blow,
Even so by love the young and tender wit
Is turn'd to folly, blasting in the bud,
Losing his verdure even in the prime
And all the fair effects of future hopes.   50
But wherefore waste I time to counsel thee
That art a votary to fond desire?
Once more adieu! my father at the road
Expects my coming, there to see me shipp'd.
Pro. And thither will I bring thee, Valentine.
Val. Sweet Proteus, no; now let us take our
leave.
To Milan let me hear from thee by letters
Of thy success in love and what news else
Betideth here in absence of thy friend;
And I likewise will visit thee with mine.   60

229

Pro. All happiness bechance to thee in Milan!
Val. As much to you at home! and so, farewell.

[*Exit.*

Pro. He after honour hunts, I after love:
He leaves his friends to dignify them more;
I leave myself, my friends, and all, for love.
Thou, Julia, thou hast metamorphosed me,
Made me neglect my studies, lose my time,
War with good counsel, set the world at nought;
Made wit with musing weak, heart sick with
      thought.

Enter SPEED.

Speed. Sir Proteus, save you! Saw you my
      master?   70
Pro. But now he parted hence, to embark for
      Milan.
Speed. Twenty to one then he is shipp'd already,
And I have play'd the sheep in losing him.
Pro. Indeed, a sheep doth very often stray,
An if the shepherd be a while away.
Speed. You conclude that my master is a shep-
      herd then and I a sheep?
Pro. I do.
Speed. Why then, my horns are his horns,
      whether I wake or sleep.   80
Pro. A silly answer and fitting well a sheep.
Speed. This proves me still a sheep.
Pro. True; and thy master a shepherd.
Speed. Nay, that I can deny by a circumstance.
Pro. It shall go hard but I'll prove it by another.
Speed. The shepherd seeks the sheep, and not
the sheep the shepherd; but I seek my master,
and my master seeks not me: therefore I am no
sheep.   91
Pro. The sheep for fodder follow the shepherd;
the shepherd for food follows not the sheep: thou
for wages followest thy master; thy master for
wages follows not thee: therefore thou art a
sheep.
Speed. Such another proof will make me cry
"baa."
Pro. But, dost thou hear? gavest thou my letter
to Julia?   100
Speed. Ay, sir: I, a lost mutton, gave your letter
to her, a laced mutton, and she, a laced mutton,
gave me, a lost mutton, nothing for my labour.
Pro. Here's too small a pasture for such store of
muttons.
Speed. If the ground be overcharged, you were
best stick her.
Pro. Nay: in that you are astray, 'twere best
pound you.   110
Speed. Nay, sir, less than a pound shall serve me
for carrying your letter.
Pro. You mistake; I mean the pound—a pinfold.

Speed. From a pound to a pin? fold it over and
over,
'Tis threefold too little for carrying a letter to
      your lover.
Pro. But what said she?
Speed. [*First nodding*] Ay.
Pro. Nod—Ay—why, that's noddy.
Speed. You mistook, sir; I say, she did nod: and
you ask me if she did nod; and I say, "Ay."
Pro. And that set together is noddy.   122
Speed. Now you have taken the pains to set it
together, take it for your pains.
Pro. No, no; you shall have it for bearing the
letter.
Speed. Well, I perceive I must be fain to bear
with you.
Pro. Why, sir, how do you bear with me?
Speed. Marry, sir, the letter, very orderly;
having nothing but the word "noddy" for my
pains.
Pro. Beshrew me, but you have a quick wit.
Speed. And yet it cannot overtake your slow
purse.
Pro. Come, come, open the matter in brief: what
said she?
Speed. Open your purse, that the money and the
matter may be both at once delivered.
Pro. Well, sir, here is for your pains. What said
she?   140
Speed. Truly, sir, I think you'll hardly win her.
Pro. Why, couldst thou perceive so much from
her?
Speed. Sir, I could perceive nothing at all from
her; no, not so much as a ducat for delivering
your letter: and being so hard to me that brought
your mind, I fear she'll prove as hard to you in
telling your mind. Give her no token but stones;
for she's as hard as steel.
Pro. What said she? nothing?   150
Speed. No, not so much as "Take this for thy
pains." To testify your bounty, I thank you, you
have testerned me; in requital whereof, henceforth carry your letters yourself: and so, sir, I'll
commend you to my master.
Pro. Go, go, be gone, to save your ship from
      wreck,
Which cannot perish having thee aboard,
Being destined to a drier death on shore.

[*Exit* SPEED.

I must go send some better messenger:
I fear my Julia would not deign my lines,   160
Receiving them from such a worthless post. [*Exit.*

SCENE II. *The same: garden of Julia's house*
Enter JULIA *and* LUCETTA.

Jul. But say, Lucetta, now we are alone,

Wouldst thou then counsel me to fall in love?

Luc. Ay, madam, so you stumble not unheedfully.

Jul. Of all the fair resort of gentlemen
That every day with parle encounter me,
In thy opinion which is worthiest love?

Luc. Please you repeat their names, I'll show my mind
According to my shallow simple skill.

Jul. What think'st thou of the fair Sir Eglamour?

Luc. As of a knight well- spoken, neat and fine;
But, were I you, he never should be mine.   *11*

Jul. What think'st thou of the rich Mercatio?

Luc. Well of his wealth; but of himself, so so.

Jul. What think'st thou of the gentle Proteus?

Luc. Lord, Lord! to see what folly reigns in us!

Jul. How now! what means this passion at his name?

Luc. Pardon, dear madam: tis a passing shame
That I, unworthy body as I am,
Should censure thus on lovely gentlemen.

Jul. Why not on Proteus, as of all the rest?   *20*

Luc. Then thus: of many good I think him best.

Jul. Your reason?

Luc. I have no other but a woman's reason;
I think him so because I think him so.

Jul. And wouldst thou have me cast my love on him?

Luc. Ay, if you thought your love not cast away.

Jul. Why he, of all the rest, hath never moved me.

Luc. Yet he, of all the rest, I think, best loves ye.

Jul. His little speaking shows his love but small.   *29*

Luc. Fire that's closest kept burns most of all.

Jul. They do not love that do not show their love.

Luc. O, they love least that let men know their love.

Jul. I would I knew his mind.

Luc. Peruse this paper, madam.

Jul. "To Julia." Say, from whom?

Luc. That the contents will show.

Jul. Say, say, who gave it thee?

Luc. Sir Valentine's page; and sent, I think, from Proteus.
He would have given it you; but I, being in the way,
Did in your name receive it: pardon the fault, I pray.   *40*

Jul. Now, by my modesty, a goodly broker!
Dare you presume to harbour wanton lines?
To whisper and conspire against my youth?
Now, trust me, 'tis an office of great worth

And you an officer fit for the place.
There, take the paper: see it be return'd;
Or else return no more into my sight.

Luc. To plead for love deserves more fee than hate.

Jul. Will ye be gone?

Luc.   That you may ruminate.
                                        [*Exit.*

Jul. And yet I would I had o'erlooked the letter: *50*
It were a shame to call her back again
And pray her to a fault for which I chid her.
What a fool is she, that knows I am a maid,
And would not force the letter to my view!
Since maids, in modesty, say "no" to that
Which they would have the profferer construe "ay."
Fie, fie, how wayward is this foolish love
That, like a testy babe, will scratch the nurse
And presently all humbled kiss the rod!
How churlishly I chid Lucetta hence,   *60*
When willingly I would have had her here!
How angerly I taught my brow to frown,
When inward joy enforced my heart to smile!
My penance is to call Lucetta back
And ask remission for my folly past.
What ho! Lucetta!

Re-enter LUCETTA.

Luc.   What would your ladyship?

Jul. Is't near dinner-time?

Luc.   I would it were,
That you might kill your stomach on your meat
And not upon your maid.

Jul. What is't that you took up so gingerly?

Luc. Nothing.   *71*

Jul. Why didst thou stoop, then?

Luc. To take a paper up that I let fall.

Jul. And is that paper nothing?

Luc. Nothing concerning me.

Jul. Then let it lie for those that it concerns.

Luc. Madam, it will not lie where it concerns,
Unless it have a false interpreter.

Jul. Some love of yours hath writ to you in rhyme.

Luc. That I might sing it, madam, to a tune.
Give me a note: your ladyship can set.   *81*

Jul. As little by such toys as may be possible.
Best sing it to the tune of "Light o' Love."

Luc. It is too heavy for so light a tune.

Jul. Heavy! belike it hath some burden then?

Luc. Ay, and melodious were it, would you sing it.

Jul. And why not you?

Luc.   I cannot reach so high.

Jul. Let's see your song. How now, minion!

Luc. Keep tune there still, so you will sing it
    out:
And yet methinks I do not like this tune.   90
    Jul. You do not?
    Luc.   No, madam; it is too sharp.
    Jul. You, minion, are too saucy.
    Luc. Nay, now you are too flat
And mar the concord with too harsh a descant:
There wanteth but a mean to fill your song.
    Jul. The mean is drown'd with your unruly bass.
    Luc. Indeed, I bid the base for Proteus.
    Jul. This babble shall not henceforth trouble me.
Here is a coil with protestation! [*Tears the letter.*]
Go get you gone, and let the papers lie: 100
You would be fingering them, to anger me.
    Luc. She makes it strange; but she would be
    best pleased
To be so anger'd with another letter.   [*Exit.*
    Jul. Nay, would I were so anger'd with the
    same!
O hateful hands, to tear such loving words!
Injurious wasps, to feed on such sweet honey
And kill the bees that yield it with your stings!
I'll kiss each several paper for amends.
Look, here is writ "kind Julia." Unkind Julia!
As in revenge of thy ingratitude,   110
I throw thy name against the bruising stones,
Trampling contemptuously on thy disdain.
And here is writ "love-wounded Proteus."
Poor wounded name! my bosom as a bed
Shall lodge thee till thy wound be throughly
    heal'd;
And thus I search it with a sovereign kiss.
But twice or thrice was "Proteus" written down.
Be calm, good wind, blow not a word away
Till I have found each letter in the letter,
Except mine own name: that some whirlwind
    bear
Unto a ragged fearful-hanging rock   121
And throw it thence into the raging sea!
Lo, here in one line is his name twice writ,
"Poor forlorn Proteus, passionate Proteus,
To the sweet Julia": that I'll tear away.
And yet I will not, sith so prettily
He couples it to his complaining names.
Thus will I fold them one upon another:
Now kiss, embrace, contend, do what you will.

Re-enter LUCETTA.

Luc. Madam,   130
Dinner is ready, and your father stays.
    Jul. Well, let us go.
    Luc. What, shall these papers lie like telltales
    here?
    Jul. If you respect them, best to take them up.
    Luc. Nay, I was taken up for laying them down:

Yet here they shall not lie, for catching cold.
    Jul. I see you have a month's mind to them.
    Luc. Ay, madam, you may say what sights you
    see;
I see things too, although you judge I wink.
    Jul. Come, come; will't please you go?   140
                                        [*Exeunt.*

SCENE III. *The same: Antonio's house.*

Enter ANTONIO *and* PANTHINO.

Ant. Tell me, Panthino, what sad talk was that
Wherewith my brother held you in the cloister?
    Pan. 'Twas of his nephew Proteus, your son.
    Ant. Why, what of him?
    Pan.   He wonder'd that your lordship
Would suffer him to spend his youth at home,
While other men, of slender reputation,
Put forth their sons to seek preferment out:
Some to the wars, to try their fortune there;
Some to discover islands far away;
Some to the studious universities.   10
For any or for all these exercises
He said that Proteus your son was meet,
And did request me to importune you
To let him spend his time no more at home,
Which would be great impeachment to his age,
In having known no travel in his youth.
    Ant. Nor need'st thou much importune me to
    that
Wheron this month I have been hammering.
I have consider'd well his loss of time
And how he cannot be a perfect man,   20
Not being tried and tutor'd in the world:
Experience is by industry achieved
And perfected by the swift course of time.
Then tell me, whither were I best to send him?
    Pan. I think your lordship is not ignorant
How his companion, youthful Valentine,
Attends the Emperor in his royal court.
    Ant. I know it well.
    Pan. 'Twere good, I think, your lordship sent
    him thither:
There shall he practise tilts and tournaments,   30
Hear sweet discourse, converse with noblemen,
And be in eye of every exercise
Worthy his youth and nobleness of birth.
    Ant. I like thy counsel; well hast thou advised:
And that thou mayst perceive how well I like it
The execution of it shall make known.
Even with the speediest expedition
I will dispatch him to the Emperor's court.
    Pan. To-morrow, may it please you, Don
    Alphonso
With other gentlemen of good esteem   40
Are journeying to salute the Emperor
And to commend their service to his will.

Ant. Good company; with them shall Proteus
 go:
And, in good time! now will we break with
 him.

Enter PROTEUS.

Pro. Sweet love! sweet lines! sweet life!
Here is her hand, the agent of her heart;
Here is her oath for love, her honour's pawn.
O, that our fathers would applaud our loves,
To seal our happiness with their consents!
O heavenly Julia!   50
 Ant. How now! what letter are you reading
  there?
 Pro. May't please your lordship, 'tis a word
  or two
Of commendations sent from Valentine,
Deliver'd by a friend that came from him.
 Ant. Lend me the letter; let me see what news.
 Pro. There is no news, my lord, but that he
  writes
How happily he lives, how well beloved
And daily graced by the Emperor;
Wishing me with him, partner of his fortune.
 Ant. And how stand you affected to his wish?
 Pro. As one relying on your lordship's will   61
And not depending on his friendly wish.
 Ant. My will is something sorted with his
  wish.
Muse not that I thus suddenly proceed;
For what I will, I will, and there an end.
I am resolved that thou shalt spend some time
With Valentinus in the Emperor's court:
What maintenance he from his friends receives,
Like exhibition thou shalt have from me.
To-morrow be in readiness to go: 70
Excuse it not, for I am peremptory.
 Pro. My lord, I cannot be so soon provided:
Please you, deliberate a day or two.
 Ant. Look, what thou want'st shall be sent
  after thee:
No more of stay! to-morrow thou must go.
Come on, Panthino: you shall be employ'd
To hasten on his expedition.
            [*Exeunt* ANTONIO *and* PANTHINO.
 Pro. Thus have I shunn'd the fire for fear of
  burning,
And drench'd me in the sea, where I am drown'd.
I fear'd to show my father Julia's letter,   80
Lest he should take exceptions to my love;
And with the vantage of mine own excuse
Hath he excepted most against my love.
O, how this spring of love resembleth
 The uncertain glory of an April day,
Which now shows all the beauty of the sun,
 And by and by a cloud takes all away!

Re-enter PANTHINO.

 Pan. Sir Proteus, your father calls for you:
He is in haste; therefore, I pray you, go.   89
 Pro. Why, this it is: my heart accords thereto,
And yet a thousand times it answers "no."
                                           [*Exeunt.*

ACT II

SCENE I. *Milan: the Duke's palace*
Enter VALENTINE *and* SPEED.

Speed. Sir, your glove.
Val.   Not mine; my gloves are on.
Speed. Why, then, this may be yours, for this
 is but one.
Val. Ha! let me see: ay, give it me, it's
 mine:
Sweet ornament that decks a thing divine!
Ah, Silvia, Silvia!
Speed. Madam Silvia! Madam Silvia!
Val. How now, sirrah?
Speed. She is not within hearing, sir.
Val. Why sir, who bade you call her?
Speed. Your worship, sir; or else I mistook.   10
Val. Well, you'll still be too forward.
Speed. And yet I was last chidden for being too
 slow.
Val. Go to, sir: tell me, do you know Madam
Silvia?
Speed. She that your worship loves?
Val. Why, how know you that I am in love?
Speed. Marry, by these special marks: first,
you have learned, like Sir Proteus, to wreathe
your arms, like a malcontent; to relish a love-
song, like a robin-redbreast; to walk alone, like
one that had the pestilence; to sigh, like a school-
boy that had lost his A B C; to weep, like a
young wench that had buried her grandam; to
fast, like one that takes diet; to watch, like one
that fears robbing; to speak puling, like a beggar at Hallowmas. You were wont, when you
laughed, to crow like a cock; when you walked,
to walk like one of the lions; when you fasted,
it was presently after dinner; when you looked
sadly, it was for want of money: and now you
are metamorphosed with a mistress, that, when
I look on you, I can hardly think you my master.
Val. Are all these things perceived in me?
Speed. They are all perceived without ye.
Val. Without me? they cannot.
Speed. Without you? nay, that's certain, for,
without you were so simple, none else would:
but you are so without these follies, that these
follies are within you and shine through you like
the water in an urinal, that not an eye that sees

you but is a physician to comment on your malady.

Val. But tell me, dost thou know my lady Silvia?

Speed. She that you gaze on so as she sits at supper?

Val. Hast thou observed that? even she, I mean.

Speed. Why, sir, I know her not. 50

Val. Dost thou know her by my gazing on her, and yet knowest her not?

Speed. Is she not hard-favoured, sir?

Val. Not so fair, boy, as well-favoured.

Speed. Sir, I know that well enough.

Val. What dost thou know?

Speed. That she is not so fair as, of you, well favoured.

Val. I mean that her beauty is exquisite, but her favour infinite. 60

Speed. That's because the one is painted and the other out of all count.

Val. How painted? and how out of count?

Speed. Marry, sir, so painted, to make her fair, that no man counts of her beauty.

Val. How esteemest thou me? I account of her beauty.

Speed. You never saw her since she was deformed.

Val. How long hath she been deformed? 70

Speed. Ever since you loved her.

Val. I have loved her ever since I saw her; and still I see her beautiful.

Speed. If you love her, you cannot see her.

Val. Why?

Speed. Because Love is blind. O, that you had mine eyes; or your own eyes had the lights they were wont to have when you chid at Sir Proteus for going ungartered!

Val. What should I see then? 80

Speed. Your own present folly and her passing deformity: for he, being in love, could not see to garter his hose, and you, being in love, cannot see to put on your hose.

Val. Belike, boy, then, you are in love; for last morning you could not see to wipe my shoes.

Speed. True, sir; I was in love with my bed: I thank you, you swinged me for my love, which makes me the bolder to chide you for yours.

Val. In conclusion, I stand affected to her. 90

Speed. I would you were set, so your affection would cease.

Val. Last night she enjoined me to write some lines to one she loves.

Speed. And have you?

Val. I have.

Speed. Are they not lamely writ?

Val. No, boy, but as well as I can do them. Peace! here she comes. 99

Speed. [*Aside*] O excellent motion! O exceeding puppet! Now will he interpret to her.

Enter SILVIA.

Val. Madam and mistress, a thousand good-morrows.

Speed [*Aside*] O, give ye good even! here's a million of manners.

Sil. Sir Valentine and servant, to you two thousand.

Speed. [*Aside*] He should give her interest, and she gives it him.

Val. As you enjoin'd me, I have writ your letter Unto the secret nameless friend of yours; 111 Which I was much unwilling to proceed in But for my duty to your ladyship.

Sil. I thank you, gentle servant: 'tis very clerkly done.

Val. Now trust me, madam, it came hardly off; For being ignorant to whom it goes I writ at random, very doubtfully.

Sil. Perchance you think too much of so much pains?

Val. No, madam; so it stead you, I will write, Please you command, a thousand times as much; And yet— 121

Sil. A pretty period! Well, I guess the sequel; And yet I will not name it; and yet I care not; And yet take this again; and yet I thank you, Meaning henceforth to trouble you no more.

Speed. [*Aside*] And yet you will; and yet another "yet."

Val. What means your ladyship? do you not like it?

Sil. Yes, yes: the lines are very quaintly writ; But since unwillingly, take them again. Nay, take them. 130

Val. Madam, they are for you.

Sil. Ay, ay: you writ them, sir, at my request; But I will none of them; they are for you; I would have had them writ more movingly.

Val. Please you, I'll write your ladyship another.

Sil. And when it's writ, for my sake read it over. And if it please you, so; if not, why, so.

Val. If it please me, madam, what then?

Sil. Why, if it please you, take it for your labour: And so, good morrow, servant. [*Exit.* 140

Speed. O jest unseen, inscrutable, invisible, As a nose on a man's face, or a weathercock on a steeple!

My master sues to her, and she hath taught her suitor,

He being her pupil, to become her tutor.
O excellent device! was there ever heard a better,
That my master, being scribe, to himself should
    write the letter?

Val. How now, sir? what are you reasoning
with yourself?

Speed. Nay, I was rhyming: 'tis you that have
the reason.   *150*

Val. To do what?

Speed. To be a spokesman from Madam Silvia.

Val. To whom?

Speed. To yourself: why, she wooes you by a
figure.

Val. What figure?

Speed. By a letter, I should say.

Val. Why, she hath not writ to me?

Speed. What need she, when she hath made you
write to yourself? Why, do you not perceive the
jest?   *160*

Val. No, believe me.

Speed. No believing you, indeed, sir. But did you
perceive her earnest?

Val. She gave me none, except an angry word.

Speed. Why, she hath given you a letter.

Val. That's the letter I writ to her friend.

Speed. And that letter hath she delivered, and
there an end.

Val. I would it were no worse.

Speed. I'll warrant you, 'tis as well: *170*
For often have you writ to her, and she, in
    modesty,
Or else for want of idle time, could not again
    reply;
Or fearing else some messenger that might her
    mind discover,
Herself hath taught her love himself to write
    unto her lover.
All this I speak in print, for in print I found it.
Why muse you, sir? 'tis dinner-time.

Val. I have dined.

Speed. Ay, but hearken, sir; though the chameleon Love can feed on the air, I am one that
am nourished by my victuals and would fain have
meat. O, be not like your mistress; be moved,
be moved.   [*Exeunt.*

SCENE II. *Verona: Julia's house*

Enter PROTEUS *and* JULIA.

Pro. Have patience, gentle Julia.

Jul. I must, where is no remedy.

Pro. When possibly I can, I will return.

Jul. If you turn not, you will return the sooner.
Keep this remembrance for thy Julia's sake.
    Giving a ring.

Pro. Why, then, we'll make exchange; here,
    take you this.

Jul. And seal the bargain with a holy kiss.

Pro. Here is my hand for my true constancy;
And when that hour o'erslips me in the day
Wherein I sigh not, Julia, for thy sake,   *10*
The next ensuing hour some foul mischance
Torment me for my love's forgetfulness!
My father stays my coming; answer not;
The tide is now: nay, not thy tide of tears;
That tide will stay me longer than I should.
Julia, farewell!   [*Exit* JULIA.
        What, gone without a word?
Ay, so true love should do: it cannot speak;
For truth hath better deeds than words to
    grace it.

Enter PANTHINO.

Pan. Sir Proteus, you are stay'd for.

Pro. Go; I come, I come.   *20*
Alas! this parting strikes poor lovers dumb.
                                                      [*Exeunt.*

SCENE III. *The same: a street*

Enter LAUNCE, *leading a dog.*

Launce. Nay, 'twill be this hour ere I have done
weeping; all the kind of the Launces have this
very fault. I have received my proportion, like
the prodigious son, and am going with Sir Proteus
to the Imperial's court. I think Crab my dog be
the sourest-natured dog that lives: my mother
weeping, my father wailing, my sister crying, our
maid howling, our cat wringing her hands, and all
our house in a great perplexity, yet did not this
cruel-hearted cur shed one tear: he is a stone, a
very pebble stone, and has no more pity in him
than a dog: a Jew would have wept to have seen
our parting; why, my grandam, having no eyes,
look you, wept herself blind at my parting. Nay,
I'll show you the manner of it. This shoe is my
father: no, this left shoe is my father: no, no, this
left shoe is my mother: nay, that cannot be so
neither: yes, it is so, it is so, it hath the worser
sole. This shoe, with the hole in it, is my mother,
and this my father; a vengeance on't there 'tis:
now, sir, this staff is my sister, for, look you,
she is as white as a lily and as small as a wand:
this hat is Nan, our maid: I am the dog: no, the
dog is himself, and I am the dog—Oh! the dog is
me, and I am myself; ay, so, so. Now come I
to my father; Father, your blessing: now should
not the shoe speak a word for weeping: now
should I kiss my father; well, he weeps on. Now
come I to my mother: O, that she could speak
now like a wood woman! Well, I kiss her; why,
there 'tis; here's my mother's breath up and
down. Now come I to my sister; mark the moan
she makes. Now the dog all this while sheds not

a tear nor speaks a word; but see how I lay the dust with my tears.

Enter PANTHINO.

Pan. Launce, away, away, aboard! thy master is shipped and thou art to post after with oars. What's the matter? why weepest thou, man? Away, ass! you'll lose the tide, if you tarry any longer.

Launce. It is no matter if the tied were lost; for it is the unkindest tied that ever any man tied.

Pan. What's the unkindest tide?

Launce. Why, he that's tied here, Crab, my dog.

Pan. Tut, man, I mean thou'lt lose the flood, and, in losing the flood, lose thy voyage, and, in losing thy voyage, lose thy master, and, in losing thy master, lose thy service, and, in losing thy service—Why dost thou stop my mouth? 51

Launce. For fear thou shouldst lose thy tongue.

Pan. Where should I lose my tongue?

Launce. In thy tale.

Pan. In thy tail!

Launce. Lose the tide, and the voyage, and the master, and the service, and the tied! Why, man, if the river were dry, I am able to fill it with my tears; if the wind were down, I could drive the boat with my sighs. 60

Pan. Come, come away, man; I was sent to call thee.

Launce. Sir, call me what thou darest.

Pan. Wilt thou go?

Launce. Well, I will go. [*Exeunt.*

SCENE IV. *Milan: the Duke's palace*

Enter SILVIA, VALENTINE, THURIO, *and* SPEED.

Sil. Servant!

Val. Mistress?

Speed. Master, Sir Thurio frowns on you.

Val. Ay, boy, it's for love.

Speed. Not of you.

Val. Of my mistress, then.

Speed. 'Twere good you knocked him. [*Exit.*

Sil. Servant, you are sad.

Val. Indeed, madam, I seem so.

Thu. Seem you that you are not? 10

Val. Haply I do.

Thu. So do counterfeits.

Val. So do you.

Thu. What seem I that I am not?

Val. Wise.

Thu. What instance of the contrary?

Val. Your folly.

Thu. And how quote you my folly?

Val. I quote it in your jerkin.

Thu. My jerkin is a doublet. 20

Val. Well, then, I'll double your folly.

Thu. How?

Sil. What, angry, Sir Thurio! do you change colour?

Val. Give him leave, madam; he is a kind of chameleon.

Thu. That hath more mind to feed on your blood than live in your air.

Val. You have said, sir.

Thu. Ay, sir, and done too, for this time. 30

Val. I know it well, sir; you always end ere you begin.

Sil. A fine volley of words, gentlemen, and quickly shot off.

Val. 'Tis indeed, madam; we thank the giver.

Sil. Who is that, servant?

Val. Yourself, sweet lady; for you gave the fire. Sir Thurio borrows his wit from your ladyship's looks, and spends what he borrows kindly in your company. 40

Thu. Sir, if you spend word for word with me, I shall make your wit bankrupt.

Val. I know it well, sir; you have an exchequer of words, and, I think, no other treasure to give your followers, for it appears, by their bare liveries, that they live by your bare words.

Sil. No more, gentlemen, no more: here comes my father.

Enter DUKE.

Duke. Now, daughter Silvia, you are hard beset. Sir Valentine, your father's in good health: 50 What say you to a letter from your friends Of much good news?

Val. My lord, I will be thankful To any happy messenger from thence.

Duke. Know ye Don Antonio, your country-man?

Val. Ay, my good lord, I know the gentleman To be of worth and worthy estimation And not without desert so well reputed.

Duke. Hath he not a son?

Val. Ay, my good lord; a son that well deserves The honour and regard of such a father. 60

Duke. You know him well?

Val. I know him as myself; for from our infancy We have conversed and spent our hours together: And though myself have been an idle truant, Omitting the sweet benefit of time To clothe mine age with angel-like perfection, Yet hath Sir Proteus, for that's his name, Made use and fair advantage of his days; His years but young, but his experience old; His head unmellow'd, but his judgement ripe; 70 And, in a word, for far behind his worth Comes all the praises that I now bestow,

He is complete in feature and in mind
With all good grace to grace a gentleman.
  Duke. Beshrew me, sir, but if he make this good,
He is as worthy for an empress' love
As meet to be an emperor's counsellor.
Well, sir, this gentleman is come to me,
With commendation from great potentates;
And here he means to spend his time awhile: *80*
I think 'tis no unwelcome news to you.
  Val. Should I have wish'd a thing, it had been he.
  Duke. Welcome him then according to his
          worth.
Silvia, I speak to you, and you, Sir Thurio;
For Valentine, I need not cite him to it:
I will send him hither to you presently.   [*Exit.*
  Val. This is the gentleman I told your ladyship
Had come along with me, but that his mistress
Did hold his eyes lock'd in her crystal looks.
  Sil. Belike that now she hath enfranchised
          them   *90*
Upon some other pawn for fealty.
  Val. Nay, sure, I think she holds them prisoners
          still.
  Sil. Nay, then he should be blind; and, being
          blind,
How could he see his way to seek out you?
  Val. Why, lady, Love hath twenty pair of eyes.
  Thu. They say that Love hath not an eye at all.
  Val. To see such lovers, Thurio, as yourself:
Upon a homely object Love can wink.
  Sil. Have done, have done; here comes the
          gentleman.   [*Exit* THURIO.

Enter PROTEUS.

  Val. Welcome, dear Proteus! Mistress, I
          beseech you,   *100*
Confirm his welcome with some special favour.
  Sil. His worth is warrant for his welcome hither,
If this be he you oft have wish'd to hear from.
  Val. Mistress, it is: sweet lady, entertain him
To be my fellow-servant to your ladyship.
  Sil. Too low a mistress for so high a servant.
  Pro. Not so, sweet lady: but too mean a servant
To have a look of such a worthy mistress.
  Val. Leave off discourse of disability:
Sweet lady, entertain him for your servant.   *110*
  Pro. My duty will I boast of; nothing else.
  Sil. And duty never yet did want his meed:
Servant, you are welcome to a worthless mistress.
  Pro. I'll die on him that says so but yourself.
  Sil. That you are welcome?
  Pro.   That you are worthless.

Re-enter THURIO.

  Thu. Madam, my lord your father would speak
with you.

  Sil. I wait upon his pleasure. Come, Sir Thurio,
Go with me. Once more, new servant, welcome:
I'll leave you to confer of home affairs;   *119*
When you have done, we look to hear from you.
  Pro. We'll both attend upon your ladyship.
          [*Exeunt* SILVIA *and* THURIO.
  Val. Now, tell me, how do all from whence
          you came?
  Pro. Your friends are well and have them much
          commended.
  Val. And how do yours?
  Pro.   I left them all in health.
  Val. How does your lady? and how thrives
          your love?
  Pro. My tales of love were wont to weary you;
I know you joy not in a love-discourse.
  Val. Ay, Proteus, but that life is alter'd now:
I have done penance for contemning Love,
Whose high imperious thoughts have punish'd
          me   *130*
With bitter fasts, with penitential groans,
With nightly tears, and daily heart-sore sighs;
For in revenge of my contempt of love,
Love hath chased sleep from my enthralled eyes
And made them watchers of mine own heart's
          sorrow.
O gentle Proteus, Love's a mighty lord
And hath so humbled me as I confess
There is no woe to his correction
Nor to his service no such joy on earth.
Now no discourse, except it be of love;   *140*
Now can I break my fast, dine, sup, and sleep,
Upon the very naked name of love.
  Pro. Enough; I read your fortune in your eye.
Was this the idol that you worship so?
  Val. Even she; and is she not a heavenly saint?
  Pro. No; but she is an earthly paragon.
  Val. Call her divine.
  Pro.   I will not flatter her.
  Val. O, flatter me; for love delights in praises.
  Pro. When I was sick, you gave me bitter pills,
And I must minister the like to you.   *150*
  Val. Then speak the truth by her; if not divine,
Yet let her be a principality,
Sovereign to all the creatures on the earth.
  Pro. Except my mistress.
  Val.   Sweet, except not any;
Except thou wilt except against my love.
  Pro. Have I not reason to prefer mine own?
  Val. And I will help thee to prefer her too:
She shall be dignified with this high honour—
To bear my lady's train, lest the base earth
Should from her vesture chance to steal a kiss *160*
And, of so great a favour growing proud,
Disdain to root the summer-swelling flower
And make rough winter everlasting.

Pro. Why, Valentine, what braggardism is
    this?
Val. Pardon me, Proteus: all I can is nothing
To her whose worth makes other worthies
    nothing;
She is alone.
    Pro.   Then let her alone.
Val. Not for the world: why, man, she is mine
    own,
And I as rich in having such a jewel
As twenty seas, if all their sand were pearl,   *170*
The water nectar, and the rocks pure gold.
Forgive me that I do not dream on thee,
Because thou see'st me dote upon my love.
My foolish rival, that her father likes
Only for his possessions are so huge,
Is gone with her along, and I must after,
For love, thou know'st, is full of jealousy.
    Pro. But she loves you?
Val. Ay, and we are bethroth'd: nay, more, our
    marriage-hour,
With all the cunning manner of our flight,   *180*
Determined of; how I must climb her window,
The ladder made of cords, and all the means
Plotted and 'greed on for my happiness.
Good Proteus, go with me to my chamber,
In these affairs to aid me with thy counsel.
    Pro. Go on before; I shall inquire you forth:
I must unto the road, to disembark
Some necessaries that I needs must use,
And then I'll presently attend you.
Val. Will you make haste?   *190*
Pro. I will.   [*Exit* VALENTINE.
Even as one heat another heat expels,
Or as one nail by strength drives out another,
So the remembrance of my former love
Is by a newer object quite forgotten.
[Is it mine, or Valentine's praise,]
Her true perfection, or my false transgression,
That makes me reasonless to reason thus?
She is fair; and so is Julia that I love—
That I did love, for now my love is thaw'd;   *200*
Which, like a waxen image 'gainst a fire,
Bears no impression of the thing it was.
Methinks my zeal to Valentine is cold,
And that I love him not as I was wont.
O, but I love his lady too too much,
And that's the reason I love him so little.
How shall I dote on her with more advice,
That thus without advice begin to love her!
'Tis but her picture I have yet beheld,
And that hath dazzled my reason's light;   *210*
But when I look on her perfections,
There is no reason but I shall be blind.
If I can check my erring love, I will;
If not, to compass her I'll use my skill.   [*Exit.*

SCENE V. *The same: a street*

Enter SPEED *and* LAUNCE *severally.*

Speed. Launce! by mine honesty, welcome to
Milan!
Launce. Forswear not thyself, sweet youth, for
I am not welcome. I reckon this always, that a
man is never undone till he be hanged, nor never
welcome to a place till some certain shot be paid
and the hostess say "Welcome!"
Speed. Come on, you madcap, I'll to the alehouse
with you presently; where, for one shot of five
pence, thou shalt have five thousand welcomes.
But, sirrah, how did thy master part with Madam
Julia?
Launce. Marry, after they closed in earnest,
they parted very fairly in jest.
Speed. But shall she marry him?
Launce. No.
Speed. How then? shall he marry her?
Launce. No, neither.
Speed. What, are they broken?
Launce. No, they are both as whole as a fish.   *20*
Speed. Why, then, how stands the matter with
them?
Launce. Marry, thus; when it stands well with
him, it stands well with her.
Speed. What an ass art thou! I understand thee not.
Launce. What a block art thou, that thou canst
not! My staff understands me.
Speed. What thou sayest?
Launce. Ay, and what I do too: look thee, I'll
but lean, and my staff understands me.   *31*
Speed. It stands under thee, indeed.
Launce. Why, stand-under and under-stand is
all one.
Speed. But tell me true, will't be a match?
Launce. Ask my dog: if he say ay, it will; if he
say no, it will; if he shake his tail and say
nothing, it will.
Speed. The conclusion is then that it will.
Launce. Thou shalt never get such a secret from
me but by a parable.   *41*
Speed. 'Tis well that I get it so. But, Launce,
how sayest thou, that my master is become a
notable lover?
Launce. I never knew him otherwise.
Speed. Than how?
Launce. A notable lubber, as thou reportest him
to be.
Speed. Why, thou whoreson ass, thou mistakest
me.   *50*
Launce. Why, fool, I meant not thee; I meant
thy master.
Speed. I tell thee, my master is become a hot
lover.

Launce. Why, I tell thee, I care not though he
burn himself in love. If thou wilt, go with me to
the alehouse; if not, thou art an Hebrew, a Jew,
and not worth the name of a Christian.

Speed. Why? 59

Launce. Because thou hast not so much charity
in thee as to go to the ale with a Christian. Wilt
thou go?

Speed. At thy service. [*Exeunt.*

SCENE VI. *The same: the Duke's palace*

Enter PROTEUS.

Pro. To leave my Julia, shall I be forsworn;
To love fair Silvia, shall I be forsworn;
To wrong my friend, I shall be much forsworn;
And even that power which gave me first my
  oath
Provokes me to this threefold perjury;
Love bade me swear and Love bids me forswear.
O sweet-suggesting Love, if thou hast sinn'd,
Teach me, thy tempted subject, to excuse it!
At first I did adore a twinkling star,
But now I worship a celestial sun. 10
Unheedful vows may heedfully be broken,
And he wants wit that wants resolved will
To learn his wit to exchange the bad for better.
Fie, fie, unreverend tongue! to call her bad,
Whose sovereignty so oft thou hast preferr'd
With twenty thousand soul-confirming oaths.
I cannot leave to love, and yet I do;
But there I leave to love where I should love.
Julia I lose and Valentine I lose:
If I keep them, I needs must lose myself; 20
If I lose them, thus find I by their loss
For Valentine myself, for Julia Silvia.
I to myself am dearer than a friend,
For love is still most precious in itself;
And Silvia—witness Heaven, that made her
  fair!—
Shows Julia but a swarthy Ethiope.
I will forget that Julia is alive,
Remembering that my love to her is dead;
And Valentine I'll hold an enemy,
Aiming at Silvia as a sweeter friend. 30
I cannot now prove constant to myself,
Without some treachery used to Valentine.
This night he meaneth with a corded ladder
To climb celestial Silvia's chamber-window,
Myself in counsel, his competitor.
Now presently I'll give her father notice
Of their disguising and pretended flight;
Who, all enraged, will banish Valentine;
For Thurio, he intends, shall wed his daughter;
But, Valentine being gone, I'll quickly cross 40
By some sly trick blunt Thurio's dull proceed-
  ing.

Love, lend me wings to make my purpose swift,
As thou hast lent me wit to plot this drift! [*Exit.*

SCENE VII. *Verona: Julia's house*

Enter JULIA and LUCETTA.

Jul. Counsel, Lucetta; gentle girl, assist me;
And even in kind love I do conjure thee,
Who art the table wherein all my thoughts
Are visibly character'd and engraved,
To lesson me and tell me some good mean
How, with my honour, I may undertake
A journey to my loving Proteus.

Luc. Alas, the way is wearisome and long!

Jul. A true-devoted pilgrim is not weary
To measure kingdoms with his feeble steps; 10
Much less shall she that hath Love's wings to fly,
And when the flight is made to one so dear,
Of such divine perfection, as Sir Proteus.

Luc. Better forbear till Proteus make return.

Jul. O, know'st thou not his looks are my soul's
  food?
Pity the dearth that I have pined in,
By longing for that food so long a time.
Didst thou but know the inly touch of love,
Thou wouldst as soon go kindle fire with snow
As seek to quench the fire of love with words. 20

Luc. I do not seek to quench your love's hot fire,
But qualify the fire's extreme rage,
Lest it should burn above the bounds of reason.

Jul. The more thou damn'st it up, the more it
  burns.
The current that with gentle murmur glides,
Thou know'st, being stopp'd, impatiently doth
  rage;
But when his fair course is not hindered,
He makes sweet music with the enamell'd stones,
Giving a gentle kiss to every sedge
He overtaketh in his pilgrimage, 30
And so by many winding nooks he strays
With willing sport to the wild ocean.
Then let me go and hinder not my course:
I'll be as patient as a gentle stream
And make a pastime of each weary step,
Till the last step have brought me to my love;
And there I'll rest, as after much turmoil
A blessed soul doth in Elysium.

Luc. But in what habit will you go along?

Jul. Not like a woman; for I would prevent 40
The loose encounters of lascivious men:
Gentle Lucetta, fit me with such weeds
As may beseem some well-reputed page.

Luc. Why, then, your ladyship must cut your
  hair.

Jul. No, girl; I'll knit it up in silken strings
With twenty odd-conceited true-love knots.
To be fantastic may become a youth

Of greater time than I shall show to be.

Luc. What fashion, madam, shall I make your
   breeches?   49

Jul. That fits as well as "Tell me, good my lord,
What compass will you wear your farthingale?"
Why even what fashion thou best likest, Lucetta.

Luc. You must needs have them with a codpiece,
   madam.

Jul. Out, out, Lucetta! that will be ill-favour'd.

Luc. A round hose, madam, now's not worth a
   pin,
Unless you have a codpiece to stick pins on.

Jul. Lucetta, as thou lovest me, let me have
What thou thinkest meet and is most mannerly.
But tell me, wench, how will the world repute
   me
For undertaking so unstaid a journey?   60
I fear me, it will make me scandalized.

Luc. If you think so, then stay at home and go
   not.

Jul. Nay, that I will not.

Luc. Then never dream on infamy, but go.
If Proteus like your journey when you come,
No matter who's displeased when you are gone:
I fear me, he will scarce be pleased withal.

Jul. That is the least, Lucetta, of my fear:
A thousand oaths, an ocean of his tears
And instances of infinite of love   70
Warrant me welcome to my Proteus.

Luc. All these are servants to deceitful men.

Jul. Base men, that use them to so base effect!
But truer stars did govern Proteus' birth;
His words are bonds, his oaths are oracles,
His love sincere, his thoughts immaculate,
His tears pure messengers sent from his heart,
His heart as far from fraud as heaven from earth.

Luc. Pray heaven he prove so, when you come
   to him!

Jul. Now, as thou lovest me, do him not that
   wrong   80
To bear a hard opinion of his truth:
Only deserve my love by loving him;
And presently go with me to my chamber,
To take a note of what I stand in need of,
To furnish me upon my longing journey.
All that is mine I leave at thy dispose,
My goods, my lands, my reputation;
Only, in lieu thereof, dispatch me hence.
Come, answer not, but to it presently!
I am impatient of my tarriance.   [*Exeunt.* 90

ACT III

SCENE I. *Milan: the Duke's palace*

Enter DUKE, THURIO, *and* PROTEUS.

Duke. Sir Thurio, give us leave, I pray, awhile;

We have some secrets to confer about.
                                      [*Exit* THURIO.
Now tell me, Proteus, what's your will with
   me?

Pro. My gracious lord, that which I would
   discover
The law of friendship bids me to conceal;
But when I call to mind your gracious favours
Done to me, undeserving as I am,
My duty pricks me on to utter that
Which else no worldly good should draw from
   me.   9
Know, worthy prince, Sir Valentine, my friend,
This night intends to steal away your daughter:
Myself am one made privy to the plot.
I know you have determined to bestow her
On Thurio, whom your gentle daughter hates;
And should she thus be stol'n away from you,
It would be much vexation to your age,
Thus, for my duty's sake, I rather chose
To cross my friend in his intended drift
Than, by concealing it, heap on your head
A pack of sorrows which would press you down,
Being unprevented, to your timeless grave.   21

Duke. Proteus, I thank thee for thine honest
   care;
Which to requite, command me while I live.
This love of theirs myself have often seen,
Haply when they have judged me fast asleep,
And oftentimes have purposed to forbid
Sir Valentine her company and my court:
But fearing lest my jealous aim might err
And so unworthily disgrace the man,
A rashness that I ever yet have shunn'd,   30
I gave him gentle looks, thereby to find
That which thyself hast now disclosed to me.
And, that thou mayst perceive my fear of this,
Knowing that tender youth is soon suggested,
I nightly lodge her in an upper tower,
The key whereof myself have ever kept;
And thence she cannot be convey'd away.

Pro. Know, noble lord, they have devised a
   mean
How he her chamber-window will ascend
And with a corded ladder fetch her down;   40
For which the youthful lover now is gone
And this way comes he with it presently;
Where, if it please you, you may intercept him.
But, good my Lord, do it so cunningly
That my discovery be not aimed at;
For love of you, not hate unto my friend,
Hath made me publisher of this pretence.

Duke. Upon mine honour, he shall never know
That I had any light from thee of this.

Pro. Adieu, my lord; Sir Valentine is coming.
                                         [*Exit.*   50

Enter VALENTINE.

Duke. Sir Valentine, whither away so fast?

Val. Please it your Grace, there is a messenger
That stays to bear my letters to my friends,
And I am going to deliver them.

Duke. Be they of much import?

Val. The tenour of them doth but signify
My health and happy being at your court.

Duke. Nay then, no matter; stay with me
     awhile;
I am to break with thee of some affairs
That touch me near, wherein thou must be secret.
'Tis not unknown to thee that I have sought   61
To match my friend Sir Thurio to my daughter.

Val. I know it well, my Lord; and, sure, the
     match
Were rich and honourable; besides, the gentle-
     man
Is full of virtue, bounty, worth, and qualities
Beseeming such a wife as your fair daughter:
Cannot your Grace win her to fancy him?

Duke. No, trust me; she is peevish, sullen,
     froward,
Proud, disobedient, stubborn, lacking duty,
Neither regarding that she is my child   70
Nor fearing me as if I were her father;
And, may I say to thee, this pride of hers,
Upon advice, hath drawn my love from her;
And, where I thought the remnant of mine age
Should have been cherish'd by her child-like duty,
I now am full resolved to take a wife
And turn her out to who will take her in:
Then let her beauty be her wedding-dower;
For me and my possessions she esteems not.

Val. What would your Grace have me to do in
     this?   80

Duke. There is a lady in Verona here
Whom I affect; but she is nice and coy
And nought esteems my aged eloquence:
Now therefore would I have thee to my tutor—
For long agone I have forgot to court;
Besides, the fashion of the time is changed—
How and which way I may bestow myself
To be regarded in her sun-bright eye.

Val. Win her with gifts, if she respect not
     words:
Dumb jewels often in their silent kind   90
More than quick words do move a woman's mind.

Duke. But she did scorn a present that I sent her.

Val. A woman sometimes scorns what best
     contents her.
Send her another; never give her o'er;
For scorn at first makes after-love the more.
If she do frown, 'tis not in hate of you,
But rather to beget more love in you:

If she do chide, 'tis not to have you gone;
For why, the fools are mad, if left alone.
Take no repulse, whatever she doth say;   100
For "get you gone," she doth not mean "away!"
Flatter and praise, commend, extol their graces;
Though ne'er so black, say they have angels'
     faces.
That man that hath a tongue, I say, is no man,
If with his tongue he cannot win a woman.

Duke. But she I mean is promised by her friends
Unto a youthful gentleman of worth,
And kept severely from resort of men,
That no man hath access by day to her.

Val. Why, then, I would resort to her by night.

Duke. Ay, but the doors be lock'd and keys
     kept safe,   111
That no man hath recourse to her by night.

Val. What lets but one may enter at her
     window?

Duke. Her chamber is aloft, far from the ground,
And built so shelving that one cannot climb it
Without apparent hazard of his life.

Val. Why then, a ladder quaintly made of
     cords,
To cast up, with a pair of anchoring hooks,
Would serve to scale another Hero's tower,
So bold Leander would adventure it.   120

Duke. Now, as thou art a gentleman of blood,
Advise me where I may have such a ladder.

Val. When would you use it? pray, sir, tell me
     that.

Duke. This very night; for Love is like a child,
That longs for every thing that he can come by.

Val. By seven o'clock I'll get you such a ladder.

Duke. But, hark thee; I will go to her alone:
How shall I best convey the ladder thither?

Val. It will be light, my lord, that you may bear
     it
Under a cloak that is of any length.   130

Duke. A cloak as long as thine will serve the
     turn?

Val. Ay, my good lord.

Duke.   Then let me see thy cloak:
I'll get me one of such another length.

Val. Why, any cloak will serve the turn, my
     lord.

Duke. How shall I fashion me to wear a cloak?
I pray thee, let me feel thy cloak upon me.
What letter is this same? What's here? "To
     Silvia"!
And here an engine fit for my proceeding.
I'll be so bold to break the seal for once. [*Reads.*
"My thoughts do harbour with my Silvia nightly,
     And slaves they are to me that send them
     flying: 141
O, could their master come and go as lightly,

Himself would lodge where senseless they
   are lying!
My herald thoughts in thy pure bosom rest them;
   While I, their king, that hither them impor-
   tune,
Do curse the grace that with such grace hath
   bless'd them,
   Because myself do want my servants' fortune:
I curse myself, for they are sent by me,
That they should harbour where their lord would
   be."
What's here?   150
   "Silvia, this night I will enfranchise thee."
'Tis so; and here's the ladder for the purpose.
Why, Phaethon—for thou art Merops' son—
Wilt thou aspire to guide the heavenly car
And with thy daring folly burn the world?
Wilt thou reach stars, because they shine on thee?
Go, base intruder! overweening slave!
Bestow thy fawning smiles on equal mates,
And think my patience, more than thy desert,
Is privilege for thy departure hence: 160
Thank me for this more than for all the favours
Which all too much I have bestow'd on thee.
But if thou linger in my territories
Longer than swiftest expedition
Will give thee time to leave our royal court,
By heaven! my wrath shall far exceed the love
I ever bore my daughter or thyself.
Be gone! I will not hear thy vain excuse;
But, as thou lovest thy life, make speed from
   hence.   [*Exit.*
  Val. And why not death rather than living
   torment?   170
To die is to be banish'd from myself;
And Silvia is myself: banish'd from her
Is self from self: a deadly banishment!
What light is light, if Silvia be not seen?
What joy is joy, if Silvia be not by?
Unless it be to think that she is by
And feed upon the shadow of perfection.
Except I be by Silvia in the night,
There is no music in the nightingale;
Unless I look on Silvia in the day,   180
There is no day for me to look upon;
She is my essence, and I leave to be,
If I be not by her fair influence
Foster'd, illumined, cherish'd, kept alive.
I fly not death, to fly his deadly doom:
Tarry I here, I but attend on death:
But, fly I hence, I fly away from life.

     Enter PROTEUS *and* LAUNCE.

Pro. Run, boy, run, run, and seek him out.
Launce. Soho, soho!
Pro. What seest thou?   190

Launce. Him we go to find: there's not a hair
on 's head but 'tis a Valentine.
  Pro. Valentine?
  Val. No.
  Pro. Who then? his spirit?
  Val. Neither.
  Pro. What then?
  Val. Nothing.
  Launce. Can nothing speak? Master, shall I
   strike?
  Pro. Who wouldst thou strike?   200
  Launce. Nothing.
  Pro. Villain, forbear.
  Launce. Why, sir, I'll strike nothing: I pray
   you—
  Pro. Sirrah, I say, forbear. Friend Valentine, a
   word.
  Val. My ears are stopt and cannot hear good
   news,
So much of bad already hath possess'd them.
  Pro. Then in dumb silence will I bury mine,
For they are harsh, untuneable and bad.
  Val. Is Silvia dead?
  Pro. No, Valentine.   210
  Val. No Valentine, indeed, for sacred Silvia.
Hath she forsworn me?
  Pro. No, Valentine.
  Val. No Valentine, if Silvia have forsworn me.
What is your news?
  Launce. Sir, there is a proclamation that you are
   vanished.
  Pro. That thou art banished—O, that's the
   news!—
From hence, from Silvia, and from me thy friend.
  Val. O, I have fed upon this woe already,
And now excess of it will make me surfeit.   220
Doth Silvia know that I am banished?
  Pro. Ay, ay; and she hath offer'd to the doom—
Which, unreversed, stands in effectual force—
A sea of melting pearl, which some call tears:
Those at her father's churlish feet she tender'd;
With them, upon her knees, her humble self;
Wringing her hands, whose whiteness so became
   them
As if but now they waxed pale for woe:
But neither bended knees, pure hands held up,
Sad sighs, deep groans, nor silver-shedding tears,
Could penetrate her uncompassionate sire;   231
But Valentine, if he be ta'en, must die.
Besides, her intercession chafed him so,
When she for thy repeal was suppliant,
That to close prison he commanded her,
With many bitter threats of biding there.
  Val. No more; unless the next word that thou
   speak'st
Have some malignant power upon my life:

If so, I pray thee, breathe it in mine ear,
As ending anthem of my endless dolour.   *240*
  Pro. Cease to lament for that thou canst not
    help,
And study help for that which thou lament'st.
Time is the nurse and breeder of all good.
Here if thou stay, thou canst not see thy love;
Besides, thy staying will abridge thy life.
Hope is a lover's staff; walk hence with that
And manage it against despairing thoughts.
Thy letters may be here, though thou art hence;
Which, being writ to me, shall be deliver'd
Even in the milk-white bosom of thy love.   *250*
The time now serves not to expostulate:
Come, I'll convey thee through the city-gate;
And, ere I part with thee, confer at large
Of all that may concern thy love-affairs.
As thou lovest Silvia, though not for thyself,
Regard thy danger, and along with me!
  Val. I pray thee, Launce, an if thou seest my
    boy,
Bid him make haste and meet me at the North-
    gate.
  Pro. Go, sirrah, find him out. Come, Valentine.
  Val. O my dear Silvia! Hapless Valentine!   *260*
          [*Exeunt* VALENTINE *and* PROTEUS.
  Launce. I am but a fool, look you; and yet I have
the wit to think my master is a kind of a knave:
but that's all one, if he be but one knave. He lives
not now that knows me to be in love; yet I am
in love; but a team of horse shall not pluck that
from me; nor who 'tis I love; and yet 'tis a
woman; but what woman, I will not tell myself;
and yet 'tis a milkmaid; yet 'tis not a maid, for
she hath had gossips; yet 'tis a maid, for she is
her master's maid, and serves for wages. She hath
more qualities than a water-spaniel; which is
much in a bare Christian. [*Pulling out a paper.*]
Here is the cate-log of her condition. "*Imprimis:*
She can fetch and carry." Why, a horse can do
no more: nay, a horse cannot fetch but only
carry; therefore is she better than a jade. "*Item:*
She can milk"; look you, a sweet virtue in a
maid with clean hands.

Enter SPEED.

  Speed. How now, Signior Launce! what news
with your mastership?   *280*
  Launce. With my master's ship? why, it is at sea.
  Speed. Well, your old vice still; mistake the
word. What news, then, in your paper?
  Launce. The blackest news that ever thou
heardest.
  Speed. Why, man, how black?
  Launce. Why, as black as ink.
  Speed. Let me read them.

  Launce. Fie on thee, jolt-head! thou canst not
read.   *291*
  Speed. Thou liest; I can.
  Launce. I will try thee. Tell me this: who begot
thee?
  Speed. Marry, the son of my grandfather.
  Launce. O illiterate loiterer! it was the son of
thy grandmother: this proves that thou canst not
read.
  Speed. Come, fool, come; try me in thy paper.
  Launce. There; and Saint Nicholas be thy
speed!   *301*
  Speed. [*Reads.*] "*Imprimis:* She can milk."
  Launce. Ay, that she can.
  Speed. "*Item:* She brews good ale."
  Launce. And thereof comes the proverb:
"Blessing of your heart, you brew good ale."
  Speed. "*Item:* She can sew."
  Launce. That's as much as to say, "Can she
so?"
  Speed. "*Item:* She can knit."   *310*
  Launce. What need a man care for a stock with
a wench, when she can knit him a stock?
  Speed. "*Item:* She can wash and scour."
  Launce. A special virtue; for then she need not
be washed and scoured.
  Speed. "*Item:* She can spin."
  Launce. Then may I set the world on wheels,
when she can spin for her living.   *319*
  Speed. "*Item:* she hath many nameless virtues."
  Launce. That's as much as to say, bastard vir-
tues; that, indeed, know not their fathers and
therefore have no names.
  Speed. "Here follow her vices."
  Launce. Close at the heels of her virtues.
  Speed. "*Item:* She is not to be kissed fasting, in
respect of her breath."
  Launce. Well, that fault may be mended with a
breakfast. Read on.
  Speed. "*Item:* She hath a sweet mouth."   *330*
  Launce. That makes amends for her sour breath.
  Speed. "*Item:* She doth talk in her sleep."
  Launce. It's no matter for that, so she sleep not
in her talk.
  Speed. "*Item:* She is slow in words."
  Launce. O villain, that set this down among her
vices! To be slow in words is a woman's only
virtue: I pray thee, out with't, and place it for
her chief virtue.   *340*
  Speed. "*Item:* she is proud."
  Launce. Out with that too; it was Eve's legacy,
and cannot be ta'en from her.
  Speed. "*Item:* She hath no teeth."
  Launce. I care not for that neither, because I
love crusts.
  Speed. "*Item:* She is curst."

Launce. Well, the best is, she hath no teeth to bite. 350

Speed. "*Item:* She will often praise her liquor."

Launce. If her liquor be good, she shall: if she will not, I will; for good things should be praised.

Speed. "*Item:* She is too liberal."

Launce. Of her tongue she cannot, for that's writ down she is slow of; of her purse she shall not, for that I'll keep shut: now, of another thing she may, and that cannot I help. Well, proceed.

Speed. "*Item:* She hath more hair than wit, and more faults than hairs, and more wealth than faults."

Launce. Stop there; I'll have her: she was mine, and not mine, twice or thrice in that last article. Rehearse that once more.

Speed. "*Item:* She hath more hair than wit"—

Launce. More hair than wit? It may be: I'll prove it. The cover of the salt hides the salt, and therefore it is more than the salt; the hair that covers the wit is more than the wit, for the greater hides the less. What's next?

Speed. "And more faults than hairs"—

Launce. That's monstrous: O, that that were out!

Speed. "And more wealth than faults."

Launce. Why, that word makes the faults gracious. Well, I'll have her: and if it be a match, as nothing is impossible—

Speed. What then? 380

Launce. Why, then will I tell thee—that thy master stays for thee at the North-gate.

Speed. For me?

Launce. For thee! ay, who art thou? he hath stayed for a better man than thee.

Speed. And must I go to him?

Launce. Thou must run to him, for thou hast stayed so long that going will scarce serve the turn.

Speed. Why didst not tell me sooner? pox of your love-letters! [*Exit.* 391

Launce. Now will he be swinged for reading my letter; an unmannerly slave, that will thrust himself into secrets! I'll after, to rejoice in the boy's correction. [*Exit.*

SCENE II. *The same: the Duke's palace*

Enter DUKE *and* THURIO.

Duke. Sir Thurio, fear not but that she will love you,
Now Valentine is banish'd from her sight.

Thu. Since his exile she hath despised me most,
Forsworn my company, and rail'd at me,
That I am desperate of obtaining her.

Duke. This weak impress of love is as a figure
Trenched in ice, which with an hour's heat

Dissolves to water and doth lose his form.
A little time will melt her frozen thoughts
And worthless Valentine shall be forgot. . 10

Enter PROTEUS.

How now, Sir Proteus! Is your countryman
According to our proclamation gone?

Pro. Gone, my good lord.

Duke. My daughter takes his going grievously.

Pro. A little time, my lord, will kill that grief.

Duke. So I believe; but Thurio thinks not so.
Proteus, the good conceit I hold of thee—
For thou hast shown some sign of good desert—
Makes me the better to confer with thee.

Pro. Longer than I prove loyal to your grace
Let me not live to look upon your Grace. 21

Duke. Thou know'st how willingly I would effect
The match between Sir Thurio and my daughter.

Pro. I do, my lord.

Duke. And also, I think, thou art not ignorant
How she opposes her against my will.

Pro. She did, my lord, when Valentine was here.

Duke. Ay, and perversely she persevers so.
What might we do to make the girl forget
The love of Valentine and love Sir Thurio? 30

Pro. The best way is to slander Valentine
With falsehood, cowardice, and poor descent,
Three things that women highly hold in hate.

Duke. Ay, but she'll think that it is spoke in hate.

Pro. Ay, if his enemy deliver it:
Therefore it must with circumstance be spoken
By one whom she esteemeth as his friend.

Duke. Then you must undertake to slander him.

Pro. And that, my lord I shall be loath to do:
'Tis an ill office for a gentleman, 40
Especially against his very friend.

Duke. Where your good word cannot advantage him,
Your slander never can endamage him;
Therefore the office is indifferent,
Being entreated to it by your friend.

Pro. You have prevail'd, my lord: if I can do it
By aught that I can speak in his dispraise,
She shall not long continue love to him.
But say this weed her love from Valentine,
It follows not that she will love Sir Thurio. 50

Thu. Therefore, as you unwind her love from him,
Lest it should ravel and be good to none,
You must provide to bottom it on me;
Which must be done by praising me as much
As you in worth dispraise Sir Valentine.

Duke. And, Proteus, we dare trust you in this kind,

Because we know, on Valentine's report,
You are already Love's firm votary
And cannot soon revolt and change your mind.
Upon this warrant shall you have access　60
Where you with Silvia may confer at large;
For she is lumpish, heavy, melancholy,
And, for your friend's sake, will be glad of
　you;
Where you may temper her by your persuasion
To hate young Valentine and love my friend.
　Pro. As much as I can do, I will effect:
But you, Sir Thurio, are not sharp enough;
You must lay lime to tangle her desires
By wailful sonnets, whose composed rhymes
Should be full-fraught with serviceable vows.　70
　Duke. Ay,
Much is the force of heaven-bred poesy.
　Pro. Say that upon the altar of her beauty
You sacrifice your tears, your sighs, your heart:
Write till your ink be dry, and with your tears
Moist it again, and frame some feeling line
That may discover such integrity:
For Orpheus' lute was strung with poets' sinews,
Whose golden touch could soften steel and stones,
Make tigers tame and huge leviathans　80
Forsake unsounded deeps to dance on sands.
After your dire-lamenting elegies,
Visit by night your lady's chamber-window
With some sweet concert; to their instruments
Tune a deploring dump: the night's dead silence
Will well become such sweet-complaining
　grievance.
This, or else nothing, will inherit her.
　Duke. This discipline shows thou hast been in
　love.
　Thu. And thy advice this night I'll put in
　practice.
Therefore, sweet Proteus, my direction-giver,
Let us into the city presently　91
To sort some gentlemen well skill'd in music.
I have a sonnet that will serve the turn
To give the onset to thy good advice.
　Duke. About it, gentlemen!
　Pro. We'll wait upon your Grace till after
　supper,
And afterward determine our proceedings.
　Duke. Even now about it! I will pardon you.
　　　　　　　　　　　　　　　　[*Exeunt.*

ACT IV

SCENE I. *The frontiers of Mantua: a forest*
Enter certain OUTLAWS.

　1st Out. Fellows, stand fast; I see a passenger.
　2nd Out. If there be ten, shrink not, but down
　with 'em.

Enter VALENTINE *and* SPEED.

　3rd Out. Stand, sir, and throw us that you have
　about ye:
If not, we'll make you sit and rifle you.
　Speed. Sir, we are undone; these are the villains
That all the travellers do fear so much.
　Val. My friends—
　1st Out. That's not so, sir: we are your enemies.
　2nd Out. Peace! we'll hear him.
　3rd Out. Ay, by my beard, will we, for he's a
　proper man.　10
　Val. Then know that I have little wealth to
　lose;
A man I am cross'd with adversity;
My riches are these poor habiliments,
Of which if you should here disfurnish me,
You take the sum and substance that I have.
　2nd Out. Whither travel you?
　Val. To Verona.
　1st Out. Whence came you?
　Val. From Milan.
　3rd Out. Have you long sojourned there?
　Val. Some sixteen months, and longer might
　have stay'd,　21
If crooked fortune had not thwarted me.
　1st Out. What, were you banish'd thence?
　Val. I was.
　2nd Out. For what offence?
　Val. For that which now torments me to re-
　hearse:
I kill'd a man, whose death I much repent;
But yet I slew him manfully in fight,
Without false vantage or base treachery.
　1st Out. Why, ne'er repent it, if it were done so.
But were you banish'd for so small a fault?　31
　Val. I was, and held me glad of such a doom.
　2nd Out. Have you the tongues?
　Val. My youthful travel therein made me
　happy,
Or else I often had been miserable.
　3rd Out. By the bare scalp of Robin Hood's fat
　friar,
This fellow were a king for our wild faction!
　1st Out. We'll have him. Sirs, a word.
　Speed. Master, be one of them; it's an honour-
　able kind of thievery.　40
　Val. Peace, villain!
　2nd Out. Tell us this: have you any thing to
　take to?
　Val. Nothing but my fortune.
　3rd Out. Know, then, that some of us are
　gentlemen,
Such as the fury of ungovern'd youth
Thrust from the company of awful men:
Myself was from Verona banished

For practising to steal away a lady,
An heir, and near allied unto the Duke.

2nd Out. And I from Mantua, for a gentle-
man,   50
Who, in my mood, I stabb'd unto the heart.

1st Out. And I for such like petty crimes as
these.
But the purpose—for we cite our faults,
That they may hold excused our lawless lives;
And partly, seeing you are beautified
With goodly shape and by your own report
A linguist and a man of such perfection
As we do in our quality much want—

2nd Out. Indeed, because you are a banish'd
man,
Therefore, above the rest, we parley to you: 60
Are you content to be our general?
To make a virtue of necessity
And live, as we do, in this wilderness?

3rd Out. What say'st thou? wilt thou be of our
consort?
Say ay, and be the captain of us all:
We'll do thee homage and be ruled by thee,
Love thee as our commander and our king.

1st Out. But if thou scorn our courtesy, thou
diest.

2nd Out. Thou shalt not live to brag what we
have offer'd.

Val. I take your offer and will live with you,
Provided that you do no outrages   71
On silly women or poor passengers.

3rd Out. No, we detest such vile base prac-
tices.
Come, go with us, we'll bring thee to our crews,
And show thee all the treasure we have got;
Which, with ourselves, all rest at thy dispose.
                                           [*Exeunt.*

SCENE II. *Milan: Outside the* DUKE'S *palace, under*
SILVIA'S *chamber*

Enter PROTEUS.

Pro. Already have I been false to Valentine
And now I must be as unjust to Thurio.
Under the colour of commending him,
I have access my own love to prefer:
But Silvia is too fair, too true, too holy,
To be corrupted with my worthless gifts.
When I protest true loyalty to her,
She twits me with my falsehood to my friend;
When to her beauty I commend my vows,
She bids me think how I have been forsworn   10
In breaking faith with Julia whom I loved:
And notwithstanding all her sudden quips,
The least whereof would quell a lover's hope,
Yet, spaniel-like, the more she spurns my love,
The more it grows and fawneth on her still.

But here comes Thurio: now must we to her
window,
And give some evening music to her ear.
                Enter THURIO *and Musicians.*

Thu. How now, Sir Proteus, are you crept
before us?

Pro. Ay, gentle Thurio: for you know that
love
Will creep in service where it cannot go.   20

Thu. Ay, but I hope, sir, that you love not here.

Pro. Sir, but I do; or else I would be hence.

Thu. Who? Silvia?

Pro.   Ay, Silvia; for your sake.

Thu. I thank you for your own. Now, gentlemen,
Let's tune, and to it lustily awhile.
        Enter, at a distance, HOST, *and* JULIA *in boy's
clothes.*

Host. Now, my young guest, methinks you're
allycholly: I pray you, why is it?

Jul. Marry, mine host, because I cannot be
merry.   25

Host. Come, we'll have you merry: I'll bring
you where you shall hear music and see the gentleman that you asked for.

Jul. But shall I hear him speak?

Host. Ay, that you shall.

Jul. That will be music.

Music plays.

Host. Hark, hark!

Jul. Is he among these?

Host. Ay: but, peace! let's hear 'em.

                       SONG

Who is Silvia? what is she,
   That all our swains commend her?
Holy, fair and wise is she;   40
   The heaven such grace did lend her,
That she might admired be.

Is she kind as she is fair?
   For beauty lives with kindness.
Love doth to her eyes repair,
   To help him of his blindness,
And, being help'd, inhabits there.

Then to Silvia let us sing,
   That Silvia is excelling;   50
She excels each mortal thing
   Upon the dull earth dwelling:
To her let us garlands bring.

Host. How now! are you sadder than you were
before? How do you, man? the music likes you
not.

Jul. You mistake; the musician likes me not.

Host. Why, my pretty youth?

Jul. He plays false, father.

Host. How? out of tune on the strings?   60

Jul. Not so; but yet so false that he grieves my
very heart-strings.

Host. You have a quick ear.

Jul. Ay, I would I were deaf; it makes me
have a slow heart.

Host. I perceive you delight not in music.

Jul. Not a whit, when it jars so.

Host. Hark, what fine change is in the music!

Jul. Ay, that change is the spite.

Host. You would have them always play but
one thing?   71

Jul. I would always have one play but one
thing.
But, host, doth this Sir Proteus that we talk on
Often resort unto this gentlewoman?

Host. I tell you what Launce, his man, told me:
he loved her out of all nick.

Jul. Where is Launce?

Host. Gone to seek his dog; which to-morrow,
by his master's command, he must carry for a
present to his lady.   80

Jul. Peace! stand aside: the company parts.

Pro. Sir Thurio, fear not you: I will so plead
That you shall say my cunning drift excels.

Thu. Where meet we?

Pro.   At Saint Gregory's well.

Thu.   Farewell.

          [*Exeunt* THURIO *and Musicians.*

Enter SILVIA *above.*

Pro. Madam, good even to your ladyship.

Sil. I thank you for your music, gentlemen.
Who is that that spake?

Pro. One, lady, if you knew his pure heart's
truth,
You would quickly learn to know him by his
voice.

Sil. Sir Proteus, as I take it.   90

Pro. Sir Proteus, gentle lady, and your servant.

Sil. What's your will?

Pro.   That I may compass yours.

Sil. You have your wish; my will is even this:
That presently you hie you home to bed.
Thou subtle, perjured, false, disloyal man!
Think'st thou I am so shallow, so conceitless,
To be seduced by thy flattery,
That hast deceived so many with thy vows?
Return, return, and make thy love amends.
For me, by this pale queen of night I swear,   100
I am so far from granting thy request
That I despise thee for thy wrongful suit,
And by and by intend to chide myself
Even for this time I spend in talking to thee.

Pro. I grant, sweet love, that I did love a lady;

But she is dead.

Jul. [*Aside*] 'Twere false, if I should speak it;
For I am sure she is not buried.

Sil. Say that she be; yet Valentine thy friend
Survives; to whom, thyself art witness,   110
I am betroth'd: and art thou not ashamed
To wrong him with thy importunacy?

Pro. I likewise hear that Valentine is dead.

Sil. And so suppose am I; for in his grave
Assure thyself my love is buried.

Pro. Sweet lady, let me rake it from the earth.

Sil. Go to thy lady's grave and call hers thence,
Or, at the least, in hers sepulchre thine.

Jul. [*Aside*] He heard not that.

Pro. Madam, if your heart be so obdurate,
Vouchsafe me yet your picture for my love,   121
The picture that is hanging in your chamber;
To that I'll speak, to that I'll sigh and weep:
For since the substance of your perfect self
Is else devoted, I am but a shadow;
And to your shadow will I make true love.

Jul. [*Aside*] If 'twere a substance, you would,
      sure, deceive it,
And make it but a shadow, as I am.

Sil. I am very loath to be your idol, sir;
But since your falsehood shall become you well
To worship shadows and adore false shapes,   131
Send to me in the morning and I'll send it:
And so, good rest.

Pro.   As wretches have o'ernight
That wait for execution in the morn.

         [*Exeunt* PROTEUS *and* SILVIA, *severally.*

Jul. Host, will you go?

Host. By my halidom, I was fast asleep.

Jul. Pray you, where lies Sir Proteus?

Host. Marry, at my house. Trust me, I think
'tis almost day.

Jul. Not so; but it hath been the longest night
That e'er I watch'd and the most heaviest.   141
                         [*Exeunt.*

SCENE III. *The same*

Enter EGLAMOUR.

Egl. This is the hour that Madam Silvia
Entreated me to call and know her mind:
There's some great matter she'ld employ me in.
Madam, madam!

Enter SILVIA *above.*

Sil.   Who calls?

Egl.   Your servant and your friend;
One that attends your ladyship's command.

Sil. Sir Eglamour, a thousand times good morrow.

Egl. As many, worthy lady, to yourself:
According to your ladyship's impose,

I am thus early come to know what service
It is your pleasure to command me in.   10
 Sil. O Eglamour, thou art a gentleman—
Think not I flatter, for I swear I do not—
Valiant, wise, remorseful, well accomplish'd:
Thou art not ignorant what dear good will
I bear unto the banish'd Valentine,
Nor how my father would enforce me marry
Vain Thurio, whom my very soul abhors.
Thyself hast loved; and I have heard thee say
No grief did ever come so near thy heart
As when thy lady and thy true love died,   20
Upon whose grave thou vow'dst pure chastity.
Sir Eglamour, I would to Valentine,
To Mantua, where I hear he makes abode;
And, for the ways are dangerous to pass,
I do desire thy worthy company,
Upon whose faith and honour I repose.
Urge not my father's anger, Eglamour,
But think upon my grief, a lady's grief,
And on the justice of my flying hence,
To keep me from a most unholy match,   30
Which heaven and fortune still rewards with
          plagues.
I do desire thee, even from a heart
As full of sorrows as the sea of sands,
To bear me company and go with me:
If not, to hide what I have said to thee,
That I may venture to depart alone.
 Egl. Madam, I pity much your grievances;
Which since I know they virtuously are placed,
I give consent to go along with you,
Recking as little what betideth me   40
As much I wish all good befortune you.
When will you go?
 Sil.   This evening coming.
 Egl. Where shall I meet you?
 Sil.   At Friar Patrick's cell,
Where I intend holy confession.
 Egl. I will not fail your ladyship. Good morrow, gentle lady.
 Sil. Good morrow, kind Sir Eglamour.
                         [*Exeunt severally.*

Scene iv. *The same*

Enter launce, *with his Dog.*

 Launce. When a man's servant shall play the
cur with him, look you, it goes hard: one that I
brought up of a puppy; one that I saved from
drowning, when three or four of his blind brothers
and sisters went to it. I have taught him, even
as one would say precisely, "thus I would teach a
dog." I was sent to deliver him as a present to
Mistress Silvia from my master; and I came no
sooner into the dining-chamber but he steps me
to her trencher and steals her capon's leg: O,
'tis a foul thing when a cur cannot keep himself
in all companies! I would have, as one should
say, one that takes upon him to be a dog indeed,
to be, as is were, a dog at all things. If I had
not had more wit than he, to take a fault upon
me that he did, I think verily he had been hanged
for't; sure as I live, he had suffered for't: you
shall judge. He thrusts me himself into the company of three or four gentlemanlike dogs, under
the Duke's table: he had not been there—bless
the mark!—a pissing while, but all the chamber
smelt him. "Out with the dog!" says one: "What
cur is that?" says another: "Whip him out" says
the third: "Hang him up" says the Duke. I,
having been acquainted with the smell before,
knew it was Crab, and goes me to the fellow that
whips the dogs: "Friend," quoth I, "you mean to
whip the dog?" "Ay, marry, do I," quoth he.
"You do him the more wrong," quoth I; "'twas
I did the thing you wot of." He makes me no
more ado, but whips me out of the chamber.
How many masters would do this for his servant?
Nay, I'll be sworn, I have sat in the stocks for
puddings he hath stolen, otherwise he had been
executed; I have stood on the pillory for geese
he hath killed, otherwise he had suffered for't.
Thou thinkest not of this now. Nay, I remember
the trick you served me when I took my leave of
Madam Silvia: did not I bid thee still mark me
and do as I do? when didst thou see me heave up
my leg and make water against a gentlewoman's
farthingale? didst thou ever see me do such a
trick?

Enter proteus *and* julia.

 Pro. Sebastian is thy name? I like thee well.
And will employ thee in some service presently.
 Jul. In what you please: I'll do what I can.
 Pro. I hope thou wilt. [*To* launce] How now,
you whoreson peasant!
Where have you been these two days loitering?
 Launce. Marry, sir, I carried Mistress Silvia
the dog you bade me.   50
 Pro. And what says she to my little jewel?
 Launce. Marry, she says your dog was a cur,
and tells you currish thanks is good enough for
such a present.
 Pro. But she received my dog?
 Launce. No, indeed, did she not: here have I
brought him back again.
 Pro. What, didst thou offer her this from me?
 Launce. Ay, sir; the other squirrel was stolen
from me by the hangman boys in the marketplace: and then I offered her mine own, who is a
dog as big as ten of yours, and therefore the gift
the greater.

Pro. Go get thee hence, and find my dog again.
Or ne'er return again into my sight.
Away, I say! stay'st thou to vex me here?
                                        [*Exit* LAUNCE.
A slave, that still an end turns me to shame!
Sebastian, I have entertained thee,
Partly that I have need of such a youth
That can with some discretion do my business, 70
For 'tis no trusting to yond foolish lout,
But chiefly for thy face and thy behaviour,
Which, if my augury deceive me not,
Witness good bringing up, fortune, and truth:
Therefore know thou, for this I entertain thee.
Go presently and take this ring with thee,
Deliver it to Madam Silvia:
She loved me well deliver'd it to me.

Jul. It seems you loved not her, to leave her
        token.
She is dead, belike?

Pro.   Not so; I think she lives.   80

Jul. Alas!

Pro. Why dost thou cry "alas"?

Jul.   I cannot choose
But pity her.

Pro.   Wherefore shouldst thou pity her?

Jul. Because methinks that she loved you as
        well
As you do love your lady Silvia:
She dreams on him that has forgot her love;
You dote on her that cares not for your love.
'Tis pity love should be so contrary;
And thinking on it makes me cry "alas!"

Pro. Well, give her that ring and therewithal 90
This letter. That's her chamber. Tell my lady
I claim the promise for her heavenly picture.
Your message done, hie home unto my chamber,
Where thou shalt find me, sad and solitary. [*Exit.*

Jul. How many women would do such a mes-
        sage?
Alas, poor Proteus! thou hast entertain'd
A fox to be the shepherd of thy lambs.
Alas, poor fool! why do I pity him
That with his very heart despiseth me?
Because he loves her, he despiseth me;   100
Because I love him, I must pity him.
This ring I gave him when he parted from me,
To bind him to remember my good will;
And now am I, unhappy messenger,
To plead for that which I would not obtain,
To carry that which I would have refused,
To praise his faith which I would have dispraised.
I am my master's true-confirmed love;
But cannot be true servant to my master,
Unless I prove false traitor to myself.   110
Yet will I woo for him, but yet so coldly
As, heaven it knows, I would not have him speed.

Enter SILVIA, *attended.*

Gentlewoman, good day! I pray you, be my mean
To being me where to speak with Madam Silvia.

Sil. What would you with her, if that I be she?

Jul. If you be she, I do entreat your patience
To hear me speak the message I am sent on.

Sil. From whom?

Jul. From my master, Sir Proteus, madam.

Sil. O, he sends you for a picture.   120

Jul. Ay, madam.

Sil. Ursula, bring my picture there.
Go give your master this: tell him from me,
One Julia, that his changing thoughts forget,
Would better fit his chamber than this shadow.

Jul. Madam, please you peruse this letter.—
Pardon me, madam; I have unadvised
Deliver'd you a paper that I should not:
This is the letter to your ladyship.

Sil. I pray thee, let me look on that again.   130

Jul. It may not be; good madam, pardon me.

Sil. There, hold!
I will not look upon your master's lines:
I know they are stuff'd with protestations
And full of new-found oaths; which he will break
As easily as I do tear his paper.

Jul. Madam, he sends your ladyship this ring.

Sil. The more shame for him that he sends it
        me;
For I have heard him say a thousand times
His Julia gave it him at his departure.   140
Though his false finger have profaned the ring,
Mine shall not do his Julia so much wrong.

Jul. She thanks you.

Sil. What say'st thou?

Jul. I thank you, madam, that you tender her.
Poor gentlewoman! my master wrongs her much.

Sil. Dost thou know her?

Jul. Almost as well as I do know myself:
To think upon her woes I do protest
That I have wept a hundred several times.   150

Sil. Belike she thinks that Proteus hath for-
        sook her.

Jul. I think she doth; and that's her cause of
        sorrow.

Sil. Is she not passing fair?

Jul. She hath been fairer, madam, than she is:
When she did think my master loved her well,
She, in my judgment, was as fair as you;
But since she did neglect her looking-glass
And threw her sun-expelling mask away,
The air hath starved the roses in her cheeks
And pinch'd the lily-tincture of her face,   160
That now she is become as black as I.

Sil. How tall was she?

Jul. About my stature; for at Pentecost,

When all our pageants of delight were play'd,
Our youth got me to play the woman's part,
And I was trimm'd in Madam Julia's gown,
Which served me as fit, by all men's judgements,
As if the garment had been made for me:
Therefore I know she is about my height.
And at that time I made her weep agood,   *170*
For I did play a lamentable part:
Madam, 'twas Ariadne passioning
For Theseus' perjury and unjust flight;
Which I so lively acted with my tears
That my poor mistress, moved therewithal,
Wept bitterly; and would I might be dead
If I in thought felt not her very sorrow!
  Sil. She is beholding to thee, gentle youth.
Alas, poor lady, desolate and left!
I weep myself to think upon thy words   *180*
Here, youth, there is my purse; I give thee this
For thy sweet mistress' sake, because thou lovest
    her.
Farewell.   [*Exit* SILVIA, *with attendants.*
  Jul. And she shall thank you for't, if e'er you
    know her.
A virtuous gentlewoman, mild and beautiful!
I hope my master's suit will be but cold,
Since she respects my mistress' love so much.
Alas, how love can trifle with itself!
Here is her picture: let me see; I think,
If I had such a tire, this face of mine   *190*
Were full as lovely as is this of hers:
And yet the painter flatter'd her a little,
Unless I flatter with myself too much.
Her hair is auburn, mine is perfect yellow:
If that be all the difference in his love,
I'll get me such a colour'd periwig.
Her eyes are grey as glass, and so are mine:
Ay, but her forehead's low, and mine's as high.
What should it be that he respects in her
But I can make respective in myself,   *200*
If this fond Love were not a blinded god?
Come, shadow, come, and take this shadow up,
For 'tis thy rival. O thou senseless form,
Thou shalt be worshipp'd, kiss'd, loved, and
    adored!
And, were there sense in his idolatry,
My substance should be statue in thy stead.
I'll use thee kindly for thy mistress' sake.
That used me so; or else, by Jove I vow,
I should have scratch'd out your unseeing eyes,
To make my master out of love with thee! [*Exit.*

ACT V

SCENE I. *Milan: an abbey*
Enter EGLAMOUR.

Egl. The sun begins to gild the western sky;

And now it is about the very hour
That Silvia, at Friar Patrick's cell, should meet
    me.
She will not fail, for lovers break not hours,
Unless it be to come before their time;
So much they spur their expedition.
See where she comes.

Enter SILVIA.

                    Lady, a happy evening!
  Sil. Amen, amen! Go on, good Eglamour,
Out at the postern by the abbey-wall:
I fear I am attended by some spies.   *10*
  Egl. Fear not: the forest is not three leagues
    off;
If we recover that, we are sure enough. [*Exeunt.*

SCENE II. *The same: the Duke's palace*
Enter THURIO, PROTEUS, *and* JULIA.

  Thu. Sir Proteus, what says Silvia to my suit?
  Pro. O, sir, I find her milder than she was;
And yet she takes exceptions at your person.
  Thu. What, that my leg is too long?
  Pro. No; that it is too little.
  Thu. I'll wear a boot, to make it somewhat
    rounder.
  Jul. [*Aside*] But love will not be spurr'd to
    what it loathes.
  Thu. What says she to my face?
  Pro. She says it is a fair one.
  Thu. Nay then, the wanton lies; my face is
    black.   *10*
  Pro. But pearls are fair; and the old saying is,
"Black men are pearls in beauteous ladies' eyes."
  Jul. [*Aside*] 'Tis true; such pearls as put out
    ladies' eyes;
For I had rather wink than look on them.
  Thu. How likes she my discourse?
  Pro. Ill, when you talk of war.
  Thu. But well, when I discourse of love and
    peace?
  Jul. [*Aside*] But better, indeed, when you hold
    your peace.
  Thu. What says she to my valour?
  Pro. O, sir, she makes no doubt of that.   *20*
  Jul. [*Aside*] She needs not, when she knows it
    cowardice.
  Thu. What says she to my birth?
  Pro. That you are well derived.
  Jul. [*Aside*] True; from a gentleman to a fool.
  Thu. Considers she my possessions?
  Pro. O, ay; and pities them.
  Thu. Wherefore?
  Jul. [*Aside*] That such an ass should owe them.
  Pro. That they are out by lease.
  Jul. Here comes the Duke.   *30*

Enter DUKE.

Duke. How now, Sir Proteus! how now, Thurio!
Which of you saw Sir Eglamour of late?
 Thu. Not I.
 Pro.   Nor I.
 Duke.   Saw you my daughter?
 Pro.   Neither.
 Duke. Why then,
She's fled unto that peasant Valentine;
And Eglamour is in her company.
'Tis true; for Friar Laurence met them both,
As he in penance wander'd through the forest;
Him he knew well, and guess'd that it was she,
But, being mask'd, he was not sure of it; *40*
Besides, she did intend confession
At Patrick's cell this even; and there she was
 not;
These likelihoods confirm her flight from hence.
Therefore, I pray you, stand not to discourse,
But mount you presently and meet with me
Upon the rising of the mountain-foot
That leads toward Mantua, whither they are fled:
Dispatch, sweet gentlemen, and follow me. [*Exit.*
 Thu. Why, this it is to be a peevish girl,
That flies her fortune when it follows her. *50*
I'll after, more to be revenged on Eglamour
Than for the love of reckless Silvia. [*Exit.*
 Pro. And I will follow, more for Silvia's love
Than hate of Eglamour that goes with her. [*Exit.*
 Jul. And I will follow, more to cross that love
Than hate for Silvia that is gone for love. [*Exit.*

SCENE III. *The frontiers of Mantua:
the forest*

Enter OUTLAWS *with* SILVIA.

1st Out. Come, come,
Be patient; we must bring you to our captain.
 Sil. A thousand more mischances than this one
Have learn'd me how to brook this patiently.
 2nd Out. Come, bring her away.
 1st Out. Where is the gentleman that was with
 her?
 3rd Out. Being nimble-footed, he hath outrun
 us,
But Moyses and Valerius follow him.
Go thou with her to the west end of the wood;
There is our captain: we'll follow him that's
 fled; *10*
The thicket is beset; he cannot 'scape.
 1st Out. Come, I must bring you to our cap-
 tain's cave:
Fear not; he bears an honourable mind,
And will not use a woman lawlessly.
 Sil. O Valentine, this I endure for thee!
           [*Exeunt.*

SCENE IV. *Another part of the forest*
Enter VALENTINE.

Val. How use doth breed a habit in a man!
This shadowy desert, unfrequented woods,
I better brook than flourishing peopled towns:
Here can I sit alone, unseen of any,
And to the nightingale's complaining notes
Tune my distresses and record my woes.
O thou that dost inhabit in my breast,
Leave not the mansion so long tenantless,
Lest, growing ruinous, the building fall
And leave no memory of what it was! *10*
Repair me with thy presence, Silvia;
Thou gentle nymph, cherish thy forlorn swain!
What halloing and what stir is this to-day?
These are my mates, that make their wills their
 law,
Have some unhappy passenger in chase.
They love me well; yet I have much to do
To keep them from uncivil outrages.
Withdraw thee, Valentine: who's this comes
 here?

Enter PROTEUS, SILVIA, *AND* JULIA.

Pro. Madam, this service I have done for you,
Though you respect not aught your servant doth,
To hazard life and rescue you from him *21*
That would have forced your honour and your
 love;
Vouchsafe me, for my meed, but one fair look;
A smaller boon than this I cannot beg
And less than this, I am sure, you cannot give.
 Val. [*Aside*] How like a dream is this I see and
 hear!
Love, lend me patience to forbear awhile.
 Sil. O miserable, unhappy that I am!
 Pro. Unhappy were you, madam, ere I came;
But by my coming I have made you happy. *30*
 Sil. By thy approach thou makest me most un-
 happy.
 Jul. [*Aside*] And me, when he approacheth to
 your presence.
 Sil. Had I been seized by a hungry lion,
I would have been a breakfast to the beast,
Rather than have false Proteus rescue me.
O, Heaven be judge how I love Valentine,
Whose life's as tender to me as my soul!
And full as much, for more there cannot be,
I do detest false perjured Proteus.
Therefore be gone; solicit me no more. *40*
 Pro. What dangerous action, stood it next to
 death,
Would I not undergo for one calm look!
O, 'tis the curse in love, and still approved,
When women cannot love where they're beloved!

Sil. When Proteus cannot love where he's be-
   loved.
Read over Julia's heart, thy first best love,
For whose dear sake thou didst then rend thy
   faith
Into a thousand oaths; and all those oaths
Descended into perjury, to love me.   49
Thou hast no faith left now, unless thou'dst two;
And that's far worse than none; better have none
Than plural faith which is too much by one:
Thou counterfeit to thy true friend!
   Pro.   In love
Who respects friend?
   Sil.   All men but Proteus.
   Pro. Nay, if the gentle spirit of moving words
Can no way change you to a milder form,
I'll woo you like a soldier, at arms' end,
And love you 'gainst the nature of love—force
   ye.
   Sil. O heaven!
   Pro.   I'll force thee yield to my desire.
   Val. Ruffian, let go that rude uncivil touch,
Thou friend of an ill fashion!
   Pro.   Valentine!   61
   Val. Thou common friend, that's without faith
   or love,
For such is a friend now; treacherous man!
Thou hast beguiled my hopes; nought but mine
   eye
Could have persuaded me: now I dare not say
I have one friend alive; thou wouldst disprove
   me.
Who should be trusted, when one's own right
   hand
Is perjured to the bosom? Proteus,
I am sorry I must never trust thee more,
But count the world a stranger for thy sake.   70
The private wound is deepest: O time most ac-
   curst,
'Mongst all foes that a friend should be the worst!
   Pro. My shame and guilt confounds me.
Forgive me, Valentine: if hearty sorrow
Be a sufficient ransom for offence,
I tender 't here; I do as truly suffer
As e'er I did commit.
   Val.   Then I am paid;
And once again I do receive thee honest.
Who by repentance is not satisfied
Is nor of heaven nor earth, for these are pleased.
By penitence the Eternal's wrath's appeased: 81
And, that my love may appear plain and free,
All that was mine in Silvia I give thee.
   Jul. O me unhappy!   [*Swoons.*]
   Pro. Look to the boy.
   Val. Why, boy! why, wag! how now! what's
the matter? Look up; speak.

   Jul. O good sir, my master charged me to de-
liver a ring to Madam Silvia, which, out of my
neglect, was never done.   90
   Pro. Where is that ring, boy?
   Jul.   Here 'tis; this is it.
   Pro. How! let me see:
Why, this is the ring I gave to Julia.
   Jul. O, cry you mercy, sir, I have mistook:
This is the ring you sent to Silvia.
   Pro. But how camest thou by this ring? At my
   depart
I gave this unto Julia.
   Jul. And Julia herself did give it me;
And Julia herself hath brought it hither.
   Pro. How! Julia!   100
   Jul. Behold her that gave aim to all thy oaths,
And entertain'd 'em deeply in her heart.
How oft hast thou with perjury cleft the root!
O Proteus, let this habit make thee blush!
Be thou ashamed that I have took upon me
Such an immodest raiment, if shame live
In a disguise of love:
It is the lesser blot, modesty finds,
Women to change their shapes than men their
   minds.
   Pro. Than men their minds! 'tis true. O heaven!
   were man   110
But constant, he were perfect. That one error
Fills him with faults; makes him run through all
   the sins:
Inconstancy falls off ere it begins.
What is in Silvia's face, but I may spy
More fresh in Julia's with a constant eye?
   Val. Come, come, a hand from either:
Let me be blest to make this happy close;
'Twere pity two such friends should be long foes.
   Pro. Bear witness, Heaven, I have my wish for
   ever.
   Jul. And I mine.   120

      Enter OUTLAWS, *with* DUKE *and* THURIO.

   Outlaws. A prize, a prize, a prize!
   Val. Forbear, forbear, I say! it is my lord the
   Duke.
Your Grace is welcome to a man disgraced,
Banished Valentine.
   Duke.   Sir Valentine!
   Thu. Yonder is Silvia; and Silvia's mine.
   Val. Thurio, give back, or else embrace thy
   death;
Come not within the measure of my wrath;
Do not name Silvia thine; if once again,
Verona shall not hold thee. Here she stands:
Take but possession of her with a touch: 130
I dare thee but to breathe upon my love.
   Thu. Sir Valentine, I care not for her, I:

I hold him but a fool that will endanger
His body for a girl that loves him not:
I claim her not, and therefore she is thine.
  Duke. The more degenerate and base art thou,
To make such means for her as thou hast done
And leave her on such slight conditions.
Now, by the honour of my ancestry,
I do applaud thy spirit, Valentine,   *140*
And think thee worthy of an empress' love:
Know then, I here forget all former griefs,
Cancel all grudge, repeal thee home again,
Plead a new state in thy unrival'd merit,
To which I thus subscribe: Sir Valentine,
Thou art a gentleman and well derived;
Take thou thy Silvia, for thou hast deserved her.
  Val. I thank your Grace; the gift hath made me
     happy.
I now beseech you, for your daughter's sake,
To grant one boon that I shall ask of you.   *150*
  Duke. I grant it, for thine own, whate'er it be.
  Val. These banish'd men that I have kept withal
Are men endued with worthy qualities:
Forgive them what they have committed here

And let them be recall'd from their exile:
They are reformed, civil, full of good,
And fit for great employment, worthy lord.
  Duke. Thou hast prevail'd; I pardon them and
     thee:
Dispose of them as thou know'st their deserts.
Come, let us go: we will include all jars   *160*
With triumphs, mirth, and rare solemnity.
  Val. And, as we walk along, I dare be bold
With our discourse to make your Grace to smile.
What think you of this page, my lord?
  Duke. I think the boy hath grace in him; he
     blushes.
  Val. I warrant you, my lord, more grace than
     boy.
  Duke. What mean you by that saying?
  Val. Please you, I'll tell you as we pass along,
That you will wonder what hath fortuned.
Come, Proteus; 'tis your penance but to hear   *170*
The story of your loves discovered:
That done, our day of marriage shall be yours;
One feast, one house, one mutual happiness.
                       [Exeunt.

❧ LOVE'S LABOUR'S LOST

DRAMATIS PERSONÆ

FERDINAND, KING OF NAVARRE
BIRON
LONGAVILLE | *lords attending on the King*
DUMAIN
BOYET
MERCADE | *lords attending on the Princess of France*
DON ADRIANO DE ARMADO, *a fantastical Spaniard*
SIR NATHANIEL, *a curate*
HOLOFERNES, *a schoolmaster*
DULL, *a constable*
COSTARD, *a clown*
MOTH, *a page to Armado*

A FORESTER
A LORD OF FRANCE

THE PRINCESS OF FRANCE
ROSALINE
MARIA | *ladies attending on the Princess*
KATHARINE
JAQUENETTA, *a country wench*

NON-SPEAKING: *Lords, Attendants, Blackamoors, &c.*

SCENE: *Navarre*

❧

ACT I

SCENE I. *The king of Navarre's park*

Enter FERDINAND, KING OF NAVARRE, BIRON,
LONGAVILLE, *and* DUMAIN.

King. Let fame, that all hunt after in their lives,
Live register'd upon our brazen tombs
And then grace us in the disgrace of death;
When, spite of cormorant devouring Time,
The endeavour of this present breath may buy
That honour which shall bate his scythe's keen
  edge
And make us heirs of all eternity.
Therefore, brave conquerors—for so you are,
That war against your own affections
And the huge army of the world's desires— 10
Our late edict shall strongly stand in force:
Navarre shall be the wonder of the world;
Our court shall be a little Academe,
Still and contemplative in living art.
You three, Biron, Dumain, and Longaville,
Have sworn for three years' term to live with me
My fellow-scholars and to keep those statutes
That are recorded in this schedule here:
Your oaths are pass'd; and now subscribe your
  names,
That his own hand may strike his honour down
That violates the smallest branch herein: 21
If you are arm'd to do as sworn to do,
Subscribe to your deep oaths, and keep it too.
  Long. I am resolved; 'tis but a three years' fast:
The mind shall banquet, though the body pine:
Fat paunches have lean pates, and dainty bits
Make rich the ribs, but bankrupt quite the wits.
  Dum. My loving lord, Dumain is mortified:
The grosser manner of these world's delights
He throws upon the gross world's baser slaves:

To love, to wealth, to pomp, I pine and die; 31
With all these living in philosophy.
  Biron. I can but say their protestation over;
So much, dear liege, I have already sworn,
That is, to live and study here three years.
But there are other strict observances;
As, not to see a woman in that term,
Which I hope well is not enrolled there;
And one day in a week to touch no food
And but one meal on every day beside, 40
The which I hope is not enrolled there;
And then, to sleep but three hours in the night,
And not be seen to wink of all the day—
When I was wont to think no harm all night
And make a dark night too of half the day—
Which I hope well is not enrolled there:
O, these are barren tasks, too hard to keep,
Not to see ladies, study, fast, not sleep!
  King. Your oath is pass'd to pass away from
  these.
  Biron. Let me say no, my liege, an if you
  please: 50
I only swore to study with your Grace
And stay here in your court for three years' space.
  Long. You swore to that, Biron, and to the rest.
  Biron. By yea and nay, sir, then I swore in jest.
What is the end of study? let me know.
  King. Why, that to know, which else we should
  not know.
  Biron. Things hid and barr'd, you mean, from
  common sense?
  King. Ay, that is study's godlike recompense.
  Biron. Come on, then; I will swear to study so,
To know the thing I am forbid to know: 60
As thus—to study where I well may dine,
  When I to feast expressly am forbid;
Or study where to meet some mistress fine,

254

When mistresses from common sense are hid;
Or, having sworn too hard a keeping oath,
Study to break it and not break my troth.
If study's gain be thus and this be so,
Study knows that which yet it doth not know:
Swear me to this, and I will ne'er say no.

King. These be the stops that hinder study
    quite   70
And train our intellects to vain delight.

Biron. Why, all delights are vain; but that most
    vain,
Which, with pain purchased, doth inherit pain:
As, painfully to pore upon a book
    To seek the light of truth; while truth the
    while
Doth falsely blind the eyesight of his look:
    Light seeking light doth light of light beguile:
So, ere you find where light in darkness lies,
Your light grows dark by losing of your eyes.
Study me how to please the eye indeed   80
    By fixing it upon a fairer eye,
Who dazzling so, that eye shall be his heed
    And give him light that it was blinded by.
Study is like the heaven's glorious sun
    That will not be deep-search'd with saucy looks:
Small have continual plodders ever won
    Save base authority from others' books.
These earthly godfathers of heaven's lights
    That give a name to every fixed star
Have no more profit of their shining nights   90
    Than those that walk and wot not what they
    are.
Too much to know is to know nought but fame;
And every godfather can give a name.

King. How well he's read, to reason against
    reading!

Dum. Proceeded well, to stop all good proceed-
    ing!

Long. He weeds the corn and still lets grow the
    weeding.

Biron. The spring is near when green geese are
    a-breeding.

Dum. How follows that?

Biron.   Fit in his place and time.

Dum. In reason nothing.

Biron.   Something then in rhyme.

King. Biron is like an envious sneaping frost
        That bites the first-born infants of the
        spring.   101

Biron. Well, say I am; why should proud sum-
        mer boast
        Before the birds have any cause to
        sing?
Why should I joy in any abortive birth?
At Christmas I no more desire a rose
Than wish a snow in May's new-fangled mirth;

But like of each thing that in season grows.
So you, to study now it is too late,
Climb o'er the house to unlock the little gate.

King. Well, sit you out: go home, Biron:
    adieu.   110

Biron. No, my good lord; I have sworn to stay
    with you:
And though I have for barbarism spoke more
    Than for that angel knowledge you can say,
Yet confident I'll keep what I have swore
    And bide the penance of each three years' day.
Give me the paper; let me read the same;
And to the strict'st decrees I'll write my name.

King. How well this yielding rescues thee from
    shame!

Biron [*reads*]. "*Item*, That no woman shall come
within a mile of my court": Hath this been proclaimed?   121

Long. Four days ago.

Biron. Let's see the penalty. [*Reads*] "On pain
of losing her tongue." Who devised this penalty?

Long. Marry, that did I.

Biron. Sweet lord, and why?

Long. To fright them hence with that dread
    penalty.

Biron. A dangerous law against gentility!
[*Reads*] "*Item*, If any man be seen to talk with a
woman within the term of three years, he shall
endure such public shame as the rest of the court
can possibly devise."
This article, my liege, yourself must break;
    For well you know here comes in embassy
The French king's daughter with yourself to
    speak—
A maid of grace and complete majesty—
About surrender up of Aquitaine
To her decrepit, sick and bedrid father:
Therefore this article is made in vain,   140
    Or vainly comes the admired princess hither.

King. What say you, lords? why, this was
    quite forgot.

Biron. So study evermore is overshot:
While it doth study to have what it would
It doth forget to do the thing it should,
And when it hath the thing it hunteth most,
'Tis won as towns with fire, so won, so lost.

King. We must of force dispense with this
    decree;
She must lie here on mere necessity.

Biron. Necessity will make us all forsworn
    Three thousand times within this three years'
    space.   151
For every man with his affects is born,
    Not by might master'd but by special grace:
If I break faith, this word shall speak for me;
I am forsworn on "mere necessity."

So to the laws at large I write my name:
  Subscribes.
And he that breaks them in the least degree
Stands in attainder of eternal shame:
Suggestions are to other as to me;
But I believe, although I seem so loath,   *160*
I am the last that will last keep his oath.
But is there no quick recreation granted?
  King. Ay, that there is. Our court, you know,
    is haunted
With a refined traveller of Spain;
A man in all the world's new fashion planted,
  That hath a mint of phrases in his brain;
One whom the music of his own vain tongue
  Doth ravish like enchanting harmony;
A man of complements, whom right and
    wrong
Have chose as umpire of their mutiny: *170*
This child of fancy that Armado hight
For interim to our studies shall relate
In high-born words the worth of many a knight
From tawny Spain lost in the world's debate.
How you delight, my lords, I know not, I;
But, I protest, I love to hear him lie
And I will use him for my minstrelsy.
  Biron. Armado is a most illustrious wight,
A man of fire-new words, fashion's own knight.
  Long. Costard the swain and he shall be our
    sport;   *180*
And so to study, three years is but short.

    Enter DULL *with a letter, and* COSTARD.

  Dull. Which is the Duke's own person?
  Biron. This, fellow: what wouldst?
  Dull. I myself reprehend his own person, for I
am his grace's tharborough: but I would see his
own person in flesh and blood.
  Biron. This is he.
  Dull. Signior Arme—Arme—commends you.
There's villainy abroad: this letter will tell you
more.   *190*
  Cost. Sir, the contempts thereof are as touching
me.
  King. A letter from the magnificent Armado.
  Biron. How low soever the matter, I hope in
God for high words.
  Long. A high hope for a low heaven: God
grant us patience!
  Biron. To hear? or forbear laughing?
  Long. To hear meekly, sir, and to laugh mod-
erately; or to forbear both.   *200*
  Biron. Well, sir, be it as the style shall give us
cause to climb in the merriness.
  Cost. The matter is to me, sir, as concerning
Jaquenetta. The manner of it is, I was taken
with the manner.

  Biron. In what manner?
  Cost. In manner and form following, sir; all
those three: I was seen with her in the manor-
house, sitting with her upon the form, and taken
following her into the park; which, put together,
is in manner and form following. Now, sir, for
the manner—it is the manner of a man to speak
to a woman: for the form—in some form.
  Biron. For the following, sir?
  Cost. As it shall follow in my correction: and
God defend the right!
  King. Will you hear this letter with attention?
  Biron. As we would hear an oracle.
  Cost. Such is the simplicity of man to hearken
after the flesh.   *220*
  King. [*reads*]. "Great deputy, the welkin's
vicegerent and sole dominator of Navarre, my
soul's earth's god, and body's fostering patron."
  Cost. Not a word of Costard yet.
  King [*reads*]. "So it is—"
  Cost. It may be so: but if he say it is so, he is,
in telling true, but so.
  King. Peace!
  Cost. Be to me and every man that dares not
fight!   *230*
  King. No words!
  Cost. Of other men's secrets, I beseech you.
  King [*reads*]. "So it is, besieged with sable-
coloured melancholy, I did commend the black-
oppressing humour to the most wholesome physic
of thy health-giving air; and, as I am a gentleman, betook myself to walk. The time when.
About the sixth hour; when beasts most graze,
birds best peck, and men sit down to that nourish-
ment which is called supper: so much for the
time when. Now for the ground which; which, I
mean, I walked upon: it is ycleped thy park.
Then for the place where; where, I mean, I did
encounter that obscene and most preposterous
event, that draweth from my snow-white pen
the ebon-coloured ink, which here thou viewest,
beholdest, surveyest, or seest: but to the place
where; it standeth north-north-east and by east
from the west corner of thy curious-knotted
garden: there did I see that low-spirited swain,
that base minnow of thy mirth"—   *251*
  Cost. Me?
  King. [*reads*]. "that unlettered small-knowing
soul"—
  Cost. Me?
  King [*reads*]. "that shallow vassal"—
  Cost. Still me?
  King [*reads*]. "which, as I remember, hight
Costard"—
  Cost. O, me!   *260*
  King [*reads*]. "sorted and consorted, contrary

to thy established proclaimed edict and continent
canon, which with—O, with—but with this I
passion to say wherewith"—

Cost. With a wench.

King [*reads*]. "with a child of our grandmother
Eve, a female; or, for thy more sweet understanding, a woman. Him I, as my ever-esteemed
duty pricks me on, have sent to thee, to receive
the meed of punishment, by thy sweet grace's
officer, Anthony Dull; a man of good repute,
carriage, bearing, and estimation."

Dull. Me, an't shall please you; I am Anthony
Dull.

King. [*reads*]. "For Jaquenetta—so is the
weaker vessel called which I apprehended with
the aforesaid swain—I keep her as a vessel of
thy law's fury; and shall, at the least of thy sweet
notice, bring her to trial. Thine, in all compli-
ments of devoted and heart-burning heat of duty.
        Don Adriano de Armado"

Biron. This is not so well as I looked for, but
the best that ever I heard.

King. Ay, the best for the worst. But, sirrah,
what say you to this?

Cost. Sir, I confess the wench.

King. Did you hear the proclamation?

Cost. I do confess much of the hearing it, but
little of the marking of it.

King. It was proclaimed a year's imprisonment, to be taken with a wench.   *290*

Cost. I was taken with none, sir: I was taken
with a damsel.

King. Well, it was proclaimed "damsel."

Cost. This was no damsel neither, sir; she was
a virgin.

King. It is so varied too; for it was proclaimed
"virgin."

Cost. If it were, I deny her virginity: I was
taken with a maid.

King. This maid will not serve your turn, sir.

Cost. This maid will serve my turn, sir.   *301*

King. Sir, I will pronounce your sentence; you
shall fast a week with bran and water.

Cost. I had rather pray a month with mutton
and porridge.

King. And Don Armado shall be your keeper.
My Lord Biron, see him deliver'd o'er:
And go we, lords, to put in practice that
Which each to other hath so strongly sworn.

        [*Exeunt* KING, LONGAVILLE, *and* DUMAIN.

Biron. I'll lay my head to any good man's hat, *310*
These oaths and laws will prove an idle scorn.
Sirrah, come on.

Cost. I suffer for the truth, sir; for true it is,
I was taken with Jaquenetta, and Jaquenetta is a
true girl; and therefore welcome the sour cup of

prosperity! Affliction may one day smile again;
and till then, sit thee down, sorrow!   [*Exeunt.*

SCENE II. *The same*

Enter ARMADO *and* MOTH.

Arm. Boy, what sign is it when a man of great
spirit grows melancholy?

Moth. A great sign, sir, that he will look sad.

Arm. Why, sadness is one and the self-same
thing, dear imp.

Moth. No, no; O Lord, sir, no.

Arm. How canst thou part sadness and melancholy, my tender juvenal?

Moth. By a familiar demonstration of the working, my tough senior.   *10*

Arm. Why tough senior? why tough senior?

Moth. Why tender juvenal? why tender juvenal?

Arm. I spoke it, tender juvenal, as a congruent
epitheton appertaining to thy young days, which
we may nominate tender.

Moth. And I, tough senior, as an appertinent
title to your old time, which we may name tough.

Arm. Pretty and apt.

Moth. How mean you, sir? I pretty, and my
saying apt? or I apt, and my saying pretty?

Arm. Thou pretty, because little.

Moth. Little pretty, because little. Wherefore
apt?

Arm. And therefore apt, because quick.

Moth. Speak you this in my praise, master?

Arm. In thy condign praise.

Moth. I will praise an eel with the same praise.

Arm. What, that an eel is ingenious?

Moth. That an eel is quick.   *30*

Arm. I do say thou art quick in answers: thou
heatest my blood.

Moth. I am answered, sir.

Arm. I love not to be crossed.

Moth. [*Aside*] He speaks the mere contrary;
crosses love not him.

Arm. I have promised to study three years
with the duke.

Moth. You may do it in an hour, sir.

Arm. Impossible.   *40*

Moth. How many is one thrice told?

Arm. I am ill at reckoning; it fitteth the spirit
of a tapster.

Moth. You are a gentleman and a gamester, sir.

Arm. I confess both; they are both the varnish
of a complete man.

Moth. Then, I am sure, you know how much
the gross sum of deuce-ace amounts to.

Arm. It doth amount to one more than two.

Moth. Which the base vulgar do call three.

Arm. True.

Moth. Why, sir, is this such a piece of study? Now here is three studied, ere ye'll thrice wink: and how easy it is to put "years" to the word "three," and study three years in two words, the dancing horse will tell you.

Arm. A most fine figure!

Moth. To prove you a cipher.   59

Arm. I will hereupon confess I am in love: and as it is base for a soldier to love, so am I in love with a base wench. If drawing my sword against the humour of affection would deliver me from the reprobate thought of it, I would take Desire prisoner, and ransom him to any French courtier for a new-devised courtesy. I think scorn to sigh: methinks I should outswear Cupid. Comfort me, boy: what great men have been in love?

Moth. Hercules, master.   69

Arm. Most sweet Hercules! More authority, dear boy, name more; and, sweet my child, let them be men of good repute and carriage.

Moth. Samson, master: he was a man of good carriage, great carriage, for he carried the town-gates on his back like a porter: and he was in love.

Arm. O well-knit Samson! strong-jointed Samson! I do excel thee in my rapier as much as thou didst me in carrying gates. I am in love too. Who was Samson's love, my dear Moth?

Moth. A woman, master.   81

Arm. Of what complexion?

Moth. Of all the four, or the three, or the two, or one of the four.

Arm. Tell me precisely of what complexion.

Moth. Of the sea-water green, sir.

Arm. Is that one of the four complexions?

Moth. As I have read, sir; and the best of them too.   89

Arm. Green indeed is the colour of lovers; but to have a love of that colour, methinks Samson had small reason for it. He surely affected her for her wit.

Moth. It was so, sir; for she had a green wit.

Arm. My love is most immaculate white and red.

Moth. Most maculate thoughts, master, are masked under such colours.

Arm. Define, define, well-educated infant.

Moth. My father's wit and my mother's tongue, assist me!   101

Arm. Sweet invocation of a child; most pretty and pathetical!

Moth. If she be made of white and red,
     Her faults will ne'er be known,
  For blushing cheeks by faults are bred
     And fears by pale white shown:
      Then if she fear, or be to blame,

     By this you shall not know,
  For still her cheeks possess the same
     Which native she doth owe.   111
A dangerous rhyme, master, against the reason of white and red.

Arm. Is there not a ballad, boy, of the King and the Beggar?

Moth. The world was very guilty of such a ballad some three ages since: but I think now 'tis not to be found; or, if it were, it would neither serve for the writing nor the tune.   119

Arm. I will have that subject newly writ o'er, that I may example my digression by some mighty precedent. Boy, I do love that country girl that I took in the park with the rational hind Costard: she deserves well.

Moth. [*Aside*] To be whipped; and yet a better love than my master.

Arm. Sing, boy; my spirit grows heavy in love.

Moth. And that's great marvel, loving a light wench.

Arm. I say, sing.   130

Moth. Forbear till this company be past.

Enter DULL, COSTARD, *and* JAQUENETTA.

Dull. Sir, the Duke's pleasure is, that you keep Costard safe: and you must suffer him to take no delight nor no penance; but a' must fast three days a week. For this damsel, I must keep her at the park: she is allowed for the day-woman. Fare you well.

Arm. I do betray myself with blushing. Maid!

Jaq. Man?

Arm. I will visit thee at the lodge.   140

Jaq. That's hereby.

Arm. I know where it is situate.

Jaq. Lord, how wise you are!

Arm. I will tell thee wonders.

Jaq. With that face?

Arm. I love thee.

Jaq. So I heard you say.

Arm. And so, farewell.

Jaq. Fair weather after you!

Dull. Come, Jaquenetta, away!   150
         [*Exeunt* DULL *and* JAQUENETTA.

Arm. Villain, thou shalt fast for thy offences ere thou be pardoned.

Cost. Well, sir, I hope, when I do it, I shall do it on a full stomach.

Arm. Thou shalt be heavily punished.

Cost. I am more bound to you than your fellows, for they are but lightly rewarded.

Arm. Take away this villain; shut him up.

Moth. Come, you transgressing slave; away!

Cost. Let me not be pent up, sir: I will fast, being loose.   161

Moth. No, sir; that were fast and loose; thou shalt to prison.

Cost. Well, if ever I do see the merry days of desolation that I have seen, some shall see.

Moth. What shall some see?

Cost. Nay, nothing, Master Moth, but what they look upon. It is not for prisoners to be too silent in their words; and therefore I will say nothing: I thank God I have as little patience as another man; and therefore I can be quiet.   *171*

[*Exeunt* MOTH *and* COSTARD.

Arm. I do affect the very ground, which is base, where her shoe, which is baser, guided by her foot, which is basest, doth tread. I shall be forsworn, which is a great argument of falsehood, if I love. And how can that be true love which is falsely attempted? Love is a familiar; Love is a devil: there is no evil angel but Love. Yet was Samson so tempted, and he had an excellent strength; yet was Solomon so seduced, and he had a very good wit. Cupid's butt-shaft is too hard for Hercules' club; and therefore too much odds for a Spaniard's rapier. The first and second cause will not serve my turn; the passado he respects not, the duello he regards not: his disgrace is to be called boy; but his glory is to subdue men. Adieu, valour! rust, rapier! be still, drum! for your manager is in love; yea, he loveth. Assist me, some extemporal god of rhyme, for I am sure I shall turn sonnet. Devise, wit; write, pen; for I am for whole volumes in folio.   [*Exit.*

ACT II

SCENE I. *The same*

Enter the PRINCESS OF FRANCE, ROSALINE, MARIA, KATHARINE, BOYET, LORDS, *and other Attendants.*

Boyet. Now, madam, summon up your dearest spirits:
Consider who the King your father sends,
To whom he sends, and what's his embassy:
Yourself, held precious in the world's esteem,
To parley with the sole inheritor
Of all perfections that a man may owe,
Matchless Navarre; the plea of no less weight
Than Aquitaine, a dowry for a queen.
Be now as prodigal of all dear grace
As Nature was in making graces dear   *10*
When she did starve the general world beside
And prodigally gave them all to you.

Prin. Good Lord Boyet, my beauty, though but mean,
Needs not the painted flourish of your praise:
Beauty is bought by judgement of the eye,
Not utter'd by base sale of chapmen's tongues:
I am less proud to hear you tell my worth
Than you much willing to be counted wise
In spending your wit in the praise of mine.
But now to task the tasker: good Boyet,   *20*
You are not ignorant, all-telling fame
Doth noise abroad, Navarre hath made a vow,
Till painful study shall outwear three years,
No woman may approach his silent court:
Therefore to's seemeth it a needful course,
Before we enter his forbidden gates,
To know his pleasure; and in that behalf,
Bold of your worthiness, we single you
As our best-moving fair solicitor.
Tell him, the daughter of the King of France,   *30*
On serious business, craving quick dispatch,
Importunes personal conference with his Grace:
Haste, signify so much; while we attend,
Like humble-visaged suitors, his high will.

Boyet. Proud of employment, willingly I go.

Prin. All pride is willing pride, and yours is so.

[*Exit* BOYET.

Who are the votaries, my loving lords,
That are vow-fellows with this virtuous Duke?

1st Lord. Lord Longaville is one.

Prin.   Know you the man?

Mar. I know him, madam: at a marriage-feast,   *40*
Between Lord Perigort and the beauteous heir
Of Jaques Falconbridge, solemnized
In Normandy, saw I this Longaville:
A man of sovereign parts he is esteem'd;
Well fitted in arts, glorious in arms:
Nothing becomes him ill that he would well.
The only soil of his fair virtue's gloss,
If virtue's gloss will stain with any soil,
Is a sharp wit match'd with too blunt a will;
Whose edge hath power to cut, whose will still wills   *50*
It should none spare that come within his power.

Prin. Some merry mocking lord, belike; is't so?

Mar. They say so most that most his humours know.

Prin. Such short-lived wits do wither as they grow.
Who are the rest?

Kath. The young Dumain, a well-accomplished youth,
Of all that virtue love for virtue loved:
Most power to do most harm, least knowing ill;
For he hath wit to make an ill shape good,
And shape to win grace though he had no wit.   *60*
I saw him at the Duke Alençon's once;
And much too little of that good I saw
Is my report to his great worthiness.

Ros. Another of these students at that time
Was there with him, if I have heard a truth.

Biron they call him; but a merrier man,
Within the limit of becoming mirth,
I never spent an hour's talk withal;
His eye begets occasion for his wit;
For every object that the one doth catch   70
The other turns to a mirth-moving jest,
Which his fair tongue, conceit's expositor,
Delivers in such apt and gracious words
That aged ears play truant at his tales
And younger hearings are quite ravished;
So sweet and voluble is his discourse.
  Prin. God bless my ladies! are they all in love,
That every one her own hath garnished
With such bedecking ornaments of praise?
  1st Lord. Here comes Boyet.

Re-enter BOYET.

  Prin.   Now, what admittance, lord?   80
  Boyet. Navarre had notice of your fair approach;
And he and his competitors in oath
Were all address'd to meet you, gentle lady,
Before I came. Marry, thus much I have learnt:
He rather means to lodge you in the field,
Like one that comes here to besiege his court,
Than seek a dispensation for his oath,
To let you enter his unpeopled house.
Here comes Navarre.

Enter KING, LONGAVILLE, DUMAIN, BIRON, *and*
Attendants.

  King. Fair princess, welcome to the court of
    Navarre.   90
  Prin. "Fair" I give you back again; and "wel-
come" I have not yet: the roof of this court is
too high to be yours; and welcome to the wide
fields too base to be mine.
  King. You shall be welcome, madam, to my
    court.
  Prin. I will be welcome, then: conduct me
    thither.
  King. Hear me, dear lady; I have sworn an oath.
  Prin. Our Lady help my lord! he'll be forsworn.
  King. Not for the world, fair madam, by my
    will.
  Prin. Why, will shall break it; will and no-
    thing else.   100
  King. Your ladyship is ignorant what it is.
  Prin. Were my lord so, his ignorance were
    wise,
Where now his knowledge must prove ignorance.
I hear your Grace hath sworn out house-keeping:
'Tis deadly sin to keep that oath, my lord,
And sin to break it.
But pardon me, I am too sudden-bold:
To teach a teacher ill beseemeth me.
Vouchsafe to read the purpose of my coming,

And suddenly resolve me in my suit.   110
  King. Madam, I will, if suddenly I may.
  Prin. You will the sooner, that I were away;
For you'll prove perjured if you make me stay.
  Biron. Did not I dance with you in Brabant
    once?
  Ros. Did not I dance with you in Brabant once?
  Biron. I know you did.
  Ros. How needless was it then to ask the ques-
    tion!
  Biron. You must not be so quick.
  Ros. 'Tis 'long of you that spur me with such
    questions.
  Biron. Your wit's too hot, it speeds too fast,
    'twill tire.   120
  Ros. Not till it leave the rider in the mire.
  Biron. What time o'day?
  Ros. The hour that fools should ask.
  Biron. Now fair befall your mask!
  Ros. Fair fall the face it covers!
  Biron. And send you many lovers!
  Ros. Amen, so you be none.
  Biron. Nay, then will I be gone.
  King. Madam, your father here doth intimate
The payment of a hundred thousand crowns; *130*
Being but the one half of an entire sum
Disbursed by my father in his wars.
But say that he or we, as neither have,
Received that sum, yet there remains unpaid
A hundred thousand more; in surety of the
  which,
One part of Aquitaine is bound to us,
Although not valued to the money's worth.
If then the King your father will restore
But that one half which is unsatisfied,
We will give up our right in Aquitaine,   *140*
And hold fair friendship wih his Majesty.
But that, it seems, he little purposeth,
For here he doth demand to have repaid
A hundred thousand crowns; and not demands,
On payment of a hundred thousand crowns,
To have his title live in Aquitaine;
Which we much rather had depart withal
And have the money by our father lent
Than Aquitaine so gelded as it is.
Dear Princess, were not his requests so far   *150*
From reason's yielding, your fair self should
  make
A yielding 'gainst some reason in my breast
And go well satisfied to France again.
  Prin. You do the King my father too much
    wrong
And wrong the reputation of your name,
In so unseeming to confess receipt
Of that which hath so faithfully been paid.
  King. I do protest I never heard of it;

And if you prove it, I'll repay it back
Or yield up Aquitaine.

Prin.   We arrest your word. *160*
Boyet, you can produce acquittances
For such a sum from special officers
Of Charles his father.

King.   Satisfy me so.

Boyet. So please your Grace, the packet is not
      come
Where that and other specialties are bound:
To-morrow you shall have a sight of them.

King. It shall suffice me: at which interview
All liberal reason I will yield unto.
Meantime receive such welcome at my hand
As honour without breach of honour may   *170*
Make tender of to thy true worthiness:
You may not come, fair Princess, in my gates;
But here without you shall be so received
As you shall deem yourself lodged in my heart,
Though so denied fair harbour in my house.
Your own good thoughts excuse me, and farewell:
To-morrow shall we visit you again.

Prin. Sweet health and fair desires consort your
      Grace!

King. Thy own wish wish I thee in every place!
                                    [*Exit.*

Biron. Lady, I will commend you to mine own
      heart.   *180*

Ros. Pray you, do my commendations; I would
be glad to see it.

Biron. I would you heard it groan.

Ros. Is the fool sick?

Biron. Sick at the heart.

Ros. Alack, let it blood.

Biron. Would that do it good?

Ros. My physic says "ay."

Biron. Will you prick't with your eye?

Ros. No point, with my knife.   *190*

Biron. Now, God save thy life!

Ros. And yours from long living!

Biron. I cannot stay thanksgiving. [*Retiring.*

Dum. Sir, I pray you, a word: what lady is that
      same?

Boyet. The heir of Alençon, Katharine her
      name.

Dum. A gallant lady. Monsieur, fare you well.
                                    [*Exit.*

Long. I beseech you a word: what is she in the
      white?

Boyet. A woman sometimes, an you saw her in
      the light.

Long. Perchance light in the light. I desire her
      name.

Boyet. She hath but one for herself; to desire
      that were a shame.   *200*

Long. Pray you, sir, whose daughter?

Boyet. Her mother's, I have heard.

Long. God's blessing on your beard!

Boyet. Good sir, be not offended.
She is an heir of Falconbridge.

Long. Nay, my choler is ended.
She is a most sweet lady.

Boyet. Not unlike, sir, that may be.
                          [*Exit* LONGAVILLE.

Biron. What's her name in the cap?

Boyet. Rosaline, by good hap.   *210*

Biron. Is she wedded or no?

Boyet. To her will, sir, or so.

Biron. You are welcome, sir: adieu.

Boyet. Farewell to me, sir, and welcome to you.
                                    [*Exit* BIRON.

Mar. That last is Biron, the merry mad-cap
      lord:
Nor a word with him but a jest.

Boyet.   And every jest but a word.

Prin. It was well done of you to take him at his
      word.

Boyet. I was as willing to grapple as he was to
      board.

Mar. Two hot sheeps, marry.

Boyet.   And wherefore not ships?
No sheep, sweet lamb, unless we feed on your
      lips.   *220*

Mar. You sheep, and I pasture: shall that finish
      the jest?

Boyet. So you grant pasture for me.
      Offering to kiss her.

Mar.   Not so, gentle beast:
My lips are no common, though several they be.

Boyet. Belonging to whom?

Mar.   To my fortunes and me.

Prin. Good wits will be jangling; but, gentles,
      agree:
This civil war of wits were much better used
On Navarre and his book-men; for here 'tis
      abused.

Boyet. If my observation, which very seldom
      lies,
By the heart's still rhetoric disclosed with eyes,
Deceive me not now, Navarre is infected.   *230*

Prin. With what?

Boyet. With that which we lovers entitle af-
      fected.

Prin. Your reason?

Boyet. Why, all his behaviours did make their
      retire
To the court of his eye, peeping thorough desire:
His heart, like an agate, with your print im-
      press'd,
Proud with his form, in his eye pride express'd:
His tongue, all impatient to speak and not see,
Did stumble with haste in his eyesight to be;

All senses to that sense did make their repair, 240
To feel only looking on fairest of fair:
Methought all his senses were lock'd in his eye,
As jewels in crystal for some prince to buy;
Who, tendering their own worth from where
they were glass'd,
Did point you to buy them, along as you pass'd:
His face's own margent did quote such amazes
That all eyes saw his eyes enchanted with gazes
I'll give you Aquitaine and all that is his,
An you give him for my sake but one loving kiss.
Prin. Come to our pavilion: Boyet is disposed.
Boyet. But to speak that in words which his eye
hath disclosed.   251
I only have made a mouth of his eye,
By adding a tongue which I know will not lie.
Ros. Thou art an old love-monger and speakest
skilfully.
Mar. He is Cupid's grandfather and learns news
of him.
Ros. Then was Venus like her mother, for her
father is but grim.
Boyet. Do you hear, my mad wenches?
Mar.   No.
Boyet.   What then, do you see?
Ros. Ay, our way to be gone.
Boyet.   You are too hard for me.
                              [*Exeunt.*

ACT III

Scene I. *The same*

Enter ARMADO *and* MOTH.

Arm. Warble, child; make passionate my sense
of hearing.
Moth. Concolinel.   [*Singing.*
Arm. Sweet air! Go, tenderness of years; take
this key, give enlargement to the swain, bring
him festinately hither: I must employ him in a
letter to my love.
Moth. Master, will you win your love with a
French brawl?   9
Arm. How meanest thou? brawling in French?
Moth. No, my complete master: but to jig off a
tune at the tongue's end, canary to it with your
feet, humour it with turning up your eyelids, sigh
a note and sing a note, sometime through the
throat, as if you swallowed love with singing
love, sometime through the nose, as if you
snuffed up love by smelling love; with your hat
penthouse-like o'er the shop of your eyes; with
your arms crossed on your thin-belly doublet like
a rabbit on a spit; or your hands in your pocket
like a man after the old painting; and keep not
too long in one tune, but a snip and away. These
are complements, these are humours; these be-

tray nice wenches, that would be betrayed with-
out these; and make them men of note—do you
note me?—that most are affected to these.
Arm. How hast thou purchased this experience?
Moth. By my penny of observation.
Arm. But O—but O—
Moth. "The hobby-horse is forgot."   30
Arm. Callest thou my love "hobby-horse"?
Moth. No, master; the hobby-horse is but a colt,
and your love perhaps a hackney. But have you
forgot your love?
Arm. Almost I had.
Moth. Negligent student! learn her **by** heart.
Arm. By heart and in heart, boy.
Moth. And out of heart, master: all those three
I will prove.
Arm. What wilt thou prove?   40
Moth. A man, if I live; and this, by, in, and
without, upon the instant: by heart you love her,
because your heart cannot come by her; in heart
you love her, because your heart is in love with
her; and out of heart you love her, being out of
heart that you cannot enjoy her.
Arm. I am all these three.
Moth. And three times as much more, and yet
nothing at all.
Arm. Fetch hither the swain: he must carry me
a letter.   51
Moth. A message well sympathized; a horse to
be ambassador for an ass.
Arm. Ha, ha! what sayest thou?
Moth. Marry, sir, you must send the ass upon
the horse, for he is very slow-gaited. But I go.
Arm. The way is but short: away!
Moth. As swift as lead, sir?
Arm. The meaning, pretty ingenious?
Is not lead a metal heavy, dull, and slow?   60
Moth. Minime, honest master; or rather, mas-
ter, no.
Arm. I say lead is slow.
Moth.   You are too swift, sir, to say so:
Is that lead slow which is fired from a gun?
Arm. Sweet smoke of rhetoric!
He reputes me a cannon; and the bullet, that's he:
I shoot thee at the swain.
Moth.   Thump then and I flee. [*Exit.*
Arm. A most acute juvenal; volable and free of
grace!
By thy favour, sweet welkin, I must sigh in thy
face:
Most rude melancholy, valour gives thee place.
My herald is return'd.   70

Re-enter MOTH *with* COSTARD.

Moth. A wonder, master! here's a costard broken in a shin.

Arm. Some enigma, some riddle: come, thy
l'envoy; begin.

Cost. No egma, no riddle, no l'envoy; no salve
in the mail, sir: O, sir, plantain, a plain plantain!
no l'envoy, no l'envoy; no salve, sir, but a plantain!

Arm. By virtue, thou enforcest laughter; thy
silly thought my spleen; the heaving of my
lungs provokes me to ridiculous smiling. O, pardon me, my stars! Doth the inconsiderate take
salve for l'envoy, and the word l'envoy for a
salve?   *80*

Moth. Do the wise think them other? is not
l'envoy a salve?

Arm. No, page: it is an epilogue or discourse,
to make plain
Some obscure precedence that hath tofore been
sain.
I will example it:
                    The fox, the ape and the humble-bee,
                    Were still at odds, being but three.
There's the moral. Now the l'envoy.

Moth. I will add the l'envoy. Say the moral
again.

Arm. The fox, the ape, the humble-bee,   *90*
                    Were still at odds, being but three.

Moth. Until the goose came out of door,
                    And stay'd the odds by adding four.
Now will I begin your moral, and do you follow
with my l'envoy.
                    The fox, the ape and the humble-bee,
                    Were still at odds, being but three.

Arm. Until the goose came out of door,
                    Staying the odds by adding four.

Moth. A good l'envoy, ending in the goose:
would you desire more?   *101*

Cost. The boy hath sold him a bargain, a goose,
that's flat.
Sir, your pennyworth is good, an your goose be
fat.
To sell a bargain well is as cunning as fast and
loose:
Let me see; a fat l'envoy; ay, that's a fat
goose.

Arm. Come hither, come hither. How did this
argument begin?

Moth. By saying that a costard was broken in a
shin.
Then call'd you for the l'envoy.

Cost. True, and I for a plantain: thus came your
argument in;
Then the boy's fat l'envoy, the goose that you
bought;   *110*
And he ended the market.

Arm. But tell me; how was there a costard broken in a shin?

Moth. I will tell you sensibly.

Cost. Thou hast no feeling of it, Moth: I will
speak that l'envoy:
                    I Costard, running out, that was safely within,
                    Fell over the threshold, and broke my shin.

Arm. We will talk no more of this matter.

Cost. Till there be more matter in the shin.

Arm. Sirrah Costard, I will enfranchise thee.

Cost. O, marry me to one Frances: I smell some
l'envoy, some goose, in this.

Arm. By my sweet soul, I mean setting thee at
liberty, enfreedoming thy person: thou wert immured, restrained, captivated, bound.

Cost. True, true; and now you will be my purgation and let me loose.

Arm. I give thee thy liberty, set thee from durance; and, in lieu thereof, impose on thee nothing
but this: bear this significant [*giving a letter*] to
the country maid Jaquenetta: there is remuneration; for the best ward of mine honour is reward-
ing my dependents. Moth, follow.   [*Exit.*

Moth. Like the sequel, I. Signior Costard, adieu.

Cost. My sweet ounce of man's flesh! my incony
Jew!   [*Exit* MOTH.
Now will I look to his remuneration. Remunera-
tion! O, that's the Latin word for three farthings:
three farthings—remuneration. "What's the
price of this inkle?" "One penny." "No, I'll give
you a remuneration" why, it carries it. Remuneration! why, it is a fairer name than French crown.
I will never buy and sell out of this word.

Enter BIRON.

Biron. O, my good knave Costard! exceedingly
well met.

Cost. Pray you, sir, how much carnation ribbon
may a man buy for a remuneration?

Biron. What is a remuneration?

Cost. Marry, sir, halfpenny farthing.   *149*

Biron. Why, then, three-farthing worth of silk.

Cost. I thank your worship: God be wi' you!

Biron. Stay, slave; I must employ thee:
As thou wilt win my favour, good my knave,
Do one thing for me that I shall entreat.

Cost. When would you have it done, sir?

Biron. This afternoon.

Cost. Well, I will do it, sir: fare you well.

Biron. Thou knowest not what it is.

Cost. I shall know, sir, when I have done it.

Biron. Why, villain, thou must know first.   *160*

Cost. I will come to your worship to-morrow
morning.

Biron. It must be done this afternoon. Hark,
slave, it is but this:
The Princess comes to hunt here in the park,
And in her train there is a gentle lady;

When tongues speak sweetly, then they name
    her name,
And Rosaline they call her: ask for her;
And to her white hand see thou do commend   *169*
This seal'd-up counsel. There's thy guerdon; go.
    Giving him a shilling.
  Cost. Gardon, O sweet gardon! better than re-
muneration, a 'leven-pence farthing better: most
sweet gardon! I will do it, sir, in print. Gardon!
Remuneration!   [*Exit.*
  Biron. And I, forsooth, in love! I, that have been
love's whip;
A very beadle to a humorous sigh;
A critic, nay, a night-watch constable;
A domineering pedant o'er the boy;
Than whom no mortal so magnificent!   *180*
This wimpled, whining, purblind, wayward boy;
This senior-junior, giant-dwarf, Dan Cupid;
Regent of love-rhymes, lord of folded arms,
The anointed sovereign of sighs and groans,
Liege of all loiterers and malcontents,
Dread prince of plackets, king of codpieces,
Sole imperator and great general
Of trotting 'paritors: O my little heart!—
And I to be a corporal of his field,
And wear his colours like a tumbler's hoop!   *190*
What, I! I love! I sue! I seek a wife!
A woman, that is like a German clock,
Still a-repairing, ever out of frame,
And never going aright, being a watch,
But being watch'd that it may still go right!
Nay, to be perjured, which is worst of all;
And, among three, to love the worst of all;
A wightly wanton with a velvet brow,
With two pitch-balls stuck in her face for eyes;
Ay, and, by heaven, one that will do the deed *200*
Though Argus were her eunuch and her guard:
And I to sigh for her! to watch for her!
To pray for her! Go to; it is a plague
That Cupid will impose for my neglect
Of his almighty dreadful little might.
Well, I will love, write, sigh, pray, sue and
    groan:
Some men must love my lady and some
    Joan.
                      [*Exit.*

ACT IV

Scene i. *The same*

Enter the princess, *and her train, a* forester,
boyet, rosaline, maria, *and* katharine.

  Prin. Was that the King, that spurr'd his horse
    so hard
Against the steep uprising of the hill?
  Boyet. I know not; but I think it was not he.

  Prin. Whoe'er a' was, a' show'd a mounting
    mind.
Well, lords, to-day we shall have our dispatch:
On Saturday we will return to France.
Then, forester, my friend, where is the bush
That we must stand and play the murderer in?
  For. Hereby, upon the edge of yonder coppice;
A stand where you make the fairest shoot.
  Prin. I thank my beauty, I am fair that shoot,
And thereupon thou speak'st the fairest shoot.
  For. Pardon me, madam, for I meant not so.
  Prin. What, what? first praise me and again say
    no?
O short-lived pride! Not fair? alack for woe!
  For. Yes, madam, fair.
  Prin.   Nay, never paint me now:
Where fair is not, praise cannot mend the brow.
Here, good my glass, take this for telling true:
Fair payment for foul words is more than due.
  For. Nothing but fair is that which you inherit.
  Prin. See, see, my beauty will be saved by
    merit!   *21*
O heresy in fair, fit for these days!
A giving hand, though foul, shall have fair praise.
But come, the bow: now mercy goes to kill,
And shooting well is then accounted ill.
Thus will I save my credit in the shoot:
Not wounding, pity would not let me do't;
If wounding, then it was to show my skill,
That more for praise than purpose meant to kill.
And out of question so it is sometimes,   *30*
Glory grows guilty of detested crimes,
When, for fame's sake, for praise, an outward
    part,
We bend to that the working of the heart;
As I for praise alone now seek to spill
The poor deer's blood, that my heart means no
    ill.
  Boyet. Do not curst wives hold that self-sover-
    eignty
Only for praise sake, when they strive to be
Lords o'er their lords?
  Prin. Only for praise: and praise we may afford
To any lady that subdues a lord.   *40*
  Boyet. Here comes a member of the common-
    wealth.

Enter costard.

  Cost. God dig-you-den all! Pray you, which is
the head lady?
  Prin. Thou shalt know her, fellow, by the rest
that have no heads.
  Cost. Which is the greatest lady, the highest?
  Prin. The thickest and the tallest.
  Cost. The thickest and the tallest! it is so; truth
is truth.

An your waist, mistress, were as slender as my
　　wit,
One o' these maids' girdles for your waist should
　　be fit.　　　　　　　　　　　　　　　　　50
Are not you the chief woman? you are the thick-
　　est here.
Prin. What's your will, sir? what's your will?
Cost. I have a letter from Monsieur Biron to one
　　Lady Rosaline.
Prin. O, thy letter, thy letter! he's a good friend
　　of mine:
Stand aside, good bearer. Boyet, you can carve;
Break up this capon.
Boyet.　　　　　　　　I am bound to serve.
This letter is mistook, it importeth none here;
It is writ to Jaquenetta.
Prin.　　　　　　　We will read it, I swear.
Break the neck of the wax, and every one give
　　ear.　　　　　　　　　　　　　　　　　59
Boyet [*reads*]. "By heaven, that thou art fair, is
most infallible; true, that thou art beauteous;
truth itself, that thou art lovely. More fairer than
fair, beautiful than beauteous, truer than truth
itself, have commiseration on thy heroical vassal!
The magnanimous and most illustrate king Cophetua set eye upon the pernicious and indubiate
beggar Zenelophon; and he it was that might
rightly say, *Veni, vidi, vici;* which to annothan-
ize in the vulgar,—O base and obscure vulgar!—
videlicet, He came, saw, and overcame: he came,
one; saw, two; overcame, three. Who came? the
king: why did he come? to see: why did he see?
to overcome: to whom came he? to the beggar:
what saw he? the beggar: who overcame he? the
beggar. The conclusion is victory: on whose
side? the king's. The captive is enriched: on
whose side? the beggar's. The catastrophe is a
nuptial: on whose side? the king's: no, on both
in one, or one in both. I am the king; for so
stands the comparison: thou the beggar; for so
witnesseth thy lowliness. Shall I command thy
love? I may: shall I enforce thy love? I could:
shall I entreat thy love? I will. What shalt thou
exchange for rags? robes; for tittles? titles; for
thyself? me. Thus, expecting thy reply, I profane my lips on thy foot, my eyes on thy picture,
and my heart on thy every part. Thine, in the
dearest design of industry,
　　　　　　　　　　Don Adriano de Armado"
Thus dost thou hear the Nemean lion roar　　90
　　'Gainst thee, thou lamb, that standest as his
　　　　prey.
Submissive fall his princely feet before,
　　And he from forage will incline to play:
But if thou strive, poor soul, what art thou then?
Food for his rage, repasture for his den.

Prin. What plume of feathers is he that indited
　　this letter?
What vane? what weathercock? did you ever
　　hear better?
Boyet. I am much deceived but I remember the
　　style.
Prin. Else your memory is bad, going o'er it
　　erewhile.
Boyet. This Armado is a Spaniard, that keeps
　　here in court;　　　　　　　　　　　　100
A phantasime, a Monarcho, and one that makes
　　sport
To the prince and his bookmates.
Prin.　　　　　　　　Thou fellow, a word:
Who gave thee this letter?
Cost.　　　　　　　I told you; my lord.
Prin. To whom shouldst thou give it?
Cost.　　　　　　From my lord to my lady.
Prin. From which lord to which lady?
Cost. From my lord Biron, a good master of
　　mine,
To a lady of France that he call'd Rosaline.
Prin. Thou hast mistaken his letter. Come,
　　lords, away.
[*To* ROSALINE] Here, sweet, put up this: 'twill be
　　thine another day.
　　　　　　　　[*Exeunt* PRINCESS *and train.*
Boyet. Who is the suitor? who is the suitor?
Ros.　　　　　　Shall I teach you to know?　110
Boyet. Ay, my continent of beauty.
Ros.　　　　　　Why, she that bears the bow.
Finely put off!
Boyet. My lady goes to kill horns; but, if thou
　　marry,
Hang me by the neck, if horns that year miscarry.
Finely put on!
Ros. Well, then, I am the shooter.
Boyet.　　　　　　　And who is your deer?
Ros. If we choose by the horns, yourself come
　　not near.
Finely put on, indeed!
Mar. You still wrangle with her, Boyet, and she
　　strikes at the brow.
Boyet. But she herself is hit lower: have I hit her
　　now?　　　　　　　　　　　　　　　120
Ros. Shall I come upon thee with an old saying,
that was a man when King Pepin of France was a
little boy, as touching the hit it?
Boyet. So I may answer thee with one as old,
that was a woman when Queen Guinever of
Britain was a little wench, as touching the hit it.
Ros.　　Thou canst not hit it, hit it, hit it,
　　　　Thou canst not hit it, my good man.
Boyet. An I cannot, cannot, cannot,
　　　　An I cannot, another can.　　　　　130
　　　　　　　[*Exeunt* ROSALINE *and* KATHARINE.

Cost. By my troth, most pleasant: how both did
    fit it!

Mar. A mark marvellous well shot, for they
    both did hit it.

Boyet. A mark! O, mark but that mark! A
    mark, says my lady!

Let the mark have a prick in't, to mete at, if it
    may be.

Mar. Wide o' the bow hand! i' faith, your hand
    is out.

Cost. Indeed, a' must shoot nearer, or he'll ne'er
    hit the clout.

Boyet. An if my hand be out, then belike your
    hand is in.

Cost. Then will she get the upshoot by cleaving
    the pin.

Mar. Come, come, you talk greasily; your lips
    grow foul.

Cost. She's too hard for you at pricks, sir: chal-
    lenge her to bowl.   140

Boyet. I fear too much rubbing. Good night, my
    good owl.   [*Exeunt* BOYET *and* MARIA.

Cost. By my soul, a swain! a most simple clown!

Lord, Lord, how the ladies and I have put him
    down!

O' my troth, most sweet jests! most incony vul-
    gar wit!

When it comes so smoothly off, so obscenely, as
    it were, so fit.

Armado o' th' one side—O, a most dainty man!

To see him walk before a lady and to bear her
    fan!

To see him kiss his hand! and how most sweetly
    a' will swear!

And his page o' t' other side, that handful of wit!

Ah, heavens, it is a most pathetical nit!   150

Sola, sola! [*Shout within. Exit* COSTARD, *running*.

SCENE II. *The same*

Enter HOLOFERNES, SIR NATHANIEL, *and* DULL.

Nath. Very reverend sport, truly; and done in
the testimony of a good conscience.

Hol. The deer was, as you know, *sanguis*, in
blood; ripe as the pomewater, who now hangeth
like a jewel in the ear of *caelo*, the sky, the welkin, the heaven; and anon falleth like a crab on
the face of *terra*, the soil, the land, the earth.

Nath. Truly, Master Holofernes, the epithets
are sweetly varied, like a scholar at the least:
but, sir, I assure ye, it was a buck of the first
head.   10

Hol. Sir Nathaniel, *haud credo*.

Dull. 'Twas not a haud credo; 'twas a pricket.

Hol. Most barbarous intimation! yet a kind of
insinuation, as it were, *in via*, in way, of explica-
tion; *facere*, as it were, replication, or rather,

ostentare, to show, as it were, his inclination, after
his undressed, unpolished, uneducated, unpruned,
untrained, or rather, unlettered, or ratherest, unconfirmed fashion, to insert again my *haud credo*
for a deer.   20

Dull. I said the deer was not a haud credo;
'twas a pricket.

Hol. Twice-sod simplicity, *bis coctus!*

O thou monster Ignorance, how deformed dost
    thou look!

Nath. Sir, he hath never fed of the dainties that
    are bred in a book;

he hath not eat paper, as it were; he hath not
drunk ink: his intellect is not replenished; he is
only an animal, only sensible in the duller parts:

And such barren plants are set before us, that we
    thankful should be,

Which we of taste and feeling are, for those parts
    that do fructify in us more than he.   30

For as it would ill become me to be vain, indis-
    creet, or a fool,

So were there a patch set on learning, to see him
    in a school:

But *omne bene*, say I; being of an old father's
    mind,

Many can brook the weather that love not the
    wind.

Dull. You two are book-men: can you tell me
    by your wit

What was a month old at Cain's birth, that's not
    five weeks old as yet?

Hol. Dictynna, goodman Dull; Dictynna, goodman Dull.

Dull. What is Dictynna?

Nath. A title to Phœbe, to Luna, to the moon.

Hol. The moon was a month old when Adam
    was no more,   40

And raught not to five weeks when he came to
    five-score.

The allusion holds in the exchange.

Dull. 'Tis true indeed; the collusion holds in
    the exchange.

Hol. God comfort thy capacity! I say, the allusion holds in the exchange.

Dull. And I say, the pollusion holds in the exchange; for the moon is never but a month old:
and I say beside that, 'twas a pricket that the
Princess killed.

Hol. Sir Nathaniel, will you hear an extemporal
epitaph on the death of the deer? And, to humour
the ignorant, call I the deer the Princess killed a
pricket.

Nath. Perge, good Master Holofernes, *perge;* so
it shall please you to abrogate scurrility.

Hol. I will something affect the letter, for it
argues facility.

The preyful Princess pierced and prick'd a pretty
    pleasing pricket;
  Some say a sore; but not a sore, till now made
    sore with shooting.
The dogs did yell: put L to sore, then sorel jumps
    from thicket;   60
  Or pricket sore, or else sorel; the people fall
    a-hooting.
If sore be sore, then L to sore makes fifty sores
    one sorel.
Of one sore I an hundred make by adding but
    one more L.

Nath. A rare talent!

Dull. [*Aside*] If a talent be a claw, look how he
claws him with a talent.

Hol. This is a gift that I have, simple, simple; a
foolish extravagant spirit, full of forms, figures,
shapes, objects, ideas, apprehensions, motions,
revolutions: these are begot in the ventricle of
memory, nourished in the womb of *pia mater*, and
delivered upon the mellowing of occasion. But
the gift is good in those in whom it is acute, and I
am thankful for it.

Nath. Sir, I praise the Lord for you: and so may
my parishioners; for their sons are well tutored
by you, and their daughters profit very greatly
under you: you are a good member of the commonwealth.   79

Hol. Mehercle, if their sons be ingenuous, they
shall want no instruction; if their daughters be
capable, I will put it to them: but *vir sapit qui
pauca loquitur;* a soul feminine saluteth us.

Enter JAQUENETTA *and* COSTARD.

Jaq. God give you good morrow, master Parson.

Hol. Master Parson, *quasi* pers-on. An if one
should be pierced, which is the one?

Cost. Marry, master schoolmaster, he that is
likest to a hogshead.

Hol. Piercing a hogshead! a good lustre of conceit in a turf of earth; fire enough for a flint, pearl
enough for a swine: 'tis pretty; it is well.   90

Jaq. Good master Parson, be so good as read me
this letter: it was given me by Costard, and sent
me from Don Armado: I beseech you, read it.

*Hol. Fauste, precor gelida quando pecus omne sub
umbra Ruminat*—and so forth. Ah, good old
Mantuan! I may speak of thee as the traveller
doth of Venice;
    Venetia, Venetia,
    Chi non ti vede non ti pretia.   *100*
Old Mantuan, old Mantuan! who understandeth
thee not, loves thee not. *Ut, re, sol, la, mi, fa.*
Under pardon, sir, what are the contents? or
rather, as Horace says in his: What, my soul,
verses?

Nath. Ay, sir, and very learned.

Hol. Let me hear a staff, a stanze, a verse; *lege,
domine.*

Nath. [*reads*]
"If love make me forsworn, how shall I swear to
    love?
  Ah, never faith could hold, if not to beauty
    vow'd!   110
Though to myself forsworn, to thee I'll faithful
    prove;
  Those thoughts to me were oaks, to thee like
    osiers bow'd.
Study his bias leaves and makes his book thine
    eyes,
  Where all those pleasures live that art would
    comprehend:
If knowledge be the mark, to know thee shall
    suffice;
  Well learned is that tongue that well can thee
    commend,
All ignorant that soul that sees thee without
    wonder;
  Which is to me some praise that I thy parts
    admire:
Thy eye Jove's lightning bears, thy voice his
    dreadful thunder,
  Which, not to anger bent, is music and sweet
    fire.   120
Celestial as thou art, O, pardon love this wrong,
That sings heaven's praise with such an earthly
    tongue."

Hol. You find not the apostraphas, and so miss
the accent: let me supervise the canzonet. Here
are only numbers ratified; but, for the elegancy,
facility, and golden cadence of poesy, *caret.* Ovid-
ius Naso was the man: and why, indeed, Naso,
but for smelling out the odoriferous flowers of
fancy, the jerks of invention? *Imitari* is nothing:
so doth the hound his master, the ape his keeper,
the tired horse his rider. But, damosella virgin,
was this directed to you?

Jaq. Ay, sir, from one Monsieur Biron, one of
the strange queen's lords.

Hol. I will overglance the superscript: "To the
snow-white hand of the most beauteous Lady
Rosaline." I will look again on the intellect of the
letter, for the nomination of the party writing to
the person written unto: "Your ladyship's in all
desired employment, *Biron.*" Sir Nathaniel, this
Biron is one of the votaries with the king; and
here he hath framed a letter to a sequent of the
stranger queen's, which accidentally, or by the
way of progression, hath miscarried. Trip and
go, my sweet; deliver this paper into the royal
hand of the King: it may concern much. Stay
not thy compliment; I forgive thy duty: adieu.

Jaq. Good Costard, go with me. Sir, God save your life!   *150*

Cost. Have with thee, my girl.

[*Exeunt* COSTARD *and* JAQUENETTA.

Nath. Sir, you have done this in the fear of God, very religiously; and, as a certain father saith—

Hol. Sir, tell not me of the father; I do fear colourable colours. But to return to the verses: did they please you, Sir Nathaniel?

Nath. Marvellous well for the pen.

Hol. I do dine to-day at the father's of a certain pupil of mine; where, if, before repast, it shall please you to gratify the table with a grace, I will, on my privilege I have with the parents of the foresaid child or pupil, undertake your *ben venuto;* where I will prove those verses to be very unlearned, neither savouring of poetry, wit, nor invention: I beseech your society.

Nath. And thank you too; for society, saith the text, is the happiness of life.

Hol. And, certes, the text most infallibly concludes it. [*To* DULL] Sir, I do invite you too; you shall not say me nay: *pauca verba.* Away! the gentles are at their game, and we will to our recreation.   [*Exeunt.*

SCENE III. *The same*

Enter BIRON, *with a paper.*

Biron. The King he is hunting the deer; I am coursing myself: they have pitched a toil; I am toiling in a pitch—pitch that defiles: defile! a foul word. Well, set thee down, sorrow! for so they say the fool said, and so say I, and I the fool: well proved, wit! By the Lord, this love is as mad as Ajax: it kills sheep; it kills me, I a sheep; well proved again o' my side! I will not love: if I do, hang me; i' faith, I will not. O, but her eye—by this light, but for her eye, I would not love her; yes, for her two eyes. Well, I do nothing in the world but lie, and lie in my throat. By heaven, I do love: and it hath taught me to rhyme and to be melancholy; and here is part of my rhyme, and here my melancholy. Well, she hath one o' my sonnets already: the clown bore it, the fool sent it, and the lady hath it: sweet clown, sweeter fool, sweetest lady! By the world, I would not care a pin, if the other three were in. Here comes one with a paper: God give him grace to groan! [*Stands aside.*   *21*

Enter the KING, *with a paper.*

King. Ay me!

Biron. [*Aside*] Shot, by heaven! Proceed, sweet Cupid: thou hast thumped him with thy bird-bolt under the left pap. In faith, secrets!

King [*reads*].

"So sweet a kiss the golden sun gives not
  To those fresh morning drops upon the rose,
As thy eye-beams, when their fresh rays have smote
  The night of dew that on my cheeks down flows:
Nor shines the silver moon one half so bright   *30*
  Through the transparent bosom of the deep,
As doth thy face through tears of mine give light;
  Thou shinest in every tear that I do weep:
No drop but as a coach doth carry thee;
  So ridest thou triumphing in my woe.
Do but behold the tears that swell in me,
  And they thy glory through my grief will show;
But do not love thyself; then thou wilt keep
My tears for glasses, and still make me weep.
O queen of queens! how far dost thou excel,   *40*
No thought can think, nor tongue of mortal tell."

How shall she know my griefs? I'll drop the paper:

Sweet leaves, shade folly. Who is he comes here?
  Steps aside.

What, Longaville! and reading! listen, ear.

Biron. Now, in thy likeness, one more fool appear!

Enter LONGAVILLE, *with a paper.*

Long. Ay me, I am forsworn!

Biron. Why, he comes in like a perjure, wearing papers.

King. In love, I hope: sweet fellowship in shame!

Biron. One drunkard loves another of the name.   *50*

Long. Am I the first that have been perjured so?

Biron. I could put thee in comfort. Not by two that I know:

Thou makest the triumviry, the corner-cap of society,

The shape of Love's Tyburn that hangs up simplicity.

Long. I fear these stubborn lines lack power to move.

O sweet Maria, empress of my love!

These numbers will I tear, and write in prose.

Biron. O, rhymes are guards on wanton Cupid's hose:

Disfigure not his slop.

Long.   This same shall go. [*Reads*].

"Did not the heavenly rhetoric of thine eye,   *60*
  'Gainst whom the world cannot hold argument,
Persuade my heart to this false perjury?
  Vows for thee broke deserve not punishment.
A woman I forswore; but I will prove,
  Thou being a goddess, I forswore not thee:
My vow was earthly, thou a heavenly love;
  Thy grace being gain'd cures all disgrace in me.

Vows are but breath, and breath a vapour is:
  Then thou, fair sun, which on my earth dost
    shine,
Exhalest this vapour-vow; in thee it is: 70
  If broken then, it is no fault of mine:
If by me broke, what fool is not so wise
To lose an oath to win a paradise?"
  Biron. This is the liver-vein, which makes
    flesh a deity,
A green goose a goddess: pure, pure idolatry.
God amend us, God amend! we are much out o'
  the way.
  Long. By whom shall I send this?—Company!
    stay.   [*Steps aside.*
  Biron. All hid, all hid; an old infant play.
Like a demigod here sit I in the sky,
And wretched fools' secrets heedfully o'er-eye. 80
More sacks to the mill! O heavens, I have my
  wish!

      Enter DUMAIN, *with a paper.*

Dumain transform'd! four woodcocks in a dish!
  Dum. O most divine Kate!
  Biron. O most profane coxcomb!
  Dum. By heaven, the wonder in a mortal eye!
  Biron. By earth, she is not, corporal, there you
    lie.
  Dum. Her amber hair for foul hath amber
    quoted.
  Biron. An amber-colour'd raven was well noted.
  Dum. As upright as the cedar.
  Biron.   Stoop, I say;
Her shoulder is with child.
  Dum.   As fair as day.   90
  Biron. Ay, as some days; but then no sun
    must shine.
  Dum. O that I had my wish!
  Long.   And I had mine!
  King. And I mine too, good Lord!
  Biron. Amen, so I had mine: is not that a good
    word?
  Dum. I would forget her; but a fever she
Reigns in my blood and will remember'd be.
  Biron. A fever in your blood! why, then incis-
    ion
Would let her out in saucers: sweet misprision!
  Dum. Once more I'll read the ode that I have
    writ.
  Biron. Once more I'll mark how love can vary
    wit.   100
  Dum. [*reads*]
    "On a day—alack the day!—
      Love, whose month is ever May,
      Spied a blossom passing fair
      Playing in the wanton air:
      Through the velvet leaves the wind,

All unseen, can passage find;
  That the lover, sick to death,
  Wish himself the heaven's breath.
  Air, quoth he, thy cheeks may blow;
  Air, would I might triumph so!   110
  But, alack, my hand is sworn
  Ne'er to pluck thee from thy thorn;
  Vow, alack, for youth unmeet,
  Youth so apt to pluck a sweet!
  Do not call it sin in me,
  That I am forsworn for thee;
  Thou for whom Jove would swear
  Juno but an Ethiope were;
  And deny himself for Jove,
  Turning mortal for thy love."   120
This will I send and something else more plain,
That shall express my true love's fasting pain.
O, would the King, Biron, and Longaville,
Were lovers too! Ill, to example ill,
Would from my forehead wipe a perjured note;
For none offend where all alike do dote.
  Long. [*advancing*]. Dumain, thy love is far from
    charity,
That in love's grief desirest society:
You may look pale, but I should blush, I know,
To be o'erheard and taken napping so.   130
  King [*advancing*]. Come, sir, you blush; as his
    your case is such;
You chide at him, offending twice as much;
You do not love Maria; Longaville
Did never sonnet for her sake compile,
Nor never lay his wreathed arms athwart
His loving bosom to keep down his heart.
I have been closely shrouded in this bush
And mark'd you both and for you both did blush:
I heard your guilty rhymes, observed your fashion,
Saw sighs reek from you, noted well your passion:
"Ay me!" says one; "O Jove!" the other
  cries;   141
One, her hairs were gold, crystal the other's eyes:
[*To* LONGAVILLE] You would for paradise break
  faith and troth;
[*To* DUMAIN] And Jove, for your love, would in-
  fringe an oath.
What will Biron say when that he shall hear
Faith so infringed, which such zeal did swear?
How will he scorn! how will he spend his wit!
How will he triumph, leap, and laugh at it!
For all the wealth that ever I did see,
I would not have him know so much by me.   150
  Biron. Now step I forth to whip hypocrisy.
    Advancing.
Ah, good my liege, I pray thee, pardon me!
Good heart, what grace hast thou, thus to reprove
These worms for loving, that art most in love?
Your eyes do make no coaches; in your tears

There is no certain princess that appears;
You'll not be perjured, 'tis a hateful thing;
Tush, none but minstrels like of sonneting!
But are you not ashamed? nay, are you not,
All three of you, to be thus much o'ershot?   *160*
You found his mote; the King your mote did see;
But I a beam do find in each of three.
O, what a scene of foolery have I seen,
Of sighs, of groans, of sorrow, and of teen!
O me, with what strict patience have I sat,
To see a king transformed to a gnat!
To see great Hercules whipping a gig,
And profound Solomon to tune a jig,
And Nestor play at push-pin with the boys,
And critic Timon laugh at idle toys!   *170*
Where lies thy grief, O, tell me, good Dumain?
And, gentle Longaville, where lies thy pain?
And where my liege's? all about the breast:
A caudle, ho!
  King.   Too bitter is thy jest.
Are we betray'd thus to thy over-view?
  Biron. Not you to me, but I betray'd by you:
I, that am honest; I, that hold it sin
To break the vow I am engaged in;
I am betray'd, by keeping company
With men like men of inconstancy.   *180*
When shall you see me write a thing in rhyme?
Or groan for love? or spend a minute's time
In pruning me? When shall you hear that I
Will praise a hand, a foot, a face, an eye,
A gait, a state, a brow, a breast, a waist,
A leg, a limb?
  King.   Soft! whither away so fast?
A true man or a thief that gallops so?
  Biron. I post from love: good lover, let me go.

     Enter JAQUENETTA *and* COSTARD.

Jaq. God bless the King!
  King.   What present hast thou there?
Cost. Some certain treason.
  King.   What makes treason here?   *190*
Cost. Nay, it makes nothing, sir.
  King.   If it mar nothing neither,
The treason and you go in peace away together.
  Jaq. I beseech your Grace, let this letter be
    read:
Our parson misdoubts it; 'twas treason, he said.
  King. Biron, read it over.
    Giving him the paper.
Where hadst thou it?
  Jaq. Of Costard.
  King. Where hadst thou it?
Cost. Of Dun Adramadio, Dun Adramadio.
  Biron tears the letter.
  King. How now! what is in you? why dost
    thou tear it?   *200*

  Biron. A toy, my liege, a toy: your Grace
    needs not fear it.
  Long. It did move him to passion, and therefore
    let's hear it.
  Dum. It is Biron's writing, and here is his name.
    [*Gathering up the pieces.*]
  Biron. [*To* COSTARD] Ah, you whoreson logger-
    head! you were born to do me shame.
Guilty, my lord, guilty! I confess, I confess.
  King. What?
  Biron. That you three fools lack'd me fool to
    make up the mess:
He, he, and you, and you, my liege, and I,
Are pick-purses in love, and we deserve to die.
O, dismiss this audience, and I shall tell you more.
  Dum. Now the number is even.   *211*
  Biron.   True, true; we are four.
Will these turtles be gone?
  King.   Hence, sirs; away!
  Cost. Walk aside the true folk, and let the
    traitors stay.
        [*Exeunt* COSTARD *and* JAQUENETTA.
  Biron. Sweet lords, sweet lovers, O, let us em-
    brace!
As true we are as flesh and blood can be:
The sea will ebb and flow, heaven show his face;
Young blood doth not obey an old decree:
We cannot cross the cause why we were born;
Therefore of all hands must we be forsworn.
  King. What, did these rent lines show some
    love of thine?   *220*
  Biron. Did they, quoth you? Who sees the
    heavenly Rosaline,
That, like a rude and savage man of Ind,
  At the first opening of the gorgeous east,
Bows not his vassal head and strucken blind
  Kisses the base ground with obedient breast?
What peremptory eagle-sighted eye
  Dares look upon the heaven of her brow,
That is not blinded by her majesty?
  King. What zeal, what fury hath inspired thee
    now?
My love, her mistress, is a gracious moon;   *230*
  She an attending star, scarce seen a light.
  Biron. My eyes are then no eyes, nor I Biron:
  O, but for my love, day would turn to night!
Of all complexions the cull'd sovereignty
  Do meet, as at a fair, in her fair cheek,
Where several worthies make one dignity,
  Where nothing wants that want itself doth seek.
Lend me the flourish of all gentle tongues—
  Fie, painted rhetoric! O, she needs it not:
To things of sale a seller's praise belongs,   *240*
  She passes praise; then praise too short doth
    blot.
A wither'd hermit, five-score winters worn,

Might shake off fifty, looking in her eye:
Beauty doth varnish age, as if new-born,
  And gives the crutch the cradle's infancy:
O, 'tis the sun that maketh all things shine.
  King. By heaven, thy love is black as ebony.
  Biron. Is ebony like her? O wood divine!
A wife of such wood were felicity.
O, who can give an oath? where is a book?   250
  That I may swear beauty doth beauty lack,
If that she learn not of her eye to look:
  No face is fair that is not full so black.
  King. O paradox! Black is the badge of hell,
  The hue of dungeons, and the suit of night;
And beauty's crest becomes the heavens well.
  Biron. Devils soonest tempt, resembling spirits
    of light.
O, if in black my lady's brows be deck'd,
  It mourns that painting and usurping hair
Should ravish doters with a false aspect;   260
  And therefore is she born to make black fair.
Her favour turns the fashion of the days,
  For native blood is counted painting now;
And therefore red, that would avoid dispraise,
Paints itself black, to imitate her brow.
  Dum. To look like her are chimney-sweepers
    black.
  Long. And since her time are colliers counted
    bright.
  King. And Ethiopes of their sweet complexion
    crack.
  Dum. Dark needs no candles now, for dark is
    light.
  Biron. Your mistresses dare never come in rain,
  For fear their colours should be wash'd away,
  King. 'Twere good, yours did; for, sir, to tell
    you plain,
  I'll find a fairer face not wash'd to-day.
  Biron. I'll prove her fair, or talk till doomsday
    here.
  King. No devil will fright thee then so much as
    she.
  Dum. I never knew man hold vile stuff so dear.
  Long. Look, here's thy love: my foot and her
    face see.
  Biron. O, if the streets were paved with thine
    eyes,
Her feet were much too dainty for such tread!
  Dum. O vile! then, as she goes, what upward
    lies   280
The street should see as she walk'd overhead.
  King. But what of this? are we not all in love?
  Biron. Nothing so sure; and thereby all for-
    sworn.
  King. Then leave this chat; and, good Biron,
    now prove
Our loving lawful, and our faith not torn.

  Dum. Ay, marry, there; some flattery for this
    evil.
  Long. O, some authority how to proceed;
Some tricks, some quillets, how to cheat the devil.
  Dum. Some salve for perjury.
  Biron.   'Tis more than need.
Have at you, then, affection's men at arms.   290
Consider what you first did swear unto,
To fast, to study, and to see no woman;
Flat treason 'gainst the kingly state of youth.
Say, can you fast? your stomachs are too young;
And abstinence engenders maladies.
And where that you have vow'd to study, lords,
In that each of you have forsworn his book,
Can you still dream and pore and thereon look?
For when would you, my lord, or you, or you,
Have found the ground of study's excellence   300
Without the beauty of a woman's face?
[From women's eyes this doctrine I derive;
They are the ground, the books, the academes
From whence doth spring the true Promethean
  fire.]
Why, universal plodding poisons up
The nimble spirits in the arteries,
As motion and long-during action tires
The sinewy vigour of the traveller.
Now, for not looking on a woman's face,
You have in that forsworn the use of eyes   310
And study too, the causer of your vow;
For where is any author in the world
Teaches such beauty as a woman's eye?
Learning is but an adjunct to ourself
And where we are our learning likewise is:
Then when ourselves we see in ladies' eyes,
Do we not likewise see our learning there?
O, we have made a vow to study, lords,
And in that vow we have forsworn our books.
For when would you, my liege, or you, or you,
In leaden contemplation have found out   321
Such fiery numbers as the prompting eyes
Of beauty's tutors have enrich'd you with?
Other slow arts entirely keep the brain;
And therefore, finding barren practisers,
Scarce show a harvest of their heavy toil:
But love, first learned in a lady's eyes,
Lives not alone immured in the brain;
But, with the motion of all elements,
Courses as swift as thought in every power,   330
And gives to every power a double power,
Above their functions and their offices.
It adds a precious seeing to the eye;
A lover's eyes will gaze an eagle blind;
A lover's ear will hear the lowest sound,
When the suspicious head of theft is stopp'd:
Love's feeling is more soft and sensible
Than are the tender horns of cockled snails;

Love's tongue proves dainty Bacchus gross in
 taste:
For valour, is not Love a Hercules,   *340*
Still climbing trees in the Hesperides?
Subtle as Sphinx; as sweet and musical
As bright Apollo's lute, strung with his hair;
And when Love speaks, the voice of all the
 gods
Make heaven drowsy with the harmony.
Never durst poet touch a pen to write
Until his ink were temper'd with Love's sighs;
O, then his lines would ravish savage ears
And plant in tyrants mild humility.
From women's eyes this doctrine I derive: *350*
They sparkle still the right Promethean fire;
They are the books, the arts, the academes,
That show, contain and nourish all the world:
Else none at all in aught proves excellent.
Then fools you were these women to forswear,
Or keeping what is sworn, you will prove fools,
For wisdom's sake, a word that all men love,
Or for love's sake, a word that loves all men,
Or for men's sake, the authors of these women,
Or women's sake, by whom we men are men, *360*
Let us once lose our oaths to find ourselves,
Or else we lose ourselves to keep our oaths.
It is religion to be thus forsworn,
For charity itself fulfils the law,
And who can sever love from charity?
 King. Saint Cupid, then! and, soldiers, to the
 field!
 Biron. Advance your standards, and upon them,
 lords;
Pell-mell, down with them! but be first advised,
In conflict that you get the sun of them. *369*
 Long. Now to plain-dealing; lay these glozes by:
Shall we resolve to woo these girls of France?
 King. And win them too: therefore let us de-
 vise
Some entertainment for them in their tents.
 Biron. First, from the park let us conduct them
 thither;
Then homeward every man attach the hand
Of his fair mistress: in the afternoon
We will with some strange pastime solace them,
Such as the shortness of the time can shape;
For revels, dances, masks, and merry hours
Forerun fair Love, strewing her way with
 flowers.   *380*
 King. Away, away! no time shall be omitted
That will betime, and may by us be fitted.
 Biron. Allons! allons! Sow'd cockle reap'd no
 corn;
And justice always whirls in equal measure.
Light wenches may prove plagues to men for-
 sworn;

If so, our copper buys no better treasure.
           [*Exeunt.*

ACT V

SCENE I. *The same*

Enter HOLOFERNES, SIR NATHANIEL, *and*
DULL.

 Hol. Satis quod sufficit.
 Nath. I praise God for you, sir: your reasons
at dinner have been sharp and sententious;
pleasant without scurrility, witty without affection, audacious without impudency, learned
without opinion, and strange without heresy. I
did converse this *quondam* day with a companion
of the king's, who is intituled, nominated, or
called, Don Adriano de Armado.
 Hol. Novi hominem tanquam te: his humour is
lofty, his discourse peremptory, his tongue
filed, his eye ambitious, his gait majestical, and
his general behaviour vain, ridiculous, and
thrasonical. He is too picked, too spruce, too
affected, too odd, as it were, too peregrinate, as
I may call it.
 Nath. A most singular and choice epithet.
 Draws out his table-book.
 Hol. He draweth out the thread of his ver-
bosity finer than the staple of his argument. I
abhor such fanatical phantasimes, such insociable
and point-devise companions; such rackers of
orthography, as to speak *dout,* fine, when he
should say *doubt; det,* when he should pronounce
debt,—d, e, b, t, not d, e, t: he clepeth a calf, *cauf;*
half, *hauf;* neighbour *vocatur nebour;* neigh abbre-
viated *ne.* This is abhominable,—which he would
call abbominable: it insinuateth me of insanie:
anne intelligis, domine? to make frantic, lunatic.
 Nath. Laus Deo, bene intelligo.   *30*
 Hol. Bon, bon, fort bon! Priscian a little
scratched, 'twill serve.
 Nath. Videsne quis venit?
 Hol. Video, et gaudeo.

Enter ARMADO, MOTH, *and* COSTARD.

 Arm. [*To* MOTH]. Chirrah!
 Hol. Quare chirrah, not sirrah?
 Arm. Men of peace, well encountered.
 Hol. Most military sir, salutation.
 Moth. [*Aside to* COSTARD] They have been at a
great feast of languages, and stolen the scraps.
 Cost. O, they have lived long on the almsbasket
of words. I marvel thy master hath not eaten
thee for a word; for thou art not so long by the
head as *honorificabilitudinitatibus:* thou art easier
swallowed than a flap-dragon.
 Moth. Peace! the peal begins.

Arm. [*To* HOLOFERNES] Monsieur, are you not lettered?

Moth. Yes, yes; he teaches boys the hornbook. What is *a, b,* spelt backward, with the horn on his head?

Hol. Ba, pueritia, with a horn added.

Moth. Ba, most silly sheep with a horn. You hear his learning.

Hol. Quis, quis, thou consonant?

Moth. The third of the five vowels, if you repeat them; or the fifth, if I.

Hol. I will repeat them—*a, e, i,*—

Moth. The sheep: the other two concludes it,—*o, u.* 60

Arm. Now, by the salt wave of the Mediterraneum, a sweet touch, a quick venue of wit! snip, snap, quick, and home! it rejoiceth my intellect: true wit!

Moth. Offered by a child to an old man; which is wit-old.

Hol. What is the figure? what is the figure?

Moth. Horns.

Hol. Thou disputest like an infant: go, whip thy gig. 70

Moth. Lend me your horn to make one, and I will whip about your infamy *circum circa*—a gig of a cuckold's horn.

Cost. An I had but one penny in the world, thou shouldst have it to buy gingerbread: hold, there is the very remuneration I had of thy master, thou halfpenny purse of wit, thou pigeonegg of discretion. O, an the heavens were so pleased that thou wert but my bastard, what a joyful father wouldst thou make me! Go to; thou hast it *ad dunghill,* at the fingers' ends, as they say.

Hol. O, I smell false Latin; *dunghill* for *unguem.*

Arm. Arts-man, preambulate, we will be singuled from the barbarous. Do you not educate youth at the charge-house on the top of the mountain?

Hol. Or *mons,* the hill.

Arm. At your sweet pleasure, for the mountain.

Hol. I do, sans question. 91

Arm. Sir, it is the King's most sweet pleasure and affection to congratulate the Princess at her pavilion in the posteriors of this day, which the rude multitude call the afternoon.

Hol. The posterior of the day, most generous sir, is liable, congruent and measurable for the afternoon: the word is well culled, chose, sweet and apt, I do assure you, sir, I do assure. 99

Arm. Sir, the King is a noble gentleman, and my familiar, I do assure ye, very good friend: for what is inward between us, let it pass. I do beseech thee, remember thy courtesy; I beseech thee, apparel thy head: and among other important and most serious designs, and of great import indeed, too, but let that pass: for I must tell thee, it will please his Grace, by the world, sometime to lean upon my poor shoulder, and with his royal finger, thus, dally with my excrement, with my mustachio; but, sweet heart, let that pass. By the world, I recount no fable: some certain special honours it pleaseth my greatness to impart to Armado, a soldier, a man of travel, that hath seen the world; but let that pass. The very all of all is—but, sweet heart, I do implore secrecy—that the King would have me present the Princess, sweet chuck, with some delightful ostentation, or show, or pageant, or antique, or firework. Now, understanding that the curate and your sweet self are good at such eruptions and sudden breaking out of mirth, as it were, I have acquainted you withal, to the end to crave your assistance.

Hol. Sir, you shall present before her the Nine Worthies. Sir, as concerning some entertainment of time, some show in the posterior of this day, to be rendered by our assistants, at the King's command, and this most gallant, illustrate, and learned gentleman, before the Princess; I say none so fit as to present the Nine Worthies. 130

Nath. Where will you find men worthy enough to present them?

Hol. Joshua, yourself; myself and this gallant gentleman, Judas Maccabæus; this swain, because of his great limb or joint, shall pass Pompey the Great; the page, Hercules—

Arm. Pardon, sir; error: he is not quantity enough for that Worthy's thumb: he is not so big as the end of his club. 139

Hol. Shall I have audience? he shall present Hercules in minority: his enter and exit shall be strangling a snake; and I will have an apology for that purpose.

Moth. An excellent device! so, if any of the audience hiss, you may cry "Well done, Hercules! now thou crushest the snake!" That is the way to make an offence gracious, though few have the grace to do it.

Arm. For the rest of the Worthies?—

Hol. I will play three myself. 150

Moth. Thrice-worthy gentleman!

Arm. Shall I tell you a thing?

Hol. We attend.

Arm. We will have, if this fadge not, an antique. I beseech you, follow.

Hol. Via, goodman Dull! thou hast spoken no word all this while.

Dull. Nor understood none neither, sir.

Hol. Allons! we will employ thee.

Dull. I'll make one in a dance, or so; or I will
play 160
On the tabor to the Worthies, and let them dance
the hay.
Hol. Most dull, honest Dull! To our sport,
away! [*Exeunt.*

SCENE II. *The same*

Enter the PRINCESS, KATHARINE, ROSALINE, *and*
MARIA.

Prin. Sweet hearts, we shall be rich ere we de-
part,
If fairings come thus plentifully in:
A lady wall'd about with diamonds!
Look you what I have from the loving King.
Ros. Madame, came nothing else along with
that?
Prin. Nothing but this! yes, as much love in
rhyme
As would be cramm'd up in a sheet of paper,
Writ o' both sides the leaf, margent and all,
That he was fain to seal on Cupid's name.
Ros. That was the way to make his godhead
wax, 10
For he hath been five thousand years a boy.
Kath. Ay, and a shrewd unhappy gallows too.
Ros. You'll ne'er be friends with him; a'kill'd
your sister.
Kath. He made her melancholy, sad, and heavy;
And so she died: had she been light, like you,
Of such a merry, nimble, stirring spirit,
She might ha' been a grandam ere she died:
And so may you; for a light heart lives long.
Ros. What's your dark meaning, mouse, of this
light word?
Kath. A light condition in a beauty dark. 20
Ros. We need more light to find your meaning
out.
Kath. You'll mar the light by taking it in snuff;
Therefore I'll darkly end the argument.
Ros. Look, what you do, you do it still i' the
dark.
Kath. So do not you, for you are a light wench.
Ros. Indeed I weigh not you, and therefore light.
Kath. You weigh me not? O, that's you care not
for me.
Ros. Great reason; for "past cure is still past
care."
Prin. Well bandied both; a set of wit well
play'd.
But, Rosaline, you have a favour too: 30
Who sent it? and what is it?
Ros. I would you knew:
An if my face were but as fair as yours,
My favour were as great; be witness this.
Nay, I have verses too, I thank Biron:

The numbers true; and, were the numbering too,
I were the fairest goddess on the ground:
I am compared to twenty thousand fairs.
O, he hath drawn my picture in his letter!
Prin. Any thing like?
Ros. Much in the letters; nothing in the praise.
Prin. Beauteous as ink; a good conclusion. 41
Kath. Fair as a text *B* in a copy-book.
Ros. 'Ware pencils, ho! let me not die your
debtor,
My red dominical, my golden letter:
O that your face were not so full of O's!
Kath. A pox of that jest! and I beshrew all
shrows.
Prin. But, Katherine, what was sent to you from
fair Dumain?
Kath. Madam, this glove.
Prin. Did he not send you twain?
Kath. Yes, madam, and moreover
Some thousand verses of a faithful lover, 50
A huge translation of hypocrisy,
Vilely compiled, profound simplicity.
Mar. This and these pearls to me sent Lon-
gaville:
The letter is too long by half a mile.
Prin. I think no less. Dost thou not wish in
heart
The chain were longer and the letter short?
Mar. Ay, or I would these hands might never
part.
Prin. We are wise girls to mock our lovers so.
Ros. They are worse fools to purchase mocking
so.
That same Biron I'll torture ere I go: 60
O that I knew he were but in by the week!
How I would make him fawn and beg and seek
And wait the season and observe the times
And spend his prodigal wits in bootless rhymes
And shape his service wholly to my hests
And make him proud to make me proud that
jests!
So perttaunt-like would I o'ersway his state
That he should be my fool and I his fate.
Prin. None are so surely caught, when they are
catch'd,
As wit turn'd fool: folly, in wisdom hatch'd, 70
Hath wisdom's warrant and the help of school
And wit's own grace to grace a learned fool.
Ros. The blood of youth burns not with such
excess
As gravity's revolt to wantonness.
Mar. Folly in fools bears not so strong a note
As foolery in the wise, when wit doth dote;
Since all the power thereof it doth apply
To prove, by wit, worth in simplicity.
Prin. Here comes Boyet, and mirth is in his face.

Enter BOYET

Boyet. O, I am stabb'd with laughter! Where's
   her Grace? 80
Prin. Thy news, Boyet?
Boyet.   Prepare, madam, prepare!
Arm, wenches, arm! encounters mounted are
Against your peace: Love doth approach dis-
   guised,
Armed in arguments; you'll be surprised:
Muster your wits; stand in your own defence;
Or hide your heads like cowards, and fly hence.
   Prin. Saint Denis to Saint Cupid! What are they
That charge their breath against us? say, scout,
   say.
   Boyet. Under the cool shade of a sycamore
I thought to close mine eyes some half an hour;
When, lo! to interrupt my purposed rest, 91
Toward that shade I might behold addrest
The King and his companions: warily
I stole into a neighbour thicket by,
And overheard what you shall overhear;
That, by and by, disguised they will be here.
Their herald is a pretty knavish page,
That well by heart hath conn'd his embassage:
Action and accent did they teach him there;
"Thus must thou speak," and "thus thy body
   bear":
And ever and anon they made a doubt 101
Presence majestical would put him out;
"For," quoth the King, "an angel shalt thou see;
Yet fear not thou, but speak audaciously."
The boy replied, "An angel is not evil;
I should have fear'd her had she been a devil."
With that, all laugh'd and clapp'd him on the
   shoulder,
Making the bold wag by their praises bolder:
One rubb'd his elbows thus, and fleer'd, and
   swore
A better speech was never spoke before; 110
Another, with his finger and his thumb,
Cried, "*Via!* we will do't, come what will come";
The third he caper'd, and cried, "All goes well";
The fourth turn'd on the toe, and down he fell.
With that, they all did tumble on the ground,
With such a zealous laughter, so profound,
That in this spleen ridiculous appears,
To check their folly, passion's solemn tears.
   Prin. But what, but what, come they to visit us?
   Boyet. They do, they do; and are apparell'd
   thus, 120
Like Muscovites or Russians as I guess.
Their purpose is to parle, to court and dance;
And every one his love-feat will advance
Unto his several mistress, which they'll know
By favours several which they did bestow.

   Prin. And will they so? the gallants shall be
   task'd;
For, ladies, we will every one be mask'd;
And not a man of them shall have the grace,
Despite of suit, to see a lady's face.
Hold, Rosaline, this favour thou shalt wear, *130*
And then the King will court thee for his dear;
Hold, take thou this, my sweet, and give me
   thine,
So shall Biron take me for Rosaline.
And change you favours too; so shall your loves
Woo contrary, deceived by these removes.
   Ros. Come on, then; wear the favours most in
   sight.
   Kath. But in this changing what is your intent?
   Prin. The effect of my intent is to cross theirs:
They do it but in mocking merriment;
And mock for mock is only my intent. *140*
Their several counsels they unbosom shall
To loves mistook, and so be mock'd withal
Upon the next occasion that we meet,
With visages display'd, to talk and greet.
   Ros. But shall we dance, if they desire us to't?
   Prin. No, to the death, we will not move a
   foot;
Nor to their penn'd speech render we no grace,
But while 'tis spoke each turn away her face.
   Boyet. Why, that contempt will kill the speak-
   er's heart,
And quite divorce his memory from his part. *150*
   Prin. Therefore I do it; and I make no doubt
The rest will ne'er come in, if he be out.
There's no such sport as sport by sport o'er-
   thrown,
To make theirs ours and ours none but our own:
So shall we stay, mocking intended game,
And they, well mock'd, depart away with shame.
   Trumpets sound within.
   Boyet. The trumpet sounds: be mask'd; the
   maskers come. [*The* LADIES *mask.*]

Enter Blackamoors with music; MOTH; *the* KING
   BIRON, LONGAVILLE, *and* DUMAIN, *in Russian
   habits, and masked.*

   Moth. All hail, the richest beauties on the
   earth!—
   Boyet. Beauties no richer than rich taffeta.
   Moth. A holy parcel of the fairest dames *160*
      [*The* LADIES *turn their backs to him.*
That ever turn'd their—backs—to mortal views!
   Biron. [*Aside to* MOTH] Their eyes, villain, their
   eyes.
   Moth. That ever turn'd their eyes to mortal
   views!—
Out—
   Boyet. True; out indeed.

Moth. Out of your favours, heavenly spirits, vouchsafe

Not to behold—

Biron. [*Aside to* MOTH] Once to behold, rogue.

Moth. Once to behold with your sun-beamed eyes,

—with your sun-beamed eyes—   *169*

Boyet. They will not answer to that epithet;

You were best call it "daughter-beamed eyes."

Moth. They do not mark me, and that brings me out.

Biron. Is this your perfectness? be gone, you rogue!   [*Exit* MOTH.

Ros. What would these strangers? know their minds, Boyet:

If they do speak our language, 'tis our will

That some plain man recount their purposes:

Know what they would.

Boyet. What would you with the Princess?

Biron. Nothing but peace and gentle visitation.

Ros. What would they, say they?   *180*

Boyet. Nothing but peace and gentle visitation.

Ros. Why, that they have; and bid them so be gone.

Boyet. She says, you have it, and you may be gone.

King. Say to her, we have measured many miles

To tread a measure with her on this grass.

Boyet. They say that they have measured many a mile

To tread a measure with you on this grass.

Ros. It is not so. Ask them how many inches

Is in one mile: if they have measured many,

The measure then of one is easily told.   *190*

Boyet. If to come hither you have measured miles,

And many miles, the Princess bids you tell

How many inches doth fill up one mile.

Biron. Tell her, we measure them by weary steps.

Boyet. She hears herself.

Ros.   How many weary steps,

Of many weary miles you have o'ergone,

Are number'd in the travel of one mile?

Biron. We number nothing that we spend for you:

Our duty is so rich, so infinite,

That we may do it still without accompt.   *200*

Vouchsafe to show the sunshine of your face,

That we, like savages, may worship it.

Ros. My face is but a moon, and clouded too.

King. Blessed are clouds, to do as such clouds do!

Vouchsafe, bright moon, and these thy stars, to shine,

Those clouds removed, upon our watery eyne.

Ros. O vain petitioner! beg a greater matter;

Thou now request'st but moonshine in the water.

King. Then, in our measure do but vouchsafe one change.

Thou bid'st me beg: this begging is not strange.

Ros. Play, music, then! Nay, you must do it soon. [*Music plays.*]   *211*

Not yet! no dance! Thus change I like the moon.

King. Will you not dance? How come you thus estranged?

Ros. You took the moon at full, but now she's changed.

King. Yet still she is the moon, and I the man.

The music plays; vouchsafe some motion to it.

Ros. Our ears vouchsafe it.

King.   But your legs should do it.

Ros. Since you are strangers and come here by chance,

We'll not be nice: take hands. We will not dance.

King. Why take we hands, then?

Ros.   Only to part friends: *220*

Curtsy, sweet hearts; and so the measure ends.

King. More measure of this measure; be not nice.

Ros. We can afford no more at such a price.

King. Prize you yourselves: what buys your company?

Ros. Your absence only.

King.   That can never be.

Ros. Then cannot we be bought: and so, adieu;

Twice to your visor, and half once to you.

King. If you deny to dance, let's hold more chat.

Ros. In private, then.

King.   I am best pleased with that.

They converse apart.

Biron. White-handed mistress, one sweet word with three.   *230*

Prin. Honey, and milk, and sugar; there is three.

Biron. Nay then, two treys, and if you grow so nice,

Metheglin, wort, and malmsey: well run, dice!

There's half-a-dozen sweets.

Prin.   Seventh sweet, adieu;

Since you can cog, I'll play no more with you.

Biron. One word in secret.

Prin.   Let it not be sweet.

Biron. Thou grievest my gall.

Prin.   Gall! bitter.

Biron   Therefore meet.

They converse apart.

Dum. Will you vouchsafe with me to change a word?

Mar. Name it.

Dum.   Fair lady—

Mar.   Say you so? Fair lord—

Take that for your fair lady.

Dum.   Please it you,   *240*
As much in private, and I'll bid adieu.

    They converse apart.

Kath. What, was your vizard made without a .
    tongue?

Long. I know the reason, lady, why you ask.

Kath. O for your reason! quickly, sir; I long.

Long. You have a double tongue within your
    mask,
And would afford my speechless vizard half.

Kath. "Veal," quoth the Dutchman. Is not
    "veal" a calf?

Long. A calf, fair lady!

Kath.   No, a fair lord calf.

Long. Let's part the word.

Kath.   No, I'll not be your half:
Take all, and wean it; it may prove an ox.   *250*

Long. Look, how you butt yourself in these
    sharp mocks!
Will you give horns, chaste lady? do not so.

Kath. Then die a calf, before your horns do
    grow.

Long. One word in private with you, ere I die.

Kath. Bleat softly then; the butcher hears you
    cry.

    They converse apart.

Boyet. The tongues of mocking wenches are as
    keen
    As is the razor's edge invisible,
Cutting a smaller hair than may be seen,
    Above the sense of sense; so sensible
Seemeth their conference; their conceits have
    wings   *260*
Fleeter than arrows, bullets, wind, thought,
    swifter things.

Ros. Not one word more, my maids; break off,
    break off.

Biron. By heaven, all dry-beaten with pure
    scoff!

King. Farewell, mad wenches; you have simple
    wits.

Prin. Twenty adieus, my frozen Muscovits.

    [*Exeunt* KING, LORDS, *and Blackamoors.*
Are these the breed of wits so wonder'd at?

Boyet. Tapers they are, with your sweet
    breaths puff'd out.

Ros. Well-liking wits they have; gross, gross;
    fat, fat.

Prin. O poverty in wit, kingly-poor flout!
Will they not, think you, hang themselves to-
    night?   *270*
    Or ever, but in vizards, show their faces?
This pert Biron was out of countenance quite.

Ros. O, they were all in lamentable cases!
The King was weeping-ripe for a good word.

Prin. Biron did swear himself out of all suit.

Mar. Dumain was at my service, and his sword:
"No point," quoth I; my servant straight was
    mute.

Kath. Lord Longaville said I came o'er his
    heart;
And trow you what he call'd me?

Prin   Qualm, perhaps.

Kath. Yes, in good faith.

Prin.   Go, sickness as thou art!   *280*

Ros. Well, better wits have worn plain statute-
    caps.
But will you hear? the King is my love sworn.

Prin. And quick Biron hath plighted faith to
    me.

Kath. And Longaville was for my service born.

Mar. Dumain is mine, as sure as bark on tree.

Boyet. Madam, and pretty mistresses, give ear:
Immediately they will again be here
In their own shapes; for it can never be
They will digest this harsh indignity.

Prin. Will they return?

Boyet. They will, they will, God knows,   *290*
And leap for joy, though they are lame with
    blows:
Therefore change favours; and, when they re-
    pair,
Blow like sweet roses in this summer air.

Prin. How blow? how blow? speak to be under-
    stood.

Boyet. Fair ladies mask'd are roses in their bud;
Dismask'd, their damask sweet commixture
    shown,
Are angels vailing clouds, or roses blown.

Prin. Avaunt, perplexity! What shall we do,
If they return in their own shapes to woo?

Ros. Good madam, if by me you'll be advised,
Let's mock them still, as well known as disguised:
Let us complain to them what fools were here,
Disguised like Muscovites, in shapeless gear;
And wonder what they were and to what end
Their shallow shows and prologue vilely penn'd
And their rough carriage so ridiculous,
Should be presented at our tent to us.

Boyet. Ladies, withdraw: the gallants are at
    hand.

Prin. Whip to our tents, as roes run o'er land.

    [*Exeunt* PRINCESS, ROSALINE, KATHARINE, *and*
                                       MARIA.

    Re-enter the KING, BIRON, LONGAVILLE, *and*
            DUMAIN, *in their proper habits.*

King. Fair sir, God save you! Where's the
    Princess?   *310*

Boyet. Gone to her tent. Please it your Majesty
Command me any service to her thither?

King. That she vouchsafe me audience for one
   word.
Boyet. I will; and so will she, I know, my lord.
                              [*Exit.*
Biron. This fellow pecks up wit as pigeons
   pease,
And utters it again when God doth please:
He is wit's pedler, and retails his wares
At wakes and wassails, meetings, markets, fairs;
And we that sell by gross, the Lord doth know,
Have not the grace to grace it with such show.
This gallant pins the wenches on his sleeve;   *321*
Had he been Adam, he had tempted Eve;
A' can carve too, and lisp: why, this is he
That kiss'd his hand away in courtesy;
This is the ape of form, monsieur the nice,
That, when he plays at tables, chides the dice
In honourable terms: nay, he can sing
A mean most meanly; and in ushering
Mend him who can: the ladies call him sweet;
The stairs, as he treads on them, kiss his feet;
This is the flower that smiles on every one,   *331*
To show his teeth as white as whale's bone;
And consciences, that will not die in debt,
Pay him the due of honey-tongued Boyet.
  King. A blister on his sweet tongue, with my -
   heart,
That put Armado's page out of his part!
Biron. See where it comes! Behaviour, what
   wert thou
Till this madman show'd thee? and what art thou
   now?

Re-enter the PRINCESS, *ushered by* BOYET; ROSA-
     LINE, MARIA, *and* KATHARINE.

  King. All hail, sweet madam, and fair time of
   day!   *339*
Prin. "Fair" in "all hail" is foul, as I conceive.
King. Construe my speeches better, if you may.
Prin. Then wish me better; I will give you leave.
King. We came to visit you, and purpose now
To lead you to our court; vouchsafe it then.
  Prin. This field shall hold me; and so hold your
   vow:
Nor God, nor I, delights in perjured men.
  King. Rebuke me not for that which you pro-
   voke:
The virtue of your eye must break my oath.
  Prin. You nickname virtue; vice you should
   have spoke;
For virtue's office never breaks men's troth.
Now by maiden honour, yet as pure   *351*
   As the unsullied lily, I protest,
A world of torments though I should endure,
   I would not yield to be your house's guest;
So much I hate a breaking cause to be

Of heavenly oaths, vow'd with integrity.
  King. O, you have lived in desolation here,
   Unseen, unvisited, much to our shame.
  Prin. Not so, my lord; it is not so, I swear;
   We have had pastimes here and pleasant
     game:
A mess of Russians left us but of late.   *361*
  King. How, madam! Russians!
  Prin.   Ay, in truth, my lord;
Trim gallants, full of courtship and of state.
  Ros. Madam, speak true. It is not so, my lord:
My lady, to the manner of the days,
In courtesy gives undeserving praise.
We four indeed confronted were with four
In Russian habit: here they stay'd an hour,
And talk'd apace; and in that hour, my lord,
They did not bless us with one happy word.   *370*
I dare not call them fools; but this I think,
When they are thirsty, fools would fain have
   drink.
  Biron. This jest is dry to me. Fair gentle sweet,
Your wit makes wise things foolish: when we
   greet,
With eyes best seeing, heaven's fiery eye,
By light we lose light: your capacity
Is of that nature that to your huge store
Wise things seem foolish and rich things but
   poor.
  Ros. This proves you wise and rich, for in my
   eye—
  Biron. I am a fool, and full of poverty.   *380*
  Ros. But that you take what doth to you belong,
It were a fault to snatch words from my tongue.
  Biron. O, I am yours, and all that I possess!
  Ros. All the fool mine?
  Biron.   I cannot give you less.
  Ros. Which of the vizards was it that you wore?
  Biron. Where? when? what vizard? why de-
   mand you this?
  Ros. There, then, that vizard; that superfluous
   case
That hid the worse and show'd the better face.
  King. We are descried; they'll mock us now
   downright.
  Dum. Let us confess and turn it to a jest.
  Prin. Amazed, my lord? why looks your High-
   ness sad?   *391*
  Ros. Help, hold his brows! he'll swoon! Why
   look you pale?
Sea-sick, I think, coming from Muscovy.
  Biron. Thus pour the stars down plagues for
   perjury.
Can any face of brass hold longer out?
Here stand I: lady, dart thy skill at me;
   Bruise me with scorn, confound me with a
    flout;

Thrust thy sharp wit quite through my igno-
    rance;
    Cut me to pieces with thy keen conceit;
And I will wish thee never more to dance,   *400*
    Nor never more in Russian habit wait.
O, never will I trust to speeches penn'd,
    Nor to the motion of a schoolboy's tongue,
Nor never come in vizard to my friend,
    Nor woo in rhyme, like a blind harper's song!
Taffeta phrases, silken terms precise,
    Three-piled hyperboles, spruce affectation,
Figures pedantical; these summer-flies
    Have blown me full of maggot ostentation:
I do forswear them; and I here protest,   *410*
    By this white glove—how white the hand,
      God knows!—
Henceforth my wooing mind shall be express'd
    In russet yeas and honest kersey noes:
And, to begin, wench—so God help me, la!—
My love to thee is sound, sans crack or flaw.
  Ros. Sans sans, I pray you.
  Biron.   Yet I have a trick
Of the old rage: bear with me, I am sick;
I'll leave it by degrees. Soft, let us see:
Write, "Lord have mercy on us" on those three;
They are infected; in their hearts it lies;   *420*
They have the plague, and caught it of your eyes;
These lords are visited; you are not free,
For the Lord's tokens on you do I see.
  Prin. No, they are free that gave these tokens to
    us.
  Biron. Our states are forfeit: seek not to undo
    us.
  Ros. It is not so; for how can this be true,
That you stand forfeit, being those that sue?
  Biron. Peace! for I will not have to do with you.
  Ros. Nor shall not, if I do as I intend.
  Biron. Speak for yourselves; my wit is at an
    end.   *430*
  King. Teach us, sweet madam, for our rude
    transgression
Some fair excuse.
  Prin.   The fairest is confession.
Were not you here but even now disguised?
  King. Madam, I was.
  Prin.   And were you well advised?
  King. I was, fair madam.
  Prin.   When you then were here,
What did you whisper in your lady's ear?
  King. That more than all the world I did re-
    spect her.
  Prin. When she shall challenge this, you will
    reject her.
  King. Upon mine honour, no.
  Prin.   Peace, peace! forbear:
Your oath once broke, you force not to forswear.

  King. Despise me, when I break this oath of
    mine.   *441*
  Prin. I will: and therefore keep it. Rosaline,
What did the Russian whisper in your ear?
  Ros. Madam, he swore that he did hold me dear
As precious eyesight, and did value me
Above this world; adding thereto moreover
That he would wed me, or else die my lover.
  Prin. God give thee joy of him! the noble lord
Most honourably doth uphold his word.
  King. What mean you, madam? by my life, my
    troth,   *450*
I never swore this lady such an oath.
  Ros. By heaven, you did; and to confirm it plain,
You gave me this: but take it, sir, again.
  King. My faith and this the Princess I did give:
I knew her by this jewel on her sleeve.
  Prin. Pardon me, sir, this jewel did she wear;
And Lord Biron, I thank him, is my dear.
What, will you have me, or your pearl again?
  Biron. Neither of either; I remit both twain.
I see the trick on't: here was a consent,   *460*
Knowing aforehand of our merriment,
To dash it like a Christmas comedy:
Some carry-tale, some please-man, some slight
    zany,
Some mumble-news, some trencher-knight, some
    Dick,
That smiles his cheek in years and knows the
    trick
To make my lady laugh when she's disposed,
Told our intents before; which once disclosed,
The ladies did change favours; and then we,
Following the signs, woo'd but the sign of she.
Now, to our perjury to add more terror,   *470*
We are again forsworn, in will and error.
Much upon this it is: and might not you
    To BOYET.
Forestall our sport, to make us thus untrue?
Do not you know my lady's foot by the squire,
    And laugh upon the apple of her eye?
And stand between her back, sir, and the fire,
    Holding a trencher, jesting merrily?
You put our page out: go, you are allow'd;
Die when you will, a smock shall be your shroud.
You leer upon me, do you? there's an eye   *480*
Wounds like a leaden sword.
  Boyet.   Full merrily
Hath this brave manage, this career, been run.
  Biron. Lo, he is tilting straight! Peace! I have
    done.

             Enter COSTARD.

Welcome, pure wit! thou partest a fair fray.
  Cost. O Lord, sir, they would know
Whether the three Worthies shall come in or no.

Biron. What, are there but three?

Cost.   No, sir; but it is vara fine,
For every one pursents three.

Biron.   And three times thrice is nine.

Cost. Not so, sir; under correction, sir; I hope it
is not so.

You cannot beg us, sir, I can assure you, sir; we
     know what we know: 490
I hope, sir, three times thrice, sir—

Biron. Is not nine.

Cost. Under correction, sir, we know whereuntil it doth amount.

Biron. By Jove, I always took three threes for
nine.

Cost. O Lord, sir, it were pity you should get
your living by reckoning, sir.

Biron. How much is it?   499

Cost. O Lord, sir, the parties themselves, the
actors, sir, will show whereuntil it doth amount:
for mine own part, I am, as they say, but to
parfect one man in one poor man, Pompion the
Great, sir.

Biron. Art thou one of the Worthies?

Cost. It pleased them to think me worthy of
Pompion the Great: for mine own part, I know
not the degree of the Worthy, but I am to stand
for him.

Biron. Go, bid them prepare.   510

Cost. We will turn it finely off, sir; we will take
some care.   [*Exit.*

King. Biron, they will shame us: let them not
approach.

Biron. We are shame-proof, my lord: and 'tis
some policy

To have one show worse than the King's and his
company.

King. I say they shall not come.

Prin. Nay, my good lord, let me o'errule you
now:

That sport best pleases that doth least know how:
Where zeal strives to content, and the contents
Dies in the zeal of that which it presents:
Their form confounded makes most form in
     mirth,   520
When great things labouring perish in their birth.

Biron. A right description of our sport, my
lord.

Enter ARMADO.

Arm. Anointed, I implore so much expense of
thy royal sweet breath as will utter a brace of
words.

     Converses apart with the KING, *and delivers him*
     a paper.

Prin. Doth this man serve God?

Biron. Why ask you?

Prin. He speaks not like a man of God's making.

Arm. That is all one, my fair, sweet, honey
monarch; for, I protest, the schoolmaster is exceeding fantastical; too too vain, too too vain:
but we will put it, as they say, to *fortuna dela
guerra.* I wish you the peace of mind, most royal
couplement!   [*Exit.*

King. Here is like to be a good presence of
Worthies. He presents Hector of Troy; the
swain, Pompey the Great; the parish curate,
Alexander; Armado's page, Hercules; the ped-
ant, Judas Maccabæus: 540
And if these four Worthies in their first show
     thrive
These four will change habits, and present the
     other five.

Biron. There is five in the first show.

King. You are deceived; 'tis not so.

Biron. The pedant, the braggart, the hedge-
priest, the fool and the boy:
Abate throw at novum, and the whole world
     again
Cannot pick out five such, take each one in his
     vein.

King. The ship is under sail, and here she comes
amain.

Enter COSTARD, *for Pompey.*

Cost. "I Pompey am"—

Boyet.   You lie, you are not he.   550

Cost. "I Pompey am"—

Boyet.   With libbard's head on knee.

Biron. Well said, old mocker: I must needs be
friends with thee.

Cost. "I Pompey am, Pompey surnamed the
Big"—

Dum. The Great.

Cost. It is, "Great," sir:—

         "Pompey surnamed the Great;
That oft in field, with targe and shield, did make
     my foe to sweat:
And travelling along this coast, I here am come
     by chance,
And lay my arms before the legs of this sweet
     lass of France."
If your ladyship would say, "Thanks, Pompey,"
     I had done.

Prin. Great thanks, great Pompey.   560

Cost. 'Tis not so much worth; but I hope I was
perfect: I made a little fault in "Great."

Biron. My hat to a halfpenny, Pompey proves
the best Worthy.

Enter SIR NATHANIEL, *for Alexander.*

Nath. "When in the world I lived, I was the
     world's commander;

By east, west, north, and south, I spread my
  conquering might:
My scutcheon plain declares that I am Alisan-
  der"—
Boyet. Your nose says, no, you are not; for it
  stands too right.
Biron. Your nose smells "no" in this, most
  tender-smelling knight.
Prin. The conqueror is dismay'd. Proceed, good
  Alexander.   570
Nath. "When in the world I lived, I was the
  world's commander"—
Boyet. Most true, 'tis right; you were so, Ali-
  sander.
Biron. Pompey the Great—
Cost. Your servant, and Costard.
Biron. Take away the conqueror, take away
Alisander.
Cost. [*To* SIR NATHANIEL] O, sir, you have overthrown Alisander the conqueror! You will be
scraped out of the painted cloth for this: your
lion, that holds his poll-axe sitting on a close-
stool, will be given to Ajax: he will be the ninth
Worthy. A conqueror, and afeard to speak! run
away for shame, Alisander. [SIR NATHANIEL *retires.*] There, an't shall please you; a foolish mild
man; an honest man, look you, and soon dashed.
He is a marvellous good neighbour, faith, and a
very good bowler: but, for Alisander—alas, you
see how 'tis—a little o'erparted. But there are
Worthies a-coming will speak their mind in some
other sort.   590
Prin. Stand aside, good Pompey.

Enter HOLOFERNES, *for Judas; and* MOTH,
  for Hercules.

Hol. "Great Hercules is presented by this imp,
  Whose club kill'd Cerberus, that three-
  headed *canus*;
  And when he was a babe, a child, a shrimp,
  Thus did he strangle serpents in his *manus*.
Quoniam he seemeth in minority,
Ergo I come with this apology."
Keep some state in thy exit, and vanish.
                              [MOTH *retires.*
"Judas I am"—
Dum. A Judas!   600
Hol. Not Iscariot, sir.
  "Judas I am, ycliped Maccabæus."
Dum. Judas Maccabæus clipt is plain Judas.
Biron. A kissing traitor. How art thou proved
Judas?
Hol. "Judas I am"—
Dum. The more shame for you, Judas.
Hol. What mean you, sir?
Boyet. To make Judas hang himself.

Hol. Begin, sir; you are my elder.
Biron. Well followed: Judas was hanged on an
  elder.   610
Hol. I will not be put out of countenance.
Biron. Because thou hast no face.
Hol. What is this?
Boyet. A cittern-head.
Dum. The head of a bodkin.
Biron. A Death's face in a ring.
Long. The face of an old Roman coin, scarce
  seen.
Boyet. The pommel of Cæsar's falchion.
Dum. The carved-bone face on a flask.
Biron. Saint George's half-cheek in a brooch.
Dum. Ay, and in a brooch of lead.   621
Biron. Ay, and worn in the cap of a tooth-
  drawer.
And now forward; for we have put thee in coun-
  tenance.
Hol. You have put me out of countenance.
Biron. False; we have given thee faces.
Hol. But you have out-faced them all.
Biron. An thou wert a lion, we would do so.
Boyet. Therefore, as he is an ass, let him go.
And so adieu, sweet Jude! nay, why dost thou
  stay?
Dum. For the latter end of his name.   630
Biron. For the ass to the Jude; give it him:
  Jud-as, away!
Hol. This is not generous, not gentle, not
  humble.
Boyet. A light for Monsieur Judas! it grows
  dark, he may stumble.   [HOLOFERNES *retires.*
Prin. Alas, poor Maccabæus, how hath he been
  baited!

Enter ARMADO, *for Hector.*

Biron. Hide thy head, Achilles: here comes
Hector in arms.
Dum. Though my mocks come home by me, I
will now be merry.
King. Hector was but a Troyan in respect of
this.   640
Boyet. But is this Hector?
King. I think Hector was not so clean-timbered.
Long. His leg is too big for Hector's.
Dum. More calf, certain.
Boyet. No; he is best indued in the small.
Biron. This cannot be Hector.
Dum. He's a god or a painter; for he makes
faces.
Arm. "The armipotent Mars, of lances the
  almighty,   650
Gave Hector a gift"—
Dum. A gilt nutmeg.
Biron. A lemon.

Long. Stuck with cloves.

Dum. No, cloven.

Arm. Peace!—

"The armipotent Mars, of lances the almighty,
    Gave Hector a gift, the heir of Ilion;
A man so breathed, that certain he would fight,
    yea
    From morn till night, out of his pavilion. 660
I am that flower"—

Dum.   That mint.

Long.   That columbine.

Arm. Sweet Lord Longaville, rein thy tongue.

Long. I must rather give it the rein, for it runs
against Hector.

Dum. Ay, and Hector's a greyhound.

Arm. The sweet war-man is dead and rotten;
sweet chucks, beat not the bones of the buried;
when he breathed, he was a man. But I will
forward with my device. [*To the* PRINCESS] Sweet
royalty, bestow on me the sense of hearing. 670

Prin. Speak, brave Hector: we are much de-
lighted.

Arm. I do adore thy sweet grace's slipper.

Boyet. [*Aside to* DUMAIN] Loves her by the foot.

Dum. [*Aside to* BOYET] He may not by the yard.

Arm. "This Hector far surmounted Hannibal"—

Cost. The party is gone, fellow Hector, she is
gone; she is two months on her way.

Arm. What meanest thou?   680

Cost. Faith, unless you play the honest Troyan,
the poor wench is cast away: she's quick; the
child brags in her belly already: 'tis yours.

Arm. Dost thou infamonize me among potentates? thou shalt die.

Cost. Then shall Hector be whipped for Jaquenetta that is quick by him and hanged for Pompey
that is dead by him.

Dum. Most rare Pompey!

Boyet. Renowned Pompey!   690

Biron. Greater than great, great, great, great
Pompey! Pompey the Huge!

Dum. Hector trembles.

Biron. Pompey is moved. More Ates, more
Ates! stir them on! stir them on!

Dum. Hector will challenge him.

Biron. Ay, if a' have no more man's blood in's
belly than will sup a flea.

Arm. By the north pole, I do challenge thee.

Cost. I will not fight with a pole, like a northern
man: I'll slash; I'll do it by the sword. I bepray
you, let me borrow my arms again.

Dum. Room for the incensed Worthies!

Cost. I'll do it in my shirt.

Dum. Most resolute Pompey!

Moth. Master, let me take you a button-hole

lower. Do you not see Pompey is uncasing for
the combat? What mean you? You will lose your
reputation.

Arm. Gentlemen and soldiers, pardon me; I
will not combat in my shirt.   711

Dum. You may not deny it: Pompey hath made
the challenge.

Arm. Sweet bloods, I both may and will.

Biron. What reason have you for't?

Arm. The naked truth of it is, I have no shirt;
I go woolward for penance.

Boyet. True, and it was enjoined him in Rome
for want of linen: since when, I'll be sworn, he
wore none but a dishclout of Jaquenetta's, and
that a' wears next his heart for a favour.

Enter MERCADE.

Mer. God save you, madam!

Prin. Welcome, Mercade;
But that thou interrupt'st our merriment.

Mer. I am sorry, madam; for the news I bring
Is heavy in my tongue. The King your father—

Prin. Dead, for my life!

Mer. Even so; my tale is told.

Biron. Worthies, away! the scene begins to
cloud.   731

Arm. For mine own part, I breathe free breath.
I have seen the day of wrong through the little
hole of discretion, and I will right myself like a
soldier.   [*Exeunt Worthies.*

King. How fares your Majesty?

Prin. Boyet, prepare; I will away to-night.

King. Madam, not so; I do beseech you, stay.

Prin. Prepare, I say. I thank you, gracious
lords,
For all your fair endeavours; and entreat, 740
Out of a new-sad soul, that you vouchsafe
In your rich wisdom to excuse or hide
The liberal opposition of our spirits,
If over-boldly we have borne ourselves
In the converse of breath: your gentleness
Was guilty of it. Farewell, worthy lord!
A heavy heart bears not a nimble tongue:
Excuse me so, coming too short of thanks
For my great suit so easily obtain'd.

King. The extreme parts of time extremely
    forms   750
All causes to the purpose of his speed,
And often at his very loose decides
That which long process could not arbitrate:
And though the mourning brow of progeny
Forbid the smiling courtesy of love
The holy suit which fain it would convince,
Yet, since love's argument was first on foot,
Let not the cloud of sorrow justle it
From what it purposed; since, to wail friends lost

Is not by much so wholesome-profitable 760
As to rejoice at friends but newly found.

Prin. I understand you not: my griefs are
double.

Biron. Honest plain words best pierce the ear
of grief;
And by these badges understand the King.
For your fair sakes have we neglected time,
Play'd foul play with our oaths: your beauty,
ladies,
Hath much deform'd us, fashioning our humours
Even to the opposed end of our intents:
And what in us hath seem'd ridiculous—
As love is full of unbefitting strains, 770
All wanton as a child, skipping and vain,
Form'd by the eye and therefore, like the eye,
Full of strange shapes, of habits and of forms,
Varying in subjects as the eye doth roll
To every varied object in his glance:
Which parti-coated presence of loose love
Put on by us, if, in your heavenly eyes,
Have misbecomed our oaths and gravities,
Those heavenly eyes, that look into these faults,
Suggested us to make. Therefore, ladies, 780
Our love being yours, the error that love makes
Is likewise yours: we to ourselves prove false,
By being once false for ever to be true
To those that make us both—fair ladies, you:
And even that falsehood, in itself a sin,
Thus purifies itself and turns to grace.

Prin. We have received your letters full of love;
Your favours, the ambassadors of love;
And, in our maiden council, rated them
At courtship, pleasant jest, and courtesy, 790
As bombast and as lining to the time:
But more devout than this in our respects
Have we not been; and therefore met your loves
In their own fashion, like a merriment.

Dum. Our letters, madam, show'd much more
than jest.

Long. So did our looks.

Ros. We did not quote them so.

King. Now, at the latest minute of the hour,
Grant us your loves.

Prin. A time, methinks, too short
To make a world-without-end bargain in.
No, no, my lord, your Grace is perjured much,
Full of dear guiltiness; and therefore this: 801
If for my love, as there is no such cause,
You will do aught, this shall you do for me:
Your oath I will not trust; but go with speed
To some forlorn and naked hermitage,
Remote from all the pleasures of the world;
There stay until the twelve celestial signs
Have brought about the annual reckoning.
If this austere insociable life

Change not your offer made in heat of blood;
If frosts and fasts, hard lodging and thin weeds
Nip not the gaudy blossoms of your love,
But that it bear this trial and last love;
Then, at the expiration of the year,
Come challenge me, challenge me by these de-
serts,
And, by this virgin palm now kissing thine,
I will be thine; and till that instant shut
My woeful self up in a mourning house,
Raining the tears of lamentation
For the remembrance of my father's death. 820
If this thou do deny, let our hands part,
Neither intitled in the other's heart.

King. If this, or more than this, I would deny,
To flatter up these powers of mine with rest,
The sudden hand of death close up mine eye!
Hence ever then my heart is in thy breast.

Biron. And what to me, my love? and what to
me?

Ros. You must be purged too, your sins are
rack'd,
You are attaint with faults and perjury:
Therefore if you my favour mean to get, 830
A twelvemonth shall you spend, and never rest,
But seek the weary beds of people sick.

Dum. But what to me, my love? but what to me?
A wife?

Kath. A beard, fair health, and honesty;
With three-fold love I wish you all these three.

Dum. O, shall I say, "I thank you, gentle
wife"?

Kath. Not so, my lord; a twelvemonth and a
day
I'll mark no words that smooth-faced wooers
say:
Come when the King doth to my lady come;
Then, if I have much love, I'll give you some. 840

Dum. I'll serve thee true and faithfully till
then.

Kath. Yet swear not, lest ye be forsworn again.

Long. What says Maria?

Mar. At the twelvemonth's end
I'll change my black gown for a faithful friend.

Long. I'll stay with patience; but the time is
long.

Mar. The liker you; few taller are so young.

Biron. Studies my lady? mistress, look on me;
Behold the window of my heart, mine eye,
What humble suit attends thy answer there:
Impose some service on me for thy love. 850

Ros. Oft have I heard of you, my Lord Biron,
Before I saw you; and the world's large tongue
Proclaims you for a man replete with mocks,
Full of comparisons and wounding flouts,
Which you on all estates will execute

That lie within the mercy of your wit.
To weed this wormwood from your fruitful
    brain,
And therewithal to win me, if you please,
Without the which I am not to be won,
You shall this twelvemonth term from day to day
Visit the speechless sick and still converse   861
With groaning wretches; and your task shall be,
With all the fierce endeavour of your wit
To enforce the pained impotent to smile.
    Biron. To move wild laughter in the throat of
    death?
It cannot be; it is impossible:
Mirth cannot move a soul in agony.
    Ros. Why, that's the way to choke a gibing
    spirit,
Whose influence is begot of that loose grace
Which shallow laughing hearers give to fools:
A jest's prosperity lies in the ear   871
Of him that hears it, never in the tongue
Of him that makes it: then, if sickly ears,
Deaf'd with the clamours of their own dear
    groans,
Will hear your idle scorns, continue then,
And I will have you and that fault withal;
Buf if they will not, throw away that spirit,
And I shall find you empty of that fault,
Right joyful of your reformation.
    Biron. A twelvemonth! well; befall what will
    befall,   880
I'll jest a twelvemonth in an hospital.
    Prin. [*To the* KING] Ay, sweet my lord; and so
    I take my leave.
    King. No, madam; we will bring you on your
    way.
    Biron. Our wooing doth not end like an old
    play;
Jack hath not Jill: these ladies' courtesy
Might well have made our sport a comedy.
    King. Come, sir, it wants a twelvemonth and a
    day,
And then 'twill end.
    Biron.   That's too long for a play.

Re-enter ARMADO.

    Arm. Sweet majesty, vouchsafe me—
    Prin. Was not that Hector?
    Dum. The worthy knight of Troy.   890
    Arm. I will kiss thy royal finger, and take
leave. I am a votary; I have vowed to Jaquenetta to hold the plough for her sweet love three
years. But, most esteemed greatness, will you
hear the dialogue that the two learned men have

compiled in praise of the owl and the cuckoo? It
should have followed in the end of our show.
    King. Call them forth quickly; we will do so.
    Arm. Holla! approach.   900

Re-enter HOLOFERNES, NATHANIEL, MOTH, COS-TARD, *and others.*

This side is Hiems, Winter, this Ver, the Spring;
the one maintained by the owl, the other by the
cuckoo. Ver, begin.

SONG

Spring.
    When daisies pied and violets blue
        And lady-smocks all silver-white
    And cuckoo-buds of yellow hue
        Do paint the meadows with delight,
    The cuckoo then, on every tree,
    Mocks married men; for thus sings he,
            "Cuckoo;   910
    Cuckoo, cuckoo"; O word of fear,
    Unpleasing to a married ear!
    When shepherds pipe on oaten straws
        And merry larks are ploughmen's clocks,
    When turtles tread, and rooks, and daws,
        And maidens bleach their summer smocks,
    The cuckoo then, on every tree,
    Mocks married men; for thus sings he,
            "Cuckoo;
    Cuckoo, cuckoo"; O word of fear,   920
    Unpleasing to a married ear!
Winter.
    When icicles hang by the wall
        And Dick the shepherd blows his nail
    And Tom bears logs into the hall
        And milk comes frozen home in pail,
    When blood is nipp'd and ways be foul,
    Then nightly sings the staring owl,
            "Tu-whit;
    Tu-who," a merry note,
    While greasy Joan doth keel the pot.   930
    When all aloud the wind doth blow
        And coughing drowns the parson's saw
    And birds sit brooding in the snow
        And Marian's nose looks red and raw,
    When roasted crabs hiss in the bowl,
    Then nightly sings the staring owl,
            "Tu-whit;
    To-who," a merry note,
    While greasy Joan doth keel the pot.   939
    Arm. The words of Mercury are harsh after
the songs of Apollo. You that way: we this
way.   [*Exeunt.*

❧ ROMEO AND JULIET

DRAMATIS PERSONÆ

ESCALUS, PRINCE OF VERONA
PARIS, *a young nobleman, kinsman to the Prince*
MONTAGUE | *heads of two houses at variance with*
CAPULET | *each other*
COUSIN TO CAPULET, *an old man*
ROMEO, *son to Montague*
MERCUTIO, *kinsman to the Prince, and friend to Romeo*
BENVOLIO, *nephew to Montague, and friend to Romeo*
TYBALT, *nephew to Lady Capulet*
FRIAR LAURENCE | *Franciscans*
FRIAR JOHN |
BALTHASAR, *servant to Romeo*
SAMPSON | *servants to Capulet*
GREGORY |
PETER, *servant to Juliet's nurse*
ABRAHAM, *servant to Montague*

AN APOTHECARY
THREE MUSICIANS
PAGE *to Paris*
THREE WATCHMEN
A CITIZEN *of Verona*
THREE SERVANTS *to Capulet*

LADY MONTAGUE, *wife to Montague*
LADY CAPULET, *wife to Capulet*
JULIET, *daughter to Capulet*
NURSE *to Juliet*
CHORUS

NON-SPEAKING: *Citizens of Verona, Maskers, Musicians, Page to Mercutio, Guards, Watchmen, and Attendants*

SCENE: *Verona and Mantua*

PROLOGUE

Two households, both alike in dignity,
  In fair Verona, where we lay our scene,
From ancient grudge break to new mutiny,
  Where civil blood makes civil hands unclean.
From forth the fatal loins of these two foes
A pair of star-cross'd lovers take their life;
Whose misadventured piteous overthrows
  Do with their death bury their parents' strife.
The fearful passage of their death-mark'd love,
  And the continuance of their parents' rage,   *10*
Which, but their children's end, nought could
    remove,
  Is now the two hours' traffic of our stage;
The which if you with patient ears attend,
What here shall miss, our toil shall strive to
    mend.

ACT I

SCENE I. *Verona: a public place*

Enter SAMPSON *and* GREGORY, *of the house of Capulet, armed with swords and bucklers.*

Sam. Gregory, o' my word, we'll not carry coals.

Gre. No, for then we should be colliers.

Sam. I mean, an we be in choler, we'll draw.

Gre. Ay, while you live, draw your neck out o' the collar.

Sam. I strike quickly, being moved.

Gre. But thou art not quickly moved to strike.

Sam. A dog of the house of Montague moves me.   *10*

Gre. To move is to stir; and to be valiant is to stand: therefore, if thou art moved, thou runn'st away.

Sam. A dog of that house shall move me to stand: I will take the wall of any man or maid of Montague's.

Gre. That shows thee a weak slave; for the weakest goes to the wall.

Sam. True; and therefore women, being the weaker vessels, are ever thrust to the wall: therefore I will push Montague's men from the wall, and thrust his maids to the wall.

Gre. The quarrel is between our masters and us their men.

Sam. 'Tis all one, I will show myself a tyrant: when I have fought with the men, I will be cruel with the maids and cut off their heads.

Gre. The heads of the maids?   *29*

Sam. Ay, the heads of the maids, or their maidenheads; take it in what sense thou wilt.

Gre. They must take it in sense that feel it.

Sam. Me they shall feel while I am able to stand: and 'tis known I am a pretty piece of flesh.

Gre. 'Tis well thou art not fish; if thou hadst, thou hadst been poor John. Draw thy tool; here comes two of the house of the Montagues.

Sam. My naked weapon is out: quarrel, I will back thee.   *40*

Gre. How! turn thy back and run?

Sam. Fear me not.

Gre. No, marry: I fear thee!

Sam. Let us take the law of our sides; let them begin.

Gre. I will frown as I pass by, and let them take it as they list.

Sam. Nay, as they dare. I will bite my thumb at them; which is a disgrace to them, if they bear it.

Enter ABRAHAM *and* BALTHASAR.

Abr. Do you bite your thumb at us, sir?   52

Sam. I do bite my thumb, sir.

Abr. Do you bite your thumb at us, sir?

Sam. [*Aside to* GREGORY] Is the law of our side, if I say ay?

Gre. No.

Sam. No, sir, I do not bite my thumb at you, sir, but I bite my thumb, sir.

Gre. Do you quarrel, sir?

Abr. Quarrel, sir! no, sir.   60

Sam. If you do, sir, I am for you: I serve as good a man as you.

Abr. No better.

Sam. Well, sir.

Gre. Say "better": here comes one of my master's kinsmen.

Sam. Yes, better, sir.

Abr. You lie.

Sam. Draw, if you be men. Gregory, remember thy swashing blow. [*They fight.*]   70

Enter BENVOLIO.

Ben. Part, fools!

Put up your swords; you know not what you do.
Beats down their swords.

Enter TYBALT.

Tyb. What, art thou drawn among these heart-less hinds?

Turn thee, Benvolio, look upon thy death.

Ben. I do but keep the peace: put up thy sword, Or manage it to part these men with me.

Tyb. What, drawn, and talk of peace! I hate the word,

As I hate hell, all Montagues, and thee:

Have at thee, coward! [*They fight.*]

Enter several of both houses, *who join the fray;* then enter CITIZENS, *with clubs.*

1st Cit. Clubs, bills, and partisans! strike! beat them down!   80

Down with the Capulets! down with the Mon-tagues!

Enter CAPULET *in his gown, and* LADY CAPULET.

Cap. What noise is this? Give me my long sword, ho!

La. Cap. A crutch, a crutch! why call you for a sword?

Cap. My sword, I say! Old Montague is come, And flourishes his blade in spite of me.

Enter MONTAGUE *and* LADY MONTAGUE.

Mon. Thou villain Capulet. Hold me not, let me go.

La. Mon. Thou shalt not stir a foot to seek a foe.

Enter PRINCE ESCALUS, *with Attendants.*

Prin. Rebellious subjects, enemies to peace,

Profaners of this neighbour-stained steel—

Will they not hear? What, ho! you men, you beasts,   90

That quench the fire of your pernicious rage

With purple fountains issuing from your veins,

On pain of torture, from those bloody hands

Throw your mistemper'd weapons to the ground,

And hear the sentence of your moved prince.

Three civil brawls, bred of an airy word,

By thee, old Capulet, and Montague,

Have thrice disturb'd the quiet of our streets,

And made Verona's ancient citizens

Cast by their grave beseeming ornaments   100

To wield old partisans, in hands as old,

Canker'd with peace, to part your canker'd hate:

If ever you disturb our streets again,

Your lives shall pay the forfeit of the peace.

For this time, all the rest depart away:

You, Capulet, shall go along with me:

And, Montague, come you this afternoon,

To know our further pleasure in this case,

To old Free-town, our common judgement-place.

Once more, on pain of death, all men depart.   110

[*Exeunt all but* MONTAGUE, LADY MONTAGUE, *and* BENVOLIO.

Mon. Who set this ancient quarrel new abroach?

Speak, nephew, were you by when it began?

Ben. Here were the servants of your adversary,

And yours, close fighting ere I did approach:

I drew to part them: in the instant came

The fiery Tybalt, with his sword prepared,

Which, as he breathed defiance to my ears,

He swung about his head and cut the winds,

Who nothing hurt withal hiss'd him in scorn: 119

While we were interchanging thrusts and blows,

Came more and more and fought on part and part,

Till the prince came, who parted either part.

La. Mon. O, where is Romeo? saw you him to-day?

Right glad I am he was not at this fray.

Ben. Madam, an hour before the worshipp'd sun

Peer'd forth the golden window of the east,

A troubled mind drave me to walk abroad;

Where, underneath the grove of sycamore
That westward rooteth from the city's side,
So early walking did I see your son: *130*
Towards him I made, but he was ware of me
And stole into the covert of the wood:
I, measuring his affections by my own,
That most are busied when they're most alone,
Pursued my humour not pursuing his,
And gladly shunn'd who gladly fled from me.
  Mon. Many a morning hath he there been seen,
With tears augmenting the fresh morning's dew,
Adding to clouds more clouds with his deep sighs;
But all so soon as the all-cheering sun   *140*
Should in the furthest east begin to draw
The shady curtains from Aurora's bed,
Away from light steals home my heavy son,
And private in his chamber pens himself,
Shuts up his windows, locks fair daylight out,
And makes himself an artificial night:
Black and portentous must this humour prove,
Unless good counsel may the cause remove.
  Ben. My noble uncle, do you know the cause?
  Mon. I neither know it nor can learn of him. *150*
  Ben. Have you importuned him by any means?
  Mon. Both by myself and many other friends:
But he, his own affections' counsellor,
Is to himself—I will not say how true—
But to himself so secret and so close,
So far from sounding and discovery,
As is the bud bit with an envious worm,
Ere he can spread his sweet leaves to the air,
Or dedicate his beauty to the sun.
Could we but learn from whence his sorrows
  grow,   *160*
We would as willingly give cure as know.

                Enter ROMEO.

  Ben. See, where he comes: so please you, step
  aside;
I'll know his grievance, or be much denied.
  Mon. I would thou wert so happy by thy stay,
To hear true shrift. Come, madam, let's away.
                    [*Exeunt* MONTAGUE *and* LADY.
  Ben. Good morrow, cousin.
  Rom.   Is the day so young?
  Ben. But new struck nine.
  Rom.   Ay me! sad hours seem long.
Was that my father that went hence so fast?
  Ben. It was. What sadness lengthens Romeo's
  hours?
  Rom. Not having that, which, having, makes
  them short.   *170*
  Ben. In love?
  Rom. Out—
  Ben. Of love?
  Rom. Out of her favour, where I am in love.

  Ben. Alas, that love, so gentle in his view,
Should be so tyrannous and rough in proof!
  Rom. Alas, that love, whose view is muffled
  still,
Should, without eyes, see pathways to his will!
Where shall we dine? O me! What fray was
  here?
Yet tell me not, for I have heard it all.   *180*
Here's much to do with hate, but more with love.
Why, then, O brawling love! O loving hate!
O any thing, of nothing first create!
O heavy lightness! serious vanity!
Mis-shapen chaos of well-seeming forms!
Feather of lead, bright smoke, cold fire, sick
  health!
Still-waking sleep, that is not what it is!
This love feel I, that feel no love in this.
Dost thou not laugh?
  Ben.   No, coz, I rather weep. *189*
  Rom. Good heart, at what?
  Ben.   At thy good heart's oppression.
  Rom. Why, such is love's transgression.
Griefs of mine own lie heavy in my breast,
Which thou wilt propagate, to have it prest
With more of thine: this love that thou hast
  shown
Doth add more grief to too much of mine own.
Love is a smoke raised with the fume of sighs;
Being purged, a fire sparkling in lovers' eyes;
Being vex'd, a sea nourish'd with lovers' tears:
What is it else? a madness most discreet,
A choking gall and a preserving sweet.   *200*
Farewell, my coz.
  Ben.   Soft! I will go along;
An if you leave me so, you do me wrong.
  Rom. Tut, I have lost myself; I am not here;
This is not Romeo, he's some other where.
  Ben. Tell me in sadness, who is that you love.
  Rom. What, shall I groan and tell thee?
  Ben.   Groan! why, no;
But sadly tell me who.
  Rom. Bid a sick man in sadness make his will:
Ah, word ill urged to one that is so ill!
In sadness, cousin, I do love a woman.   *210*
  Ben. I aim'd so near, when I supposed you loved.
  Rom. A right good mark-man! And she's fair
  I love.
  Ben. A right fair mark, fair coz, is soonest hit.
  Rom. Well, in that hit you miss: she'll not be hit
With Cupid's arrow; she hath Dian's wit;
And, in strong proof of chastity well arm'd,
From love's weak childish bow she lives
  unharm'd.
She will not stay the siege of loving terms,
Nor bide the encounter of assailing eyes,
Nor ope her lap to saint-seducing gold: *220*

O, she is rich in beauty, only poor
That, when she dies, with beauty dies her store.
Ben. Then she hath sworn that she will still live
    chaste?
Rom. She hath, and in that sparing makes huge
    waste,
For beauty starved with her severity
Cuts beauty off from all posterity.
She is too fair, too wise, wisely too fair,
To merit bliss by making me despair:
She hath forsworn to love, and in that vow
Do I live dead that live to tell it now.   *230*
  Ben. Be ruled by me, forget to think of her.
  Rom. O, teach me how I should forget to think.
  Ben. By giving liberty unto thine eyes;
Examine other beauties.
  Rom.   'Tis the way
To call hers exquisite, in question more:
These happy masks that kiss fair ladies' brows
Being black put us in mind they hide the fair;
He that is strucken blind cannot forget
The precious treasure of his eyesight lost:
Show me a mistress that is passing fair,   *240*
What doth her beauty serve, but as a note
Where I may read who pass'd that passing fair?
Farewell: thou canst not teach me to forget.
  Ben. I'll pay that doctrine, or else die in debt.
                          [*Exeunt.*

Scene ii. *A street*

Enter CAPULET, PARIS, *and* SERVANT.

Cap. But Montague is bound as well as I,
In penalty alike; and 'tis not hard, I think,
For men so old as we to keep the peace.
  Par. Of honourable reckoning are you both;
And pity 'tis you lived at odds so long.
But now, my lord, what say you to my suit?
  Cap. But saying o'er what I have said before:
My child is yet a stranger in the world;
She hath not seen the change of fourteen years;
Let two more summers wither in their pride, *10*
Ere we may think her ripe to be a bride.
  Par. Younger than she are happy mothers made.
  Cap. And too soon marr'd are those so early
    made.
The earth hath swallow'd all my hopes but she,
She is the hopeful lady of my earth:
But woo her, gentle Paris, get her heart,
My will to her consent is but a part;
An she agree, within her scope of choice
Lies my consent and fair according voice.
This night I hold an old accustom'd feast, *20*
Whereto I have invited many a guest,
Such as I love; and you, among the store,
One more, most welcome, makes my number
  more,

At my poor house look to behold this night
Earth-treading stars that make dark heaven light:
Such comfort as do lusty young men feel
When well-apparell'd April on the heel
Of limping winter treads, even such delight
Among fresh female buds shall you this night
Inherit at my house; hear all, all see,   *30*
And like her most whose merit most shall be:
Which on more view, of many mine being one
May stand in number, though in reckoning none.
Come, go with me.[*To* SERVANT, *giving a paper.*]
  Go, sirrah, trudge about
Through fair Verona; find those persons out
Whose names are written there, and to them say,
My house and welcome on their pleasure stay.
             [*Exeunt* CAPULET *and* PARIS.
  Serv. Find them out whose names are written
here! It is written, that the shoemaker should
meddle with his yard, and the tailor with his last,
the fisher with his pencil, and the painter with his
nets; but I am sent to find those persons whose
names are here writ, and can never find what
names the writing person hath here writ. I must
to the learned.—In good time.

    Enter BENVOLIO *and* ROMEO.

  Ben. Tut, man, one fire burns out another's
    burning,
  One pain is lessen'd by another's anguish;
Turn giddy, and be holp by backward turning;
  One desperate grief cures with another's lan-
    guish:
Take thou some new infection to thy eye, *50*
And the rank poison of the old will die.
  Rom. Your plaintain-leaf is excellent for that.
  Ben. For what, I pray thee?
  Rom.   For your broken shin.
  Ben. Why, Romeo, art thou mad?
  Rom. Not mad, but bound more than a madman
    is;
Shut up in prison, kept without my food,
Whipp'd and tormented and—God-den, good
    fellow.
  Serv. God gi' god-den. I pray, sir, can you read?
  Rom. Ay, mine own fortune in my misery. *60*
  Serv. Perhaps you have learned it without book:
but, I pray, can you read anything you see?
  Rom. Ay, if I know the letters and the language.
  Serv. Ye say honestly: rest you merry!
  Rom. Stay, fellow; I can read. [*Reads.*]
  "Signior Martino and his wife and daughters;
County Anselme and his beauteous sisters; the
lady widow of Vitruvio; Signior Placentio and
his lovely nieces; Mercutio and his brother
Valentine; mine uncle Capulet, his wife, and
daughters; my fair niece Rosaline; Livia; Signior

Valentio and his cousin Tybalt; Lucio and the
lively Helena."
A fair assembly: whither should they come?
  Serv. Up.
  Rom. Whither?
  Serv. To supper; to our house.
  Rom. Whose house?
  Serv. My master's.   80
  Rom. Indeed, I should have ask'd you that
    before.
  Serv. Now I'll tell you without asking: my
master is the great rich Capulet; and if you be
not of the house of Montagues, I pray, come and
crush a cup of wine. Rest you merry!   [*Exit.*
  Ben. At this same ancient feast of Capulet's
Sups the fair Rosaline whom thou so lovest,
With all the admired beauties of Verona:
Go thither; and, with unattained eye,   90
Compare her face with some that I shall show,
And I will make thee think thy swan a crow.
  Rom. When the devout religion of mine eye
    Maintains such falsehood, then turn tears to
    fires;
And these, who often drown'd could never die,
    Transparent heretics, be burnt for liars!
One fairer than my love! the all-seeing sun
Ne'er saw her match since first the world begun.
  Ben. Tut, you saw her fair, none else being by,
Herself poised with herself in either eye: 100
But in that crystal scales let there be weigh'd
Your lady's love against some other maid
That I will show you shining at this feast,
And she shall scant show well that now shows
    best.
  Rom. I'll go along, no such sight to be shown,
But to rejoice in splendour of mine own.
                                          [*Exeunt.*

SCENE III. *A room in Capulet's house*
Enter LADY CAPULET *and* NURSE.

  La. Cap. Nurse, where's my daughter? call her
    forth to me.
  Nurse. Now, by my maidenhead at twelve year
    old,
I bade her come. What, lamb! what, lady-bird!
God forbid! Where's this girl? What, Juliet!

Enter JULIET.

  Jul. How now! who calls?
  Nurse.   Your mother.
  Jul.   Madam, I am here.
What is your will?
  La. Cap. This is the matter:—Nurse, give
    leave awhile,
We must talk in secret:—nurse, come back
    again;

I have remember'd me, thou's hear our counsel.
Thou know'st my daughter's of a pretty age.   10
  Nurse. Faith, I can tell her age unto an hour.
  La. Cap. She's not fourteen.
  Nurse.   I'll lay fourteen of my teeth—
And yet, to my teen be it spoken, I have but
    four—
She is not fourteen. How long is it now
To Lammas-tide?
  La. Cap.   A fortnight and odd days.
  Nurse. Even or odd, of all days in the year,
Come Lammas-eve at night shall she be fourteen.
Susan and she—God rest all Christian souls!—
Were of an age: well, Susan is with God;
She was too good for me: but, as I said,   20
On Lammas-eve at night shall she be fourteen;
That shall she, marry; I remember it well.
'Tis since the earthquake now eleven years:
And she was wean'd—I never shall forget it—
Of all the days of the year, upon that day:
For I had then laid wormwood to my dug,
Sitting in the sun under the dove-house wall;
My lord and you were then at Mantua—
Nay, I do bear a brain— but, as I said,
When it did taste the wormwood on the nipple
Of my dug and felt it bitter, pretty fool,   31
To see it tetchy and fall out with the dug!
"Shake" quoth the dove-house: 'twas no need, I
    trow,
To bid me trudge:
And since that time it is eleven years;
For then she could stand alone; nay, by the rood,
She could have run and waddled all about;
For even the day before, she broke her brow:
And then my husband—God be with his soul!
A' was a merry man—took up the child: 40
"Yea," quoth he, "dost thou fall upon thy face?
Thou wilt fall backward when thou hast more
    wit;
Wilt thou not, Jule?" and, by my holidame,
The pretty wretch left crying and said "Ay."
To see, now, how a jest shall come about!
I warrant, an I should live a thousand years,
I never should forget it: "Wilt thou not, Jule?"
    quoth he;
And, pretty fool, it stinted and said, "Ay."
  La. Cap. Enough of this; I pray thee, hold thy
    peace.
  Nurse. Yes, madam: yet I cannot choose but
    laugh,   50
To think it should leave crying and say, "Ay."
And yet, I warrant, it had upon its brow
A bump as big as a young cockerel's stone;
A parlous knock; and it cried bitterly:
"Yea," quoth my husband, "fall'st upon thy face?

Thou wilt fall backward when thou comest to
    age;
Wilt thou not, Jule?" it stinted and said, "Ay."
Jul. And stint thou too, I pray thee, nurse, say I.
Nurse. Peace, I have done. God mark thee to
    his grace!
Thou wast the prettiest babe that e'er I nursed:
An I might live to see thee married once,   61
I have my wish.
  La. Cap. Marry, that "marry" is the very theme
I came to talk of. Tell me, daughter Juliet,
How stands your disposition to be married?
Jul. It is an honour that I dream not of.
Nurse. An honour! were not I thine only nurse,
I would say thou hadst suck'd wisdom from thy
    teat.
  La. Cap. Well, think of marriage now; younger
    than you,
Here in Verona, ladies of esteem,   70
Are made already mothers: by my count,
I was your mother much upon these years
That you are now a maid. Thus then in brief:
The valiant Paris seeks you for his love.
  Nurse. A man, young lady! lady, such a man
As all the world—why, he's a man of wax.
  La. Cap. Verona's summer hath not such a
    flower.
  Nurse. Nay, he's a flower; in faith, a very
    flower.
  La. Cap. What say you? can you love the
    gentleman?
This night you shall behold him at our feast;   80
Read o'er the volume of young Paris' face
And find delight writ there with beauty's pen;
Examine every married lineament
And see how one another lends content,
And what obscured in this fair volume lies
Find written in the margent of his eyes.
This precious book of love, this unbound lover,
To beautify him, only lacks a cover:
The fish lives in the sea, and 'tis much pride
For fair without the fair within to hide: 90
That book in many's eyes doth share the glory,
That in gold clasps locks in the golden story;
So shall you share all that he doth possess,
By having him, making yourself no less.
  Nurse. No less! nay, bigger; women grow by
    men.
  La. Cap. Speak briefly, can you like of Paris'
    love?
Jul. I'll look to like, if looking liking move:
But no more deep will I endart mine eye
Than your consent gives strength to make it fly.

        Enter a SERVANT.

Serv. Madam, the guests are come, supper

served up, you called, my young lady asked for,
the nurse cursed in the pantry, and everything in
extremity. I must hence to wait; I beseech you,
follow straight.
  La. Cap.   We follow thee. [*Exit* SERVANT.
    Juliet, the County stays.
  Nurse. Go, girl, seek happy nights to happy
    days.   [*Exeunt.*

       SCENE IV. *A street*

Enter ROMEO, MERCUTIO, BENVOLIO, *with five
or six Maskers, Torch-bearers, and others.*

  Rom. What, shall this speech be spoke for our
    excuse?
Or shall we on without apology?
  Ben. The date is out of such prolixity:
We'll have not Cupid hoodwink'd with a scarf,
Bearing a Tartar's painted bow of lath,
Scaring the ladies like a crow-keeper;
Nor no without-book prologue, faintly spoke
After the prompter, for our entrance:
But let them measure us by what they will;
We'll measure them a measure and be gone.   10
  Rom. Give me a torch: I am not for this
    ambling;
Being but heavy, I will bear the light.
  Mer. Nay, gentle Romeo, we must have you
    dance.
  Rom. Not I, believe me: you have dancing shoes
With nimble soles: I have a soul of lead
So stakes me to the ground I cannot move.
  Mer. You are a lover; borrow Cupid's wings,
And soar with them above a common bound.
  Rom. I am too sore enpierced with his shaft
To soar with his light feathers, and so bound   20
I cannot bound a pitch above dull woe:
Under love's heavy burden do I sink.
  Mer. And, to sink in it, should you burden love;
Too great oppression for a tender thing.
  Rom. Is love a tender thing? it is too rough,
Too rude, too boisterous, and it pricks like
    thorn.
  Mer. If love be rough with you, be rough with
    love;
Prick love for pricking, and you beat love down.
Give me a case to put my visage in!
A visor for a visor! what care I   30
What curious eye doth quote deformities?
Here are the beetle brows shall blush for me.
  Ben. Come, knock and enter; and no sooner in,
But every man betake him to his legs.
  Rom. A torch for me: let wantons light of
    heart
Tickle the senseless rushes with their heels,
For I am proverb'd with a grandsire phrase;
I'll be a candle-holder, and look on.

The game was ne'er so fair, and I am done.

Mer. Tut, dun's the mouse, the constable's own
    word: 40
If thou art Dun, we'll draw thee from the mire
Of this sir-reverence love, wherein thou stick'st
Up to the ears. Come, we burn daylight, ho!

Rom. Nay, that's not so.

Mer.   I mean, sir, in delay
We waste our lights in vain, like lamps by day.
Take our good meaning, for our judgment sits
Five times in that ere once in our five wits.

Rom. And we mean well in going to this mask;
But 'tis no wit to go.

Mer.   Why, may one ask?

Rom. I dream'd a dream to-night.

Mer.   And so did I.   50

Rom. Well, what was yours?

Mer.   That dreamers often lie.

Rom. In bed asleep, while they do dream
    things true.

Mer. O, then, I see Queen Mab hath been with
    you.
She is the fairies' midwife, and she comes
In shape no bigger than an agate-stone
On the fore-finger of an alderman,
Drawn with a team of little atomies
Athwart men's noses as they lie asleep;
Her waggon-spokes made of long spinners' legs,
The cover of the wings of grasshoppers,   60
The traces of the smallest spider's web,
The collars of the moonshine's watery beams,
Her whip of cricket's bone, the lash of film,
Her waggoner a small grey-coated gnat,
Not half so big as a round little worm
Prick'd from the lazy finger of a maid;
Her chariot is an empty hazel-nut
Made by the joiner squirrel or old grub,
Time out o' mind the fairies' coachmakers.
And in this state she gallops night by night   70
Through lovers' brains, and then they dream of
    love;
O'er courtiers' knees, that dream on court'sies
    straight,
O'er lawyers' fingers, who straight dream on
    fees,
O'er ladies' lips, who straight on kisses dream,
Which oft the angry Mab with blisters plagues,
Because their breaths with sweetmeats tainted
    are:
Sometime she gallops o'er a courtier's nose,
And then dreams he of smelling out a suit;
And sometime comes she with a tithe-pig's tail
Tickling a parson's nose as a' lies asleep,   80
Then dreams he of another benefice:
Sometime she driveth o'er a soldier's neck,
And then dreams he of cutting foreign throats,

Of breaches, ambuscadoes, Spanish blades,
Of healths five-fathom deep; and then anon
Drums in his ear, at which he starts and wakes,
And being thus frighted swears a prayer or two
And sleeps again. This is that very Mab
That plats the manes of horses in the night,
And bakes the elf-locks in foul sluttish hairs,   90
Which once untangled much misfortune bodes:
This is the hag, when maids lie on their backs,
That presses them and learns them first to bear,
Making them women of good carriage:
This is she—

Rom.   Peace, peace, Mercutio, peace!
Thou talk'st of nothing.

Mer.   True, I talk of dreams,
Which are the children of an idle brain,
Begot of nothing but vain fantasy,
Which is as thin of substance as the air
And more inconstant than the wind, who
    wooes
Even now the frozen bosom of the north,   101
And, being anger'd, puffs away from thence,
Turning his face to the dew-dropping south.

Ben. This wind, you talk of, blows us from
    ourselves;
Supper is done, and we shall come too late.

Rom. I fear, too early: for my mind misgives
Some consequence yet hanging in the stars
Shall bitterly begin his fearful date
With this night's revels and expire the term
Of a despised life closed in my breast   110
By some vile forfeit of untimely death.
But He, that hath the steerage of my course,
Direct my sail! On, lusty gentlemen.

Ben. Strike, drum.   [*Exeunt.*

SCENE V. *A hall in Capulet's house*

Musicians waiting. Enter SERVINGMEN, *with
napkins.*

1st Serv. Where's Potpan, that he helps not to
take away? He shift a trencher? he scrape a
trencher!

2nd Serv. When good manners shall lie all in
one or two men's hands and they unwashed too,
'tis a foul thing.

1st. Serv. Away with the joint-stools, remove
the court-cupboard, look to the plate. Good thou,
save me a piece of marchpane; and, as thou lovest
me, let the porter let in Susan Grindstone and
Nell. Antony, and Potpan!   11

2nd Serv. Ay, boy, ready.

1st Serv. You are looked for and called for,
asked for and sought for, in the greater chamber.

2nd Serv. We cannot be here and there too.
Cheerly, boys; be brisk awhile, and the longer
liver take all.

Enter CAPULET, *with* JULIET, *and others of his
house, meeting the Guests and Maskers.*

Cap. Welcome, gentlemen! ladies that have
    their toes
Unplagued with corns will have a bout with you.
Ah ha, my mistresses! which of you all   20
Will now deny to dance? she that makes dainty,
She, I'll swear, hath corns; am I come near ye
    now?
Welcome, gentlemen! I have seen the day
That I have worn a visor and could tell
A whispering tale in a fair lady's ear,
Such as would please: 'tis gone, 'tis gone, 'tis
    gone:
You are welcome, gentlemen! Come, musicians,
    play.
A hall, a hall! give room! and foot it, girls.
    Music plays, and they dance.
More light, you knaves; and turn the tables up,
And quench the fire, the room is grown too hot.
Ah, sirrah, this unlook'd-for sport comes well. 31
Nay, sit, nay, sit, good cousin Capulet;
For you and I are past our dancing days:
How long is't now since last yourself and I
Were in a mask?
   Cousin Cap. By'r lady, thirty years.
  Cap. What, man! 'tis not so much, 'tis not so
    much:
'Tis since the nuptial of Lucentio,
Come pentecost as quickly as it will,
Some five and twenty years; and then we mask'd.
   Cousin Cap. 'Tis more, 'tis more: his son is
    elder, sir;   40
His son is thirty.
  Cap.   Will you tell me that?
His son was but a ward two years ago.
  Rom. [*To a* SERVINGMAN] What lady is that,
    which doth enrich the hand
Of yonder knight?
  Serv. I know not, sir.
  Rom. O, she doth teach the torches to burn
    bright!
It seems she hangs upon the cheek of night
Like a rich jewel in an Ethiope's ear;
Beauty too rich for use, for earth too dear!
So shows a snowy dove trooping with crows, 50
As yonder lady o'er her fellows shows.
The measure done, I'll watch her place of stand,
And, touching hers, make blessed my rude hand.
Did my heart love till now? forswear it, sight!
For I ne'er saw true beauty till this night.
  Tyb. This, by his voice, should be a Montague.
Fetch me my rapier, boy. What dares the slave
Come hither, cover'd with an antic face,
To fleet and scorn at our solemnity?

Now, by the stock and honour of my kin,   60
To strike him dead I hold it not a sin.
  Cap. Why, how now, kinsman! wherefore
    storm you so?
  Tyb. Uncle, this is a Montague, our foe,
A villain that is hither come in spite,
To scorn at our solemnity this night.
  Cap. Young Romeo is it?
  Tyb.   'Tis he, that villain Romeo.
  Cap. Content thee, gentle coz, let him alone;
He bears him like a portly gentleman;
And, to say truth, Verona brags of him
To be a virtuous and well govern'd youth: 70
I would not for the wealth of all the town
Here in my house do him disparagement:
Therefore be patient, take no note of him:
It is my will, the which if thou respect,
Show a fair presence and put off these frowns,
An ill-beseeming semblance for a feast.
  Tyb. It fits, when such a villain is a guest:
I'll not endure him.
  Cap.   He shall be endured:
What, goodman boy! I say, he shall: go to;
Am I the master here, or you? go to.   80
You'll not endure him! God shall mend my soul!
You'll make a mutiny among my guests!
You will set cock-a-hoop! you'll be the man!
  Tyb. Why, uncle, 'tis a shame.
  Cap.   Go to, go to;
You are a saucy boy: is't so, indeed?
This trick may chance to scathe you, I know
    what:
You must contrary me! marry, 'tis time.
Well said, my hearts! You are a princox; go:
Be quiet, or—More light, more light! For shame!
I'll make you quiet. What, cheerly, my hearts!
  Tyb. Patience perforce with wilful choler
    meeting
Makes my flesh tremble in their different
    greeting.
I will withdraw: but this intrusion shall
Now seeming sweet convert to bitter gall. [*Exit.*
  Rom. [*To* JULIET] If I profane with my un-
    worthiest hand
    This holy shrine, the gentle fine is this:
My lips, two blushing pilgrims, ready stand
    To smooth that rough touch with a tender kiss.
  Jul. Good pilgrim, you do wrong your hand too
    much,
    Which mannerly devotion shows in this;   100
For saints have hands that pilgrims' hands do
    touch,
    And palm to palm is holy palmers' kiss.
  Rom. Have not saints lips, and holy palmers too?
  Jul. Ay, pilgrim, lips that they must use in
    prayer.

Rom. O, then, dear saint, let lips do what hands
    do;
  They pray, grant thou, lest faith turn to
    despair.
Jul. Saints do not move, though grant for
    prayers' sake.
Rom. Then move not, while my prayer's effect
    I take.
Thus from my lips, by yours, my sin is purged.
Jul. Then have my lips the sin that they have
    took.   *110*
Rom. Sin from my lips? O trespass sweetly
    urged!
  Give me my sin again.
Jul.   You kiss by the book.
Nurse. Madam, your mother craves a word
    with you.
Rom. What is her mother?
Nurse.   Marry, bachelor,
Her mother is the lady of the house,
And a good lady, and a wise and virtuous:
I nursed her daughter, that you talk'd withal;
I tell you, he that can lay hold of her
Shall have the chinks.
Rom.   Is she a Capulet?
O dear account! my life is my foe's debt.   *120*
Ben. Away, be gone; the sport is at the best.
Rom. Ay, so I fear; the more is my unrest.
Cap. Nay, gentlemen, prepare not to be gone;
We have a trifling foolish banquet towards.
Is it e'en so? why, then, I thank you all;
I thank you, honest gentlemen; good night.
More torches here! Come on then, let's to bed.
Ah, sirrah, by my fay, it waxes late:
I'll to my rest.
              [*Exeunt all but* JULIET *and* NURSE.
Jul. Come hither, nurse. What is yond gentle-
    man?   *130*
Nurse. The son and heir of old Tiberio.
Jul. What's he that now is going out of door?
Nurse. Marry, that, I think, be young Petruchio.
Jul. What's he that follows there, that would
    not dance?
Nurse. I know not.
Jul. Go, ask his name: if he be married,
My grave is like to be my wedding bed.
Nurse. His name is Romeo, and a Montague;
The only son of your great enemy.
Jul. My only love sprung from my only hate!
Too early seen unknown, and known too late! *141*
Prodigious birth of love it is to me
That I must love a loathed enemy.
Nurse. What's this? what's this?
Jul.   A rhyme I learn'd even now
Of one I danced withal.
    One calls within, "Juliet."

Nurse.   Anon, anon!
Come, let's away; the strangers all are gone.
                            [*Exeunt.*

ACT II

PROLOGUE

Enter CHORUS.

Chor. Now old desire doth in his death-bed lie,
  And young affection gapes to be his heir;
That fair for which love groan'd for and would
    die,
  With tender Juliet match'd, is now not fair.
Now Romeo is beloved and loves again,
  Alike bewitched by the charm of looks,
But to his foe supposed he must complain,
  And she steal love's sweet bait from fearful
    hooks.
Being held a foe, he may not have access
  To breathe such vows as lovers use to swear;
And she as much in love, her means much less *11*
  To meet her new-beloved anywhere:
But passion lends them power, time means, to
    meet,
Tempering extremities with extreme sweet.
                            [*Exit.*

SCENE I. *A lane by the wall of Capulet's orchard*
              Enter ROMEO.

Rom. Can I go forward when my heart is here?
Turn back, dull earth, and find thy centre out.
   He climbs the wall, and leaps down within it.

     Enter BENVOLIO *and* MERCUTIO.

Ben. Romeo! my cousin Romeo!
Mer.   He is wise;
And, on my life, hath stol'n him home to bed.
Ben. He ran this way, and leap'd this orchard
    wall:
Call, good Mercutio.
Mer.   Nay, I'll conjure too.
Romeo! humours! madman! passion! lover!
Appear thou in the likeness of a sigh:
Speak but one rhyme, and I am satisfied;
Cry but "Ay me!" pronounce but "love" and
    "dove";   *10*
Speak to my gossip Venus one fair word,
One nick-name for her purblind son and heir,
Young Adam Cupid, he that shot so trim,
When King Cophetua loved the beggar-maid!
He heareth not, he stirreth not, he moveth not;
The ape is dead, and I must conjure him.
I conjure thee by Rosaline's bright eyes,
By her high forehead and her scarlet lip,
By her fine foot, straight leg, and quivering
    thigh

And the demesnes that there adjacent lie,   20
That in thy likeness thou appear to us!
 Ben. An if he hear thee, thou wilt anger him.
 Mer. This cannot anger him: 'twould anger him
To raise a spirit in his mistress' circle
Of some strange nature, letting it there stand
Till she had laid it and conjured it down;
That were some spite: my invocation
Is fair and honest, and in his mistress' name
I conjure only but to raise up him.
 Ben. Come, he hath hid himself among these
  trees,   30
To be consorted with the humorous night:
Blind is his love and best befits the dark.
 Mer. If love be blind, love cannot hit the mark.
Now will he sit under a medlar tree,
And wish his mistress were that kind of fruit
As maids call medlars, when they laugh alone.
O, Romeo, that she were, O, that she were
An open *et cætera*, thou a poperin pear!
Romeo, good night: I'll to my truckle-bed;
This field-bed is too cold for me to sleep: 40
Come, shall we go?
 Ben.   Go, then; for 'tis in vain
To seek him here that means not to be found.
          [Exeunt.

Scene II. *Capulet's orchard*
Enter ROMEO.

 Rom. He jests at scars that never felt a wound.
 JULIET *appears above at a window.*
But, soft! what light through yonder window
 breaks?
It is the east, and Juliet is the sun.
Arise, fair sun, and kill the envious moon,
Who is already sick and pale with grief,
That thou her maid art far more fair than she:
Be not her maid, since she is envious;
Her vestal livery is but sick and green
And none but fools do wear it; cast it off.
It is my lady, O, it is my love!   10
O, that she knew she were!
She speaks, yet she says nothing: what of that?
Her eye discourses; I will answer it.
I am too bold, 'tis not to me she speaks:
Two of the fairest stars in all the heaven,
Having some business, do entreat her eyes
To twinkle in their spheres till they return.
What if her eyes were there, they in her head?
The brightness of her cheek would shame those
 stars,
As daylight doth a lamp; her eyes in heaven   20
Would through the airy region stream so bright
That birds would sing and think it were not
 night.
See, how she leans her cheek upon her hand!

O, that I were a glove upon that hand,
That I might touch that cheek!
 Jul.   Ay me!
 Rom.   She speaks:
O, speak again, bright angel! for thou art
As glorious to this night, being o'er my head,
As is a winged messenger of heaven
Unto the white-upturned wondering eyes
Of mortals that fall back to gaze on him   30
When he bestrides the lazy-pacing clouds
And sails upon the bosom of the air.
 Jul. O Romeo, Romeo! wherefore art thou
  Romeo?
Deny thy father and refuse thy name;
Or, if thou wilt not, be but sworn my love,
And I'll no longer be a Capulet.
 Rom. [*Aside*] Shall I hear more, or shall I speak
  at this?
 Jul. 'Tis but thy name that is my enemy;
Thou art thyself, though not a Montague.
What's Montague? it is nor hand, nor foot,   40
Nor arm, nor face, nor any other part
Belonging to a man. O, be some other name!
What's in a name? that which we call a rose
By any other name would smell as sweet;
So Romeo would, were he not Romeo call'd,
Retain that dear perfection which he owes
Without that title. Romeo, doff thy name,
And for that name which is no part of thee
Take all myself.
 Rom.   I take thee at thy word:
Call me but love, and I'll be new baptized;   50
Henceforth I never will be Romeo.
 Jul. What man art thou that thus bescreen'd
  in night
So stumblest on my counsel?
 Rom.   By a name
I know not how to tell thee who I am:
My name, dear saint, is hateful to myself,
Because it is an enemy to thee;
Had I it written, I would tear the word.
 Jul. My ears have not yet drunk a hundred
  words
Of that tongue's utterance, yet I know the sound:
Art thou not Romeo and a Montague?   60
 Rom. Neither, fair saint, if either thee dislike.
 Jul. How camest thou hither, tell me, and
  wherefore?
The orchard walls are high and hard to climb,
And the place death, considering who thou art,
If any of my kinsmen find thee here.
 Rom. With love's light wings did I o'er-perch
  these walls;
For stony limits cannot hold love out,
And what love can do that dares love attempt;
Therefore thy kinsmen are no let to me.

Jul. If they do see thee, they will murder
   thee.   70
Rom. Alack, there lies more peril in thine eye
Than twenty of their swords: look thou but
   sweet,
And I am proof against their enmity.
Jul. I would not for the world they saw thee
   here.
Rom. I have night's cloak to hide me from
   their sight;
And but thou love me, let them find me here:
My life were better ended by their hate,
Than death prorogued, wanting of thy love.
Jul. By whose direction found'st thou out this
   place?
Rom. By love, who first did prompt me to
   inquire;   80
He lent me counsel and I lent him eyes.
I am no pilot; yet, wert thou as far
As that vast shore wash'd with the farthest sea,
I would adventure for such merchandise.
Jul. Thou know'st the mask of night is on my
   face,
Else would a maiden blush bepaint my cheek
For that which thou hast heard me speak to-night.
Fain would I dwell on form, fain, fain deny
What I have spoke: but farewell compliment! 89
Dost thou love me? I know thou wilt say "Ay,"
And I will take thy word: yet, if thou swear'st,
Thou mayst prove false; at lovers' perjuries,
They say, Jove laughs. O gentle Romeo,
If thou dost love, pronounce it faithfully:
Or if thou think'st I am too quickly won,
I'll frown and be perverse and say thee nay,
So thou wilt woo; but else, not for the world.
In truth, fair Montague, I am too fond,
And therefore thou mayst think my 'haviour
   light:
But trust me, gentleman, I'll prove more true 100
Than those that have more cunning to be strange.
I should have been more strange, I must confess,
But that thou overheard'st, ere I was ware,
My true love's passion: therefore pardon me,
And not impute this yielding to light love,
Which the dark night hath so discovered.
Rom. Lady, by yonder blessed moon I swear
That tips with silver all these fruit-tree tops—
Jul. O, swear not by the moon, the inconstant
   moon,
That monthly changes in her circled orb,   110
Lest that thy love prove likewise variable.
Rom. What shall I swear by?
Jul.   Do not swear at all;
Or, if thou wilt, swear by thy gracious self,
Which is the god of my idolatry,
And I'll believe thee.

Rom.   If my heart's dear love—
Jul. Well, do not swear: although I joy in thee,
I have no joy of this contract to-night:
It is too rash, too unadvised, too sudden;
Too like the lightning, which doth cease to be
Ere one can say "It lightens." Sweet, good night!
This bud of love, by summer's ripening breath,
May prove a beauteous flower when next we
   meet.   122
Good night, good night! as sweet repose and rest
Come to thy heart as that within my breast!
Rom. O, wilt thou leave me so unsatisfied?
Jul. What satisfaction canst thou have to-
   night?
Rom. The exchange of thy love's faithful vow
   for mine.
Jul. I gave thee mine before thou didst request
   it:
And yet I would it were to give again.
Rom. Wouldst thou withdraw it? for what
   purpose, love?   130
Jul. But to be frank, and give it thee again.
And yet I wish but for the thing I have:
My bounty is as boundless as the sea,
My love as deep; the more I give to thee,
The more I have, for both are infinite.
   Nurse calls within.
I hear some noise within; dear love, adieu!
Anon, good nurse! Sweet Montague, be true.
Stay but a little, I will come again. [*Exit, above.*
Rom. O blessed, blessed night! I am afeard,
Being in night, all this is but a dream,   140
Too flattering-sweet to be substantial.

     Re-enter JULIET, *above.*

Jul. Three words, dear Romeo, and good night
   indeed.
If that thy bent of love be honourable,
Thy purpose marriage, send me word to-morrow,
By one that I'll procure to come to thee,
Where and what time thou wilt perform the rite;
And all my fortunes at thy foot I'll lay
And follow thee my lord throughout the world.
   Nurse [*Within*] Madam!
Jul. I come, anon.—But if thou mean'st not
   well,   150
I do beseech thee—
   Nurse. [*Within*] Madam!
Jul.   By and by, I come:—
To cease thy suit, and leave me to my grief:
To-morrow will I send.
Rom.   So thrive my soul—
Jul. A thousand times good night!
                       [*Exit, above.*
Rom. A thousand times the worse, to want thy
   light.

Love goes toward love, as schoolboys from their
  books,
But love from love, toward school with heavy
  looks.   [*Retiring.*

Re-enter JULIET, *above.*

Jul. Hist! Romeo, hist! O, for a falconer's
  voice,
To lure this tassel-gentle back again!   160
Bondage is hoarse, and may not speak aloud;
Else would I tear the cave where Echo lies,
And make her airy tongue more hoarse than mine,
With repetition of my Romeo's name.
  Rom. It is my soul that calls upon my name:
How silver-sweet sound lovers' tongues by night,
Like softest music to attending ears!
  Jul. Romeo!
  Rom.   My dear?
  Jul.   At what o'clock to-morrow
Shall I send to thee?
  Rom.   At the hour of nine.   169
  Jul. I will not fail: 'tis twenty years till then.
I have forgot why I did call thee back.
  Rom. Let me stand here till thou remember it.
  Jul. I shall forget, to have thee still stand there,
Remembering how I love thy company.
  Rom. And I'll still stay, to have thee still forget,
Forgetting any other home but this.
  Jul. 'Tis almost morning; I would have thee
  gone:
And yet no further than a wanton's bird;
Who lets it hop a little from her hand,
Like a poor prisoner in his twisted gyves,   180
And with a silk thread plucks it back again,
So loving-jealous of his liberty.
  Rom. I would I were thy bird.
  Jul.   Sweet, so would I:
Yet I should kill thee with much cherishing.
Good night, good night! parting is such sweet
  sorrow,
That I shall say good night till it be morrow.
                                    [*Exit above.*
  Rom. Sleep dwell upon thine eyes, peace in thy
  breast!
Would I were sleep and peace, so sweet to rest!
Hence will I to my ghostly father's cell,   189
His help to crave, and my dear hap to tell. [*Exit.*

SCENE III. *Friar Laurence's cell*

Enter FRIAR LAURENCE, *with a basket.*

Fri. L. The grey-eyed morn smiles on the
  frowning night,
Chequering the eastern clouds with streaks of
  light,
And flecked darkness like a drunkard reels
From forth day's path and Titan's fiery wheels:

Now, ere the sun advance his burning eye,
The day to cheer and night's dank dew to dry,
I must up-fill this osier cage of ours
With baleful weeds and precious-juiced flowers.
The earth that's nature's mother is her tomb;
What is her burying grave that is her womb,   10
And from her womb children of divers kind
We sucking on her natural bosom find,
Many for many virtues excellent,
None but for some, and yet all different.
O, mickle is the powerful grace that lies
In herbs, plants, stones, and their true qualities:
For nought so vile that on the earth doth live
But to the earth some special good doth give,
Nor aught so good but strain'd from that fair use
Revolts from true birth, stumbling on abuse: 20
Virtue itself turns vice, being misapplied;
And vice sometimes by action dignified.
Within the infant rind of this small flower
Poison hath residence and medicine power:
For this, being smelt, with that part cheers each
  part;
Being tasted, slays all senses with the heart.
Two such opposed kings encamp them still
In man as well as herbs, grace and rude will;
And where the worser is predominant,
Full soon the canker death eats up that plant. 30

Enter ROMEO.

  Rom. Good morrow, father.
  Fri. L.   *Benedicite!*
What early tongue so sweet saluteth me?
Young son, it argues a distemper'd head
So soon to bid good morrow to thy bed:
Care keeps his watch in every old man's eye,
And where care lodges, sleep will never lie;
But where unbruised youth with unstuff'd brain
Doth couch his limbs, there golden sleep doth
  reign:
Therefore thy earliness doth me assure
Thou art up-roused by some distemperature;   40
Or if not so, then here I hit it right,
Our Romeo hath not been in bed to-night.
  Rom. That last is true; the sweeter rest was
  mine.
  Fri. L. God pardon sin! wast thou with Rosa-
  line?
  Rom. With Rosaline, my ghostly father? no;
I have forgot that name, and that name's woe.
  Fri. L. That's my good son: but where hast
  thou been, then?
  Rom. I'll tell thee, ere thou ask it me again.
I have been feasting with mine enemy,
Where on a sudden one hath wounded me,   50
That's by me wounded: both our remedies
Within thy help and holy physic lies:

I bear no hatred, blessed man, for, lo,
My intercession likewise steads my foe.
 Fri. L. Be plain, good son, and homely in thy
   drift;
Riddling confession finds but riddling shrift.
 Rom. Then plainly know my heart's dear love
   is set
On the fair daughter of rich Capulet:
As mine on hers so hers is set on mine;   59
And all combined, save what thou must combine
By holy marriage: when and where and how
We met, we woo'd, and made exchange of vow,
I'll tell thee as we pass; but this I pray,
That thou consent to marry us to-day.
 Fri. L. Holy Saint Francis, what a change is
   here!
Is Rosaline, whom thou didst love so dear,
So soon forsaken? young men's love then lies
Not truly in their hearts, but in their eyes.
Jesu Maria, what a deal of brine
Hath wash'd thy sallow cheeks for Rosaline!   70
How much salt water thrown away in waste,
To season love, that of it doth not taste!
The sun not yet thy sighs from heaven clears,
Thy old groans ring yet in my ancient ears;
Lo, here upon thy cheek the stain doth sit
Of an old tear that is not wash'd off yet:
If e'er thou wast thyself and these woes thine,
Thou and these woes were all for Rosaline:
And art thou changed? pronounce this sentence
   then: 79
Women may fall, when there's no strength in
   men.
 Rom. Thou chid'st me oft for loving Rosaline.
 Fri. L. For doting, not for loving, pupil mine.
 Rom. And bad'st me bury love.
 Fri. L.   Not in a grave,
To lay one in, another out to have.
 Rom. I pray thee, chide not: she whom I love
   now
Doth grace for grace and love for love allow;
The other did not so.
 Fri. L.   O, she knew well
Thy love did read by rote and could not spell.
But come, young waverer, come, go with me,
In one respect I'll thy assistant be;   90
For this alliance may so happy prove,
To turn your households' rancour to pure love.
 Rom. O, let us hence; I stand on sudden haste.
 Fri. L. Wisely and slow; they stumble that run
   fast.   [*Exeunt.*

Scene IV. *A street*

Enter BENVOLIO *and* MERCUTIO.

 Mer. Where the devil should this Romeo be?
Came he not home to-night?

 Ben. Not to his father's; I spoke with his
   man.
 Mer. Ah, that same pale hard-hearted wench,
   that Rosaline,
Torments him so, that he will sure run mad.
 Ben. Tybalt, the kinsman of old Capulet,
Hath sent a letter to his father's house.
 Mer. A challenge, on my life.
 Ben. Romeo will answer it.
 Mer. Any man that can write may answer a
   letter.   10
 Ben. Nay, he will answer the letter's master,
how he dares, being dared.
 Mer. Alas, poor Romeo! he is already dead;
stabbed with a white wench's black eye; shot
thorough the ear with a love-song; the very pin
of his heart cleft with the blind bow-boy's butt-
shaft: and is he a man to encounter Tybalt?
 Ben. Why, what is Tybalt?
 Mer. More than prince of cats, I can tell you.
O, he is the courageous captain of complements.
He fights as you sing prick-song, keeps time,
distance, an proportion; rests me his minim
rest, one, two, and the third in your bosom: the
very butcher of a silk button, a duellist, a duellist; a gentleman of the very first house, of the
first and second cause: ah, the immortal *passado!*
the *punto reverso!* the *hai!*
 Ben. The what?
 Mer. The pox of such antic, lisping, affecting
fantasticoes; these new tuners of accents! "By
Jesu, a very good blade! a very tall man! a very
good whore!" Why, is not this a lamentable
thing, grandsire, that we should be thus afflicted
with these strange flies, these fashion-mongers,
these *perdona-mi's,* who stand so much on the
new form, that they cannot sit at ease on the old
bench? O, their bones, their bones!

Enter ROMEO.

 Ben. Here comes Romeo, here comes Romeo.
 Mer. Without his roe, like a dried herring: O
flesh, flesh, how art thou fishified! Now is he
for the numbers that Petrarch flowed in: Laura
to his lady was but a kitchen-wench; marry,
she had a better love to be-rhyme her; Dido a
dowdy; Cleopatra a gipsy; Helen and Hero
hildings and harlots; Thisbe a grey eye or so,
but not to the purpose. Signior Romeo, *bon
jour!* there's a French salutation to your French
slop. You gave us the counterfeit fairly last
night.
 Rom. Good morrow to you both. What counterfeit did I give you?   50
 Mer. The slip, sir, the slip; can you not conceive?

Rom. Pardon, good Mercutio, my business was great; and in such a case as mine a man may strain courtesy.

Mer. That's as much as to say, such a case as yours constrains a man to bow in the hams.

Rom. Meaning, to court'sy.

Mer. Thou hast most kindly hit it.

Rom. A most courteous exposition.   60

Mer. Nay, I am the very pink of courtesy.

Rom. Pink for flower.

Mer. Right.

Rom. Why, then is my pump well flowered.

Mer. Well said: follow me this jest now till thou hast worn out thy pump, that when the single sole of it is worn, the jest may remain after the wearing sole singular.

Rom. O single-soled jest, solely singular for the singleness!   70

Mer. Come between us, good Benvolio; my wits faint.

Rom. Switch and spurs, switch and spurs; or I'll cry a match.

Mer. Nay, if thy wits run the wild-goose chase, I have done, for thou hast more of the wild-goose in one of thy wits than, I am sure, I have in my whole five: was I with you there for the goose?

Rom. Thou wast never with me for any thing when thou wast not there for the goose.   80

Mer. I will bite thee by the ear for that jest.

Rom. Nay, good goose, bite not.

Mer. Thy wit is a very bitter sweeting; it is a most sharp sauce.

Rom. And is it not well served in to a sweet goose?

Mer. O, here's a wit of cheveril, that stretches from an inch narrow to an ell broad!

Rom. I stretch it out for that word "broad"; which added to the goose, proves thee far and wide a broad goose.   91

Mer. Why, is not this better now than groaning for love? now art thou sociable, now art thou Romeo; now art thou what thou art, by art as well as by nature: for this drivelling love is like a great natural, that runs lolling up and down to hide his bauble in a hole.

Ben. Stop there, stop there.

Mer. Thou desirest me to stop in my tale against the hair.   100

Ben. Thou wouldst else have made thy tale large.

Mer. O, thou art deceived; I would have made it short: for I was come to the whole depth of my tale; and meant, indeed, to occupy the argument no longer.

Rom. Here's goodly gear!

Enter NURSE *and* PETER.

Mer. A sail, a sail!

Ben. Two, two; a shirt and a smock.

Nurse. Peter!   110

Peter. Anon!

Nurse. My fan, Peter.

Mer. Good Peter, to hide her face; for her fan's the fairer face.

Nurse. God ye good morrow, gentlemen.

Mer. God ye good den, fair gentlewoman.

Nurse. Is it good den?

Mer. 'Tis no less, I tell you, for the bawdy hand of the dial is now upon the prick of noon.

Nurse. Out upon you! what a man are you!   120

Rom. One, gentlewoman, that God hath made for himself to mar.

Nurse. By my troth, it is well said; "for himself to mar," quoth a'? Gentlemen, can any of you tell me where I may find the young Romeo?

Rom. I can tell you; but young Romeo will be older when you have found him than he was when you sought him: I am the youngest of that name, for fault of a worse.

Nurse. You say well.   130

Mer. Yea, is the worst well? very well took, i' faith; wisely, wisely.

Nurse. If you be he, sir, I desire some confidence with you.

Ben. She will indite him to some supper.

Mer. A bawd, a bawd, a bawd! So ho!

Rom. What hast thou found?

Mer. No hare, sir; unless a hare, sir, in a lenten pie, that is something stale and hoar ere it be spent. [*Sings.*]   140

> An old hare hoar,
> And an old hare hoar,
> Is very good meat in lent:
> But a hare that is hoar
> Is too much for a score,
> When it hoars ere it be spent.

Romeo, will you come to your father's? we'll to dinner, thither.

Rom. I will follow you.

Mer. Farewell, ancient lady; farewell, [*singing*] "lady, lady, lady."   151

[*Exeunt* MERCUTIO *and* BENVOLIO.

Nurse. Marry, farewell! I pray you, sir, what saucy merchant was this, that was so full of his ropery?

Rom. A gentleman, nurse, that loves to hear himself talk, and will speak more in a minute than he will stand to in a month.

Nurse. An a' speak any thing against me, I'll take him down, an a' were lustier than he is, and twenty such Jacks; and if I cannot, I'll find those that shall. Scurvy knave! I am none of his flirt-gills; I am none of his skains-mates. And thou must stand by too, and suffer every knave to use me at his pleasure?

Peter. I saw no man use you at his pleasure: if I had, my weapon should quickly have been out, I warrant you: I dare draw as soon as another man, if I see occasion in a good quarrel, and the law on my side.   *169*

Nurse. Now, afore God, I am so vexed, that every part about me quivers. Scurvy knave! Pray you, sir, a word: and as I told you, my young lady bade me inquire you out; what she bade me say, I will keep to myself: but first let me tell ye, if ye should lead her into a fool's paradise, as they say, it were a very gross kind of behaviour, as they say: for the gentlewoman is young; and, therefore, if you should deal double with her, truly it were an ill thing to be offered to any gentlewoman, and very weak dealing.   *181*

Rom. Nurse, commend me to thy lady and mistress. I protest unto thee—

Nurse. Good heart, and, i' faith, I will tell her as much: Lord, Lord, she will be a joyful woman.

Rom. What wilt thou tell her, nurse? thou dost not mark me.

Nurse. I will tell her, sir, that you do protest; which, as I take it, is a gentlemanlike offer.

Rom. Bid her devise   *191*
Some means to come to shrift this afternoon;
And there she shall at Friar Laurence' cell
Be shrived and married. Here is for thy pains.

Nurse. No, truly, sir; not a penny.

Rom. Go to; I say you shall.

Nurse. This afternoon, sir? well, she shall be there.

Rom. And stay, good nurse, behind the abbey
wall:
Within this hour my man shall be with thee,   *200*
And bring thee cords made like a tackled stair;
Which to the high top-gallant of my joy
Must be my convoy in the secret night.
Farewell; be trusty, and I'll quit thy pains:
Farewell; commend me to thy mistress.

Nurse. Now God in heaven bless thee! Hark
you, sir.

Rom. What say'st thou, my dear nurse?

Nurse. Is your man secret? Did you ne'er hear
say,
"Two may keep counsel, putting one away"?

Rom. I warrant thee, my man's as true as
steel.   *210*

Nurse. Well, sir; my mistress is the sweetest lady—Lord, Lord! when 'twas a little prating thing:— O, there is a nobleman in town, one

Paris, that would fain lay knife aboard, but she, good soul, had as lief see a toad, a very toad, as see him. I anger her sometimes and tell her that Paris is the properer man; but, I'll warrant you, when I say so, she looks as pale as any clout in the versal world. Doth not rosemary and Romeo begin both with a letter?   *220*

Rom. Ay, nurse; what of that? both with an R.

Nurse. Ah, mocker! that's the dog's name; R is for the—No; I know it begins with some other letter:— and she hath the prettiest sententious of it, of you and rosemary, that it would do you good to hear it.

Rom. Commend me to thy lady.

Nurse. Ay, a thousand times. [*Exit* ROMEO.]
Peter!   *230*

Pet. Anon!

Nurse. Peter, take my fan, and go before, and apace.   [*Exeunt.*

SCENE V. *Capulet's orchard*

Enter JULIET.

Jul. The clock struck nine when I did send the
nurse;
In half an hour she promised to return.
Perchance she cannot meet him: that's not so.
O, she is lame! love's heralds should be thoughts,
Which ten times faster glide than the sun's beams,
Driving back shadows over louring hills:
Therefore do nimble-pinion'd doves draw love,
And therefore hath the wind-swift Cupid wings.
Now is the sun upon the highmost hill
Of this day's journey, and from nine till twelve
Is three long hours, yet she is not come.   *11*
Had she affections and warm youthful blood,
She would be as swift in motion as a ball;
My words would bandy her to my sweet love,
And his to me:
But old folks, many feign as they were dead;
Unwieldy, slow, heavy, and pale as lead.
O God, she comes!

Enter NURSE *and* PETER.

O honey nurse, what news?
Hast thou met with him? Send thy man away.

Nurse. Peter, stay at the gate. [*Exit* PETER.

Jul. Now, good sweet nurse—O Lord, why
look'st thou sad?   *21*
Though news be sad, yet tell them merrily;
If good, thou shamest the music of sweet news
By playing it to me with so sour a face.

Nurse. I am a-weary, give me leave awhile:
Fie, how my bones ache! what a jaunt have I
had!

Jul. I would thou hadst my bones, and I thy
news.

Nay, come, I pray thee, speak; good, good
   nurse, speak.
Nurse. Jesu, what haste? can you not stay
   awhile?
Do you not see that I am out of breath?   30
Jul. How art thou out of breath, when thou hast
   breath
To say to me that thou art out of breath?
The excuse that thou dost make in this delay
Is longer than the tale thou dost excuse.
Is thy news good, or bad? answer to that;
Say either, and I'll stay the circumstance:
Let me be satisfied, is't good or bad?
Nurse. Well, you have made a simple choice;
you know not how to choose a man: Romeo! no,
not he; though his face be better than any man's,
yet his leg excels all men's; and for a hand, and a
foot, and a body, though they be not to be talked
on, yet they are past compare: he is not the
flower of courtesy, but, I'll warrant him, as
gentle as a lamb. Go thy ways, wench; serve
God. What, have you dined at home?
Jul. No, no: but all this did I know before.
What says he of our marriage? what of that?
Nurse. Lord, how my head aches! what a head
have I!
It beats as it would fall in twenty pieces.   50
My back o' t' other side—O, my back, my back!
Beshrew your heart for sending me about
To catch my death with jaunting up and down!
Jul. I' faith, I am sorry that thou art not well.
Sweet, sweet, sweet nurse, tell me, what says my
   love?
Nurse. Your love says, like an honest gentle-
man, and a courteous, and a kind, and a hand-
some, and, I warrant, a virtuous—Where is your
mother?
Jul. Where is my mother! why, she is
   within;   60
Where should she be? How oddly thou repliest!
"Your love says, like an honest gentleman,
'Where is your mother?'"
Nurse.   O God's lady dear!
Are you so hot? marry, come up, I trow;
Is this the poultice for my aching bones?
Henceforward do your messages yourself.
Jul. Here's such a coil! come, what says
   Romeo?
Nurse. Have you got leave to go to shrift
   to-day?
Jul. I have.
Nurse. Then hie you hence to Friar Laurence'
   cell;   70
There stays a husband to make you a wife:
Now comes the wanton blood up in your cheeks,
They'll be in scarlet straight at any news.

Hie you to church; I must another way,
To fetch a ladder, by the which your love
Must climb a bird's nest soon when it is dark:
I am the drudge and toil in your delight,
But you shall bear the burden soon at night.
Go; I'll to dinner; hie you to the cell.
Jul. Hie to high fortune! Honest nurse,
   farewell.   [*Exeunt.*   80

SCENE VI. *Friar Laurence's cell*

Enter FRIAR LAURENCE *and* ROMEO.

Fri. L. So smile the heavens upon this holy act,
That after hours with sorrow chide us not!
Rom. Amen, amen! but come what sorrow can,
It cannot countervail the exchange of joy
That one short minute gives me in her sight:
Do thou but close our hands with holy words,
Then love-devouring death do what he dare;
It is enough I may call her mine.
Fri. L. These violent delights have violent
   ends
And in their triumph die, like fire and powder,   10
Which as they kiss consume: the sweetest honey
Is loathesome in his own deliciousness
And in the taste confounds the appetite:
Therefore love moderately; long love doth so;
Too swift arrives as tardy as too slow.

Enter JULIET.

Here comes the lady: O, so light a foot
Will ne'er wear out the everlasting flint:
A lover may bestride the gossamer
That idles in the wanton summer air,
And yet not fall; so light is vanity.   20
Jul. Good even to my ghostly confessor.
Fri. L. Romeo shall thank thee, daughter, for us
   both.
Jul. As much to him, else is his thanks too
   much.
Rom. Ah, Juliet, if the measure of thy joy
Be heap'd like mine and that thy skill be more
To blazon it, then sweeten with thy breath
This neighbour air, and let rich music's tongue
Unfold the imagined happiness that both
Receive in either by this dear encounter.
Jul. Conceit, more rich in matter than in
   words,
Brags of his substance, not of ornament: 31
They are but beggars that can count their worth;
But my true love is grown to such excess
I cannot sum up sum of half my wealth.
Fri. L. Come, come with me, and we will
   make short work;
For, by your leaves, you shall not stay alone
Till holy church incorporate two in one.
                                       [*Exeunt.*

ACT III

SCENE I. *A public place*

Enter MERCUTIO, BENVOLIO, *Page, and Servants.*

Ben. I pray thee, good Mercutio, let's retire:
The day is hot, the Capulets abroad,
And, if we meet, we shall not scape a brawl;
For now, these hot days, is the mad blood
    stirring.
Mer. Thou art like one of those fellows that
when he enters the confines of a tavern claps me
his sword upon the table and says, "God send
me no need of thee!" and by the operation of the
second cup draws it on the drawer, when indeed
there is no need.   *10*
Ben. Am I like such a fellow?
Mer. Come, come, thou art as hot a Jack in thy
mood as any in Italy, and as soon moved to be
moody, and as soon moody to be moved.
Ben. And what to?
Mer. Nay, an there were two such, we should
have none shortly, for one would kill the other.
Thou! why, thou wilt quarrel with a man that
hath a hair more, or a hair less, in his beard than
thou hast: thou wilt quarrel with a man for
cracking nuts, having no other reason but because thou hast hazel eyes: what eye but such
an eye would spy out such a quarrel? Thy head
is as full of quarrels as an egg is full of meat, and
yet thy head hath been beaten as addle as an egg
for quarrelling: thou hast quarrelled with a man
for coughing in the street, because he hath
wakened thy dog that hath lain asleep in the sun:
didst thou not fall out with a tailor for wearing
his new doublet before Easter? with another, for
tying his new shoes with old riband? and yet
thou wilt tutor me from quarrelling!
Ben. An I were so apt to quarrel as thou art, any
man should buy the fee-simple of my life for an
hour and a quarter.
Mer. The fee-simple—O simple!
Ben. By my head, here come the Capulets.
Mer. By my heel, I care not.   *39*

Enter TYBALT *and others.*

Tyb. Follow me close, for I will speak to them.
Gentlemen, good den: a word with one of you.
Mer. And but one word with one of us? couple
it with something; make it a word and a blow.
Tyb. You shall find me apt enough to that, sir,
an you will give me occasion.
Mer. Could you not take some occasion with-
out giving?
Tyb. Mercutio, thou consort'st with Romeo—
Mer. Consort! what, dost thou make us min-
strels? an thou make minstrels of us, look to hear
nothing but discords: here's my fiddlestick;
here's that shall make you dance. 'Zounds,
consort!
Ben. We talk here in the public haunt of men:
Either withdraw unto some private place,
And reason coldly of your grievances,
Or else depart; here all eyes gaze on us.
Mer. Men's eyes were made to look, and let
    them gaze;
I will not budge for no man's pleasure, I.

Enter ROMEO.

Tyb. Well, peace be with you, sir: here comes
    my man.
Mer. But I'll be hang'd, sir, if he wear your
    livery: *60*
Marry, go before to field, he'll be your follower;
Your worship in that sense may call him "man."
Tyb. Romeo, the hate I bear thee can afford
No better term than this: thou art a villain.
Rom. Tybalt, the reason that I have to love
    thee
Doth much excuse the appertaining rage
To such a greeting: villain am I none;
Therefore farewell; I see thou know'st me not.
Tyb. Boy, this shall not excuse the injuries
That thou hast done me; therefore turn and draw.
Rom. I do protest I never injured thee,   *71*
But love thee better than thou canst devise,
Till thou shalt know the reason of my love:
And so, good Capulet—which name I tender
As dearly as my own—be satisfied.
Mer. O calm, dishonourable, vile submission!
Alla stoccata carries it away. [*Draws.*]
Tybalt, you rat-catcher, will you walk?
Tyb. What wouldst thou have with me?   *79*
Mer. Good king of cats, nothing but one of your
nine lives; that I mean to make bold withal, and,
as you shall use me hereafter, dry-beat the rest of
the eight. Will you pluck your sword out of his
pilcher by the ears? make haste, lest mine be
about your ears ere it be out.
Tyb. I am for you. [*Drawing.*]
Rom. Gentle Mercutio, put thy rapier up.
Mer. Come, sir, your *passado*. [*They fight.*]
Rom. Draw, Benvolio; beat down their weapons.
Gentlemen, for shame, forbear this outrage!   *90*
Tybalt, Mercutio, the prince expressly hath
Forbidden bandying in Verona streets:
Hold, Tybalt! good Mercutio!
    [TYBALT *under* ROMEO's *arm stabs* MERCUTIO,
                    and flies with his followers.
Mer.   I am hurt.
A plague o' both your houses! I am sped.
Is he gone, and hath nothing?
Ben.   What, art thou hurt?

Mer. Ay, ay, a scratch, a scratch; marry, 'tis enough.

Where is my page? Go, villain, fetch a surgeon.

[*Exit* PAGE.

Rom. Courage, man; the hurt cannot be much.

Mer. No, 'tis not so deep as a well, nor so wide as a church-door; but 'tis enough, 'twill serve: ask for me to-morrow, and you shall find me a grave man. I am peppered, I warrant, for this world. A plague o' both your houses! 'Zounds, a dog, a rat, a mouse, a cat, to scratch a man to death! a braggart, a rogue, a villain, that fights by the book of arithmetic! Why the devil came you between us? I was hurt under your arm.

Rom. I thought all for the best.   109

Mer. Help me into some house, Benvolio,
Or I shall faint. A plague o' both your houses!
They have made worms' meat of me: I have it,
And soundly too: your houses!

[*Exeunt* MERCUTIO *and* BENVOLIO.

Rom. This gentleman, the Prince's near ally,
My very friend, hath got his mortal hurt
In my behalf; my reputation stain'd
With Tybalt's slander— Tybalt, that an hour
Hath been my kinsman! O sweet Juliet,
Thy beauty hath made me effeminate
And in my temper soften'd valour's steel!   120

Re-enter BENVOLIO.

Ben. O Romeo, Romeo, brave Mercutio's dead!
That gallant spirit hath aspired the clouds,
Which too untimely here did scorn the earth.

Rom. This day's black fate on more days doth depend;
This but begins the woe others must end.

Ben. Here comes the furious Tybalt back again.

Rom. Alive, in triumph! and Mercutio slain!
Away to heaven, respective lenity,
And fire-eyed fury be my conduct now!

Re-enter TYBALT.

Now, Tybalt, take the "villain" back again   130
That late thou gavest me; for Mercutio's soul
Is but a little way above our heads,
Staying for thine to keep him company:
Either thou, or I, or both, must go with him.

Tyb. Thou, wretched boy, that didst consort him here,
Shalt with him hence.

Rom.   This shall determine that.

They fight; TYBALT *falls.*

Ben. Romeo away, be gone!
The citizens are up, and Tybalt slain.
Stand not amazed: the Prince will doom thee death,
If thou art taken: hence, be gone, away!   140

Rom. O, I am fortune's fool!

Ben.   Why dost thou stay?

[*Exit* ROMEO.

Enter CITIZENS, &c.

1st Cit. Which way ran he that kill'd Mercutio?
Tybalt, that murderer, which way ran he?

Ben. There lies that Tybalt.

1st Cit.   Up, sir, go with me;
I charge thee in the Prince's name, obey.

Enter PRINCE, *attended;* MONTAGUE, CAPULET, *their* WIVES, *and others.*

Prin. Where are the vile beginners of this fray?

Ben. O noble Prince, I can discover all
The unlucky manage of this fatal brawl:
There lies the man, slain by young Romeo,
That slew thy kinsman, brave Mercutio.   150

La. Cap. Tybalt, my cousin! O my brother's child!
O Prince! O cousin! husband! O, the blood is spilt
Of my dear kinsman! Prince, as thou art true,
For blood of ours, shed blood of Montague.
O cousin, cousin!

Prin. Benvolio, who began this bloody fray?

Ben. Tybalt, here slain, whom Romeo's hand did slay;
Romeo that spoke him fair, bade him bethink
How nice the quarrel was, and urged withal
Your high displeasure: all this uttered   160
With gentle breath, calm look, knees humbly bow'd,
Could not take truce with the unruly spleen
Of Tybalt deaf to peace, but that he tilts
With piercing steel at bold Mercutio's breast,
Who, all as hot, turns deadly point to point,
And, with a martial scorn, with one hand beats
Cold death aside, and with the other sends
It back to Tybalt, whose dexterity
Retorts it: Romeo he cried aloud,
"Hold, friends! friends, part!" and, swifter than his tongue,   170
His agile arm beats down their fatal points,
And 'twixt them rushes; underneath whose arm
An envious thrust from Tybalt hit the life
Of stout Mercutio, and then Tybalt fled;
But by and by comes back to Romeo,
Who had but newly entertain'd revenge,
And to't they go like lightning, for, ere I
Could draw to part them, was stout Tybalt slain,
And, as he fell, did Romeo turn and fly.
This is the truth, or let Benvolio die.   180

La. Cap. He is a kinsman to the Montague;
Affection makes him false; he speaks not true:
Some twenty of them fought in this black strife,

And all those twenty could but kill one life.
I beg for justice, which thou, Prince, must give;
Romeo slew Tybalt, Romeo must not live.
Prin. Romeo slew him, he slew Mercutio;
Who now the price of his dear blood doth owe?
Mon. Not Romeo, Prince, he was Mercutio's
friend;   *189*
His fault concludes but what the law should end,
The life of Tybalt.
Prin.   And for that offence
Immediately we do exile him hence:
I have an interest in your hate's proceeding,
My blood for your rude brawls doth lie a-bleed-
ing;
But I'll amerce you with so strong a fine
That you shall all repent the loss of mine:
I will be deaf to pleading and excuses;
Nor tears nor prayers shall purchase out abuses:
Therefore use none: let Romeo hence in haste,
Else, when he's found, that hour is his last.   *200*
Bear hence this body and attend our will:
Mercy but murders, pardoning those that kill.
                                              [*Exeunt.*

SCENE II. *Capulet's orchard*
Enter JULIET.

Jul. Gallop apace, you fiery-footed steeds,
Towards Phœbus' lodging: such a waggoner
As Phaethon would whip you to the west,
And bring in cloudy night immediately.
Spread thy close curtain, love-performing night,
That runaways' eyes may wink, and Romeo
Leap to these arms, untalk'd of and unseen.
Lovers can see to do their amorous rites
By their own beauties; or, if love be blind,
It best agrees with night. Come, civil night,   *10*
Thou sober-suited matron, all in black,
And learn me how to lose a winning match,
Play'd for a pair of stainless maidenhoods:
Hood my unmann'd blood, bating in my cheeks,
With thy black mantle; till strange love, grown
bold,
Think true love acted simple modesty.
Come, night; come, Romeo; come, thou day in
night;
For thou wilt lie upon the wings of night
Whiter than new snow on a raven's back.
Come, gentle night, come, loving, black-brow'd
night,   *20*
Give me my Romeo; and, when he shall die,
Take him and cut him out in little stars,
And he will make the face of heaven so fine
That all the world will be in love with night
And pay no worship to the garish sun.
O, I have bought the mansion of a love,
But not possess'd it, and, though I am sold,

Not yet enjoy'd: so tedious is this day
As is the night before some festival
To an impatient child that hath new robes   *30*
And may not wear them. O, here comes my
nurse,
And she brings news; and every tongue that
speaks
But Romeo's name speaks heavenly eloquence.

Enter NURSE, *with cords.*

Now, nurse, what news? What hast thou there?
the cords
That Romeo bid thee fetch?
Nurse.   Ay, ay, the cords.
    Throws them down.
Jul. Ay me! what news? why dost thou wring
thy hands?
Nurse. Ah, well-a-day! he's dead, he's dead!
We are undone, lady, we are undone!
Alack the day! he's gone, he's kill'd, he's dead!
Jul. Can heaven be so envious?
Nurse.   Romeo can,   *40*
Though heaven cannot: O Romeo, Romeo!
Who ever would have thought it? Romeo!
Jul. What devil art thou, that dost torment me
thus?
This torture should be roar'd in dismal hell.
Hath Romeo slain himself? say thou but ay,
And that bare vowel I shall poison more
Than the death-darting eye of cockatrice:
I am not I, if there be such an ay,
Or those eyes shut, that make thee answer ay.
If he be slain, say ay; or if not, no: *50*
Brief sounds determine of my weal or woe.
Nurse. I saw the wound, I saw it with mine
eyes—
God save the mark!—here on his manly breast:
A piteous corse, a bloody piteous corse;
Pale, pale as ashes, all bedaub'd in blood,
All in gore-blood; I swounded at the sight.
Jul. O, break, my heart! poor bankrupt, break
at once!
To prison, eyes, ne'er look on liberty!
Vile earth, to earth resign; end motion here;
And thou and Romeo press one heavy bier!   *60*
Nurse. O Tybalt, Tybalt, the best friend I
had!
O courteous Tybalt! honest gentleman!
That ever I should live to see thee dead!
Jul. What storm is this that blows so contrary?
Is Romeo slaughter'd, and is Tybalt dead?
My dear-loved cousin, and my dearer lord?
Then, dreadful trumpet, sound the general doom!
For who is living, if those two are gone?
Nurse. Tybalt is gone, and Romeo banished;
Romeo that kill'd him, he is banished.   *70*

Jul. O God! did Romeo's hand shed Tybalt's
 blood?
Nurse. It did, it did; alas the day, it did!
Jul. O serpent heart, hid with a flowering face!
Did ever dragon keep so fair a cave?
Beautiful tyrant! fiend angelical!
Dove-feather'd raven! wolvish-ravening lamb!
Despised substance of divinest show!
Just opposite to what thou justly seem'st,
A damned saint, an honourable villain!
O nature, what hadst thou to do in hell,   80
When thou didst bower the spirit of a fiend
In mortal paradise of such sweet flesh?
Was ever book containing such vile matter
So fairly bound? O, that deceit should dwell
In such a gorgeous palace!
Nurse.   There's no trust,
No faith, no honesty in men; all perjured,
All forsworn, all naught, all dissemblers.
Ah, where's my man? give me some *aqua vitæ:*
These griefs, these woes, these sorrows make me
 old.
Shame come to Romeo!
Jul.   Blister'd be thy tongue   90
For such a wish! he was not born to shame:
Upon his brow shame is ashamed to sit;
For 'tis a throne where honour may be crown'd
Sole monarch of the universal earth.
O, what a beast was I to chide at him!
Nurse. Will you speak well of him that kill'd
 your cousin?
Jul. Shall I speak ill of him that is my husband?
Ah, poor my lord, what tongue shall smooth thy
 name,
When I, thy three-hours wife, have mangled it?
But, wherefore, villain, didst thou kill my
 cousin?   100
That villain cousin would have kill'd my husband:
Back, foolish tears, back to your native spring;
Your tributary drops belong to woe,
Which you, mistaking, offer up to joy.
My husband lives, that Tybalt would have slain;
And Tybalt's dead, that would have slain my
 husband:
All this is comfort; wherefore weep I then?
Some word there was, worser than Tybalt's death,
That murder'd me: I would forget it fain;
But, O, it presses to my memory,   110
Like damned guilty deeds to sinners' minds:
"Tybalt is dead, and Romeo—banished";
That "banished," that one word "banished,"
Hath slain ten thousand Tybalts. Tybalt's death
Was woe enough, if it had ended there:
Or, if sour woe delights in fellowship
And needly will be rank'd with other griefs,

Why follow'd not, when she said "Tybalt's
 dead,"
Thy father, or thy mother, nay, or both,   119
Which modern lamentation might have moved?
But with a rearward following Tybalt's death,
"Romeo is banished," to speak that word,
Is father, mother, Tybalt, Romeo, Juliet,
All slain, all dead. "Romeo is banished!"
There is no end, no limit, measure, bound,
In that word's death; no words can that woe
 sound.
Where is my father and my mother, nurse?
Nurse. Weeping and wailing over Tybalt's
 corse:
Will you go to them? I will bring you thither.
Jul. Wash they his wounds with tears: mine
 shall be spent,   130
When theirs are dry, for Romeo's banishment.
Take up those cords: poor ropes, you are
 beguiled,
Both you and I; for Romeo is exiled:
He made you for a highway to my bed;
But I, a maid, die maiden-widowed.
Come, cords, come, nurse; I'll to my wedding-
 bed;
And death, not Romeo, take my maidenhead!
Nurse. Hie to your chamber: I'll find Romeo
To comfort you: I wot well where he is.
Hark ye, your Romeo will be here at night: 140
I'll to him; he is hid at Laurence' cell.
Jul. O, find him! give this ring to my true
 knight,
And bid him come to take his last farewell.
                                        [*Exeunt.*

SCENE III. *Friar Laurence's cell*
Enter FRIAR LAURENCE.

Fri. L. Romeo, come forth; come forth, thou
 fearful man:
Affliction is enamour'd of thy parts,
And thou art wedded to calamity.

Enter ROMEO.

Rom. Father, what news? what is the Prince's
 doom?
What sorrow craves acquaintance at my hand,
That I yet know not?
Fri. L.   Too familiar
Is my dear son with such sour company:
I bring thee tidings of the Prince's doom.
Rom. What less than dooms-day is the Prince's
 doom?
Fri. L. A gentler judgement vanish'd from his
 lips,   10
Not body's death, but body's banishment.

Rom. Ha, banishment! be merciful, say
  "death";
For exile hath more terror in his look,
Much more than death: do not say "banishment."
  Fri. L. Hence from Verona art thou banished:
Be patient, for the world is broad and wide.
  Rom. There is no world without Verona walls,
But purgatory, torture, hell itself.
Hence-banished is banish'd from the world,
And world's exile is death: then "banished"   20
Is death mis-term'd: calling death "banishment,"
Thou cutt'st my head off with a golden axe,
And smilest upon the stroke that murders me.
  Fri. L. O deadly sin! O rude unthankfulness!
Thy fault our law calls death; but the kind prince,
Taking thy part, hath rush'd aside the law,
And turn'd that black word "death" to "banish-
  ment":
This is dear mercy, and thou seest it not.
  Rom. 'Tis torture, and not mercy: heaven is
  here,
Where Juliet lives; and every cat and dog   30
And little mouse, every unworthy thing,
Live here in heaven and may look on her;
But Romeo may not: more validity,
More honourable state, more courtship lives
In carrion-flies than Romeo: they may seize
On the white wonder of dear Juliet's hand
And steal immortal blessing from her lips,
Who, even in pure and vestal modesty,
Still blush, as thinking their own kisses sin;
But Romeo may not; he is banished: 40
Flies may do this, but I from this must fly:
They are free men, but I am banished:
And say'st thou yet that exile is not death?
Hadst thou no poison mix'd, no sharp-ground
  knife,
No sudden mean of death, though ne'er so mean,
But "banished" to kill me?—"banished"?
O friar, the damned use that word in hell;
Howlings attend it: how hast thou the heart,
Being a divine, a ghostly confessor,
A sin-absolver, and my friend profess'd,   50
To mangle me with that word "banished"?
  Fri. L. Thou fond mad man, hear me but speak
  a word.
  Rom. O, thou wilt speak again of banishment.
  Fri. L. I'll give thee armour to keep off that
  word;
Adversity's sweet milk, philosophy,
To comfort thee, though thou art banished.
  Rom. Yet "banished"? Hang up philosophy!
Unless philosophy can make a Juliet,
Displant a town, reverse a prince's doom,
It helps not, it prevails not: talk no more.   60
  Fri. L. O, then I see that madmen have no ears.

  Rom. How should they, when that wise men
  have no eyes?
  Fri. L. Let me dispute with thee of thy estate.
  Rom. Thou canst not speak of that thou dost
  not feel:
Wert thou as young as I, Juliet thy love,
An hour but married, Tybalt murdered,
Doting like me and like me banished,
Then mightst thou speak, then mightst thou tear
  thy hair,
And fall upon the ground, as I do now,
Taking the measure of an unmade grave.   70
  Knocking within.
  Fri. L. Arise; one knocks; good Romeo, hide
  thyself.
  Rom. Not I; unless the breath of heart-sick
  groans,
Mist-like, infold me from the search of eyes.
  Knocking.
  Fri. L. Hark, how they knock! Who's there?
  Romeo, arise;
Thou wilt be taken. Stay awhile! Stand up;
  Knocking.
Run to my study. By and by! God's will,
What simpleness is this! I come, I come!
  Knocking.
Who knocks so hard? whence come you? what's
  your will?
  Nurse. [*Within*] Let me come in, and you shall
  know my errand;
I come from Lady Juliet.
  Fri. L.   Welcome, then.   80

Enter NURSE.

  Nurse. O holy friar, O, tell me, holy friar,
Where is my lady's lord, where's Romeo?
  Fri. L. There on the ground, with his own tears
  made drunk.
  Nurse. O, he is even in my mistress' case,
Just in her case! O woeful sympathy!
Piteous predicament! Even so lies she,
Blubbering and weeping, weeping and blubbering.
Stand up, stand up, stand, an you be a man:
For Juliet's sake, for her sake, rise and stand;
Why should you fall into so deep an O?   90
  Rom. Nurse!
  Nurse. Ah sir! ah sir! Well, death's the end of
  all.
  Rom. Spakest thou of Juliet? how is it with her?
Doth she not think me an old murderer,
Now I have stain'd the childhood of our joy
With blood removed but little from her own?
Where is she? and how doth she? and what says
My conceal'd lady to our cancell'd love?
  Nurse. O, she says nothing, sir, but weeps and
  weeps;

And now falls on her bed, and then starts up,   *100*
And Tybalt calls; and then on Romeo cries,
And then down falls again.
  Rom.   As if that name,
Shot from the deadly level of a gun,
Did murder her; as that name's cursed hand
Murder'd her kinsman. O, tell me, friar, tell me,
In what vile part of this anatomy
Doth my name lodge? tell me, that I may sack
The hateful mansion. [*Drawing his sword.*]
  Fri. L.   Hold thy desperate hand:
Art thou a man? thy form cries out thou art:
Thy tears are womanish; thy wild acts denote
The unreasonable fury of a beast: *111*
Unseemly woman in a seeming man!
Or ill-beseeming beast in seeming both!
Thou hast amazed me: by my holy order,
I thought thy disposition better temper'd.
Hast thou slain Tybalt? wilt thou slay thyself?
And slay thy lady too that lives in thee,
By doing damned hate upon thyself?
Why rail'st thou on thy birth, the heaven, and
    earth?
Since birth, and heaven, and earth, all three do
    meet   *120*
In thee at once; which thou at once wouldst lose.
Fie, fie, thou shamest thy shape, thy love, thy
    wit;
Which, like a usurer, abound'st in all,
And usest none in that true use indeed
Which should bedeck thy shape, thy love, thy
    wit:
Thy noble shape is but a form of wax,
Digressing from the valour of a man;
Thy dear love sworn but hollow perjury,
Killing that love which thou hast vow'd to
    cherish;
Thy wit, that ornament to shape and love,   *130*
Mis-shapen in the conduct of them both,
Like powder in a skilless soldier's flask,
Is set a-fire by thine own ignorance,
And thou dismember'd with thine own defence.
What, rouse thee, man! thy Juliet is alive,
For whose dear sake thou wast but lately dead;
There art thou happy: Tybalt would kill thee,
But thou slew'st Tybalt; there art thou happy
    too:
The law that threaten'd death becomes thy friend
And turns it to exile; there art thou happy: *140*
A pack of blessings lights upon thy back;
Happiness courts thee in her best array;
But, like a misbehaved and sullen wench,
Thou pout'st upon thy fortune and thy love:
Take heed, take heed, for such die miserable.
Go, get thee to thy love, as was decreed,
Ascend her chamber, hence and comfort her;

But look thou stay not till the watch be set,
For then thou canst not pass to Mantua;
Where thou shalt live, till we can find a time   *150*
To blaze your marriage, reconcile your friends,
Beg pardon of the Prince, and call thee back
With twenty hundred thousand times more joy
Than thou went'st forth in lamentation.
Go before, nurse: commend me to thy lady;
And bid her hasten all the house to bed,
Which heavy sorrow makes them apt unto:
Romeo is coming.
  Nurse. O Lord, I could have stay'd here all the
    night
To hear good counsel: O, what learning is!   *160*
My lord, I'll tell my lady you will come.
  Rom. Do so, and bid my sweet prepare to chide.
  Nurse. Here, sir, a ring she bid me give you, sir:
Hie you, make haste, for it grows very late.
                          [*Exit.*
  Rom. How well my comfort is revived by this!
  Fri. L. Go hence; good night; and here stands
    all your state:
Either be gone before the watch be set,
Or by the break of day disguised from hence:
Sojourn in Mantua; I'll find out your man,
And he shall signify from time to time   *170*
Every good hap to you that chances here:
Give me thy hand; 'tis late: farewell; good
    night.
  Rom. But that a joy past joy calls out on me,
It were a grief, so brief to part with thee:
Farewell.   [*Exeunt.*

        Scene IV. *A room in Capulet's house*
    Enter CAPULET, LADY CAPULET, *and* PARIS.

  Cap. Things have fall'n out, sir, so unluckily,
That we have had no time to move our daughter:
Look you, she loved her kinsman Tybalt dearly,
And so did I. Well, we were born to die.
'Tis very late, she'll not come down to-night:
I promise you, but for your company,
I would have been a-bed an hour ago.
  Par. These times of woe afford no time to woo.
Madam, good night: commend me to your
    daughter.
  La. Cap. I will, and know her mind early to-
    morrow;   *10*
To-night she is mew'd up to her heaviness.
  Cap. Sir Paris, I will make a desperate tender
Of my child's love: I think she will be ruled
In all respects by me; nay, more, I doubt it not.
Wife, go you to her ere you go to bed;
Acquaint her here of my son Paris' love;
And bid her, mark you me, on Wednesday next—
But, soft! what day is this?
  Par.   Monday, my lord.

Cap. Monday! ha, ha! Well, Wednesday is too
soon,
O' Thursday let it be: o' Thursday, tell her, 20
She shall be married to this noble earl.
Will you be ready? do you like this haste?
We'll keep no great ado—a friend or two;
For, hark you, Tybalt being slain so late,
It may be thought we held him carelessly,
Being our kinsman, if we revel much:
Therefore we'll have some half a dozen friends,
And there an end. But what say you to Thursday?
Par. My lord, I would that Thursday were to-
morrow.
Cap. Well, get you gone: o' Thursday be it,
then. 30
Go you to Juliet ere you go to bed,
Prepare her, wife, against this wedding-day.
Farewell, my lord. Light to my chamber, ho!
Afore me! it is so very very late,
That we may call it early by and by.
Good night. [*Exeunt.*

SCENE V. *Capulet's orchard*

Enter ROMEO *and* JULIET *above, at the window.*

Jul. Wilt thou be gone? it is not yet near day:
It was the nightingale, and not the lark,
That pierced the fearful hollow of thine ear;
Nightly she sings on yon pomegranate-tree:
Believe me, love, it was the nightingale.
Rom. It was the lark, the herald of the morn,
No nightingale: look, love, what envious streaks
Do lace the severing clouds in yonder east:
Night's candles are burnt out, and jocund day
Stands tiptoe on the misty mountain tops. 10
I must be gone and live, or stay and die.
Jul. Yon light is not day-light, I know it, I:
It is some meteor that the sun exhales,
To be to thee this night a torch-bearer,
And light thee on thy way to Mantua:
Therefore stay yet; thou need'st not to be gone.
Rom. Let me be ta'en, let me be put to death;
I am content, so thou wilt have it so.
I'll say yon grey is not the morning's eye,
'Tis but the pale reflex of Cynthia's brow; 20
Nor that is not the lark, whose notes do beat
The vaulty heaven so high above our heads:
I have more care to stay than will to go:
Come, death, and welcome! Juliet wills it so.
How is't, my soul? let's talk; it is not day.
Jul. It is, it is: hie hence, be gone, away!
It is the lark that sings so out of tune,
Straining harsh discords and unpleasing sharps.
Some say the lark makes sweet division;
This doth not so, for she divideth us: 30
Some say the lark and loathed toad change eyes;
O, now I would they had changed voices too!

Since arm from arm that voice doth us affray,
Hunting thee hence with hunt's-up to the day.
O, now be gone; more light and light it grows.
Rom. More light and light; more dark and dark
our woes!

Enter NURSE, *to the chamber.*

Nurse. Madam!
Jul. Nurse?
Nurse. Your lady mother is coming to your
chamber:
The day is broke; be wary, look about. [*Exit.* 40
Jul. Then, window, let day in, and let life out.
Rom. Farewell, farewell! one kiss, and I'll
descend. [*He goeth down.*
Jul. Art thou gone so? love, lord, ay, husband,
friend!
I must hear from thee every day in the hour,
For in a minute there are many days:
O, by this count I shall be much in years
Ere I again behold my Romeo!
Rom. Farewell!
I will omit no opportunity
That may convey my greetings, love, to thee. 50
Jul. O, think'st thou we shall ever meet again?
Rom. I doubt it not; and all these woes shall
serve
For sweet discourses in our time to come.
Jul. O God, I have an ill-divining soul!
Methinks I see thee, now thou art below,
As one dead in the bottom of a tomb:
Either my eyesight fails, or thou look'st pale.
Rom. And trust me, love, in my eye so do
you:
Dry sorrow drinks our blood. Adieu, adieu!
[*Exit.*
Jul. O Fortune, Fortune! all men call thee
fickle: 60
If thou art fickle, what dost thou with him
That is renown'd for faith? Be fickle, Fortune;
For then, I hope, thou wilt not keep him long,
But send him back.
La. Cap. [*Within*] Ho, daughter! are you up?
Jul. Who is't that calls? is it my lady mother?
Is she not down so late, or up so early?
What unaccustom'd cause procures her hither?

Enter LADY CAPULET.

La. Cap. Why, how now, Juliet!
Jul. Madam, I am not well.
La. Cap. Evermore weeping for your cousin's
death? 70
What, wilt thou wash him from his grave with
tears?
An if thou couldst, thou couldst not make him
live;

Therefore, have done: some grief shows much of
   love;
But much of grief shows still some want of wit.
  Jul. Yet let me weep for such a feeling loss.
  La. Cap. So shall you feel the loss, but not the
   friend
Which you weep for.
  Jul.   Feeling so the loss,
I cannot choose but ever weep the friend.
  La. Cap. Well, girl, thou weep'st not so much
   for his death,
As that the villain lives which slaughter'd him.
  Jul. What villain, madam?   *81*
  La. Cap.   That same villain, Romeo.
  Jul. [*Aside*] Villain and he be many miles
   asunder.—
God pardon him! I do, with all my heart;
And yet no man like he doth grieve my heart.
  La. Cap. That is, because the traitor murderer
   lives.
  Jul. Ay, madam, from the reach of these my
   hands:
Would none but I might venge my cousin's death!
  La. Cap. We will have vengeance for it, fear
   thou not:
Then weep no more. I'll send to one in Mantua,
Where that same banish'd runagate doth live,
Shall give him such an unaccustom'd dram,   *91*
That he shall soon keep Tybalt company:
And then, I hope, thou wilt be satisfied.
  Jul. Indeed, I never shall be satisfied
With Romeo, till I behold him—dead—
Is my poor heart so for a kinsman vex'd:
Madam, if you could find out but a man
To bear a poison, I would temper it;
That Romeo should, upon receipt thereof,
Soon sleep in quiet. O, how my heart abhors *100*
To hear him named, and cannot come to him,
To wreak the love I bore my cousin
Upon his body that hath slaughter'd him!
  La. Cap. Find thou the means, and I'll find such
   a man.
But now I'll tell thee joyful tidings, girl.
  Jul. And joy comes well in such a needy time:
What are they, I beseech your ladyship?
  La. Cap. Well, well, thou hast a careful father,
   child;
One who, to put thee from thy heaviness,
Hath sorted out a sudden day of joy,   *110*
That thou expect'st not nor I look'd not for.
  Jul. Madam, in happy time, what day is that?
  La. Cap. Marry, my child, early next Thursday
   morn,
The gallant, young and noble gentleman,
The County Paris, at Saint Peter's Church,
Shall happily make thee there a joyful bride.

  Jul. Now, by Saint Peter's Church and Peter
   too,
He shall not make me there a joyful bride.
I wonder at this haste; that I must wed
Ere he, that should be husband, comes to woo.
I pray you, tell my lord and father, madam, *121*
I will not marry yet; and, when I do, I swear,
It shall be Romeo, whom you know I hate,
Rather than Paris. These are news indeed!
  La. Cap. Here comes your father; tell him so
   yourself,
And see how he will take it at your hands.

         Enter CAPULET *and* NURSE.

  Cap. When the sun sets, the air doth drizzle
   dew;
But for the sunset of my brother's son
It rains downright.
How now! a conduit, girl? what, still in tears?
Evermore showering? In one little body *131*
Thou counterfeit'st a bark, a sea, a wind;
For still thy eyes, which I may call the sea,
Do ebb and flow with tears; the bark thy body is,
Sailing in this salt flood; the winds, thy sighs;
Who, raging with thy tears, and they with them,
Without a sudden calm, will overset
Thy tempest-tossed body. How now, wife!
Have you deliver'd to her our decree?
  La. Cap. Ay, sir; but she will none, she gives
   you thanks.   *140*
I would the fool were married to her grave!
  Cap. Soft! take me with you, take me with you,
   wife.
How! will she none? doth she not give us thanks?
Is she not proud? doth she not count her blest,
Unworthy as she is, that we have wrought
So worthy a gentleman to be her bridegroom?
  Jul. Not proud you have; but thankful that you
   have:
Proud can I never be of what I hate;
But thankful even for hate that is meant love.
  Cap. How now, how now, chop-logic! What is
   this?   *150*
"Proud," and "I thank you," and "I thank you
   not";
And yet "not proud": mistress minion, you,
Thank me no thankings, nor proud me no prouds,
But fettle your fine joints 'gainst Thursday next,
To go with Paris to Saint Peter's Church,
Or I will drag thee on a hurdle thither.
Out, you green-sickness carrion! out, you bag-
   gage!
You tallow-face!
  La. Cap.   Fie, fie! what, are you mad?
  Jul. Good father, I beseech you on my knees,
Hear me with patience but to speak a word. *160*

Cap. Hang thee, young baggage! disobedient
    wretch!
I tell thee what: get thee to church o' Thursday,
Or never after look me in the face:
Speak not, reply not, do not answer me;
My fingers itch. Wife, we scarce thought us
    blest
That God had lent us but this only child;
But now I see this one is one too much,
And that we have a curse in having her:
Out on her, hilding!
    Nurse.   God in heaven bless her!
You are to blame, my lord, to rate her so.   *170*
    Cap. And why, my lady Wisdom? hold your
    tongue,
Good prudence; smatter with your gossips, go.
    Nurse. I speak no treason.
    Cap.   O, God ye god-den.
    Nurse. May not one speak?
    Cap.   Peace, you mumbling fool!
Utter your gravity o'er a gossip's bowl;
For here we need it not.
    La. Cap.   You are too hot.
    Cap. God's bread! it makes me mad:
Day, night, hour, tide, time, work, play,
Alone, in company, still my care hath been   *179*
To have her match'd: and having now provided
A gentleman of noble parentage,
Of fair demesnes, youthful, and nobly train'd,
Stuff'd, as they say, with honourable parts,
Proportion'd as one's thought would wish a man;
And then to have a wretched puling fool,
A whining mammet, in her fortune's tender,
To answer "I'll not wed; I cannot love,
I am too young; I pray you, pardon me."
But, an you will not wed, I'll pardon you:
Graze where you will, you shall not house with
    me: *190*
Look to't, think on't, I do not use to jest.
Thursday is near; lay hand on heart, advise:
An you be mine, I'll give you to my friend;
An you be not, hang, beg, starve, die in the
    streets,
For, by my soul, I'll ne'er acknowledge thee,
Nor what is mine shall never do thee good:
Trust to't, bethink you; I'll not be forsworn.
                                       [*Exit.*
    Jul. Is there no pity sitting in the clouds,
That sees into the bottom of my grief?
O, sweet my mother, cast me not away!   *200*
Delay this marriage for a month, a week;
Or, if you do not, make the bridal bed
In that dim monument where Tybalt lies.
    La. Cap Talk not to me, for I'll not speak a
    word:
Do as thou wilt, for I have done with thee. [*Exit.*

    Jul. O God!—O nurse, how shall this be pre-
    vented?
My husband is on earth, my faith in heaven;
How shall that faith return again to earth,
Unless that husband send it me from heaven
By leaving earth? comfort me, counsel me.   *210*
Alack, alack, that heaven should practise strata-
    gems
Upon so soft a subject as myself!
What say'st thou? hast thou not a word of joy?
Some comfort, nurse.
    Nurse.   Faith, here it is.
Romeo is banish'd; and all the world to nothing
That he dares ne'er come back to challenge you;
Or, if he do, it needs must be by stealth.
Then, since the case so stands as now it doth,
I think it best you married with the County.
O, he's a lovely gentleman!   *220*
Romeo's a dishclout to him: an eagle, madam,
Hath not so green, so quick, so fair an eye
As Paris hath. Beshrew my very heart,
I think you are happy in this second match,
For it excels your first: or if it did not,
Your first is dead; or 'twere as good he were
As living here and you no use of him.
    Jul. Speakest thou from thy heart?
    Nurse.   And from my soul too;
Or else beshrew them both.
    Jul.   Amen!
    Nurse.   What?
    Jul. Well, thou hast comforted me marvellous
    much.   *230*
Go in; and tell my lady I am gone,
Having displeased my father, to Laurence' cell,
To make confession and to be absolved.
    Nurse. Marry, I will; and this is wisely done.
                                         [*Exit.*
    Jul. Ancient damnation! O most wicked fiend!
Is it more sin to wish me thus forsworn,
Or to dispraise my lord with that same tongue
Which she hath praised him with above compare
So many thousand times? Go, counsellor;   *239*
Thou and my bosom henceforth shall be twain.
I'll to the friar, to know his remedy:
If all else fail, myself have power to die. [*Exit.*

ACT IV

SCENE I. *Friar Laurence's cell*

Enter FRIAR LAURENCE *and* PARIS.

    Fri. L. On Thursday, sir? the time is very
    short.
    Par. My father Capulet will have it so;
And I am nothing slow to slack his haste.
    Fri. L. You say you do not know the lady's
    mind:

Uneven is the course, I like it not.
 Par. Immoderately she weeps for Tybalt's
  death,
And therefore have I little talk'd of love;
For Venus smiles not in a house of tears.
Now, sir, her father counts it dangerous
That she doth give her sorrow so much sway, *10*
And in his wisdom hastes our marriage,
To stop the inundation of her tears;
Which, too much minded by herself alone,
May be put from her by society:
Now do you know the reason of this haste.
 Fri. L. [*Aside*] I would I knew not why it
  should be slow'd.
Look, sir, here comes the lady towards my cell.

    Enter JULIET.

 Par. Happily met, my lady and my wife!
 Jul. That may be, sir, when I may be a wife.
 Par. That may be must be, love, on Thursday
  next.   *20*
 Jul. What must be shall be.
 Fri. L.   That's a certain text.
 Par. Come you to make confession to this
  father?
 Jul. To answer that, I should confess to you.
 Par. Do not deny to him that you love me.
 Jul. I will confess to you that I love him.
 Par. So will ye, I am sure, that you love me.
 Jul. If I do so, it will be of more price,
Being spoke behind your back, than to your face.
 Par. Poor soul, thy face is much abused with
  tears.
 Jul. The tears have got small victory by that;
For it was bad enough before their spite. *31*
 Par. Thou wrong'st it, more than tears, with
  that report.
 Jul. That is no slander, sir, which is a truth;
And what I spake, I spake it to my face.
 Par. Thy face is mine, and thou hast slander'd it.
 Jul. It may be so, for it is not mine own.
Are you at leisure, holy father, now;
Or shall I come to you at evening mass?
 Fri. L. My leisure serves me, pensive daughter,
  now.
My lord, we must entreat the time alone. *40*
 Par. God shield I should disturb devotion!
Juliet, on Thursday early will I rouse ye:
Till then, adieu; and keep this holy kiss. [*Exit.*
 Jul. O, shut the door! and when thou hast done
  so,
Come weep with me; past hope, past cure, past
  help!
 Fri. L. Ah, Juliet, I already know thy grief;
It strains me past the compass of my wits:
I hear thou must, and nothing may prorogue it,

On Thursday next be married to this County.
 Jul. Tell me not, friar, that thou hear'st of this,
Unless thou tell me how I may prevent it: *51*
If, in thy wisdom, thou canst give no help,
Do thou but call my resolution wise,
And with this knife I'll help it presently.
God join'd my heart and Romeo's, thou our
  hands;
And ere this hand, by thee to Romeo seal'd,
Shall be the label to another deed,
Or my true heart with treacherous revolt
Turn to another, this shall slay them both:
Therefore, out of thy long-experienced time, *60*
Give me some present counsel, or, behold,
'Twixt my extremes and me this bloody knife
Shall play the umpire, arbitrating that
Which the commission of thy years and art
Could to no issue of true honour bring.
Be not so long to speak; I long to die,
If what thou speak'st speak not of remedy.
 Fri. L. Hold, daughter: I do spy a kind of hope,
Which craves as desperate an execution
As that is desperate which we would prevent. *70*
If, rather than to marry County Paris,
Thou hast the strength of will to slay thyself,
Then is it likely thou wilt undertake
A thing like death to chide away this shame,
That copest with death himself to scape from it;
And, if thou darest, I'll give thee remedy.
 Jul. O, bid me leap, rather than marry Paris,
From off the battlements of yonder tower;
Or walk in thievish ways; or bid me lurk
Where serpents are; chain me with roaring bears;
Or shut me nightly in a charnel-house, *81*
O'er-cover'd quite with dead men's rattling
  bones,
With reeky shanks and yellow chapless skulls;
Or bid me go into a new-made grave
And hide me with a dead man in his shroud;
Things that, to hear them told, have made me
  tremble;
And I will do it without fear or doubt,
To live an unstain'd wife to my sweet love.
 Fri. L. Hold, then; go home, be merry, give
  consent
To marry Paris: Wednesday is to-morrow: *90*
To-morrow night look that thou lie alone;
Let not thy nurse lie with thee in thy chamber:
Take thou this vial, being then in bed,
And this distilled liquor drink thou off;
When presently through all thy veins shall run
A cold and drowsy humour, for no pulse
Shall keep his native progress, but surcease:
No warmth, no breath, shall testify thou livest;
The roses in thy lips and cheeks shall fade
To paly ashes, thy eyes' windows fall, *100*

Like death, when he shuts up the day of life;
Each part, deprived of supple government,
Shall, stiff and stark and cold, appear like death:
And in this borrow'd likeness of shrunk death
Thou shalt continue two and forty hours,
And then awake as from a pleasant sleep.
Now, when the bridegroom in the morning comes
To rouse thee from thy bed, there art thou dead:
Then, as the manner of our country is,
In thy best robes uncover'd on the bier   110
Thou shalt be borne to that same ancient vault
Where all the kindred of the Capulets lie.
In the mean time, against thou shalt awake,
Shall Romeo by my letters know our drift,
And hither shall he come: and he and I
Will watch thy waking, and that very night
Shall Romeo bear thee hence to Mantua.
And this shall free thee from this present shame;
If no inconstant toy, nor womanish fear,
Abate thy valour in the acting it.   120
  Jul. Give me, give me! O, tell not me of fear!
  Fri. L. Hold; get you gone, be strong and
    prosperous
In this resolve: I'll send a friar with speed
To Mantua, with my letters to thy lord.
  Jul. Love give me strength! and strength shall
    help afford.
Farewell, dear father!   [*Exeunt.*

SCENE II. *Hall in Capulet's house*

Enter CAPULET, LADY CAPULET, NURSE, *and*
TWO SERVINGMEN.

  Cap. So many guests invite as here are writ.
                          [*Exit* 1ST SERVANT.
Sirrah, go hire me twenty cunning cooks.
  2nd Serv. You shall have none ill, sir; for I'll try
if they can lick their fingers.
  Cap. How canst thou try them so?
  2nd Serv. Marry, sir, 'tis an ill cook that can-
not lick his own fingers: therefore he that can-
not lick his fingers goes not with me.
  Cap. Go, be gone.   [*Exit* 2ND SERVANT.
We shall be much unfurnish'd for this time.   10
What, is my daughter gone to Friar Laurence?
  Nurse. Ay, forsooth.
  Cap. Well, he may chance to do some good on
    her:
A peevish self-will'd harlotry it is.
  Nurse. See where she comes from shrift with
    merry look.

Enter JULIET.

  Cap. How now, my headstrong! where have
    you been gadding?
  Jul. Where I have learn'd me to repent the sin
Of disobedient opposition

To you and your behests, and am enjoin'd
By holy Laurence to fall prostrate here,   20
And beg your pardon: pardon, I beseech you!
Henceforward I am ever ruled by you.
  Cap. Send for the County; go tell him of this:
I'll have this knot knit up to-morrow morning.
  Jul. I met the youthful lord at Laurence' cell;
And gave him what becomed love I might,
Not stepping o'er the bounds of modesty.
  Cap. Why, I am glad on't; this is well: stand
    up:
This is as't should be. Let me see the County;
Ay, marry, go, I say, and fetch him hither.   30
Now, afore God! this reverend holy friar,
All our whole city is much bound to him.
  Jul. Nurse, will go with me into my closet,
To help me sort such needful ornaments
As you think fit to furnish me to-morrow?
  La. Cap. No, not till Thursday; there is time
    enough.
  Cap. Go nurse, go with her: we'll to church
    to-morrow.   [*Exeunt* JULIET *and* NURSE.
  La. Cap. We shall be short in our provision:
'Tis now near night.
  Cap.   Tush, I will stir about,
And all things shall be well, I warrant thee, wife:
Go thou to Juliet, help to deck up her;   41
I'll not to bed to-night; let me alone;
I'll play the housewife for this once. What, ho!
They are all forth. Well, I will walk myself
To County Paris, to prepare him up
Against to-morrow: my heart is wondrous light,
Since this same wayward girl is so reclaim'd.
                          [*Exeunt.*

SCENE III. *Juliet's chamber*

Enter JULIET *and* NURSE.

  Jul. Ay, those attires are best: but, gentle
    nurse,
I pray thee, leave me to myself to-night;
For I have need of many orisons
To move the heavens to smile upon my state,
Which, well thou know'st, is cross and full of
    sin.

Enter LADY CAPULET.

  La. Cap. What, are you busy, ho? need you
    my help?
  Jul. No, madam; we have cull'd such neces-
    saries
As are behoveful for our state to-morrow:
So please you, let me now be left alone,
And let the nurse this night sit up with you;   10
For, I am sure, you have your hands full all,
In this so sudden business.
  La. Cap.   Good night:

Get thee to bed, and rest; for thou hast need.
    [*Exeunt* LADY CAPULET *and* NURSE.
Jul. Farewell! God knows when we shall meet
 again.
I have a faint cold fear thrills though my
 veins,
That almost freezes up the heat of life:
I'll call them back again to comfort me:
Nurse! What should she do here?
My dismal scene I needs must act alone.
Come, vial.   20
What if this mixture do not work at all?
Shall I be married then to-morrow morning?
No, no: this shall forbid it: lie thou there.
  Laying down her dagger.
What if it be a poison, which the friar
Subtly hath minister'd to have me dead,
Lest in this marriage he should be dishonour'd,
Because he married me before to Romeo?
I fear it is: and yet, methinks, it should not,
For he hath still been tried a holy man.
How if, when I am laid into the tomb,   30
I wake before the time that Romeo
Come to redeem me? there's a fearful point!
Shall I not, then, be stifled in the vault,
To whose foul mouth no healthsome air breathes
 in,
And there die strangled ere my Romeo comes?
Or, if I live, is it not very like,
The horrible conceit of death and night,
Together with the terror of the place—
As in a vault, an ancient receptacle,
Where, for these many hundred years, the
 bones
Of all my buried ancestors are pack'd: 41
Where bloody Tybalt, yet but green in earth,
Lies festering in his shroud; where, as they
 say,
At some hours in the night spirits resort—
Alack, alack, is it not like that I,
So early waking, what with loathsome smells,
And shrieks like mandrakes' torn out of the
 earth,
That living mortals, hearing them, run mad:
O, if I wake, shall I not be distraught,
Environed with all these hideous fears?   50
And madly play with my forefathers' joints?
And pluck the mangled Tybalt from his shroud?
And, in this rage, with some great kinsman's
 bone,
As with a club, dash out my desperate brains?
O, look! methinks I see my cousin's ghost
Seeking out Romeo, that did spit his body
Upon a rapier's point: stay, Tybalt, stay!
Romeo, I come! this do I drink to thee.
  [*She falls upon her bed, within the curtains.*

SCENE IV. *Hall in Capulet's house*
  Enter LADY CAPULET *and* NURSE.

La. Cap. Hold, take these keys, and fetch more
 spices nurse.
Nurse. They call for dates and quinces in the
 pastry.
    Enter CAPULET.
Cap. Come, stir, stir, stir! the second cock hath
 crow'd,
The curfew-bell hath rung, 'tis three o'clock:
Look to the baked meats, good Angelica:
Spare not for cost.
Nurse.   Go, you cot-quean, go,
Get you to bed; faith, you'll be sick to-morrow
For this night's watching.
 Cap. No, not a whit: what! I have watch'd ere
 now
All night for lesser cause, and ne'er been sick. 10
La. Cap. Ay, you have been a mouse-hunt in
 your time;
But I will watch you from such watching now.
    [*Exeunt* LADY CAPULET *and* NURSE.
Cap. A jealous-hood, a jealous-hood!

Enter three or four SERVINGMEN, *with spits, logs,
and baskets.*

          Now, fellow,
What's there?
 1st Serv. Things for the cook, sir; but I know
 not what.
 Cap. Make haste, make haste. [*Exit* FIRST
 SERVANT] Sirrah, fetch drier logs:
Call Peter, he will show thee where they are.
 2nd Serv. I have a head, sir, that will find out logs,
And never trouble Peter for the matter. [*Exit.*
 Cap. Mass, and well said; a merry whoreson, ha!
Thou shalt be logger-head. Good faith, 'tis day:
The County will be here with music straight, 21
For so he said he would: I hear him near.
 Music within.
Nurse! Wife, What, ho! What, nurse, I say!

    Re-enter NURSE.

Go waken Juliet, go and trim her up;
I'll go and chat with Paris: hie, make haste,
Make haste; the bridegroom he is come already:
Make haste, I say.   [*Exeunt.*

SCENE V. *Juliet's chamber*
    Enter NURSE.

Nurse. Mistress! what, mistress! Juliet! fast,
 I warrant her, she:
Why, lamb! why, lady! fie, you slug-a-bed!
Why, love, I say! madam! sweet-heart! why,
 bride!

What, not a word? you take your pennyworths
  now;
Sleep for a week; for the next night, I warrant,
The County Paris hath set up his rest,
That you shall rest but little. God forgive me,
Marry, and amen, how sound is she asleep!
I must needs wake her. Madam, madam, madam!
Ay, let the County take you in your bed;   10
He'll fright you up, i' faith. Will it not be?
    Undraws the curtains.
What, dress'd! and in your clothes! and down
  again!
I must needs wake you: Lady! lady! lady!
Alas, alas! Help, help! my lady's dead!
O, well-a-day, that ever I was born!
Some *aqua vitæ*, ho! My lord! my lady!

Enter LADY CAPULET.

La. Cap. What noise is here?
Nurse.   O lamentable day!
La. Cap. What is the matter?
Nurse.   Look, look! O heavy day!
La Cap. O me, O me! My child, my only life,
Revive, look up, or I will die with thee!   20
Help, help! Call help.

Enter CAPULET.

Cap. For shame, bring Juliet forth; her lord is
  come.
Nurse. She's dead, deceased, she's dead; alack
  the day!
La. Cap. Alack the day, she's dead, she's dead,
  she's dead!
Cap. Ha! let me see her: out, alas! she's cold;
Her blood is settled, and her joints are stiff;
Life and these lips have long been separated:
Death lies on her like an untimely frost
Upon the sweetest flower of all the field.
Nurse. O lamentable day!
La. Cap.   O woeful time! 30
Cap. Death, that hath ta'en her hence to make
  me wail,
Ties up my tongue and will not let me speak.

Enter FRIAR LAURENCE *and* PARIS,
        with MUSICIANS.

Fri. L. Come, is the bride ready to go to church?
Cap. Ready to go, but never to return.
O son! the night before thy wedding-day
Hath Death lain with thy wife. There she lies,
Flower as she was, deflowered by him.
Death is my son-in-law, Death is my heir;
My daughter he hath wedded: I will die,
And leave him all; life, living, all is Death's. 40
Par. Have I thought long to see this morning's
  face,

And doth it give me such a sight as this?
    La. Cap. Accursed, unhappy, wretched hateful
      day!
Most miserable hour that e'er time saw
In lasting labour of his pilgrimage!
But one, poor one, one poor and loving child,
But one thing to rejoice and solace in,
And cruel death hath catch'd it from my sight!
    Nurse. O woe! O woeful, woeful, woeful day!
Most lamentable day, most woeful day,   50
That ever, ever, I did yet behold!
O day! O day! O day! O hateful day!
Never was seen so black a day as this:
O woeful day, O woeful day!
    Par. Beguiled, divorced, wronged, spited, slain
Most detestable death, by thee beguiled,
By cruel cruel thee quite overthrown!
O love! O life! not life, but love in death!
    Cap. Despised, distressed, hated, martyr'd,
      kill'd!
Uncomfortable time, why camest thou now   60
To murder, murder our solemnity?
O child! O child! my soul, and not my child!
Dead art thou! Alack! my child is dead:
And with my child my joys are buried.
    Fri. L. Peace, ho, for shame! confusion's cure
      lives not
In these confusions. Heaven and yourself
Had part in this fair maid; now heaven hath all,
And all the better is it for the maid:
Your part in her you could not keep from death,
But heaven keeps his part in eternal life.   70
The most you sought was her promotion;
For 'twas your heaven she should be advanced:
And weep ye now, seeing she is advanced
Above the clouds, as high as heaven itself?
O, in this love, you love your child so ill
That you run mad, seeing that she is well:
She's not well married that lives married long;
But she's best married that dies married young.
Dry up your tears, and stick your rosemary
On this fair corse; and, as the custom is,   80
In all her best array bear her to church:
For though fond nature bids us all lament,
Yet nature's tears are reason's merriment.
    Cap. All things that we ordained festival,
Turn from their office to black funeral;
Our instruments to melancholy bells,
Our wedding cheer to a sad burial feast,
Our solemn hymns to sullen dirges change,
Our bridal flowers serve for a buried corse,
And all things change them to the contrary.   90
    Fri. L. Sir, go you in; and, madam, go with him;
And go, Sir Paris; every one prepare
To follow this fair corse unto her grave:
The heavens do lour upon you for some ill;

Move them no more by crossing their high will.

        [*Exeunt* CAPULET, LADY CAPULET,
           PARIS, *and* FRIAR.

1st Mus. Faith, we may put up our pipes and be gone.

Nurse. Honest good fellows, ah, put up, put up;
For, well you know, this is a pitiful case.   [*Exit.*

1st Mus. Ay, by my troth, the case may be amended.   *101*

Enter PETER.

Pet. Musicians, O, musicians, "Heart's ease,
Heart's ease": O, an you will have me live, play
"Heart's ease."

1st Mus. Why "Heart's ease"?

Pet. O, musicians, because my heart itself plays
"My heart is full of woe": O, play me some
merry dump, to comfort me.

1st Mus. Not a dump we; 'tis no time to play
now.   *110*

Pet. You will not, then?

1st Mus. No.

Pet. I will then give it you soundly.

1st Mus. What will you give us?

Pet. No money, on my faith, but the gleek; I
will give you the minstrel.

1st Mus. Then will I give you the serving-
creature.

Pet. Then will I lay the serving-creature's
dagger on your pate. I will carry no crotchets:
I'll *re* you, I'll *fa* you; do you note me?   *121*

1st Mus. An you *re* us and *fa* us, you note us.

2nd Mus. Pray you, put up your dagger, and
put out your wit.

Pet. Then have at you with my wit! I will dry-
beat you with an iron wit, and put up my iron
dagger. Answer me like men:

  "When griping grief the heart doth wound,
    And doleful dumps the mind oppress,
  Then music with her silver sound"—   *130*
why "silver sound"? why "music with her silver sound"? What say you, Simon Catling?

1st Mus. Marry, sir, because silver hath a sweet
sound.

Pet. Pretty! What say you, Hugh Rebeck?

2nd Mus. I say "silver sound," because musicians sound for silver.

Pet. Pretty too! What say you, James Sound-
post?   *139*

3rd Mus. Faith, I know not what to say.

Pet. O, I cry you mercy; you are the singer:
I will say for you. It is "music with her silver
sound," because musicians have no gold for
sounding:

  "Then music with her silver sound
    With speedy help doth lend redress."   [*Exit.*

1st Mus. What a pestilent knave is this same!

2nd Mus. Hang him, Jack! Come, we'll in here;
tarry for the mourners, and stay dinner.

              [*Exeunt.*

ACT V

SCENE I. *Mantua: a street*
Enter ROMEO.

Rom. If I may trust the flattering truth of sleep,
My dreams presage some joyful news at hand:
My bosom's lord sits lightly in his throne;
And all this day an unaccustom'd spirit
Lifts me above the ground with cheerful thoughts.
I dreamt my lady came and found me dead—
Strange dream, that gives a dead man leave to
    think!—
And breathed such life with kisses in my lips,
That I revived, and was an emperor.
Ah me! how sweet is love itself possess'd,   *10*
When but love's shadows are so rich in joy!

Enter BALTHASAR, *booted.*

News from Verona!—How now, Balthasar!
Dost thou not bring me letters from the friar?
How doth my lady? Is my father well?
How fares my Juliet? that I ask again;
For nothing can be ill, if she be well.

Bal. Then she is well, and nothing can be ill:
Her body sleeps in Capel's monument,
And her immortal part with angels lives.
I saw her laid low in her kindred's vault,   *20*
And presently took post to tell it you:
O, pardon me for bringing these ill news,
Since you did leave it for my office, sir.

Rom. Is it even so? then I defy you, stars!
Thou know'st my lodging: get me ink and paper,
And hire post-horses; I will hence to-night.

Bal. I do beseech you, sir, have patience:
Your looks are pale and wild, and do import
Some misadventure.

Rom.   Tush, thou art deceived:
Leave me, and do the thing I bid thee do.   *30*
Hast thou no letters to me from the friar?

Bal. No, my good lord.

Rom.   No matter: get thee gone,
And hire those horses; I'll be with thee straight.

          [*Exit* BALTHASAR.

Well, Juliet, I will lie with thee to-night.
Let's see for means: O mischief, thou art swift
To enter in the thoughts of desperate men!
I do remember an apothecary—
And hereabouts he dwells—which late I noted
In tatter'd weeds, with overwhelming brows,
Culling of simples; meagre were his looks,   *40*
Sharp misery had worn him to the bones:

And in his needy shop a tortoise hung,
An alligator stuff'd, and other skins
Of ill-shaped fishes; and about his shelves
A beggarly account of empty boxes,
Green earthen pots, bladders and musty seeds,
Remnants of packthread and old cakes of roses,
Were thinly scatter'd, to make up a show.
Noting this penury, to myself I said
"An if a man did need a poison now,   50
Whose sale is present death in Mantua,
Here lives a caitiff wretch would sell it him."
O, this same thought did but forerun my need;
And this same needy man must sell it me.
As I remember, this should be the house.
Being holiday, the beggar's shop is shut.
What, ho! apothecary!

Enter APOTHECARY.

Ap.   Who calls so loud?
Rom. Come hither, man. I see that thou art
    poor:
Hold, there is forty ducats: let me have
A dram of poison, such soon-speeding gear   60
As will disperse itself through all the veins
That the life-weary taker may fall dead
And that the trunk may be discharged of breath
As violently as hasty powder fired
Doth hurry from the fatal cannon's womb.
Ap. Such mortal drugs I have; but Mantua's law
Is death to any he that utters them.
Rom. Art thou so bare and full of wretchedness,
And fear'st to die? famine is in thy cheeks,
Need and oppression starveth in thine eyes,   70
Contempt and beggary hangs upon thy back;
The world is not thy friend nor the world's law;
The world affords no law to make thee rich;
Then be not poor, but break it, and take this.
Ap. My poverty, but not my will, consents.
Rom. I pay thy poverty, and not thy will.
Ap. Put this in any liquid thing you will,
And drink it off; and, if you had the strength
Of twenty men, it would dispatch you straight.
Rom. There is thy gold, worse poison to men's
    souls,   80
Doing more murders in this loathsome world
Than these poor compounds that thou mayst not
    sell.
I sell thee poison; thou hast sold me none.
Farewell: buy food, and get thyself in flesh.
Come, cordial and not poison, go with me
To Juliet's grave; for there must I use thee.
                       [*Exeunt.*

SCENE II. *Friar Laurence's cell*
Enter FRIAR JOHN.

Fri. J. Holy Franciscan friar! brother, ho!

Enter FRIAR LAURENCE.

Fri. L. This same should be the voice of Friar
    John.
Welcome from Mantua: what says Romeo?
Or, if his mind be writ, give me his letter.
Fri. J. Going to find a bare-foot brother out,
One of our order, to associate me,
Here in this city visiting the sick,
And finding him, the searchers of the town,
Suspecting that we both were in a house
Where the infectious pestilence did reign,   10
Seal'd up the doors, and would not let us forth;
So that my speed to Mantua there was stay'd.
Fri. L. Who bare my letter, then, to Romeo?
Fri. J. I could not send it—here it is again—
Nor get a messenger to bring it thee,
So fearful were they of infection.
Fri. L. Unhappy fortune! by my brother-
    hood,
The letter was not nice but full of charge
Of dear import, and the neglecting it
May do much danger. Friar John, go hence;   20
Get me an iron crow, and bring it straight
Unto my cell.
Fri. J. Brother, I'll go and bring it thee.   [*Exit.*
Fri. L. Now must I to the monument alone;
Within this three hours will fair Juliet wake:
She will beshrew me much that Romeo
Hath had no notice of these accidents;
But I will write again to Mantua,
And keep her at my cell till Romeo come;
Poor living corse, closed in a dead man's tomb!
                       [*Exit.*

SCENE III. *A churchyard; in it a tomb
belonging to the Capulets*
Enter PARIS, *and his* PAGE *bearing flowers
and a torch.*

Par. Give me thy torch, boy: hence, and stand
    aloof:
Yet put it out, for I would not be seen.
Under yond yew-trees lay thee all along,
Holding thine ear close to the hollow ground;
So shall no foot upon the churchyard tread,
Being loose, unfirm, with digging up of graves,
But thou shalt hear it: whistle then to me,
As signal that thou hear'st something approach.
Give me those flowers. Do as I bid thee, go.
Page. [*Aside*] I am almost afraid to stand alone
Here in the churchyard; yet I will adventure.   11
                       [*Retires.*
Par. Sweet flower, with flowers thy bridal bed
    I strew—
    O woe! thy canopy is dust and stones—
Which with sweet water nightly I will dew,

Or, wanting that, with tears distill'd by
  moans:
The obsequies that I for thee will keep
Nightly shall be to strew thy grave and weep.
  The PAGE *whistles.*
The boy gives warning something doth approach.
What cursed foot wanders this way to-night,
To cross my obsequies and true love's rite?   20
What, with a torch! muffle me, night, awhile.
                             [*Retires.*

    Enter ROMEO *and* BALTHASAR, *with a torch,*
              mattock, &c.

Rom. Give me that mattock and the wrenching
  iron.
Hold, take this letter; early in the morning
See thou deliver it to my lord and father.
Give me the light: upon thy life, I charge thee,
Whate'er thou hear'st or seest, stand all aloof,
And do not interrupt me in my course.
Why I descend into this bed of death,
Is partly to behold my lady's face;   29
But chiefly to take thence from her dead finger
A precious ring, a ring that I must use
In dear employment: therefore hence, be gone:
But if thou, jealous, dost return to pry
In what I further shall intend to do,
By heaven, I will tear thee joint by joint
And strew this hungry churchyard with thy
  limbs:
The time and my intents are savage-wild,
More fierce and more inexorable far
Than empty tigers or the roaring sea.   39
  Bal. I will be gone, sir, and not trouble you.
  Rom. So shalt thou show me friendship. Take
  thou that:
Live, and be prosperous: and farewell, good
  fellow.
  Bal. [*Aside*] For all this same, I'll hide me
  hereabout:
His looks I fear, and his intents I doubt.
                            [*Retires.*
  Rom. Thou detestable maw, thou womb of
  death,
Gorged with the dearest morsel of the earth,
Thus I enforce thy rotten jaws to open,
And, in despite, I'll cram thee with more food!
  Opens the tomb.
  Par. This is that banish'd haughty Montague, 49
That murder'd my love's cousin, with which
  grief,   50
It is supposed, the fair creature died;
And here is come to do some villainous shame
To the dead bodies: I will apprehend him.
  Comes forward.
Stop thy unhallow'd toil, vile Montague!

Can vengeance be pursued further than death?
Condemned villain, I do apprehend thee:
Obey, and go with me; for thou must die.
  Rom. I must indeed; and therefore came I hither.
Good gentle youth, tempt not a desperate man;
Fly hence, and leave me: think upon these gone;
Let them affright thee. I beseech thee, youth,
Put not another sin upon my head,
By urging me to fury: O, be gone!
By heaven, I love thee better than myself;
For I come hither arm'd against myself:
Stay not, be gone; live, and hereafter say,
A madman's mercy bade thee run away.
  Par. I do defy thy conjurations,
And apprehend thee for a felon here.
  Rom. Wilt thou provoke me? then have at thee,
  boy! [*They fight.*]   70
  Page. O Lord, they fight! I will go call the
  watch.   [*Exit.*
  Par. O, I am slain! [*Falls.*] If thou be merciful,
Open the tomb, lay me with Juliet.   [*Dies.*
  Rom. In faith, I will. Let me peruse this face.
Mercutio's kinsman, noble County Paris!
What said my man, when my betossed soul
Did not attend him as we rode? I think
He told me Paris should have married Juliet:
Said he not so? or did I dream it so?
Or am I mad, hearing him talk of Juliet,   80
To think it was so? O, give me thy hand,
One writ with me in sour misfortune's book!
I'll bury thee in a triumphant grave;
A grave? O, no! a lantern, slaughter'd youth,
For here lies Juliet, and her beauty makes
This vault a feasting presence full of light.
Death, lie thou there, by a dead man interr'd.
  Laying Paris in the tomb.
How oft when men are at the point of death
Have they been merry! which their keepers call
A lightning before death: O, how may I   90
Call this a lightning? O my love! my wife!
Death, that hath suck'd the honey of thy breath,
Hath had no power yet upon thy beauty:
Thou art not conquer'd; beauty's ensign yet
Is crimson in thy lips and in thy cheeks,
And death's pale flag is not advanced there.
Tybalt, liest thou there in thy bloody sheet?
O, what more favour can I do to thee,
Than with that hand that cut thy youth in twain
To sunder his that was thine enemy?   100
Forgive me, cousin! Ah, dear Juliet,
Why art thou yet so fair? shall I believe
That unsubstantial death is amorous,
And that the lean abhorred monster keeps
Thee here in dark to be his paramour?
For fear of that, I still will stay with thee;
And never from this palace of dim night

Depart again: here, here will I remain
With worms that are thy chamber-maids; O,
    here
Will I set up my everlasting rest,   *110*
And shake the yoke of inauspicious stars
From this world-wearied flesh. Eyes, look your
    last!
Arms, take your last embrace! and, lips, O you
The doors of breath, seal with a righteous kiss
A dateless bargain to engrossing death!
Come, bitter conduct, come, unsavoury guide!
Thou desperate pilot, now at once run on
The dashing rocks thy sea-sick weary bark!
Here's to my love! [*Drinks.*] O true apothecary!
Thy drugs are quick. Thus with a kiss I die. *120*
                                                    [*Dies.*

Enter, at the other end of the churchyard, FRIAR
LAURENCE, *with a lantern, crow, and spade.*

Fri. L. Saint Francis be my speed! how oft
    to-night
Have my old feet stumbled at graves! Who's
    there?
Bal. Here's one, a friend, and one that knows
    you well.
Fri. L. Bliss be upon you! Tell me, good my
    friend,
What torch is yond, that vainly lends his light
To grubs and eyeless skulls? as I discern,
It burneth in the Capels' monument.
Bal. It doth so, holy sir; and there's my master,
One that you love.
Fri. L.   Who is it?
Bal.   Romeo.
Fri. L. How long hath he been there?
Bal.   Full half an hour. *130*
Fri. L. Go with me to the vault.
Bal.   I dare not, sir:
My master knows not but I am gone hence;
And fearfully did menace me with death,
If I did stay to look on his intents.
Fri. L. Stay, then; I'll go alone. Fear comes
    upon me:
O, much I fear some ill unlucky thing.
Bal. As I did sleep under this yew-tree here,
I dreamt my master and another fought,
And that my master slew him.
Fri. L.   Romeo!
    Advances.
Alack, alack, what blood is this, which stains
The stony entrance of this sepulchre?   *141*
What mean these masterless and gory swords
To lie discolour'd by this place of peace?
    Enters the tomb.
Romeo! O, pale! Who else? what, Paris too?
And steep'd in blood? Ah, what an unkind hour

Is guilty of this lamentable chance!
The lady stirs.
    JULIET *wakes.*
Jul. O comfortable friar! where is my lord?
I do remember well where I should be,
And there I am. Where is my Romeo?   *150*
    Noise within.
Fri. L. I hear some noise. Lady, come from that
    nest
Of death, contagion, and unnatural sleep:
A greater power than we can contradict
Hath thwarted our intents. Come, come away.
Thy husband in thy bosom there lies dead;
And Paris too. Come, I'll dispose of thee
Among a sisterhood of holy nuns:
Stay not to question, for the watch is coming;
Come, go, good Juliet [*Noise again*], I dare no
    longer stay.   *159*
Jul. Go, get thee hence, for I will not away.
                                    [*Exit* FRIAR LAURENCE.
What's here? a cup, closed in my true love's
    hand?
Poison, I see, hath been his timeless end:
O churl! drunk all, and left no friendly drop
To help me after? I will kiss thy lips;
Haply some poison yet doth hang on them,
To make me die with a restorative. [*Kisses him.*
Thy lips are warm.
1st Watch. [*Within*] Lead, boy: which way?
Jul. Yea, noise? then I'll be brief. O happy
    dagger! [*Snatching Romeo's dagger.*]
This is thy sheath [*Stabs herself*]; there rust, and
    let me die.   *170*
                        [*Falls on Romeo's body, and dies.*

Enter FIRST WATCH, *with the* PAGE *of* PARIS.

Page. This is the place; there, where the torch
    doth burn.
1st Watch. The ground is bloody; search about
    the churchyard:
Go, some of you, whoe'er you find attach.
Pitiful sight! here lies the County slain;
And Juliet bleeding, warm, and newly dead,
Who here hath lain these two days buried.
Go, tell the Prince: run to the Capulets:
Raise up the Montagues: some others search:
We see the ground whereon these woes do
    lie;
But the true ground of all these piteous woes *180*
We cannot without circumstance descry.

Re-enter some of the WATCH, *with* BALTHASAR.

2nd Watch. Here's Romeo's man; we found
    him in the churchyard.
1st Watch. Hold him in safety, till the Prince
    come hither.

Re-enter others of the WATCH, *with* FRIAR
LAURENCE.

3rd Watch. Here is a friar, that trembles, sighs,
and weeps:
We took this mattock and this spade from him,
As he was coming from this churchyard side.
1st Watch. A great suspicion: stay the friar too.

Enter PRINCE *and Attendants.*

Prince. What misadventure is so early up,
That calls our person from our morning's rest?

Enter CAPULET, LADY CAPULET, *and others.*

Cap. What should it be, that they so shriek
abroad?   *190*
L. Cap. The people in the street cry "Romeo,"
Some "Juliet," and some "Paris"; and all run,
With open outcry, toward our monument.
Prince. What fear is this which startles in our
ears?
1st Watch. Sovereign, here lies the County
Paris slain;
And Romeo dead; and Juliet, dead before,
Warm and new kill'd.
Prince. Search, seek, and know how this foul
murder comes.
First Watch. Here is a friar, and slaughter'd
Romeo's man;
With instruments upon them, fit to open   *200*
These dead men's tombs.
Cap. O heavens! O wife, look how our daugh-
ter bleeds!
This dagger hath mista'en—for, lo, his house
Is empty on the back of Montague—
And it mis-sheathed in my daughter's bosom!
La. Cap. O me! this sight of death is as a bell,
That warns my old age to a sepulchre.

Enter MONTAGUE *and others.*

Prince. Come, Montague; for thou art early up,
To see thy son and heir more early down.   *209*
Mon. Alas, my liege, my wife is dead to-night;
Grief of my son's exile hath stopp'd her breath:
What further woe conspires against mine age?
Prince. Look, and thou shalt see.
Mon. O thou untaught! what manners is in this,
To press before thy father to a grave?
Prince. Seal up the mouth of outrage for a while,
Till we can clear these ambiguities,
And know their spring, their head, their true
descent;
And then will I be general of your woes   *219*
And lead you even to death: meantime forbear,
And let mischance be slave to patience.
Bring forth the parties of suspicion.

Fri. L. I am the greatest, able to do least,
Yet most suspected, as the time and place
Doth make against me, of this direful murder;
And here I stand, both to impeach and purge
Myself condemned and myself excused.
Prince. Then say at once what thou dost know
in this.
Fri. L. I will be brief, for my short date of
breath
Is not so long as is a tedious tale.   *230*
Romeo, there dead, was husband to that Juliet;
And she, there dead, that Romeo's faithful wife:
I married them; and their stol'n marriage-day
Was Tybalt's dooms-day, whose untimely death
Banish'd the new-made bridegroom from this
city,
For whom, and not for Tybalt, Juliet pined.
You, to remove that siege of grief from her,
Betroth'd and would have married her perforce
To County Paris: then comes she to me,   *239*
And, with wild looks, bid me devise some mean
To rid her from this second marriage,
Or in my cell there would she kill herself.
Then gave I her, so tutor'd by my art,
A sleeping potion; which so took effect
As I intended, for it wrought on her
The form of death: meantime I writ to Romeo,
That he should hither come as this dire night,
To help to take her from her borrow'd grave,
Being the time the potion's force should cease.
But he which bore my letter, Friar John,   *250*
Was stay'd by accident, and yesternight
Return'd my letter back. Then all alone
At the prefixed hour of her waking,
Came I to take her from her kindred's vault;
Meaning to keep her closely at my cell,
Till I conveniently could send to Romeo:
But when I came, some minute ere the time
Of her awaking, here untimely lay
The noble Paris and true Romeo dead.
She wakes; and I entreated her come forth,   *260*
And bear this work of heaven with patience:
But then a noise did scare me from the tomb;
And she, too desperate, would not go with me,
But, as it seems, did violence on herself.
All this I know; and to the marriage
Her nurse is privy; and, if aught in this
Miscarried by my fault, let my old life
Be sacrificed, some hour before his time,
Unto the rigour of severest law.
Prince. We still have known thee for a holy
man.   *270*
Where's Romeo's man? what can he say in this?
Bal. I brought my master news of Juliet's death;
And then in post he came from Mantua
To this same place, to this same monument.

This letter he early bid me give his father,
And threaten'd me with death, going in the vault,
If I departed not and left him there.
 Prince. Give me the letter; I will look on it.
Where is the County's page, that raised the
  watch?
Sirrah, what made your master in this place? *280*
 Page. He came with flowers to strew his lady's
  grave;
And bid me stand aloof, and so I did:
Anon comes one with light to ope the tomb;
And by and by my master drew on him;
And then I ran away to call the watch.
 Prince. This letter doth make good the friar's
  words,
Their course of love, the tidings of her death:
And here he writes that he did buy a poison
Of a poor 'pothecary, and therewithal
Came to this vault to die, and lie with Juliet. *290*
Where be these enemies? Capulet! Montague!
See, what a scourge is laid upon your hate,

That heaven finds means to kill your joys with
  love.
And I for winking at your discords too
Have lost a brace of kinsmen: all are punish'd.
 Cap. O brother Montague, give me thy hand:
This is my daughter's jointure, for no more
Can I demand.
 Mon.   But I can give thee more:
For I will raise her statue in pure gold;
That while Verona by that name is known, *300*
There shall no figure at such rate be set
As that of true and faithful Juliet.
 Cap. As rich shall Romeo's by his lady's lie;
Poor sacrifices of our enmity!
 Prince. A glooming peace this morning with it
  brings;
The sun, for sorrow, will not show his head:
Go hence, to have more talk of these sad things;
 Some shall be pardon'd, and some punished:
For never was a story of more woe
Than this of Juliet and her Romeo. [*Exeunt. 310*

The Tragedy of
KING RICHARD II

DRAMATIS PERSONÆ

KING RICHARD THE SECOND
JOHN OF GAUNT, DUKE OF LANCASTER | *uncles to*
EDMUND OF LANGLEY, DUKE OF YORK | *the King*
HENRY, *surnamed* BOLINGBROKE, DUKE OF HERE-
    FORD, *son to John of Gaunt; afterwards* KING
    HENRY IV
DUKE OF AUMERLE, *son to the Duke of York*
THOMAS MOWBRAY, DUKE OF NORFOLK
DUKE OF SURREY
EARL OF SALISBURY
LORD BERKELEY
BUSHY |
BAGOT | *servants to King Richard*
GREEN |
EARL OF NORTHUMBERLAND
HENRY PERCY, *surnamed* HOTSPUR, *his son*
LORD ROSS
LORD WILLOUGHBY
LORD FITZWATER
BISHOP OF CARLISLE
ABBOT OF WESTMINSTER

LORD MARSHAL
SIR STEPHEN SCROOP
SIR PIERCE OF EXTON
CAPTAIN *to a band of Welshmen*
TWO HERALDS
ANOTHER LORD
GARDENER
GROOM OF THE STABLE
KEEPER
TWO SERVANTS *to York*
SERVANT *to Exton*

QUEEN *to King Richard*
DUCHESS OF YORK
DUCHESS OF GLOUCESTER
LADY *attending on the Queen*

NON-SPEAKING: *Lords, Ladies, Officers, Soldiers,
    Gardeners, Guards, and other Attendants*

SCENE: *England and Wales*

ACT I

SCENE I. *London: King Richard's palace*

Enter KING RICHARD, JOHN OF GAUNT, *with
other Nobles and Attendants.*

K. Rich. Old John of Gaunt, time-honour'd
    Lancaster,
Hast thou, according to thy oath and band,
Brought hither Henry Hereford thy bold son,
Here to make good the boisterous late appeal,
Which then our leisure would not let us hear,
Against the Duke of Norfolk, Thomas Mow-
    bray?
Gaunt. I have, my liege.
K. Rich. Tell me, moreover, hast thou sounded
    him,
If he appeal the Duke on ancient malice;
Or worthily, as a good subject should,   10
On some known ground of treachery in him?
Gaunt. As near as I could sift him on that argu-
    ment,
On some apparent danger seen in him
Aim'd at your Highness, no inveterate malice.
K. Rich. Then call them to our presence; face to
    face,
And frowning brow to brow, ourselves will hear
The accuser and the accused freely speak:

High-stomach'd are they both, and full of ire,
In rage deaf as the sea, hasty as fire.

Enter BOLINGBROKE *and* MOWBRAY.

Boling. Many years of happy days befall   20
My gracious sovereign, my most loving liege!
Mow. Each day still better other's happiness;
Until the heavens, envying earth's good hap,
Add an immortal title to your crown!
K. Rich. We thank you both: yet one but flat-
    ters us,
As well appeareth by the cause you come;
Namely, to appeal each other of high treason.
Cousin of Hereford, what dost thou object
Against the Duke of Norfolk, Thomas Mow-
    bray?
Boling. First, heaven be the record to my
    speech!   30
In the devotion of a subject's love,
Tendering the precious safety of my prince,
And free from other misbegotten hate,
Come I appellant to this princely presence.
Now, Thomas Mowbray, do I turn to thee,
And mark my greeting well; for what I speak
My body shall make good upon this earth,
Or my divine soul answer it in heaven.
Thou art a traitor and a miscreant,

320

Too good to be so and too bad to live,   *40*
Since the more fair and crystal is the sky,
The uglier seem the clouds that in it fly.
Once more, the more to aggravate the note,
With a foul traitor's name stuff I thy throat;
And wish, so please my sovereign, ere I move,
What my tongue speaks my right drawn sword
   may prove.
  Mow. Let not my cold words here accuse my
   zeal:
'Tis not the trial of a woman's war,
The bitter clamour of two eager tongues,
Can arbitrate this cause betwixt us twain;   *50*
The blood is hot that must be cool'd for this:
Yet can I not of such tame patience boast
As to be hush'd and nought at all to say:
First, the fair reverence of your Highness curbs
  me
From giving reins and spurs to my free speech;
Which else would post until it had return'd
These terms of treason doubled down his throat.
Setting aside his high blood's royalty,
And let him be no kinsman to my liege,
I do defy him, and I spit at him;   *60*
Call him a slanderous coward and a villain:
Which to maintain I would allow him odds,
And meet him, were I tied to run afoot
Even to the frozen ridges of the Alps,
Or any other ground inhabitable
Where ever Englishman durst set his foot.
Meantime let this defend my loyalty,
By all my hopes, most falsely doth he lie.
  Boling. Pale trembling coward, there I throw
   my gage,
Disclaiming here the kindred of the King,   *70*
And lay aside my high blood's royalty,
Which fear, not reverence, makes thee to ex-
  cept.
If guilty dread have left thee so much strength
As to take up mine honour's pawn, then stoop:
By that and all the rites of knighthood else,
Will I make good against thee, arm to arm,
What I have spoke or thou canst worse devise.
  Mow. I take it up; and by that sword I swear
Which gently laid my knighthood on my shoul-
  der,
I'll answer thee in any fair degree,   *80*
Or chivalrous design of knightly trial:
And when I mount, alive may I not light,
If I be traitor or unjustly fight!
  K. Rich. What doth our cousin lay to Mow-
  bray's charge?
It must be great that can inherit us
So much as of a thought of ill in him.
  Boling. Look, what I speak, my life shall prove
  it true;

That Mowbray hath received eight thousand
  nobles
In name of lendings for your Highness' soldiers,
The which he hath detain'd for lewd employ-
  ments,
Like a false traitor and injurious villain.   *91*
Besides I say and will in battle prove,
Or here or elsewhere to the furthest verge
That ever was survey'd by English eye,
That all the treasons for these eighteen years
Complotted and contrived in this land
Fetch from false Mowbray their first head and
  spring.
Further I say and further will maintain
Upon his bad life to make all this good,
That he did plot the Duke of Gloucester's death,
Suggest his soon-believing adversaries,   *101*
And consequently, like a traitor coward,
Sluiced out his innocent soul through streams of
  blood:
Which blood, like sacrificing Abel's, cries,
Even from the tongueless caverns of the earth,
To me for justice and rough chastisement;
And, by the glorious worth of my descent,
This arm shall do it, or this life be spent.
  K. Rich. How high a pitch his resolution soars!
Thomas of Norfolk, what say'st thou to this?   *110*
  Mow. O, let my sovereign turn away his face
And bid his ears a little while be deaf,
Till I have told this slander of his blood,
How God and good men hate so foul a liar.
  K. Rich. Mowbray, impartial are our eyes and
  ears:
Were he my brother, nay, my kingdom's heir,
As he is but my father's brother's son,
Now, by my sceptre's awe, I make a vow,
Such neighbour nearness to our sacred blood
Should nothing privilege him, nor partialize   *120*
The unstooping firmness of my upright soul:
He is our subject, Mowbray; so art thou:
Free speech and fearless I to thee allow.
  Mow. Then, Bolingbroke, as low as to thy
  heart,
Through the false passage of thy throat, thou
  liest.
Three parts of that receipt I had for Calais
Disbursed I duly to his Highness' soldiers;
The other part reserved I by consent,
For that my sovereign liege was in my debt
Upon remainder of a dear account,   *130*
Since last I went to France to fetch his queen:
Now swallow down that lie. For Gloucester's
  death,
I slew him not; but to my own disgrace
Neglected my sworn duty in that case.
For you, my noble Lord of Lancaster,

The honourable father to my foe,
Once did I lay an ambush for your life,
A trespass that doth vex my grieved soul;
But ere I last received the sacrament
I did confess it, and exactly begg'd   140
Your Grace's pardon, and I hope I had it.
This is my fault: as for the rest appeal'd,
It issues from the rancour of a villain,
A recreant and most degenerate traitor:
Which in myself I boldly will defend;
And interchangeably hurl down my gage
Upon this overweening traitor's foot,
To prove myself a loyal gentleman
Even in the best blood chamber'd in his bosom.
In haste whereof, most heartily I pray   150
Your Highness to assign our trial day.
  K. Rich. Wrath-kindled gentlemen, be ruled by
    me;
Let's purge this choler without letting blood:
This we prescribe, though no physician;
Deep malice makes too deep incision;
Forget, forgive; conclude and be agreed;
Our doctors say this is no month to bleed.
Good uncle, let this end where it begun;
We'll calm the Duke of Norfolk, you your son.
  Gaunt. To be a make-peace shall become my
    age: 160
Throw down, my son, the Duke of Norfolk's
    gage.
  K. Rich. And, Norfolk, throw down his.
  Gaunt.   When, Harry, when?
Obedience bids I should not bid again.
  K. Rich. Norfolk, throw down, we bid; there is
    no boot.
  Mow. Myself I throw, dread sovereign, at thy
    foot.
My life thou shalt command, but not my shame:
The one my duty owes; but my fair name,
Despite of death that lives upon my grave,
To dark dishonour's use thou shalt not have.
I am disgraced, impeach'd and baffled here,   170
Pierced to the soul with slander's venom'd spear,
The which no balm can cure but his heart-blood
Which breathed this poison.
  K. Rich.   Rage must be withstood:
Give me his gage: lions make leopards tame.
  Mow. Yea, but not change his spots: take but
    my shame,
And I resign my gage. My dear dear lord,
The purest treasure mortal times afford
Is spotless reputation: that away,
Men are but gilded loam or painted clay.
A jewel in a ten-times-barr'd-up chest   180
Is a bold spirit in a loyal breast.
Mine honour is my life; both grow in one;
Take honour from me, and my life is done:

Then, dear my liege, mine honour let me try;
In that I live and for that will I die.
  K. Rich. Cousin, throw up your gage; do you
    begin.
  Boling. O, God defend my soul from such deep
    sin!
Shall I seem crest-fall'n in my father's sight?
Or with pale beggar-fear impeach my height   189
Before this out-dared dastard? Ere my tongue
Shall wound my honour with such feeble wrong,
Or sound so base a parle, my teeth shall tear
The slavish motive of recanting fear,
And spit it bleeding in his high disgrace,
Where shame doth harbour, even in Mowbray's
    face.   [*Exit* GAUNT.
  K. Rich. We were not born to sue, but to com-
    mand;
Which since we cannot do to make you friends,
Be ready, as your lives shall answer it,
At Coventry, upon Saint Lambert's day:
There shall your swords and lances arbitrate   200
The swelling difference of your settled hate:
Since we can not atone you, we shall see
Justice design the victor's chivalry.
Lord marshal, command our officers at arms
Be ready to direct these home alarms.   [*Exeunt.*

SCENE II. *The Duke of Lancaster's palace*
Enter JOHN OF GAUNT *with the* DUCHESS
OF GLOUCESTER.

  Gaunt. Alas, the part I had in Woodstock's blood
Doth more solicit me than your exclaims
To stir against the butchers of his life!
But since correction lieth in those hands
Which made the fault that we cannot correct,
Put we our quarrel to the will of heaven;
Who, when they see the hours ripe on earth,
Will rain hot vengeance on offenders' heads.
  Duch. Finds brotherhood in thee no sharper
    spur?
Hath love in thy old blood no living fire?   10
Edward's seven sons, whereof thyself art one,
Were as seven vials of his sacred blood,
Or seven fair branches springing from one root:
Some of those seven are dried by nature's course,
Some of those branches by the Destinies cut;
But Thomas, my dear lord, my life, my Glou-
    cester,
One vial full of Edward's sacred blood,
One flourishing branch of his most royal root,
Is crack'd, and all the precious liquor spilt,
Is hack'd down, and his summer leaves all faded,
By Envy's hand and Murder's bloody axe.   21
Ah, Gaunt, his blood was thine! that bed, that
    womb,
That metal, that self mould, that fashion'd thee

Made him a man; and though thou livest and
    breathest,
Yet art thou slain in him: thou dost consent
In some large measure to thy father's death,
In that thou seest thy wretched brother die,
Who was the model of thy father's life.
Call it not patience, Gaunt; it is despair:
In suffering thus thy brother to be slaughter'd, 30
Thou showest the naked pathway to thy life,
Teaching stern murder how to butcher thee:
That which in mean men we entitle patience
Is pale cowardice in noble breasts.
What shall I say? to safeguard thine own life,
The best way is to venge my Gloucester's death.
  Gaunt. God's is the quarrel; for God's substi-
    tute,
His deputy anointed in His sight,
Hath caused his death: the which if wrongfully,
Let heaven revenge; for I may never lift   40
An angry arm against His minister.
  Duch. Where then, alas, may I complain my-
    self?
  Gaunt. To God, the widow's champion and de-
    fence.
  Duch. Why, then, I will. Farewell, old Gaunt.
Thou goest to Coventry, there to behold
Our cousin Hereford and fell Mowbray fight:
O, sit my husband's wrongs on Hereford's spear,
That it may enter butcher Mowbray's breast!
Or, if misfortune miss the first career,
Be Mowbray's sins so heavy in his bosom   50
That they may break his foaming courser's back,
And throw the rider headlong in the lists,
A caitiff recreant to my cousin Hereford!
Farewell, old Gaunt: thy sometimes brother's
    wife
With her companion grief must end her life.
  Gaunt. Sister, farewell; I must to Coventry:
As much good stay with thee as go with me!
  Duch. Yet one word more: grief boundeth
    where it falls,
Not with the empty hollowness, but weight:
I take my leave before I have begun,   60
For sorrow ends not when it seemeth done.
Commend me to thy brother, Edmund York.
Lo, this is all:—nay, yet depart not so;
Though this be all, do not so quickly go;
I shall remember more. Bid him—ah, what?—
With all good speed at Plashy visit me.
Alack, and what shall good old York there see
But empty lodgings and unfurnish'd walls,
Unpeopled offices, untrodden stones?
And what hear there for welcome but my
    groans?   70
Therefore commend me; let him not come there,
To seek out sorrow that dwells everywhere.

Desolate, desolate, will I hence and die:
The last leave of thee takes my weeping eye.

                               [Exeunt.

       SCENE III. *The lists at Coventry*

  Enter the LORD MARSHAL *and the* DUKE OF
                AUMERLE.

  Mar. My Lord Aumerle, is Harry Hereford
    arm'd?
  Aum. Yea, at all points; and longs to enter in.
  Mar. The Duke of Norfolk, sprightfully and
    bold,
Stays but the summons of the appellant's trumpet.
  Aum. Why, then, the champions are prepared,
    and stay
For nothing but his Majesty's approach.

The trumpets sound, and the KING *enters with his*
  nobles, GAUNT, BUSHY, BAGOT, GREEN, *and*
  others. When they are set, enter MOWBRAY *in*
  arms, defendant, with a HERALD.

  K. Rich. Marshal, demand of yonder champion
The cause of his arrival here in arms:
Ask him his name and orderly proceed
To swear him in the justice of his cause.   10
  Mar. In God's name and the King's, say who
    thou art
And why thou comest thus knightly clad in arms,
Against what man thou comest, and what thy
    quarrel:
Speak truly, on thy knighthood and thy oath;
As so defend thee heaven and thy valour!
  Mow. My name is Thomas Mowbray, Duke of
    Norfolk;
Who hither come engaged by my oath—
Which God defend a knight should violate!—
Both to defend my loyalty and truth
To God, my King, and my succeeding issue,   20
Against the Duke of Hereford that appeals me;
And, by the grace of God and this mine arm,
To prove him, in defending of myself,
A traitor to my God, my King, and me:
And as I truly fight, defend me heaven!

    The trumpets sound. Enter BOLINGBROKE,
      appellant, in armour, with a HERALD.

  K. Rich. Marshal, ask yonder knight in arms,
Both who he is and why he cometh hither
Thus plated in habiliments of war,
And formally, according to our law,
Depose him in the justice of his cause.   30
  Mar. What is thy name? and wherefore comest
    thou hither,
Before King Richard in his royal lists?
Against whom comest thou? and what's thy
    quarrel?

Speak like a true knight, so defend thee heaven!

Boling. Harry of Hereford, Lancaster, and
  Derby
Am I; who ready here do stand in arms,
To prove, by God's grace and my body's valour,
In lists, on Thomas Mowbray, Duke of Norfolk,
That he is a traitor, foul and dangerous,
To God of heaven, King Richard, and to me;   40
And as I truly fight, defend me heaven!

Mar. On pain of death, no person be so bold
Or daring-hardy as to touch the lists,
Except the Marshal and such officers
Appointed to direct these fair designs.

Boling. Lord Marshal, let me kiss my
  sovereign's hand,
And bow my knee before his Majesty:
For Mowbray and myself are like two men
That vow a long and weary pilgrimage;
Then let us take a ceremonious leave   50
And loving farewell of our several friends.

Mar. The appellant in all duty greets your
  Highness,
And craves to kiss your hand and take his leave.

K. Rich. We will descend and fold him in our
  arms.
Cousin of Hereford, as thy cause is right,
So be thy fortune in this royal fight!
Farewell, my blood; which if to-day thou shed,
Lament we may, but not revenge thee dead.

Boling. O, let no noble eye profane a tear
For me, if I be gored with Mowbray's spear: 60
As confident as is the falcon's flight
Against a bird, do I with Mowbray fight.
My loving lord, I take my leave of you;
Of you, my noble cousin, Lord Aumerle;
Not sick, although I have to do with death,
But lusty, young, and cheerly drawing breath.
Lo, as at English feasts, so I regreet
The daintiest last, to make the end most sweet:
O thou, the earthly author of my blood,
Whose youthful spirit, in me regenerate,   70
Doth with a twofold vigour lift me up
To reach at victory above my head,
Add proof unto mine armour with thy prayers;
And with thy blessings steel my lance's point,
That it may enter Mowbray's waxen coat,
And furbish new the name of John o' Gaunt,
Even in the lusty haviour of his son.

Gaunt. God in thy good cause make thee pros-
  perous!
Be swift like lightning in the execution;
And let thy blows, doubly redoubled,   80
Fall like amazing thunder on the casque
Of thy adverse pernicious enemy:
Rouse up thy youthful blood, be valiant, and
  live.

Boling. Mine innocency and Saint George to
  thrive!

Mow. However God or fortune cast my lot,
There lives or dies, true to King Richard's
  throne,
A loyal, just, and upright gentleman:
Never did captive with a freer heart
Cast off his chains of bondage and embrace
His golden uncontroll'd enfranchisement,   90
More than my dancing soul doth celebrate
This feast of battle with mine adversary.
Most mighty liege, and my companion peers,
Take from my mouth the wish of happy years:
As gentle and as jocund as to jest
Go I to fight: truth hath a quiet breast.

K. Rich. Farewell, my lord: securely I espy
Virtue with valour couched in thine eye.
Order the trial, Marshal, and begin.

Mar. Harry of Hereford, Lancaster, and
  Derby,   100
Receive thy lance; and God defend the right!

Boling. Strong as a tower in hope, I cry amen.

Mar. Go bear this lance to Thomas, Duke of
  Norfolk.

1st Her. Harry of Hereford, Lancaster, and
  Derby,
Stands here for God, his sovereign, and himself,
On pain to be found false and recreant,
To prove the Duke of Norfolk, Thomas Mow-
  bray,
A traitor to his God, his King, and him;
And dares him to set forward to the fight.

2nd Her. Here standeth Thomas Mowbray,
  Duke of Norfolk,   110
On pain to be found false and recreant,
Both to defend himself and to approve
Henry of Hereford, Lancaster, and Derby,
To God, his sovereign, and to him disloyal;
Courageously and with a free desire
Attending but the signal to begin.

Mar. Sound, trumpets; and set forward, combatants.

  A charge sounded.
Stay, the King hath thrown his warder down.

K. Rich. Let them lay by their helmets and their
  spears,
And both return back to their chairs again: 120
Withdraw with us: and let the trumpets sound
While we return these Dukes what we decree.

  A long flourish.
Draw near,
And list what with our council we have done.
For that our kingdom's earth should not be
  soil'd
With that dear blood which it hath fostered;
And for our eyes do hate the dire aspect

Of civil wounds plough'd up with neighbours'
    sword;
And for we think the eagle-winged pride
Of sky-aspiring and ambitious thoughts,   *130*
With rival-hating envy, set on you
To wake our peace, which in our country's
    cradle
Draws the sweet infant breath of gentle sleep;
Which so roused up with boisterous untuned
    drums,
With harsh-resounding trumpets' dreadful bray,
And grating shock of wrathful iron arms,
Might from our quiet confines fright fair peace
And make us wade even in our kindred's blood;
Therefore, we banish you our territories:
You, cousin Hereford, upon pain of life,   *140*
Till twice five summers have enrich'd our fields
Shall not regreet our fair dominions,
But tread the stranger paths of banishment.
  Boling. Your will be done: this must my com-
    fort be,
That sun that warms you here shall shine on
    me;
And those his golden beams to you here lent
Shall point on me and gild my banishment.
  K. Rich. Norfolk, for thee remains a heavier
    doom,
Which I with some unwillingness pronounce:
The sly slow hours shall not determinate   *150*
The dateless limit of thy dear exile;
The hopeless word of "never to return"
Breathe I against thee, upon pain of life.
  Mow. A heavy sentence, my most sovereign
    liege,
And all unlook'd for from your Highness' mouth:
A dearer merit, not so deep a maim
As to be cast forth in the common air,
Have I deserved at your Highness' hands.
The language I have learn'd these forty years,
My native English, now I must forego: *160*
And now my tongue's use is to me no more
Than an unstringed viol or a harp,
Or like a cunning instrument cased up,
Or, being open, put into his hands
That knows no touch to tune the harmony:
Within my mouth you have engaol'd my tongue,
Doubly portcullis'd with my teeth and lips;
And dull unfeeling barren ignorance
Is made my gaoler to attend on me.
I am too old to fawn upon a nurse,   *170*
Too far in years to be a pupil now:
What is thy sentence then but speechless death,
Which robs my tongue from breathing native
    breath?
  K. Rich. It boots thee not to be compassionate:
After our sentence plaining comes too late.

  Mow. Then thus I turn me from my country's
    light,
To dwell in solemn shades of endless night.
  K. Rich. Return again, and take an oath with
    thee.
Lay on our royal sword your banish'd hands;
Swear by the duty that you owe to God—   *180*
Our part therein we banish with yourselves—
To keep the oath that we administer:
You never shall, so help you truth and God!
Embrace each other's love in banishment;
Nor never look upon each other's face;
Nor never write, regreet, nor reconcile
This louring tempest of your home-bred hate;
Nor never by advised purpose meet
To plot, contrive, or complot any ill
'Gainst us, our state, our subjects, or our land.*190*
  Boling. I swear.
  Mow. And I, to keep all this.
  Boling. Norfolk, so far as to mine enemy:—
By this time, had the King permitted us,
One of our souls had wander'd in the air,
Banish'd this frail sepulchre of our flesh,
As now our flesh is banish'd from this land:
Confess thy treasons ere thou fly the realm;
Since thou hast far to go, bear not along
The clogging burthen of a guilty soul.   *200*
  Mow. No, Bolingbroke: if ever I were traitor,
My name be blotted from the book of life,
And I from heaven banish'd as from hence!
But what thou art, God, thou, and I do know;
And all too soon, I fear, the King shall rue.
Farewell, my liege. Now no way can I stray;
Save back to England, all the world's my way.
                            [Exit.
  K. Rich. Uncle, even in the glasses of thine eyes
I see thy grieved heart: thy sad aspect
Hath from the number of his banish'd years   *210*
Pluck'd four away. [*To* BOLINGBROKE] Six frozen
    winters spent,
Return with welcome home from banishment.
  Boling. How long a time lies in one little word!
Four lagging winters and four wanton springs
End in a word: such is the breath of Kings.
  Gaunt. I thank my liege, that in regard of me
He shortens four years of my son's exile:
But little vantage shall I reap thereby;
For, ere the six years that he hath to spend
Can change their moons and bring their times
    about,   *220*
My oil-dried lamp and time-bewasted light
Shall be extinct with age and endless night;
My inch of taper will be burnt and done,
And blindfold death not let me see my son.
  K. Rich. Why, uncle, thou hast many years to
    live.

Gaunt. But not a minute, King, that thou canst
  give:
Shorten my days thou canst with sullen sorrow,
And pluck nights from me, but not lend a mor-
  row;
Thou canst help time to furrow me with age,
But stop no wrinkle in his pilgrimage;   *230*
Thy word is current with him for my death,
But dead, thy kingdom cannot buy my breath.
  K. Rich. Thy son is banish'd upon good advice,
Whereto thy tongue a party-verdict gave:
Why at our justice seem'st thou then to lour?
  Gaunt. Things sweet to taste prove in digestion
  sour.
You urged me as a judge; but I had rather
You would have bid me argue like a father.
O, had it been a stranger, not my child,
To smooth his fault I should have been more
  mild:
A partial slander sought I to avoid,   *241*
And in the sentence my own life destroy'd.
Alas, I look'd when some of you should say,
I was too strict to make mine own away;
But you gave leave to my unwilling tongue
Against my will to do myself this wrong.
  K. Rich. Cousin, farewell; and, uncle, bid him
  so:
Six years we banish him, and he shall go.
    [*Flourish. Exeunt* KING RICHARD *and train.*
  Aum. Cousin, farewell: what presence must not
  know,
From where you do remain let paper show.   *250*
  Mar. My lord, no leave take I; for I will ride,
As far as land will let me, by your side.
  Gaunt. O, to what purpose dost thou hoard thy
  words,
That thou return'st no greeting to thy friends?
  Boling. I have too few to take my leave of you,
When the tongue's office should be prodigal
To breathe the abundant dolour of the heart.
  Gaunt. Thy grief is but thy absence for a time.
  Boling. Joy absent, grief is present for that time.
  Gaunt. What is six winters? they are quickly
  gone.   *260*
  Boling. To men in joy; but grief makes one hour
  ten.
  Gaunt. Call it a travel that thou takest for pleas-
  ure.
  Boling. My heart will sigh when I miscall it so,
Which finds it an enforced pilgrimage.
  Gaunt. The sullen passage of thy weary steps
Esteem as foil wherein thou art to set
The precious jewel of thy home return.
  Boling. Nay, rather, every tedious stride I make
Will but remember me what a deal of world
I wander from the jewels that I love.   *270*

Must I not serve a long apprenticehood
To foreign passages, and in the end,
Having my freedom, boast of nothing else
But that I was a journeyman to grief?
  Gaunt. All places that the eye of heaven visits
Are to a wise man ports and happy havens.
Teach thy necessity to reason thus;
There is no virtue like necessity.
Think not the King did banish thee,
But thou the King. Woe doth the heavier sit, *280*
Where it perceives it is but faintly borne.
Go, say I sent thee forth to purchase honour
And not the King exiled thee; or suppose
Devouring pestilence hangs in our air
And thou art flying to a fresher clime:
Look, what thy soul holds dear, imagine it
To lie that way thou go'st, not whence thou
  comest:
Suppose the singing birds musicians,
The grass whereon thou tread'st the presence
  strew'd,
The flowers fair ladies, and thy steps no more
Than a delightful measure or a dance;   *291*
For gnarling sorrow hath less power to bite
The man that mocks at it and sets it light.
  Boling. O, who can hold a fire in his hand
By thinking on the frosty Caucasus?
Or cloy the hungry edge of appetite
By bare imagination of a feast?
Or wallow naked in December snow
By thinking on fantastic summer's heat?
O, no! the apprehension of the good   *300*
Gives but the greater feeling to the worse:
Fell sorrow's tooth doth never rankle more
Than when he bites, but lanceth not the sore.
  Gaunt. Come, come, my son, I'll bring thee on
  thy way:
Had I thy youth and cause, I would not stay.
  Boling. Then, England's ground, farewell;
  sweet soil, adieu;
My mother, and my nurse, that bears me yet!
Where'er I wander, boast of this I can,
Though banish'd, yet a trueborn Englishman.
                           [*Exeunt.*

SCENE IV. *The court*

Enter the KING, *with* BAGOT *and* GREEN *at one
door; and the* DUKE OF AUMERLE *at another.*

  K. Rich. We did observe. Cousin Aumerle,
How far brought you high Hereford on his
  way?
  Aum. I brought high Hereford, if you call him
  so,
But to the next highway, and there I left him.
  K. Rich. And say, what store of parting tears
  were shed?

Aum. Faith, none for me; except the northeast
 wind,
Which then blew bitterly against our faces,
Awaked the sleeping rheum, and so by chance
Did grace our hollow parting with a tear.
 K. Rich. What said our cousin when you parted
 with him?   *10*
 Aum. "Farewell":
And, for my heart disdained that my tongue
Should so profane the word, that taught me craft
To counterfeit oppression of such grief
That words seem'd buried in my sorrow's
 grave.
Marry, would the word "farewell" have length-
 en'd hours
And added years to his short banishment,
He should have had a volume of farewells;
But since it would not, he had none of me.
 K. Rich. He is our cousin, cousin; but 'tis
 doubt,   *20*
When time shall call him from banishment,
Whether our kinsman come to see his friends.
Ourself and Bushy, Bagot here and Green
Observed his courtship to the common people;
How he did seem to dive into their hearts
With humble and familiar courtesy,
What reverence he did throw away on slaves,
Wooing poor craftsmen with the craft of smiles
And patient underbearing of his fortune,
As 'twere to banish their affects with him. *30*
Off goes his bonnet to an oyster-wench;
A brace of draymen bid God speed him well
And had the tribute of his supple knee,
With "Thanks, my countrymen, my loving
 friends";
As were our England in reversion his,
And he our subjects' next degree in hope.
 Green. Well, he is gone; and with him go these
 thoughts.
Now for the rebels which stand out in Ireland,
Expedient manage must be made, my liege,
Ere further leisure yield them further means *40*
For their advantage and your Highness' loss.
 K. Rich. We will ourself in person to this war:
And, for our coffers, with too great a court
And liberal largess, are grown somewhat light,
We are inforced to farm our royal realm;
The revenue whereof shall furnish us
For our affairs in hand: if that come short,
Our substitutes at home shall have blank char-
 ters;
Whereto, when they shall know what men are
 rich,
They shall subscribe them for large sums of gold
And send them after to supply our wants; *51*
For we will make for Ireland presently.

Enter BUSHY.

Bushy, what news?
 Bushy. Old John of Gaunt is grievous sick, my
 lord,
Suddenly taken; and hath sent post haste
To entreat your Majesty to visit him.
 K. Rich. Where lies he?
 Bushy. At Ely House.
 K. Rich. Now put it, God, in the physician's
 mind
To help him to his grave immediately! *50*
The lining of his coffers shall make coats
To deck our soldiers for these Irish wars.
Come, gentlemen, let's all go visit him:
Pray God we may make haste, and come too late!
 All. Amen.   *[Exeunt.*

ACT II

Scene I. *Ely House*

Enter JOHN OF GAUNT *sick, with the* DUKE OF
YORK, &c.

 Gaunt. Will the King come, that I may breathe
 my last
In wholesome counsel to his unstaid youth?
 York. Vex not yourself, nor strive not with your
 breath,
For all in vain comes counsel to his ear.
 Gaunt. O, but they say the tongues of dying
 men
Enforce attention like deep harmony:
Where words are scarce, they are seldom spent
 in vain,
For they breathe truth that breathe their words
 in pain.
He that no more must say is listen'd more
 Than they whom youth and ease have taught
 to glose;   *10*
More are men's ends mark'd than their lives be-
 fore:
 The setting sun, and music at the close,
As the last taste of sweets, is sweetest last,
Writ in remembrance more than things long
 past:
Though Richard my life's counsel would not
 hear,
My death's sad tale may yet undeaf his ear.
 York. No; it is stopp'd with other flattering
 sounds,
As praises, of whose taste the wise are fond,
Lascivious metres, to whose venom sound
The open ear of youth doth always listen; *20*
Report of fashions in proud Italy,
Whose manners still our tardy apish nation
Limps after in base imitation.

Where doth the world thrust forth a vanity—
So it be new, there's no respect how vile—
That is not quickly buzz'd into his ears?
Then all too late comes counsel to be heard,
Where will doth mutiny with wit's regard.
Direct not him whose way himself will choose:
'Tis breath thou lack'st, and that breath wilt thou
    lose.   30

Gaunt. Methinks I am a prophet new inspired
And thus expiring do foretell of him:
His rash fierce blaze of riot cannot last,
For violent fires soon burn out themselves;
Small showers last long, but sudden storms are
    short;
He tires betimes that spurs too fast betimes;
With eager feeding food doth choke the feeder:
Light vanity, insatiate cormorant,
Consuming means, soon preys upon itself.
This royal throne of kings, this scepter'd isle,   40
This earth of majesty, this seat of Mars,
This other Eden, demi-paradise,
This fortress built by Nature for herself
Against infection and the hand of war,
This happy breed of men, this little world,
This precious stone set in the silver sea,
Which serves it in the office of a wall
Or as a moat defensive to a house,
Against the envy of less happier lands,
This blessed plot, this earth, this realm, this Eng-
    land,   50
This nurse, this teeming womb of royal kings,
Fear'd by their breed and famous by their birth,
Renowned for their deeds as far from home,
For Christian service and true chivalry,
As is the sepulchre in stubborn Jewry
Of the world's ransom, blessed Mary's Son,
This land of such dear souls, this dear dear land,
Dear for her reputation through the world,
Is now leased out, I die pronouncing it,
Like to a tenement or pelting farm: 60
England, bound in with the triumphant sea,
Whose rocky shore beats back the envious siege
Of watery Neptune, is now bound in with shame,
With inky blots and rotten parchment bonds:
That England, that was wont to conquer others,
Hath made a shameful conquest of itself.
Ah, would the scandal vanish with my life,
How happy then were my ensuing death!

Enter KING RICHARD *and* QUEEN, AUMERLE, BUSHY,
    GREEN, BAGOT, ROSS, *and* WILLOUGHBY.

York. The King is come: deal mildly with his
    youth;   69
For young hot colts being raged do rage the
    more.
Queen. How fares our noble uncle, Lancaster?

K. Rich. What comfort, man? how is't with
    aged Gaunt?
Gaunt. O, how that name befits my composi-
    tion!
Old Gaunt indeed, and gaunt in being old:
Within me grief hath kept a tedious fast;
And who abstains from meat that is not gaunt?
For sleeping England long time have I watch'd;
Watching breeds leanness, leanness is all gaunt:
The pleasure that some fathers feed upon,
Is my strict fast; I mean, my children's looks;   80
And therein fasting, hast thou made me gaunt:
Gaunt am I for the grave, gaunt as a grave,
Whose hollow womb inherits nought but bones.
K. Rich. Can sick men play so nicely with their
    names?
Gaunt. No, misery makes sport to mock itself:
Since thou dost seek to kill my name in me,
I mock my name, great King, to flatter thee.
K. Rich. Should dying men flatter with those
    that live?
Gaunt. No, no, men living flatter those that die.
K. Rich. Thou, now a-dying, say'st thou flatter-
    est me.   90
Gaunt. O, no! thou diest, though I the sicker be.
K. Rich. I am in health, I breathe, and see thee
    ill.
Gaunt. Now He that made me knows I see thee
    ill;
Ill in myself to see, and in thee seeing ill.
Thy death-bed is no lesser than thy land
Wherein thou liest in reputation sick;
And thou, too careless patient as thou art,
Commit'st thy anointed body to the cure
Of those physicians that first wounded thee:
A thousand flatterers sit within thy crown,   100
Whose compass is no bigger than thy head;
And yet, incaged in so small a verge,
The waste is no whit lesser than thy land.
O, had thy grandsire with a prophet's eye
Seen how his son's son should destroy his sons,
From forth thy reach he would have laid thy
    shame,
Deposing thee before thou wert possess'd,
Which art possess'd now to depose thyself.
Why, cousin, wert thou regent of the world,
It were a shame to let this land by lease;   110
But for thy world enjoying but this land,
Is it not more than shame to shame it so?
Landlord of England art thou now, not king:
Thy state of law is bondslave to the law;
And thou—
K. Rich. A lunatic lean-witted fool,
Presuming on an ague's privilege,
Darest with thy frozen admonition
Make pale our cheek, chasing the royal blood

With fury from his native residence.
Now, by my seat's right royal majesty,   120
Wert thou not brother to great Edward's son,
This tongue that runs so roundly in thy head
Should run thy head from thy unreverent shoul-
    ders.
    Gaunt. O, spare me not, my brother Edward's
    son,
For that I was his father Edward's son;
That blood already, like the pelican,
Hast thou tapp'd out and drunkenly caroused:
My brother Gloucester, plain well-meaning soul,
Whom fair befall in heaven 'mongst happy souls!
May be a precedent and witness good   130
That thou respect'st not spilling Edward's blood:
Join with the present sickness that I have;
And thy unkindness be like crooked age,
To crop at once a too long wither'd flower.
Live in thy shame, but die not shame with thee!
These words hereafter thy tormentors be!
Convey me to my bed, then to my grave:
Love they to live that love and honour have,
    [*Exit, borne off by his Attendants.*
    K. Rich. And let them die that age and sullens
    have;
For both hast thou, and both become the grave.
    York. I do beseech your majesty, impute his
    words   141
To wayward sickliness and age in him:
He loves you, on my life, and holds you dear
As Harry Duke of Hereford, were he here.
    K. Rich. Right, you say true: as Hereford's
    love, so his;
As theirs, so mine; and all be as it is.

    Enter NORTHUMBERLAND.

    North. My liege, old Gaunt commends him to
    your Majesty.
    K. Rich. What says he?
    North.   Nay, nothing; all is said:
His tongue is now a stringless instrument;
Words, life and all, old Lancaster hath spent.   150
    York. Be York the next that must be bankrupt
    so!
Though death be poor, it ends a mortal woe.
    K. Rich. The ripest fruit first falls, and so doth
    he;
His time is spent, our pilgrimage must be.
So much for that. Now for our Irish wars:
We must supplant those rough rug-headed kerns,
Which live like venom where no venom else
But only they have privilege to live.
And for these great affairs do ask some charge,
Towards our assistance we do seize to us   160
The plate, coin, revenues and moveables,
Whereof our uncle Gaunt did stand possess'd.

    York. How long shall I be patient? ah, how long
Shall tender duty make me suffer wrong?
Not Gloucester's death, nor Hereford's banish-
    ment,
Not Gaunt's rebukes, nor England's private
    wrongs,
Nor the prevention of poor Bolingbroke
About his marriage, nor my own disgrace,
Have ever made me sour my patient cheek,
Or bend one wrinkle on my sovereign's face.   170
I am the last of noble Edward's sons,
Of whom thy father, Prince of Wales, was first:
In war was never lion raged more fierce,
In peace was never gentle lamb more mild,
Than was that young and princely gentleman.
His face thou hast, for even so look'd he,
Accomplish'd with the number of thy hours;
But when he frown'd, it was against the French
And not against his friends; his noble hand
Did win what he did spend and spent not that   180
Which his triumphant father's hand had won;
His hands were guilty of no kindred blood,
But bloody with the enemies of his kin.
O Richard! York is too far gone with grief,
Or else he never would compare between.
    K. Rich. Why, uncle, what's the matter?
    York.   O my liege,
Pardon me, if you please; if not, I, pleased
Not to be pardon'd, am content withal.
Seek you to seize and gripe into your hands   189
The royalties and rights of banish'd Hereford?
Is not Gaunt dead, and doth not Hereford live?
Was not Gaunt just, and is not Harry true?
Did not the one deserve to have an heir?
Is not his heir a well-deserving son?
Take Hereford's rights away, and take from
    Time
His charters and his customary rights;
Let not to-morrow then ensue to-day;
Be not thyself; for how art thou a king
But by fair sequence and succession?
Now, afore God—God forbid I say true!—   200
If you do wrongfully seize Hereford's rights,
Call in the letters patents that he hath
By his attorneys-general to sue
His livery, and deny his offer'd homage,
You pluck a thousand dangers on your head,
You lose a thousand well-disposed hearts
And prick my tender patience to those thoughts
Which honour and allegiance cannot think.
    K. Rich. Think what you will, we seize into our
    hands
His plate, his goods, his money, and his lands.
    York. I'll not be by the while: my liege, fare-
    well: 211
What will ensue hereof, there's none can tell;

But by bad courses may be understood
That their events can never fall out good.   [*Exit.*
  K. Rich. Go, Bushy, to the Earl of Wiltshire
    straight:
Bid him repair to us to Ely House
To see this business. To-morrow next
We will for Ireland; and 'tis time, I trow:
And we create, in absence of ourself,
Our uncle York lord governor of England;   *220*
For he is just and always loved us well.
Come on, our queen: to-morrow must we part;
Be merry, for our time of stay is short.
        [*Flourish. Exeunt* KING, QUEEN, AUMERLE,
                BUSHY, GREEN, *and* BAGOT.
  North. Well, lords, the Duke of Lancaster is
    dead.
  Ross. And living too; for now his son is duke.
  Willo. Barely in title, not in revenues.
  North. Richly in both, if justice had her
    right.
  Ross. My heart is great; but it must break with
    silence,
Ere't be disburden'd with a liberal tongue.
  North. Nay, speak thy mind; and let him ne'er
    speak more   *230*
That speaks thy words again to do thee harm!
  Willo. Tends that thou wouldst speak to the
    Duke of Hereford?
If it be so, out with it boldly, man;
Quick is mine ear to hear of good towards him.
  Ross. No good at all that I can do for him;
Unless you call it good to pity him,
Bereft and gelded of his patrimony.
  North. Now, afore God, 'tis shame such wrongs
    are borne
In him, a royal prince, and many moe
Of noble blood in this declining land.   *240*
The King is not himself, but basely led
By flatterers; and what they will inform,
Merely in hate, 'gainst any of us all,
That will the King severely prosecute
'Gainst us, our lives, our children, and our heirs.
  Ross. The commons hath he pill'd with grievous
    taxes,
And quite lost their hearts: the nobles hath he
    fined
For ancient quarrels, and quite lost their hearts.
  Willo. And daily new exactions are devised,
As blanks, benevolences, and I wot not what: *250*
But what, o' God's name, doth become of this?
  North. Wars have not wasted it, for warr'd he
    hath not,
But basely yielded upon compromise
That which his noble ancestors achieved with
    blows:
More hath he spent in peace than they in wars.

  Ross. The Earl of Wiltshire hath the realm in
    farm.
  Willo. The King's grown bankrupt, like a bro-
    ken man.
  North. Reproach and dissolution hangeth over
    him.
  Ross. He hath not money for these Irish wars,
His burthenous taxations notwithstanding,   *260*
But by the robbing of the banish'd Duke.
  North. His noble kinsman: most degenerate
    king!
But, lords, we hear this fearful tempest sing,
Yet seek no shelter to avoid the storm;
We see the wind sit sore upon our sails,
And yet we strike not, but securely perish.
  Ross. We see the very wreck that we must
    suffer;
And unavoided is the danger now,
For suffering so the causes of our wreck.
  North. Not so; even through the hollow eyes of
    death   *270*
I spy life peering; but I dare not say
How near the tidings of our comfort is.
  Willo. Nay, let us share thy thoughts, as thou
    dost ours.
  Ross. Be confident to speak, Northumberland:
We three are but thyself; and, speaking so,
Thy words are but as thoughts; therefore, be
    bold.
  North. Then thus: I have from Port le Blanc, a
    bay
In Brittany, received intelligence
That Harry Duke of Hereford, Rainold Lord
    Cobham,
. . . . *280*
That late broke from the Duke of Exeter,
His brother, Archbishop late of Canterbury,
Sir Thomas Erpingham, Sir John Ramston,
Sir John Norbery, Sir Robert Waterton and
    Francis Quoint,
All these well furnish'd by the Duke of Bretagne
With eight tall ships, three thousand men of war,
Are making hither with all due expedience
And shortly mean to touch our northern shore:
Perhaps they had ere this, but that they stay
The first departing of the King for Ireland.   *290*
If then we shall shake off our slavish yoke,
Imp out our drooping country's broken wing,
Redeem from broking pawn the blemish'd crown,
Wipe off the dust that hides our sceptre's gilt
And make high majesty look like itself,
Away with me in post to Ravenspurgh;
But if you faint, as fearing to do so,
Stay and be secret, and myself will go.
  Ross. To horse, to horse! urge doubts to them
    that fear.

Willo. Hold out my horse, and I will first be
    there.   *[Exeunt. 300*

SCENE II. *Windsor Castle*

Enter QUEEN, BUSHY, *and* BAGOT.

Bushy. Madam, your majesty is too much sad:
You promised, when you parted with the King,
To lay aside life-harming heaviness
And entertain a cheerful disposition.
  Queen. To please the King I did; to please my-
    self
I cannot do it; yet I know no cause
Why I should welcome such a guest as grief,
Save bidding farewell to so sweet a guest
As my sweet Richard: yet again, methinks,
Some unborn sorrow, ripe in fortune's womb,   *11*
Is coming towards me, and my inward soul
With nothing trembles: at some thing it grieves,
More than with parting from my lord the king.
  Bushy. Each substance of a grief hath twenty
    shadows,
Which shows like grief itself, but is not so;
For sorrow's eye, glazed with blinding tears,
Divides one thing entire to many objects;
Like perspectives, which rightly gazed upon
Show nothing but confusion, eyed awry
Distinguish form: so your sweet Majesty,   *20*
Looking awry upon your lord's departure,
Find shapes of grief, more than himself, to wail;
Which, look'd on as it is, is nought but shadows
Of what it is not. Then, thrice-gracious Queen,
More than your lord's departure weep not:
    more's not seen;
Or if it be, 'tis with false sorrow's eye,
Which for things true weeps things imaginary.
  Queen. It may be so; but yet my inward soul
Persuades me it is otherwise: howe'er it be,
I cannot but be sad; so heavy sad   *30*
As, though on thinking on no thought I think,
Makes me with heavy nothing faint and shrink.
  Bushy. 'Tis nothing but conceit, my gracious
    lady.
  Queen. 'Tis nothing less: conceit is still derived
From some forefather grief; mine is not so,
For nothing hath begot my something grief;
Or something hath the nothing that I grieve:
'Tis in reversion that I do possess;
But what it is, that is not yet known; what
I cannot name; 'tis nameless woe, I wot.   *40*

Enter GREEN

Green. God save your Majesty! and well met,
    gentlemen:
I hope the King is not yet shipp'd for Ireland.
  Queen. Why hopest thou so? 'tis better hope
    he is;

For his designs crave haste, his haste good hope:
Then wherefore dost thou hope he is not shipp'd?
  Green. That he, our hope, might have retired
    his power,
And driven into despair an enemy's hope,
Who strongly hath set footing in this land:
The banish'd Bolingbroke repeals himself,
And with uplifted arms is safe arrived   *50*
At Ravenspurgh.
  Queen.   Now God in heaven forbid!
  Green. Ah, madam, 'tis too true: and that is
    worse,
The Lord Northumberland, his son young Henry
    Percy,
The Lords of Ross, Beaumond, and Willoughby,
With all their powerful friends, are fled to him.
  Bushy. Why have you not proclaim'd North-
    umberland
And all the rest revolted faction traitors?
  Green. We have: whereupon the Earl of Wor-
    cester
Hath broke his staff, resign'd his stewardship,
And all the household servants fled with him   *60*
To Bolingbroke.
  Queen. So, Green, thou art the midwife to my
    woe,
And Bolingbroke my sorrow's dismal heir:
Now hath my soul brought forth her prodigy,
And I, a gasping new-deliver'd mother,
Have woe to woe, sorrow to sorrow join'd.
  Bushy. Despair not, madam.
  Queen.   Who shall hinder me?
I will despair, and be at enmity
With cozening hope: he is a flatterer,
A parasite, a keeper back of death,   *70*
Who gently would dissolve the bands of life,
Which false hope lingers in extremity.

Enter YORK.

Green. Here comes the Duke of York.
  Queen. With signs of war about his aged neck:
O, full of careful business are his looks!
Uncle, for God's sake, speak comfortable words.
  York. Should I do so, I should belie my thoughts:
Comfort's in heaven; and we are on the earth,
Where nothing lives but crosses, cares and
    grief.
Your husband, he is gone to save far off,   *80*
Whilst others come to make him lose at home:
Here am I left to underprop his land,
Who, weak with age, cannot support myself:
Now comes the sick hour that his surfeit made;
Now shall he try his friends that flatter'd him.

Enter a SERVANT.

Serv. My lord, you son was gone before I came.

York. He was? Why, so! go all which way it
    will!
The nobles they are fled, the commons they are
    cold,
And will, I fear, revolt on Hereford's side.
Sirrah, get thee to Plashy, to my sister Glou-
    cester;   90
Bid her send me presently a thousand pound:
Hold, take my ring.
    Serv. My lord, I had forgot to tell your lord-
    ship,
To-day, as I came by, I called there;
But I shall grieve you to report the rest.
    York. What is't, knave?
    Serv. An hour before I came, the Duchess died.
    York. God for his mercy! what a tide of woes
Comes rushing on this woeful land at once!
I know not what to do: I would to God,   100
So my untruth had not provoked him to it,
The King had cut off my head with my brother's.
What, are there no posts dispatch'd for Ireland?
How shall we do for money for these wars?
Come, sister—cousin, I would say—pray, par-
    don me.
Go, fellow, get thee home, provide some carts
And bring away the armour that is there.
                                    [*Exit Servant.*
Gentlemen, will you go muster men?
If I know how or which way to order these affairs
Thus thrust disorderly into my hands,   110
Never believe me. Both are my kinsmen:
The one is my sovereign, whom both my oath
And duty bids defend; the other again
Is my kinsman, whom the King hath wrong'd,
Whom conscience and my kindred bids to right.
Well, somewhat we must do. Come, cousin, I'll
Dispose of you.
Gentlemen, go, muster up your men,
And meet me presently at Berkeley.
I should to Plashy too;   120
But time will not permit: all is uneven,
And every thing is left at six and seven.
                            [*Exeunt* YORK *and* QUEEN.
    Bushy. The wind sits fair for news to go to
    Ireland,
But none returns. For us to levy power
Proportionable to the enemy
Is all unpossible.
    Green. Besides, our nearness to the King in love
Is near the hate of those love not the King.
    Bagot. And that's the wavering commons: for
    their love
Lies in their purses, and whoso empties them 130
By so much fills their hearts with deadly hate.
    Bushy. Wherein the King stands generally con-
    demn'd.

    Bagot. If judgement lie in them, then so do we,
Because we ever have been near the King.
    Green. Well, I will for refuge straight to Bristol
    castle:
The Earl of Wiltshire is already there.
    Bushy. Thither will I with you; for little office
The hateful commons will perform for us,
Except like curs to tear us all to pieces.
Will you go along with us?   140
    Bagot. No; I will to Ireland to his Majesty.
Farewell: if heart's presages be not vain,
We three here part that ne'er shall meet again.
    Bushy. That's as York thrives to beat back Bol-
    ingbroke.
    Green. Alas, poor duke! the task he undertakes
Is numbering sands and drinking oceans dry:
Where one on his side fights, thousands will fly.
Farewell at once, for once, for all, and ever.
    Bushy. Well, we may meet again.
    Bagot.   I fear me, never.
                                            [*Exeunt.*

SCENE III. *Wilds in Gloucestershire*

Enter BOLINGBROKE *and* NORTHUMBERLAND, *with
                        Forces.*

    Boling. How far is it, my lord, to Berkeley
    now?
    North. Believe me, noble lord,
I am a stranger here in Gloucestershire:
These high wild hills and rough uneven ways
Draws out our miles, and makes them weari-
    some;
And yet your fair discourse hath been as sugar,
Making the hard way sweet and delectable.
But I bethink me what a weary way
From Ravenspurgh to Cotswold will be found
In Ross and Willoughby, wanting your company,
Which, I protest, hath very much beguiled   11
The tediousness and process of my travel:
But theirs is sweetened with the hope to have
The present benefit which I possess;
And hope to joy is little less in joy
Than hope enjoy'd: by this the weary lords
Shall make their way seem short, as mine hath
    done
By sight of what I have, your noble company.
    Boling. Of much less value is my company
Than your good words. But who comes here?

Enter HENRY PERCY.

    North. It is my son, young Harry Percy,   21
Sent from my brother Worcester, whencesoever.
Harry, how fares your uncle?
    Percy. I had thought, my lord, to have learn'd
    his health of you.
    North. Why, is he not with the Queen?

Percy. No, my good Lord; he hath forsook the court,
Broken his staff of office and dispersed
The household of the King.
North.   What was his reason?
He was not so resolved when last we spake to-
gether.
Percy. Because your lordship was proclaimed
traitor.   *30*
But he, my lord, is gone to Ravenspurgh,
To offer service to the Duke of Hereford,
And sent me over by Berkeley, to discover
What power the Duke of York had levied there;
Then with directions to repair to Ravenspurgh.
North. Have you forgot the Duke of Hereford,
boy?
Percy. No, my good lord, for that is not forgot
Which ne'er I did remember: to my knowledge,
I never in my life did look on him.
North. Then learn to know him now; this is
the Duke.   *40*
Percy. My gracious lord, I tender you my serv-
ice.
Such as it is, being tender, raw and young;
Which elder days shall ripen and confirm
To more approved service and desert.
Boling. I thank thee, gentle Percy; and be sure
I count myself in nothing else so happy
As in a soul remembering my good friends;
And, as my fortune ripens with thy love,
It shall be still thy true love's recompense:
My heart this covenant makes, my hand thus
seals it.   *50*
North. How far is it to Berkeley? and what stir
Keeps good old York there with his men of war?
Percy. There stands the castle, by yon tuft of
trees,
Mann'd with three hundred men, as I have heard:
And in it are the Lords of York, Berkeley, and
Seymour;
None else of name and noble estimate.

Enter ROSS *and* WILLOUGHBY.

North. Here come the Lords of Ross and
Willoughby,
Bloody with spurring, fiery-red with haste.
Boling. Welcome, my lords. I wot your love
pursues
A banish'd traitor: all my treasury   *60*
Is yet but unfelt thanks, which more enrich'd
Shall be your love and labour's recompense.
Ross. Your presence makes us rich, most noble
lord.
Willo. And far surmounts our labour to attain it.
Boling. Evermore thanks, the exchequer of the
poor;

Which, till my infant fortune comes to years,
Stands for my bounty. But who comes here?

Enter BERKELEY.

North. It is my Lord of Berkeley, as I guess.
Berk. My Lord of Hereford, my message is to
you.   *69*
Boling. My lord, my answer is—to Lancaster;
And I am come to seek that name in England;
And I must find that title in your tongue,
Before I make reply to aught you say.
Berk. Mistake me not, my lord; 'tis not my
meaning
To raze one title of your honour out:
To you, my lord, I come, what lord you will,
From the most gracious regent of this land,
The Duke of York, to know what pricks you on
To take advantage of the absent time
And fright our native peace with self-born arms.

Enter YORK *attended*.

Boling. I shall not need transport my words by
you;   *81*
Here comes his Grace in person.
                              My noble uncle! [*Kneels.*
York. Show me thy humble heart, and not thy
knee,
Whose duty is deceiveable and false.
Boling. My gracious uncle—
York. Tut, tut!
Grace me no grace, nor uncle me no uncle:
I am no traitor's uncle; and that word "grace"
In an ungracious mouth is but profane.
Why have those banish'd and forbidden legs   *90*
Dared once to touch a dust of England's ground?
But then more "why?" Why have they dared to
march
So many miles upon her peaceful bosom,
Frighting her pale-faced villages with war
And ostentation of despised arms?
Comest thou because the anointed King is hence?
Why, foolish boy, the King is left behind,
And in my loyal bosom lies his power.
Were I but now the lord of such hot youth
As when brave Gaunt, thy father, and myself *100*
Rescued the Black Prince, that young Mars of
men,
From forth the ranks of many thousand French,
O, then how quickly should this arm of mine,
Now prisoner to the palsy, chastise thee
And minister correction to thy fault!
Boling. My gracious uncle, let me know my
fault:
On what condition stands it and wherein?
York. Even in condition of the worst degree,
In gross rebellion and detested treason:

Thou art a banish'd man, and here art come *110*
Before the expiration of thy time,
In braving arms against thy sovereign.
  Boling. As I was banish'd, I was banish'd Here-
    ford;
But as I come, I come for Lancaster.
And, noble uncle, I beseech your Grace
Look on my wrongs with an indifferent eye:
You are my father, for methinks in you
I see old Gaunt alive; O, then, my father,
Will you permit that I shall stand condemn'd
A wandering vagabond; my rights and royalties
Pluck'd from my arms perforce and given away
To upstart unthrifts? Wherefore was I born?
If that my cousin king be King of England,
It must be granted I am Duke of Lancaster.
You have a son, Aumerle, my noble cousin;
Had you first died, and he been thus trod down,
He should have found his uncle Gaunt a father,
To rouse his wrongs and chase them to the bay.
I am denied to sue my livery here,
And yet my letters-patents give me leave: *130*
My father's goods are all distrain'd and sold,
And these and all are all amiss employ'd.
What would you have me do? I am a subject,
And I challenge law: attorneys are denied me;
And therefore personally I lay my claim
To my inheritance of free descent.
  North. The noble Duke hath been too much
    abused.
  Ross. It stands your Grace upon to do him
    right.
  Willo. Base men by his endowments are made
    great.
  York. My lords of England, let me tell you this:
I have had feeling of my cousin's wrongs *141*
And labour'd all I could to do him right;
But in this kind to come, in braving arms,
Be his own carver and cut out his way,
To find out right with wrong, it may not be;
And you that do abet him in this kind
Cherish rebellion and are rebels all.
  North. The noble Duke hath sworn his coming
    is
But for his own; and for the right of that
We all have strongly sworn to give him aid; *150*
And let him ne'er see joy that breaks that oath!
  York. Well, well, I see the issue of these arms:
I cannot mend it, I must needs confess,
Because my power is weak and all ill left:
But if I could, by Him that gave me life,
I would attach you all and make you stoop
Unto the sovereign mercy of the King;
But since I cannot, be it known to you
I do remain as neuter. So, fare you well;
Unless you please to enter in the castle *160*

And there repose you for this night.
  Boling. An offer, uncle, that we will accept:
But we must win your Grace to go with us
To Bristol castle, which they say is held
By Bushy, Bagot, and their complices,
The caterpillars of the commonwealth,
Which I have sworn to weed and pluck away.
  York. It may be I will go with you: but yet I'll
    pause;
For I am loath to break our country's laws.
Nor friends nor foes, to me welcome you are: *170*
Things past redress are now with me past care.
                       [*Exeunt.*

Scene iv. *A camp in Wales*

Enter salisbury *and a* welsh captain.

  Cap. My Lord of Salisbury, we have stay'd ten
    days,
And hardly kept our countrymen together,
And yet we hear no tidings from the King;
Therefore we will disperse ourselves: farewell.
  Sal. Stay yet another day, thou trusty Welsh-
    man:
The King reposeth all his confidence in thee.
  Cap. 'Tis thought the King is dead; we will not
    stay.
The bay-trees in our country are all wither'd
And meteors fright the fixed stars of heaven;
The pale-faced moon looks bloody on the earth *10*
And lean-look'd prophets whisper fearful change;
Rich men look sad and ruffians dance and leap,
The one in fear to lose what they enjoy,
The other to enjoy by rage and war:
These signs forerun the death or fall of kings.
Farewell: our countrymen are gone and fled,
As well assured Richard their king is dead.
                       [*Exit.*
  Sal. Ah, Richard, with the eyes of heavy mind
I see thy glory like a shooting star
Fall to the base earth from the firmament. *20*
Thy sun sets weeping in the lowly west,
Witnessing storms to come, woe, and unrest:
Thy friends are fled to wait upon thy foes,
And crossly to thy good all fortune goes. [*Exit.*

ACT III

Scene i. *Bristol: before the castle*

Enter bolingbroke, york, northumberland,
ross, percy, willoughby, *with* bushy *and*
green, *prisoners.*

  Boling. Bring forth these men.
Bushy and Green, I will not vex your souls—
Since presently your souls must part your
    bodies—
With too much urging your pernicious lives,

For 'twere no charity; yet, to wash your blood
From off my hands, here in the view of men
I will unfold some causes of your deaths.
You have misled a prince, a royal king,
A happy gentleman in blood and lineaments,
By you unhappied and disfigured clean: 10
You have in manner with your sinful hours
Made a divorce betwixt his queen and him,
Broke the possession of a royal bed
And stain'd the beauty of a fair queen's cheeks
With tears drawn from her eyes by your foul
    wrongs.
Myself, a prince by fortune of my birth,
Near to the King in blood, and near in love
Till you did make him misinterpret me,
Have stoop'd my neck under your injuries,
And sigh'd my English breath in foreign clouds,
Eating the bitter bread of banishment;   21
Whilst you have fed upon my signories,
Dispark'd my parks and fell'd my forest woods,
From my own windows torn my household
    coat,
Razed out my imprese, leaving me no sign,
Save men's opinions and my living blood,
To show the world I am a gentleman.
This and much more, much more than twice all
    this,
Condemns you to the death. See them deliver'd
    over
To execution and the hand of death.   30
  Bushy. More welcome is the stroke of death to
    me
Than Bolingbroke to England. Lords, farewell.
  Green. My comfort is that heaven will take our
    souls
And plague injustice with the pains of hell.
  Boling. My Lord Northumberland, see them
    dispatch'd.
    [*Exeunt* NORTHUMBERLAND *and others,*
                        with the prisoners.
Uncle, you say the Queen is at your house;
For God's sake, fairly let her be entreated:
Tell her I send to her my kind commends;
Take special care my greetings be deliver'd.
  York. A gentleman of mine I have dispatch'd
With letters of your love to her at large.   41
  Boling. Thanks, gentle uncle. Come, lords,
    away,
To fight with Glendower and his complices:
Awhile to work, and after holiday.   [*Exeunt.*

SCENE II. *The coast of Wales: a castle in view*
Drums: flourish and colours. Enter KING RICHARD,
the BISHOP OF CARLISLE, AUMERLE, *and Soldiers.*

  K. *Rich.* Barkloughly castle call they this at
    hand?

  Aum. Yea, my lord. How brooks your Grace
    the air,
After your late tossing on the breaking seas?
  K. *Rich.* Needs must I like it well: I weep for
    joy
To stand upon my kingdom once again.
Dear earth, I do salute thee with my hand,
Though rebels wound thee with their horses'
    hoofs:
As a long-parted mother with her child
Plays fondly with her tears and smiles in meeting,
So, weeping, smiling, greet I thee, my earth,   10
And do thee favours with my royal hands.
Feed not thy sovereign's foe, my gentle earth,
Nor with thy sweets comfort his ravenous sense;
But let thy spiders, that suck up thy venom,
And heavy-gaited toads lie in their way,
Doing annoyance to the treacherous feet
Which with usurping steps do trample thee:
Yield stinging nettles to mine enemies;
And when they from thy bosom pluck a flower,
Guard it, I pray thee, with a lurking adder   20
Whose double tongue may with a mortal touch
Throw death upon thy sovereign's enemies.
Mock not my senseless conjuration, lords:
This earth shall have a feeling and these stones
Prove armed soldiers, ere her native king
Shall falter under foul rebellion's arms.
  Car. Fear not, my lord: that Power that made
    you king
Hath power to keep you king in spite of all.
The means that heaven yields must be embraced,
And not neglected; else, if heaven would,   30
And we will not, heaven's offer we refuse,
The proffer'd means of succour and redress.
  Aum. He means, my lord, that we are too
    remiss;
Whilst Bolingbroke, through our security,
Grows strong and great in substance and in
    power.
  K. *Rich.* Discomfortable cousin! know'st thou
    not
That when the searching eye of heaven is hid,
Behind the globe, that lights the lower world,
Then thieves and robbers range abroad unseen
In murders and in outrage, boldly here;   40
But when from under this terrestrial ball
He fires the proud tops of the eastern pines
And darts his light through every guilty hole,
Then murders, treasons, and detested sins,
The cloak of night being pluck'd from off their
    backs,
Stand bare and naked, trembling at themselves?
So when this thief, this traitor, Bolingbroke,
Who all this while hath revell'd in the night
Whilst we were wandering with the antipodes,

Shall see us rising in our throne, the east,   50
His treasons will sit blushing in his face,
Not able to endure the sight of day,
But self-affrighted tremble at his sin.
Not all the water in the rough rude sea
Can wash the balm off from an anointed king;
The breath of worldly men cannot depose
The deputy elected by the Lord:
For every man that Bolingbroke hath press'd
To lift shrewd steel against our golden crown,
God for his Richard hath in heavenly pay   60
A glorious angel: then, if angels fight,
Weak men must fall, for heaven still guards the
    right.

Enter SALISBURY.

Welcome, my lord: how far off lies your power?
   Sal. Nor near nor farther off, my gracious lord,
Than this weak arm: discomfort guides my
    tongue
And bids me speak of nothing but despair.
One day too late, I fear me, noble lord,
Hath clouded all thy happy days on earth:
O, call back yesterday, bid time return,
And thou shalt have twelve thousand fighting
    men!   70
To-day, to-day, unhappy day, too late,
O'erthrows thy joys, friends, fortune, and thy
    state:
For all the Welshmen, hearing thou wert dead,
Are gone to Bolingbroke, dispersed and fled;
   Aum. Comfort, my liege: why looks your
    grace so pale?
   K. Rich. But now the blood of twenty thousand
    men
Did triumph in my face, and they are fled;
And, till so much blood thither come again,
Have I not reason to look pale and dead?
All souls that will be safe fly from my side,   80
For time hath set a blot upon my pride.
   Aum. Comfort, my liege; remember who you
    are.
   K. Rich. I had forgot myself: am I not king?
Awake, thou coward majesty! thou sleepest.
Is not the King's name twenty thousand names?
Arm, arm, my name! a puny subject strikes
At thy great glory. Look not to the ground,
Ye favourites of a king: are we not high?
High be our thoughts: I know my uncle York
Hath power enough to serve our turn. But who
    comes here?   90

Enter SCROOP.

   Scroop. More health and happiness betide my
    liege
Than can my care-tuned tongue deliver him!

   K. Rich. Mine ear is open and my heart pre-
    pared:
The worst is worldly loss thou canst unfold.
Say, is my kingdom lost? why, 'twas my care;
And what loss is it to be rid of care?
Strives Bolingbroke to be as great as we?
Greater he shall not be; if he serve God,
We'll serve Him too and be his fellow so:
Revolt our subjects? that we cannot mend;   100
They break their faith to God as well as us:
Cry woe, destruction, ruin, and decay;
The worst is death, and death will have his day.
   Scroop. Glad am I that your Highness is so
    arm'd
To bear the tidings of calamity.
Like an unseasonable stormy day,
Which makes the silver rivers drown their shores,
As if the world were all dissolved to tears,
So high above his limits swells the rage
Of Bolingbroke, covering your fearful land   110
With hard bright steel and hearts harder than
    steel.
White-beards have arm'd their thin and hairless
    scalps
Against thy Majesty; boys, with women's voices,
Strive to speak big and clap their female joints
In stiff unwieldy arms against thy crown:
Thy very beadsmen learn to bend their bows
Of double-fatal yew against thy state;
Yea, distaff-women manage rusty bills
Against thy seat: both young and old rebel,
And all goes worse than I have power to tell.   120
   K. Rich. Too well, too well thou tell'st a tale
    so ill.
Where is the Earl of Wiltshire? where is Bagot?
What is become of Bushy? where is Green?
That they have let the dangerous enemy
Measure our confines with such peaceful steps?
If we prevail, their heads shall pay for it:
I warrant they have made peace with Boling-
    broke.
   Scroop. Peace have they made with him indeed,
    my lord.
   K. Rich. O villains, vipers, damn'd without
    redemption!
Dogs, easily won to fawn on any man!   130
Snakes, in my heart-blood warm'd, that sting my
    heart!
Three Judases, each one thrice worse than
    Judas!
Would they make peace? terrible hell make war
Upon their spotted souls for this offence!
   Scroop. Sweet love, I see, changing his prop-
    erty,
Turns to the sourest and most deadly hate:
Again uncurse their souls; their peace is made

With heads, and not with hands: those whom
  you curse
Have felt the worst of death's destroying wound
And lie full low, graved in the hollow ground.
  Aum. Is Bushy, Green, and the Earl of Wilt-
  shire dead?   *141*
  Scroop. Ay, all of them at Bristol lost their
  heads.
  Aum. Where is the Duke my father with his
  power?
  K. Rich. No matter where; of comfort no man
  speak:
Let's talk of graves, of worms and epitaphs;
Make dust our paper and with rainy eyes
Write sorrow on the bosom of the earth,
Let's choose executors and talk of wills:
And yet no so, for what can we bequeath
Save our deposed bodies to the ground?   *150*
Our lands, our lives, and all are Bolingbroke's,
And nothing can we call our own but death
And that small model of the barren earth
Which serves as paste and cover to our bones.
For God's sake, let us sit upon the ground
And tell sad stories of the death of kings:
How some have been deposed; some slain in
  war;
Some haunted by the ghosts they have deposed;
Some poison'd by their wives; some sleeping
  kill'd;
All murder'd: for within the hollow crown   *160*
That rounds the mortal temples of a king
Keeps Death his court and there the antic sits,
Scoffing his state and grinning at his pomp,
Allowing him a breath, a little scene,
To monarchize, be fear'd, and kill with looks,
Infusing him with self and vain conceit,
As if this flesh which walls about our life
Were brass impregnable, and humour'd thus
Comes at the last and with a little pin   *169*
Bores through his castle wall, and farewell king!
Cover your heads and mock not flesh and blood
With solemn reverence: throw away respect,
Tradition, form, and ceremonious duty,
For you have but mistook me all this while:
I live with bread like you, feel want,
Taste grief, need friends: subjected thus,
How can you say to me I am a king?
  Car. My lord, wise men ne'er sit and wail their
  woes,
But presently prevent the ways to wail.   *179*
To fear the foe, since fear oppresseth strength,
Gives in your weakness strength unto your foe,
And so your follies fight against yourself.
Fear, and be slain; no worse can come to fight:
And fight and die is death destroying death;
Where fearing dying pays death servile breath.

  Aum. My father hath a power; inquire of him,
And learn to make a body of a limb.
  K. Rich. Thou chidest me well: proud Boling-
  broke, I come
To change blows with thee for our day of doom.
This ague fit of fear is over-blown;   *190*
An easy task it is to win our own.
Say, Scroop, where lies our uncle with his power?
Speak sweetly, man, although thy looks be sour.
  Scroop. Men judge by the complexion of the
  sky
The state and inclination of the day:
So may you by my dull and heavy eye,
  My tongue hath but a heavier tale to say.
I play the torturer, by small and small
To lengthen out the worst that must be spoken:
Your uncle York is join'd with Bolingbroke,   *200*
And all your northern castles yielded up,
And all your southern gentlemen in arms
Upon his party.
  K. Rich. Thou hast said enough.
Beshrew thee, cousin, which didst lead me forth
  To AUMERLE.
Of that sweet way I was in to despair!
What say you now? what comfort have we now?
By heaven, I'll hate him everlastingly
That bids me be of comfort any more.
Go to Flint castle: there I'll pine away;
A king, woe's slave, shall kingly woe obey.   *210*
That power I have, discharge; and let them go
To ear the land that hath some hope to grow,
For I have none: let no man speak again
To alter this, for counsel is but vain.
  Aum. My liege, one word.
  K. Rich.   He does me double wrong
That wounds me with the flatteries of his tongue.
Discharge my followers: let them hence away,
From Richard's night to Bolingbroke's fair day.
                          [Exeunt.

SCENE III. *Wales: before Flint castle*

Enter, with drum and colours, BOLINGBROKE,
YORK, NORTHUMBERLAND, *Attendants, and forces.*

  Boling. So that by this intelligence we learn
The Welshmen are dispersed, and Salisbury
Is gone to meet the King, who lately landed
With some few private friends upon this coast.
  North. The news is very fair and good, my
  lord:
Richard not far from hence hath hid his head.
  York. It would beseem the Lord Northumber-
  land
To say "King Richard": alack the heavy day
When such a sacred king should hide his head.
  North. Your Grace mistakes; only to be brief,
Left I his title out.

York.   The time hath been,   *11*
Would you have been so brief with him, he would
Have been so brief with you, to shorten you,
For taking so the head, your whole head's length.
  Boling. Mistake not, uncle, further than you
    should.
  York. Take not, good cousin, further than you
    should,
Lest you mistake the heavens are o'er our heads.
  Boling. I know it, uncle, and oppose not myself
Against their will. But who comes here?   *19*

Enter PERCY.

Welcome, Harry: what, will not this castle yield?
  Percy. The castle royally is mann'd, my lord,
Against thy entrance.
  Boling. Royally!
Why, it contains no king?
  Percy.   Yes, my good lord,
It doth contain a king; King Richard lies
Within the limits of yon lime and stone:
And with him are the Lord Aumerle, Lord Salis-
    bury,
Sir Stephen Scroop, besides a clergyman
Of holy reverence; who, I cannot learn.
  North. O, belike it is the Bishop of Carlisle.
  Boling. Noble lords,   *31*
Go to the rude ribs of that ancient castle;
Through brazen trumpet send the breath of parley
Into his ruin'd ears, and thus deliver:
Henry Bolingbroke
On both his knees doth kiss King Richard's hand
And sends allegiance and true faith of heart
To his most royal person, hither come
Even at his feet to lay my arms and power,
Provided that my banishment repeal'd   *40*
And lands restored again be freely granted:
If not, I'll use the advantage of my power
And lay the summer's dust with showers of blood
Rain'd from the wounds of slaughter'd English-
    men:
The which, how far off from the mind of Boling-
    broke
It is, such crimson tempest should bedrench
The fresh green lap of fair King Richard's land,
My stooping duty tenderly shall show.
Go, signify as much, while here we march
Upon the grassy carpet of this plain.   *50*
Let's march without the noise of threatening
    drum,
That from this castle's tatter'd battlements
Out fair appointments may be well perused.
Methinks King Richard and myself should meet
With no less terror than the elements
Of fire and water, when their thundering shock
At meeting tears the cloudy cheeks of heaven.

Be he the fire, I'll be the yielding water:
The rage be his, whilst on the earth I rain
My waters; on the earth, and not on him.   *60*
March on, and mark King Richard how he looks.

Parle without, and answer within. Then a flourish.
  Enter on the walls, KING RICHARD, *the* BISHOP OF
    CARLISLE, AUMERLE, SCROOP, *and* SALISBURY.

See, see, King Richard doth himself appear,
As doth the blushing discontented sun
From out the fiery portal of the east,
When he perceives the envious clouds are bent
To dim his glory and to stain the track
Of his bright passage to the occident.
  York. Yet looks he like a king: behold, his eye,
As bright as is the eagle's, lightens forth
Controlling majesty: alack, alack, for woe,   *70*
That any harm should stain so fair a show!
  K. Rich. We are amazed; and thus long have we
    stood
To watch the fearful bending of thy knee,
  To NORTHUMBERLAND.
Because we thought ourself thy lawful king:
And if we be, how dare thy joints forget
To pay their awful duty to our presence?
If we be not, show us the hand of God
That hath dismiss'd us from our stewardship;
For well we know, no hand of blood and bone
Can gripe the sacred handle of our sceptre,   *80*
Unless he do profane, steal, or usurp.
And though you think that all, as you have done,
Have torn their souls by turning them from us,
And we are barren and bereft of friends;
Yet know, my master, God omnipotent,
Is mustering in his clouds on our behalf
Armies of pestilence; and they shall strike
Your children yet unborn and unbegot,
That lift your vassal hands against my head
And threat the glory of my precious crown.   *90*
Tell Bolingbroke—for yond methinks he
    stands—
That every stride he makes upon my land
Is dangerous treason: he is come to open
The purple testament of bleeding war;
But ere the crown he looks for live in peace,
Ten thousand bloody crowns of mothers' sons
Shall ill become the flower of England's face,
Change the complexion of her maid-pale peace
To scarlet indignation and bedew
Her pastures' grass with faithful English blood.
  North. The King of heaven forbid our lord
    the King   *101*
Should so with civil and uncivil arms
Be rush'd upon! Thy thrice noble cousin
Harry Bolingbroke doth humbly kiss thy hand;
And by the honourable tomb he swears,

That stands upon your royal grandsire's bones,
And by the royalties of both your bloods,
Currents that spring from one most gracious
    head,
And by the buried hand of warlike Gaunt,
And by the worth and honour of himself,   *110*
Comprising all that may be sworn or said,
His coming hither hath no further scope
Than for his lineal royalties, and to beg
Enfranchisement immediate on his knees:
Which on thy royal party granted once,
His glittering arms he will commend to rust,
His barbed steeds to stables, and his heart
To faithful service of your Majesty.
This swears he, as he is a prince, is just;
And, as I am a gentleman, I credit him.   *120*
  K. Rich. Northumberland, say thus the King
    returns:
His noble cousin is right welcome hither;
And all the number of his fair demands
Shall be accomplish'd without contradiction:
With all the gracious utterance thou hast
Speak to his gentle hearing kind commends.
We do debase ourselves, cousin, do we not,
  To AUMERLE.
To look so poorly and to speak so fair?
Shall we call back Northumberland, and send
Defiance to the traitor, and so die?   *130*
  Aum. No, good my lord; let's fight with gentle
    words
Till time lend friends and friends their helpful
    swords.
  K. Rich. O God, O God! that e'er this tongue
    of mine,
That laid the sentence of dread banishment
On yon proud man, should take it off again
With words of sooth! O that I were as great
As is my grief, or lesser than my name!
Or that I could forget what I have been,
Or not remember what I must be now!
Swell'st thou, proud heart? I'll give thee scope
    to beat,   *140*
Since foes have scope to beat both thee and me.
  Aum. Northumberland comes back from Bo-
    lingbroke.
  K. Rich. What must the King do now? must he
    submit?
The King shall do it: must he be deposed?
The King shall be contented: must he lose
The name of king? o' God's name, let it go:
I'll give my jewels for a set of beads,
My gorgeous palace for a hermitage,
My gay apparel for an almsman's gown,
My figured goblets for a dish of wood,   *150*
My sceptre for a palmer's walking-staff,
My subjects for a pair of carved saints

And my large kingdom for a little grave,
A little little grave, an obscure grave;
Or I'll be buried in the King's highway,
Some way of common trade, where subjects' feet
May hourly trample on their sovereign's head;
For on my heart they tread now whilst I live;
And buried once, why not upon my head?
Aumerle, thou weep'st, my tender-hearted cousin!
We'll make foul weather with despised tears; *161*
Our sighs and they shall lodge the summer corn,
And make a dearth in this revolting land.
Or shall we play the wantons with our woes,
And make some pretty match with shedding
    tears?
As thus, to drop them still upon one place,
Till they have fretted us a pair of graves
Within the earth; and, therein laid—there lies
Two kinsmen digg'd their graves with weeping
    eyes.
Would not this ill do well? Well, well, I see *170*
I talk but idly, and you laugh at me.
Most mighty prince, my Lord Northumberland,
What says King Bolingbroke? will his majesty
Give Richard leave to live till Richard die?
You make a leg, and Bolingbroke says ay.
  North. My lord, in the base court he doth
    attend
To speak with you; may it please you to come
    down.
  K. Rich. Down, down I come; like glist'ring
    Phaethon,
Wanting the manage of unruly jades.
In the base court? Base court, where kings grow
    base,   *180*
To come at traitors' calls and do them grace.
In the base court? Come down? Down, court!
    down, king!
For night-owls shriek where mounting larks
    should sing.   [*Exeunt from above.*
  Boling. What says his majesty?
  North.   Sorrow and grief of heart
Makes him speak fondly, like a frantic man:
Yet he is come.

  Enter KING RICHARD *and his attendants below.*

  Boling. Stand all apart,
And show fair duty to his majesty.
  He kneels down.
My gracious lord—
  K. Rich. Fair cousin, you debase your princely
    knee   *190*
To make the base earth proud with kissing it:
Me rather had my heart might feel your love
Than my unpleased eye see your courtesy.
Up, cousin, up; your heart is up, I know,
Thus high at least, although your knee be low.

Boling. My gracious lord, I come but for mine
  own.
K. Rich. Your own is yours, and I am yours,
  and all.
Boling. So far be mine, my most redoubted
  lord,
As my true service shall deserve your love.
K. Rich. Well you deserve: they well deserve
  to have   200
That know the strong'st and surest way to get.
Uncle, give me your hands: nay, dry your eyes;
Tears show their love, but want their remedies.
Cousin, I am too young to be your father,
Though you are old enough to be my heir.
What you will have, I'll give, and willing too;
For do we must what force will have us do.
Set on towards London, cousin, is it so?
  Boling. Yea, my good lord.
  K. Rich.   Then I must not say no.
                                    [*Flourish. Exeunt.*

SCENE IV. *Langley: the* DUKE OF YORK'S
                    garden.

Enter the QUEEN *and* TWO LADIES.

'*Queen.* What sport shall we devise here in this
  garden
To drive away the heavy thought of care?
Lady. Madam, we'll play at bowls.
Queen. 'Twill make me think the world is full
  of rubs,
And that my fortune runs against the bias.
Lady. Madam, we'll dance.
Queen. My legs can keep no measure in de-
  light,
When my poor heart no measure keeps in
  grief:
Therefore, no dancing, girl; some other sport.
Lady. Madam, we'll tell tales.   10
Queen. Of sorrow or of joy?
Lady.   Of either, madam.
Queen. Of neither, girl:
For if of joy, being altogether wanting,
It doth remember me the more of sorrow;
Or if of grief, being altogether had,
It adds more sorrow to my want of joy:
For what I have I need not to repeat;
And what I want it boots not to complain.
Lady. Madam, I'll sing.
Queen.   'Tis well that thou has cause;
But thou shouldst please me better, wouldst thou
  weep.   20
Lady. I could weep, madam, would it do you
  good.
Queen. And I could sing, would weeping do me
  good,
And never borrow any tear of thee.

Enter a GARDENER, *and two* SERVANTS.

But stay, here come the gardeners:
Let's step into the shadow of these trees.
My wretchedness unto a row of pins,
They'll talk of state; for every one doth so
Against a change; woe is forerun with woe.
                        [QUEEN *and* LADIES *retire.*
Gard. Go, bind thou up yon dangling apricocks,
Which, like unruly children, make their sire   30
Stoop with oppression of their prodigal weight:
Give some supportance to the bending twigs.
Go thou, and like an executioner,
Cut off the heads of too fast growing sprays,
That look too lofty in our commonwealth:
All must be even in our government.
You thus employ'd, I will go root away
The noisome weeds, which without profit suck
The soil's fertility from wholesome flowers.
Serv. Why should we in the compass of a pale
Keep law and form and due proportion,   41
Showing, as in a model, our firm estate,
When our sea-walled garden, the whole land,
Is full of weeds, her fairest flowers choked up,
Her fruit-trees all unpruned, her hedges ruin'd,
Her knots disorder'd and her wholesome herbs
Swarming with caterpillars?
Gard.   Hold thy peace:
He that hath suffer'd this disorder'd spring
Hath now himself met with the fall of leaf:
The weeds which his broad-spreading leaves did
  shelter,   50
That seem'd in eating him to hold him up,
Are pluck'd up root and all by Bolingbroke,
I mean the Earl of Wiltshire, Bushy, Green.
Serv. What, are they dead?
Gard.   They are; and Bolingbroke
Hath seized the wasteful king. O, what pity is it
That he had not so trimm'd and dress'd his land
As we this garden! We at time of year
Do wound the bark, the skin of our fruit-trees,
Lest, being over-proud in sap and blood,
With too much riches it confound itself: 60
Had he done so to great and growing men,
They might have lived to bear and he to taste
Their fruits of duty: superfluous branches
We lop away, that bearing boughs may live:
Had he done so, himself had borne the crown,
Which waste of idle hours hath quite thrown
  down.
Serv. What, think you then the King shall be
  deposed?
Gard. Depress'd he is already, and deposed
'Tis doubt he will be: letters came last night
To a dear friend of the good Duke of York's,   70
That tell black tidings.

Queen. O, I am press'd to death through want
of speaking! [*Coming forward.*]
Thou, old Adam's likeness, set to dress this
garden,
How dares thy harsh rude tongue sound this un-
pleasing news?
What Eve, what serpent, hath suggested thee
To make a second fall of cursed man?
Why dost thou say King Richard is deposed?
Darest thou, thou little better thing than earth,
Divine his downfall? Say, where, when, and how,
Camest thou by this ill tidings? speak, thou
wretch.   *80*
Gard. Pardon me, madam: little joy have I
To breathe this news; yet what I say is true.
King Richard, he is in the mighty hold
Of Bolingbroke: their fortunes both are weigh'd:
In your lord's scale is nothing but himself,
And some few vanities that make him light;
But in the balance of great Bolingbroke,
Besides himself, are all the English peers,
And with that odds he weighs King Richard
down.
Post you to London, and you will find it so;   *90*
I speak no more than every one doth know.
Queen. Nimble mischance, that art so light of
foot,
Doth not thy embassage belong to me,
And am I last that knows it? O, thou think'st
To serve me last, that I may longest keep
Thy sorrow in my breast. Come, ladies, go,
To meet at London London's king in woe.
What, was I born to this, that my sad look
Should grace the triumph of great Bolingbroke?
Gardener, for telling me these news of woe, *100*
Pray God the plants thou graft'st may never
grow.
                         [*Exeunt* QUEEN *and* LADIES.
Gard. Poor queen! so that thy state might be no
worse,
I would my skill were subject to thy curse.
Here did she fall a tear; here in this place
I'll set a bank of rue, sour herb of grace:
Rue, even for ruth, here shortly shall be seen,
In the remembrance of a weeping queen. [*Exeunt.*

ACT IV

SCENE I. *Westminster Hall*

Enter, as to the Parliament, BOLINGBROKE, AU-
MERLE, NORTHUMBERLAND, PERCY, FITZWATER,
SURREY, *the* BISHOP OF CARLISLE, *the* ABBOT OF
WESTMINSTER, *and another* LORD, *Herald, Offi-
cers, and* BAGOT.

Boling. Call forth Bagot.
Now, Bagot, freely speak thy mind;

What thou dost know of noble Gloucester's
death,
Who wrought it with the King, and who per-
form'd
The bloody office of his timeless end.
Bagot. Then set before my face the Lord
Aumerle.
Boling. Cousin, stand forth, and look upon that
man.
Bagot. My Lord Aumerle, I know your daring
tongue
Scorns to unsay what once it hath deliver'd.
In that dead time when Gloucester's death was
plotted,   *10*
I heard you say, "Is not my arm of length,
That reacheth from the restful English court
As far as Calais, to mine uncle's head?"
Amongst much other talk, that very time,
I heard you say that you had rather refuse
The offer of an hundred thousand crowns
Than Bolingbroke's return to England;
Adding withal, how blest this land would be
In this your cousin's death.
Aum.   Princes and noble lords,
What answer shall I make to this base man? *20*
Shall I so much dishonour my fair stars,
On equal terms to give him chastisement?
Either I must, or have mine honour soil'd
With the attainder of his slanderous lips.
There is my gage, the manual seal of death,
That marks thee out for hell: I say, thou liest,
And will maintain what thou hast said is false
In thy heart-blood, though being all too base
To stain the temper of my knightly sword.
Boling. Bagot, forbear; thou shalt not take it
up.   *30*
Aum. Excepting one, I would he were the best
In all this presence that hath moved me so.
Fitz. If that thy valour stand on sympathy,
There is my gage, Aumerle, in gage to thine:
By that fair sun which shows me where thou
stand'st,
I heard thee say, and vauntingly thou spakest it,
That thou wert cause of noble Gloucester's death.
If thou deny'st it twenty times, thou liest;
And I will turn thy falsehood to thy heart,
Where it was forged, with my rapier's point. *40*
Aum. Thou darest not, coward, live to see that
day.
Fitz. Now, by my soul, I would it were this
hour.
Aum. Fitzwater, thou art damn'd to hell for
this.
Percy. Aumerle, thou liest; his honour is as true
In this appeal as thou art all unjust;
And that thou art so, there I throw my gage,

To prove it on thee to the extremest point
Of mortal breathing: seize it, if thou darest.
  Aum. An if I do not, may my hands rot off
And never brandish more revengeful steel   50
Over the glittering helmet of my foe!
  Another Lord. I task the earth to the like, for-
    sworn Aumerle;
And spur thee on with full as many lies
As may be holloa'd in thy treacherous ear
From sun to sun: there is my honour's pawn;
Engage it to the trial, if thou darest.
  Aum. Who sets me else? by heaven, I'll throw
    at all:
I have a thousand spirits in one breast,
To answer twenty thousand such as you.
  Surrey. My Lord Fitzwater, I do remember
    well   60
The very time Aumerle and you did talk.
  Fitz. 'Tis very true: you were in presence then;
And you can witness with me this is true.
  Surrey. As false, by heaven, as heaven itself is
    true.
  Fitz. Surrey, thou liest.
  Surrey.   Dishonourable boy!
That lie shall lie so heavy on my sword,
That it shall render vengeance and revenge
Till thou the lie-giver and that lie do lie
In earth as quiet as thy father's skull:
In proof whereof, there is my honour's pawn; 70
Engage it to the trial, if thou darest.
  Fitz. How fondly dost thou spur a forward
    horse!
If I dare eat, or drink, or breathe, or live,
I dare meet Surrey in a wilderness,
And spit upon him, whilst I say he lies,
And lies, and lies: there is my bond of faith,
To tie thee to my strong correction.
As I intend to thrive in this new world,
Aumerle is guilty of my true appeal:
Besides, I heard the banish'd Norfolk say   80
That thou, Aumerle, didst send two of thy men
To execute the noble duke at Calais.
  Aum. Some honest Christian trust me with a
    gage,
That Norfolk lies: here do I throw down this,
If he may be repeal'd, to try his honour.
  Boling. These differences shall all rest under
    gage
Till Norfolk be repeal'd: repeal'd he shall be,
And, though mine enemy, restored again
To all his lands and signories: when he's re-
    turn'd,
Against Aumerle we will enforce his trial.   90
  Car. That honourable day shall ne'er be seen.
Many a time hath banish'd Norfolk fought
For Jesu Christ in glorious Christian field,

Streaming the ensign of the Christian cross
Against black pagans, Turks, and Saracens;
And toil'd with works of war, retired himself
To Italy; and there at Venice gave
His body to that pleasant country's earth,
And his pure soul unto his captain Christ,
Under whose colours he had fought so long.   100
  Boling. Why, bishop, is Norfolk dead?
  Car. As surely as I live, my lord.
  Boling. Sweet peace conduct his sweet soul to
    the bosom
Of good old Abraham! Lords appellants,
Your differences shall all rest under gage
Till we assign you to your days of trial.

Enter YORK, *attended.*

  York. Great Duke of Lancaster, I come to thee
From plume-pluck'd Richard; who with willing
    soul
Adopts thee heir, and his high sceptre yields
To the possession of thy royal hand: 110
Ascend his throne, descending now from him;
And long live Henry, fourth of that name!
  Boling. In God's name, I'll ascend the regal
    throne.
  Car. Marry, God forbid!
Worst in this royal presence may I speak,
Yet best beseeming me to speak the truth.
Would God that any in this noble presence
Were enough noble to be upright judge
Of noble Richard! then true noblesse would
Learn him forbearance from so foul a wrong. 120
What subject can give sentence on his king?
And who sits here that is not Richard's subject?
Thieves are not judged but they are by to hear,
Although apparent guilt be seen in them;
And shall the figure of God's majesty,
His captain, steward, deputy-elect,
Anointed, crowned, planted many years,
Be judged by subject and inferior breath,
And he himself not present? O, forfend it, God,
That in a Christian climate souls refined   130
Should show so heinous, black, obscene a deed!
I speak to subjects, and a subject speaks,
Stirr'd up by God, thus boldly for his king.
My Lord of Hereford here, whom you call king,
Is a foul traitor to proud Hereford's king:
And if you crown him, let me prophesy:
The blood of English shall manure the ground,
And future ages groan for this foul act;
Peace shall go sleep with Turks and infidels,
And in this seat of peace tumultuous wars   140
Shall kin with kin and kind with kind confound;
Disorder, horror, fear, and mutiny
Shall here inhabit, and this land be call'd
The field of Golgotha and dead men's skulls.

O, if you raise this house against this house,
It will the woefullest division prove
That ever fell upon this cursed earth.
Prevent it, resist it, let it not be so,
Lest child, child's children, cry against you
      "woe!"
    North. Well have you argued, sir; and, for your
      pains,   150
Of capital treason we arrest you here.
My Lord of Westminster, be it your charge
To keep him safely till his day of trial.
May it please you, lords, to grant the commons'
      suit.
    Boling. Fetch hither Richard, that in common
      view
He may surrender; so we shall proceed
Without suspicion.
    York.   I will be his conduct.   [*Exit.*
    Boling. Lords, you that here are under our
      arrest,
Procure your sureties for your days of answer.
Little are we beholding to your love,   160
And little look'd for at your helping hands.

Re-enter YORK, *with* RICHARD, *and Officers
      bearing the regalia.*

    K. Rich. Alack, why am I sent for to a king,
Before I have shook off the regal thoughts
Wherewith I reign'd? I hardly yet have learn'd
To insinuate, flatter, bow, and bend my limbs:
Give sorrow leave awhile to tutor me
To this submission. Yet I well remember
The favours of these men: were they not mine?
Did they not sometime cry, "all hail!" to me?
So Judas did to Christ: but he, in twelve,   170
Found truth in all but one; I, in twelve thousand,
      none.
God save the King! Will no man say amen?
Am I both priest and clerk? well then, amen.
God save the King! although I be not he;
And yet, amen, if heaven do think him me.
To do what service am I sent for hither?
    York. To do that office of thine own good
      will
Which tired majesty did make thee offer,
The resignation of thy state and crown
To Henry Bolingbroke.   180
    K. Rich. Give me the crown. Here, cousin,
      seize the crown;
Here cousin;
On this side my hand, and on that side yours.
Now is this golden crown like a deep well
That owes two buckets, filling one another,
The emptier ever dancing in the air,
The other down, unseen, and full of water:
That bucket down and full of tears am I,

Drinking my griefs, whilst you mount up on
      high.
    Boling. I thought you had been willing to resign.
    K. Rich. My crown I am; but still my griefs are
      mine: 191
You may my glories and my state depose,
But not my griefs; still am I king of those.
    Boling. Part of your cares you give me with
      your crown.
    K. Rich. Your cares set up do not pluck my
      cares down.
My care is loss of care, by old care done;
Your care is gain of care, by new care won:
The cares I give I have, though given away;
They tend the crown, yet still with me they stay.
    Boling. Are you contented to resign the
      crown?   200
    K. Rich. Ay, no; no, ay; for I must nothing be;
Therefore no no, for I resign to thee.
Now mark me, how I will undo myself:
I give this heavy weight from off my head
And this unwieldly sceptre from my hand,
The pride of kingly sway from out my heart;
With mine own tears I wash away my balm,
With mine own hands I give away my crown,
With mine own tongue deny my sacred state,
With mine own breath release all duty's rites:
All pomp and majesty I do forswear;   211
My manors, rents, revenues I forego;
My acts, decrees, and statutes I deny:
God pardon all oaths that are broke to me!
God keep all vows unbroke that swear to thee!
Make me, that nothing have, with nothing
      grieved,
And thou with all pleased, that hast all achieved!
Long mayst thou live in Richard's seat to sit,
And soon lie Richard in an earthy pit!
God save King Harry, unking'd Richard says,
And send him many years of sunshine days!   221
What more remains?
    North.   No more, but that you read
These accusations and these grievous crimes
Committed by your person and your followers
Against the state and profit of this land;
That, by confessing them, the souls of men
May deem that you are worthily deposed.
    K. Rich. Must I do so? and must I ravel out
My weaved-up folly? Gentle Northumberland,
If thy offences were upon record,   230
Would it not shame thee in so fair a troop
To read a lecture of them? If thou wouldst,
There shouldst thou find one heinous article,
Containing the deposing of a king
And cracking the strong warrant of an oath,
Mark'd with a blot, damn'd in the book of
      heaven:

Nay, all of you that stand and look upon,
Whilst that my wretchedness doth bait myself,
Though some of you with Pilate wash your
    hands
Showing an outward pity; yet you Pilates   240
Have here deliver'd me to my sour cross,
And water cannot wash away your sin.
    North. My lord, dispatch; read o'er these
    articles.
    K. Rich. Mine eyes are full of tears, I cannot
    see:
And yet salt water blinds them not so much
But they can see a sort of traitors here.
Nay, if I turn mine eyes upon myself,
I find myself a traitor with the rest;
For I have given here my soul's consent
To undeck the pompous body of a king;   250
Made glory base and sovereignty a slave,
Proud majesty a subject, state a peasant.
    North. My lord—
    K. Rich. No lord of thine, thou haught insulting
    man,
Nor no man's lord; I have no name, no title,
No, not that name was given me at the font,
But 'tis usurp'd: alack the heavy day,
That I have worn so many winters out,
And know not now what name to call myself!
O that I were a mockery king of snow,   260
Standing before the sun of Bolingbroke,
To melt myself away in water-drops!
Good king, great king, and yet not greatly good,
An if my word be sterling yet in England,
Let it command a mirror hither straight,
That it may show me what a face I have
Since it is bankrupt of his majesty.
    Boling. Go some of you and fetch a looking-
    glass.   [*Exit an attendant.*
    North. Read o'er this paper while the glass doth
    come.
    K. Rich. Fiend, thou torment'st me ere I come
    to hell!   270
    Boling. Urge it no more, my Lord Northumber-
    land.
    North. The commons will not then be satisfied.
    K. Rich. They shall be satisfied: I'll read
    enough,
When I do see the very book indeed
Where all my sins are writ, and that's myself.

Re-enter Attendant, with a glass.

Give me the glass, and therein will I read.
No deeper wrinkles yet? hath sorrow struck
So many blows upon this face of mine,
And made no deeper wounds? O flattering glass,
Like to my followers in prosperity,   280
Thou dost beguile me! Was this face the face

That every day under his household roof
Did keep ten thousand men? was this the face
That, like the sun, did make beholders wink?
Was this the face that faced so many follies,
And was at last out-faced by Bolingbroke?
A brittle glory shineth in this face:
As brittle as the glory is the face;
    Dashes the glass against the ground.
For there it is, crack'd in a hundred shivers.
Mark, silent king, the moral of this sport,   290
How soon my sorrow hath destroy'd my face.
    Boling. The shadow of your sorrow hath de-
    stroy'd
The shadow of your face.
    K. Rich.   Say that again.
The shadow of my sorrow! ha! let's see:
'Tis very true, my grief lies all within;
And these external manners of laments
Are merely shadows to the unseen grief
That swells with silence in the tortured soul;
There lies the substance: and I thank thee,
    King,
For thy great bounty, that not only givest   300
Me cause to wail but teachest me the way
How to lament the cause. I'll beg one boon,
And then be gone and trouble you no more.
Shall I obtain it?
    Boling.   Name it, fair cousin.
    K. Rich. "Fair cousin"? I am greater than a
    king:
For when I was a king, my flatterers
Were then but subjects; being now a subject,
I have a king here to my flatterer.
Being so great, I have no need to beg.
    Boling. Yet ask.   310
    K. Rich. And shall I have?
    Boling. You shall.
    K. Rich. Then give me leave to go.
    Boling. Whither?
    K. Rich. Whither you will, so I were from
    your sights.
    Boling. Go, some of you convey him to the
    Tower.
    K. Rich. O, good! convey? conveyers are you
    all,
That rise thus nimbly by a true king's fall.
                    [*Exeunt* KING RICHARD, *some Lords,*
                                        and a Guard.
    Boling. On Wednesday next we solemnly set
    down
Our coronation: lords, prepare yourselves.   320
        [*Exeunt all except the* BISHOP OF CARLISLE, *the*
            ABBOT OF WESTMINSTER, *and* AUMERLE.
    Abbot. A woeful pageant have we here beheld.
    Car. The woe's to come; the children yet un-
    born

Shall feel this day as sharp to them as thorn.

Aum. You holy clergymen, is there no plot
To rid the realm of this pernicious blot?

Abbot. My lord,
Before I freely speak my mind herein,
You shall not only take the sacrament
To bury mine intents, but also to effect
Whatever I shall happen to devise.   *330*
I see your brows are full of discontent,
Your hearts of sorrow, and your eyes of tears:
Come home with me to supper; and I'll lay
A plot shall show us all a merry day.   [*Exeunt.*

ACT V

SCENE I. *London: a street leading to the Tower*
Enter QUEEN *and* LADIES.

Queen. This way the King will come; this is
    the way
To Julius Cæsar's ill-erected tower,
To whose flint bosom my condemned lord
Is doom'd a prisoner by proud Bolingbroke:
Here let us rest, if this rebellious earth
Have any resting for her true king's queen.

Enter RICHARD *and Guard.*

But soft, but see, or rather do not see,
My fair rose wither: yet look up, behold,
That you in pity may dissolve to dew   *9*
And wash him fresh again with true-love tears.
Ah, thou, the model where old Troy did stand.
Thou map of honour, thou King Richard's tomb,
And not King Richard; thou most beauteous inn,
Why should hard-favour'd grief be lodged in
    thee,
When triumph is become an alehouse guest?

K. Rich. Join not with grief, fair woman, do
    not so,
To make my end too sudden: learn, good soul,
To think our former state a happy dream;
From which awaked, the truth of what we are
Shows us but this: I am sworn brother, sweet, *20*
To grim Necessity, and he and I
Will keep a league till death. Hie thee to France
And cloister thee in some religious house:
Our holy lives must win a new world's crown,
Which our profane hours here have stricken
    down.

Queen. What, is my Richard both in shape and
    mind
Transform'd and weaken'd? hath Bolingbroke
    deposed
Thine intellect? hath he been in thy heart?
The lion dying thrusteth forth his paw,
And wounds the earth, if nothing else, with rage
To be o'erpower'd; and wilt thou, pupil-like, *31*

Take thy correction mildly, kiss the rod,
And fawn on rage with base humility,
Which art a lion and a king of beasts?

K. Rich. A king of beasts, indeed; if aught but
    beasts,
I had been still a happy king of men.
Good sometime queen, prepare thee hence for
    France:
Think I am dead and that even here thou takest,
As from my death-bed, thy last living leave.
In winter's tedious nights sit by the fire   *40*
With good old folks and let them tell thee tales
Of woeful ages long ago betid;
And ere thou bid good night, to quit their
    griefs,
Tell thou the lamentable tale of me
And send the hearers weeping to their beds:
For why the senseless brands will sympathize
The heavy accent of thy moving tongue
And in compassion weep the fire out;
And some will mourn in ashes, some coal-black,
For the deposing of a rightful king.   *50*

Enter NORTHUMBERLAND *and others.*

North. My lord, the mind of Bolingbroke is
    changed;
You must to Pomfret, not unto the Tower.
And, madam, there is order ta'en for you;
With all swift speed you must away to France.

K. Rich. Northumberland, thou ladder where-
    withal
The mounting Bolingbroke ascends my throne,
The time shall not be many hours of age
More than it is ere foul sin gathering head
Shall break into corruption: thou shalt think
Though he divide the realm and give thee half,
It is too little, helping him to all;   *61*
And he shall think that thou, which know'st the
    way
To plant unrightful kings, wilt know again,
Being ne'er so little urged, another way
To pluck him headlong from the usurped throne.
The love of wicked men converts to fear;
That fear to hate, and hate turns one or both
To worthy danger and deserved death.

North. My guilt be on my head, and there an
    end.
Take leave and part; for you must part forth-
    with.   *70*

K. Rich. Doubly divorced! Bad men, you vio-
    late
A twofold marriage, 'twixt my crown and me,
And then betwixt me and my married wife.
Let me unkiss the oath 'twixt thee and me;
And yet not so, for with a kiss 'twas made.
Part us, Northumberland; I towards the north,

Where shivering cold and sickness pines the
    clime;
My wife to France: from whence, set forth in
    pomp,
She came adorned hither like sweet May,
Sent back like Hallowmas or short'st of day. 80
  Queen. And must we be divided? must we part?
  K. Rich. Ay, hand from hand, my love, and
    heart from heart.
  Queen. Banish us both and send the King with
    me.
  North. That were some love but little policy.
  Queen. Then whither he goes, thither let me go.
  K. Rich. So two, together weeping, make one
    woe.
Weep thou for me in France, I for thee here;
Better far off than near, be ne'er the near.
Go, count thy way with sighs; I mine with
    groans.
  Queen. So longest way shall have the longest
    moans.   90
  K. Rich. Twice for one step I'll groan, the way
    being short,
And piece the way out with a heavy heart.
Come, come, in wooing sorrow let's be brief,
Since, wedding it, there is such length in grief:
One kiss shall stop our mouths, and dumbly part;
Thus give I mine, and thus take I thy heart.
  Queen. Give me mine own again; 'twere no
    good part
To take on me to keep and kill thy heart.
So, now I have mine own again, be gone,
That I may strive to kill it with a groan.   100
  K. Rich. We make woe wanton with this fond
    delay:
Once more, adieu; the rest let sorrow say.
                                          [*Exeunt.*

SCENE II. *The Duke of York's palace*
        Enter YORK *and his* DUCHESS.

  Duch. My lord, you told me you would tell the
    rest,
When weeping made you break the story off,
Of our two cousins coming into London.
  York. Where did I leave?
  Duch.   At that sad stop, my lord,
Where rude misgovern'd hands from windows'
    tops
Threw dust and rubbish on King Richard's head.
  York. Then, as I said, the Duke, great Boling-
    broke,
Mounted upon a hot and fiery steed
Which his aspiring rider seem'd to know,
With slow but stately pace kept on his course, 10
Whilst all tongues cried "God save thee, Boling-
    broke!"

You would have thought the very windows spake,
So many greedy looks of young and old
Through casements darted their desiring eyes
Upon his visage, and that all the walls
With painted imagery had said at once
"Jesu preserve thee! Welcome, Bolingbroke!"
Whilst he, from the one side to the other turning,
Bareheaded, lower than his proud steed's neck,
Bespake them thus: "I thank you, countrymen:"
And thus still doing, thus he pass'd along.   21
  Duch. Alack, poor Richard! where rode he the
    whilst?
  York. As in a theatre, the eyes of men,
After a well-graced actor leaves the stage,
Are idly bent on him that enters next,
Thinking his prattle to be tedious;
Even so, or with much more contempt, men's
    eyes
Did scowl on gentle Richard; no man cried "God
    save him!"
No joyful tongue gave him his welcome home:
But dust was thrown upon his sacred head;   30
Which with such gentle sorrow he shook off,
His face still combating with tears and smiles,
The badges of his grief and patience,
That had not God, for some strong purpose, steel'd
The hearts of men, they must perforce have
    melted
And barbarism itself have pitied him.
But heaven hath a hand in these events,
To whose high will we bound our calm con-
    tents.
To Bolingbroke are we sworn subjects now,
Whose state and honour I for aye allow.   40
  Duch. Here comes my son Aumerle.
  York.   Aumerle that was;
But that is lost for being Richard's friend,
And madam, you must call him Rutland now:
I am in parliament pledge for his truth
And lasting fealty to the new-made king.

        Enter AUMERLE.

  Duch. Welcome, my son: who are the violets
    now
That strew the green lap of the new come spring?
  Aum. Madam, I know not, nor I greatly care
    not:
God knows I had as lief be none as one.
  York. Well, bear you well in this new spring of
    time,   50
Lest you be cropp'd before you come to prime.
What news from Oxford? hold those jousts and
    triumphs?
  Aum. For aught I know, my lord, they do.
  York. You will be there, I know.
  Aum. If God prevent not, I purpose so.

York. What seal is that, that hangs without
        thy bosom?
Yea, look'st thou pale? let me see the writing.
Aum. My lord, 'tis nothing.
York.   No matter, then, who see it:
I will be satisfied; let me see the writing.
Aum. I do beseech your Grace to pardon me: 61
It is a matter of small consequence,
Which for some reasons I would not have seen.
York. Which for some reasons, sir, I mean
        to see.
I fear, I fear— .
Duch.   What should you fear?
'Tis nothing but some bond that he is enter'd
        into
For gay apparel 'gainst the triumph day.
York. Bound to himself! what doth he with a
        bond
That he is bound to? Wife, thou art a fool.
Boy, let me see the writing.
Aum. I do beseech you, pardon me; I may
        not show it.   70
York. I will be satisfied; let me see it, I say.
        He plucks it out of his bosom and reads it.
Treason! foul treason! Villain! traitor! slave!
Duch. What is the matter, my lord?
York. Ho! who is within there?

                Enter a SERVANT.

                        Saddle my horse.
God for his mercy, what treachery is here!
Duch. Why, what is it, my lord?
York. Give me my boots, I say; saddle my
        horse.   [*Exit* SERVANT.
Now, by mine honour, by my life, by my troth,
I will appeach the villain.
Duch.   What is the matter?
York. Peace, foolish woman.   80
Duch. I will not peace. What is the matter,
        Aumerle?
Aum. Good mother, be content; it is no more
Than my poor life must answer.
Duch.   Thy life answer!
York. Bring me my boots: I will unto the King.

        Re-enter SERVANT *with boots.*

Duch. Strike him, Aumerle. Poor boy, thou
        art amazed.
Hence, villain! never more come in my sight.
York. Give me my boots, I say.
Duch. Why, York, what wilt thou do?
Wilt thou not hide the trespass of thine own?
Have we more sons? or are we like to have?   90
Is not my teeming date drunk up with time?
And wilt thou pluck my fair son from mine age,
And rob me of a happy mother's name?

Is he not like thee? is he not thine own?
York. Thou fond mad woman,
Wilt thou conceal this dark conspiracy?
A dozen of them here have ta'en the sacrament,
And interchangeably set down their hands,
To kill the King at Oxford.
Duch.   He shall be none;   99
We'll keep him here: then what is that to him?
York. Away, fond woman! were he twenty
        times my son,
I would appeach him.
Duch.   Hadst thou groan'd for him
As I have done, thou wouldst be more pitiful.
But now I know thy mind; thou dost suspect
That I have been disloyal to thy bed,
And that he is a bastard, not thy son:
Sweet York, sweet husband, be not of that mind:
He is as like thee as a man may be,
Not like to me, or any of my kin,
And yet I love him.
York.   Make way, unruly woman!   110
                                        [*Exit.*
Duch. After, Aumerle! mount thee upon his
        horse;
Spur post, and get before him to the King,
And beg thy pardon ere he do accuse thee.
I'll not be long behind; though I be old,
I doubt not but to ride as fast as York.
And never will I rise up from the ground
Till Bolingbroke have pardon'd thee. Away, be
        gone!   [*Exeunt.*

        SCENE III. *A royal palace*

Enter BOLINGBROKE, PERCY, *and other Lords.*
Boling. Can no man tell me of my unthrifty
        son?
'Tis full three months since I did see him last:
If any plague hang over us, 'tis he.
I would to God, my lords, he might be found:
Inquire at London, 'mongst the taverns there,
For there, they say, he daily doth frequent,
With unrestrained loose companions,
Even such, they say, as stand in narrow lanes,
And beat our watch, and rob our passengers;
Which he, young wanton and effeminate boy,   10
Takes on the point of honour to support
So dissolute a crew.
Percy. My lord, some two days since I saw the
        prince,
And told him of those triumphs held at Oxford.
Boling. And what said the gallant?
Percy. His answer was, he would unto the
        stews,
And from the common'st creature pluck a glove,
And wear it as a favour; and with that
He would unhorse the lustiest challenger.

Boling. As dissolute as desperate; yet through both   20
I see some sparks of better hope, which elder years
May happily bring forth. But who comes here?

Enter Aumerle.

Aum. Where is the King?
Boling. What means our cousin, that he stares and looks
So wildly?
Aum. God save your Grace! I do beseech your Majesty,
To have some conference with your Grace alone.
Boling. Withdraw yourselves, and leave us here alone.   [*Exeunt* PERCY *and Lords.*
What is the matter with our cousin now?
Aum. For ever may my knees grow to the earth,   30
My tongue cleave to my roof within my mouth,
Unless a pardon ere I rise or speak.
Boling. Intended or committed was this fault?
If on the first, how heinous e'er it be,
To win thy after-love I pardon thee.
Aum. Then give me leave that I may turn the key,
That no man enter till my tale be done.
Boling. Have thy desire.
AUMERLE *locks the door.* YORK *knocks at the door and crieth.*
York. [*Within*] My liege, beware: look to thyself;
Thou hast a traitor in thy presence there.   40
Boling. Villain, I'll make thee safe.
Drawing.
Aum. Stay thy revengeful hand; thou hast no cause to fear.
York. [*Within*] Open the door, secure, fool-hardy King:
Shall I for love speak treason to thy face?
Open the door, or I will break it open.

Enter YORK.

Boling. What is the matter, uncle? speak;
Recover breath; tell us how near is danger,
That we may arm us to encounter it.
York. Peruse this writing here, and thou shalt know
The treason that my haste forbids me show.   50
Aum. Remember, as thou read'st, thy promise pass'd:
I do repent me; read not my name there;
My heart is not confederate with my hand.
York. It was, villain, ere thy hand did set it down.
I tore it from the traitor's bosom, King;

Fear, and not love, begets his penitence:
Forget to pity him, lest thy pity prove
A serpent that will sting thee to the heart.
Boling. O heinous, strong and bold conspiracy!
O loyal father of a treacherous son!   60
Thou sheer, immaculate, and silver fountain,
From whence this stream through muddy passages
Hath held his current and defiled himself!
Thy overflow of good converts to bad,
And thy abundant goodness shall excuse
This deadly blot in thy digressing son.
York. So shall my virtue be his vice's bawd;
And he shall spend mine honour with his shame,
As thriftless sons their scraping fathers' gold.
Mine honour lives when his dishonour dies,   70
Or my shamed life in his dishonour lies:
Thou kill's me in this life; giving him breath,
The traitor lives, the true man's put to death.
Duch. [*Within*] What ho, my liege! for God's sake, let me in.
Boling. What shrill-voiced suppliant makes this eager cry?
Duch. A woman, and thy aunt, great King; 'tis I.
Speak with me, pity me, open the door:
A begger begs that never begg'd before.
Boling. Our scene is alter'd from a serious thing,
And now changed to "The Beggar and the King."
My dangerous cousin, let your mother in: 81
I know she is come to pray for your foul sin.
York. If thou do pardon, whosoever pray,
More sins for this forgiveness prosper may.
This fester'd joint cut off, the rest rest sound;
This let alone will all the rest confound;

Enter DUCHESS.

Duch. O King, believe not this hard-hearted man!
Love loving not itself none other can.
York. Thou frantic woman, what dost thou make here?
Shall thy old dugs once more a traitor rear?   90
Duch. Sweet York, be patient. Hear me, gentle liege. [*Kneels.*]
Boling. Rise up, good aunt.
Duch.   Not yet, I thee beseech:
For ever will I walk upon my knees,
And never see day that the happy sees,
Till thou give joy; until thou bid me joy,
By pardoning Rutland, my transgressing boy.
Aum. Unto my mother's prayers I bend my knee.
York. Against them both my true joints bended be.
Ill mayst thou thrive, if thou grant any grace!

Duch. Pleads he in earnest? look upon his
    face;   *100*
His eyes do drop no tears, his prayers are in jest:
His words come from his mouth, ours from our
    breast:
He prays but faintly and would be denied;
We pray with heart and soul and all beside:
His weary joints would gladly rise, I know;
Our knees shall kneel till to the ground they
    grow:
His prayers are full of false hypocrisy;
Ours of true zeal and deep integrity.
Our prayers do out-pray his; then let them have
That mercy which true prayer ought to have. *110*
    Boling. Good aunt, stand up.
    Duch.   Nay, do not say, "Stand up";
Say "Pardon" first, and afterwards "Stand up."
An if I were thy nurse, thy tongue to teach,
"Pardon" should be the first word of thy speech.
I never long'd to hear a word till now;
Say "pardon," King; let pity teach thee how:
The word is short, but not so short as sweet;
No word like "pardon" for kings' mouths so
    meet.
    York. Speak it in French, King; say *Pardonne
    moi.*
    Duch. Dost thou teach pardon pardon to de-
    stroy?   *120*
Ah, my sour husband, my hard-hearted lord,
That set'st the word itself against the word!
Speak "pardon" as 'tis current in our land;
The chopping French we do not understand.
Thine eye begins to speak; set thy tongue there;
Or in thy piteous heart plant thou thine ear;
That hearing how our plaints and prayers do
    pierce,
Pity may move thee "pardon" to rehearse.
    Boling. Good aunt, stand up.
    Duch.   I do not sue to stand;
Pardon is all the suit I have in hand.   *130*
    Boling. I pardon him, as God shall pardon me.
    Duch. O happy vantage of a kneeling knee!
Yet am I sick for fear: speak it again;
Twice saying "pardon" doth not pardon twain,
But makes one pardon strong.
    Boling.   With all my heart
I pardon him.
    Duch.   A god on earth thou art.
    Boling. But for our trusty brother-in-law and
    the abbot,
With all the rest of that consorted crew,
Destruction straight shall dog them at the heels.
Good uncle, help to order several powers   *140*
To Oxford, or where'er these traitors are:
They shall not live within this world, I swear,
But I will have them, if I once know where.

Uncle, farewell: and, cousin too, adieu:
Your mother well hath pray'd, and prove you
    true.
    Duch. Come, my old son: I pray God make thee
    new.   [*Exeunt.*

SCENE IV. *The same*

Enter EXTON *and* SERVANT.

    Exton. Didst thou not mark the King, what
    words he spake,
"Have I no friend will rid me of this living fear?"
Was it not so?
    Ser.   These were his very words.
    Exton. "Have I no friend?" quoth he: he spake
    it twice,
And urged it twice together, did he not?
    Serv. He did.
    Exton. And speaking, it, he wistly look'd on
    me;
As who should say, "I would thou wert the man
That would divorce this terror from my heart";
Meaning the king at Pomfret. Come, let's go: *10*
I am the king's friend, and will rid his foe.
                         [*Exeunt.*

SCENE V. *Pomfret castle*

Enter KING RICHARD.

    K. Rich. I have been studying how I may com-
    pare
This prison where I live unto the world:
And for because the world is populous
And here is not a creature but myself,
I cannot do it; yet I'll hammer it out.
My brain I'll prove the female to my soul,
My soul the father; and these two beget
A generation of still-breeding thoughts,
And these same thoughts people this little world,
In humours like the people of this world,   *10*
For no thought is contented. The better sort,
As thoughts of things divine, are intermix'd
With scruples and do set the word itself
Against the word:
As thus, "Come, little ones," and then again,
"It is as hard to come as for a camel
To thread the postern of a small needle's eye."
Thoughts tending to ambition, they do plot
Unlikely wonders; how these vain weak nails
May tear a passage through the flinty ribs   *20*
Of this hard world, my ragged prison walls,
And, for they cannot, die in their own pride.
Thoughts tending to content flatter themselves
That they are not the first of fortune's slaves,
Nor shall not be the last; like silly beggars
Who sitting in the stocks refuge their shame,
That many have and others must sit there;
And in this thought they find a kind of ease,

Bearing their own misfortunes on the back
Of such as have before endured the like.   30
Thus play I in one person many people,
And none contented: sometimes am I king;
Then treasons make me wish myself a beggar,
And so I am: then crushing penury
Persuades me I was better when a king;
Then am I king'd again: and by and by
Think that I am unking'd by Bolingbroke,
And straight am nothing: but whate'er I be,
Nor I nor any man that but man is
With nothing shall be pleased, till he be eased 40
With being nothing. Music do I hear? [*Music.*
Ha, ha! keep time: how sour sweet music is,
When time is broke and no proportion kept!
So is it in the music of men's lives.
And here have I the daintiness of ear
To check time broke in a disorder'd strong;
But for the concord of my state and time
Had not an ear to hear my true time broke.
I wasted time, and now doth time waste me;
For now hath time made me his numbering
     clock: 50
My thoughts are minutes; and with sighs they
     jar
Their watches on unto mine eyes, the outward
     watch,
Whereto my finger, like a dial's point,
Is pointing still, in cleansing them from tears.
Now sir, the sound that tells what hour it is
Are clamorous groans, which strike upon my
     heart,
Which is the bell: so sighs and tears and groans
Show minutes, times, and hours: but my time
Runs posting on in Bolingbroke's proud joy,
While I stand fooling here, his Jack o' the clock.
This music mads me; let it sound no more;   61
For though it have holp madmen to their wits,
In me it seems it will make wise men mad.
Yet blessing on his heart that gives it me!
For 'tis a sign of love; and love to Richard
Is a strange brooch in this all-hating world.

Enter a GROOM OF THE STABLE

Groom. Hail, royal prince!
K. Rich.   Thanks, noble peer;
The cheapest of us is ten groats too deer.
What art thou? and how comest thou hither,
Where no man never comes but that sad dog 70
That brings me food to make misfortune live?
Groom. I was a poor groom of thy stable, King,
When thou wert king; who, travelling towards
     York,
With much ado at length have gotten leave
To look upon my sometimes royal master's face.
O, how it yearn'd my heart when I beheld

In London streets, that coronation-day,
When Bolingbroke rode on roan Barbary,
That horse that thou so often hast bestrid,
That horse that I so carefully have dress'd!   80
K. Rich. Rode he on Barbary? Tell me, gentle
     friend,
How went he under him?
Groom. So proudly as if he disdain'd the ground.
K. Rich. So proud that Bolingbroke was on his
     back!
That jade hath eat bread from my royal hand;
This hand hath made him proud with clapping
     him.
Would he not stumble? would he not fall down,
Since pride must have a fall, and break the neck
Of that proud man that did usurp his back?
Forgiveness, horse! why do I rail on thee,   90
Since thou, created to be awed by man,
Wast born to bear? I was not made a horse;
And yet I bear a burthen like an ass,
Spurr'd, gall'd, and tired by jauncing Boling-
     broke.

Enter KEEPER, *with a dish.*

Keep. Fellow, give place; here is no longer
     stay.
K. Rich. If thou love me, 'tis time thou wert
     away.
Groom. What my tongue dares not, that my
     heart shall say.   [*Exit.*
Keep. My lord, will't please you to fall to?
K. Rich. Taste of it first, as thou art wont to
     do.   99
Keep. My lord, I dare not: Sir Pierce of Ex-
ton, who lately came from the King, commands
the contrary.
K. Rich. The devil take Henry of Lancaster
     and thee!
Patience is stale, and I am weary of it.
Beats the keeper.
Keep. Help, help, help!

Enter EXTON *and servants, armed.*

K. Rich. How now! what means death in this
     rude assault?
Villain, thy own hand yields thy death's instru-
     ment.
Snatching an axe from a Servant and killing him.
Go thou, and fill another room in hell.
He kills another, Then EXTON *strikes him down.*
That hand shall burn in never-quenching fire
That staggers thus my person. Exton, thy fierce
     hand   110
Hath with the King's blood stain'd the King's
     own land.
Mount, mount, my soul! thy seat is up on high;

Whilst my gross flesh sinks downward, here to
   die.   [*Dies.*
Exton. As full of valour as of royal blood:
Both have I spill'd; O would the deed were
   good!
For now the devil, that told me I did well,
Says that this deed is chronicled in hell.
This dead king to the living king I'll bear:
Take hence the rest, and give them burial here.
                                       [*Exeunt.*

SCENE VI. *Windsor castle*

Flourish. Enter BOLINGBROKE, YORK, *with other
Lords, and Attendants.*

Boling. Kind uncle York, the latest news we
   hear
Is that the rebels have consumed with fire
Out town of Cicester in Gloucestershire;
But whether they be ta'en or slain we hear not.

Enter NORTHUMBERLAND.

Welcome, my lord: what is the news?
   North. First, to thy sacred state wish I all
   happiness.
The next news is, I have to London sent
The heads of Oxford, Salisbury, Blunt, and Kent:
The manner of their taking may appear
At large discoursed in this paper here.   *10*
   Boling. We thank thee, gentle Percy, for thy
   pains;
And to thy worth will add right worthy gains.

Enter FITZWATER.

Fitz. My lord, I have from Oxford sent to
   London
The heads of Brocas and Sir Bennet Seely,
Two of the dangerous consorted traitors
That sought at Oxford thy dire overthrow.
   Boling. Thy pains, Fitzwater, shall not be
   forgot;
Right noble is thy merit, well I wot.

Enter PERCY, *and the* BISHOP OF CARLISLE

Percy. The grand conspirator, Abbot of West-
   minster,
With clog of conscience and sour melancholy *20*
Hath yielded up his body to the grave;
But here is Carlisle living, to abide
Thy kingly doom and sentence of his pride.
   Boling. Carlisle, this is your doom:
Choose out some secret place, some reverend
   room,
More than thou hast, and with it joy thy life;
So as thou livest in peace, die free from strife;
For though mine enemy thou hast ever been,
High sparks of honour in thee have I seen.

Enter EXTON, *with persons bearing a coffin.*

Exton. Great King, within this coffin I pre-
   sent   *30*
Thy buried fear: herein all breathless lies
The mightiest of thy greatest enemies,
Richard of Bordeaux, by me hither brought.
   Boling. Exton, I thank thee not; for thou hast
   wrought
A deed of slander with thy fatal hand
Upon my head and all this famous land.
   Exton. From your own mouth, my lord, did I
   this deed.
   Boling. They love not poison that do poison
   need,
Nor do I thee: though I did wish him dead,
I hate the murderer, love him murdered.   *40*
The guilt of conscience take thou for thy labour,
But neither my good word nor princely favour:
With Cain go wander through shades of night,
And never show thy head by day nor light.
Lords, I protest, my soul is full of woe,
That blood should sprinkle me to make me grow:
Come, mourn with me for that I do lament,
And put on sullen black incontinent:
I'll make a voyage to the Holy Land,
To wash this blood off from my guilty hand: *50*
March sadly after; grace my mournings here;
In weeping after this untimely bier.   [*Exeunt.*

❧ A MIDSUMMER-NIGHT'S DREAM

DRAMATIS PERSONÆ

THESEUS, *Duke of Athens*
EGEUS, *father to Hermia*
LYSANDER | *in love with Hermia*
DEMETRIUS |
PHILOSTRATE, *master of the revels to Theseus*
QUINCE, *a carpenter*
SNUG, *a joiner*
BOTTOM, *a weaver*
FLUTE, *a bellows-mender*
SNOUT, *a tinker*
STARVELING, *a tailor*

HIPPOLYTA, *Queen of the Amazons, betrothed to Theseus*
HERMIA, *daughter to Egeus, in love with Lysander*

HELENA, *in love with Demetrius*

OBERON, *King of the fairies*
TITANIA, *Queen of the fairies*
PUCK, *or Robin Goodfellow*
PEASEBLOSSOM
COBWEB
MOTH | *fairies*
MUSTARDSEED
TWO FAIRIES |

NON-SPEAKING: *Attendants on Theseus and Hippolyta; fairies attending their King and Queen.*

SCENE: *Athens, and a wood near it*

❧

ACT I

SCENE I. *Athens: the palace of Theseus*

Enter THESEUS, HIPPOLYTA, PHILOSTRATE, *and Attendants.*

The. Now, fair Hippolyta, our nuptial hour
Draws on apace; four happy days bring in
Another moon: but, O, methinks, how slow
This old moon wanes! she lingers my desires,
Like to a step-dame or a dowager
Long withering out a young man's revenue.
Hip. Four days will quickly steep themselves in night;
Four nights will quickly dream away the time;
And then the moon, like to a silver bow
New-bent in heaven, shall behold the night   10
Of our solemnities.
The.   Go, Philostrate,
Stir up the Athenian youth to merriments;
Awake the pert and nimble spirit of mirth:
Turn melancholy forth to funerals;
The pale companion is not for our pomp.
                [*Exit* PHILOSTRATE.
Hippolyta, I woo'd thee with my sword,
And won thy love, doing thee injuries;
But I will wed thee in another key,
With pomp, with triumph, and with revelling.

Enter EGEUS, HERMIA, LYSANDER, *and* DEMETRIUS.

Ege. Happy be Theseus, our renowned Duke!

The. Thanks, good Egeus: what's the news with thee?   21
Ege. Full of vexation come I, with complaint
Against my child, my daughter Hermia.
Stand forth, Demetrius. My noble lord,
This man hath my consent to marry her.
Stand forth, Lysander: and, my gracious Duke,
This man hath bewitch'd the bosom of my child:
Thou, thou, Lysander, thou hast given her rhymes
And interchanged love-tokens with my child:
Thou hast by moonlight at her window sung   30
With feigning voice verses of feigning love,
And stolen the impression of her fantasy
With bracelets of thy hair, rings, gawds, conceits,
Knacks, trifles, nosegays, sweetmeats, messengers
Of strong prevailment in unharden'd youth:
With cunning hast thou filch'd my daughter's heart,
Turn'd her obedience, which is due to me,
To stubborn harshness: and, my gracious Duke,
Be it so she will not here before your Grace
Consent to marry with Demetrius,   40
I beg the ancient privilege of Athens,
As she is mine, I may dispose of her:
Which shall be either to this gentleman
Or to her death, according to our law
Immediately provided in that case.
The. What say you, Hermia? be advised, **fair** maid:

To you your father should be as a god;
One that composed your beauties, yea, and one
To whom you are but as a form in wax
By him imprinted and within his power   50
To leave the figure or disfigure it.
Demetrius is a worthy gentleman.
  Her. So is Lysander.
  The.   In himself he is;
But in this kind, wanting your father's voice,
The other must be held the worthier.
  Her. I would my father look'd but with my eyes.
  The. Rather your eyes must with his judge-
      ment look.
  Her. I do entreat your Grace to pardon me.
I know not by what power I am made bold,
Nor how it may concern my modesty,   60
In such a presence here to plead my thoughts;
But I beseech your Grace that I may know
The worst that may befall me in this case,
If I refuse to wed Demetrius.
  The. Either to die the death or to abjure
For ever the society of men.
Therefore, fair Hermia, question your desires;
Know of your youth, examine well your blood,
Whether, if you yield not to your father's choice,
You can endure the livery of a nun,   70
For aye to be in shady cloister mew'd,
To live a barren sister all your life,
Chanting faint hymns to the cold fruitless moon.
Thrice-blessed they that master so their blood
To undergo such maiden pilgrimage;
But earthlier happy is the rose distill'd
Than that which withering on the virgin thorn
Grows, lives, and dies in single blessedness.
  Her. So will I grow, so live, so die, my lord,
Ere I will yield my virgin patent up   80
Unto his lordship, whose unwished yoke
My soul consents not to give sovereignty.
  The. Take time to pause; and, by the next new
      moon—
The sealing-day betwixt my love and me,
For everlasting bond of fellowship—
Upon that day either prepare to die
For disobedience to your father's will,
Or else to wed Demetrius, as he would;
Or on Diana's altar to protest
For aye austerity and single life.   90
  Dem. Relent, sweet Hermia: and, Lysander,
      yield
Thy crazed title to my certain right.
  Lys. You have her father's love, Demetrius;
Let me have Hermia's: do you marry him.
  Ege. Scornful Lysander! true, he hath my love,
And what is mine my love shall render him.
And she is mine, and all my right of her
I do estate unto Demetrius.

  Lys. I am, my lord, as well derived as he,
As well possess'd; my love is more than his;   100
My fortunes every way as fairly rank'd,
If not with vantage, as Demetrius';
And, which is more than all these boasts can be,
I am beloved of beauteous Hermia:
Why should not I then prosecute my right?
Demetrius, I'll avouch it to his head,
Made love to Nedar's daughter, Helena,
And won her soul; and she, sweet lady, dotes,
Devoutly dotes, dotes in idolatry,
Upon this spotted and inconstant man.   110
  The. I must confess that I have heard so much,
And with Demetrius thought to have spoke
      thereof;
But, being over-full of self-affairs,
My mind did lose it. But, Demetrius, come;
And come, Egeus; you shall go with me,
I have some private schooling for you both.
For you, fair Hermia, look you arm yourself
To fit your fancies to your father's will;
Or else the law of Athens yields you up—
Which by no means we may extenuate—
To death, or to a vow of single life.
Come, my Hippolyta: what cheer, my love?
Demetrius and Egeus, go along:
I must employ you in some business
Against our nuptial and confer with you
Of something nearly that concerns yourselves.
  Ege. With duty and desire we follow you.
            [*Exeunt all but* LYSANDER *and* HERMIA.
  Lys. How now, my love! why is your cheek so
      pale?
How chance the roses there do fade so fast?
  Her. Belike for want of rain, which I could
      well   130
Beteem them from the tempest of my eyes.
  Lys. Ay me! for aught that I could ever read,
Could ever hear by tale or history,
The course of true love never did run smooth;
But, either it was different in blood—
  Her. O cross! too high to be enthrall'd to low.
  Lys. Or else misgraffed in respect of years—
  Her. O spite! too old to be engaged to young.
  Lys. Or else it stood upon the choice of friends—
  Her. O hell! to choose love by another's eyes.
  Lys. Or, if there were a sympathy in choice,
War, death, or sickness did lay siege to it,
Making it momentany as a sound,
Swift as a shadow, short as any dream;
Brief as the lightning in the collied night,
That, in a spleen, unfolds both heaven and earth,
And ere a man hath power to say "Behold!"
The jaws of darkness do devour it up:
So quick bright things come to confusion.
  Her. If then true lovers have been ever cross'd,

It stands as an edict in destiny: 151
Then let us teach our trial patience,
Because it is a customary cross,
As due to love as thoughts and dreams and sighs,
Wishes and tears, poor Fancy's followers.
  Lys. A good persuasion: therefore, hear me,
    Hermia.
I have a widow aunt, a dowager
Of great revenue, and she hath no child:
From Athens is her house remote seven leagues;
And she respects me as her only son.   160
There, gentle Hermia, may I marry thee;
And to that place the sharp Athenian law
Cannot pursue us. If thou lovest me then,
Steal forth thy father's house to-morrow night;
And in the wood, a league without the town,
Where I did meet thee once with Helena
To do observance to a morn of May,
There will I stay for thee.
  Her.   My good Lysander!
I swear to thee, by Cupid's strongest bow,
By his best arrow with the golden head,   170
By the simplicity of Venus' doves,
By that which knitteth souls and prospers loves,
And by that fire which burn'd the Carthage
    queen,
When the false Troyan under sail was seen,
By all the vows that ever men have broke,
In number more than ever women spoke,
In that same place thou hast appointed me,
To-morrow truly will I meet with thee.
  Lys. Keep promise, love. Look, here comes
    Helena.

Enter HELENA.

  Her. God speed fair Helena! whither away?
  Hel. Call you me fair? that fair again unsay.
Demetrius loves your fair: O happy fair!
Your eyes are lode-stars; and your tongue's
    sweet air
More tuneable than lark to shepherd's ear,
When wheat is green, when hawthorn buds ap-
    pear.
Sickness is catching: O, were favour so,
Yours would I catch, fair Hermia, ere I go;
My ear should catch your voice, my eye your
    eye,
My tongue should catch your tongue's sweet me-
    lody.
Were the world mine, Demetrius being bated,
The rest I'ld give to be to you translated.   191
O, teach me how you look, and with what art
You sway the motion of Demetrius' heart.
  Her. I frown upon him, yet he loves me still.
  Hel. O that your frowns would teach my
    smiles such skill!

  Her. I give him curses, yet he gives me love.
  Hel. O that my prayers could such affection
    move!
  Her. The more I hate, the more he follows me.
  Hel. The more I love, the more he hateth me.
  Her. His folly, Helena, is no fault of mine.
  Hel. None, but your beauty: would that fault
    were mine!   201
  Her. Take comfort: he no more shall see my
    face;
Lysander and myself will fly this place.
Before the time I did Lysander see,
Seem'd Athens as a paradise to me:
O, then, what graces in my love do dwell,
That he hath turn'd a heaven unto a hell!
  Lys. Helen, to you our minds we will unfold:
To-morrow night, when Phœbe doth behold
Her silver visage in the watery glass,   210
Decking with liquid pearl the bladed grass,
A time that lovers' flights doth still conceal,
Through Athens' gates have we devised to steal.
  Her. And in the wood, where often you and I
Upon faint primrose-beds were wont to lie,
Emptying our bosoms of their counsel sweet,
There my Lysander and myself shall meet;
And thence from Athens turn away our eyes,
To seek new friends and stranger companies.
Farewell, sweet playfellow: pray thou for us;
And good luck grant thee thy Demetrius!   221
Keep word, Lysander: we must starve our sight
From lovers' food till morrow deep midnight.
  Lys. I will, my Hermia.   [*Exit Hermia.*
                  Helena, adieu:
As you on him, Demetrius dote on you!   [*Exit.*
  Hel. How happy some o'er other some can be!
Through Athens I am thought as fair as she.
But what of that? Demetrius thinks not so;
He will not know what all but he do know:
And as he errs, doting on Hermia's eyes,   230
So I, admiring of his qualities:
Things base and vile, holding no quantity,
Love can transpose to form and dignity:
Love looks not with the eyes, but with the mind;
And therefore is wing'd Cupid painted blind:
Nor hath Love's mind of any judgement taste;
Wings and no eyes figure unheedy haste:
And therefore is Love said to be a child,
Because in choice he is so oft beguiled.
As waggish boys in game themselves for-
    swear,   240
So the boy Love is perjured every where:
For ere Demetrius look'd on Hermia's eyne,
He hail'd down oaths that he was only mine;
And when this hail some heat from Hermia felt,
So he dissolved, and showers of oaths did melt.
I will go tell him of fair Hermia's flight:

Then to the wood will he to-morrow night
Pursue her; and for this intelligence
If I have thanks, it is a dear expense:
But herein mean I to enrich my pain,   250
To have his sight thither and back again.   [*Exit.*

SCENE II. *Athens: Quince's huose.*

Enter QUINCE, SNUG, BOTTOM, FLUTE, SNOUT, *and*
STARVELING.

Quin. Is all our company here?

Bot. You were best to call them generally,
man by man, according to the scrip.

Quin. Here is the scroll of every man's name,
which is thought fit, through all Athens, to play
in our interlude before the Duke and the Duchess,
on his wedding-day at night.

Bot. First, good Peter Quince, say what the
play treats on, then read the names of the actors,
and so grow to a point.

Quin. Marry, our play is *The most lamentable
comedy, and most cruel death of Pyramus and
Thisby.*

Bot. A very good piece of work, I assure you,
and a merry. Now, good Peter Quince, call
forth your actors by the scroll. Masters, spread
yourselves.

Quin. Answer as I call you. Nick Bottom, the
weaver.

Bot. Ready. Name what part I am for, and proceed.   21

Quin. You, Nick Bottom, are set down for
Pyramus.

Bot. What is Pyramus? a lover, or a tyrant?

Quin. A lover, that kills himself most gallant
for love.

Bot. That will ask some tears in the true per-
forming of it: if I do it, let the audience look to
their eyes; I will move storms, I will condole in
some measure. To the rest: yet my chief humour
is for a tyrant: I could play Ercles rarely, or a
part to tear a cat in, to make all split.
            "The raging rocks
              And shivering shocks
            Shall break the locks
                Of prison gates;
            And Phibbus' car
            Shall shine from far
            And make and mar
                The foolish Fates."   40
This was lofty! Now name the rest of the
players. This is Ercles' vein, a tyrant's vein; a
lover is more condoling.

Quin. Francis Flute, the bellows-mender.

Flu. Here, Peter Quince.

Quin. Flute, you must take Thisby on you.

Flu. What is Thisby? a wandering knight?

Quin. It is the lady that Pyramus must love.

Flu. Nay, faith, let not me play a woman; I
have a beard coming.   50

Quin. That's all one: you shall play it in a
mask, and you may speak as small as you will.

Bot. An I may hide my face, let me play
Thisby too, I'll speak in a monstrous little voice,
"Thisne, Thisne"; "Ah Pyramus, my lover
dear! thy Thisby dear, and lady dear!"

Quin. No, no; you must play Pyramus: and,
Flute, you Thisby.

Bot. Well, proceed.

Quin. Robin Starveling, the tailor.   60

Star. Here, Peter Quince.

Quin. Robin Starveling, you must play Thisby's
mother. Tom Snout, the tinker.

Snout. Here, Peter Quince.

Quin. You, Pyramus' father: myself, Thisby's
father. Snug, the joiner; you, the lion's part:
and, I hope, here is a play fitted.

Snug. Have you the lion's part written? pray
you, if it be, give it me, for I am slow of study.

Quin. You may do it extempore, for it is nothing but roaring.   71

Bot. Let me play the lion too: I will roar, that
I will do any man's heart good to hear me;
I will roar, that I will make the Duke say, "Let
him roar again, let him roar again."

Quin. An you should do it too terribly, you
would fright the Duchess and the ladies, that
they would shriek; and that were enough to hang
us all.

All. That would hang us, every mother's son.

Bot. I grant you, friends, if that you should
fright the ladies out of their wits, they would
have no more discretion but to hang us: but I
will aggravate my voice so that I will roar you
as gently as any sucking dove; I will roar you
an 'twere any nightingale.

Quin. You can play no part but Pyramus; for
Pyramus is a sweet-faced man; a proper man, as
one shall see in a summer's day; a most lovely
gentleman-like man: therefore you must needs
play Pyramus.   91

Bot. Well, I will undertake it. What beard were
I best to play it in?

Quin. Why, what you will.

Bot. I will discharge it in either your straw-
colour beard, your orange-tawny beard, your
purple-in-grain beard, or your French-crown-
colour beard, your perfect yellow.

Quin. Some of your French crowns have no hair
at all, and then you will play barefaced. But,
masters, here are your parts: and I am to entreat you, request you and desire you, to con
them by to-morrow night; and meet me in the

palace wood, a mile without the town, by moonlight; there will we rehearse, for if we meet in
the city, we shall be dogged with company, and
our devices known. In the meantime I will draw
a bill of properties, such as our play wants. I
pray you, fail me not.   *109*

Bot. We will meet; and there we may rehearse
most obscenely and courageously. Take pains;
be perfect: adieu.

Quin. At the Duke's oak we meet.

Bot. Enough; hold or cut bow-strings.

                                        [*Exeunt.*

ACT II

Scene i. *A wood near Athens*

Enter, from opposite sides, a FAIRY, *and* PUCK.

Puck. How now, spirit! whither wander you?

Fai. Over hill, over dale,
 Thorough bush, thorough brier,
 Over park, over pale,
 Thorough flood, thorough fire,
I do wander every where,
Swifter than the moon's sphere;
And I serve the fairy Queen,
To dew her orbs upon the green.
The cowslips tall her pensioners be: *10*
In their gold coats spots you see;
Those be rubies, fairy favours,
In those freckles live their savours:
I must go seek some dewdrops here
And hang a pearl in every cowslip's ear.
Farewell, thou lob of spirits; I'll be gone:
Our Queen and all her elves come here
 anon.

Puck. The King doth keep his revels here to-
 night:
Take heed the Queen come not within his sight;
For Oberon is passing fell and wrath, *20*
Because that she as her attendant hath
A lovely boy, stolen from an Indian king;
She never had so sweet a changeling;
And jealous Oberon would have the child
Knight of his train, to trace the forests wild;
But she perforce withholds the loved boy,
Crowns him with flowers and makes him all her
 joy:
And now they never meet in grove or green,
By fountain clear, or spangled starlight sheen,
But they do square, that all their elves for fear *30*
Creep into acorn-cups and hide them there.

Fai. Either I mistake your shape and making
 quite,
Or else you are that shrewd and knavish sprite
Call'd Robin Goodfellow: are not you he
That frights the maidens of the villagery;
Skim milk, and sometimes labour in the quern

And bootless make the breathless housewife
 churn;
And sometime make the drink to bear no barm;
Mislead night-wanderers, laughing at their
 harm?
Those that Hobgoblin call you and sweet Puck,
You do their work, and they shall have good
 luck:
Are not you he?

Puck.   Thou speak'st aright;
I am that merry wanderer of the night.
I jest to Oberon and make him smile
When I a fat and bean-fed horse beguile,
Neighing in likeness of a filly foal:
And sometime lurk I in a gossip's bowl,
In very likeness of a roasted crab,
And when she drinks, against her lips I bob
And on her wither'd dewlap pour the ale. *50*
The wisest aunt, telling the saddest tale,
Sometime for three-foot stool mistaketh me;
Then slip I from her bum, down topples she,
And "tailor" cries, and falls into a cough;
And then the whole quire hold their hips and
 laugh,
And waxen in their mirth and neeze and swear
A merrier hour was never wasted there.
But, room, fairy! here comes Oberon.

Fai. And here my mistress. Would that he were
 gone!

Enter, from one side, OBERON, *with his train;
from the other,* TITANIA, *with hers.*

Obe. Ill met by moonlight, proud Titania. *60*

Tita. What, jealous Oberon! Fairies, skip
 hence:
I have forsworn his bed and company.

Obe. Tarry, rash wanton: am not I thy lord?

Tita. Then I must be thy lady: but I know
When thou hast stolen away from fairy land,
And in the shape of Corin sat all day,
Playing on pipes of corn and versing love
To amorous Phillida. Why art thou here,
Come from the farthest steppe of India?
But that, forsooth, the bouncing Amazon, *70*
Your buskin'd mistress and your warrior love,
To Theseus must be wedded, and you come
To give their bed joy and prosperity.

Obe. How canst thou thus for shame, Titania,
Glance at my credit with Hippolyta,
Knowing I know thy love to Theseus?
Didst thou not lead him through the glimmering
 night
From Perigenia, whom he ravished?
And make him with fair Ægle break his faith,
With Ariadne and Antiopa? *80*

Tita. These are the forgeries of jealousy:

And never, since the middle summer's spring,
Met we on hill, in dale, forest or mead,
By paved fountain or by rushy brook,
Or in the beached margent of the sea,
To dance our ringlets to the whistling wind,
But with thy brawls thou hast disturb'd our
     sport.
Therefore the winds, piping to us in vain,
As in revenge, have suck'd up from the sea
Contagious fogs; which falling in the land   90
Have every pelting river made so proud
That they have overborne their continents:
The ox hath therefore stretch'd his yoke in vain,
The ploughman lost his sweat, and the green corn
Hath rotted ere his youth attain'd a beard;
The fold stands empty in the drowned field,
And crows are fatted with the murrion flock;
The nine men's morris is fill'd up with mud,
And the quaint mazes in the wanton green
For lack of tread are undistinguishable: 100
The human mortals want their winter here;
No night is now with hymn or carol blest:
Therefore the moon, the governess of floods,
Pale in her anger, washes all the air,
That rheumatic diseases do abound:
And thorough this distemperature we see
The seasons alter: hoary-headed frosts
Fall in the fresh lap of the crimson rose,
And on old Hiems' thin and icy crown
An odorous chaplet of sweet summer buds   110
Is, as in mockery, set: the spring, the summer,
The childing autumn, angry winter, change
Their wonted liveries, and the mazed world,
By their increase, now knows not which is
     which:
And this same progeny of evils comes
From our debate, from our dissension;
We are their parents and original.
  Obe. Do you amend it then; it lies in you:
Why should Titania cross her Oberon?
I do but beg a little changeling boy   120
To be my henchman.
  Tita.   Set your heart at rest:
The fairy land buys not the child of me.
His mother was a votaress of my order:
And, in the spiced Indian air, by night,
Full often hath she gossip'd by my side,
And sat with me on Neptune's yellow sands,
Marking the embarked traders on the flood,
When we have laugh'd to see the sails conceive
And grow big-bellied with the wanton wind;
Which she, with pretty and with swimming gait
Following—her womb then rich with my young
     squire—   131
Would imitate, and sail upon the land,
To fetch me trifles, and return again,

As from a voyage, rich with merchandise.
But she, being mortal, of that boy did die;
And for her sake do I rear up her boy,
And for her sake I will not part with him.
  Obe. How long within this wood intend you
     stay?
  Tita. Perchance till after Theseus' wedding-
     day.
If you will patiently dance in our round   140
And see our moonlight revels, go with us;
If not, shun me, and I will spare your haunts.
  Obe. Give me that boy, and I will go with thee.
  Tita. Not for thy fairy kingdom. Fairies, away!
We shall chide downright, if I longer stay.
          [*Exit* TITANIA *with her train.*
  Obe. Well, go thy way: thou shalt not from
     this grove
Till I torment thee for this injury.
My gentle Puck, come hither. Thou remem-
     b'rest
Since once I sat upon a promontory,
And heard a mermaid on a dolphin's back   150
Uttering such dulcet and harmonious breath
That the rude sea grew civil at her song
And certain stars shot madly from their spheres,
To hear the sea-maid's music.
  Puck.   I remember.
  Obe. That very time I saw, but thou couldst not,
Flying between the cold moon and the earth,
Cupid all arm'd: a certain aim he took
At a fair vestal throned by the west,
And loosed his love-shaft smartly from his bow,
As it should pierce a hundred thousand hearts;160
But I might see young Cupid's fiery shaft
Quench'd in the chaste beams of the watery
     moon,
And the imperial votaress passed on,
In maiden meditation, fancy-free.
Yet mark'd I where the bolt of Cupid fell:
It fell upon a little western flower,
Before milk-white, now purple with love's
     wound,
And maidens call it love-in-idleness.
Fetch me that flower; the herb I shew'd thee
     once:
The juice of it on sleeping eye-lids laid   170
Will make or man or woman madly dote
Upon the next live creature that it sees.
Fetch me this herb; and be thou here again
Ere the leviathan can swim a league.
  Puck. I'll put a girdle round about the earth
In forty minutes.   [*Exit.*
  Obe.   Having once this juice,
I'll watch Titania when she is asleep,
And drop the liquor of it in her eyes.
The next thing then she waking looks upon,

Be it on lion, bear, or wolf, or bull,   *180*
On meddling monkey, or on busy ape,
She shall pursue it with the soul of love:
And ere I take this charm from off her sight,
As I can take it with another herb,
I'll make her render up her page to me.
But who comes here? I am invisible;
And I will overhear their conference.

Enter DEMETRIUS, HELENA *following him.*

Dem. I love thee not, therefore pursue me not.
Where is Lysander and fair Hermia?
The one I'll slay, the other slayeth me.   *190*
Thou told'st me they were stolen unto this wood;
And here am I, and wood within this wood,
Because I cannot meet my Hermia.
Hence, get thee gone, and follow me no more.

Hel. You draw me, you hard-hearted adamant;
But yet you draw not iron, for my heart
Is true as steel: leave you your power to draw,
And I shall have no power to follow you.

Dem. Do I entice you? do I speak you fair?
Or, rather, do I not in plainest truth   *200*
Tell you, I do not, nor I cannot love you?

Hel. And even for that do I love you the more.
I am your spaniel; and, Demetrius,
The more you beat me, I will fawn on you:
Use me but as your spaniel, spurn me, strike me,
Neglect me, lose me; only give me leave,
Unworthy as I am, to follow you.
What worser place can I beg in your love—
And yet a place of high respect with me—
Than to be used as you use your dog?   *210*

Dem. Tempt not too much the hatred of my
     spirit,
For I am sick when I do look on thee.

Hel. And I am sick when I look not on you.

Dem. You do impeach your modesty too much,
To leave the city and commit yourself
Into the hands of one that loves you not;
To trust the opportunity of night
And the ill counsel of a desert place
With the rich worth of your virginity.

Hel. Your virtue is my privilege: for that   *220*
It is not night when I do see your face,
Therefore I think I am not in the night;
Nor doth this wood lack worlds of company,
For you in my respect are all the world:
Then how can it be said I am alone,
When all the world is here to look on me?

Dem. I'll run from thee and hide me in the
     brakes,
And leave thee to the mercy of wild beasts.

Hel. The wildest hath not such a heart as you.
Run when you will, the story shall be changed:
Apollo flies, and Daphne holds the chase;   *231*

The dove pursues the griffin; the mild hind
Makes speed to catch the tiger; bootless speed,
When cowardice pursues and valour flies.

Dem. I will not stay thy questions; let me go:
Or, if thou follow me, do not believe
But I shall do thee mischief in the wood.

Hel. Ay, in the temple, in the town, the field,
You do me mischief. Fie, Demetrius!
Your wrongs do set a scandal on my sex: *240*
We cannot fight for love, as men may do;
We should be woo'd and were not made to woo.
                              [*Exit* DEMETRIUS.

I'll follow thee and make a heaven of hell,
To die upon the hand I love so well.   [*Exit.*

Obe. Fare thee well, nymph: ere he do leave
     this grove,
Thou shalt fly him and he shall seek thy love.

Re-enter PUCK.

Hast thou the flower there? Welcome, wanderer.

Puck. Ay, there it is.

Obe.   I pray thee, give it me.
I know a bank where the wild thyme blows,
Where oxlips and the nodding violet grows,   *250*
Quite over-canopied with luscious woodbine,
With sweet musk-roses and with eglantine:
There sleeps Titania sometime of the night,
Lull'd in these flowers with dances and delight;
And there the snake throws her enamell'd skin,
Weed wide enough to wrap a fairy in:
And with the juice of this I'll streak her eyes,
And make her full of hateful fantasies.
Take thou some of it, and seek through this
     grove:
A sweet Athenian lady is in love   *260*
With a disdainful youth: anoint his eyes;
But do it when the next thing he espies
May be the lady; thou shalt know the man
By the Athenian garments he hath on.
Effect it with some care that he may prove
More fond on her than she upon her love:
And look thou meet me ere the first cock crow.

Puck. Fear not, my lord, your servant shall do
so.   [*Exeunt.*

SCENE II. *Another part of the wood*
Enter TITANIA, *with her train.*

Tita. Come, now a roundel and a fairy song;
Then, for the third part of a minute, hence;
Some to kill cankers in the musk-rose buds,
Some war with rere-mice for their leathern
     wings,
To make my small elves coats, and some keep
     back
The clamorous owl that nightly hoots and won-
     ders

At our quaint spirits. Sing me now asleep;
Then to your offices and let me rest.

The FAIRIES *sing.*

1st Fai. You spotted snakes with double tongue,
          Thorny hedgehogs, be not seen;   *10*
        Newts and blind-worms, do no wrong,
          Come not near our fairy queen.
Chorus. Philomel, with melody
          Sing in our sweet lullaby;
        Lulla, lulla, lullaby, lulla, lulla, lullaby:
          Never harm,
          Nor spell nor charm,
          Come our lovely lady nigh;
        So, good night, with lullaby.

1st Fai. Weaving spiders, come not here;   *20*
          Hence, you long-legg'd spinners,
            hence!
        Beetles black, approach not near;
          Worm nor snail, do no offence.
Chorus. Philomel, with melody, &c.

2nd Fai. Hence, away! now all is well:
          One aloof stand sentinel.
            [*Exeunt* FAIRIES. TITANIA *sleeps.*

Enter OBERON, *and squeezes the flower on*
        TITANIA'S *eyelids.*

Obe. What thou seest when thou dost wake,
        Do it for thy true-love take,
        Love and languish for his sake:
        Be it ounce, or cat, or bear,   *30*
        Pard, or boar with bristled hair,
        In thy eye that shall appear
        When thou wakest, it is thy dear:
        Wake when some vile thing is near. [*Exit.*

Enter LYSANDER *and* HERMIA.

Lys. Fair love, you faint with wandering in the
        wood;
    And to speak troth, I have forgot our way:
We'll rest us, Hermia, if you think it good,
    And tarry for the comfort of the day.
Her. Be it so, Lysander: find you out a bed;
For I upon this bank will rest my head.   *40*
Lys. One turf shall serve as pillow for us both;
One heart, one bed, two bosoms, and one troth.
Her. Nay, good Lysander; for my sake, my
        dear,
Lie further off yet, do not lie so near.
Lys. O, take the sense, sweet, of my innocence!
Love takes the meaning in love's conference.
I mean, that my heart unto yours is knit
So that but one heart we can make of it;
Two bosoms interchained with an oath;

So then two bosoms and a single troth.   *50*
Then by your side no bed-room me deny;
For lying so, Hermia, I do not lie.
    Her. Lysander riddles very prettily:
Now much beshrew my manners and my pride,
If Hermia meant to say Lysander lied.
But, gentle friend, for love and courtesy
Lie further off; in human modesty,
Such separation as may well be said
Becomes a virtuous bachelor and a maid,
So far be distant; and, good night, sweet friend:
Thy love ne'er alter till thy sweet life end!   *61*
    Lys. Amen, amen, to that fair prayer, say I;
And then end life when I end loyalty!
Here is my bed: sleep give thee all his rest!
    Her. With half that wish the wisher's eyes be
        press'd!   [*They sleep.*

Enter PUCK.

Puck. Through the forest have I gone,
        But Athenian found I none,
        On whose eyes I might approve
        This flower's force in stirring love.
        Night and silence.—Who is here?   *70*
        Weeds of Athens he doth wear:
        This is he, my master said,
        Despised the Athenian maid;
        And here the maiden, sleeping sound,
        On the dank and dirty ground.
        Pretty soul! she durst not lie
        Near this lack-love, this kill-courtesy.
        Churl, upon thy eyes I throw
        All the power this charm doth owe.
        When thou wakest, let love forbid   *80*
        Sleep his seat on thy eyelid:
        So awake when I am gone;
        For I must now to Oberon.   [*Exit.*

Enter DEMETRIUS *and* HELENA, *running.*

Hel. Stay, though thou kill me, sweet Deme-
        trius.
Dem. I charge thee, hence, and do not haunt me
        thus.
Hel. O, wilt thou darkling leave me? do not so.
Dem. Stay, on thy peril: I alone will go.
                        [*Exit.*
    Hel. O, I am out of breath in this fond chase!
The more my prayer, the lesser is my grace.
Happy is Hermia, wheresoe'er she lies;   *90*
For she hath blessed and attractive eyes.
How came her eyes so bright? Not with salt
        tears:
If so, my eyes are oftener wash'd than hers.
No, no, I am as ugly as a bear;
For beasts that meet me run away for fear:
Therefore no marvel though Demetrius

Do, as a monster, fly my presence thus.
What wicked and dissembling glass of mine
Made me compare with Hermia's sphery eyne?
But who is here? Lysander! on the ground!   *100*
Dead? or asleep? I see no blood, no wound.
Lysander, if you live, good sir, awake.
  Lys. [*Awaking*] And run through fire I will
       for thy sweet sake.
Transparent Helena! Nature shows art,
That through thy bosom makes me see thy heart.
Where is Demetrius? O, how fit a word
Is that vile name to perish on my sword!
  Hel. Do not say so, Lysander; say not so.
What though he love your Hermia? Lord, what
       though?
Yet Hermia still loves you: then be content.   *110*
  Lys. Content with Hermia! No; I do repent
The tedious minutes I with her have spent.
Not Hermia but Helena I love:
Who will not change a raven for a dove?
The will of man is by his reason sway'd;
And reason says you are the worthier maid.
Things growing are not ripe until their season:
So I, being young, till now ripe not to reason;
And touching now the point of human skill,
Reason becomes the marshal to my will   *120*
And leads me to your eyes, where I o'erlook
Love's stories written in love's richest book.
  Hel. Wherefore was I to this keen mockery
       born?
When at your hands did I deserve this scorn?
Is't not enough, is't not enough, young man,
That I did never, no, nor never can,
Deserve a sweet look from Demetrius' eye,
But you must flout my insufficiency?
Good troth, you do me wrong, good sooth, you
       do,
In such disdainful manner me to woo.   *130*
But fare you well: perforce I must confess
I thought you lord of more true gentleness.
O, that a lady, of one man refused,
Should of another therefore be abused!   [*Exit.*
  Lys. She sees not Hermia. Hermia, sleep thou
       there:
And never mayst thou come Lysander near!
For as a surfeit of the sweetest things
The deepest loathing to the stomach brings,
Or as the heresies that men do leave
Are hated most of those they did deceive,   *140*
So thou, my surfeit and my heresy,
Of all be hated, but the most of me!
And, all my powers, address your love and might
To honour Helen and to be her knight!   [*Exit.*
  Her. [*Awaking*] Help me, Lysander, help me!
       do thy best
To pluck this crawling serpent from my breast!

Ay me, for pity! what a dream was here!
Lysander, look how I do quake with fear:
Methought a serpent eat my heart away,
And you sat smiling at his cruel prey.   *150*
Lysander! what, removed? Lysander! lord!
What, out of hearing? gone? no sound, no word?
Alack, where are you? speak, an if you hear;
Speak, of all loves! I swoon almost with fear.
No? then I well perceive you are not nigh:
Either death or you I'll find immediately.   [*Exit.*

ACT III

SCENE I. *The wood:* TITANIA *lying asleep*

Enter QUINCE, SNUG, BOTTOM, FLUTE, SNOUT,
and STARVELING.

  Bot. Are we all met?
  Quin. Pat, pat; and here's a marvellous convenient place for our rehearsal. This green plot shall
be our stage, this hawthorn-brake our tiring-
house; and we will do it in action as we will do it
before the Duke.
  Bot. Peter Quince,—
  Quin. What sayest thou, bully Bottom?
  Bot. There are things in this comedy of Pyramus and Thisby that will never please. First,
Pyramus must draw a sword to kill himself,
which the ladies cannot abide. How answer you
that?
  Snout. By'r lakin, a parlous fear.
  Star. I believe we must leave the killing out,
when all is done.
  Bot. Not a whit: I have a device to make all
well. Write me a prologue; and let the prologue
seem to say, we will do no harm with our swords
and that Pyramus is not killed indeed; and, for
the more better assurance, tell them that I Pyramus am not Pyramus, but Bottom the weaver:
this will put them out of fear.
  Quin. Well, we will have such a prologue; and
it shall be written in eight and six.
  Bot. No, make it two more; let it be written in
eight and eight.
  Snout. Will not the ladies be afeard of the lion?
  Star. I fear it, I promise you.   *29*
  Bot. Masters, you ought to consider with yourselves: to bring in—God shield us!—a lion among
ladies, is a most dreadful thing; for there is not a
more fearful wild-fowl than your lion living; and
we ought to look to 't.
  Snout. Therefore another prologue must tell he
is not a lion.
  Bot. Nay, you must name his name, and half his
face must be seen through the lion's neck; and he
himself must speak through, saying thus, or to
the same defect, "Ladies," or "Fair ladies, I

would wish you," or "I would request you," or "I would entreat you, not to fear, not to tremble: my life for yours. If you think I come hither as a lion, it were a pity of my life: no, I am no such thing; I am a man as other men are"; and there indeed let him name his name, and tell them plainly he is Snug the joiner.

Quin. Well, it shall be so. But there is two hard things; that is, to bring the moonlight into a chamber; for, you know, Pyramus and Thisby meet by moonlight.   *51*

Snout. Doth the moon shine that night we play our play?

Bot. A calendar, a calendar! look in the almanac; find out moonshine, find out moonshine.

Quin. Yes, it doth shine that night.

Bot. Why, then may you leave a casement of the great chamber window, where we play, open, and the moon may shine in at the casement.

Quin. Ay; or else one must come in with a bush of thorns and a lanthorn, and say he comes to disfigure, or to present, the person of Moonshine. Then, there is another thing: we must have a wall in the great chamber; for Pyramus and Thisby, says the story, did talk through the chink of a wall.

Snout. You can never bring in a wall. What say you, Bottom?

Bot. Some man or other must present Wall: and let him have some plaster, or some loam, or some rough-cast about him, to signify wall; and let him hold his fingers thus, and through that cranny shall Pyramus and Thisby whisper.

Quin. If that may be, then all is well. Come, sit down, every mother's son, and rehearse your parts. Pyramus, you begin: when you have spoken your speech, enter into that brake: and so every one according to his cue.

Enter PUCK *behind.*

Puck. What hempen home-spuns have we swaggering here,
So near the cradle of the fairy queen?   *80*
What, a play toward! I'll be an auditor;
An actor too perhaps, if I see cause.

Quin. Speak, Pyramus. Thisby, stand forth.

Bot. "Thisby, the flowers of odious savours sweet"—

Quin. Odours, odours.

Bot. —"odours savours sweet:
So hath thy breath, my dearest Thisby dear.
But hark, a voice! stay thou but here awhile,
And by and by I will to thee appear."   [*Exit.*

Puck. A stranger Pyramus than e'er played here.   [*Exit.* *90*

Flu. Must I speak now?

Quin. Ay, marry, must you; for you must understand he goes but to see a noise that he heard, and is to come again.

Flu. "Most radiant Pyramus, most lily-white of hue,
   Of colour like the red rose on triumphant brier,
Most brisky juvenal and eke most lovely Jew,
   As true as truest horse that yet would never tire,
I'll meet thee, Pyramus, at Ninny's tomb."   *99*

Quin. "Ninus' tomb," man: why, you must not speak that yet; that you answer to Pyramus: you speak all your part at once, cues and all. Pyramus enter: your cue is past; it is, "never tire."

Flu. O,—"As true as truest horse, that yet would never tire."

Re-enter PUCK, *and* BOTTOM *with an ass's head.*

Bot. "If I were fair, Thisby, I were only thine."

Quin. O monstrous! O strange! we are haunted. Pray, masters! fly, masters! Help!
            [*Exeunt* QUINCE, SNUG, FLUTE, SNOUT, *and*
                                   STARVELING.

Puck. I'll follow you, I'll lead you about a round,
   Through bog, through bush, through brake, through brier: *110*
Sometime a horse I'll be, sometime a hound,
   A hog, a headless bear, sometime a fire;
And neigh, and bark, and grunt, and roar, and burn,
Like horse, hound, hog, bear, fire, at every turn.
                                          [*Exit.*

Bot. Why do they run away? this is a knavery of them to make me afeard.

Re-enter SNOUT.

Snout. O Bottom, thou art changed! what do I see on thee?

Bot. What do you see? you see an ass-head of your own, do you?   [*Exit* SNOUT. *120*

Re-enter QUINCE.

Quin. Bless thee, Bottom! bless thee! thou art translated.   [*Exit.*

Bot. I see their knavery: this is to make an ass of me; to fright me, if they could. But I will not stir from this place, do what they can: I will walk up and down here, and I will sing, that they shall hear I am not afraid. [*Sings.*]
   "The ousel cock so black of hue,
      With orange-tawny bill,
   The throstle with his note so true,   *130*
      The wren with little quill"—

Tita. [*Awaking*] What angel wakes me from
   my flowery bed?
   Bot. [*Sings*]
      "The finch, the sparrow and the lark,
         The plain-song cuckoo gray,
      Whose note full many a man doth mark,
         And dares not answer nay"—
for, indeed, who would set his wit to so foolish a
bird? who would give a bird the lie, though he
cry "cuckoo" never so?
   Tita. I pray thee, gentle mortal, sing again:
Mine ear is much enamour'd of thy note;   *141*
So is mine eye enthralled to thy shape;
And thy fair virtue's force perforce doth move
   me
On the first view to say, to swear, I love thee.
   Bot. Methinks, mistress, you should have little
reason for that: and yet, to say the truth, reason
and love keep little company together now-a-
days; the more the pity that some honest neigh-
bours will not make them friends. Nay, I can
gleek upon occasion.   *150*
   Tita. Thou art as wise as thou art beautiful.
   Bot. Not so, neither: but if I had wit enough to
get out of this wood, I have enough to serve mine
own turn.
   Tita. Out of this wood do not desire to go:
Thou shalt remain here, whether thou wilt or no.
I am a spirit of no common rate:
The summer still doth tend upon my state;
And I do love thee: therefore, go with me;
I'll give thee fairies to attend on thee,   *160*
And they shall fetch thee jewels from the deep,
And sing while thou on pressed flowers dost
   sleep:
And I will purge thy mortal grossness so
That thou shalt like an airy spirit go.
Peaseblossom! Cobweb! Moth! and Mustard-
   seed!

   Enter PEASEBLOSSOM, COBWEB, MOTH, *and*
            MUSTARDSEED.

Peas. Ready.
Cob.   And I.
Moth.   And I.
Mus.   And I.
All.   Where shall we go?
   Tita. Be kind and courteous to this gentleman;
Hop in his walks and gambol in his eyes;
Feed him with apricocks and dewberries,
With purple grapes, green figs, and mulberries;
The honey-bags steal from the humble-bees,   *171*
And for night-tapers crop their waxen thighs
And light them at the fiery glow-worm's eyes,
To have my love to bed and to arise;
And pluck the wings from painted butterflies

To fan the moonbeams from his sleeping eyes:
Nod to him, elves, and do him courtesies.
   Peas. Hail, mortal!
   Cob. Hail!
   Moth. Hail!   *180*
   Mus. Hail!
   Bot. I cry your worships mercy, heartily: I be-
seech your worship's name.
   Cob. Cobweb.
   Bot. I shall desire you of more acquaintance,
good Master Cobweb: if I cut my finger, I shall
make bold with you. Your name, honest gentle-
man?
   Peas. Peaseblossom.
   Bot. I pray you, commend me to Mistress
Squash, your mother, and to Master Peascod,
your father. Good Master Peaseblossom, I shall
desire you of more acquaintance too. Your name,
I beseech you, sir?
   Mus. Mustardseed.
   Bot. Good Master Mustardseed, I know your
patience well: that same cowardly, giant-like ox-
beef hath devoured many a gentleman of your
house: I promise you your kindred hath made
my eyes water ere now. I desire your more ac-
quaintance, good Master Mustardseed.   *201*
   Tita. Come, wait upon him; lead him to my
      bower.
   The moon methinks looks with a watery
      eye;
And when she weeps, weeps every little flower,
   Lamenting some enforced chastity.
Tie up my love's tongue, bring him silently.
                                          [*Exeunt.*

SCENE II. *Another part of the wood*
         Enter OBERON.

Obe. I wonder if Titania be awaked;
Then, what it was that next came in her eye,
Which she must dote on in extremity.

         Enter PUCK.

Here comes my messenger.
                           How now, mad spirit!
What night-rule now about this haunted grove?
   Puck. My mistress with a monster is in love.
Near to her close and consecrated bower,
While she was in her dull and sleeping hour,
A crew of patches, rude mechanicals,
That work for bread upon Athenian stalls,   *10*
Were met together to rehearse a play
Intended for great Theseus' nuptial-day.
The shallowest thick-skin of that barren sort,
Who Pyramus presented, in their sport
Forsook his scene and enter'd in a brake:
When I did him at this advantage take,

An ass's nole I fixed on his head:
Anon his Thisbe must be answered,
And forth my mimic comes. When they him spy,
As wild geese that the creeping fowler eye,   20
Or russet-pated choughs, many in sort,
Rising and cawing at the gun's report,
Sever themselves and madly sweep the sky,
So, at his sight, away his fellows fly;
And, at our stamp, here o'er and o'er one falls;
He murder cries and help from Athens calls.
Their sense thus weak, lost with their fears thus
    strong,
Made senseless things begin to do them wrong;
For briers and thorns at their apparel snatch;
Some sleeves, some hats, from yielders all things
    catch.   30
I led them on in this distracted fear,
And left sweet Pyramus translated there:
When in that moment, so it came to pass,
Titania waked and straightway loved an ass.
  Obe. This falls out better than I could devise.
But hast thou yet latch'd the Athenian's eyes
With the love-juice, as I did bid thee do?
  Puck. I took him sleeping—that is finish'd too—
And the Athenian woman by his side;
That, when he waked, of force she must be   40
    eyed.

    Enter HERMIA *and* DEMETRIUS.

  Obe. Stand close: this is the same Athenian.
  Puck. This is the woman, but not this the man.
  Dem. O, why rebuke you him that loves you so?
Lay breath so bitter on your bitter foe.
  Her. Now I but chide; but I should use thee
    worse,
For thou, I fear, hast given me cause to curse.
If thou hast slain Lysander in his sleep,
Being o'er shoes in blood, plunge in the deep,
And kill me too.
The sun was not so true unto the day   50
As he to me: would he have stolen away
From sleeping Hermia? I'll believe as soon
This whole earth may be bored and that the
    moon
May through the centre creep and so displease
Her brother's noontide with the Antipodes.
It cannot be but thou hast murder'd him;
So should a murderer look, so dead, so grim.
  Dem. So should the murder'd look, and so
    should I,
Pierced through the heart with your stern cruelty:
Yet you, the murderer, look as bright, as clear,
As yonder Venus in her glimmering sphere.   61
  Her. What's this to my Lysander? where is he?
Ah, good Demetrius, wilt thou give him me?
  Dem. I had rather give his carcass to my hounds.

  Her. Out, dog! out, cur! thou drivest me past
    the bounds
Of maiden's patience. Hast thou slain him, then?
Henceforth be never number'd among men!
O, once tell true, tell true, even for my sake!
Durst thou have look'd upon him being awake,
And hast thou kill'd him sleeping? O brave
    touch!   70
Could not a worm, an adder, do so much?
An adder did it; for with doubler tongue
Than thine, thou serpent, never adder stung.
  Dem. You spend your passion on a misprised
    mood:
I am not guilty of Lysander's blood;
Nor is he dead, for aught that I can tell.
  Her. I pray thee, tell me than that he is well.
  Dem. An if I could, what should I get therefore?
  Her. A privilege never to see me more.
And from thy hated presence part I so: 80
See me no more, whether he be dead or no. [*Exit.*
  Dem. There is no following her in this fierce
    vein:
Here therefore for a while I will remain.
So sorrow's heaviness doth heavier grow
For debt that bankrupt sleep doth sorrow owe;
Which now in some slight measure it will pay,
If for his tender here I make some stay.
    Lies down and sleeps.
  Obe. What hast thou done? thou hast mistaken
    quite
And laid the love-juice on some true-love's sight:
Of thy misprision must perforce ensue   90
Some true love turn'd and not a false turn'd true.
  Puck. Then fate o'er-rules, that, one man hold-
    ing troth,
A million fail, confounding oath on oath.
  Obe. About the wood go swifter than the wind,
And Helena of Athens look thou find:
All fancy-sick she is and pale of cheer,
With sighs of love, that costs the fresh blood
    dear:
By some illusion see thou bring her here:
I'll charm his eyes against she do appear.
  Puck. I go, I go; look how I go,   100
Swifter than arrow from the Tartar's bow. [*Exit.*
  Obe. Flower of this purple dye,
    Hit with Cupid's archery,
    Sink in apple of his eye.
    When his love he doth espy,
    Let her shine as gloriously
    As the Venus of the sky.
    When thou wakest, if she **be by**,
    Beg of her for remedy.

    Re-enter PUCK.

  Puck. Captain of our fairy band,   110

Helena is here at hand;
And the youth, mistook by me,
Pleading for a lover's fee.
Shall we their fond pageant see?
Lord, what fools these mortals be!

Obe. Stand aside: the noise they make
Will cause Demetrius to awake.

Puck. Then will two at once woo one;
That must needs be sport alone;
And those things do best please me　　120
That befall preposterously.

Enter LYSANDER *and* HELENA.

Lys. Why should you think that I should woo in
　　scorn?
Scorn and derision never come in tears:
Look, when I vow, I weep; and vows so born,
In their nativity all truth appears.
How can these things in me seem scorn to you,
Bearing the badge of faith, to prove them true?

Hel. You do advance your cunning more and
　　more.
When truth kills truth, O devilish-holy fray!
These vows are Hermia's: will you give her
　　o'er?
Weigh oath with oath, and you will nothing
　　weigh:　　131
Your vows to her and me, put in two scales,
Will even weigh, and both as light as tales.

Lys. I had no judgement when to her I swore.

Hel. Nor none, in my mind, now you give her
　　o'er.

Lys. Demetrius loves her, and he loves not you.

Dem. [*Awaking*] O Helen, goddess, nymph,
　　perfect, divine!
To what, my love, shall I compare thine eyne?
Crystal is muddy. O, how ripe in show
Thy lips, those kissing cherries, tempting grow!
That pure congealed white, high Taurus' snow,
Fann'd with the eastern wind, turns to a crow
When thou hold'st up thy hand: O, let me kiss
This princess of pure white, this seal of bliss!

Hel. O spite! O hell! I see you all are bent
To set against me for your merriment:
If you were civil and knew courtesy,
You would not do me thus much injury.
Can you not hate me, as I know you do,
But you must join in souls to mock me too?　　150
If you were men, as men you are in show,
You would not use a gentle lady so;
To vow, and swear, and superpraise my parts,
When I am sure you hate me with your hearts.
You both are rivals, and love Hermia;
And now both rivals, to mock Helena:
A trim exploit, a manly enterprise,
To conjure tears up in a poor maid's eyes

With your derision! none of noble sort
Would so offend a virgin and extort　　160
A poor soul's patience, all to make you sport.

Lys. You are unkind, Demetrius; be not so;
For you love Hermia; this you know I know:
And here, with all good will, with all my heart,
In Hermia's love I yield you up my part;
And yours of Helena to me bequeath,
Whom I do love and will do till my death.

Hel. Never did mockers waste more idle breath.

Dem. Lysander, keep thy Hermia; I will none:
If e'er I loved her, all that love is gone.　　170
My heart to her but as guest-wise sojourn'd,
And now to Helen is it home return'd,
There to remain.

Lys.　　　　Helen, it is not so.

Dem. Disparage not the faith thou dost not
　　know,
Lest, to thy peril, thou aby it dear.
Look, where thy love comes; yonder is thy dear.

Re-enter HERMIA.

Her. Dark night, that from the eye his function
　　takes,
The ear more quick of apprehension makes;
Wherein it doth impair the seeing sense,
It pays the hearing double recompense.　　180
Thou art not by mine eye, Lysander, found;
Mine ear, I thank it, brought me to thy sound.
But why unkindly didst thou leave me so?

Lys. Why should he stay, whom love doth press
　　to go?

Her. What love could press Lysander from my
　　side?

Lys. Lysander's love, that would not let him
　　bide,
Fair Helena, who more engilds the night
Than all yon fiery oes and eyes of light.
Why seek'st thou me? could not this make thee
　　know,
The hate I bear thee made me leave thee so?　　190

Her. You speak not as you think: it cannot be.

Hel. Lo, she is one of this confederacy!
Now I perceive they have conjoin'd all three
To fashion this false sport, in spite of me.
Injurious Hermia! most ungrateful maid!
Have you conspired, have you with these con-
　　trived
To bait me with this foul derision?
Is all the counsel that we two have shared,
The sisters' vows, the hours that we have spent,
When we have chid the hasty-footed time　　200
For parting us—O, is it all forgot?
All school-days' friendship, childhood innocence?
We, Hermia, like two artificial gods,
Have with our needles created both one flower,

Both on one sampler, sitting on one cushion,
Both warbling of one song, both in one key,
As if our hands, our sides, voices and minds,
Had been incorporate. So we grew together,
Like to a double cherry, seeming parted,
But yet an union in partition;   *210*
Two lovely berries moulded on one stem;
So, with two seeming bodies, but one heart;
Two of the first, like coats in heraldry,
Due but to one and crowned with one crest.
And will you rend our ancient love asunder,
To join with men in scorning your poor friend?
It is not friendly, 'tis not maidenly:
Our sex, as well as I, may chide you for it,
Though I alone do feel the injury.
   Her. I am amazed at your passionate words.
I scorn you not: it seems that you scorn me.   *221*
   Hel. Have you not set Lysander, as in scorn,
To follow me and praise my eyes and face?
And made your other love, Demetrius,
Who even but now did spurn me with his foot,
To call me goddess, nymph, divine and rare,
Precious, celestial? Wherefore speaks he this
To her he hates? and wherefore doth Lysander
Deny your love, so rich within his soul,
And tender me, forsooth, affection,   *230*
But by your setting on, by your consent?
What though I be not so in grace as you,
So hung upon with love, so fortunate,
But miserable most, to love unloved?
This you should pity rather than despise.
   Her. I understand not what you mean by this.
   Hel. Ay, do, persever, counterfeit sad looks,
Make mouths upon me when I turn my back;
Wink each at other; hold the sweet jest up:
This sport, well carried, shall be chronicled.   *240*
If you have any pity, grace, or manners,
You would not make me such an argument.
But fare ye well: 'tis partly my own fault;
Which death or absence soon shall remedy.
   Lys. Stay, gentle Helena; hear my excuse:
My love, my life, my soul, fair Helena!
   Hel. O excellent!
   Her.   Sweet, do not scorn her so.
   Dem. If she cannot entreat, I can compel.
   Lys. Thou canst compel no more than she entreat:
Thy threats have no more strength than her weak
     prayers.   *250*
Helen, I love thee, by my life, I do:
I swear by that which I will lose for thee,
To prove him false that says I love thee not.
   Dem. I say I love thee more than he can do.
   Lys. If thou say so, withdraw, and prove it too.
   Dem. Quick, come!
   Her.   Lysander, whereto tends all this?

   Lys. Away, you Ethiope!
   Dem.   No, no; he'll but
Seem to break loose; take on as you would
     follow,
But yet come not: you are a tame man, go!
   Lys. Hang off, thou cat, thou burr! vile thing,
     let loose,   *260*
Or I will shake thee from me like a serpent!
   Her. Why are you grown so rude? what change
     is this?
Sweet love—
   Lys.   Thy love! out, tawny Tartar, out!
Out, loathed medicine! hated potion, hence!
   Her. Do you not jest?
   Hel.   Yes, sooth; and so do you.
   Lys. Demetrius, I will keep my word with thee.
   Dem. I would I had your bond, for I perceive
A weak bond holds you: I'll not trust your word.
   Lys. What, should I hurt her, strike her, kill
     her dead?
Although I hate her, I'll not harm her so.   *270*
   Her. What, can you do me greater harm than
     hate?
Hate me! wherefore? O me! what news, my
     love!
Am not I Hermia? are not you Lysander?
I am as fair now as I was erewhile.
Since night you loved me; yet since night you
     left me:
Why, then you left me—O, the gods forbid!—
In earnest, shall I say?
   Lys.   Ay, by my life;
And never did desire to see thee more.
Therefore be out of hope, of question, of doubt;
Be certain, nothing truer; 'tis no jest   *280*
That I do hate thee and love Helena.
   Her. O me! you juggler! you canker-blossom!
You thief of love! what, have you come by night
And stolen my love's heart from him?
   Hel.   Fine, i'faith!
Have you no modesty, no maiden shame,
No touch of bashfulness? What, will you tear
Impatient answers from my gentle tongue?
Fie, fie! you counterfeit, you puppet, you!
   Her. "Puppet"? why so? ay, that way goes the
     game.
Now I perceive that she hath made compare   *290*
Between our statures; she hath urged her height;
And with her personage, her tall personage,
Her height, forsooth, she hath prevail'd with
     him.
And are you grown so high in his esteem,
Because I am so dwarfish and so low?
How low am I, thou painted maypole? speak;
How low am I? I am not yet so low
But that my nails can reach unto thine eyes.

Hel. I pray you, though you mock me, gentle-
men,
Let her not hurt me: I was never curst;   300
I have no gift at all in shrewishness;
I am a right maid for my cowardice:
Let her not strike me. You perhaps may think,
Because she is something lower than myself,
That I can match her.
      Her.   "Lower"! hark, again.
Hel. Good Hermia, do not be so bitter with me.
I evermore did love you, Hermia,
Did ever keep your counsels, never wrong'd you;
Save that, in love unto Demetrius,
I told him of your stealth unto this wood.   310
He follow'd you; for love I follow'd him;
But he hath chid me hence and threaten'd me
To strike me, spurn me, nay, to kill me too:
And now, so you will let me quiet go,
To Athens will I bear my folly back
And follow you no further: let me go:
You see how simple and how fond I am.
      Her. Why, get you gone: who is't that hinders
you?
Hel. A foolish heart, that I leave here behind.
Her. What, with Lysander?
Hel.   With Demetrius.   320
Lys. Be not afraid; she shall not harm thee,
Helena.
Dem. No, sir, she shall not, though you take her
part.
Hel. O, when she's angry, she is keen and
shrewd!
She was a vixen when she went to school;
And though she be but little, she is fierce.
      Her. "Little" again! nothing but "low" and
"little"!
Why will you suffer her to flout me thus?
Let me come to her.
      Lys.   Get you gone, you dwarf;
You minimus, of hindering knot-grass made;
You bead, you acorn.
      Dem.   You are too officious   330
In her behalf that scorns your services.
Let her alone: speak not of Helena;
Take not her part; for, if thou dost intend
Never so little show of love to her,
Thou shalt aby it.
      Lys.   Now she holds me not;
Now follow, if thou darest, to try whose right,
Of thine or mine, is most in Helena.
Dem. Follow! nay, I'll go with thee, cheek
      by jole.   [*Exeunt* LYSANDER *and* DEMETRIUS.
Her. You, mistress, all this coil is 'long of you:
Nay, go not back.
      Hel.   I will not trust you, I,   340
Nor longer stay in your curst company.

Your hands than mine are quicker for a fray,
My legs are longer though, to run away.   [*Exit.*
      Her. I am amazed, and know not what to say.
                                                    [*Exit.*
      Obe. This is thy negligence: still thou mistak-
est,
Or else committ'st thy knaveries wilfully.
      Puck. Believe me, king of shadows, I mistook.
Did not you tell me I should know the man
By the Athenian garments he had on?
And so far blameless proves my enterprise,   350
That I have 'nointed an Athenian's eyes;
And so far am I glad it so did sort
As this their jangling I esteem a sport.
      Obe. Thou see'st these lovers seek a place to
      fight:
Hie therefore, Robin, overcast the night;
The starry welkin cover thou anon
With drooping fog as black as Acheron,
And lead these testy rivals so astray
As one come not within another's way.
Like to Lysander sometime frame thy tongue,
Then stir Demetrius up with bitter wrong;   361
And sometime rail thou like Demetrius;
And from each other look thou lead them thus,
Till o'er their brows death-counterfeiting sleep
With leaden legs and batty wings doth creep:
Then crush this herb into Lysander's eye;
Whose liquor hath this virtuous property,
To take from thence all error with his might,
And make his eyeballs roll with wonted sight.
When they next wake, all this derision   370
Shall seem a dream and fruitless vision,
And back to Athens shall the lovers wend,
With league whose date till death shall never
      end.
Whiles I in this affair do thee employ,
I'll to my queen and beg her Indian boy;
And then I will her charmed eye release
From monster's view, and all things shall be
      peace.
      Puck. My fairy lord, this must be done with
      haste,
For night's swift dragons cut the clouds full fast,
And yonder shines Aurora's harbinger;   380
At whose approach, ghosts, wandering here and
      there,
Troop home to churchyards: damned spirits all,
That in crossways and floods have burial,
Already to their wormy beds are gone;
For fear lest day should look their shames upon,
They wilfully themselves exile from light
And must for aye consort with black-brow'd
      night.
      Obe. But we are spirits of another sort:
I with the morning's love have oft made sport,

And, like a forester, the groves may tread,   *390*
Even till the eastern gate, all fiery-red,
Opening on Neptune with fair blessed beams,
Turns into yellow gold his salt green streams.
But, notwithstanding, haste; make no delay:
We may effect this business yet ere day.   [*Exit.*
  Puck. Up and down, up and down,
     I will lead them up and down:
     I am fear'd in field and town:
     Goblin, lead them up and down.
Here comes one.   *400*

Re-enter LYSANDER.

  Lys. Where art thou, proud Demetrius? speak
    thou now.
  Puck. Here, villain; drawn and ready. Where
    art thou?
  Lys. I will be with thee straight.
  Puck.   Follow me, then,
To plainer ground.
      [*Exit* LYSANDER, *as following the voice.*

Re-enter DEMETRIUS.

  Dem.   Lysander! speak again:
Thou runaway, thou coward, art thou fled?
Speak! In some bush? Where dost thou hide thy
    head?
  Puck. Thou coward, art thou bragging to the
    stars,
Telling the bushes that thou look'st for wars,
And wilt not come? Come, recreant; come, thou
    child;
I'll whip thee with a rod: he is defiled   *410*
That draws a sword on thee.
  Dem.   Yea, art thou there?
  Puck. Follow my voice: we'll try no manhood
    here.   [*Exeunt.*

Re-enter LYSANDER.

  Lys. He goes before me and still dares me on:
When I come where he calls, then he is gone.
The villain is much lighter-heel'd than I:
I follow'd fast, but faster he did fly;
That fallen am I in dark uneven way,
And here will rest me. [*Lies down.*] Come, thou
    gentle day!
For if but once thou show me thy grey light,
I'll find Demetrius and revenge this spite. [*Sleeps.*

Re-enter PUCK *and* DEMETRIUS.

  Puck. Ho, ho, ho! Coward, why comest thou
    not?   *421*
  Dem. Abide, me, if thou darest; for well I wot
Thou runn'st before me, shifting every place,
And darest not stand, nor look me in the face.
Where art thou now?

  Puck.   Come hither: I am here.
  Dem. Nay, then, thou mock'st me. Thou shalt
    buy this dear,
If ever I thy face by daylight see:
Now, go thy way. Faintness constraineth me
To measure out my length on this cold bed.
By day's approach look to be visited.   *430*
    Lies down and sleeps.

Re-enter HELENA.

  Hel. O weary night, O long and tedious night,
    Abate thy hours! Shine comforts from the east,
That I may back to Athens by daylight,
    From these that my poor company detest:
And sleep, that sometimes shuts up sorrow's eye,
Steal me awhile from mine own company.
    Lies down and sleeps.
  Puck. Yet but three? Come one more;
     Two of both kinds makes up four.
     Here she comes, curst and sad:
     Cupid is a knavish lad,   *440*
     Thus to make poor females mad.

Re-enter HERMIA.

  Her. Never so weary, never so in woe,
    Bedabbled with the dew and torn with briers,
I can no further crawl, no further go;
    My legs can keep no pace with my desires.
Here will I rest me till the break of day.
Heavens shield Lysander, if they mean a fray!
    Lies down and sleeps.
  Puck.   On the ground
     Sleep sound:
     I'll apply   *450*
     To your eye,
  Gentle lover, remedy.
    Squeezing the juice on Lysander's eyes.
     When thou wakest,
     Thou takest
     True delight
     In the sight
     Of thy former lady's eye:
     And the country proverb known,
     That every man should take his own,
     In your waking shall be shown: *460*
     Jack shall have Jill;
     Nought shall go ill;
The man shall have his mare again, and all shall
    be well.   [*Exit.*

ACT IV

SCENE I. *The same:* LYSANDER, DEMETRIUS, HEL-
    ENA, *and* HERMIA *lying asleep*

Enter TITANIA *and* BOTTOM; PEASEBLOSSOM, COB-
  WEB, MOTH, MUSTARDSEED, *and other Fairies*
  attending; OBERON *behind unseen.*

Tita. Come, sit thee down upon this flowery
    bed,
While I thy amiable cheeks do coy,
And stick musk-roses in thy sleek smooth
    head,
And kiss thy fair large ears, my gentle
    joy.
Bot. Where's Peaseblossom?
Peas. Ready.
Bot. Scratch my head, Peaseblossom. Where's
Mounsieur Cobweb?
Cob. Ready.
Bot. Mounsieur Cobweb, good mounsieur, get
you your weapons in your hand, and kill me a
red-hipped humble-bee on the top of a thistle;
and, good mounsieur, bring me the honey-bag.
Do not fret yourself too much in the action,
mounsieur; and, good mounsieur, have a care the
honey-bag break not; I would be loath to have
you overflown with a honey-bag, signior. Where's
Mounsieur Mustardseed?
  Mus. Ready.   *19*
Bot. Give me your neaf, Mounsieur Mustard-
seed. Pray you, leave your courtesy, good moun-
sieur.
  Mus. What's your will?
Bot. Nothing, good mounsieur, but to help
Cavalery Cobweb to scratch. I must to the bar-
ber's, mounsieur; for methinks I am marvellous
hairy about the face; and I am such a tender ass,
if my hair do but tickle me, I must scratch.
Tita. What, wilt thou hear some music, my
    sweet love?
Bot. I have a reasonable good ear in music.
Let's have the tongs and the bones.   *31*
Tita. Or say, sweet love, what thou desirest
    to eat.
Bot. Truly, a peck of provender: I could
munch your good dry oats. Methinks I have a
great desire to a bottle of hay: good hay, sweet
hay, hath no fellow.
Tita. I have a venturous fairy that shall seek
The squirrel's hoard, and fetch thee new nuts.
Bot. I had rather have a handful or two of dried
peas. But, I pray you, let none of your people
stir me: I have an exposition of sleep come upon
me.   *42*
Tita. Sleep thou, and I will wind thee in my
    arms.
Fairies, be gone, and be all ways away.
                     [*Exeunt fairies.*
So doth the woodbine the sweet honeysuckle
Gently entwist; the female ivy so
Enrings the barky fingers of the elm.
O, how I love thee! how I dote on thee!
They sleep.

Enter Puck

Obe. [*Advancing*] Welcome, good Robin.
    See'st thou this sweet sight?
Her dotage now I do begin to pity:
For, meeting her of late behind the wood,
Seeking sweet favours for this hateful fool,
I did upbraid her and fall out with her;
For she his hairy temples then had rounded
With coronet of fresh and fragrant flowers;
And that same dew, which sometime on the buds
Was wont to swell like round and orient pearls,
Stood now within the pretty flowerets' eyes
Like tears that did their own disgrace bewail.
When I had at my pleasure taunted her   *60*
And she in mild terms begg'd my patience,
I then did ask her of her changeling child;
Which straight she gave me, and her fairy sent
To bear him to my bower in fairy land.
And now I have the boy, I will undo
This hateful imperfection of her eyes:
And, gentle Puck, take this transformed scalp
From off the head of this Athenian swain;
That, he awaking when the other do,
May all to Athens back again repair   *70*
And think no more of this night's accidents
But as the fierce vexation of a dream.
But first I will release the fairy queen. [*Touching
    her eyes.*]
       Be as thou wast wont to be;
       See as thou wast wont to see:
       Dian's bud o'er Cupid's flower
       Hath such force and blessed power.
Now, my Titania; wake you, my sweet queen.
  Tita. My Oberon! what visions have I seen!
Methought I was enamour'd of an ass.   *80*
  Obe. There lies your love.
  Tita.   How came these things to pass?
O, how mine eyes do loathe his visage now!
  Obe. Silence awhile. Robin, take off this head.
Titania, music call; and strike more dead
Than common sleep of all these five the sense.
  Tita. Music, ho! music, such as charmeth sleep!
Music, still.
  Puck. Now, when thou wakest, with thine own
    fool's eyes peep.
  Obe. Sound, music! Come, my queen, take
    hands with me,   *89*
And rock the ground whereon these sleepers be.
Now thou and I are new in amity
And will to-morrow midnight solemnly
Dance in Duke Theseus' house triumphantly
And bless it to all fair prosperity:
There shall the pairs of faithful lovers be
Wedded, with Theseus, all in jollity.
  Puck. Fairy king, attend, and mark:

I do hear the morning lark.

Obe. Then, my queen, in silence sad,
Trip we after night's shade:
We the globe can compass soon,   100
Swifter than the wandering moon.

Tita. Come, my lord, and in our flight
Tell me how it came this night
That I sleeping here was found
With these mortals on the ground.

[*Exeunt.*

Horns winded within.

Enter THESEUS, HIPPOLYTA, EGEUS, *and train.*

The. Go, one of you, find out the forester;
For now our observation is perform'd;
And since we have the vaward of the day,
My love shall hear the music of my hounds.   110
Uncouple in the western valley; let them go:
Dispatch, I say, and find the forester.

[*Exit an Attendant.*

We will, fair queen, up to the mountain's top
And mark the musical confusion
Of hounds and echo in conjunction.

Hip. I was with Hercules and Cadmus once,
When in a wood of Crete they bay'd the bear
With hounds of Sparta: never did I hear
Such gallant chiding; for, besides the groves,
The skies, the fountains, every region near   120
Seem'd all one mutual cry: I never heard
So musical a discord, such sweet thunder.

The. My hounds are bred out of the Spartan
kind,
So flew'd, so sanded, and their heads are hung
With ears that sweep away the morning dew;
Crook-knee'd, and dew-lapp'd like Thessalian
bulls;
Slow in pursuit, but match'd in mouth like bells,
Each under each. A cry more tuneable
Was never holla'd to, nor cheer'd with horn,
In Crete, in Sparta, nor in Thessaly: 130
Judge when you hear. But, soft! what nymphs
are these?

Ege. My lord, this is my daughter here asleep;
And this, Lysander; this Demetrius is;
This Helena, old Nedar's Helena:
I wonder of their being here together.

The. No doubt they rose up early to observe
The rite of May, and, hearing our intent,
Came here in grace of our solemnity.
But speak, Egeus; is not this the day
That Hermia should give answer of her choice?

Ege. It is, my lord.   141

The. Go, bid the huntsmen wake them with
their horns. *Horns and shout within.*

LYSANDER, DEMETRIUS, HELENA, *and* HERMIA,
wake and start up.

Good morrow, friends. Saint Valentine is past:
Begin these wood-birds but to couple now?

Lys. Pardon, my lord.

The.   I pray you all, stand up.
I know you two are rival enemies:
How comes this gentle concord in the world,
That hatred is so far from jealousy
To sleep by hate and fear no enmity?

Lys. My lord, I shall reply amazedly,   150
Half sleep, half waking: but as yet, I swear,
I cannot truly say how I came here;
But, as I think—for truly would I speak,
And now I do bethink me, so it is—
I came with Hermia hither: our intent
Was to be gone from Athens, where we might,
Without the peril of the Athenian law—

Ege. Enough, enough, my lord; you have
enough:
I beg the law, the law, upon his head.
They would have stolen away; they would,
Demetrius,   160
Thereby to have defeated you and me,
You of your wife and me of my consent,
Of my consent that she should be your wife.

Dem. My lord, fair Helen told me of their
stealth,
Of this their purpose hither to this wood;
And I in fury hither follow'd them,
Fair Helena in fancy following me.
But, my good lord, I wot not by what power—
But by some power it is—my love to Hermia,
Melted as the snow, seems to me now   170
As the remembrance of an idle gawd
Which in my childhood I did dote upon;
And all the faith, the virtue of my heart,
The object and the pleasure of mine eye,
Is only Helena. To her, my lord,
Was I betroth'd ere I saw Hermia:
But like in sickness did I loathe this food;
But, as in health, come to my natural taste,
Now I do wish it, love it, long for it,
And will for evermore be true to it.   180

The. Fair lovers, you are fortunately met:
Of this discourse we more will hear anon.
Egeus, I will overbear your will;
For in the temple, by and by, with us
These couples shall eternally be knit:
And, for the morning now is something worn,
Our purposed hunting shall be set aside.
Away with us to Athens; three and three,
We'll hold a feast in great solemnity.
Come, Hippolyta.   190

[*Exeunt* THESEUS, HIPPOLYTA, EGEUS, *and train.*

Dem. These things seem small and undistinguishable,
Like far-off mountains turned into clouds.

Her. Methinks I see these things with parted
  eye,
When every thing seems double.
  Hel.   So methinks:
And I have found Demetrius like a jewel,
Mine own, and not mine own.
  Dem.   Are you sure
That we are awake? It seems to me
That yet we sleep, we dream. Do not you think
The Duke was here, and bid us follow him?   *199*
  Her. Yea; and my father.
  Hel.   And Hippolyta.
  Lys. And he did bid us follow to the temple.
  Dem. Why, then, we are awake: let's follow
  him;
And by the way let us recount our dreams.
                                    [*Exeunt.*

  Bot. [*Awaking*] When my cue comes, call me,
and I will answer: my next is, "Most fair Pyramus." Heigh-ho! Peter Quince! Flute, the bellows-mender! Snout, the tinker! Starveling! God's
my life, stolen hence, and left me asleep! I have
had a most rare vision. I have had a dream, past
the wit of man to say what dream it was: man is
but an ass, if he go about to expound this dream.
Methought I was—there is no man can tell
what. Methought I was—and methought I had—
but man is but a patched fool, if he will offer to
say what methought I had. The eye of man hath
not heard, the ear of man hath not seen, man's
hand is not able to taste, his tongue to conceive,
nor his heart to report, what my dream was. I
will get Peter Quince to write a ballad of this
dream: it shall be called "Bottom's Dream,"
because it hath no bottom; and I will sing it in
the latter end of a play, before the Duke: peradventure, to make it the more gracious, I shall
sing it at her death.   [*Exit.*

SCENE II. *Athens: Quince's house*

Enter QUINCE, FLUTE, SNOUT, *and*
                    STARVELING.

  Quin. Have you sent to Bottom's house? is he
come home yet?
  Star. He cannot be heard of. Out of doubt
he is transported.
  Flu. If he come not, then the play is marred:
it goes not forward, doth it?
  Quin. It is not possible: you have not a man
in all Athens able to discharge Pyramus but he.
  Flu. No, he hath simply the best wit of any
handicraft man in Athens.   *10*
  Quin. Yea, and the best person too; and he is a
very paramour for a sweet voice.
  Flu. You must say "paragon": a paramour is,
God bless us, a thing of naught.

Enter SNUG.

  Snug. Masters, the Duke is coming from the
temple, and there is two or three lords and ladies
more married: if our sport had gone forward, we
had all been made men.
  Flu. O sweet bully Bottom! Thus hath he lost
sixpence a day during his life; he could not have
'scaped sixpence a day: an the Duke had not
given him sixpence a day for playing Pyramus,
I'll be hanged; he would have deserved it: sixpence a day in Pyramus, or nothing.

Enter BOTTOM.

  Bot. Where are these lads? where are these
hearts?
  Quin. Bottom! O most courageous day! O most
happy hour!
  Bot. Masters, I am to discourse wonders: but
ask me not what: for if I tell you, I am no true
Athenian. I will tell you everything, right as it
fell out.
  Quin. Let us hear, sweet Bottom.
  Bot. Not a word of me. All that I will tell you
is, that the Duke hath dined. Get your apparel
together, good strings to your beards, new rib-
bons to your pumps; meet presently at the palace; every man look o'er his part; for the short
and the long is, our play is preferred. In any
case, let Thisby have clean linen; and let not
him that plays the lion pare his nails, for they
shall hang out for the lion's claws. And, most
dear actors, eat no onions nor garlic, for we are
to utter sweet breath; and I do not doubt but to
hear them say, it is a sweet comedy. No more
words: away! go, away!   [*Exeunt.*

ACT V

SCENE I. *Athens: the palace of Theseus*

Enter THESEUS, HIPPOLYTA, PHILOSTRATE, *Lords,
              and Attendants.*

  Hip. 'Tis strange, my Theseus, that these
  lovers speak of.
  The. More strange than true: I never may be-
  lieve
These antique fables, nor these fairy toys.
Lovers and madmen have such seething brains,
Such shaping fantasies, that apprehend
More than cool reason ever comprehends.
The lunatic, the lover, and the poet
Are of imagination all compact:
One sees more devils than vast hell can hold,
That is, the madman: the lover, all as frantic,   *10*
Sees Helen's beauty in a brow of Egypt:
The poet's eye, in a fine frenzy rolling,

Doth glance from heaven to earth, from earth to
     heaven;
And as imagination bodies forth
The forms of things unknown, the poet's pen
Turns them to shapes and gives to airy nothing
A local habitation and a name.
Such tricks hath strong imagination,
That, if it would but apprehend some joy,
It comprehends some bringer of that joy;   20
Or in the night, imagining some fear,
How easy is a bush supposed a bear!
  Hip. But all the story of the night told over,
And all their minds transfigured so together,
More witnesseth than fancy's images
And grows to something of great constancy;
But, howsoever, strange and admirable.
  The. Here come the lovers, full of joy and
mirth.

Enter LYSANDER, DEMETRIUS, HERMIA, *and*
                    HELENA.

Joy, gentle friends! joy and fresh days of love
Accompany your hearts!
  Lys.   More than to us   30
Wait in your royal walks, your board, your bed!
  The. Come now; what masques, what dances
     shall we have,
To wear away this long age of three hours
Between our after-supper and bed-time?
Where is our usual manager of mirth?
What revels are in hand? Is there no play,
To ease the anguish of a torturing hour?
Call Philostrate.
  Phil.   Here, mighty Theseus.
  The. Say, what abridgement have you for this
     evening?
What masque? what music? How shall we be-
     guile   40
The lazy time, if not with some delight?
  Phil. There is a brief how many sports are ripe:
Make choice of which your highness will see
     first.
Giving a paper.
  The. [*Reads*] "The battle with the Centaurs, to
     be sung
By an Athenian eunuch to the harp."
We'll none of that: that have I told my love,
In glory of my kinsman Hercules.
"The riot of the tipsy Bacchanals,
Tearing the Thracian singer in their rage."
That is an old device; and it was play'd   50
When I from Thebes came last a conqueror.
"The thrice three Muses mourning for the death
Of learning, late deceased in beggary."
That is some satire, keen and critical,
Not sorting with a nuptial ceremony.

"A tedious brief scene of young Pyramus
And his love Thisby; very tragical mirth."
Merry and tragical! tedious and brief!
That is, hot ice and wondrous strange snow.
How shall we find the concord of this discord? 60
  Phil. A play there is, my lord, some ten words
     long,
Which is as brief as I have known a play;
But by ten words, my lord, it is too long,
Which makes it tedious; for in all the play
There is not one word apt, one player fitted:
And tragical, my noble lord, it is;
For Pyramus therein doth kill himself.
Which, when I saw rehearsed, I must confess,
Made mine eyes water; but more merry tears
The passion of loud laughter never shed.   70
  The. What are they that do play it?
  Phil. Hard-handed men that work in Athens
     here,
Which never labour'd in their minds till now,
And now have toil'd their unbreathed memories
With this same play, against your nuptial.
  The. And we will hear it.
  Phil.   No, my noble lord;
It is not for you: I have heard it over,
And it is nothing, nothing in the world;
Unless you can find sport in their intents,
Extremely stretch'd and conn'd with cruel pain, 80
To do you service.
  The.   I will hear that play;
For never anything can be amiss,
When simpleness and duty tender it.
Go, bring them in: and take your places ladies.
                              [*Exit* PHILOSTRATE.
  Hip. I love not to see wretchedness o'ercharged
And duty in his service perishing.
  The. Why, gentle sweet, you shall see no such
     thing.
  Hip. He says they can do nothing in this kind.
  The. The kinder we, to give them thanks for
     nothing.
Our sport shall be to take what they mistake: 90
And what poor duty cannot do, noble respect
Takes it in might, not merit.
Where I have come, great clerks have purposed
To greet me with premeditated welcomes;
Where I have seen them shiver and look pale,
Make periods in the midst of sentences,
Throttle their practised accent in their fears
And in conclusion dumbly have broke off,
Not paying me a welcome. Trust me, sweet,
Out of this silence yet I pick'd a welcome;   100
And in the modesty of fearful duty
I read as much as from the rattling tongue
Of saucy and audacious eloquence.
Love, therefore, and tongue-tied simplicity

In least speak most, to my capacity.

Re-enter PHILOSTRATE.

Phil. So please your grace, the Prologue is address'd.

The. Let him approach. [*Flourish of trumpets.*

Enter QUINCE *for the* PROLOGUE.

Pro. If we offend, it is with our good will.
  That you should think, we come not to offend,
But with good will. To show our simple skill, *110*
  That is the true beginning of our end.
Consider then we come but in despite.
  We do not come as minding to content you,
Our true intent is. All for your delight
  We are not here. That you should here repent you,
The actors are at hand and by their show
You shall know all that you are like to know.

The. This fellow doth not stand upon points.

Lys. He hath rid his prologue like a rough colt; he knows not the stop. A good moral, my lord: it is not enough to speak, but to speak true.

Hip. Indeed he hath played on his prologue like a child on a recorder; a sound, but not in government.

The. His speech was like a tangled chain; nothing impaired, but all disordered. Who is next?

Enter PYRAMUS *and* THISBE, WALL, MOONSHINE, *and* LION.

Pro. Gentles, perchance you wonder at this show;
But wonder on, till truth make all things plain.
This man is Pyramus, if you would know; *130*
  This beauteous lady Thisby is certain.
This man, with lime and rough-cast, doth present
  Wall, that vile Wall which did these lovers sunder;
And through Wall's chink, poor souls, they are content
  To whisper. At the which let no man wonder.
This man, with lanthorn, dog, and bush of thorn,
  Presenteth Moonshine; for, if you will know,
By moonshine did these lovers think no scorn
  To meet at Ninus' tomb, there, there to woo.
This grisly beast, which Lion hight by name, *140*
  The trusty Thisby, coming first by night,
Did scare away, or rather did affright;
  And, as she fled, her mantle she did fall,
Which Lion vile with bloody mouth did stain.
Anon comes Pyramus, sweet youth and tall,
  And finds his trusty Thisby's mantle slain:
Whereat, with blade, with bloody blameful blade,
  He bravely broach'd his boiling bloody breast;

And Thisby, tarrying in mulberry shade,
  His dagger drew, and died. For all the rest,
Let Lion, Moonshine, Wall, and lovers twain *151*
  At large discourse, while here they do remain.

[*Exeunt* PROLOGUE, PYRAMUS, THISBE, LION, *and* MOONSHINE.

The. I wonder if the lion be to speak.

Dem. No wonder, my lord: one lion may, when many asses do.

Wall. In this same interlude it doth befall
That I, one Snout by name, present a wall;
And such a wall, as I would have you think,
That had in it a crannied hole or chink,
Through which the lovers, Pyramus and Thisby,
Did whisper often very secretly.   *161*
This loam, this rough-cast, and this stone doth show
That I am that same wall; the truth is so:
And this the cranny is, right and sinister,
Through which the fearful lovers are to whisper.

The. Would you desire lime and hair to speak better?

Dem. It is the wittiest partition that ever I heard discourse, my lord.

Re-enter PYRAMUS.

The. Pyramus draws near the wall: silence!

Pyr. O grim-look'd night! O night with hue so black!   *171*
O night, which ever art when day is not!
O night, O night! alack, alack, alack,
  I fear my Thisby's promise is forgot!
And thou, O wall, O sweet, O lovely wall,
  That stand'st between her father's ground and mine!
Thou wall, O wall, O sweet and lovely wall,
  Show me thy chink, to blink through with mine eyne!   [WALL *holds up his fingers.*
Thanks, courteous wall: Jove shield thee well for this!
But what see I? No Thisby do I see.   *180*
O wicked wall, through whom I see no bliss!
Curs'd be thy stones for thus deceiving me!

The. The wall, methinks, being sensible, should curse again.

Pyr. No, in truth, sir, he should not. "Deceiving me" is Thisby's cue: she is to enter now, and I am to spy her through the wall. You shall see, it will fall pat as I told you. Yonder she comes.

Re-enter THISBE.

This. O wall, full often hast thou heard my moans,   *190*
  For parting my fair Pyramus and me!
My cherry lips have often kiss'd thy stones,

Thy stones with lime and hair knit up in thee.

Pyr. I see a voice: now will I to the chink,
To spy an I can hear my Thisby's face.
Thisby!

This. My love thou art, my love I think.

Pyr. Think what thou wilt, I am thy lover's
grace;
And, like Limander, am I trusty still.

This. And I like Helen, till the Fates me kill.

Pyr. Not Shafalus to Procrus was so true.   *200*

This. As Shafalus to Procrus, I to you.

Pyr. O, kiss me through the hole of this vile
wall!

This. I kiss the wall's hole, not your lips at all.

Pyr. Wilt thou at Ninny's tomb meet me
straightway?

This. 'Tide life, 'tide death, I come without
delay.   [*Exeunt* PYRAMUS *and* THISBE.

Wall. Thus have I, Wall, my part discharged
so;
And, being done, thus Wall away doth go. [*Exit.*

The. Now is the mural down between the two
neighbours.

Dem. No remedy, my lord, when walls are so
wilful to hear without warning.   *211*

Hip. This is the silliest stuff that ever I heard.

The. The best in this kind are but shadows; and
the worst are no worse, if imagination amend
them.

Hip. It must be your imagination then, and not
theirs.

The. If we imagine no worse of them than they
of themselves, they may pass for excellent men.
Here come two noble beasts in, a man and a
lion.   *221*

Re-enter LION *and* MOONSHINE.

Lion. You, ladies, you, whose gentle hearts do
fear
The smallest monstrous mouse that creeps on
floor,
May now perchance both quake and tremble here,
When lion rough in wildest rage doth roar.
Then know that I, one Snug the joiner, am
A lion fell, nor else no lion's dam;
For, if I should as lion come in strife
Into this place, 'twere pity on my life.

The. A very gentle beast, and of a good conscience.   *231*

Dem. The very best at a beast, my lord, that
e'er I saw.

Lys. This lion is a very fox for his valour.

The. True; and a goose for his discretion.

Dem. Not so, my lord; for his valour cannot
carry his discretion; and the fox carries the
goose.

The. His discretion, I am sure, cannot carry
his valour; for the goose carries not the fox. It is
well: leave it to his discretion, and let us listen to
the moon.

Moon. This lanthorn doth the horned moon
present—

Dem. He should have worn the horns on his
head.

The. He is no crescent, and his horns are invisible within the circumference.

Moon. This lanthorn doth the horned moon
present;
Myself the man i' the moon do seem to be.

The. This is the greatest error of all the rest:
the man should be put into the lanthorn. How is
it else the man i' the moon?

Dem. He dares not come there for the candle;
for, you see, it is already in snuff.

Hip. I am aweary of this moon: would he
would change!

The. It appears, by his small light of discretion, that he is in the wane; but yet, in courtesy,
in all reason, we must stay the time.

Lys. Proceed, Moon.   *260*

Moon. All that I have to say, is, to tell you that
the lanthorn is the moon; I, the man in the moon;
this thorn-bush, my thorn-bush; and this dog, my
dog.

Dem. Why, all these should be in the lanthorn;
for all these are in the moon. But, silence! here
comes Thisbe.

Re-enter THISBE.

This. This is old Ninny's tomb. Where is my
love?

Lion. [*Roaring*] Oh—   [THISBE *runs off.*

Dem. Well roared, Lion.   *270*

The. Well run, Thisbe.

Hip. Well shone, Moon. Truly, the moon
shines with a good grace.

[*The* LION *shakes* THISBE'S *mantle, and exit.*

The. Well moused, Lion.

Lys. And so the lion vanished.

Dem. And then came Pyramus.

Re-enter PYRAMUS.

Pyr. Sweet Moon, I thank thee for thy sunny
beams;
I thank thee, Moon, for shining now so bright;
For, by thy gracious, golden, glittering gleams,
I trust to take of truest Thisby sight.   *280*
        But stay, O spite!
        But mark, poor knight,
    What dreadful dole is here!
        Eyes, do you see?
        How can it be?

O dainty duck! O dear!
    Thy mantle good,
    What, stain'd with blood!
    Approach, ye Furies fell!
        O Fates, come, come,   290
        Cut thread and thrum;
        Quail, crush, conclude, and quell!
The. This passion, and the death of a dear
friend, would go near to make a man look sad.
Hip. Beshrew my heart, but I pity the man.
Pyr. O wherefore, Nature, didst thou lions
frame?
Since lion vile hath here deflower'd my dear:
Which is—no, no—which was the fairest dame
That lived, that loved, that liked, that look'd
    with cheer.
        Come, tears, confound;   300
        Out, sword, and wound
    The pap of Pyramus;
        Ay, that left pap,
        Where heart doth hop: [*Stabs him-
        self.*]
Thus die I, thus, thus, thus.
        Now am I dead,
        Now am I fled;
My soul is in the sky:
    Tongue, lose thy light;   309
    Moon take thy flight: [*Exit* MOON-
SHINE.
    Now die, die, die, die, die.   [*Dies.*
Dem. No die, but an ace, for him; for he is but
one.
Lys. Less than an ace, man; for he is dead; he
is nothing.
The. With the help of a surgeon he might yet
recover, and prove an ass.
Hip. How chance Moonshine is gone before
Thisbe comes back and finds her lover?
The. She will find him by starlight. Here she
comes; and her passion ends the play.   321

Re-enter THISBE.

Hip. Methinks she should not use a long one
for such a Pyramus: I hope she will be brief.
Dem. A mote will turn the balance, which
Pyramus, which Thisbe, is the better; he for a
man, God warrant us; she for a woman, God
bless us.
Lys. She hath spied him already with those
sweet eyes.
Dem. And thus she moans, *videlicet*—   330
This.   Asleep, my love?
        What, dead, my dove?
    O Pyramus, arise!
        Speak, speak. Quite dumb?
        Dead, dead? A tomb

    Must cover thy sweet eyes.
        These lily lips,
        This cherry nose,
    These yellow cowslip cheeks,
        Are gone, are gone:
    Lovers, make moan:
His eyes were green as leeks.
        O Sisters Three,
    Come, come to me,
With hands as pale as milk;
        Lay them in gore,
        Since you have shore
With shears his thread of silk.
    Tongue, not a word:
    Come, trusty sword;   350
    Come, blade, my breast imbrue:
Stabs herself.
        And, farewell, friends;
        Thus Thisby ends:
    Adieu, adieu, adieu.   [*Dies.*
The. Moonshine and Lion are left to bury the
dead.
Dem. Ay, and Wall too.
Bot. [*Starting up*] No, I assure you; the wall
is down that parted their fathers. Will it please
you to see the epilogue, or to hear a Bergomask
dance between two of our company?   361
The. No epilogue, I pray you; for your play
needs no excuse. Never excuse; for when the
players are all dead, there need none to be blamed.
Marry, if he that writ it had played Pyramus and
hanged himself in Thisbe's garter, it would have
been a fine tragedy: and so it is, truly; and very
notably discharged. But, come, your Bergo-
mask: let your epilogue alone.
A dance.
The iron tongue of midnight hath told twelve:
Lovers, to bed; 'tis almost fairy time.   371
I fear we shall out-sleep the coming morn
As much as we this night have overwatch'd.
This palpable-gross play hath well beguiled
The heavy gait of night. Sweet friends, to bed.
A fortnight hold we this solemnity,
In nightly revels and new jollity.   [*Exeunt.*

Enter PUCK.

Puck. Now the hungry lion roars,
    And the wolf behowls the moon;
Whilst the heavy ploughman snores,   380
    All with weary task fordone.
Now the wasted brands do glow,
    Whilst the screech-owl, screeching loud,
Puts the wretch that lies in woe
    In remembrance of a shroud.
Now it is the time of night
    That the graves all gaping wide,

Every one lets forth his sprite,
  In the church-way paths to glide:
And we fairies, that do run   *390*
  By the triple Hecate's team,
From the presence of the sun,
  Following darkness like a dream,
Now are frolic: not a mouse
Shall disturb this hallow'd house:
I am sent with broom before,
To sweep the dust behind the door.

Enter OBERON *and* TITANIA *with their train.*

Obe. Through the house give glimmering light,
  By the dead and drowsy fire:
Every elf and fairy sprite
  Hop as light as bird from brier;
And this ditty, after me,
Sing, and dance it trippingly.
Tita. First, rehearse your song by rote,
  To each word a warbling note:
Hand in hand, with fairy grace,
Will we sing, and bless this place.
  Song and dance.
Obe. Now, until the break of day,
  Through this house each fairy stray.
To the best bride-bed will we,   *410*
  Which by us shall blessed be;
And the issue there create
  Ever shall be fortunate.
So shall all the couples three
Ever true in loving be;

And the blots of Nature's hand
Shall not in their issue stand;
Never mole, hare lip, nor scar,
  Nor mark prodigious, such as are
Despised in nativity,   *420*
  Shall upon their children be.
With this field-dew consecrate,
Every fairy take his gait;
And each several chamber bless,
Through this palace, with sweet peace;
And the owner of it blest
Ever shall in safety rest.
Trip away; make no stay;
Meet me all by break of day.
              [*Exeunt* OBERON, TITANIA, *and train.*
Puck. If we shadows have offended,   *430*
  Think but this, and all is mended,
That you have but slumber'd here
  While these visions did appear.
And this weak and idle theme,
  No more yielding but a dream,
Gentles, do not reprehend:
  If you pardon, we will mend:
And, as I am an honest Puck,
  If we have unearned luck
Now to 'scape the serpent's tongue,   *440*
  We will make amends ere long;
Else the Puck a liar call:
  So, good night unto you all.
Give me your hands, if we be friends,
And Robin shall restore amends.   [*Exit.*

❧ The Life and Death of
KING JOHN

DRAMATIS PERSONÆ

KING JOHN
PRINCE HENRY, *son to the King*
ARTHUR, *Duke of Bretagne, nephew to the King*
EARL OF PEMBROKE
EARL OF ESSEX
EARL OF SALISBURY
LORD BIGOT
HUBERT DE BURGH
ROBERT FAULCONBRIDGE, *son to Sir Robert Faulcon-*
   bridge
PHILIP THE BASTARD, *his half-brother, later dubbed*
   Richard Plantagenet
JAMES GURNEY, *servant to Lady Faulconbridge*
PETER OF POMFRET, *a prophet*
EXECUTIONER
TWO MESSENGERS
ENGLISH HERALD

PHILIP, *King of France*
LEWIS, *the Dauphin*
LYMOGES, DUKE OF AUSTRIA
CARDINAL PANDULPH, *the Pope's legate*
MELUN, *a French Lord*
CHATILLON, *ambassador from France to King John*
CITIZEN *of Angiers*
FRENCH HERALD

QUEEN ELINOR, *mother to King John*
CONSTANCE, *mother to Arthur*
BLANCH *of Spain, niece to King John*
LADY FAULCONBRIDGE

NON-SPEAKING: *Lords, Citizens of Angiers, Sheriff,*
   Officers, Soldiers and other Attendants

SCENE: *Partly in England, and partly in France*

❧

ACT I

SCENE I. *King John's palace*

Enter KING JOHN, QUEEN ELINOR, PEMBROKE,
ESSEX, SALISBURY, *and others, with* CHATILLON.

K. John. Now, say, Chatillon, what would
   France with us?
Chat. Thus, after greeting, speaks the King
   of France
In my behaviour to the majesty,
The borrow'd majesty, of England here.
Eli. A strange beginning: "borrow'd majesty!"
K. John. Silence, good mother; hear the em-
   bassy.
Chat. Philip of France, in right and true behalf
Of thy deceased brother Geoffrey's son,
Arthur Plantagenet, lays most lawful claim
To this fair island and the territories,   *10*
To Ireland, Poictiers, Anjou, Touraine, Maine,
Desiring thee to lay aside the sword
Which sways usurpingly these several titles,
And put the same into young Arthur's hand,
Thy nephew and right royal sovereign.
K. John. What follows if we disallow of this?
Chat. The proud control of fierce and bloody
   war,
To enforce these rights so forcibly withheld.
K. John. Here have we war for war and blood
   for blood,

Controlment for controlment: so answer France.
Chat. Then take my king's defiance from my
   mouth,   *21*
The farthest limit of my embassy.
K. John. Bear mine to him, and so depart in
   peace:
Be thou as lightning in the eyes of France;
For ere thou canst report I will be there,
The thunder of my cannon shall be heard:
So hence! Be thou the trumpet of our wrath
And sullen presage of your own decay.
An honourable conduct let him have:
Pembroke, look to't. Farewell, Chatillon.   *30*
   [*Exeunt* CHATILLON *and* PEMBROKE.
Eli. What now, my son! have I not ever said
How that ambitious Constance would not cease
Till she had kindled France and all the world
Upon the right and party of her son?
This might have been prevented and made whole
With very easy arguments of love,
Which now the manage of two kingdoms must
With fearful bloody issue arbitrate.
K. John. Our strong possession and our right
   for us.
Eli. Your strong possession much more than
   your right,
Or else it must go wrong with you and me:
So much my conscience whispers in your ear,
Which none but heaven and you and I shall hear.

Enter a Sheriff.

Essex. My liege, here is the strangest contro-
versy
Come from the country to be judged by you
That e'er I heard: shall I produce the men?
K. John. Let them approach.
Our abbeys and our priories shall pay
This expedition's charge.

Enter ROBERT FAULCONBRIDGE, *and* PHILIP THE
BASTARD.
                    What men are you?
Bast. Your faithful subject I, a gentleman   50
Born in Northamptonshire and eldest son,
As I suppose, to Robert Faulconbridge,
A soldier, by the honour-giving hand
Of Cœur-de-lion knighted in the field.
K. John. What art thou?
Rob. The son and heir to that same Faulcon-
bridge.
K. John. Is that the elder, and art thou the heir?
You came not of one mother then, it seems.
Bast. Most certain of one mother, mighty king;
That is well known; and, as I think, one father:
But for the certain knowledge of that truth   61
I put you o'er to heaven and to my mother:
Of that I doubt, as all men's children may.
Eli. Out on thee, rude man! thou dost shame
thy mother
And wound her honour with this diffidence.
Bast. I, madam? no, I have no reason for it;
That is my brother's plea and none of mine;
The which if he can prove, a' pops me out
At least from fair five hundred pound a year:
Heaven guard my mother's honour and my land!
K. John. A good blunt fellow. Why, being
younger born,   71
Doth he lay claim to thine inheritance?
Bast. I know not why, except to get the land.
But once he slander'd me with bastardy:
But whether I be as true begot or no,
That still I lay upon my mother's head,
But that I am as well begot, my liege—
Fair fall the bones that took the pains for me!—
Compare our faces and be judge yourself.
If old sir Robert did beget us both   80
And were our father and this son like him,
O old sir Robert, father, on my knee
I give heaven thanks I was not like to thee!
K. John. Why, what a madcap hath heaven lent
us here!
Eli. He hath a trick of Cœur-de-lion's face;
The accent of his tongue affecteth him.
Do you not read some tokens of my son
In the large composition of this man?

K. John. Mine eye hath well examined his parts
And finds them perfect Richard. Sirrah, speak, 90
What doth move you to claim your brother's
land?
Bast. Because he hath a half-face, like my
father.
With half that face would he have all my land:
A half-faced groat five hundred pound a year!
Rob. My gracious liege, when that my father
lived,
Your brother did employ my father much—
Bast. Well, sir, by this you cannot get my land:
Your tale must be how he employ'd my mother.
Rob. And once dispatch'd him in an embassy
To Germany, there with the Emperor   100
To treat of high affairs touching that time.
The advantage of his absence took the king
And in the mean time sojourn'd at my father's;
Where how he did prevail I shame to speak,
But truth is truth: large lengths of seas and
shores
Between my father and my mother lay,
As I have heard my father speak himself,
When this same lusty gentleman was got.
Upon his death-bed he by will bequeath'd
His lands to me, and took it on his death   110
That this my mother's son was none of his;
And if he were, he came into the world
Full fourteen weeks before the course of time.
Then, good my liege, let me have what is mine,
My father's land, as was my father's will.
K. John. Sirrah, your brother is legitimate;
Your father's wife did after wedlock bear him,
And if she did play false, the fault was hers;
Which fault lies on the hazards of all husbands
That marry wives. Tell me, how if my brother,
Who, as you say, took pains to get this son, 121
Had of your father claim'd this son for his?
In sooth, good friend, your father might have
kept
This calf bred from his cow from all the world;
In sooth he might; then, if he were my brother's,
My brother might not claim him; nor your father,
Being none of his, refuse him: this concludes;
My mother's son did get your father's heir;
Your father's heir must have your father's land.
Rob. Shall then my father's will be of no
force   130
To dispossess that child which is not his?
Bast. Of no more force to dispossess me, sir,
Than was his will to get me, as I think.
Eli. Whether hadst thou rather be a Faulcon-
bridge
And like thy brother, to enjoy thy land,
Or the reputed son of Cœur-de-lion,
Lord of thy presence and no land beside?

Bast. Madam, an if my brother had my shape,
And I had his, Sir Robert's his, like him;
And if my legs were two such riding-rods,   *140*
My arms such eel-skins stuff'd, my face so thin
That in mine ear I durst not stick a rose
Lest men should say "Look, where three-farth-
    ings goes!"
And, to his shape, were heir to all this land,
Would I might never stir from off this place,
I would give it every foot to have this face;
I would not be Sir Nob in any case.
    Eli. I like thee well: wilt thou forsake thy
    fortune,
Bequeath thy land to him and follow me?
I am a soldier and now bound to France.   *150*
    Bast. Brother, take you my land, I'll take my
    chance.
Your face hath got five hundred pound a year,
Yet sell your face for five pence and 'tis dear.
Madam, I'll follow you unto the death.
    Eli. Nay, I would have you go before me
    thither.
    Bast. Our country manners give our betters
    way.
K. John. What is thy name?
    Bast. Philip, my liege, so is my name begun;
Philip, good old Sir Robert's wife's eldest son.
    K. John. From henceforth bear his name whose
    form thou bear'st: *160*
Kneel thou down Philip, but rise more great,
Arise Sir Richard and Plantagenet.
    Bast. Brother by the mother's side, give me
    your hand:
My father gave me honour, yours gave land.
Now blessed be the hour, by night or day,
When I was got, Sir Robert was away!
    Eli. The very spirit of Plantagenet!
I am thy grandam, Richard; call me so.
    Bast. Madam, by chance but not by truth;
    what though?
Something about, a little from the right,   *170*
In at the window, or else o'er the hatch:
Who dares not stir by day must walk by night,
    And have is have, however men do catch:
Near or far off, well won is still well shot,
And I am I, howe'er I was begot.
    K. John. Go, Faulconbridge: now hast thou thy
    desire;
A landless knight makes thee a landed squire.
Come, madam, and come, Richard, we must
    speed
For France, for France, for it is more than need.
    Bast. Brother, adieu: good fortune come to
    thee!   *180*
For thou wast got i' the way of honesty.

    [Exeunt all but BASTARD.

A foot of honour better than I was;
But many a many foot of land the worse.
Well, now can I make any Joan a lady.
"Good den, sir Richard!" "God-a-mercy, fel-
    low!"
And if his name be George, I'll call him Peter;
For new-made honour doth forget men's names;
'Tis too respective and too sociable
For your conversion. Now your traveller,
He and his toothpick at my worship's mess,   *190*
And when my knightly stomach is sufficed,
Why then I suck my teeth and catechize
My picked man of countries: "My dear sir,"
Thus, leaning on mine elbow, I begin,
"I shall beseech you"—that is question now;
And then comes answer like an Absey book:
"O sir," says answer, "at your best command;
At your employment; at your service, sir":
"No, sir," says question, "I, sweet sir, at
    yours":
And so, ere answer knows what question would,
Saving in dialogue of compliment,   *201*
And talking of the Alps and Apennines,
The Pyrenean and the river Po,
It draws toward supper in conclusion so.
But this is worshipful society
And fits the mounting spirit like myself,
For he is but a bastard to the time
That doth not smack of observation;
And so am I, whether I smack or no;
And not alone in habit and device,   *210*
Exterior form, outward accoutrement,
But from the inward motion to deliver
Sweet, sweet, sweet poison for the age's tooth:
Which, though I will not practise to deceive,
Yet, to avoid deceit, I mean to learn;
For it shall strew the footsteps of my rising.
But who comes in such haste in riding-robes?
What woman-post is this? hath she no husband
That will take pains to blow a horn before her?

Enter LADY FAULCONBRIDGE *and* JAMES GURNEY.

O me! it is my mother, How now, good lady!
What brings you here to court so hastily?   *221*
    Lady. F. Where is that slave, thy brother,
    where is he,
That holds in chase mine honour up and down?
    Bast. My brother Robert? old Sir Robert's
    son?
Colbrand the giant, that same mighty man?
Is it Sir Robert's son that you seek so?
    Lady F. Sir Robert's son! Ay, thou unreverend
    boy,
Sir Robert's son: why scorn'st thou at Sir
    Robert?
He is Sir Robert's son, and so art thou.

Bast. James Gurney, wilt thou give us leave
    awhile?   *230*

Gur. Good leave, good Philip.

Bast.   Philip! sparrow: James,
There's toys abroad: anon I'll tell thee more.
                      [Exit GURNEY.

Madam, I was not old Sir Robert's son:
Sir Robert might have eat his part in me
Upon Good-Friday and ne'er broke his fast:
Sir Robert could do well: marry, to confess,
Could he get me? Sir Robert could not do it:
We know his handiwork: therefore, good
    mother,
To whom am I beholding for these limbs?
Sir Robert never holp to make this leg.   *240*

Lady F. Hast thou conspired with thy bro-
    ther too,
That for thine own gain shouldst defend mine
    honour?
What means this scorn, thou most untoward
    knave?

Bast. "Knight, knight," good mother, Basilisco-
    like.
What! I am dubb'd! I have it on my shoulder.
But, mother, I am not Sir Robert's son;
I have disclaim'd Sir Robert and my land;
Legitimation, name, and all is gone:
Then, good my mother, let me know my father;
Some proper man, I hope: who was it, mother?

Lady F. Hast thou denied thyself a Faulcon-
    bridge?

Bast. As faithfully as I deny the devil.

Lady F. King Richard Cœur-de-lion was thy
    father:
By long and vehement suit I was seduced
To make room for him in my husband's bed:
Heaven lay not my transgression to my charge!
Thou are the issue of my dear offence,
Which was so strongly urged past my defence.

Bast. Now, by this light, were I to get again,
Madam, I would not wish a better father.   *260*
Some sins do bear their privilege on earth,
And so doth yours; your fault was not your folly:
Needs must you lay your heart at his dispose,
Subjected tribute to commanding love,
Against whose fury and unmatched force
The aweless lion could not wage the fight,
Nor keep his princely heart from Richard's hand.
He that perforce robs lions of their hearts
May easily win a woman's. Ay, my mother,
With all my heart I thank thee for my father! *270*
Who lives and dares but say thou didst not well
When I was got, I'll send his soul to hell.
Come, lady, I will show thee to my kin;
  And they shall say, when Richard me begot,
If thou hadst said him nay, it had been sin:

Who says it was, he lies; I say 'twas not.
                      [Exeunt.

ACT II

SCENE I. *France: before Angiers*

Enter AUSTRIA *and forces, drums, etc. on one side:
on the other* KING PHILIP *of France and his power;*
LEWIS, ARTHUR, CONSTANCE *and attendants.*

Lew. Before Angiers well met, brave Austria.
Arthur, that great forerunner of thy blood,
Richard, that robb'd the lion of his heart
And fought the holy wars in Palestine,
By this brave duke came early to his grave:
And for amends to his posterity,
At our importance hither is he come,
To spread his colours, boy, in thy behalf,
And to rebuke the usurpation
Of thy unnatural uncle, English John: *10*
Embrace him, love him, give him welcome hither.

Arth. God shall forgive you Cœur-de-lion's
    death
The rather that you give his offspring life,
Shadowing their right under your wings of war:
I give you welcome with a powerless hand,
But with a heart full of unstained love;
Welcome before the gates of Angiers, Duke.

Lew. A noble boy! Who would not do thee
    right?

Aust. Upon thy cheek lay I this zealous kiss
As seal to this indenture of my love   *20*
That to my home I will no more return
Till Angiers and the right thou hast in France,
Together with that pale, that white-faced shore,
Whose foot spurns back the ocean's roaring tides
And coops from other lands her islanders,
Even till that England, hedged in with the main,
That water-walled bulwark, still secure
And confident from foreign purposes,
Even till that utmost corner of the west
Salute thee for her king: till then, fair boy, *30*
Will I not think of home, but follow arms.

Const. O, take his mother's thanks, a widow's
    thanks,
Till your strong hand shall help to give him
    strength
To make a more requital to your love!

Aust. The peace of heaven is theirs that lift
    their swords
In such a just and charitable war.

K. Phi. Well then, to work: our cannon shall be
    bent
Against the brows of this resisting town.
Call for our chiefest men of discipline,
To cull the plots of best advantages: *40*
We'll lay before this town our royal bones,

Wade to the market-place in Frenchmen's blood,
But we will make it subject to this boy.

Const. Stay for an answer to your embassy,
Lest unadvised you stain your swords with
      blood:
My Lord Chatillon may from England bring
That right in peace which here we urge in war,
And then we shall repent each drop of blood
That hot rash haste so indirectly shed.

Enter CHATILLON.

K. Phi. A wonder, lady! lo, upon thy wish,
Our messenger Chatillon is arrived!   51
What England says, say briefly, gentle lord;
We coldly pause for thee; Chatillon, speak.

Chat. Then turn your forces from this paltry
      siege
And stir them up against a mightier task.
England, impatient of your just demands,
Hath put himself in arms: the adverse winds,
Whose leisure I have stay'd, have given him
      time
To land his legions all as soon as I;
His marches are expedient to this town,   60
His forces strong, his soldiers confident.
With him along is come the mother-queen,
An Ate, stirring him to blood and strife;
With her her niece, the Lady Blanch of Spain;
With them a bastard of the king's deceased;
And all the unsettled humours of the land,
Rash, inconsiderate, fiery voluntaries,
With ladies' faces and fierce dragons' spleens,
Have sold their fortunes at their native homes,
Bearing their birthrights proudly on their backs,
To make a hazard of new fortunes here: 71
In brief, a braver choice of dauntless spirits
Than now the English bottoms have waft o'er
Did never float upon the swelling tide,
To do offence and scath in Christendom.
      Drum beats.
The interruption of their churlish drums
Cuts off more circumstance: they are at hand
To parley or to fight; therefore prepare.

K. Phi. How much unlook'd for is this expedi-
      tion!

Aust. By how much unexpected, by so much
We must awake endeavour for defence;   81
For courage mounteth with occasion:
Let them be welcome then; we are prepared.

Enter KING JOHN, ELINOR, BLANCH, *the*
BASTARD, *Lords, and forces.*

K. John. Peace be to France, if France in peace
      permit
Our just and lineal entrance to our own;
If not, bleed France, and peace ascend to heaven,

Whiles we, God's wrathful agent, do correct
Their proud contempt that beats His peace to
      heaven.

K. Phi. Peace be to England, if that war return
From France to England, there to live in peace.
England we love; and for that England's sake   91
With burden of our armour here we sweat.
This toil of ours should be a work of thine;
But thou from loving England art so far,
That thou hast under-wrought his lawful king,
Cut off the sequence of posterity,
Out-faced infant state, and done a rape
Upon the maiden virtue of the crown.
Look here upon thy brother Geoffrey's face;
These eyes, these brows, were moulded out of
      his: 100
This little abstract doth contain that large
Which died in Geoffrey, and the hand of time
Shall draw this brief into as huge a volume.
That Geoffrey was thy elder brother born,
And this his son; England was Geoffrey's right
And this is Geoffrey's: in the name of God
How comes it then that thou art call'd a king,
When living blood doth in these temples beat,
Which owe the crown that thou o'ermasterest?

K. John. From whom hast thou this great com-
      mission, France,   110
To draw my answer from thy articles?

K. Phi. From that supernal judge, that stirs good
      thoughts
In any breast of strong authority,
To look into the blots and stains of right:
That judge hath made me guardian to this boy:
Under whose warrant I impeach thy wrong
And by whose help I mean to chastise it.

K. John. Alack, thou dost usurp authority.

K. Phi. Excuse, it is to beat usurping down.

Eli. Who is it thou dost call usurper, France?

Const. Let me make answer; thy usurping son.

Eli. Out, insolent! thy bastard shall be king
That thou mayst be a queen, and check the
      world!

Const. My bed was ever to thy son as true
As thine was to thy husband; and this boy
Liker in feature to his father Geoffrey
Than thou and John in manners; being as like
As rain to water, or devil to his dam.
My boy a bastard! By my soul, I think
His father never was so true begot: 130
It cannot be, an if thou wert his mother.

Eli. There's a good mother, boy, that blots thy
      father.

Const. There's a good grandam, boy, that would
      blot thee.

Aust. Peace!

Bast.   Hear the crier.

Aust.   What the devil art thou?
Bast. One that will play the devil, sir, with you,
An a' may catch your hide and you alone:
You are the hare of whom the proverb goes,
Whose valour plucks dead lions by the beard:
I'll smoke your skin-coat, an I catch you right;
Sirrah, look to 't; i' faith, I will, i' faith.   *140*
   Blanch. O, well did he become that lion's robe
That did disrobe the lion of that robe!
   Bast. It lies as sightly on the back of him
As great Alcides' shows upon an ass:
But, ass, I'll take that burthen from your back,
Or lay on that shall make your shoulders crack.
   Aust. What cracker is this same that deafs our
     ears
With this abundance of superfluous breath?
   K. Phi. Lewis, determine what we shall do
     straight.
   Lew. Women and fools, break off your con-
     ference.   *150*
King John, this is the very sum of all;
England and Ireland, Anjou, Touraine, Maine,
In right of Arthur do I claim of thee:
Wilt thou resign them and lay down thy arms?
   K. John. My life as soon: I do defy thee,
     France.
Arthur of Bretagne, yield thee to my hand;
And out of my dear love I'll give thee more
Than e'er the coward hand of France can win:
Submit thee, boy.
   Eli.   Come to thy grandam, child.
   Const. Do, child, go to it grandam, child;   *160*
Give grandam kingdom, and it grandam will
Give it a plum, a cherry, and a fig:
There's a good grandam.
   Arth.   Good my mother, peace!
I would that I were low laid in my grave:
I am not worth this coil that's made for me.
   Eli. His mother shames him so, poor boy, he
     weeps.
   Const. Now shame upon you, whether she does
     or no!
His grandam's wrongs, and not his mother's
     shames,
Draws those heaven-moving pearls from his poor
     eyes,
Which heaven shall take in nature of a fee;   *170*
Ay, with these crystal beads heaven shall be
     bribed
To do him justice and revenge on you.
   Eli. Thou monstrous slanderer of heaven and
     earth!
   Const. Thou monstrous injurer of heaven and
     earth!
Call not me slanderer; thou and thine usurp
The dominations, royalties, and rights

Of this oppressed boy: this is thy eld'st son's son,
Infortunate in nothing but in thee:
Thy sins are visited in this poor child;
The canon of the law is laid on him,   *180*
Being but the second generation
Removed from thy sin-conceiving womb.
   K. John. Bedlam, have done.
   Const.   I have but this to say,
That he is not only plagued for her sin,
But God hath made her sin and her the plague
On this removed issue, plagued for her
And with her plague; her sin his injury,
Her injury the beadle to her sin,
All punish'd in the person of this child,
And all for her; a plague upon her!   *190*
   Eli. Thou unadvised scold, I can produce
A will that bars the title of thy son.
   Const. Ay, who doubts that? a will! a wicked
     will;
A woman's will; a canker'd grandam's will!
   K. Phi. Peace, lady! pause, or be more tem-
     perate:
It ill beseems this presence to cry aim
To these ill-tuned repetitions.
Some trumpet summon hither to the walls
These men of Angiers: let us hear them speak
Whose title they admit, Arthur's or John's.   *200*

     Trumpet sounds. Enter a CITIZEN *upon*
           the walls, attended.

   Cit. Who is it that hath warn'd us to the walls?
   K. Phi. 'Tis France, for England.
   K. John.   England, for itself.
You men of Angiers, and my loving subjects—
   K. Phi. You loving men of Angiers, Arthur's
     subjects,
Our trumpet call'd you to this gentle parle—
   K. John. For our advantage; therefore hear us
     first.
These flags of France, that are advanced here
Before the eye and prospect of your town,
Have hither march'd to your endamagement:
The cannons have their bowels full of wrath,   *210*
And ready mounted are they to spit forth
Their iron indignation 'gainst your walls:
All preparation for a bloody siege
And merciless proceeding by these French
Confronts your city's eyes, your winking gates;
And but for our approach those sleeping stones,
That as a waist doth girdle you about,
By the compulsion of their ordinance
By this time from their fixed beds of lime
Had been dishabited, and wide havoc made   *220*
For bloody power to rush upon your peace.
But on the sight of us your lawful king,
Who painfully with much expedient march

Have brought a countercheck before your gates,
To save unscratch'd your city's threatened
   cheeks,
Behold, the French amazed vouchsafe a parle;
And now, instead of bullets wrapp'd in fire,
To make a shaking fever in your walls,
They shoot but calm words folded up in smoke,
To make a faithless error in your ears: 230
Which trust accordingly kind citizens,
And let us in, your king, whose labour'd spirits,
Forwearied in this action of swift speed,
Crave harbourage within your city walls.
   K. Phi. When I have said, make answer to us
   both.
Lo, in this right hand, whose protection
Is most divinely vow'd upon the right
Of him it holds, stands young Plantagenet,
Son to the elder brother of this man,
And king o'er him and all that he enjoys: 240
For this down-trodden equity, we tread
In warlike march these greens before your town,
Being no further enemy to you
Than the constraint of hospitable zeal
In the relief of this oppressed child
Religiously provokes. Be pleased then
To pay that duty which you truly owe
To him that owes it, namely this young prince:
And then our arms, like to a muzzled bear,
Save in aspect, hath all offence seal'd up;   250
Our cannons' malice vainly shall be spent
Against the invulnerable clouds of heaven;
And with a blessed and unvex'd retire,
With unhack'd swords and helmets all unbruised,
We will bear home that lusty blood again
Which here we came to spout against your town,
And leave your children, wives, and you in peace.
But if you fondly pass our proffer'd offer,
'Tis not the roundure of your old-faced walls
Can hide you from our messengers of war,   260
Though all these English and their discipline
Were harbour'd in their rude circumference.
Then tell us, shall your city call us lord,
In that behalf which we have challenged it?
Or shall we give the signal to our rage
And stalk in blood to our possession?
   Cit. In brief, we are the King of England's sub-
   jects:
For him, and in his right, we hold this town.
   K. John. Acknowledge then the King, and let
   me in.
   Cit. That can we not; but he that proves the
   King,   270
To him will we prove loyal: till that time
Have we ramm'd up our gates against the world.
   K. John. Doth not the crown of England prove
   the King?

And if not that, I bring you witnesses,
Twice fifteen thousand hearts of England's
   breed—
   Bast. Bastards, and else.
   K. John. To verify our title with their lives.
   K. Phi. As many and as well-born bloods as
   those—
   Bast. Some bastards too.
   K. Phi. Stand in his face to contradict his claim.
   Cit. Till you compound whose right is worthi-
   est,   281
We for the worthiest hold the right from both.
   K. John. Then God forgive the sin of all those
   souls
That to their everlasting residence,
Before the dew of evening fall, shall fleet,
In dreadful trial of our kingdom's king!
   K. Phi. Amen, amen! Mount, chevaliers! to
   arms!
   Bast. Saint George, that swinged the dragon,
   and e'er since
Sits on his horse back at mine hostess' door,
Teach us some fence! [*To* AUSTRIA] Sirrah, were
   I at home,   290
At your den, sirrah, with your lioness,
I would set an ox-head to your lion's hide,
And make a monster of you.
   Aust.   Peace! no more.
   Bast. O, tremble, for you hear the lion roar.
   K. John. Up higher to the plain; where we'll
   set forth
In best appointment all our regiments.
   Bast. Speed then, to take advantage of the field.
   K. Phi. It shall be so; and at the other hill
Command the rest to stand. God and our right!
                        [*Exeunt.*

Here after excursions, enter the HERALD OF
   FRANCE, *with trumpets, to the gates.*

   F. Her. You men of Angiers, open wide your
   gates,   300
And let young Arthur, Duke of Bretagne, in,
Who by the hand of France this day hath made
Much work for tears in many an English mother,
Whose sons lie scattered on the bleeding ground;
Many a widow's husband grovelling lies,
Coldly embracing the discolour'd earth;
And victory, with little loss, doth play
Upon the dancing banners of the French,
Who are at hand, triumphantly display'd,
To enter conquerors and to proclaim   310
Arthur of Bretagne England's king and yours.

Enter ENGLISH HERALD, *with trumpet.*

   E. Her. Rejoice, you men of Angiers, ring your
   bells;

King John, your king and England's, doth approach,
Commander of this hot malicious day:
Their armours, that march'd hence so silver-bright,
Hither return all gilt with Frenchmen's blood;
There stuck no plume in any English crest
That is removed by a staff of France;
Our colours do return in those same hands
That did display them when we first march'd forth;
And, like a jolly troop of huntsmen, come   321
Our lusty English, all with purpled hands,
Dyed in the dying slaughter of their foes:
Open your gates and give the victors way.
    Cit. Heralds, from off our towers we might behold,
From first to last, the onset and retire
Of both your armies; whose equality
By our best eyes cannot be censured:
Blood hath bought blood and blows have answer'd blows;
Strength match'd with strength, and power confronted power: 330
Both are alike; and both alike we like.
One must prove greatest: while they weigh so even,
We hold our town for neither, yet for both.

Re-enter the two KINGS, *with their powers,
severally.*

    K. John. France, hast thou yet more blood to cast away?
Say, shall the current of our right run on?
Whose passage, vex'd with thy impediment,
Shall leave his native channel and o'erswell
With course disturb'd even thy confining shores,
Unless thou let his silver water keep
A peaceful progress to the ocean.   340
    K. Phi. England, thou hast not saved one drop of blood,
In this hot trial, more than we of France;
Rather, lost more. And by this hand I swear,
That sways the earth this climate overlooks,
Before we will lay down our just-borne arms,
We'll put thee down, 'gainst whom these arms we bear,
Or add a royal number to the dead,
Gracing the scroll that tells of this war's loss
With slaughter coupled to the name of kings.
    Bast. Ha, majesty! how high thy glory towers,
When the rich blood of kings is set on fire!   351
O, now doth Death line his dead chaps with steel;
The swords of soldiers are his teeth, his fangs;
And now he feasts, mousing the flesh of men,
In undetermined differences of kings.

Why stand these royal fronts amazed thus?
Cry, "havoc!" kings; back to the stained field,
You equal potents, fiery kindled spirits!
Then let confusion of one part confirm
The other's peace; till then, blows, blood, and death!   360
    K. John. Whose party do the townsmen yet admit?
    K. Phi. Speak, citizens, for England; who's your king?
    Cit. The King of England, when we know the King.
    K. Phi. Know him in us, that here hold up his right.
    K. John. In us, that are our own great deputy,
And bear possession of our person here,
Lord of our presence, Angiers, and of you.
    Cit. A greater power than we denies all this;
And till it be undoubted, we do lock
Our former scruple in our strong-barr'd gates;
King'd of our fears, until our fears, resolved,   371
Be by some certain king purged and deposed.
    Bast. By heaven, these scroyles of Angiers flout you, kings,
And stand securely on their battlements
As in a theatre, whence they gape and point
At your industrious scenes and acts of death.
Your royal presences be ruled by me:
Do like the mutines of Jerusalem,
Be friends awhile and both conjointly bend
Your sharpest deeds of malice on this town: 380
By east and west let France and England mount
Their battering cannon charged to the mouths,
Till their soul-fearing clamours have brawl'd down
The flinty ribs of this contemptuous city:
I'ld play incessantly upon these jades,
Even till unfenced desolation
Leave them as naked as the vulgar air.
That done, dissever your united strengths,
And part your mingled colours once again;
Turn face to face and bloody point to point;   390
Then, in a moment, Fortune shall cull forth
Out of one side her happy minion,
To whom in favour she shall give the day,
And kiss him with a glorious victory.
How like you this wild counsel, mighty states?
Smacks it not something of the policy?
    K. John. Now, by the sky that hangs above our heads,
I like it well. France, shall we knit our powers
And lay this Angiers even with the ground;
Then after fight who shall be king of it?   400
    Bast. An if thou hast the mettle of a king,
Being wrong'd as we are by this peevish town,
Turn thou the mouth of thy artillery,

As we will ours, against these saucy walls;
And when that we have dash'd them to the
    ground,
Why then defy each other, and pell-mell
Make work upon ourselves, for heaven or hell.

  K. Phi. Let it be so. Say, where will you as-
    sault?

  K. John. We from the west will send destruc-
    tion
Into this city's bosom.   410

  Aust. I from the north.

  K. Phi.   Our thunder from the south
Shall rain their drift of bullets on this town.

  Bast. O prudent discipline! From north to south:
Austria and France shoot in each other's mouth:
I'll stir them to it. Come, away, away!

  Cit. Hear us, great kings: vouchsafe awhile to
    stay,
And I shall show you peace and fair-faced league
Win you this city without stroke or wound;
Rescue those breathing lives to die in beds,
That here come sacrifices for the field: 420
Persever not, but hear me, mighty kings.

  K. John. Speak on with favour; we are bent to
    hear.

  Cit. That daughter there of Spain, the Lady
    Blanch,
Is niece to England: look upon the years
Of Lewis the Dauphin and that lovely maid:
If lusty love should go in quest of beauty,
Where should he find it fairer than in Blanch?
If zealous love should go in search of virtue,
Where should he find it purer than in Blanch?
If love ambitious sought a match of birth, 430
Whose veins bound richer blood than Lady
    Blanch?
Such as she is, in beauty, virtue, birth,
Is the young Dauphin every way complete:
If not complete of, say he is not she;
And she again wants nothing, to name want,
If want it be not that she is not he:
He is the half part of a blessed man,
Left to be finished by such as she;
And she a fair divided excellence,
Whose fulness of perfection lies in him. 440
O, two such silver currents, when they join,
Do glorify the banks that bound them in;
And two such shores to two such streams made
    one,
Two such controlling bounds shall you be, kings,
To these two princes, if you marry them.
This union shall do more than battery can
To our fast-closed gates; for at this match,
With swifter spleen than powder can enforce,
The mouth of passage shall we fling wide ope,
And give you entrance: but without this match,

The sea enraged is not half so deaf,   451
Lions more confident, mountains and rocks
More free from motion, no, not Death himself
In mortal fury half so peremptory,
As we to keep this city.

  Bast.   Here's a stay
That shakes the rotten carcass of old Death
Out of his rags! Here's a large mouth, indeed,
That spits forth death and mountains, rocks and
    seas,
Talks as familiarly of roaring lions
As maids of thirteen do of puppy-dogs! 460
What cannoneer begot this lusty blood?
He speaks plain cannon fire, and smoke and
    bounce;
He gives the bastinado with his tongue:
Our ears are cudgell'd; not a word of his
But buffets better than a fist of France:
Zounds! I was never so bethump'd with words
Since I first called my brother's father dad.

  Eli. Son, list to this conjunction, make this
    match;
Give with our niece a dowry large enough:
For by this knot thou shalt so surely tie 470
Thy now unsured assurance to the crown,
That yon green boy shall have no sun to ripe
The bloom that promiseth a mighty fruit.
I see a yielding in the looks of France;
Mark, how they whisper: urge them while their
    souls
Are capable of this ambition,
Lest zeal, now melted by the windy breath
Of soft petitions, pity, and remorse,
Cool and congeal again to what it was.

  Cit. Why answer not the double majesties 480
This friendly treaty of our threaten'd town?

  K. Phi. Speak England first, that hath been for-
    ward first
To speak unto this city: what say you?

  K. John. If that the Dauphin there, thy princely
    son,
Can in this book of beauty read "I love,"
Her dowry shall weigh equal with a queen:
For Anjou and fair Touraine, Maine, Poictiers,
And all that we upon this side the sea,
Except this city now by us besieged,
Find liable to our crown and dignity,   490
Shall gild her bridal bed and make her rich
In titles, honours, and promotions,
As she in beauty, education, blood,
Holds hand with any princess of the world.

  K. Phi. What say'st thou, boy? look in the
    lady's face.

  Lew. I do, my lord; and in her eye I find
A wonder, or a wondrous miracle,
The shadow of myself form'd in her eye;

Which, being but the shadow of your son,
Becomes a sun and makes your son a shadow: *500*
I do protest I never loved myself
Till now infixed I beheld myself
Drawn in the flattering table of her eye.
    Whispers with BLANCH.
 Bast. Drawn in the flattering table of her eye!
  Hang'd in the frowning wrinkle of her brow!
And quarter'd in her heart! he doth espy
  Himself love's traitor: this is pity now,
That, hang'd and drawn and quarter'd, there
    should be
In such a love so vile a lout as he.
 Blanch. My uncle's will in this respect is
    mine:
If he see aught in you that makes him like,   *511*
That anything he sees, which moves his liking,
I can with ease translate it to my will;
Or if you will, to speak more properly,
I will enforce it easily to my love.
Further I will not flatter you, my lord,
That all I see in you is worthy love,
Than this; that nothing do I see in you,
Though churlish thoughts themselves should be
    your judge,
That I can find should merit any hate.   *520*
 K. John. What say these young ones? What say
  you, my niece?
 Blanch. That she is bound in honour still to do
What you in wisdom still vouchsafe to say.
 K. John. Speak then, Prince Dauphin; can you
  love this lady?
 Lew. Nay, ask me if I can refrain from love;
For I do love her most unfeignedly.
 K. John. Then do I give Volquessen, Touraine,
  Maine,
Poictiers and Anjou, these five provinces,
With her to thee; and this addition more,
Full thirty thousand marks of English coin.   *530*
Philip of France, if thou be pleased withal,
Command thy son and daughter to join hands.
 K. Phi. It likes us well; young princes, close
  your hands.
 Aust. And your lips too; for I am well assured
That I did so when I was first assured.
 K. Phi. Now, citizens of Angiers, ope your
  gates,
Let in that amity which you have made;
For at Saint Mary's chapel presently
The rites of marriage shall be solemnized.
Is not the Lady Constance in this troop?   *540*
I know she is not, for this match made up
Her presence would have interrupted much:
Where is she and her son? tell me, who knows.
 Lew. She is sad and passionate at your High-
  ness' tent.

 K. Phil. And, by my faith, this league that we
  have made
Will give her sadness very little cure.
Brother of England, how may we content
This widow lady? In her right we came;
Which we, God knows, have turn'd another way,
To our own vantage.
 K. John.   We will heal up all;   *550*
For we'll create young Arthur Duke of Bretagne
And Earl of Richmond; and this rich fair town
We make him lord of. Call the Lady Constance;
Some speedy messenger bid her repair
To our solemnity: I trust we shall,
If not fill up the measure of her will,
Yet in some measure satisfy her so
That we shall stop her exclamation.
Go we, as well as haste will suffer us,
To this unlook'd for, unprepared pomp.   *560*
    [*Exeunt all but the* BASTARD.
 Bast. Mad world! mad kings! mad composition!
John, to stop Arthur's title in the whole,
Hath willingly departed with a part,
And France, whose armour conscience buckled
    on,
Whom zeal and charity brought to the field
As God's own soldier, rounded in the ear
With that same purpose-changer, that sly devil,
That broker, that still breaks the pate of faith,
That daily break-vow, he that wins of all,
Of kings, of beggars, old men, young men, maids,
Who, having no external thing to lose   *571*
But the word "maid," cheats the poor maid of
    that,
That smooth-faced gentleman, tickling Com-
    modity,
Commodity, the bias of the world,
The world, who of itself is peised well,
Made to run even upon even ground,
Till this advantage, this vile-drawing bias,
This sway of motion, this Commodity,
Makes it take head from all indifferency,
From all direction, purpose, course, intent: *580*
And this same bias, this Commodity,
This bawd, this broker, this all-changing word,
Clapp'd on the outward eye of fickle France,
Hath drawn him from his own determined aid,
From a resolved and honourable war,
To a most base and vile-concluded peace.
And why rail I on this Commodity?
But for because he hath not woo'd me yet:
Not that I have the power to clutch my hand,
When his fair angels would salute my palm;   *590*
But for my hand, as unattempted yet,
Like a poor beggar, raileth on the rich.
Well, whiles I am a beggar, I will rail
And say there is no sin but to be rich;

And being rich, my virtue then shall be
To say there is no vice but beggary.
Since kings break faith upon Commodity,
Gain, be my lord, for I will worship thee.   [*Exit.*

ACT III

SCENE I. *The French King's pavilion*

Enter CONSTANCE, ARTHUR, *and* SALISBURY.

Const. Gone to be married! gone to swear a
    peace!
False blood to false blood join'd! gone to be
    friends!
Shall Lewis have Blanch, and Blanch those prov-
    inces?
It is not so; thou hast misspoke, misheard;
Be well advised, tell o'er thy tale again:
It cannot be; thou dost but say 'tis so:
I trust I may not trust thee; for thy word
Is but the vain breath of a common man:
Believe me, I do not believe thee, man;
I have a king's oath to the contrary.   10
Thou shalt be punish'd for thus frighting me,
For I am sick and capable of fears,
Oppress'd with wrongs and therefore full of
    fears,
A widow, husbandless, subject to fears,
A woman, naturally born to fears;
And though thou now confess thou didst but jest,
With my vex'd spirits I cannot take a truce,
But they will quake and tremble all this day.
What dost thou mean by shaking of thy head?
Why dost thou look so sadly on my son?   20
What means that hand upon that breast of thine?
Why holds thine eye that lamentable rheum,
Like a proud river peering o'er his bounds?
Be these sad signs confirmers of thy words?
Then speak again; not all thy former tale,
But this one word, whether thy tale be true.
Sal. As true as I believe you think them false
That give you cause to prove my saying true.
Const. O, if thou teach me to believe this sorrow,
Teach thou this sorrow how to make me die,   30
And let belief and life encounter so
As doth the fury of two desperate men
Which in the very meeting fall and die.
Lewis marry Blanch! O boy, then where art thou?
France friend with England, what becomes of
    me?
Fellow, be gone: I cannot brook thy sight:
This news hath made thee a most ugly man.
Sal. What other harm have I, good lady, done,
But spoke the harm that is by others done?
Const. Which harm within itself so heinous is
As it makes harmful all that speak of it.   41
Arth. I do beseech you, madam, be content.

Const. If thou, that bid'st me be content, wert
    grim,
Ugly, and slanderous to thy mother's womb,
Full of unpleasing blots and sightless stains,
Lame, foolish, crooked, swart, prodigious,
Patch'd with foul moles and eye-offending marks,
I would not care, I then would be content,
For then I should not love thee, no, nor thou
Become thy great birth nor deserve a crown.   50
But thou art fair, and at thy birth, dear boy,
Nature and Fortune join'd to make thee great:
Of Nature's gifts thou mayst with lilies boast
And with the half-blown rose. But Fortune, O,
She is corrupted, changed, and won from thee;
She adulterates hourly with thine uncle John,
And with her golden hand hath pluck'd on France
To tread down fair respect of sovereignty,
And made his majesty the bawd to theirs.
France is a bawd to Fortune and King John,   60
That strumpet Fortune, that usurping John!
Tell me, thou fellow, is not France forsworn?
Envenom him with words, or get thee gone
And leave those woes alone which I alone
Am bound to under-bear.
Sal.   Pardon me, madam,
I may not go without you to the kings.
Const. Thou mayst, thou shalt; I will not go
    with thee:
I will instruct my sorrows to be proud;
For grief is proud and makes his owner stoop.
To me and to the state of my great grief   70
Let kings assemble; for my grief's so great
That no supporter but the huge firm earth
Can hold it up: here I and sorrows sit;
Here is my throne, bid kings come bow to it.
    Seats herself on the ground.

Enter KING JOHN, KING PHILIP, LEWIS, BLANCH,
ELINOR, *the* BASTARD, AUSTRIA, *and Attendants.*

K. Phi. 'Tis true, fair daughter; and this blessed
    day
Ever in France shall be kept festival:
To solemnize this day the glorious sun
Stays in his course and plays the alchemist,
Turning with splendour of his precious eye
The meagre cloddy earth to glittering gold: 80
The yearly course that brings this day about
Shall never see it but a holiday.
Const. A wicked day, and not a holy day!
    Rising.
What hath this day deserved? what hath it done,
That it in golden letters should be set
Among the high tides in the calendar?
Nay, rather turn this day out of the week,
This day of shame, oppression, perjury.
Or, if it must stand still, let wives with child

Pray that their burthens may not fall this day, *90*
Lest that their hopes prodigiously be cross'd:
But on this day let seamen fear no wreck;
No bargains break that are not this day made:
This day, all things begun come to ill end,
Yea, faith itself to hollow falsehood change!
  K. Phi. By heaven, lady, you shall have no
    cause
To curse the fair proceedings of this day:
Have I not pawn'd to you my majesty?
  Const. You have beguiled me with a counterfeit
Resembling majesty, which, being touch'd and
    tried,   *100*
Proves valueless: you are forsworn, forsworn;
You came in arms to spill mine enemies' blood,
But now in arms you strengthen it with yours:
The grappling vigour and rough frown of war
Is cold in amity and painted peace,
And our oppression hath made up this league.
Arm, arm, you heavens, against these perjured
    kings!
A widow cries; be husband to me, heavens!
Let not the hours of this ungodly day
Wear out the day in peace; but, ere sunset,   *110*
Set armed discord 'twixt these perjured kings!
Hear me, O, hear me!
  Aust.   Lady Constance, peace!
  Const. War! war! no peace! peace is to me a
    war.
O Lymoges! O Austria! thou dost shame
That bloody spoil: thou slave, thou wretch, thou
    coward!
Thou little valiant, great in villainy!
Thou ever strong upon the stronger side!
Thou Fortune's champion that dost never fight
But when her humorous ladyship is by
To teach thee safety! thou art perjured too, *120*
And soothest up greatness. What a fool art thou,
A ramping fool, to brag and stamp and swear
Upon my party! Thou cold-blooded slave,
Hast thou not spoke like thunder on my side,
Been sworn my soldier, bidding me depend
Upon thy stars, thy fortune, and thy strength,
And dost thou now fall over to my foes?
Thou wear a lion's hide! doff it for shame,
And hang a calf's-skin on those recreant limbs,
  Aust. O, that a man should speak those words
    to me!   *130*
  Bast. And hang a calf's-skin on those recreant
    limbs.
  Aust. Thou darest not say so, villain, for thy
    life.
  Bast. And hang a calf's-skin on those recreant
    limbs.
  K. John. We like not this; thou dost forget
    thyself.

Enter PANDULPH.

  K. Phi. Here comes the holy legate of the
    Pope.
  Pand. Hail, you anointed deputies of heaven!
To thee, King John, my holy errand is.
I Pandulph, of fair Milan cardinal,
And from Pope Innocent the legate here,
Do in his name religiously demand   *140*
Why thou against the church, our holy mother,
So wilfully dost spurn; and force perforce
Keep Stephen Langton, chosen Archbishop
Of Canterbury, from that holy see?
This, in our foresaid Holy Father's name,
Pope Innocent, I do demand of thee.
  K. John. What earthly name to interrogatories
Can task the free breath of a sacred king?
Thou canst not, Cardinal, devise a name
So slight, unworthy, and ridiculous,   *150*
To charge me to an answer, as the Pope.
Tell him this tale; and from the mouth of England
Add thus much more, that no Italian priest
Shall tithe or toll in our dominions;
But as we, under heaven, are supreme head,
So under Him that great supremacy,
Where we do reign, we will alone uphold,
Without the assistance of a mortal hand:
So tell the Pope, all reverence set apart
To him and his usurp'd authority.   *160*
  K. Phi. Brother of England, you blaspheme
    in this.
  K. John. Though you and all the kings of
    Christendom
Are led so grossly by this meddling priest,
Dreading the curse that money may buy out;
And by the merit of vile gold, dross, dust,
Purchase corrupted pardon of a man,
Who in that sale sells pardon from himself,
Though you and all the rest so grossly led
This juggling witchcraft with revenue cherish,
Yet I alone, alone do me oppose   *170*
Against the Pope and count his friends my foes.
  Pand. Then, by the lawful power that I have,
Thou shalt stand cursed and excommunicate:
And blessed shall he be that doth revolt
From his allegiance to an heretic;
And meritorious shall that hand be call'd,
Canonized and worshipp'd as a saint,
That takes away by any secret course
Thy hateful life.
  Const.   O, lawful let it be
That I have room with Rome to curse awhile! *180*
Good father Cardinal, cry thou amen
To my keen curses: for without my wrong
There is no tongue hath power to curse him
    right.

Pand. There's law and warrant, lady, for my
    curse.

Const. And for mine too: when law can do
    no right,
Let it be lawful that law bar no wrong:
Law cannot give my child his kingdom here,
For he that holds his kingdom holds the law;
Therefore, since law itself is perfect wrong,
How can the law forbid my tongue to curse?

Pand. Philip of France, on peril of a curse,
Let go the hand of that arch-heretic;
And raise the power of France upon his head,
Unless he do submit himself to Rome.

Eli. Look'st thou pale, France? do not let go
    thy hand.

Const. Look to that, devil; lest that France re-
    pent,
And, by disjoining hands, hell lose a soul.

Aust. King Philip, listen to the Cardinal.

Bast. And hang a calf's-skin on his recreant
    limbs.

Aust. Well, ruffian, I must pocket up these
    wrongs,   *200*
Because—

Bast. Your breeches best may carry them.

K. John. Philip, what say'st thou to the Car-
    dinal?

Const. What should he say, but as the Car-
    dinal?

Lew. Bethink you, father; for the difference
Is purchase of a heavy curse from Rome,
Or the light loss of England for a friend:
Forego the easier.

Blanch.   That's the curse of Rome.

Const. O Lewis, stand fast! the devil tempts thee
    here
In likeness of a new untrimmed bride.

Blanch. The Lady Constance speaks not from
    her faith,   *210*
But from her need.

Const.   O, if thou grant my need,
Which only lives but by the death of faith,
That need must needs infer this principle,
That faith would live again by death of
    need.
O then, tread down my need, and faith mounts
    up;
Keep my need up, and faith is trodden down!

K. John. The King is moved, and answers not
    to this.

Const. O, be removed from him, and answer
    well!

Aust. Do so, King Philip; hang no more in
    doubt.

Bast. Hang nothing but a calf's-skin, most
    sweet lout.   *220*

K. Phi. I am perplex'd, and know not what to
    say.

Pand. What canst thou say but will perplex thee
    more,
If thou stand excommunicate and cursed?

K. Phi. Good reverend father, make my person
    yours,
And tell me how you would bestow yourself.
This royal hand and mine are newly knit,
And the conjunction of our inward souls
Married in league, coupled, and link'd together
With all religious strength of sacred vows;
The latest breath that gave the sound of words *230*
Was deep-sworn faith, peace, amity, true love
Between our kingdoms and our royal selves,
And even before this truce, but new before,
No longer than we well could wash our hands
To clap this royal bargain up of peace,
Heaven knows, they were besmear'd and over-
    stain'd
With slaughter's pencil, where revenge did paint
The fearful difference of incensed kings:
And shall these hands, so lately purged of blood,
So newly join'd in love, so strong in both,   *240*
Unyoke this seizure and this kind regreet?
Play fast and loose with faith? so jest with
    heaven,
Make such unconstant children of ourselves,
As now again to snatch our palm from palm,
Unswear faith sworn, and on the marriage-bed
Of smiling peace to march a bloody host,
And make a riot on the gentle brow
Of true sincerity? O, holy sir,
My reverend father, let it not be so!
Out of your grace, devise, ordain, impose   *250*
Some gentle order; and then we shall be blest
To do your pleasure and continue friends.

Pand. All form is formless, order orderless,
Save what is opposite to England's love.
Therefore to arms! be champion of our church,
Or let the church, our mother, breathe her curse,
A mother's curse, on her revolting son.
France, thou mayst hold a serpent by the tongue,
A chafed lion by the mortal paw,
A fasting tiger safer by the tooth,   *260*
Than keep in peace that hand which thou dost
    hold.

K. Phi. I may disjoin my hand, but not my
    faith.

Pand. So makest thou faith an enemy to faith;
And like a civil war set'st oath to oath,
Thy tongue against thy tongue. O, let thy vow
First made to heaven, first be to heaven per-
    form'd,
That is, to be the champion of our church!
What since thou sworest is sworn against thyself

And may not be performed by thyself,
For that which thou hast sworn to do amiss   270
Is not amiss when it is truly done,
And being not done, where doing tends to ill,
The truth is then most done not doing it:
The better act of purposes mistook
Is to mistake again; though indirect,
Yet indirection thereby grows direct,
And falsehood falsehood cures, as fire cools fire
Within the scorched veins of one new-burn'd.
It is religion that doth make vows kept;
But thou hast sworn against religion,   280
By what thou swear'st against the thing thou
    swear'st,
And makest an oath the surety for thy truth
Against an oath: the truth thou art unsure
To swear, swears only not to be forsworn;
Else what a mockery should it be to swear!
But thou dost swear only to be forsworn;
And most forsworn, to keep what thou dost
    swear.
Therefore thy later vows against thy first
Is in thyself rebellion to thyself;
And better conquest never canst thou make   290
Than arm thy constant and thy nobler parts
Against these giddy loose suggestions:
Upon which better part our prayers come in,
If thou vouchsafe them. But if not, then know
The peril of our curses light on thee
So heavy as thou shalt not shake them off,
But in despair die under their black weight.
    Aust. Rebellion, flat rebellion!
    Bast.   Will't not be?
Will not a calf's-skin stop that mouth of thine?
    Lew. Father, to arms!
    Blanch.   Upon thy wedding day?   300
Against the blood that thou hast married?
What, shall our feast be kept with slaughter'd
    men?
Shall braying trumpets and loud churlish drums,
Clamours of hell, be measures to our pomp?
O husband, hear me! ay, alack, how new
Is husband in my mouth! even for that name,
Which till this time my tongue did ne'er pro-
    nounce,
Upon my knee I beg, go not to arms
Against mine uncle.
    Const.   O, upon my knee,
Made hard with kneeling, I do pray to thee,   310
Thou virtuous Dauphin, alter not the doom
Forethought by heaven!
    Blanch. Now shall I see thy love: what mo-
    tive may
Be stronger with thee than the name of wife?
    Const. That which upholdeth him that thee
    upholds,

His honour: O, thine honour, Lewis, thine
    honour!
    Lew. I muse your Majesty doth seem so cold,
When such profound respects do pull you on.
    Pand. I will denounce a curse upon his head.
    K. Phi. Thou shalt not need. England, I will fall
    from thee.   320
    Const. O fair return of banish'd majesty!
    Eli. O foul revolt of French inconstancy!
    K. John. France, thou shalt rue this hour within
    this hour.
    Bast. Old Time the clock-setter, that bald sex-
    ton Time,
Is it as he will? well then, France shall rue.
    Blanch. The sun's o'ercast with blood: fair day,
    adieu!
Which is the side that I must go withal?
I am with both: each army hath a hand;
And in their rage, I having hold of both,
They whirl asunder and dismember me.   330
Husband, I cannot pray that thou mayst win;
Uncle, I needs must pray that thou mayst
    lose;
Father, I may not wish the fortune thine;
Grandam, I will not wish thy wishes thrive:
Whoever wins, on that side shall I lose;
Assured loss before the match be play'd.
    Lew. Lady, with me, with me thy fortune lies.
    Blanch. There where my fortune lives, there my
    life dies.
    K. John. Cousin, go draw our puissance to-
    gether.   [*Exit* BASTARD.
France, I am burn'd up with inflaming wrath;   340
A rage whose heat hath this condition,
That nothing can allay, nothing but blood,
The blood, and dearest-valued blood, of France.
    K. Phi. Thy rage shall burn thee up, and thou
    shalt turn
To ashes, ere our blood shall quench that fire:
Look to thyself, thou art in jeopardy.
    K. John. No more than he that threats. To arms
    let's hie!   [*Exeunt.*

SCENE II. *The same: plains near Angiers*

Alarums, excursions. Enter the BASTARD, *with*
AUSTRIA'S *head.*

    Bast. Now, by my life, this day grows won-
    drous hot;
Some airy devil hovers in the sky
And pours down mischief. Austria's head lie
    there,
While Philip breathes.

    Enter KING JOHN, ARTHUR, *and* HUBERT.

    K. John. Hubert, keep this boy. Philip, make
    up:

My mother is assailed in our tent,
And ta'en, I fear.
   Bast.   My lord, I rescued her;
Her Highness is in safety, fear you not:
But on, my liege; for very little pains
Will bring this labour to an happy end.   [*Exeunt.*

SCENE III. *The same*

Alarums, excursions, retreat. Enter KING JOHN,
ELINOR, ARTHUR, *the* BASTARD, HUBERT, *and*
Lords.

   K. John. [*To* ELINOR] So shall it be; your Grace
     shall stay behind
So strongly guarded. [*To* ARTHUR] Cousin, look
     not sad:
Thy grandam loves thee; and thy uncle will
As dear be to thee as thy father was.
   Arth. O, this will make my mother die with
     grief!
   K. John. [*To the* BASTARD] Cousin, away for
     England! haste before:
And, ere our coming, see thou shake the bags
Of hoarding abbots; imprisoned angels
Set at liberty: the fat ribs of peace
Must by the hungry now be fed upon: *10*
Use our commission in his utmost force.
   Bast. Bell, book, and candle shall not drive me
     back,
When gold and silver becks me to come on.
I leave your highness. Grandam, I will pray,
If ever I remember to be holy,
For your fair safety; so, I kiss your hand.
   Eli. Farewell, gentle cousin.
   K. John.   Coz, farewell.   [*Exit* BASTARD.
   Eli. Come hither, little kinsman; hark, a word.
   K. John. Come hither, Hubert. O my gentle
     Hubert,
We owe thee much! within this wall of flesh   *20*
There is a soul counts thee her creditor
And with advantage means to pay thy love:
And, my good friend, thy voluntary oath
Lives in this bosom, dearly cherished.
Give me thy hand. I had a thing to say,
But I will fit it with some better time.
By heaven, Hubert, I am almost ashamed
To say what good respect I have of thee.
   Hub. I am much bounden to your Majesty.
   K. John. Good friend, thou hast no cause to say
     so yet,   *30*
But thou shalt have; and creep time ne'er so slow,
Yet it shall come for me to do thee good.
I had a thing to say, but let it go:
The sun is in the heaven, and the proud day,
Attended with the pleasures of the world,
Is all too wanton and too full of gawds
To give me audience: if the midnight bell

Did, with his iron tongue and brazen mouth,
Sound on into the drowsy race of night;
If this same were a churchyard where we stand,
And thou possessed with a thousand wrongs,   *41*
Or if that surly spirit, melancholy,
Had baked thy blood and made it heavy-thick,
Which else runs tickling up and down the veins,
Making that idiot, laughter, keep men's eyes
And strain their cheeks to idle merriment,
A passion hateful to my purposes,
Or if that thou couldst see me without eyes,
Hear me without thine ears, and make reply
Without a tongue, using conceit alone,   *50*
Without eyes, ears, and harmful sound of words;
Then, in despite of brooded watchful day,
I would into thy bosom pour my thoughts:
But, ah, I will not! yet I love thee well;
And, by my troth, I think thou lovest me well.
   Hub. So well, that what you bid me undertake,
Though that my death were adjunct to my act,
By heaven, I would do it.
   K. John.   Do not I know thou wouldst?
Good Hubert, Hubert, Hubert, throw thine eye
On yon young boy: I'll tell thee what, my
     friend,   *60*
He is a very serpent in my way;
And wheresoe'er this foot of mine doth tread,
He lies before me: dost thou understand me?
Thou art his keeper.
   Hub.   And I'll keep him so,
That he shall not offend your Majesty.
   K. John.   Death.
   Hub. My lord?
   K. John.   A grave.
   Hub.   He shall not live.
   K. John.   Enough.
I could be merry now. Hubert, I love thee;
Well, I'll not say what I intend for thee:
Remember. Madam, fare you well:
I'll send those powers o'er to your Majesty.   *70*
   Eli. My blessing go with thee!
   K. John.   For England, cousin, go:
Hubert shall be your man, attend on you
With all true duty. On toward Calais, ho!
                         [*Exeunt.*

SCENE IV. *The same: the French King's tent.*

Enter KING PHILIP, LEWIS, PANDULPH, *and Attendants.*

   K. Phi. So, by a roaring tempest on the flood,
A whole armado of convicted sail
Is scatter'd and disjoin'd from fellowship.
   Pand. Courage and comfort! all shall yet go
     well.
   K. Phil. What can go well, when we have run
     so ill?

Are we not beaten? Is not Angiers lost?
Arthur ta'en prisoner? divers dear friends slain?
And bloody England into England gone,
O'erbearing interruption, spite of France?
  Lew. What he hath won, that hath he forti-
    fied: 10
So hot a speed with such advice disposed,
Such temperate order in so fierce a cause,
Doth want example: who hath read or heard
Of any kindred action like to this?
  K. Phi. Well could I bear that England had this
    praise,
So we could find some pattern of our shame.

                Enter CONSTANCE.

Look, who comes here! a grave unto a soul;
Holding the eternal spirit, against her will,
In the vile prison of afflicted breath.
I prithee, lady, go away with me.   20
  Const. Lo, now! now see the issue of your peace.
  K. Phi. Patience, good lady! comfort, gentle
    Constance!
  Const. No, I defy all counsel, all redress,
But that which ends all counsel, true redress,
Death, death; O amiable lovely death!
Thou odoriferous stench! sound rottenness!
Arise forth from the couch of lasting night,
Thou hate and terror to prosperity,
And I will kiss thy detestable bones
And put my eyeballs in thy vaulty brows   30
And ring these fingers with thy household worms
And stop this gap of breath with fulsome dust
And be a carrion monster like thyself:
Come, grin on me, and I will think thou smilest
And buss thee as thy wife. Misery's love,
O, come to me!
  K. Phi.   O fair affliction, peace!
  Const. No, no, I will not, having breath to cry:
O, that my tongue were in the thunder's mouth!
Then with a passion would I shake the world;
And rouse from sleep that fell anatomy   40
Which cannot hear a lady's feeble voice,
Which scorns a modern invocation.
  Pand. Lady, you utter madness, and not sorrow.
  Const. Thou art not holy to belie me so;
I am not mad: this hair I tear is mine;
My name is Constance; I was Geoffrey's wife;
Young Arthur is my son, and he is lost:
I am not mad: I would to heaven I were!
For then, 'tis like I should forget myself:
O, if I could, what grief should I forget!   50
Preach some philosophy to make me mad,
And thou shalt be canonized, Cardinal;
For being not mad but sensible of grief,
My reasonable part produces reason
How I may be deliver'd of these woes,

And teaches me to kill or hang myself:
If I were mad, I should forget my son,
Or madly think a babe of clouts were he:
I am not mad; too well, too well I feel
The different plague of each calamity.   60
  K. Phi. Bind up those tresses. O, what love
    I note
In the fair multitude of those her hairs!
Where but by chance a silver drop hath fallen,
Even to that drop ten thousand wiry friends
Do glue themselves in sociable grief,
Like true, inseparable, faithful loves,
Sticking together in calamity.
  Const. To England, if you will,
  K. Phi.   Bind up your hairs.
  Const. Yes, that I will; and wherefore will I
    do it?
I tore them from their bonds and cried aloud   70
"O that these hands could so redeem my son
As they have given these hairs their liberty!"
But now I envy at their liberty,
And will again commit them to their bonds,
Because my poor child is a prisoner.
And, father Cardinal, I have heard you say
That we shall see and know our friends in
    heaven:
If that be true, I shall see my boy again;
For since the birth of Cain, the first male child,
To him that did but yesterday suspire,   80
There was not such a gracious creature born.
But now will canker sorrow eat my bud
And chase the native beauty from his cheek
And he will look as hollow as a ghost,
As dim and meagre as an ague's fit,
And so he'll die; and, rising so again,
When I shall meet him in the court of heaven
I shall not know him: therefore never, never
Must I behold my pretty Arthur more.
  Pand. You hold too heinous a respect of grief. 90
  Const. He talks to me that never had a son.
  K. Phi. You are as fond of grief as of your
    child.
  Const. Grief fills the room up of my absent
    child,
Lies in his bed, walks up and down with me,
Puts on his pretty looks, repeats his words,
Remembers me of all his gracious parts,
Stuffs out his vacant garments with his form;
Then, have I reason to be fond of grief?
Fare you well: had you such a loss as I,
I could give better comfort than you do.   100
I will not keep this form upon my head [*tearing
                                          her hair*]
When there is such disorder in my wit.
O Lord! my boy, my Arthur, my fair son!
My life, my joy, my food, my all the world!

My widow-comfort, and my sorrows' cure!
[*Exit.*
K. Phi. I fear some outrage, and I'll follow her.
[*Exit.*
Lew. There's nothing in this world can make
me joy:
Life is as tedious as a twice-told tale
Vexing the dull ear of a drowsy man;
And bitter shame hath spoil'd the sweet world's
taste, *110*
That it yields nought but shame and bitterness.
Pand. Before the curing of a strong disease,
Even in the instant of repair and health,
The fit is strongest; evils that take leave,
On their departure most of all show evil:
What have you lost by losing of this day?
Lew. All days of glory, joy, and happiness.
Pand. If you had won it, certainly you had.
No, no; when Fortune means to men most
good,
She looks upon them with a threatening eye. *120*
'Tis strange to think how much King John hath
lost
In this which he accounts so clearly won:
Are not you grieved that Arthur is his prisoner?
Lew. As heartily as he is glad he hath him.
Pand. Your mind is all as youthful as your
blood.
Now hear me speak with a prophetic spirit;
For even the breath of what I mean to speak
Shall blow each dust, each straw, each little rub,
Out of the path which shall directly lead
Thy foot to England's throne; and therefore
mark.
John hath seized Arthur; and it cannot be *131*
That, whiles warm life plays in that infant's
veins,
The misplaced John should entertain an hour,
One minute, nay, one quiet breath of rest.
A sceptre snatch'd with an unruly hand
Must be as boisterously maintain'd as gain'd;
And he that stands upon a slippery place
Makes nice of no vile hold to stay him up:
That John may stand, then Arthur needs must
fall;
So be it, for it cannot be but so. *140*
Lew. But what shall I gain by young Arthur's
fall?
Pand. You, in the right of Lady Blanch your
wife,
May then make all the claim that Arthur did.
Lew. And lose it, life and all, as Arthur did.
Pand. How green you are and fresh in this old
world!
John lays you plots; the times conspire with
you;

For he that steeps his safety in true blood
Shall find but bloody safety and untrue.
This act so evilly born shall cool the hearts
Of all his people and freeze up their zeal, *150*
That none so small advantage shall step forth
To check his reign, but they will cherish it;
No natural exhalation in the sky,
No scope of nature, no distemper'd day,
No common wind, no customed event,
But they will pluck away his natural cause
And call them meteors, prodigies, and signs,
Abortives, presages, and tongues of heaven,
Plainly denouncing vengeance upon John.
Lew. May be he will not touch young Arthur's
life, *160*
But hold himself safe in his prisonment.
Pand. O, sir, when he shall hear of your ap-
proach,
If that young Arthur be not gone already,
Even at that news he dies; and then the hearts
Of all his people shall revolt from him
And kiss the lips of unacquainted change
And pick strong matter of revolt and wrath
Out of the bloody fingers' ends of John.
Methinks I see this hurly all on foot:
And, O, what better matter breeds for you *170*
Than I have named! The bastard Faulconbridge
Is now in England, ransacking the church,
Offending charity: if but a dozen French
Were there in arms, they would be as a call
To train ten thousand English to their side,
Or as a little snow, tumbled about,
Anon becomes a mountain. O noble Dauphin,
Go with me to the King: 'tis wonderful
What may be wrought out of their discontent,
Now that their souls are topfull of offence. *180*
For England go: I will whet on the King.
Lew. Strong reasons make strong actions:
let us go:
If you say ay, the King will not say no. [*Exeunt.*

ACT IV

Scene i. *A room in a castle*

Enter HUBERT *and* EXECUTIONERS.

Hub. Heat me these irons hot; and look thou
stand
Within the arras: when I strike my foot
Upon the bosom of the ground, rush forth
And bind the boy which you shall find with me
Fast to the chair: be heedful: hence, and watch.
1st Exec. I hope your warrant will bear out the
deed.
Hub. Uncleanly scruples! fear not you: look
to't. [*Exeunt* EXECUTIONERS.
Young lad, come forth; I have to say with you.

Enter ARTHUR.

Arth. Good morrow, Hubert.

Hub.　　　　　　Good morrow, little prince.

Arth. As little prince, having so great a title
To be more prince, as may be. You are sad.　　*11*

Hub. Indeed, I have been merrier.

Arth.　　　　　　　　　Mercy on me!
Methinks no body should be sad but I:
Yet, I remember, when I was in France,
Young gentlemen would be as sad as night,
Only for wantonness. By my christendom,
So I were out of prison and kept sheep,
I should be as merry as the day is long;
And so I would be here, but that I doubt
My uncle practises more harm to me:　　*20*
He is afraid of me and I of him:
Is it my fault that I was Geoffrey's son?
No, indeed, is't not; and I would to heaven
I were your son, so you would love me, Hubert.

Hub. [*Aside*] If I talk to him, with his innocent
　　prate
He will awake my mercy which lies dead:
Therefore I will be sudden and dispatch.

Arth. Are you sick, Hubert? you look pale
　　to-day:
In sooth, I would you were a little sick,
That I might sit all night and watch with you:　*30*
I warrant I love you more than you do me.

Hub. [*Aside*] His words do take possession of
　　my bosom.
Read here, young Arthur. [*Showing a paper.*]
　　　　　　[*Aside*] How now, foolish rheum!
Turning dispiteous torture out of door!
I must be brief, lest resolution drop
Out at mine eyes in tender womanish tears.
Can you not read it? is it not fair writ?

Arth. Too fairly, Hubert, for so foul effect:
Must you with hot irons burn out both mine eyes?

Hub. Young boy, I must.

Arth.　　　　　　And will you?

Hub.　　　　　　　　And I will.　*40*

Arth. Have you the heart? When your head did
　　but ache,
I knit my handkercher about your brows,
The best I had, a princess wrought it me,
And I did never ask it you again;
And with my hand at midnight held your head,
And like the watchful minutes to the hour,
Still and anon cheer'd up the heavy time,
Saying, "What lack you?" and "Where lies your
　　grief?"
Or "What good love may I perform for you?"
Many a poor man's son would have lien still　*50*
And ne'er have spoke a loving word to you;
But you at your sick service had a prince.

Nay, you may think my love was crafty love
And call it cunning: do, an if you will:
If heaven be pleased that you must use me ill,
Why then you must. Will you put out mine eyes?
These eyes that never did nor never shall
So much as frown on you.

Hub.　　　　　　I have sworn to do it;
And with hot irons must I burn them out.

Arth. Ah, none but in this iron age would do
　　it!　　*60*
The iron of itself, though heat red-hot,
Approaching near these eyes, would drink my
　　tears
And quench his fiery indignation
Even in the matter of mine innocence;
Nay, after that, consume away in rust,
But for containing fire to harm mine eye.
Are you more stubborn-hard than hammer'd
　　iron?
An if an angel should have come to me
And told me Hubert should put out mine eyes,
I would not have believed him—no tongue but
　　Hubert's.　　*70*

Hub. Come forth. [*Stamps.*]

Re-enter EXECUTIONERS, *with a cord, irons, &c.*

Do as I bid you do.

Arth. O, save me, Hubert, save me! my eyes
　　are out
Even with the fierce looks of these bloody men.

Hub. Give me the iron, I say, and bind him
　　here.

Arth. Alas, what need you be so boisterous-
　　rough?
I will not struggle, I will stand stone-still.
For heaven sake, Hubert, let me not be bound!
Nay, hear me, Hubert, drive these men away,
And I will sit as quiet as a lamb;　　*80*
I will not stir, nor wince, nor speak a word,
Nor look upon the iron angerly:
Thrust but these men away, and I'll forgive you,
Whatever torment you do put me to.

Hub. Go, stand within; let me alone with him.

1st Exec. I am best pleased to be from such a
　　deed.　　　　[*Exeunt* EXECUTIONERS.

Arth. Alas, I then have chid away my friend!
He hath a stern look, but a gentle heart:
Let him come back, that his compassion may
Give life to yours.

Hub.　　　　Come, boy, prepare yourself.　*90*

Arth. Is there no remedy?

Hub.　　　　　None, but to lose your eyes.

Arth. O heaven, that there were but a mote in
　　yours,
A grain, a dust, a gnat, a wandering hair,
Any annoyance in that precious sense!

Then feeling what small things are boisterous
  there,
Your vile intent must needs seem horrible.
  Hub. Is this your promise? go to, hold your
  tongue.
  Arth. Hubert, the utterance of a brace of
  tongues
Must needs want pleading for a pair of eyes:
Let me not hold my tongue, let me not, Hubert;
Or, Hubert, if you will, cut out my tongue,   *101*
So I may keep mine eyes: O, spare mine eyes,
Though to no use but still to look on you!
Lo, by my troth, the instrument is cold
And would not harm me.
  Hub.   I can heat it, boy.
  Arth. No, in good sooth; the fire is dead with
  grief,
Being create for comfort, to be used
In undeserved extremes: see else yourself;
There is no malice in this burning coal;
The breath of heaven hath blown his spirit
  out   *110*
And strew'd repentant ashes on his head.
  Hub. But with my breath I can revive it, boy.
  Arth. An if you do, you will but make it blush
And glow with shame of your proceedings, Hu-
  bert:
Nay, it perchance will sparkle in your eyes;
And like a dog that is compell'd to fight,
Snatch at his master that doth tarre him on.
All things that you should use to do me wrong
Deny their office: only you do lack
That mercy which fierce fire and iron extends, *120*
Creatures of note for mercy-lacking uses.
  Hub. Well, see to live; I will not touch thine eye
For all the treasure that thine uncle owes:
Yet am I sworn and I did purpose, boy,
With this same very iron to burn them out.
  Arth. O, now you look like Hubert! all this
  while
You were disguised.
  Hub.   Peace; no more. Adieu.
Your uncle must not know but you are dead;
I'll fill these dogged spies with false reports:
And, pretty child, sleep doubtless and secure *130*
That Hubert, for the wealth of all the world,
Will not offend thee.
  Arth.   O heaven! I thank you, Hubert.
  Hub. Silence; no more: go closely in with me:
Much danger do I undergo for thee.   [*Exeunt.*

SCENE II. KING JOHN's *palace.*

Enter KING JOHN, PEMBROKE, SALISBURY, *and
  other Lords.*

  K. John. Here once again we sit, once again
  crown'd,

And looked upon, I hope, with cheerful eyes.
  Pem. This "once again," but that your High-
  ness pleased,
Was once superfluous: you were crown'd before,
And that high royalty was ne'er pluck'd off,
The faiths of men ne'er stained with revolt;
Fresh expectation troubled not the land
With any long'd-for change or better state.
  Sal. Therefore, to be possess'd with double
  pomp,
To guard a title that was rich before,   *10*
To gild refined gold, to paint the lily,
To throw a perfume on the violet,
To smooth the ice, or add another hue
Unto the rainbow, or with taper-light
To seek the beauteous eye of heaven to garnish,
Is wasteful and ridiculous excess.
  Pem. But that your royal pleasure must be
  done,
This act is as an ancient tale new told,
And in the last repeating troublesome,
Being urged at a time unseasonable.   *20*
  Sal. In this the antique and well noted face
Of plain old form is much disfigured;
And, like a shifted wind unto a sail,
It makes the course of thoughts to fetch about,
Startles and frights consideration,
Makes sound opinion sick and truth suspected,
For putting on so new a fashion'd robe.
  Pem. When workmen strive to do better than
  well,
They do confound their skill in covetousness;
And oftentimes excusing of a fault   *30*
Doth make the fault the worse by the excuse,
As patches set upon a little breach
Discredit more in hiding of the fault
Than did the fault before it was so patch'd.
  Sal. To this effect, before you were new
  crown'd,
We breathed our counsel: but it pleased your
  highness
To overbear it, and we are all well pleased,
Since all and every part of what we would
Doth make a stand at what your Highness will.
  K. John. Some reasons of this double corona-
  tion   *40*
I have possess'd you with and think them strong;
And more, more strong, then lesser is my fear,
I shall indue you with: meantime but ask
What you would have reform'd that is not well,
And well shall you perceive how willingly
I will both hear and grant you your requests.
  Pem. Then I, as one that am the tongue of
  these
To sound the purposes of all their hearts,
Both for myself and them, but, chief of all,

Your safety, for the which myself and them   50
Bend their best studies, heartily request
The enfranchisement of Arthur; whose restraint
Doth move the murmuring lips of discontent
To break into this dangerous argument—
If what in rest you have in right you hold,
Why then your fears, which, as they say, attend
The steps of wrong, should move you to mew up
Your tender kinsman and to choke his days
With barbarous ignorance and deny his youth
The rich advantage of good exercise?   60
That the time's enemies may not have this
To grace occasions, let it be our suit
That you have bid us ask his liberty;
Which for our goods we do no further ask
Than whereupon our weal, on you depending,
Counts it your weal he have his liberty.

Enter HUBERT.

K. John. Let it be so: I do commit his youth
To your direction. Hubert, what news with you?
    [*Taking him apart.*]
Pem. This is the man should do the bloody
    deed;
He show'd his warrant to a friend of mine: 70
The image of a wicked heinous fault
Lives in his eye; that close aspect of his
Does show the mood of a much troubled breast;
And I do fearfully believe 'tis done,
What we so fear'd he had a charge to do.
Sal. The colour of the King doth come and go
Between his purpose and his conscience,
Like heralds 'twixt two dreadful battles set:
His passion is so ripe, it needs must break.
Pem. And when it breaks, I fear will issue
    thence   80
The foul corruption of a sweet child's death.
K. John. We cannot hold mortality's strong
    hand:
Good lords, although my will to give is living,
The suit which you demand is gone and dead:
He tells us Arthur is deceased to-night.
Sal. Indeed we fear'd his sickness was past cure.
Pem. Indeed we heard how near his death he
    was
Before the child himself felt he was sick:
Thus must be answer'd either here or hence.
K. John. Why do you bend such solemn brows
    on me?   90
Think you I bear the shears of destiny?
Have I commandment on the pulse of life?
Sal. It is apparent foul play; and 'tis shame
That greatness should so grossly offer it:
So thrive it in your game! and so, farewell.
Pem. Stay yet, Lord Salisbury; I'll go with
    thee,

And find the inheritance of this poor child,
His little kingdom of a forced grave.
That blood which owed the breadth of all
    this isle,   99
Three foot of it doth hold: bad world the while!
This must not be thus borne: this will break out
To all our sorrows, and ere long I doubt.
        [*Exeunt Lords.*
K. John. They burn in indignation. I repent:
There is no sure foundation set on blood,
No certain life achieved by others' death.

Enter a MESSENGER.

A fearful eye thou hast: where is that blood
That I have seen inhabit in those cheeks?
So foul a sky clears not without a storm:
Pour down thy weather: how goes all in France?
Mess. From France to England. Never such a
    power   110
For any foreign preparation
Was levied in the body of a land.
The copy of your speed is learn'd by them;
For when you should be told they do prepare,
The tidings come that they are all arrived.
K. John. O, where hath our intelligence been
    drunk?
Where hath it slept? Where is my mother's care,
That such an army could be drawn in France,
And she not hear of it?
Mess.   My liege, her ear
Is stopp'd with dust; the first of April died   120
Your noble mother: and, as I hear, my lord,
The Lady Constance in a frenzy died
Three days before: but this from rumour's
    tongue
I idly heard; if true or false I know not.
K. John. Withhold thy speed, dreadful occa-
    sion!
O, make a league with me, till I have pleased
My discontented peers! What! mother dead!
How wildly then walks my estate in France!
Under whose conduct came those powers of
    France
That thou for truth givest out are landed here?
Mess. Under the Dauphin.
K. John.   Thou hast made me giddy   131
With these ill tidings.

Enter the BASTARD *and* PETER OF POMFRET.

                Now, what says the world
To your proceedings? do not seek to stuff
My head with more ill news, for it is full.
Bast. But if you be afeard to hear the worst,
Then let the worst unheard fall on your head.
K. John. Bear with me, cousin; for I was
    amazed

Under the tide: but now I breathe again
Aloft the flood, and can give audience
To any tongue, speak it of what it will.   *140*
    Bast. How I have sped among the clergymen,
The sums I have collected shall express.
But as I travell'd hither through the land,
I find the people strangely fantasied;
Possess'd with rumours, full of idle dreams,
Not knowing what they fear, but full of fear:
And here's a prophet, that I brought with me
From forth the streets of Pomfret, whom I found
With many hundreds treading on his heels:
To whom he sung, in rude harsh-sounding
    rhymes,
That, ere the next Ascension-day at noon,   *151*
Your highness should deliver up your crown.
    K. John. Thou idle dreamer, wherefore didst
    thou so?
    Peter. Foreknowing that the truth will fall out
    so.
    K. John. Hubert, away with him, imprison him;
And on that day at noon, whereon he says
I shall yield up my crown, let him be hang'd.
Deliver him to safety; and return,
For I must use thee. [*Exit* HUBERT *with* PETER.
            O my gentle cousin,
Hear'st thou the news abroad, who are arrived?
    Bast. The French, my lord; men's mouths are
    full of it: *161*
Besides, I met Lord Bigot and Lord Salisbury,
With eyes as red as new-enkindled fire,
And others more, going to seek the grave
Of Arthur, whom they say is kill'd to-night
On your suggestion.
    K. John.   Gentle kinsman, go,
And thrust thyself into their companies:
I have a way to win their loves again;
Bring them before me.
    Bast.   I will seek them out.
    K. John. Nay, but make haste; the better foot
    before.   *170*
O, let me have no subject enemies,
When adverse foreigners affright my towns
With dreadful pomp of stout invasion!
Be Mercury, set feathers to thy heels,
And fly like thought from them to me again.
    Bast. The spirit of the time shall teach me
    speed.   [*Exit.*
    K. John. Spoke like a sprightful noble gentle-
man.
Go after him; for he perhaps shall need
Some messenger betwixt me and the peers;
And be thou he.
    Mess.   With all my heart, my liege.   *180*
                [*Exit.*
    K. John. My mother dead!

Re-enter HUBERT.

    Hub. My lord, they say five moons were seen
    to-night;
Four fixed; and the fifth did whirl about
The other four in wondrous motion.
    K. John. Five moons!
    Hub.   Old men and beldams in the streets
Do prophesy upon it dangerously:
Young Arthur's death is common in their mouths:
And when they talk of him, they shake their heads
And whisper one another in the ear;
And he that speaks doth gripe the hearer's wrist,
Whilst he that hears makes fearful action,   *191*
With wrinkled brows, with nods, with rolling
    eyes.
I saw a smith stand with his hammer, thus,
The whilst his iron did on the anvil cool,
With open mouth swallowing a tailor's news;
Who, with his shears and measure in his hand,
Standing on slippers, which his nimble haste
Had falsely thrust upon contrary feet,
Told of a many thousand warlike French
That were embattailed and rank'd in Kent: *200*
Another lean unwash'd artificer
Cuts off his tale and talks of Arthur's death.
    K. John. Why seek'st thou to possess me with
    these fears?
Why urgest thou so oft young Arthur's death?
Thy hand hath murder'd him: I had a mighty
    cause
To wish him dead, but thou hadst none to kill
    him.
    Hub. No had, my lord! why, did you not pro-
    voke me?
    K. John. It is the curse of kings to be attended
By slaves that take their humours for a warrant
To break within the bloody house of life,   *210*
And on the winking of authority
To understand a law, to know the meaning
Of dangerous majesty, when perchance it frowns
More upon humour than advised respect.
    Hub. Here is your hand and seal for what I
    did.
    K. John. O, when the last account 'twixt
    heaven and earth
Is to be made, then shall this hand and seal
Witness against us to damnation!
How oft the sight of means to do ill deeds
Make deeds ill done! Hadst not thou been by,
A fellow by the hand of nature mark'd,   *221*
Quoted and sign'd to do a deed of shame,
This murder had not come into my mind:
But taking note of thy abhorr'd aspect,
Finding thee fit for bloody villainy,
Apt, liable to be employ'd in danger,

I faintly broke with thee of Arthur's death;
And thou, to be endeared to a king,
Made it no conscience to destroy a prince.
  Hub. My lord—   230
  K. John. Hadst thou but shook thy head or
    made a pause
When I spake darkly what I purposed,
Or turn'd an eye of doubt upon my face,
As bid me tell my tale in express words,
Deep shame had struck me dumb, made me
    break off,
And those thy fears might have wrought fears in
    me:
But thou didst understand me by my signs
And didst in signs again parley with sin;
Yea, without stop, didst let thy heart consent,
And consequently thy rude hand to act   240
The deed, which both our tongues held vile to
    name.
Out of my sight, and never see me more!
My nobles leave me; and my state is braved,
Even at my gates, with ranks of foreign powers:
Nay, in the body of this fleshly land,
This kingdom, this confine of blood and breath,
Hostility and civil tumult reigns
Between my conscience and my cousin's death.
  Hub. Arm you against your other enemies,
I'll make a peace between your soul and you. *250*
Young Arthur is alive: this hand of mine
Is yet a maiden and an innocent hand,
Not painted with the crimson spots of blood.
Within this bosom never enter'd yet
The dreadful motion of a murderous thought;
And you have slander'd nature in my form,
Which, howsoever rude exteriorly,
Is yet the cover of a fairer mind
Than to be butcher of an innocent child.
  K. John. Doth Arthur live? O, haste thee to the
    peers,   260
Throw this report on their incensed rage,
And make them tame to their obedience!
Forgive the comment that my passion made
Upon thy feature; for my rage was blind,
And foul imaginary eyes of blood
Presented thee more hideous than thou art.
O, answer not, but to my closet bring
The angry lords with all expedient haste.
I conjure thee but slowly; run more fast.
                                              [*Exeunt.*

        Scene iii. *Before the castle*
        Enter arthur, *on the walls.*

  Arth. The wall is high, and yet will I leap
    down:
Good ground, be pitiful and hurt me not!
There's few or none do know me: if they did,

This ship-boy's semblance hath disguised me
    quite.
I am afraid; and yet I'll venture it.
If I get down, and do not break my limbs,
I'll find a thousand shifts to get away:
As good to die and go, as die and stay.
    Leaps down.
O me! my uncle's spirit is in these stones:
Heaven take my soul, and England keep my
    bones!   [*Dies.* 10

    Enter pembroke, salisbury, *and* bigot.

  Sal. Lords, I will meet him at Saint Edmunds-
    bury:
It is our safety, and we must embrace
This gentle offer of the perilous time.
  Pem. Who brought that letter from the Card-
    inal?
  Sal. The Count Melun, a noble lord of France;
Whose private with me of the Dauphin's love
Is much more general than these lines import.
  Big. To-morrow morning let us meet him then.
  Sal. Or rather then set forward; for 'twill be
Two long days' journey, lords, or ere we meet. *20*

            Enter the bastard.

  Bast. Once more to-day well met, distemper'd
    lords!
The King by me requests your presence straight.
  Sal. The King hath dispossess'd himself of us:
We will not line his thin bestained cloak
With our pure honours, nor attend the foot
That leaves the print of blood where'er it walks.
Return and tell him so: we know the worst.
  Bast. Whate'er you think, good words, I
    think, were best.
  Sal. Our griefs, and not our manners, reason
    now.   29
  Bast. But there is little reason in your grief;
Therefore 'twere reason you had manners now.
  Pem. Sir, sir, impatience hath his privilege.
  Bast. 'Tis true, to hurt his master, no man else.
  Sal. This is the prison. What is he lies here?
    Seeing arthur.
  Pem. O death, made proud with pure and prince-
    ly beauty!
The earth had not a hole to hide this deed.
  Sal. Murder, as hating what himself hath done,
Doth lay it open to urge on revenge.
  Big. Or, when he doom'd this beauty to a
    grave,
Found it too precious-princely for a grave.   40
  Sal. Sir Richard, what think you? have you be-
    held,
Or have
You read or heard? or could you think?
Or do you almost think, although you see,

That you do see? could thought, without this
    object,
Form such another? This is the very top,
The height, the crest, or crest unto the crest,
Of murder's arms: this is the bloodiest shame,
The wildest savagery, the vilest stroke,
That ever wall-eyed wrath or staring rage
Presented to the tears of soft remorse.   *50*
  Pem. All murders past do stand excused in this:
And this, so sole and so unmatchable,
Shall give a holiness, a purity,
To the yet unbegotten sin of times;
And prove a deadly bloodshed but a jest,
Exampled by this heinous spectacle.
  Bast. It is a damned and a bloody work;
The graceless action of a heavy hand,
If that it be the work of any hand.
  Sal. If that it be the work of any hand!   *60*
We had a kind of light what would ensue:
It is the shameful work of Hubert's hand;
The practice and the purpose of the King:
From whose obedience I forbid my soul,
Kneeling before this ruin of sweet life,
And breathing to his breathless excellence
The incense of a vow, a holy vow,
Never to taste the pleasures of the world,
Never to be infected with delight,
Nor conversant with ease and idleness,   *70*
Till I have set a glory to this hand,
By giving it the worship of revenge.
  Pem.⎱ Our souls religiously confirm thy
  Big.⎰   words.

    Enter HUBERT.

  Hub. Lords, I am hot with haste in seeking you:
Arthur doth live; the King hath sent for you.
  Sal. O, he is bold and blushes not at death.
Avaunt, thou hateful villain, get thee gone!
  Hub. I am no villain.
  Sal.   Must I rob the law?
    Drawing his sword.
  Bast. Your sword is bright, sir; put it up again.
  Sal. Not till I sheathe it in a murderer's skin.   *80*
  Hub. Stand back, Lord Salisbury, stand back, I
  say;
By heaven, I think my sword's as sharp as yours:
I would not have you, lord, forget yourself,
Nor tempt the danger of my true defence;
Lest I, by marking of your rage, forget
Your worth, your greatness and nobility.
  Big. Out, dunghill! darest thou brave a noble-
  man?
  Hub. Not for my life: but yet I dare defend
My innocent life against an emperor.
  Sal. Thou art a murderer.
  Hub.   Do not prove me so;   *90*

Yet I am none: whose tongue soe'er speaks false,
Not truly speaks; who speaks not truly, lies.
  Pem. Cut him to pieces.
  Bast.   Keep the peace, I say.
  Sal. Stand by, or I shall gall you, Faulcon-
  bridge.
  Bast. Thou wert better gall the devil, Salisbury:
If thou but frown on me, or stir thy foot,
Or teach thy hasty spleen to do me shame,
I'll strike thee dead. Put up thy sword betime;
Or I'll so maul you and your toasting-iron,
That you shall think the devil is come from hell.
  Big. What wilt thou do, renowned Faulcon-
  bridge?   *101*
Second a villain and a murderer?
  Hub. Lord Bigot, I am none.
  Big.   Who kill'd this prince?
  Hub. 'Tis not an hour since I left him well:
I honour'd him, I loved him, and will weep
My date of life out for his sweet life's loss.
  Sal. Trust not those cunning waters of his eyes,
For villainy is not without such rheum;
And he, long traded in it, makes it seem
Like rivers of remorse and innocency.   *110*
Away with me, all you whose souls abhor
The uncleanly savours of a slaughter-house;
For I am stifled with this smell of sin.
  Big. Away toward Bury, to the Dauphin there!
  Pem. There tell the King he may inquire us out.
                   [*Exeunt Lords.*
  Bast. Here's a good world! Knew you of this
  fair work?
Beyond the infinite and boundless reach
Of mercy, if thou didst this deed of death,
Art thou damn'd, Hubert.
  Hub.   Do but hear me, sir.
  Bast. Ha! I'll tell thee what;   *120*
Thou'rt damn'd as black—nay, nothing is so
  black;
Thou art more deep damn'd than Prince Lucifer:
There is not yet so ugly a fiend of hell
As thou shalt be, if thou didst kill this child.
  Hub. Upon my soul—
  Bast.   If thou didst but consent
To this most cruel act, do but despair;
And if thou want'st a cord, the smallest thread
That ever spider twisted from her womb
Will serve to strangle thee; a rush will be a
  beam
To hang thee on; or wouldst thou drown thyself,
Put but a little water in a spoon,   *131*
And it shall be as all the ocean,
Enough to stifle such a villain up.
I do suspect thee very grievously.
  Hub. If I in act, consent, or sin of thought,
Be guilty of the stealing that sweet breath

Which was embounded in this beauteous clay,
Let hell want pains enough to torture me.
I left him well.
  Bast.   Go, bear him in thine arms.
I am amazed, methinks, and lose my way   140
Among the thorns and dangers of this world.
How easy dost thou take all England up!
From forth this morsel of dead royalty,
The life, the right, and truth of all this realm
Is fled to heaven; and England now is left
To tug and scamble and to part by the teeth
The unowed interest of proud-swelling state.
Now for the bare-pick'd bone of majesty
Doth dogged war bristle his angry crest
And snarleth in the gentle eyes of peace: 150
Now powers from home and discontents at home
Meet in one line; and vast confusion waits,
As doth a raven on a sick-fall'n beast,
The imminent decay of wrested pomp.
Now happy he whose cloak and cincture can
Hold out this tempest. Bear away that child
And follow me with speed: I'll to the King:
A thousand businesses are brief in hand,
And heaven itself doth frown upon the land.
                              [*Exeunt.*

ACT V

SCENE I. *King John's palace*
Enter KING JOHN, PANDULPH, *and Attendants.*

  K. John. Thus have I yielded up into your hand
The circle of my glory. [*Giving the crown.*
  Pand.   Take again
From this my hand, as holding of the Pope
Your sovereign greatness and authority.
  K. John. Now keep your holy word: go meet
    the French,
And from his Holiness use all your power
To stop their marches 'fore we are inflamed.
Our discontented counties do revolt;
Our people quarrel with obedience,
Swearing allegiance and the love of soul   10
To stranger blood, to foreign royalty.
This inundation of mistemper'd humour
Rests by you only to be qualified:
Then pause not; for the present time's so sick,
That present medicine must be minister'd,
Or overthrow incurable ensues.
  Pand. It was my breath that blew this tempest
    up,
Upon your stubborn usage of the Pope;
But since you are a gentle convertite,
My tongue shall hush again this storm of war   20
And make fair weather in your blustering land.
On this Ascension-day, remember well,
Upon your oath of service to the Pope,

Go I to make the French lay down their arms.
                              [*Exit.*
  K. John. Is this Ascension-day? Did not the
    prophet
Say that before Ascension-day at noon
My crown I should give off? Even so I have:
I did suppose it should be on constraint;
But, heaven be thank'd, it is but voluntary.

Enter the BASTARD.

  Bast. All Kent hath yielded; nothing there holds
    out   30
But Dover castle: London hath received,
Like a kind host, the Dauphin and his powers:
Your nobles will not hear you, but are gone
To offer service to your enemy,
And wild amazement hurries up and down
The little number of your doubtful friends.
  K. John. Would not my lords return to me
    again,
After they heard young Arthur was alive?
  Bast. They found him dead and cast into the
    streets,
An empty casket, where the jewel of life   40
By some damn'd hand was robb'd and ta'en
    away.
  K. John. That villain Hubert told me he did live.
  Bast. So, on my soul, he did, for aught he knew.
But wherefore do you droop? why look you sad?
Be great in act, as you have been in thought;
Let not the world see fear and sad distrust
Govern the motion of a kingly eye:
Be stirring as the time; be fire with fire;
Threaten the threatener and outface the brow
Of bragging horror: so shall inferior eyes,   50
That borrow their behaviours from the great,
Grow great by your example and put on
The dauntless spirit of resolution.
Away, and glister like the god of war,
When he intendeth to become the field:
Show boldness and aspiring confidence.
What, shall they seek the lion in his den,
And fright him there? and make him tremble
    there?
O, let it not be said: forage, and run
To meet displeasure father from the doors,   60
And grapple with him ere he come so nigh.
  K. John. The legate of the Pope hath been with
    me,
And I have made a happy peace with him;
And he hath promised to dismiss the powers
Led by the Dauphin.
  Bast.   O inglorious league!
Shall we, upon the footing of our land,
Send fair-play orders and make compromise,
Insinuation, parley and base truce

To arms invasive? shall a beardless boy,
A cocker'd silken wanton, brave our fields,   70
And flesh his spirit in a warlike soil,
Mocking the air with colours idly spread,
And find no check? Let us, my liege, to arms:
Perchance the Cardinal cannot make your peace;
Or if he do, let it at least be said
They saw we had a purpose of defence.
  K. John. Have thou the ordering of this present
    time.
  Bast. Away, then, with good courage! yet, I
    know,
Our party may well meet a prouder foe. [*Exeunt.*

SCENE II. *The Dauphin's camp at Saint
Edmundsbury*

Enter, in arms, LEWIS, SALISBURY, MELUN,
PEMBROKE, BIGOT, *and Soldiers.*

  Lew. My Lord Melun, let this be copied out,
And keep it safe for our remembrance:
Return the precedent to these lords again;
That, having our fair order written down,
Both they and we, perusing o'er these notes,
May know wherefore we took the sacrament
And keep our faiths firm and inviolable.
  Sal. Upon our sides it never shall be broken.
And, noble Dauphin, albeit we swear
A voluntary zeal and an unurged faith   10
To your proceedings; yet believe me, Prince,
I am not glad that such a sore of time
Should seek a plaster by contemn'd revolt,
And heal the inveterate canker of one wound
By making many. O, it grieves my soul,
That I must draw this metal from my side
To be a widow-maker! O, and there
Where honourable rescue and defence
Cries out upon the name of Salisbury!
But such is the infection of the time,   20
That, for the health and physic of our right,
We cannot deal but with the very hand
Of stern injustice and confused wrong.
And is't not pity, O my grieved friends,
That we, the sons and children of this isle,
Were born to see so sad an hour as this;
Wherein we step after a stranger march
Upon her gentle bosom, and fill up
Her enemies' ranks—I must withdraw and
    weep
Upon the spot of this enforced cause—   30
To grace the gentry of a land remote,
And follow unacquainted colours here?
What, here? O nation, that thou couldst remove!
That Neptune's arms, who clippeth thee about,
Would bear thee from the knowledge of thyself,
And grapple thee unto a pagan shore;

Where these two Christian armies might com-
    bine
The blood of malice in a vein of league,
And not to spend it so unneighbourly!
  Lew. A noble temper dost thou show in this;
And great affections wrestling in thy bosom   41
Doth make an earthquake of nobility.
O, what a noble combat hast thou fought
Between compulsion and a brave respect!
Let me wipe off this honourable dew,
That silverly doth progress on thy cheeks:
My heart hath melted at a lady's tears,
Being an ordinary inundation;
But this effusion of such manly drops,
This shower, blown up by tempest of the soul,   50
Startles mine eyes, and makes me more amazed
Than had I seen the vaulty top of heaven
Figured quite o'er with burning meteors.
Lift up thy brow, renowned Salisbury,
And with a great heart heave away this storm:
Commend these waters to those baby eyes
That never saw the giant world enraged;
Nor met with fortune other than at feasts,
Full of warm blood, of mirth, of gossiping.
Come, come; for thou shalt thrust thy hand as
    deep   60
Into the purse of rich prosperity
As Lewis himself: so, nobles, shall you all,
That knit your sinews to the strength of mine.
And even there, methinks, an angel spake:

Enter PANDULPH.

Look, where the holy legate comes apace,
To give us warrant from the hand of heaven,
And on our actions set the name of right
With holy breath.
  Pand.   Hail, noble prince of France!
The next is this, King John hath reconciled
Himself to Rome; his spirit is come in,   70
That so stood out against the Holy Church,
The great metropolis and see of Rome:
Therefore thy threatening colours now wind up;
And tame the savage spirit of wild war,
That, like a lion foster'd up at hand,
It may lie gently at the foot of peace,
And be no further harmful than in show.
  Lew. Your Grace shall pardon me, I will not
    back:
I am too high-born to be propertied,
To be a secondary at control,   80
Or useful serving-man and instrument,
To any sovereign state throughout the world.
Your breath first kindled the dead coal of wars
Between this chastised kingdom and myself,
And brought in matter that should feed this fire;
And now 'tis far too huge to be blown out

With that same weak wind which enkindled it.
You taught me how to know the face of right,
Acquainted me with interest to this land,
Yea, thrust this enterprise into my heart;   90
And come ye now to tell me John hath made
His peace with Rome? What is that peace to me?
I, by the honour of my marriage-bed,
After young Arthur, claim this land for mine;
And, now it is half-conquer'd, must I back
Because that John hath made his peace with
    Rome?
Am I Rome's slave? What penny hath Rome
    borne,
What men provided, what munition sent,
To underprop this action? Is't not I
That undergo this charge? who else but I,   100
And such as to my claim are liable,
Sweat in this business and maintain this war?
Have I not heard these islanders shout out
Vive le roi! as I have bank'd their towns?
Have I not here the best cards for the game,
To win this easy match play'd for a crown?
And shall I now give o'er the yielded set?
No, no, on my soul, it never shall be said.
    Pand. You look but on the outside of this work.
    Lew. Outside or inside, I will not return   110
Till my attempt so much be glorified
As to my ample hope was promised
Before I drew this gallant head of war,
And cull'd these fiery spirits from the world, .
To outlook conquest and to win renown
Even in the jaws of danger and of death.
    Trumpet sounds.
What lusty trumpet thus doth summon us?

Enter the BASTARD, attended.

    Bast. According to the fair play of the world,
Let me have audience; I am sent to speak:
My holy lord of Milan, from the King   120
I come, to learn how you have dealt for him;
And, as you answer, I do know the scope
And warrant limited unto my tongue.
    Pand. The Dauphin is too wilful-opposite,
And will not temporize with my entreaties;
He flatly says he'll not lay down his arms.
    Bast. By all the blood that ever fury breathed,
The youth says well. Now hear our English
    King;
For thus his royalty doth speak in me.
He is prepared, and reason too he should: 130
This apish and unmannerly approach,
This harness'd masque and unadvised revel,
This unhair'd sauciness and boyish troops,
The King doth smile at; and is well prepared
To whip this dwarfish war, these pigmy arms,
From out the circle of his territories.

That hand which had the strength, even at your
    door,
To cudgel you and make you take the hatch,
To dive like buckets in concealed wells,
To crouch in litter of your stable planks,   140
To lie like pawns lock'd up in chests and trunks,
To hug with swine, to seek sweet safety out
In vaults and prisons, and to thrill and shake
Even at the crying of your nation's crow,
Thinking his voice an armed Englishman;
Shall that victorious hand be feebled here,
That in your chambers gave you chastisement?
No: know the gallant monarch is in arms
And like an eagle o'er his aery towers,
To souse annoyance that comes near his nest.   150
And you degenerate, you ingrate revolts,
You bloody Neroes, ripping up the womb
Of your dear mother England, blush for shame;
For your own ladies and pale-visaged maids
Like Amazons come tripping after drums,
Their thimbles into armed gauntlets change,
Their needles to lances, and their gentle hearts
To fierce and bloody inclination.
    Lew. There end thy brave, and turn thy face in
    peace;
We grant thou canst outscold us: fare thee well;
We hold our time too precious to be spent   161
With such a brabbler.
    Pand.   Give me leave to speak.
    Bast. No, I will speak.
    Lew.   We will attend to neither.
Strike up the drums; and let the tongue of war
Plead for our interest and our being here.
    Bast. Indeed, your drums, being beaten, will cry
    out;
And so shall you, being beaten: do but start
An echo with the clamour of thy drum,
And even at hand a drum is ready braced
That shall reverberate all as loud as thine;   170
Sound but another, and another shall
As loud as thine rattle the welkin's ear
And mock the deep-mouth'd thunder: for at hand,
Not trusting to this halting legate here,
Whom he hath used rather for sport than need,
Is warlike John; and in his forehead sits
A bare-ribb'd death, whose office is this day
To feast upon whole thousands of the French.
    Lew. Strike up our drums, to find this danger
    out.
    Bast. And thou shalt find it, Dauphin, do not
    doubt.   [*Exeunt.* 180

SCENE III. *The field of battle*

Alarums. Enter KING JOHN *and* HUBERT.

    K. John. How goes the day with us? O, tell me,
    Hubert.

Hub. Badly, I fear. How fares your Majesty?
K. John. This fever, that hath troubled me so
    long,
Lies heavy on me; O, my heart is sick!

Enter a MESSENGER.

Mess. My lord, your valiant kinsman, Faulcon-
    bridge,
Desires your Majesty to leave the field
And send him word by me which way you go.
    K. John. Tell him, toward Swinstead, to the
    abbey there.
    Mess. Be of good comfort; for the great supply
That was expected by the Dauphin here,   10
Are wreck'd three nights ago on Goodwin Sands.
This news was brought to Richard but even now:
The French fight coldly, and retire themselves.
    K. John. Ay me! this tyrant fever burns me
    up,
And will not let me welcome this good news.
Set on toward Swinstead: to my litter straight;
Weakness possesseth me, and I am faint.
                                    [*Exeunt.*

SCENE IV. *Another part of the field*

Enter SALISBURY, PEMBROKE, *and* BIGOT.

Sal. I did not think the King so stored with
    friends.
Pem. Up once again; put spirit in the French:
If they miscarry, we miscarry too.
Sal. That misbegotten devil, Faulconbridge,
In spite of spite, alone upholds the day.
Pem. They say King John sore sick hath left the
    field.

Enter MELUN, *wounded.*

Mel. Lead me to the revolts of England here.
Sal. When we were happy we had other names.
Pem. It is the Count Melun.
Sal.   Wounded to death.
Mel. Fly, noble English, you are bought and
    sold;   10
Unthread the rude eye of rebellion
And welcome home again discarded faith.
Seek out King John and fall before his feet;
For if the French be lords of this loud day,
He means to recompense the pains you take
By cutting off your heads: thus hath he sworn
And I with him, and many moe with me,
Upon the altar at Saint Edmundsbury;
Even on that altar where we swore to you
Dear amity and everlasting love.   20
Sal. May this be possible? may this be true?
Mel. Have I not hideous death within my
    view,
Retaining but a quantity of life,

Which bleeds away, even as a form of wax
Resolveth from his figure 'gainst the fire?
What in the world should make me now de-
    ceive,
Since I must lose the use of all deceit?
Why should I then be false, since it is true
That I must die here and live hence by truth?
I say again, if Lewis do win the day,   30
He is forsworn, if e'er those eyes of yours
Behold another day break in the east:
But even this night, whose black contagious
    breath
Already smokes about the burning crest
Of the old, feeble, and day-wearied sun,
Even this ill night, your breathing shall expire,
Paying the fine of rated treachery
Even with a treacherous fine of all your lives,
If Lewis by your assistance win the day.
Commend me to one Hubert with your king: 40
The love of him, and this respect besides,
For that my grandsire was an Englishman,
Awakes my conscience to confess all this.
In lieu whereof, I pray you, bear me hence
From forth the noise and rumour of the field,
Where I may think the remnant of my thoughts
In peace, and part this body and my soul
With contemplation and devout desires.
    Sal. We do believe thee: and beshrew my soul
But I do love the favour and the form   50
Of this most fair occasion, by the which
We will untread the steps of damned flight,
And like a bated and retired flood,
Leaving our rankness and irregular course,
Stoop low within those bounds we have o'er-
    look'd
And calmly run on in obedience
Even to our ocean, to our great King John.
My arm shall give thee help to bear thee hence;
For I do see the cruel pangs of death
Right in thine eye. Away, my friends! New
    flight;   60
And happy newness, that intends old right.
                    [*Exeunt, leading off* MELUN.

SCENE V. *The French camp*

Enter LEWIS *and his train.*

Lew. The sun of heaven methought was loath
    to set,
But stay'd and made the western welkin blush,
When English measure backward their own
    ground
In faint retire. O, bravely came we off,
When with a volley of our needless shot,
After such bloody toil, we bid good night;
And wound out tattering colours clearly up,
Last in the field, and almost lords of it!

Enter a MESSENGER.

Mess. Where is my prince, the Dauphin?
Lew.   Here: what news?
Mess. The Count Melun is slain; the English
    lords   10
By his persuasion are again fall'n off,
And your supply, which you have wish'd so long,
Are cast away and sunk on Goodwin Sands.
    Lew. Ah, foul shrewd news! beshrew thy very
    heart!
I did not think to be so sad to-night
As this hath made me. Who was he that said
King John did fly an hour or two before
The stumbling night did part our weary powers?
    Mess. Whoever spoke it, it is true, my lord.
    Lew. Well; keep good quarter and good care
    to-night: 20
The day shall not be up so soon as I,
To try the fair adventure of to-morrow. [*Exeunt.*

SCENE VI. *An open place in the neighbourhood
of Swinstead Abbey*

Enter the BASTARD *and* HUBERT, *severally.*

    Hub. Who's there? speak, ho! speak quickly,
    or I shoot.
    Bast. A friend. What art thou?
    Hub.   Of the part of England.
    Bast. Whither dost thou go?
    Hub. What's that to thee? why may not I de-
    mand
Of thine affairs, as well as thou of mine?
    Bast. Hubert, I think?
    Hub.   Thou hast a perfect thought:
I will upon all hazards well believe
Thou art my friend, that know'st my tongue so
    well.
Who art thou?
    Bast.   Who thou wilt: and if thou please,
Thou mayst befriend me so much as to think   10
I come one way of the Plantagenets.
    Hub. Unkind remembrance! thou and eyeless
    night
Have done me shame: brave soldier, pardon me,
That any accent breaking from thy tongue
Should 'scape the true acquaintance of mine ear.
    Bast. Come, come; sans compliment, what news
    abroad?
    Hub. Why, here walk I in the black brow of
    night,
To find you out.
    Bast. Brief, then; and what's the news?
    Hub. O, my sweet sir, news fitting to the night,
Black, fearful, comfortless, and horrible.   20
    Bast. Show me the very wound of this ill news:
I am no woman, I'll not swoon at it.

    Hub. The King, I fear, is poison'd by a monk:
I left him almost speechless; and broke out
To acquaint you with this evil, that you might
The better arm you to the sudden time,
Than if you had at leisure known of this.
    Bast. How did he take it? who did taste to him?
    Hub. A monk, I tell you; a resolved villain,
Whose bowels suddenly burst out: the King   30
Yet speaks and peradventure may recover.
    Bast. Who didst thou leave to tend his Majesty?
    Hub. Why, know you not? the lords are all
    come back,
And brought Prince Henry in their company;
At whose request the King hath pardon'd them,
And they are all about his Majesty.
    Bast. Withhold thine indignation, mighty heav-
    en,
And tempt us not to bear above our power!
I'll tell thee, Hubert, half my power this night,
Passing these flats, are taken by the tide;   40
These Lincoln Washes have devoured them;
Myself, well mounted, hardly have escaped.
Away before: conduct me to the King;
I doubt he will be dead or ere I come.   [*Exeunt.*

SCENE VII. *The orchard in Swinstead Abbey*

Enter PRINCE HENRY, SALISBURY, *and* BIGOT.

    P. Hen. It is too late: the life of all his blood
Is touch'd corruptibly, and his pure brain,
Which some suppose the soul's frail dwelling-
    house,
Doth by the idle comments that it makes
Foretell the ending of mortality.

Enter PEMBROKE.

    Pem. His Highness yet doth speak, and holds
    belief
That, being brought into the open air,
It would allay the burning quality
Of that fell poison which assaileth him.
    P. Hen. Let him be brought into the orchard
    here.   10
Doth he still rage?   [*Exit* BIGOT.
    Pem.   He is more patient
Than when you left him; even now he sung.
    P. Hen. O vanity of sickness! fierce extremes
In their continuance will not feel themselves.
Death, having prey'd upon the outward parts,
Leaves them invisible, and his siege is now
Against the mind, the which he pricks and
    wounds
With many legions of strange fantasies,
Which, in their throng and press to that last hold,
Confound themselves. 'Tis strange that death
    should sing.   20
I am the cygnet to this pale faint swan,

Who chants a doleful hymn to his own death,
And from the organ-pipe of frailty sings
His soul and body to their lasting rest.

  Sal. Be of good comfort, Prince; for you are born
To set a form upon that indigest
Which he hath left so shapeless and so rude.

Enter Attendants, and BIGOT, *carrying* KING JOHN
in a chair.

  K. John. Ay, marry, now my soul hath elbow-room;
I would not out at windows nor at doors.
There is so hot a summer in my bosom,   30
That all my bowels crumble up to dust:
I am a scribbled form, drawn with a pen
Upon a parchment, and against this fire
Do I shrink up.
  P. Hen.   How fares your Majesty?
  K. John. Poison'd—ill fare—dead, forsook, cast off:
And none of you will bid the winter come
To thrust his icy fingers in my maw,
Nor let my kingdom's rivers take their course
Through my burn'd bosom, nor entreat the north
To make his bleak winds kiss my parched lips 40
And comfort me with cold. I do not ask you much,
I beg cold comfort; and you are so strait
And so ingrateful, you deny me that.
  P. Hen. O that there were some virtue in my tears,
That might relieve you!
  K. John.   The salt in them is hot.
Within me is a hell; and there the poison
Is as a fiend confined to tyrannize
On unreprievable condemned blood.

Enter the BASTARD.

  Bast. O, I am scalded with my violent motion,
And spleen of speed to see your Majesty!   50
  K. John. O cousin, thou art come to set mine eye:
The tackle of my heart is crack'd and burn'd,
And all the shrouds wherewith my life should sail
Are turned to one thread, one little hair:
My heart hath one poor string to stay it by,
Which holds but till thy news be uttered;
And then all this thou seest is but a clod
And module of confounded royalty.
  Bast. The Dauphin is preparing hitherward,
Where heaven He knows how we shall answer him;   60
For in a night the best part of my power,

As I upon advantage did remove,
Were in the Washes all unwarily
Devoured by the unexpected flood.

                           [The king dies.

  Sal. You breathe these dead news in as dead an ear.
My liege! my lord! but now a king, now thus.
  P. Hen. Even so must I run on, and even so stop.
What surety of the world, what hope, what stay,
When this was now a king, and now is clay?
  Bast. Art thou gone so? I do but stay behind 70
To do the office for thee of revenge,
And then my soul shall wait on thee to heaven,
As it on earth hath been thy servant still.
Now, now, you stars that move in your right spheres,
Where be your powers? show now your mended faiths,
And instantly return with me again,
To push destruction and perpetual shame
Out of the weak door of our fainting land.
Straight let us seek, or straight we shall be sought;
The Dauphin rages at our very heels.   80
  Sal. It seems you know not, then, so much as we:
The Cardinal Pandulph is within at rest,
Who half an hour since came from the Dauphin,
And brings from him such offers of our peace
As we with honour and respect may take,
With purpose presently to leave this war.
  Bast. He will the rather do it when he sees
Ourselves well sinewed to our defence.
  Sal. Nay, it is in a manner done already;
For many carriages he hath dispatch'd   90
To the sea-side, and put his cause and quarrel
To the disposing of the Cardinal:
With whom yourself, myself, and other lords,
If you think meet, this afternoon will post
To consummate this business happily.
  Bast. Let it be so: and you, my noble prince,
With other princes that may best be spared,
Shall wait upon your father's funeral.
  P. Hen. At Worcester must his body be interr'd;
For so he will'd it.
  Bast.   Thither shall it then: 100
And happily may your sweet self put on
The lineal state and glory of the land!
To whom, with all submission, on my knee
I do bequeath my faithful services
And true subjection everlastingly.
  Sal. And the like tender of our love we make,

To rest without a spot for evermore.

   P. Hen. I have a kind soul that would give you thanks

And knows not how to do it but with tears.

   Bast. O, let us pay the time but needful woe,

Since it hath been beforehand with our griefs. *111*

This England never did, nor never shall,

Lie at the proud foot of a conqueror,

But when it first did help to wound itself.

Now these her princes are come home again,

Come the three corners of the world in arms,

And we shall shock them. Nought shall make us rue,

If England to itself do rest but true.   [*Exeunt.*

❧ THE MERCHANT OF VENICE

DRAMATIS PERSONÆ

THE DUKE OF VENICE
PRINCE OF MOROCCO ⎤ *suitors to Portia*
PRINCE OF ARRAGON ⎦
ANTONIO, *a merchant of Venice*
BASSANIO, *his friend, suitor likewise to Portia*
SALANIO ⎤
SALARINO ⎥ *friends to Antonio and Bassanio*
GRATIANO ⎥
SALERIO ⎦
LORENZO, *in love with Jessica*
SHYLOCK, *a rich Jew*
TUBAL, *a Jew, his friend*
LAUNCELOT GOBBO, *the clown, servant to Shylock*
OLD GOBBO, *father to Launcelot*
LEONARDO, *servant to Bassanio*

BALTHASAR ⎤ *servants to Portia*
STEPHANO ⎦
SERVANT *to Antonio*
SERVANT *to Portia*

PORTIA, *a rich heiress*
NERISSA, *her waiting-maid*
JESSICA, *daughter to Shylock*

NON-SPEAKING: *Magnificoes of Venice, Officers of the Court of Justice, Gaoler, Musicians, Servants to Portia, and other Attendants*

SCENE: *Partly in Venice, and partly at Belmont, the seat of Portia, on the continent*

ACT I

SCENE I. *Venice: a street*

Enter ANTONIO, SALARINO, *and* SALANIO.

Ant. In sooth, I know not why I am so sad:
It wearies me; you say it wearies you;
But how I caught it, found it, or came by it,
What stuff 'tis made of, whereof it is born,
I am to learn;
And such a want-wit sadness makes of me,
That I have much ado to know myself.

Salar. Your mind is tossing on the ocean;
There, where your argosies with portly sail,
Like signiors and rich burghers on the flood,   10
Or, as it were, the pageants of the sea,
Do overpeer the petty traffickers
That curtsy to them, do them reverence,
As they fly by them with their woven wings.

Salan. Believe me, sir, had I such venture forth,
The better part of my affections would
Be with my hopes abroad. I should be still
Plucking the grass, to know where sits the wind,
Peering in maps for ports and piers and roads;
And every object that might make me fear   20
Misfortune to my ventures, out of doubt
Would make me sad.

Salar.   My wind cooling my broth
Would blow me to an ague, when I thought
What harm a wind too great at sea might do.
I should not see the sandy hour-glass run,
But I should think of shallows and of flats,
And see my wealthy Andrew dock'd in sand,
Vailing her high-top lower than her ribs
To kiss her burial. Should I go to church

And see the holy edifice of stone,   30
And not bethink me straight of dangerous rocks,
Which touching but my gentle vessel's side,
Would scatter all her spices on the stream,
Enrobe the roaring waters with my silks,
And, in a word, but even now worth this,
And now worth nothing? Shall I have the thought
To think on this, and shall I lack the thought
That such a thing bechanced would make me sad?
But tell not me; I know, Antonio
Is sad to think upon his merchandise.   40

Ant. Believe me, no: I thank my fortune for it,
My ventures are not in one bottom trusted,
Nor to one place; nor is my whole estate
Upon the fortune of this present year:
Therefore my merchandise makes me not sad.

Salar. Why, then you are in love.

Ant.   Fie, fie!

Salar. Not in love neither? Then let us say you
      are sad,
Because you are not merry: and 'twere as easy
For you to laugh and leap and say you are merry,
Because you are not sad. Now, by two-headed
      Janus,   50
Nature hath framed strange fellows in her time:
Some that will evermore peep through their eyes
And laugh like parrots at a bag-piper,
And other of such vinegar aspect
That they'll not show their teeth in way of smile,
Though Nestor swear the jest be laughable.

Enter BASSANIO, LORENZO, *and* GRATIANO.

Salan. Here comes Bassanio, your most noble
      kinsman,

Gratiano, and Lorenzo. Fare ye well:
We leave you now with better company.

Salar. I would have stay'd till I had made you
     merry   60
If worthier friends had not prevented me.

Ant. Your worth is very dear in my regard.
I take it, your own business calls on you
And you enbrace the occasion to depart.

Salar. Good morrow, my good lords.

Bass. Good signiors both, when shall we laugh?
     say, when?
You grow exceeding strange; must it be so?

Salar. We'll make our leisures to attend on
     yours.
         [*Exeunt* SALARINO *and* SALANIO.

Lor. My lord Bassanio, since you have found
     Antonio,
We two will leave you: but at dinner-time,   70
I pray you, have in mind where we must meet.

Bass. I will not fail you.

Gra. You look not well, Signior Antonio;
You have too much respect upon the world:
They lose it that do buy it with much care:
Believe me, you are marvellously changed.

Ant. I hold the world but as the world, Gratiano;
A stage where every man must play a part,
And mine a sad one.

Gra.   Let me play the fool:
With mirth and laughter let old wrinkles come,
And let my liver rather heat with wine   81
Than my heart cool with mortifying groans.
Why should a man, whose blood is warm within,
Sit like his grandsire cut in alabaster?
Sleep when he wakes and creep into the jaundice
By being peevish? I tell thee what, Antonio—
I love thee, and it is my love that speaks—
There are a sort of men whose visages
Do cream and mantle like a standing pond,
And do a wilful stillness entertain,   90
With purpose to be dress'd in an opinion
Of wisdom, gravity, profound conceit,
As who should say, "I am Sir Oracle,
And when I ope my lips let no dog bark!"
O my Antonio, I do know of these
That therefore only are reputed wise
For saying nothing, when, I am very sure,
If they should speak, would almost damn those
     ears
Which, hearing them, would call their brothers
     fools.
I'll tell thee more of this another time: 100
But fish not, with this melancholy bait,
For this fool gudgeon, this opinion.
Come, good Lorenzo. Fare ye well awhile:
I'll end my exhortation after dinner.

Lor. Well, we will leave you then till dinnertime:

I must be one of these same dumb wise men,
For Gratiano never lets me speak.

Gra. Well, keep me company but two years
     moe,
Thou shalt not know the sound of thine own
     tongue.   109

Ant. Farewell: I'll grow a talker for this gear.

Gra. Thanks, i' faith, for silence is only com-
     mendable
In a neat's tongue dried and a maid not vendible.
         [*Exeunt* GRATIANO *and* LORENZO.

Ant. Is that any thing now?

Bass. Gratiano speaks an infinite deal of nothing,
more than any man in all Venice. His reasons are
as two grains of wheat hid in two bushels of chaff:
you shall seek all day ere you find them, and
when you have them, they are not worth the
search.

Ant. Well, tell me now what lady is the same
To whom you swore a secret pilgrimage,   120
That you to-day promised to tell me of?

Bass. 'Tis not unknown to you, Antonio,
How much I have disabled mine estate,
By something showing a more swelling port
Than my faint means would grant continuance:
Nor do I now make moan to be abridged
From such a noble rate; but my chief care
Is to come fairly off from the great debts
Wherein my time something too prodigal
Hath left me gaged. To you, Antonio,   130
I owe the most, in money and in love,
And from your love I have a warranty
To unburden all my plots and purposes
How to get clear of all the debts I owe.

Ant. I pray you, good Bassanio, let me know it;
And if it stand, as you yourself still do,
Within the eye of honour, be assured,
My purse, my person, my extremest means,
Lie all unlock'd to your occasions.

Bass. In my school-days, when I had lost one
     shaft,   140
I shot his fellow of the self-same flight
The self-same way with more advised watch,
To find the other forth, and by adventuring both
I oft found both: I urge this childhood proof,
Because what follows is pure innocence.
I owe you much, and, like a wilful youth,
That which I owe is lost; but if you please
To shoot another arrow that self way
Which you did shoot the first, I do not doubt,
As I will watch the aim, or to find both   150
Or bring your latter hazard back again
And thankfully rest debtor for the first.

Ant. You know me well, and herein spend but
     time
To wind about my love with circumstance;

And out of doubt you do me now more wrong
In making question of my uttermost
Than if you had made waste of all I have:
Then do but say to me what I should do
That in your knowledge may by me be done,
And I am prest unto it: therefore, speak.   160
  Bass. In Belmont is a lady richly left;
And she is fair and, fairer than that word,
Of wondrous virtues: sometimes from her eyes
I did receive fair speechless messages:
Her name is Portia, nothing undervalued
To Cato's daughter, Brutus' Portia:
Nor is the wide world ignorant of her worth,
For the four winds blow in from every coast
Renowned suitors, and her sunny locks
Hang on her temples like a golden fleece;   170
Which makes her seat of Belmont Colchos'
    strand,
And many Jasons come in quest of her.
O my Antonio, had I but the means
To hold a rival place with one of them,
I have a mind presages me such thrift,
That I should questionless be fortunate!
  Ant. Thou know'st that all my fortunes are at
    sea;
Neither have I money nor commodity
To raise a present sum: therefore go forth;
Try what my credit can in Venice do: 180
That shall be rack'd, even to the uttermost,
To funish thee to Belmont, to fair Portia.
Go, presently inquire, and so will I,
Where money is, and I no question make
To have it of my trust or for my sake.   [*Exeunt.*

SCENE II. *Belmont: a room in Portia's house*
        Enter PORTIA *and* NERISSA.

  Por. By my troth, Nerissa, my little body is
aweary of this great world.
  Ner. You would be, sweet madam, if your
miseries were in the same abundance as your
good fortunes are: and yet, for aught I see, they
are as sick that surfeit with too much as they that
starve with nothing. It is no mean happiness
therefore, to be seated in the mean: superfluity
comes sooner by white hairs, but competency
lives longer.   10
  Por. Good sentences and well pronounced.
  Ner. They would be better, if well followed.
  Por. If to do were as easy as to know what were
good to do, chapels had been churches and poor
men's cottages princes' palaces. It is a good
divine that follows his own instructions: I can
easier teach twenty what were good to be done,
than be one of the twenty to follow mine own
teaching. The brain may devise laws for the
blood, but a hot temper leaps o'er a cold decree:

such a hare is madness the youth, to skip o'er the
meshes of good counsel the cripple. But this
reasoning is not the fashion to choose me a
husband. O me, the word "choose!" I may neither choose whom I would nor refuse whom I
dislike; so is the will of a living daughter curbed
by the will of a dead father. Is it not hard,
Nerissa, that I cannot choose one nor refuse
none?   29
  Ner. Your father was ever virtuous; and holy
men at their death have good inspirations: therefore the lottery, that he hath devised in these
three chests of gold, silver, and lead, whereof
who chooses his meaning chooses you, will, no
doubt, never be chosen by any rightly but one
who shall rightly love. But what warmth is there
in your affection towards any of these princely
suitors that are already come?
  Por. I pray thee, over-name them; and as thou
namest them, I will describe them; and, according to my description, level at my affection.
  Ner. First, there is the Neapolitan prince.
  Por. Ay, that's a colt indeed, for he doth nothing
but talk of his horse; and he makes it a great
appropriation to his own good parts, that he can
shoe him himself. I am much afeard my lady his
mother played false with a smith.
  Ner. Then there is the County Palatine.
  Por. He doth nothing but frown, as who should
say "If you will not have me, choose": he hears
merry tales and smiles not: I fear he will prove
the weeping philosopher when he grows old,
being so full of unmannerly sadness in his youth.
I had rather be married to a death's-head with
a bone in his mouth than to either of these. God
defend me from these two!
  Ner. How say you by the French lord, Monsieur Le Bon?   59
  Por. God made him, and therefore let him pass
for a man. In truth, I know it is a sin to be a
mocker: but, he! why, he hath a horse better than
the Neapolitan's, a better bad habit of frowning
than the Count Palatine; he is every man in no
man; if a throstle sing, he falls straight a capering: he will fence with his own shadow: if I
should marry him, I should marry twenty husbands. If he would despise me, I would forgive
him, for if he love me to madness, I shall never
requite him.   70
  Ner. What say you, then, to Falconbridge, the
young baron of England?
  Por. You know I say nothing to him, for he
understands not me, nor I him: he hath neither
Latin, French, nor Italian, and you will come
into the court and swear that I have a poor
pennyworth in the English. He is a proper man's

picture, but, alas, who can converse with a dumb-show? How oddly he is suited! I think he bought his doublet in Italy, his round hose in France, his bonnet in Germany and his behaviour every-where.

Ner. What think you of the Scottish lord, his neighbour?

Por. That he hath a neighbourly charity in him, for he borrowed a box of the ear of the English-man and swore he would pay him again when he was able: I think the Frenchman became his surety and sealed under for another.

Ner. How like you the young German, the Duke of Saxony's nephew?   *91*

Por. Very vilely in the morning, when he is sober, and most vilely in the afternoon, when he is drunk: when he is best, he is a little worse than a man, and when he is worst, he is little better than a beast: an the worst fall that ever fell, I hope I shall make shift to go without him.

Ner. If he should offer to choose, and choose the right casket, you should refuse to perform your father's will, if you should refuse to accept him.

Por. Therefore, for fear of the worst, I pray thee, set a deep glass of rhenish wine on the contrary casket, for if the devil be within and that temptation without, I know he will choose it. I will do anything, Nerissa, ere I'll be married to a sponge.

Ner. You need not fear, lady, the having any of these lords: they have acquainted me with their determinations; which is, indeed, to return suit, unless you may be won by some other sort than your father's imposition depending on the caskets.

Por. If I live to be as old as Sibylla, I will die as chaste as Diana, unless I be obtained by the manner of my father's will. I am glad this parcel of wooers are so reasonable, for there is not one among them but I dote on his very absence, and I pray God grant them a fair departure.

Ner. Do you not remember, lady, in your father's time, a Venetian, a scholar and a soldier, that came hither in company of the Marquis of Montferrat?

Por. Yes, yes, it was Bassanio; as I think, he was so called.

Ner. True, madam: he, of all the men that ever my foolish eyes looked upon, was the best deserving a fair lady.   *131*

Por. I remember him well, and I remember him worthy of thy praise.

Enter a SERVING-MAN.

How now! what news?

Serv. The four strangers seek for you, madam, to take their leave: and there is a forerunner come from a fifth, the Prince of Morocco, who brings word the Prince his master will be here to-night.   *139*

Por. If I could bid the fifth welcome with so good a heart as I can bid the other four farewell, I should be glad of his approach; if he have the condition of a saint and the complexion of a devil, I had rather he should shrive me than wive me.

Come, Nerissa. Sirrah, go before.

Whiles we shut the gates upon one wooer, another knocks at the door.   [*Exeunt.*

SCENE III. *Venice: a public place*

Enter BASSANIO *and* SHYLOCK.

Shy. Three thousand ducats; well.

Bass. Ay, sir, for three months.

Shy. For three months; well.

Bass. For the which, as I told you, Antonio shall be bound.

Shy. Antonio shall become bound; well.

Bass. May you stead me? will you pleasure me? shall I know your answer?

Shy. Three thousand ducats for three months and Antonio bound.   *10*

Bass. Your answer to that.

Shy. Antonio is a good man.

Bass. Have you heard any imputation to the contrary?

Shy. Oh, no, no, no, no: my meaning in saying he is a good man is to have you understand me that he is sufficient. Yet his means are in supposi-tion: he hath an argosy bound to Tripolis, an-other to the Indies; I understand, moreover, upon the Rialto, he hath a third at Mexico, a fourth for England, and other ventures he hath, squan-dered abroad. But ships are but boards, sailors but men: there be land-rats and water-rats, water-thieves and land-thieves, I mean pirates, and then there is the peril of waters, winds, and rocks. The man is, notwithstanding, sufficient. Three thousand ducats; I think I may take his bond.

Bass. Be assured you may.

Shy. I will be assured I may; and, that I may be assured, I will bethink me. May I speak with Antonio?

Bass. If it please you to dine with us.

Shy. Yes, to smell pork; to eat of the habitation which your prophet the Nazarite conjured the devil into. I will buy with you, sell with you, talk with you, walk with you, and so following, but I will not eat with you, drink with you, nor pray with you. What news on the Rialto? Who is he comes here?   *40*

Enter ANTONIO.

Bass. This is Signior Antonio.

Shy. [*Aside*] How like a fawning publican he
  looks!
I hate him for he is a Christian,
But more for that in low simplicity
He lends out money gratis and brings down
The rate of usance here with us in Venice.
If I can catch him once upon the hip,
I will feed fat the ancient grudge I bear him.
He hates our sacred nation, and he rails,
Even there where merchants most do congregate,
On me, my bargains, and my well-won thrift,   51
Which he calls interest. Cursed be my tribe,
If I forgive him!

Bass.   Shylock, do you hear?

Shy. I am debating of my present store,
And, by the near guess of my memory,
I cannot instantly raise up the gross
Of full three thousand ducats. What of that?
Tubal, a wealthy Hebrew of my tribe,
Will furnish me. But soft! how many months
Do you desire? [*To* ANTONIO] Rest you fair, good
  signior;   60
Your worship was the last man in our mouths.

Ant. Shylock, although I neither lend nor
  borrow
By taking nor by giving of excess,
Yet, to supply the ripe wants of my friend,
I'll break a custom. Is he yet possess'd
How much ye would?

Shy.   Ay, ay, three thousand ducats.

Ant. And for three months.

Shy. I had forgot; three months; you told me so.
Well then, your bond; and let me see; but hear
  you;
Methought you said you neither lend nor borrow
Upon advantage.

Ant.   I do never use it.   71

Shy. When Jacob grazed his uncle Laban's
  sheep—
This Jacob from our holy Abram was,
As his wise mother wrought in his behalf,
The third possessor; ay, he was the third—

Ant. And what of him? did he take interest?

Shy. No, not take interest, not, as you would
  say,
Directly interest: mark what Jacob did.
When Laban and himself were compromised
That all the eanlings which were streak'd and
  pied   80
Should fall as Jacob's hire, the ewes, being rank,
In the end of autumn turned to the rams,
And, when the work of generation was
Between these wooly breeders in the act,

The skilful shepherd peel'd me certain wands
And, in the doing of the deed of kind,
He stuck them up before the fulsome ewes,
Who then conceiving did in eaning time
Fall parti-colour'd lambs, and those were Jacob's.
This was a way to thrive, and he was blest: 90
And thrift is blessing, if men steal it not.

Ant. This was a venture, sir, that Jacob served
  for;
A thing not in his power to bring to pass,
But sway'd and fashion'd by the hand of heaven.
Was this inserted to make interest good?
Or is your gold and silver ewes and rams?

Shy. I cannot tell; I make it breed as fast:
But note me, signior.

Ant.   Mark you this Bassanio,
The devil can cite Scripture for his purpose.
An evil soul producing holy witness   100
Is like a villain with a smiling cheek,
A goodly apple rotten at the heart:
O, what a goodly outside falsehood hath!

Shy. Three thousand ducats; 'tis a good round
  sum.
Three months from twelve; then, let me see; the
  rate—

Ant. Well, Shylock, shall we be beholding to
  you?

Shy. Signior Antonio, many a time and oft
In the Rialto you have rated me
About my moneys and my usances:
Still have I borne it with a patient shrug,   110
For sufferance is the badge of all our tribe.
You call me misbeliever, cut-throat dog,
And spit upon my Jewish gaberdine,
And all for use of that which is mine own.
Well then, it now appears you need my help:
Go to, then; you come to me, and you say
"Shylock, we would have moneys": you say so;
You, that did void your rheum upon my beard
And foot me as you spurn a stranger cur
Over your threshold: moneys is your suit.   120
What should I say to you? Should I not say
"Hath a dog money? is it possible
A cur can lend three thousand ducats?" Or
Shall I bend low and in a bondman's key,
With bated breath and whispering humbleness,
Say this;
"Fair sir, you spit on me on Wednesday last;
You spurn'd me such a day; another time
You call'd me dog; and for these courtesies
I'll lend you thus much moneys"?   130

Ant. I am as like to call thee so again,
To spit on thee again, to spurn thee too.
If thou wilt lend this money, lend it not
As to thy friends; for when did friendship take
A breed for barren metal of his friend?

But lend it rather to thine enemy,
Who, if he break, thou mayst with better face
Exact the penalty.

Shy. Why, look you, how you storm!
I would be friends with you and have your love,
Forget the shames that you have stain'd me
with,
Supply your present wants and take no doit   *141*
Of usance for my moneys, and you'll not hear
me:
This is kind I offer.

Bass. This were kindness.

Shy. This kindness will I show.
Go with me to a notary, seal me there
Your single bond; and, in a merry sport,
If you repay me not on such a day,
In such a place, such sum or sums as are
Express'd in the condition, let the forfeit
Be nominated for an equal pound   *150*
Of your fair flesh, to be cut off and taken
In what part of your body pleaseth me.

Ant. Content, i' faith: I'll seal to such a bond
And say there is much kindness in the Jew.

Bass. You shall not seal to such a bond for me:
I'll rather dwell in my necessity.

Ant. Why, fear not, man; I will not forfeit it:
Within these two months, that's a month be-
fore
This bond expires, I do expect return
Of thrice three times the value of this bond.   *160*

Shy. O father Abram, what these Christians
are,
Whose own hard dealings teaches them suspect
The thoughts of others! Pray you, tell me this;
If he should break his day, what should I gain
By the exaction of the forfeiture?
A pound of man's flesh taken from a man
Is not so estimable, profitable neither,
As flesh of muttons, beefs, or goats. I say,
To buy his favour, I extend this friendship:
If he will take it, so; if not, adieu;   *170*
And, for my love, I pray you wrong me not.

Ant. Yes, Shylock, I will seal unto this bond.

Shy. Then meet me forthwith at the notary's;
Give him direction for this merry bond,
And I will go and purse the ducats straight,
See to my house, left in the fearful guard
Of an unthrifty knave, and presently
I will be with you.

Ant. Hie thee, gentle Jew.   [*Exit* SHYLOCK.
The Hebrew will turn Christian: he grows
kind.

Bass. I like not fair terms and a villain's mind.

Ant. Come on: in this there can be no dismay;
My ships come home a month before the day.

                        [*Exeunt.*

ACT II

SCENE I. *Belmont: a room in Portia's house*

Flourish of cornets. Enter the PRINCE OF MOROCCO
and his train; PORTIA, NERISSA, *and others
attending.*

Mor. Mislike me not for my complexion,
The shadow'd livery of the burnish'd sun,
To whom I am a neighbour and near bred.
Bring me the fairest creature northward born,
Where Phœbus' fire scarce thaws the icicles,
And let us make incision for your love,
To prove whose blood is reddest, his or mine.
I tell thee, lady, this aspect of mine
Hath fear'd the valiant: by my love, I swear
The best-regarded virgins of our clime   *10*
Have loved it too: I would not change this hue,
Except to steal your thoughts, my gentle queen.

Por. In terms of choice I am not solely led
By nice direction of a maiden's eyes;
Besides, the lottery of my destiny
Bars me the right of voluntary choosing:
But if my father had not scanted me
And hedged me by his wit, to yield myself
His wife who wins me by that means I told you,
Yourself, renowned Prince, then stood as fair   *20*
As any comer I have look'd on yet
For my affection.

Mor. Even for that I thank you:
Therefore, I pray you, lead me to the caskets
To try my fortune. By this scimitar
That slew the Sophy and a Persian prince
That won three fields of Sultan Solyman,
I would outstare the sternest eyes that look,
Outbrave the heart most daring on the earth,
Pluck the young sucking cubs from the she-bear,
Yea, mock the lion when he roars for prey,   *30*
To win thee, lady. But, alas the while!
If Hercules and Lichas play at dice
Which is the better man, the greater throw
May turn by fortune from the weaker hand:
So is Alcides beaten by his page;
And so may I, blind fortune leading me,
Miss that which one unworthier may attain,
And die with grieving.

Por. You must take your chance,
And either not attempt to choose at all
Or swear before you choose, if you choose
wrong
Never to speak to lady afterward   *41*
In way of marriage: therefore be advised.

Mor. Nor will not. Come, bring me unto my
chance.

Por. First, forward to the temple: after dinner
Your hazard shall be made.

Mor. Good fortune then!

To make me blest or cursed'st among men.

[*Cornets, and exeunt.*

SCENE II. *Venice: a street*

Enter LAUNCELOT.

Laun. Certainly my conscience will serve me to run from this Jew my master. The fiend is at mine elbow and tempts me saying to me "Gobbo, Launcelot Gobbo, good Launcelot," or "good Gobbo," or "good Launcelot Gobbo, use your legs, take the start, run away." My conscience says "No; take heed, honest Launcelot; take heed, honest Gobbo," or, as aforesaid, "honest Launcelot Gobbo; do not run; scorn running with thy heels." Well, the most courageous fiend bids me pack: "Via!" says the fiend; "away!" says the fiend; "for the heavens, rouse up a brave mind," says the fiend, "and run." Well, my conscience, hanging about the neck of my heart, says very wisely to me, "My honest friend Launcelot, being an honest man's son," or rather an honest woman's son; for, indeed, my father did something smack, something grow to, he had a kind of taste; well, my conscience says, "Launcelot, budge not." "Budge," says the fiend. "Budge not," says my conscience. "Conscience," say I, "you counsel well"; "Fiend," say I, "you counsel well": to be ruled by my conscience, I should stay with the Jew my master, who, God bless the mark, is a kind of devil; and, to run away from the Jew, I should be ruled by the fiend, who, saving your reverence, is the devil himself. Certainly the Jew is the very devil incarnal; and, in my conscience, my conscience is but a kind of hard conscience, to offer to counsel me to stay with the Jew. The fiend gives the more friendly counsel: I will run, fiend; my heels are at your command; I will run.

Enter OLD GOBBO, *with a basket.*

Gob. Master young man, you, I pray you, which is the way to master Jew's?

Laun. [*Aside*] O heavens, this is my true-begotten father! who, being more than sand-blind, high-gravel blind, knows me not: I will try confusions with him.

Gob. Master young gentleman, I pray you, which is the way to master Jew's?　　　　*41*

Laun. Turn up on your right hand at the next turning, but, at the next turning of all, on your left; marry, at the very next turning, turn of no hand, but turn down indirectly to the Jew's house.

Gob. By God's sonties, 'twill be a hard way to hit. Can you tell me whether one Launcelot, that dwells with him, dwell with him or no?　　　*49*

Laun. Talk you of young Master Launcelot?

[*Aside*] Mark me now; now will I raise the waters. Talk you of young Master Launcelot?

Gob. No master, sir, but a poor man's son: his father, though I say it, is an honest exceeding poor man and, God be thanked, well to live.

Laun. Well, let his father be what a' will, we talk of young Master Launcelot.

Gob. Your worship's friend and Launcelot, sir.

Laun. But I pray you, ergo, old man, ergo, I beseech you, talk you of young Master Launcelot?　　　　*60*

Gob. Of Launcelot, an't please your mastership.

Laun. Ergo, Master Launcelot. Talk not of Master Launcelot, father; for the young gentleman, according to Fates and Destinies and such odd sayings, the Sisters Three and such branches of learning, is indeed deceased, or, as you would say in plain terms, gone to heaven.

Gob. Marry, God forbid! the boy was the very staff of my age, my very prop.　　　　*70*

Laun. Do I look like a cudgel or a hovelpost, a staff or a prop? Do you know me, father?

Gob. Alack the day, I know you not, young gentleman: but, I pray you, tell me, is my boy, God rest his soul, alive or dead?

Laun. Do you not know me, father?

Gob. Alack, Sir, I am sand-blind; I know you not.

Laun. Nay, indeed, if you had your eyes, you might fail of the knowing me: it is a wise father that knows his own child. Well, old man, I will tell you news of your son: give me your blessing: truth will come to light; murder cannot be hid long; a man's son may, but at the length truth will out.

Gob. Pray you, sir, stand up: I am sure you are not Launcelot, my boy.

Laun. Pray you, let's have no more fooling about it, but give me your blessing: I am Launcelot, your boy that was, your son that is, your child that shall be.　　　　*91*

Gob. I cannot think you are my son.

Laun. I know not what I shall think of that: but I am Launcelot, the Jew's man, and I am sure Margery your wife is my mother.

Gob. Her name is Margery, indeed: I'll be sworn, if thou be Launcelot, thou art mine own flesh and blood. Lord worshipped might he be! what a beard hast thou got! thou hast got more hair on thy chin than Dobbin my fill-horse has on his tail.　　　　*101*

Laun. It should seem, then, that Dobbin's tail grows backward: I am sure he had more hair of his tail than I have of my face when I last saw him.

Gob. Lord, how art thou changed! How dost

thou and thy master agree? I have brought him
a present. How 'gree you now?

Laun. Well, well: but, for mine own part, as I
have set up my rest to run away, so I will not
rest till I have run some ground. My master's a
very Jew: give him a present! give him a halter:
I am famished in his service; you may tell every
finger I have with my ribs. Father, I am glad you
are come: give me your present to one Master
Bassanio, who, indeed, gives rare new liveries:
if I serve not him, I will run as far as God has
any ground. O rare fortune! here comes the man:
to him, father; for I am a Jew, if I serve the Jew
any longer.   *120*

Enter BASSANIO, *with* LEONARDO *and other*
followers.

Bass. You may do so; but let it be so hasted that
supper be ready at the farthest by five of the
clock. See these letters delivered; put the liveries
to making, and desire Gratiano to come anon to
my lodging.   [*Exit a Servant.*

Laun. To him, father.

Gob. God bless your worship!

Bass. Gramercy! wouldst thou aught with me?

Gob. Here's my son, sir, a poor boy—   *129*

Laun. Not a poor boy, sir, but the rich Jew's
man; that would, sir, as my father shall specify—

Gob. He hath a great infection, sir, as one
would say, to serve—

Laun. Indeed, the short and the long is, I serve
the Jew, and have a desire, as my father shall
specify—

Gob. His master and he, saving your worship's
reverence, are scarce cater-cousins—   *139*

Laun. To be brief, the very truth is that the Jew,
having done me wrong, doth cause me, as my father,
being, I hope, an old man, shall frutify unto you—

Gob. I have here a dish of doves that I would
bestow upon your worship, and my suit is—

Laun. In very brief, the suit is impertinent to
myself, as your worship shall know by this
honest old man; and, though I say it, though old
man, yet poor man, my father.

Bass. One speak for both. What would you?

Laun. Serve you, sir.   *151*

Gob. That is the very defect of the matter, sir.

Bass. I know thee well; thou hast obtain'd thy
suit:
Shylock thy master spoke with me this day,
And hath preferr'd thee, if it be preferment
To leave a rich Jew's service, to become
The follower of so poor a gentleman.

Laun. The old proverb is very well parted
between my master Shylock and you, sir: you
have the grace of God, sir, and he hath enough.

Bass. Thou speak'st it well. Go, father, with
thy son.
Take leave of thy old master and inquire
My lodging out. Give him a livery
More guarded than his fellows': see it done.

Laun. Father, in. I cannot get a service, no; I
have ne'er a tongue in my head. Well, if any man
in Italy have a fairer table which doth offer to
swear upon a book, I shall have good fortune. Go
to, here's a simple line of life: here's a small trifle
of wives: alas, fifteen wives is nothing! eleven
widows and nine maids is a simple coming-in for
one man: and then to 'scape drowning thrice, and
to be in peril of my life with the edge of a feather-
bed; here are simple scapes. Well, if Fortune be
a woman, she's a good wench for this gear.
Father, come; I'll take my leave of the Jew in
the twinkling of an eye.

                  [*Exeunt* LAUNCELOT *and* OLD GOBBO.

Bass. I pray thee, good Leonardo, think on this:
These things being bought and orderly bestow'd,
Return in haste, for I do feast to-night   *180*
My best-esteem'd acquaintance: hie thee, go.

Leon. My best endeavours shall be done herein.

Enter GRATIANO.

Gra. Where is your master?

Leon.   Yonder, sir, he walks. [*Exit.*

Gra. Signior Bassanio!

Bass. Gratiano!

Gra. I have a suit to you.

Bass.   You have obtain'd it.

Gra. You must not deny me: I must go with you
to Belmont.

Bass. Why, then you must. But hear thee, Gra-
tiano;
Thou art too wild, too rude, and bold of voice;
Parts that become thee happily enough   *191*
And in such eyes as ours appear not faults;
But where thou art not known, why, there they
show
Something too liberal. Pray thee, take pain
To allay with some cold drops of modesty
Thy skipping spirit, lest through thy wild be-
haviour
I be misconstrued in the place I go to
And lose my hopes.

Gra.   Signior Bassanio, hear me:
If I do not put on a sober habit,   *199*
Talk with respect and swear but now and then,
Wear prayer-books in my pocket, look demurely,
Nay more, while grace is saying, hood mine eyes
Thus with my hat, and sigh and say "amen,"
Use all the observance of civility,
Like one well studied in a sad ostent
To please his grandam, never trust me more.

Bass. Well, we shall see your bearing.

Gra. Nay, but I bar to-night: you shall not
    gauge me
By what we do to-night.
  Bass.   No, that were pity:
I would entreat you rather to put on   *210*
Your boldest suit of mirth, for we have friends
That purpose merriment. But fare you well:
I have some business.
  Gra. And I must to Lorenzo and the rest:
But we will visit you at supper-time.   [*Exeunt.*

Scene iii. *The same: a room in Shylock's house*

Enter JESSICA *and* LAUNCELOT.

Jes. I am sorry thou wilt leave my father so:
Our house is hell, and thou, a merry devil,
Didst rob it of some taste of tediousness.
But fare thee well, there is a ducat for thee:
And, Launcelot, soon at supper shalt thou see
Lorenzo, who is thy new master's guest:
Give him this letter; do it secretly;
And so farewell: I would not have my father
See me in talk with thee.   *9*
  Laun. Adieu! tears exhibit my tongue. Most
beautiful pagan, most sweet Jew! if a Christian
did not play the knave and get thee, I am much
deceived. But, adieu: these foolish drops do
something drown my manly spirit: adieu.
  Jes. Farewell, good Launcelot.
                  [*Exit* LAUNCELOT.
Alack, what heinous sin is it in me
To be ashamed to be my father's child!
But though I am a daughter to his blood,
I am not to his manners. O Lorenzo,
If thou keep promise, I shall end this strife, *20*
Become a Christian and thy loving wife.   [*Exit.*

Scene iv. *The same: a street*

Enter GRATIANO, LORENZO, SALARINO, *and*
SALANIO.

Lor. Nay, we will slink away in supper-time,
Disguise us at my lodging and return,
All in an hour.
  Gra. We have not made good preparation.
  Salar. We have not spoke us yet of torch-
    bearers.
  Salan. 'Tis vile, unless it may be quaintly
    order'd,
And better in my mind not undertook.
  Lor. 'Tis now but four o'clock: we have two
    hours
To furnish us.

Enter LAUNCELOT, *with a letter.*

          Friend Launcelot, what's the news?
  Laun. An it shall please you to break up this,
it shall seem to signify.   *11*

Lor. I know the hand: in faith, 'tis a fair hand;
And whiter than the paper it writ on
Is the fair hand that writ.
  Gra.   Love-news, in faith.
  Laun. By your leave, sir.
  Lor. Whither goest thou?
  Laun. Marry, sir, to bid my old master the Jew
to sup to-night with my new master the Christian.
  Lor. Hold here, take this: tell gentle Jessica I
will not fail her; speak it privately.   *21*
Go, gentlemen,   [*Exit* LAUNCELOT.
Will you prepare you for this masque to-night?
I am provided of a torch-bearer.
  Salar. Ay, marry, I'll be gone about it straight.
  Salan. And so will I.
  Lor.   Meet me and Gratiano
At Gratiano's lodging some hour hence.
  Salar. 'Tis good we do so.
           [*Exeunt* SALARINO *and* SALANIO.
  Gra. Was not that letter from fair Jessica?
  Lor. I must needs tell thee all. She hath directed
How I shall take her from her father's house, *31*
What gold and jewels she is furnish'd with,
What page's suit she hath in readiness.
If e'er the Jew her father come to heaven,
It will be for his gentle daughter's sake:
And never dare misfortune cross her foot,
Unless she do it under this excuse,
That she is issue to a faithless Jew.
Come, go with me; peruse this as thou goest:
Fair Jessica shall be my torch-bearer.   [*Exeunt.*

Scene v. *The same: before Shylock's house*

Enter SHYLOCK *and* LAUNCELOT.

Shy. Well, thou shalt see, thy eyes shall be thy
    judge,
The difference of old Shylock and Bassanio:—
What, Jessica!—thou shalt not gormandise,
As thou hast done with me:—What Jessica!—
And sleep and snore, and rend apparel out;—
Why, Jessica, I say!
  Laun.   Why, Jessica!
  Shy. Who bids thee call? I do not bid thee call.
  Laun. Your worship was wont to tell me that
I could do nothing without bidding.

Enter JESSICA.

  Jes. Call you? what is your will?   *10*
  Shy. I am bid forth to supper, Jessica:
There are my keys. But wherefore should I go?
I am not bid for love; they flatter me:
But yet I'll go in hate, to feed upon
The prodigal Christian. Jessica, my girl,
Look to my house. I am right loath to go:
There is some ill a-brewing towards my rest,
For I did dream of money-bags to-night.

Laun. I beseech you, sir, go: my young master
doth expect your reproach.   20
Shy. So do I his.
Laun. And they have conspired together, I will
not say you shall see a masque; but if you do,
then it was not for nothing that my nose fell
a-bleeding on Black-Monday last at six o'clock i'
the morning, falling out that year on Ash-Wed-
nesday was four year, in the afternoon.
Shy. What, are there masques? Hear you me,
  Jessica:
Lock up my doors; and when you hear the drum
And the vile squealing of the wry-neck'd fife,   30
Clamber not you up to the casements then,
Nor thrust your head into the public street
To gaze on Christian fools with varnish'd faces,
But stop my house's ears, I mean my casements:
Let not the sound of shallow foppery enter
My sober house. By Jacob's staff, I swear,
I have no mind of feasting forth to-night:
But I will go. Go you before me, sirrah;
Say I will come.
Laun. I will go before, sir. Mistress, look out at
window, for all this;   41
     There will come a Christian by,
     Will be worth a Jewess' eye.   [*Exit.*
Shy. What says that fool of Hagar's offspring,
  ha?
Jes. His words were "Farewell mistress";
  nothing else.
Shy. The patch is kind enough, but a huge
  feeder;
Snail-slow in profit, and he sleeps by day
More than the wild-cat: drones hive not with me;
Therefore I part with him, and part with him
To one that I would have him help to waste   50
His borrow'd purse. Well, Jessica, go in:
Perhaps I will return immediately:
Do as I bid you; shut doors after you:
Fast bind, fast find;
A proverb never stale in thrifty mind.   [*Exit.*
Jes. Farewell; and if my fortune be not crost,
I have a father, you a daughter, lost.   [*Exit.*

SCENE VI. *The same*

Enter GRATIANO *and* SALARINO, *masqued.*

Gra. This is the pent-house under which
  Lorenzo
Desired us to make stand.
Salar.   His hour is almost past.
Gra. And it is marvel he out-dwells his hour,
For lovers ever run before the clock.
Salar. O, ten times faster Venus' pigeons fly
To seal love's bonds new-made, than they are
  wont
To keep obliged faith unforfeited!

Gra. That ever holds: who riseth from a feast
With that keen appetite that he sits down?
Where is the horse that doth untread again   10
His tedious measures with the unbated fire
That he did pace them first? All things that are,
Are with more spirit chased than enjoy'd.
How like a younker or a prodigal
The scarfed bark puts from her native bay,
Hugg'd and embraced by the strumpet wind!
How like the prodigal doth she return,
With over-weather'd ribs and ragged sails,
Lean, rent and beggar'd by the strumpet wind!
Salar. Here comes Lorenzo: more of this
  hereafter.   20

Enter LORENZO.

Lor. Sweet friends, your patience for my long
  abode;
Not I, but my affairs, have made you wait:
When you shall please to play the thieves for
  wives,
I'll watch as long for you then. Approach;
Here dwells my father Jew. Ho! who's within?

Enter JESSICA, *above, in boy's clothes.*

Jes. Who are you? Tell me, for more certainty,
Albeit I'll swear that I do know your tongue.
Lor. Lorenzo, and thy love.
Jes. Lorenzo, certain, and my love indeed,
For who love I so much? And now who knows
But you, Lorenzo, whether I am yours?   31
Lor. Heaven and thy thoughts are witness that
  thou art.
Jes. Here, catch this casket; it is worth the
  pains.
I am glad 'tis night, you do not look on me,
For I am much ashamed of my exchange:
But love is blind and lovers cannot see
The pretty follies that themselves commit;
For if they could, Cupid himself would blush
To see me thus transformed to a boy.
Lor. Descend, for you must be my torch-
  bearer.   40
Jes. What, must I hold a candle to my shames?
They in themselves, good sooth, are too too light.
Why, 'tis an office of discovery, love;
And I should be obscured.
Lor.   So are you, sweet,
Even in the lovely garnish of a boy.
But come at once;
For the close night doth play the runaway,
And we are stay'd for at Bassanio's feast.
Jes. I will make fast the doors, and gild myself
With some more ducats, and be with you
  straight.   [*Exit above.* 50
Gra. Now, by my hood, a Gentile and no Jew.

Lor. Beshrew me but I love her heartily;
For she is wise, if I can judge of her,
And fair she is, if that mine eyes be true,
And true she is, as she hath proved herself,
And therefore, like herself, wise, fair, and true,
Shall she be placed in my constant soul.

Enter JESSICA, *below.*

What, art thou come? On, gentlemen; away!
Our masquing mates by this time for us stay.
[*Exit with* JESSICA *and* SALARINO.

Enter ANTONIO.

Ant. Who's there?   60
Gra. Signior Antonio!
Ant. Fie, fie, Gratiano! where are all the rest?
'Tis nine o'clock: our friends all stay for you.
No masque to-night: the wind is come about;
Bassanio presently will go aboard:
I have sent twenty out to seek for you.
Gra. I am glad on't: I desire no more delight
Than to be under sail and gone to-night. [*Exeunt.*

SCENE VII. *Belmont: a room in Portia's house.*

Flourish of cornets. Enter PORTIA, *with the* PRINCE
OF MOROCCO, *and their trains.*

Por. Go draw aside the curtains and discover
The several caskets to this noble prince.
Now make your choice.
Mor.   The first, of gold, who this inscription
bears,
"Who chooseth me shall gain what many men
desire";
The second, silver, which this promise carries,
"Who chooseth me shall get as much as he de-
serves";
This third, dull lead, with warning all as blunt,
"Who chooseth me must give and hazard all he
hath."
How shall I know if I do choose the right?   *10*
Por. The one of them contains my picture,
Prince:
If you choose that, then I am yours withal.
Mor. Some god direct my judgement! Let me
see;
I will survey the inscriptions back again.
What says this leaden casket?
"Who chooseth me must give and hazard all he
hath."
Must give: for what? for lead? hazard for
lead?
This casket threatens. Men that hazard all
Do it in hope of fair advantages:
A golden mind stoops not to shows of dross; *20*
I'll then nor give hazard aught for lead.
What says the silver with her virgin hue?

"Who chooseth me shall get as much as he de-
serves."
As much as he deserves! Pause there, Morocco,
And weigh thy value with an even hand:
If thou be'st rated by thy estimation,
Thou dost deserve enough; and yet enough
May not extend so far as to the lady:
And yet to be afeard of my deserving
Were but a weak disabling of myself.   *30*
As much as I deserve! Why, that's the lady:
I do in birth deserve her, and in fortunes,
In graces, and in qualities of breeding;
But more than these, in love I do deserve.
What if I stray'd no further, but chose here?
Let's see once more this saying graved in gold;
"Who chooseth me shall gain what many men
desire."
Why, that's the lady; all the world desires her;
From the four corners of the earth they come,
To kiss this shrine, this mortal-breathing saint:
The Hyrcanian deserts and the vasty wilds   *41*
Of wide Arabia are as throughfares now
For princes to come view fair Portia:
The watery kingdom, whose ambitious head
Spits in the face of heaven, is no bar
To stop the foreign spirits, but they come,
As o'er a brook, to see fair Portia.
One of these three contains her heavenly picture.
Is't like that lead contains her? 'Twere damnation
To think so base a thought: it were too gross *50*
To rib her cerecloth in the obscure grave.
Or shall I think in silver she's immured,
Being ten times undervalued to tried gold?
O sinful thought! Never so rich a gem
Was set in worse than gold. They have in Eng-
land
A coin that bears the figure of an angel
Stamped in gold, but that's insculp'd upon;
But here an angel in a golden bed
Lies all within. Deliver me the key:
Here do I choose, and thrive I as I may!   *60*
Por. There, take it, Prince; and if my form lie
there,
Then I am yours. [*He unlocks the golden casket.*]
Mor.   O hell! what have we here?
A carrion Death, within whose empty eye
There is a written scroll! I'll read the writing.
[*Reads*] "All that glisters is not gold;
       Often have you heard that told:
       Many a man his life hath sold
       But my outside to behold:
       Gilded tombs do worms infold.
       Had you been as wise as bold,   *70*
       Young in limbs, in judgement old,
       Your answer had not been inscroll'd:
       Fare you well; your suit is cold."

Cold, indeed; and labour lost:
Then, farewell, heat, and welcome, frost!
Portia, adieu. I have too grieved a heart
To take a tedious leave: thus losers part.
         [Exit with his train. Flourish of cornets.
Por. A gentle riddance. Draw the curtains, go.
Let all of his complexion choose me so.   *[Exeunt.*

SCENE VIII. *Venice: a street*
Enter SALARINO *and* SALANIO.

Salar. Why, man, I saw Bassanio under sail:
With him is Gratiano gone along;
And in their ship I am sure Lorenzo is not.
  Salan. The villain Jew with outcries raised the
    Duke,
Who went with him to search Bassanio's ship.
  Salar. He came too late, the ship was under sail:
But there the Duke was given to understand
That in a gondola were seen together
Lorenzo and his amorous Jessica:
Besides, Antonio certified the Duke   10
They were not with Bassanio in his ship.
  Salan. I never heard a passion so confused,
So strange, outrageous, and so variable,
As the dog Jew did utter in the streets:
"My daughter! O my ducats! O my daughter!
Fled with a Christian! O my Christian ducats!
Justice! the law! my ducats, and my daughter!
A sealed bag, two sealed bags of ducats,
Of double ducats, stolen from me by my daugh-
    ter!
And jewels, two stones, two rich and precious
    stones,   20
Stolen by my daughter! Justice! find the girl;
She hath the stones upon her, and the ducats."
  Salar. Why, all the boys in Venice follow him,
Crying, "His stones, his daughter, and his
    ducats."
  Salan. Let good Antonio look he keep his day,
Or he shall pay for this.
  Salar.   Marry, well remember'd.
I reason'd with a Frenchman yesterday,
Who told me, in the narrow seas that part
The French and English, there miscarried
A vessel of our country richly fraught: 30
I thought upon Antonio when he told me;
And wish'd in silence that it were not his.
  Salan. You were best to tell Antonio what you
    hear;
Yet do not suddenly, for it may grieve him.
  Salar. A kinder gentleman treads not the earth.
I saw Bassanio and Antonio part:
Bassanio told him he would make some speed
Of his return: he answer'd, "Do not so;
Slubber not business for my sake, Bassanio,
But stay the very riping of the time;   40

And for the Jew's bond which he hath of me,
Let it not enter in your mind of love:
Be merry, and employ your chiefest thoughts
To courtship and such fair ostents of love
As shall conveniently become you there":
And even there, his eye being big with tears,
Turning his face, he put his hand behind him,
And with affection wondrous sensible
He wrung Bassanio's hand; and so they parted.
  Salan. I think he only loves the world for him.
I pray thee, let us go and find him out   51
And quicken his embraced heaviness
With some delight or other.
  Salar.   Do we so. *[Exeunt.*

SCENE IX. *Belmont: a room in Portia's house*
Enter NERISSA *with a Servitor.*

Ner. Quick, quick, I pray thee; draw the cur-
    tain straight:
The Prince of Arragon hath ta'en his oath,
And comes to his election presently.

Flourish of cornets. Enter the PRINCE OF ARRAGON,
    PORTIA, *and their trains.*

  Por. Behold, there stand the caskets, noble
    Prince:
If you choose that wherein I am contain'd,
Straight shall our nuptial rites be solemnized:
But if you fail, without more speech, my lord,
You must be gone from hence immediately.
  Ar. I am enjoin'd by oath to observe three
    things:
First, never to unfold to any one   10
Which casket 'twas I chose; next, if I **fail**
Of the right casket, never in my life
To woo a maid in way of marriage:
Lastly,
If I do fail in fortune of my choice,
Immediately to leave you and be gone.
  Por. To these injunctions every one doth swear
That comes to hazard for my worthless self.
  Ar. And so have I address'd me. Fortune now
To my heart's hope! Gold; silver; and base lead.
"Who chooseth me must give and hazard all he
    hath."   21
You shall look fairer, ere I give or hazard.
What says the golden chest? ha, let me see:
"Who chooseth me shall gain what many men
    desire."
What many men desire! that "many" may be
    meant
By the fool multitude, that choose by show,
Not learning more than the fond eye doth teach;
Which pries not to the interior, but, like the
    martlet,
Builds in the weather on the outward wall,

Even in the force and road of casualty.   30
I will not choose what many men desire,
Because I will not jump with common spirits
And rank me with the barbarous multitudes.
Why, then to thee, thou silver treasure-house;
Tell me once more what title thou dost bear:
"Who chooseth me shall get as much as he de-
    serves":
And well said too; for who shall go about
To cozen fortune and be honourable
Without the stamp of merit? Let none presume
To wear an undeserved dignity.   40
O, that estates, degrees, and offices
Were not derived corruptly, and that clear
    honour
Were purchased by the merit of the wearer!
How many then should cover that stand bare!
How many be commanded that command!
How much low peasantry would then be glean'd
From the true seed of honour! and how much
    honour
Pick'd from the chaff and ruin of the times
To be new-varnish'd! Well, but to my choice:
"Who chooseth me shall get as much as he de-
    serves."   50
I will assume desert. Give me a key for this,
And instantly unlock my fortunes here.
    He opens the silver casket.
    Por. Too long a pause for that which you find
    there.
    Ar. What's here? the portrait of a blinking
    idiot,
Presenting me a schedule! I will read it.
How much unlike art thou to Portia!
How much unlike my hopes and my deservings!
"Who chooseth me shall have as much as he de-
    serves."
Did I deserve no more than a fool's head?
Is that my prize? are my deserts no better?   60
    Por. To offend, and judge, are distinct offices
And of opposed natures.
    Ar.   What is here?
[*Reads*] "The fire seven times tried this:
    Seven times tried that judgement is,
    That did never choose amiss.
    Some there be that shadows kiss;
    Such have but a shadow's bliss:
    There be fools alive, I wis,
    Silver'd o'er; and so was this.
    Take what wife you will to bed,   70
    I will ever be your head:
    So be gone: you are sped."
Still more fool I shall appear
By the time I linger here:
With one fool's head I came to woo,
But I go away with two.

Sweet, adieu. I'll keep my oath,
Patiently to bear my wroth.
                    [*Exeunt* ARRAGON *and train.*
    Por. Thus hath the candle singed the moth.
O, these deliberate fools! when they do choose,
They have the wisdom by their wit to lose.   81
    Ner. The ancient saying is no heresy,
Hanging and wiving goes by destiny.
    Por. Come, draw the curtain, Nerissa.

                    Enter a SERVANT.

    Serv. What is my lady?
    Por.   Here: what would my lord?
    Serv. Madam, there is alighted at your gate
A young Venetian, one that comes before
To signify the approaching of his lord;
From whom he bringeth sensible regreets,
To wit, besides commends and courteous breath,
Gifts of rich value. Yet I have not seen   91
So likely an ambassador of love:
A day in April never came so sweet,
To show how costly summer was at hand,
As this fore-spurrer comes before his lord.
    Por. No more, I pray thee: I am half afeard
Thou wilt say anon he is some kin to thee,
Thou spend'st such high-day wit in praising him.
Come, come, Nerissa; for I long to see
Quick Cupid's post that comes so mannerly.   100
    Ner. Bassanio, lord Love, if thy will it be!
                    [*Exeunt.*

ACT III

SCENE I. *Venice: a street*
Enter SALANIO *and* SALARINO.

    Salan. Now, what news on the Rialto?
    Salar. Why, yet it lives there unchecked that
Antonio hath a ship of rich lading wrecked on the
narrow seas; the Goodwins, I think they call the
place; a very dangerous flat and fatal, where the
carcases of many a tall ship lie buried, as they say,
if my gossip Report be an honest woman of her
word.
    Salan. I would she were as lying a gossip in that
as ever knapped ginger or made her neighbours
believe she wept for the death of a third husband.
But it is true, without any slips of prolixity or
crossing the plain highway of talk, that the good
Antonio, the honest Antonio—O that I had a
title good enough to keep his name company!—
    Salar. Come, the full stop.
    Salan. Ha! what sayest thou? Why, the end is,
he hath lost a ship.
    Salar. I would it might prove the end of his
losses.   21
    Salan. Let me say "amen" betimes, lest the

devil cross my prayer, for here he comes in the likeness of a Jew.

Enter SHYLOCK.

How now, Shylock! what news among the merchants?

Shy. You knew, none so well, none so well as you, of my daughter's flight.

Salar. That's certain: I, for my part, knew the tailor that made the wings she flew withal. 30

Salan. And Shylock, for his own part, knew the bird was fledged; and then it is the complexion of them all to leave the dam.

Shy. She is damned for it.

Salar. That's certain, if the devil may be her judge.

Shy. My own flesh and blood to rebel!

Salan. Out upon it, old carrion! rebels it at these years? 39

Shy. I say, my daughter is my flesh and blood.

Salar. There is more difference between thy flesh and hers than between jet and ivory; more between your bloods than there is between red wine and rhenish. But tell us, do you hear whether Antonio have had any loss at sea or no?

Shy. There I have another bad match: a bankrupt, a prodigal, who dare scarce show his head on the Rialto: a beggar, that was used to come so smug upon the mart; let him look to his bond: he was wont to call me usurer; let him look to his bond: he was wont to lend money for a Christian courtesy; let him look to his bond.

Salar. Why, I am sure, if he forfeit, thou wilt not take his flesh: what's that good for?

Shy. To bait fish withal: if it will feed nothing else, it will feed my revenge. He hath disgraced me, and hindered me half a million; laughed at my losses, mocked at my gains, scorned my nation, thwarted my bargains, cooled my friends, heated mine enemies; and what's his reason? I am a Jew. Hath not a Jew eyes? hath not a Jew hands, organs, dimensions, senses, affections, passions? fed with the same food, hurt with the same weapons, subject to the same diseases, healed by the same means, warmed and cooled by the same winter and summer, as a Christian is? If you prick us, do we not bleed? if you tickle us, do we not laugh? if you poison us, do we not die? and if you wrong us, shall we not revenge? If we are like you in the rest, we will resemble you in that. If a Jew wrong a Christian, what is his humility? Revenge. If a Christian wrong a Jew, what should his sufferance be by Christian example? Why, revenge. The villany you teach me, I will execute, and it shall go hard but I will better the instruction.

Enter a SERVANT.

Serv. Gentlemen, my master Antonio is at his house and desires to speak with you both.

Salar. We have been up and down to seek him.

Enter TUBAL.

Salan. Here comes another of the tribe: a third cannot be matched, unless the devil himself turn Jew. [*Exeunt* SALANIO, SALARINO, *and* SERVANT.

Shy. How now, Tubal! what news from Genoa? hast thou found my daughter?

Tub. I often came where I did hear of her, but cannot find her.

Shy. Why, there, there, there, there! a diamond gone, cost me two thousand ducats in Frankfort! The curse never fell upon our nation till now; I never felt it till now: two thousand ducats in that; and other precious, precious jewels. I would my daughter were dead at my foot, and the jewels in her ear! would she were hearsed at my foot, and the ducats in her coffin! No news of them? Why, so: and I know not what's spent in the search: why, thou loss upon loss! the thief gone with so much, and so much to find the thief; and no satisfaction, no revenge: nor no ill luck stirring but what lights on my shoulders; no sighs but of my breathing; no tears but of my shedding. 101

Tub. Yes, other men have ill luck too: Antonio, as I heard in Genoa—

Shy. What, what, what? ill luck, ill luck?

Tub. Hath an argosy cast away, coming from Tripolis.

Shy. I thank God, I thank God. Is't true, is't true?

Tub. I spoke with some of the sailors that escaped the wreck. 110

Shy. I thank thee, good Tubal: good news, good news! ha, ha! where? in Genoa?

Tub. Your daughter spent in Genoa, as I heard, in one night fourscore ducats.

Shy. Thou stickest a dagger in me: I shall never see my gold again: fourscore ducats at a sitting! fourscore ducats!

Tub. There came divers of Antonio's creditors in my company to Venice, that swear he cannot choose but break. 120

Shy. I am very glad of it: I'll plague him; I'll torture him: I am glad of it.

Tub. One of them showed me a ring that he had of your daughter for a monkey.

Shy. Out upon her! Thou torturest me, Tubal: it was my turquoise; I had it of Leah when I was a bachelor: I would not have given it for a wilderness of monkeys.

Tub. But Antonio is certainly undone.   *129*

Shy. Nay, that's true, that's very true. Go, Tubal, fee me an officer; bespeak him a fortnight before. I will have the heart of him, if he forfeit; for, were he out of Venice, I can make what merchandise I will. Go, go, Tubal, and meet me at our synagogue; go, good Tubal; at our synagogue, Tubal.   [*Exeunt*.

SCENE II. *Belmont: a room in Portia's house*

Enter BASSANIO, PORTIA, GRATIANO, NERISSA, *and Attendants*.

Por. I pray you, tarry: pause a day or two
Before you hazard; for, in choosing wrong,
I lose your company: therefore forbear awhile.
There's something tells me, but it is not love,
I would not lose you; and you know yourself,
Hate counsels not in such a quality.
But lest you should not understand me well—
And yet a maiden hath no tongue but thought—
I would detain you here some month or two
Before you venture for me. I could teach you
How to choose right, but I am then forsworn;   *11*
So will I never be: so may you miss me;
But if you do, you'll make me wish a sin,
That I had been forsworn. Beshrew your eyes,
They have o'erlook'd me and divided me;
One half of me is yours, the other half yours,
Mine own, I would say; but if mine, then yours,
And so all yours. O, these naughty times
Put bars between the owners and their rights!
And so, though yours, not yours. Prove it so,
Let fortune go to hell for it, not I.   *21*
I speak too long; but 'tis to peize the time,
To eke it, and to draw it out in length,
To stay you from election.

Bass.   Let me choose;
For as I am, I live upon the rack.

Por. Upon the rack, Bassanio! then confess
What treason there is mingled with your love.

Bass. None but that ugly treason of mistrust,
Which makes me fear the enjoying of my love:
There may as well be amity and life   *30*
'Tween snow and fire, as treason and my love.

Por. Ay, but I fear you speak upon the rack,
Where men enforced do speak anything.

Bass. Promise me life, and I'll confess the truth.

Por. Well then, confess and live.

Bass.   "Confess" and "love"
Had been the very sum of my confession:
O happy torment, when my torturer
Doth teach me answers for deliverance!
But let me to my fortune and the caskets.

Por. Away, then! I am lock'd in one of them: *40*
If you do love me, you will find me out.
Nerissa and the rest, stand all aloof.

Let music sound while he doth make his choice;
Then, if he lose, he makes a swan-like end,
Fading in music: that the comparison
May stand more proper, my eye shall be the
    stream
And watery death-bed for him. He may win;
And what is music then? Then music is
Even as the flourish when true subjects bow
To a new-crowned monarch: such it is   *50*
As are those dulcet sounds in break of day
That creep into the dreaming bridegroom's ear
And summon him to marriage. Now he goes,
With no less presence, but with much more love,
Than young Alcides, when he did redeem
The virgin tribute paid by howling Troy
To the sea-monster: I stand for sacrifice;
The rest aloof are the Dardanian wives,
With bleared visages, come forth to view
The issue of the exploit. Go, Hercules!   *60*
Live thou, I live: with much much more dismay
I view the fight than thou that makest the fray.

Music, whilst BASSANIO *comments on the caskets
to himself*.

SONG

Tell me where is fancy bred,
Or in the heart or in the head?
How begot, how nourished?
    Reply, reply.
It is engender'd in the eyes,
With gazing fed; and fancy dies
In the cradle where it lies.
    Let us all ring fancy's knell: *70*
    I'll begin it—Ding, dong, bell.

All. Ding, dong, bell.

Bass. So may the outward shows be least themselves:
The world is still deceived with ornament.
In law, what plea so tainted and corrupt
But, being season'd with a gracious voice,
Obscures the show of evil? In religion,
What damned error, but some sober brow
Will bless it and approve it with a text,
Hiding the grossness with fair ornament?   *80*
There is no vice so simple but assumes
Some mark of virtue on his outward parts:
How many cowards, whose hearts are all as false
As stairs of sand, wear yet upon their chins
The beards of Hercules and frowning Mars,
Who, inward search'd, have livers white as milk;
And these assume but valour's excrement
To render them redoubted! Look on beauty,
And you shall see 'tis purchased by the weight;
Which therein works a miracle in nature,   *90*
Making them lightest that wear most of it:
So are those crisped snaky golden locks

Which make such wanton gambols with the wind,
Upon supposed fairness, often known
To be the dowry of a second head,
The skull that bred them in the sepulchre.
Thus ornament is but the guiled shore
To a most dangerous sea; the beauteous scarf
Veiling an Indian beauty; in a word,   *99*
The seeming truth which cunning times put on
To entrap the wisest. Therefore, thou gaudy gold,
Hard food for Midas, I will none of thee;
Nor none of thee, thou pale and common drudge
'Tween man and man: but thou, thou meagre lead.
Which rather threatenest than dost promise aught,
Thy paleness moves me more than eloquence;
And here choose I: joy be the consequence!
  Por. [*Aside*] How all the other passions fleet to air,
As doubtful thoughts, and rash-embraced despair,
And shuddering fear, and green-eyed jealousy!
O love,   *111*
Be moderate; allay thy ecstasy;
In measure rein thy joy; scant this excess.
I feel too much thy blessing; make it less,
For fear I surfeit.
  Bass.   What find I here?
  Opening the leaden casket.
Fair Portia's counterfeit! What demi-god
Hath come so near creation? Move these eyes?
Or whether, riding on the balls of mine,
Seem they in motion? Here are sever'd lips,
Parted with sugar breath: so sweet a bar   *120*
Should sunder such sweet friends. Here in her hairs
The painter plays the spider and hath woven
A golden mesh to entrap the hearts of men
Faster than gnats in cobwebs: but her eyes—
How could he see to do them? having made one,
Methinks it should have power to steal both his
And leave itself unfurnish'd. Yet look, how far
The substance of my praise doth wrong this shadow
In underprizing it, so far this shadow
Doth limp behind the substance. Here's the scroll,   *130*
The continent and summary of my fortune.
  [*Reads*] "You that choose not by the view,
          Chance as fair and choose as true!
          Since this fortune falls to you,
          Be content and seek no new.
          If you be well pleased with this
          And hold your fortune for your bliss,
          Turn you where your lady is
          And claim her with a loving kiss."
A gentle scroll. Fair lady, by your leave;   *140*

I come by note, to give and to receive.
Like one of two contending in a prize,
That thinks he hath done well in people's eyes,
Hearing applause and universal shout,
Giddy in spirit, still gazing in a doubt
Whether those peals of praise be his or no;
So, thrice-fair lady, stand I, even so;
As doubtful whether what I see be true,
Until confirm'd, sign'd, ratified by you.
  Por. You see me, Lord Bassanio, where I stand,
Such as I am: though for myself alone   *151*
I would not be ambitious in my wish,
To wish myself much better; yet, for you
I would be trebled twenty times myself;
A thousand times more fair, ten thousand times
More rich;
That only to stand high in your account,
I might in virtues, beauties, livings, friends,
Exceed account; but the full sum of me
Is sum of something, which, to term in gross,
Is an unlesson'd girl, unschool'd, unpractised;   *161*
Happy in this, she is not yet so old
But she may learn; happier than this,
She is not bred so dull but she can learn;
Happiest of all is that her gentle spirit
Commits itself to yours to be directed,
As from her lord, her governor, her king.
Myself and what is mine to you and yours
Is now converted: but now I was the lord
Of this fair mansion, master of my servants,   *170*
Queen o'er myself; and even now, but now,
This house, these servants, and this same myself
Are yours, my lord: I give them with this ring;
Which when you part from, lose, or give away,
Let it presage the ruin of your love
And be my vantage to exclaim on you.
  Bass. Madam, you have bereft me of all words,
Only my blood speaks to you in my veins;
And there is such confusion in my powers,
As, after some oration fairly spoke   *180*
By a beloved prince, there doth appear
Among the buzzing pleased multitude;
Where every something, being blent together,
Turns to a wild of nothing, save of joy,
Express'd and not express'd. But when this ring
Parts from this finger, then parts life from hence:
O, then be bold to say Bassanio's dead!
  Ner. My lord and lady, it is now our time,
That have stood by and seen our wishes prosper,
To cry, good joy: good joy, my lord and lady!
  Gra. My lord Bassanio and my gentle lady,
I wish you all the joy that you can wish;
For I am sure you can wish none from me:
And when your honours mean to solemnize
The bargain of your faith, I do beseech you,
Even at that time I may be married too.

Bass. With all my heart, so thou canst get a wife.

Gra. I thank your lordship, you have got me one.
My eyes, my lord, can look as swift as yours:
You saw the mistress, I beheld the maid;   200
You loved, I loved for intermission.
No more pertains to me, my lord, than you.
Your fortune stood upon the casket there,
And so did mine too, as the matter falls;
For wooing here until I sweat again,
And swearing till my very roof was dry
With oaths of love, at last, if promise last,
I got a promise of this fair one here
To have her love, provided that your fortune
Achieved her mistress.

Por.   Is this true, Nerissa?   210

Ner. Madam, it is , so you stand pleased withal.

Bass. And do you, Gratiano, mean good faith?

Gra. Yes, faith, my lord.

Bass. Our feast shall be much honour'd in your
marriage.

Gra. We'll play with them the first boy for a
thousand ducats.

Ner. What, and stake down?

Gra. No; we shall ne'er win at that sport, and
stake down.   220
But who comes here? Lorenzo and his infidel?
What, and my old Venetian friend Salerio?

Enter LORENZO, JESSICA, *and* SALERIO,
a Messenger from Venice.

Bass. Lorenzo and Salerio, welcome hither;
If that the youth of my new interest here
Have power to bid you welcome. By your **leave,**
I bid my friends and countrymen,
Sweet Portia, welcome.

Por.   So do I, my lord:
They are entirely welcome.

Lor. I thank your honour. For my part, my lord,
My purpose was not to have seen you here;   230
But meeting with Salerio by the way,
He did intreat me, past all saying nay,
To come with him along.

Saler.   I did, my lord;
And I have reason for it. Signor Antonio
Commends him to you. [*Gives* BASSANIO *a letter.*]

Bass.   Ere I ope his letter,
I pray you, tell me how my good friend doth.

Saler. Not sick, my lord, unless it be in mind;
Nor well, unless in mind: his letter there
Will show you his estate.

Gra. Nerissa, cheer yon stranger; bid her
welcome.   240
Your hand, Salerio: what's the news from
Venice?
How doth that royal merchant, good Antonio?
I know he will be glad of our success;
We are the Jasons, we have won the fleece.

Saler. I would you had won the fleece that he
hath lost.

Por. There are some shrewd contents in yon
same paper,
That steals the colour from Bassanio's cheek:
Some dear friend dead; else nothing in the world
Could turn so much the constitution
Of any constant man. What, worse and worse!
With leave, Bassanio; I am half yourself,   251
And I must freely have the half of anything
That this same paper brings you.

Bass.   O sweet Portia,
Here are a few of the unpleasant'st words
That ever blotted paper! Gentle lady,
When I did first impart my love to you,
I freely told you, all the wealth I had
Ran in my veins, I was a gentleman;
And then I told you true: and yet, dear lady,
Rating myself at nothing, you shall see
How much I was a braggart. When I told you
My state was nothing, I should then have told
you
That I was worse than nothing; for, indeed,
I have engaged myself to a dear friend,
Engaged my friend to his mere enemy,
To feed my means. Here is a letter, lady;
The paper as the body of my friend,
And every word in it a gaping wound,
Issuing life-blood. But is it true, Salerio?
Have all his ventures fail'd? What, not one hit?
From Tripolis, from Mexico, and England,   271
From Lisbon, Barbary, and India?
And not one vessel 'scape the dreadful touch
Of merchant-marring rocks?

Saler.   Not one, my lord.
Besides, it should appear, that if he had
The present money to discharge the Jew,
He would not take it. Never did I know
A creature that did bear the shape of man
So keen and greedy to confound a man:
He plies the Duke at morning and at night,   280
And doth impeach the freedom of the state,
If they deny him justice: twenty merchants,
The Duke himself, and the magnificoes
Of greatest port, have all persuaded with him;
But none can drive him from the envious plea
Of forfeiture, of justice, and his bond.

Jes. When I was with him I have heard him
swear
To Tubal and to Chus, his countrymen,
That he would rather have Antonio's flesh
Than twenty times the value of the sum   290
That he did owe him: and I know, my lord,
If law, authority and power deny not,
It will go hard with poor Antonio.

Por. Is it your dear friend that is thus in trouble?

Bass. The dearest friend to me, the kindest man,
The best-condition'd and unwearied spirit
In doing courtesies, and one in whom
The ancient Roman honour more appears
Than any that draws breath in Italy.

Por. What sum owes he the Jew?   *300*

Bass. For me three thousand ducats.

Por.   What, no more?
Pay him six thousand, and deface the bond;
Double six thousand, and then treble that,
Before a friend of this description
Shall lose a hair through Bassanio's fault.
First go with me to church and call me wife,
And then away to Venice to your friend;
For never shall you lie by Portia's side
With an unquiet soul. You shall have gold
To pay the petty debt twenty times over: *310*
When it is paid, bring your true friend along.
My maid Nerissa and myself meantime
Will live as maids and widows. Come, away!
For you shall hence upon your wedding-day:
Bid your friends welcome, show a merry cheer:
Since you are dear bought, I will love you dear.
But let me hear the letter of your friend.

Bass. [*Reads*] "Sweet Bassanio, my ships have all
miscarried, my creditors grow cruel, my estate
is very low, my bond to the Jew is forfeit; and
since in paying it, it is impossible I should live,
all debts are cleared between you and I, if I might
but see you at my death. Notwithstanding, use
your pleasure: if your love do not persuade you
to come, let not my letter."

Por. O love, dispatch all business, and be gone!

Bass. Since I have your good leave to go away,
I will make haste: but, till I come again,
No bed shall e'er be guilty of my stay,
No rest be interposer 'twixt us twain.   *330*
                  [*Exeunt.*

SCENE III. *Venice: a street*

Enter SHYLOCK, SALARINO, ANTONIO, *and Gaoler.*

Shy. Gaoler, look to him: tell not me of
    mercy;
This is the fool that lent out money gratis:
Gaoler, look to him.

Ant.   Hear me yet, good Shylock.

Shy. I'll have my bond; speak not against my
    bond:
I have sworn an oath that I will have my bond.
Thou call'dst me dog before thou hadst a cause;
But, since I am a dog, beware my fangs:
The Duke shall grant me justice. I do wonder,
Thou naughty gaoler, that thou art so fond
To come abroad with him at his request.   *10*

Ant. I pray thee, hear me speak.

Shy. I'll have my bond; I will not hear thee
    speak:
I'll have my bond; and therefore speak no more.
I'll not be made a soft and dull-eyed fool,
To shake the head, relent, and sigh, and yield
To Christian intercessors. Follow not;
I'll have no speaking: I will have my bond.
                  [*Exit.*

Salar. It is most impenetrable cur
That ever kept with men.

Ant.   Let him alone:
I'll follow him no more with bootless prayers. *20*
He seeks my life; his reason well I know:
I oft deliver'd from his forfeitures
Many that have at times made moan to me;
Therefore he hates me.

Salar.   I am sure the Duke
Will never grant this forfeiture to hold.

Ant. The Duke cannot deny the course of law:
For the commodity that strangers have
With us in Venice, if it be denied,
Will much impeach the justice of his state;
Since that the trade and profit of the city   *30*
Consisteth of all nations. Therefore, go:
These griefs and losses have so bated me,
That I shall hardly spare a pound of flesh
To-morrow to my bloody creditor.
Well, gaoler, on. Pray God, Bassanio come
To see me pay his debt, and then I care not!
                  [*Exeunt.*

SCENE IV. *Belmont: a room in Portia's house*

Enter PORTIA, NERISSA, LORENZO, JESSICA,
and BALTHASAR.

Lor. Madam, although I speak it in your
    presence,
You have a noble and a true conceit
Of god-like amity; which appears most strongly
In bearing thus the absence of your lord.
But if you knew to whom you show this honour,
How true a gentleman you send relief,
How dear a lover of my lord your husband,
I know you would be prouder of the work
Than customary bounty can enforce you.

Por. I never did repent for doing good,   *10*
Nor shall not now: for in companions
That do converse and waste the time together,
Whose souls do bear an equal yoke of love,
There must be needs a like proportion
Of lineaments, of manners, and of spirit;
Which makes me think that this Antonio,
Being the bosom lover of my lord,
Must needs be like my lord. If it be so,
How little is the cost I have bestow'd
In purchasing the semblance of my soul   *20*
From out the state of hellish misery!

This comes too near the praising of myself;
Therefore no more of it: hear other things.
Lorenzo, I commit into your hands
The husbandry and manage of my house
Until my lord's return: for mine own part,
I have toward heaven breathed a secret vow
To live in prayer and contemplation,
Only attended by Nerissa here,
Until her husband and my lord's return: 30
There is a monastery two miles off;
And there will we abide. I do desire you
Not to deny this imposition;
The which my love and some necessity
Now lays upon you.
    Lor.   Madam, with all my heart;
I shall obey you in all fair commands.
    Por. My people do already know my mind,
And will acknowledge you and Jessica
In place of Lord Bassanio and myself.
And so farewell, till we shall meet again.   40
    Lor. Fair thoughts and happy hours attend on
        you!
    Jes. I wish your ladyship all heart's content.
    Por. I thank you for your wish, and am well
        pleased
To wish it back on you: fare you well, Jessica.
                    [*Exeunt* JESSICA *and* LORENZO.
Now, Balthasar,
As I have ever found thee honest-true,
So let me find thee still. Take this same letter,
And use thou all the endeavour of a man
In speed to Padua: see thou render this
Into my cousin's hand, Doctor Bellario;   50
And, look, what notes and garments he doth
        give thee,
Bring them, I pray thee, with imagined speed
Unto the tranect, to the common ferry
Which trades to Venice. Waste no time in words,
But get thee gone: I shall be there before thee.
    Balth. Madam, I go with all convenient speed.
                    [*Exit.*
    Por. Come on, Nerissa; I have work in hand
That you yet know not of: we'll see our
        husbands
Before they think of us.
    Ner.   Shall they see us?
    Por. They shall, Nerissa; but in such a habit,   60
That they shall think we are accomplished
With that we lack. I'll hold thee any wager,
When we are both accoutred like young men,
I'll prove the prettier fellow of the two,
And wear my dagger with the braver grace,
And speak between the change of man and boy
With a reed voice, and turn two mincing steps
Into a manly stride, and speak of frays
Like a fine bragging youth, and tell quaint lies,

How honourable ladies sought my love,   70
Which I denying, they fell sick and died;
I could not do withal; then I'll repent,
And wish, for all that, that I had not kill'd them;
And twenty of these puny lies I'll tell,
That men shall swear I have discontinued school
Above a twelvemonth. I have within my mind
A thousand raw tricks of these bragging Jacks,
Which I will practise.
    Ner.   Why, shall we turn to men?
    Por. Fie, what a question's that,
If thou wert near a lewd interpreter!   80
But come, I'll tell thee all my whole device
When I am in my coach, which stays for us
At the park gate; and therefore haste away,
For we must measure twenty miles to-day.
                    [*Exeunt.*

SCENE V. *The same: a garden*

Enter LAUNCELOT *and* JESSICA.

    Laun. Yes, truly; for, look you, the sins of the
father are to be laid upon the children: therefore,
I promise ye, I fear you. I was always plain with
you, and so now I speak my agitation of the
matter: therefore be of good cheer, for truly I
think you are damned. There is but one hope in
it can do you any good; and that is but a kind of
bastard hope neither.
    Jes. And what hope is that. I pray thee?   10
    Laun. Marry, you may partly hope that your
father got you not, that you are not the Jew's
daughter.
    Jes. That were a kind of bastard hope, indeed:
so the sins of my mother should be visited upon
me.
    Laun. Truly then I fear you are damned both
by father and mother: thus when I shun Scylla,
your father, I fall into Charybdis, your mother:
well, you are gone both ways.   20
    Jes. I shall be saved by my husband; he hath
made me a Christian.
    Laun. Truly, the more to blame he: we were
Christians enow before; e'en as many as could
well live, one by another. This making of Christians will raise the price of hogs: if we grow all
to be pork-eaters, we shall not shortly have a
rasher on the coals for money.

Enter LORENZO.

    Jes. I'll tell my husband, Launcelot, what you
say: here he comes.   30
    Lor. I shall grow jealous of you shortly, Laun-
celot, if you thus get my wife into corners.
    Jes. Nay, you need not fear us, Lorenzo: Laun-
celot and I are out. He tells me flatly, there is no
mercy for me in heaven, because I am a Jew's

daughter: and he says, you are no good member
of the commonwealth, for in converting Jews to
Christians, you raise the price of pork.   39

Lor. I shall answer that better to the commonwealth than you can the getting up of the negro's
belly: the Moor is with child by you, Launcelot.

Laun. It is much that the Moor should be more
than reason: but if she be less than an honest
woman, she is indeed more than I took her for.

Lor. How every fool can play upon the word!
I think the best grace of wit will shortly turn into
silence, and discourse grow commendable in none
only but parrots. Go in, sirrah; bid them prepare
for dinner.

Laun. That is done, sir; they have all stomachs.

Lor. Goodly Lord, what a wit-snapper are you!
then bid them prepare dinner.

Laun. That is done too, sir; only "cover" is the
word.

Lor. Will you cover then, sir?

Laun. Not so, sir, neither; I know my duty.   59

Lor. Yet more quarrelling with occasion! Wilt
thou show the whole wealth of thy wit in an instant? I pray thee, understand a plain man in his
plain meaning: go to thy fellows; bid them cover
the table, serve in the meat, and we will come in
to dinner.

Laun. For the table, sir, it shall be served in; for
the meat, sir, it shall be covered; for your coming in to dinner, sir, why, let it be as humours
and conceits shall govern.   [*Exit.*

Lor. O dear discretion, how his words are
          suited!   70
The fool hath planted in his memory
An army of good words; and I do know
A many fools, that stand in better place,
Garnish'd like him, that for a tricksy word
Defy the matter. How cheer'st thou, Jessica?
And now, good sweet, say thy opinion,
How dost thou like the Lord Bassanio's wife?

Jes. Past all expressing. It is very meet
The Lord Bassanio live an upright life;
For, having such a blessing in his lady,   80
He finds the joys of heaven here on earth;
And if on earth he do not mean it, then
In reason he should never come to heaven.
Why, if two gods should play some heavenly
          match
And on the wager lay two earthly women,
And Portia one, there must be something else
Pawn'd with the other, for the poor rude world
Hath not her fellow.

Lor.   Even such a husband
Hast thou of me as she is for a wife.

Jes. Nay, but ask my opinion too of that.   90

Lor. I will anon: first, let us go to dinner.

Jes. Nay, let me praise you while I have a
          stomach.

Lor. No, pray thee, let it serve for table-talk;
Then, howsoe'er thou speak'st, 'mong other
          things
I shall digest it.

Jes.   Well, I'll set you forth. [*Exeunt.*

ACT IV

Scene i. *Venice: a court of justice*

Enter the DUKE, *the Magnificoes,* ANTONIO,
BASSANIO, GRATIANO, SALERIO, *and others.*

Duke. What, is Antonio here?

Ant. Ready, so please your Grace.

Duke. I am sorry for thee: thou art come to
          answer
A stony adversary, an inhuman wretch
Uncapable of pity, void and empty
From any dram of mercy.

Ant.   I have heard
Your Grace hath ta'en great pains to qualify
His rigorous course; but since he stands obdurate
And that no lawful means can carry me
Out of his envy's reach, I do oppose   10
My patience to his fury, and am arm'd
To suffer, with a quietness of spirit,
The very tyranny and rage of his.

Duke. Go one, and call the Jew into the court.

Saler. He is ready at the door: he comes, my
          lord.

Enter SHYLOCK.

Duke. Make room, and let him stand before our
          face.
Shylock, the world thinks, and I think so too,
That thou but lead'st this fashion of thy malice
To the last hour of act; and then 'tis thought
Thou'lt show thy mercy and remorse more
          strange
Than is thy strange apparent cruelty;   21
And where thou now exact'st the penalty,
Which is a pound of this poor merchant's flesh,
Thou wilt not only loose the forfeiture,
But, touch'd with human gentleness and love,
Forgive a moiety of the principal;
Glancing an eye of pity on his losses,
That have of late so huddled on his back,
Enow to press a royal merchant down
And pluck commiseration of his state   30
From brassy bosoms and rough hearts of flint,
From stubborn Turks and Tartars, never train'd
To offices of tender courtesy.
We all expect a gentle answer, Jew.

Shy. I have possess'd your Grace of what I
          purpose;

And by our holy Sabbath have I sworn
To have the due and forfeit of my bond:
If you deny it, let the danger light
Upon your charter and your city's freedom.
You'll ask me, why I rather choose to have   40
A weight of carrion flesh than to receive
Three thousand ducats: I'll not answer that:
But say it is my humour: is it answer'd?
What if my house be troubled with a rat
And I be pleased to give ten thousand ducats
To have it baned? What, are you answer'd yet?
Some men there are love not a gaping pig;
Some, that are mad if they behold a cat;
And others, when the bagpipe sings i' the nose,
Cannot contain their urine: for affection,   50
Mistress of passion, sways it to the mood
Of what it likes or loathes. Now, for your
     answer:
As there is no firm reason to be render'd,
Why he cannot abide a gaping pig;
Why he, a harmless necessary cat;
Why he, a woollen bag-pipe; but of force
Must yield to such inevitable shame
As to offend, himself being offended;
So can I give no reason, nor I will not,
More than a lodged hate and a certain loathing
I bear Antonio, that I follow thus   61
A losing suit against him. Are you answer'd?
     Bass. This is no answer, thou unfeeling man,
To excuse the current of thy cruelty.
     Shy. I am not bound to please thee with my
     answers.
     Bass. Do all men kill the things they do not love?
     Shy. Hates any man the thing he would not kill?
     Bass. Every offence is not a hate at first.
     Shy. What, wouldst thou have a serpent sting
     thee twice?
     Ant. I pray you, think you question with the
     Jew: 70
You may as well go stand upon the beach
And bid the main flood bate his usual height;
You may as well use question with the wolf
Why he hath made the ewe bleat for the lamb;
You may as well forbid the mountain pines
To wag their high tops and to make no noise,
When they are fretten with the gusts of heaven;
You may as well do any thing most hard,
As seek to soften that—than which what's hard-
     er?—
His Jewish heart: therefore, I do beseech you,   80
Make no more offers, use no farther means,
But with all brief and plain conveniency
Let me have judgement and the Jew his will.
     Bass. For thy three thousand ducats here is six.
     Shy. If every ducat in six thousand ducats
Were in six parts and every part a ducat,

I would not draw them; I would have my bond.
     Duke. How shalt thou hope for mercy, render-
     ing none?
     Shy. What judgement shall I dread, doing no
     wrong?
You have among you many a purchased slave,   90
Which, like your asses and your dogs and mules,
You use in abject and in slavish parts,
Because you bought them: shall I say to you,
Let them be free, marry them to your heirs?
Why sweat they under burthens? let their beds
Be made as soft as yours and let their palates
Be season'd with such viands? You will answer
"The slaves are ours": so do I answer you:
The pound of flesh, which I demand of him,
Is dearly bought; 'tis mine and I will have it.   100
If you deny me, fie upon your law!
There is no force in the decrees of Venice.
I stand for judgement: answer; shall I have it?
     Duke. Upon my power I may dismiss this court,
Unless Bellario, a learned doctor,
Whom I have sent for to determine this,
Come here to-day.
     Saler.   My lord, here stays without
A messenger with letters from the doctor,
New come from Padua.
     Duke. Bring us the letters; call the messenger.
     Bass. Good cheer, Antonio! What, man,
     courage yet!   111
The Jew shall have my flesh, blood, bones, and
     all,
Ere thou shalt lose for me one drop of blood.
     Ant. I am a tainted wether of the flock,
Meetest for death: the weakest kind of fruit
Drops earliest to the ground; and so let me:
You cannot better be employ'd, Bassanio,
Than to live still and write mine epitaph.

     Enter NERISSA, *dressed like a lawyer's clerk.*

     Duke. Came you from Padua, from Bellario?
     Ner. From both, my lord. Bellario greets your
     Grace. [*Presenting a letter.*]   120
     Bass. Why dost thou whet thy knife so
     earnestly?
     Shy. To cut the forfeiture from that bankrupt
     there.
     Gra. Not on thy sole, but on thy soul, harsh
     Jew,
Thou makest thy knife keen; but no metal can,
No, not the hangman's axe, bear half the keenness
Of thy sharp envy. Can no prayers pierce thee?
     Shy. No, none that thou hast wit enough to
     make.
     Gra. O, be thou damn'd, inexecrable dog!
And for thy life let justice be accused.
Thou almost makest me waver in my faith   130

To hold opinion with Pythagoras,
That souls of animals infuse themselves
Into the trunks of men: thy currish spirit
Govern'd a wolf, who, hang'd for human
    slaughter,
Even from the gallows did his fell soul fleet,
And, whilst thou lay'st in thy unhallow'd dam,
Infused itself in thee; for thy desires
Are wolvish, bloody, starved, and ravenous.
  Shy. Till thou canst rail the seal from off my
    bond,
Thou but offend'st thy lungs to speak so loud:
Repair thy wit, good youth, or it will fall   *141*
To cureless ruin. I stand here for law.
  Duke. This letter from Bellario doth commend
A young and learned doctor to our court.
Where is he?
  Ner.   He attendeth here hard by.
To know your answer, whether you'll admit him.
  Duke. With all my heart. Some three or four
    of you
Go give him courteous conduct to this place.
Meantime the court shall hear Bellario's letter.
  Clerk [*Reads*] "Your Grace shall understand
that at the receipt of your letter I am very sick:
but in the instant that your messenger came, in
loving visitation was with me a young doctor of
Rome; his name is Balthasar. I acquainted him
with the cause in controversy between the Jew
and Antonio the merchant: we turned o'er many
books together: he is furnished with my opinion;
which, bettered with his own learning, the greatness whereof I cannot enough commend, comes
with him, at my importunity, to fill up your
Grace's request in my stead. I beseech you, let
his lack of years be no impediment to let him lack
a reverend estimation; for I never knew so young
a body with so old a head. I leave him to your
gracious acceptance, whose trial shall better publish his commendation."
  Duke. You hear the learn'd Bellario, what he
    writes:
And here, I take it, is the doctor come.

    Enter PORTIA, *dressed like a doctor of laws.*

Give me your hand. Come you from old Bellario?
  Por. I did, my lord.
  Duke.   You are welcome: take your place.
Are you acquainted with the difference   *171*
That holds this present question in the court?
  Por. I am informed throughly of the cause.
Which is the merchant here, and which the Jew?
  Duke. Antonio and old Shylock, both stand
    forth.
  Por. Is your name Shylock?
  Shy.   Shylock is my name.

  Por. Of a strange nature is the suit you follow;
Yet in such rule that the Venetian law
Cannot impugn you as you do proceed.
You stand within his danger, do you not?   *180*
  Ant. Ay, so he says.
  Por.   Do you confess the bond?
  Ant. I do.
  Por.   Then must the Jew be merciful.
  Shy. On what compulsion must I? tell me that.
  Por. The quality of mercy is not strain'd,
It droppeth as the gentle rain from heaven
Upon the place beneath: it is twice blest;
It blesseth him that gives and him that takes:
'Tis mightiest in the mightiest: it becomes
The throned monarch better than his crown;
His sceptre shows the force of temporal power,
The attribute to awe and majesty,   *191*
Wherein doth sit the dread and fear of kings;
But mercy is above this sceptred sway;
It is enthroned in the hearts of kings,
It is an attribute to God himself;
And earthly power doth then show likest God's
When mercy seasons justice. Therefore, Jew,
Though justice be thy plea, consider this,
That, in the course of justice, none of us
Should see salvation: we do pray for mercy;   *200*
And that same prayer doth teach us all to render
The deeds of mercy. I have spoke thus much
To mitigate the justice of thy plea;
Which if thou follow, this strict court of Venice
Must needs give sentence 'gainst the merchant
    there.
  Shy. My deeds upon my head! I crave the law,
The penalty and forfeit of my bond.
  Por. Is he not able to discharge the money?
  Bass. Yes, here I tender it for him in the court;
Yea, twice the sum: if that will not suffice,   *210*
I will be bound to pay it ten times o'er,
On forfeit of my hands, my head, my heart:
If this will not suffice, it must appear
That malice bears down truth. And I beseech you,
Wrest once the law to your authority:
To do a great right, do a little wrong,
And curb this cruel devil of his will.
  Por. It must not be; there is no power in Venice
Can alter a decree established:
'Twill be recorded for a precedent,   *220*
And many an error by the same example
Will rush into the state: it cannot be.
  Shy. A Daniel come to judgement! yea, a
    Daniel!
O wise young judge, how I do honour thee!
  Por. I pray you, let me look upon the bond.
  Shy. Here 'tis, most reverend doctor, here it is.
  Por. Shylock, there's thrice thy money offer'd
    thee.

Shy. An oath, an oath, I have an oath in heaven:
Shall I lay perjury upon my soul?
No, not for Venice.

Por.   Why, this bond is forfeit;   *230*
And lawfully by this the Jew may claim
A pound of flesh, to be by him cut off
Nearest the merchant's heart. Be merciful:
Take thrice thy money; bid me tear the bond.

Shy. When it is paid according to the tenour.
It doth appear you are a worthy judge;
You know the law, your exposition
Hath been most sound: I charge you by the law,
Whereof you are a well-deserving pillar,
Proceed to judgement: by my soul I swear   *240*
There is no power in the tongue of man
To alter me: I stay here on my bond.

Ant. Most heartily I do beseech the court
To give the judgement.

Por.   Why then, thus it is:
You must prepare your bosom for his knife.

Shy. O noble judge! O excellent young man!

Por. For the intent and purpose of the law
Hath full relation to the penalty,
Which here appeareth due upon the bond.

Shy. 'Tis very true: O wise and upright
    judge!   *250*
How much more elder art thou than thy looks!

Por. Therefore lay bare your bosom.

Shy.   Ay, his breast:
So says the bond: doth it not, noble judge?
"Nearest his heart": those are the very words.

Por. It is so. Are there balance here to weigh
The flesh?

Shy. I have them ready.

Por. Have by some surgeon, Shylock, on your
    charge,
To stop his wounds, lest he do bleed to death.

Shy. Is it so nominated in the bond?

Por. It is not so express'd: but what of that?
'Twere good you do so much for charity.   *261*

Shy. I cannot find it; 'tis not in the bond.

Por. You, merchant, have you any thing to say?

Ant. But little: I am arm'd and well prepared.
Give me your hand, Bassanio: fare you well!
Grieve not that I am fallen to this for you;
For herein Fortune shows herself more kind
Than is her custom: it is still her use
To let the wretched man outlive his wealth,
To view with hollow eye and wrinkled brow   *270*
An age of poverty; from which lingering penance
Of such misery doth she cut me off.
Commend me to your honourable wife:
Tell her the process of Antonio's end;
Say how I loved you, speak me fair in death;
And, when the tale is told, bid her be judge
Whether Bassanio had not once a love.

Repent but you that you shall lose your friend,
And he repents not that he pays your debt;
For if the Jew do cut but deep enough,   *280*
I'll pay it presently with all my heart.

Bass. Antonio, I am married to a wife
Which is as dear to me as life itself;
But life itself, my wife, and all the world,
Are not with me esteem'd above thy life:
I would lose all, sacrifice them all
Here to this devil, to deliver you.

Por. Your wife would give you little thanks for
    that,
If she were by, to hear you make the offer.

Gra. I have a wife, whom, I protest, I love:
I would she were in heaven, so she could   *291*
Entreat some power to change this currish Jew.

Ner. 'Tis well you offer it behind her back;
The wish would make else an unquiet house.

Shy. These be the Christian husbands. I have
    a daughter;
Would any of the stock of Barrabas
Had been her husband rather than a Christian!
                                        [*Aside.*]
We trifle time: I pray thee, pursue sentence.

Por. A pound of that same merchant's flesh is
    thine:
The court awards it, and the law doth give it.

Shy. Most rightful judge!   *301*

Por. And you must cut this flesh from off his
    breast:
The law allows it, and the court awards it.

Shy. Most learned judge! A sentence! Come,
    prepare!

Por. Tarry a little; there is something else.
This bond doth give thee here no jot of blood;
The words expressly are "a pound of flesh":
Take then thy bond, take thou thy pound of flesh;
But, in the cutting it, if thou dost shed
One drop of Christian blood, thy lands and goods
Are, by the laws of Venice, confiscate   *311*
Unto the state of Venice.

Gra. O upright judge! Mark, Jew: O learned
    judge!

Shy. Is that the law?

Por.   Thyself shalt see the act:
For, as thou urgest justice, be assured
Thou shalt have justice, more than thou desirest.

Gra. O learned judge! Mark, Jew: a learned
    judge!

Shy. I take this offer, then; pay the bond thrice
And let the Christian go.

Bass.   Here is the money.

Por. Soft!   *320*
The Jew shall have all justice; soft! no haste:
He shall have nothing but the penalty.

Gra. O Jew! an upright judge, a learned judge!

Por. Therefore prepare thee to cut off the flesh.
Shed thou no blood, nor cut thou less nor more
But just a pound of flesh: if thou cut'st more
Or less than a just pound, be it but so much
As makes it light or heavy in the substance,
Or the division of the twentieth part
Of one poor scruple, nay, if the scale do turn   330
But in the estimation of a hair,
Thou diest and all thy goods are confiscate.
  Gra. A second Daniel, a Daniel, Jew!
Now, infidel, I have you on the hip.
  Por. Why doth the Jew pause? take thy for-
      feiture.
  Shy. Give me my principal, and let me go.
  Bass. I have it ready for thee; here it is.
  Por. He hath refused it in the open court:
He shall have merely justice and his bond.   339
  Gra. A Daniel, still say I, a second Daniel!
I thank thee, Jew, for teaching me that word.
  Shy. Shall I not have barely my principal?
  Por. Thou shalt have nothing but the forfeiture,
To be so taken at thy peril, Jew.
  Shy. Why, then the devil give him good of it!
I'll stay no longer question.
  Por.   Tarry, Jew:
The law hath yet another hold on you.
It is enacted in the laws of Venice,
If it be proved against an alien
That by direct or indirect attempts   350
He seek the life of any citizen,
The party 'gainst the which he doth contrive
Shall seize one half his goods; the other half
Comes to the privy coffer of the state;
And the offender's life lies in the mercy
Of the Duke only, 'gainst all other voice.
In which predicament, I say, thou stand'st:
For it appears, by manifest proceeding,
That indirectly and directly too
Thou hast contrived against the very life
Of the defendant; and thou hast incurr'd
The danger formerly by me rehearsed.
Down therefore and beg mercy of the Duke.
  Gra. Beg that thou mayst have leave to hang
      thyself:
And yet, thy wealth being forfeit to the state,
Thou hast not left the value of a cord;
Therefore thou must be hang'd at the state's
      charge.
  Duke. That thou shalt see the difference of our
      spirits,
I pardon thee thy life before thou ask it:
For half thy wealth, it is Antonio's;   370
The other half comes to the general state,
Which humbleness may drive unto a fine.
  Por. Ay, for the state, not for Antonio.
  Shy. Nay, take my life and all; pardon not that:

You take my house when you do take the prop
That doth sustain my house; you take my life
When you do take the means whereby I live.
  Por. What mercy can you render him, Antonio?
  Gra. A halter gratis; nothing else, for God's
      sake.
  Ant. So please my lord the Duke and all the
      court   380
To quit the fine for one half of his goods,
I am content; so he will let me have
The other half in use, to render it,
Upon his death, unto the gentleman
That lately stole his daughter:
Two things provided more, that, for this favour,
He presently become a Christian;
The other, that he do record a gift,
Here in the court, of all he dies possess'd,
Unto his son Lorenzo and his daughter.   390
  Duke. He shall do this, or else I do recant
The pardon that I late pronounced here.
  Por. Art thou contented, Jew? what dost thou
      say?
  Shy. I am content.
  Por.   Clerk, draw a deed of gift.
  Shy. I pray you, give me leave to go from hence;
I am not well: send the deed after me,
And I will sign it.
  Duke.   Get thee gone, but do it.
  Gra. In christening shalt thou have two god-
      fathers:
Had I been judge, thou shouldst have had ten
      more,
To bring thee to the gallows, not the font.   400
                                    [*Exit* SHYLOCK.
  Duke. Sir, I entreat you home with me to dinner.
  Por. I humbly do desire your Grace of pardon:
I must away this night toward Padua,
And it is meet I presently set forth.
  Duke. I am sorry that your leisure serves you
      not.
Antonio, gratify this gentleman,
For, in my mind, you are much bound to him.
                        [*Exeunt* DUKE *and his train.*
  Bass. Most worthy gentleman, I and my friend
Have by your wisdom been this day acquitted
Of grievous penalties; in lieu whereof,   410
Three thousand ducats, due unto the Jew,
We freely cope your courteous pains withal.
  Ant. And stand indebted, over and above,
In love and service to you evermore.
  Por. He is well paid that is well satisfied;
And I, delivering you, am satisfied
And therein do account myself well paid:
My mind was never yet more mercenary.
I pray you, know me when we meet again:
I wish you well, and so I take my leave   420

Bass. Dear sir, of force I must attempt you
        further:
Take some remembrance of us, as a tribute,
Not as a fee, grant me two things, I pray
        you,
Not to deny me, and to pardon me.
   Por. You press me far, and therefore I will
        yield.
[*To* ANTONIO] Give me your gloves, I'll wear
        them for your sake;
[*To* BASSANIO] And, for your love, I'll take this
        ring from you:
Do not draw back your hand; I'll take no
        more;
And you in love shall not deny me this.
   Bass. This ring, good sir, alas, it is a trifle!
I will not shame myself to give you this.   431
   Por. I will have nothing else but only this;
And now methinks I have a mind to it.
   Bass. There's more depends on this than on the
        value.
The dearest ring in Venice will I give you,
And find it out by proclamation:
Only for this, I pray you, pardon me,
   Por. I see, sir, you are liberal in offers:
You taught me first to beg; and now methinks
You teach me how a beggar should be answer'd.
   Bass. Good sir, this ring was given me by my
        wife;   441
And when she put it on, she made me vow
That I should neither sell nor give nor lose it.
   Por. That 'scuse serves many men to save their
        gifts.
An if your wife be not a mad-woman,
And know how well I have deserved the ring,
She would not hold out enemy for ever,
For giving it to me. Well, peace be with you!
        [*Exeunt* PORTIA *and* NERISSA.
   Ant. My Lord Bassanio, let him have the ring:
Let his deservings and my love withal   450
Be valued 'gainst your wife's commandment.
   Bass. Go, Gratiano, run and overtake him;
Give him the ring, and bring him, if thou canst,
Unto Antonio's house: away! make haste.
        [*Exit* GRATIANO.
Come, you and I will thither presently;
And in the morning early will we both
Fly toward Belmont: come, Antonio.   [*Exeunt.*

SCENE II. *The same: a street*

Enter PORTIA *and* NERISSA.

   Por. Inquire the Jew's house out, give him this
        deed
And let him sign it: we'll away to-night
And be a day before our husbands home:
This deed will be well welcome to Lorenzo.

Enter GRATIANO.

   Gra. Fair sir, you are well o'erta'en:
My Lord Bassanio upon more advice
Hath sent you here this ring, and doth entreat
Your company at dinner.
   Por.   That cannot be:
His ring I do accept most thankfully:
And so, I pray you, tell him: furthermore,   10
I pray you, show my youth old Shylock's house.
   Gra. That will I do.
   Ner.   Sir, I would speak with you.
[*Aside to* PORTIA] I'll see if I can get my husband's
        ring,
Which I did make him swear to keep for ever.
   Por. [*Aside to* NERISSA] Thou mayst, I warrant.
        We shall have old swearing
That they did give the rings away to men;
But we'll outface them, and outswear them too.
[*Aloud*] Away! make haste: thou know'st where
        I will tarry.
   Ner. Come, good sir, will you show me to this
        house?   [*Exeunt.*

ACT V

SCENE I. *Belmont: avenue to Portia's house*

Enter LORENZO *and* JESSICA.

   Lor. The moon shines bright: in such a night
        as this,
When the sweet wind did gently kiss the trees
And they did make no noise, in such a night
Troilus methinks mounted the Troyan walls
And sigh'd his soul toward the Grecian tents,
Where Cressid lay that night.
   Jes.   In such a night
Did Thisbe fearfully o'ertrip the dew
And saw the lion's shadow ere himself
And ran dismay'd away.
   Lor.   In such a night
Stood Dido with a willow in her hand   10
Upon the wild sea banks, and waft her love
To come again to Carthage.
   Jes.   In such a night
Medea gather'd the enchanted herbs
That did renew old Æson.
   Lor.   In such a night
Did Jessica steal from the wealthy Jew,
And with an unthrift love did run from Venice
As far as Belmont.
   Jes.   In such a night
Did young Lorenzo swear he loved her well,
Stealing her soul with many vows of faith
And ne'er a true one.
   Lor.   In such a night   20
Did pretty Jessica, like a little shrew,

Slander her love, and he forgave it her.

Jes. I would out-night you, did no body come;
But, hark, I hear the footing of a man.

Enter STEPHANO.

Lor. Who comes so fast in silence of the night?
Steph. A friend.
Lor. A friend! what friend? your name, I pray
   you, friend?
Steph. Stephano is my name; and I bring word
My mistress will before the break of day
Be here at Belmont: she doth stray about   30
By holy crosses, where she kneels and prays
For happy wedlock hours.
Lor.   Who comes with her?
Steph. None but a holy hermit and her maid.
I pray you, is my master yet return'd?
Lor. He is not, nor we have not heard from him.
But go we in, I pray thee, Jessica,
And ceremoniously let us prepare
Some welcome for the mistress of the house.

Enter LAUNCELOT.

Laun. Sola, sola! wo ha, ho! sola, sola!
Lor. Who calls?   40
Laun. Sola! did you see Master Lorenzo? Mas-
ter Lorenzo, sola,sola!
Lor. Leave hollaing, man: here.
Laun. Sola! where? where?
Lor. Here.
Laun. Tell him there's a post come from my
master, with his horn full of good news: my mas-
ter will be here ere morning.   [*Exit.*
Lor. Sweet soul, let's in, and there expect
   their coming.
And yet no matter: why should we go in?   50
My friend Stephano, signify, I pray you,
Within the house, your mistress is at hand;
And bring your music forth into the air.
                         [*Exit* STEPHANO.
How sweet the moonlight sleeps upon this bank!
Here will we sit and let the sounds of music
Creep in our ears: soft stillness and the night
Become the touches of sweet harmony.
Sit, Jessica. Look how the floor of heaven
Is thick inlaid with patines of bright gold:
There's not the smallest orb which thou behold'st
But in his motion like an angel sings,   61
Still quiring to the young-eyed cherubins;
Such harmony is in immortal souls;
But whilst this muddy vesture of decay
Doth grossly close it in, we cannot hear it.

Enter Musicians.

Come, ho! and wake Diana with a hymn:
With sweetest touches pierce your mistress' ear

And draw her home with music.
   Music.
Jes. I am never merry when I hear sweet music.
Lor. The reason is, your spirits are attentive:
For do but note a wild and wanton herd,   71
Or race of youthful and unhandled colts,
Fetching mad bounds, bellowing, and neighing
   loud,
Which is the hot condition of their blood;
If they but hear perchance a trumpet sound,
Or any air of music touch their ears,
You shall perceive them make a mutual stand,
Their savage eyes turn'd to a modest gaze
By the sweet power of music: therefore the poet
Did feign that Orpheus drew trees, stones and
   floods;   80
Since nought so stockish, hard, and full of rage,
But music for the time doth change his nature.
The man that hath no music in himself,
Nor is not moved with concord of sweet sounds,
Is fit for treasons, stratagems and spoils;
The motions of his spirit are dull as night
And his affections dark as Erebus:
Let no such man be trusted. Mark the music.

Enter PORTIA *and* NERISSA.

Por. That light we see is burning in my hall.
How far that little candle throws his beams!   90
So shines a good deed in a naughty world.
Ner. When the moon shone, we did not see the
   candle.
Por. So doth the greater glory dim the less:
A substitute shines brightly as a king
Until a king be by, and then his state
Empties itself, as doth an inland brook
Into the main of waters. Music! hark!
Ner. It is your music, madam, of the house.
Por. Nothing is good, I see, without respect:
Methinks it sounds much sweeter than by day.
Ner. Silence bestows that virtue on it, madam.
Por. The crow doth sing as sweetly as the lark
When neither is attended, and I think
The nightingale, if she should sing by day,
When every goose is cackling, would be thought
No better a musician than the wren.
How many things by season season'd are
To their right praise and true perfection!
Peace, ho! the moon sleeps with Endymion
And would not be awaked.
   Music ceases.
Lor.   That is the voice,   110
Or I am much deceived, of Portia.
Por. He knows me as the blind man knows the
   cuckoo,
By the bad voice.
Lor.   Dear lady, welcome home.

Por. We have been praying for our husbands'
    healths,
Which speed, we hope, the better for our words.
Are they return'd?
    Lor.   Madam, they are not yet;
But there is come a messenger before,
To signify their coming.
    Por.   Go in, Nerissa;
Give order to my servants that they take
No note at all of our being absent hence;   *120*
Nor you, Lorenzo; Jessica, nor you.
    A tucket sounds.
    Lor. Your husband is at hand; I hear his
    trumpet:
We are no tell-tales, madam; fear you not.
    Por. This night methinks is but the daylight
    sick;
It looks a little paler: 'tis a day,
Such as the day is when the sun is hid.

    Enter BASSANIO, ANTONIO, GRATIANO, *and*
        their followers.

    Bass. We should hold day with the Antipodes,
If you would walk in absence of the sun.
    Por. Let me give light, but let me not be light;
For a light wife doth make a heavy husband,   *130*
And never be Bassanio so for me:
But God sort all! You are welcome home, my
    lord.
    Bass. I thank you, madam. Give welcome to my
    friend.
This is the man, this is Antonio,
To whom I am so infinitely bound.
    Por. You should in all sense be much bound to
    him,
For, as I hear, he was much bound for you.
    Ant. No more than I am well acquitted of.
    Por. Sir, you are very welcome to our house:
It must appear in other ways than words,   *140*
Therefore I scant this breathing courtesy.
    Gra. [*To* NERISSA] By yonder moon I swear you
    do me wrong;
In faith, I gave it to the judge's clerk:
Would he were gelt that had it, for my part,
Since you do take it, love, so much at heart.
    Por. A quarrel, ho, already! what's the matter?
    Gra. About a hoop of gold, a paltry ring
That she did give me, whose posy was
For all the world like cutler's poetry
Upon a knife, "Love me, and leave me not."   *150*
    Ner. What talk you of the posy or the value?
You swore to me, when I did give it you,
That you would wear it till your hour of death
And that it should lie with you in your grave:
Though not for me, yet for your vehement oaths,
You should have been respective and have kept it.

Gave it a judge's clerk! no, God's my judge,
The clerk will ne'er wear hair on's face that had
    it.
    Gra. He will, an if he live to be a man.
    Ner. Ay, if a woman live to be a man.   *160*
    Gra. Now, by this hand, I gave it to a youth,
A kind of boy, a little scrubbed boy,
No higher than thyself, the judge's clerk,
A prating boy, that begg'd it as a fee:
I could not for my heart deny it him.
    Por. You were to blame, I must be plain with
    you,
To part so slightly with your wife's first gift;
A thing stuck on with oaths upon your finger
And so riveted with faith unto your flesh.
I gave my love a ring and made him swear   *170*
Never to part with it; and here he stands;
I dare be sworn for him he would not leave it
Nor pluck it from his finger, for the wealth
That the world masters. Now, in faith, Gratiano,
You give your wife too unkind a cause of grief:
An 'twere to me. I should be mad at it.
    Bass. [*Aside*] Why, I were best to cut my left
    hand off
And swear I lost the ring defending it.
    Gra. My Lord Bassanio gave his ring away
Unto the judge that begg'd it and indeed   *180*
Deserved it too; and then the boy, his clerk,
That took some pains in writing, he begg'd mine;
And neither man nor master would take aught
But the two rings.
    Por.   What ring gave you, my lord?
Not that, I hope, which you received of me.
    Bass. If I could add a lie unto a fault,
I would deny it; but you see my finger
Hath not the ring upon it; it is gone.
    Por. Even so void is your false heart of truth.
By heaven, I will ne'er come in your bed   *190*
Until I see the ring.
    Ner.   Nor I in yours
Till I again see mine.
    Bass.   Sweet Portia,
If you did know to whom I gave the ring,
If you did know for whom I gave the ring,
And would conceive for what I gave the ring,
And how unwillingly I left the ring,
When nought would be accepted but the ring,
You would abate the strength of your displeasure.
    Por. If you had known the virtue of the ring,
Or half her worthiness that gave the ring,   *200*
Or your own honour to contain the ring,
You would not then have parted with the ring.
What man is there so much unreasonable,
If you had pleased to have defended it
With any terms of zeal, wanted the modesty
To urge the thing held as a ceremony?

Nerissa teaches me what to believe:
I'll die for't but some woman had the ring.

Bass. No, by my honour, madam, by my soul,
No woman had it, but a civil doctor,   *210*
Which did refuse three thousand ducats of me
And begg'd the ring; the which I did deny him
And suffer'd him to go displeased away;
Even he that did uphold the very life
Of my dear friend. What should I say, sweet lady?
I was enforced to send it after him;
I was beset with shame and courtesy;
My honour would not let ingratitude
So much besmear it. Pardon me, good lady;
For, by these blessed candles of the night,   *220*
Had you been there, I think you would have
          begg'd
The ring of me to give the worthy doctor.

Por. Let not that doctor e'er come near my
          house:
Since he hath got the jewel that I loved,
And that which you did swear to keep for me,
I will become as liberal as you;
I'll not deny him any thing I have,
No, not my body, nor my husband's bed:
Know him I shall, I am well sure of it:
Lie not a night from home; watch me like Argus:
If you do not, if I be left alone,   *231*
Now, by mine honour, which is yet mine own,
I'll have that doctor for my bedfellow.

Ner. And I his clerk; therefore be well advised
How you do leave me to mine own protection.

Gra. Well, do you so: let not me take him, then;
For if I do, I'll mar the young clerk's pen.

Ant. I am the unhappy subject of these quarrels.

Por. Sir, grieve not you; you are welcome not-
          withstanding.

Bass. Portia, forgive me this enforced wrong;
And, in the hearing of these many friends,   *241*
I swear to thee, even by thine own fair eyes,
Wherein I see myself—

Por.   Mark you but that!
In both my eyes he doubly sees himself;
In each eye, one: swear by your double self,
And there's an oath of credit.

Bass.   Nay, but hear me:
Pardon this fault, and by my soul I swear
I never more will break an oath with thee.

Ant. I once did lend my body for his wealth;
Which, but for him that had your husband's ring,
Had quite miscarried: I dare be bound again,
My soul upon the forfeit, that your lord
Will never more break faith advisedly.

Por. Then you shall be his surety. Give him this
And bid him keep it better than the other.

Ant. Here, Lord Bassanio; swear to keep this
          ring.

Bass. By heaven, it is the same I gave the doctor!

Por. I had it of him: pardon me, Bassanio;
For, by this ring, the doctor lay with me.   *259*

Ner. And pardon me, my gentle Gratiano;
For that same scrubbed boy, the doctor's clerk,
In lieu of this last night did lie with me.

Gra. Why, this is like the mending of highways
In summer, where the ways are fair enough:
What, are we cuckolds ere we have deserved it?

Por. Speak not so grossly. You are all amazed:
Here is a letter; read it at your leisure;
It comes from Padua, from Bellario:
There you shall find that Portia was the doctor,
Nerissa there her clerk: Lorenzo here   *270*
Shall witness I set forth as soon as you
And even but now return'd; I have not yet
Enter'd my house. Antonio, you are welcome;
And I have better news in store for you
Than you expect: unseal this letter soon;
There you shall find three of your argosies
Are richly come to harbour suddenly:
You shall not know by what strange accident
I chanced on this letter.

Ant.   I am dumb.

Bass. Were you the doctor and I knew you not?

Gra. Were you the clerk that is to make me
          cuckold?   *281*

Ner. Ay, but the clerk that never means to do it,
Unless he live until he be a man.

Bass. Sweet doctor, you shall be my bedfellow:
When I am absent, then lie with my wife.

Ant. Sweet lady, you have given me life and
          living;
For here I read for certain that my ships
Are safely come to road.

Por.   How now, Lorenzo!
My clerk hath some good comforts too for you.

Ner. Ay, and I'll give them him without a fee.
There do I give to you and Jessica,   *291*
From the rich Jew, a special deed of gift,
After his death, of all he dies possess'd of.

Lor. Fair ladies, you drop manna in the way
Of starved people.

Por.   It is almost morning,
And yet I am sure you are not satisfied
Of these events at full. Let us go in;
And charge us there upon inter'gatories,
And we will answer all things faithfully.

Gra. Let it be so: the first inter'gatory   *300*
That my Nerissa shall be sworn on is,
Whether till the next night she had rather stay,
Or go to bed now, being two hours to day:
But were the day come, I should wish it dark,
That I were couching with the doctor's clerk.
Well, while I live I'll fear no other thing
So sore as keeping safe Nerissa's ring.   [*Exeunt.*

❧ The First Part of
KING HENRY THE FOURTH

DRAMATIS PERSONÆ

KING HENRY THE FOURTH
HENRY, PRINCE OF WALES ⎫
JOHN OF LANCASTER ⎬ *sons to the King*
EARL OF WESTMORELAND
SIR WALTER BLUNT
THOMAS PERCY, EARL OF WORCESTER
HENRY PERCY, EARL OF NORTHUMBERLAND
HENRY PERCY, *surnamed* HOTSPUR, *his son*
EDMUND MORTIMER, EARL OF MARCH
RICHARD SCROOP, ARCHBISHOP OF YORK
ARCHIBALD, EARL OF DOUGLAS
OWEN GLENDOWER
SIR RICHARD VERNON
SIR JOHN FALSTAFF
SIR MICHAEL, *a friend to the Archbishop of York*
POINS
GADSHILL
PETO
BARDOLPH

TWO CARRIERS
OSTLER
A CHAMBERLAIN
SEVERAL TRAVELLERS
A VINTNER
FRANCIS, *the drawer*
SHERIFF
TWO MESSENGERS
SERVANT *to Hotspur*

LADY PERCY, *wife to Hotspur, and sister to* MORTIMER
LADY MORTIMER, *daughter to Glendower, and wife to*
  Mortimer
MISTRESS QUICKLY, *hostess of a tavern in Eastcheap*

NON-SPEAKING: *Lords, Officers, Drawers, Travellers*
  and Attendants

SCENE: *England*

ACT I

SCENE I. *London: the palace*

Enter KING HENRY, LORD JOHN OF LANCASTER,
the EARL OF WESTMORELAND, SIR WALTER
BLUNT, *and others.*

King. So shaken as we are, so wan with care,
Find we a time for frighted peace to pant,
And breathe short-winded accents of new broils
To be commenced in strands afar remote.
No more the thirsty entrance of this soil
Shall daub her lips with her own children's blood;
No more shall trenching war channel her fields,
Nor bruise her flowers with the armed hoofs
Of hostile paces: those opposed eyes,
Which, like the meteors of a troubled heaven, *10*
All of one nature, of one substance bred,
Did lately meet in the intestine shock
And furious close of civil butchery
Shall now, in mutual well-beseeming ranks,
March all one way and be no more opposed
Against acquaintance, kindred and allies:
The edge of war, like an ill-sheathed knife,
No more shall cut his master. Therefore, friends,
As far as to the sepulchre of Christ,
Whose soldier now, under whose blessed cross *20*
We are impressed and engaged to fight,

Forthwith a power of English shall we levy;
Whose arms were moulded in their mothers'
  womb
To chase these pagans in those holy fields
Over whose acres walk'd those blessed feet
Which fourteen hundred years ago were nail'd
For our advantage on the bitter cross.
But this our purpose now is twelve month old,
And bootless 'tis to tell you we will go:
Therefore we meet not now. Then let me hear *30*
Of you, my gentle cousin Westmoreland,
What yesternight our council did decree
In forwarding this dear expedience.
  West. My liege, this haste was hot in question,
And many limits of the charge set down
But yesternight: when all athwart there came
A post from Wales loaden with heavy news;
Whose worst was that the noble Mortimer,
Leading the men of Herefordshire to fight
Against the irregular and wild Glendower, *40*
Was by the rude hands of that Welshman taken,
A thousand of his people butchered;
Upon whose dead corpse there was such misuse,
Such beastly shameless transformation,
By those Welshwomen done as may not be
Without much shame retold or spoken of.
  King. It seems then that the tidings of this broil

434

Brake off our business for the Holy Land.

West. This match'd with other did, my gracious
    lord;
For more uneven and unwelcome news   50
Came from the north and thus it did import:
On Holy-rood day, the gallant Hotspur there,
Young Harry Percy and brave Archibald,
That ever-valiant and approved Scot,
At Holmedon met,
Where they did spend a sad and bloody hour;
As by discharge of their artillery,
And shape of likelihood, the news was told;
For he that brought them, in the very heat
And pride of their contention did take horse,   60
Uncertain of the issue any way.

King. Here is a dear, a true industrious friend,
Sir Walter Blunt, new lighted from his horse,
Stain'd with the variation of each soil
Betwixt that Holmedon and this seat of ours;
And he hath brought us smooth and welcome
    news.
The Earl of Douglas is discomfited:
Ten thousand bold Scots, two and twenty
    knights,
Balk'd in their own blood did Sir Walter see
On Holmedon's plains. Of prisoners, Hotspur
    took   70
Mordake the Earl of Fife, and eldest son
To beaten Douglas; and the Earl of Athol,
Of Murray, Angus, and Menteith:
And is not this an honourable spoil?
A gallant prize? ha, cousin, is it not?

West. In faith,
It is a conquest for a prince to boast of.

King. Yea, there thou makest me sad and mak-
    est me sin
In envy that my Lord Northumberland
Should be the father to so blest a son,   80
A son who is the theme of Honour's tongue;
Amongst a grove, the very straightest plant;
Who is sweet Fortune's minion and her pride:
Whilst I, by looking on the praise of him,
See riot and dishonour stain the brow
Of my young Harry. O that it could be proved
That some night-tripping fairy had exchanged
In cradle-clothes our children where they lay,
And call'd mine Percy, his Plantagenet!
Then would I have his Harry, and he mine.   90
But let him from my thoughts. What think you,
    coz,
Of this young Percy's pride? the prisoners,
Which he in this adventure hath surprised,
To his own use he keeps; and sends me word,
I shall have none but Mordake Earl of Fife.

West. This is his uncle's teaching: this is Wor-
    cester,

Malevolent to you in all aspects;
Which makes him prune himself, and bristle up
The crest of youth against your dignity.

King. But I have sent for him to answer this;
And for this cause awhile we must neglect   101
Our holy purpose to Jerusalem.
Cousin, on Wednesday next our council we
Will hold at Windsor; so inform the lords:
But come yourself with speed to us again;
For more is to be said and to be done
Than out of anger can be uttered.

West. I will, my liege.   [*Exeunt.*

SCENE II. *London: an apartment of the Prince's*

Enter *the* PRINCE OF WALES *and* FALSTAFF.

Fal. Now, Hal, what time of day is it, lad?

Prince. Thou art so fat-witted, with drinking
of old sack and unbuttoning thee after supper
and sleeping upon benches after noon, that thou
hast forgotten to demand that truly which thou
wouldst truly know. What a devil hast thou to
do with the time of the day? Unless hours were
cups of sack and minutes capons and clocks the
tongues of bawds and dials the signs of leaping-
houses and the blessed sun himself a fair hot
wench in flame-coloured taffeta, I see no reason
why thou shouldst be so superfluous to demand
the time of the day.

Fal. Indeed, you come near me now, Hal;
for we that take purses go by the moon and the
seven stars, and not by Phœbus, he "that wandering knight so fair." And, I prithee, sweet
wag, when thou art king, as, God save thy
Grace—Majesty I should say, for grace thou
wilt have none—   20

Prince. What, none?

Fal. No, by my troth, not so much as will serve
to be prologue to an egg and butter.

Prince. Well, how then? come, roundly,
roundly.

Fal. Marry, then, sweet wag, when thou art
king, let not us that are squires of the night's
body be called thieves of the day's beauty: let
us be Diana's foresters, gentlemen of the shade,
minions of the moon; and let men say we be men
of good government, being governed, as the sea
is, by our noble and chaste mistress the moon,
under whose countenance we steal.

Prince. Thou sayest well, and it holds well too;
for the fortune of us that are the moon's men
doth ebb and flow like the sea, being governed,
as the sea is, by the moon. As, for proof, now:
a purse of gold most resolutely snatched on
Monday night and most dissolutely spent on
Tuesday morning; got with swearing "Lay by"
and spent with crying "Bring in"; now in as low

an ebb as the foot of the ladder and by and by in as high a flow as the ridge of the gallows.

Fal. By the Lord thou sayest true, lad. And is not my hostess of the tavern a most sweet wench?

Prince. As the honey of Hybla, my old lad of the castle. And is not a buff jerkin a most sweet robe of durance? 49

Fal. How now, how now, mad wag! what, in thy quips and thy quiddities? what a plague have I to do with a buff jerkin?

Prince. Why, what a pox have I to do with my hostess of the tavern?

Fal. Well, thou hast called her to a reckoning many a time and oft.

Prince. Did I ever call for thee to pay thy part?

Fal. No; I'll give thee thy due, thou hast paid all there. 60

Prince. Yea, and elsewhere, so far as my coin would stretch; and where it would not, I have used my credit.

Fal. Yea, and so used it that, were it not here apparent that thou art heir apparent—But, I prithee, sweet wag, shall there be gallows standing in England when thou art king? and resolution thus fobbed as it is with the rusty curb of old father antic the law? Do not thou, when thou art king, hang a thief. 70

Prince. No; thou shalt.

Fal. Shall I? O rare! By the Lord, I'll be a brave judge.

Prince. Thou judgest false already: I mean, thou shalt have the hanging of the thieves and so become a rare hangman.

Fal. Well, Hal, well; and in some sort it jumps with my humour as well as waiting in the court, I can tell you.

Prince. For obtaining of suits? 80

Fal. Yea, for obtaining of suits, whereof the hangman hath no lean wardrobe. 'Sblood, I am as melancholy as a gib cat or a lugged bear.

Prin. Or an old lion, or a lover's lute.

Fal. Yea, or the drone of a Lincolnshire bagpipe.

Prince. What sayest thou to a hare, or the melancholy of Moor-ditch?

Fal. Thou hast the most unsavoury similes and art indeed the most comparative, rascalliest, sweet young prince. But, Hal, I prithee, trouble me no more with vanity. I would to God thou and I knew where a commodity of good names were to be bought. An old lord of the council rated me the other day in the street about you, sir, but I marked him not; and yet he talked very wisely, but I regarded him not; and yet he talked wisely, and in the street too.

Prince. Thou didst well; for wisdom cries out

in the streets, and no man regards it. 100

Fal. O, thou hast damnable iteration and art indeed able to corrupt a saint. Thou hast done much harm upon me, Hal; God forgive thee for it! Before I knew thee, Hal, I knew nothing; and now am I, if a man should speak truly, little better than one of the wicked. I must give over this life, and I will give it over: by the Lord, an I do not, I am a villain: I'll be damned for never a king's son in Christendom.

Prince. Where shall we take a purse to-morrow, Jack? 111

Fal. 'Zounds, where thou wilt, lad; I'll make one; an I do not, call me villain and baffle me.

Prince. I see a good amendment of life in thee; from praying to purse-taking.

Fal. Why, Hal, 'tis my vocation, Hal; 'tis no sin for a man to labour in his vocation.

Enter POINS.

Poins! Now shall we know if Gadshill have set a match. O, if men were to be saved by merit, what hole in hell were hot enough for him? This is the most omnipotent villain that ever cried "Stand" to a true man.

Prince. Good morrow, Ned.

Poins. Good morrow, sweet Hal. What says Monsieur Remorse? what says Sir John Sack and Sugar? Jack! how agrees the devil and thee about thy soul, that thou soldest him on Good-Friday last for a cup of Madeira and a cold capon's leg? 129

Prince. Sir John stands to his word, the devil shall have his bargain; for he was never yet a breaker of proverbs: he will give the devil his due.

Poins. Then art thou damned for keeping thy word with the devil.

Prince. Else he had been damned for cozening the devil.

Poins. But, my lads, my lads, to-morrow morning, by four o'clock, early at Gadshill! there are pilgrims going to Canterbury with rich offerings, and traders riding to London with fat purses: I have vizards for you all; you have horses for yourselves: Gadshill lies to-night in Rochester: I have bespoke supper to-morrow night in Eastcheap: we may do it as secure as sleep. If you will go, I will stuff your purses full of crowns; if you will not, tarry at home and be hanged.

Fal. Hear ye, Yedward; if I tarry at home and go not, I'll hang you for going. 150

Poins. You will, chops?

Fal. Hal, wilt thou make one?

Prince. Who, I rob? I a thief? not I, by my faith.

Fal. There's neither honesty, manhood, nor good fellowship in thee, nor thou camest not of the blood royal, if thou darest not stand for ten shillings.

Prince. Well then, once in my days I'll be a madcap.   *160*

Fal. Why, that's well said.

Prince. Well, come what will, I'll tarry at home.

Fal. By the Lord, I'll be a traitor then, when thou art king.

Prince. I care not.

Poins. Sir John, I prithee, leave the Prince and me alone: I will lay him down such reasons for this adventure that he shall go.   *169*

Fal. Well, God give thee the spirit of persuasion and him the ears of profiting, that what thou speakest may move and what he hears may be believed, that the true prince may, for recreation sake, prove a false thief; for the poor abuses of the time want countenance. Farewell: you shall find me in Eastcheap.

Prince. Farewell, thou latter spring! farewell, All-hallown summer!   [*Exit* FALSTAFF.

Poins. Now, my good sweet honey lord, ride with us to-morrow: I have a jest to execute that I cannot manage alone. Falstaff, Bardolph, Peto and Gadshill shall rob those men that we have already waylaid; yourself and I will not be there; and when they have the booty, if you and I do not rob them, cut this head off from my shoulders.

Prince. How shall we part with them in setting forth?

Poins. Why, we will set forth before or after them, and appoint them a place of meeting, wherein it is at our pleasure to fail, and then will they adventure upon the exploit themselves; which they shall have no sooner achieved, but we'll set upon them.

Prince. Yea, but 'tis like that they will know us by our horses, by our habits and by every other appointment, to be ourselves.

Poins. Tut! our horses they shall not see; I'll tie them in the wood; our vizards we will change after we leave them: and, sirrah, I have cases of buckram for the nonce, to immask our noted outward garments.

Prince. Yea, but I doubt they will be too hard for us.

Poins. Well, for two of them, I know them to be as true-bred cowards as ever turned back; and for the third, if he fight longer than he sees reason, I'll forswear arms. The virtue of this jest will be the incomprehensible lies that this same fat rogue will tell us when we meet at supper:

how thirty, at least, he fought with; what wards, what blows, what extremities he endured; and in the reproof of this lies the jest.

Prince. Well, I'll go with thee: provide us all things necessary and meet me to-morrow night in Eastcheap; there I'll sup. Farewell.

Poins. Farewell, my lord.   [*Exit.*

Prince. I know you all, and will awhile uphold
The unyoked humour of your idleness:
Yet herein will I imitate the sun,   *220*
Who doth permit the base contagious clouds
To smother up his beauty from the world,
That, when he please again to be himself,
Being wanted, he may be more wonder'd at,
By breaking through the foul and ugly mists
Of vapours that did seem to strangle him.
If all the year were playing holidays,
To sport would be as tedious as to work;
But when they seldom come, they wish'd for come,
And nothing pleaseth but rare accidents.   *230*
So, when this loose behaviour I throw off
And pay the debt I never promised,
By how much better than my word I am,
By so much shall I falsify men's hopes;
And like bright metal on a sullen ground,
My reformation, glittering o'er my fault,
Shall show more goodly and attract more eyes
Than that which hath no foil to set it off.
I'll so offend, to make offence a skill;
Redeeming time when men think least I will. *240*
          [*Exit.*

SCENE III. *London: the palace*

Enter the KING, NORTHUMBERLAND, WORCESTER,
          HOTSPUR, SIR WALTER BLUNT, *with others.*

King. My blood hath been too cold and temperate,
Unapt to stir at these indignities,
And you have found me; for accordingly
You tread upon my patience: but be sure
I will from henceforth rather be myself,
Mighty and to be fear'd, than my condition;
Which hath been smooth as oil, soft as young down,
And therefore lost that title of respect
Which the proud soul ne'er pays but to the proud.

Wor. Our house, my sovereign liege, little deserves   *10*
The scourge of greatness to be used on it;
And that same greatness too which our own hands
Have holp to make so portly.

North. My lord—

King. Worcester, get thee gone; for I do see

Danger and disobedience in thine eye:
O, sir, your presence is too bold and peremptory,
And majesty might never yet endure
The moody frontier of a servant brow.
You have good leave to leave us: when we need
Your use and counsel, we shall send for you. 21
                  [*Exit* WORCESTER.
You were about to speak. [*To* NORTHUMBERLAND.
  North.   Yea, my good lord.
Those prisoners in your Highness' name demanded,
Which Harry Percy here at Holmedon took,
Were, as he says, not with such strength denied
As is deliver'd to your Majesty:
Either envy, therefore, or misprision
Is guilty of this fault and not my son.
  Hot. My liege, I did deny no prisoners.
But I remember, when the fight was done, 30
When I was dry with rage and extreme toil,
Breathless and faint, leaning upon my sword,
Came there a certain lord, neat, and trimly
    dress'd,
Fresh as a bridegroom; and his chin new reap'd
Show'd like a stubble-land at harvest-home;
He was perfumed like a milliner;
And 'twixt his finger and his thumb he held
A pouncet-box, which ever and anon
He gave his nose and took't away again: 39
Who therewith angry, when it next came there,
Took it in snuff; and still he smiled and talk'd,
And as the soldiers bore dead bodies by,
He call'd them untaught knaves, unmannerly,
To bring a slovenly unhandsome corse
Betwixt the wind and his nobility.
With many holiday and lady terms
He question'd me; amongst the rest, demanded
My prisoners in your Majesty's behalf.
I then, all smarting with my wounds being cold,
To be so pester'd with a popinjay, 50
Out of my grief and my impatience,
Answer'd neglectingly I know not what,
He should, or he should not; for he made me
    mad
To see him shine so brisk and smell so sweet
And talk so like a waiting-gentlewoman
Of guns and drums and wounds—God save the
    mark!—
And telling me the sovereign'st thing on earth
Was parmaceti for an inward bruise;
And that it was great pity, so it was,
This villainous salt-petre should be digg'd 60
Out of the bowels of the harmless earth,
Which many a good tall fellow had destroy'd
So cowardly; and but for these vile guns,
He would himself have been a soldier.
This bald unjointed chat of his, my lord,

I answer'd indirectly, as I said;
And I beseech you, let not his report
Come current for an accusation
Betwixt my love and your high Majesty.
  Blunt. The circumstance consider'd, good my
    lord,   70
Whate'er Lord Harry Percy then had said
To such a person and in such a place,
At such a time, with all the rest retold,
May reasonably die and never rise
To do him wrong or any way impeach
What then he said, so he unsay it now.
  King. Why, yet he doth deny his prisoners,
But with proviso and exception,
That we at our own charge shall ransom straight
His brother-in-law, the foolish Mortimer; 80
Who, on my soul, hath wilfully betray'd
The lives of those that he did lead to fight
Against that great magician, damn'd Glendower,
Whose daughter, as we hear, the Earl of March
Hath lately married. Shall our coffers, then,
Be emptied to redeem a traitor home?
Shall we buy treason? and indent with fears,
When they have lost and forfeited themselves?
No, on the barren mountains let him starve;
For I shall never hold that man my friend 90
Whose tongue shall ask me for one penny cost
To ransom home revolted Mortimer.
  Hot. Revolted Mortimer!
He never did fall off, my sovereign liege,
But by the chance of war: to prove that true
Needs no more but one tongue for all those
    wounds,
Those mouthed wounds, which valiantly he took,
When on the gentle Severn's sedgy bank,
In single opposition, hand to hand,
He did confound the best part of an hour 100
In changing hardiment with great Glendower:
Three times they breathed and three times did
    they drink,
Upon agreement, of swift Severn's flood;
Who then, affrighted with their bloody looks,
Ran fearfully among the trembling reeds,
And hid his crisp head in the hollow bank
Bloodstained with these valiant combatants.
Never did base and rotten policy
Colour her working with such deadly wounds:
Nor never could the noble Mortimer 110
Receive so many, and all willingly:
Then let not him be slander'd with revolt.
  King. Thou dost belie him, Percy, thou dost
    belie him;
He never did encounter with Glendower:
I tell thee,
He durst as well have met the devil alone
As Owen Glendower for an enemy.

Art thou not ashamed? But, sirrah, henceforth
Let me not hear you speak of Mortimer:
Send me your prisoners with the speediest means,
Or you shall hear in such a kind from me   *121*
As will displease you. My Lord Northumber-
    land,
We license your departure with your son.
Send us your prisoners, or you'll hear of it.
        [*Exeunt* KING HENRY, BLUNT, *and train.*
    Hot. An if the devil come and roar for them,
I will not send them: I will after straight
And tell him so; for I will ease my heart,
Albeit I make a hazard of my head.
    North. What, drunk with choler? stay and
        pause awhile:
Here comes your uncle.

                Re-enter WORCESTER.

    Hot.   Speak of Mortimer! *130*
'Zounds, I will speak of him; and let my soul
Want mercy, if I do not join with him:
Yea, on his part I'll empty all these veins,
And shed my dear blood drop by drop in the dust,
But I will lift the down-trod Mortimer
As high in the air as this unthankful king,
As this ingrate and canker'd Bolingbroke.
    North. Brother, the King hath made your
        nephew mad.
    Wor. Who struck this heat up after I was
        gone?   *139*
    Hot. He will, forsooth, have all my prisoners;
And when I urged the ransom once again
Of my wife's brother, then his cheek look'd pale,
And on my face he turn'd an eye of death,
Trembling even at the name of Mortimer.
    Wor. I cannot blame him: was not he pro-
        claim'd
By Richard, that dead is, the next of blood?
    North. He was; I heard the proclamation:
And then it was when the unhappy king—
Whose wrongs in us God pardon!—did set forth
Upon his Irish expedition;   *150*
From whence he intercepted did return
To be deposed and shortly murdered.
    Wor. And for whose death we in the world's
        wide mouth
Live scandalized and foully spoken of.
    Hot. But, soft, I pray you; did King Richard then
Proclaim my brother Edmund Mortimer
Heir to the crown?
    North.   He did; myself did hear it.
    Hot. Nay, then I cannot blame his cousin king,
That wish'd him on the barren mountains starve.
But shall it be that you, that set the crown   *160*
Upon the head of this forgetful man
And for his sake wear the detested blot

Of murderous subornation, shall it be
That you a world of curses undergo,
Being the agents, or base second means,
The cords, the ladder, or the hangman rather?
O, pardon me that I descend so low
To show the line and the predicament
Wherein you range under this subtle king;
Shall it for shame be spoken in these days,   *170*
Or fill up chronicles in time to come,
That men of your nobility and power
Did gage them both in an unjust behalf,
As both of you—God pardon it!—have done,
To put down Richard, that sweet lovely rose,
And plant this thorn, this canker, Bolingbroke?
And shall it in more shame be further spoken
That you are fool'd, discarded and shook off
By him for whom these shames ye underwent?
No; yet time serves wherein you may redeem *180*
Your banish'd honours and restore yourselves
Into the good thoughts of the world again,
Revenge the jeering and disdain'd contempt
Of this proud king, who studies day and night
To answer all the debt he owes to you
Even with the bloody payment of your deaths:
Therefore, I say—
    Wor.   Peace, cousin, say no more:
And now I will unclasp a secret book,
And to your quick-conceiving discontents
I'll read you matter deep and dangerous,   *190*
As full of peril and adventurous spirit
As to o'er-walk a current roaring loud
On the unsteadfast footing of a spear.
    Hot. If he fall in, good night! or sink or swim:
Send Danger from the east unto the west,
So Honour cross it from the north to south,
And let them grapple: O, the blood more stirs
To rouse a lion than to start a hare!
    North. Imagination of some great exploit
Drives him beyond the bounds of patience.   *200*
    Hot. By heaven, methinks it were an easy leap,
To pluck bright Honour from the pale-faced
        moon,
Or dive into the bottom of the deep,
Where fathom-line could never touch the
        ground,
And pluck up drowned Honour by the locks;
So he that doth redeem her thence might wear
Without corrival all her dignities:
But out upon this half-faced fellowship!
    Wor. He apprehends a world of figures here,
But not the form of what he should attend.   *210*
Good cousin, give me audience for a while.
    Hot. I cry you mercy.
    Wor.   Those same noble Scots
That are your prisoners—
    Hot.   I'll keep them all;

By God, he shall not have a Scot of them;
No, if a Scot would save his soul, he shall not:
I'll keep them, by this hand.
  Wor.   You start away
And lend no ear unto my purposes.
Those prisoners you shall keep.
  Hot.   Nay, I will; that's flat:
He said he would not ransom Mortimer;
Forbade my tongue to speak of Mortimer; *220*
But I will find him when he lies asleep,
And in his ear I'll holla "Mortimer!"
Nay,
I'll have a starling shall be taught to speak
Nothing but "Mortimer," and give it him,
To keep his anger still in motion.
  Wor. Hear you, cousin; a word.
  Hot. All studies here I solemnly defy,
Save how to gall and pinch this Bolingbroke:
And that same sword-and-buckler Prince of
    Wales, *230*
But that I think his father loves him not
And would be glad he met with some mischance,
I would have him poison'd with a pot of ale.
  Wor. Farewell, kinsman: I'll talk to you
When you are better temper'd to attend.
  North. Why, what a wasp-stung and impatient
    fool
Art thou to break into this woman's mood,
Tying thine ear to no tongue but thine own!
  Hot. Why, look you, I am whipp'd and
    scourged with rods,
Nettled and stung with pismires, when I hear
Of this vile politician, Bolingbroke. *241*
In Richard's time—what do you call the place?—
A plague upon it, it is in Gloucestershire;
'Twas where the madcap duke his uncle kept,
His uncle York; where I first bow'd my knee
Unto this king of smiles, this Bolingbroke—
'Sblood!—
When you and he came back from Ravenspurgh.
  North. At Berkley castle.
  Hot. You say true: *250*
Why, what a candy deal of courtesy
This fawning greyhound then did proffer me!
Look, "when his infant fortune came to age,"
And "gentle Harry Percy," and "kind cousin";
O, the devil take such cozeners! God forgive me!
Good uncle, tell your tale; I have done.
  Wor. Nay, if you have not, to it again;
We will stay your leisure.
  Hot.   I have done, i' faith.
  Wor. Then once more to your Scottish prison-
    ers.
Deliver them up without their ransom straight,
And make the Douglas' son your only mean *261*
For powers in Scotland; which, for divers reasons

Which I shall send you written, be assured,
Will easily be granted. You, my lord,
    To NORTHUMBERLAND.
Your son in Scotland being thus employ'd,
Shall secretly into the bosom creep
Of that same noble prelate, well beloved,
The Archbishop.
  Hot. Of York, is it not?
  Wor. True; who bears hard *270*
His brother's death at Bristol, the Lord Scroop.
I speak not this in estimation,
As what I think might be, but what I know
Is ruminated, plotted, and set down,
And only stays but to behold the face
Of that occasion that shall bring it on.
  Hot. I smell it: upon my life, it will do well.
  North. Before the game is afoot, thou still let'st
    slip.
  Hot. Why, it cannot choose but be a noble plot;
And then the power of Scotland and of York, *280*
To join with Mortimer, ha?
  Wor.   And so they shall.
  Hot. In faith, it is exceedingly well aim'd.
  Wor. And 'tis no little reason bids us speed,
To save our heads by raising of a head;
For, bear ourselves as even as we can,
The King will always think him in our debt,
And think we think ourselves unsatisfied,
Till he hath found a time to pay us home:
And see already how he doth begin
To make us strangers to his looks of love. *290*
  Hot. He does, he does: we'll be revenged on
    him.
  Wor. Cousin, farewell: no further go in this
Than I by letters shall direct your course.
When time is ripe, which will be suddenly,
I'll steal to Glendower and Lord Mortimer;
Where you and Douglas and our powers at once,
As I will fashion it, shall happily meet,
To bear our fortunes in our own strong arms,
Which now we hold at much uncertainty.
  North. Farewell, good brother: we shall thrive,
    I trust. *300*
  Hot. Uncle, adieu: O, let the hours be short
Till fields and blows and groans applaud our
    sport!   [*Exeunt.*

ACT II

SCENE 1. *Rochester: an inn yard*

Enter a CARRIER *with a lantern in his hand.*

  1st Car. Heigh-ho! an it be not four by the day,
I'll be hanged: Charles' wain is over the new
chimney, and yet our horse not packed. What,
ostler!
  Ost. [*Within*] Anon, anon.

1st Car. I prithee, Tom, beat Cut's saddle, put a few flocks in the point; poor jade, is wrung in the withers out of all cess.

Enter a SECOND CARRIER.

2nd Car. Peas and beans are as dank here as a dog, and that is the next way to give poor jades the bots: this house is turned upside down since Robin Ostler died.

1st Car. Poor fellow, never joyed since the price of oats rose; it was the death of him.

2nd Car. I think this be the most villainous house in all London road for fleas: I am stung like a tench.

1st Car. Like a tench! by the mass, there is ne'er a king christen could be better bit than I have been since the first cock.   20

2nd Car. Why, they will allow us ne'er a jordan, and then we leak in your chimney; and your chamber-lie breeds fleas like a loach.

1st Car. What, ostler! come away and be hanged! come away.

2nd Car. I have a gammon of bacon and two razes of ginger, to be delivered as far as Charing-cross.

1st Car. God's body! the turkeys in my pannier are quite starved. What, ostler! A plague on thee! hast thou never an eye in thy head? canst not hear? An 'twere not as good deed as drink, to break the pate on thee, I am a very villain. Come, and be hanged! hast no faith in thee?

Enter GADSHILL.

Gads. Good morrow, carriers. What's o'clock?

1st Car. I think it be two o'clock.

Gads. I prithee, lend me thy lantern, to see my gelding in the stable.

1st Car. Nay, by God, soft; I know a trick worth two of that, i' faith.   41

Gads. I pray thee, lend me thine.

2nd Car. Ay, when? canst tell? Lend me thy lantern, quoth he? marry, I'll see thee hanged first.

Gads. Sirrah carrier, what time do you mean to come to London?

2nd Car. Time enough to go to bed with a candle, I warrant thee. Come, neighbour Mugs, we'll call up the gentlemen: they will along with company, for they have great charge.   51

[*Exeunt* CARRIERS.

Gads. What, ho! chamberlain!

Cham. [*Within*] At hand, quoth pick-purse.

Gads. That's even as fair as—at hand, quoth the chamberlain; for thou variest no more from picking of purses than giving direction doth from labouring; thou layest the plot how.

Enter CHAMBERLAIN.

Cham. Good morrow, Master Gadshill. It holds current that I told you yesternight: there's a franklin in the Wild of Kent hath brought three hundred marks with him in gold: I heard him tell it to one of his company last night at supper; a kind of auditor; one that hath abundance of charge too, God knows what. They are up already, and call for eggs and butter: they will away presently.

Gads. Sirrah, if they meet not with Saint Nicholas' clerks, I'll give thee this neck.   69

Cham. No, I'll none of it: I pray thee, keep that for the hangman; for I know thou worshippest Saint Nicholas as truly as a man of falsehood may.

Gads. What talkest thou to me of the hangman? if I hang, I'll make a fat pair of gallows; for if I hang, old Sir John hangs with me, and thou knowest he is no starveling. Tut! there are other Trojans that thou dreamest not of, the which for sport sake are content to do the profession some grace; that would, if matters should be looked into, for their own credit sake, make all whole. I am joined with no foot land-rakers, no long-staff sixpenny strikers, none of these mad mustachio purple-hued malt-worms; but with nobility and tranquility, burgomasters and great oneyers, such as can hold in, such as will strike sooner than speak, and speak sooner than drink, and drink sooner than pray: and yet, 'zounds, I lie; for they pray continually to their saint, the commonwealth; or rather, not pray to her, but prey on her, for they ride up and down on her and make her their boots.   91

Cham. What, the commonwealth their boots? will she hold out water in foul way?

Gads. She will, she will; justice hath liquored her. We steal as in a castle, cock-sure; we have the receipt of fern-seed, we walk invisible.

Cham. Nay, by my faith, I think you are more beholding to the night than to fern-seed for your walking invisible.

Gads. Give me thy hand: thou shalt have a share in our purchase, as I am a true man.   101

Cham. Nay, rather let me have it, as you are a false thief.

Gads. Go to; *homo* is a common name to all men. Bid the ostler bring my gelding out of the stable. Farewell, you muddy knave.   [*Exeunt.*

SCENE II. *The highway, near Gadshill*

Enter PRINCE HENRY *and* POINS.

Poins. Come, shelter, shelter: I have removed

Falstaff's horse, and he frets like a gummed velvet.

Prince. Stand close.

Enter FALSTAFF.

Fal. Poins! Poins, and be hanged! Poins!

Prince. Peace, ye fat-kidneyed rascal! what a brawling dost thou keep!

Fal. Where's Poins, Hal?

Prince. He is walked up to the top of the hill: I'll go seek him.   9

Fal. I am accursed to rob in that thief's company: the rascal hath removed my horse, and tied him I know not where. If I travel but four foot by the squire further afoot, I shall break my wind. Well, I doubt not but to die a fair death for all this, if I 'scape hanging for killing that rogue. I have forsworn his company hourly any time this two and twenty years, and yet I am bewitched with the rogue's company. If the rascal have not given me medicines to make me love him, I'll be hanged; it could not be else; I have drunk medicines. Poins! Hal! a plague upon you both! Bardolph! Peto! I'll starve ere I'll rob a foot further. An 'twere not as good a deed as drink, to turn true man and to leave these rogues, I am the veriest varlet that ever chewed with a tooth. Eight yards of uneven ground is three-score and ten miles afoot with me; and the stony-hearted villains know it well enough: a plague upon it when thieves cannot be true one to another! [*They whistle.*] Whew! A plague upon you all! Give me my horse, you rogues; give me my horse, and be hanged!

Prince. Peace, ye fat-guts! lie down; lay thine ear close to the ground and list if thou canst hear the tread of travellers.

Fal. Have you any levers to lift me up again, being down? 'Sblood, I'll not bear mine own flesh so far afoot again for all the coin in thy father's exchequer. What a plague mean ye to colt me thus?   40

Prince. Thou liest; thou art not colted, thou art uncolted.

Fal. I prithee, good Prince Hal, help me to my horse, good king's son.

Prince. Out, ye rogue! shall I be your ostler?

Fal. Go hang thyself in thine own heir-apparent garters! If I be ta'en, I'll peach for this. An I have not ballads made on you all and sung to filthy tunes, let a cup of sack be my poison: when a jest is so forward, and afoot too! I hate it.

Enter GADSHILL, BARDOLPH *and* PETO *with him.*

Gads. Stand.

Fal. So I do, against my will.

Poins. O, 'tis our setter: I know his voice. Bardolph, what news?

Bard. Case ye, case ye; on with your vizards: there's money of the King's coming down the hill; 'tis going to the King's exchequer.

Fal. You lie, ye rogue; 'tis going to the King's tavern.

Gads. There's enough to make us all.   60

Fal. To be hanged.

Prince. Sirs, you four shall front them in the narrow lane; Ned Poins and I will walk lower: if they 'scape from your encounter, then they light on us.

Peto. How many be there of them?

Gads. Some eight or ten.

Fal. 'Zounds, will they not rob us?

Prince. What, a coward, Sir John Paunch?

Fal. Indeed, I am not John of Gaunt, your grandfather; but yet no coward, Hal.   71

Prince. Well, we leave that to the proof.

Poins. Sirrah Jack, thy horse stands behind the hedge: when thou needest him, there thou shalt find him. Farewell, and stand fast.

Fal. Now cannot I strike him, if I should be hanged.

Prince. Ned, where are our disguises?

Poins. Here, hard by: stand close.

[*Exeunt* PRINCE *and* POINS.

Fal. Now, my masters, happy man be his dole, say I; every man to his business.

Enter the TRAVELLERS.

1st Trav. Come, neighbour: the boy shall lead our horses down the hill; we'll walk afoot awhile, and ease our legs.

Thieves. Stand!

Travellers. Jesus bless us!

Fal. Strike; down with them; cut the villains' throats: ah! whoreson caterpillars! bacon-fed knaves! they hate us youth: down with them: fleece them.

Travellers. O, we are undone, both we and ours for ever!

Fal. Hang ye, gorbellied knaves, are ye undone? No, ye fat chuffs; I would your store were here! On, bacons, on! What, ye knaves! young men must live. You are grandjurors, are ye? we'll jure ye, 'faith.

[*Here they rob them and bind them. Exeunt.*

Re-enter PRINCE HENRY *and* POINS *in buckram.*

Prince. The thieves have bound the true men. Now could thou and I rob the thieves and go merrily to London, it would be argument for a week, laughter for a month and a good jest for ever.

Poins. Stand close; I hear them coming.

    Enter the THIEVES *again.*

Fal. Come, my masters, let us share, and then
to horse before day. An the Prince and Poins be
not two arrant cowards, there's no equity stirring: there's no more valour in that Poins than in
a wild-duck.

Prince. Your money!

Poins. Villains!   *110*

    As they are sharing, the PRINCE *and* POINS *set
    upon them; they all run away; and* FALSTAFF,
    *after a blow or two, runs away too, leaving the
    booty behind them.*

Prince. Got with much ease. Now merrily to
    horse:
The thieves are all scatter'd and possess'd with
    fear
So strongly that they dare not meet each other;
Each takes his fellow for an officer.
Away, good Ned. Falstaff sweats to death,
And lards the lean earth as he walks along:
Were 't not for laughing, I should pity him.

Poins. How the rogue roar'd!   [*Exeunt.*

    SCENE III. *Warkworth castle*

    Enter HOTSPUR, *solus, reading a letter.*

Hot. "But, for mine own part, my lord, I could
be well contented to be there, in respect of the
love I bear your house." He could be contented:
why is he not, then? In respect of the love he
bears our house: he shows in this, he loves his
own barn better than he loves our house. Let me
see some more. "The purpose you undertake is
dangerous"; why, that's certain: 'tis dangerous
to take a cold, to sleep, to drink; but I tell you,
my lord fool, out of this nettle, danger, we pluck
this flower, safety. "The purpose you undertake
is dangerous; the friends you have named uncertain; the time itself unsorted; and your whole
plot too light for the counterpoise of so great an
opposition." Say you so, say you so? I say unto
you again, you are a shallow cowardly hind, and
you lie. What a lack-brain is this! By the Lord,
our plot is a good plot as ever was laid; our
friends true and constant: a good plot, good
friends, and full of expectation; an excellent plot,
very good friends. What a frosty-spirited rogue
is this! Why, my lord of York commends the
plot and the general course of the action. 'Zounds,
an I were now by this rascal, I could brain him
with his lady's fan. Is there not my father, my
uncle and myself? lord Edmund Mortimer, my
lord of York and Owen Glendower? is there not
besides the Douglas? have I not all their letters
to meet me in arms by the ninth of next month?

and are they not some of them set forward already? What a pagan rascal is this! an infidel!
Ha! you shall see now in very sincerity of fear
and cold heart, will he to the King and lay open
all our proceedings. O, I could divide myself and
go to buffets, for moving such a dish of skim
milk with so honourable an action! Hang him!
let him tell the King: we are prepared. I will set
forward to-night.

    Enter LADY PERCY.

How now, Kate! I must leave you within these
    two hours.

    Lady. O, my good lord, why are you thus
      alone?   *40*
For what offence have I this fortnight been
A banish'd woman from my Harry's bed?
Tell me, sweet lord, what is't that takes from
    thee
Thy stomach, pleasure, and thy golden sleep?
Why dost thou bend thine eyes upon the earth,
And start so often when thou sit'st alone?
Why hast thou lost the fresh blood in thy cheeks;
And given my treasures and my rights of thee
To thick-eyed musing and cursed melancholy?
In thy faint slumbers I by thee have watch'd,   *50*
And heard thee murmur tales of iron wars;
Speak terms of manage to thy bounding steed;
Cry "Courage! to the field!" And thou hast
    talk'd
Of sallies and retires, of trenches, tents,
Of palisadoes, frontiers, parapets,
Of basilisks, of cannon, culverin,
Of prisoners' ransom, and of soldiers slain,
And all the currents of a heady fight.
Thy spirit within thee hath been so at war
And thus hath so bestirr'd thee in thy sleep,   *60*
That beads of sweat have stood upon thy brow,
Like bubbles in a late-disturbed stream;
And in thy face strange motions have appear'd,
Such as we see when men restrain their breath
On some great sudden hest. O, what portents are
    these?
Some heavy business hath my lord in hand,
And I must know it, else he loves me not.

    Hot. What, ho!

    Enter SERVANT.

                Is Gilliams with the packet gone?

Serv. He is, my lord, an hour ago.

Hot. Hath Butler brought those horses from the
    sheriff?   *70*

Serv. One horse, my lord, he brought even now.

Hot. What horse? a roan, a crop-ear, is it not?

Serv. It is, my lord.

Hot.   That roan shall be my throne.

Well, I will back him straight: O *esperance!*
Bid Butler lead him forth into the park.
                                    [*Exit* SERVANT.

Lady. But hear you, my lord.
Hot. What say'st thou, my lady?
Lady. What is it carries you away?
Hot. Why, my horse, my love, my horse.
Lady. Out, you mad-headed ape!   80
A weasel hath not such a deal of spleen
As you are toss'd with. In faith,
I'll know your business, Harry, that I will.
I fear my brother Mortimer doth stir
About his title, and hath sent for you
To line his enterprize: but if you go—
Hot. So far afoot, I shall be weary, love.
Lady. Come, come, you paraquito, answer me
Directly unto this question that I ask:
In faith, I'll break thy little finger, Harry,   90
An if thou wilt not tell me all things true.
Hot. Away,
Away, you trifler! Love! I love thee not,
I care not for thee, Kate: this is no world
To play with mammets and to tilt with lips:
We must have bloody noses and crack'd crowns,
And pass them current too. God's me, my horse!
What say'st thou, Kate? what would'st thou
      have with me?
Lady. Do you not love me? do you not, indeed?
Well, do not then; for since you love me not, 100
I will not love myself. Do you not love me?
Nay, tell me if you speak in jest or no.
Hot. Come, wilt thou see me ride?
And when I am o' horseback, I will swear
I love thee infinitely. But hark you, Kate;
i must not have you henceforth question me
Whither I go, nor reason whereabout:
Whither I must, I must; and, to conclude,
This evening must I leave you, gentle Kate.
I know you wise, but yet no farther wise   110
Than Harry Percy's wife: constant you are,
But yet a woman: and for secrecy,
No lady closer; for I well believe
Thou wilt not utter what thou dost not know;
And so far will I trust thee, gentle Kate.
Lady. How! so far?
Hot. Not an inch further. But hark you, Kate:
Whither I go, thither shall you go too;
To-day will I set forth, to-morrow you.
Will this content you, Kate?
Lady.   It must of force. [*Exeunt.* 120

SCENE IV. *The Boar's-Head Tavern, Eastcheap*
      Enter the PRINCE, *and* POINS.

Prince. Ned, prithee, come out of that fat room,
and lend me thy hand to laugh a little.
Poins. Where hast been, Hal?

Prince. With three or four loggerheads amongst
three or four score hogsheads. I have sounded
the very base-string of humility. Sirrah, I am
sworn brother to a leash of drawers; and can
call them all by their christen names, as Tom, Dick,
and Francis. They take it already upon their salvation, that though I be but Prince of Wales, yet
I am the king of courtesy; and tell me flatly I am
no proud Jack, like Falstaff, but a Corinthian, a
lad of mettle, a good boy, by the Lord, so they
call me, and when I am King of England, I shall
command all the good lads in Eastcheap. They
call drinking deep, dyeing scarlet; and when you
breathe in your watering, they cry "hem!" and
bid you play it off. To conclude, I am so good a
proficient in one quarter of an hour, that I can
drink with any tinker in his own language during
my life. I tell thee, Ned, thou hast lost much
honour, that thou wert not with me in this action.
But, sweet Ned—to sweeten which name of Ned,
I give thee this pennyworth of sugar, clapped
even now into my hand by an under-skinker, one
that never spake other English in his life than
"Eight shillings and sixpence," and "You are
welcome," with this shrill addition, "Anon,
anon, sir! Score a pint of bastard in the Half-
moon," or so. But, Ned, to drive away the time
till Falstaff come, I prithee, do thou stand in
some by-room, while I question my puny drawer
to what end he gave me the sugar; and do thou
never leave calling "Francis," that his tale to me
may be nothing but "Anon." Step aside, and I'll
show thee a precedent.
Poins. Francis!
Prince. Thou art perfect.
Poins. Francis!   [*Exit* POINS. 40

            Enter FRANCIS.

Fran. Anon, anon, sir. Look down into the
Pomgarnet, Ralph.
Prince. Come hither, Francis.
Fran. My lord?
Prince. How long hast thou to serve, Francis?
Fran. Forsooth, five years, and as much as to—
Poins. [*Within*] Francis!
Fran. Anon, anon, sir.   49
Prince. Five year! by'r lady, a long lease for the
clinking of pewter. But, Francis, darest thou be
so valiant as to play the coward with thy inden-
ture and show it a fair pair of heels and run from
it?
Fran. O Lord, sir, I'll be sworn upon all the
books in England, I could find in my heart.
Poins. [*Within*] Francis!
Fran. Anon, sir.
Prince. How old art thou, Francis?

Fran. Let me see—about Michaelmas next I shall be—   *61*

Poins. [*Within*] Francis!

Fran. Anon, sir. Pray stay a little, my lord.

Prince. Nay, but hark you, Francis: for the sugar thou gavest me, 'twas a pennyworth, was't not?

Fran. O Lord, I would it had been two!

Prince. I will give thee for it a thousand pound: ask me when thou wilt, and thou shalt have it. *70*

Poins. [*Within*] Francis!

Fran. Anon, anon.

Prince. Anon, Francis? No, Francis; but to-morrow, Francis; or Francis, o' Thursday; or indeed, Francis, when thou wilt. But, Francis!

Fran. My lord?

Prince. Wilt thou rob this leathern jerkin, crystal-button, not-pated, agate-ring, puke-stocking, caddis-garter, smooth-tongue, Spanish-pouch,—

Fran. O Lord, sir, who do you mean?   *81*

Prince. Why, then, your brown bastard is your only drink; for look you, Francis, your white canvas doublet will sully: in Barbary, sir, it cannot come to so much.

Fran. What, sir?

Poins. [*Within*] Francis!

Prince. Away, you rogue! dost thou not hear them call? [*Here they both call him; the drawer stands amazed, not knowing which way to go.*

Enter VINTNER.

Vint. What, standest thou still, and hearest such a calling? Look to the guests within. [*Exit FRANCIS.*] My lord, old Sir John, with half-a-dozen more, are at the door: shall I let them in?

Prince. Let them alone awhile, and then open the door. [*Exit VINTNER.*] Poins!

Re-enter POINS.

Poins. Anon, anon, sir.

Prince. Sirrah, Falstaff and the rest of the thieves are at the door: shall we be merry?   *99*

Poins. As merry as crickets, my lad. But hark ye; what cunning match have you made with this jest of the drawer? come, what's the issue?

Prince. I am now of all humours that have showed themselves humours since the old days of goodman Adam to the pupil age of this present twelve o'clock at midnight.

Re-enter FRANCIS.

What's o'clock, Francis?

Fran. Anon, anon, sir.   [*Exit.* *109*

Prince. That ever this fellow should have fewer words than a parrot, and yet the son of a woman!

His industry is up-stairs and down-stairs; his eloquence the parcel of a reckoning. I am not yet of Percy's mind, the Hotspur of the north; he that kills me some six or seven dozen of Scots at a breakfast, washes his hands, and says to his wife, "Fie upon this quiet life! I want work." "O, my sweet Harry," says she, "how many hast thou killed to-day?" "Give my roan horse a drench," says he; and answers "Some fourteen," an hour after; "a trifle, a trifle." I prithee, call in Falstaff: I'll play Percy, and that damned brawn shall play Dame Mortimer his wife. "Rivo!" says the drunkard. Call in ribs, call in tallow.

Enter FALSTAFF, GADSHILL, BARDOLPH, *and* PETO; FRANCIS *following with wine.*

Poins. Welcome, Jack: where hast thou been?

Fal. A plague of all cowards, I say, and a vengeance too! marry, and amen! Give me a cup of sack, boy. Ere I lead this life long, I'll sew nether stocks and mend them and foot them too. A plague of all cowards! Give me a cup of sack, rogue. Is there no virtue extant?

He drinks.

Prince. Didst thou never see Titan kiss a dish of butter? pitiful-hearted Titan, that melted at the sweet tale of the sun's! if thou didst, then behold that compound.

Fal. You rogue, here's lime in this sack too: there is nothing but roguery to be found in villainous man: yet a coward is worse than a cup of sack with lime in it. A villainous coward! Go thy ways, old Jack; die when thou wilt, if manhood, good manhood, be not forgot upon the face of the earth, then am I a shotten herring. There live not three good men unhanged in England; and one of them is fat and grows old: God help the while! a bad world, I say. I would I were a weaver; I could sing psalms or anything. A plague of all cowards, I say still.

Prince. How now, wool-sack! what mutter you?   *149*

Fal. A king's son! If I do not beat thee out of thy kingdom with a dagger of lath, and drive all thy subjects afore thee like a flock of wild-geese, I'll never wear hair on my face more. You Prince of Wales!

Prince. Why, you whoreson round man, what's the matter?

Fal. Are not you a coward? answer me to that: and Poins there?

Poins. 'Zounds, ye fat paunch, an ye call me coward, by the Lord, I'll stab thee.   *160*

Fal. I call thee coward! I'll see thee damned ere I call thee coward: but I would give a thousand pound I could run as fast as thou canst. You are straight enough in the shoulders, you care not who sees your back: call you that backing of your friends? A plague upon such backing! give me them that will face me. Give me a cup of sack: I am a rogue, if I drunk to-day.

Prince. O villain! thy lips are scarce wiped since thou drunkest last. 171

Fal. All's one for that. [*He drinks.*] A plague of all cowards, still say I.

Prince. What's the matter?

Fal. What's the matter! there be four of us here have ta'en a thousand pound this day morning.

Prince. Where is it, Jack? where is it?

Fal. Where is it! taken from us it is: a hundred upon poor four of us. 180

Prince. What, a hundred, man?

Fal. I am a rogue, if I were not at half-sword with a dozen of them two hours together. I have 'scaped by miracle. I am eight times thrust through the doublet, four through the hose; my buckler cut through and through; my sword hacked like a hand-saw—*ecce signum!* I never dealt better since I was a man: all would not do. A plague of all cowards! Let them speak: if they speak more or less than truth, they are villains and the sons of darkness. 191

Prince. Speak, sirs; how was it?

Gads. We four set upon some dozen—

Fal. Sixteen at least, my lord.

Gads. And bound them.

Peto. No, no, they were not bound.

Fal. You rogue, they were bound, every man of them; or I am a Jew else, an Ebrew Jew.

Gads. As we were sharing, some six or seven fresh men set upon us— 200

Fal. And unbound the rest, and then come in the other.

Prince. What, fought you with them all?

Fal. All! I know not what you call all; but if I fought not with fifty of them, I am a bunch of radish: if there were not two or three and fifty upon poor old Jack, then am I no two-legged creature.

Prince. Pray God you have not murdered some of them. 210

Fal. Nay, that's past praying for: I have peppered two of them; two I am sure I have paid, two rogues in buckram suits. I tell thee what, Hal, if I tell thee a lie, spit in my face, call me horse. Thou knowest my old ward; here I lay, and thus I bore my point. Four rogues in buckram let drive at me—

Prince. What, four? thou saidst but two even now.

Fal. Four, Hal; I told thee four. 220

Poins. Ay, ay, he said four.

Fal. These four came all a-front, and mainly thrust at me. I made me no more ado but took all their seven points in my target, thus.

Prince. Seven? why, there were but four even now.

Fal. In buckram?

Poins. Ay, four, in buckram suits.

Fal. Seven, by these hilts, or I am a villain else.

Prince. Prithee, let him alone; we shall have more anon. 232

Fal. Dost thou hear me, Hal?

Prince. Ay, and mark thee too, Jack.

Fal. Do so, for it is worth the listening to. These nine in buckram that I told thee of—

Prince. So, two more already.

Fal. Their points being broken—

Poins. Down fell their hose. 239

Fal. Began to give me ground: but I followed me close, came in foot and hand; and with a thought seven of the eleven I paid.

Prince. O monstrous! eleven buckram men grown out of two!

Fal. But, as the devil would have it, three misbegotten knaves in Kendal green came at my back and let drive at me; for it was so dark, Hal, that thou couldst not see thy hand.

Prince. These lies are like their father that begets them; gross as a mountain, open, palpable. Why, thou clay-brained guts, thou knotty-pated fool, thou whoreson, obscene, greasy tallowcatch—

Fal. What, art thou mad? art thou mad? is not the truth the truth?

Prince. Why, how couldst thou know these men in Kendal green, when it was so dark thou couldst not see thy hand? come, tell us your reason: what sayest thou to this? 259

Poins. Come, your reason, Jack, your reason.

Fal. What, upon compulsion? 'Zounds, an I were at the strappado, or all the racks in the world, I would not tell you on compulsion. Give you a reason on compulsion! if reasons were as plentiful as blackberries, I would give no man a reason upon compulsion, I.

Prince. I'll be no longer guilty of this sin; this sanguine coward, this bed-presser, this horseback-breaker, this huge hill of flesh— 269

Fal. 'Sblood, you starveling, you elf-skin, you dried neat's tongue, you bull's pizzle, you stockfish! O for breath to utter what is like thee! you tailor's-yard, you sheath, you bow-case, you vile standing-tuck—

Prince. Well, breathe awhile, and then to it again: and when thou hast tired thyself in base comparisons, hear me speak but this.

Poins. Mark, Jack.

Prince. We two saw you four set on four and bound them, and were masters of their wealth. Mark now, how a plain tale shall put you down. Then did we two set on you four; and, with a word, out-faced you from your prize, and have it; yea, and can show it you here in the house: and, Falstaff, you carried your guts away as nimbly, with as quick dexterity, and roared for mercy and still run and roared, as ever I heard bull-calf. What a slave art thou, to hack thy sword as thou hast done, and then say it was in fight! What trick, what device, what starting-hole, canst thou now find out to hide thee from this open and apparent shame?

Poins. Come, let's hear, Jack; what trick hast thou now?

Fal. By the Lord, I knew ye as well as he that made ye. Why, hear you, my masters: was it for me to kill the heir-apparent? should I turn upon the true prince? why, thou knowest I am as valiant as Hercules: but beware instinct; the lion will not touch the true prince. Instinct is a great matter; I was now a coward on instinct. I shall think the better of myself and thee during my life; I for a valiant lion, and thou for a true prince. But, by the Lord, lads, I am glad you have the money. Hostess, clap to the doors: watch to-night, pray to-morrow. Gallants, lads, boys, hearts of gold, all the titles of good fellowship come to you! What, shall we be merry? shall we have a play extempore?

Prince. Content; and the argument shall be thy running away.   *311*

Fal. Ah, no more of that, Hal, an thou lovest me!

Enter MISTRESS QUICKLY, *the Hostess.*

Quick. O Jesu, my lord the prince!

Prince. How now, my lady the hostess! what sayest thou to me?

Quick. Marry, my lord, there is a nobleman of the court at door would speak with you: he says he comes from your father.   *319*

Prince. Give him as much as will make him a royal man, and send him back again to my mother.

Fal. What manner of man is he?

Quick. An old man.

Fal. What doth gravity out of his bed at midnight? Shall I give him his answer?

Prince. Prithee, do, Jack.

Fal. 'Faith, and I'll send him packing.   [*Exit.*

Prince. Now, sirs: by'r lady, you fought fair; so did you, Peto; so did you, Bardolph: you are

lions too, you ran away upon instinct, you will not touch the true prince; no, fie!

Bard. 'Faith, I ran when I saw others run.

Prince. 'Faith, tell me now in earnest, how came Falstaff's sword so hacked?

Peto. Why, he hacked it with his dagger, and said he would swear truth out of England but he would make you believe it was done in fight, and persuaded us to do the like.   *339*

Bard. Yea, and to tickle our noses with spear-grass to make them bleed, and then to beslubber our garments with it and swear it was the blood of true men. I did that I did not this seven year before, I blushed to hear his monstrous devices.

Prince. O villain, thou stolest a cup of sack eighteen years ago, and wert taken with the manner, and ever since thou hast blushed extempore. Thou hadst fire and sword on thy side, and yet thou rannest away: what instinct hadst thou for it?   *350*

Bard. My lord, do you see these meteors? do you behold these exhalations?

Prince. I do.

Bard. What think you they portend?

Prince. Hot livers and cold purses.

Bard. Choler, my lord, if rightly taken.

Prince. No, if rightly taken, halter.

Re-enter FALSTAFF.

Here comes lean Jack, here comes bare-bone. How now, my sweet creature of bombast! How long is't ago, Jack, since thou sawest thine own knee?   *361*

Fal. My own knee! when I was about thy years, Hal, I was not an eagle's talon in the waist; I could have crept into any alderman's thumb-ring: a plague of sighing and grief! it blows a man up like a bladder. There's villainous news abroad: here was Sir John Bracy from your father; you must to the court in the morning. That same mad fellow of the north, Percy, and he of Wales, that gave Amamon the bastinado and made Lucifer cuckold and swore the devil his true liegeman upon the cross of a Welsh hook—what a plague call you him?

Poins. O, Glendower.

Fal. Owen, Owen, the same; and his son-in-law Mortimer, and old Northumberland, and that sprightly Scot of Scots, Douglas, that runs o' horseback up a hill perpendicular—

Prince. He that rides at high speed and with his pistol kills a sparrow flying.   *380*

Fal. You have hit it.

Prince. So did he never the sparrow.

Fal. Well, that rascal hath good mettle in him; he will not run.

Prince. Why, what a rascal art thou then, to praise him so for running!

Fal. O' horseback, ye cuckoo; but afoot he will not budge a foot.

Prince. Yes, Jack, upon instinct.   389

Fal. I grant ye, upon instinct. Well, he is there too, and one Mordake, and a thousand blue-caps more: Worcester is stolen away to-night; thy father's beard is turned white with the news: you may buy land now as cheap as stinking mackerel.

Prince. Why, then, it is like, if there come a hot June and this civil buffeting hold, we shall buy maidenheads as they buy hob-nails, by the hundreds.   399

Fal. By the mass, lad, thou sayest true; it is like we shall have good trading that way. But tell me, Hal, art not thou horrible afeard? thou being heir-apparent, could the world pick thee out three such enemies again as that fiend Douglas, that spirit Percy, and that devil Glendower? Art thou not horribly afraid? doth not thy blood thrill at it?

Prince. Not a whit, i' faith; I lack some of thy instinct.   409

Fal. Well, thou wilt be horribly chid to-morrow when thou comest to thy father: if thou love me, practise an answer.

Prince. Do thou stand for my father, and examine me upon the particulars of my life?

Fal. Shall I? content: this chair shall be my state, this dagger my sceptre, and this cushion my crown.

Prince. Thy state is taken for a joined-stool, thy golden sceptre for a leaden dagger, and thy precious rich crown for a pitiful bald crown!   420

Fal. Well, an the fire of grace be not quite out of thee, now shalt thou be moved. Give me a cup of sack to make my eyes look red, that it may be thought I have wept; for I must speak in passion, and I will do it in King Cambyses' vein.

Prince. Well, here is my leg.

Fal. And here is my speech. Stand aside, nobility.   429

Quick. O Jesu, this is excellent sport, i' faith!

Fal. Weep not, sweet queen; for trickling tears are vain.

Quick. O, the father, how he holds his countenance!

Fal. For God's sake, lords, convey my tristful queen;
For tears do stop the flood-gates of her eyes.

Quick. O Jesu, he doth it as like one of these harlotry players as ever I see!

Fal. Peace, good pint-pot; peace, good ticklebrain. Harry, I do not only marvel where thou spendest thy time, but also how thou art accompanied: for though the camomile, the more it is trodden on the faster it grows, yet youth, the more it is wasted the sooner it wears. That thou art my son, I have partly thy mother's word, partly my own opinion, but chiefly a villainous trick of thine eye and a foolish hanging of thy nether lip, that doth warrant me. If then thou be son to me, here lies the point; why, being son to me, art thou so pointed at? Shall the blessed sun of heaven prove a micher and eat blackberries? a question not to be asked. Shall the son of England prove a thief and take purses? a question to be asked. There is a thing, Harry, which thou hast often heard of and it is known to many in our land by the name of pitch: this pitch, as ancient writers do report, doth defile; so doth the company thou keepest: for, Harry, now I do not speak to thee in drink but in tears, not in pleasure but in passion, not in words only, but in woes also: and yet there is a virtuous man whom I have often noted in thy company, but I know not his name.   461

Prince. What manner of man, an it like your Majesty?

Fal. A goodly portly man, i' faith, and a corpulent; of a cheerful look, a pleasing eye, and a most noble carriage; and, as I think, his age some fifty, or, by'r lady, inclining to three score; and now I remember me, his name is Falstaff: if that man should be lewdly given, he deceiveth me; for, Harry, I see virtue in his looks. If then the tree may be known by the fruit, as the fruit by the tree, then peremptorily I speak it, there is virtue in that Falstaff: him keep with, the rest banish. And tell me now, thou naughty varlet, tell me, where hast thou been this month?

Prince. Dost thou speak like a king? Do thou stand for me, and I'll play my father.

Fal. Depose me? if thou dost it half so gravely, so majestically, both in word and matter, hang me up by the heels for a rabbit-sucker or a poulter's hare.   481

Prince. Well, here I am set.

Fal. And here I stand: judge, my masters.

Prince. Now, Harry, whence come you?

Fal. My noble lord, from Eastcheap.

Prince. The complaints I hear of thee are grievous.

Fal. 'Sblood, my lord, they are false: nay, I'll tickle ye for a young prince, i' faith.   489

Prince. Swearest thou, ungracious boy? henceforth ne'er look on me. Thou art violently carried away from grace: there is a devil haunts thee in the likeness of an old fat man; a tun of man is thy companion. Why dost thou converse with that trunk of humours, that bolting-hutch of beastliness, that swollen parcel of dropsies, that huge bombard of sack, that stuffed cloak-bag of guts, that roasted Manningtree ox with the pudding in his belly, that reverend vice, that grey iniquity, that father ruffian, that vanity in years? Wherein is he good, but to taste sack and drink it? wherein neat and cleanly, but to carve a capon and eat it? wherein cunning, but in craft? wherein crafty, but in villainy? wherein villainous, but in all things? wherein worthy, but in nothing?

Fal. I would your Grace would take me with you: whom means your Grace?

Prince. That villainous abominable misleader of youth, Falstaff, that old white-bearded Satan.

Fal. My lord, the man I know.   *510*

Prince. I know thou dost.

Fal. But to say I know more harm in him than in myself, were to say more than I know. That he is old, the more the pity, his white hairs do witness it; but that he is, saving your reverence, a whoremaster, that I utterly deny. If sack and sugar be a fault, God help the wicked! if to be old and merry be a sin, then many an old host that I know is damned: if to be fat be to be hated, then Pharaoh's lean kine are to be loved. No, my good lord; banish Peto, banish Bardolph, banish Poins: but for sweet Jack Falstaff, kind Jack Falstaff, true Jack Falstaff, valiant Jack Falstaff, and therefore more valiant, being, as he is, old Jack Falstaff, banish not him thy Harry's company, banish not him thy Harry's company: banish plump Jack, and banish all the world.

Prince. I do, I will. [*A knocking heard. Exeunt* MISTRESS QUICKLY, FRANCIS, *and* BARDOLPH.

Re-enter BARDOLPH, *running.*

Bard. O, my lord, my lord! the sheriff with a most monstrous watch is at the door.   *530*

Fal. Out, ye rogue! Play out the play; I have much to say in the behalf of that Falstaff.

Re-enter MISTRESS QUICKLY.

Quick. O Jesu, my lord, my lord!

Prince. Heigh, heigh! the devil rides upon a fiddlestick: what's the matter?

Quick. The sheriff and all the watch are at the door: they are come to search the house. Shall I let them in?

Fal. Dost thou hear, Hal? never call a true piece of gold a counterfeit: thou art essentially mad, without seeming so.   *541*

Prince. And thou a natural coward, without instinct.

Fal. I deny your major: if you will deny the sheriff, so; if not, let him enter: if I become not a cart as well as another man, a plague on my

bringing up! I hope I shall as soon be strangled with a halter as another.

Prince. Go, hide thee behind the arras: the rest walk up above. Now, my masters, for a true face and good conscience.   *551*

Fal. Both which I have had: but their date is out, and therefore I'll hide me.

Prince. Call in the sheriff.

     [*Exeunt all except the* PRINCE *and* PETO.

Enter SHERIFF *and the* FIRST CARRIER.

Now, master sheriff, what is your will with me?

Sher. First, pardon me, my lord. A hue and cry Hath follow'd certain men unto this house.

Prince. What men?

Sher. One of them is well known, my gracious lord,
A gross fat man.

1st Car.   As fat as butter.   *560*

Prince. The man, I do assure you, is not here;
For I myself at this time have employ'd him.
And, sheriff, I will engage my word to thee
That I will, by to-morrow dinner-time,
Send him to answer thee, or any man,
For anything he shall be charged withal:
And so let me entreat you leave the house.

Sher. I will, my lord. There are two gentlemen
Have in this robbery lost three hundred marks.

Prince. It may be so: if he have robb'd these men,   *570*
He shall be answerable; and so farewell.

Sher. Good night, my noble lord.

Prince. I think it is good morrow, is it not?

Sher. Indeed, my lord, I think it be two o'clock.

     [*Exeunt* SHERIFF *and* FIRST CARRIER.

Prince. This oily rascal is known as well as Paul's. Go, call him forth.

Peto. Falstaff!—Fast asleep behind the arras, and snorting like a horse.

Prince. Hark, how hard he fetches breath. Search his pockets. [*He searcheth his pockets, and findeth certain papers.*] What hast thou found?

Peto. Nothing but papers, my lord.

Prince. Let's see what they be: read them.

Peto. [*Reads*] "Item, A capon, .   . 2s. 2d.
         Item, Sauce,   .   . 4d.
         Item, Sack, two gallons, . 5s. 8d.
         Item, Anchovies and sack
             after supper,   . 2s. 6d.
         Item, Bread,   .   . ob."

Prince. O monstrous! but one half-penny-worth of bread to this intolerable deal of sack! What there is else, keep close; we'll read it at more advantage: there let him sleep till day. I'll to the court in the morning. We must all to the wars, and thy place shall be honourable. I'll procure

this fat rogue a charge of foot; and I know his
death will be a march of twelve-score. The
money shall be paid back again with advantage.
Be with me betimes in the morning; and so, good
morrow, Peto.   *601*

Peto. Good morrow, good my lord.   [*Exeunt.*

ACT III

Scene i. *Bangor: The Archdeacon's house*

Enter HOTSPUR, WORCESTER, MORTIMER, *and*
                    GLENDOWER

Mort. These promises are fair, the parties sure,
And our induction full of prosperous hope.

Hot. Lord Mortimer, and cousin Glendower,
Will you sit down?
And Uncle Worcester: a plague upon it!
I have forgot the map.

Glend.   No, here it is.
Sit, cousin Percy; sit, good cousin Hotspur,
For by that name as oft as Lancaster
Doth speak of you, his cheek looks pale and with
A rising sigh he wisheth you in heaven.   *10*

Hot. And you in hell, as oft as he hears Owen
Glendower spoke of.

Glend. I cannot blame him: at my nativity
The front of heaven was full of fiery shapes,
Of burning cressets; and at my birth
The frame and huge foundation of the earth
Shaked like a coward.

Hot. Why, so it would have done at the same
season, if your mother's cat had but kittened,
though yourself had never been born.   *20*

Glend. I say the earth did shake when I was
born.

Hot. And I say the earth was not of my mind,
If you suppose as fearing you it shook.

Glend. The heavens were all on fire, the earth
did tremble.

Hot. O, then the earth shook to see the heavens
on fire,
And not in fear of your nativity.
Diseased nature oftentimes breaks forth
In strange eruptions; oft the teeming earth
Is with a kind of colic pinch'd and vex'd
By the imprisoning of unruly wind   *30*
Within her womb; which, for enlargement striv-
ing,
Shakes the old beldam earth and topples down
Steeples and moss-grown towers. At your birth
Our grandam earth, having this distemperature,
In passion shook.

Glend.   Cousin, of many men
I do not bear these crossings. Give me leave
To tell you once again that at my birth
The front of heaven was full of fiery shapes,

The goats ran from the mountains, and the herds
Were strangely clamorous to the frighted fields.
These signs have mark'd me extraordinary;
And all the courses of my life do show
I am not in the roll of common men.
Where is he living, clipp'd in with the sea
That chides the banks of England, Scotland,
    Wales,
Which calls me pupil, or hath read to me?
And bring him out that is but woman's son
Can trace me in the tedious ways of art
And hold me pace in deep experiments.

Hot. I think there's no man speaks better
Welsh. I'll to dinner.   *51*

Mort. Peace, cousin Percy; you will make him
mad.

Glend. I can call spirits from the vasty deep.

Hot. Why, so can I, or so can any man;
But will they come when you do call for them?

Glend. Why, I can teach you, cousin, to command
The devil.

Hot. And I can teach thee, coz, to shame the
devil
By telling truth: tell truth and shame the devil.
If thou have power to raise him, bring him
hither,
And I'll be sworn I have power to shame him
hence.   *61*
O, while you live, tell truth and shame the devil!

Mort. Come, come, no more of this unprofitable
chat.

Glend. Three times hath Henry Bolingbroke
made head
Against my power; thrice from the banks of Wye
And sandy-bottom'd Severn have I sent him
Bootless home and weather-beaten back.

Hot. Home without boots, and in foul weather
too!
How 'scapes he agues, in the devil's name?

Glend. Come, here's the map: shall we divide
our right   *70*
According to our threefold order ta'en?

Mort. The Archdeacon hath divided it
Into three limits very equally:
England, from Trent and Severn hitherto,
By south and east is to my part assign'd:
All westward, Wales beyond the Severn shore,
And all the fertile land within that bound,
To Owen Glendower: and, dear coz, to you
The remnant northward, lying off from Trent.
And our indentures tripartite are drawn;   *80*
Which being sealed interchangeably,
A business that this night may execute,
To-morrow, cousin Percy, you and I
And my good Lord of Worcester will set forth

To meet your father and the Scottish power,
As is appointed us, at Shrewsbury.
My father Glendower is not ready yet,
Nor shall we need his help these fourteen days.
Within that space you may have drawn together
Your tenants, friends, and neighbouring gentle-
    men.   90
  Glend. A shorter time shall send me to you,
    lords:
And in my conduct shall your ladies come;
From whom you now must steal and take no
    leave,
For there will be a world of water shed
Upon the parting of your wives and you.
  Hot. Methinks my moiety, north from Burton
    here,
In quantity equals not one of yours:
See how this river comes me cranking in,
And cuts me from the best of all my land
A huge half-moon, a monstrous cantle out.   100
I'll have the current in this place damm'd up;
And here the smug and silver Trent shall run
In a new channel, fair and evenly;
It shall not wind with such a deep indent,
To rob me of so rich a bottom here.
  Glend. Not wind? it shall, it must; you see it
    doth.
  Mort. Yea, but
Mark how he bears his course, and runs me up
With like advantage on the other side;
Gelding the opposed continent as much   110
As on the other side it takes from you.
  Wor. Yea, but a little charge will trench him
    here
And on this north side win this cape of land;
And then he runs straight and even.
  Hot. I'll have it so: a little charge will do it.
  Glend. I'll not have it alter'd.
  Hot.   Will not you?
  Glend. No, nor you shall not.
  Hot.   Who shall say me nay?
  Glend. Why, that will I.
  Hot. Let me not understand you, then; speak it
in Welsh.   120
  Glend. I can speak English, lord, as well as you;
For I was train'd up in the English court;
Where, being but young, I framed to the harp
Many an English ditty lovely well
And gave the tongue a helpful ornament,
A virtue that was never seen in you.
  Hot. Marry,
And I am glad of it with all my heart:
I had rather be a kitten and cry mew
Than one of these same metre ballad-mongers;
I had rather hear a brazen canstick turn'd,   131
Or a dry wheel grate on the axle-tree;

And that would set my teeth nothing on edge,
Nothing so much as mincing poetry:
'Tis like the forced gait of a shuffling nag.
  Glend. Come, you shall have Trent turn'd.
  Hot. I do not care: I'll give thrice so much land
To any well-deserving friend;
But in the way of bargain, mark ye me,
I'll cavil on the ninth part of a hair.   140
Are the indentures drawn? shall we be gone?
  Glend. The moon shines fair; you may away
    by night:
I'll haste the writer and withal
Break with your wives of your departure hence:
I am afraid my daughter will run mad,
So much she doteth on her Mortimer.   [Exit.
  Mort. Fie, cousin Percy! how you cross my
    father!
  Hot. I cannot choose: sometime he angers me
With telling me of the moldwarp and the ant,
Of the dreamer Merlin and his prophecies,   150
And of a dragon and a finless fish,
A clip-wing'd griffin and a moulten raven,
A couching lion and a ramping cat,
And such a deal of skimble-skamble stuff
As puts me from my faith. I tell you what;
He held me last night at least nine hours
In reckoning up the several devils' names
That were his lackeys: I cried "hum," and
    "well, go to,"
But mark'd him not a word. O, he is as tedious
As a tired horse, a railing wife;   160
Worse than a smoky house: I had rather live
With cheese and garlic in a windmill, far,
Than feed on cates and have him talk to me
In any summer-house in Christendom.
  Mort. In faith, he is a worthy gentleman,
Exceedingly well read, and profited
In strange concealments, valiant as a lion
And wondrous affable and as bountiful
As mines of India. Shall I tell you, cousin?
He holds your temper in a high respect   170
And curbs himself even of his natural scope
When you come 'cross his humour; faith, he
    does:
I warrant you, that man is not alive
Might so have tempted as you have done,
Without the taste of danger and reproof:
But do not use it oft, let me entreat you.
  Wor. In faith, my lord, you are too wilful-
    blame;
And since your coming hither have done enough
To put him quite beside his patience.
You must needs learn, lord, to amend this fault:
Though sometimes it show greatness, courage,
    blood—   181
And that's the dearest grace it renders you—

Yet oftentimes it doth present harsh rage,
Defect of manners, want of government,
Pride, haughtiness, opinion, and disdain:
The least of which haunting a nobleman
Loseth men's hearts and leaves behind a stain
Upon the beauty of all parts besides,
Beguiling them of commendation.
  Hot. Well, I am school'd: good manners be
    your speed!   *190*
Here comes our wives, and let us take our leave.

    Re-enter GLENDOWER *with* THE LADIES.

  Mort. This is the deadly spite that angers me;
My wife can speak no English, I no Welsh.
  Glend. My daughter weeps: she will not part
    with you;
She'll be a soldier too, she'll to the wars.
  Mort. Good father, tell her that she and my
    aunt Percy
Shall follow in your conduct speedily.
  GLENDOWER *speaks to* LADY MORTIMER *in Welsh,*
           and she answers him in the same.
  Glend. She is desperate here; a peevish self-
will'd harlotry, one that no persuasion can do
good upon.
    The LADY MORTIMER *speaks in Welsh.*
  Mort. I understand thy looks: that pretty
    Welsh   *201*
Which thou pour'st down from these swelling
    heavens
I am too perfect in; and, but for shame,
In such a parley should I answer thee.
    The LADY MORTIMER *speaks again in Welsh.*
I understand thy kisses and thou mine,
And that's a feeling disputation:
But I will never be a truant, love,
Till I have learn'd thy language; for thy tongue
Makes Welsh as sweet as ditties highly penn'd,
Sung by a fair queen in a summer's bower,   *210*
With ravishing division, to her lute.
  Glend. Nay, if you melt, then will she run mad.
    The LADY MORTIMER *speaks again in Welsh.*
  Mort. O, I am ignorance itself in this!
  Glend. She bids you on the wanton rushes
    lay you down
And rest your gentle head upon her lap,
And she will sing the song that pleaseth you
And on your eyelids crown the god of sleep,
Charming your blood with pleasing heaviness,
Making such difference 'twixt wake and sleep
As is the difference betwixt day and night   *220*
The hour before the heavenly-harness'd team
Begins his golden progress in the east.
  Mort. With all my heart I'll sit and hear her sing:
By that time will our book, I think, be drawn.
  Glend. Do so;

And those musicians that shall play to you
Hang in the air a thousand leagues from hence,
And straight they shall be here: sit, and attend.
  Hot. Come, Kate, thou art perfect in lying
down: come, quick, quick, that I may lay my
head in thy lap.   *231*
  Lady P. Go, ye giddy goose.
    The music plays.
  Hot. Now I perceive the devil understands
    Welsh;
And 'tis no marvel he is so humorous.
By'r, lady, he is a good musician.
  Lady. P. Then should you be nothing but
musical, for you are altogether governed by hu-
mours. Lie still, ye thief, and hear the lady sing
in Welsh.
  Hot. I had rather hear Lady, my brach, howl
in Irish.   *241*
  Lady P. Wouldst thou have thy head broken?
  Hot. No.
  Lady. P. Then be still.
  Hot. Neither; 'tis a woman's fault.
  Lady. P. Now God help thee!
  Hot. To the Welsh lady's bed.
  Lady P. What's that?
  Hot. Peace! she sings.
    Here the LADY MORTIMER *sings a Welsh song.*
  Hot. Come, Kate, I'll have your song too.
  Lady P. Not mine, in good sooth.   *251*
  Hot. Not yours, in good sooth! Heart! you
swear like a comfit-maker's wife. "Not you, in
good sooth," and "as true as I live," and "as
God shall mend me," and "as sure as day,"
And givest such sarcenet surety for thy oaths
As if thou never walk'st further than Finsbury.
Swear me, Kate, like a lady as thou art,
A good mouth-filling oath, and leave "in sooth,"
And such protest of pepper-gingerbread,   *260*
To velvet-guards and Sunday-citizens.
Come, sing.
  Lady P. I will not sing.
  Hot. 'Tis the next way to turn tailor, or be
red-breast teacher. An the indentures be drawn,
I'll away within these two hours; and so, come
in when ye will.   [*Exit.*
  Glend. Come, come, Lord Mortimer; you are
    as slow
As hot Lord Percy is on fire to go.
By this our book is drawn; we'll but seal,   *270*
And then to horse immediately.
  Mort.   With all my heart.   [*Exeunt.*

      SCENE II. *London: the palace*

Enter the KING, PRINCE OF WALES, *and others.*
  King. Lords, give us leave; the Prince of
    Wales and I

Must have some private conference: but be near
    at hand,
For we shall presently have need of you.
                              [*Exeunt Lords.*
I know not whether God will have it so,
For some displeasing service I have done,
That, in his secret doom, out of my blood
He'll breed revengement and a scourge for me;
But thou dost in thy passages of life
Make me believe that thou art only mark'd
For the hot vengeance and the rod of heaven   *10*
To punish my mistreadings. Tell me else,
Could such inordinate and low desires,
Such poor, such bare, such lewd, such mean
    attempts,
Such barren pleasures, rude society,
As thou art match'd withal and grafted to,
Accompany the greatness of thy blood
And hold their level with thy princely heart?
  Prince. So please your Majesty, I would I
    could
Quit all offences with as clear excuse
As well as I am doubtless I can purge   *20*
Myself of many I am charged withal:
Yet such extenuation let me beg,
As, in reproof of many tales devised,
Which oft the ear of greatness needs must hear,
By smiling pick-thanks and base newsmongers,
I may, for some things true, wherein my youth
Hath faulty wander'd and irregular,
Find pardon on my true submission.
  King. God pardon thee! yet let me wonder,
    Harry,
At thy affections, which do hold a wing   *30*
Quite from the flight of all thy ancestors.
Thy place in council thou hast rudely lost,
Which by thy younger brother is supplied,
And art almost an alien to the hearts
Of all the court and princes of my blood:
The hope and expectation of thy time
Is ruin'd, and the soul of every man
Prophetically doth forethink thy fall.
Had I so lavish of my presence been,
So common-hackney'd in the eyes of men,   *40*
So stale and cheap to vulgar company,
Opinion, that did help me to the crown,
Had still kept loyal to possession
And left me in reputeless banishment,
A fellow of no mark nor likelihood.
By being seldom seen, I could not stir
But like a comet I was wonder'd at;
That men would tell their children "This is he";
Others would say "Where, which is Boling-
    broke?"
And then I stole all courtesy from heaven,   *50*
And dress'd myself in such humility

That I did pluck allegiance from men's hearts,
Loud shouts and salutations from their mouths,
Even in the presence of the crowned King.
Thus did I keep my person fresh and new;
My presence, like a robe pontifical,
Ne'er seen but wonder'd at: and so my state,
Seldom but sumptuous, showed like a feast
And won by rareness such solemnity.
The skipping King, he ambled up and down   *60*
With shallow jesters and rash bavin wits,
Soon kindled and soon burnt; carded his state,
Mingled his royalty with capering fools,
Had his great name profaned with their scorns
And gave his countenance, against his name,
To laugh at gibing boys and stand the push
Of every beardless vain comparative,
Grew a companion to the common streets,
Enfeoff'd himself to popularity;
That, being daily swallow'd by men's eyes,   *70*
They surfeited with honey and began
To loathe the taste of sweetness, whereof a little
More than a little is by much too much.
So when he had occasion to be seen,
He was but as the cuckoo is in June,
Heard, not regarded; seen, but with such eyes
As sick and blunted with community,
Afford no extraordinary gaze,
Such as is bent on sun-like majesty
When it shines seldom in admiring eyes;   *80*
But rather drowsed and hung their eyelids down,
Slept in his face and render'd such aspect
As cloudy men use to their adversaries,
Being with his presence glutted, gorged, and full.
And in that very line, Harry, standest thou;
For thou hast lost thy princely privilege
With vile participation: not an eye
But is a-weary of thy common sight,
Save mine, which hath desired to see thee more;
Which now doth that I would not have it do,   *90*
Make blind itself with foolish tenderness.
  Prince. I shall hereafter, my thrice gracious
    lord,
Be more myself.
  King.   For all the world
As thou art to this hour was Richard then
When I from France set foot at Ravenspurgh,
And even as I was then is Percy now.
Now, by my sceptre and my soul to boot,
He hath more worthy interest to the state
Than thou the shadow of succession;
For of no right, nor colour like to right,   *100*
He doth fill fields with harness in the realm,
Turns head against the lion's armed jaws,
And, being no more in debt to years than thou,
Leads ancient lords and reverend bishops on
To bloody battles and to bruising arms.

What never-dying honour hath he got
Against renowned Douglas! whose high deeds,
Whose hot incursions and great name in arms
Holds from all soldiers chief majority
And military title capital   *110*
Through all the kingdoms that acknowledge
    Christ:
Thrice hath this Hotspur, Mars in swathling
    clothes,
This infant warrior, in his enterprises
Discomfited great Douglas, ta'en him once,
Enlarged him and made a friend of him,
To fill the mouth of deep defiance up
And shake the peace and safety of our throne.
And what say you to this? Percy, Northumber-
    land,
The Archbishop's grace of York, Douglas, Mor-
    timer,
Capitulate against us and are up.   *120*
But wherefore do I tell these news to thee?
Why, Harry, do I tell thee of my foes,
Which art my near'st and dearest enemy?
Thou that art like enough, through vassal **fear,**
Base inclination, and the start of spleen,
To fight against me under Percy's pay,
To dog his heels and curtsy at his frowns,
To show how much thou art degenerate.
    Prince. Do not think so; you shall not find it so:
And God forgive them that so much have sway'd
Your Majesty's good thoughts away from me! *131*
I will redeem all this on Percy's head
And in the closing of some glorious day
Be bold to tell you that I am your son;
When I will wear a garment all of blood
And stain my favours in a bloody mask,
Which, wash'd away, shall scour my shame **with**
    it:
And that shall be the day, whene'er it lights,
That this same child of honour and renown,
This gallant Hotspur, this all-praised knight, *140*
And your unthought-of Harry chance to meet.
For every honour sitting on his helm,
Would they were multitudes, and on my head
My shames redoubled! for the time will come
That I shall make this northern youth exchange
His glorious deeds for my indignities.
Percy is but my factor, good my lord,
To engross up glorious deeds on my behalf;
And I will call him to so strict account
That he shall render every glory up,   *150*
Yea, even the slightest worship of his time,
Or I will tear the reckoning from his heart. •
This, in the name of God, I promise here:
The which if He be pleased I shall perform,
I do beseech your Majesty may salve
The long-grown wounds of my intemperance:

If not, the end of life cancels all bands;
And I will die a hundred thousand deaths
Ere break the smallest parcel of this vow.
    King. A hundred thousand rebels die in this:
Thou shalt have charge and sovereign trust
    herein.

Enter BLUNT.

How now, good Blunt? thy looks are full of
    speed.
    Blunt. So hath the business that I come to
    speak of.
Lord Mortimer of Scotland hath sent word
That Douglas and the English rebels met
The eleventh of this month at Shrewsbury:
A mighty and a fearful head they are,
If promises be kept on every hand,
As ever offer'd foul play in a state.
    King. The Earl of Westmoreland set forth
    to-day;   *170*
With him my son, Lord John of Lancaster;
For this advertisement is five days old:
On Wednesday next, Harry, you shall set for-
    ward;
On Thursday we ourselves will march: our
    meeting
Is Bridgenorth: and, Harry, you shall march
Through Gloucestershire; by which account,
Our business valued, some twelve days hence
Our general forces at Bridgenorth shall meet.
Our hands are full of business: let's away;
Advantage feeds him fat, while men delay.   *180*
                                                                    [*Exeunt.*

SCENE III. *Eastcheap: the Boar's-Head Tavern*
        Enter FALSTAFF *and* BARDOLPH.

Fal. Bardolph, am I not fallen away vilely
since this last action? do I not bate? do I not
dwindle? Why, my skin hangs about me like an
old lady's loose gown; I am withered like an old
apple-john. Well, I'll repent, and that suddenly,
while I am in some liking; I shall be out of heart
shortly, and then I shall have no strength to
repent. An I have not forgotten what the inside
of a church is made of, I am a peppercorn, a
brewer's horse: the inside of a church! Company, villainous company, hath been the spoil of
me.
    Bard. Sir John, you are so fretful, you cannot
live long.
    Fal. Why, there is it: come sing me a bawdy
song; make me merry. I was as virtuously given
as a gentleman need to be; virtuous enough;
swore little; diced not above seven times a week;
went to a bawdy-house not above once in a
quarter—of an hour; paid money that I bor-

rowed, three or four times; lived well and in good compass: and now I live out of all order, out of all compass.

Bard. Why, you are so fat, Sir John, that you must needs be out of all compass, out of all reasonable compass, Sir John.

Fal. Do thou amend thy face, and I'll amend my life: thou art our admiral, thou bearest the lantern in the poop, but 'tis in the nose of thee; thou art the Knight of the Burning Lamp.   30

Bard. Why, Sir John, my face does you no harm.

Fal. No, I'll be sworn; I make as good use of it as many a man doth of a Death's-head or a *memento mori:* I never see thy face but I think upon hell-fire and Dives that lived in purple; for there he is in his robes, burning, burning. If thou wert any way given to virtue, I would swear by thy face; my oath should be, "By this fire that's God's angel:" but thou art altogether given over; and wert indeed, but for the light in thy face, the son of utter darkness. When thou rannest up Gadshill in the night to catch my horse, if I did not think thou hadst been an *ignis fatuus* or a ball of wildfire, there's no purchase in money. O, thou art a perpetual triumph, an everlasting bonfire-light! Thou hast saved me a thousand marks in links and torches, walking with thee in the night betwixt tavern and tavern: but the sack that thou hast drunk me would have bought me lights as good cheap at the dearest chandler's in Europe. I have maintained that salamander of yours with fire any time this two and thirty years; God reward me for it!

Bard. 'Sblood, I would my face were in your belly!

Fal. God-a-mercy! so should I be sure to be heart-burned.

Enter MISTRESS QUICKLY.

How now, Dame Partlet the hen! have you inquired yet who picked my pocket?   61

Quick. Why, Sir John, what do you think, Sir John? do you think I keep thieves in my house? I have searched, I have inquired, so has my husband, man by man, boy by boy, servant by servant: the tithe of a hair was never lost in my house before.

Fal. Ye lie, hostess: Bardolph was shaved and lost many a hair; and I'll be sworn my pocket was picked. Go to, you are a woman, go.

Quick. Who, I? no; I defy thee: God's light, I was never called so in mine own house before.

Fal. Go to, I know you well enough.

Quick. No, Sir John; you do not know me, Sir John. I know you, Sir John: you owe me money, Sir John; and now you pick a quarrel to beguile me of it: I bought you a dozen of shirts to your back.

Fal. Dowlas, filthy dowlas: I have given them away to bakers' wives, and they have made bolters of them.   81

Quick. Now, as I am a true woman, holland of eight shillings an ell. You owe money here besides, Sir John, for your diet and by-drinkings, and money lent you, four and twenty pound.

Fal. He had his part of it; let him pay.

Quick. He? alas, he is poor; he hath nothing.

Fal. How! poor? look upon his face; what call you rich? let them coin his nose, let them coin his cheeks: I'll not pay a denier. What, will you make a younker of me? shall I not take mine ease in mine inn but I shall have my pocket picked? I have lost a seal-ring of my grandfather's worth forty mark.

Quick. O Jesu, I have heard the Prince tell him, I know not how oft, that that ring was copper!

Fal. How! the Prince is a Jack, a sneak-cup: 'sblood, an he were here, I would cudgel him like a dog, if he would say so.   101

Enter the PRINCE *and* PETO, *marching, and* FALSTAFF, *meets them playing on his truncheon like a fife.*

How now, lad! is the wind in that door, i' faith? must we all march?

Bard. Yea, two and two, Newgate fashion.

Quick. My lord, I pray you, hear me.

Prince. What sayest thou, Mistress Quickly? How doth thy husband? I love him well; he is an honest man.

Quick. Good my lord, hear me.

Fal. Prithee, let her alone, and list to me.

Prince. What sayest thou, Jack?   111

Fal. The other night I fell asleep here behind the arras and had my pocket picked: this house is turned bawdy-house; they pick pockets.

Prince. What didst thou lose, Jack?

Fal. Wilt thou believe me, Hal? three or four bonds of forty pound a-piece, and a seal-ring of my grandfather's.

Prince. A trifle, some eight-penny matter.

Quick. So I told him, my lord; and I said I heard your Grace say so: and, my lord, he speaks most vilely of you, like a foul-mouthed man as he is; and said he would cudgel you.

Prince. What! he did not?

Quick. There's neither faith, truth, nor womanhood in me else.

Fal. There's no more faith in thee than in a stewed prune; nor no more truth in thee than in a drawn fox; and for womanhood, Maid Marian may be the deputy's wife of the ward to thee. Go, you thing, go.   *131*

Quick. Say, what thing? what thing?

Fal. What thing! why, a thing to thank God on.

Quick. I am no thing to thank God on, I would thou shouldst know it; I am an honest man's wife; and, setting thy knighthood aside, thou art a knave to call me so.

Fal. Setting thy womanhood aside, thou art a beast to say otherwise.   *140*

Quick. Say, what beast, thou knave, thou?

Fal. What beast! why, an otter.

Prince. An otter, Sir John! why an otter?

Fal. Why, she's neither fish nor flesh; a man knows not where to have her.

Quick. Thou art an unjust man in saying so: thou or any man knows where to have me, thou knave, thou!

Prince. Thou sayest true, hostess; and he slanders thee most grossly.   *150*

Quick. So he doth you, my lord; and said this other day you ought him a thousand pound.

Prince. Sirrah, do I owe you a thousand pound?

Fal. A thousand pound, Hal! a million: thy love is worth a million: thou owest me thy love.

Quick. Nay, my lord, he called you Jack, and said he would cudgel you.

Fal. Did I, Bardolph?   *160*

Bard. Indeed, Sir John, you said so.

Fal. Yea, if he said my ring was copper.

Prince. I say 'tis copper: darest thou be as good as thy word now?

Fal. Why, Hal, thou knowest, as thou art but man, I dare: but as thou art Prince, I fear thee as I fear the roaring of the lion's whelp.

Prince. And why not as the lion?

Fal. The King himself is to be feared as the lion: dost thou think I'll fear thee as I fear thy father? nay, an I do, I pray God my girdle break.

Prince. O, if it should, how would thy guts fall about thy knees! But, sirrah, there's no room for faith, truth, nor honesty in this bosom of thine; it is all filled up with guts and midriff. Charge an honest woman with picking thy pocket! why, thou whoreson, impudent, embossed rascal, if there were anything in thy pocket but tavern-reckonings, memorandums of bawdy-houses, and one poor penny-worth of sugar-candy to make thee long-winded, if thy pocket were enriched with any other injuries but these, I am a villain: and yet you will stand to it; you will not pocket up wrong: art thou not ashamed?

Fal. Dost thou hear, Hal? thou knowest in the state of innocency Adam fell; and what should poor Jack Falstaff do in the days of villainy? Thou seest I have more flesh than another man, and therefore more frailty. You confess then, you picked my pocket?   *190*

Prince. It appears so by the story.

Fal. Hostess, I forgive thee: go, make ready breakfast; love thy husband, look to thy servants, cherish thy guests: thou shalt find me tractable to any honest reason: thou seest I am pacified still. Nay, prithee, be gone. [*Exit* MISTRESS QUICKLY.] Now, Hal, to the news at court: for the robbery, lad, how is that answered?

Prince. O, my sweet beef, I must still be good angel to thee: the money is paid back again.   *200*

Fal. O, I do not like that paying back; 'tis a double labour.

Prince. I am good friends with my father and may do anything.

Fal. Rob me the exchequer the first thing thou doest, and do it with unwashed hands too.

Bard. Do, my lord.

Prince. I have procured thee, Jack, a charge of foot.   *209*

Fal. I would it had been of horse. Where shall I find one that can steal well? O, for a fine thief, of the age of two and twenty or thereabouts! I am heinously unprovided. Well, God be thanked for these rebels, they offend none but the virtuous: I laud them, I praise them.

Prince. Bardolph!

Bard. My lord?

Prince. Go bear this letter to Lord John of Lancaster, to my brother John; this to my Lord of Westmoreland. [*Exit* BARDOLPH.] Go, Peto, to horse, to horse; for thou and I have thirty miles to ride yet ere dinner time. [*Exit* PETO.] Jack, meet me to-morrow in the Temple hall at two o'clock in the afternoon.

There shalt thou know thy charge; and there receive

Money and order for their furniture.

The land is burning; Percy stands on high;

And either we or they must lower lie.   [*Exit*.

Fal. Rare words! brave world! Hostess, my breakfast, come!   *229*

O, I could wish this tavern were my drum! [*Exit*.

ACT IV

SCENE I. *The rebel camp near Shrewsbury*

Enter HOTSPUR, WORCESTER, *and* DOUGLAS.

Hot. Well said, my noble Scot: if speaking truth

In this fine age were not thought flattery,

Such attribution should the Douglas have

As not a soldier of this season's stamp
Should go so general current through the world.
By God, I cannot flatter; I do defy
The tongues of soothers; but a braver place
In my heart's love hath no man than yourself:
Nay, task me to my word; approve me, lord.
  Doug. Thou are the king of honour: *10*
No man so potent breathes upon the ground
But I will beard him.
  Hot.   Do so, and 'tis well.

Enter a MESSENGER *with letters.*

What letters hast thou there?—I can but thank
    you.
  Mess. These letters come from your father.
  Hot. Letters from him! why comes he not
    himself?
  Mess. He cannot come, my lord; he is grievous
    sick.
  Hot. 'Zounds! how has he the leisure to be sick
In such a justling time? Who leads his power?
Under whose government come they along?   *19*
  Mess. His letters bear his mind, not I, my
    lord.
  Wor. I prithee, tell me, doth he keep his bed?
  Mess. He did, my lord, four days ere I set forth;
And at the time of my departure thence
He was much fear'd by his physicians.
  Wor. I would the state of time had first been
    whole
Ere he by sickness had been visited:
His health was never better worth than now.
  Hot. Sick now! droop now! this sickness doth
    infect
The very life-blood of our enterprise;
'Tis catching hither, even to our camp.   *30*
He writes me here, that inward sickness—
And that his friends by deputation could not
So soon be drawn, nor did he think it meet
To lay so dangerous and dear a trust
On any soul removed but on his own.
Yet doth he give us bold advertisement
That with our small conjunction we should on
To see how fortune is disposed to us;
For, as he writes, there is no quailing now,
Because the King is certainly possess'd   *40*
Of all our purposes. What say you to it?
  Wor. Your father's sickness is a maim to us.
  Hot. A perilous gash, a very limb lopp'd off:
And yet, in faith, it is not; his present want
Seems more than we shall find it: were it good
To set the exact wealth of all our states
All at one cast? to set so rich a main
On the nice hazard of one doubtful hour?
It were not good; for therein should we read
The very bottom and the soul of hope,   *50*

The very list, the very utmost bound
Of all our fortunes.
  Doug.   'Faith, and so we should;
Where now remains a sweet reversion:
We may boldly spend upon the hope of what
Is to come in:
A comfort of retirement lives in this.
  Hot. A rendezvous, a home to fly unto,
If that the devil and mischance look big
Upon the maidenhead of our affairs.
  Wor. But yet I would your father had been
    here.   *60*
The quality and hair of our attempt
Brooks no division: it will be thought
By some, that know not why he is away,
That wisdom, loyalty, and mere dislike
Of our proceedings kept the earl from hence:
And think how such an apprehension
May turn the tide of fearful faction
And breed a kind of question in our cause;
For well you know we of the offering side
Must keep aloof from strict arbitrement,   *70*
And stop all sight-holes, every loop from whence
The eye of reason may pry in upon us:
This absence of your father's draws a curtain,
That shows the ignorant a kind of fear
Before not dreamt of.
  Hot.   You strain too far.
I rather of his absence make this use:
It lends a lustre and more great opinion,
A larger dare to our great enterprise,
Than if the earl were here; for men must think,
If we without his help can make a head   *80*
To push against a kingdom, with his help
We shall o'erturn it topsy-turvy down.
Yet all goes well, yet all our joints are whole.
  Doug. As heart can think: there is not such a
    word
Spoke of in Scotland as this term of fear.

Enter SIR RICHARD VERNON.

  Hot. My cousin Vernon! welcome, by my soul.
  Ver. Pray God my news be worth a welcome,
    lord.
The Earl of Westmoreland, seven thousand
    strong,
Is marching hitherwards; with him Prince John.
  Hot. No harm: what more?
  Ver.   And further, I have learn'd,   *90*
The King himself in person is set forth,
Or hitherwards intended speedily,
With strong and mighty preparation.
  Hot. He shall be welcome too. Where is his son,
The nimble-footed madcap Prince of Wales,
And his comrades, that daff'd the world aside,
And bid it pass?

Ver. All furnish'd, all in arms;
All plumed like estridges that with the wind
Baited like eagles having lately bathed;
Glittering in golden coats, like images; *100*
As full of spirit as the month of May,
And gorgeous as the sun at midsummer;
Wanton as youthful goats, wild as young bulls.
I saw young Harry, with his beaver on,
His cuisses on his thighs, gallantly arm'd,
Rise from the ground like feather'd Mercury,
And vaulted with such ease into his seat,
As if an angel dropp'd down from the clouds,
To turn and wind a fiery Pegasus
And witch the world with noble horsemanship.

Hot. No more, no more: worse than the sun in
March, *111*
This praise doth nourish agues. Let them come;
They come like sacrifices in their trim,
And to the fire-eyed maid of smoky war
All hot and bleeding will we offer them:
The mailed Mars shall on his altar sit
Up to the ears in blood. I am on fire
To hear this rich reprisal is so nigh
And yet not ours. Come, let me taste my horse,
Who is to bear me like a thunderbolt *120*
Against the bosom of the Prince of Wales:
Harry to Harry shall, hot horse to horse,
Meet and ne'er part till one drop down a corse.
O that Glendower were come!

Ver. There is more news:
I learn'd in Worcester, as I rode along,
He cannot draw his power this fourteen days.

Doug. That's the worst tidings that I hear of
yet.

Wor. Ay, by my faith, that bears a frosty
sound.

Hot. What may the King's whole battle reach
unto?

Ver. To thirty thousand.

Hot. Forty let it be: *130*
My father and Glendower being both away,
The powers of us may serve so great a day.
Come, let us take a muster speedily:
Doomsday is near; die all, die merrily.

Doug. Talk not of dying: I am out of fear
Of death or death's hand for this one-half year.
[*Exeunt.*

SCENE II. *A public road near Coventry*

Enter FALSTAFF *and* BARDOLPH.

Fal. Bardolph, get thee before to Coventry;
fill me a bottle of sack: our soldiers shall march
through; we'll to Sutton Cophill to-night.

Bard. Will you give me money, captain?

Fal. Lay out, lay out.

Bard. This bottle makes an angel.

Fal. An if it do, take it for thy labour; and if it
make twenty, take them all; I'll answer the
coinage. Bid my lieutenant Peto meet me at
town's end. *10*

Bard. I will, captain: farewell. [*Exit.*

Fal. If I be not ashamed of my soldiers, I am
a soused gurnet. I have misused the King's press
damnably. I have got, in exchange of a hundred
and fifty soldiers, three hundred and odd pounds.
I press me none but good householders, yeomen's
sons; inquire me out contracted bachelors, such
as had been asked twice on the banns; such a
commodity of warm slaves, as had as lieve hear
the devil as a drum; such as fear the report of a
caliver worse than a struck fowl or a hurt wild-
duck. I pressed me none but such toasts-and-
butter, with hearts in their bellies no bigger than
pins' heads, and they have bought out their services; and now my whole charge consists of
ancients, corporals, lieutenants, gentlemen of
companies, slaves as ragged as Lazarus in the
painted cloth, where the glutton's dogs licked his
sores; and such as indeed were never soldiers,
but discarded unjust serving-men, younger sons
to younger brothers, revolted tapsters and ostlers
trade-fallen, the cankers of a calm world and a
long peace, ten times more dishonourable ragged
than an old faced ancient: and such have I, to
fill up the rooms of them that have bought out
their services, that you would think that I had a
hundred and fifty tattered prodigals lately come
from swine-keeping, from eating draff and husks.
A mad fellow met me on the way and told me I
had unloaded all the gibbets and pressed the
dead bodies. No eye hath seen such scarecrows.
I'll not march through Coventry with them,
that's flat: nay, and the villains march wide
betwixt the legs, as if they had gyves on; for
indeed I had the most of them out of prison.
There's but a shirt and a half in all my company;
and the half shirt is two napkins tacked together
and thrown over the shoulders like a herald's
coat without sleeves; and the shirt, to say the
truth, stolen from my host at Saint Alban's, or
the red-nose innkeeper of Daventry. But that's
all one; they'll find linen enough on every hedge.

Enter the PRINCE *and* WESTMORELAND.

Prince. How now, blown Jack! how now,
quilt!

Fal. What, Hal! how now, mad wag! what
a devil dost thou in Warwickshire? My good
Lord of Westmoreland, I cry you mercy: I
thought your honour had already been at Shrewsbury. *59*

West. Faith, Sir John, 'tis more than time that

I were there, and you too; but my powers are there already. The King, I can tell you, looks for us all: we must away all night.

Fal. Tut, never fear me: I am as vigilant as a cat to steal cream.

Prince. I think, to steal cream indeed, for thy theft hath already made thee butter. But tell me, Jack, whose fellows are these that come after?

Fal. Mine, Hal, mine.   69

Prince. I did never see such pitiful rascals.

Fal. Tut, tut; good enough to toss; food for powder, food for powder; they'll fill a pit as well as better: tush, man, mortal men, mortal men.

West. Ay, but, Sir John, methinks they are exceeding poor and bare, too beggarly.

Fal. 'Faith, for their poverty, I know not where they had that; and for their bareness, I am sure they never learned that of me.

Prince. No, I'll be sworn; unless you call three fingers on the ribs bare. But, sirrah, make haste: Percy is already in the field.   81

Fal. What, is the King encamped?

West. He is, Sir John: I fear we shall stay too long.

Fal. Well,
To the latter end of a fray and the beginning of a
    feast
Fits a dull fighter and a keen guest.   [*Exeunt.*

SCENE III. *The rebel camp near Shrewsbury*

Enter HOTSPUR, WORCESTER, DOUGLAS, *and*
    VERNON.

Hot. We'll fight with him to-night.

Wor.   It may not be.

Doug. You give him then advantage.

Ver.   Not a whit.

Hot. Why say you so? looks he not for supply?

Ver. So do we.

Hot.   His is certain, ours is doubtful.

Wor. Good cousin, be advised; stir not tonight.

Ver. Do not, my lord.

Doug.   You do not counsel well:
You speak it out of fear and cold heart.

Ver. Do me no slander, Douglas: by my life,
And I dare well maintain it with my life,
If well-respected honour bid me on,   10
I hold as little counsel with weak fear
As you, my lord, or any Scot that this day lives:
Let it be seen to-morrow in the battle
Which of us fears.

Doug.   Yea, or to-night.

Ver.   Content.

Hot. To-night, say I.

Ver. Come, come, it may not be. I wonder
    much,
Being men of such great leading as you are,

That you foresee not what impediments
Drag back our expedition: certain horse
Of my cousin Vernon's are not yet come up: 20
Your uncle Worcester's horse came but to-day;
And now their pride and mettle is asleep,
Their courage with hard labour tame and dull,
That not a horse is half the half of himself.

Hot. So are the horses of the enemy
In general, journey-bated and brought low:
The better part of ours are full of rest.

Wor. The number of the King exceedeth ours:
For God's sake, cousin, stay till all come in.
    The trumpet sounds a parley.

Enter SIR WALTER BLUNT.

Blunt. I come with gracious offers from the
    King.   30
If you vouchsafe me hearing and respect.

Hot. Welcome, Sir Walter Blunt; and would to
    God
You were of our determination!
Some of us love you well; and even those some
Envy your great deservings and good name,
Because you are not of our quality,
But stand against us like an enemy.

Blunt. And God defend but still I should stand
    so,
So long as out of limit and true rule
You stand against anointed majesty.   40
But to my charge. The King hath sent to know
The nature of your griefs, and whereupon
You conjure from the breast of civil peace
Such bold hostility, teaching his duteous land
Audacious cruelty. If that the King
Have any way your good deserts forgot,
Which he confesseth to be manifold,
He bids you name your griefs; and with all speed
You shall have your desires with interest
And pardon absolute for yourself and these   50
Herein misled by your suggestion.

Hot. The King is kind; and well we know the
    King
Knows at what time to promise, when to pay.
My father and my uncle and myself
Did give him that same royalty he wears;
And when he was not six and twenty strong,
Sick in the world's regard, wretched and low,
A poor unminded outlaw sneaking home,
My father gave him welcome to the shore;
And when he heard him swear and vow to God
He came but to be Duke of Lancaster,   61
To sue his livery and beg his peace,
With tears of innocency and terms of zeal,
My father, in kind heart and pity moved,
Swore him assistance and perform'd it too.
Now when the lords and barons of the realm

Perceived Northumberland did lean to him,
The more and less came in with cap and knee;
Met him in boroughs, cities, villages,
Attended him on bridges, stood in lanes,   70
Laid gifts before him, proffer'd him their oaths,
Gave him their heirs, as pages follow'd him
Even at the heels in golden multitudes.
He presently, as greatness knows itself,
Steps me a little higher than his vow
Made to my father, while his blood was poor,
Upon the naked shore at Ravenspurgh;
And now, forsooth, takes on him to reform
Some certain edicts and some strait decrees
That lie too heavy on the commonwealth,   80
Cries out upon abuses, seems to weep
Over his country's wrongs; and by this face,
This seeming brow of justice, did he win
The hearts of all that he did angle for;
Proceeded further; cut me off the heads
Of all the favourites that the absent King
In deputation left behind him here,
When he was personal in the Irish war.

Blunt. Tut, I came not to hear this.

Hot.   Then to the point.
In short time after, he deposed the King;   90
Soon after that, deprived him of his life;
And in the neck of that, task'd the whole state;
To make that worse, suffer'd his kinsman March,
Who is, if every owner were well placed,
Indeed his king, to be engaged in Wales,
There without ransom to lie forfeited;
Disgraced me in my happy victories,
Sought to entrap me by intelligence;
Rated mine uncle from the council-board;
In rage dismiss'd my father from the court;   100
Broke oath on oath, committed wrong on wrong,
And in conclusion drove us to seek out
This head of safety; and withal to pry
Into his title, the which we find
Too indirect for long continuance.

Blunt. Shall I return this answer to the King?

Hot. Not so, Sir Walter: we'll withdraw awhile.
Go to the King; and let there be impawn'd
Some surety for a safe return again,
And in the morning early shall my uncle   110
Bring him our purposes: and so farewell.

Blunt. I would you would accept of grace and
      love.

Hot. And may be so we shall.

Blunt.   Pray God you do.
                              [*Exeunt.*

SCENE IV. *York: The Archbishop's palace*

Enter the ARCHBISHOP OF YORK *and* SIR MICHAEL.

Arch. Hie, good Sir Michael; bear this sealed
      brief

With winged haste to the Lord Marshal;
This to my cousin Scroop, and all the rest
To whom they are directed. If you knew
How much they do import, you would make
      haste.

Sir M. My good lord,
I guess their tenour.

Arch.   Like enough you do.
To-morrow, good Sir Michael, is a day
Wherein the fortune of ten thousand men
Must bide the touch; for, sir, at Shrewsbury,   10
As I am truly given to understand,
The King with mighty and quick-raised power
Meets with Lord Harry: and, I fear, Sir Michael,
What with the sickness of Northumberland,
Whose power was in the first proportion,
And what with Owen Glendower's absence
      thence,
Who with them was a rated sinew too
And comes not in, o'er-ruled by prophecies,
I fear the power of Percy is too weak
To wage an instant trial with the King.   20

Sir M. Why, my good lord, you need not fear;
There is Douglas and Lord Mortimer.

Arch. No, Mortimer is not there.

Sir M. But there is Mordake, Vernon, Lord
      Harry Percy,
And there is my Lord of Worcester and a head
Of gallant warriors, noble gentlemen.

Arch. And so there is: but yet the King hath
      drawn
The special head of all the land together:
The Prince of Wales, Lord John of Lancaster,
The noble Westmoreland, and warlike Blunt;   30
And many moe corrivals and dear men
Of estimation and command in arms.

Sir M. Doubt not, my lord, they shall be well
      opposed.

Arch. I hope no less, yet needful 'tis to fear;
And, to prevent the worst, Sir Michael, speed:
For if Lord Percy thrive not, ere the King
Dismiss his power, he means to visit us,
For he hath heard of our confederacy,
And 'tis but wisdom to make strong against him:
Therefore make haste. I must go write again
To other friends; and so farewell, Sir Michael.
                              [*Exeunt.*

ACT V

SCENE I. *The King's camp near Shrewsbury*

Enter the KING, PRINCE OF WALES, LORD JOHN OF
      LANCASTER, EARL OF WESTMORELAND, SIR WAL-
      TER BLUNT, *and* FALSTAFF.

King. How bloodily the sun begins to peer
Above yon busky hill! the day looks pale
At his distemperature.

Prince.   The southern wind
Doth play the trumpet to his purposes,
And by his hollow whistling in the leaves
Foretells a tempest and a blustering day.
King. Then with the losers let it sympathise,
For nothing can seem foul to those that win.
   The trumpet sounds.

   Enter WORCESTER *and* VERNON.

How now, my Lord of Worcester! 'tis not well
That you and I should meet upon such terms   10
As now we meet. You have deceived our trust,
And made us doff our easy robes of peace,
To crush our old limbs in ungentle steel:
This is not well, my lord, this is not well.
What say you to it? will you again unknit
This churlish knot of all-abhorred war?
And move in that obedient orb again
Where you did give a fair and natural light,
And be no more an exhaled meteor,
A prodigy of fear and a portent   20
Of broached mischief to the unborn times?
  Wor. Hear me, my liege:
For mine own part, I could be well content
To entertain the lag-end of my life
With quiet hours; for I do protest,
I have not sought the day of this dislike.
  King. You have not sought it! how comes it,
    then?
  Fal. Rebellion lay in his way, and he found it.
  Prince. Peace, chewet, peace!
  Wor. It pleased your Majesty to turn your
    looks   30
Of favour from myself and all our house;
And yet I must remember you, my lord,
We were the first and dearest of your friends.
For you my staff of office did I break
In Richard's time; and posted day and night
To meet you on the way, and kiss your hand,
When yet you were in place and in account
Nothing so strong and fortunate as I.
It was myself, my brother, and his son,
That brought you home and boldly did outdare
The dangers of the time. You swore to us,   41
And you did swear that oath at Doncaster,
That you did nothing purpose 'gainst the state;
Nor claim no further than your new-fall'n right,
The seat of Gaunt, dukedom of Lancaster:
To this we swore our aid. But in short space
It rain'd down fortune showering on your head;
And such a flood of greatness fell on you,
What with our help, what with the absent King,
What with the injuries of a wanton time,   50
The seeming sufferances that you had borne,
And the contrarious winds that held the King
So long in his unlucky Irish wars

That all in England did repute him dead:
And from this swarm of fair advantages
You took occasion to be quickly woo'd
To gripe the general sway into your hand;
Forgot your oath to us at Doncaster;
And being fed by us you used us so
As that ungentle gull, the cuckoo's bird,   60
Useth the sparrow; did oppress our nest;
Grew by our feeding to so great a bulk
That even our love durst not come near your
    sight
For fear of swallowing; but with nimble wing
We were enforced, for safety sake, to fly
Out of your sight and raise this present head;
Whereby we stand opposed by such means
As you yourself have forged against yourself
By unkind usage, dangerous countenance,
And violation of all faith and troth   70
Sworn to us in your younger enterprise.
  King. These things indeed you have articulate,
Proclaim'd at market-crosses, read in churches,
To face the garment of rebellion
With some fine colour that may please the eye
Of fickle changelings and poor discontents,
Which gape and rub the elbow at the news
Of hurlyburly innovation:
And never yet did insurrection want
Such water-colours to impaint his cause;   80
Nor moody beggars, starving for a time
Of pellmell havoc and confusion.
  Prince. In both your armies there is many a soul
Shall pay full dearly for this encounter,
If once they join in trial. Tell your nephew,
The Prince of Wales doth join with all the world
In praise of Henry Percy: by my hopes,
This present enterprise set off his head,
I do not think a braver gentleman,
More active-valiant or more valiant-young,   90
More daring or more bold, is now alive
To grace this latter age with noble deeds.
For my part, I may speak it to my shame,
I have a truant been to chivalry;
And so I hear he doth account me too;
Yet this before my father's majesty—
I am content that he shall take the odds
Of his great name and estimation,
And will, to save the blood on either side,
Try fortune with him in a single fight.   100
  King. And, Prince of Wales, so dare we venture
    thee,
Albeit considerations infinite
Do make against it. No, good Worcester, no,
We love our people well; even those we love
That are misled upon your cousin's part;
And, will they take the offer of our grace,
Both he and they and you, yea, every man

Shall be my friend again and I'll be his:
So tell your cousin, and bring me word
What he will do: but if he will not yield,   *110*
Rebuke and dread correction wait on us
And they shall do their office. So, be gone;
We will not now be troubled with reply:
We offer fair; take it advisedly.
                    [*Exeunt* WORCESTER *and* VERNON.
  Prince. It will not be accepted, on my life:
The Douglas and the Hotspur both together
Are confident against the world in arms.
  King. Hence, therefore, every leader to his
          charge;
For, on their answer, will we set on them:
And God befriend us, as our cause is just!   *120*
          [*Exeunt all but the* PRINCE OF WALES
                              and FALSTAFF.
  Fal. Hal, if thou see me down in the battle and
bestride me, so; 'tis a point of friendship.
  Prince. Nothing but a colossus can do thee that
friendship. Say thy prayers, and farewell.
  Fal. I would 'twere bed-time, Hal, and all well.
  Prince. Why, thou owest God a death.
                                        [*Exit.*
  Fal. 'Tis not due yet; I would be loath to pay
him before his day. What need I be so forward
with him that calls not on me? Well, 'tis no
matter; honour pricks me on. Yea, but how if
honour prick me off when I come on? how then?
Can honour set to a leg? no: or an arm? no: or
take away the grief of a wound? no. Honour
hath no skill in surgery, then? no. What is honour? a word. What is in that word honour? what
is that honour? air. A trim reckoning! Who hath
it? he that died o' Wednesday. Doth he feel it?
no. Doth he hear it? no. 'Tis insensible, then?
Yea, to the dead. But will it not live with the
living? no. Why? detraction will not suffer it.
Therefore I'll none of it. Honour is a mere
scutcheon: and so ends my catechism.   [*Exit.*

SCENE II. *The rebel camp*
Enter WORCESTER *and* VERNON.

  Wor. O, no, my nephew must not know, Sir
          Richard,
The liberal and kind offer of the King.
  Ver. 'Twere best he did.
  Wor.   Then are we all undone.
It is not possible, it cannot be,
The King should keep his word in loving us;
He will suspect us still and find a time
To punish this offence in other faults:
Suspicion all our lives shall be stuck full of eyes;
For treason is but trusted like the fox,
Who, ne'er so tame, so cherish'd, and lock'd up,
Will have a wild trick of his ancestors.   *11*

Look how we can, or sad or merrily,
Interpretation will misquote our looks,
And we shall feed like oxen at a stall,
The better cherish'd, still the nearer death.
My nephew's trespass may be well forgot;
It hath the excuse of youth and heat of blood,
And an adopted name of privilege,
A hare-brain'd Hotspur, govern'd by a spleen:
All his offences live upon my head   *20*
And on his father's; we did train him on,
And, his corruption being ta'en from us,
We, as the spring of all, shall pay for all.
Therefore, good cousin, let not Harry know,
In any case, the offer of the King.
  Ver. Deliver what you will; I'll say 'tis so.
Here comes your cousin.

Enter HOTSPUR *and* DOUGLAS.

  Hot. My uncle is return'd:
Deliver up my Lord of Westmoreland.
Uncle, what news?   *30*
  Wor. The King will bid you battle presently.
  Doug. Defy him by the Lord of Westmoreland.
  Hot. Lord Douglas, go you and tell him so.
  Doug. Marry, and shall, and very willingly.
                                        [*Exit.*
  Wor. There is no seeming mercy in the King.
  Hot. Did you beg any? God forbid!
  Wor. I told him gently of our grievances,
Of his oath-breaking; which he mended thus,
By now forswearing that he is forsworn:
He calls us rebels, traitors; and will scourge   *40*
With haughty arms this hateful name in us.

Re-enter DOUGLAS.

  Doug. Arm, gentlemen; to arms! for I have
          thrown
A brave defiance in King Henry's teeth,
And Westmoreland, that was engaged, did bear
          it;
Which cannot choose but bring him quickly on.
  Wor. The Prince of Wales stepp'd forth before
          the King,
And, nephew, challenged you to single fight.
  Hot. O, would the quarrel lay upon our heads,
And that no man might draw short breath to-day
But I and Harry Monmouth! Tell me, tell me,   *50*
How show'd his tasking? seem'd it in contempt?
  Ver. No, by my soul; I never in my life
Did hear a challenge urged more modestly,
Unless a brother should a brother dare
To gentle exercise and proof of arms.
He gave you all the duties of a man;
Trimm'd up your praises with a princely tongue,
Spoke your deservings like a chronicle,
Making you ever better than his praise

By still dispraising praise valued with you;   60
And, which became him like a prince indeed,
He made a blushing cital of himself;
And chid his truant youth with such a grace
As if he master'd there a double spirit
Of teaching and of learning instantly.
There did he pause: but let me tell the world,
If he outlive the envy of this day,
England did never owe so sweet a hope,
So much misconstrued in his wantonness.

  Hot. Cousin, I think thou art enamoured   70
On his follies: never did I hear
Of any prince so wild a libertine.
But be he as he will, yet once ere night
I will embrace him with a soldier's arm,
That he shall shrink under my courtesy.
Arm, arm with speed: and, fellows, soldiers,
    friends,
Better consider what you have to do
Than I, that have not well the gift of tongue,
Can lift your blood up with persuasion.

        Enter a MESSENGER.

  Mess. My lord, here are letters for you.   80
  Hot. I cannot read them now.
O gentlemen, the time of life is short!
To spend that shortness basely were too long,
If life did ride upon a dial's point,
Still ending at the arrival of an hour.
An if we live, we live to tread on kings;
If die, brave death, when princes die with us!
Now, for our consciences, the arms are fair,
When the intent of bearing them is just.

        Enter another MESSENGER.

  Mess. My lord, prepare; the King comes on
    apace.   90
  Hot. I thank him, that he cuts me from my tale,
For I profess not talking; only this—
Let each man do his best: and here draw I
A sword, whose temper I intend to stain
With the best blood that I can meet withal
In the adventure of this perilous day.
Now, *Esperance!* Percy! and set on.
Sound all the lofty instruments of war,
And by that music let us all embrace;
For, heaven to earth, some of us never shall   *100*
A second time do such a courtesy.
  [*The trumpets sound. They embrace, and exeunt.*

    SCENE III. *Plain between the camps*

The KING *enters with his power. Alarum to the
battle. Then enter* DOUGLAS *and* SIR WALTER BLUNT.

  Blunt. What is thy name, that in the battle thus
Thou crossest me? what honour dost thou seek
Upon my head?

  Doug.   Know then, my name is Douglas;
And I do haunt thee in the battle thus
Because some tell me that thou art a king.
  Blunt. They tell thee true.
  Doug. The Lord of Stafford dear to-day hath
    bought
Thy likeness, for instead of thee, King Harry,
This sword hath ended him: so shall it thee,
Unless thou yield thee as my prisoner.   10
  Blunt. I was not born a yielder, thou proud Scot;
And thou shalt find a king that will revenge
Lord Stafford's death.

    They fight. DOUGLAS *kills* BLUNT.

        Enter HOTSPUR.

  Hot. O Douglas, hadst thou fought at Holme-
    don thus,
I never had triumph'd upon a Scot.
  Doug. All's done, all's won; here breathless lies
    the King.
  Hot. Where?
  Doug. Here.
  Hot. This, Douglas? no: I know this face full
    well:
A gallant knight he was, his name was Blunt;   20
Semblably furnish'd like the King himself.
  Doug. A fool go with thy soul, whither it goes!
A borrow'd title hast thou bought too dear:
Why didst thou tell me that thou wert a king?
  Hot. The King hath many marching in his coats.
  Doug. Now, by my sword, I will kill all his
    coats;
I'll murder all his wardrobe, piece by piece,
Until I meet the King.
  Hot.   Up, and away!
Our soldiers stand full fairly for the day.   29
                  [*Exeunt.*

    Alarum. Enter FALSTAFF, *solus.*

  Fal. Though I could 'scape shot-free at London,
I fear the shot here; here's no scoring but upon
the pate. Soft! who are you? Sir Walter Blunt:
there's honour for you! here's no vanity! I am as
hot as molten lead, and as heavy too: God keep
lead out of me! I need no more weight than mine
own bowels. I have led my ragamuffins where
they are peppered: there's not three of my hundred and fifty left alive; and they are for the
town's end, to beg during life. But who comes
here?   40

        Enter the PRINCE.

  Prince. What, stand'st thou idle here? lend me
    thy sword:
Many a nobleman lies stark and stiff
Under the hoofs of vaunting enemies,

Whose deaths are yet unrevenged: I prithee, lend
  me thy sword.

Fal. O Hal, I prithee, give me leave to breathe
awhile. Turk Gregory never did such deeds in
arms as I have done this day. I have paid Percy,
I have made him sure.

Prince. He is, indeed; and living to kill thee.
I prithee, lend me thy sword.   50

Fal. Nay, before God, Hal, if Percy be alive,
thou get'st not my sword; but take my pistol, if
thou wilt.

Prince. Give it me: what, is it in the case?

Fal. Ay, Hal; 'tis hot, 'tis hot; there's that will
sack a city.

    *The Prince draws it out, and finds it to be a bottle
      of sack.*

Prince. What, is it a time to jest and dally now?

    [*He throws the bottle at him.*   *Exit.*

Fal. Well, if Percy be alive, I'll pierce him. If
he do come in my way, so: if he do not, if I come
in his willingly, let him make a carbonado of me.
I like not such grinning honour as Sir Walter
hath: give me life: which if I can save, so; if not,
honour comes unlooked for, and there's an end.

                              [*Exit.*

    Scene iv. *Another part of the field*

Alarum. Excursions. Enter the KING, *the* PRINCE,
    LORD JOHN OF LANCASTER, *and* EARL OF WEST-
    MORELAND.

King. I prithee,
Harry, withdraw thyself; thou bleed'st too
  much.
Lord John of Lancaster, go you with him.

Lan. Not I, my lord, unless I did bleed too.

Prince. I beseech your Majesty, make up,
Lest your retirement do amaze your friends.

King. I will do so.
My Lord of Westmoreland, lead him to his tent.

West. Come, my lord, I'll lead you to your tent.

Prince. Lead me, my lord? I do not need your
  help: 10
And God forbid a shallow scratch should drive
The Prince of Wales from such a field as this,
Where stain'd nobility lies trodden on,
And rebels' arms triumph in massacres!

Lan. We breathe too long: come, cousin Westmoreland,
Our duty this way lies; for God's sake, come.

    [*Exeunt* PRINCE JOHN *and* WESTMORELAND.

Prince. By God, thou hast deceived me, Lan-
  caster;
I did not think thee lord of such a spirit:
Before, I loved thee as a brother, John;
But now, I do respect thee as my soul.   20

King. I saw him hold Lord Percy at the point

With lustier maintenance than I did look for
Of such an ungrown warrior.

Prince.   O, this boy
Lends mettle to us all!   [*Exit.*

           Enter DOUGLAS.

Doug. Another king! they grow like Hydra's
  heads:
I am the Douglas, fatal to all those
That wear those colours on them: what art thou,
That counterfeit'st the person of a king?

King. The King himself; who, Douglas, grieves
  at heart
So many of his shadows thou hast met   30
And not the very King. I have two boys
Seek Percy and thyself about the field:
But, seeing thou fall'st on me so luckily,
I will assay thee: so, defend thyself.

Doug. I fear thou art another counterfeit;
And yet, in faith, thou bear'st thee like a king:
But mine I am sure thou art, whoe'er thou be,
And thus I win thee.

    They fight; the KING *being in danger, re-enter*
      PRINCE OF WALES.

Prince. Hold up thy head, vile Scot, or thou art
  like
Never to hold it up again! the spirits   40
Of valiant Shirley, Stafford, Blunt, are in my
  arms:
It is the Prince of Wales that threatens thee;
Who never promiseth but he means to pay.

    They fight: DOUGLAS *flies.*
Cheerly, my lord: how fares your Grace?
Sir Nicholas Gawsey hath for succour sent,
And so hath Clifton: I'll to Clifton straight.

King. Stay, and breathe awhile:
Thou hast redeem'd thy lost opinion,
And show'd thou makest some tender of my life
In this fair rescue thou hast brought to me.   50

Prince. O God! they did me too much injury
That ever said I hearken'd for your death.
If it were so, I might have let alone
The insulting hand of Douglas over you,
Which would have been as speedy in your end
As all the poisonous potions in the world
And saved the treacherous labour of your son.

King. Make up to Clifton: I'll to Sir Nicholas
  Gawsey.   [*Exit.*

           Enter HOTSPUR.

Hot. If I mistake not, thou art Harry Monmouth.

Prince. Thou speak'st as if I would deny my
  name.   60

Hot. My name is Harry Percy.

Prince.   Why, then I see
A very valiant rebel of the name.
I am the Prince of Wales; and think not, Percy,
To share with me in glory any more:
Two stars keep not their motion in one sphere;
Nor can one England brook a double reign,
Of Harry Percy and the Prince of Wales.

Hot. Nor shall it, Harry; for the hour is come
To end the one of us; and would to God
Thy name in arms were now as great as mine! *70*

Prince. I'll make it greater ere I part from thee;
And all the budding honours on thy crest
I'll crop, to make a garland for my head.

Hot. I can no longer brook thy vanities.

        They fight.

        Enter FALSTAFF.

Fal. Well said, Hal! to it, Hal! Nay, you shall
find no boy's play here, I can tell you.

Re-enter DOUGLAS; *he fights with* FALSTAFF, *who
falls down as if he were dead, and exit* DOUGLAS.
HOTSPUR *is wounded, and falls.*

Hot. O, Harry, thou hast robb'd me of my
        youth!
I better brook the loss of brittle life
Than those proud titles thou hast won of me;
They wound my thoughts worse than thy sword
        my flesh: *80*
But thought's the slave of life, and life time's fool;
And time, that takes survey of all the world,
Must have a stop. O, I could prophesy,
But that the earthy and cold hand of death
Lies on my tongue: no, Percy, thou art dust,
And food for—   [*Dies.*

Prince. For worms, brave Percy: fare thee well,
        great heart!
Ill-weaved ambition, how much art thou shrunk!
When that this body did contain a spirit,
A kingdom for it was too small a bound;   *90*
But now two paces of the vilest earth
Is room enough: this earth that bears thee dead
Bears not **alive** so stout a gentleman.
If thou wert sensible of courtesy,
I should not make so dear a show of zeal:
But let my favours hide thy mangled face;
And, even in thy behalf, I'll thank myself
For doing these fair rites of tenderness.
Adieu, and take thy praise with thee to heaven!
Thy ignominy sleep with thee in the grave, *100*
But not remember'd in thy epitaph!

        He spieth FALSTAFF *on the ground.*

What, old acquaintance! could not all this flesh
Keep in a little life? Poor Jack, farewell!
I could have better spared a better man:

O, I should have a heavy miss of thee,
If I were much in love with vanity!
Death hath not struck so fat a deer to-day,
Though many dearer, in this bloody fray.
Embowell'd will I see thee by and by:
Till then in blood by noble Percy lie. [*Exit.* *110*

Fal. [*Rising up*] Embowelled! if thou embowel
me to-day, I'll give you leave to powder me and
eat me too to-morrow. 'Sblood, 'twas time to
counterfeit, or that hot termagant Scot had paid
me scot and lot too. Counterfeit? I lie, I am no
counterfeit: to die, is to be a counterfeit; for he
is but the counterfeit of a man who hath not the
life of a man: but to counterfeit dying, when a
man thereby liveth, is to be no counterfeit, but
the true and perfect image of life indeed. The
better part of valour is discretion; in the which
better part I have saved my life. 'Zounds, I am
afraid of this gunpowder Percy, though he be
dead: how, if he should counterfeit too and rise?
by my faith, I am afraid he would prove the
better counterfeit. Therefore I'll make him sure;
yea, and I'll swear I killed him. Why may not he
rise as well as I? Nothing confutes me but eyes,
and nobody sees me. Therefore, sirrah [*stabbing
him*], with a new wound in your thigh, come you
along with me. [*Takes up* HOTSPUR *on his back.*]

Re-enter the PRINCE OF WALES *and* LORD JOHN
        OF LANCASTER.

Prince. Come, brother John; full bravely hast
        thou flesh'd
Thy maiden sword.

Lan.   But, soft! whom have we here?
Did you not tell me this fat man was dead?

Prince. I did; I saw him dead,
Breathless and bleeding on the ground. Art thou
        alive?
Or is it fantasy that plays upon our eyesight?
I prithee, speak; we will not trust our eyes   *139*
Without our ears: thou art not what thou seem'st.

Fal. No, that's certain; I am not a double man:
but if I be not Jack Falstaff, then am I a Jack.
There is Percy [*throwing the body down*]: if your
father will do me any honour, so; if not, let him
kill the next Percy himself. I look to be either
earl or duke, I can assure you.

Prince. Why, Percy I killed myself and saw
        thee dead.

Fal. Didst thou? Lord, Lord, how this world is
given to lying! I grant you I was down and out of
breath; and so was he: but we rose both at an
instant and fought a long hour by Shrewsbury
clock. If I may be believed, so; if not, let them
that should reward valour bear the sin upon their
own heads. I'll take it upon my death, I gave him

this wound in the thigh: if the man were alive
and would deny it, 'zounds, I would make him
eat a piece of my sword.

Lan. This is the strangest tale that ever I heard.

Prince. This is the strangest fellow, brother
John.   *159*
Come, bring your luggage nobly on your back:
For my part, if a lie may do thee grace,
I'll gild it with the happiest terms I have.

A retreat is sounded.

The trumpet sounds retreat; the day is ours.
Come, brother, let us to the highest of the field,
To see what friends are living, who are dead.

        [Exeunt PRINCE OF WALES *and* LANCASTER.

Fal. I'll follow, as they say, for reward. He that
rewards me, God reward him! If I do grow great,
I'll grow less; for I'll purge, and leave sack, and
live cleanly as a nobleman should do.   *[Exit.*

Scene v. *Another part of the field*

The trumpets sound. Enter the KING, PRINCE OF
WALES, LORD JOHN OF LANCASTER, EARL OF
WESTMORELAND, *with* WORCESTER *and* VERNON
prisoners.

King. Thus ever did rebellion find rebuke.
Ill-spirited Worcester! did not we send grace,
Pardon, and terms of love to all of you?
And wouldst thou turn our offers contrary?
Misuse the tenour of thy kinsman's trust?
Three knights upon our party slain to-day,
A noble earl, and many a creature else
Had been alive this hour,
If like a Christian thou hadst truly borne
Betwixt our armies true intelligence.   *10*

Wor. What I have done my safety urged me to;
And I embrace this fortune patiently,
Since not to be avoided it falls on me.

King. Bear Worcester to the death and Vernon
  too:
Other offenders we will pause upon.

      [Exeunt WORCESTER *and* VERNON, *guarded.*

How goes the field?

Prince. The noble Scot, Lord Douglas, when he
  saw
The fortune of the day quite turn'd from him,
The noble Percy slain, and all his men
Upon the foot of fear, fled with the rest;   *20*
And falling from a hill, he was so bruised
That the pursuers took him. At my tent
The Douglas is; and I beseech your Grace
I may dispose of him.

King.   With all my heart.

Prince. Then, brother John of Lancaster, to you
This honourable bounty shall belong:
Go to the Douglas, and deliver him
Up to his pleasure, ransomless and free:
His valour shown upon our crests to-day
Hath taught us how to cherish such high deeds
Even in the bosom of our adversaries.   *31*

Lan. I thank your Grace for this high courtesy,
Which I shall give away immediately.

King. Then this remains, that we divide our
  power.
You, son John, and my cousin Westmoreland
Towards York shall bend you with your dearest
  speed,
To meet Northumberland and the prelate Scroop,
Who, as we hear, are busily in arms:
Myself and you, son Harry, will towards Wales,
To fight with Glendower and the Earl of March.
Rebellion in this land shall lose his sway,   *41*
Meeting the check of such another day:
And since this business so fair is done,
Let us not leave till all our own be won.   *[Exeunt.*

The Second Part of
KING HENRY THE FOURTH

DRAMATIS PERSONÆ

King Henry the Fourth
Henry, Prince of Wales,
   afterwards King Henry V
Thomas, Duke of Clarence | *his sons*
Prince John of Lancaster
Prince Humphrey of Gloucester
Earl of Warwick
Earl of Westmoreland
Gower
Harcourt
Lord Chief Justice *of the King's Bench*
A Servant *of the Chief Justice*
Earl of Northumberland
Scroop, Archbishop of York
Lord Mowbray
Lord Hastings
Lord Bardolph
Sir John Coleville
Travers | *retainers of Northumberland*
Morton
Sir John Falstaff
Page *to Falstaff*
Bardolph
Pistol
Poins
Peto

Shallow | *country justices*
Silence
Davy, *servant to Shallow*
Mouldy
Shadow
Wart | *recruits*
Feeble
Bullcalf
Fang | *sheriff's officers*
Snare
A Porter
Two Drawers
A Messenger
A Beadle
Two Grooms
Rumour, *the Presenter*
A Dancer, *speaker of the Epilogue*

Lady Northumberland
Lady Percy
Mistress Quickly, *hostess of a tavern in Eastcheap*
Doll Tearsheet

Non-Speaking: *Earl of Surrey, Blunt, Lords, Beadles, Musicians, and Attendants*

Scene: *England*

INDUCTION

Warkworth: before the castle
Enter rumour, *painted full of tongues.*

Rum. Open your ears; for which of you will
   stop
The vent of hearing when loud Rumour speaks?
I, from the orient to the drooping west,
Making the wind my post-horse, still unfold
The acts commenced on this ball of earth:
Upon my tongues continual slanders ride,
The which in every language I pronounce,
Stuffing the ears of men with false reports.
I speak of peace, while covert enmity
Under the smile of safety wounds the world: *10*
And who but Rumour, who but only I,
Make fearful musters and prepared defence,
Whiles the big year, swoln with some other
   grief,
Is thought with child by the stern tyrant war,
And no such matter? Rumour is a pipe
Blown by surmises, jealousies, conjectures,

And of so easy and so plain a stop
That the blunt monster with uncounted heads,
The still-discordant wavering multitude,
Can play upon it. But what need I thus   *20*
My well-known body to anatomize
Among my household? Why is Rumour here?
I run before King Harry's victory;
Who in a bloody field by Shrewsbury
Hath beaten down young Hotspur and his troops,
Quenching the flame of bold rebellion
Even with the rebels' blood. But what mean I
To speak so true at first? my office is
To noise abroad that Harry Monmouth fell
Under the wrath of noble Hotspur's sword,   *30*
And that the king before the Douglas' rage
Stoop'd his anointed head as low as death.
This have I rumour'd through the peasant towns
Between the royal field of Shrewsbury
And this worm-eaten hold of ragged stone,
Where Hotspur's father, old Northumberland,
Lies crafty-sick: the posts come tiring on,
And not a man of them brings other news

Than they have learn'd of me: from Rumour's
        tongues
They bring smooth comforts false, worse than
        true wrongs.   [*Exit.*   40

ACT I

SCENE I. *The same*

Enter LORD BARDOLPH.

L. Bard. Who keeps the gate here, ho?

The PORTER *opens the gate.*

                            Where is the Earl?
Port. What shall I say you are?
L. Bard.   Tell thou the Earl
That the Lord Bardolph doth attend him here.
Port. His lordship is walk'd forth into the or-
        chard:
Please it your honour, knock but at the gate,
And he himself will answer.

Enter NORTHUMBERLAND.

L. Bard.   Here comes the Earl.
                            [*Exit* PORTER.
North. What news, Lord Bardolph? every min-
        ute now
Should be the father of some stratagem:
The times are wild; contention, like a horse
Full of high feeding, madly hath broke loose   10
And bears down all before him.
L. Bard.   Noble Earl,
I bring you certain news from Shrewsbury.
North. Good, an God will!
L. Bard.   As good as heart can wish:
The King is almost wounded to the death;
And, in the fortune of my lord your son,
Prince Harry slain outright; and both the
        Blunts
Kill'd by the hand of Douglas; young Prince
        John
And Westmoreland and Stafford fled the field;
And Harry Monmouth's brawn, the hulk Sir
        John,
Is prisoner to your son: O, such a day,   20
So fought, so follow'd, and so fairly won,
Came not till now to dignify the times,
Since Cæsar's fortunes!
North.   How is this derived?
Saw you the field? came you from Shrewsbury?
L. Bard. I spake with one, my lord, that came
        from thence,
A gentleman well bred and of good name,
That freely render'd me these news for true.
North. Here comes my servant Travers, whom
        I sent
On Tuesday last to listen after news.

Enter TRAVERS.

L. Bard. My lord, I over-rode him on the way;
And he is furnish'd with no certainties   31
More than he haply may retail from me.
North. Now, Travers, what good tidings comes
        with you?
Tra. My lord, Sir John Umfrevile turn'd me
        back
With joyful tidings; and, being better horsed,
Out-rode me. After him came spurring hard
A gentleman, almost forspent with speed,
That stopp'd by me to breathe his bloodied horse.
He ask'd the way to Chester; and of him
I did demand what news from Shrewsbury: 40
He told me that rebellion had bad luck
And that young Harry Percy's spur was cold.
With that, he gave his able horse the head,
And bending forward struck his armed heels
Against the panting sides of his poor jade
Up to the rowel-head, and starting so
He seem'd in running to devour the way,
Staying no longer question.
North.   Ha! Again:
Said he young Harry Percy's spur was cold?
Of Hotspur Coldspur? that rebellion   50
Had met ill luck?
L. Bard.   My lord, I'll tell you what;
If my young lord your son have not the day,
Upon mine honour, for a silken point
I'll give my barony: never talk of it.
North. Why should that gentleman that rode by
        Travers
Give then such instances of loss?
L. Bard.   Who, he?
He was some hilding fellow that had stolen
The horse he rode on, and, upon my life,
Spoke at a venture. Look, here comes more news.

Enter MORTON.

North. Yea, this man's brow, like to a title-leaf,
Foretells the nature of a tragic volume: 60
So looks the strand whereon the imperious flood
Hath left a witness'd usurpation.
Say, Morton, didst thou come from Shrewsbury?
Mor. I ran from Shrewsbury, my noble lord;
Where hateful death put on his ugliest mask
To fright our party.
North.   How doth my son and brother?
Thou tremblest; and the whiteness in thy cheek
Is apter than thy tongue to tell thy errand.
Even such a man, so faint, so spiritless,   70
So dull, so dead in look, so woe-begone,
Drew Priam's curtain in the dead of night,
And would have told him half his Troy was
        burnt;

But Priam found the fire ere he his tongue,
And I my Percy's death ere thou report'st it.
This thou wouldst say, "Your son did thus and
    thus;
Your brother thus: so fought the noble Douglas":
Stopping my greedy ear with their bold deeds:
But in the end, to stop my ear indeed,
Thou hast a sigh to blow away this praise,   *80*
Ending with "Brother, son, and all are dead."
  Mor. Douglas is living, and your brother, yet;
But, for my lord your son—
  North.   Why, he is dead.
See what a ready tongue suspicion hath!
He that but fears the thing he would not know
Hath by instinct knowledge from others' eyes
That what he fear'd is chanced. Yet speak,
    Morton;
Tell thou an earl his divination lies,
And I will take it as a sweet disgrace
And make thee rich for doing me such wrong.   *90*
  Mor. You are too great to be by me gainsaid:
Your spirit is too true, your fears too certain.
  North. Yet, for all this, say not that Percy's
    dead.
I see a strange confession in thine eye:
Thou shakest thy head and hold'st it fear or sin
To speak a truth. If he be slain, say so;
The tongue offends not that reports his death:
And he doth sin that doth belie the dead,
Not he which says the dead is not alive.
Yet the first bringer of unwelcome news   *100*
Hath but a losing office, and his tongue
Sounds ever after as a sullen bell,
Remember'd tolling a departing friend.
  L. Bard. I cannot think, my lord, your son is
    dead.
  Mor. I am sorry I should force you to believe
That which I would to God I had not seen;
But these mine eyes saw him in bloody state,
Rendering faint quittance, wearied and out-
    breathed,
To Harry Monmouth; whose swift wrath beat
    down
The never-daunted Percy to the earth,   *110*
From whence with life he never more sprung up.
In few, his death, whose spirit lent a fire
Even to the dullest peasant in his camp,
Being bruited once, took fire and heat away
From the best-temper'd courage in his troops;
For from his metal was his party steel'd;
Which once in him abated, all the rest
Turn'd on themselves, like dull and heavy lead:
And as the thing that's heavy in itself
Upon enforcement flies with greatest speed,   *120*
So did our men, heavy in Hotspur's loss,
Lend to this weight such lightness with their fear

That arrows fled not swifter toward their aim
Than did our soldiers, aiming at their safety,
Fly from the field. Then was that noble Wor-
    cester
Too soon ta'en prisoner; and that furious Scot,
The bloody Douglas, whose well-labouring
    sword
Had three times slain the appearance of the King,
'Gan vail his stomach and did grace the shame
Of those that turn'd their backs, and in his flight,
Stumbling in fear, was took. The sum of all   *131*
Is that the King hath won, and hath sent out
A speedy power to encounter you, my lord,
Under the conduct of young Lancaster
And Westmoreland. This is the news at full.
  North. For this I shall have time enough to
    mourn.
In poison there is physic; and these news,
Having been well, that would have made me sick,
Being sick, have in some measure made me well:
And as the wretch, whose fever-weaken'd joints,
Like strengthless hinges, buckle under life,   *141*
Impatient of his fit, breaks like a fire
Out of his keeper's arms, even so my limbs,
Weaken'd with grief, being now enraged with
    grief,
Are thrice themselves. Hence, therefore, thou
    nice crutch!
A scaly gauntlet now with joints of steel
Must glove this hand: and hence, thou sickly
    quoif!
Thou art a guard too wanton for the head
Which princes, flesh'd with conquest, aim to hit.
Now bind my brows with iron; and approach *150*
The ragged'st hour that time and spite dare bring
To frown upon the enraged Northumberland!
Let heaven kiss earth! now let not Nature's hand
Keep the wild flood confined! let order die!
And let this world no longer be a stage
To feed contention in a lingering act;
But let one spirit of the first-born Cain
Reign in all bosoms, that, each heart being set
On bloody courses, the rude scene may end,
And darkness be the burier of the dead!   *160*
  Tra. This strained passion doth you wrong,
    my lord.
  L. Bard. Sweet Earl, divorce not wisdom from
    your honour.
  Mor. The lives of all your loving complices
Lean on your health; the which, if you give o'er
To stormy passion, must perforce decay.
You cast the event of war, my noble lord,
And summ'd the account of chance, before you
    said
"Let us make head." It was your presurmise
That, in the dole of blows, your son might drop:

You knew he walk'd o'er perils, on an edge,   *170*
More likely to fall in than to get o'er;
You were advised his flesh was capable
Of wounds and scars and that his forward spirit
Would lift him where most trade of danger
    ranged:
Yet did you say, "Go forth"; and none of this,
Though strongly apprehended, could restrain
The stiff-borne action: what hath then befallen,
Or what hath this bold enterprise brought forth,
More than that being which was like to be?

L. Bard. We all that are engaged to this loss   *180*
Knew that we ventured on such dangerous seas
That if we wrought out life 'twas ten to one;
And yet we ventured, for the gain proposed
Choked the respect of likely peril fear'd;
And since we are o'erset, venture again.
Come, we will all put forth, body and goods.

Mor. 'Tis more than time: and, my most noble
    lord,
I hear for certain, and do speak the truth,
The gentle Archbishop of York is up
With well-appointed powers: he is a man   *190*
Who with a double surety binds his followers.
My lord your son had only but the corpse,
But shadows and the shows of men, to fight;
For that same word, "rebellion," did divide
The action of their bodies from their souls;
And they did fight with queasiness, constrain'd,
As men drink potions, that their weapons only
Seem'd on our side; but, for their spirits and
    souls,
This word, "rebellion," it had froze them up,
As fish are in a pond. But now the Bishop   *200*
Turns insurrection to religion:
Supposed sincere and holy in his thoughts,
He's followed both with body and with mind;
And doth enlarge his rising with the blood
Of fair King Richard, scraped from Pomfret
    stones;
Derives from heaven his quarrel and his cause;
Tells them he doth bestride a bleeding land,
Gasping for life under great Bolingbroke;
And more and less do flock to follow him.

North. I knew of this before; but, to speak
    truth,   *210*
This present grief had wiped it from my mind.
Go in with me; and counsel every man
The aptest way for safety and revenge:
Get posts and letters, and make friends with
    speed:
Never so few, and never yet more need. [*Exeunt.*

SCENE II. *London: a street*

Enter FALSTAFF, *with his* PAGE *bearing his
sword and buckler.*

Fal. Sirrah, you giant, what says the doctor to
my water?

Page. He said, sir, the water itself was a good
healthy water; but, for the party that owed it, he
might have more diseases than he knew for.

Fal. Men of all sorts take a pride to gird at me:
the brain of this foolish-compounded clay, man,
is not able to invent any thing that tends to laughter, more than I invent or is invented on me: I
am not only witty in myself, but the cause that
wit is in other men. I do here walk before thee
like a sow that hath overwhelmed all her litter
but one. If the Prince put thee into my service
for any other reason than to set me off, why then
I have no judgement. Thou whoreson mandrake,
thou art fitter to be worn in my cap than to wait
at my heels. I was never manned with an agate
till now: but I will inset you neither in gold nor
silver, but in vile apparel, and send you back
again to your master, for a jewel—the juvenal,
the Prince your master, whose chin is not yet
fledged. I will sooner have a beard grow in the
palm of my hand than he shall get one on his
cheek; and yet he will not stick to say his face is
a face-royal: God may finish it when he will, 'tis
not a hair amiss yet: he may keep it still at a face-
royal, for a barber shall never earn sixpence out
of it; and yet he'll be crowing as if he had writ
man ever since his father was a bachelor. He
may keep his own grace, but he's almost out of
mine, I can assure him. What said Master Dom-
bledon about the satin for my short cloak and my
slops?

Page. He said, sir, you should procure him better
assurance than Bardolph: he would not take his
band and yours; he liked not the security.

Fal. Let him be damned, like the glutton! pray
God his tongue be hotter! A whoreson Achito-
phel! a rascally yea-forsooth knave! to bear a
gentleman in hand, and then stand upon security!
The whoreson smooth-pates do now wear nothing but high shoes, and bunches of keys at their
girdles; and if a man is through with them in
honest taking up, then they must stand upon security. I had as lief they would put ratsbane in
my mouth as offer to stop it with security. I
looked a' should have sent me two and twenty
yards of satin, as I am a true knight, and he sends
me security. Well, he may sleep in security; for
he hath the horn of abundance, and the lightness
of his wife shines through it: and yet cannot he
see, though he have his own lanthorn to light
him. Where's Bardolph?

Page. He's gone into Smithfield to buy your
worship a horse.

Fal. I bought him in Paul's, and he'll buy me a

horse in Smithfield: an I could get me but a wife in the stews, I were manned, horsed, and wived.

Enter the LORD CHIEF JUSTICE *and* SERVANT.

Page. Sir, here comes the nobleman that committed the Prince for striking him about Bardolph.

Fal. Wait close; I will not see him.

Ch. Just. What's he that goes there?

Serv. Falstaff, an't please your lordship.

Ch. Just. He that was in question for the robbery?   69

Serv. He, my lord: but he hath since done good service at Shrewsbury; and, as I hear, is now going with some charge to the Lord John of Lancaster.

Ch. Just. What, to York? Call him back again.

Serv. Sir John Falstaff!

Fal. Boy, tell him I am deaf.

Page. You must speak louder; my master is deaf.

Ch. Just. I am sure he is, to the hearing of anything good. Go, pluck him by the elbow; I must speak with him.

Serv. Sir John!

Fal. What! a young knave, and begging! Is there not wars? is there not employment? doth not the King lack subjects? do not the rebels need soldiers? Though it be a shame to be on any side but one, it is worse shame to beg than to be on the worst side, were it worse than the name of rebellion can tell how to make it.   90

Serv. You mistake me, sir.

Fal. Why, sir, did I say you were an honest man? setting my knighthood and my soldiership aside, I had lied in my throat, if I had said so.

Serv. I pray you, sir, then set your knighthood and your soldiership aside; and give me leave to tell you, you lie in your throat, if you say I am any other than an honest man.

Fal. I give thee leave to tell me so! I lay aside that which grows to me! If thou gettest any leave of me, hang me; if thou takest leave, thou wert better be hanged. You hunt counter: hence! avaunt!

Serv. Sir, my lord would speak with you.

Ch. Just. Sir John Falstaff, a word with you.

Fal. My good lord! God give your lordship good time of day. I am glad to see your lordship abroad: I heard say your lordship was sick: I hope your lordship goes abroad by advice. Your lordship, though not clean past your youth, hath yet some smack of age in you, some relish of the saltness of time; and I most humbly beseech your lordship to have a reverent care of your health.

Ch. Just. Sir John, I sent for you before your expedition to Shrewsbury.

Fal. An't please your lordship, I hear his Majesty is returned with some discomfort from Wales.

Ch. Just. I talk not of his Majesty: you would not come when I sent for you.   121

Fal. And I hear, moreover, his Highness is fallen into this same whoreson apoplexy.

Ch. Just. Well, God mend him! I pray you, let me speak with you.

Fal. This apoplexy is, as I take it, a kind of lethargy, an't please your lordship; a kind of sleeping in the blood, a whoreson tingling.

Ch. Just. What tell you me of it? be it as it is.   130

Fal. It hath it original from much grief, from study and perturbation of the brain: I have read the cause of his effects in Galen: it is a kind of deafness.

Ch. Just. I think you are fallen into the disease; for you hear not what I say to you.

Fal. Very well, my lord, very well: rather, an't please you, it is the disease of not listening, the malady of not marking, that I am troubled withal.   140

Ch. Just. To punish you by the heels would amend the attention of your ears; and I care not if I do become your physician.

Fal. I am as poor as Job, my lord, but not so patient: your lordship may minister the potion of imprisonment to me in respect of poverty; but how I should be your patient to follow your prescriptions, the wise may make some dram of a scruple, or indeed a scruple itself.

Ch. Just. I sent for you, when there were matters against you for your life, to come speak with me.

Fal. As I was then advised by my learned counsel in the laws of this land-service, I did not come.

Ch. Just. Well, the truth is, Sir John, you live in great infamy.

Fal. He that buckles him in my belt cannot live in less.

Ch. Just. Your means are very slender, and your waste is great.   160

Fal. I would it were otherwise; I would my means were greater, and my waist slenderer.

Ch. Just. You have misled the youthful Prince.

Fal. The young Prince hath misled me: I am the fellow with the great belly, and he my dog.

Ch. Just. Well, I am loath to gall a new-healed wound: your day's service at Shrewsbury hath a little gilded over your night's exploit on Gadshill: you may thank the unquiet time for your quiet o'er-posting that action.   171

Fal. My lord?

Ch. Just. But since all is well, keep it so: wake not a sleeping wolf.

Fal. To wake a wolf is as bad as to smell a fox.

Ch. Just. What! you are as a candle, the better part burnt out.

Fal. A wassail candle, my lord, all tallow: if I did say of wax, my growth would approve the truth. *181*

Ch. Just. There is not a white hair on your face but should have his effect of gravity.

Fal. His effect of gravy, gravy, gravy.

Ch. Just. You follow the young Prince up and down, like his ill angel.

Fal. Not so, my lord; your ill angel is light; but I hope he that looks upon me will take me without weighing: and yet, in some respects, I grant, I cannot go: I cannot tell. Virtue is of so little regard in these costermonger times that true valour is turned bear-herd: pregnancy is made a tapster, and hath his quick wit wasted in giving reckonings: all the other gifts appertinent to man, as the malice of this age shapes them, are not worth a gooseberry. You that are old consider not the capacities of us that are young; you do measure the heat of our livers with the bitterness of your galls: and we that are in the vaward of our youth, I must confess, are wags too. *200*

Ch. Just. Do you set down your name in the scroll of youth, that are written down old with all the characters of age? Have you not a moist eye? a dry hand? a yellow cheek? a white beard? a decreasing leg? an increasing belly? is not your voice broken? your wind short? your chin double? your wit single? and every part about you blasted with antiquity? and will you yet call yourself young? Fie, fie, fie, Sir John! *209*

Fal. My lord, I was born about three of the clock in the afternoon, with a white head and something a round belly. For my voice, I have lost it with halloing and singing of anthems. To approve my youth further, I will not: the truth is, I am only old in judgement and understanding; and he that will caper with me for a thousand marks, let him lend me the money, and have at him! For the box of the ear that the Prince gave you, he gave it like a rude prince, and you took it like a sensible lord. I have checked him for it, and the young lion repents; marry, not in ashes and sackcloth, but in new silk and old sack.

Ch. Just. Well, God send the Prince a better companion!

Fal. God send the companion a better prince! I cannot rid my hands of him.

Ch. Just. Well, the King hath severed you and Prince Harry: I hear you are going with Lord John of Lancaster against the Archbishop and the Earl of Northumberland. *230*

Fal. Yea; I thank your pretty sweet wit for it. But look you pray, all you that kiss my lady Peace at home, that our armies join not in a hot day; for, by the Lord, I take but two shirts out with me, and I mean not to sweat extraordinarily: if it be a hot day, and I brandish anything but a bottle, I would I might never spit white again. There is not a dangerous action can peep out his head but I am thrust upon it: well, I cannot last ever: but it was alway yet the trick of our English nation, if they have a good thing, to make it too common. If ye will needs say I am an old man, you should give me rest. I would to God my name were not so terrible to the enemy as it is: I were better to be eaten to death with a rust than to be scoured to nothing with perpetual motion.

Ch. Just. Well, be honest, be honest; and God bless your expedition!

Fal. Will your lordship lend me a thousand pound to furnish me forth? *251*

Ch. Just. Not a penny, not a penny; you are too impatient to bear crosses. Fare you well: commend me to my cousin Westmoreland.

[*Exeunt* CHIEF JUSTICE *and* SERVANT.

Fal. If I do, fillip me with a three-man beetle. A man can no more separate age and covetousness than a' can part young limbs and lechery: but the gout galls the one, and the pox pinches the other; and so both the degrees prevent my curses. Boy! *260*

Page. Sir?

Fal. What money is in my purse?

Page. Seven groats and two pence.

Fal. I can get no remedy against this consumption of the purse: borrowing only lingers and lingers it out, but the disease is incurable. Go bear this letter to my Lord of Lancaster; this to the Prince; this to the Earl of Westmoreland; and this to old Mistress Ursula, whom I have weekly sworn to marry since I perceived the first white hair on my chin. About it: you know where to find me. [*Exit* PAGE.] A pox of this gout! or, a gout of this pox! for the one or the other plays the rogue with my great toe. 'Tis no matter if I do halt; I have the wars for my colour, and my pension shall seem the more reasonable. A good wit will make use of anything: I will turn diseases to commodity. [*Exit.*

SCENE III. *York: the Archbishop's palace*

Enter the ARCHBISHOP, *the* LORDS HASTINGS, MOW-
BRAY, *and* BARDOLPH.

Arch. Thus have you heard our cause and known our means;

And, my most noble friends, I pray you all,
Speak plainly your opinions of our hopes:
And first, Lord Marshal, what say you to it?

Mowb. I well allow the occasion of our arms;
But gladly would be better satisfied
How in our means we should advance ourselves
To look with forehead bold and big enough
Upon the power and puissance of the King.

Hast. Our present musters grow upon the file 10
To five and twenty thousand men of choice;
And our supplies live largely in the hope
Of great Northumberland, whose bosom burns
With an incensed fire of injuries.

L. Bard. The question then, Lord Hastings,
    standeth thus;
Whether our present five and twenty thousand
May hold up head without Northumberland?

Hast. With him, we may.

L. Bard.   Yea, marry, there's the point:
But if without him we be thought too feeble,
My judgement is, we should not step too far 20
Till we had his assistance by the hand;
For in a theme so bloody-faced as this
Conjecture, expectation, and surmise
Of aids incertain should not be admitted.

Arch. 'Tis very true, Lord Bardolph; for indeed
It was young Hotspur's case at Shrewsbury.

L. Bard. It was, my lord; who lined himself
    with hope,
Eating the air on promise of supply,
Flattering himself in project of a power
Much smaller than the smallest of his thoughts:
And so, with great imagination 31
Proper to madmen, led his powers to death
And winking leap'd into destruction.

Hast. But, by your leave, it never yet did hurt
To lay down likelihoods and forms of hope.

L. Bard. Yes, if this present quality of war,
Indeed the instant action: a cause on foot
Lives so in hope as in an early spring
We see the appearing buds; which to prove fruit,
Hope gives not so much warrant as despair 40
That frosts will bite them. When we mean to
    build,
We first survey the plot, then draw the model;
And when we see the figure of the house,
Then must we rate the cost of the erection;
Which if we find outweighs ability,
What do we then but draw anew the model
In fewer offices, or at last desist
To build at all? Much more, in this great work,
Which is almost to pluck a kingdom down
And set another up, should we survey 50
The plot of situation and the model,
Consent upon a sure foundation,
Question surveyors, know our own estate,

How able such a work to undergo,
To weigh against his opposite; or else
We fortify in paper and in figures,
Using the names of men instead of men:
Like one that draws the model of a house
Beyond his power to build it; who, half through,
Gives o'er and leaves his part-created cost 60
A naked subject to the weeping clouds
And waste for churlish winter's tyranny.

Hast. Grant that our hopes, yet likely of fair
    birth,
Should be still-born, and that we now possess'd
The utmost man of expectation,
I think we are a body strong enough,
Even as we are, to equal with the King.

L. Bard. What, is the King but five and twenty
    thousand?

Hast. To us no more; nay, not so much, Lord
    Bardolph.
For his divisions, as the times do brawl, 70
Are in three heads: one power against the French,
And one against Glendower; perforce a third
Must take up us: so is the unfirm King
In three divided; and his coffers sound
With hollow poverty and emptiness.

Arch. That he should draw his several strengths
    together
And come against in full puissance,
Need not be dreaded.

Hast.   If he should do so,
He leaves his back unarm'd, the French and Welsh
Baying him at the heels: never fear that. 80

L. Bard. Who is it like should lead his forces
    hither?

Hast. The Duke of Lancaster and Westmore-
    land;
Against the Welsh, himself and Harry Monmouth.
But who is substituted 'gainst the French,
I have no certain notice.

Arch.   Let us on,
And publish the occasion of our arms.
The commonwealth is sick of their own choice;
Their over-greedy love hath surfeited:
An habitation giddy and unsure
Hath he that buildeth on the vulgar heart. 90
O thou fond many, with what loud applause
Didst thou beat heaven with blessing Bolingbroke,
Before he was what thou wouldst have him be!
And being now trimm'd in thine own desires,
Thou, beastly feeder, art so full of him
That thou provokest thyself to cast him up.
So, so, thou common dog, didst thou disgorge
Thy glutton bosom of the royal Richard;
And now thou wouldst eat thy dead vomit up,
And howl'st to find it. What trust is in these
    times?

They that, when Richard lived, would have him
 die, *101*
Are now become enamour'd on his grave:
Thou, that threw'st dust upon his goodly head
When through proud London he came sighing on
After the admired heels of Bolingbroke,
Criest now, "O earth, yield us that king again,
And take thou this!" O thoughts of men accursed!
Past and to come seems best; things present
 worst.

Mowb. Shall we go draw our numbers and set
 on?

Hast. We are time's subjects, and time bids be
 gone.   [*Exeunt. 110*

ACT II

Scene i. *London: a street*

Enter mistress quickly, fang *and his Boy with
her, and* snare *following*.

Quick. Master Fang, have you entered the
action?

Fang. It is entered.

Quick. Where's your yeoman? Is't a lusty
yeoman? will a' stand to't?

Fang. Sirrah, where's Snare?

Quick. O Lord, ay! good Master Snare.

Snare. Here, here.

Fang. Snare, we must arrest Sir John Falstaff.

Quick. Yea, good Master Snare; I have entered him and all. *11*

Snare. It may chance cost some of us our lives,
for he will stab.

Quick. Alas the day! take heed of him; he
stabbed me in mine own house, and that most
beastly: in good faith, he cares not what mischief
he does, if his weapon be out: he will foin like
any devil; he will spare neither man, woman,
nor child.

Fang. If I can close with him, I care not for
his thrust. *21*

Quick. No, nor I neither: I'll be at your elbow.

Fang. An I but fist him once: an a' come but
within my vice—

Quick. I am undone by his going; I warrant
you, he's an infinitive thing upon my score. Good
Master Fang, hold him sure: good Master Snare,
let him not 'scape. A' comes continuantly to Pie-
corner—saving your manhoods—to buy a saddle;
and he is indited to dinner to the Lubber's-head
in Lumbert street, to Master Smooth's the silk-
man: I pray ye, since my exion is entered and
my case so openly known to the world, let him
be brought in to his answer. A hundred mark is
a long one for a poor lone woman to bear: and
I have borne, and borne, and borne, and have

been fubbed off, and fubbed off, and fubbed off,
from this day to that day, that it is a shame to
be thought on. There is no honesty in such
dealing; unless a woman should be made an ass
and a beast, to bear every knave's wrong. Yonder
he comes; and that arrant malmsey-nose knave,
Bardolph, with him. Do your offices, do your
offices: Master Fang and Master Snare, do me,
do me, do me your offices.

Enter falstaff, page, *and* bardolph.

Fal. How now! whose mare's dead? what's
the matter?

Fang. Sir John, I arrest you at the suit of Mistress Quickly. *49*

Fal. Away, varlets! Draw, Bardolph: cut me off
the villain's head: throw the quean in the channel.

Quick. Throw me in the channel! I'll throw
thee in the channel. Wilt thou? wilt thou? thou
bastardly rogue! Murder, murder! Ah, thou
honey-suckle villain! wilt thou kill God's officers
and the king's? Ah, thou honey-seed rogue! thou
art a honey-seed, a man-queller, and a woman-
queller.

Fal. Keep them off, Bardolph. *60*

Fang. A rescue! a rescue!

Quick. Good people, bring a rescue or two.
Thou wo't, wo't thou? thou wo't, wo't ta? do,
do, thou rogue! do, thou hemp-seed!

Fal. Away, you scullion! you rampallian! you
fustilarian! I'll tickle your catastrophe.

Enter the lord chief justice, *and his men*.

Ch. Just. What is the matter? keep the peace
here, ho!

Quick. Good my lord, be good to me. I beseech you, stand to me. *70*

Ch. Just. How now, Sir John! what are you
 brawling here?
Doth this become your place, your time, and
 business?
You should have been well on your way to York.
Stand from him, fellow: wherefore hang'st upon
 him?

Quick. O my most worshipful lord, an't please
your Grace, I am a poor widow of Eastcheap,
and he is arrested at my suit.

Ch. Just. For what sum?

Quick. It is more than for some, my lord; it is
for all, all I have. He hath eaten me out of house
and home; he hath put all my substance into that
fat belly of his: but I will have some of it out
again, or I will ride thee o'nights like the mare.

Fal. I think I am as like to ride the mare, if I
have any vantage of ground to get up.

Ch. Just. How comes this, Sir John? Fie!

what man of good temper would endure this tempest of exclamation? Are you not ashamed to
enforce a poor widow to so rough a course to
come by her own?   90

Fal. What is the gross sum that I owe thee?

Quick. Marry, if thou wert an honest man,
thyself and the money too. Thou didst swear to
me upon a parcel-gilt goblet, sitting in my Dol-
phin-chamber, at the round table, by a sea-coal
fire, upon Wednesday in Wheeson week, when
the Prince broke thy head for liking his father to
a singing-man of Windsor, thou didst swear to
me then, as I was washing thy wound, to marry
me and make me my lady thy wife. Canst thou
deny it? Did not goodwife Keech, the butcher's
wife, come in then and call me gossip Quickly?
coming in to borrow a mess of vinegar; telling us
she had a good dish of prawns; whereby thou
didst desire to eat some; whereby I told thee they
were ill for a green wound? And didst thou not,
when she was gone downstairs, desire me to be
no more so familiarity with such poor people;
saying that ere long they should call me madam?
And didst thou not kiss me and bid me fetch thee
thirty shillings? I put thee now to thy book-
oath: deny it, if thou canst.

Fal. My lord, this is a poor mad soul; and
she says up and down the town that her eldest
son is like you: she hath been in good case, and
the truth is, poverty hath distracted her. But
for these foolish officers, I beseech you I may
have redress against them.

Ch. Just. Sir John, Sir John, I am well acquainted
with your manner of wrenching the true cause
the false way. It is not a confident brow, nor
the throng of words that come with such more
than impudent sauciness from you, can thrust
me from a level consideration: you have, as it
appears to me, practised upon the easy-yielding
spirit of this woman, and made her serve your
uses both in purse and in person.

Quick. Yea, in truth, my lord.

Ch. Just. Pray thee, peace. Pay her the debt
you owe her, and unpay the villainy you have
done her: the one you may do with sterling
money, and the other with current repentance.

Fal. My lord, I will not undergo this sneap
without reply. You call honourable boldness
impudent sauciness: if a man will make courtesy
and say nothing, he is virtuous: no, my lord, my
humble duty remembered, I will not be your
suitor. I say to you, I do desire deliverance from
these officers, being upon hasty employment in
the King's affairs.   140

Ch. Just. You speak as having power to do
wrong: but answer in the effect of your reputation, and satisfy the poor woman.

Fal. Come hither, hostess.

Enter GOWER.

Ch. Just. Now, Master Gower, what news?

Gow. The King, my lord, and Harry Prince of
    Wales
Are near at hand: the rest the paper tells.

Fal. As I am a gentleman.

Quick. Faith, you said so before.

Fal. As I am a gentleman. Come, no more
words of it.   151

Quick. By this heavenly ground I tread on, I
must be fain to pawn both my plate and the
tapestry of my dining-chambers.

Fal. Glasses, glasses, is the only drinking:
and for thy walls, a pretty slight drollery, or the
story of the Prodigal, or the German hunting in
water-work, is worth a thousand of these bed-
hangings and these fly-bitten tapestries. Let it
be ten pound, if thou canst. Come, an 'twere not
for thy humours, there's not a better wench in
England. Go, wash thy face, and draw the action.
Come, thou must not be in this humour with me;
dost not know me? come, come, I know thou
wast set on to this.

Quick. Pray thee, Sir John, let it be but twenty
nobles: i' faith, I am loath to pawn my plate, so
God save me, la!

Fal. Let it alone; I'll make other shift: you'll
be a fool still.   170

Quick. Well, you shall have it, though I pawn
my gown. I hope you'll come to supper. You'll
pay me all together?

Fal. Will I live? [*To* BARDOLPH] Go, with her,
with her; hook on, hook on.

Quick. Will you have Doll Tearsheet meet you
at supper?

Fal. No more words; let's have her.

[*Exeunt* MISTRESS QUICKLY, BARDOLPH, *Officers
    and Boy.*

Ch. Just. I have heard better news.

Fal. What's the news, my lord?   180

Ch. Just. Where lay the King last night?

Gow. At Basingstoke, my lord.

Fal. I hope, my lord, all's well: what is the
news, my lord?

Ch. Just. Come all his forces back?

Gow. No; fifteen hundred foot, five hundred
    horse,
Are march'd up to my Lord of Lancaster,
Against Northumberland and the Archbishop.

Fal. Comes the King back from Wales, my
    noble lord?

Ch. Just. You shall have letters of me presently: 190

Come, go along with me, good Master Gower.

Fal. My lord!

Ch. Just. What's the matter?

Fal. Master Gower, shall I entreat you with me to dinner?

Gow. I must wait upon my good lord here; I thank you, good Sir John.

Ch. Just. Sir John, you loiter here too long, being you are to take soldiers up in counties as you go.   200

Fal. Will you sup with me, Master Gower?

Ch. Just. What foolish master taught you these manners, Sir John?

Fal. Master Gower, if they become me not, he was a fool that taught them me. This is the right fencing grace, my lord; tap for tap, and so part fair.

Ch. Just. Now the Lord lighten thee! thou art a great fool.   [*Exeunt.*

SCENE II. *London: another street*

Enter PRINCE HENRY *and* POINS.

Prince. Before God, I am exceeding weary.

Poins. Is't come to that? I had thought weariness durst not have attached one of so high blood.

Prince. Faith, it does me; though it discolours the complexion of my greatness to acknowledge it. Doth it not show vilely in me to desire small beer?

Poins. Why, a prince should not be so loosely studied as to remember so weak a composition.

Prince. Belike then my appetite was not princely got; for, by my troth, I do now remember the poor creature, small beer. But, indeed, these humble considerations make me out of love with my greatness. What a disgrace is it to me to remember thy name! or to know thy face to-morrow! or to take note how many pair of silk stockings thou hast, viz. these, and those that were thy peach-coloured ones! or to bear the inventory of thy shirts, as, one for superfluity, and another for use! But that the tennis-court-keeper knows better than I; for it is a low ebb of linen with thee when thou keepest not racket there; as thou hast not done a great while, because the rest of thy low countries have made a shift to eat up thy holland: and God knows, whether those that bawl out the ruins of thy linen shall inherit his kingdom: but the mid-wives say the children are not in the fault; whereupon the world increases, and kindreds are mightily strengthened.

Poins. How ill it follows, after you have laboured so hard, you should talk so idly! Tell me, how many good young princes would do so, their fathers being so sick as yours at this time is?

Prince. Shall I tell thee one thing, Poins?

Poins. Yes, faith; and let it be an excellent good thing.

Prince. It shall serve among wits of no higher breeding than thine.

Poins. Go to; I stand the push of your one thing that you will tell.   41

Prince. Marry, I tell thee, it is not meet that I should be sad, now my father is sick: albeit I could tell to thee, as to one it pleases me, for fault of a better, to call my friend, I could be sad, and sad indeed too.

Poins. Very hardly upon such a subject.

Prince. By this hand, thou thinkest me as far in the devil's book as thou and Falstaff for obduracy and persistency: let the end try the man. But I tell thee, my heart bleeds inwardly that my father is so sick: and keeping such vile company as thou art hath in reason taken from me all ostentation of sorrow.

Poins. The reason?

Prince. What wouldst thou think of me, if I should weep?

Poins. I would think thee a most princely hypocrite.   59

Prince. It would be every man's thought; and thou art a blessed fellow to think as every man thinks: never a man's thought in the world keeps the road-way better than thine: every man would think me an hypocrite indeed. And what accites your most worshipful thought to think so?

Poins. Why, because you have been so lewd and so much engraffed to Falstaff.

Prince. And to thee.

Poins. By this light, I am well spoke on; I can hear it with mine own ears: the worst that they can say of me is that I am a second brother and that I am a proper fellow of my hands; and those two things, I confess, I cannot help. By the mass, here comes Bardolph.

Enter BARDOLPH *and* PAGE.

Prince. And the boy that I gave Falstaff: a' had him from me Christian; and look, if the fat villain have not transformed him ape.

Bard. God save your Grace!

Prince. And yours, most noble Bardolph!   79

Bard. Come, you virtuous ass, you bashful fool, must you be blushing? wherefore blush you now? What a maidenly man-at-arms are you become! Is't such a matter to get a pottle-pot's maidenhead?

Page. A' calls e'en now, my lord, through a red lattice, and I could discern no part of his face from the window: at last I spied his eyes, and methought he had made two holes in the ale-wife's new petticoat and so peeped through.

Prince. Has not the boy profited?   90

Bard. Away, you whoreson upright rabbit, away!

Page. Away, you rascally Althæa's dream, away!

Prince. Instruct us, boy; what dream, boy?

Page. Marry, my lord, Althæa dreamed she was delivered of a fire-brand; and therefore I call him her dream.

Prince. A crown's worth of good interpretation: there 'tis, boy.   100

Poins. O, that this good blossom could be kept from cankers! Well, there is sixpence to preserve thee.

Bard. An you do not make him hanged among you, the gallows shall have wrong.

Prince. And how doth thy master, Bardolph?

Bard. Well, my lord. He heard of your Grace's coming to town: there's a letter for you.

Poins. Delivered with good respect. And how doth the martlemas, your master?   110

Bard. In bodily health, sir.

Poins. Marry, the immortal part needs a physician; but that moves not him: though that be sick, it dies not.

Prince. I do allow this wen to be as familiar with me as my dog; and he holds his place; for look you how he writes.

Poins. [*Reads*] "John Falstaff, knight"—every man must know that, as oft as he has occasion to name himself: even like those that are kin to the King; for they never prick their finger but they say, "There's some of the King's blood spilt." "How comes that?" says he, that takes upon him not to conceive. The answer is as ready as a borrower's cap, "I am the King's poor cousin, sir."

Prince. Nay, they will be kin to us, or they will fetch it from Japhet. But to the letter:

Poins. [*Reads*] "Sir John Falstaff, knight, to the son of the King, nearest his father, Harry Prince of Wales, greeting." Why, this is a certificate.

Prince. Peace!

Poins. [*Reads*] "I will imitate the honourable Romans in brevity": he sure means brevity in breath, short-winded. "I commend me to thee, I commend thee, and I leave thee. Be not too familiar with Poins; for he misuses thy favours so much that he swears thou art to marry his sister Nell. Repent at idle times as thou mayest; and so, farewell.   141

"Thine, by yea and no, which is as much as to say, as thou usest him, *Jack Falstaff* with my familiars, *John* with my

brothers and sisters, and *Sir John* with all Europe."

My lord, I'll steep this letter in sack and make him eat it.

Prince. That's to make him eat twenty of his words. But do you use me thus, Ned? must I marry your sister?   151

Poins. God send the wench no worse fortune! But I never said so.

Prince. Well, thus we play the fools with the time, and the spirits of the wise sit in the clouds and mock us. Is your master here in London?

Bard. Yea, my lord.

Prince. Where sups he? doth the old boar feed in the old frank?   160

Bard. At the old place, my lord, in Eastcheap.

Prince. What company?

Page. Ephesians, my lord, of the old church.

Prince. Sup any women with him?

Page. None, my lord, but old Mistress Quickly and Mistress Doll Tearsheet.

Prince. What pagan may that be?

Page. A proper gentlewoman, sir, and a kinswoman of my master's.   170

Prince. Even such kin as the parish heifers are to the town bull. Shall we steal upon them, Ned, at supper?

Poins. I am your shadow, my lord; I'll follow you.

Prince. Sirrah, you boy, and Bardolph, no word to your master that I am yet come to town: there's for your silence.

Bard. I have no tongue, sir.

Page. And for mine, sir, I will govern it.   180

Prince. Fare you well; go. [*Exeunt* BARDOLPH *and* PAGE.] This Doll Tearsheet should be some road.

Poins. I warrant you, as common as the way between Saint Alban's and London.

Prince. How might we see Falstaff bestow himself to-night in his true colours, and not ourselves be seen?

Poins. Put on two leathern jerkins and aprons and wait upon him at his table as drawers.   191

Prince. From a God to a bull? a heavy descension! it was Jove's case. From a prince to a prentice? a low transformation! that shall be mine; for in every thing the purpose must weigh with the folly. Follow me, Ned.   [*Exeunt.*

SCENE III. *Warkworth: before the castle*

Enter NORTHUMBERLAND, LADY NORTHUMBERLAND, *and* LADY PERCY.

North. I pray thee, loving wife, and gentle daughter,

Give even way unto my rough affairs:
Put not you on the visage of the times
And be like them to Percy troublesome.

Lady N. I have given over, I will speak no
more:
Do what you will; your wisdom be your guide.

North. Alas, sweet wife, my honour is at
pawn;
And, but my going, nothing can redeem it.

Lady P. O yet, for God's sake, go not to
these wars!
The time was, father, that you broke your word,
When you were more endear'd to it than now; 11
When your own Percy, when my heart's dear
Harry,
Threw many a northward look to see his father
Bring up his powers; but he did long in vain.
Who then persuaded you to stay at home?
There were two honours lost, yours and your
son's.
For yours, the God of heaven brighten it!
For his, is stuck upon him as the sun
In the grey vault of heaven, and by his light
Did all the chivalry of England move   20
To do brave acts: he was indeed the glass
Wherein the noble youth did dress themselves:
He had no legs that practised not his gait;
And speaking thick, which nature made his
blemish,
Became the accents of the valiant;
For those that could speak low and tardily
Would turn their own perfection to abuse
To seem like him: so that in speech, in gait,
In diet, in affections of delight,
In military rules, humours of blood,   30
He was the mark and glass, copy and book,
That fashion'd others. And him, O wondrous
him!
O miracle of men! him did you leave,
Second to none, unseconded by you,
To look upon the hideous god of war
In disadvantage; to abide a field
Where nothing but the sound of Hotspur's name
Did seem defensible: so you left him.
Never, O never, do his ghost the wrong
To hold your honour more precise and nice   40
With others than with him! let them alone:
The Marshal and the Archbishop are strong:
Had my sweet Harry had but half their numbers,
To-day might I, hanging on Hotspur's neck,
Have talk'd of Monmouth's grave.

North.   Beshrew your heart,
Fair daughter, you do draw my spirits from me
With new lamenting ancient oversights.
But I must go and meet with danger there,
Or it will seek me in another place

And find me worse provided.

Lady N.   O, fly to Scotland,   50
Till that the nobles and the armed commons
Have of their puissance made a little taste.

Lady P. If they get ground and vantage of the
King,
Then join you with them, like a rib of steel,
To make strength stronger; but, for all our loves,
First let them try themselves. So did your son;
He was so suffer'd: so came I a widow;
And never shall have length of life enough
To rain upon remembrance with mine eyes,
That it may grow and sprout as high as heaven,
For recordation to my noble husband.   61

North. Come, come, go in with me. 'Tis with
my mind
As with the tide swell'd up unto his height,
That makes a still-stand, running neither way:
Fain would I go to meet the Archbishop,
But many thousand reasons hold me back.
I will resolve for Scotland: there am I,
Till time and vantage crave my company.
                                        [*Exeunt.*

SCENE IV. *London: the Boar's-head Tavern in Eastcheap*

Enter TWO DRAWERS.

1st Draw. What the devil hast thou brought
there? Apple-johns? thou knowest Sir John cannot endure an apple-john.

2nd Draw. Mass, thou sayest true. The
Prince once set a dish of apple-johns before him,
and told him there were five more Sir Johns,
and, putting off his hat, said, "I will now take my
leave of these six dry, round, old, withered
knights." It angered him to the heart: but he
hath forgot that.   10

1st Draw. Why, then, cover, and set them
down: and see if thou canst find out Sneak's
noise; Mistress Tearsheet would fain hear some
music. Dispatch: the room where they supped
is too hot; they'll come in straight.

2nd Draw. Sirrah, here will be the Prince and
Master Poins anon; and they will put on two of
our jerkins and aprons; and Sir John must not
know of it: Bardolph hath brought word.   20

1st Draw. By the mass, here will be old utis:
it will be an excellent stratagem.

2nd Draw. I'll see if I can find out Sneak. [*Exit.*

Enter MISTRESS QUICKLY, *the Hostess and* DOLL
TEARSHEET.

Quick. I' faith, sweetheart, methinks now you
are in an excellent good temperality: your pul-
sidge beats as extraordinarily as heart would
desire; and your colour, I warrant you, is as

red as any rose, in good truth, la! But, i' faith,
you have drunk too much canaries; and that's
a marvellous searching wine, and it perfumes
the blood ere one can say "What's this?" How
do you now?

Dol. Better than I was: hem!

Quick. Why, that's well said; a good heart's
worth gold. Lo, here comes Sir John.

Enter FALSTAFF.

Fal. [*Singing*] "When Arthur first in court"
—Empty the jordan. [*Exit* FIRST DRAWER].—
[*Singing*] "And was a worthy king." How now,
Mistress Doll!

Quick. Sick of a calm: yea, good faith.   40

Fal. So is all her sect; an they be once in a
calm, they are sick.

Dol. You muddy rascal, is that all the comfort
you give me?

Fal. You make fat rascals, Mistress Doll.

Dol. I make them! gluttony and diseases make
them; I make them not.

Fal. If the cook help to make the gluttony,
you help to make the diseases, Doll: we catch
of you, Doll, we catch of you; grant that, my
poor virtue, grant that.   51

Dol. Yea, joy, our chains and our jewels.

Fal. "Your brooches, pearls, and ouches":
for to serve bravely is to come halting off, you
know: to come off the breach with his pike bent
bravely, and to surgery bravely; to venture upon
the charged chambers bravely—

Dol. Hang yourself, you muddy conger, hang
yourself!   59

Quick. By my troth, this is the old fashion; you
two never meet but you fall to some discord:
you are both, i' good truth, as rheumatic as two
dry toasts; you cannot one bear with another's
confirmities. What the good-year! one must
bear, and that must be you: you are the weaker
vessel, as they say, the emptier vessel.

Dol. Can a weak empty vessel bear such a
huge full hogshead? there's a whole merchant's
venture of Bourdeaux stuff in him; you have not
seen a hulk better stuffed in the hold. Come,
I'll be friends with thee, Jack: thou art going
to the wars; and whether I shall ever see thee
again or no, there is nobody cares.

Re-enter FIRST DRAWER.

1st Draw. Sir, Ancient Pistol's below, and
would speak with you.

Dol. Hang him, swaggering rascal! let him
not come hither: it is the foul-mouthed'st rogue
in England.

Quick. If he swagger, let him not come here:

no, by my faith; I must live among my neighbours; I'll no swaggerers: I am in good name
and fame with the very best: shut the door;
there comes no swaggerers here: I have not
lived all this while, to have swaggering now:
shut the door, I pray you.

Fal. Dost thou hear, hostess?

Quick. Pray ye, pacify yourself, Sir, John: there
comes no swaggerers here.

Fal. Dost thou hear? it is mine ancient.   89

Quick. Tilly-fally, Sir John, ne'er tell me:
your ancient swaggerer comes not in my doors.
I was before Master Tisick, the deputy, t'other
day; and, as he said to me, 'twas no longer ago
than Wednesday last, "I' good faith, neighbour
Quickly," says he; Master Dumbe, our minister,
was by then; "neighbour Quickly," says he,
"receive those that are civil; for," said he, "you
are in an ill name": now a' said so, I can tell
whereupon; "for," says he, "you are an honest
woman, and well thought on; therefore take
heed what guests you receive: receive," says he,
"no swaggering companions." There comes none
here: you would bless you to hear what he said:
no, I'll no swaggerers.

Fal. He's no swaggerer, hostess; a tame
cheater, i' faith; you may stroke him as gently
as a puppy greyhound: he'll not swagger with a
Barbary hen, if her feathers turn back in any
show of resistance. Call him up, drawer.

[*Exit* FIRST DRAWER.

Quick. Cheater, call you him? I will bar no
honest man from my house, nor no cheater: but
I do not love swaggering, by my troth; I am the
worse, when one says swagger: feel, masters,
how I shake; look you, I warrant you.

Dol. So you do, hostess.

Quick. Do I? yea, in very truth, do I, an
'twere an aspen leaf: I cannot abide swaggerers.

Enter PISTOL, BARDOLPH, *and* PAGE.

Pist. God save you, Sir John!   119

Fal. Welcome, Ancient Pistol. Here, Pistol,
I charge you with a cup of sack: do you discharge
upon mine hostess.

Pist. I will discharge upon her, Sir John, with
two bullets.

Fal. She is pistol-proof, sir; you shall hardly
offend her.

Quick. Come, I'll drink no proofs nor no bullets: I'll drink no more than will do me good,
for no man's pleasure, I.

Pist. Then to you, Mistress Dorothy; I will
charge you.   131

Dol. Charge me! I scorn you, scurvy companion. What! you poor, base, rascally, cheating, lack-linen mate! Away, you mouldy rogue, away! I am meat for your master.

Pist. I know you, Mistress Dorothy.

Dol. Away, you cut-purse rascal! you filthy bung, away! by this wine, I'll thrust my knife in your mouldy chaps, an you play the saucy cuttle with me. Away, you bottle-ale rascal! you basket-hilt stale juggler, you! Since when, I pray you, sir? God's light, with two points on your shoulder? much!

Pist. God let me not live, but I will murder your ruff for this.

Fal. No more, Pistol; I would not have you go off here: discharge yourself of our company, Pistol.

Quick. No, good Captain Pistol; not here, sweet captain.   150

Dol. Captain! thou abominable damned cheater, art thou not ashamed to be called captain? An captains were of my mind, they would truncheon you out, for taking their names upon you before you have earned them. You a captain: you slave, for what? for tearing a poor whore's ruff in a bawdy-house? He a captain! hang him, rogue! he lives upon mouldy stewed prunes and dried cakes. A captain! God's light, these villains will make the word as odious as the word "occupy"; which was an excellent good word before it was ill sorted: therefore captains had need look to't.

Bard. Pray thee, go down, good ancient.

Fal. Hark thee hither, Mistress Doll.

Pist. Not I: I tell thee what, Corporal Bardolph, I could tear her: I'll be revenged of her.

Page. Pray thee, go down.

Pist. I'll see her damned first; to Pluto's damned lake, by this hand, to the infernal deep, with Erebus and tortures vile also. Hold hook and line, say I. Down, down, dogs! down, faitors! Have we not Hiren here?

Quick. Good Captain Peesel, be quiet; 'tis very late, i' faith: I beseek you now, aggravate your choler.

Pist. These be good humors, indeed! Shall pack-horses
And hollow pamper'd jades of Asia,
Which cannot go but thirty mile a-day,
Compare with Cæsars, and with Cannibals,   180
And Trojan Greeks? nay, rather damn them with King Cerberus; and let the welkin roar.
Shall we fall foul for toys?

Quick. By my troth, captain, these are very bitter words.

Bard. Be gone, good ancient: this will grow to a brawl anon.

Pist. Die men like dogs! give crowns like pins! Have we not Hiren here?   189

Quick. O' my word, captain, there's none such here. What the good-year! do you think I would deny her? For God's sake, be quiet.

Pist. Then feed, and be fat, my fair Calipolis. Come, give's some sack.
Si fortune me tormente, sperato me contento.
Fear we broadsides? no, let the fiend give fire:
Give me some sack: and, sweetheart, lie thou there. [*Laying down his sword.*]
Come we to full points here; and are etceteras nothing?

Fal. Pistol, I would be quiet.

Pist. Sweet knight, I kiss thy neif: what! we have seen the seven stars.   201

Dol. For God's sake, thrust him downstairs: I cannot endure such a fustian rascal.

Pist. Thrust him downstairs! know we not Galloway nags?

Fal. Quoit him down, Bardolph, like a shove-groat shilling: nay, and a' do nothing but speak nothing, a' shall be nothing here.

Bard. Come, get you downstairs.

Pist. What! shall we have incision? shall we imbrue? [*Snatching up his sword.*]   210
Then death rock me asleep, abridge my doleful days!
Why, then, let grievous, ghastly, gaping wounds
Untwine the Sisters Three! Come, Atropos, I say!

Quick. Here's goodly stuff toward!

Fal. Give me my rapier, boy.

Dol. I pray thee, Jack, I pray thee, do not draw.

Fal. Get you down stairs.

Drawing and driving PISTOL *out.*

Quick. Here's a goodly tumult! I'll forswear keeping house, afore I'll be in these tirrits and frights. So; murder, I warrant now. Alas, alas! put up your naked weapons, put up your naked weapons. [*Exeunt* PISTOL *and* BARDOLPH.

Dol. I pray thee, Jack, be quiet; the rascal's gone. Ah, you whoreson little valiant villain, you!

Quick. Are you not hurt i' the groin? methought a' made a shrewd thrust at your belly.

Re-enter BARDOLPH.

Fal. Have you turned him out o'doors?

Bard. Yea, sir. The rascal's drunk: you have hurt him, sir, i' the shoulder.   231

Fal. A rascal! to brave me!

Dol. Ah, you sweet little rogue, you! Alas, poor ape, how thou sweatest! come, let me wipe thy face; come on, you whoreson chops: ah, rogue! i' faith, I love thee: thou art as valorous as Hector of Troy, worth five of Agamemnon, and ten times better than the Nine Worthies: ah, villain!

Fal. A rascally slave! I will toss the rogue in a blanket.   *241*

Dol. Do, an thou darest for thy heart: an thou dost, I'll canvass thee between a pair of sheets.

Enter Music.

Page. The music is come, sir.

Fal. Let them play. Play, sirs. Sit on my knee, Doll. A rascal bragging slave! the rogue fled from me like quicksilver.

Dol. I' faith, and thou followedst him like a church. Thou whoreson little tidy Bartholomew boar-pig, when wilt thou leave fighting o'days and foining o' nights, and begin to patch up thine old body for heaven?

Enter, behind, PRINCE HENRY and POINS, *disguised.*

Fal. Peace, good Doll! do not speak like a death's-head; do not bid me remember mine end.

Dol. Sirrah, what humour's the Prince of?

Fal. A good shallow young fellow: a' would have made a good pantler, a' would ha' chipped bread well.

Dol. They say Poins has a good wit.   *260*

Fal. He a good wit? hang him, baboon! his wit's as thick as Tewksbury mustard; there's no more conceit in him than is in a mallet.

Dol. Why does the Prince love him so, then?

Fal. Because their legs are both of a bigness, and a' plays at quoits well, and eats conger and fennel, and drinks off candles' ends for flap-dragons, and rides the wild-mare with the boys, and jumps upon joined-stools, and swears with a good grace, and wears his boots very smooth, like unto the sign of the leg, and breeds no bate with telling of discreet stories; and such other gambol faculties a' has, that show a weak mind and an able body, for the which the Prince admits him: for the Prince himself is such another; the weight of a hair will turn the scales between their avoirdupois.

Prince. Would not this nave of a wheel have his ears cut off?

Poins. Let's beat him before his whore.   *280*

Prince. Look, whether the withered elder hath not his poll clawed like a parrot.

Poins. Is it not strange that desire should so many years outlive performance?

Fal. Kiss me, Doll.

Prince. Saturn and Venus this year in conjunction! what says the almanac to that?

Poins. And, look, whether the fiery Trigon, his

man, be not lisping to his master's old tables, his note-book, his counsel-keeper.   *290*

Fal. Thou dost give me flattering busses.

Dol. By my troth, I kiss thee with a most constant heart.

Fal. I am old, I am old.

Dol. I love thee better than I love e'er a scurvy young boy of them all.

Fal. What stuff wilt have a kirtle of? I shall receive money o' Thursday: shalt have a cap to-morrow. A merry song, come: it grows late; we'll to bed. Thou'lt forget me when I am gone.

Dol. By my troth, thou'lt set me a-weeping, an thou sayest so: prove that ever I dress myself handsome till thy return: well, hearken at the end.

Fal. Some sack, Francis.

Prince.⎱ Anon, anon, sir. [*Coming forward.*
Poins.⎰

Fal. Ha! a bastard son of the King's? And art not thou Poins his brother?

Prince. Why, thou globe of sinful continents, what a life dost thou lead!   *310*

Fal. A better than thou: I am a gentleman; thou art a drawer.

Prince. Very true, sir; and I come to draw you out by the ears.

Quick. O, the Lord preserve thy good Grace! by my troth, welcome to London. Now, the Lord bless that sweet face of thine! O Jesu, are you come from Wales?

Fal. Thou whoreson mad compound of majesty, by this light flesh and corrupt blood, thou art welcome.   *321*

Dol. How, you fat fool! I scorn you.

Poins. My lord, he will drive you out of your revenge and turn all to a merriment, if you take not the heat.

Prince. You whoreson candle-mine, you, how vilely did you speak of me even now before this honest, virtuous, civil gentlewoman!

Quick. God's blessing of your good heart! and so she is, by my troth.   *330*

Fal. Didst thou hear me?

Prince. Yea, and you knew me, as you did when you ran away by Gadshill: you knew I was at your back, and spoke it on purpose to try my patience.

Fal. No, no, no; not so; I did not think thou wast within hearing.

Prince. I shall drive you then to confess the wilful abuse; and then I know how to handle you.

Fal. No abuse, Hal, o' mine honour; no abuse.

Prince. Not to dispraise me, and call me pantler and bread-chipper and I know not what?

Fal. No abuse, Hal.

Poins. No abuse?

Fal. No abuse, Ned, i' the world; honest Ned, none. I dispraised him before the wicked, that the wicked might not fall in love with him; in which doing, I have done the part of a careful friend and a true subject, and thy father is to give me thanks for it. No abuse, Hal: none, Ned, none: no, faith, boys, none.   351

Prince. See now, whether pure fear and entire cowardice doth not make thee wrong this virtuous gentlewoman to close with us. Is she of the wicked? is thine hostess here of the wicked? or is thy boy of the wicked? or honest Bardolph, whose zeal burns in his nose, of the wicked?

Poins. Answer, thou dead elm, answer.

Fal. The fiend hath pricked down Bardolph, irrecoverable; and his face is Lucifer's privy-kitchen, where he doth nothing but roast malt-worms. For the boy, there is a good angel about him; but the devil outbids him too.

Prince. For the women?

Fal. For one of them, she is in hell already, and burns poor souls. For the other, I owe her money; and whether she be damned for that, I know not.

Quick. No, I warrant you.   369

Fal. No, I think thou art not; I think thou are quit for that. Marry, there is another indictment upon thee, for suffering flesh to be eaten in thy house, contrary to the law; for the which I think thou wilt howl.

Quick. All victuallers do so: what's a joint of mutton or two in a whole Lent?

Prince. You, gentlewoman—

Dol. What says your Grace?

Fal. His Grace says that which his flesh rebels against.

Knocking within.   380

Quick. Who knocks so loud at door? Look to the door there, Francis.

Enter PETO.

Prince. Peto, how now! what news?

Peto. The King your father is at Westminster;
And there are twenty weak and wearied posts
Come from the north: and, as I came along,
I met and overtook a dozen captains,
Bare-headed, sweating, knocking at the taverns,
And asking every one for Sir John Falstaff.

Prince. By heaven, Poins, I feel me much to blame,   390
So idly to profane the precious time,
When tempest of commotion, like the south
Borne with black vapour, doth begin to melt
And drop upon our bare unarmed heads.

Give me my sword and cloak. Falstaff, goodnight.
        [*Exeunt* PRINCE HENRY, POINS, PETO,
                and BARDOLPH.

Fal. Now comes in the sweetest morsel of the the night, and we must hence and leave it unpicked. [*Knocking within.*] More knocking at the door!

Re-enter BARDOLPH.

How now! what's the matter?   400

Bard. You must away to court, sir, presently;
A dozen captains stay at door for you.

Fal. [*To the* PAGE] Pay the musicians, sirrah. Farewell, hostess; farewell, Doll. You see, my good wenches, how men of merit are sought after: the undeserver may sleep, when the man of action is called on. Farewell, good wenches: if I be not sent away post, I will see you again ere I go.

Dol. I cannot speak; if my heart be not ready to burst—well, sweet Jack, have a care of thyself.

Fal. Farewell, farewell. [*Exeunt* FALSTAFF *and
                BARDOLPH.*

Quick. Well, fare thee well: I have known thee these twenty nine years, come peascod-time; but an honester and truer-hearted man—well, fare thee well.

Bard. [*Within*] Mistress Tearsheet!

Quick. What's the matter?

Bard. [*Within*] Bid Mistress Tearsheet come to my master.   419

Quick. O, run, Doll, run; run, good Doll: come. [*She comes blubbered.*] Yea, will you come, Doll?
        [*Exeunt.*

ACT III

SCENE I. *Westminster: the palace.*

Enter the KING *in his nightgown, with a Page.*

King. Go call the Earls of Surrey and of Warwick;
But, ere they come, bid them o'er-read these letters,
And well consider of them: make good speed.
        [*Exit Page.*
How many thousand of my poorest subjects
Are at this hour asleep! O Sleep, O gentle Sleep,
Nature's soft nurse, how have I frighted thee
That thou no more wilt weigh my eyelids down
And steep my senses in forgetfulness?
Why rather, Sleep, liest thou in smoky cribs,
Upon uneasy pallets stretching thee   10
And hush'd with buzzing night-flies to thy slumber,
Than in the perfumed chambers of the great,
Under the canopies of costly state,
And lull'd with sound of sweetest melody?

O thou dull god, why liest thou with the vile
In loathsome beds, and leavest the kingly couch
A watch-case or a common 'larum-bell?
Wilt thou upon the high and giddy mast
Seal up the ship-boy's eyes, and rock his brains
In cradle of the rude imperious surge   20
And in the visitation of the winds,
Who take the ruffian billows by the top,
Curling their monstrous heads and hanging them
With deafening clamour in the slippery clouds,
That, with the hurly, death itself awakes?
Canst thou, O partial Sleep, give thy repose
To the wet sea-boy in an hour so rude,
And in the calmest and most stillest night,
With all appliances and means to boot,
Deny it to a king? Then happy low, lie down!   30
Uneasy lies the head that wears a crown.

Enter WARWICK *and* SURREY.

War. Many good morrows to your Majesty!
King. Is it good morrow, lords?
War. 'Tis one o'clock, and past.
King. Why, then, good morrow to you all, my
      lords.
Have you read o'er the letters that I sent you?
War. We have, my liege.
King. Then you perceive the body of our
      kingdom
How foul it is; what rank diseases grow,
And with what danger, near the heart of it.   40
War. It is but as a body yet distemper'd;
Which to his former strength may be restored
With good advice and little medicine:
My Lord Northumberland will soon be cool'd.
King. O God! that one might read the book of
      fate,
And see the revolution of the times
Make mountains level, and the continent,
Weary of solid firmness, melt itself
Into the sea! and, other times, to see
The beachy girdle of the ocean   50
Too wide for Neptune's hips; how chances mock,
And changes fill the cup of alteration
With divers liquors! O, if this were seen,
The happiest youth, viewing his progress through,
What perils past, what crosses to ensue,
Would shut the book, and sit him down and die.
'Tis not ten years gone
Since Richard and Northumberland, great friends,
Did feast together, and in two years after
Were they at wars: it is but eight years since   60
This Percy was the man nearest my soul,
Who like a brother toil'd in my affairs
And laid his love and life under my foot,
Yea, for my sake, even to the eyes of Richard
Gave him defiance. But which of you was by—

You, cousin Nevil, as I may remember—
      To WARWICK.
When Richard, with his eye brimful of tears,
Then check'd and rated by Northumberland,
Did speak these words, now proved a prophecy?
"Northumberland, thou ladder by the which   70
My cousin Bolingbroke ascends my throne";
Though then, God knows, I had no such intent,
But that necessity so bow'd the state
That I and greatness were compell'd to kiss:
"The time shall come," thus did he follow it,
"The time will come, that foul sin, gathering
      head,
Shall break into corruption": so went on,
Foretelling this same time's condition
And the division of our amity.
War. There is a history in all men's lives,   80
Figuring the nature of the times deceased;
The which observed, a man may prophesy,
With a near aim, of the main chance of things
As yet not come to life, which in their seeds
And weak beginnings lie intreasured.
Such things become the hatch and brood of time;
And by necessary form of this
King Richard might create a perfect guess
That great Northumberland, then false to him,
Would of that seed grow to a greater falseness;
Which should not find a ground to root upon,   91
Unless on you.
King.   Are these things then necessities?
Then let us meet them like necessities:
And that same word even now cries out on us:
They say the Bishop and Northumberland
Are fifty thousand strong.
War.   It cannot be, my lord;
Rumour doth double, like the voice and echo,
The numbers of the fear'd. Please it your Grace
To go to bed. Upon my soul, my lord,
The powers that you already have sent forth   100
Shall bring this prize in very easily.
To comfort you the more, I have received
A certain instance that Glendower is dead.
Your Majesty hath been this fortnight ill,
And these unseason'd hours perforce must add
Unto your sickness.
King.   I will take your counsel:
And were these inward wars once out of hand,
We would, dear lords, unto the Holy Land.
                                    [*Exeunt.*

SCENE II. *Gloucestershire: before Justice Shallow's
      house*

Enter SHALLOW *and* SILENCE, *meeting;* MOULDY,
SHADOW, WART, FEEBLE, BULLCALF, *a Servant or
two with them.*

Shal. Come on, come on, come on, sir; give

me your hand, sir, give me your hand, sir: an
early stirrer, by the rood! And how doth my
good cousin Silence?

Sil. Good morrow, good cousin Shallow.

Shal. And how doth my cousin, your bedfellow? and your fairest daughter and mine, my
god-daughter Ellen?

Sil. Alas, a black ousel, cousin Shallow!   9

Shal. By yea and nay, sir, I dare say my
cousin William is become a good scholar: he is at
Oxford still, is he not?

Sil. Indeed, sir, to my cost.

Shal. A'must, then, to the Inns o'Court shortly.
I was once of Clement's Inn, where I think they
will talk of mad Shallow yet.

Sil. You were called "lusty Shallow" then,
cousin.

Shal. By the mass, I was called any thing;
and I would have done anything indeed too, and
roundly too. There was I, and little John Doit
of Staffordshire, and black George Barnes, and
Francis Pickbone, and Will Squele, a Cotswold
man; you had not four such swinge-bucklers in
all the Inns o'Court again: and I may say to you,
we knew where the bona-robas were and had the
best of them all at commandment. Then was
Jack Falstaff, now Sir John, a boy, and page to
Thomas Mowbray, Duke of Norfolk.

Sil. This Sir John, cousin, that comes hither
anon about soldiers?   31

Shal. The same Sir John, the very same. I
see him break Skogan's head at the court-gate,
when a' was a crack not thus high: and the very
same day did I fight with one Sampson Stockfish,
a fruiterer, behind Gray's Inn. Jesu, Jesu, the
mad days that I have spent! and to see how many
of my old acquaintance are dead!

Sil. We shall all follow, cousin.   39

Shal. Certain, 'tis certain; very sure, very
sure: death, as the Psalmist saith, is certain to
all; all shall die. How a good yoke of bullocks
at Stamford fair?

Sil. By my troth, I was not there.

Shal. Death is certain. Is old Double of your
town living yet?

Sil. Dead, sir.

Shal. Jesu, Jesu, dead! a' drew a good bow;
and dead! a' shot a fine shoot: John a Gaunt
loved him well, and betted much money on his
head. Dead! a' would have clapped i' the clout
at twelve score; and carried you a forehand shaft
a fourteen and fourteen and a half, that it would
have done a man's heart good to see. How a
score of ewes now?

Sil. Thereafter as they be: a score of good
ewes may be worth ten pounds.

Shal. And is old Double dead?

Sil. Here come two of Sir John Falstaff's men,
as I think.   60

Enter BARDOLPH *and one with him.*

Bard. Good morrow, honest gentlemen: I
beseech you, which is Justice Shallow?

Shal. I am Robert Shallow, sir; a poor esquire
of this county, and one of the King's justices of
the peace: what is your good pleasure with me?

Bard. My captain, sir, commends him to you;
my captain, Sir John Falstaff, a tall gentleman,
by heaven, and a most gallant leader.

Shal. He greets me well, sir. I knew him a
good backsword man. How doth the good knight?
may I ask how my lady his wife doth?   71

Bard. Sir, pardon; a soldier is better accommodated than with a wife.

Shal. It is well said, in faith, sir; and it is well
said indeed too. Better accommodated! it is good;
yea, indeed, is it: good phrases are surely, and
ever were, very commendable. Accommodated!
it comes of *accommodo*: very good, a good
phrase.   79

Bard. Pardon me, sir; I have heard the word.
Phrase call you it? by this good day, I know not
the phrase; but I will maintain the word with
my sword to be a soldier-like word, and a word
of exceeding good command, by heaven. Accommodated; that is, when a man is, as they say,
accommodated; or when a man is, being, whereby a' may be thought to be accommodated; which
is an excellent thing.

Shal. It is very just.   89

Enter FALSTAFF.

Look, here comes good Sir John. Give me your
good hand, give me your worship's good hand:
by my troth, you like well and bear your years
very well: welcome, good Sir John.

Fal. I am glad to see you well, good Master
Robert Shallow: Master Surecard, as I think?

Shal. No, Sir John; it is my cousin Silence, in
commission with me.

Fal. Good Master Silence, it well befits you
should be of the peace.

Sil. Your good worship is welcome.   100

Fal. Fie! this is hot weather, gentlemen. Have
you provided me here half a dozen sufficient
men?

Shal. Marry, have we sir. Will you sit?

Fal. Let me see them, I beseech you.

Shal. Where's the roll? where's the roll?
where's the roll? Let me see, let me see, let me
see. So, so, so, so, so, so, so: yea, marry, sir:
Ralph Mouldy! Let them appear as I call; let

them do so, let them do so. Let me see; where is
Mouldy?   *111*

Moul. Here, an't please you.

Shal. What think you, Sir John? a good-limbed
fellow; young, strong, and of good friends.

Fal. Is thy name Mouldy?

Moul. Yea, an't please you.

Fal. 'Tis the more time thou wert used.

Shal. Ha, ha, ha! most excellent, i' faith! things
that are mouldy lack use: very singular good! in
faith, well said, Sir John, very well said.

Fal. Prick him.   *121*

Moul. I was pricked well enough before, an
you could have let me alone: my old dame will
be undone now for one to do her husbandry
and her drudgery: you need not to have pricked
me; there are other men fitter to go out
than I.

Fal. Go to: peace, Mouldy; you shall go.
Mouldy, it is time you were spent.

Moul. Spent!   *129*

Shal. Peace, fellow, peace; stand aside: know
you where you are? For the other, Sir John: let
me see: Simon Shadow!

Fal. Yea, marry, let me have him to sit under:
he's like to be a cold soldier.

Shal. Where's Shadow?

Shad. Here, sir.

Fal. Shadow, whose son art thou?

Shad. My mother's son, sir.

Fal. Thy mother's son! like enough, and thy
father's shadow: so the son of the female is the
shadow of the male: it is often so, indeed; but
much of the father's substance!

Shal. Do you like him, Sir John?

Fal. Shadow will serve for summer; prick him,
for we have a number of shadows to fill up the
muster-book.

Shal. Thomas Wart!

Fal. Where's he.

Wart. Here, sir.

Fal. Is thy name Wart?   *150*

Wart. Yea, sir.

Fal. Thou art a very ragged wart.

Shal. Shall I prick him down, Sir John?

Fal. It were superfluous; for his apparel is built
upon his back and the whole frame stands upon
pins: prick him no more.

Shal. Ha, ha, ha! you can do it, sir; you can do
it: I commend you well. Francis Feeble!

Fee. Here, sir.

Fal. What trade art thou, Feeble?   *160*

Fee. A woman's tailor, sir.

Shal. Shall I prick him, sir?

Fal. You may: but if he had been a man's tailor,
he'ld ha' pricked you. Wilt thou make as many
holes in an enemy's battle as thou hast done in a
woman's petticoat?

Fee. I will do my good will, sir: you can have
no more.

Fal. Well said, good woman's tailor! well said,
courageous Feeble! thou wilt be as valiant as the
wrathful dove or most magnanimous mouse.
Prick the woman's tailor: well, Master Shallow;
deep, Master Shallow.

Fee. I would Wart might have gone, sir.

Fal. I would thou wert a man's tailor, that thou
mightest mend him and make him fit to go. I
cannot put him to a private soldier that is the
leader of so many thousands: let that suffice,
most forcible Feeble.

Fee. It shall suffice, sir.   *180*

Fal. I am bound to thee, reverend Feeble. Who
is next?

Shal. Peter Bullcalf o' the green!

Fal. Yea, marry, let's see Bullcalf.

Bull. Here, sir.

Fal. 'Fore God, a likely fellow! Come, prick
me Bullcalf till he roar again.

Bull. O Lord! good my lord captain—

Fal. What, dost thou roar before thou art
pricked?   *190*

Bull. O Lord, sir! I am a diseased man.

Fal. What disease hast thou?

Bull. A whoreson cold, sir, a cough, sir, which
I caught with ringing in the King's affairs upon
his coronation-day, sir.

Fal. Come, thou shalt go to the wars in a gown;
we will have away thy cold; and I will take such
order that thy friends shall ring for thee. Is here
all?   *199*

Shal. Here is two more called than your number; you must have but four here, sir: and so, I
pray you, go in with me to dinner.

Fal. Come, I will go drink with you, but I cannot tarry dinner. I am glad to see you, by my
troth, Master Shallow.

Shal. O, Sir John, do you remember since we
lay all night in the windmill in Saint George's
field?

Fal. No more of that, good Master Shallow, no
more of that.

Shal. Ha! 'twas a merry night. And is Jane
Nightwork alive?   *211*

Fal. She lives, Master Shallow.

Shal. She never could away with me.

Fal. Never, never; she would always say she
could not abide Master Shallow.

Shal. By the mass, I could anger her to the
heart. She was then a bona-roba. Doth she hold
her own well?

Fal. Old, old, Master Shallow.   *219*

Shal. Nay, she must be old; she cannot choose but be old; certain she's old; and had Robin Nightwork by old Nightwork before I came to Clement's Inn.

Sil. That's fifty five year ago.

Shal. Ha, cousin Silence, that thou hadst seen that that this knight and I have seen! Ha, Sir John, said I well?

Fal. We have heard the chimes at midnight, Master Shallow.   *229*

Shal. That we have, that we have, that we have; in faith, Sir John, we have: our watchword was "Hem, boys!" Come, let's to dinner; come, let's to dinner: Jesus, the days that we have seen! Come, come.

    [*Exeunt* FALSTAFF *and the* JUSTICES.

Bull. Good Master Corporate Bardolph, stand my friend; and here's four Harry ten shillings in French crowns for you. In very truth, sir, I had as lief be hanged, sir, as go: and yet, for mine own part, sir, I do not care; but rather, because I am unwilling, and, for mine own part, have a desire to stay with my friends; else, sir, I did not care, for mine own part, so much.

Bard. Go to; stand aside.

Moul. And, good master corporal captain, for my old dame's sake, stand my friend: she has nobody to do anything about her when I am gone; and she is old, and cannot help herself: you shall have forty, sir.

Bard. Go to; stand aside.   *249*

Fee. By my troth, I care not; a man can die but once: we owe God a death: I'll ne'er bear a base mind: an't be my destiny, so; an't be not, so: no man is too good to serve's prince; and let it go which way it will, he that dies this year is quit for the next.

Bard. Well said; thou'rt a good fellow.

Fee. Faith, I'll bear no base mind.

Re-enter FALSTAFF *and the* JUSTICES.

Fal. Come, sir, which men shall I have?

Shal. Four of which you please.

Bard. Sir, a word with you: I have three pound to free Mouldy and Bullcalf.   *261*

Fal. Go to; well.

Shal. Come, Sir John, which four will you have?

Fal. Do you choose for me.

Shal. Marry, then, Mouldy, Bullcalf, Feeble and Shadow.

Fal. Mouldy and Bullcalf: for you, Mouldy, stay at home till you are past service: and for your part, Bullcalf, grow till you come unto it: I will none of you.   *271*

Shal. Sir John, Sir John, do not yourself wrong:

they are your likeliest men, and I would have you served with the best.

Fal. Will you tell me, Master Shallow, how to choose a man? Care I for the limb, the thewes, the stature, bulk, and big assemblance of a man! Give me the spirit, Master Shallow. Here's Wart; you see what a ragged appearance it is: a' shall charge you and discharge you with the motion of a pewterer's hammer, come off and on swifter than he that gibbets on the brewer's bucket. And this same half-faced fellow, Shadow; give me this man: he presents no mark to the enemy; the foeman may with as great aim level at the edge of a penknife. And for a retreat; how swiftly will this Feeble the woman's tailor run off! O, give me the spare men, and spare me the great ones. Put me a caliver into Wart's hand, Bardolph.   *290*

Bard. Hold, Wart, traverse; thus, thus, thus.

Fal. Come, manage me your caliver. So: very well: go to: very good, exceeding good. O, give me always a little, lean, old, chapt, bald shot. Well said, i' faith, Wart; thou'rt a good scab: hold, there's a tester for thee.

Shal. He is not his craft's master; he doth not do it right. I remember at Mile-end Green, when I lay at Clement's Inn—I was then Sir Dagonet in Arthur's show—there was a little quiver fellow, and a' would manage you his piece thus; and a' would about and about, and come you in and come you in: "rah, tah, tah," would a' say, "bounce" would a' say; and away again would a' go, and again would a' come: I shall ne'er see such a fellow.

Fal. These fellows will do well, Master Shallow. God keep you, Master Silence: I will not use many words with you. Fare you well, gentlemen both: I thank you: I must a dozen mile to-night. Bardolph, give the soldiers coats.   *311*

Shal. Sir John, the Lord bless you! God prosper your affairs! God send us peace! At your return visit our house; let our old acquaintance be renewed: peradventure I will with ye to the court.

Fal. 'Fore God, I would you would, Master Shallow.

Shal. Go to; I have spoke at a word. God keep you.   *320*

Fal. Fare you well, gentle gentlemen. [*Exeunt* JUSTICES.] On, Bardolph; lead the men away. [*Exeunt* BARDOLPH, RECRUITS, *&c.*] As I return, I will fetch off these justices: I do see the bottom of Justice Shallow. Lord, Lord, how subject we old men are to this vice of lying! This same starved justice hath done nothing but prate to me of the wildness of his youth, and the feats he hath done about Turnbull Street; and every third

word a lie, duer paid to the hearer than the
Turk's tribute. I do remember him at Clement's
Inn like a man made after supper of a cheese-
paring: when a' was naked, he was, for all the
world, like a forked radish, with a head fantastically carved upon it with a knife: a' was so forlorn, that his dimensions to any thick sight were
invincible: a' was the very genius of famine; yet
lecherous as a monkey, and the whores called
him mandrake: a' came ever in the rearward of
the fashion, and sung those tunes to the over-
scutched huswives that he heard the carmen
whistle, and sware they were his fancies or his
good-nights. And now is this Vice's dagger become a squire, and talks as familiarly of John a
Gaunt as if he had been sworn brother to him;
and I'll be sworn a' ne'er saw him but once in the
Tilt-yard; and then he burst his head for crowding among the marshal's men. I saw it, and told
John a Gaunt he beat his own name; for you
might have thrust him and all his apparel into an
eel-skin; the case of a treble hautboy was a mansion for him, a court: and now has he land and
beefs. Well, I'll be acquainted with him, if I
return; and it shall go hard but I will make him
a philosopher's two stones to me: if the young
dace be a bait for the old pike, I see no reason in
the law of nature but I may snap at him. Let
time shape, and there an end.   [*Exit.*

ACT IV

Scene I. *Yorkshire: Gaultree Forest*

Enter the archbishop of york, mowbray,
hastings, *and others.*

Arch. What is this forest call'd?
Hast. 'Tis Gaultree Forest, an't shall please
  your Grace.
Arch. Here stand, my lords; and send discover-
  ers forth
To know the numbers of our enemies.
Hast. We have sent forth already.
Arch.   'Tis well done.
My friends and brethren in these great affairs,
I must acquaint you that I have received
New-dated letters from Northumberland;
Their cold intent, tenour, and substance, thus:
Here doth he wish his person, with such powers
As might hold sortance with his quality,   *11*
The which he could not levy; whereupon
He is retired, to ripe his growing fortunes,
To Scotland: and concludes in hearty prayers
That your attempts may overlive the hazard
And fearful meeting of their opposite.
Mowb. Thus do the hopes we have in him
  touch ground

And dash themselves to pieces.

Enter a messenger.

Hast.   Now, what news?
Mess. West of this forest, scarcely off a mile,
In goodly form comes on the enemy;   *20*
And, by the ground they hide, I judge their
  number
Upon or near the rate of thirty thousand.
Mowb. The just proportion that we gave them
  out.
Let us sway on and face them in the field.
Arch. What well-appointed leader fronts us
  here?

Enter westmoreland.

Mowb. I think it is my Lord of Westmoreland.
West. Health and fair greeting from our general,
The Prince, Lord John and Duke of Lancaster.
Arch. Say on, my Lord of Westmoreland, in
  peace:
What doth concern your coming?
West.   Then, my lord,   *30*
Unto your Grace do I in chief address
The substance of my speech. If that rebellion
Came like itself, in base and abject routs,
Led on by bloody youth, guarded with rags,
And countenanced by boys and beggary,
I say, if damn'd commotion so appear'd,
In his true, native, and most proper shape,
You, reverend father, and these noble lords
Had not been here, to dress the ugly form
Of base and bloody insurrection   *40*
With your fair honours. You, Lord Archbishop,
Whose see is by a civil peace maintain'd,
Whose beard the silver hand of peace hath
  touch'd,
Whose learning and good letters peace hath
  tutor'd,
Whose white investments figure innocence,
The dove and very blessed spirit of peace,
Wherefore do you so ill translate yourself
Out of the speech of peace that bears such grace,
Into the harsh and boisterous tongue of war;
Turning your books to graves, your ink to blood,
Your pens to lances and your tongue divine   *51*
To a loud trumpet and a point of war?
Arch. Wherefore do I this? so the question
  stands.
Briefly to this end: we are all diseased,
And with our surfeiting and wanton hours
Have brought ourselves into a burning fever,
And we must bleed for it; of which disease
Our late king, Richard, being infected, died.
But, my most noble Lord of Westmoreland,
I take not on me here as a physician,   *60*

Nor do I as an enemy to peace
Troop in the throngs of military men;
But rather show awhile like fearful war,
To diet rank minds sick of happiness
And purge the obstructions which begin to stop
Our very veins of life. Hear me more plainly.
I have in equal balance justly weigh'd
What wrongs our arms may do, what wrongs we
    suffer,
And find our griefs heavier than our offences.
We see which way the stream of time doth run,
And are enforced from our most quiet there   71
By the rough torrent of occasion;
And have the summary of all our griefs,
When time shall serve, to show in articles;
Which long ere this we offer'd to the King,
And might by no suit gain our audience:
When we are wrong'd and would unfold our
    griefs,
We are denied access unto his person
Even by those men that most have done us
    wrong.
The dangers of the days but newly gone,   80
Whose memory is written on the earth
With yet appearing blood, and the examples
Of every minute's instance, present now,
Hath put us in these ill-beseeming arms,
Not to break peace or any branch of it,
But to establish here a peace indeed,
Concurring both in name and quality.
    West. When ever yet was your appeal denied?
Wherein have you been galled by the King?
What peer hath been suborn'd to grate on you 90
That you should seal this lawless bloody book
Of forged rebellion with a seal divine
And consecrate commotion's bitter edge?
    Arch. My brother general, the commonwealth,
To brother born an household cruelty,
I make my quarrel in particular.
    West. There is no need of any such redress;
Or if there were, it not belongs to you.
    Mowb. Why not to him in part, and to us all
That feel the bruises of the days before,   100
And suffer the condition of these times
To lay a heavy and unequal hand
Upon our honours?
    West.   O, my good Lord Mowbray,
Construe the times to their necessities,
And you shall say indeed, it is the time,
And not the King, that doth you injuries.
Yet for your part, it not appears to me
Either from the King or in the present time
That you should have an inch of any ground
To build a grief on: were you not restored   110
To all the Duke of Norfolk's signories,
Your noble and right well remember'd father's?

    Mowb. What thing, in honour, had my father
    lost,
That need to be revived and breathed in me?
The King that loved him, as the state stood
    then,
Was force perforce compell'd to banish him:
And then that Henry Bolingbroke and he,
Being mounted and both roused in their seats,
Their neighing coursers daring of the spur,   119
Their armed staves in charge, their beavers
    down,
Their eyes of fire sparkling through sights of
    steel
And the loud trumpet blowing them together,
Then, then, when there was nothing could have
    stay'd
My father from the breast of Bolingbroke,
O, when the King did throw his warder down,
His own life hung upon the staff he threw;
Then threw he down himself and all their lives
That by indictment and by dint of sword
Have since miscarried under Bolingbroke.
    West. You speak, Lord Mowbray, now you
    know not what.   130
The Earl of Hereford was reputed then
In England the most valiant gentleman:
Who knows on whom Fortune would then have
    smiled?
But if your father had been victor there,
He ne'er had borne it out of Coventry:
For all the country in a general voice
Cried hate upon him; and all their prayers and
    love
Were set on Hereford, whom they doted on
And bless'd and graced indeed, more than the
    King.
But this is mere digression from my purpose. 140
Here come I from our princely general
To know your griefs; to tell you from his Grace
That he will give you audience; and wherein
It shall appear that your demands are just,
You shall enjoy them, everything set off
That might so much as think you enemies.
    Mowb. But he hath forced us to compel this
    offer;
And it proceeds from policy, not love.
    West. Mowbray, you overween to take it so;
This offer comes from mercy, not from fear: 150
For, lo! within a ken our army lies,
Upon mine honour, all too confident
To give admittance to a thought of fear.
Our battle is more full of names than yours,
Our men more perfect in the use of arms,
Our armour all as strong, our cause the best;
Then reason will our hearts should be as good:
Say you not then our offer is compell'd.

Mowb. Well, by my will we shall admit no
    parley.

West. That argues but the shame of your of-
    fence: *160*
A rotten case abides no handling.

Hast. Hath the Prince John a full commission,
In very ample virtue of his father,
To hear and absolutely to determine
Of what conditions we shall stand upon?

West. That is intended in the general's name:
I muse you make so slight a question.

Arch. Then take, my Lord of Westmoreland,
    this schedule,
For this contains our general grievances:
Each several article herein redress'd,   *170*
All members of our cause, both here and hence,
That are insinew'd to this action,
Acquitted by a true substantial form
And present execution of our wills
To us and to our purposes confined,
We come within our awful banks again
And knit our powers to the arm of peace.

West. This will I show the general. Please you,
    lords,
In sight of both our battles we may meet;
And either end in peace, which God so frame! *180*
Or to the place of difference call the swords
Which must decide it.

Arch. My lord, we will do so.

                    [*Exit* WESTMORELAND.

Mowb. There is a thing within my bosom tells
    me
That no conditions of our peace can stand.

Hast. Fear you not that: if we can make our
    peace
Upon such large terms and so absolute
As our conditions shall consist upon,
Our peace shall stand as firm as rocky mountains.

Mowb. Yea, but our valuation shall be such
That every slight and false-derived cause, *190*
Yea, every idle, nice, and wanton reason
Shall to the King taste of this action;
That, were our royal faiths martyrs in love,
We shall be winnow'd with so rough a wind
That even our corn shall seem as light as chaff
And good from bad find no partition.

Arch. No, no, my lord. Note this; the King is
    weary
Of dainty and such picking grievances:
For he hath found to end one doubt by death
Revives two greater in the heirs of life,   *200*
And therefore will he wipe his tables clean
And keep no tell-tale to his memory
That may repeat and history his loss
To new remembrance; for full well he knows
He cannot so precisely weed this land

As his misdoubts present occasion:
His foes are so enrooted with his friends
That, plucking to unfix an enemy,
He doth unfasten so and shake a friend:
So that this land, like an offensive wife *210*
That hath enraged him on to offer strokes,
As he is striking, holds his infant up
And hangs resolved correction in the arm
That was uprear'd to execution.

Hast. Besides, the King hath wasted all his rods
On late offenders, that he now doth lack
The very instruments of chastisement:
So that his power, like to a fangless lion,
May offer, but not hold.

Arch.   'Tis very true:
And therefore be assured, my good Lord Mar-
    shal,
If we do now make our atonement well, *221*
Our peace will, like a broken limb united,
Grow stronger for the breaking.

Mowb.   Be it so.
Here is return'd my Lord of Westmoreland.

          Re-enter WESTMORELAND.

West. The Prince is here at hand: pleaseth your
    lordship
To meet his Grace just distance 'tween our
    armies.

Mowb. Your Grace of York, in God's name,
    then, set forward.

Arch. Before, and greet his Grace: my lord, we
    come.   [*Exeunt.*

      SCENE II. *Another part of the forest*

Enter, from one side, MOWBRAY, *attended; after-*
    wards the ARCHBISHOP, HASTINGS, *and others:*
    from the other side, PRINCE JOHN OF LANCASTER,
    and WESTMORELAND; *Officers, and others with*
    them.

Lan. You are well encounter'd here, my cousin
    Mowbray:
Good day to you, gentle Lord Archbishop;
And so to you, Lord Hastings, and to all.
My Lord of York, it better show'd with you
When that your flock, assembled by the bell,
Encircled you to hear with reverence
Your exposition on the holy text
Than now to see you here an iron man,
Cheering a rout of rebels with your drum,
Turning the Word to sword and life to death. *10*
That man that sits within a monarch's heart
And ripens in the sunshine of his favour,
Would he abuse the countenance of the King,
Alack, what mischiefs might be set abroach
In shadow of such greatness! With you, Lord
    Bishop,

It is even so. Who hath not heard it spoken
How deep you were within the books of God?
To us the speaker in His parliament;
To us the imagined voice of God himself;
The very opener and intelligencer   20
Between the grace, the sanctities of Heaven
And our dull workings. O, who shall believe
But you misuse the reverence of your place,
Employ the countenance and grace of Heaven,
As a false favourite doth his prince's name,
In deeds dishonourable? You have ta'en up,
Under the counterfeited zeal of God,
The subjects of His substitute, my father,
And both against the peace of Heaven and him
Have here up-swarm'd them.
    Arch.   Good my Lord of Lancaster, *30*
I am not here against your father's peace;
But, as I told my Lord of Westmoreland,
The time misorder'd doth, in common sense,
Crowd us and crush us to this monstrous form
To hold our safety up. I sent your Grace
The parcels and particulars of our grief,
The which hath been with scorn shoved from the
    court,
Whereon this Hydra son of war is born;
Whose dangerous eyes may well be charm'd
    asleep
With grant of our most just and right desires, *40*
And true obedience, of this madness cured,
Stoop tamely to the foot of majesty.
    Mowb. If not, we ready are to try our fortunes
To the last man.
    Hast.   And though we here fall down,
We have supplies to second our attempt:
If they miscarry, theirs shall second them;
And so success of mischief shall be born
And heir from heir shall hold this quarrel up
Whiles England shall have generation.
    Lan. You are too shallow, Hastings, much too
    shallow,   *50*
To sound the bottom of the after-times.
    West. Pleaseth your Grace to answer them
    directly
How far forth you do like their articles?
    Lan. I like them all, and do allow them well,
And swear here, by the honour of my blood,
My father's purposes have been mistook,
And some about him have too lavishly
Wrested his meaning and authority.
My lord, these griefs shall be with speed re-
    dress'd;
Upon my soul, they shall. If this may please you,
Discharge your powers unto their several coun-
    ties,
As we will ours: and here between the armies
Let's drink together friendly and embrace,

That all their eyes may bear those tokens home
Of our restored love and amity.
    Arch. I take your princely word for these re-
    dresses.
    Lan. I give it you, and will maintain my word:
And thereupon I drink unto your Grace.
    Hast. Go, captain, and deliver to the army   *69*
This news of peace: let them have pay, and part:
I know it will well please them. Hie thee, cap-
    tain.   [*Exit Officer.*
    Arch. To you, my noble Lord of Westmore-
    land.
    West. I pledge your Grace; and, if you knew
    what pains
I have bestow'd to breed this present peace,
You would drink freely: but my love to ye
Shall show itself more openly hereafter.
    Arch. I do not doubt you.
    West.   I am glad of it.
Health to my lord and gentle cousin, Mowbray.
    Mowb. You wish me health in very happy
    season;
For I am, on the sudden, something ill.   *80*
    Arch. Against ill chances men are ever merry;
But heaviness foreruns the good event.
    West. Therefore be merry, coz; since sudden
    sorrow
Serves to say thus, "some good thing comes to-
    morrow."
    Arch. Believe me, I am passing light in spirit.
    Mowb. So much the worse, if your own rule be
    true.
    Shouts within.
    Lan. The word of peace is render'd: hark, how
    they shout!
    Mowb. This had been cheerful after victory.
    Arch. A peace is of the nature of a conquest;
For then both parties nobly are subdued,   *90*
And neither party loser.
    Lan.   Go, my lord,
And let our army be discharged too.
                [*Exit* WESTMORELAND.
And, good my lord, so please you, let our trains
March by us, that we may peruse the men
We should have coped withal.
    Arch.   Go, good Lord Hastings,
And, ere they be dismiss'd, let them march by.
                [*Exit* HASTINGS.
    Lan. I trust, lords, we shall lie to-night to-
    gether.

Re-enter WESTMORELAND.

Now cousin, wherefore stands our army still?
    West. The leaders, having charge from you to
    stand,
Will not go off until they hear you speak.   *100*

Lan. They know their duties.

Re-enter HASTINGS.

Hast. My lord, our army is dispersed already:
Like youthful steers unyoked, they take their
     courses
East, west, north, south; or, like a school broke
     up,
Each hurries toward his home and sporting-place.
   West. Good tidings, my Lord Hastings; for the
     which
I do arrest thee, traitor, of high treason:
And you, Lord Archbishop, and you, Lord
     Mowbray,
Of capital treason I attach you both.
   Mowb. Is this proceeding just and honourable?
   West. Is your assembly so?   *111*
   Arch. Will you thus break your faith?
   Lan.   I pawn'd thee none:
I promised you redress of these same grievances
Whereof you did complain; which, by mine
     honour,
I will perform with a most Christian care.
But for you, rebels, look to taste the due
Meet for rebellion and such acts as yours.
Most shallowly did you these arms commence,
Fondly brought here and foolishly sent hence.
Strike up our drums, pursue the scatter'd stray:
God, and not we, hath safely fought to-day.   *121*
Some guard these traitors to the block of death,
Treason's true bed and yielder up of breath.
                                        [*Exeunt.*

SCENE III. *Another part of the forest*
   Alarum. Excursions. Enter FALSTAFF
             and COLEVILLE, *meeting.*

   Fal. What's your name, sir? of what condition
are you, and of what place, I pray?
   Cole. I am a knight, sir; and my name is Cole-
ville of the Dale.
   Fal. Well, then, Coleville is your name, a
knight is your degree, and your place the Dale:
Coleville shall be still your name, a traitor your
degree, and the dungeon your place, a place deep
enough; so shall you be still Coleville of the
Dale.   *10*
   Cole. Are not you Sir John Falstaff?
   Fal. As good a man as he, sir, whoe'er I am.
Do ye yield, sir? or shall I sweat for you? If I
do sweat, they are the drops of thy lovers, and
they weep for thy death: therefore rouse up fear
and trembling, and do observance to my mercy.
   Cole. I think you are Sir John Falstaff, and in
that thought yield me.   *19*
   Fal. I have a whole school of tongues in this
belly of mine, and not a tongue of them all

speaks any other word but my name. An I had
but a belly of any indifferency, I were simply
the most active fellow in Europe: my womb,
my womb, my womb, undoes me. Here comes
our general.

   Enter PRINCE JOHN OF LANCASTER, WESTMORE-
            LAND, BLUNT, *and others.*

   Lan. The heat is past; follow no further now:
Call in the powers, good cousin Westmoreland.
                          [*Exit* WESTMORELAND.
Now, Falstaff, where have you been all this
     while?
When everything is ended, then you come: *30*
These tardy tricks of yours will, on my life,
One time or other break some gallows' back.
   Fal. I would be sorry, my lord, but it should
be thus: I never knew yet but rebuke and check
was the reward of valour. Do you think me a
swallow, an arrow, or a bullet? have I, in my
poor and old motion, the expedition of thought?
I have speeded hither with the very extremest
inch of possibility; I have foundered nine score
and odd posts: and here, travel-tainted as I am,
have, in my pure and immaculate valour, taken
Sir John Coleville of the Dale, a most furious
knight and valorous enemy. But what of that?
he saw me, and yielded; that I may justly say,
with the hook-nosed fellow of Rome, "I came,
I saw, and overcame."
   Lan. It was more of his courtesy than your deserving.
   Fal. I know not: here he is, and here I yield
him: and I beseech your Grace, let it be booked
with the rest of this day's deeds; or, by the Lord,
I will have it in a particular ballad else, with
mine own picture on the top on't, Coleville
kissing my foot: to the which course if I be
enforced, if you do not all show like gilt two-
pences to me, and I in the clear sky of fame
o'ershine you as much as the full moon doth the
cinders of the element, which show like pins'
heads to her, believe not the word of the noble:
therefore let me have right, and let desert
mount   *61*
   Lan. Thine's too heavy to mount.
   Fal. Let it shine, then.
   Lan. Thine's too thick to shine.
   Fal. Let it do something, my good lord, that
may do me good, and call it what you will.
   Lan. Is thy name Coleville?
   Cole. It is, my lord.
   Lan. A famous rebel art thou, Coleville.
   Fal. And a famous true subject took him.   *70*
   Cole. I am, my lord, but as my betters are
That led me hither: had they been ruled by me,

You should have won them dearer than you have.

Fal. I know not how they sold themselves: but thou, like a kind fellow, gavest thyself away gratis; and I thank thee for thee.

Re-enter WESTMORELAND.

Lan. Now, have you left pursuit?

West. Retreat is made and execution stay'd.

Lan. Send Coleville with his confederates
To York, to present execution: 80
Blunt, lead him hence; and see you guard him sure.

       [*Exeunt* BLUNT *and others with* COLEVILLE.

And now dispatch we toward the court, my lords;
I hear the King my father is sore sick:
Our news shall go before us to his Majesty,
Which, cousin, you shall bear to comfort him,
And we with sober speed will follow you.

Fal. My lord, I beseech you, give me leave to go
Through Gloucestershire: and, when you come to court,
Stand my good lord, pray, in your good report.

Lan. Fare you well, Falstaff: I, in my condition,   90
Shall better speak of you than you deserve.

       [*Exeunt all but* FALSTAFF.

Fal. I would you had but the wit: 'twere better than your dukedom. Good faith, this same young sober-blooded boy doth not love me; nor a man cannot make him laugh; but that's no marvel, he drinks no wine. There's never none of these demure boys come to any proof; for thin drink doth so over-cool their blood, and making many fish-meals, that they fall into a kind of male green-sickness; and then, when they marry, they get wenches: they are generally fools and cowards; which some of us should be too, but for inflammation. A good sherris-sack hath a two-fold operation in it. It ascends me into the brain; dries me there all the foolish and dull and crudy vapours which environ it; makes it apprehensive, quick, forgetive, full of nimble, fiery, and delectable shapes; which, delivered o'er to the voice, the tongue, which is the birth, becomes excellent wit. The second property of your excellent sherris is the warming of the blood; which, before cold and settled, left the liver white and pale, which is the badge of pusillanimity and cowardice; but the sherris warms it and makes it course from the inwards to the parts extreme: it illumineth the face, which as a beacon gives warning to all the rest of this little kingdom, man, to arm; and then the vital commoners and inland petty spirits muster me all to their captain, the heart, who, great and puffed up with this retinue, doth any deed of courage; and this valour comes of sherris. So that skill in the weapon is nothing without sack, for that sets it a-work; and learning a mere hoard of gold kept by a devil, till sack commences it and sets it in act and use. Hereof comes it that Prince Harry is valiant; for the cold blood he did naturally inherit of his father, he hath, like lean, sterile, and bare land, manured, husbanded, and tilled with excellent endeavour of drinking good and good store of fertile sherris, that he is become very hot and valiant. If I had a thousand sons, the first humane principle I would teach them should be to forswear thin potations and to addict themselves to sack.

Enter BARDOLPH.

How now, Bardolph?

Bard. The army is discharged all and gone.

Fal. Let them go. I'll through Gloucestershire; and there will I visit Master Robert Shallow, esquire: I have him already tempering between my finger and my thumb, and shortly will I seal with him. Come away.   [*Exeunt.*

SCENE IV. *Westminster: the Jerusalem Chamber*

Enter the KING, *the* PRINCES THOMAS OF CLARENCE *and* HUMPHREY OF GLOUCESTER, WARWICK, *and others.*

King. Now, lords, if God doth give successful end
To this debate that bleedeth at our doors,
We will our youth lead on to higher fields
And draw no swords but what are sanctified.
Our navy is address'd, our power collected,
Our substitutes in absence well invested,
And everything lies level to our wish:
Only, we want a little personal strength;
And pause us, till these rebels, now afoot,
Come underneath the yoke of government.   10

War. Both which we doubt not but your Majesty
Shall soon enjoy.

King.   Humphrey, my son of Gloucester,
Where is the Prince your brother?

Glou. I think he's gone to hunt, my lord, at Windsor.

King. And how accompanied?

Glou.   I do not know, my lord.

King. Is not his brother, Thomas of Clarence, with him?

Glou. No, my good lord; he is in presence here.

Clar. What would my lord and father?

King. Nothing but well to thee, Thomas of Clarence.

How chance thou art not with the Prince thy
    brother?   20
He loves thee, and thou dost neglect him,
    Thomas;
Thou hast a better place in his affection
Than all thy brothers: cherish it, my boy,
And noble offices thou mayst effect
Of mediation, after I am dead,
Between his greatness and thy other brethren:
Therefore omit him not; blunt not his love,
Nor lose the good advantage of his grace
By seeming cold or careless of his will;
For he is gracious, if he be observed: 30
He hath a tear for pity and a hand
Open as day for melting charity:
Yet notwithstanding, being incensed, he's flint,
As humorous as winter and as sudden
As flaws congealed in the spring of day.
His temper, therefore, must be well observed:
Chide him for faults, and do it reverently,
When you perceive his blood inclined to mirth;
But, being moody, give him line and scope,
Till that his passions, like a whale on ground, 40
Confound themselves with working. Learn this,
    Thomas,
And thou shalt prove a shelter to thy friends,
A hoop of gold to bind thy brothers in,
That the united vessel of their blood,
Mingled with venom of suggestion—
As, force perforce, the age will pour it in—
Shall never leak, though it do work as strong
As aconitum or rash gunpowder.
  Clar. I shall observe him with all care and love.
  King. Why art thou not at Windsor with him,
    Thomas?   50
  Clar. He is not there to-day; he dines in
    London.
  King. And how accompanied? canst thou tell
    that?
  Clar. With Poins, and other his continual fol-
  lowers.
  King. Most subject is the fattest soil to weeds;
And he, the noble image of my youth,
Is overspread with them: therefore my grief
Stretches itself beyond the hour of death:
The blood weeps from my heart when I do shape
In forms imaginary the unguided days
And rotten times that you shall look upon   60
When I am sleeping with my ancestors.
For when his headstrong riot hath no curb,
When rage and hot blood are his counsellors,
When means and lavish manners meet together,
O, with what wings shall his affections fly
Towards fronting peril and opposed decay!
  War. My gracious lord, you look beyond him
  quite:

The Prince but studies his companions
Like a strange tongue, wherein, to gain the lan-
  guage,
'Tis needful that the most immodest word   70
Be look'd upon and learn'd; which once attain'd,
Your Highness knows, comes to no further use
But to be known and hated. So, like gross terms,
The Prince will in the perfectness of time
Cast off his followers; and their memory
Shall as a pattern or a measure live,
By which his Grace must mete the lives of others,
Turning past evils to advantages.
  King. 'Tis seldom when the bee doth leave her
  comb
In the dead carrion.

Enter WESTMORELAND.

         Who's here? Westmoreland?   80
  West. Health to my sovereign, and new happi-
  ness
Added to that that I am to deliver!
Prince John your son doth kiss your Grace's
  hand:
Mowbray, the Bishop Scroop, Hastings, and all
Are brought to the correction of your law;
There is not now a rebel's sword unsheathed,
But Peace puts forth her olive everywhere.
The manner how this action hath been borne
Here at more leisure may your Highness read,
With every course in his particular.   90
  King. O Westmoreland, thou art a summer bird,
Which ever in the haunch of winter sings
The lifting up of day.

Enter HARCOURT.

         Look, here's more news.
  Har. From enemies heaven keep your Majesty;
And, when they stand against you, may they fall
As those that I am come to tell you of!
The Earl Northumberland and the Lord Bar-
  dolph,
With a great power of English and of Scots,
Are by the sheriff of Yorkshire overthrown:
The manner and true order of the fight   100
This packet, please it you, contains at large.
  King. And wherefore should these good news
  make me sick?
Will Fortune never come with both hands full,
But write her fair words still in foulest letters?
She either gives a stomach and no food;
Such are the poor, in health; or else a feast
And takes away the stomach; such are the rich,
That have abundance and enjoy it not.
I should rejoice now at this happy news;
And now my sight fails, and my brain is giddy:
O me! come near me; now I am much ill.   *111*

Glou. Comfort, your Majesty!
Clar.   O my royal father!
West. My sovereign lord, cheer up yourself, look up.
War. Be patient, Princes; you do know, these fits
Are with his Highness very ordinary.
Stand from him, give him air; he'll straight be well.
Clar. No, no, he cannot long hold out these pangs:
The incessant care and labour of his mind
Hath wrought the mure that should confine it in
So thin that life looks through and will break out.
Glou. The people fear me; for they do observe
Unfather'd heirs and loathly births of nature:
The seasons change their manners, as the year
Had found some months asleep and leap'd them over.
Clar. The river hath thrice flow'd, no ebb between;
And the old folk, time's doting chronicles,
Say it did so a little time before
That our great-grandsire, Edward, sick'd and died.
War. Speak lower, Princes, for the King recovers.
Glou. This apoplexy will certain be his end. *130*
King. I pray you, take me up, and bear me hence
Into some other chamber: softly, pray. [*Exeunt.*

SCENE V. *Another chamber*

The KING *lying on a bed:* CLARENCE, GLOUCESTER, WARWICK, *and others in attendance.*

King. Let there be no noise made, my gentle friends;
Unless some dull and favourable hand
Will whisper music to my weary spirit.
War. Call for the music in the other room.
King. Set me the crown upon my pillow here.
Clar. His eye is hollow, and he changes much.
War. Less noise, less noise!

Enter PRINCE HENRY.

Prince.   Who saw the Duke of Clarence?
Clar. I am here, brother, full of heaviness.
Prince. How now! rain within doors, and none abroad!
How doth the King?   *10*
Glou. Exceeding ill.
Prince.   Heard he the good news yet?
Tell it him.
Glou. He alter'd much upon the hearing it.
Prince. If he be sick with joy, he'll recover without physic.

War. Not so much noise, my lords: sweet prince, speak low;
The King your father is disposed to sleep.
Clar. Let us withdraw into the other room.
War. Will't please your Grace to go along with us?
Prince. No; I will sit and watch here by the King.   [*Exeunt all but the* PRINCE   *20*
Why doth the crown lie there upon his pillow,
Being so troublesome a bedfellow?
O polish'd perturbation! golden care!
That keep'st the ports of slumber open wide
To many a watchful night! sleep with it now!
Yet not so sound and half so deeply sweet
As he whose brow with homely biggen bound
Snores out the watch of night. O majesty!
When thou dost pinch thy bearer, thou dost sit
Like a rich armour worn in heat of day,   *30*
That scalds with safety. By his gates of breath
There lies a downy feather which stirs not:
Did he suspire, that light and weightless down
Perforce must move. My gracious lord! my father!
This sleep is sound indeed; this is a sleep
That from this golden rigol hath divorced
So many English kings. Thy due from me
Is tears and heavy sorrows of the blood,
Which nature, love, and filial tenderness
Shall, O dear father, pay thee plenteously: *40*
My due from thee is this imperial crown,
Which, as immediate from thy place and blood,
Derives itself to me. [*Puts on the crown.*] Lo, here it sits,
Which God shall guard: and put the world's whole strength
Into one giant arm, it shall not force
This lineal honour from me: this from thee
Will I to mine leave, as 'tis left to me.   [*Exit.*
King. Warwick! Gloucester! Clarence!

Re-enter WARWICK, GLOUCESTER, CLARENCE, *and the rest.*

Clar. Doth the King call?
War. What would your Majesty? How fares your Grace?   *50*
King. Why did you leave me here alone, my lords?
Clar. We left the Prince my brother here, my liege,
Who undertook to sit and watch by you.
King. The Prince of Wales! Where is he? let me see him:
He is not here.
War. This door is open; he is gone this way.
Glou. He came not through the chamber where we stay'd.

King. Where is the crown? who took it from
   my pillow?
War. When we withdrew, my liege, we left it
   here.
King. The Prince hath ta'en it hence: go, seek
   him out.   60
Is he so hasty that he doth suppose
My sleep my death?
Find him, my Lord of Warwick; chide him
   hither.   [*Exit* WARWICK.
This part of his conjoins with my disease,
And helps to end me. See, sons, what things you
   are!
How quickly nature falls into revolt
When gold becomes her object!
For this the foolish over-careful fathers
Have broke their sleep with thoughts, their
   brains with care,
Their bones with industry;   70
For this they have engross'd and piled up
The canker'd heaps of strange-achieved gold;
For this they have been thoughtful to invest
Their sons with arts and martial exercises:
When, like the bee, culling from every flower
The virtuous sweets,
Our thighs pack'd with wax, our mouths with
   honey,
We bring it to the hive, and, like the bees,
Are murdered for our pains. This bitter taste
Yield his engrossments to the ending father. 80

Re-enter WARWICK.

Now, where is he that will not stay so long
Till his friend sickness hath determined me?
War. My lord, I found the Prince in the next
   room,
Washing with kindly tears his gentle cheeks,
With such a deep demeanour in great sorrow
That tyranny, which never quaff'd but blood,
Would, by beholding him, have wash'd his knife
With gentle eye-drops. He is coming hither.
King. But wherefore did he take away the
   crown?

Re-enter PRINCE HENRY.

Lo, where he comes. Come hither to me, Harry.
Depart the chamber, leave us here along.   91
              [*Exeunt* WARWICK *and the rest.*
Prince. I never thought to hear you speak again.
King. Thy wish was father, Harry, to that
   thought:
I stay too long by thee, I weary thee.
Dost thou so hunger for mine empty chair
That thou wilt needs invest thee with my hon-
   ours
Before thy hour be ripe? O foolish youth!

Thou seek'st the greatness that will overwhelm
   thee.
Stay but a little; for my cloud of dignity
Is held from falling with so weak a wind   *100*
That it will quickly drop: my day is dim.
Thou hast stolen that which after some few
   hours
Were thine without offense; and at my death
Thou hast seal'd up my expectation:
Thy life did manifest thou lovedst me not,
And thou wilt have me die assured of it.
Thou hidst a thousand daggers in thy thoughts,
Which thou hast whetted on thy stony heart
To stab at half an hour of my life.   *109*
What! canst thou not forbear me half an hour?
Then get thee gone and dig my grave thyself,
And bid the merry bells ring to thine ear
That thou art crowned, not that I am dead.
Let all the tears that should bedew my hearse
Be drops of balm to sanctify thy head:
Only compound me with forgotten dust;
Give that which gave thee life unto the worms.
Pluck down my officers, break my decrees;
For now a time is come to mock at form:
Harry the Fifth is crown'd: up, vanity!   *120*
Down, royal state! all you sage counsellors,
   hence!
And to the English court assemble now,
From every region, apes of idleness!
Now, neighbour confines, purge you of your
   scum:
Have you a ruffian that will swear, drink, dance,
Revel the night, rob, murder, and commit
The oldest sins the newest kind of ways?
Be happy, he will trouble you no more;
England shall double gild his treble guilt,
England shall give him office, honour, might; *130*
For the fifth Harry from curb'd license plucks
The muzzle of restraint, and the wild dog
Shall flesh his tooth on every innocent.
O my poor kingdom, sick with civil blows!
When that my care could not withhold thy riots,
What wilt thou do when riots is thy care?
O, thou wilt be a wilderness again,
Peopled with wolves, thy old inhabitants!
Prince. O, pardon me, my liege! but for my
   tears,
The moist impediments unto my speech,   *140*
I had forestall'd this dear and deep rebuke
Ere you with grief had spoke and I had heard
The course of it so far. There is your crown;
And He that wears the crown immortally
Long guard it yours! If I affect it more
Than as your honour and as your renown,
Let me no more from this obedience rise,
Which my most inward, true, and duteous spirit

Teacheth, this prostrate and exterior bending.
God witness with me, when I here came in,   *150*
And found no course of breath within your Majesty,
How cold it struck my heart! If I do feign,
O, let me in my present wildness die
And never live to show the incredulous world
The noble change that I have purposed!
Coming to look on you, thinking you dead.
And dead almost, my liege, to think you were,
I spake unto this crown as having sense,
And thus upbraided it: "The care on thee depending
Hath fed upon the body of my father;   *160*
Therefore, thou best of gold art worst of gold:
Other, less fine in carat, is more precious,
Preserving life in medicine potable;
But thou, most fine, most honour'd, most renown'd,
Hast eat thy bearer up." Thus, my most royal liege,
Accusing it, I put it on my head,
To try with it, as with an enemy
That had before my face murder'd my father,
The quarrel of a true inheritor.
But if it did infect my blood with joy,   *170*
Or swell my thoughts to any strain of pride;
If any rebel or vain spirit of mine
Did with the least affection of a welcome
Give entertainment to the might of it,
Let God for ever keep it from my head
And make me as the poorest vassal is
That doth with awe and terror kneel to it!
    King. O my son,
God put it in thy mind to take it hence,
That thou mightst win the more thy father's love,   *180*
Pleading so wisely in excuse of it!
Come hither, Harry, sit thou by my bed;
And hear, I think, the very latest counsel
That ever I shall breathe. God knows, my son,
By what by-paths and indirect crook'd ways
I met this crown; and I myself know well
How troublesome it sat upon my head.
To thee it shall descend with better quiet,
Better opinion, better confirmation;
For all the soil of the achievement goes   *190*
With me into the earth. It seem'd in me
But as an honour snatch'd with boisterous hand
And I had many living to upbraid
My gain of it by their assistances;
Which daily grew to quarrel and to bloodshed,
Wounding supposed peace: all these bold fears
Thou see'st with peril I have answered;
For all my reign hath been but as a scene

Acting that argument: and now my death
Changes the mode; for what in me was purchased,   *200*
Falls upon thee in a more fairer sort;
So thou the garland wear'st successively.
Yet, though thou stand'st more sure than I could do,
Thou art not firm enough, since griefs are green;
And all my friends, which thou must make thy friends,
Have but their stings and teeth newly ta'en out,
By whose fell working I was first advanced
And by whose power I well might lodge a fear
To be again displaced: which to avoid,
I cut them off; and had a purpose now   *210*
To lead out many to the Holy Land,
Lest rest and lying still might make them look
Too near unto my state. Therefore, my Harry,
Be it thy course to busy giddy minds
With foreign quarrels; that action, hence borne out,
May waste the memory of the former days.
More would I, but my lungs are wasted so
That strength of speech is utterly denied me.
How I came by the crown, O God forgive;
And grant it may with thee in true peace live!
    Prince. My gracious liege,   *221*
You won it, wore it, kept it, gave it me;
Then plain and right must my possession be:
Which I with more than with a common pain
'Gainst all the world will rightfully maintain.

Enter LORD JOHN OF LANCASTER.

    King. Look, look, here comes my John of Lancaster.
    Lan. Health, peace, and happiness to my royal father!
    King. Thou bring'st me happiness and peace, son John;
But health, alack, with youthful wings is flown
From this bare wither'd trunk: upon thy sight
My worldly business makes a period.   *231*
Where is my Lord of Warwick?
    Prince.   My Lord of Warwick!

Re-enter WARWICK, *and others.*

    King. Doth any name particular belong
Unto the lodging where I first did swoon?
    War. 'Tis call'd Jerusalem, my noble lord.
    King. Laud be to God! even there my life must end.
It hath been prophesied to me many years,
I should not die but in Jerusalem;
Which vainly I supposed the Holy Land:
But bear me to that chamber; there I'll lie;   *240*
In that Jerusalem shall Harry die.   [*Exeunt.*

ACT V

Scene I. *Gloucestershire: Shallow's house*

Enter SHALLOW, FALSTAFF, BARDOLPH, *and* PAGE.

Shal. By cock and pie, sir, you shall not away
to-night. What, Davy, I say!

Fal. You must excuse me, Master Robert
Shallow.

Shal. I will not excuse you; you shall not be
excused; excuses shall not be admitted; there is
no excuse shall serve; you shall not be excused.
Why, Davy!

Enter DAVY.

Davy. Here, sir.   9

Shal. Davy, Davy, Davy, Davy, let me see,
Davy; let me see, Davy; let me see: yea, marry,
William cook bid him come hither. Sir John,
you shall not be excused.

Davy. Marry, sir, thus; those precepts cannot
be served: and, again, sir, shall we sow the
headland with wheat?

Shal. With red wheat, Davy. But for William
cook: are there no young pigeons?

Davy. Yes, sir. Here is now the smith's note
for shoeing and plough-irons.   20

Shal. Let it be cast and paid. Sir John, you shall
not be excused.

Davy. Now, sir, a new link to the bucket
must needs be had: and, sir, do you mean to stop
any of William's wages, about the sack he lost
the other day at Hinckley fair?

Shal. A' shall answer it. Some pigeons, Davy,
a couple of short-legged hens, a joint of mutton,
and any pretty little tiny kickshaws, tell William
cook.   30

Davy. Doth the man of war stay all night, sir?

Shal. Yea, Davy. I will use him well: a friend
i' the court is better than a penny in purse. Use
his men well, Davy; for they are arrant knaves,
and will backbite.

Davy. No worse than they are backbitten, sir;
for they have marvellous foul linen.

Shal. Well conceited, Davy: about thy business,
Davy.   40

Davy. I beseech you, sir, to countenance
William Visor of Woncot against Clement
Perkes of the hill.

Shal. There is many complaints, Davy, against
that Visor: that Visor is an arrant knave, on my
knowledge.

Davy. I grant your worship that he is a knave,
sir; but yet, God forbid, sir, but a knave should
have some countenance at his friend's request.
An honest man, sir, is able to speak for himself,

when a knave is not. I have served your worship truly, sir, this eight years; and if I cannot
once or twice in a quarter bear out a knave against
an honest man, I have but a very little credit with
your worship. The knave is mine honest friend,
sir; therefore, I beseech your worship, let him be
countenanced.

Shal. Go to; I say he shall have no wrong.
Look about, Davy. [*Exit* DAVY.] Where are
you, Sir John? Come, come, come, off with
your boots. Give me your hand, Master Bardolph.

Bard. I am glad to see your worship.

Shal. I thank thee with all my heart, kind
Master Bardolph: and welcome, my tall fellow
[*to the* PAGE]. Come, Sir John.

Fal. I'll follow you, good Master Robert
Shallow. [*Exit* SHALLOW.] Bardolph, look to
our horses. [*Exeunt* BARDOLPH *and* PAGE.] If
I were sawed into quantities, I should make four
dozen of such bearded hermits' staves as Master
Shallow. It is a wonderful thing to see the semblable coherence of his men's spirits and his: they
by observing of him, do bear themselves like
foolish justices; he, by conversing with them, is
turned into a justice-like serving-man: their
spirits are so married in conjunction with the
participation of society that they flock together
in consent, like so many wild-geese. If I had a
suit to Master Shallow, I would humour his men
with the imputation of being near their master: if
to his men, I would curry with Master Shallow
that no man could better command his servants.
It is certain that either wise bearing or ignorant
carriage is caught, as men take diseases, one of
another: therefore let men take heed of their
company. I will devise matter enough out of
this Shallow to keep Prince Harry in continual
laughter the wearing out of six fashions, which is
four terms, or two actions, and a' shall laugh
without intervallums. O, it is much that a lie
with a slight oath and a jest with a sad brow will
do with a fellow that never had the ache in his
shoulders! O, you shall see him laugh till his
face be like a wet cloak ill laid up!

Shal. [*Within*] Sir John!

Fal. I come, Master Shallow; I come, Master
Shallow.   [*Exit.*

Scene II. *Westminster: the Palace*

Enter WARWICK *and the* LORD CHIEF JUSTICE,
meeting.

War. How now, my Lord Chief Justice,
whither away?

Ch. Just. How doth the King?

War. Exceeding well; his cares are now all
  ended.
  Ch. Just. I hope, not dead.
  War.   He's walk'd the way of nature;
And to our purposes he lives no more.
  Ch. Just. I would his Majesty had call'd me
  with him:
The service that I truly did his life
Hath left me open to all injuries.
  War. Indeed I think the young King loves you
  not.
  Ch. Just. I know he doth not, and do arm my-
  self   10
To welcome the condition of the time,
Which cannot look more hideously upon me
Than I have drawn it in my fantasy.

Enter LANCASTER, CLARENCE, GLOUCESTER, WEST-
MORELAND *and others.*

  War. Here come the heavy issue of dead Harry:
O that the living Harry had the temper
Of him, the worst of these three gentlemen!
How many nobles then should hold their places,
That must strike sail to spirits of vile sort!
  Ch. Just. O God, I fear all will be overturn'd!
  Lan. Good morrow, cousin Warwick, good
  morrow.   20
  Glou. ⎱
  Clar. ⎰ Good morrow, cousin.
  Lan. We meet like men that had forgot to
  speak.
  War. We do remember; but our argument
Is all too heavy to admit much talk.
  Lan. Well, peace be with him that hath made
  us heavy!
  Ch. Just. Peace be with us, lest we be heavier!
  Glou. O, good my lord, you have lost a friend
  indeed;
And I dare swear you borrow not that face
Of seeming sorrow, it is sure your own.
  Lan. Though no man be assured what Grace
  to find,   30
You stand in coldest expectation:
I am the sorrier; would 'twere otherwise.
  Clar. Well, you must now speak Sir John
  Falstaff fair;
Which swims against your stream of quality.
  Ch. Just. Sweet Princes, what I did, I did in
  honour,
Led by the impartial conduct of my soul:
And never shall you see that I will beg
A ragged and forestall'd remission.
If truth and upright innocency fail me,
I'll to the King my master that is dead,   40
And tell him who hath sent me after him.
  War. Here comes the Prince.

Enter KING HENRY THE FIFTH, *attended.*

  Ch. Just. Good morrow; and God save your
  Majesty!
  King. This new and gorgeous garment, ma-
  jesty,
Sits not so easy on me as you think.
Brothers, you mix your sadness with some fear:
This is the English, not the Turkish court;
Not Amurath an Amurath succeeds,
But Harry Harry. Yet be sad, good brothers,
For, by my faith, it very well becomes you: 50
Sorrow so royally in you appears
That I will deeply put the fashion on
And wear it in my heart: why then, be sad;
But entertain no more of it, good brothers,
Than a joint burden laid upon us all.
For me, by heaven, I bid you be assured,
I'll be your father and your brother too;
Let me but bear your love, I'll bear your cares:
Yet weep that Harry's dead; and so will I;
But Harry lives, that shall convert those tears   60
By number into hours of happiness.
  Princes. We hope no other from your Majesty.
  King. You all look strangely on me: and you
  most;
You are, I think, assured I love you not.
  Ch. Just. I am assured, if I be measured rightly,
Your Majesty hath no just cause to hate me.
  King. No!
How might a prince of my great hopes forget
So great indignities you laid upon me?   69
What! rate, rebuke, and roughly send to prison
The immediate heir of England! Was this easy?
May this be wash'd in Lethe, and forgotten?
  Ch. Just. I then did use the person of your
  father;
The image of his power lay then in me:
And, in the administration of his law,
Whiles I was busy for the commonwealth,
Your Highness pleased to forget my place,
The majesty and power of law and justice,
The image of the King whom I presented,
And struck me in my very seat of judgement;   80
Whereon, as an offender to your father,
I gave bold way to my authority
And did commit you. If the deed were ill,
Be you contented, wearing now the garland,
To have a son set your decrees at nought,
To pluck down justice from your awful bench,
To trip the course of law and blunt the sword
That guards the peace and safety of your person;
Nay, more, to spurn at your most royal image
And mock your workings in a second body.   90
Question your royal thoughts, make the case
  yours;

Be now the father and propose a son,
Hear your own dignity so much profaned,
See your most dreadful laws so loosely slighted,
Behold yourself so by a son disdain'd;
And then imagine me taking your part
And in your power soft silencing your son:
After this cold consideration, sentence me;
And, as you are a king, speak in your state
What I have done that misbecame my place, *100*
My person, or my liege's sovereignty.

  King. You are right, Justice, and you weigh
    this well;
Therefore still bear the balance and the sword:
And I do wish your honours may increase,
Till you do live to see a son of mine
Offend you and obey you, as I did.
So shall I live to speak my father's words:
"Happy am I, that have a man so bold,
That dares do justice on my proper son;
And not less happy, having such a son, *110*
That would deliver up his greatness so
Into the hands of justice." You did commit me:
For which, I do commit into your hand
The unstained sword that you have used to bear;
With this remembrance, that you use the same
With the like bold, just and impartial spirit
As you have done 'gainst me. There is my hand.
You shall be as a father to my youth:
My voice shall sound as you do prompt mine ear,
And I will stoop and humble my intents *120*
To your well-practised wise directions.
And, Princes all, believe me, I beseech you;
My father is gone wild into his grave,
For in his tomb lie my affections,
And with his spirit sadly I survive,
To mock the expectation of the world,
To frustrate prophecies, and to raze out
Rotten opinion, who hath writ me down
After my seeming. The tide of blood in me
Hath proudly flow'd in vanity till now: *130*
Now doth it turn and ebb back to the sea,
Where it shall mingle with the state of floods
And flow henceforth in formal majesty.
Now call we our high court of parliament:
And let us choose such limbs of noble counsel,
That the great body of our state may go
In equal rank with the best govern'd nation;
That war, or peace, or both at once, may be
As things acquainted and familiar to us;
In which you, father, shall have foremost hand.
Our coronation done, we will accite, *141*
As I before remember'd, all our state:
And, God consigning to my good intents,
No prince nor peer shall have just cause to say,
God shorten Harry's happy life one day!
                         [Exeunt.

SCENE III. *Gloucestershire: Shallow's
orchard*

Enter FALSTAFF, SHALLOW, SILENCE, DAVY, BAR-
DOLPH, *and the* PAGE.

  Shal. Nay, you shall see my orchard, where,
in an arbour, we will eat a last year's pippin
of my own graffing, with a dish of caraways,
and so forth: come, cousin Silence: and then to
bed.

  Fal. 'Fore God, you have here a goodly
dwelling and a rich.

  Shal. Barren, barren, barren; beggars all,
beggars all, Sir John: marry, good air. Spread,
Davy; spread, Davy: well said, Davy. *10*

  Fal. This Davy serves you for good uses; he
is your serving-man and your husband.

  Shal. A good varlet, a good varlet, a very good
varlet, Sir John: by the mass, I have drunk too
much sack at supper: a good varlet. Now sit
down, now sit down: come, cousin.

  Sil. Ah, sirrah! quoth-a, we shall [*Singing.*]
"Do nothing but eat, and make good cheer,
  And praise God for the merry year;
When flesh is cheap and females dear, *20*
  And lusty lads roam here and there
          So merrily,
  And ever among so merrily."

  Fal. There's a merry heart! Good Master
Silence, I'll give you a health for that anon.

  Shal. Give Master Bardolph some wine,
Davy.

  Davy. Sweet sir, sit; I'll be with you anon;
most sweet sir, sit. Master page, good master
page, sit. Proface! What you want in meat,
we'll have in drink: but you must bear; the
heart's all.   *[Exit.*

  Shal. Be merry, Master Bardolph; and, my
little soldier there, be merry.

  Sil. [*Singing.*] "Be merry, be merry, my wife
    has all;
For women are shrews, both short and tall:
'Tis merry in hall when beards wag all,
    And welcome merry Shrove-tide.
Be merry, be merry."

  Fal. I did not think Master Silence had been a
man of this mettle. *41*

  Sil. Who, I? I have been merry twice and once
ere now.

Re-enter DAVY.

  Davy. There's a dish of leather-coats for you.
                        [To BARDOLPH.

  Shal. Davy!

  Davy. Your worship! I'll be with you straight
[*to* BARDOLPH]. A cup of wine, sir?

Sil. [*Singing.*] "A cup of wine that's brisk and
  fine,
    And drink unto the leman mine;
      And a merry heart lives long-a."   *50*

Fal. Well said, Master Silence.

Sil. An we shall be merry, now comes in the
sweet o' the night.

Fal. Health and long life to you, Master Silence.

Sil. [*Singing.*] "Fill the cup, and let it come;
    I'll pledge you a mile to the
      bottom."

Shal. Honest Bardolph, welcome: if thou
wantest anything, and wilt not call, beshrew thy
heart. Welcome, my little tiny thief [*to the*
PAGE], and welcome indeed too. I'll drink to
Master Bardolph, and to all the cavaleros about
London.

Davy. I hope to see London once ere I die.

Bard. An I might see you there, Davy—

Shal. By the mass, you'll crack a quart together, ha! will you not, Master Bardolph?

Bard. Yea, sir, in a pottle-pot.

Shal. By God's liggens, I thank thee: the
knave will stick by thee, I can assure thee that.
A' will not out; he is true bred.   *71*

Bard. And I'll stick by him, sir.

Shal. Why, there spoke a king. Lack nothing:
be merry. [*Knocking within.*] Look who's at
door there, ho! who knocks?

                    [*Exit* DAVY.

Fal. Why, now you have done me right.

To SILENCE, *seeing him take off a bumper.*

Sil. [*Singing.*] "Do me right,
    And dub me knight:
      Samingo."

Is't not so?   *80*

Fal. 'Tis so.

Sil. Is't so? Why then, say an old man can do
somewhat.

Re-enter DAVY.

Davy. An't please your worship, there's one
Pistol come from the court with news.

Fal. From the court! let him come in.

Enter PISTOL.

How now, Pistol!

Pist. Sir John, God save you!

Fal. What wind blew you hither, Pistol?   *89*

Pist. Not the ill wind which blows no man to
good. Sweet knight, thou art now one of the
greatest men in this realm.

Sil. By'r lady, I think a' be, but goodman
Puff of Barson.

Pist. Puff!

Puff in thy teeth, most recreant coward base!

Sir John, I am thy Pistol and thy friend,
And helter-skelter have I rode to thee,
And tidings do I bring and lucky joys
And golden times and happy news of price.   *100*

Fal. I pray thee now, deliver them like a man
of this world.

Pist. A foutre for the world and worldlings
  base!

I speak of Africa and golden joys.

Fal. O base Assyrian knight, what is thy news?
Let King Cophetua know the truth thereof.

Sil. [*Singing.*] "And Robin Hood, Scarlet, and
    John."

Pist. Shall dunghill curs confront the Helicons?
And shall good news be baffled?
Then, Pistol, lay thy head in Furies' lap.   *110*

Shal. Honest gentleman, I know not your
breeding.

Pist. Why then, lament therefore.

Shal. Give me pardon, sir: if, sir, you come
with news from the court, I take it there's but
two ways, either to utter them, or to conceal
them. I am, sir, under the King, in some authority.

Pist. Under which king, Besonian? speak, or
  die.

Shal. Under King Harry.

Pist.   Harry the Fourth? or Fifth?

Shal. Harry the Fourth.

Pist.   A foutre for thine office!   *121*

Sir John, thy tender lambkin now is king;
Harry the Fifth's the man. I speak the truth:
When Pistol lies, do this; and fig me, like
The bragging Spaniard.

Fal. What, is the old king dead?

Pist. As nail in door: the things I speak are just.

Fal. Away, Bardolph! saddle my horse. Master
Robert Shallow, choose what office thou wilt in
the land, 'tis thine. Pistol, I will double-charge
thee with dignities.   *131*

Bard. O joyful day!

I would not take a knighthood for my fortune.

Pist. What! I do bring good news.

Fal. Carry Master Silence to bed. Master
Shallow, my Lord Shallow—be what thou wilt;
I am fortune's steward—get on thy boots: we'll
ride all night. O sweet Pistol! Away, Bardolph!
[*Exit* BARDOLPH.] Come, Pistol, utter more to
me; and withal devise something to do thyself
good. Boot, boot, Master Shallow: I know the
young king is sick for me. Let us take any
man's horses; the laws of England are at my
commandment. Blessed are they that have been
my friends; and woe to my Lord Chief Justice!

Pist. Let vultures vile seize on his lungs also!
"Where is the life that late I led?" say they:

Why, here it is; welcome these pleasant days!

[*Exeunt.*

SCENE IV. *London: a street.*

Enter BEADLES, *dragging in* MISTRESS QUICKLY
and DOLL TEARSHEET.

Quick. No, thou arrant knave; I would to God
that I might die, that I might have thee hanged:
thou hast drawn my shoulder out of joint.

1st Bead. The constables have delivered her
over to me; and she shall have whipping-cheer
enough, I warrant her: there hath been a man or
two lately killed about her.

Dol. Nut-hook, nut-hook, you lie. Come on;
I'll tell thee what, thou damned tripe-visaged
rascal, an the child I now go with do miscarry,
thou wert better thou hadst struck thy mother,
thou paper-faced villain.

Quick. O the Lord, that Sir John were come!
he would make this a bloody day to somebody.
But I pray God the fruit of her womb miscarry!

1st Bead. If it do, you shall have a dozen of
cushions again; you have but eleven now. Come,
I charge you both go with me; for the man is
dead that you and Pistol beat amongst you.   19

Dol. I'll tell you what, you thin man in a censer,
I will have you as soundly swinged for this—
you blue-bottle rogue, you filthy famished
correctioner, if you be not swinged, I'll forswear
half-kirtles.

1st Bead. Come, come, you she knight-errant,
come.

Quick. O God, that right should thus overcome
might! Well, of sufferance comes ease.

Dol. Come, you rogue, come; bring me to a
justice.   30

Quick. Ay, come, you starved blood-hound.

Dol. Goodman death, goodman bones!

Quick. Thou atomy, thou!

Dol. Come, you thin thing; some, you rascal.

1st Bead. Very well.   [*Exeunt.*

SCENE V. *A public place near Westminster Abbey*

Enter TWO GROOMS, *strewing rushes.*

1st Groom. More rushes, more rushes.

2nd Groom. The trumpets have sounded twice.

1st Groom. 'Twill be two o'clock ere they come
from the coronation: dispatch, dispatch.

[*Exeunt.*

Enter FALSTAFF, SHALLOW, PISTOL, BARDOLPH,
and PAGE.

Fal. Stand here by me, Master Robert Shallow; I will make the King do you grace: I will
leer upon him as a' comes by; and do but mark
the countenance that he will give me.

Pist. God bless thy lungs, good knight.   9

Fal. Come here, Pistol; stand behind me. O,
if I had had time to have made new liveries,
I would have bestowed the thousand pound I
borrowed of you. But 'tis no matter; this poor
show doth better: this doth infer the zeal I had
to see him.

Shal. It doth so.

Fal. It shows my earnestness of affection—

Shal. It doth so.

Fal. My devotion—

Shal. It doth, it doth, it doth.   20

Fal. As it were, to ride day and night; and not
to deliberate, not to remember, not to have
patience to shift me—

Shal. It is best, certain.

Fal. But to stand stained with travel and sweating with desire to see him; thinking of nothing
else, putting all affairs else in oblivion, as if there
were nothing else to be done but to see him.   29

Pist. 'Tis *semper idem,* for *obsque hoc nihil est:*
'tis all in every part.

Shal. 'Tis so, indeed.

Pist. My knight, I will inflame thy noble liver,
And make thee rage.
Thy Doll, and Helen of thy noble thoughts,
Is in base durance and contagious prison;
Haled thither
By most mechanical and dirty hand:
Rouse up revenge from ebon den with fell
　　Alecto's snake,   39
For Doll is in. Pistol speaks nought but truth.

Fal. I will deliver her.

Shouts within and the trumpets sound.

Pist. There roar'd the sea, and trumpet-clangor
sounds.

Enter the KING *and his train, the* LORD CHIEF
JUSTICE *among them.*

Fal. God save thy Grace, King Hal! my royal
Hal!

Pist. The heavens thee guard and keep, most
royal imp of fame!

Fal. God save thee, my sweet boy!

King. My Lord Chief Justice, speak to that vain
man.

Ch. Just. Have you your wits? know you what
'tis you speak?

Fal. My King! my Jove! I speak to thee, my
heart!   50

King. I know thee not, old man: fall to thy
prayers;
How ill white hairs become a fool and jester!
I have long dream'd of such a kind of man,
So surfeit-swell'd, so old, and so profane;
But, being awaked, I do despise my dream.

Make less thy body hence, and more thy grace;
Leave gormandizing; know the grave doth gape
For thee thrice wider than for other men.
Reply not to me with a fool-born jest:
Presume not that I am the thing I was;   60
For God doth know, so shall the world perceive,
That I have turn'd away my former self;
So will I those that kept me company.
When thou dost hear I am as I have been,
Approach me, and thou shalt be as thou wast,
The tutor and the feeder of my riots:
Till then, I banish thee, on pain of death,
As I have done the rest of my misleaders,
Not to come near our person by ten mile.
For competence of life I will allow you,   70
That lack of means enforce you not to evil:
And, as we hear you do reform yourselves,
We will, according to your strengths and quali-
    ties,
Give you advancement. Be it your charge, my
    lord,
To see perform'd the tenour of our word.
Set on.   [*Exeunt* KING, &c.
    Fal. Master Shallow, I owe you a thousand
pound.
    Shal. Yea, marry, Sir John; which I beseech you
to let me have home with me.   80
    Fal. That can hardly be, Master Shallow. Do
not you grieve at this; I shall be sent for in private to him: look you, he must seem thus to the
world: fear not your advancements; I will be the
man yet that shall make you great.
    Shal. I cannot well perceive how, unless you
should give me your doublet and stuff me out
with straw. I beseech you, good Sir John, let me
have five hundred of my thousand.
    Fal. Sir, I will be as good as my word: this that
you heard was but a colour.   91
    Shal. A colour that I fear you will die in, Sir
John.
    Fal. Fear no colours: go with me to dinner:
come, Lieutenant Pistol; come, Bardolph: I shall
be sent for soon at night.

Re-enter PRINCE JOHN, *the* LORD CHIEF JUSTICE;
    Officers with them.

    Ch. Just. Go, carry Sir John Falstaff to the
    Fleet:
Take all his company along with him.
    Fal. My lord, my lord—
    Ch. Just. I cannot now speak: I will hear you
    soon.   100
Take them away.
    Pist. Si fortuna me tormenta, spero contenta.
                [*Exeunt all but* PRINCE JOHN *and the*
                                   CHIEF JUSTICE.

    Lan. I like this fair proceeding of the King's:
He hath intent his wonted followers
Shall all be very well provided for;
But all are banish'd till their conversations
Appear more wise and modest to the world.
    Ch. Just. And so they are.
    Lan. The King hath call'd his parliament, my
    lord.
    Ch. Just. He hath.   110
    Lan. I will lay odds that, ere this year expire,
We bear our civil swords and native fire
As far as France: I heard a bird so sing,
Whose music, to my thinking, pleased the
    King.
Come, will you hence?   [*Exeunt.*

EPILOGUE
Spoken by a DANCER.

First my fear; then my courtesy; last my
speech. My fear is, your displeasure; my courtesy, my duty; and my speech, to beg your pardons. If you look for a good speech now, you
undo me: for what I have to say is of mine own
making; and what indeed I should say will, I
doubt, prove mine own marring. But to the purpose, and so to the venture. Be it known to you,
as it is very well, I was lately here in the end of
a displeasing play, to pray your patience for it
and to promise you a better. I meant indeed to
pay you with this; which, if like an ill venture it
come unluckily home, I break, and you, my
gentle creditors, lose. Here I promised you I
would be and here I commit my body to your
mercies: bate me some and I will pay you some
and, as most debtors do, promise you infinitely.

If my tongue cannot entreat you to acquit me,
will you command me to use my legs? and yet
that were but light payment, to dance out of your
debt. But a good conscience will make any possible satisfaction, and so would I. All the gentlewomen here have forgiven me: if the gentlemen
will not, then the gentlemen do not agree with
the gentlewomen, which was never seen before
in such an assembly.

One word more, I beseech you. If you be not
too much cloyed with fat meat, our humble author will continue the story, with Sir John in it,
and make you merry with fair Katharine of
France: where, for anything I know, Falstaff
shall die of a sweat, unless already a' be killed
with your hard opinions; for Oldcastle died a
martyr, and this is not the man. My tongue is
weary; when my legs are too, I will bid you good
night: and so kneel down before you; but, indeed,
to pray for the Queen.

❧ MUCH ADO ABOUT NOTHING

DRAMATIS PERSONÆ

DON PEDRO, *Prince of Arragon*
DON JOHN, *his bastard brother*
CLAUDIO, *a young lord of Florence*
BENEDICK, *a young lord of Paudua*
LEONATO, *Governor of Messina*
ANTONIO, *his brother*
BALTHASAR, *attendant on Don Pedro*
CONRADE
BORACHIO } *followers of Don John*
FRIAR FRANCIS
DOGBERRY, *a constable*
VERGES, *a headborough*
A SEXTON
A BOY

TWO MESSENGERS
TWO WATCHMEN
A LORD

HERO, *daughter to Leonato*
BEATRICE, *niece to Leonato*
MARGARET
URSULA } *gentlewomen attending on Hero*

NON-SPEAKING: *Messengers, Watch, Attendants, and Musicians*

SCENE: *Messina*

ACT I

SCENE I. *Before Leonato's house*

Enter LEONATO, HERO, *and* BEATRICE, *with a* MESSENGER.

Leon. I learn in this letter that Don Peter of Arragon comes this night to Messina.

Mess. He is very near by this: he was not three leagues off when I left him.

Leon. How many gentlemen have you lost in this action?

Mess. But few of any sort, and none of name.

Leon. A victory is twice itself when the achiever brings home full numbers. I find here that Don Peter hath bestowed much honour on a young Florentine called Claudio. 11

Mess. Much deserved on his part and equally remembered by Don Pedro: he hath borne himself beyond the promise of his age, doing, in the figure of a lamb, the feats of a lion: he hath indeed better bettered expectation than you must expect of me to tell you how.

Leon. He hath an uncle here in Messina will be very much glad of it. 19

Mess. I have already delivered him letters, and there appears much joy in him; even so much that joy could not show itself modest enough without a badge of bitterness.

Leon. Did he break out into tears?

Mess. In great measure.

Leon. A kind overflow of kindness: there are no faces truer than those that are so washed. How much better is it to weep at joy than to joy at weeping!

Beat. I pray you, is Signior Mountanto returned from the wars or no? 31

Mess. I know none of that name, lady: there was none such in the army of any sort.

Leon. What is he that you ask for, niece?

Hero. My cousin means Signior Benedick of Padua.

Mess. O, he's returned; and as pleasant as ever he was.

Beat. He set up his bills here in Messina and challenged Cupid at the flight; and my uncle's fool, reading the challenge, subscribed for Cupid, and challenged him at the bird-bolt. I pray you, how many hath he killed and eaten in these wars? But how many hath he killed? for indeed I promised to eat all of his killing.

Leon. Faith, niece, you tax Signior Benedick too much; but he'll be meet with you, I doubt it not.

Mess. He hath done good service, lady, in these wars. 49

Beat. You had musty victual, and he hath holp to eat it: he is a very valiant trencherman; he hath an excellent stomach.

Mess. And a good soldier too, lady.

Beat. And a good soldier to a lady: but what is he to a lord?

Mess. A lord to a lord, a man to a man; stuffed with all honourable virtues.

Beat. It is so, indeed; he is no less than a stuffed man: but for the stuffing—well, we are all mortal. 60

Leon. You must not, sir, mistake my niece. There is a kind of merry war betwixt Signior Benedick and her: they never meet but there's a skirmish of wit between them.

Beat. Alas! he gets nothing by that. In our last

503

conflict four of his five wits went halting off, and now is the whole man governed with one: so that if he have wit enough to keep himself warm, let him bear it for a difference between himself and his horse; for it is all the wealth that he hath left, to be known a reasonable creature. Who is his companion now? He hath every month a new sworn brother.

Mess. Is't possible?

Beat. Very easily possible: he wears his faith but as the fashion of his hat; it ever changes with the next block.

Mess. I see, lady, the gentleman is not in your books. 79

Beat. No; an he were, I would burn my study. But, I pray you, who is his companion? Is there no young squarer now that will make a voyage with him to the devil?

Mess. He is most in the company of the right noble Claudio.

Beat. O Lord, he will hang upon him like a disease: he is sooner caught than the pestilence, and the taker runs presently mad. God help the noble Claudio! if he have caught the Benedick, it will cost him a thousand pound ere a' be cured.

Mess. I will hold friends with you, lady. 91

Beat. Do, good friend.

Leon. You will never run mad, niece.

Beat. No, not till a hot January.

Mess. Don Pedro is approached.

Enter DON PEDRO, DON JOHN, CLAUDIO, BENEDICK, *and* BALTHASAR.

D. Pedro. Good Signior Leonato, you are come to meet your trouble: the fashion of the world is to avoid cost, and you encounter it.

Leon. Never came trouble to my house in the likeness of your Grace: for trouble being gone, comfort should remain; but when you depart from me, sorrow abides and happiness takes his leave.

D. Pedro. You embrace your charge too willingly. I think this is your daughter.

Leon. Her mother hath many times told me so.

Bene. Were you in doubt, sir, that you asked her?

Leon. Signior Benedick, no; for then were you a child. 109

D. Pedro. You have it full, Benedick: we may guess by this what you are, being a man. Truly, the lady fathers herself. Be happy, lady; for you are like an honourable father.

Bene. If Signior Leonato be her father, she would not have his head on her shoulders for all Messina, as like him as she is.

Beat. I wonder that you will still be talking, Signior Benedick: nobody marks you.

Bene. What, my dear Lady Disdain! are you yet living? 120

Beat. Is it possible disdain should die while she hath such meet food to feed it as Signior Benedick? Courtesy itself must convert to disdain if you come in her presence.

Bene. Then is courtesy a turncoat. But it is certain I am loved of all ladies, only you excepted: and I would I could find in my heart that I had not a hard heart; for, truly, I love none.

Beat. A dear happiness to women: they would else have been troubled with a pernicious suitor. I thank God and my cold blood, I am of your humour for that: I had rather hear my dog bark at a crow than a man swear he loves me.

Bene. God keep your ladyship still in that mind! so some gentleman or other shall 'scape a predestinate scratched face.

Beat. Scratching could not make it worse, an 'twere such a face as yours were.

Bene. Well, you are a rare parrot-teacher.

Beat. A bird of my tongue is better than a beast of yours. 141

Bene. I would my horse had the speed of your tongue, and so good a continuer. But keep your way, i' God's name; I have done.

Beat. You always end with a jade's trick: I know you of old.

D. Pedro. That is the sum of all, Leonato. Signior Claudio and Signior Benedick, my dear friend Leonato hath invited you all. I tell him we shall stay here at the least a month; and he heartily prays some occasion may detain us longer. I dare swear he is no hypocrite, but prays from his heart.

Leon. If you swear, my lord, you shall not be forsworn. [*To* DON JOHN] Let me bid you welcome, my lord: being reconciled to the Prince your brother, I owe you all duty.

D. John. I thank you: I am not of many words, but I thank you.

Leon. Please it your Grace lead on? 160

D. Pedro. Your hand, Leonato; we will go together.

[*Exeunt all except* BENEDICK *and* CLAUDIO.

Claud. Benedick, didst thou note the daughter of Signior Leonato?

Bene. I noted her not; but I looked on her.

Claud. Is she not a modest young lady?

Bene. Do you question me, as an honest man should do, for my simple true judgement; or would you have me speak after my custom, as being a professed tyrant to their sex? 170

Claud. No; I pray thee speak in sober judgement.

Bene. Why, i' faith, methinks she's too low for

a high praise, too brown for a fair praise and too little for a great praise: only this commendation I can afford her, that were she other than she is, she were unhandsome; and being no other but as she is, I do not like her.

Claud. Thou thinkest I am in sport: I pray thee tell me truly how thou likest her.   *180*

Bene. Would you buy her, that you inquire after her?

Claud. Can the world buy such a jewel?

Bene. Yea, and a case to put it into. But speak you this with a sad brow? or do you play the flouting Jack, to tell us Cupid is a good hare-finder and Vulcan a rare carpenter? Come, in what key shall a man take you, to go in the song?

Claud. In mine eye she is the sweetest lady that ever I looked on.   *190*

Bene. I can see yet without spectacles and I see no such matter: there's her cousin, an she were not possessed with a fury, exceeds her as much in beauty as the first of May doth the last of December. But I hope you have no intent to turn husband, have you?

Claud. I would scarce trust myself, though I had sworn the contrary, if Hero would be my wife.

Bene. Is't come to this? In faith, hath not the world one man but he will wear his cap with suspicion? Shall I never see a bachelor of threescore again? Go to, i' faith; an thou wilt needs thrust thy neck into a yoke, wear the print of it and sigh away Sundays. Look; Don Pedro is returned to seek you.

Re-enter DON PEDRO.

D. Pedro. What secret hath held you here, that you followed not to Leonato's?

Bene. I would your Grace would constrain me to tell.

D. Pedro. I charge thee on thy allegiance.

Bene. You hear, Count Claudio: I can be secret as a dumb man; I would have you think so; but, on my allegiance, mark you this, on my allegiance. He is in love. With who? now that is your Grace's part. Mark how short his answer is—With Hero, Leonato's short daughter.

Claud. If this were so, so were it uttered.

Bene. Like the old tale, my lord: "It is not so, nor 'twas not so, but, indeed, God forbid it should be so."   *220*

Claud. If my passion change not shortly, God forbid it should be otherwise.

D. Pedro. Amen, if you love her; for the lady is very well worthy.

Claud. You speak this to fetch me in, my lord.

D. Pedro. By my troth, I speak my thought.

Claud. And, in faith, my lord, I spoke mine.

Bene. And, by my two faiths and troths, my lord, I spoke mine.

Claud. That I love her, I feel.   *230*

D. Pedro. That she is worthy, I know.

Bene. That I neither feel how she should be loved nor know how she should be worthy, is the opinion that fire cannot melt out of me: I will die in it at the stake.

D. Pedro. Thou wast ever an obstinate heretic in the despite of beauty.

Claud. And never could maintain his part but in the force of his will.

Bene. That a woman conceived me, I thank her; that she brought me up, I likewise give her most humble thanks: but that I will have a recheat winded in my forehead, or hang my bugle in an invisible baldrick, all women shall pardon me. Because I will not do them the wrong to mistrust any, I will do myself the right to trust none; and the fine is, for the which I may go the finer, I will live a bachelor.

D. Pedro. I shall see thee, ere I die, look pale with love.   *250*

Bene. With anger, with sickness, or with hunger, my lord, not with love: prove that ever I lose more blood with love than I will get again with drinking, pick out mine eyes with a ballad-maker's pen and hang me up at the door of a brothel-house for the sign of blind Cupid.

D. Pedro. Well, if ever thou dost fall from this faith, thou wilt prove a notable argument.

Bene. If I do, hang me in a bottle like a cat and shoot at me; and he that hits me, let him be clapped on the shoulder, and called Adam.   *261*

D. Pedro. Well, as time shall try: "In time the savage bull doth bear the yoke."

Bene. The savage bull may; but if ever the sensible Benedick bear it, pluck off the bull's horns and set them in my forehead: and let me be vilely painted, and in such great letters as they write "Here is good horse to hire," let them signify under my sign "Here you may see Benedick the married man."   *270*

Claud. If this should ever happen, thou wouldst be horn-mad.

D. Pedro. Nay, if Cupid have not spent all his quiver in Venice, thou wilt quake for this shortly.

Bene. I look for an earthquake too, then.

D. Pedro. Well, you will temporize with the hours. In the meantime, good Signior Benedick, repair to Leonato's: commend me to him and tell him I will not fail him at supper; for indeed he hath made great preparation.   *280*

Bene. I have almost matter enough in me for such an embassage; and so I commit you—

Claud. To the tuition of God: From my house, if I had it—

D. Pedro. The sixth of July: Your loving friend, Benedick.

Bene. Nay, mock not, mock not. The body of your discourse is sometime guarded with fragments, and the guards are but slightly basted on neither: ere you flout old ends any further, examine your conscience: and so I leave you. [*Exit.* 291

Claud. My liege, your Highness now may do me good.

D. Pedro. My love is thine to teach: teach it but how,
And thou shalt see how apt it is to learn
Any hard lesson that may do thee good.

Claud. Hath Leonato any son, my lord?

D. Pedro. No child but Hero; she's his only heir.
Dost thou affect her, Claudio?

Claud.   O, my lord,
When you went onward on this ended action,
I look'd upon her with a soldier's eye,   300
That liked, but had a rougher task in hand
Than to drive liking to the name of love:
But now I am return'd and that war-thoughts
Have left their places vacant, in their rooms
Come thronging soft and delicate desires,
All prompting me how fair young Hero is,
Saying, I liked her ere I went to wars.

D. Pedro. Thou wilt be like a lover presently
And tire the hearer with a book of words.
If thou dost love fair Hero, cherish it,   310
And I will break with her and with her father
And thou shalt have her. Was't not to this end
That thou began'st to twist so fine a story?

Claud. How sweetly you do minister to love,
That know love's grief by his complexion!
But lest my liking might too sudden seem,
I would have salved it with a longer treatise.

D. Pedro. What need the bridge much broader than the flood?
The fairest grant is the necessity.
Look, what will serve is fit: 'tis once, thou lovest,   320
And I will fit thee with the remedy.
I know we shall have revelling to-night:
I will assume thy part in some disguise
And tell fair Hero I am Claudio,
And in her bosom I'll unclasp my heart
And take her hearing prisoner with the force
And strong encounter of my amorous tale;
Then after to her father will I break;
And the conclusion is, she shall be thine.
In practice let us put it presently.   [*Exeunt.* 330

Scene II. *A room in Leonato's house*

Enter LEONATO *and* ANTONIO, *meeting.*

Leon. How now, brother! Where is my cousin, your son? hath he provided this music?

Ant. He is very busy about it. But, brother, I can tell you stranger news that you yet dreamt not of.

Leon. Are they good?

Ant. As the event stamps them: but they have a good cover; they show well outward. The Prince and Count Claudio, walking in a thick-pleached alley in mine orchard, were thus much overheard by a man of mine: the Prince discovered to Claudio that he loved my niece your daughter and meant to acknowledge it this night in a dance; and if he found her accordant, he meant to take the present time by the top and instantly break with you of it.

Leon. Hath the fellow any wit that told you this?

Ant. A good sharp fellow: I will send for him; and question him yourself.   20

Leon. No, no; we will hold it as a dream till it appear itself: but I will acquaint my daughter withal, that she may be the better prepared for an answer, if peradventure this be true. Go you and tell her of it. [*Enter attendants.*] Cousins, you know what you have to do. O, I cry you mercy, friend; go you with me, and I will use your skill. Good cousin, have a care this busy time.   [*Exeunt.*

Scene III. *The same*

Enter DON JOHN *and* CONRADE.

Con. What the good-year, my lord! why are you thus out of measure sad?

D. John. There is no measure in the occasion that breeds; therefore the sadness is without limit.

Con. You should hear reason.

D. John. And when I have heard it, what blessing brings it?

Con. If not a present remedy, at least a patient sufferance.   10

D. John. I wonder that thou, being, as thou sayest thou art, born under Saturn, goest about to apply a moral medicine to a mortifying mischief. I cannot hide what I am: I must be sad when I have cause and smile at no man's jests, eat when I have stomach and wait for no man's leisure, sleep when I am drowsy and tend on no man's business, laugh when I am merry and claw no man in his humour.

Con. Yea, but you must not make the full show of this till you may do it without controlment.

You have of late stood out against your brother,
and he hath ta'en you newly into his grace;
where it is impossible you should take true root
but by the fair weather that you make yourself:
it is needful that you frame the season for your
own harvest.

D. John. I had rather be a canker in a hedge than
a rose in his grace, and it better fits my blood to
be disdained of all than to fashion a carriage to
rob love from any: in this, though I cannot be
said to be a flattering honest man, it must not be
denied but I am a plain-dealing villain. I am
trusted with a muzzle and enfranchised with a
clog; therefore I have decreed not to sing in
my cage. If I had my mouth, I would bite; if
I had my liberty, I would do my liking: in the
meantime let me be that I am and seek not to
alter me.

Con. Can you make no use of your discontent?   40

D. John. I make all use of it, for I use it only.
Who comes here?

Enter BORACHIO,

What news, Borachio?

Bora. I came yonder from a great supper: the
Prince your brother is royally entertained by
Leonato; and I can give you intelligence of an
intended marriage.

D. John. Will it serve for any model to build
mischief on? What is he for a fool that betroths
himself to unquietness?   50

Bora. Marry, it is your brother's right hand.

D. John. Who? the most exquisite Claudio?

Bora. Even he.

D. John. A proper squire! And who, and who?
which way looks he?

Bora. Marry, on Hero, the daughter and heir of
Leonato.

D. John. A very forward March-chick! How
came you to this?

Bora. Being entertained for a perfumer, as I was
smoking a musty room, comes me the Prince and
Claudio, hand in hand, in sad conference: I whipt
me behind the arras; and there heard it agreed
upon that the Prince should woo Hero for himself, and having obtained her, give her to Count
Claudio.

D. John. Come, come, let us thither: this may
prove food to my displeasure. That young start-
up hath all the glory of my overthrow: if I can
cross him any way, I bless myself every way.
You are both sure, and will assist me?   71

Con. To the death, my lord.

D. John. Let us to the great supper: their cheer
is the greater that I am subdued. Would the cook

were of my mind! Shall we go prove what's to
be done?

Bora. We'll wait upon your lordship.   [*Exeunt.*

ACT II

SCENE I. *A hall in Leonato's house*

Enter LEONATO, ANTONIO, HERO, BEATRICE,
and others.

Leon. Was not Count John here at supper?

Ant. I saw him not.

Beat. How tartly that gentleman looks! I never
can see him but I am heart-burned an hour after.

Hero. He is of a very melancholy disposition.

Beat. He were an excellent man that were made
just in the midway between him and Benedick:
the one is too like an image and says nothing, and
the other too like my lady's eldest son, evermore
tattling.   12

Leon. Then half Signior Benedick's tongue in
Count John's mouth, and half Count John's
melancholy in Signior Benedick's face—

Beat. With a good leg and a good foot, uncle,
and money enough in his purse, such a man would
win any woman in the world, if a' could get her
good-will.

Leon. By my troth, niece, thou wilt never get
thee a husband, if thou be so shrewd of thy
tongue.   21

Ant. In faith, she's too curst.

Beat. Too curst is more than curst: I shall lessen
God's sending that way; for it is said, "God
sends a curst cow short horns," but to a cow
too curst he sends none.

Leon. So, by being too curst, God will send
you no horns.

Beat. Just, if he send me no husband; for the
which blessing I am at him upon my knees every
morning and evening. Lord, I could not endure
a husband with a beard on his face: I had rather
lie in the woollen.

Leon. You may light on a husband that hath no
beard.

Beat. What should I do with him? dress him in
my apparel and make him my waiting-gentlewoman? He that hath a beard is more than a
youth, and he that hath no beard is less than a
man: and he that is more than a youth is not for
me, and he that is less than a man, I am not for
him: therefore I will even take sixpence in earnest of the bear-ward, and lead his apes into hell.

Leon. Well, then, go you into hell?

Beat. No, but to the gate; and there will the
devil meet me, like an old cuckold, with horns
on his head, and say "Get you to heaven, Beatrice, get you to heaven: here's no place for you
maids": so deliver I up my apes, and away to

Saint Peter for the heavens; he shows me where the bachelors sit, and there live we as merry as the day is long.

Ant. [*To* HERO] Well, niece, I trust you will be ruled by your father.

Beat. Yes, faith; it is my cousin's duty to make curtsy and say, "Father, as it please you." But yet for all that, cousin, let him be a handsome fellow, or else make another curtsy and say, "Father, as it please me."

Leon. Well, niece, I hope to see you one day fitted with a husband. 　　　　61

Beat. Not till God make men of some other metal than earth. Would it not grieve a woman to be overmastered with a piece of valiant dust? to make an account of her life to a clod of wayward marl? No, uncle, I'll none: Adam's sons are my brethren; and, truly, I hold it a sin to match in my kindred.

Leon. Daughter, remember what I told you: if the Prince do solicit you in that kind, you know your answer. 　　　　71

Beat. The fault will be in the music, cousin, if you be not wooed in good time: if the Prince be too important, tell him there is measure in everything and so dance out the answer. For, hear me, Hero: wooing, wedding, and repenting, is as a Scotch jig, a measure, and a cinque pace: the first suit is hot and hasty, like a Scotch jig, and full as fantastical; the wedding, mannerly-modest, as a measure, full of state and ancientry; and then comes repentance and, with his bad legs, falls into the cinque pace faster and faster, till he sink into his grave.

Leon. Cousin, you apprehend passing shrewdly.

Beat. I have a good eye, uncle; I can see a church by daylight.

Leon. The revellers are entering, brother: make good room. 　　　[*All put on their masks.*

Enter DON PEDRO, CLAUDIO, BENEDICK, BALTHASAR, DON JOHN, BORACHIO, MARGARET, URSULA, *and others, masked.*

D. Pedro. Lady, will you walk about with your friend? 　　　　90

Hero. So you walk softly and look sweetly and say nothing, I am yours for the walk; and especially when I walk away.

D. Pedro. With me in your company?

Hero. I may say so, when I please.

D. Pedro. And when please you to say so?

Hero. When I like your favour; for God defend the lute should be like the case!

D. Pedro. My visor is Philemon's roof; within the house is Jove. 　　　　100

Hero. Why, then, your visor should be thatched.

D. Pedro. Speak low, if you speak love.
　　Drawing her aside.

Balth. Well, I would you did like me.

Marg. So would not I, for your own sake; for I have many ill qualities.

Balth. Which is one?

Marg. I say my prayers aloud.

Balth. I love you the better: the hearers may cry, Amen. 　　　　110

Marg. God match me with a good dancer!

Balth. Amen.

Marg. And God keep him out of my sight when the dance is done! Answer, clerk.

Balth. No more words: the clerk is answered.

Urs. I know you well enough; you are Signior Antonio.

Ant. At a word, I am not.

Urs. I know you by the waggling of your head.

Ant. To tell you true, I counterfeit him. 　　121

Urs. You could never do him so ill-well, unless you were the very man. Here's his dry hand up and down: you are he, you are he.

Ant. At a word, I am not.

Urs. Come, come, do you think I do not know you by your excellent wit? can virtue hide itself? Go to, mum, you are he. Graces will appear, and there's an end.

Beat. Will you not tell me who told you so?

Bene. No, you shall pardon me. 　　　131

Beat. Nor will you not tell me who you are?

Bene. Not now.

Beat. That I was disdainful, and that I had my good wit out of the "Hundred Merry Tales": well, this was Signior Benedick that said so.

Bene. What's he?

Beat. I am sure you know him well enough.

Bene. Not I, believe me.

Beat. Did he never make you laugh? 　　140

Bene. I pray you, what is he?

Beat. Why, he is the Prince's jester: a very dull fool; only his gift is in devising impossible slanders: none but libertines delight in him; and the commendation is not in his wit, but in his villainy; for he both pleases men and angers them, and then they laugh at him and beat him. I am sure he is in the fleet: I would he had boarded me.

Bene. When I know the gentleman, I'll tell him what you say. 　　　151

Beat. Do, do: he'll but break a comparison or two on me; which, peradventure not marked or not laughed at, strikes him into melancholy; and then there's a partridge wing saved, for the fool will eat no supper that night. [*Music.*] We must follow the leaders.

Bene. In every good thing.

Beat. Nay, if they lead to any ill, I will leave them at the next turning.   *160*

[*Dance. Then exeunt all except* DON
JOHN, BORACHIO, *and* CLAUDIO.

D. John. Sure my brother is amorous on Hero and hath withdrawn her father to break with him about it. The ladies follow her and but one visor remains.

Bora. And that is Claudio: I know him by his bearing.

D. John. Are not you Signior Benedick?

Claud. You know me well; I am he.

D. John. Signior, you are very near my brother in his love: he is enamoured on Hero; I pray you, dissuade him from her: she is no equal for his birth: you may do the part of an honest man in it.

Claud. How know you he loves her?

D. John. I heard him swear his affection.

Bora. So did I too; and he swore he would marry her to-night.

D. John. Come, let us to the banquet.

[*Exeunt* DON JOHN *and* BORACHIO.

Claud. Thus answer I in name of Benedick,
But hear these ill news with the ears of Claudio.
'Tis certain so; the Prince wooes for himself. *181*
Friendship is constant in all other things
Save in the office and affairs of love:
Therefore all hearts in love use their own
    tongues;
Let every eye negotiate for itself
And trust no agent; for beauty is a witch
Against whose charms faith melteth into blood.
This is an accident of hourly proof,
Which I mistrusted not. Farewell, therefore,
    Hero!

Re-enter BENEDICK.

Bene. Count Claudio?   *190*

Claud. Yea, the same.

Bene. Come, will you go with me?

Claud. Whither?

Bene. Even to the next willow, about your own business, County. What fashion will you wear the garland of? about your neck, like an usurer's chain? or under your arm, like a lieutenant's scarf? You must wear it one way, for the Prince hath got your Hero.

Claud. I wish him joy of her.   *200*

Bene. Why, that's spoken like an honest drovier: so they sell bullocks. But did you think the Prince would have served you thus?

Claud. I pray you, leave me.

Bene. Ho! now you strike like the blind man: 'twas the boy that stole your meat, and you'll beat the post.

Claud. If it will not be, I'll leave you.   [*Exit.*

Bene. Alas, poor hurt fowl! now will he creep into sedges. But that my Lady Beatrice should know me, and not know me! the Prince's fool! Ha? It may be I go under that title because I am merry. Yea, but so I am apt to do myself wrong; I am not so reputed: it is the base, though bitter, disposition of Beatrice that puts the world into her person, and so gives me out. Well, I'll be revenged as I may.

Re-enter DON PEDRO.

D. Pedro. Now, signior, where's the Count? did you see him?   *219*

Bene. Troth, my lord, I have played the part of Lady Fame. I found him here as melancholy as a lodge in a warren: I told him, and I think I told him true, that your Grace had got the good will of this young lady; and I offered him my company to a willow-tree, either to make him a garland, as being forsaken, or to bind him up a rod, as being worthy to be whipped.

D. Pedro. To be whipped! What's his fault?

Bene. The flat transgression of a school-boy, who, being overjoyed with finding a birds' nest shows it his companion, and he steals it.   *231*

D. Pedro. Wilt thou make a trust a transgression? The transgression is in the stealer.

Bene. Yet it had not been amiss the rod had been made, and the garland too; for the garland he might have worn himself, and the rod he might have bestowed on you, who, as I take it, have stolen his birds' nest.

D. Pedro. I will but teach them to sing, and restore them to the owner.   *240*

Bene. If their singing answer your saying, by my faith, you say honestly.

D. Pedro. The Lady Beatrice hath a quarrel to you: the gentleman that danced with her told her she is much wronged by you.

Bene. O, she misused me past the endurance of a block! an oak but with one green leaf on it would have answered her; my very visor began to assume life and scold with her. She told me, not thinking I had been myself, that I was the Prince's jester, that I was duller than a great thaw; huddling jest upon jest with such impossible conveyance upon me that I stood like a man at a mark, with a whole army shooting at me. She speaks poniards, and every word stabs: if her breath were as terrible as her terminations, there were no living near her; she would infect to the north star. I would not marry her, though she were endowed with all that Adam had left him before he transgressed: she would have made Hercules have turned spit, yea, and have cleft his club to make the fire too. Come, talk not of her:

you shall find her the infernal Ate in good apparel. I would to God some scholar would conjure her; for certainly, while she is here, a man may live as quiet in hell as in a sanctuary; and people sin upon purpose, because they would go thither; so, indeed, all disquiet, horror, and perturbation follows her.

D. Pedro. Look, here she comes.   270

Re-enter CLAUDIO, BEATRICE, HERO, *and* LEONATO.

Bene. Will your Grace command me any service to the world's end? I will go on the slightest errand now to the Antipodes that you can devise to send me on; I will fetch you a toothpicker now from the furthest inch of Asia, bring you the length of Prester John's foot, fetch you a hair off the great Cham's beard, do you any embassage to the Pigmies, rather than hold three words' conference with this harpy. You have no employment for me?   280

D. Pedro. None, but to desire your good company.

Bene. O God, sir, here's a dish I love not: I cannot endure my Lady Tongue.   [*Exit.*

D. Pedro. Come, lady, come; you have lost the heart of Signior Benedick.

Beat. Indeed, my lord, he lent it me awhile; and I gave him use for it, a double heart for his single one: marry, once before he won it of me with false dice, therefore your Grace may well say I have lost it.   291

D. Pedro. You have put him down, lady, you have put him down.

Beat. So I would not he should do me, my lord, lest I should prove the mother of fools. I have brought Count Claudio, whom you sent me to seek.

D. Pedro. Why, how now, Count! wherefore are you sad?

Claud. Not sad, my lord.   300

D. Pedro. How then? sick?

Claud. Neither, my lord.

Beat. The Count is neither sad, nor sick, nor merry, nor well; but civil Count, civil as an orange, and something of that jealous complexion.

D. Pedro. I' faith, lady, I think your blazon to be true; though, I'll be sworn, if he be so, his conceit is false. Here, Claudio, I have wooed in thy name, and fair Hero is won: I have broke with her father, and his good will obtained: name the day of marriage, and God give thee joy!

Leon. Count, take of me my daughter, and with her my fortunes: his Grace hath made the match, and all grace say "Amen" to it.

Beat. Speak, Count, 'tis your cue.

Claud. Silence is the perfectest herald of joy: I were but little happy, if I could say how much. Lady, as you are mine, I am yours: I give away myself for you and dote upon the exchange.   320

Beat. Speak, cousin; or, if you cannot, stop his mouth with a kiss, and let not him speak neither.

D. Pedro. In faith, lady, you have a merry heart.

Beat. Yea, my lord; I thank it, poor fool, it keeps on the windy side of care. My cousin tells him in his ear that he is in her heart.

Claud. And so she doth, cousin.

Beat. Good Lord, for alliance! Thus goes every one to the world but I, and I am sunburnt; I may sit in a corner and cry heigh-ho for a husband!

D. Pedro. Lady Beatrice, I will get you one.

Beat. I would rather have one of your father's getting. Hath your Grace ne'er a brother like you? Your father got excellent husbands, if a maid could come by them.

D. Pedro. Will you have me, lady?   339

Beat. No, my lord, unless I might have another for working-days: your Grace is too costly to wear every day. But, I beseech your Grace, pardon me: I was born to speak all mirth and no matter.

D. Pedro. Your silence most offends me, and to be merry best becomes you; for, out of question, you were born in a merry hour.

Beat. No, sure, my lord, my mother cried; but then there was a star danced, and under that was I born. Cousins, God give you joy!   350

Leon. Niece, will you look to those things I told you of?

Beat. I cry you mercy, uncle. By your Grace's pardon.   [*Exit.*

D. Pedro. By my troth, a pleasant-spirited lady.

Leon. There's little of the melancholy element in her, my lord: she is never sad but when she sleeps, and not ever sad then; for I have heard my daughter say, she hath often dreamed of unhappiness and waked herself with laughing.

D. Pedro. She cannot endure to hear tell of a husband.

Leon. O, by no means: she mocks all her wooers out of suit.

D. Pedro. She were an excellent wife for Benedick.

Leon. O Lord, my lord, if they were but a week married, they would talk themselves mad.

D. Pedro. County Claudio, when mean you to go to church?   371

Claud. To-morrow, my lord: time goes on crutches till love have all his rites.

Leon. Not till Monday, my dear son, which is hence a just seven-night; and a time too brief, too, to have all things answer my mind.

D. Pedro. Come, you shake the head at so long a breathing: but, I warrant thee, Claudio, the time shall not go dully by us. I will in the interim undertake one of Hercules' labours; which is, to bring Signior Benedick and the Lady Beatrice into a mountain of affection the one with the other. I would fain have it a match, and I doubt not but to fashion it, if you three will but minister such assistance as I shall give you direction.

Leon. My lord, I am for you, though it cost me ten night's watchings.

Claud. And I, my lord.

D. Pedro. And you too, gentle Hero?

Hero. I will do any modest office, my lord, to help my cousin to a good husband.   *391*

D. Pedro. And Benedick is not the unhopefullest husband that I know. Thus far can I praise him; he is of a noble strain, of approved valour and confirmed honesty. I will teach you how to humour your cousin, that she shall fall in love with Benedick; and I, with your two helps, will so practice on Benedick that, in despite of his quick wit and his queasy stomach, he shall fall in love with Beatrice. If we can do this, Cupid is no longer an archer: his glory shall be ours, for we are the only love-gods. Go in with me, and I will tell you my drift.   [*Exeunt.*

Scene II. *The same*

Enter DON JOHN *and* BORACHIO.

D. John. It is so; the Count Claudio shall marry the daughter of Leonato.

Bora. Yea, my lord; but I can cross it.

D. John. Any bar, any cross, any impediment will be medicinable to me: I am sick in displeasure to him, and whatsoever comes athwart his affection ranges evenly with mine. How canst thou cross this marriage?

Bora. Not honestly, my lord; but so covertly that no dishonesty shall appear in me.   *10*

D. John. Show me briefly how.

Bora. I think I told your lordship a year since, how much I am in the favour of Margaret, the waiting gentlewoman to Hero.

D. John. I remember.

Bora. I can, at any unseasonable instant of the night, appoint her to look out at her lady's chamber window.

D. John. What life is in that, to be the death of this marriage?   *20*

Bora. The poison of that lies in you to temper. Go you to the Prince your brother; spare not to tell him that he hath wronged his honour in marrying the renowned Claudio—whose estimation do you mightily hold up—to a contaminated stale, such a one as Hero.

D. John. What proof shall I make of that?

Bora. Proof enough to misuse the Prince, to vex Claudio, to undo Hero, and kill Leonato. Look you for any other issue?   *30*

D. John. Only to despite them, I will endeavour anything.

Bora. Go, then; find me a meet hour to draw Don Pedro and the Count Claudio alone: tell them that you know that Hero loves me; intend a kind of zeal both to the Prince and Claudio, as —in love of your brother's honour, who hath made this match, and his friend's reputation, who is thus like to be cozened with the semblance of a maid— that you have discovered thus. They will scarcely believe this without trial: offer them instances; which shall bear no less likelihood than to see me at her chamber-window, hear me call Margaret Hero, hear Margaret term me Claudio; and bring them to see this the very night before the intended wedding—for in the meantime I will so fashion the matter that Hero shall be absent—and there shall appear such seeming truth of Hero's disloyalty that jealousy shall be called assurance and all the preparation overthrown.   *51*

D. John. Grow this to what adverse issue it can, I will put it in practice. Be cunning in the working this, and thy fee is a thousand ducats.

Bora. Be you constant in the accusation, and my cunning shall not shame me.

D. John. I will presently go learn their day of marriage.   [*Exeunt.*

Scene III. *Leonato's orchard*

Enter BENEDICK.

Bene. Boy!

Enter BOY.

Boy. Signior?

Bene. In my chamber-window lies a book: bring it hither to me in the orchard.

Boy. I am here already, sir.

Bene. I know that; but I would have thee hence, and here again. [*Exit* BOY.] I do much wonder that one man, seeing how much another man is a fool when he dedicates his behaviours to love, will, after he hath laughed at such shallow follies in others, become the argument of his own scorn by falling in love: and such a man is Claudio. I have known when there was no music with him but the drum and the fife; and now had he rather hear the tabor and the pipe: I have known when he would have walked ten mile a-foot to see a good armour; and now will he lie ten nights awake, carving the fashion of a new doublet. He was wont to speak plain and

to the purpose, like an honest man and a soldier;
and now is he turned orthography; his words are
a very fantastical banquet, just so many strange
dishes. May I be so converted and see with these
eyes? I cannot tell; I think not: I will not be
sworn but love may transform me to an oyster;
but I'll take my oath on it, till he have made an
oyster of me, he shall never make me such a fool.
One woman is fair, yet I am well; another is
wise, yet I am well; another virtuous, yet I am
well; but till all graces be in one woman, one
woman shall not come in my grace. Rich she
shall be, that's certain; wise, or I'll none; virtuous, or I'll never cheapen her; fair, or I'll never
look on her; mild, or come not near me; noble,
or not I for an angel; of good discourse, an
excellent musician, and her hair shall be of what
colour it please God. Ha! the Prince and Monsieur Love! I will hide me in the arbour.

[*Withdraws.*

Enter DON PEDRO, CLAUDIO, *and* LEONATO.

D. Pedro. Come, shall we hear this music?
Claud. Yea, my good lord. How still the
evening is,   40
As hush'd on purpose to grace harmony!
D. Pedro. See you where Benedick hath hid him-
self?
Claud. O, very well, my lord: the music ended,
We'll fit the kid-fox with a pennyworth.

Enter BALTHASAR *with Music.*

D. Pedro. Come, Balthasar, we'll hear that song
again.
Balth. O, good my lord, tax not so bad a voice
To slander music any more than once.
D. Pedro. It is the witness still of excellency
To put a strange face on his own perfection.
I pray thee, sing, and let me woo no more.   50
Balth. Because you talk of wooing, I will sing;
Since many a wooer doth commence his suit
To her he thinks not worthy, yet he wooes,
Yet will he swear he loves.
D. Pedro.   Now, pray thee, come;
Or, if thou wilt hold longer argument,
Do it in notes.
Balth.   Note this before my notes;
There's not a note of mine that's worth the
noting.
D. Pedro. Why, these are very crotchets that
he speaks;
Note, notes, forsooth, and nothing.   [*Air.*]
Bene. Now, divine air! now is his soul ravished!
Is it not strange that sheeps' guts should hale
souls out of men's bodies? Well, a horn for my
money, when all's done.

Balth. Sigh no more, ladies, sigh no more,
    Men were deceivers ever,
One foot in sea and one on shore,
    To one thing constant never:
Then sigh not so, but let them go,
    And be you blithe and bonny,
Converting all your sounds of woe   70
    Into Hey nonny, nonny.

Sing no more ditties, sing no moe,
    Of dumps so dull and heavy;
The fraud of men was ever so,
    Since summer first was leavy:
    Then sigh not so, &c.

D. Pedro. By my troth, a good song.
Balth. And an ill singer, my lord.
D. Pedro. Ha, no, no, faith; thou singest well
enough for a shift.   80
Bene. An he had been a dog that should have
howled thus, they would have hanged him: and
I pray God his bad voice bode no mischief. I had
as lief have heard the night-raven, come what
plague could have come after it.
D. Pedro. Yea, marry, dost thou hear, Baltha-
sar? I pray thee, get us some excellent music; for
to-morrow night we would have it at the Lady
Hero's chamber-window.
Balth. The best I can, my lord.   90
D. Pedro. Do so: farewell. [*Exit* BALTHASAR.]
Come hither, Leonato. What was it you told me
of to-day, that your niece Beatrice was in love
with Signior Benedick?
Claud. O, ay: stalk on, stalk on; the fowl sits.
I did never think that lady would have loved any
man.
Leon. No, nor I neither; but most wonderful
that she should so dote on Signior Benedick,
whom she hath in all outward behaviours seemed
ever to abhor.   101
Bene. Is't possible? Sits the wind in that corner?
Leon. By my troth, my lord, I cannot tell what
to think of it but that she loves him with an
enraged affection; it is past the infinite of
thought.
D. Pedro. May be she doth but counterfeit.
Claud. Faith, like enough.
Leon. O God, counterfeit! There was never
counterfeit of passion came so near the life of
passion as she discovers it.   111
D. Pedro. Why, what effects of passion shows
she?
Claud. Bait the hook well; this fish will bite.
Leon. What effects, my lord? She will sit you,
you heard my daughter tell you how.

Claud. She did, indeed.

D. Pedro. How, how, I pray you? You amaze me: I would have thought her spirit had been invincible against all assaults of affection.   *120*

Leon. I would have sworn it had, my lord; especially against Benedick.

Bene. I should think this a gull, but that the white-bearded fellow speaks it: knavery cannot, sure, hide himself in such reverence.

Claud. He hath ta'en the infection: hold it up.

D. Pedro. Hath she made her affection known to Benedick?

Leon. No; and swears she never will: that's her torment.   *130*

Claud. 'Tis true, indeed; so your daughter says: "Shall I," says she, "that have so oft encountered him with scorn, write to him that I love him?"

Leon. This says she now when she is beginning to write to him; for she'll be up twenty times a night, and there will she sit in her smock till she have writ a sheet of paper: my daughter tells us all.

Claud. Now you talk of a sheet of paper, I remember a pretty jest your daughter told us of.

Leon. O, when she had writ it and was reading it over, she found Benedick and Beatrice between the sheet?

Claud. That.

Leon. O, she tore the letter into a thousand halfpence; railed at herself, that she should be so immodest to write to one that she knew would flout her; "I measure him," says she, "by my own spirit; for I should flout him, if he writ to me; yea, though I love him, I should."   *151*

Claud. Then down upon her knees she falls, weeps, sobs, beats her heart, tears her hair, prays, curses; "O sweet Benedick! God give me patience!"

Leon. She doth indeed; my daughter says so: and the ecstasy hath so much overborne her that my daughter is sometime afeard she will do a desperate outrage to herself: it is very true.

D. Pedro. It were good that Benedick knew of it by some other, if she will not discover it.   *161*

Claud. To what end? He would make but a sport of it and torment the poor lady worse.

D. Pedro. An he should, it were an alms to hang him. She's an excellent sweet lady; and, out of all suspicion, she is virtuous.

Claud. And she is exceeding wise.

D. Pedro. In everything but in loving Benedick.

Leon. O, my lord, wisdom and blood combating in so tender a body, we have ten proofs to one that blood hath the victory. I am sorry for her, as I have just cause, being her uncle and her guardian.

D. Pedro. I would she had bestowed this dotage on me: I would have daffed all other respects and made her half myself. I pray you, tell Benedick of it, and hear what a' will say.

Leon. Were it good, think you?   *179*

Claud. Hero thinks surely she will die; for she says she will die, if he love her not, and she will die, ere she make her love known, and she will die, if he woo her, rather than she will bate one breath of her accustomed crossness.

D. Pedro. She doth well: if she should make tender of her love, 'tis very possible he'll scorn it; for the man, as you know all, hath a contemptible spirit.

Claud. He is a very proper man.

D. Pedro. He hath indeed a good outward happiness.   *191*

Claud. Before God! and, in my mind, very wise.

D. Pedro. He doth indeed show some sparks that are like wit.

Claud. And I take him to be valiant.

D. Pedro. As Hector, I assure you: and in the managing of quarrels you may say he is wise; for either he avoids them with great discretion, or undertakes them with a most Christian-like fear.

Leon. If he do fear God, a' must necessarily keep peace: if he break the peace, he ought to enter into a quarrel with fear and trembling.

D. Pedro. And so will he do; for the man doth fear God, howsoever it seems not in him by some large jests he will make, Well, I am sorry for your niece. Shall we go seek Benedick, and tell him of her love?

Claud. Never tell him, my lord: let her wear it out with good counsel.

Leon. Nay, that's impossible: she may wear her heart out first.   *210*

D. Pedro. Well, we will hear further of it by your daughter: let it cool the while. I love Benedick well; and I could wish he would modestly examine himself, to see how much he is unworthy so good a lady.

Leon. My lord, will you walk? dinner is ready.

Claud. If he do not dote on her upon this, I will never trust my expectation.   *220*

D. Pedro. Let there be the same net spread for her; and that must your daughter and her gentlewomen carry. The sport will be, when they hold one an opinion of another's dotage, and no such matter: that's the scene that I would see, which will be merely a dumb-show. Let us send her to call him in to dinner.

    [*Exeunt* DON PEDRO, CLAUDIO, *and* LEONATO.

Bene. [*Coming forward*] This can be no trick:

the conference was sadly borne. They have the truth of this from Hero. They seem to pity the lady: it seems her affections have their full bent. Love me! why, it must be requited. I hear how I am censured: they say I will bear myself proudly, if I perceive the love come from her; they say too that she will rather die than give any sign of affection. I did never think to marry: I must not seem proud: happy are they that hear their detractions and can put them to mending. They say the lady is fair; 'tis a truth, I can bear them witness; and virtuous; 'tis so, I cannot reprove it; and wise, but for loving me; by my troth, it is no addition to her wit, nor no great argument of her folly, for I will be horribly in love with her. I may chance have some odd quirks and remnants of wit broken on me, because I have railed so long against marriage: but doth not the appetite alter? a man loves the meat in his youth that he cannot endure in his age. Shall quips and sentences and these paper bullets of the brain awe a man from the career of his humour? No, the world must be peopled. When I said I would die a bachelor, I did not think I should live till I were married. Here comes Beatrice. By this day! she's a fair lady: I do spy some marks of love in her.

Enter BEATRICE.

Beat. Against my will I am sent to bid you come in to dinner.

Bene. Fair Beatrice, I thank you for your pains.

Beat. I took no more pains for those thanks than you take pains to thank me: if it had been painful, I would not have come.   *261*

Bene. You take pleasure then in the message?

Beat. Yea, just so much as you may take upon a knife's point and choke a daw withal. You have no stomach, signior: fare you well.
                                                  [*Exit.*

Bene. Ha! "Against my will I am sent to bid you come in to dinner"; there's a double meaning in that. "I took no more pains for those thanks than you took pains to thank me"; that's as much as to say, "Any pains that I take for you is as easy as thanks." If I do not take pity of her, I am a villain; if I do not love her, I am a Jew. I will go get her picture.   [*Exit.*

ACT III

SCENE I. *Leonato's garden*

Enter HERO, MARGARET, *and* URSULA.

Hero. Good Margaret, run thee to the parlour;
There shalt thou find my cousin Beatrice
Proposing with the Prince and Claudio:

Whisper her ear and tell her, I and Ursula
Walk in the orchard and our whole discourse
Is all of her; say that thou overheard'st us;
And bid her steal into the pleached bower,
Where honeysuckles, ripen'd by the sun,
Forbid the sun to enter, like favourites,
Made proud by princes, that advance their pride
Against that power that bred it: there will she
          hide her,   11
To listen our purpose. This is thy office;
Bear thee well in it and leave us alone.

Marg. I'll make her come, I warrant you,
          presently.   [*Exit.*

Hero. Now, Ursula, when Beatrice doth come,
As we do trace alley up and down,
Our talk must only be of Benedick.
When I do name him, let it be thy part
To praise him more than ever man did merit:
My talk to thee must be how Benedick   20
Is sick in love with Beatrice. Of this matter
Is little Cupid's crafty arrow made,
That only wounds by hearsay.

Enter BEATRICE, *behind.*

                                        Now begin;
For look where Beatrice, like a lapwing, runs
Close by the ground, to hear our conference.

Urs. The pleasant'st angling is to see the fish
Cut with her golden oars the silver stream,
And greedily devour the treacherous bait:
So angle we for Beatrice; who even now
Is couched in the woodbine coverture.   30
Fear you not my part of the dialogue.

Hero. Then go we near her, that her ear lose
          nothing
Of the false sweet bait that we lay for it.

Approaching the bower.

No, truly, Ursula, she is too disdainful;
I know her spirits are as coy and wild
As haggerds of the rock.

Urs.   But are you sure
That Benedick loves Beatrice so entirely?

Hero. So says the Prince and my new-trothed
          lord.

Urs. And did they bid you tell her of it, madam?

Hero. They did entreat me to acquaint her of it;
But I persuaded them if they loved Benedick,   41
To wish him wrestle with affection,
And never to let Beatrice know of it.

Urs. Why did you so? Doth not the gentleman
Deserve as full as fortunate a bed
As ever Beatrice shall couch upon?

Hero. O god of love! I know he doth deserve
As much as may be yielded to a man:
But Nature never framed a woman's heart
Of prouder stuff than that of Beatrice;   50

Disdain and scorn ride sparkling in her eyes,
Misprising what they look on, and her wit
Values itself so highly that to her
All matter else seems weak: she cannot love,
Nor take no shape nor project of affection,
She is so self-endeared.

   Urs.   Sure, I think so;
And therefore certainly it were not good
She knew his love, lest she make sport at it.

   Hero. Why, you speak truth. I never yet saw man,
How wise, how noble, young, how rarely fea-
   tured,   60
But she would spell him backward: if fair-faced,
She would swear the gentleman should be her
   sister;
If black, why, Nature, drawing of an antique,
Made a foul blot; if tall, a lance ill-headed;
If low, an agate very vilely cut;
If speaking, why, a vane blown with all winds;
If silent, why, a block moved with none.
So turns she every man the wrong side out
And never gives to truth and virtue that
Which simpleness and merit purchaseth.   70

   Urs. Sure, sure, such carping is not commendable.

   Hero. No, not to be so odd and from all fashions
As Beatrice is, cannot be commendable:
But who dare tell her so? If I should speak,
She would mock me into air; O, she would laugh me
Out of myself, press me to death with wit.
Therefore let Benedick, like cover'd fire,
Consume away in sighs, waste inwardly:
It were a better death than die with mocks,
Which is as bad as die with tickling.   80

   Urs. Yet tell her of it: hear what she will say.

   Hero. No; rather I will go to Benedick
And counsel him to fight against his passion.
And, truly, I'll devise some honest slanders
To stain my cousin with: one doth not know
How much an ill word may empoison liking.

   Urs. O, do not do your cousin such a wrong.
She cannot be so much without true judgement—
Having so swift and excellent a wit
As she is prized to have—as to refuse   90
So rare a gentleman as Signior Benedick.

   Hero. He is the only man of Italy,
Always excepted my dear Claudio.

   Urs. I pray you, be not angry with me, madam,
Speaking my fancy: Signior Benedick,
For shape, for bearing, argument, and valour,
Goes foremost in report through Italy.

   Hero. Indeed, he hath an excellent good name.

   Urs. His excellence did earn it, ere he had it.
When are you married, madam?   100

   Hero. Why, every day, to-morrow. Come, go in:
I'll show thee some attires, and have thy counsel
Which is the best to furnish me to-morrow.

   Urs. She's limed, I warrant you: we have
   caught her, madam.

   Hero. If it prove so, then loving goes by haps:
Some Cupid kills with arrows, some with traps.
                    [Exeunt HERO *and* URSULA.

   Beat. [*Coming forward*] What fire is in mine
   ears? Can this be true?
Stand I condemn'd for pride and scorn so
   much?
Contempt, farewell! and maiden pride, adieu!
No glory lives behind the back of such.   110
And, Benedick, love on; I will requite thee,
Taming my wild heart to thy loving hand:
If thou dost love, my kindness shall incite thee
To bind our loves up in a holy band;
For others say thou dost deserve, and I
Believe it better than reportingly.   *[Exit.*

SCENE II. *A room in Leonato's house*

Enter DON PEDRO, CLAUDIO, BENEDICK, *and*
LEONATO.

   D. Pedro. I do but stay till your marriage be
consummate, and then go I toward Arragon.

   Claud. I'll bring you thither, my lord, if you'll
vouchsafe me.

   D. Pedro. Nay, that would be as great a soil in
the new gloss of your marriage as to show a child
his new coat and forbid him to wear it. I will
only be bold with Benedick for his company; for,
from the crown of his head to the sole of his foot,
he is all mirth: he hath twice or thrice cut Cupid's
bow-string and the little hangman dare not shoot
at him; he hath a heart as sound as a bell and his
tongue is the clapper, for what his heart thinks
his tongue speaks.

   Bene. Gallants, I am not as I have been.

   Leon. So say I: methinks you are sadder.

   Claud. I hope he be in love.

   D. Pedro. Hang him, truant! there's no true drop
of blood in him, to be truly touched with love: if
he be sad, he wants money.   20

   Bene. I have the toothache.

   D. Pedro. Draw it.

   Bene. Hang it!

   Claud. You must hang it first, and draw it afterwards.

   D. Pedro. What! sigh for the toothache?

   Leon. Where is but a humour or a worm.

   Bene. Well, every one can master a grief but he
that has it.

   Claud. Yet say I, he is in love.   30

   D. Pedro. There is no appearance of fancy in

him, unless it be a fancy that he hath to strange disguises; as, to be a Dutchman to-day, a Frenchman to-morrow, or in the shape of two countries at once, as, a German from the waist downward, all slops, and a Spaniard from the hip upward, no doublet. Unless he have a fancy to this foolery, as it appears he hath, he is no fool for fancy, as you would have it appear he is.

Claud. If he be not in love with some woman, there is no believing old signs: a' brushes his hat o' mornings; what should that bode?   *42*

D. Pedro. Hath any man seen him at the barber's?

Claud. No, but the barber's man hath been seen with him, and the old ornament of his cheek hath already stuffed tennis-balls.

Leon. Indeed, he looks younger than he did, by the loss of a beard.

D. Pedro. Nay, a' rubs himself with civet: can you smell him out by that?   *51*

Claud. That's as much as to say, the sweet youth's in love.

D. Pedro. The greatest note of it is his melancholy.

Claud. And when was he wont to wash his face?

D. Pedro. Yea, or to paint himself? for the which, I hear what they say of him.

Claud. Nay, but his jesting spirit; which is now crept into a lute-string and now governed by stops.

D. Pedro. Indeed, that tells a heavy tale for him: conclude, conclude he is in love.

Claud. Nay, but I know who loves him.

D. Pedro. That would I know too: I warrant, one that knows him not.

Claud. Yes, and his ill conditions; and, in despite of all, dies for him.

D. Pedro. She shall be buried with her face upwards.   *71*

Bene. Yet is this no charm for the toothache. Old signior, walk aside with me: I have studied eight or nine wise words to speak to you, which these hobby-horses must not hear.

     [*Exeunt* BENEDICK *and* LEONATO.

D. Pedro. For my life, to break with him about Beatrice.

Claud. 'Tis even so. Hero and Margaret have by this played their parts with Beatrice; and then the two bears will not bite one another when they meet.   *81*

Enter DON JOHN.

D. John. My lord and brother, God save you!

D. Pedro. Good den, brother.

D. John. If your leisure served, I would speak with you.

D. Pedro. In private?

D. John. If it please you: yet Count Claudio may hear; for what I would speak of concerns him.

D. Pedro. What's the matter?   *90*

D. John. [*To* CLAUDIO] Means your lordship to be married to-morrow?

D. Pedro. You know he does.

D. John. I know not that, when he knows what I know.

Claud. If there be any impediment, I pray you discover it.

D. John. You may think I love you not: let that appear hereafter, and aim better at me by that I now will manifest. For my brother, I think he holds you well, and in dearness of heart hath holp to effect your ensuing marriage—surely suit ill spent and labour ill bestowed.

D. Pedro. Why, what's the matter?

D. John. I came hither to tell you; and, circumstances shortened, for she has been too long a talking of, the lady is disloyal.

Claud. Who, Hero?

D. John. Even she; Leonato's Hero, your Hero, every man's Hero.   *110*

Claud. Disloyal?

D. John. The word is too good to paint out her wickedness; I could say she were worse: think you of a worse title, and I will fit her to it. Wonder not till further warrant: go but with me to-night, you shall see her chamber-window entered, even the night before her wedding-day: if you love her then, to-morrow wed her; but it would better fit your honour to change your mind.

Claud. May this be so?   *120*

D. Pedro. I will not think it.

D. John. If you dare not trust that you see, confess not that you know: if you will follow me, I will show you enough; and when you have seen more and heard more, proceed accordingly.

Claud. If I see anything to-night why I should not marry her to-morrow, in the congregation, where I should wed, there will I shame her.

D. Pedro. And, as I wooed for thee to obtain her, I will join with thee to disgrace her.   *130*

D. John. I will disparage her no farther till you are my witnesses: bear it coldly but till midnight, and let the issue show itself.

D. Pedro. O day untowardly turned!

Claud O mischief strangely thwarting!

D. John. O plague right well prevented! so will you say when you have seen the sequel.

     [*Exeunt.*

SCENE III. *A street*

Enter DOGBERRY *and* VERGES *with* THE WATCH.

Dog. Are you good men and true?

Verg. Yea, or else it were pity but they should suffer salvation, body and soul.

Dog. Nay, that were a punishment too good for them, if they should have any allegiance in them, being chosen for the Prince's watch.

Verg. Well, give them their charge, neighbour Dogberry.

Dog. First, who think you the most desartless man to be constable?   *10*

1st Watch. Hugh Otecake, sir, or George Seacole; for they can write and read.

Dog. Come hither, neighbour Seacole. God hath blessed you with a good name: to be a well-favoured man is the gift of fortune; but to write and read comes by nature.

2nd Watch. Both which, master constable—

Dog. You have: I knew it would be your answer. Well, for your favour, sir, why, give God thanks, and make no boast of it; and for your writing and reading, let that appear when there is no need of such vanity. You are thought here to be the most senseless and fit man for the constable of the watch; therefore bear you the lantern. This is your charge: you shall comprehend all vagrom men; you are to bid any man stand, in the Prince's name.

2nd Watch. How if a' will not stand?

Dog. Why, then, take no note of him, but let him go; and presently call the rest of the watch together and thank God you are rid of a knave.

Verg. If he will not stand when he is bidden, he is none of the Prince's subjects.

Dog. True, and they are to meddle with none but the Prince's subjects. You shall also make no noise in the streets; for for the watch to babble and to talk is most tolerable and not to be endured.

2nd Watch. We will rather sleep than talk: we know what belongs to a watch.   *40*

Dog. Why, you speak like an ancient and most quiet watchman; for I cannot see how sleeping should offend: only, have a care that your bills be not stolen. Well, you are to call at all the alehouses, and bid those that are drunk get them to bed.

2nd Watch. How if they will not?

Dog. Why, then, let them alone till they are sober: if they make you not then the better answer, you may say they are not the men you took them for.   *51*

2nd Watch. Well, sir.

Dog. If you meet a thief, you may suspect him, by virtue of your office, to be no true man; and, for such kind of men, the less you meddle or make with them, why, the more is for your honesty.

2nd Watch. If we know him to be a thief, shall we not lay hands on him?

Dog. Truly, by your office, you may; but I think they that touch pitch will be defiled: the most peaceable way for you, if you do take a thief, is to let him show himself what he is and steal out of your company.

Verg. You have been always called a merciful man, partner.

Dog. Truly, I would not hang a dog by my will, much more a man who hath honesty in him.

Verg. If you hear a child cry in the night, you must call to the nurse and bid her still it.   *70*

2nd Watch. How if the nurse be asleep and will not hear us?

Dog. Why, then, depart in peace, and let the child wake her with crying; for the ewe that will not hear her lamb when it baes will never answer a calf when he bleats.

Verg. 'Tis very true.

Dog. This is the end of the charge: you, constable, are to present the Prince's own person: if you meet the Prince in the night, you may stay him.   *81*

Verg. Nay, by'r lady, that I think a' cannot.

Dog. Five shillings to one on't, with any man that knows the statues, he may stay him: marry, not without the Prince be willing; for, indeed, the watch ought to offend no man; and it is an offence to stay a man against his will.

Verg. By'r lady, I think it be so.   *89*

Dog. Ha, ah, ha! Well, masters, good night: an there be any matter of weight chances, call up me: keep your fellows' counsels and your own; and good night. Come, neighbour.

2nd Watch. Well, masters, we hear our charge: let us go sit here upon the church-bench till two, and then all to bed.

Dog. One word more, honest neighbours. I pray you, watch about Signior Leonato's door; for the wedding being there to-morrow, there is a great coil to-night. Adieu: be vigitant, I beseech you.   [*Exeunt* DOGBERRY *and* VERGES. *101*

Enter BORACHIO *and* CONRADE.

Bora. What, Conrade!

2nd Watch. [*Aside*] Peace! stir not.

Bora. Conrade, I say!

Con. Here, man; I am at thy elbow.

Bora. Mass, and my elbow itched; I thought there would a scab follow.

Con. I will owe thee an answer for that: and now forward with thy tale.   109

Bora. Stand thee close, then, under this penthouse, for it drizzles rain; and I will, like a true drunkard, utter all to thee.

2nd Watch. [*Aside*] Some treason, masters: yet stand close.

Bora. Therefore know I have earned of Don John a thousand ducats.

Con. Is it possible that any villainy should be so dear?

Bora. Thou shouldst rather ask if it were possible any villainy should be so rich; for when rich villains have need of poor ones, poor ones may make what price they will.

Con. I wonder at it.

Bora. That shows thou art unconfirmed. Thou knowest that the fashion of a doublet, or a hat, or a cloak, is nothing to a man.

Con. Yes, it is apparel.

Bora. I mean, the fashion.

Con. Yes, the fashion is the fashion.   129

Bora. Tush! I may as well say the fool's the fool. But seest thou not what a deformed thief this fashion is?

2nd Watch. [*Aside*] I know that Deformed; a' has been a vile thief this seven year; a' goes up and down like a gentleman: I remember his name.

Bora. Didst thou not hear somebody?

Con. No; 'twas the vane on the house.

Bora. Seest thou not, I say, what a deformed thief this fashion is? how giddily a' turns about all the hot bloods between fourteen and five-and-thirty? sometimes fashioning them like Pharaoh's soldiers in the reechy painting, sometime like god Bel's priests in the old church-window, sometime like the shaven Hercules in the smirched worm-eaten tapestry, where his codpiece seems as massy as his club?

Con. All this I see; and I see that the fashion wears out more apparel than the man. But art not thou thyself giddy with the fashion too, that thou hast shifted out of thy tale into telling me of the fashion?

Bora. Not so, neither: but know that I have to-night wooed Margaret, the Lady Hero's gentlewoman, by the name of Hero: she leans me out at her mistress' chamber-window, bids me a thousand times good night—I tell this tale vilely. I should first tell thee how the Prince, Claudio and my master, planted and placed and possessed by my master Don John, saw afar off in the orchard this amiable encounter.   161

Con. And thought they Margaret was Hero?

Bora. Two of them did, the Prince and Claudio; but the devil my master knew she was Margaret; and partly by his oaths, which first possessed them, partly by the dark night, which did deceive them, but chiefly by my villainy, which did confirm any slander that Don John had made, away went Claudio enraged; swore he would meet her, as he was appointed, next morning at the temple, and there, before the whole congregation, shame her with what he saw o'er night and send her home again without a husband.

1st Watch. We charge you, in the Prince's name, stand!

2nd Watch. Call up the right master constable. We have here recovered the most dangerous piece of lechery that ever was known in the commonwealth.   181

1st Watch. And one Deformed is one of them: I know him; a' wears a lock.

Con. Masters, masters—

2nd Watch. You'll be made bring Deformed forth, I warrant you.

Con. Masters—

1st Watch. Never speak: we charge you let us obey you to go with us.

Bora. We are like to prove a goodly commodity, being taken up of these men's bills.   191

Con. A commodity in question, I warrant you. Come, we'll obey you.   [*Exeunt.*

SCENE IV. *Hero's apartment*

Enter HERO, MARGARET, *and* URSULA.

Hero. Good Ursula, wake my cousin Beatrice, and desire her to rise.

Urs. I will, lady.

Hero. And bid her come hither.

Urs. Well.   [*Exit.*

Marg. Troth, I think your other rabato were better.

Hero. No, pray thee, good Meg, I'll wear this.

Marg. By my troth, 's not so good; and I warrant your cousin will say so.   10

Hero. My cousin's a fool, and thou art another: I'll wear none but this.

Marg. I like the new tire within excellently, if the hair were a thought browner; and your gown's a most rare fashion, i' faith. I saw the Duchess of Milan's gown that they praise so.

Hero. O, that exceeds, they say.

Marg. By my troth, 's but a night-gown in respect of yours: cloth o' gold, and cuts, and laced with silver, set with pearls, down sleeves, side sleeves, and skirts, round underborne with a bluish tinsel: but for a fine, quaint, graceful, and excellent fashion, yours is worth ten on't.

Hero. God give me joy to wear it! for my heart is exceeding heavy.

Marg. 'Twill be heavier soon by the weight of a man.

Hero. Fie upon thee! art not ashamed?

Marg. Of what, lady? of speaking honourably? Is not marriage honourable in a beggar? Is not your lord honourable without marriage? I think you would have me say, "saving your reverence, a husband": an bad thinking do not wrest true speaking, I'll offend nobody: is there any harm in "the heavier for a husband"? None, I think, an it be the right husband and the right wife; otherwise 'tis light, and not heavy: ask my Lady Beatrice else; here she comes.

Enter BEATRICE.

Hero. Good morrow, coz.

Beat. Good morrow, sweet Hero.   *40*

Hero. Why, how now? do you speak in the sick tune?

Beat. I am out of all other tune, methinks.

Marg. Clap's into "Light o' love"; that goes without a burden: do you sing it, and I'll dance it.

Beat. Ye light o' love, with your heels! then, if your husband have stables enough, you'll see he shall lack no barns.

Marg. O illegitimate construction! I scorn that with my heels.   *51*

Beat. 'Tis almost five o'clock, cousin; 'tis time you were ready. By my troth, I am exceeding ill: heigh-ho!

Marg. For a hawk, a horse, or a husband?

Beat. For the letter that begins them all, H.

Marg. Well, an you be not turned Turk, there's no more sailing by the star.

Beat. What means the fool, trow?

Marg. Nothing I; but God send every one their heart's desire!   *61*

Hero. These gloves the Count sent me; they are an excellent perfume.

Beat. I am stuffed, cousin; I cannot smell.

Marg. A maid, and stuffed! there's goodly catching of cold.

Beat. O, God help me! God help me! how long have you professed apprehension?

Marg. Ever since you left it. Doth not my wit become me rarely?   *70*

Beat. It is not seen enough, you should wear it in your cap. By my troth, I am sick.

Marg. Get you some of this distilled Carduus Benedictus, and lay it to your heart: it is the only thing for a qualm.

Hero. There thou prickest her with a thistle.

Beat. Benedictus! why Benedictus? you have some moral in this Benedictus.

Marg. Moral! no, by my troth, I have no moral meaning! I meant, plain holy-thistle. You may

think perchance that I think you are in love: nay, by'r lady, I am not such a fool to think what I list, nor I list not to think what I can, nor indeed I cannot think, if I would think my heart out of thinking, that you are in love or that you will be in love or that you can be in love. Yet Benedick was such another, and now is he become a man: he swore he would never marry, and yet now, in despite of his heart, he eats his meat without grudging: and how you may be converted I know not, but methinks you look with your eyes as other women do.

Beat. What pace is this that thy tongue keeps?

Marg. Not a false gallop.

Re-enter URSULA.

Urs. Madam, withdraw: the Prince, the Count, Signior Benedick, Don John, and all the gallants of the town, are come to fetch you to church.

Hero. Help to dress me, good coz, good Meg, good Ursula.   [*Exeunt.*

SCENE V. *Another room in Leonato's house*

Enter LEONATO, *with* DOGBERRY *and* VERGES.

Leon. What would you with me, honest neighbour?

Dog. Marry, sir, I would have some confidence with you that decerns you nearly.

Leon. Brief, I pray you; for you see it is a busy time with me.

Dog. Marry, this it is, sir.

Verg. Yes, truth it is, sir.

Leon. What is it, my good friends?

Dog. Goodman Verges, sir, speaks a little off the matter: an old man, sir, and his wits are not so blunt as, God help, I would desire they were; but, in faith, honest as the skin between his brows.

Verg. Yes, I thank God I am as honest as any man living that is an old man and no honester than I.

Dog. Comparisons are odorous: palabras, neighbour Verges.

Leon. Neighbours, you are tedious.   *20*

Dog. It pleases your worship to say so, but we are the poor Duke's officers; but truly, for mine own part, if I were as tedious as a king, I could find it in my heart to bestow it all of your worship.

Leon. All thy tediousness on me, ah?

Dog. Yea, an 'twere a thousand pound more than 'tis; for I hear as good exclamation on your worship as of any man in the city; and though I be but a poor man, I am glad to hear it.   *30*

Verg. And so am I.

Leon. I would fain know what you have to say.

Verg. Marry, sir, our watch to-night, excepting your worship's presence, ha' ta'en a couple of as arrant knaves as any in Messina.

Dog. A good old man, sir; he will be talking: as they say, "When the age is in, the wit is out." God help us! it is a world to see. Well said, i' faith, neighbour Verges: well, God's a good man; an two men ride of a horse, one must ride behind. An honest soul, i' faith, sir; by my troth he is, as ever broke bread; but God is to be worshipped; all men are not alike; alas, good neighbour!

Leon. Indeed, neighbour, he comes too short of you.

Dog. Gifts that God gives.

Leon. I must leave you.

Dog. One word, sir: our watch, sir, have indeed comprehended two aspicious persons, and we would have them this morning examined before your worship.

Leon. Take their examination yourself and bring it me: I am now in great haste, as it may appear unto you.

Dog. It shall be suffigance.

Leon. Drink some wine ere you go: fare you well.

Enter a MESSENGER.

Mess. My lord, they stay for you to give your daughter to her husband.   60

Leon. I'll wait upon them: I am ready.

[*Exeunt* LEONATO *and* MESSENGER.

Dog. Go, good partner, go, get you to Francis Seacole; bid him bring his pen and inkhorn to the gaol: we are now to examination these men.

Verg. And we must do it wisely.

Dog. We will spare for no wit, I warrant you; here's that shall drive some of them to a noncome: only get the learned writer to set down our excommunication and meet me at the gaol.

[*Exeunt.*

ACT IV

Scene I. *A church*

Enter DON PEDRO, DON JOHN, LEONATO, FRIAR FRANCIS, CLAUDIO, BENEDICK, HERO, BEATRICE, *and attendants.*

Leon. Come, Friar Francis, be brief; only to the plain form of marriage, and you shall recount their particular duties afterwards.

Friar. You come hither, my lord, to marry this lady.

Claud. No.

Leon. To be married to her: friar, you come to marry her.

Friar. Lady, you come hither to be married to this Count.   10

Hero. I do.

Friar. If either of you know any inward impediment why you should not be conjoined, I charge you, on your souls, to utter it.

Claud. Know you any, Hero?

Hero. None, my lord.

Friar. Know you any, Count?

Leon. I dare make his answer, none.

Claud. O, what men dare do! what men may do! what men daily do, not knowing what they do!   21

Bene. How now! interjections? Why, then, some be of laughing, as, ah, ha, he!

Claud. Stand thee by, friar. Father, by your leave:

Will you with free and unconstrained soul
Give me this maid, your daughter?

Leon. As freely, son, as God did give her me.

Claud. And what have I to give you back, whose worth
May counterpoise this rich and precious gift?

D. Pedro. Nothing, unless you render her again.

Claud. Sweet Prince, you learn me noble thankfulness.   31

There, Leonato, take her back again:
Give not this rotten orange to your friend;
She's but the sign and semblance of her honour.
Behold how like a maid she blushes here!
O, what authority and show of truth
Can cunning sin cover itself withal!
Comes not that blood as modest evidence
To witness simple virtue? Would you not swear,
All you that see her, that she were a maid,   40
By these exterior shows? But she is none:
She knows the heat of a luxurious bed;
Her blush is guiltiness, not modesty.

Leon. What do you mean, my lord?

Claud.   Not to be married,
Not to knit my soul to an approved wanton.

Leon. Dear my lord, if you, in your own proof,
Have vanquish'd the resistance of her youth,
And made defeat of her virginity—

Claud. I know what you would say: if I have known her,
You will say she did embrace me as a husband,
And so extenuate the 'forehand sin: 51
No, Leonato,
I never tempted her with word too large;
But, as a brother to his sister, show'd
Bashful sincerity and comely love.

Hero. And seem'd I ever otherwise to you?

Claud. Out on thee! Seeming! I will write against it:
You seem to me as Dian in her orb,
As chaste as is the bud ere it be blown;

But you are more intemperate in your blood   60
Than Venus, or those pamper'd animals
That rage in savage sensuality.
 Hero. Is my lord well, that he doth speak so
  wide?
 Leon. Sweet Prince, why speak not you?
 D. Pedro.   What should I speak?
I stand dishonour'd, that have gone about
To link my dear friend to a common stale.
 Leon. Are these things spoken, or do I but dream?
 D. John. Sir, they are spoken, and these things
  are true.
 Bene. This looks not like a nuptial.
 Hero.   True! O God!
 Claud. Leonato, stand I here?   70
Is this the Prince? is this the Prince's brother?
Is this face Hero's? are our eyes our own?
 Leon. All this is so: but what of this, my lord?
 Claud. Let me but move one question to your
  daughter;
And, by that fatherly and kindly power
That you have in her, bid her answer truly.
 Leon. I charge thee do so, as thou art my child.
 Hero. O, God defend me! how am I beset!
What kind of catechising call you this?
 Claud. To make you answer truly to your
  name.   80
 Hero. Is it not Hero? Who can blot that name
With any just reproach?
 Claud.   Marry, that can Hero;
Hero itself can blot out Hero's virtue.
What man was he talk'd with you yesternight
Out at your window betwixt twelve and one?
Now, if you are a maid, answer to this.
 Hero. I talk'd with no man at that hour, my lord.
 D. Pedro. Why, then are you no maiden.
  Leonato,
I am sorry you must hear: upon mine honour,
Myself, my brother and this grieved Count   90
Did see her, hear her, at that hour last night
Talk with a ruffian at her chamber-window;
Who hath indeed, most like a liberal villain,
Confess'd the vile encounters they have had
A thousand times in secret.
 D. John. Fie, fie! they are not to be named, my
  lord,
Not to be spoke of:
There is not chastity enough in language
Without offence to utter them. Thus, pretty lady,
I am sorry for thy much misgovernment.   100
 Claud. O Hero, what a Hero hadst thou been,
If half thy outward graces had been placed
About thy thoughts and counsels of thy heart!
But fare thee well, most foul, most fair! farewell,
Thou pure impiety and impious purity!
For thee I'll lock up all the gates of love,

And on my eyelids shall conjecture hang,
To turn all beauty into thoughts of harm,
And never shall it more be gracious.
 Leon. Hath no man's dagger here a point for
  me?   110
 [*Hero swoons.*]
 Beat. Why, how now, cousin! wherefore sink
  you down?
 D. John. Come, let us go. These things, come
  thus to light,
Smother her spirits up.
   [*Exeunt* DON PEDRO, DON JOHN, *and* CLAUDIO.
 Bene. How doth the lady?
 Beat.   Dead, I think. Help, uncle!
Hero! why, Hero! Uncle! Signior Benedick!
  Friar!
 Leon. O Fate! take not away thy heavy hand.
Death is the fairest cover for her shame
That may be wish'd for.
 Beat.   How now, cousin Hero!
 Friar. Have comfort, lady.
 Leon. Dost thou look up?   120
 Friar. Yea, wherefore should she not?
 Leon. Wherefore! Why, doth not every earthly
  thing
Cry shame upon her? Could she here deny
The story that is printed in her blood?
Do not live, Hero; do not ope thine eyes:
For, did I think thou wouldst not quickly die,
Thought I thy spirits were stronger than thy
  shames,
Myself would, on the rearward of reproaches,
Strike at thy life. Grieved I, I had but one?
Chid I for that at frugal nature's frame?   130
O, one too much by thee! Why had I one?
Why ever wast thou lovely in my eyes?
Why had I not with charitable hand
Took up a beggar's issue at my gates,
Who smirched thus and mired with infamy,
I might have said "No part of it is mine;
This shame derives itself from unknown loins"?
But mine and mine I loved and mine I praised
And mine that I was proud on, mine so much
That I myself was to myself not mine,   140
Valuing of her—why, she, O, she is fallen
Into a pit of ink, that the wide sea
Hath drops too few to wash her clean again
And salt too little which may season give
To her foul-tainted flesh!
 Bene.   Sir, sir, be patient.
For my part, I am so attired in wonder,
I know not what to say.
 Beat. O, on my soul, my cousin is belied!
 Bene. Lady, were you her bedfellow last night?
 Beat. No, truly not; although, until last night,
I have this twelvemonth been her bedfellow.   151

Leon. Confirm'd, confirm'd! O, that is stronger
  made
Which was before barr'd up with ribs of iron!
Would the two Princes lie, and Claudio lie,
Who loved her so, that, speaking of her foulness,
Wash'd it with tears? Hence from her! let her
  die.
  Friar. Hear me a little; for I have only been
Silent so long and given way unto
This course of fortune,
By noting of the lady. I have mark'd   *160*
A thousand blushing apparitions
To start into her face, a thousand innocent
  shames
In angel whiteness beat away those blushes;
And in her eye there hath appear'd a fire,
To burn the errors that these Princes hold
Against her maiden truth. Call me a fool;
Trust not my reading nor my observations,
Which with experimental seal doth warrant
The tenour of my book; trust not my age,
My reverence, calling, nor divinity,   *170*
If this sweet lady lie not guiltless here
Under some biting error.
  Leon.   Friar, it cannot be.
Thou seest that all the grace that she hath left
Is that she will not add to her damnation
A sin of perjury; she not denies it:
Why seek'st thou then to cover with excuse
That which appears in proper nakedness?
  Friar. Lady, what man is he you are accused of?
  Hero. They know that do accuse me; I know
  none:
If I know more of any man alive   *180*
Than that which maiden modesty doth warrant,
Let all my sins lack mercy! O my father,
Prove you that any man with me conversed
At hours unmeet, or that I yesternight
Maintain'd the change of words with any
  creature,
Refuse me, hate me, torture me to death!
  Friar. There is some strange misprision in the
  Princes.
  Bene. Two of them have the very bent of
  honour;
And if their wisdoms be misled in this,
The practice of it lives in John the Bastard, *190*
Whose spirits toil in frame of villainies.
  Leon. I know not. If they speak but truth of her,
These hands shall tear her; if they wrong her
  honour,
The proudest of them shall well hear of it.
Time hath not yet so dried this blood of mine,
Nor age so eat up my invention,
Nor fortune made such havoc of my means,
Nor my bad life reft me so much of friends,

But they shall find, awaked in such a kind,
Both strength of limb and policy of mind,   *200*
Ability in means and choice of friends,
To quit me of them throughly.
  Friar   Pause awhile,
And let my counsel sway you in this case.
Your daughter here the Princes left for dead:
Let her awhile be secretly kept in,
And publish it that she is dead indeed;
Maintain a mourning ostentation
And on your family's old monument
Hang mournful epitaphs and do all rites
That appertain unto a burial.   *210*
  Leon. What shall become of this? what will this
  do?
  Friar. Marry, this well carried shall on her
  behalf
Change slander to remorse; that is some good:
But not for that dream I on this strange course,
But on this travail look for greater birth.
She dying, as it must be so maintain'd,
Upon the instant that she was accused,
Shall be lamented, pitied, and excused
Of every hearer: for it so falls out
That what we have we prize not to the worth *220*
Whiles we enjoy it, but being lack'd and lost,
Why, then we rack the value, then we find
The virtue that possession would not show us
Whiles it was ours. So will it fare with Claudio:
When he shall hear she died upon his words,
The idea of her life shall sweetly creep
Into his study of imagination,
And every lovely organ of her life
Shall come apparell'd in more precious habit,
More moving-delicate and full of life,   *230*
Into the eye and prospect of his soul,
Than when she lived indeed; then shall he mourn,
If ever love had interest in his liver,
And wish he had not so accused her,
No, though he thought his accusation true.
Let this be so, and doubt not but success
Will fashion the event in better shape
Than I can lay it down in likelihood.
But if all aim but this be levell'd false,
The supposition of the lady's death   *240*
Will quench the wonder of her infamy:
And if it sort not well, you may conceal her,
As best befits her wounded reputation,
In some reclusive and religious life,
Out of all eyes, tongues, minds and injuries.
  Bene. Signior Leonato, let the friar advise you:
And though you know my inwardness and love
Is very much unto the Prince and Claudio,
Yet, by mine honour, I will deal in this
As secretly and justly as your soul   *250*
Should with your body.

Leon.   Being that I flow in grief,
The smallest twine may lead me.

Friar. 'Tis well consented: presently away;
For to strange sores strangely they strain the
    cure.
Come, lady, die to live: this wedding-day
Perhaps is but prolong'd: have patience and
    endure.

[*Exeunt all but* BENEDICK *and* BEATRICE.

Bene. Lady Beatrice, have you wept all this
    while?

Beat. Yea, and I will weep a while longer.

Bene. I will not desire that.

Beat. You have no reason; I do it freely.   260

Bene. Surely I do believe your fair cousin is
wronged.

Beat. Ah, how much might the man deserve of
me that would right her!

Bene. Is there any way to show such friendship?

Beat. A very even way, but no such friend.

Bene. May a man do it?

Beat. It is a man's office, but not yours.

Bene. I do love nothing in the world so well as
you: is not that strange?   270

Beat. As strange as the thing I know not. It were
as possible for me to say I loved nothing so well
as you: but believe me not; and yet I lie not; I
confess nothing, nor I deny nothing. I am sorry
for my cousin.

Bene. By my sword, Beatrice, thou lovest me.

Beat. Do not swear, and eat it.

Bene. I will swear by it that you love me; and I
will make him eat it that says I love not you.

Beat. Will you not eat your word?   280

Bene. With no sauce that can be devised to it.
I protest I love thee.

Beat. Why, then, God forgive me!

Bene. What offence, sweet Beatrice?

Beat. You have stayed me in a happy hour: I was
about to protest I loved you.

Bene. And do it with all thy heart.

Beat. I love you with so much of my heart that
none is left to protest.

Bene. Come, bid me do anything for thee.   290

Beat. Kill Claudio.

Bene. Ha! not for the wide world.

Beat. You kill me to deny it. Farewell.

Bene. Tarry, sweet Beatrice.

Beat. I am gone, though I am here: there is no
love in you: nay, I pray you, let me go.

Bene. Beatrice—

Beat. In faith, I will go.

Bene. We'll be friends first.

Beat. You dare easier be friends with me than
fight with mine enemy.   301

Bene. Is Claudio thine enemy?

Beat. Is he not approved in the height a villain,
that hath slandered, scorned, dishonoured my
kinswoman? O that I were a man! What, bear
her in hand until they come to take hands; and
then, with public accusation, uncovered slander,
unmitigated rancour—O God, that I were a man!
I would eat his heart in the market-place.

Bene. Hear me, Beatrice—   310

Beat. Talk with a man out at a window! A
proper saying!

Bene. Nay, but, Beatrice—

Beat. Sweet Hero! She is wronged, she is
slandered, she is undone.

Bene. Beat—

Beat. Princes and counties! Surely, a princely
testimony, a goodly count, Count Comfect; a
sweet gallant, surely! O that I were a man for
his sake! or that I had any friend would be a man
for my sake! But manhood is melted into courtesies, valour into compliment, and men are only
turned into tongue, and trim ones too: he is now
as valiant as Hercules that only tells a lie and
swears it. I cannot be a man with wishing, therefore I will die a woman with grieving.

Bene. Tarry, good Beatrice. By this hand, I love
thee.

Beat. Use it for my love some other way than
swearing by it.   330

Bene. Think you in your soul the Count Claudio
hath wronged Hero?

Beat. Yea, as sure as I have a thought or a
soul.

Bene. Enough, I am engaged; I will challenge
him. I will kiss your hand, and so I leave you.
By this hand, Claudio shall render me a dear
account. As you hear of me, so think of me. Go,
comfort your cousin: I must say she is dead; and
so, farewell.   [*Exeunt.* 340

SCENE II. *A prison*

Enter DOGBERRY, VERGES, *and* SEXTON, *in gowns;
and the* WATCH, *with* CONRADE *and* BORACHIO.

Dog. Is our whole dissembly appeared?

Verg. O, a stool and a cushion for the sexton.

Sex. Which be the malefactors?

Dog. Marry, that am I and my partner.

Verg. Nay, that's certain; we have the exhibition to examine.

Sex. But which are the offenders that are to be
examined? let them come before master constable.

Dog. Yea, marry, let them come before me.
What is your name, friend?   11

Bora. Borachio.

Dog. Pray, write down, Borachio. Yours,
sirrah?

Con. I am a gentleman, sir, and my name is Conrade.

Dog. Write down, master gentleman Conrade. Masters, do you serve God?

Con. ⎫
Bora. ⎭ Yea, sir, we hope.

Dog. Write down, that they hope they serve God: and write God first; for God defend but God should go before such villains! Masters, it is proved already that you are little better than false knaves; and it will go near to be thought so shortly. How answer you for yourselves?

Con. Marry, sir, we say we are none.

Dog. A marvellous witty fellow, I assure you; but I will go about with him. Come you hither, sirrah; a word in your ear: sir, I say to you, it is thought you are false knaves.   *30*

Bora. Sir, I say to you we are none.

Dog. Well, stand aside. 'Fore God, they are both in a tale. Have you writ down, that they are none?

Sex. Master constable, you go not the way to examine: you must call forth the watch that are their accusers.

Dog. Yea, marry, that's the eftest way. Let the watch come forth. Masters I charge you, in the Prince's name, accuse these men.   *40*

1st Watch. This man said, sir, that Don John, the Prince's brother, was a villain.

Dog. Write down Prince John a villain. Why, this is flat perjury, to call a Prince's brother villain.

Bora. Master constable—

Dog. Pray thee, fellow, peace: I do not like thy look, I promise thee.

Sex. What heard you him say else?

2nd Watch. Marry, that he had received a thousand ducats of Don John for accusing the Lady Hero wrongfully.   *51*

Dog. Flat burglary as ever was committed.

Verg. Yea, by mass, that it is.

Sex. What else, fellow?

1st Watch. And that Count Claudio did mean, upon his words, to disgrace Hero before the whole assembly, and not marry her.

Dog. O villain! thou wilt be condemned into everlasting redemption for this.

Sex. What else?   *60*

1st Watch. This is all.

Sex. And this is more, masters, than you can deny. Prince John is this morning secretly stolen away; Hero was in this manner accused, in this very manner refused, and upon the grief of this suddenly died. Master constable, let these men be bound, and brought to Leonato's: I will go before and show him their examination.   [*Exit.*

Dog. Come, let them be opinioned.

Verg. Let them be in the hands—   *70*

Con. Off, coxcomb!

Dog. God's my life, where's the sexton? let him write down the Prince's officer coxcomb. Come, bind them. Thou naughty varlet!

Con. Away! you are an ass, you are an ass.

Dog. Dost thou not suspect my place? dost thou not suspect my years? O that he were here to write me down an ass! But, masters, remember that I am an ass; though it be not written down, yet forget not that I am an ass. No, thou villain, thou art full of piety, as shall be proved upon thee by good witness. I am a wise fellow, and, which is more, an officer, and, which is more, a householder, and, which is more, as pretty a piece of flesh as any is in Messina, and one that knows the law, go to; and a rich fellow enough, go to; and a fellow that hath had losses, and one that hath two gowns and everything handsome about him. Bring him away. O that I had been writ down an ass!   [*Exeunt.* *90*

ACT V

Scene i. *Before Leonato's house*

Enter LEONATO *and* ANTONIO.

Ant. If you go on thus, you will kill yourself;
And 'tis not wisdom thus to second grief
Against yourself.

Leon.   I pray thee, cease thy counsel,
Which falls into mine ears as profitless
As water in a sieve: give not me counsel;
Nor let no comforter delight mine ear
But such a one whose wrongs do suit with
    mine.
Bring me a father that so loved his child,
Whose joy of her is overwhelm'd like mine,
And bid him speak of patience;   *10*
Measure his woe the length and breadth of mine
And let it answer every strain for strain,
As thus for thus and such a grief for such,
In every lineament, branch, shape, and form:
If such a one will smile and stroke his beard,
Bid sorrow wag, cry "hem"! when he should
    groan,
Patch grief with proverbs, make misfortune
    drunk
With candle-wasters; bring him yet to me,
And I of him will gather patience.
But there is no such man: for, brother, men   *20*
Can counsel and speak comfort to that grief
Which they themselves not feel; but, tasting it,
Their counsel turns to passion, which before
Would give preceptial medicine to rage,
Fetter strong madness in a silken thread,

Charm ache with air and agony with words:
No, no; 'tis all men's office to speak patience
To those that wring under the load of sorrow,
But no man's virtue nor sufficiency
To be so moral when he shall endure   30
The like himself. Therefore give me no counsel:
My griefs cry louder than advertisement.
    Ant. Therein do men from children nothing
        differ.
    Leon. I pray thee, peace. I will be flesh and
        blood;
For there was never yet philosopher
That could endure the toothache patiently,
However they have writ the style of gods
And made a push at chance and sufferance.
    Ant. Yet bend not all the harm upon yourself;
Make those that do offend you suffer too.   40
    Leon. There thou speak'st reason: nay, I will
        do so.
My soul doth tell me Hero is belied;
And that shall Claudio know; so shall the Prince
And all of them that thus dishonour her.
    Ant. Here comes the Prince and Claudio hastily.

Enter DON PEDRO *and* CLAUDIO.

    D. Pedro. Good den, good den.
    Claud.   Good day to both of you.
    Leon. Hear you, my lords—
    D. Pedro.   We have some haste, Leonato.
    Leon. Some haste, my lord! well, fare you well,
        my lord:
Are you so hasty now? well, all is one.
    D. Pedro. Nay, do not quarrel with us, good
        old man.   50
    Ant. If he could right himself with quarrelling,
Some of us would lie low.
    Claud.   Who wrongs him?
    Leon. Marry, thou dost wrong me; thou dis-
        sembler, thou:—
Nay, never lay thy hand upon thy sword;
I fear thee not.
    Claud.   Marry, beshrew my hand,
If it should give your age such cause of fear:
In faith, my hand meant nothing to my sword.
    Leon. Tush, tush, man; never fleer and jest at
        me:
I speak not like a dotard nor a fool,
As under privilege of age to brag   60
What I have done being young, or what would do
Were I not old. Know, Claudio, to thy head,
Thou hast wrong'd mine innocent child and
        me
That I am forced to lay my reverence by
And, with grey hairs and bruise of many days,
Do challenge thee to trial of a man.
I say thou hast belied mine innocent child;

Thy slander hath gone through and through her
        heart,
And she lies buried with her ancestors;
O, in a tomb where never scandal slept,   70
Save this of hers, framed by thy villainy!
    Claud. My villainy?
    Leon.   Thine, Claudio; thine, I say.
    D. Pedro. You say not right, old man.
    Leon.   My lord, my lord,
I'll prove it on his body, if he dare,
Despite his nice fence and his active practice,
His May of youth and bloom of lustihood.
    Claud. Away! I will not have to do with you.
    Leon. Canst thou so daff me? Thou hast kill'd
        my child:
If thou kill'st me, boy, thou shalt kill a man.
    Ant. He shall kill two of us, and men indeed:
But that's no matter; let him kill one first;   81
Win me and wear me; let him answer me.
Come, follow me, boy; come, sir boy, come, fol-
        low me:
Sir boy, I'll whip you from your foining fence;
Nay, as I am a gentleman, I will.
    Leon. Brother—
    Ant. Content yourself. God knows I loved my
        niece;
And she is dead, slander'd to death by villains,
That dare as well answer a man indeed
As I dare take a serpent by the tongue: 90
Boys, apes, braggarts, Jacks, milksops!
    Leon.   Brother Antony—
    Ant. Hold you content. What, man! I know
        them, yea,
And what they weigh, even to the utmost
        scruple—
Scrambling, out-facing, fashion-monging boys,
That lie and cog and flout, deprave and slander,
Go anticly, show outward hideousness,
And speak off half a dozen dangerous words,
How they might hurt their enemies, if they durst;
And this is all.
    Leon. But, brother Antony—
    Ant.   Come, 'tis no matter: 100
Do not you meddle; let me deal in this.
    D. Pedro. Gentlemen both, we will not wake
        your patience.
My heart is sorry for your daughter's death:
But, on my honour, she was charged with noth-
        ing
But what was true and very full of proof.
    Leon. My lord, my lord—
    D. Pedro. I will not hear you.
    Leon. No? Come, brother; away! I will be
        heard.
    Ant. And shall, or some of us will smart for it.
                [Exeunt LEONATO *and* ANTONIO.

D. Pedro. See, see; here comes the man we went to seek.   *110*

Enter BENEDICK.

Claud. Now, signior, what news?

Bene. Good day, my lord.

D. Pedro. Welcome, signior: you are almost come to part almost a fray.

Claud. We had like to have had our two noses snapped off with two old men without teeth.

D. Pedro. Leonato and his brother. What thinkest thou? Had we fought, I doubt we should have been too young for them.

Bene. In a false quarrel there is no true valour. I came to seek you both.   *121*

Claud. We have been up and down to seek thee; for we are high-proof melancholy and would fain have it beaten away. Wilt thou use thy wit?

Bene. It is in my scabbard: shall I draw it?

D. Pedro. Dost thou wear thy wit by thy side?

Claud. Never any did so, though very many have been beside their wit. I will bid thee draw, as we do the minstrels; draw, to pleasure us.

D. Pedro. As I am an honest man, he looks pale. Art thou sick, or angry?   *131*

Claud. What, courage, man! What though care killed a cat, thou hast mettle enough in thee to kill care.

Bene. Sir, I shall meet your wit in the career, an you charge it against me. I pray you choose another subject.

Claud. Nay, then, give him another staff: this last was broke cross.

D. Pedro. By this light, he changes more and more: I think he be angry indeed.   *141*

Claud. If he be, he knows how to turn his girdle.

Bene. Shall I speak a word in your ear?

Claud. God bless me from a challenge!

Bene. [*Aside to* CLAUDIO] You are a villain; I jest not: I will make it good how you dare, with what you dare, and when you dare. Do me right, or I will protest your cowardice. You have killed a sweet lady, and her death shall fall heavy on you. Let me hear from you.   *151*

Claud. Well, I will meet you, so I may have good cheer.

D. Pedro. What, a feast, a feast?

Claud. I' faith, I thank him; he hath bid me to a calf's head and a capon; the which if I do not carve most curiously, say my knife's naught. Shall I not find a woodcock too?

Bene. Sir, your wit ambles well; it goes easily.

D. Pedro. I'll tell thee how Beatrice praised thy wit the other day. I said, thou hadst a fine wit: "True," said she, "a fine little one." "No," said I, "a great wit": "Right" says she, "a great gross one." "Nay," said I, "a good wit": "Just," said she, "it hurts nobody." "Nay," said I, "the gentleman is wise": "Certain," said she, "a wise gentleman." "Nay," said I, "he hath the tongues": "That I believe," said she, "for he swore a thing to me on Monday night, which he forswore on Tuesday morning; there's a double tongue; there's two tongues." Thus did she, an hour together, trans-shape thy particular virtues: yet at last she concluded with a sigh, thou wast the properest man in Italy.

Claud. For the which she wept heartily and said she cared not.

D. Pedro. Yea, that she did; but yet, for all that, an if she did not hate him deadly, she would love him dearly: the old man's daughter told us all.   *180*

Claud. All, all; and, moreover, God saw him when he was hid in the garden.

D. Pedro. But when shall we set the savage bull's horns on the sensible Benedick's head?

Claud. Yea, and text underneath, "Here dwells Benedick the married man"?

Bene. Fare you well, boy: you know my mind. I will leave you now to your gossip-like humour: you break jests as braggarts do their blades, which, God be thanked, hurt not. My lord, for your many courtesies I thank you: I must discontinue your company: your brother the bastard is fled from Messina: you have among you killed a sweet and innocent lady. For my Lord Lackbeard there, he and I shall meet: and, till then, peace be with him.   [*Exit.*

D. Pedro. He is earnest.

Claud. In most profound earnest; and, I'll warrant you, for the love of Beatrice.

D. Pedro. And hath challenged thee.   *200*

Claud. Most sincerely.

D. Pedro. What a pretty thing man is when he goes in his doublet and hose and leaves off his wit!

Claud. He is then a giant to an ape; but then is an ape a doctor to such a man.

D. Pedro. But, soft you, let me be: pluck up, my heart, and be sad. Did he not say, my brother was fled?

Enter DOGBERRY, VERGES, *and the* WATCH, *with* CONRADE *and* BORACHIO.

Dog. Come you, sir: if justice cannot tame you, she shall ne'er weigh more reasons in her balance: nay, an you be a cursing hypocrite once, you must be looked to.

D. Pedro. How now? two of my brother's men bound! Borachio one!

Claud. Hearken after their offence, my lord.

D. Pedro. Officers, what offence have these men done?

Dog. Marry, sir, they have committed false report; moreover, they have spoken untruths; secondarily, they are slanders; sixth and lastly, they have belied a lady; thirdly, they have verified unjust things; and, to conclude, they are lying knaves.

D. Pedro. First, I ask thee what they have done; thirdly, I ask thee what's their offence; sixth and lastly, why they are committed; and, to conclude, what you lay to their charge.

Claud. Rightly reasoned, and in his own division; and, by my troth, there's one meaning well suited.   231

D. Pedro. Who have you offended, masters, that you are thus bound to your answer? this learned constable is too cunning to be understood: what's your offence?

Bora. Sweet Prince, let me go no farther to mine answer: do you hear me, and let this Count kill me. I have deceived even your very eyes: what your wisdoms could not discover, these shallow fools have brought to light; who in the night overheard me confessing to this man how Don John your brother incensed me to slander the Lady Hero, how you were brought into the orchard and saw me court Margaret in Hero's garments, how you disgraced her, when you should marry her: my villainy they have upon record; which I had rather seal with my death than repeat over to my shame. The lady is dead upon mine and my master's false accusation; and, briefly, I desire nothing but the reward of a villain.   251

D. Pedro. Runs not this speech like iron through your blood?

Claud. I have drunk poison whiles he utter'd it.

D. Pedro. But did my brother set thee on to this?

Bora. Yea, and paid me richly for the practice of it.

D. Pedro. He is composed and framed of treachery:
And fled he is upon this villainy.

Claud. Sweet Hero! now thy image doth appear
In the rare semblance that I loved it first.   260

Dog. Come, bring away the plaintiffs: by this time our sexton hath reformed Signior Leonato of the matter: and, masters, do not forget to specify, when time and place shall serve, that I am an ass.

Verg. Here, here comes master Signior Leonato, and the sexton too.

Re-enter LEONATO *and* ANTONIO, *with the* SEXTON.

Leon. Which is the villain? let me see his eyes,
That, when I note another man like him,   270
I may avoid him: which of these is he?

Bora. If you would know your wronger, look on me.

Leon. Art thou the slave that with thy breath hast kill'd
Mine innocent child?

Bora.   Yea, even I alone.

Leon. No, not so, villain; thou beliest thyself:
Here stand a pair of honourable men;
A third is fled, that had a hand in it.
I thank you, Princes, for my daughter's death:
Record it with your high and worthy deeds:
'Twas bravely done, if you bethink you of it.

Claud. I know not how to pray your patience;
Yet I must speak. Choose your revenge yourself;
Impose me to what penance your invention
Can lay upon my sin: yet sinn'd I not
But in mistaking.

D. Pedro.   By my soul, nor I:
And yet, to satisfy this good old man,
I would bend under any heavy weight
That he'll enjoin me to.

Leon. I cannot bid you bid my daughter live;
That were impossible; but, I pray you both,
Possess the people in Messina here   291
How innocent she died; and if your love
Can labour aught in sad invention,
Hang her an epitaph upon her tomb
And sing it to her bones, sing it to-night:
To-morrow morning come you to my house,
And since you could not be my son-in-law,
Be yet my nephew: my brother hath a daughter,
Almost the copy of my child that's dead,
And she alone is heir to both of us: 300
Give her the right you should have given her cousin,
And so dies my revenge.

Claud.   O noble sir,
Your over-kindness doth wring tears from me!
I do embrace your offer; and dispose
For henceforth of poor Claudio.

Leon. To-morrow then I will expect your coming;
To-night I take my leave. This naughty man
Shall face to face be brought to Margaret,
Who I believe was pack'd in all this wrong,
Hired to it by your brother.

Bora.   No, by my soul, she was not,
Nor knew not what she did when she spoke to me,
But always hath been just and virtuous   312
In any thing that I do know by her.

Dog. Moreover, sir, which indeed is not under white and black, this plaintiff here, the offender, did call me ass: I beseech you, let it be remembered in his punishment. And also, the watch heard them talk of one Deformed: they say he wears a key in his ear and a lock hanging by it, and borrows money in God's name, the which he hath used so long and never paid that now men grow hard-hearted and will lend nothing for God's sake: pray you, examine him upon that point.

Leon. I thank thee for thy care and honest pains.

Dog. Your worship speaks like a most thankful and reverend youth; and I praise God for you.

Leon. There's for thy pains.

Dog. God save the foundation!

Leon. Go, I discharge thee of thy prisoner, and I thank thee.   *330*

Dog. I leave an arrant knave with your worship; which I beseech your worship to correct yourself, for the example of others. God keep your worship! I wish your worship well; God restore you to health! I humbly give you leave to depart; and if a merry meeting may be wished, God prohibit it! Come, neighbour.

                    [*Exeunt* DOGBERRY *and* VERGES.

Leon. Until to-morrow morning, lords, farewell.

Ant. Farewell, my lords: we look for you to-morrow.

D. Pedro. We will not fail.

Claud.   To-night I'll mourn with Hero.

Leon. [*To the* WATCH] Bring you these fellows on. We'll talk with Margaret,   *341*
How her acquaintance grew with this lewd fellow.

                    [*Exeunt severally.*

SCENE II. *Leonato's garden*

Enter BENEDICK *and* MARGARET, *meeting.*

Bene. Pray thee, sweet Mistress Margaret, deserve well at my hands by helping me to the speech of Beatrice.

Marg. Will you then write me a sonnet in praise of my beauty?

Bene. In so high a style, Margaret, that no man living shall come over it; for, in most comely truth, thou deservest it.

Marg. To have no man come over me! why, shall I always keep below stairs?   *10*

Bene. Thy wit is as quick as the greyhound's mouth; it catches.

Marg. And yours as blunt as the fencer's foils, which hit, but hurt not.

Bene. A most manly wit, Margaret; it will not hurt a woman: and so, I pray thee, call Beatrice: I give thee the bucklers.

Marg. Give us the swords; we have bucklers of our own.

Bene. If you use them, Margaret, you must put in the pikes with a vice; and they are dangerous weapons for maids.

Marg. Well, I will call Beatrice to you, who I think hath legs.

Bene. And therefore will come.

                    [*Exit* MARGARET.

[*Sings*]   The god of love,
                    That sits above,
          And knows me, and knows me,
              How pitiful I deserve—

I mean in singing; but in loving, Leander the good swimmer, Troilus the first employer of pandars, and a whole bookful of these quondam carpet-mongers, whose names yet run smoothly in the even road of a blank verse, why, they were never so truly turned over and over as my poor self in love. Marry, I cannot show it in rhyme; I have tried: I can find out no rhyme to "lady" but "baby," an innocent rhyme; for "scorn," "horn," a hard rhyme; for "school," "fool," a babbling rhyme; very ominous endings: no, I was not born under a rhyming planet, nor I cannot woo in festival terms.   *41*

Enter BEATRICE.

Sweet Beatrice, wouldst thou come when I called thee?

Beat. Yea, signior, and depart when you bid me.

Bene. O, stay but till then!

Beat. "Then" is spoken; fare you well now: and yet, ere I go, let me go with that I came; which is, with knowing what hath passed between you and Claudio.

Bene. Only foul words; and thereupon I will kiss thee.   *51*

Beat. Foul words is but foul wind, and foul wind is but foul breath, and foul breath is noisome; therefore I will depart unkissed.

Bene. Thou hast frighted the word out of his right sense, so forcible is thy wit. But I must tell thee plainly, Claudio undergoes my challenge; and either I must shortly hear from him, or I will subscribe him a coward. And, I pray thee now, tell me for which of my bad parts didst thou first fall in love with me?   *61*

Beat. For them all together; which maintained so politic a state of evil that they will not admit any good part to intermingle with them. But for which of my good parts did you first suffer love for me?

Bene. Suffer love! a good epithet! I do suffer love indeed, for I love thee against my will.

Beat. In spite of your heart, I think; alas, poor heart! If you spite it for my sake, I will spite it for yours; for I will never love that which my friend hates.

Bene. Thou and I are too wise to woo peaceably.

Beat. It appears not in this confession: there's not one wise man among twenty that will praise himself.

Bene. An old, an old instance, Beatrice, that lived in the time of good neighbours. If a man do not erect in this age his own tomb ere he dies, he shall live no longer in monument than the bell rings and the widow weeps.

Beat. And how long is that, think you?

Bene, Question: why, an hour in clamour and a quarter in rheum: therefore is it most expedient for the wise, if Don Worm, his conscience, find no impediment to the contrary, to be the trumpet of his own virtues, as I am to myself. So much for praising myself, who, I myself will bear witness, is praiseworthy: and now tell me, how doth your cousin?   *91*

Beat. Very ill.

Bene. And how do you?

Beat. Very ill too.

Bene. Serve God, love me, and mend. There will I leave you too, for here comes one in haste.

Enter URSULA.

Urs. Madam, you must come to your uncle. Yonder's old coil at home: it is proved my Lady Hero hath been falsely accused, the Prince and Claudio mightily abused; and Don John is the author of all, who is fled and gone. Will you come presently?

Beat. Will you go hear this news, signior?

Bene. I will live in thy heart, die in thy lap, and be buried in thy eyes; and moreover I will go with thee to thy uncle's.   [*Exeunt.*

SCENE III. *A church*

Enter DON PEDRO, CLAUDIO, *and three or four with tapers.*

Claud. Is this the monument of Leonato?

A Lord. It is, my lord.

Claud. [*Reading out of a scroll*]
"Done to death by slanderous tongues
     Was the Hero that here lies:
Death, in guerdon of her wrongs,
     Gives her fame which never dies.
So the life that died with shame
     Lives in death with glorious fame."

Hang thou there upon the tomb,
     Praising her when I am dumb.   *10*
Now, music, sound, and sing your solemn hymn.

SONG

"Pardon, goddess of the night,
Those that slew thy virgin knight;

For the which, with songs of woe,
Round about her tomb they go.
     Midnight, assist our moan;
Help us to sigh and groan,
     Heavily, heavily:
Graves, yawn and yield your dead,
Till death be uttered,   *20*
     Heavily, heavily."

Claud. Now, unto thy bones good night!
     Yearly will I do this rite.

D. Pedro. Good morrow, masters; put your torches out:
The wolves have prey'd; and look, the gentle day,
Before the wheels of Phœbus, round about
Dapples the drowsy east with spots of grey.
Thanks to you all, and leave us: fare you well.

Claud. Good morrow, masters: each his several way.

D. Pedro. Come, let us hence, and put on other weeds;   *30*
And then to Leonato's we will go.

Claud. And Hymen now with luckier issue speed's
Than this for whom we render'd up this woe.
     [*Exeunt.*

SCENE IV. *A room in Leonato's house*

Enter LEONATO, ANTONIO, BENEDICK, BEATRICE, MARGARET, URSULA, FRIAR FRANCIS, *and* HERO.

Friar. Did I not tell you she was innocent?

Leon. So are the Prince and Claudio, who accused her
Upon the error that you heard debated:
But Margaret was in some fault for this,
Although against her will, as it appears
In the true course of all the question.

Ant. Well, I am glad that all things sort so well.

Bene. And so am I, being else by faith enforced.
To call young Claudio to a reckoning for it.

Leon. Well, daughter, and you gentlewomen all,
Withdraw into a chamber by yourselves,   *11*
And when I send for you, come hither mask'd.
     [*Exeunt* LADIES.
The Prince and Claudio promised by this hour
To visit me. You know your office, brother:
You must be father to your brother's daughter,
And give her to young Claudio.

Ant. Which I will do with comfirm'd countenance.

Bene. Friar, I must entreat your pains, I think.

Friar. To do what, signior?

Bene. To bind me, or undo me; one of them.
Signior Leonato, truth it is, good signior,   *21*

Your niece regards me with an eye of favour.

Leon. That eye my daughter lent her: 'tis most
true.

Bene. And I do with an eye of love requite her.

Leon. The sight whereof I think you had from
me,
From Claudio and the Prince: but what's your
will?

Bene. Your answer, sir, is enigmatical:
But, for my will, my will is your good will
May stand with ours, this day to be conjoin'd
In the state of honourable marriage: 30
In which, good friar, I shall desire your help.

Leon. My heart is with your liking.

Friar.   And my help.
Here comes the Prince and Claudio.

Enter DON PEDRO *and* CLAUDIO, *and two or
three others.*

D. Pedro. Good morrow to this fair assembly.

Leon. Good morrow, Prince; good morrow,
Claudio:
We here attend you. Are you yet determined
To-day to marry with my brother's daughter?

Claud. I'll hold my mind, were she an Ethiope.

Leon. Call her forth, brother; here's the friar
ready.   [*Exit* ANTONIO.

D. Pedro. Good morrow, Benedick. Why,
what's the matter,   40
That you have such a February face,
So full of frost, of storm, and cloudiness?

Claud. I think he thinks upon the savage bull.
Tush, fear not, man; we'll tip thy horns with
gold
And all Europa shall rejoice at thee,
As once Europa did at lusty Jove,
When he would play the noble beast in love.

Bene. Bull Jove, sir, had an amiable low;
And some such strange bull leap'd your father's
cow,
And got a calf in that same noble feat   50
Much like to you, for you have just his bleat.

Claud. For this I owe you: here comes other
reckonings.

Re-enter ANTONIO, *with the* LADIES *masked.*

Which is the lady I must seize upon?

Ant. This same is she, and I do give you her.

Claud. Why, then she's mine. Sweet, let me see
your face.

Leon. No, that you shall not, till you take her
hand
Before this friar and swear to marry her.

Claud. Give me your hand: before this holy
friar,

I am your husband, if you like of me.

Hero. And when I lived, I was your other
wife: [*Unmasking.*   60
And when you loved, you were my other husband.

Claud. Another Hero!

Hero.   Nothing certainer:
One Hero died defiled, but I do live,
And surely as I live, I am a maid.

D. Pedro. The former Hero! Hero that is dead!

Leon. She died, my lord, but whiles her slander
lived.

Friar. All this amazement can I qualify;
When after that the holy rites are ended,
I'll tell you largely of fair Hero's death:
Meantime let wonder seem familiar,   70
And to the chapel let us presently.

Bene. Soft and fair, friar. Which is Beatrice?

Beat. [*Unmasking*] I answer to that name.
What is your will?

Bene. Do not you love me?

Beat.   Why, no; no more than reason.

Bene. Why, then your uncle and the Prince and
Claudio
Have been deceived; they swore you did.

Beat. Do not you love me?

Bene.   Troth, no; no more than reason.

Beat. Why, then my cousin Margaret and
Ursula
Are much deceived; for they did swear you did.

Bene. They swore that you were almost sick
for me.   80

Beat. They swore that you were well-nigh
dead for me.

Bene. 'Tis no such matter. Then you do not
love me?

Beat. No, truly, but in friendly recompense.

Leon. Come, cousin, I am sure you love the
gentleman.

Claud. And I'll be sworn upon't that he loves
her;
For here's a paper written in his hand,
A halting sonnet of his own pure brain,
Fashion'd to Beatrice.

Hero.   And here's another
Writ in my cousin's hand, stolen from her pocket,
Containing her affection unto Benedick.   90

Bene. A miracle! here's our own hands against
our hearts. Come, I will have thee; but, by this
light, I take thee for pity.

Beat. I would not deny you; but, by this good
day, I yield upon great persuasion; and partly
to save your life, for I was told you were in a
consumption.

Bene. Peace! I will stop your mouth.
Kissing her.

D. Pedro. How dost thou, Benedick, the married man?   *100*

Bene. I'll tell thee what, Prince; a college of wit-crackers cannot flout me out of my humour. Dost thou think I care for a satire or an epigram? No: if a man will be beaten with brains, a' shall wear nothing handsome about him. In brief, since I do purpose to marry, I will think nothing to any purpose that the world can say against it; and therefore never flout at me for what I have said against it; for man is a giddy thing, and this is my conclusion. For thy part, Claudio, I did think to have beaten thee; but in that thou art like to be my kinsman, live unbruised and love my cousin.

Claud. I had well hoped thou wouldst have denied Beatrice, that I might have cudgelled thee out of thy single life, to make thee a double dealer; which, out of question, thou wilt be, if my cousin do not look exceeding narrowly to thee.

Bene. Come, come, we are friends: let's have a dance ere we are married, that we may lighten our own hearts and our wives' heels.   *121*

Leon. We'll have dancing afterward.

Bene. First, of my word; therefore play, music. Prince, thou art sad; get thee a wife, get thee a wife: there is no staff more reverend than one tipped with horn.

Enter a MESSENGER.

Mess. My lord, your brother John is ta'en in flight,
And brought with armed men back to Messina.

Bene. Think not on him till to-morrow: I'll devise thee brave punishments for him. Strike up, pipers.   *131*

Dance.   [*Exeunt.*

The Life of
KING HENRY THE FIFTH

DRAMATIS PERSONÆ

KING HENRY THE FIFTH
DUKE OF GLOUCESTER |
DUKE OF BEDFORD | *brothers to the King*
DUKE OF EXETER, *Uncle to the King*
DUKE OF YORK, *cousin to the King*
EARL OF SALISBURY
EARL OF WESTMORELAND
EARL OF WARWICK
ARCHBISHOP OF CANTERBURY
BISHOP OF ELY
EARL OF CAMBRIDGE
LORD SCROOP
SIR THOMAS GREY
SIR THOMAS ERPINGHAM |
GOWER |
FLUELLEN | *officers in King Henry's army*
MACMORRIS |
JAMY |
BATES |
COURT | *soldiers in King Henry's army*
WILLIAMS |
PISTOL
NYM
BARDOLPH
BOY
A HERALD

THREE MESSENGERS
CHARLES THE SIXTH, *King of France*
LEWIS, THE DAUPHIN
DUKE OF BURGUNDY
DUKE OF ORLEANS
DUKE OF BOURBON
THE CONSTABLE OF FRANCE
RAMBURES |
GRANDPRÉ | *French Lords*
GOVERNOR OF HARFLEUR
MONTJOY, *a French Herald*
AMBASSADOR *to the King of England*
FRENCH PRISONER

ISABEL, *Queen of France*
KATHARINE, *daughter to Charles and Isabel*
ALICE, *a lady attending on her*.
HOSTESS *of a tavern in Eastcheap, formerly* MISTRESS
QUICKLY, *and now married to Pistol*

CHORUS

NON-SPEAKING: *Lords, Ladies, Officers, Soldiers,*
Citizens, and Attendants

SCENE: *England; afterwards France*

PROLOGUE

Enter CHORUS.

Chor. O for a Muse of fire, that would ascend
The brightest heaven of invention
A kingdom for a stage, princes to act
And monarchs to behold the swelling scene!
Then should the warlike Harry, like himself,
Assume the port of Mars; and at his heels,
Leash'd in like hounds, should famine, sword,
    and fire
Crouch for employment. But pardon, gentles
    all,
The flat unraised spirits that have dared
On this unworthy scaffold to bring forth   *10*
So great an object: can this cockpit hold
The vasty fields of France? or may we cram
Within this wooden O the very casques
That did affright the air at Agincourt?
O, pardon! since a crooked figure may
Attest in little place a million;
And let us, ciphers to this great accompt,
On your imaginary forces work.
Suppose within the girdle of these walls
Are now confined two mighty monarchies,   *20*
Whose high upreared and abutting fronts
The perilous narrow ocean parts asunder:
Piece out our imperfections with your
    thoughts;
Into a thousand parts divide one man,
And make imaginary puissance:
Think, when we talk of horses, that you see
    them
Printing their proud hoofs i' the receiving
    earth;
For 'tis your thoughts that now must deck our
    kings,
Carry them here and there; jumping o'er
    times,
Turning the accomplishment of many years   *30*
Into an hour-glass: for the which supply,
Admit me Chorus to this history;
Who, prologue-like, your humble patience pray,
Gently to hear, kindly to judge, our play. [*Exit.*

ACT I

SCENE I. *London: an ante-chamber in the King's palace*

Enter the ARCHBISHOP OF CANTERBURY, *and the* BISHOP OF ELY.

Cant. My lord, I'll tell you; that self bill is urged,
Which in the eleventh year of the last king's reign
Was like, and had indeed against us pass'd,
But that the scambling and unquiet time
Did push it out of farther question.
  Ely. But how, my lord, shall we resist it now?
  Cant. It must be thought on. If it pass against us,
We lose the better half of our possession:
For all the temporal lands which men devout
By testament have given to the Church   10
Would they strip from us; being valued thus:
As much as would maintain, to the King's honour,
Full fifteen earls and fifteen hundred knights,
Six thousand and two hundred good esquires;
And, to relief of lazars and weak age,
Of indigent faint souls past corporal toil,
A hundred almshouses right well supplied;
And to the coffers of the King beside,
A thousand pounds by the year: thus runs the bill.
  Ely. This would drink deep.
  Cant.   'Twould drink the cup and all.   20
  Ely. But what prevention?
  Cant. The King is full of grace and fair regard.
  Ely. And a true lover of the holy Church.
  Cant. The courses of his youth promised it not.
The breath no sooner left his father's body,
But that his wildness, mortified in him,
Seem'd to die too; yea, at that very moment
Consideration, like an angel, came
And whipp'd the offending Adam out of him,
Leaving his body as a paradise,   30
To envelope and contain celestial spirits.
Never was such a sudden scholar made;
Never came reformation in a flood
With such a heady currance, scouring faults;
Nor never Hydra-headed wilfulness
So soon did lose his seat and all at once
As in this King.
  Ely.   We are blessed in the change.
  Cant. Hear him but reason in divinity,
And all-admiring with an inward wish
You would desire the King were made a prelate:
Hear him debate of commonwealth affairs,   41
You would say it hath been all in all his study:
List his discourse of war, and you shall hear
A fearful battle render'd you in music:
Turn him to any cause of policy,
The Gordian knot of it he will unloose,
Familiar as his garter: that, when he speaks,
The air, a charter'd libertine, is still,
And the mute wonder lurketh in men's ears,
To steal his sweet and honey'd sentences;   50
So that the art and practic part of life
Must be the mistress to this theoric:
Which is a wonder how his Grace should glean it,
Since his addiction was to courses vain,
His companies unletter'd, rude, and shallow,
His hours fill'd up with riots, banquets, sports,
And never noted in him any study,
Any retirement, any sequestration
From open haunts and popularity.
  Ely. The strawberry grows underneath the nettle   60
And wholesome berries thrive and ripen best
Neighbour'd by fruit of baser quality:
And so the Prince obscured his contemplation
Under the veil of wildness; which, no doubt,
Grew like the summer grass, fastest by night,
Unseen, yet crescive in his faculty.
  Cant. It must be so; for miracles are ceased;
And therefore we must needs admit the means
How things are perfected.
  Ely.   But, my good lord,
How now for mitigation of this bill   70
Urged by the commons? Doth his Majesty
Incline to it, or no?
  Cant.   He seems indifferent,
Or rather swaying more upon our part
Than cherishing the exhibiters against us;
For I have made an offer to his Majesty,
Upon our spiritual convocation
And in regard of causes now in hand,
Which I have open'd to his Grace at large,
As touching France, to give a greater sum
Than ever at one time the clergy yet   80
Did to his predecessors part withal.
  Ely. How did this offer seem received, my lord?
  Cant. With good acceptance of his Majesty;
Save that there was not time enough to hear,
As I perceived his Grace would fain have done,
The severals and unhidden passages
Of his true titles to some certain dukedoms
And generally to the crown and seat of France
Derived from Edward, his great-grandfather.
  Ely. What was the impediment that broke this off?   90
  Cant. The French ambassador upon that instant
Craved audience; and the hour, I think, is come
To give him hearing: is it four o'clock?
  Ely. It is.
  Cant. Then go we in, to know his embassy;
Which I could with a ready guess declare,
Before the Frenchman speak a word of it.
  Ely. I'll wait upon you, and I long to hear it.
                                          [*Exeunt.*

SCENE II. *The same: the presence chamber*

Enter KING HENRY, GLOUCESTER, BEDFORD, EXE-
TER, WARWICK, WESTMORELAND, *and Attendants.*

K. Hen. Where is my gracious Lord of Canterbury?

Exe. Not here in presence.

K. Hen.   Send for him, good uncle.

West. Shall we call in the ambassador, my liege?

K. Hen. Not yet, my cousin: we would be
resolved,
Before we hear him, of some things of weight
That task our thoughts, concerning us and France.

Enter the ARCHBISHOP OF CANTERBURY, *and the*
BISHOP OF ELY.

Cant. God and his angels guard your sacred
throne
And make you long become it!

K. Hen.   Sure, we thank you.
My learned lord, we pray you to proceed
And justly and religiously unfold   *10*
Why the law Salique that they have in France
Or should, or should not, bar us in our claim:
And God forbid, my dear and faithful lord,
That you should fashion, wrest, or bow your
reading,
Or nicely charge your understanding soul
With opening titles miscreate, whose right
Suits not in native colours with the truth;
For God doth know how many now in health
Shall drop their blood in approbation
Of what your reverence shall incite us to.   *20*
Therefore take heed how you impawn our
person,
How you awake our sleeping sword of war:
We charge you, in the name of God, take heed;
For never two such kingdoms did contend
Without much fall of blood; whose guiltless drops
Are every one a woe, a sore complaint
'Gainst him whose wrongs give edge unto the
swords
That make such waste in brief mortality.
Under this conjuration speak, my lord;
For we will hear, note, and believe in heart   *30*
That what you speak is in your conscience
wash'd
As pure as sin with baptism.

Cant. Then hear me, gracious sovereign, and
you peers,
That owe yourselves, your lives, and services
To this imperial throne. There is no bar
To make against your Highness' claim to France
But this, which they produce from Pharamond,
In terram Salicam mulieres ne succedant:
"No woman shall succeed in Salique land":

Which Salique land the French unjustly glose   *40*
To be the realm of France, and Pharamond
The founder of this law and female bar.
Yet their own authors faithfully affirm
That the land Salique is in Germany,
Between the floods of Sala and of Elbe;
Where Charles the Great, having subdued the
Saxons,
There left behind and settled certain French;
Who, holding in disdain the German women
For some dishonest manners of their life,
Establish'd then this law; to wit, no female   *50*
Should be inheritrix in Salique land:
Which Salique, as I said, 'twixt Elbe and Sala,
Is at this day in Germany call'd Meisen.
Then doth it well appear the Salique law
Was not devised for the realm of France;
Nor did the French possess the Salique land
Until four hundred one and twenty years
After defunction of King Pharamond,
Idly supposed the founder of this law;
Who died within the year of our redemption   *60*
Four hundred twenty-six; and Charles the Great
Subdued the Saxons, and did seat the French
Beyond the river Sala, in the year
Eight hundred five. Besides, their writers say,
King Pepin, which deposed Childeric,
Did, as heir general, being descended
Of Blithild, which was daughter to King Clothair,
Make claim and title to the crown of France.
Hugh Capet also, who usurp'd the crown   *69*
Of Charles the Duke of Lorraine, sole heir male
Of the true line and stock of Charles the Great,
To find his title with some shows of truth,
Though, in pure truth, it was corrupt and naught,
Convey'd himself as heir to the Lady Lingare,
Daughter to Charlemain, who was the son
To Lewis the Emperor, and Lewis the son
Of Charles the Great. Also King Lewis the
Tenth,
Who was sole heir to the usurper Capet,
Could not keep quiet in his conscience,
Wearing the crown of France, till satisfied   *80*
That fair Queen Isabel, his grandmother,
Was lineal of the Lady Ermengare,
Daughter to Charles the foresaid Duke of
Lorraine,
By the which marriage the line of Charles the
Great
Was re-united to the crown of France.
So that, as clear as is the summer's sun,
King Pepin's title and Hugh Capet's claim,
King Lewis his satisfaction, all appear
To hold in right and title of the female:
So do the kings of France unto this day;   *90*
Howbeit they would hold up this Salique law

To bar your Highness claiming from the female,
And rather choose to hide them in a net
Than amply to imbar their crooked titles
Usurp'd from you and your progenitors.
  K. Hen. May I with right and conscience make
    this claim?
  Cant. The sin upon my head, dread sovereign!
For in the book of Numbers is it writ,
"When the man dies, let the inheritance
Descend unto the daughter." Gracious lord, *100*
Stand for your own; unwind your bloody flag;
Look back into your mighty ancestors:
Go, my dread lord, to your great-grandsire's
    tomb,
From whom you claim; invoke his warlike spirit,
And your great-uncle's Edward the Black
    Prince,
Who on the French ground play'd a tragedy,
Making defeat on the full power of France,
Whiles his most mighty father on a hill
Stood smiling to behold his lion's whelp
Forage in blood of French nobility.   *110*
O noble English, that could entertain
With half their forces the full pride of France
And let another half stand laughing by,
All out of work and cold for action!
  Ely. Awake remembrance of these valiant dead
And with your puissant arm renew their feats:
You are their heir; you sit upon their throne;
The blood and courage that renowned them
Runs in your veins; and my thrice-puissant liege
Is in the very May-morn of his youth,   *120*
Ripe for exploits and mighty enterprises.
  Exe. Your brother kings and monarchs of the
    earth
Do all expect that you should rouse yourself,
As did the former lions of your blood.
  West. They know your Grace hath cause and
    means and might;
So hath your Highness; never King of England
Had nobles richer and more loyal subjects,
Whose hearts have left their bodies here in Eng-
    land
And lie pavilion'd in the fields of France.   *129*
  Cant. O, let their bodies follow, my dear liege,
With blood and sword and fire to win your
    right;
In aid whereof we of the spiritualty
Will raise your Highness such a mighty sum
As never did the clergy at one time
Bring in to any of your ancestors.
  K. Hen. We must not only arm to invade the
    French,
But lay down our proportions to defend
Against the Scot, who will make road upon us
With all advantages.

  Cant. They of those marches, gracious
    sovereign,   *140*
Shall be a wall sufficient to defend
Our inland from the pilfering borderers.
  K. Hen. We do not mean the coursing snatchers
    only,
But fear the main intendment of the Scot,
Who hath been still a giddy neighbour to us;
For you shall read that my great-grandfather
Never went with his forces into France
But that the Scot on his unfurnish'd kingdom
Came pouring, like the tide into a breach,
With ample and brim fulness of his force,   *150*
Galling the gleaned land with hot assays,
Girding with grievous siege castles and towns;
That England, being empty of defence,
Hath shook and trembled at the ill neighbour-
    hood.
  Cant. She hath been then more fear'd than
    harm'd, my liege;
For hear her but exampled by herself:
When all her chivalry hath been in France
And she a mourning widow of her nobles,
She hath herself not only well defended
But taken and impounded as a stray   *160*
The King of Scots; whom she did send to France,
To fill King Edward's fame with prisoner kings
And make her chronicle as rich with praise
As is the ooze and bottom of the sea
With sunken wreck and sumless treasuries.
  West. But there's a saying very old and true,
    "If that you will France win,
      Then with Scotland first begin":
For once the eagle England being in prey,
To her unguarded nest the weasel Scot   *170*
Comes sneaking and so sucks her princely eggs,
Playing the mouse in absence of the cat,
To tear and havoc more than she can eat.
  Exe. It follows then the cat must stay at home:
Yet that is but a crush'd necessity,
Since we have locks to safeguard necessaries,
And pretty traps to catch the petty thieves.
While that the armed hand doth fight abroad,
The advised head defends itself at home;
For government, though high and low and lower,
Put into parts, doth keep in one consent,   *181*
Congreeing in a full and natural close,
Like music.
  Cant.   Therefore doth heaven divide
The state of man in divers functions,
Setting endeavour in continual motion;
To which is fixed, as an aim or butt,
Obedience: for so work the honey-bees,
Creatures that by a rule in nature teach
The act of order to a peopled kingdom.
They have a king and officers of sorts;   *190*

Where some, like magistrates, correct at home,
Others, like merchants, venture trade abroad,
Others, like soldiers, armed in their stings,
Make boot upon the summer's velvet buds,
Which pillage they with merry march bring
     home
To the tent-royal of their emperor;
Who, busied in his majesty, surveys
The singing masons building roofs of gold,
The civil citizens kneading up the honey,
The poor mechanic porters crowding in   200
Their heavy burdens at his narrow gate,
The sad-eyed justice, with his surly hum,
Delivering o'er to executors pale
The lazy yawning drone. I this infer,
That many things, having full reference
To one consent, may work contrariously:
As many arrows, loosed several ways,
Come to one mark; as many ways meet in one
     town;
As many fresh streams meet in one salt sea;
As many lines close in the dial's centre;   210
So may a thousand actions, once afoot,
End in one purpose, and be all well borne
Without defeat. Therefore to France, my liege.
Divide your happy England into four;
Whereof take you one quarter into France,
And you withal shall make all Gallia shake.
If we, with thrice such powers left at home,
Cannot defend our own doors from the dog,
Let us be worried and our nation lose
The name of hardiness and policy.   220
     K. Hen. Call in the messengers sent from the
     Dauphin.   [*Exeunt some Attendants.*
Now are we well resolved; and, by God's help,
And yours, the noble sinews of our power,
France being ours, we'll bend it to our awe,
Or break it all to pieces: or there we'll sit,
Ruling in large and ample empery
O'er France and all her almost kingly dukedoms,
Or lay these bones in an unworthy urn,
Tombless, with no remembrance over them:
Either our history shall with full mouth   230
Speak freely of our acts, or else our grave,
Like Turkish mute, shall have a tongueless
     mouth,
Not worshipp'd with a waxen epitaph.

Enter AMBASSADORS *of France.*

Now are we well prepared to know the pleasure
Of our fair cousin Dauphin; for we hear
Your greeting is from him, not from the King.
     1st Amb. May't please your Majesty to give us
     leave
Freely to render what we have in charge;
Or shall we sparingly show you far off

The Dauphin's meaning and our embassy?   240
     K. Hen. We are no tyrant, but a Christian
     king:
Unto whose grace our passion is as subject
As are our wretches fetter'd in our prisons:
Therefore with frank and with uncurbed plain-
     ness
Tell us the Dauphin's mind.
     1st Amb.   Thus, then, in few.
Your Highness, lately sending into France,
Did claim some certain dukedoms, in the right
Of your great predecessor, King Edward the
     Third.
In answer of which claim, the Prince our master
Says that you savour too much of your youth,
And bids you be advised there's nought in
     France   251
That can be with a nimble galliard won;
You cannot revel into dukedoms there.
He therefore sends you, meeter for your spirit,
This tun of treasure; and, in lieu of this,
Desires you let the dukedoms that you claim
Hear no more of you. This the Dauphin speaks.
     K. Hen. What treasure, uncle?
     Exe.   Tennis-balls, my liege.
     K. Hen. We are glad the Dauphin is so pleasant
     with us;
His present and your pains we thank you for:
When we have match'd our rackets to these
     balls,   261
We will, in France, by God's grace, play a set
Shall strike his father's crown into the hazard.
Tell him he hath made a match with such a
     wrangler
That all the courts of France will be disturb'd
With chaces. And we understand him well,
How he comes o'er us with our wilder days,
Not measuring what use we made of them.
We never valued this poor seat of England;
And therefore, living hence, did give ourself   270
To barbarous license; as 'tis ever common
That men are merriest when they are from home.
But tell the Dauphin I will keep my state,
Be like a king and show my sail of greatness
When I do rouse me in my throne of France:
For that I have laid by my majesty
And plodded like a man for working-days,
But I will rise there with so full a glory
That I will dazzle all the eyes of France,
Yea, strike the Dauphin blind to look on us.   280
And tell the pleasant prince this mock of his
Hath turn'd his balls to gun-stones; and his soul
Shall stand sore charged for the wasteful venge-
     ance
That shall fly with them: for many a thousand
     widows

Shall this his mock mock out of their dear hus-
    bands;
Mock mothers from their sons, mock castles
    down;
And some are yet ungotten and unborn
That shall have cause to curse the Dauphin's
    scorn.
But this lies all within the will of God,
To whom I do appeal; and in whose name   290
Tell you the Dauphin I am coming on,
To venge me as I may and to put forth
My rightful hand in a well-hallow'd cause.
So get you hence in peace; and tell the Dauphin
His jest will savour but of shallow wit,
When thousands weep more than did laugh at it.
Convey them with safe conduct. Fare you well.
                         [*Exeunt* AMBASSADORS.
  Exe. This was a merry message.
  K. Hen. We hope to make the sender blush
    at it.
Therefore, my lord, omit no happy hour   300
That may give furtherance to our expedition;
For we have now no thought in us but France,
Save those to God, that run before our business.
Therefore let our proportions for these wars
Be soon collected and all things thought upon
That may with reasonable swiftness add
More feathers to our wings; for, God before,
We'll chide this Dauphin at his father's door.
Therefore let every man now task his thought,
That this fair action may on foot be brought. *310*
                         [*Exeunt. Flourish.*

ACT II
PROLOGUE

Flourish. Enter CHORUS.

  Chor. Now all the youth of England are on fire,
And silken dalliance in the wardrobe lies:
Now thrive the armourers, and honour's thought
Reigns solely in the breast of every man:
They sell the pasture now to buy the horse,
Following the mirror of all Christian kings
With winged heels, as English Mercuries.
For now sits Expectation in the air,
And hides a sword from hilts unto the point
With crowns imperial, crowns, and coronets, *10*
Promised to Harry and his followers.
The French, advised by good intelligence
Of this most dreadful preparation,
Shake in their fear and with pale policy
Seek to divert the English purposes.
O England! model to thy inward greatness,
Like little body with a mighty heart,
What mightst thou do, that honour would thee
    do,

Were all thy children kind and natural!
But see thy fault! France hath in thee found out
A nest of hollow bosoms, which he fills   20
With treacherous crowns; and three corrupted
    men,
One, Richard Earl of Cambridge, and the second,
Henry Lord Scroop of Masham, and the third,
Sir Thomas Grey, knight, of Northumberland,
Have, for the gilt of France—O guilt indeed!—
Confirm'd conspiracy with fearful France;
And by their hands this grace of kings must die,
If hell and treason hold their promises,
Ere he take ship for France, and in Southampton,
Linger your patience on; and we'll digest   31
The abuse of distance; force a play:
The sum is paid; the traitors are agreed;
The King is set from London; and the scene
Is now transported, gentles, to Southampton;
There is the playhouse now, there must you sit:
And thence to France shall we convey you safe,
And bring you back, charming the narrow seas
To give you gentle pass; for, if we may,
We'll not offend one stomach with our play.   40
But, till the King come forth, and not till then,
Unto Southampton do we shift our scene.   [*Exit.*

SCENE I. *London: a street*

Enter CORPORAL NYM *and* LIEUTENANT BARDOLPH.

  Bard. Well met, Corporal Nym.
  Nym. Good morrow, Lieutenant Bardolph.
  Bard. What, are Ancient Pistol and you friends
yet?
  Nym. For my part, I care not: I say little; but
when time shall serve, there shall be smiles; but
that shall be as it may. I dare not fight; but I will
wink and hold out mine iron: it is a simple one;
but what though? it will toast cheese, and it will
endure cold as another man's sword will: and
there's an end.   *11*
  Bard. I will bestow a breakfast to make you
friends; and we'll be all three sworn brothers to
France: let it be so, good Corporal Nym.
  Nym. Faith, I will live so long as I may, that's
the certain of it; and when I cannot live any
longer, I will do as I may: that is my rest, that
is the rendezvous of it.
  Bard. It is certain, corporal, that he is married
to Nell Quickly: and certainly she did you
wrong; for you were troth-plight to her.   *21*
  Nym. I cannot tell: things must be as they may:
men may sleep, and they may have their throats
about them at that time; and some say knives
have edges. It must be as it may: though
patience be a tired mare, yet she will plod. There
must be conclusions. Well, I cannot tell.

Enter PISTOL *and* MISTRESS QUICKLY, *the hostess.*

Bard. Here comes Ancient Pistol and his wife:
good corporal, be patient here. How now, mine
host Pistol!   30

Pist. Base tike, call'st thou me host?
Now, by this hand, I swear, I scorn the term;
Nor shall my Nell keep lodgers.

Quick. No, by my troth, not long, for we cannot lodge and board a dozen or fourteen gentlewomen that live honestly by the prick of their
needles, but it will be thought we keep a bawdy
house straight. [NYM *and* PISTOL *draw.*] O well a
day, Lady, if he be not drawn now! we shall see
wilful adultery and murder committed.   40

Bard. Good lieutenant! good corporal! offer
nothing here.

Nym. Pish!

Pist. Pish for thee, Iceland dog! thou prick-ear'd
cur of Iceland!

Quick. Good Corporal Nym, show thy valour,
and put up your sword.

Nym. Will you shog off? I would have you
solus.

Pist. "Solus," egregious dog? O viper vile!
The "solus" in thy most mervailous face;   50
The "solus" in thy teeth, and in thy throat,
And in thy hateful lungs, yea, in thy maw, perdy,
And, which is worse, within thy nasty mouth!
I do retort the "solus" in thy bowels;
For I can take, and Pistol's cock is up,
And flashing fire will follow.

Nym. I am not Barbason; you cannot conjure
me. I have an humour to knock you indifferently
well. If you grow foul with me, Pistol, I will
scour you with my rapier, as I may, in fair terms:
if you would walk off, I would prick your guts a
little, in good terms, as I may: and that's the
humour of it.

Pist. O braggart vile and damned furious wight!
The grave doth gape, and doting death is near;
Therefore exhale.

Bard. Hear me, hear me what I say: he that
strikes the first stroke, I'll run him up to the hilts,
as I am a soldier. [*Draws.*]

Pist. An oath of mickle might; and fury shall
abate.   70
Give me thy fist, thy fore-foot to me give:
Thy spirits are most tall.

Nym. I will cut thy thoat, one time or other, in
fair terms: that is the humour of it.

Pist. "Couple a gorge!"
That is the word. I thee defy again.
O hound of Crete, think'st thou my spouse to get?
No; to the spital go,
And from the powdering-tub of infamy

Fetch forth the lazar kite of Cressid's kind,   80
Doll Tearsheet she by name, and her espouse:
I have, and I will hold, the quondam Quickly
For the only she; and—*pauca*, there's enough.
Go to.

Enter the BOY.

Boy. Mine host Pistol, you must come to my
master, and you, hostess: he is very sick, and
would to bed. Good Bardolph, put thy face
between his sheets, and do the office of a warm-
ing-pan. Faith, he's very ill.

Bard. Away, you rogue!   90

Quick. By my troth, he'll yield the crow a
pudding one of these days. The King has killed
his heart. Good husband, come home presently.
[*Exeunt* MISTRESS QUICKLY *and* BOY.

Bard. Come, shall I make you two friends? We
must to France together: why the devil should
we keep knives to cut one another's throats?

Pist. Let floods o'erswell, and fiends for food
howl on!

Nym. You'll pay me the eight shillings I won of
you at betting?

Pist. Base is the slave that pays.   100

Nym. That now I will have: that's the humour
of it.

Pist. As manhood shall compound: push home.
They draw.

Bard. By this sword, he that makes the first
thrust, I'll kill him; by this sword, I will.

Pist. Sword is an oath, and oaths must have
their course.

Bard. Corporal Nym, an thou wilt be friends, be
friends: an thou wilt not, why, then, be enemies
with me too. Prithee, put up.

Nym. I shall have my eight shillings I won of
you at betting?   111

Pist. A noble shalt thou have, and present pay;
And liquor likewise will I give to thee,
And friendship shall combine, and brotherhood:
I'll live by Nym, and Nym shall live by me;
Is not this just? for I shall sutler be
Unto the camp, and profits will accrue.
Give me thy hand.

Nym. I shall have my noble?

Pist. In cash most justly paid.   120

Nym. Well, then, that's the humour of't.

Re-enter MISTRESS QUICKLY.

Quick. As ever you came of women, come in
quickly to Sir John. Ah, poor heart! he is so
shaked of a burning quotidian tertian, that it is
most lamentable to behold. Sweet men, come to
him.

Nym. The King hath run bad humours on the

knight; that's the even of it.

Pist. Nym, thou hast spoke the right;
His heart is fracted and corroborate.   *130*

Nym. The King is a good King: but it must be
as it may; he passes some humours and careers.

Pist. Let us condole the knight; for, lambkins,
we will live.

SCENE II. *Southampton: a council-chamber*

Enter EXETER, BEDFORD, *and* WESTMORELAND.

Bed. 'Fore God, his Grace is bold, to trust these
traitors.

Exe. They shall be apprehended by and by.

West. How smooth and even they do bear
themselves!
As if allegiance in their bosoms sat,
Crowned with faith and constant loyalty.

Bed. The King hath note of all that they intend,
By interception which they dream not of.

Exe. Nay, but the man that was his bedfellow,
Whom he hath dull'd and cloy'd with gracious
favours,
That he should, for a foreign purse, so sell   *10*
His sovereign's life to death and treachery.

Trumpets sound. Enter KING HENRY, SCROOP,
CAMBRIDGE, GREY, *and Attendants.*

K. Hen. Now sits the wind fair, and we will
aboard.
My Lord of Cambridge, and my kind Lord of
Masham,
And you, my gentle knight, give me your
thoughts:
Think you not that the powers we bear with us
Will cut their passage through the force of
France,
Doing the execution and the act
For which we have in head assembled them?

Scroop. No doubt, my liege, if each man do his
best.

K. Hen. I doubt not that: since we are well
persuaded   *20*
We carry not a heart with us from hence
That grows not in a fair consent with ours,
Nor leave not one behind that doth not wish
Success and conquest to attend on us.

Cam. Never was monarch better fear'd and
loved
Than is your Majesty: there's not, I think, a
subject
That sits in heart-grief and uneasiness
Under the sweet shade of your government.

Grey. True: those that were your father's
enemies
Have steep'd their galls in honey and do serve
you   *30*

With hearts create of duty and of zeal.

K. Hen. We therefore have great cause of
thankfulness;
And shall forget the office of our hand
Sooner than quittance of desert and merit
According to the weight and worthiness.

Scroop. So service shall with steeled sinews toil,
And labour shall refresh itself with hope,
To do your Grace incessant services.

K. Hen. We judge no less. Uncle of Exeter,
Enlarge the man committed yesterday,   *40*
That rail'd against our person: we consider
It was excess of wine that set him on;
And on his more advice we pardon him.

Scroop. That's mercy, but too much security:
Let him be punish'd, sovereign, lest example
Breed, by his sufferance, more of such a kind.

K. Hen. O, let us yet be merciful.

Cam. So may your Highness, and yet punish too.

Grey. Sir,
You show great mercy, if you give him life   *50*
After the taste of much correction.

K. Hen. Alas, your too much love and care of
me
Are heavy orisons 'gainst this poor wretch!
If little faults, proceeding on distemper,
Shall not be wink'd at, how shall we stretch our
eye
When capital crimes, chew'd, swallow'd, and
digested,
Appear before us? We'll yet enlarge that man,
Though Cambridge, Scroop, and Grey, in their
dear care
And tender preservation of our person,
Would have him punish'd. And now to our
French causes: *60*
Who are the late commissioners?

Cam. I one, my lord:
Your Highness bade me ask for it to-day.

Scroop. So did you me, my liege.

Grey. And I, my royal sovereign.

K. Hen. Then, Richard Earl of Cambridge,
there is yours;
There yours, Lord Scroop of Masham; and, sir
knight,
Grey of Northumberland, this same is yours:
Read them; and know I know your worthiness.
My Lord of Westmoreland, and uncle Exeter,   *70*
We will aboard to night. Why, how now, gen-
tlemen!
What see you in those papers that you lose
So much complexion? Look ye, how they change!
Their cheeks are paper. Why, what read you
there,
That hath so cowarded and chased your blood
Out of appearance?

Cam.   I do confess my fault;
And do submit me to your Highness' mercy.
Grey. }
Scroop. } To which we all appeal.
K. Hen. The mercy that was quick in us but
          late,
By your own counsel is suppress'd and kill'd: *80*
You must not dare, for shame, to talk of mercy;
For your own reasons turn into your bosoms,
As dogs upon their masters, worrying you.
See you, my princes and my noble peers,
These English monsters! My Lord of Cambridge
          here,
You know how apt our love was to accord
To furnish him with all appertinents
Belonging to his honour; and this man
Hath, for a few light crowns, lightly conspired,
And sworn unto the practices of France,   *90*
To kill us here in Hampton: to the which
This knight, no less for bounty bound to us
Than Cambridge is, hath likewise sworn. But, O,
What shall I say to thee, Lord Scroop? thou
          cruel,
Ingrateful, savage, and inhuman creature!
Thou that didst bear the key of all my counsels,
That knew'st the very bottom of my soul,
That almost mightst have coin'd me into gold,
Wouldst thou have practised on me for thy use!
May it be possible that foreign hire   *100*
Could out of thee extract one spark of evil
That might annoy my finger? 'Tis so strange,
That, though the truth of it stands off as gross
As black and white, my eye will scarcely see it.
Treason and murder ever kept together,
As two yoke-devils sworn to either's purpose,
Working so grossly in a natural cause
That admiration did not hoop at them:
But thou, 'gainst all proportion, didst bring in
Wonder to wait on treason and on murder: *110*
And whatsoever cunning fiend it was
That wrought upon thee so preposterously
Hath got the voice in hell for excellence:
All other devils that suggest by treasons
Do botch and bungle up damnation
With patches, colours, and with forms being
          fetch'd
From glistering semblances of piety;
But he that temper'd thee bade thee stand up,
Gave thee no instance why thou shouldst do
          treason,
Unless to dub thee with the name of traitor.   *120*
If that same demon that hath gull'd thee thus
Should with his lion gait walk the whole world,
He might return to vasty Tartar back,
And tell the legions, "I can never win
A soul so easy as that Englishman's."

O, how hast thou with jealousy infected
The sweetness of affiance! Show men dutiful?
Why, so didst thou: seem they grave and
          learned?
Why, so didst thou: come they of noble family?
Why, so didst thou: seem they religious?   *130*
Why, so didst thou: or are they spare in diet,
Free from gross passion or of mirth or anger,
Constant in spirit, not swerving with the blood,
Garnish'd and deck'd in modest complement,
Not working with the eye without the ear,
And but in purged judgement trusting neither?
Such and so finely bolted didst thou seem:
And thus thy fall hath left a kind of blot,
To mark the full-fraught man and best indued
With some suspicion. I will weep for thee;   *140*
For this revolt of thine, methinks, is like
Another fall of man. Their faults are open:
Arrest them to the answer of the law;
And God acquit them of their practices!
Exe. I arrest thee of high treason, by the name
of Richard Earl of Cambridge.
I arrest thee of high treason, by the name of
Henry Lord Scroop of Masham.
I arrest thee of high treason, by the name of
Thomas Grey, knight, of Northumberland.   *150*
Scroop. Our purposes God justly hath dis-
          cover'd;
And I repent my fault more than my death;
Which I beseech your Highness to forgive,
Although my body pay the price of it.
Cam. For me, the gold of France did not seduce;
Although I did admit it as a motive
The sooner to effect what I intended:
But God be thanked for prevention;
Which I in sufferance heartily will rejoice,
Beseeching God and you to pardon me.   *160*
Grey. Never did faithful subject more rejoice
At the discovery of most dangerous treason
Than I do at this hour joy o'er myself,
Prevented from a damned enterprise:
My fault, but not my body, pardon, sovereign.
K. Hen. God quit you in his mercy! Hear your
          sentence.
You have conspired against our royal person,
Join'd with an enemy proclaim'd, and from his
          coffers
Received the golden earnest of our death;
Wherein you would have sold your King to
          slaughter,   *170*
His princes and his peers to servitude,
His subjects to oppression and contempt,
And his whole kingdom into desolation.
Touching our person seek we no revenge;
But we our kingdom's safety must so tender,
Whose ruin you have sought, that to her laws

We do deliver you. Get you therefore hence,
Poor miserable wretches, to your death:
The taste whereof, God of his mercy give
You patience to endure, and true repentance   *180*
Of all your dear offences! Bear them hence.

[*Exeunt* CAMBRIDGE, SCROOP *and* GREY,
guarded.

Now, lords, for France; the enterprise whereof
Shall be to you, as us, like glorious.
We doubt not of a fair and lucky war,
Since God so graciously hath brought to light
This dangerous treason lurking in our way
To hinder our beginnings. We doubt not now
But every rub is smoothed on our way.
Then forth, dear countrymen: let us deliver
Our puissance into the hand of God,   *190*
Putting it straight in expedition.
Cheerly to sea; the signs of war advance:
No king of England, if not king of France.

[*Exeunt.*

SCENE III. *London: before a tavern*

Enter PISTOL, MISTRESS QUICKLY, NYM, BARDOLPH,
and BOY.

Quick. Prithee, honey-sweet husband, let me
bring thee to Staines.

Pist. No; for my manly heart doth yearn.
Bardolph, be blithe: Nym, rouse thy vaunting
veins:
Boy, bristle thy courage up; for Falstaff he is
dead,
And we must yearn therefore.

Bard. Would I were with him, wheresome'er he
is, either in heaven or in hell!

Quick. Nay, sure, he's not in hell: he's in
Arthur's bosom, if ever man went to Arthur's
bosom. A' made a finer end and went away an
it had been any christom child; a' parted even
just between twelve and one, even at the turning
o' the tide: for after I saw him fumble with the
sheets and play with flowers and smile upon his
fingers' ends, I knew there was but one way; for
his nose was as sharp as a pen, and a' babbled of
green fields. "How now, Sir John!" quoth I:
"what, man! be o'good cheer." So a' cried out
"God, God, God!" three or four times. Now I,
to comfort him, bid him a' should not think of
God; I hoped there was no need to trouble himself with any such thoughts yet. So a' bade me
lay more clothes on his feet: I put my hand into
the bed and felt them, and they were as cold as
any stone; then I felt to his knees, an they were
as cold as any stone, and so upward and upward,
an all was as cold as any stone.

Nym. They say he cried out of sack.

Quick. Ay, that a' did.   *30*

Bard. And of women.

Quick. Nay, that a' did not.

Boy. Yes, that a' did; and said they were devils
incarnate.

Quick. A' could never abide carnation; 'twas a
colour he never liked.

Boy. A' said once, the devil would have him
about women.

Quick. A' did in some sort, indeed, handle
women; but then he was rheumatic, and talked
of the whore of Babylon.   *41*

Boy. Do you not remember, a' saw a flea stick
upon Bardolph's nose, and a' said it was a black
soul burning in hell-fire?

Bard. Well, the fuel is gone that maintained that
fire: that's all the riches I got in his service.

Nym. Shall we shog? the King will be gone
from Southampton.

Pist. Come, let's away. My love, give me
thy lips.
Look to my chattels and my movables: *50*
Let senses rule; the word is "Pitch and Pay":
Trust none;
For oaths are straws, men's faiths are wafer-
cakes,
And hold-fast is the only dog, my duck:
Therefore, *Caveto* be thy counsellor.
Go, clear thy crystals. Yoke-fellows in arms,
Let us to France; like horse-leeches, my boys,
To suck, to suck, the very blood to suck!

Boy. And that's but unwholesome food, they
say.   *60*

Pist. Touch her soft mouth, and march.

Bard. Farewell, hostess. [*Kissing her.*]

Nym. I cannot kiss, that is the humour of it;
but, adieu.

Pist. Let housewifery appear: keep close, I thee
command.

Quick. Farewell; adieu.   [*Exeunt.*

SCENE IV. *France: the King's palace*

Flourish. Enter the FRENCH KING, *the* DAUPHIN, *the*
DUKES OF BERRI *and* BRETAGNE, *the* CONSTABLE,
and others.

Fr. King. Thus comes the English with full
power upon us;
And more than carefully it us concerns
To answer royally in our defences.
Therefore the Dukes of Berri and of Bretagne,
Of Brabant and of Orleans, shall make forth,
And you, Prince Dauphin, with all swift dispatch,
To line and new repair our towns of war
With men of courage and with means defendant;
For England his approaches makes as fierce
As waters to the sucking of a gulf.   *10*
It fits us then to be as provident

As fear may teach us out of late examples
Left by the fatal and neglected English
Upon our fields.
  Dau.   My most redoubted father,
It is most meet we arm us 'gainst the foe;
For peace itself should not so dull a kingdom,
Though war nor no known quarrel were in question,
But that defences, musters, preparations,
Should be maintain'd, assembled, and collected,
As were a war in expectation.   20
Therefore, I say 'tis meet we all go forth
To view the sick and feeble parts of France:
And let us do it with no show of fear;
No, with no more than if we heard that England
Were busied with a Whitsun morris-dance:
For, my good liege, she is so idly king'd,
Her sceptre so fantastically borne
By a vain, giddy, shallow, humorous youth,
That fear attends her not.
  Con.   O peace, Prince Dauphin!
You are too much mistaken in this king: 30
Question your Grace the late ambassadors,
With what great state he heard their embassy,
How well supplied with noble counsellors,
How modest in exception, and withal
How terrible in constant resolution,
And you shall find his vanities forespent
Were but the outside of the Roman Brutus,
Covering discretion with a coat of folly,
As gardeners do with ordure hide those roots
That shall first spring and be most delicate.   40
  Dau. Well, 'tis not so, my Lord High Constable;
But though we think it so, it is no matter:
In cases of defence 'tis best to weigh
The enemy more mighty than he seems:
So the proportions of defence are fill'd;
Which of a weak and niggardly projection
Doth, like a miser, spoil his coat with scanting
A little cloth.
  Fr. King. Think we King Harry strong;
And, Princes, look you strongly arm to meet him.
The kindred of him hath been flesh'd upon us;   50
And he is bred out of that bloody strain
That haunted us in our familiar paths:
Witness our too much memorable shame
When Cressy battle fatally was struck,
And all our princes captived by the hand
Of that black name, Edward, Black Prince of
    Wales;
Whiles that his mountain sire, on mountain
    standing,
Up in the air, crown'd with the golden sun,
Saw his heroical seed, and smiled to see him,
Mangle the work of nature and deface   60

The patterns that by God and by French fathers
Had twenty years been made. This is a stem
Of that victorious stock; and let us fear
The native mightiness and fate of him.

Enter a MESSENGER.

  Mess. Ambassadors from Harry King of England
Do crave admittance to your Majesty.
  Fr. King. We'll give them present audience.
    Go, and bring them.
              [*Exeunt* MESSENGER *and certain Lords.*
You see this chase is hotly follow'd, friends.
  Dau. Turn head, and stop pursuit; for coward
    dogs
Most spend their mouths when what they seem
    to threaten   70
Runs far before them. Good my sovereign,
Take up the English short, and let them know
Of what a monarchy you are the head:
Self-love, my liege, is not so vile a sin
As self-neglecting.

Re-enter Lords, with EXETER *and train.*

  Fr. King.   From our brother England?
  Exe. From him; and thus he greets your
    Majesty.
He wills you, in the name of God Almighty,
That you divest yourself, and lay apart
The borrow'd glories that by gift of heaven,
By law of nature and of nations, 'long   80
To him and to his heirs; namely, the crown
And all wide-stretched honours that pertain
By custom and the ordinance of times
Unto the crown of France. That you may know
'Tis no sinister nor no awkward claim,
Pick'd from the worm-holes of long-vanish'd
    days,
Nor from the dust of old oblivion raked,
He sends you this most memorable line,
In every branch truly demonstrative;
Willing you overlook this pedigree: 90
And when you find him evenly derived
From his most famed of famous ancestors,
Edward the Third, he bids you then resign
Your crown and kingdom, indirectly held
From him the native and true challenger.
  Fr. King. Or else what follows?
  Exe. Bloody constraint; for if you hide the
    crown
Even in your hearts, there will he rake for it:
Therefore in fierce tempest is he coming,
In thunder and in earthquake, like a Jove,   100
That, if requiring fail, he will compel;
And bids you, in the bowels of the Lord,
Deliver up the crown, and to take mercy

On the poor souls for whom this hungry war
Opens his vasty jaws; and on your head
Turning the widows' tears, the orphans' cries,
The dead men's blood, the pining maidens'
groans,
For husbands, fathers, and betrothed lovers,
That shall be swallow'd in this controversy.
This is his claim, his threatening, and my mes-
sage; 110
Unless the Dauphin be in presence here,
To whom expressly I bring greeting too.

  Fr. King. For us, we will consider of this
further:
To-morrow shall you bear our full intent
Back to our brother England.

  Dau.   For the Dauphin,
I stand here for him: what to him from England?

  Exe. Scorn and defiance; slight regard, con-
tempt,
And anything that may not misbecome
The mighty sender, doth he prize you at.
Thus says my king; an if your father's high-
ness
Do not, in grant of all demands at large, 121
Sweeten the bitter mock you sent his Majesty,
He'll call you to so hot an answer of it
That caves and womby vaultages of France
Shall chide your trespass and return your mock
In second accent of his ordnance.

  Dau. Say, if my father render fair return,
It is against my will; for I desire
Nothing but odds with England: to that end,
As matching to his youth and vanity, 130
I did present him with the Paris balls.

  Exe. He'll make your Paris Louvre shake
for it,
Were it the mistress-court of mighty Europe:
And, be assured, you'll find a difference,
As we his subjects have in wonder found,
Between the promise of his greener days
And these he masters now: now he weighs
time
Even to the utmost grain: that you shall read
In your own losses, if he stay in France.

  Fr. King. To-morrow shall you know our
mind at full. 140

  Exe. Dispatch us with all speed, lest that our
king
Come here himself to question our delay;
For he is footed in this land already.

  Fr. King. You shall be soon dispatch'd with
fair conditions;
A night is but small breath and little pause
To answer matters of this consequence.
[*Flourish. Exeunt.*

ACT III

PROLOGUE

Enter CHORUS.

  Chor. Thus with imagined wing our swift scene
flies
In motion of no less celerity
Than that of thought. Suppose that you have seen
The well-appointed king at Hampton pier
Embark his royalty; and his brave fleet
With silken streamers the young Phœbus
fanning:
Play with your fancies, and in them behold
Upon the hempen tackle ship-boys climbing;
Hear the shrill whistle which doth order give
To sounds confused; behold the threaden sails,
Borne with the invisible and creeping wind, 11
Draw the huge bottoms through the furrow'd sea,
Breasting the lofty surge: O, do but think
You stand upon the rivage and behold
A city on the inconstant billows dancing;
For so appears this fleet majestical,
Holding due course to Harfleur. Follow, follow:
Grapple your minds to sternage of this navy,
And leave your England, as dead midnight still,
Guarded with grandsires, babies, and old women
Either past or not arrived to pith and puissance;
For who is he, whose chin is but enrich'd
With one appearing hair, that will not follow
These cull'd and choice-drawn cavaliers to
France?
Work, work your thoughts, and therein see a
siege;
Behold the ordnance on their carriages,
With fatal mouths gaping on girded Harfleur.
Suppose the ambassador from the French comes
back;
Tells Harry that the King doth offer him
Katharine his daughter, and with her, to dowry,
Some petty and unprofitable dukedoms. 31
The offer likes not: and the nimble gunner
With linstock now the devilish cannon touches,
    Alarum, and chambers go off.
And down goes all before them. Still be kind,
And eke out our performance with your mind.
[*Exit.*

SCENE I. *France: before Harfleur*

Alarum. Enter KING HENRY, EXETER, BEDFORD,
GLOUCESTER, *and Soldiers, with scaling-ladders.*

  K. Hen. Once more unto the breach, dear
friends, once more;
Or close the wall up with our English dead.
In peace there's nothing so becomes a man
As modest stillness and humility:

But when the blast of war blows in our ears,
Then imitate the action of the tiger;
Stiffen the sinews, summon up the blood,
Disguise fair nature with hard-favour'd rage;
Then lend the eye a terrible aspect;
Let it pry through the portage of the head   10
Like the brass cannon; let the brow o'erwhelm it
As fearfully as doth a galled rock
O'erhang and jutty his confounded base,
Swill'd with the wild and wasteful ocean.
Now set the teeth and stretch the nostril wide,
Hold hard the breath and bend up every spirit
To his full height. On, on, you noblest English,
Whose blood is fet from fathers of war-proof!
Fathers that, like so many Alexanders,   19
Have in these parts from morn till even fought
And sheathed their swords for lack of argument:
Dishonour not your mothers; now attest
That those whom you call'd fathers did beget you.
Be copy now to men of grosser blood,
And teach them how to war. And you, good
      yeoman,
Whose limbs were made in England, show us
      here
The mettle of your pasture; let us swear
That you are worth your breeding; which I
      doubt not;
For there is none of you so mean and base,
That hath not noble lustre in your eyes.   30
I see you stand like greyhounds in the slips,
Straining upon the start. The game's afoot:
Follow your spirit, and upon this charge
Cry "God for Harry, England, and Saint
      George!"
      [Exeunt. Alarum, and chambers go off.

SCENE II. The same

Enter NYM, BARDOLPH, PISTOL, and BOY.

Bard. On, on, on, on, on! to the breach, to the
breach!

Nym. Pray thee, corporal, stay: the knocks are
too hot; and, for mine own part, I have not a case
of lives: the humour of it is too hot, that is the
very plain-song of it.

Pist. The plain-song is most just; for humours
do abound:
"Knocks go and come; God's vassals drop and
      die;
      And sword and shield,
      In bloody field,   10
      Doth win immortal fame."

Boy. Would I were in an alehouse in London!
I would give all my fame for a pot of ale and
safety.

Pist. And I:
      "If wishes would prevail with me,

My purpose should not fail with me,
      But thither would I hie."

Boy. "As duly, but not as truly,
      As bird doth sing on bough."   20

Enter FLUELLEN.

Flu. Up to the breach, you dogs! avaunt, you
cullions! [Driving them forward.]

Pist. Be merciful, great Duke, to men of mould.
Abate thy rage, abate thy manly rage,
Abate thy rage, great Duke!
Good bawcock, bate thy rage; use lenity, sweet
      chuck!

Nym. These be good humours! your honour
wins bad humours.   [Exeunt all but BOY.

Boy. As young as I am, I have observed these
three swashers. I am boy to them all three: but
all they three, though they would serve me, could
not be man to me; for indeed three such antics
do not amount to a man. For Bardolph, he is
white-livered and red-faced; by the means whereof a' faces it out, but fights not. For Pistol, he
hath a killing tongue and a quiet sword; by the
means whereof a' breaks words, and keeps whole
weapons. For Nym, he hath heard that men of
few words are the best men; and therefore he
scorns to say his prayers, lest a' should be thought
a coward: but his few bad words are matched
with as few good deeds; for a' never broke any
man's head but his own, and that was against a
post when he was drunk. They will steal any
thing, and call it purchase. Bardolph stole a lute-
case, bore it twelve leagues, and sold it for three
half-pence. Nym and Bardolph are sworn brothers in filching, and in Calais they stole a fire-
shovel: I knew by that piece of service the men
would carry coals. They would have me as
familiar with men's pockets as their gloves or
their handkerchers: which makes much against
my manhood, if I should take from another's
pocket to put into mine; for it is plain pocketing
up of wrongs. I must leave them, and seek some
better service: their villainy goes against my weak
stomach, and therefore I must cast it up.   [Exit.

Re-enter FLUELLEN, GOWER following.

Gow. Captain Fluellen, you must come presently to the mines; the Duke of Gloucester
would speak with you.   60

Flu. To the mines! tell you the Duke, it is not
so good to come to the mines; for, look you, the
mines is not according to the disciplines of the
war: the concavities of it is not sufficient; for,
look you, th' athversary, you may discuss unto
the Duke, look you, is digt himself four yard
under the countermines: by Cheshu, I think a'

will plow up all, if there is not better directions.

Gow. The Duke of Gloucester, to whom the order of the siege is given, is altogether directed by an Irishman, a very valiant gentleman, i' faith.

Flu. It is Captain Macmorris, is it not?

Gow. I think it be.

Flu. By Cheshu, he is an ass, as in the world: I will verify as much in his beard: he has no more directions in the true disciplines of the wars, look you, of the Roman disciplines, than is a puppy-dog.

Enter MACMORRIS *and* CAPTAIN JAMY.

Gow. Here a' comes; and the Scots captain, Captain Jamy, with him.   80

Flu. Captain Jamy is a marvellous falorous gentleman, that is certain; and of great expedition and knowledge in th' aunchient wars, upon my particular knowledge of his directions: by Cheshu, he will maintain his argument as well as any military man in the world, in the disciplines of the pristine wars of the Romans.

Jamy. I say gud-day, Captain Fluellen.

Flu. God-den to your worship, good Captain James.   90

Gow. How now, Captain Macmorris! have you quit the mines? have the pioners given o'er?

Mac. By Chrish, la! tish ill done: the work ish give over, the trompet sound the retreat. By my hand, I swear, and my father's soul, the work ish ill done; it ish give over: I would have blowed up the town, so Chrish save me, la! in an hour: O, tish ill done, tish ill done; by my hand, tish ill done!   99

Flu. Captain Macmorris, I beseech you now, will you voutsafe me, look you, a few disputations with you, as partly touching or concerning the disciplines of the war, the Roman wars, in the way of argument, look you, and friendly communication; partly to satisfy my opinion, and partly for the satisfaction, look you, of my mind, as touching the direction of the military discipline; that is the point.

Jamy. It sall be vary gud, gud feith, gud captains bath: and I sall quit you with gud leve, as I may pick occasion; that sall I, marry.   111

Mac. It is no time to discourse, so Chrish save me: the day is hot, and the weather, and the wars, and the King, and the Dukes: it is no time to discourse. The town is beseeched, and the trumpet call us to the breach; and we talk, and, be Chrish, do nothing: 'tis shame for us all: so God sa' me, 'tis shame to stand still; it is shame, by my hand: and there is throats to be cut, and works to be done; and there ish nothing done, so Chrish sa' me, la!   121

Jamy. By the mess, ere theise eyes of mine take themselves to slomber, ay'll de gud service, or ay'll lig i' the grund for it; ay, or go to death; and ay'll pay 't as valorously as I may, that sall I suerly do, that is the breff and the long. Marry, I wad full fain hear some question 'tween you tway.

Flu. Captain Macmorris, I think, look you, under your correction, there is not many of your nation—   131

Mac. Of my nation! What ish my nation? Ish a villain, and a bastard, and a knave, and a rascal— What ish my nation? Who talks of my nation?

Flu. Look you, if you take the matter otherwise than is meant, Captain Macmorris, peradventure I shall think you do not use me with that affability as in discretion you ought to use me, look you; being as good a man as yourself, both in the disciplines of war, and in the derivation of my birth, and in other particularities.

Mac. I do not know you so good a man as myself: so Chrish save me, I will cut off your head.

Gow. Gentlemen both, you will mistake each other.

Jamy. A! that's a foul fault.

A parley sounded.

Gow. The town sounds a parley.   149

Flu. Captain Macmorris, when there is more better opportunity to be required, look you, I will be so bold as to tell you I know the disciplines of war; and there is an end.   [*Exeunt.*

SCENE III. *The same: before the gates*

The GOVERNOR *and some Citizens on the walls; the*
English forces below. Enter KING HENRY *and his*
train.

K. Hen. How yet resolves the governor of the
        town?
This is the latest parle we will admit:
Therefore to our best mercy give yourselves;
Or like to men proud of destruction
Defy us to our worst: for, as I am a soldier,
A name that in my thoughts becomes me best,
If I begin the battery once again,
I will not leave the half-achieved Harfleur
Till in her ashes she lie buried.
The gates of mercy shall be all shut up.   10
And the flesh'd soldier, rough and hard of heart,
In liberty of bloody hand shall range
With conscience wide as hell, mowing like grass
Your fresh-fair virgins and your flowering
        infants.
What is it then to me, if impious war,
Array'd in flames like to the prince of fiends,
Do, with his smirch'd complexion, all fell feats
Enlink'd to waste and desolation?

What is't to me, when you yourselves are
     cause,
If your pure maidens fall into the hand   20
Of hot and forcing violation?
What rein can hold licentious wickedness
When down the hill he holds his fierce career?
We may as bootless spend our vain command
Upon the enraged soldiers in their spoil
As send precepts to the leviathan
To come ashore. Therefore, you men of Harfleur,
Take pity of your town and of your people,
Whiles yet my soldiers are in my command;
Whiles yet the cool and temperate wind of
     grace
O'erblows the filthy and contagious clouds   31
Of heady murder, spoil, and villainy.
If not, why, in a moment look to see
The blind and bloody soldier with foul hand
Defile the locks of your shrill-shrieking
     daughters;
Your fathers taken by the silver beards,
And their most reverend heads dash'd to the
     walls,
Your naked infants spitted upon pikes,
Whiles the mad mothers with their howls con-
     fused
Do break the clouds, as did the wives of Jewry
At Herod's bloody-hunting slaughtermen.   41
What say you? will you yield and this avoid,
Or, guilty in defence, be thus destroy'd?

  Gov. Our expectation hath this day an end:
The Dauphin, whom of succours we entreated,
Returns us that his powers are yet not ready
To raise so great a siege. Therefore, great
     King,
We yield our town and lives to thy soft mercy.
Enter our gates; dispose of us and ours;
For we no longer are defensible.   50

  K. Hen. Open your gates. Come, uncle Exeter,
Go you and enter Harfleur; there remain,
And fortify it strongly 'gainst the French:
Use mercy to them all. For us, dear uncle,
The winter coming on and sickness growing
Upon our soldiers, we will retire to Calais.
To-night in Harfleur will we be your guest;
To-morrow for the march are we addrest.

          [*Flourish. The* KING *and his train enter*
                                        the town.

     SCENE IV. *The French King's palace*
          Enter KATHARINE *and* ALICE.

  Kath. Alice, *tu as été en Angleterre, et tu parles*
bien le langage.
  Alice. Un peu, madame.
  Kath. Je te prie, m'enseignez; il faut que j'apprenne
à parler. Comment appelez-vous la main en Anglois?

  Alice. La main? elle est appelée de hand.
  Kath. De hand. *Et les doigts?*
  Alice. Les doigts? ma foi, j'oublie les doigts; mais
je me souviendrai. Les doigts? je pense qu'ils sont
appelés de fingres; *oui, de* fingres.   11
  Kath. La main, de hand; *les doigts, de* fingres.
Je pense que je suis le bon écolier; j'ai gagné deux
mots d'Anglois vîtement. Comment appelez-vous les
ongles?
  Alice. Les ongles? nous les appelons de nails.
  Kath. De nails. *Écoutez; dites-moi, si je parle*
bien: de hand, *de* fingres, *et de* nails.
  Alice. C'est bien dit, madame; il est fort bon
Anglois.   20
  Kath. Dites-moi l'Anglois pour le bras.
  Alice. De arm, *madame.*
  Kath. Et le coude?
  Alice. De elbow.
  Kath. De elbow. *Je m'en fais la répétition de tous*
les mots que vous m'avez appris dès à présent.
  Alice. Il est trop difficile, madame, comme je pense.
  Kath. Excusez-moi, Alice; écoutez: de hand, *de*
fingres, *de* nails, *de* arma, *de* bilbow.   31
  Alice. De elbow, *madame.*
  Kath. O Seigneur Dieu, je m'en oublie! de elbow.
Comment appelez-vous le col?
  Alice. De nick, *madame.*
  Kath. De nick. *Et le menton?*
  Alice. De chin.
  Kath. De sin. *Le col, de* nick; *le menton, de* sin.39
  Alice. Oui. Sauf votre honneur, en vérité, vous
prononcez les mots aussi droit que les natifs d'Angle-
terre.
  Kath. Je ne doute point d'apprendre, par la grace de
Dieu, et en peu de temps.
  Alice. N'avez vous pas déjà oublié ce que je vous ai
enseigné?
  Kath. Non, je reciterai à vous promptement: de
hand, *de* fingres, *de* mails—
  Alice. De nails, *madame.*
  Kath. De nails, *de* arm, *de* ilbow.   50
  Alice. Sauf votre honneur, de elbow.
  Kath. Ainsi dis-je; de elbow, *de* nick, *et de* sin.
Comment appelez-vous le pied et la robe?
  Alice. De foot, *madame; et de* coun.
  Kath. De foot *et de* coun! *O Seigneur Dieu! ce sont*
mots de son mauvais, corruptible, gros, et impudique,
et non pour les dames d'honneur d'user: je ne voudrais
prononcer ces mots devant les seigneurs de France
pour tout le monde. Foh! le foot *et le* coun! *Néan-*
moins, je réciterai une autre fois ma leçon en-
semble: de hand, *de* fingres, *de* nails, *de* arm, *de*
elbow, *de* nick, *de* sin, *de* foot, *de* coun.
  Alice. Excellent, madame!
  Kath. C'est assez pour une fois: allons-nous à dîner.
                                        [*Exeunt.*

SCENE V. *The same*

Enter the KING OF FRANCE, *the* DAUPHIN, *the* DUKE
OF BOURBON, *the* CONSTABLE OF FRANCE, *and
others.*

Fr. King. 'Tis certain he hath pass'd the river
 Somme.

Con. And if he be not fought withal, my lord,
Let us not live in France; let us quit all
And give our vineyards to a barbarous people.

Dau. O Dieu vivant! shall a few sprays of us,
The emptying of our father's luxury,
Our scions put in wild and savage stock,
Spirit up so suddenly into the clouds
And overlook their grafters?

Bour. Normans, but bastard Normans, Norman
 bastards!   *10*
Mort de ma vie! if they march along
Unfought withal, but I will sell my dukedom,
To buy a slobbery and a dirty farm
In that nook-shotten isle of Albion.

Con. Dieu de batailles! where have they this
 mettle?
Is not their climate foggy, raw, and dull,
On whom, as in despite, the sun looks pale,
Killing their fruit with frowns? Can sodden
 water,
A drench for sur-rein'd jades, their barley-broth,
Decoct their cold blood to such valiant heat? *20*
And shall our quick blood, spirited with wine,
Seem frosty? O, for honour of our land,
Let us not hang like roping icicles
Upon our houses' thatch, whiles a more frosty
 people
Sweat drops of gallant youth in our rich fields!
Poor we may call them in their native lords.

Dau. By faith and honour,
Our madams mock at us, and plainly say
Our mettle is bred out and they will give
Their bodies to the lust of English youth *30*
To new-store France with bastard warriors.

Bour. They bid us to the English dancing-
 schools,
And teach lavoltas high and swift corantos;
Saying our grace is only in our heels,
And that we are most lofty runaways.

Fr. King. Where is Montjoy the herald?
 speed him hence:
Let him greet England with our sharp defiance.
Up, princes! and, with spirit of honour edged
More sharper than your swords, hie to the field:
Charles Delabreth, High Constable of France;
You Dukes of Orleans, Bourbon, and of Berri, *41*
Alençon, Brabant, Bar, and Burgundy;
Jaques, Chatillon, Rambures, Vaudemont,
Beaumont, Grandpré, Roussi, and Fauconberg,

Foix, Lestrale, Bouciqualt, and Charolois;
High dukes, great princes, barons, lords, and
 knights,
For your great seats now quit you of great
 shames.
Bar Harry England, that sweeps through our land
With pennons painted in the blood of Harfleur:
Rush on his host, as doth the melted snow *50*
Upon the valleys, whose low vassal seat
The Alps doth spit and void his rheum upon:
Go down upon him, you have power enough,
And in a captive chariot into Rouen
Bring him our prisoner.

Con.   This becomes the great.
Sorry am I his numbers are so few,
His soldiers sick and famish'd in their march,
For I am sure, when he shall see our army,
He'll drop his heart into the sink of fear
And for achievement offer us his ransom. *60*

Fr. King. Therefore, Lord Constable, haste on
 Montjoy,
And let him say to England that we send
To know what willing ransom he will give.
Prince Dauphin, you shall stay with us in Rouen.

Dau. Not so, I do beseech your Majesty.

Fr. King. Be patient, for you shall remain with
 us.
Now forth, Lord Constable and princes all,
And quickly bring us word of England's fall.
             [Exeunt.

SCENE VI. *The English camp in Picardy*

Enter GOWER *and* FLUELLEN, *meeting.*

Gow. How now, Captain Fluellen! come you
from the bridge?

Flu. I assure you, there is very excellent services committed at the bridge.

Gow. Is the Duke of Exeter safe?

Flu. The Duke of Exeter is as magnanimous as
Agamemnon; and a man that I love and honour
with my soul, and my heart, and my duty, and
my life, and my living, and my uttermost power:
he is not—God be praised and blessed!—any
hurt in the world; but keeps the bridge most
valiantly, with excellent discipline. There is an
aunchient lieutenant there at the pridge, I think
in my very conscience he is as valiant a man as
Mark Antony; and he is a man of no estimation
in the world; but I did see him do as gallant
service.

Gow. What do you call him?

Flu. He is called Aunchient Pistol.

Gow. I know him not.   *20*

Enter PISTOL.

Flu. Here is the man.

Pist. Captain, I thee beseech to do me favours:
The Duke of Exeter doth love thee well.

Flu. Ay, I praise God; and I have merited some
love at his hands.

Pist. Bardolph, a soldier, firm and sound of
    heart,
And of buxom valour, hath, by cruel fate,
And giddy Fortune's furious fickle wheel,
That goddess blind,
That stands upon the rolling restless stone—   *30*

Flu. By your patience, Aunchient Pistol. Fortune is painted blind, with a muffler afore her
eyes, to signify to you that Fortune is blind; and
she is painted also with a wheel, to signify to you,
which is the moral of it, that she is turning, and
inconstant, and mutability, and variation: and
her foot, look you, is fixed upon a spherical stone,
which rolls, and rolls, and rolls: in good truth,
the poet makes a most excellent description of it:
Fortune is an excellent moral.   *40*

Pist. Fortune is Bardolph's foe, and frowns on
    him;
For he hath stolen a pax, and hanged must a'
    be:
A damned death!
Let gallows gape for dog; let man go free
And let not hemp his wind-pipe suffocate:
But Exeter hath given the doom of death
For pax of little price.
Therefore, go speak: the Duke will hear thy
    voice;
And let not Bardolph's vital thread be cut
With edge of penny cord and vile reproach: *50*
Speak, captain, for his life, and I will thee
    requite.

Flu. Aunchient Pistol, I do partly understand
your meaning.

Pist. Why then, rejoice therefore.

Flu. Certainly, aunchient, it is not a thing to
rejoice at: for if, look you, he were my brother,
I would desire the Duke to use his good pleasure,
and put him to execution; for discipline ought to
be used.

Pist. Die and be damn'd! and *figo* for thy friendship!   *60*

Flu. It is well.

Pist. The fig of Spain!   [*Exit.*

Flu. Very good.

Gow. Why, this is an arrant counterfeit rascal;
I remember him now; a bawd, a cutpurse.

Flu. I'll assure you, a' uttered as prave words at
the pridge as you shall see in a summer's day.
But it is very well; what he has spoke to me, that
is well, I warrant you, when time is serve.   *69*

Gow. Why, 'tis a gull, a fool, a rogue, that now
and then goes to the wars, to grace himself at his

return into London under the form of a soldier.
And such fellows are perfect in the great commander's names: and they will learn you by rote
where services were done; at such and such a
sconce, at such a breach, at such a convoy; who
came off bravely, who was shot, who disgraced,
what terms the enemy stood on; and this they
con perfectly in the phrase of war, which they
trick up with new-tuned oaths: and what a beard
of the general's cut and a horrid suit of the camp
will do among foaming bottles and ale-washed
wits, is wonderful to be thought on. But you must
learn to know such slanders of the age, or else
you may be marvellously mistook.

Flu. I tell you what, Captain Gower; I do perceive he is not the man that he would gladly make
show to the world he is: if I find a hole in his
coat, I will tell him my mind. [*Drum heard.*]
Hark you, the King is coming, and I must speak
with him from the pridge.   *91*

     Drum and colours. Enter KING HENRY,
        GLOUCESTER, *and Soldiers.*

God pless your Majesty!

K. Hen. How now, Fluellen! camest thou from
    the bridge?

Flu. Ay, so please your Majesty. The Duke of
Exeter has very gallantly maintained the pridge:
the French is gone off, look you; and there is
gallant and most prave passages; marry, th' athversary was have possession of the pridge; but
he is enforced to retire, and the Duke of Exeter
is master of the pridge: I can tell your Majesty,
the Duke is a prave man.   *101*

K. Hen. What men have you lost, Fluellen?

Flu. The perdition of th' athversary hath been
very great, reasonable great: marry, for my part,
I think the Duke hath lost never a man, but one
that is like to be executed for robbing a church,
one Bardolph, if your Majesty know the man:
his face is all bubukles, and whelks, and knobs,
and flames o' fire: and his lips blows at his nose,
and it is like a coal of fire, sometimes plue and
sometimes red; but his nose is executed, and his
fire's out.

K. Hen. We would have all such offenders so
cut off: and we give express charge, that in our
marches through the country, there be nothing
compelled from the villages, nothing taken but
paid for, none of the French upbraided or abused
in disdainful language; for when lenity and
cruelty play for a kingdom, the gentler gamester
is the soonest winner.   *120*

      Tucket. Enter MONTJOY.

Mont. You know me by my habit.

K. Hen. Well then I know thee: what shall I
know of thee?

Mont. My master's mind.

K. Hen. Unfold it.

Mont. Thus says my king: "Say thou to Harry
of England: Though we seemed dead, we did but
sleep: advantage is a better soldier than rashness.
Tell him we could have rebuked him at Harfleur,
but that we thought not good to bruise an injury
till it were full ripe: now we speak upon our cue,
and our voice is imperial: England shall repent
his folly, see his weakness, and admire our sufferance. Bid him therefore consider of his ransom;
which must proportion the losses we have borne,
the subjects we have lost, the disgrace we have
digested; which in weight to re-answer, his petti-
ness would bow under. For our losses, his exchequer is too poor; for the effusion of our blood, the
muster of his kingdom too faint a number; and
for our disgrace, his own person, kneeling at our
feet, but a weak and worthless satisfaction. To
this add defiance: and tell him, for conclusion, he
hath betrayed his followers, whose condemnation
is pronounced." So far my King and master; so
much my office.

K. Hen. What is thy name? I know thy quality.

Mont. Montjoy.

K. Hen. Thou dost thy office fairly. Turn thee
back,

And tell thy King I do not seek him now;
But could be willing to march on to Calais   *150*
Without impeachment: for, to say the sooth,
Though 'tis no wisdom to confess so much
Unto an enemy of craft and vantage,
My people are with sickness much enfeebled,
My numbers lessen'd, and those few I have
Almost no better than so many French;
Who when they were in health, I tell thee, herald,
I thought upon one pair of English legs
Did march three Frenchmen. Yet, forgive me,
    God,   *159*
That I do brag thus! This your air of France
Hath blown that vice in me; I must repent.
Go therefore, tell thy master here I am;
My ransom is this frail and worthless trunk,
My army but a weak and sickly guard;
Yet, God before, tell him we will come on,
Though France himself and such another neigh-
    bour
Stand in our way. There's for thy labour, Mont-
    joy.
Go, bid thy master well advise himself:
If we may pass, we will; if we be hinder'd,   *169*
We shall your tawny ground with your red blood
Discolour: and so, Montjoy, fare you well.
The sum of all our answer is but this:

We would not seek a battle, as we are;
Nor, as we are, we say we will not shun it:
So tell your master.

Mont. I shall deliver so. Thanks to your
    Highness.   [*Exit.*

Glou. I hope they will not come upon us now.

K. Hen. We are in God's hand, brother, not in
theirs.

March to the bridge; it now draws toward night:
Beyond the river we'll encamp ourselves,   *180*
And on to-morrow bid them march away.

                               [*Exeunt.*

SCENE VII. *The French camp, near Agincourt*

Enter the CONSTABLE OF FRANCE, *the* LORD RAM-
BURES, ORLEANS, DAUPHIN, *with others.*

Con. Tut! I have the best armour of the world.
Would it were day!

Orl. You have an excellent armour; but let my
horse have his due.

Con. It is the best horse of Europe.

Orl. Will it never be morning?

Dau. My Lord of Orleans, and my Lord High
Constable, you talk of horse and armour?

Orl. You are as well provided of both as any
prince in the world.   *10*

Dau. What a long night is this! I will not change
my horse with any that treads but on four pas-
terns. *Ca, ha!* he bounds from the earth, as if his
entrails were hairs; *le cheval volant,* the Pegasus,
chez les narines de feu! When I bestride him, I
soar, I am a hawk: he trots the air; the earth
sings when he touches it; the basest horn of his
hoof is more musical than the pipe of Hermes.

Orl. He's of the colour of the nutmeg.   *20*

Dau. And of the heat of the ginger. It is a beast
for Perseus: he is pure air and fire; and the dull
elements of earth and water never appear in him,
but only in patient stillness while his rider mounts
him: he is indeed a horse; and all other jades you
may call beasts.

Con. Indeed, my lord, it is a most absolute and
excellent horse.

Dau. It is the prince of palfreys; his neigh is
like the bidding of a monarch and his countenance enforces homage.   *31*

Orl. No more, cousin.

Dau. Nay, the man hath no wit that cannot,
from the rising of the lark to the lodging of the
lamb, vary deserved praise on my palfrey: it is a
theme as fluent as the sea: turn the sands into
eloquent tongues, and my horse is argument for
them all: 'tis a subject for a sovereign to reason
on, and for a sovereign's sovereign to ride on;
and for the world, familiar to us and unknown, to
lay apart their particular functions and wonder at

him. I once writ a sonnet in his praise and began
thus: "Wonder of nature"—

Orl. I have heard a sonnet begin so to one's mistress.

Dau. Then did they imitate that which I composed to my courser, for my horse is my mistress.

Orl. Your mistress bears well.

Dau. Me well; which is the prescript praise and
perfection of a good and particular mistress.

Con. Nay, for methought yesterday your mistress shrewdly shook your back.

Dau. So perhaps did yours.

Con. Mine was not bridled.

Dau. O then belike she was old and gentle; and
you rode, like a kern of Ireland, your French
hose off, and in your strait strossers.

Con. You have good judgement in horseman-
ship.   59

Dau. Be warned by me, then: they that ride so
and ride not warily, fall into foul bogs. I had
rather have my horse to my mistress.

Con. I had as lief have my mistress a jade.

Dau. I tell thee, Constable, my mistress wears
his own hair.

Con. I could make as true a boast as that, if I
had a sow to my mistress.

Dau. *Le chien est retourné à son propre vomisse-
ment, et la truie lavée au bourbier:* thou makest
use of anything.   70

Con. Yet do I not use my horse for my mistress,
or any such proverb so little kin to the purpose.

Ram. My Lord Constable, the armour that I
saw in your tent to-night, are those stars or suns
upon it?

Con. Stars, my lord.

Dau. Some of them will fall to-morrow, I hope.

Con. And yet my sky shall not want.

Dau. That may be, for you bear a many super-
fluously, and 'twere more honour some were
away.   81

Con. Even as your horse bears your praises;
who would trot as well, were some of your brags
dismounted.

Dau. Would I were able to load him with his
desert! Will it never be day? I will trot to-
morrow a mile, and my way shall be paved with
English faces.

Con. I will not say so, for fear I should be faced
out of my way: but I would it were morning;
for I would fain be about the ears of the English.

Ram. Who will go to hazard with me for twenty
prisoners?

Con. You must first go yourself to hazard, ere
you have them.

Dau. 'Tis midnight; I'll go arm myself.   [*Exit.*

Orl. The Dauphin longs for morning.

Ram. He longs to eat the English.

Con. I think he will eat all he kills.   100

Orl. By the white hand of my lady, he's a gallant
prince.

Con. Swear by her foot, that she may tread out
the oath.

Orl. He is simply the most active gentleman of
France.

Con. Doing is activity; and he will still be doing.

Orl. He never did harm, that I heard of.

Con. Nor will do none to-morrow· he will keep
that good name still.   111

Orl. I know him to be valiant.

Con. I was told that by one that knows him
better than you.

Orl. What's he?

Con. Marry, he told me so himself; and he said
he cared not who knew it.

Orl. He needs not; it is no hidden virtue in
him.   119

Con. By my faith, sir, but it is ; never any body
saw it but his lackey: 'tis a hooded valour; and
when it appears, it will bate.

Orl. Ill will never said well.

Con. I will cap that proverb with "There is
flattery in friendship."

Orl. And I will take up that with "Give the
devil his due."

Con. Well placed: there stands your friend for
the devil: have at the very eye of that proverb
with "A pox of the devil."   130

Orl. You are the better at proverbs, by how
much "A fool's bolt is soon shot."

Con. You have shot over.

Orl. 'Tis not the first time you were overshot.

Enter a MESSENGER.

Mess. My Lord High Constable, the English lie
within fifteen hundred paces of your tents.

Con. Who hath measured the ground?

Mess. The Lord Grandpré.

Con. A valiant and most expert gentleman.
Would it were day! Alas, poor Harry of England! he longs not for the dawning as we do.   141

Orl. What a wretched and peevish fellow is
this King of England, to mope with his fat-
brained followers so far out of his knowledge!

Con. If the English had any apprehension, they
would run away.

Orl. That they lack; for if their heads had any
intellectual armour, they could never wear such
heavy head-pieces.   149

Ram. That island of England breeds very valiant
creatures; their mastiffs are of unmatchable
courage.

Orl. Foolish curs, that run winking into the

mouth of a Russian bear and have their heads crushed like rotten apples! You may as well say, that's a valiant flea that dare eat his breakfast on the lip of a lion.

Con. Just, just; and the men do sympathize with the mastiffs in robustious and rough coming on, leaving their wits with their wives: and then give them great meals of beef and iron and steel, they will eat like wolves and fight like devils.

Orl. Ay, but these English are shrewdly out of beef.

Con. Then shall we find to-morrow they have only stomachs to eat and none to fight. Now is it time to arm: come, shall we about it?

Orl. It is now two o'clock: but, let me see, by ten

We shall have each a hundred Englishmen.

                                      [Exeunt.

ACT IV
PROLOGUE

Enter CHORUS.

Chor. Now entertain conjecture of a time
When creeping murmur and the poring dark
Fills the wide vessel of the universe.
From camp to camp through the foul womb of
    night
The hum of either army stilly sounds,
That the fix'd sentinels almost receive
The secret whispers of each other's watch:
Fire answers fire, and through their paly flames
Each battle sees the other's umber'd face;   9
Steed threatens steed, in high and boastful neighs
Piercing the night's dull ear; and from the tents
The armourers, accomplishing the knights,
With busy hammers closing rivets up,
Give dreadful note of preparation:
The country cocks do crow, the clocks do toll,
And the third hour of drowsy morning name.
Proud of their numbers and secure in soul,
The confident and over-lusty French
Do the low-rated English play at dice;
And chide the cripple tardy-gaited night   20
Who, like a foul and ugly witch, doth limp
So tediously away. The poor condemned English,
Like sacrifices, by their watchful fires
Sit patiently and inly ruminate
The morning's danger, and their gesture sad
Investing lank-lean cheeks and war-worn coats
Presenteth them unto the gazing moon
So many horrid ghosts. O now, who will behold
The royal captain of this ruin'd band
Walking from watch to watch, from tent to tent,
Let him cry, "Praise and glory on his head!"   31
For forth he goes and visits all his host,
Bids them good morrow with a modest smile

And calls them brothers, friends, and country-
    men.
Upon his royal face there is no note
How dread an army hath enrounded him;
Nor doth he dedicate one jot of colour
Unto the weary and all-watched night,
But freshly looks and over-bears attaint
With cheerful semblance and sweet majesty;   40
That every wretch, pining and pale before,
Beholding him, plucks comfort from his looks:
A largess universal like the sun
His liberal eye doth give to every one,
Thawing cold fear, that mean and gentle all
Behold, as may unworthiness define,
A little touch of Harry in the night.
And so our scene must to the battle fly;
Where—O for pity!—we shall much disgrace
With four or five most vile and ragged foils,   50
Right ill-disposed in brawl ridiculous,
The name of Agincourt. Yet sit and see,
Minding true things by what their mockeries be.
                                        [Exit.

SCENE I. *The English camp at Agincourt*

Enter KING HENRY, BEDFORD, *and* GLOUCESTER.

K. Hen. Gloucester, 'tis true that we are in
    great danger;
The greater therefore should our courage be.
Good morrow, brother Bedford. God Almighty!
There is some soul of goodness in things evil,
Would men observingly distil it out.
For our bad neighbour makes us early stirrers,
Which is both healthful and good husbandry:
Besides, they are our outward consciences,
And preachers to us all, admonishing
That we should dress us fairly for our end.   10
Thus may we gather honey from the weed,
And make a moral of the devil himself.

Enter ERPINGHAM.

Good morrow, old Sir Thomas Erpingham:
A good soft pillow for that good white head
Were better than a churlish turf of France.

Erp. Not so, my liege: this lodging likes me
    better,
Since I may say, "Now lie I like a king."

K. Hen. 'Tis good for men to love their present
    pains
Upon example; so the spirit is eased:
And when the mind is quicken'd, out of doubt,
The organs, though defunct and dead before,   21
Break up their drowsy grave and newly move,
With casted slough and fresh legerity.
Lend me thy cloak, Sir Thomas. Brothers both,
Commend me to the princes in our camp;
Do my good morrow to them, and anon

Desire them all to my pavilion.

Glou. We shall, my liege.

Erp. Shall I attend your Grace?

K. Hen.   No, my good knight;
Go with my brothers to my lords of England: *30*
I and my bosom must debate a while,
And then I would no other company.

Erp. The Lord in heaven bless thee, noble
   Harry!   [*Exeunt all but* KING.

K. Hen. God-a-mercy, old heart! thou speak'st
   cheerfully.

Enter PISTOL.

Pist. Qui va là?

K. Hen. A friend.

Pist. Discuss unto me; art thou officer?
Or art thou base, common, and popular?

K. Hen. I am a gentleman of a company.

Pist. Trail'st thou the puissant pike?   *40*

K. Hen. Even so. What are you?

Pist. As good a gentleman as the Emperor.

K. Hen. Then you are a better than the King.

Pist. The King's a bawcock, and a heart of
   gold,
A lad of life, an imp of fame;
Of parents good, of fist most valiant.
I kiss his dirty shoe, and from heart-string
I love the lovely bully. What is thy name?

K. Hen. Harry le Roy.

Pist. Le Roy! a Cornish name: art thou of
   Cornish crew?   *50*

K. Hen. No, I am a Welshman.

Pist. Know'st thou Fluellen?

K. Hen. Yes.

Pist. Tell him, I'll knock his leek about his pate
Upon Saint Davy's day.

K. Hen. Do not you wear your dagger in your
cap that day, lest he knock that about yours.

Pist. Art thou his friend?

K. Hen. And his kinsman too.

Pist The *figo* for thee, then!   *60*

K. Hen. I thank you: God be with you!

Pist. My name is Pistol call'd.   [*Exit.*

K. Hen. It sorts well with your fierceness.

Enter FLUELLEN *and* GOWER.

Gow. Captain Fluellen!

Flu. So! in the name of Jesus Christ, speak
lower. It is the greatest admiration in the universal world, when the true and aunchient pre-
rogatifes and laws of the wars is not kept: if you
would take the pains but to examine the wars of
Pompey the Great, you shall find, I warrant you,
that there is no tiddle taddle nor pibble pabble in
Pompey's camp; I warrant you, you shall find
the ceremonies of the wars, and the cares of it,

and the forms of it, and the sobriety of it, and the
modesty of it, to be otherwise.

Gow. Why, the enemy is loud; you hear him all
night.

Flu. If the enemy is an ass and a fool and a
prating coxcomb, is it meet, think you, that we
should also, look you, be an ass and a fool
and a prating coxcomb? in your own conscience,
now?

Gow. I will speak lower.

Flu. I pray you and beseech you that you will.
           [*Exeunt* GOWER *and* FLUELLEN.

K. Hen. Though it appear a little out of fashion,
There is much care and valour in this Welshman.

Enter three soldiers, JOHN BATES, ALEXANDER
COURT, *and* MICHAEL WILLIAMS.

Court. Brother John Bates, is not that the morning which breaks yonder?

Bates. I think it be: but we have no great cause
to desire the approach of day.   *90*

Will. We see yonder the beginning of the day,
but I think we shall never see the end of it. Who
goes there?

K. Hen. A friend.

Will. Under what captain serve you?

K. Hen. Under Sir Thomas Erpingham.

Will. A good old commander and a most kind
gentleman: I pray you, what thinks he of our
estate?

K. Hen. Even as men wrecked upon a sand, that
look to be washed off the next tide.   *101*

Bates. He hath not told his thought to the King?

K. Hen. No; nor it is not meet he should. For,
though I speak it to you, I think the King is but a
man, as I am: the violet smells to him as it doth
to me; the element shows to him as it doth to me;
all his senses have but human conditions: his
ceremonies laid by, in his nakedness he appears
but a man; and though his affections are higher
mounted than ours, yet, when they stoop, they
stoop with the like wing. Therefore when he sees
reason of fears, as we do, his fears, out of doubt,
be of the same relish as ours are: yet, in reason,
no man should possess him with any appearance
of fear, lest he, by showing it, should dishearten
his army.

Bates. He may show what outward courage he
will; but I believe, as cold a night as 'tis, he could
wish himself in Thames up to the neck; and so I
would he were, and I by him, at all adventures,
so we were quit here.

K. Hen. By my troth, I will speak my conscience of the King: I think he would not wish
himself any where but where he is.

Bates. Then I would he were here alone; so

should he be sure to be ransomed, and a many poor men's lives saved.

K. Hen. I dare say you love him not so ill, to wish him here alone, howsoever you speak this to feel other men's minds: methinks I could not die anywhere so contented as in the King's company; his cause being just and his quarrel honourable.

Will. That's more than we know.

Bates. Ay, or more than we should seek after; for we know enough, if we know we are the King's subjects: if his cause be wrong, our obedience to the King wipes the crime of it out of us.

Will. But if the cause be not good, the King himself hath a heavy reckoning to make, when all those legs and arms and heads, chopped off in a battle, shall join together at the latter day and cry all, "We died at such a place"; some swearing, some crying for a surgeon, some upon their wives left poor behind them, some upon the debts they owe, some upon their children rawly left. I am afeard there are few die well that die in a battle; for how can they charitably dispose of anything, when blood is their argument? Now, if these men do not die well, it will be a black matter for the King that led them to it; whom to disobey were against all proportion of subjection.

K. Hen. So, if a son that is by his father sent about merchandise do sinfully miscarry upon the sea, the imputation of his wickedness, by your rule, should be imposed upon his father that sent him: or if a servant, under his master's command transporting a sum of money, be assailed by robbers and die in many irreconciled iniquities, you may call the business of the master the author of the servant's damnation: but this is not so: the King is not bound to answer the particular endings of his soldiers, the father of his son, nor the master of his servant; for they purpose not their death, when they purpose their services. Besides, there is no king, be his cause never so spotless, if it come to the arbitrement of swords, can try it out with all unspotted soldiers: some peradventure have on them the guilt of premeditated and contrived murder; some, of beguiling virgins with the broken seals of perjury; some, making the wars their bulwark, that have before gored the gentle bosom of peace with pillage and robbery. Now, if these men have defeated the law and outrun native punishment, though they can outstrip men, they have no wings to fly from God: war is his beadle, war is his vengeance; so that here men are punished for before-breach of the King's laws in now the King's quarrel: where they feared the death, they have borne life away; and where they would be safe, they perish: then

if they die unprovided, no more is the King guilty of their damnation than he was before guilty of those impieties for the which they are now visited. Every subject's duty is the King's; but every subject's soul is his own. Therefore should every soldier in the wars do as every sick man in his bed, wash every mote out of his conscience: and dying so, death is to him advantage; or not dying, the time was blessedly lost wherein such preparation was gained: and in him that escapes, it were not sin to think that, making God so free an offer, He let him outlive that day to see His greatness and to teach others how they should prepare.

Will. 'Tis certain, every man that dies ill, the ill upon his own head, the King is not to answer it.   199

Bates. I do not desire he should answer for me; and yet I determine to fight lustily for him.

K. Hen. I myself heard the King say he would not be ransomed.

Will. Ay, he said so, to make us fight cheerfully: but when our throats are cut, he may be ransomed, and we ne'er the wiser.

K. Hen. If I live to see it, I will never trust his word after.

Will. You pay him then. That's a perilous shot out of an elder-gun, that a poor and a private displeasure can do against a monarch! you may as well go about to turn the sun to ice with fanning in his face with a peacock's feather. You'll never trust his word after! come, 'tis a foolish saying.

K. Hen. Your reproof is something too round: I should be angry with you, if the time were convenient.

Will. Let it be a quarrel between us, if you live.

K. Hen. I embrace it.   221

Will. How shall I know thee again?

K. Hen. Give me any gage of thine, and I will wear it in my bonnet: then, if ever thou darest acknowledge it, I will make it my quarrel.

Will. Here's my glove: give me another of thine.

K. Hen. There.

Will. This will I also wear in my cap: if ever thou come to me and say, after to-morrow, "This is my glove," by this hand, I will take thee a box on the ear.

K. Hen. If ever I live to see it, I will challenge it.

Will. Thou darest as well be hanged.

K. Hen. Well, I will do it, though I take thee in the King's company.

Will. Keep thy word: fare thee well.

Bates. Be friends, you English fools, be friends: we have French quarrels enow, if you could tell how to reckon.   241

K. Hen. Indeed, the French may lay twenty

French crowns to one, they will beat us; for they
bear them on their shoulders: but it is no English
treason to cut French crowns, and to-morrow the
King himself will be a clipper.

[*Exeunt* SOLDIERS.

Upon the King! let us our lives, our souls,
Our debts, our careful wives,
Our children, and our sins lay on the King!
We must bear all. O hard condition,   250
Twin-born with greatness, subject to the breath
Of every fool, whose sense no more can feel
But his own wringing! What infinite heart's-ease
Must kings neglect, that private men enjoy!
And what have kings, that privates have not too,
Save ceremony, save general ceremony?
And what art thou, thou idol Ceremony?
What kind of god art thou, that suffer'st more
Of mortal griefs than do thy worshippers?
What are thy rents? what are thy comings in?
O Ceremony, show me but thy worth!   261
What is thy soul of adoration?
Art thou aught else but place, degree, and form,
Creating awe and fear in other men?
Wherein thou art less happy being fear'd
Than they in fearing.
What drink'st thou oft, instead of homage sweet,
But poison'd flattery? O, be sick, great greatness,
And bid thy Ceremony give thee cure!
Think'st thou the fiery fever will go out   270
With titles blown from adulation?
Will it give place to flexure and low bending?
Canst thou, when thou command'st the beggar's
    knee,
Command the health of it? No, thou proud dream,
That play'st so subtly with a king's repose;
I am a king that find thee, and I know
'Tis not the balm, the sceptre, and the ball,
The sword, the mace, the crown imperial,
The intertissued robe of gold and pearl,
The farced title running 'fore the King,   280
The throne he sits on, nor the tide of pomp
That beats upon the high shore of this world,
No, not all these, thrice-gorgeous Ceremony,
Not all these, laid in bed majestical,
Can sleep so soundly as the wretched slave,
Who with a body fill'd and vacant mind
Gets him to rest, cramm'd with distressful
    bread;
Never sees horrid night, the child of hell,
But, like a lackey, from the rise to set
Sweats in the eye of Phœbus and all night   290
Sleeps in Elysium; next day after dawn,
Doth rise and help Hyperion to his horse,
And follows so the ever-running year,
With profitable labour, to his grave:
And, but for ceremony, such a wretch,

Winding up days with toil and nights with sleep,
Had the fore-hand and vantage of a king.
The slave, a member of the country's peace,
Enjoys it; but in gross brain little wots
What watch the King keeps to maintain the
    peace,
Whose hours the peasant best advantages.   301

Re-enter ERPINGHAM.

Erp. My lord, your nobles, jealous of your
    absence,
Seek through your camp to find you.
K. Hen.   Good old knight,
Collect them all together at my tent:
I'll be before thee.
  Erp.   I shall do't, my lord.   [*Exit.*
  K. Hen. O God of battles! steel my soldiers'
    hearts;
Possess them not with fear; take from them
    now
The sense of reckoning, if the opposed numbers
Pluck their hearts from them. Not to-day, O
    Lord,
O, not to-day, think not upon the fault   310
My father made in compassing the crown!
I Richard's body have interred new;
And on it have bestow'd more contrite tears
Than from it issued forced drops of blood:
Five hundred poor I have in yearly pay,
Who twice a-day their wither'd hands hold up
Toward heaven, to pardon blood; and I have
    built
Two chantries, where the sad and solemn priests
Sing still for Richard's soul. More will I do;
Though all that I can do is nothing worth,   320
Since that my penitence comes after all,
Imploring pardon.

Re-enter GLOUCESTER.

  Glou. My liege!
  K. Hen. My brother Gloucester's voice? Ay;
I know thy errand, I will go with thee:
The day, my friends, and all things stay for me.

[*Exeunt.*

SCENE II. *The French camp*

Enter the DAUPHIN, ORLEANS, RAMBURES,
    and others.

  Orl. The sun doth gild our armour; up, my
    lords!
  Dau. Montez à cheval! My horse! varlet! *laquais!*
    ha!
  Orl. O brave spirit!
  Dau. Via! les eaux et la terre.
  Orl. Rien puis? l'air et le feu.
  Dau. Ciel, cousin Orleans.

Enter CONSTABLE.

Now, my Lord Constable!

Con. Hark, how our steeds for present service
  neigh!

Dau. Mount them, and make incision in their
  hides,
That their hot blood may spin in English eyes, *10*
And dout them with superfluous courage, ha!

Ram. What, will you have them weep our
  horses' blood?
How shall we, then, behold their natural tears?

Enter a MESSENGER.

Mess. The English are embattled, you French
  peers.

Con. To horse, you gallant princes! straight to
  horse!
Do but behold yon poor and starved band,
And your fair show shall suck away their souls,
Leaving them but the shales and husks of men.
There is not work enough for all our hands;
Scarce blood enough in all their sickly veins *20*
To give each naked curtle-axe a stain,
That our French gallants shall to-day draw out
And sheathe for lack of sport: let us but blow on
  them,
The vapour of our valour will o'erturn them.
'Tis positive 'gainst all exceptions, lords,
That our superfluous lackeys and our peasants,
Who in unnecessary action swarm
About our squares of battle, were enow
To purge this field of such a hilding foe,
Though we upon this mountain's basis by *30*
Took stand for idle speculation:
But that our honours must not. What's to say?
A very little little let us do,
And all is done. Then let the trumpets sound
The tucket sonance and the note to mount;
For our approach shall so much dare the field
That England shall couch down in fear and yield.

Enter GRANDPRÉ.

Grand. Why do you stay so long, my lords of
  France?
Yon island carrions, desperate of their bones,
Ill-favouredly become the morning field: *40*
Their ragged curtains poorly are let loose,
And our air shakes them passing scornfully:
Big Mars seems bankrupt in their beggar'd host
And faintly through a rusty beaver peeps:
The horsemen sit like fixed candlesticks,
With torch-staves in their hand; and their poor
  jades
Lob down their heads, dropping the hides and hips,
The gum down-roping from their pale-dead eyes,

And in their pale dull mouths the gimmal bit
Lies foul with chew'd grass, still and motionless;
And their executors, the knavish crows, *51*
Fly o'er them, all impatient for their hour.
Description cannot suit itself in words
To demonstrate the life of such a battle
In life so lifeless as it shows itself.

Con. They have said their prayers, and they
  stay for death.

Dau. Shall we go send them dinners and fresh
  suits
And give their fasting horses provender,
And after fight with them?

Con. I stay but for my guidon: to the field!
I will the banner from a trumpet take, *61*
And use it for my haste. Come, come, away!
The sun is high, and we outwear the day.
                       [Exeunt.

SCENE III. *The English camp*

Enter GLOUCESTER, BEDFORD, EXETER, ERPING-
HAM, *with all his host:* SALISBURY *and* WEST-
MORELAND.

Glou. Where is the King?

Bed. The King himself is rode to view their
  battle.

West. Of fighting men they have full three
  score thousand.

Exe. There's five to one; besides, they all are
  fresh.

Sal. God's arm strike with us! 'tis a fearful odds.
God be wi' you, princes all; I'll to my charge:
If we no more meet till we meet in heaven,
Then, joyfully, my noble Lord of Bedford,
My dear Lord Gloucester, and my good Lord
  Exeter,
And my kind kinsman, warriors all, adieu! *10*

Bed. Farewell, good Salisbury; and good luck
  go with thee!

Exe. Farewell, kind lord; fight valiantly to-day:
And yet I do thee wrong to mind thee of it,
For thou art framed of the firm truth of valour.
               [Exit SALISBURY.

Bed. He is as full of valour as of kindness;
Princely in both.

Enter the KING.

West.   O that we now had here
But one ten thousand of those men in England
That do no work to-day!

K. Hen.   What's he that wishes so?
My cousin Westmoreland? No, my fair cousin:
If we are mark'd to die, we are enow *20*
To do our country loss; and if to live,
The fewer men, the greater share of honour.
God's will! I pray thee, wish not one man more.

By Jove, I am not covetous for gold,
Nor care I who doth feed upon my cost;
It yearns me not if men my garments wear;
Such outward things dwell not in my desires:
But if it be a sin to covet honour,
I am the most offending soul alive.   29
No, faith, my coz, wish not a man from England:
God's peace! I would not lose so great an honour
As one man more, methinks, would share from
    me
For the best hope I have. O, do not wish one
    more!
Rather proclaim it, Westmoreland, through my
    host,
That he which hath no stomach to this fight,
Let him depart; his passport shall be made
And crowns for convoy put into his purse:
We would not die in that man's company
That fears his fellowship to die with us.
This day is call'd the feast of Crispian: 40
He that outlives this day and comes safe home
Will stand a tip-toe when this day is named,
And rouse him at the name of Crispian.
He that shall live this day and see old age,
Will yearly on the vigil feast his neighbours,
And say, "To-morrow is Saint Crispian":
Then will he strip his sleeve and show his scars,
And say, "These wounds I had on Crispin's
    day."
Old men forget; yet all shall be forgot,
But he'll remember with advantages   50
What feats he did that day: then shall our names,
Familiar in his mouth as household words,
Harry the King, Bedford and Exeter,
Warwick and Talbot, Salisbury and Gloucester,
Be in their flowing cups freshly remember'd.
This story shall the good man teach his son;
And Crispin Crispian shall ne'er go by,
From this day to the ending of the world,
But we in it shall be remembered;
We few, we happy few, we band of brothers; 60
For he to-day that sheds his blood with me
Shall be my brother; be he ne'er so vile,
This day shall gentle his condition:
And gentlemen in England now a-bed
Shall think themselves accursed they were not
    here,
And hold their manhoods cheap whiles any
    speaks
That fought with us upon Saint Crispin's day.

Re-enter SALISBURY.

Sal. My sovereign lord, bestow yourself with
    speed:
The French are bravely in their battles set,
And will with all expedience charge on us.   70

K. Hen. All things are ready, if our minds be so.
West. Perish the man whose mind is backward
    now!
K. Hen. Thou dost not wish more help from
    England, coz?
West. God's will! my liege, would you and I
    alone,
Without more help, could fight this royal battle!
K. Hen. Why, now thou hast unwish'd five
    thousand men;
Which likes me better than to wish us one.
You know your places: God be with you all!

Tucket. Enter MONTJOY.

Mont. Once more I come to know of thee, King
    Harry,
If for thy ransom thou wilt now compound,   80
Before thy most assured overthrow:
For certainly thou art so near the gulf,
Thou needs must be englutted. Besides, in mercy,
The Constable desires thee thou wilt mind
Thy followers of repentance; that their souls
May make a peaceful and a sweet retire
From off these fields, where, wretches, their
    poor bodies
Must lie and fester.
K. Hen.   Who hath sent thee now?
Mont. The Constable of France.
K. Hen. I pray thee, bear my former answer
    back: 90
Bid them achieve me and then sell my bones.
Good God! why should they mock poor fellows
    thus?
The man that once did sell the lion's skin
While the beast lived, was killed with hunting
    him.
A many of our bodies shall no doubt
Find native graves; upon the which, I trust,
Shall witness live in brass of this day's work:
And those that leave their valiant bones in
    France,
Dying like men, though buried in your dunghills,
They shall be famed; for there the sun shall greet
    them,   100
And draw their honours reeking up to heaven;
Leaving their earthly parts to choke your clime,
The smell whereof shall breed a plague in
    France.
Mark then abounding valour in our English,
That being dead, like to the bullet's grazing,
Break out into a second course of mischief,
Killing in relapse of mortality.
Let me speak proudly: tell the Constable
We are but warriors for the working-day;
Our gayness and our gilt are all besmirch'd   110
With rainy marching in the painful field;

There's not a piece of feather in our host—
Good argument, I hope, we will not fly—
And time hath worn us into slovenry:
But, by the mass, our hearts are in the trim;
And my poor soldiers tell me, yet ere night
They'll be in fresher robes, or they will pluck
The gay new coats o'er the French soldiers'
　　　heads
And turn them out of service. If they do this—
As, if God please, they shall—my ransom then
Will soon be levied. Herald, save thou thy
　　　labour;　　　　　　　　　　　　　　　121
Come thou no more for ransom, gentle herald:
They shall have none, I swear, but these my
　　　joints;
Which if they have as I will leave 'em them,
Shall yield them little, tell the Constable.

　Mont. I shall, King Harry. And so fare thee
　　　well:
Thou never shalt hear herald any more.　　*[Exit.*
　K. Hen. I fear thou'lt once more come again for
　　　ransom.

Enter YORK.

　York. My lord, most humbly on my knee I beg
The leading of the vaward.　　　　　　　　130
　K. Hen. Take it, brave York. Now, soldiers,
　　　march away:
And how thou pleasest, God, dispose the day!
　　　　　　　　　　　　　　　　[Exeunt.

SCENE IV. *The field of battle*

Alarum. Excursions. Enter PISTOL, FRENCH
SOLDIER, *and* BOY.

　Pist. Yield, cur!
　*Fr. Sol. Je pense que vous êtes gentilhomme de
bonne qualité.*
　Pist. Qualtitie calmie custure me! Art thou a gen-
tleman? what is thy name? discuss.
　Fr. Sol. O Seigneur Dieu!
　Pist. O, Signieur Dew should be a gentleman:
Perpend my words, O Signieur Dew, and mark;
O Signieur Dew, thou diest on point of fox,
Except, O signieur, thou do give to me　　　10
Egregious ransom.
　Fr. Sol. O, prenez miséricorde! ayez pitié de moi!
　Pist. Moy shall not serve; I will have forty
moys;
Or I will fetch thy rim out at thy throat
In drops of crimson blood.
　*Fr. Sol. Est-il impossible d'échapper la force de ton
bras?*
　Pist. Brass, cur!
Thou damned and luxurious mountain goat,　　20
Offer'st me brass?
　Fr. Sol. O pardonnez moi!

　Pist. Say'st thou me so? is that a ton of moys?
Come hither, boy: ask me this slave in French
What is his name.
　Boy. Écoutez: comment êtes-vous appelé?
　Fr. Sol. Monsieur le Fer.
　Boy. He says his name is Master Fer.
　Pist. Master Fer! I'll fer him, and firk him, and
ferret him: discuss the same in French unto him.
　Boy. I do not know the French for fer, and
ferret, and firk.　　　　　　　　　　　　32
　Pist. Bid him prepare; for I will cut his throat.
　Fr. Sol. Que dit-il, monsieur?
　*Boy. Il me commande de vous dire que vous faites
vous prêt; car ce soldat ici est disposé tout à cette heure
de couper votre gorge.*
　Pist. Owy, cuppele gorge, permafoy,
Peasant, unless thou give me crowns, brave
　　　crowns;　　　　　　　　　　　　　　　40
Or mangled shalt thou be by this my sword.
　*Fr. Sol. O, je vous supplie, pour l'amour de Dieu,
me pardonner! Je suis gentilhomme de bonne maison:
gardez ma vie, et je vous donnerai deux cents écus.*
　Pist. What are his words?
　Boy. He prays you to save his life: he is a gentleman of a good house; and for his ransom he
will give you two hundred crowns.
　Pist. Tell him my fury shall abate, and I　　50
The crowns will take.
　Fr. Sol. Petit monsieur, que dit-il?
　*Boy. Encore qu'il est contre son jurement de par-
donner aucun prisonnier, néanmoins, pour les écus
que vous l'avez promis, il est content de vous donner
la liberté, le franchisement.*
　*Fr. Sol. Sur mes genoux je vous donne mille remer-
cîmens: et je m'estime heureux que je suis tombé
entre les mains d'un chevalier, je pense, le plus brave,
vaillant, et très distingué seigneur d'Angleterre.　61*
　Pist. Expound unto me, boy.
　Boy. He gives you, upon his knees, a thousand
thanks; and he esteems himself happy that he
hath fallen into the hands of one, as he thinks, the
most brave, valorous, and thrice-worthy seigneur
of England.
　Pist. As I suck blood, I will some mercy show.
Follow me!　　　　　　　　　　　　　　　69
　Boy. Suivez-vous le grand capitaine. [Exeunt PIS-
TOL, *and* FRENCH SOLDIER.] I did never know so
full a voice issue from so empty a heart: but the
saying is true, "The empty vessel makes the
greatest sound." Bardolph and Nym had ten
times more valour than this roaring devil i' the
old play, that every one may pare his nails with a
wooden dagger: and they are both hanged; and
so would this be, if he durst steal anything ad-
venturously. I must stay with the lackeys, with
the luggage of our camp: the French might have

a good prey of us, if he knew of it; for there is
none to guard it but boys.   [*Exit.*

SCENE V. *Another part of the field*

Enter CONSTABLE, ORLEANS, BOURBON,
DAUPHIN, *and* RAMBURES.

Con. O diable!
Orl. O seigneur! le jour est perdu, tout est perdu!
Dau. Mort de ma vie! all is confounded, all!
Reproach and everlasting shame
Sits mocking in our plumes. O méchante fortune!
Do not run away.
  A short alarum.
Con.   Why, all our ranks are broke.
Dau. O perdurable shame! let's stab ourselves.
Be these the wretches that we play'd at dice for?
Orl. Is this the king we sent to for his ransom?
Bour. Shame and eternal shame, nothing but
  shame!   10
Let us die in honour: once more back again;
And he that will not follow Bourbon now,
Let him go hence, and with his cap in hand,
Like a base pandar, hold the chamber-door
Whilst by a slave, no gentler than my dog,
His fairest daughter is contaminated.
  Con. Disorder, that hath spoil'd us, friend us
  now!
Let us on heaps go offer up our lives.
  Orl. We are enow yet living in the field
To smother up the English in our throngs,   20
If any order might be thought upon.
  Bour. The devil take order now! I'll to the
  throng:
Let life be short; else shame will be too long.
                        [*Exeunt.*

SCENE VI. *Another part of the field*

Alarums. Enter KING HENRY *and forces,*
EXETER, *and others.*

K. Hen. Well have we done, thrice valiant
  countrymen:
But all's not done; yet keep the French the field.
  Exe. The Duke of York commends him to your
  Majesty.
  K. Hen. Lives he, good uncle? thrice within this
  hour
I saw him down; thrice up again, and fighting;
From helmet to the spur all blood he was.
  Exe. In which array, brave soldier, doth he lie,
Larding the plain; and by his bloody side,
Yoke-fellow to his honour-owing wounds,
The noble Earl of Suffolk also lies.   10
Suffolk first died: and York, all haggled over,
Comes to him, where in gore he lay insteep'd,
And takes him by the beard; kisses the gashes
That bloodily did yawn upon his face;

And cries aloud, "Tarry, dear cousin Suffolk!
My soul shall thine keep company to heaven;
Tarry, sweet soul, for mine, then fly abreast,
As in this glorious and well-foughten field
We kept together in our chivalry!"
Upon these words I came and cheer'd him up: 20
He smiled me in the face, raught me his hand,
And, with a feeble gripe, says, "Dear my lord,
Commend my service to my sovereign."
So did he turn and over Suffolk's neck
He threw his wounded arm and kiss'd his lips;
And so espoused to death, with blood he seal'd
A testament of noble-ending love.
The pretty and sweet manner of it forced
Those waters from me which I would have
  stopp'd;
But I had not so much of man in me,   30
And all my mother came into mine eyes
And gave me up to tears.
  K. Hen.   I blame you not;
For, hearing this, I must perforce compound
With mistful eyes, or they will issue too.
  Alarum.
But, hark! what new alarum is this same?
The French have reinforced their scatter'd men:
Then every soldier kill his prisoners:
Give the word through.   [*Exeunt.*

SCENE VII. *Another part of the field*

Enter FLUELLEN *and* GOWER.

Flu. Kill the poys and the luggage! 'tis expressly
against the law of arms: 'tis as arrant a piece of
knavery, mark you now, as can be offer't; in
your conscience, now, is it not?
  Gow. 'Tis certain there's not a boy left alive;
and the cowardly rascals that ran from the battle
ha' done this slaughter: besides, they have
burned and carried away all that was in the
King's tent; wherefore the King, most worthily,
hath caused every soldier to cut his prisoner's
throat. O, 'tis a gallant king!   11
  Flu. Ay, he was porn at Monmouth, Captain
Gower. What call you the town's name where
Alexander the Pig was born!
  Gow. Alexander the Great.
  Flu. Why, I pray you, is not pig great? the pig,
or the great, or the mighty, or the huge, or the
magnanimous, are all one reckonings, save the
phrase is a little variations.   19
  Gow. I think Alexander the Great was born in
Macedon: his father was called Phillip of Macedon, as I take it.
  Flu. I think it is in Macedon where Alexander
is porn. I tell you, captain, if you look in the
maps of the 'orld, I warrant you sall find, in the
comparisons between Macedon and Monmouth,

that the situations, look you, is both alike. There
is a river in Macedon; and there is also moreover
a river at Monmouth: it is called Wye at Monmouth; but it is out of my prains what is the
name of the other river; but 'tis all one, 'tis alike
as my fingers is to my fingers, and there is sal-
mons in both. If you mark Alexander's life well,
Harry of Monmouth's life is come after it indifferent well; for there is figures in all things.
Alexander, God knows, and you know, in his
rages, and his furies, and his wraths, and his
cholers, and his moods, and his displeasures, and
his indignations, and also being a little intoxicates
in his prains, did, in his ales and his angers, look
you, kill his best friend, Cleitus.   *41*

Gow. Our King is not like him in that: he never
killed any of his friends.

Flu. It is not well done, mark you now, to take
the tales out of my mouth, ere it is made and
finished. I speak but in the figures and comparisons of it: as Alexander killed his friend Cleitus,
being in his ales and his cups; so also Harry
Monmouth, being in his right wits and his good
judgements, turned away the fat knight with the
great-belly doublet: he was full of jests, and
gipes, and knaveries, and mocks; I have forgot
his name.

Gow. Sir John Falstaff.

Flu. That is he: I'll tell you there is good men
porn at Monmouth.

Gow. Here comes his Majesty.

Alarum. Enter KING HENRY, *and forces;* WARWICK,
GLOUCESTER, EXETER, *and others.*

K. Hen. I was not angry since I came to France
Until this instant. Take a trumpet, herald;
Ride thou unto the horsemen on yon hill: *60*
If they will fight with us, bid them come down,
Or void the field; they do offend our sight:
If they'll do neither, we will come to them
And make them skirr away, as swift as stones
Enforced from the old Assyrian slings:
Besides, we'll cut the throats of those we have,
And not a man of them that we shall take
Shall taste our mercy. Go and tell them so.

Enter MONTJOY.

Exe. Here comes the herald of the French, my
liege.

Glo. His eyes are humbler than they used to be.

K. Hen. How now! what means this, herald?
know'st thou not   *71*
That I have fined these bones of mine for ransom?
Comest thou again for ransom?

Mont.   No, great King:
I come to thee for charitable license,

That we may wander o'er this bloody field
To look our dead, and then to bury them;
To sort our nobles from our common men.
For many of our princes—woe the while!—
Lie drown'd and soak'd in mercenary blood;
So do our vulgar drench their peasant limbs   *80*
In blood of princes; and their wounded steeds
Fret fetlock deep in gore and with wild rage
Yerk out their armed heels at their dead masters,
Killing them twice. O, give us leave, great King,
To view the field in safety and dispose
Of their dead bodies!

K. Hen.   I tell thee truly, herald,
I know not if the day be ours or no;
For yet a many of your horsemen peer
And gallop o'er the field.

Mont.   The day is yours.

K. Hen. Praised be God, and not our strength,
for it!   *90*
What is this castle call'd that stands hard by?

Mont. They call it Agincourt.

K. Hen. Then call we this the field of Agincourt,
Fought on the day of Crispin Crispianus.

Flu. Your Grandfather of famous memory, an't
please your Majesty, and your great-uncle Edward the Plack Prince of Wales, as I have read
in the chronicles, fought a most prave pattle here
in France.

K. Hen. They did, Fluellen.   *100*

Flu. Your Majesty says very true: if your
Majesties is remembered of it, the Welshmen did
good service in a garden where leeks did grow,
wearing leeks in their Monmouth caps; which,
your Majesty know, to this hour is an honourable
badge of the service; and I do believe your Majesty takes no scorn to wear the leek upon Saint
Tavy's day.

K. Hen. I wear it for a memorable honour;
For I am Welsh, you know, good countryman.

Flu. All the water in Wye cannot wash your
Majesty's Welsh plood out of your pody, I can
tell you that: God pless it and preserve it, as long
as it pleases His Grace, and His Majesty too!

K. Hen. Thanks, good my countryman.

Flu. By Jeshu, I am your Majesty's countryman, I care not who know it; I will confess it to
all the 'orld: I need not be ashamed of your Majesty, praised be God, so long as your Majesty is
an honest man.   *120*

K. Hen. God keep me so! Our heralds go with
him:
Bring me just notice of the numbers dead
On both our parts. Call yonder fellow hither.
          [*Points to* WILLIAMS. *Exeunt Heralds*
                    with MONTJOY.

Exe. Soldier, you must come to the King.

K. Hen. Soldier, why wearest thou that glove in thy cap?

Will. An't please your Majesty, 'tis the gage of one that I should fight withal, if he be alive.

K. Hen. An Englishman? 129

Will. An't please your Majesty, a rascal that swaggered with me last night; who, if alive and ever dare to challenge this glove, I have sworn to take him a box o' th' ear: or if I can see my glove in his cap, which he swore, as he was a soldier, he he would wear if alive, I will strike it out soundly.

K. Hen. What think you, Captain Fluellen? is it fit this soldier keep his oath?

Flu. He is a craven and a villain else, an't please your Majesty, in my conscience. 140

K. Hen. It may be his enemy is a gentleman of great sort, quite from the answer of his degree.

Flu. Though he be as good a gentleman as the devil is, as Lucifer and Belzebub himself, it is necessary, look your Grace, that he keep his vow and his oath: if he be perjured, see you now, his reputation is as arrant a villain and a Jacksauce, as ever his black shoe trod upon God's ground and his earth, in my conscience, la! 150

K. Hen. Then keep thy vow, sirrah, when thou meetest the fellow.

Will. So I will, my liege, as I live.

K. Hen. Who servest thou under?

Will. Under Captain Gower, my liege.

Flu. Gower is a good captain, and is good knowledge and literatured in the wars.

K. Hen. Call him hither to me, soldier.

Will. I will, my liege. [*Exit.*

K. Hen. Here, Fluellen; wear thou this favour for me and stick it in thy cap: when Alençon and myself were down together, I plucked this glove from his helm: if any man challenge this, he is a friend to Alençon, and an enemy to our person; if thou encounter any such, apprehend him, an thou dost me love.

Flu. Your Grace doo's me as great honours as can be desired in the hearts of his subjects: I would fain see the man, that has but two legs, that shall find himself aggriefed at this glove; that is all; but I would fain see it once, an please God of His grace that I might see.

K. Hen. Knowest thou Gower?

Flu. He is my dear friend, an please you.

K. Hen. Pray thee, go seek him, and bring him to my tent.

Flu. I will fetch him. [*Exit.*

K. Hen. My Lord of Warwick, and my brother Gloucester,

Follow Fluellen closely at the heels:

The glove which I have given him for a favour

May haply purchase him a box o' th' ear; 181

It is the soldier's; I by bargain should

Wear it myself. Follow, good cousin Warwick:

If that the soldier strike him, as I judge

By his blunt bearing he will keep his word,

Some sudden mischief may arise of it;

For I do know Fluellen valiant

And, touch'd with choler, hot as gunpowder,

And quickly will return an injury: 189

Follow, and see there be no harm between them.

Go you with me, uncle of Exeter. [*Exeunt.*

SCENE VIII. *Before King Henry's pavilion*

Enter GOWER *and* WILLIAMS.

Will. I warrant it is to knight you, captain.

Enter FLUELLEN.

Flu. God's will and his pleasure, captain, I beseech you now, come apace to the King: there is more good toward you peradventure than is in your knowledge to dream of.

Will. Sir, know you this glove?

Flu. Know the glove! I know the glove is a glove.

Will. I know this; and thus I challenge it.

Strikes him.

Flu. 'Sblood! an arrant traitor as any is in the universal world, or in France, or in England! 11

Gow. How now, sir! you villain!

Will. Do you think I'll be forsworn?

Flu. Stand away, Captain Gower; I will give treason his payment into plows, I warrant you.

Will. I am no traitor.

Flu. That's a lie in thy throat. I charge you in his Majesty's name, apprehend him: he's a friend of the Duke of Alençon's. 19

Enter WARWICK *and* GLOUCESTER.

War. How now, how now! what's the matter?

Flu. My Lord of Warwick, here is—praised be God for it!—a most contagious treason come to light, look you, as you shall desire in a summer's day. Here is his Majesty.

Enter KING HENRY *and* EXETER.

K. Hen. How now! what's the matter?

Flu. My liege, here is a villain and a traitor, that, look your Grace, has struck the glove which your Majesty is take out of the helmet of Alençon.

Will. My liege, this was my glove; here is the fellow of it; and he that I gave it to in change promised to wear it in his cap: I promised to strike him, if he did: I met this man with my glove in his cap, and I have been as good as my word.

Flu. Your Majesty hear now, saying your Ma-

jesty's manhood, what an arrant, rascally, beggarly, lousy knave it is: I hope your Majesty is
pear me testimony and witness, and will avouch-
ment, that this is the glove of Alençon, that your
Majesty is give me; in your conscience, now.   *40*

K. Hen. Give me thy glove, soldier: look, here
is the fellow of it.
'Twas I, indeed, thou promised'st to strike;
And thou hast given me most bitter terms.

Flu. And please your Majesty, let his neck
answer for it, if there is any martial law in the
world.

K. Hen. How canst thou make me satisfaction?

Will. All offences, my lord, come from the
heart: never came any from mine that might
offend your Majesty.   *51*

K. Hen. It was ourself thou didst abuse.

Will. Your Majesty came not like yourself: you
appeared to me but as a common man; witness
the night, your garments, your lowliness; and
what your Highness suffered under that shape, I
beseech you take it for your own fault and not
mine: for had you been as I took you for, I made
no offence; therefore, I beseech your Highness,
pardon me.   *60*

K. Hen. Here, uncle Exeter, fill this glove with
crowns,
And give it to this fellow. Keep it, fellow;
And wear it for an honour in thy cap
Till I do challenge it. Give him the crowns:
And, captain, you must needs be friends with
him.

Flu. By this day and this light, the fellow has
mettle enough in his belly. Hold, there is twelve
pence for you; and I pray you to serve God, and
keep you out of prawls, and prabbles, and quarrels, and dissensions, and, I warrant you, it is the
better for you.   *71*

Will. I will none of your money.

Flu. It is with a good will; I can tell you, it will
serve you to mend your shoes: come, wherefore
should you be so pashful? your shoes is not so
good: 'tis a good silling, I warrant you, or I will
change it.

Enter an ENGLISH HERALD.

K. Hen. Now, herald, are the dead number'd?

Her. Here is the number of the slaughter'd
French.

K. Hen. What prisoners of good sort are taken,
uncle?   *80*

Exe. Charles Duke of Orleans, nephew to the
King;
John Duke of Bourbon, and Lord Bouciqualt:
Of other lords and barons, knights and squires,
Full fifteen hundred, besides common men.

K. Hen. This note doth tell me of ten thousand
French
That in the field lie slain: of princes, in this
number,
And nobles bearing banners, there lie dead
One hundred twenty six: added to these,
Of knights, esquires, and gallant gentlemen,   *89*
Eight thousand and four hundred; of the which,
Five hundred were but yesterday dubb'd knights:
So that, in these ten thousand they have lost,
There are but sixteen hundred mercenaries;
The rest are princes, barons, lords, knights,
squires,
And gentlemen of blood and quality.
The names of those their nobles that lie dead:
Charles Delabreth, High Constable of France;
Jacques of Chatillon, admiral of France;
The master of the cross-bows, Lord Rambures;
Great Master of France, the brave Sir Guichard
Dolphin,   *100*
John Duke of Alençon, Anthony Duke of Brabant,
The brother to the Duke of Burgundy,
And Edward Duke of Bar: of lusty earls,
Grandpré and Roussi, Fauconberg and Foix,
Beaumont and Marle, Vaudemont and Lestrale.
Here was a royal fellowship of death!
Where is the number of our English dead?
Herald shews him another paper.
Edward the Duke of York, the Earl of Suffolk,
Sir Richard Ketly, Davy Gam, esquire:
None else of name; and of all other men   *110*
But five and twenty. O God, thy arm was here;
And not to us, but to thy arm alone,
Ascribe we all! When, without stratagem,
But in plain shock and even play of battle,
Was ever known so great and little loss
On one part and on the other? Take it, God,
For it is none but thine!

Exe.   'Tis wonderful!

K. Hen. Come, go we in procession to the
village:
And be it death proclaimed through our host
To boast of this or take that praise from God   *120*
Which is his only.

Flu. Is it not lawful, an please your Majesty, to
tell how many is killed?

K. Hen. Yes, captain; but with this acknow-
ledgement,
That God fought for us.

Flu. Yes, my conscience, he did us great good.

K. Hen. Do we all holy rites;
Let there be sung *Non nobis* and *Te Deum*;
The dead with charity enclosed in clay:
And then to Calais; and to England then;   *130*
Where ne'er from France arrived more happy
men.   [*Exeunt.*

ACT V

PROLOGUE

Enter CHORUS.

Chor. Vouchsafe to those that have not read the
    story,
That I may prompt them: and of such as have,
I humbly pray them to admit the excuse
Of time, of numbers, and due course of things,
Which cannot in their huge and proper life
Be here presented. Now we bear the King
Toward Calais: grant him there; there seen,
Heave him away upon your winged thoughts
Athwart the sea. Behold, the English beach   9
Pales in the flood with men, with wives and
    boys,
Whose shouts and claps out-voice the deep-
    mouth'd sea,
Which like a mighty whiffler 'fore the King
Seems to prepare his way: so let him land,
And solemnly see him set on to London.
So swift a pace hath thought that even now
You may imagine him upon Blackheath;
Where that his lords desire him to have borne
His bruised helmet and his bended sword
Before him through the city: he forbids it,   19
Being free from vainness and self-glorious pride;
Giving full trophy, signal, and ostent
Quite from himself to God. But now behold,
In the quick forge and working-house of thought,
How London doth pour out her citizens!
The mayor and all his brethren in best sort,
Like to the senators of the antique Rome,
With the plebeians swarming at their heels,
Go forth and fetch their conquering Cæsar in:
As, by a lower but loving likelihood,
Were now the general of our gracious Empress,
As in good time he may, from Ireland coming,   31
Bringing rebellion broached on his sword,
How many would the peaceful city quit,
To welcome him! much more, and much more
    cause,
Did they this Harry. Now in London place him;
As yet the lamentation of the French
Invites the King of England's stay at home;
The Emperor's coming in behalf of France,
To order peace between them; and omit
All the occurrences, whatever chanced,   40
Till Harry's back-return again to France:
There must we bring him; and myself have
    play'd
The interim, by remembering you 'tis past.
Then brook abridgement, and your eyes advance
After your thoughts, straight back again to
    France.   [*Exit.*

SCENE I. *France: the English camp*

Enter FLUELLEN *and* GOWER.

Gow. Nay, that's right; but why wear you
your leek to-day? Saint Davy's day is past.

Flu. There is occasions and causes why and
wherefore in all things: I will tell you, asse my
friend, Captain Gower: the rascally, scauld, beggarly, lousy, pragging knave, Pistol, which you
and yourself and all the world know to be no
petter than a fellow, look you now, of no merits,
he is come to me and prings me pread and salt
yesterday, look you, and bid me eat my leek: it
was in a place where I could not breed no contention with him; but I will be so bold as to wear it
in my cap till I see him once again, and then I will
tell him a little piece of my desires.

Enter PISTOL.

Gow. Why, here he comes, swelling like a
turkey-cock.

Flu. 'Tis no matter for his swellings nor his
turkey-cocks. God pless you, Aunchient Pistol!
you scurvy, lousy knave, God pless you!

Pist. Ha! art thou bedlam? dost thou thirst,
    base Trojan,   20
To have me fold up Parca's fatal web?
Hence! I am qualmish at the smell of leek.

Flu. I peseech you heartily, scurvy, lousy knave,
at my desires, and my requests, and my petitions,
to eat, look you, this leek: because, look you,
you do not love it, nor your affections and your
appetites and your disgestions doo's not agree
with it, I would desire you to eat it.

Pist. Not for Cadwallader and all his goats.

Flu. There is one goat for you. [*Strikes him.*]
Will you be so good, scauld knave, as eat it?   31

Pist. Base Trojan, thou shalt die.

Flu. You say very true, scauld knave, when
God's will is: I will desire you to live in the mean
time, and eat your victuals: come, there is sauce
for it. [*Strikes him.*] You called me yesterday
mountain-squire; but I will make you to-day a
squire of low degree. I pray you, fall to: if you
can mock a leek, you can eat a leek.

Gow. Enough, captain: you have astonished
him.   41

Flu. I say, I will make him eat some part of my
leek, or I will peat his pate four days. Bite, I
pray you; it is good for your green wound and
your ploody coxcomb.

Pist. Must I bite?

Flu. Yes, certainly, and out of doubt and out of
question too, and ambiguities.

Pist. By this leek, I will most horribly revenge:
I eat and eat, I swear—   50

Flu. Eat, I pray you: will you have some more sauce to your leek? there is not enough leek to swear by.

Pist. Quiet thy cudgel; thou dost see I eat.

Flu. Much good do you, scauld knave, heartily. Nay, pray you, throw none away; the skin is good for your broken coxcomb. When you take occasions to see leeks hereafter, I pray you, mock at 'em; that is all.

Pist. Good.   60

Flu. Ay, leeks is good: hold you, there is a groat to heal your pate.

Flu. Yes, verily and in truth, you shall take it; or I have another leek in my pocket, which you shall eat.

Pist. I take thy groat in earnest of revenge.

Flu. If I owe you anything, I will pay you in cudgels: you shall be a woodmonger, and buy nothing of me but cudgels. God b' wi' you, and keep you, and heal your pate.   [*Exit*. 71

Pist. All hell shall stir for this.

Gow. Go, go; you are a counterfeit cowardly knave. Will you mock at an ancient tradition, begun upon an honourable respect, and worn as a memorable trophy of predeceased valour and dare not avouch in your deeds any of your words? I have seen you gleeking and galling at this gentleman twice or thrice. You thought, because he could not speak English in the native garb, he could not therefore handle an English cudgel: you find it otherwise; and henceforth let a Welsh correction teach you a good English condition. Fare ye well.   [*Exit*.

Pist. Doth Fortune play the huswife with me now?

News have I, that my Nell is dead i' the spital Of malady of France;
And there my rendezvous is quite cut off.
Old I do wax; and from my weary limbs
Honour is cudgelled. Well, bawd I'll turn,   90
And something learn to cutpurse of quick hand.
To England will I steal, and there I'll steal:
And patches will I get unto these cudgell'd scars,
And swear I got them in the Gallia wars.   [*Exit*.

SCENE II. *France: a royal palace*

Enter, at one door, KING HENRY, EXETER, BEDFORD, GLOUCESTER, WARWICK, WESTMORELAND, *and other Lords; at another, the* FRENCH KING, QUEEN ISABEL, *the* PRINCESS KATHARINE, ALICE *and other Ladies; the* DUKE OF BURGUNDY, *and his train.*

K. Hen. Peace to this meeting, wherefore we are met!

Unto our brother France, and to our sister,
Health and fair time of day; joy and good wishes
To our most fair and princely cousin Katharine;
And, as a branch and member of this royalty,
By whom this great assembly is contrived,
We do salute you, Duke of Burgundy;
And, princes French, and peers, health to you all!

Fr. King. Right joyous are we to behold your face,

Most worthy brother England; fairly met: 10
So are you, princes English, every one.

Q. Isa. So happy be the issue, brother England, Of this good day and of this gracious meeting, As we are now glad to behold your eyes;
Your eyes, which hitherto have borne in them
Against the French that met them in their bent
The fatal balls of murdering basilisks:
The venom of such looks, we fairly hope,
Have lost their quality, and that this day
Shall change all griefs and quarrels into love.   20

K. Hen. To cry amen to that, thus we appear.

Q. Isa. You English princes all, I do salute you.

Bur. My duty to you both, on equal love,
Great Kings of France and England! That I have labour'd,
With all my wits, my pains, and strong endeavours
To bring your most imperial Majesties
Unto this bar and royal interview,
Your mightiness on both parts best can witness.
Since then my office hath so far prevail'd
That, face to face and royal eye to eye,   30
You have congreeted, let it not disgrace me,
If I demand, before this royal view,
What rub or what impediment there is,
Why that naked, poor, and mangled Peace,
Dear nurse of arts, plenties, and joyful births,
Should not in this best garden of the world,
Our fertile France, put up her lovely visage?
Alas, she hath from France too long been chased,
And all her husbandry doth lie on heaps,
Corrupting in its own fertility.   40
Her vine, the merry cheerer of the heart,
Unpruned dies; her hedges even-pleach'd,
Like prisoners wildly overgrown with hair,
Put forth disorder'd twigs; her fallow leas
The darnel, hemlock, and rank fumitory
Doth root upon, while that the coulter rusts
That should deracinate such savagery;
The even mead, that erst brought sweetly forth
The freckled cowslip, burnet, and green clover,
Wanting the scythe, all uncorrected, rank,   50
Conceives by idleness and nothing teems
But hateful docks, rough thistles, kecksies, burs,
Losing both beauty and utility.
And as our vineyards, fallows, meads, and hedges,
Defective in their natures, grow to wildness,

Even so our houses and ourselves and children
Have lost, or do not learn for want of time,
The sciences that should become our country;
But grow like savages—as soldiers will
That nothing do but meditate on blood—   60
To swearing and stern looks, diffused attire
And everything that seems unnatural.
Which to reduce into our former favour
You are assembled: and my speech entreats
That I may know the let why gentle Peace
Should not expel these inconveniences
And bless us with her former qualities.
  K. Hen. If, Duke of Burgundy, you would the
        peace,
Whose want gives growth to the imperfections
Which you have cited, you must buy that peace
With full accord to all our just demands;   71
Whose tenours and particular effects
You have enscheduled briefly in your hands.
  Bur. The King hath heard them; to the which
        as yet
There is no answer made.
  K. Hen.   Well then the peace,
Which you before so urged, lies in his answer.
  Fr. King. I have but with a cursorary eye
O'erglanced the articles: pleaseth your Grace
To appoint some of your council presently
To sit with us once more, with better heed   80
To re-survey them, we will suddenly
Pass our accept and peremptory answer.
  K. Hen. Brother, we shall. Go, uncle Exeter,
And brother Clarence, and you, brother Glou·
        cester.
Warwick and Huntingdon, go with the King;
And take with you free power to ratify,
Augment, or alter, as your wisdoms best
Shall see advantageable for our dignity,
Anything in or out of our demands,
And we'll consign thereto. Will you, fair
        sister,
Go with the princes, or stay here with us?   91
  Q. Isa. Our gracious brother, I will go with
        them:
Haply a woman's voice may do some good,
When articles too nicely urged be stood on.
  K. Hen. Yet leave our cousin Katharine here
        with us:
She is our capital demand, comprised
Within the fore-rank of our articles.
  Q. Isa. She hath good leave.
        [Exeunt all except HENRY, KATHARINE,
                and ALICE.
  K. Hen.   Fair Katharine, and most fair,
Will you vouchsafe to teach a soldier terms
Such as will enter at a lady's ear   100
And plead his love-suit to her gentle heart?

  Kath. Your Majesty shall mock at me; I cannot speak your England.
  K. Hen. O fair Katharine, if you will love me
soundly with your French heart, I will be glad to
hear you confess it brokenly with your English
tongue. Do you like me, Kate?
  Kath. Pardonnez-moi, I cannot tell vat is "like
me."
  K. Hen. An angel is like you, Kate, and you are
like an angel.   111
  Kath. Que dit-il? que je suis semblable à les anges?
  Alice. Oui, vraiment, sauf votre grace, ainsi dit-il.
  K. Hen. I said so, dear Katharine; and I must
not blush to affirm it.
  Kath. O bon Dieu! les langues des hommes sont
pleines de tromperies.
  K. Hen. What says she, fair one? that the tongues of men are full of deceits?   121
  Alice. Oui, dat de tongues of de mans is be full
of deceits: dat is de princess.
  K. Hen. The princess is the better English-
woman. I' faith, Kate, my wooing is fit for thy
understanding: I am glad thou canst speak no
better English: for, if thou couldst, thou wouldst
find me such a plain king that thou wouldst think
I had sold my farm to buy my crown. I know
no ways to mince it in love, but directly to say
"I love you": then if you urge me farther than to
say "do you in faith?" I wear out my suit. Give
me your answer; i' faith, do: and so clap hands
and a bargain: how say you, lady?
  Kath. Sauf votre honneur, me understand vell.
  K. Hen. Marry, if you would put me to verses
or to dance for your sake, Kate, why you undid
me: for the one, I have neither words nor measure, and for the other, I have no strength in
measure, yet a reasonable measure in strength.
If I could win a lady at leap-frog, or by vaulting
into my saddle with my armour on my back,
under the correction of bragging be it spoken, I
should quickly leap into a wife. Or if I might
buffet for my love, or bound my horse for her
favours, I could lay on like a butcher and sit like
a jack-an-apes, never off. But, before God, Kate,
I cannot look greenly nor gasp out my eloquence,
nor I have no cunning in protestation; only downright oaths, which I never use till urged, nor
never break for urging. If thou canst love a
fellow of this temper, Kate, whose face is not
worth sun-burning, that never looks in his glass
for love of anything he sees there, let thine eye
be thy cook. I speak to thee plain soldier: if
thou canst love me for this take me; if not, to
say to thee that I shall die, is true; but for thy
love, by the Lord, no; yet I love thee too. And
while thou livest, dear Kate, take a fellow of

plain and uncoined constancy; for he perforce must do thee right, because he hath not the gift to woo in other places: for these fellows of infinite tongue, that can rhyme themselves into ladies' favours, they do always reason themselves out again. What! a speaker is but a prater; a rhyme is but a ballad. A good leg will fall; a straight back will stoop; a black beard will turn white; a curled pate will grow bald; a fair face will wither; a full eye will wax hollow: but a good heart, Kate, is the sun and the moon; or rather the sun and not the moon; for it shines bright and never changes, but keeps his course truly. If thou would have such a one, take me; and take me, take a soldier; take a soldier, take a king. And what sayest thou then to my love? speak, my fair, and fairly, I pray thee.

Kath. Is it possible dat I sould love de enemy of France?   *179*

K. Hen. No; it is not possible you should love the enemy of France, Kate: but, in loving me, you should love the friend of France; for I love France so well that I will not part with a village of it; I will have it all mine: and, Kate, when France is mine and I am yours, then yours is France and you are mine.

Kath. I cannot tell vat is dat.

K. Hen. No, Kate? I will tell thee in French; which I am sure will hang upon my tongue like a new-married wife about her husband's neck, hardly to be shook off. *Je quand sur le possession de France, et quand vous avez le possession de moi—* let me see, what then? Saint Denis be my speed!—*donc votre est France et vous êtes mienne.* It is easy for me, Kate, to conquer the kingdom as to speak so much more French: I shall never move thee in French, unless it be to laugh at me.

Kath. Sauf votre honneur, le François que vous parlez, il est meilleur que l'Anglois lequel je parle.   201

K. Hen. No, faith, is't not, Kate: but thy speaking of my tongue, and I thine, most truly-falsely, must needs be granted to be much at one. But, Kate, dost thou understand thus much English: canst thou love me?

Kath. I cannot tell.

K. Hen. Can any of your neighbours tell, Kate? I'll ask them. Come, I know thou lovest me: and at night, when you come into your closet, you'll question this gentlewoman about me; and I know Kate, you will to her dispraise those parts in me that you love with your heart: but, good Kate, mock me mercifully; the rather, gentle princess, because I love thee cruelly. If ever thou beest mine, Kate, as I have a saving faith within me tells me thou shalt, I get thee with scambling, and thou must therefore needs prove a good

soldier-breeder: shall not thou and I, between Saint Denis and Saint George, compound a boy, half French, half English, that shall go to Constantinople and take the Turk by the beard? shall we not? what sayest thou, my fair flower-de-luce?

Kath. I do not know dat.

K. Hen. No; 'tis hereafter to know, but now to promise: do but now promise, Kate, you will endeavour for your French part of such a boy; and for my English moiety take the word of a king and bachelor. How answer you, *la plus belle Katharine du monde, mon très cher et devin déesse?*

Kath. Your majestee ave fausse French enough to deceive de most sage demoiselle dat is en France.

K. Hen. Now, fie upon my false French! By mine honour, in true English, I love thee, Kate: by which honour I dare not swear thou lovest me; yet my blood begins to flatter me that thou dost, notwithstanding the poor and untempering effect of my visage. Now, beshrew my father's ambition! he was thinking of civil wars when he got me: therefore was I created with a stubborn outside, with an aspect of iron, that, when I come to woo ladies, I fright them. But, in faith, Kate, the elder I wax, the better I shall appear: my comfort is, that old age, that ill layer up of beauty, can do no more spoil upon my face: thou hast me, if thou hast me, at the worst; and thou shalt wear me, if thou wear me, better and better: and therefore tell me, most fair Katharine, will you have me? Put off your maiden blushes; avouch the thoughts of your heart with the looks of an empress; take me by the hand, and say, "Harry of England, I am thine": which word thou shalt no sooner bless mine ear withal, but I will tell thee aloud, "England is thine, Ireland is thine, France is thine, and Henry Plantagenet is thine"; who, though I speak it before his face, if he be not fellow with the best king, thou shalt find the best king of good fellows. Come, your answer in broken music; for thy voice is music and thy English broken; therefore, queen of all, Katharine, break thy mind to me in broken English; wilt thou have me?

Kath. Dat is as it sall please de *roi mon père.*

K. Hen. Nay, it will please him well, Kate; it shall please him, Kate.

Kath. Den it sall also content me.   *270*

K. Hen. Upon that I kiss your hand, and I call you my queen.

Kath. Laissez, mon seigneur, laissez, laissez: ma foi, je ne veux point que vous abaissiez votre grandeur en baisant la main d'une de votre seigneurie indigne serviteur; excusez-moi, je vous supplie, mon très-puissant seigneur.

K. Hen. Then I will kiss your lips, Kate.

Kath. Les dames et demoiselles pour être baisées devant leur noces, il n'est pas la coutume de France.
281

K. Hen. Madam my interpreter, what says she?

Alice. Dat it is not be de fashion *pour les* ladies of France—I cannot tell vat is *baiser* en Anglish.

K. Hen. To kiss.

Alice. Your Majesty *entendre* bettre *que moi.*

K. Hen. It is not a fashion for the maids in France to kiss before they are married, would she say?

Alice. Oui, vraiment.

K. Hen. O Kate, nice customs curtsy to great kings. Dear Kate, you and I cannot be confined within the weak list of a country's fashion: we are the makers of manners, Kate; and the liberty that follows our places stops the mouth of all find-faults; as I will do yours, for upholding the nice fashion of your country in denying me a kiss: therefore, patiently and yielding. [*Kissing her.*] You have witchcraft in your lips, Kate: there is more eloquence in a sugar touch of them than in the tongues of the French council; and they should sooner persuade Harry of England than a general petition of monarchs. Here comes your father.

Re-enter the FRENCH KING *and his* QUEEN, BURGUNDY, *and other Lords.*

Bur. God save your Majesty! my royal cousin, teach you our princess English?

K. Hen. I would have her learn, my fair cousin, how perfectly I love her; and that is good English.

Bur. Is she not apt?

K. Hen. Our tongue is rough, coz, and my condition is not smooth; so that, having neither the voice nor the heart of flattery about me, I cannot so conjure up the spirit of love in her, that he will appear in his true likeness.

Bur. Pardon the frankness of my mirth, if I answer you for that. If you would conjure in her, you must make a circle; if conjure up love in her in his true likeness, he must appear naked and blind. Can you blame her then, being a maid yet rosed over with the virgin crimson of modesty, if she deny the appearance of a naked blind boy in her naked seeing self? It were, my lord, a hard condition for a maid to consign to.

K. Hen. Yet they do wink and yield, as love is blind and enforces.

Bur. They are then excused, my lord, when they see not what they do.　330

K. Hen. Then, good my lord, teach your cousin to consent winking.

Bur. I will wink on her to consent, my lord, if you will teach her to know my meaning: for maids, well summered and warm kept, are like flies at Bartholomew-tide, blind, though they have their eyes; and then they will endure handling, which before would not abide looking on.

K. Hen. This moral ties me over to time and a hot summer; and so I shall catch the fly, your cousin, in the latter end and she must be blind too.

Bur. As love is, my lord, before it loves.

K. Hen. It is so: and you may, some of you, thank love for my blindness, who cannot see many a fair French city for one fair French maid that stands in my way.

Fr. King. Yes, my lord, you see them perspectively, the cities turned into a maid; for they are all girdled with maiden walls that war hath never entered.　350

K. Hen. Shall Kate be my wife?

Fr. King. So please you.

K. Hen. I am content; so the maiden cities you talk of may wait on her: so the maid that stood in the way for my wish shall show me the way to my will.

Fr. King. We have consented to all terms of reason.

K. Hen. Is't so, my lords of England?　359

West. The king hath granted every article:
His daughter first, and then in sequel all,
According to their firm proposed natures.

Exe. Only he hath not yet subscribed this:
Where your Majesty demands, that the King of France, having any occasion to write for matter of grant, shall name your Highness in this form and with this addition, in French, *Notre très-cher fils Henri, Roi d'Angleterre, Héritier de France;* and thus in Latin, *Præclarissimus filius noster Henricus, Rex Angliæ, et Hæres Franciæ.*

Fr. King. Nor this I have not, brother, so denied,
But your request shall make me let it pass.

K. Hen. I pray you then, in love and dear alliance,
Let that one article rank with the rest;
And thereupon give me your daughter.

Fr. King. Take her, fair son, and from her blood raise up
Issue to me; that the contending kingdoms
Of France and England, whose very shores look pale
With envy of each other's happiness,

May cease their hatred, and this dear conjunc-
    tion   *380*
Plant neighbourhood and Christian-like accord
In their sweet bosoms, that never war advance
His bleeding sword 'twixt England and fair
    France.
All. Amen!
K. Hen. Now, welcome, Kate: and bear me
    witness all,
That here I kiss her as my sovereign queen.
                           [Flourish.
Q. Isa. God, the best maker of all marriages,
Combine your hearts in one, your realms in one!
As man and wife, being two, are one in love,
So be there 'twixt your kingdoms such a spousal
That never may ill office, or fell jealousy,
Which troubles oft the bed of blessed marriage,
Thrust in between the paction of these kingdoms,
To make divorce of their incorporate league;
That English may as French, French English-
    men,
Receive each other. God speak this Amen!
All. Amen!
K. Hen. Prepare we for our marriage: on which
    day,
My Lord of Burgundy, we'll take your oath,

And all the peers', for surety of our leagues.   *400*
Then shall I swear to Kate, and you to me;
And may our oaths well kept and prosperous be!
                       [Sennet. Exeunt.

EPILOGUE

Enter CHORUS.

Chor. Thus far, with rough and all-unable pen,
    Our bending author hath pursued the story,
In little room confining mighty men,
    Mangling by starts the full course of their
        glory.
Small time, but in that small most greatly lived
    This star of England: Fortune made his sword;
By which the world's best garden he achieved,
    And of it left his son imperial lord.
Henry the Sixth, in infant bands crown'd King
    Of France and England, did this king suc-
        ceed;   *10*
Whose state so many had the managing,
    That they lost France and made his England
        bleed:
Which oft our stage hath shown; and, for their
    sake,
In your fair minds let this acceptance take.
                               [Exit.

❧ JULIUS CÆSAR

DRAMATIS PERSONÆ

JULIUS CÆSAR, *later as a* GHOST
OCTAVIUS CÆSAR ⎫
MARCUS ANTONIUS ⎬ *Triumvirs after the death*
M. ÆMILIUS LEPIDUS ⎭ *of Julius Cæsar*
CICERO
PUBLIUS ⎫ *Senators*
POPILIUS LENA ⎭
MARCUS BRUTUS
CASSIUS
CASCA
TREBONIUS ⎫ *conspirators against Julius*
LIGARIUS ⎬ *Cæsar*
DECIUS BRUTUS
METELLUS CIMBER
CINNA
FLAVIUS ⎫ *Tribunes*
MARULLUS ⎭
ARTEMIDORUS OF CNIDOS, *a teacher of rhetoric*
A SOOTHSAYER
CINNA, *a poet*
ANOTHER POET
LUCILIUS
TITINIUS
MESSALA ⎬ *friends to Brutus and Cassius*
YOUNG CATO
VOLUMNIUS

VARRO ⎫
CLITUS
CLAUDIUS
STRATO ⎬ *servants to Brutus*
LUCIUS
DARDANIUS ⎭
PINDARUS, *servant to Cassius*
TWO COMMONERS
A SERVANT *to Cæsar*
A SERVANT *to Antony*
A SERVANT *to Octavius*
FOUR CITIZENS
THREE SOLDIERS
A MESSENGER

CALPURNIA, *wife to Cæsar*
PORTIA, *wife to Brutus*

NON-SPEAKING: *Senators, Citizens, Guards, Soldiers, and Attendants*

SCENE: *Rome, the neighborhood of Sardis, and the neighborhood of Philippi*

❧

ACT I

SCENE I. *Rome: a street*

Enter FLAVIUS, MARULLUS, *and certain* COMMONERS.

Flav. Hence! home, you idle creatures, get you home:
Is this a holiday? what! know you not,
Being mechanical, you ought not walk
Upon a labouring day without the sign
Of your profession? Speak, what trade art thou?
1st Com. Why, sir, a carpenter.
Mar. Where is thy leather apron and thy rule?
What dost thou with thy best apparel on?
You, sir, what trade are you?
2nd Com. Truly, sir, in respect of a fine workman, I am but, as you would say, a cobbler. 11
Mar. But what trade art thou? answer me directly.
2nd Com. A trade, sir, that I hope I may use with a safe conscience; which is, indeed, sir, a mender of bad soles.
Mar. What trade, thou knave? thou naughty knave, what trade?
2nd Com. Nay, I beseech you, sir, be not out with me: yet, if you be out, sir, I can mend you.

Mar. What meanest thou by that? mend me thou saucy fellow! 21
2nd Com. Why, sir, cobble you.
Flav. Thou art a cobbler, art thou?
2nd Com. Truly, sir, all that I live by is with the awl: I meddle with no tradesman's matters, nor women's matters, but with awl. I am, indeed, sir, a surgeon to old shoes; when they are in great danger, I recover them. As proper men as ever trod upon neat's leather have gone upon my handiwork. 30
Flav. But wherefore art not in thy shop today?
Why dost thou lead these men about the streets?
2nd Com. Truly, sir, to wear out their shoes, to get myself into more work. But, indeed, sir, we make holiday, to see Cæsar and to rejoice in his triumph.
Mar. Wherefore rejoice? What conquest brings he home?
What tributaries follow him to Rome
To grace in captive bonds his chariot-wheels?
You blocks, you stones, you worse than senseless things! 40
O you hard hearts, you cruel men of Rome,
Knew you not Pompey? Many a time and oft
Have you climb'd up to walls and battlements,

To towers and windows, yea, to chimney-tops,
Your infants in your arms, and there have sat
The live-long day, with patient expectation,
To see great Pompey pass the streets of Rome:
And when you saw his chariot but appear,
Have you not made an universal shout,
That Tiber trembled underneath her banks   50
To hear the replication of your sounds
Made in her concave shores?
And do you now put on your best attire?
And do you now cull out a holiday?
And do you now strew flowers in his way
That comes in triumph over Pompey's blood?
Be gone!
Run to your houses, fall upon your knees,
Pray to the gods to intermit the plague
That needs must light on this ingratitude.   60
   Flav. Go, to, good countrymen, and, for this
     fault,
Assemble all the poor men of your sort;
Draw them to Tiber banks, and weep your tears
Into the channel, till the lowest stream
Do kiss the most exalted shores of all.
                [*Exeunt all the* COMMONERS.
See, whether their basest metal be not moved;
They vanish tongue-tied in their guiltiness.
Go you down that way towards the Capitol;
This way will I: disrobe the images,
If you do find them deck'd with ceremonies.   70
   Mar. May we do so?
You know it is the feast of Lupercal.
   Flav. It is no matter; let no images
Be hung with Cæsar's trophies. I'll about
And drive away the vulgar from the streets:
So do you too, where you perceive them thick.
These growing feathers pluck'd from Cæsar's
     wing
Will make him fly an ordinary pitch,
Who else would soar above the view of men   79
And keep us all in servile fearfulness.   [*Exeunt.*

SCENE II. *A public place*

Flourish. Enter CÆSAR; ANTONY, *for the course;*
CALPURNIA, PORTIA, DECIUS, CICERO, BRUTUS,
CASSIUS, *and* CASCA; *a great crowd following,
among them a* SOOTHSAYER.

   Cæs. Calpurnia!
   Casca.   Peace, ho! Cæsar speaks.
   Cæs.   Calpurnia!
   Cal. Here, my lord.
   Cæs. Stand you directly in Antonius' way,
When he doth run his course. Antonius!
   Ant. Cæsar, my lord?
   Cæs. Forget not, in your speed, Antonius,
To touch Calpurnia; for our elders say,
The barren, touched in this holy chase,

Shake off their sterile curse.
   Ant.   I shall remember:
When Cæsar says "do this," it is perform'd.   10
   Cæs. Set on; and leave no ceremony out.
     Flourish.
   Sooth. Cæsar!
   Cæs. Ha! who calls?
   Casca. Bid every noise be still: peace yet again!
   Cæs. Who is it in the press that calls on me?
I hear a tongue, shriller than all the music,
Cry "Cæsar!" Speak; Cæsar is turn'd to hear.
   Sooth. Beware the ides of March.
   Cæs.   What man is that?
   Bru. A soothsayer bids you beware the ides of
     March.   19
   Cæs. Set him before me; let me see his face.
   Cas. Fellow, come from the throng; look upon
     Cæsar.
   Cæs. What say'st thou to me now? speak once
     again.
   Sooth. Beware the ides of March.
   Cæs. He is a dreamer; let us leave him: pass.
               [*Sennet. Exeunt all except*
                   BRUTUS *and* CASSIUS.
   Cas. Will you go see the order of the course?
   Bru. Not I.
   Cas. I pray you, do.
   Bru. I am not gamesome: I do lack some part
Of that quick spirit that is in Antony.
Let me not hinder, Cassius, your desires;   30
I'll leave you.
   Cas. Brutus, I do observe you now of late:
I have not from your eyes that gentleness
And show of love as I was wont to have:
You bear too stubborn and too strange a hand
Over your friend that loves you.
   Bru.   Cassius,
Be not deceived: if I have veil'd my look,
I turn the trouble of my countenance
Merely upon myself. Vexed I am
Of late with passions of some difference,   40
Conceptions only proper to myself,
Which give some soil perhaps to my behaviours;
But let not therefore my good friends be grieved—
Among which number, Cassius, be you one—
Nor construe any further my neglect,
Than that poor Brutus, with himself at war,
Forgets the shows of love to other men.
   Cas. Then, Brutus, I have much mistook your
     passion;
By means whereof this breast of mine hath buried
Thoughts of great value, worthy cogitations.   50
Tell me, good Brutus, can you see your face?
   Bru. No, Cassius; for the eye sees not itself
But by reflection, by some other things.
   Cas. 'Tis just:

And it is very much lamented, Brutus,
That you have no such mirrors as will turn
Your hidden worthiness into your eye
That you might see your shadow. I have heard,
Where many of the best respect in Rome,
Except immortal Cæsar, speaking of Brutus   60
And groaning underneath this age's yoke,
Have wish'd that noble Brutus had his eyes.
   Bru. Into what dangers would you lead me,
    Cassius,
That you would have me seek into myself
For that which is not in me?
   Cas. Therefore, good Brutus, be prepared to
    hear:
And since you know you cannot see yourself
So well as by reflection, I, your glass,
Will modestly discover to yourself
That of yourself which you yet know not of.   70
And be not jealous on me, gentle Brutus:
Were I a common laugher, or did use
To stale with ordinary oaths my love
To every new protester; if you know
That I do fawn on men and hug them hard
And after scandal them, or if you know
That I profess myself in banqueting
To all the rout, then hold me dangerous.
   Flourish, and shout.
   Bru. What means this shouting? I do fear, the
    people
Choose Cæsar for their king.
   Cas.   Ay, do you fear it?   80
Then must I think you would not have it so.
   Bru. I would not, Cassius; yet I love him well.
But wherefore do you hold me here so long?
What is it that you would impart to me?
If it be aught toward the general good,
Set honour in one eye and death i' the other,
And I will look on both indifferently:
For let the gods so speed me as I love
The name of honour more than I fear death.   89
   Cas. I know that virtue to be in you, Brutus,
As well as I do know your outward favour.
Well, honour is the subject of my story.
I cannot tell what you and other men
Think of this life; but, for my single self,
I had as lief not be as live to be
In awe of such a thing as I myself.
I was born free as Cæsar; so were you:
We both have fed as well, and we can both
Endure the winter's cold as well as he:
For once, upon a raw and gusty day,   100
The troubled Tiber chafing with her shores,
Cæsar said to me, "Darest thou, Cassius, now
Leap in with me into this angry flood,
And swim to yonder point?" Upon the word,
Accoutred as I was, I plunged in

And bade him follow; so indeed he did.
The torrent roar'd, and we did buffet it
With lusty sinews, throwing it aside
And stemming it with hearts of controversy;
But ere we could arrive the point proposed,   110
Cæsar cried, "Help me, Cassius, or I sink!"
I, as Æneas, our great ancestor,
Did from the flames of Troy upon his shoulder
The old Anchises bear, so from the waves of
    Tiber
Did I the tired Cæsar. And this man
Is now become a god, and Cassius is
A wretched creature and must bend his body,
If Cæsar carelessly but nod on him.
He had a fever when he was in Spain,
And when the fit was on him, I did mark   120
How he did shake: 'tis true, this god did shake:
His coward lips did from their colour fly,
And that same eye whose bend doth awe the
    world
Did lose his lustre: I did hear him groan:
Ay, and that tongue of his that bade the Romans
Mark him and write his speeches in their books,
Alas, it cried, "Give me some drink, Titinius,"
As a sick girl. Ye gods, it doth amaze me
A man of such a feeble temper should
So get the start of the majestic world   130
And bear the palm alone.
   Shout. Flourish.
   Bru. Another general shout!
I do believe that these applauses are
For some new honours that are heap'd on Cæsar.
   Cas. Why, man, he doth bestride the narrow
    world
Like a Colossus, and we petty men
Walk under his huge legs and peep about
To find ourselves dishonourable graves.
Men at some time are masters of their fates:
The fault, dear Brutus, is not in our stars,   140
But in ourselves, that we are underlings.
Brutus and Cæsar: what should be in that
    "Cæsar"?
Why should that name be sounded more than
    yours?
Write them together, yours is as fair a name;
Sound them, it doth become the mouth as well;
Weigh them, it is as heavy; conjure with 'em,
Brutus will start a spirit as soon as Cæsar.
Now, in the names of all the gods at once,
Upon what meat doth this our Cæsar feed   149
That he is grown so great? Age, thou art shamed!
Rome, thou hast lost the breed of noble bloods!
When went there by an age, since the great flood,
But it was famed with more than with one man?
When could they say till now, that talk'd of
    Rome,

That her wide walls encompass'd but one man?
Now is it Rome indeed and room enough,
When there is in it but one only man.
O, you and I have heard our fathers say
There was a Brutus once that would have brook'd
The eternal devil to keep his state in Rome   *160*
As easily as a king.

Bru. That you do love me, I am nothing jealous;
What you would work me to, I have some aim:
How I have thought of this and of these times,
I shall recount hereafter; for this present,
I would not, so with love I might entreat you,
Be any further moved. What you have said
I will consider; what you have to say
I will with patience hear, and find a time   *169*
Both meet to hear and answer such high things.
Till then, my noble friend, chew upon this:
Brutus had rather be a villager
Than to repute himself a son of Rome
Under these hard conditions as this time
Is like to lay upon us.

Cas. I am glad that my weak words
Have struck but thus much show of fire from
    Brutus.

Bru. The games are done and Cæsar is re-
    turning.

Cas. As they pass by, pluck Casca by the sleeve;
And he will, after his sour fashion, tell you   *180*
What hath proceeded worthy note to-day.

     Re-enter CÆSAR *and his Train.*

Bru. I will do so. But, look you, Cassius,
The angry spot doth glow on Cæsar's brow,
And all the rest look like a chidden train:
Calpurnia's cheek is pale; and Cicero
Looks with such ferret and such fiery eyes
As we have seen him in the Capitol,
Being cross'd in conference by some senators.

Cas. Casca will tell us what the matter is.

Cæs. Antonius!   *190*

Ant. Cæsar?

Cæs. Let me have men about me that are fat;
Sleek-headed men and such as sleep o'nights:
Yond Cassius has a lean and hungry look;
He thinks too much: such men are dangerous.

Ant. Fear him not, Cæsar; he's not dangerous;
He is a noble Roman and well given.

Cæs. Would he were fatter! But I fear him not:
Yet if my name were liable to fear,
I do not know the man I should avoid   *200*
So soon as that spare Cassius. He reads much;
He is a great observer and he looks
Quite through the deeds of men; he loves no plays,
As thou dost, Antony; he hears no music;
Seldom he smiles, and smiles in such a sort
As if he mock'd himself and scorn'd his spirit

That could be moved to smile at anything.
Such men as he be never at heart's ease
Whiles they behold a greater than themselves,
And therefore are they very dangerous.   *210*
I rather tell thee what is to be fear'd
Than what I fear; for always I am Cæsar.
Come on my right hand, for this ear is deaf,
And tell me truly what thou think'st of him.
        [*Sennet. Exeunt* CÆSAR *and all his*
                         Train, but CASCA.

Casca. You pull'd me by the cloak; would you
    speak with me?

Bru. Ay, Casca; tell us what hath chanced
    to-day
That Cæsar looks so sad.

Casca. Why, you were with him, were you not?

Bru. I should not then ask Casca what had
    chanced.   *219*

Casca. Why, there was a crown offered him:
and being offered him, he put it by with the back
of his hand, thus; and then the people fell a-shout-
ing.

Bru. What was the second noise for?

Casca. Why, for that too.

Cas. They shouted thrice: what was the last
    cry for?

Casca. Why, for that too.

Bru. Was the crown offered him thrice?

Casca. Ay, marry, was't, and he put it by
thrice, every time gentler than other, and at
every putting-by mine honest neighbours shouted.

Cas. Who offered him the crown?

Casca. Why, Antony.

Bru. Tell us the manner of it, gentle Casca.

Casca. I can as well be hanged as tell the manner
of it: it was mere foolery; I did not mark it. I
saw Mark Antony offer him a crown; yet 'twas
not a crown neither, 'twas one of these coronets;
and, as I told you, he put it by once: but, for all
that, to my thinking, he would fain have had it.
Then he offered it to him again; then he put it
by again: but, to my thinking, he was very loath
to lay his fingers off it. And then he offered it the
third time; he put it the third time by: and still
as he refused, the rabblement hooted and clapped
their chopped hands and threw up their sweaty
night-caps and uttered such a deal of stinking
breath because Cæsar refused the crown that it
had almost choked Cæsar; for he swounded and
fell down at it: and for mine own part, I durst
not laugh, for fear of opening my lips and receiving the bad air.

Cas. But, soft, I pray you: what, did Cæsar
    swound?

Casca. He fell down in the market-place, and
foamed at mouth, and was speechless.

Bru. 'Tis very like: he hath the falling sickness.

Cas. No, Cæsar hath it not; but you and I
And honest Casca, we have the falling sickness.

Casca. I know not what you mean by that; but,
I am sure, Cæsar fell down. If the tag-rag
people did not clap him and hiss him, according
as he pleased and displeased them, as they use to
do the players in the theatre, I am no true man.

Bru. What said he when he came unto himself?

Casca. Marry, before he fell down, when he
perceived the common herd was glad he refused
the crown, he plucked me ope his doublet and
offered them his throat to cut. An I had been a
man of any occupation, if I would not have taken
him at a word, I would I might go to hell among
the rogues. And so he fell. When he came to
himself again, he said, if he had done or said any
thing amiss, he desired their worships to think it
was his infirmity. Three or four wenches, where
I stood, cried, "Alas, good soul!" and forgave
him with all their hearts: but there's no heed to
be taken of them; if Cæsar had stabbed their
mothers, they would have done no less.

Bru. And after that, he came, thus sad, away?

Casca. Ay.   *280*

Cas. Did Cicero say anything?

Casca. Ay, he spoke Greek.

Cas. To what effect?

Casca. Nay, an I tell you that, I'll ne'er look
you i' the face again: but those that understood
him smiled at one another and shook their heads;
but, for mine own part, it was Greek to me. I
could tell you more news too: Marullus and
Flavius, for pulling scarfs off Cæsar's images, are
put to silence. Fare you well. There was more
foolery yet, if I could remember it.   *291*

Cas. Will you sup with me to-night, Casca?

Casca. No, I am promised forth.

Cas. Will you dine with me to-morrow?

Casca. Ay, if I be alive and your mind hold and
your dinner worth the eating.

Cas. Good: I will expect you.

Casca. Do so. Farewell, both.   [*Exit.*

Bru. What a blunt fellow is this grown to be!
He was quick mettle when he went to school. *300*

Cas. So is he now in execution
Of any bold or noble enterprise,
However he puts on this tardy form.
This rudeness is a sauce to his good wit,
Which gives men stomach to digest his words
With better appetite.

Bru. And so it is. For this time I will leave you:
To-morrow, if you please to speak with me,
I will come home to you; or, if you will,
Come home to me, and I will wait for you.   *310*

Cas. I will do so: till then, think of the world.

[*Exit* BRUTUS.

Well, Brutus, thou art noble; yet, I see,
Thy honourable metal may be wrought
From that it is disposed: therefore it is meet
That noble minds keep ever with their likes;
For who so firm that cannot be seduced?
Cæsar doth bear me hard; but he loves Brutus:
If I were Brutus now and he were Cassius,
He should not humour me. I will this night,
In several hands, in at his windows throw,   *320*
As if they came from several citizens,
Writings all tending to the great opinion
That Rome holds of his name; wherein obscurely
Cæsar's ambition shall be glanced at:
And after this let Cæsar seat him sure;
For we will shake him, or worse days endure.

[*Exit.*

SCENE III. *The same: a street*

Thunder and lightning. Enter, from opposite sides,
CASCA, *with his sword drawn, and* CICERO.

Cic. Good even, Casca: brought you Cæsar
home?
Why are you breathless? and why stare you so?

Casca. Are not you moved, when all the sway of
earth
Shakes like a thing unfirm? O Cicero,
I have seen tempests, when the scolding winds
Have rived the knotty oaks, and I have seen
The ambitious ocean swell and rage and foam,
To be exalted with the threatening clouds:
But never till to-night, never till now,
Did I go through a tempest dropping fire.   *10*
Either there is a civil strife in heaven,
Or else the world, too saucy with the gods,
Incenses them to send destruction.

Cic. Why, saw you anything more wonderful?

Casca. A common slave—you know him well by
sight—
Held up his left hand, which did flame and burn
Like twenty torches join'd, and yet his hand,
Not sensible of fire, remain'd unscorch'd.
Besides—I ha' not since put up my sword—
Against the Capitol I met a lion,   *20*
Who glared upon me, and went surly by
Without annoying me: and there were drawn
Upon a heap a hundred ghastly women,
Transformed with their fear, who swore they saw
Men all in fire walk up and down the streets.
And yesterday the bird of night did sit
Even at noon-day upon the market-place,
Hooting and shrieking. When these prodigies
Do so conjointly meet, let not men say
"These are their reasons; they are natural";   *30*
For, I believe, they are portentous things

Unto the climate that they point upon.

Cic. Indeed, it is a strange-disposed time:
But men may construe things after their fashion,
Clean from the purpose of the things themselves.
Comes Cæsar to the Capitol to-morrow?

Casca. He doth; for he did bid Antonius
Send word to you he would be there to-morrow.

Cic. Good night then, Casca: this disturbed sky
Is not to walk in.

Casca. Farewell, Cicero. [*Exit* CICERO.   40

Enter CASSIUS.

Cas. Who's there?

Casca.   A Roman.

Cas.   Casca, by your voice.

Casca. Your ear is good. Cassius, what night is
this!

Cas. A very pleasing night to honest men.

Casca. Who ever knew the heavens menace so?

Cas. Those that have known the earth so full of
faults.
For my part, I have walk'd about the streets,
Submitting me unto the perilous night,
And, thus unbraced, Casca, as you see,
Have bared my bosom to the thunder-stone;
And when the cross blue lightning seem'd to open
The breast of heaven, I did present myself   51
Even in the aim and very flash of it.

Casca. But wherefore did you so much tempt
the heavens?
It is the part of men to fear and tremble
When the most mighty gods by tokens send
Such dreadful heralds to astonish us.

Cas. You are dull, Casca, and those sparks of
life
That should be in a Roman you do want,
Or else you use not. You look pale and gaze
And put on fear and cast yourself in wonder   60
To see the strange impatience of the heavens:
But if you would consider the true cause
Why all these fires, why all these gliding ghosts,
Why birds and beasts from quality and kind,
Why old men fool and children calculate,
Why all these things change from their ordinance
Their natures and preformed faculties
To monstrous quality, why, you shall find
That heaven hath infused them with these spirits
To make them instruments of fear and warning 70
Unto some monstrous state.
Now could I, Casca, name to thee a man
Most like this dreadful night,
That thunders, lightens, opens graves, and roars
As doth the lion in the Capitol,
A man no mightier than thyself or me
In personal action, yet prodigious grown
And fearful, as these strange eruptions are.

Casca. 'Tis Cæsar that you mean; is it not,
Cassius?

Cas. Let it be who it is: for Romans now   80
Have thews and limbs like to their ancestors;
But, woe the while! our fathers' minds are dead,
And we are govern'd with our mothers' spirits;
Our yoke and sufferance show us womanish.

Casca. Indeed, they say the senators to-morrow
Mean to establish Cæsar as a king;
And he shall wear his crown by sea and land,
In every place, save here in Italy.

Cas. I know where I will wear this dagger then;
Cassius from bondage will deliver Cassius: 90
Therein, ye gods, you make the weak most
strong;
Therein, ye gods, you tyrants do defeat:
Nor stony tower, nor walls of beaten brass,
Nor airless dungeon, nor strong links of iron,
Can be retentive to the strength of spirit;
But life, being weary of these worldly bars,
Never lacks power to dismiss itself.
If I know this, know all the world besides,
That part of tyranny that I do bear
I can shake off at pleasure.   [*Thunder still.*

Casca.   So can I: 100
So every bondman in his own hand bears
The power to cancel his captivity.

Cas. And why should Cæsar be a tyrant then?
Poor man! I know he would not be a wolf,
But that he sees the Romans are but sheep:
He were no lion, were not Romans hinds.
Those that with haste will make a mighty fire
Begin it with weak straws: what trash is Rome,
What rubbish, and what offal, when it serves
For the base matter to illuminate   110
So vile a thing as Cæsar! But, O grief,
Where hast thou led me? I perhaps speak this
Before a willing bondman; then I know
My answer must be made. But I am arm'd,
And dangers are to me indifferent.

Casca. You speak to Casca, and such a man
That is no fleering tell-tale. Hold, my hand:
Be factious for redress of all these griefs,
And I will set this foot of mine as far
As who goes farthest.

Cas.   There's a bargain made. 120
Now know you, Casca, I have moved already
Some certain of the noblest-minded Romans
To undergo with me an enterprise
Of honourable-dangerous consequence;
And I do know, by this, they stay for me
In Pompey's porch: for now, this fearful night,
There is no stir or walking in the streets;
And the complexion of the element
In favour's like the work we have in hand,
Most bloody, fiery, and most terrible.   130

Casca. Stand close awhile, for here comes one in
  haste.
Cas. 'Tis Cinna; I do know him by his gait;
He is a friend.

Enter CINNA.

          Cinna, where haste you so?
Cin. To find out you. Who's that? Metellus
  Cimber?
Cas. No, it is Casca; one incorporate
To our attempts. Am I not stay'd for, Cinna?
Cin. I am glad on't. What a fearful night is this!
There's two or three of us have seen strange
  sights.
Cas. Am I not stay'd for? tell me.
Cin.   Yes, you are.
O Cassius, if you could   *140*
But win the noble Brutus to our party—
Cas. Be you content: good Cinna, take this
  paper,
And look you lay it in the prætor's chair,
Where Brutus may but find it; and throw this
In at his window; set this up with wax
Upon old Brutus' statue: all this done,
Repair to Pompey's porch, where you shall find
  us.
Is Decius Brutus and Trebonius there?
Cin. All but Metellus Cimber; and he's gone
To seek you at your house. Well, I will hie,   *150*
And so bestow these papers as you bade me.
Cas. That done, repair to Pompey's theatre.
                              [*Exit* CINNA.
Come, Casca, you and I will yet ere day
See Brutus at his house: three parts of him
Is ours already, and the man entire
Upon the next encounter yields him ours.
Casca. O, he sits high in all the people's hearts:
And that which would appear offence in us,
His countenance, like richest alchemy,
Will change to virtue and to worthiness.   *160*
Cas. Him and his worth and our great need of
  him
You have right well conceited. Let us go,
For it is after midnight; and ere day
We will awake him and be sure of him.   [*Exeunt.*

ACT II

SCENE I. *Rome: Brutus's orchard*

Enter BRUTUS.

Bru. What, Lucius, ho!
I cannot by the progress of the stars
Give guess how near to day. Lucius, I say!
I would it were my fault to sleep so soundly.
When, Lucius, when? awake, I say! what,
  Lucius!

Enter LUCIUS.

Luc. Call'd you, my lord?
Bru. Get me a taper in my study, Lucius:
When it is lighted, come and call me here.
Luc. I will, my lord.   [*Exit.*
Bru. It must be by his death: and for my part,
I know no personal cause to spurn at him   *11*
But for the general. He would be crown'd:
How that might change his nature, there's the
  question.
It is the bright day that brings forth the adder;
And that craves wary walking. Crown him?
  That—
And then, I grant, we put a sting in him
That at his will he may do danger with.
The abuse of greatness is when it disjoins
Remorse from power: and, to speak truth of
  Cæsar,
I have not known when his affections sway'd   *20*
More than his reason. But 'tis a common proof
That lowliness is young ambition's ladder,
Whereto the climber-upward turns his face;
But when he once attains the upmost round,
He then unto the ladder turns his back,
Looks in the clouds, scorning the base degrees
By which he did ascend. So Cæsar may.
Then, lest he may, prevent. And, since the
  quarrel
Will bear no colour for the thing he is,
Fashion it thus; that what he is, augmented.   *30*
Would run to these and these extremities:
And therefore think him as a serpent's egg
Which, hatch'd, would, as his kind, grow mis-
  chievous,
And kill him in the shell.

Re-enter LUCIUS.

Luc. The taper burneth in your closet, sir.
Searching the window for a flint, I found
This paper, thus seal'd up; and I am sure
It did not lie there when I went to bed.
     Gives him the letter.
Bru. Get you to bed again; it is not day.
Is not to-morrow, boy, the ides of March?   *40*
Luc. I know not, sir.
Bru. Look in the calendar, and bring me word.
Luc. I will, sir.   [*Exit.*
Bru. The exhalations whizzing in the air
Give so much light that I may read by them.
     Opens the letter and reads.
"Brutus, thou sleep'st: awake, and see thyself.
Shall Rome, &c. Speak, strike, redress!
Brutus, thou sleep'st: awake!"
Such instigations have been often dropp'd
Where I have took them up.   *50*

"Shall Rome, &c." Thus must I piece it out:
Shall Rome stand under one man's awe? What,
　　Rome?
My ancestors did from the streets of Rome
The Tarquin drive, when he was call'd a king.
"Speak, strike, redress!" Am I entreated
To speak and strike? O Rome, I make thee
　　promise;
If the redress will follow, thou receivest
Thy full petition at the hand of Brutus!

Re-enter LUCIUS.

Luc. Sir, March is wasted fourteen days.
　　Knocking within.
Bru. 'Tis good. Go to the gate; somebody
　　knocks.　　　　　　　　　[*Exit Lucius　60*
Since Cassius first did whet me against Cæsar,
I have not slept.
Between the acting of a dreadful thing
And the first motion, all the interim is
Like a phantasma or a hideous dream:
The Genius and the mortal instruments
Are then in council; and the state of man,
Like to a little kingdom, suffers then
The nature of an insurrection.

Re-enter LUCIUS.

Luc. Sir, 'tis your brother Cassius at the door,
Who doth desire to see you.
　Bru.　　　　　　　Is he alone?　　*71*
Luc. No, sir, there are more with him.
　Bru.　　　　　Do you know them?
Luc. No, sir; their hats are pluck'd about their
　　ears,
And half their faces buried in their cloaks,
That by no means I may discover them
By any mark of favour.
　Bru.　　　　Let 'em enter. [*Exit* LUCIUS.
They are the faction. O Conspiracy,
Shamest thou to show thy dangerous brow by
　　night,
When evils are most free? O, then by day
Where wilt thou find a cavern dark enough　*80*
To mask thy monstrous visage? Seek none con-
　　spiracy;
Hide it in smiles and affability:
For if thou path, thy native semblance on,
Not Erebus itself were dim enough
To hide thee from prevention.

Enter the conspirators, CASSIUS, CASCA, DECIUS,
CINNA, METELLUS CIMBER *and,* TREBONIUS.

Cas. I think we are too bold upon your rest:
Good morrow, Brutus; do we trouble you?
　Bru. I have been up this hour, awake all night.
Know I these men that come along with you?

Cas. Yes, every man of them, and no man
　　here　　　　　　　　　　　　　　　*90*
But honours you; and every one doth wish
You had but that opinion of yourself
Which every noble Roman bears of you.
This is Trebonius.
　Bru.　　　　　　He is welcome hither.
Cas. This, Decius Brutus.
　Bru.　　　　　　He is welcome too.
Cas. This, Casca; this, Cinna; and this, Me-
　　tellus Cimber.
Bru. They are all welcome.
What watchful cares do interpose themselves
Betwixt your eyes and night?
　Cas. Shall I entreat a word?　　　　　*100*
　　BRUTUS *and* CASSIUS *whisper.*
Dec. Here lies the east: doth not the day break
　　here?
Casca. No.
Cin. O, pardon, sir, it doth; and yon gray lines
That fret the clouds are messengers of day.
Casca. You shall confess that you are both de-
　　ceived.
Here, as I point my sword, the sun arises,
Which is a great way growing on the south,
Weighing the youthful season of the year.
Some two months hence up higher toward the
　　north
He first presents his fire, and the high east　*110*
Stands, as the Capitol, directly here.
　Bru. Give me your hands all over, one by one.
　Cas. And let us swear our resolution.
　Bru. No, not an oath: if not the face of men,
The sufferance of our souls, the time's abuse—
If these be motives weak, break off betimes,
And every man hence to his idle bed;
So let high-sighted tyranny range on,
Till each man drop by lottery. But if these,
As I am sure they do, bear fire enough　　*120*
To kindle cowards and to steel with valour
The melting spirits of women, then, countrymen,
What need we any spur but our own cause
To prick us to redress? what other bond
Than secret Romans, that have spoke the word
And will not palter? and what other oath
Than honesty to honesty engaged
That this shall be, or we will fall for it?
Swear priests and cowards and men cautelous,
Old feeble carrions and such suffering souls　*130*
That welcome wrongs; unto bad causes swear
Such creatures as men doubt; but do not stain
The even virtue of our enterprise,
Nor the insuppressive mettle of our spirits,
To think that or our cause or our performance
Did need an oath; when every drop of blood
That every Roman bears, and nobly bears,

Is guilty of a several bastardy,
If he do break the smallest particle
Of any promise that hath pass'd from him.　　*140*
　Cas. But what of Cicero? shall we sound him?
I think he will stand very strong with us.
　Casca. Let us not leave him out.
　Cin.　　　　　　　　No, by no means.
　Met. O, let us have him, for his silver hairs
Will purchase us a good opinion
And buy men's voices to commend our deeds:
It shall be said his judgement ruled our hands;
Our youths and wildness shall no whit appear,
But all be buried in his gravity.
　Bru. O, name him not: let us not break with
　　him;　　　　　　　　　　　　　　　*150*
For he will never follow any thing
That other men begin.
　Cas.　　　　　Then leave him out.
　Casca. Indeed he is not fit.
　Dec. Shall no man else be touch'd but only
　　Cæsar?
　Cas. Decius, well urged: I think it is not meet,
Mark Antony, so well beloved of Cæsar,
Should outlive Cæsar: we shall find of him
A shrewd contriver; and, you know, his means,
If he improve them, may well stretch so far
As to annoy us all: which to prevent,　　*160*
Let Antony and Cæsar fall together.
　Bru. Our course will seem too bloody, Caius
　　Cassius,
To cut the head off and then hack the limbs,
Like wrath in death and envy afterwards;
For Antony is but a limb of Cæsar:
Let us be sacrificers, but not butchers, Caius.
We all stand up against the spirit of Cæsar;
And in the spirit of men there is no blood:
O, that we then could come by Cæsar's spirit,
And not dismember Cæsar! But, alas,　　*170*
Cæsar must bleed for it! And, gentle friends,
Let's kill him boldly, but not wrathfully;
Let's carve him as a dish fit for the gods,
Not hew him as a carcass fit for hounds:
And let our hearts, as subtle masters do,
Stir up their servants to an act of rage,
And after seem to chide 'em. This shall make
Our purpose necessary and not envious:
Which so appearing to the common eyes,
We shall be call'd purgers, not murderers.　*180*
And for Mark Antony, think not of him;
For he can do no more than Cæsar's arm
When Cæsar's head is off.
　Cas.　　　　　　Yet I fear him;
For in the ingrafted love he bears to Cæsar—
　Bru. Alas, good Cassius, do not think of him:
If he love Cæsar, all that he can do
Is to himself, take thought and die for Cæsar:

And that were much he should; for he is given
To sports, to wildness, and much company.
　Treb. There is no fear in him; let him not die;
For he will live, and laugh at this hereafter.　*191*
　　Clock strikes.
　Bru. Peace! count the clock.
　Cas.　　　　　The clock hath stricken three.
　Treb. 'Tis time to part.
　Cas.　　　　　　But it is doubtful yet
Whether Cæsar will come forth today or no;
For he is superstitious grown of late,
Quite from the main opinion he held once
Of fantasy, of dreams, and ceremonies:
It may be these apparent prodigies,
The unaccustom'd terror of this night,
And the persuasion of his augurers,　　*200*
May hold him from the Capitol to-day.
　Dec. Never fear that: if he be so resolved,
I can o'ersway him; for he loves to hear
That unicorns may be betray'd with trees,
And bears with glasses, elephants with holes,
Lions with toils, and men with flatterers;
But when I tell him he hates flatterers,
He says he does, being then most flattered.
Let me work;
For I can give his humour the true bent,　*210*
And I will bring him to the Capitol.
　Cas. Nay, we will all of us be there to fetch him.
　Bru. By the eighth hour: is that the uttermost?
　Cin. Be that the uttermost, and fail not then.
　Met. Caius Ligarius doth bear Cæsar hard,
Who rated him for speaking well of Pompey:
I wonder none of you have thought of him.
　Bru. Now, good Metellus, go along by him:
He loves me well, and I have given him reasons;
Send him but hither, and I'll fashion him.　*220*
　Cas. The morning comes upon's: we'll leave
　　you, Brutus.
And, friends, disperse yourselves; but all re-
　　member
What you have said, and show yourselves true
　　Romans.
　Bru. Good gentlemen, look fresh and merrily:
Let not our looks put on our purposes,
But bear it as our Roman actors do,
With untired spirits and formal constancy:
And so good morrow to you every one.
　　　　　　　　　　　[*Exeunt all but* BRUTUS.
Boy! Lucius! Fast asleep? It is no matter;
Enjoy the honey-heavy dew of slumber:　*230*
Thou hast no figures nor no fantasies,
Which busy care draws in the brains of men;
Therefore thou sleep'st so sound.

　　　　　　　　Enter PORTIA.

　Por.　　　　　　　Brutus, my lord!

Bru. Portia, what mean you? wherefore rise
    you now?
It is not for your health thus to commit
Your weak condition to the raw cold morning.
  Por. Nor for yours neither. You've ungently,
    Brutus,
Stole from my bed: and yesternight, at supper,
You suddenly arose and walk'd about,
Musing and sighing, with your arms across,   *240*
And when I ask'd you what the matter was,
You stared upon me with ungentle looks;
I urged you further; then you scratch'd your
    head
And too impatiently stamp'd with your foot;
Yet I insisted, yet you answer'd not,
But, with an angry wafture of your hand,
Gave sign for me to leave you: so I did;
Fearing to strengthen that impatience
Which seem'd too much enkindled, and withal
Hoping it was but an effect of humour,   *250*
Which sometime hath his hour with every man.
It will not let you eat, nor talk, nor sleep,
And could it work so much upon your shape
As it hath much prevail'd on your condition,
I should not know you, Brutus. Dear my lord,
Make me acquainted with your cause of grief.
  Bru. I am not well in health, and that is all.
  Por. Brutus is wise, and, were he not in health,
He would embrace the means to come by it.
  Bru. Why, so I do. Good Portia, go to bed.
  Por. Is Brutus sick? and is it physical   *261*
To walk unbraced and suck up the humours
Of the dank morning? What, is Brutus sick,
And will he steal out of his wholesome bed
To dare the vile contagion of the night
And tempt the rheumy and unpurged air
To add unto his sickness? No, my Brutus;
You have some sick offence within your mind,
Which, by the right and virtue of my place,
I ought to know of: and, upon my knees,   *270*
I charm you, by my once-commended beauty,
By all your vows of love and that great vow
Which did incorporate and make us one,
That you unfold to me, yourself, your half,
Why you are heavy, and what men to-night
Have had resort to you: for here have been
Some six or seven, who did hide their faces
Even from darkness,
  Bru.   Kneel not, gentle Portia.
  Por. I should not need, if you were gentle
    Brutus.
Within the bond of marriage, tell me, Brutus,   *280*
Is it excepted I should know no secrets
That appertain to you? Am I yourself
But, as it were, in sort or limitation,
To keep with you at meals, comfort your bed,
And talk to you sometimes? Dwell I but in the
    suburbs
Of your good pleasure? If it be no more,
Portia is Brutus' harlot, not his wife.
  Bru. You are my true and honourable wife,
As dear to me as are the ruddy drops
That visit my sad heart.   *290*
  Por. If this were true, then should I know this
    secret.
I grant I am a woman; but withal
A woman that Lord Brutus took to wife:
I grant I am a woman; but withal
A woman well-reputed, Cato's daughter.
Think you I am no stronger than my sex,
Being so father'd and so husbanded?
Tell me your counsels, I will not disclose 'em:
I have made strong proof of my constancy.
Giving myself a voluntary wound   *300*
Here, in the thigh: can I bear that with patience,
And not my husband's secrets?
  Bru.   O ye gods,
Render me worthy of this noble wife!
    Knocking within.
Hark, hark! one knocks: Portia, go in awhile;
And by and by thy bosom shall partake
The secrets of my heart.
All my engagements I will construe to thee,
All the charactery of my sad brows:
Leave me with haste. [*Exit* PORTIA] Lucius,
    who's that knocks?

                Re-enter LUCIUS *with* LIGARIUS.

  Luc. Here is a sick man that would speak with
    you.   *310*
  Bru. Caius Ligarius, that Metellus spake of.
Boy, stand aside. Caius Ligarius! how?
  Lig. Vouchsafe good morrow from a feeble
    tongue.
  Bru. O, what a time have you chose out, brave
    Caius,
To wear a kerchief! Would you were not sick!
  Lig. I am not sick, if Brutus have in hand
Any exploit worthy the name of honour.
  Bru. Such an exploit have I in hand, Ligarius,
Had you a healthful ear to hear of it.
  Lig. By all the gods that Romans bow before,
I here discard my sickness! Soul of Rome!   *321*
Brave son, derived from honourable loins!
Thou, like an exorcist, hast conjured up
My mortified spirit. Now bid me run,
And I will strive with things impossible;
Yea, get the better of them. What's to do?
  Bru. A piece of work that will make sick men
    whole.
  Lig. But are not some whole that we must make
    sick?

Bru. That must we also, What it is, my Caius,
I shall unfold to thee as we are going   330
To whom it must be done.
  Lig.   Set on your foot,
And with a heart new-fired I follow you,
To do I know not what: but it sufficeth
That Brutus leads me on.
  Bru.   Follow me, then.   [*Exeunt.*

Scene ii. *Cæsar's house*

Thunder and lightning. Enter CÆSAR, *in his night-
gown.*

  Cæs. Nor heaven nor earth have been at peace
    to-night:
Thrice hath Calpurnia in her sleep cried out,
"Help, ho! they murder Cæsar!" Who's within?

Enter a SERVANT.

  Serv. My lord?
  Cæs. Go bid the priests do present sacrifice
And bring me their opinions of success.
  Serv. I will, my lord.   [*Exit.*

Enter CALPURNIA.

  Cal. What mean you, Cæsar? think you to
    walk forth?
You shall not stir out of your house to-day.
  Cæs. Cæsar shall forth: the things that threat-
    en'd me   10
Ne'er look'd but on my back; when they shall see
The face of Cæsar, they are vanished.
  Cal. Cæsar, I never stood on ceremonies,
Yet now they fright me. There is one within,
Besides the things that we have heard and seen,
Recounts most horrid sights seen by the watch.
A lioness hath whelped in the streets;
And graves have yawn'd, and yielded up their
    dead;
Fierce fiery warriors fought upon the clouds
In ranks and squadrons and right form of war, 20
Which drizzled blood upon the Capitol;
The noise of battle hurtled in the air,
Horses did neigh, and dying men did groan,
And ghosts did shriek and squeal about the
    streets.
O Cæsar! these things are beyond all use,
And I do fear them.
  Cæs.   What can be avoided
Whose end is purposed by the mighty gods?
Yet Cæsar shall go forth; for these predictions
Are to the world in general as to Cæsar.
  Cal. When beggars die, there are no comets
    seen;   30
The heavens themselves blaze forth the death of
    princes.

  Cæs. Cowards die many times before their
    deaths;
The valiant never taste of death but once.
Of all the wonders that I yet have heard,
It seems to me most strange that men should fear;
Seeing that death, a necessary end,
Will come when it will come.

Re-enter SERVANT.

                    What say the augurers?
  Serv. They would not have you to stir forth
    to-day,
Plucking the entrails of an offering forth,
They could not find a heart within the beast. 40
  Cæs. The gods do this in shame of cowardice:
Cæsar should be a beast without a heart,
If he should stay at home to-day for fear.
No, Cæsar shall not: Danger knows full well
That Cæsar is more dangerous than he:
We are two lions litter'd in one day,
And I the elder and more terrible:
And Cæsar shall go forth.
  Cal.   Alas, my lord,
Your wisdom is consumed in confidence.
Do not go forth to-day: call it my fear   50
That keeps you in the house, and not your own.
We'll send Mark Antony to the senate-house;
And he shall say you are not well to-day:
Let me, upon my knee, prevail in this.
  Cæs. Mark Antony shall say I am not well;
And, for thy humour, I will stay at home.

Enter DECIUS.

Here's Decius Brutus, he shall tell them so.
  Dec. Cæsar, all hail! good morrow, worthy
    Cæsar:
I come to fetch you to the senate-house.
  Cæs. And you are come in very happy time, 60
To bear my greeting to the senators
And tell them that I will not come to-day:
Cannot, is false, and that I dare not, falser:
I will not come to-day: tell them so, Decius.
  Cal. Say he is sick.
  Cæs.   Shall Cæsar send a lie?
Have I in conquest stretch'd mine arm so far,
To be afeard to tell graybeards the truth?
Decius, go tell them Cæsar will not come.
  Dec. Most mighty Cæsar, let me know some
    cause,
Lest I be laugh'd at when I tell them so.   70
  Cæs. The cause is in my will: I will not come;
That is enough to satisfy the senate.
But for your private satisfaction,
Because I love you, I will let you know:
Calpurnia here, my wife, stays me at home:
She dreamt to-night she saw my statua,

Which, like a fountain with an hundred spouts,
Did run pure blood; and many lusty Romans
Came smiling and did bathe their hands in it:
And these does she apply for warnings, and
    portents,   80
And evils imminent; and on her knee
Hath begg'd that I will stay at home to-day.
  Dec. This dream is all amiss interpreted;
It was a vision fair and fortunate:
Your statue spouting blood in many pipes,
In which so many smiling Romans bathed,
Signifies that from you great Rome shall suck
Reviving blood, and that great men shall press
For tinctures, stains, relics, and cognizance.
This by Calpurnia's dream is signified.   90
  Cæs. And this way have you well expounded it.
  Dec. I have, when you have heard what I can
    say:
And know it now: the senate have concluded
To give this day a crown to mighty Cæsar.
If you shall send them word you will not come,
Their minds may change. Besides, it were a
    mock
Apt to be render'd, for some one to say,
"Break up the senate till another time,
When Cæsar's wife shall meet with better
    dreams."
If Cæsar hide himself, shall they not whisper *100*
"Lo, Cæsar is afraid"?
Pardon me, Cæsar; for my dear dear love
To your proceeding bids me tell you this;
And reason to my love is liable.
  Cæs. How foolish do your fears seem now, Cal-
    purnia!
I am ashamed I did yield to them.
Give me my robe, for I will go.

Enter PUBLIUS, BRUTUS, LIGARIUS, METELLUS,
    CASCA, TREBONIUS, *and* CINNA.

And look where Publius is come to fetch me.
  Pub. Good morrow, Cæsar.
  Cæs.   Welcome, Publius.
What, Brutus, are you stirr'd so early too?   *110*
Good morrow, Casca. Caius Ligarius,
Cæsar was ne'er so much your enemy
As that same ague which hath made you lean.
What is 't o'clock?
  Bru.   Cæsar, 'tis strucken eight.
  Cæs. I thank you for your pains and courtesy.

Enter ANTONY.

See! Antony, that revels long o'nights,
Is notwithstanding up. Good morrow, Antony.
  Ant. So to most noble Cæsar.
  Cæs.   Bid them prepare within:
I am to blame to be thus waited for.

Now, Cinna: now, Metellus: what, Trebonius!
I have an hour's talk in store for you;   *121*
Remember that you call on me to-day:
Be near me, that I may remember you.
  Treb. Cæsar, I will: [*Aside*] and so near will I
    be
That your best friends shall wish I had been
    further.
  Cæs. Good friends, go in, and taste some wine
    with me;
And we, like friends, will straightway go to-
    gether.
  Bru. [*Aside*] That every like is not the same, O
    Cæsar,
The heart of Brutus yearns to think upon!
                      [*Exeunt.*

SCENE III. *A street near the Capitol*

Enter ARTEMIDORUS, *reading a paper.*

  Art. "Cæsar, beware of Brutus; take heed of
Cassius; come not near Casca; have an eye to
Cinna; trust not Trebonius; mark well Me-
tellus Cimber: Decius Brutus loves thee not:
thou hast wronged Caius Ligarius. There is
but one mind in all these men, and it is bent
against Cæsar. If thou beest not immortal, look
about you: security gives way to conspiracy.
The mighty gods defend thee! Thy lover,
                         "Artemidorus"
Here will I stand till Cæsar pass along,   *11*
And as a suitor will I give him this.
My heart laments that virtue cannot live
Out of the teeth of emulation.
If thou read this, O Cæsar, thou mayst live;
If not, the Fates with traitors do contrive.   [*Exit.*

SCENE IV. *Another part of the same street, before
the house of Brutus*

Enter PORTIA *and* LUCIUS.

  Por. I prithee, boy, run to the senate-house;
Stay not to answer me, but get thee gone:
Why dost thou stay?
  Luc.   To know my errand, madam.
  Por. I would have had thee there, and here
    again,
Ere I can tell thee what thou shouldst do there.
O constancy, be strong upon my side,
Set a huge mountain 'tween my heart and tongue!
I have a man's mind, but a woman's might.
How hard it is for women to keep counsel!
Art thou here yet?
  Luc.   Madam, what should I do?   *10*
Run to the Capitol, and nothing else?
And so return to you, and nothing else?
  Por. Yes, bring me word, boy, if thy lord look
    well,

For he went sickly forth: and take good note
What Cæsar doth, what suitors press to him.
Hark, boy! what noise is that?
Luc. I hear none, madam.
Por.   Prithee, listen well;
I heard a bustling rumour, like a fray,
And the wind brings it from the Capitol.
Luc. Sooth, madam, I hear nothing.   20

Enter the SOOTHSAYER.

Por. Come hither, fellow: which way hast thou
been?
Sooth. At mine own house, good lady.
Por. What is't o'clock?
Sooth.   About the ninth hour, lady.
Por. Is Cæsar yet gone to the Capitol?
Sooth. Madam, not yet: I go to take my stand,
To see him pass on to the Capitol.
Por. Thou hast some suit to Cæsar, hast thou
not?
Sooth. That I have, lady: if it will please Cæsar
To be so good to Cæsar as to hear me,
I shall beseech him to befriend himself.   30
Por. Why know'st thou any harm's intended
towards him?
Sooth. None that I know will be, much that I fear
may chance.
Good morrow to you. Here the street is narrow:
The throng that follows Cæsar at the heels,
Of senators, of prætors, common suitors,
Will crowd a feeble man almost to death:
I'll get me to a place more void, and there
Speak to great Cæsar as he comes along.   [*Exit.*
Por. I must go in. Ay me, how weak a thing
The heart of woman is! O Brutus,   40
The heavens speed thee in thine enterprise!
Sure, the boy heard me: Brutus hath a suit
That Cæsar will not grant. O, I grow faint.
Run, Lucius, and commend me to my lord;
Say I am merry: come to me again,
And bring me word what he doth say to thee.
                                        [*Exeunt severally.*

ACT III

SCENE I. *Rome: Before the Capitol; the Senate
sitting above*

A crowd of people; among them ARTEMIDORUS *and
the* SOOTHSAYER. *Flourish. Enter* CÆSAR, BRUTUS,
CASSIUS, CASCA, DECIUS, METELLUS, TREBONIUS,
CINNA, ANTONY, LEPIDUS, POPILIUS, PUBLIUS,
and others.
Cæs. [*To the* SOOTHSAYER] The ides of March
are come.
Sooth. Ay, Cæsar; but not gone.
Art. Hail, Cæsar! read this schedule.
Dec. Trebonius doth desire you to o'er-read,

At your best leisure, this his humble suit.
Art. O Cæsar, read mine first; for mine's a
suit
That touches Cæsar nearer: read it, great Cæsar.
Cæs. What touches us ourself shall be last
served.
Art. Delay not, Cæsar; read it instantly.
Cæs. What, is the fellow mad?
Pub.   Sirrah, give place.   10
Cas. What, urge you your petitions in the
street?
Come to the Capitol.

CÆSAR *goes up to the Senate-House, the rest
following.*

Pop. I wish your enterprise to-day may thrive.
Cas. What enterprise, Popilius?
Pop.   Fare you well.
  Advances to CÆSAR.
Bru. What said Popilius Lena?
Cas. He wish'd to-day our enterprise might
thrive.
I fear our purpose is discovered.
Bru. Look, how he makes to Cæsar: mark him.
Cas. Casca, be sudden, for we fear prevention.
Brutus, what shall be done? If this be known,   20
Cassius or Cæsar never shall turn back,
For I will slay myself.
Bru.   Cassius, be constant:
Popilius Lena speaks not of our purposes;
For, look, he smiles, and Cæsar doth not change.
Cas. Trebonius knows his time; for, look you,
Brutus,
He draws Mark Antony out of the way.
                          [*Exeunt* ANTONY *and* TREBONIUS.
Dec. Where is Metellus Cimber? Let him go
And presently prefer his suit to Cæsar.
Bru. He is address'd: press near and second
him.
Cin. Casca, you are the first that rears your
hand.   30
Cæs. Are we all ready? What is now amiss
That Cæsar and his senate must redress?
Met. Most high, most mighty, and most puis-
sant Cæsar,
Metellus Cimber throws before thy seat
An humble heart—[*Kneeling*].
Cæs.   I must prevent thee, Cimber.
These couchings and these lowly courtesies
Might fire the blood of ordinary men,
And turn pre-ordinance and first decree
Into the law of children. Be not fond,
To think that Cæsar bears such rebel blood   40
That will be thaw'd from the true quality
With that which melteth fools; I mean, sweet
words,

Low-crooked court'sies, and base spaniel-fawn-
   ing.
Thy brother by decree is banished:
If thou dost bend and pray and fawn for him,
I spurn thee like a cur out of my way.
Know, Cæsar doth not wrong, nor without cause
Will he be satisfied.
  Met. Is there no voice more worthy than my
   own,
To sound more sweetly in great Cæsar's ear   *50*
For the repealing of my banish'd brother?
  Bru. I kiss thy hand, but not in flattery, Cæsar;
Desiring thee that Publius Cimber may
Have an immediate freedom of repeal.
  Cæs. What, Brutus!
  Cas.   Pardon, Cæsar; Cæsar, pardon:
As low as to thy foot doth Cassius fall,
To beg enfranchisement for Publius Cimber.
  Cæs. I could be well moved, if I were as you;
If I could pray to move, prayers would move me:
But I am constant as the northern star,   *60*
Of whose true-fix'd and resting quality
There is no fellow in the firmament.
The skies are painted with unnumber'd sparks,
They are all fire and every one doth shine,
But there's but one in all doth hold his place:
So in the world; 'tis furnish'd well with men,
And men are flesh and blood, and apprehensive;
Yet in the number I do know but one
That unassailable holds on his rank,
Unshaked of motion: and that I am he,   *70*
Let me a little show it, even in this;
That I was constant Cimber should be banish'd,
And constant do remain to keep him so.
  Cin. O Cæsar—
  Cæs.   Hence! wilt thou lift up Olympus?
  Dec. Great Cæsar—
  Cæs.   Doth not Brutus bootless kneel?
  Casca. Speak, hands, for me!
  CASCA *first, then the other Conspirators and*
        MARCUS BRUTUS *stab Cæsar.*
  Cæs. Et tu, Brute! Then fall, Cæsar!   [*Dies.*
  Cin. Liberty! Freedom! Tyranny is dead!
Run hence, proclaim, cry it about the streets.
  Cas. Some to the common pulpits, and cry out
"Liberty, freedom, and enfranchisement!"   *81*
  Bru. People and senators, be not affrighted;
Fly not; stand still: ambition's debt is paid.
  Casca. Go to the pulpit, Brutus.
  Dec.   And Cassius too.
  Bru. Where's Publius?
  Cin. Here, quite confounded with this mutiny.
  Met. Stand fast together, lest some friend of
   Cæsar's
Should chance—
  Bru. Talk not of standing. Publius, good cheer;

There is no harm intended to your person,   *90*
Nor to no Roman else: so tell them, Publius.
  Cas. And leave us, Publius; lest that the people,
Rushing on us, should do your age some mischief.
  Bru. Do so: and let no man abide this deed,
But we the doers.

Re-enter TREBONIUS.

  Cas.   Where is Antony?
  Tre. Fled to his house amazed:
Men, wives, and children stare, cry out and run
As it were doomsday.
  Bru.   Fates, we will know your pleasures:
That we shall die, we know; 'tis but the time
And drawing days out that men stand upon.   *100*
  Cas. Why, he that cuts off twenty years of life
Cuts off so many years of fearing death.
  Bru. Grant that, and then is death a benefit:
So are we Cæsar's friends, that have abridged
His time of fearing death. Stoop, Romans, stoop,
And let us bathe our hands in Cæsar's blood
Up to the elbows, and besmear our swords:
Then walk we forth, even to the market-place,
And, waving our red weapons o'er our heads,
Let's all cry, "Peace, freedom, and liberty!"   *110*
  Cas. Stoop, then, and wash. How many ages
   hence
Shall this our lofty scene be acted over
In states unborn and accents yet unknown!
  Bru. How many times shall Cæsar bleed in
   sport,
That now on Pompey's basis lies along
No worthier than the dust!
  Cas.   So oft as that shall be,
So often shall the knot of us be call'd
The men that gave their country liberty.
  Dec. What, shall we forth?
  Cas.   Ay, every man away:
Brutus shall lead; and we will grace his heels   *120*
With the most boldest and best hearts of Rome.

Enter a SERVANT.

  Bru. Soft! who comes here? A friend of An-
   tony's.
  Serv. Thus, Brutus, did my master bid me
   kneel;
Thus did Mark Antony bid me fall down;
And, being prostrate, thus he bade me say:
Brutus is noble, wise, valiant, and honest;
Cæsar was mighty, bold, royal, and loving:
Say I love Brutus, and I honour him;
Say I fear'd Cæsar, honour'd him, and loved him.
If Brutus will vouchsafe that Antony   *130*
May safely come to him, and be resolved
How Cæsar hath deserved to lie in death,
Mark Antony shall not love Cæsar dead

So well as Brutus living; but will follow
The fortunes and affairs of noble Brutus
Thorough the hazards of this untrod state
With all true faith. So says my master Antony.

Bru. Thy master is a wise and valiant Roman;
I never thought him worse.
Tell him, so please him come unto this place, *140*
He shall be satisfied; and, by my honour,
Depart untouch'd.

Serv. I'll fetch him presently. [*Exit.*

Bru. I know that we shall have him well to
　　friend.

Cas. I wish we may: but yet have I a mind
That fears him much; and my misgiving still
Falls shrewdly to the purpose.

Bru. But here comes Antony.

Re-enter ANTONY.

Welcome, Mark Antony.

Ant. O mighty Cæsar! dost thou lie so low?
Are all thy conquests, glories, triumphs, spoils,
Shrunk to this little measure? Fare thee well.
I know not, gentlemen, what you intend, *151*
Who else must be let blood, who else is rank:
If I myself, there is no hour so fit
As Cæsar's death's hour, nor no instrument
Of half that worth as those your swords, made
　　rich
With the most noble blood of all this world.
I do beseech ye, if you bear me hard,
Now, whilst your purpled hands do reek and
　　smoke,
Fulfil your pleasure. Live a thousand years,
I shall not find myself so apt to die: *160*
No place will please me so, no mean of death,
As here by Cæsar, and by you cut off,
The choice and master spirits of this age.

Bru. O Antony, beg not your death of us.
Though now we must appear bloody and cruel,
As, by our hands and this our present act,
You see we do, yet see you but our hands
And this the bleeding business they have done:
Our hearts you see not; they are pitiful;
And pity to the general wrong of Rome— *170*
As fire drives out fire, so pity pity—
Hath done this deed on Cæsar. For your part,
To you our swords have leaden points, Mark
　　Antony:
Our arms, in strength of malice, and our hearts
Of brothers' temper, do receive you in
With all kind love, good thoughts, and reverence.

Cas. Your voice shall be as strong as any man's
In the disposing of new dignities.

Bru. Only be patient till we have appeased
The multitude, beside themselves with fear, *180*
And then we will deliver you the cause

Why I, that did love Cæsar when I struck him,
Have thus proceeded.

Ant. I doubt not of your wisdom.
Let each man render me his bloody hand:
First, Marcus Brutus, will I shake with you;
Next, Caius Cassius, do I take your hand;
Now, Decius Brutus, yours; now yours, Me-
　　tellus;
Yours, Cinna; and, my valiant Casca, yours;
Though last, not least in love, yours, good Tre-
　　bonius.
Gentlemen all—alas, what shall I say? *190*
My credit now stands on such slippery ground
That one of two bad ways you must conceit me,
Either a coward or a flatterer.
That I did love thee, Cæsar, O, 'tis true:
If then thy spirit look upon us now,
Shall it not grieve thee dearer than thy death,
To see thy Antony making his peace,
Shaking the bloody fingers of thy foes,
Most noble! in the presence of thy corse?
Had I as many eyes as thou hast wounds, *200*
Weeping as fast as they stream forth thy blood,
It would become me better than to close
In terms of friendship with thine enemies.
Pardon me, Julius! Here wast thou bay'd, brave
　　hart;
Here didst thou fall; and here thy hunters stand,
Sign'd in thy spoil, and crimson'd in thy lethe.
O world, thou wast the forest to this hart;
And this, indeed, O world, the heart of thee.
How like a deer, strucken by many princes,
Dost thou here lie! *210*

Cas. Mark Antony—

Ant. Pardon me, Caius Cassius:
The enemies of Cæsar shall say this;
Then, in a friend, it is cold modesty.

Cas. I blame you not for praising Cæsar so;
But what compact mean you to have with us?
Will you be prick'd in number of our friends;
Or shall we on, and not depend on you?

Ant. Therefore I took your hands, but was,
　　indeed,
Sway'd from the point, by looking down on
　　Cæsar.
Friends am I with you all and love you all, *220*
Upon this hope, that you shall give me reasons
Why and wherein Cæsar was dangerous.

Bru. Or else were this a savage spectacle:
Our reasons are so full of good regard
That were you, Antony, the son of Cæsar,
You should be satisfied.

Ant. That's all I seek:
And am moreover suitor that I may
Produce his body to the market-place;
And in the pulpit, as becomes a friend,

Speak in the order of his funeral.   *230*
Bru. You shall, Mark Antony.
Cas.   Brutus, a word with you.
[*Aside to* BRUTUS] You know not what you do: do
     not consent
That Antony speak in his funeral:
Know you how much the people may be moved
By that which he will utter?
Bru.   By your pardon;
I will myself into the pulpit first
And show the reason of our Cæsar's death:
What Antony shall speak, I will protest
He speaks by leave and by permission,
And that we are contented Cæsar shall   *240*
Have all true rites and lawful ceremonies.
It shall advantage more than do us wrong.
Cas. I know not what may fall; I like it not.
Bru. Mark Antony, here, take you Cæsar's
     body.
You shall not in your funeral speech blame us,
But speak all good you can devise of Cæsar,
And say you do't by our permission;
Else shall you not have any hand at all
About his funeral: and you shall speak
In the same pulpit whereto I am going,   *250*
After my speech is ended.
Ant.   Be it so;
I do desire no more.
Bru. Prepare the body then, and follow us.
                    [*Exeunt all but* ANTONY.
Ant. O, pardon me, thou bleeding piece of
     earth,
That I am meek and gentle with these butchers!
Thou are the ruins of the noblest man
That ever lived in the tide of times.
Woe to the hand that shed this costly blood!
Over thy wounds now do I prophesy—   *259*
Which, like dumb mouths, do ope their ruby lips
To beg the voice and utterance of my tongue—
A curse shall light upon the limbs of men;
Domestic fury and fierce civil strife
Shall cumber all the parts of Italy;
Blood and destruction shall be so in use
And dreadful objects so familiar
That mothers shall but smile when they behold
Their infants quarter'd with the hands of war;
All pity choked with custom of fell deeds:
And Cæsar's spirit, ranging for revenge,   *270*
With Ate by his side come hot from hell,
Shall in these confines with a monarch's voice
Cry "Havoc," and let slip the dogs of war;
That this foul deed shall smell above the earth
With carrion men, groaning for burial.

Enter a SERVANT.

You serve Octavius Cæsar, do you not?

Serv. I do, Mark Antony.
Ant. Cæsar did write for him to come to Rome.
Serv. He did receive his letters, and is coming;
And bid me say to you by word of mouth—   *280*
O Cæsar!—[*Seeing the body.*]
Ant. Thy heart is big, get thee apart and weep.
Passion, I see, is catching; for mine eyes,
Seeing those beads of sorrow stand in thine,
Began to water. Is thy master coming?
Serv. He lies to-night within seven leagues of
     Rome.
Ant. Post back with speed, and tell him what
     hath chanced:
Here is a mourning Rome, a dangerous Rome,
No Rome of safety for Octavius yet;   *289*
Hie hence, and tell him so. Yet, stay awhile;
Thou shalt not back till I have borne this corse
Into the market-place: there shall I try,
In my oration, how the people take
The cruel issue of these bloody men;
According to the which, thou shalt discourse
To young Octavius of the state of things.
Lend me your hand.   [*Exeunt with* CÆSAR's *body*.

SCENE II. *The Forum.*

Enter BRUTUS *and* CASSIUS, *and a throng*
of CITIZENS.

Citizens. We will be satisfied; let us be satisfied.
Bru. Then follow me, and give me audience,
     friends.
Cassius, go you into the other street,
And part the numbers.
Those that will hear me speak, let 'em stay here;
Those that will follow Cassius, go with him;
And public reasons shall be rendered
Of Cæsar's death.
1st Cit. I will hear Brutus speak.
2nd Cit. I will hear Cassius; and compare their
     reasons
When severally we hear them rendered.   *10*
          [*Exit* CASSIUS, *with some of the* CITIZENS.
                    BRUTUS *goes into the pulpit.*
3rd Cit. The noble Brutus is ascended: silence!
Bru. Be patient till the last.
Romans, countrymen, and lovers! hear me for my
cause, and be silent, that you may hear: believe
me for mine honour, and have respect to mine
honour, that you may believe: censure me in
your wisdom, and awake your senses, that you
may the better judge. If there be any in this
assembly, any dear friend of Cæsar's, to him I say,
that Brutus' love to Cæsar was no less than his.
If then that friend demand why Brutus rose
against Cæsar, this is my answer: Not that I
loved Cæsar less, but that I loved Rome more.
Had you rather Cæsar were living and die all

slaves, than that Cæsar were dead, to live all free men? As Cæsar loved me, I weep for him; as he was fortunate, I rejoice at it; as he was valiant, I honour him: but, as he was ambitious, I slew him. There is tears for his love; joy for his fortune; honour for his valour; and death for his ambition. Who is here so base that would be a bondman? If any, speak; for him have I offended. Who is here so rude that would not be a Roman? If any, speak; for him have I offended. Who is here so vile that will not love his country? If any, speak; for him have I offended. I pause for a reply.

All. None, Brutus, none.

Bru. Then none have I offended. I have done no more to Cæsar than you shall do to Brutus. The question of his death is enrolled in the Capitol; his glory not extenuated, wherein he was worthy, nor his offences enforced, for which he suffered death.

Enter ANTONY *and others, with* CÆSAR's *body.*

Here comes his body, mourned by Mark Antony: who, though he had no hand in his death, shall receive the benefit of his dying, a place in the commonwealth; as which of you shall not? With this I depart, that, as I slew my best lover for the good of Rome, I have the same dagger for myself, when it shall please my country to need my death.

All. Live, Brutus! live, live!

1st Cit. Bring him with triumph home unto his house.

2nd Cit. Give him a statue with his ancestors.

3rd Cit. Let him be Cæsar.

4th Cit.   Cæsar's better parts Shall be crown'd in Brutus.

1st Cit.   We'll bring him to his house With shouts and clamours.

Bru.   My countrymen—

2nd Cit. Peace, silence! Brutus speaks.

1st Cit.   Peace, ho!

Bru. Good countrymen, let me depart alone, And, for my sake, stay here with Antony: 61 Do grace to Cæsar's corpse, and grace his speech Tending to Cæsar's glories; which Mark Antony, By our permission, is allow'd to make. I do entreat you, not a man depart Save I alone, till Antony have spoke.   [*Exit.*

1st Cit. Stay, ho! and let us hear Mark Antony.

3rd Cit. Let him go up into the public chair; We'll hear him. Noble Antony, go up.

Ant. For Brutus' sake, I am beholding to you.

          [*Goes into the pulpit.*]   70

4th Cit. What does he say of Brutus?

3rd Cit.   He says, for Brutus' sake,

He finds himself beholding to us all.

4th Cit. 'Twere best he speak no harm of Brutus here.

1st Cit. This Cæsar was a tyrant.

3rd Cit.   Nay, that's certain: We are blest that Rome is rid of him.

2nd Cit. Peace! let us hear what Antony can say.

Ant. You gentle Romans—

Citizens.   Peace, ho! let us hear him.

Ant. Friends, Romans, countrymen, lend me your ears; I come to bury Cæsar, not to praise him. The evil that men do lives after them;   80 The good is oft interred with their bones; So let it be with Cæsar. The noble Brutus Hath told you Cæsar was ambitious: If it were so, it was a grievous fault, And grievously hath Cæsar answer'd it. Here, under leave of Brutus and the rest— For Brutus is an honourable man; So are they all, all honourable men— Come I to speak in Cæsar's funeral. He was my friend, faithful and just to me: 90 But Brutus says he was ambitious; And Brutus is an honourable man. He hath brought many captives home to Rome, Whose ransoms did the general coffers fill: Did this in Cæsar seem ambitious? When that the poor have cried, Cæsar hath wept: Ambition should be made of sterner stuff: Yet Brutus says he was ambitious; And Brutus is an honourable man. You all did see that on the Lupercal   100 I thrice presented him a kingly crown, Which he did thrice refuse: was this ambition? Yet Brutus says he was ambitious; And, sure, he is an honourable man. I speak not to disprove what Brutus spoke, But here I am to speak what I do know. You all did love him once, not without cause: What cause withholds you then to mourn for him? O judgement! thou art fled to brutish beasts,   109 And men have lost their reason. Bear with me; My heart is in the coffin there with Cæsar, And I must pause till it come back to me.

1st Cit. Methinks there is much reason in his sayings.

2nd Cit. If thou consider rightly of the matter, Cæsar has had great wrong.

3rd Cit   Has he, masters? I fear there will a worse come in his place.

4th Cit. Mark'd ye his words? He would not take the crown; Therefore 'tis certain he was not ambitious.

1st Cit. If it be found so, some will dear abide it.

2nd Cit. Poor soul! his eyes are red as fire with
　weeping.　　　　　　　　　　　　　　　　　*120*

3rd Cit. There's not a nobler man in Rome
　than Antony.

4th Cit. Now mark him, he begins again to
　speak.

Ant. But yesterday the word of Cæsar might
Have stood against the world; now lies he there,
And none so poor to do him reverence.
O masters, if I were disposed to stir
Your hearts and minds to mutiny and rage,
I should do Brutus wrong, and Cassius wrong,
Who, you all know, are honourable men:
I will not do them wrong; I rather choose　　*130*
To wrong the dead, to wrong myself and you,
Than I will wrong such honourable men.
But here's a parchment with the seal of Cæsar;
I found it in his closet, 'tis his will:
Let but the commons hear this testament—
Which, pardon me, I do not mean to read—
And they would go and kiss dead Cæsar's wounds
And dip their napkins in his sacred blood,
Yea, beg a hair of him for memory,
And, dying, mention it within their wills,　　*140*
Bequeathing it as a rich legacy
Unto their issue.

4th Cit. We'll hear the will: read it, Mark
　Antony.

All. The will, the will! we will hear Cæsar's
　will.

Ant. Have patience, gentle friends, I must not
　read it;
It is not meet you know how Cæsar loved you.
You are not wood, you are not stones, but men;
And, being men, hearing the will of Cæsar,
It will inflame you, it will make you mad:　　*149*
'Tis good you know not that you are his heirs;
For, if you should, O, what would come of it!

4th Cit. Read the will; we'll hear it, Antony;
You shall read us the will, Cæsar's will.

Ant. Will you be patient? will you stay awhile?
I have o'ershot myself to tell you of it:
I fear I wrong the honourable men
Whose daggers have stabb'd Cæsar; I do fear it.

4th Cit. They were traitors: honourable men!

All. The will! the testament!

2nd Cit. They were villains, murderers: the
will! read the will.　　　　　　　　　　　　*160*

Ant. You will compel me, then, to read the will?
Then make a ring about the corpse of Cæsar,
And let me show you him that made the will.
Shall I descend? and will you give me leave?

Several Cit. Come down.

2nd Cit. Descend.

3rd Cit. You shall have leave.

　　　　　　　　　　　　[ANTONY *comes down.*

4th Cit. A ring; stand round.

1st Cit. Stand from the hearse, stand from the
　body.　　　　　　　　　　　　　　　　　*169*

2nd Cit. Room for Antony, most noble Antony.

Ant. Nay, press not so upon me; stand far off.

Several Cit. Stand back; room; bear back.

Ant. If you have tears, prepare to shed them
　now.
You all do know this mantle: I remember
The first time ever Cæsar put it on;
'Twas on a summer's evening, in his tent,
That day he overcame the Nervii:
Look, in this place ran Cassius' dagger through:
See what a rent the envious Casca made:
Through this the well-beloved Brutus stabb'd;
And as he pluck'd his cursed steel away,　　*181*
Mark how the blood of Cæsar follow'd it,
As rushing out of doors, to be resolved
If Brutus so unkindly knock'd or no;
For Brutus, as you know, was Cæsar's angel:
Judge, O you gods, how dearly Cæsar loved
　him!
This was the most unkindest cut of all;
For when the noble Cæsar saw him stab,
Ingratitude, more strong than traitors' arms,
Quite vanquish'd him: then burst his mighty
　heart;　　　　　　　　　　　　　　　　*190*
And, in his mantle muffling up his face,
Even at the base of Pompey's statua,
Which all the while ran blood, great Cæsar fell.
O, what a fall was there, my countrymen!
Then I, and you, and all of us fell down,
Whilst bloody treason flourish'd over us.
O, now you weep; and, I perceive, you feel
The dint of pity: these are gracious drops.
Kind souls, what, weep you when you but behold
Our Cæsar's vesture wounded? Look you here

　　　　　[*lifting* CÆSAR'S *mantle.*]　　*200*
Here is himself, marr'd, as you see, with traitors.

1st Cit. O piteous spectacle!

2nd Cit. O noble Cæsar!

3rd Cit. O woeful day!

4th Cit. O traitors, villains!

1st Cit. O most bloody sight!

2nd Cit. We will be revenged.

All. Revenge! About! Seek! Burn! Fire! Kill!
Slay! Let not a traitor live!

Ant. Stay, countrymen.　　　　　　　　*210*

1st Cit. Peace there! hear the noble Antony.

2nd Cit. We'll hear him, we'll follow him,
we'll die with him.

Ant. Good friends, sweet friends, let me not
　stir you up
To such a sudden flood of mutiny.
They that have done this deed are honourable:
What private griefs they have, alas, I know not,

That made them do it: they are wise and honour-
able
And will, no doubt, with reasons answer you.
I come not, friends, to steal away your hearts:
I am no orator, as Brutus is;   221
But, as you know me all, a plain blunt man,
That love my friend; and that they know full
well
That gave me public leave to speak of him:
For I have neither wit, nor words, nor worth,
Action, nor utterance, nor the power of
speech,
To stir men's blood: I only speak right on;
I tell you that which you yourselves do know;
Show you sweet Cæsar's wounds, poor poor dumb
mouths,   229
And bid them speak for me: but were I Brutus,
And Brutus Antony, there were an Antony
Would ruffle up your spirits and put a tongue
In every wound of Cæsar that should move
The stones of Rome to rise and mutiny.
    All. We'll mutiny.
    1st Cit. We'll burn the house of Brutus.
    3rd Cit. Away, then! come, seek the conspira-
tors.
    Ant. Yet hear me, countrymen; yet hear me
speak.
    All. Peace, ho! Hear Antony. Most noble
Antony!
    Ant. Why, friends, you go to do you know not
what: 240
Wherein hath Cæsar thus deserved your loves?
Alas, you know not: I must tell you, then:
You have forgot the will I told you of.
    All. Most true. The will! Let's stay and hear
the will.
    Ant. Here is the will, and under Cæsar's seal.
To every Roman citizen he gives,
To every several man, seventy five drachmas.
    2nd Cit. Most noble Cæsar! We'll revenge his
death.
    3rd Cit. O royal Cæsar!
    Ant. Hear me with patience.   250
    All. Peace, ho!
    Ant. Moreover, he hath left you all his walks,
His private arbours and new-planted orchards,
On this side Tiber; he hath left them you
And to your heirs for ever, common pleasures,
To walk abroad and recreate yourselves.
Here was a Cæsar! when comes such another?
    1st Cit. Never, never. Come, away, away!
We'll burn his body in the holy place,
And with the brands fire the traitors' houses. 260
Take up the body.
    2nd Cit. Go fetch fire.
    3rd Cit. Pluck down benches.

    4th Cit. Pluck down forms, windows, anything.
                    [*Exeunt* CITIZENS *with the body.*
    Ant. Now let it work. Mischief, thou art afoot,
Take thou what course thou wilt!

                Enter a SERVANT.

                            How now, fellow!
    Serv. Sir, Octavius is already come to Rome.
    Ant. Where is he?
    Serv. He and Lepidus are at Cæsar's house.
    Ant. And thither will I straight to visit him:
He comes upon a wish. Fortune is merry,   271
And in this mood will give us anything.
    Serv. I heard him say, Brutus and Cassius
Are rid like madmen through the gates of Rome.
    Ant. Belike they had some notice of the people,
How I had moved them. Bring me to Octavius.
                                            [*Exeunt.*

            SCENE III. *A street*
            Enter CINNA *the poet.*

    Cin. I dreamt to-night that I did feast with
Cæsar,
And things unluckily charge my fantasy:
I have no will to wander forth of doors,
Yet something leads me forth.

                Enter CITIZENS.

    1st Cit. What is your name?
    2nd Cit. Whither are you going?
    3rd Cit. Where do you dwell?
    4th Cit. Are you a married man or a bachelor?
    2nd Cit. Answer every man directly.   10
    1st Cit. Ay, and briefly.
    4th Cit. Ay, and wisely.
    3rd Cit. Ay, and truly, you were best.
    Cin. What is my name? Whither am I going?
Where do I dwell? Am I a married man or a
bachelor? Then, to answer every man directly
and briefly, wisely and truly: wisely I say, I am
a bachelor.
    2nd Cit. That's as much as to say, they are
fools that marry: you'll bear me a bang for that,
I fear. Proceed; directly.   21
    Cin. Directly, I am going to Cæsar's funeral.
    1st Cit. As a friend or an enemy?
    Cin. As a friend.
    2nd Cit. That matter is answered directly.
    4th Cit. For your dwelling—briefly.
    Cin. Briefly, I dwell by the Capitol.
    3rd Cit. Your name, sir, truly.
    Cin. Truly, my name is Cinna.
    1st Cit. Tear him to pieces; he's a conspirator. 30
    Cin. I am Cinna the poet, I am Cinna the poet.
    4th Cit. Tear him for his bad verses, tear him
for his bad verses.

Cin. I am not Cinna the conspirator.

4th Cit. It is no matter, his name's Cinna; pluck but his name out of his heart, and turn him going.

3rd Cit. Tear him, tear him! Come, brands, ho! fire-brands: to Brutus', to Cassius'; burn all: some to Decius' house, and some to Casca's; some to Ligarius': away, go!   [*Exeunt.*

ACT IV

SCENE I. *A house in Rome*

ANTONY, OCTAVIUS, *and* LEPIDUS, *seated at a table.*

Ant. These many, then, shall die; their names are prick'd.

Oct. Your brother too must die; consent you, Lepidus?

Lep. I do consent—

Oct.   Prick him down, Antony.

Lep. Upon condition Publius shall not live, Who is your sister's son, Mark Antony.

Ant. He shall not live; look, with a spot I damn him.

But, Lepidus, go you to Cæsar's house; Fetch the will hither, and we shall determine How to cut off some charge in legacies.

Lep. What, shall I find you here?   10

Oct. Or here, or at the Capitol.

                          [*Exit* LEPIDUS.

Ant. This is a slight unmeritable man, Meet to be sent on errands: is it fit, The three-fold world divided, he should stand One of the three to share it?

Oct.   So you thought him; And took his voice who should be prick'd to die, In our black sentence and proscription.

Ant. Octavius, I have seen more days than you: And though we lay these honours on this man To ease ourselves of divers slanderous loads,   20 He shall but bear them as the ass bears gold, To groan and sweat under the business, Either led or driven, as we point the way; And having brought our treasure where we will; Then take we down his load, and turn him off, Like to the empty ass, to shake his ears And graze in commons.

Oct.   You may do your will; But he's a tried and valiant soldier.

Ant. So is my horse, Octavius; and for that I do appoint him store of provender: 30 It is a creature that I teach to fight, To wind, to stop, to run directly on, His corporal motion govern'd by my spirit. And, in some taste, is Lepidus but so; He must be taught and train'd and bid go forth; A barren-spirited fellow; one that feeds

On abjects, orts, and imitations, Which, out of use and staled by other men, Begin his fashion: do not talk of him But as a property. And now, Octavius,   40 Listen great things: Brutus and Cassius Are levying powers: we must straight make head: Therefore let our alliance be combined, Our best friends made, our means stretch'd; And let us presently go sit in council How covert matters may be best disclosed And open perils surest answered.

Oct. Let us do so: for we are at the stake And bay'd about with many enemies;   49 And some that smile have in their hearts, I fear, Millions of mischiefs.   [*Exeunt.*

SCENE II. *Camp near Sardis: before Brutus's tent*

Drum. Enter BRUTUS, LUCILIUS, LUCIUS, *and* SOLDIERS; TITINIUS *and* PINDARUS *meeting them.*

Bru. Stand, ho!

Lucil. Give the word, ho! and stand.

Bru. What now, Lucilius! is Cassius near?

Lucil. He is at hand; and Pindarus is come To do you salutation from his master.

Bru. He greets me well. Your master, Pindarus, In his own change, or by ill officers, Hath given me some worthy cause to wish Things done, undone: but, if he be at hand, I shall be satisfied.

Pin.   I do not doubt   10 But that my noble master will appear Such as he is, full of regard and honour.

Bru. He is not doubted. A word, Lucilius; How he received you, let me be resolved.

Lucil. With courtesy and with respect enough; But not with such familiar instances, Nor with such free and friendly conference, As he hath used of old.

Bru.   Thou hast described A hot friend cooling: ever note, Lucilius, When love begins to sicken and decay   20 It useth an enforced ceremony. There are no tricks in plain and simple faith; But hollow men, like horses hot at hand, Make gallant show and promise of their mettle; But when they should endure the bloody spur, They fall their crests, and, like deceitful jades, Sink in the trial. Comes his army on?

Lucil. They mean this night in Sardis to be quarter'd; The greater part, the horse in general, Are come with Cassius.

Bru.   Hark! he is arrived.   30

Low march within.

March gently on to meet him.

Enter CASSIUS *and his powers.*

Cas. Stand, ho!

Bru. Stand, ho! Speak the word along.

1st Sol. Stand!

2nd Sol. Stand!

3rd Sol. Stand!

Cas. Most noble brother, you have done me wrong.

Bru. Judge me, you gods! wrong I mine enemies?
And, if not so, how should I wrong a brother?

Cas. Brutus, this sober form of yours hides wrongs;   40
And when you do them—

Bru.   Cassius, be content;
Speak your griefs softly: I do know you well.
Before the eyes of both our armies here,
Which should perceive nothing but love from us,
Let us not wrangle: bid them move away;
Then in my tent, Cassius, enlarge your griefs,
And I will give you audience.

Cas.   Pindarus,
Bid our commanders lead their charges off
A little from this ground.

Bru. Lucilius, do you the like; and let no man   50
Come to our tent till we have done our conference.
Let Lucius and Titinius guard our door. [*Exeunt.*

SCENE III. *Brutus' tent*

Enter BRUTUS *and* CASSIUS.

Cas. That you have wrong'd me doth appear in this:
You have condemn'd and noted Lucius Pella
For taking bribes here of the Sardians;
Wherein my letters, praying on his side,
Because I knew the man, were slighted off.

Bru. You wrong'd yourself to write in such a case.

Cas. In such a time as this it is not meet
That every nice offence should bear his comment.

Bru. Let me tell you, Cassius, you yourself
Are much condemn'd to have an itching palm;   10
To sell and mart your offices for gold
To undeservers.

Cas.   I an itching palm!
You know that you are Brutus that speak this,
Or, by the gods, this speech were else your last.

Bru. The name of Cassius honours this corruption,
And chastisement doth therefore hide his head.

Cas. Chastisement!

Bru. Remember March, the ides of March remember:
Did not great Julius bleed for justice' sake?
What villain touch'd his body, that did stab   20

And not for justice? What, shall one of us,
That struck the foremost man of all this world
But for supporting robbers, shall we now
Contaminate our fingers with base bribes,
And sell the mighty space of our large honours
For so much trash as may be grasped thus?
I had rather be a dog, and bay the moon,
Than such a Roman.

Cas.   Brutus, bay not me;
I'll not endure it: you forget yourself
To hedge me in; I am a soldier, I,   30
Older in practice, abler than yourself
To make conditions.

Bru.   Go to; you are not, Cassius.

Cas. I am.

Bru. I say you are not.

Cas. Urge me no more, I shall forget myself;
Have mind upon your health, tempt me no farther.

Bru. Away, slight man!

Cas. Is't possible?

Bru.   Hear me, for I will speak.
Must I give way and room to your rash choler?
Shall I be frighted when a madman stares?   40

Cas. O ye gods, ye gods! must I endure all this?

Bru. All this! ay, more: fret till your proud heart break;
Go show your slaves how choleric you are,
And make your bondmen tremble. Must I budge?
Must I observe you? must I stand and crouch
Under your testy humour? By the gods,
You shall digest the venom of your spleen,
Though it do split you; for, from this day forth,
I'll use you for my mirth, yea, for my laughter,
When you are waspish.

Cas.   Is it come to this?   50

Bru. You say you are a better soldier:
Let it appear so; make your vaunting true,
And it shall please me well: for mine own part,
I shall be glad to learn of noble men.

Cas. You wrong me every way; you wrong me, Brutus;
I said, an elder soldier, not a better:
Did I say "better"?

Bru.   If you did, I care not.

Cas. When Cæsar lived, he durst not thus have moved me.

Bru. Peace, peace! you durst not so have tempted him.

Cas. I durst not!   60

Bru. No.

Cas. What, durst not tempt him!

Bru.   For your life you durst not.

Cas. Do not presume too much upon my love;
I may do that I shall be sorry for.

Bru. You have done that you should be sorry for.

There is no terror, Cassius, in your threats,
For I am arm'd so strong in honesty
That they pass by me as the idle wind,
Which I respect not. I did send to you
For certain sums of gold, which you denied me:
For I can raise no money by vile means: 71
By heaven, I had rather coin my heart
And drop my blood for drachmas than to wring
From the hard hands of peasants their vile trash
By any indirection: I did send
To you for gold to pay my legions,
Which you denied me: was that done like Cas-
    sius?
Should I have answer'd Caius Cassius so?
When Marcus Brutus grows so covetous
To lock such rascal counters from his friends, 80
Be ready, gods, with all your thunderbolts;
Dash him to pieces!
    Cas.   I denied you not.
    Bru. You did.
    Cas. I did not: he was but a fool that brought
My answer back. Brutus hath rived my heart:
A friend should bear his friend's infirmities,
But Brutus makes mine greater than they are.
    Bru. I do not, till you practise them on me.
    Cas. You love me not.
    Bru.   I do not like your faults.
    Cas. A friendly eye could never see such faults.
    Bru. A flatterer's would not, though they do
    appear   91
As huge as high Olympus.
    Cas. Come, Antony, and young Octavius, come,
Revenge yourselves alone on Cassius,
For Cassius is aweary of the world;
Hated by one he loves; braved by his brother;
Check'd like a bondman; all his faults observed,
Set in a note-book, learn'd, and conn'd by rote,
To cast into my teeth. O, I could weep
My spirit from mine eyes! There is my dagger,
And here my naked breast; within a heart   101
Dearer than Plutus' mine, richer than gold:
If that thou be'st a Roman, take it forth;
I, that denied thee gold, will give my heart:
Strike, as thou didst at Cæsar; for, I know,
When thou didst hate him worst, thou lovedst
    him better
Than ever thou lovedst Cassius.
    Bru.   Sheathe your dagger:
Be angry when you will, it shall have scope;
Do what you will, dishonour shall be humour.
O Cassius, you are yoked with a lamb   110
That carries anger as the flint bears fire;
Who, much enforced, shows a hasty spark,
And straight is cold again.
    Cas.   Hath Cassius lived
To be but mirth and laughter to his Brutus,

When grief and blood ill-temper'd vexeth him?
    Bru. When I spoke that, I was ill-temper'd too.
    Cas. Do you confess so much? Give me your
    hand.
    Bru. And my heart too.
    Cas.   O Brutus!
    Bru.   What's the matter?
    Cas. Have not you love enough to bear with
    me,
When that rash humour which my mother gave
    me,
Makes me forgetful?
    Bru.   Yes, Cassius; and, from henceforth,
When you are over-earnest with your Brutus,
He'll think your mother chides, and leave you so.
    Poet. [*Within*] Let me go in to see the generals;
There is some grudge between 'em, 'tis not meet
They be alone.
    Lucil. [*Within*] You shall not come to them.
    Poet. [*Within*] Nothing but death shall stay me.

Enter POET, *followed by* LUCILIUS, TITINIUS, *and*
                    LUCIUS.

    Cas. How now! what's the matter?
    Poet. For shame, you generals! what do you
    mean?   130
Love, and be friends, as two such men should be;
For I have seen more years, I'm sure, than ye.
    Cas. Ha, ha! how vilely doth this cynic rhyme!
    Bru. Get you hence, sirrah; saucy fellow,
    hence!
    Cas. Bear with him, Brutus; 'tis his fashion.
    Bru. I'll know his humour, when he knows his
    time:
What should the wars do with these jigging
    fools?
Companion, hence!
    Cas.   Away, away, be gone!
                                    [*Exit* POET.
    Bru. Lucilius and Titinius, bid the commanders
Prepare to lodge their companies to-night.   140
    Cas. And come yourselves, and bring Messala
    with you
Immediately to us.
                    [*Exeunt* LUCILIUS *and* TITINIUS.
    Bru. Lucius, a bowl of wine! [*Exit* LUCIUS.
    Cas. I did not think you could have been so
    angry.
    Bru. O Cassius, I am sick of many griefs.
    Cas. Of your philosophy you make no use.
If you give place to accidental evils.
    Bru. No man bears sorrow better. Portia is
    dead.
    Cas. Ha! Portia!
    Bru. She is dead.
    Cas. How 'scaped I killing when I cross'd you so?

O insupportable and touching loss!   151
Upon what sickness?
    Bru.   Impatient of my absence,
And grief that young Octavius with Mark An-
    tony
Have made themselves so strong—for with her
    death
That tidings came—with this she fell distract,
And, her attendants absent, swallow'd fire.
    Cas. And died so?
    Bru.   Even so.
    Cas.   O ye immortal gods!

        Re-enter LUCIUS, *with wine and taper.*

    Bru. Speak no more of her. Give me a bowl
    of wine.
In this I bury all unkindness, Cassius.
    Cas. My heart is thirsty for that noble pledge.
Fill, Lucius, till the wine o'erswell the cup;   161
I cannot drink too much of Brutus' love.
    Bru. Come in Titinius!   [*Exit* LUCIUS.

        Re-enter TITINIUS, *with* MESSALA.

                        Welcome, good Messala.
Now sit we close about this taper here
And call in question our necessities.
    Cas. Portia, art thou gone?
    Bru.   No more, I pray you.
Messala, I have here received letters
That young Octavius and Mark Antony
Come down upon us with a mighty power,
Bending their expedition toward Philippi.   170
    Mes. Myself have letters of the selfsame tenour.
    Bru. With what addition?
    Mes. That by proscription and bills of outlawry,
Octavius, Antony, and Lepidus,
Have put to death an hundred senators.
    Bru. Therein our letters do not well agree;
Mine speak of seventy senators that died
By their proscriptions, Cicero being one.
    Cas. Cicero one!
    Mes.   Cicero is dead,
And by that order of proscription.   180
Had you your letters from your wife, my lord?
    Bru. No, Messala.
    Mes. Nor nothing in your letters writ of her.
    Bru. Nothing, Messala.
    Mes.   That, methinks, is strange.
    Bru. Why ask you? hear you aught of her in
    yours?
    Mes. No, my lord.
    Bru. Now, as you are a Roman, tell me true.
    Mes. Then like a Roman bear the truth I tell:
For certain she is dead, and by strange manner.
    Bru. Why, farewell, Portia. We must die,
    Messala: 190

With meditating that she must die once,
I have the patience to endure it now.
    Mes. Even so great men great losses should en-
    dure.
    Cas. I have as much of this in art as you,
But yet my nature could not bear it so.
    Bru. Well, to our work alive. What do you think
Of marching to Philippi presently?
    Cas. I do not think it good.
    Bru.   Your reason?
    Cas.   This it is:
'Tis better that the enemy seek us: 199
So shall he waste his means, weary his soldiers,
Doing himself offence; whilst we, lying still,
Are full of rest, defence, and nimbleness.
    Bru. Good reasons must, of force, give place to
    better.
The people 'twixt Philippi and this ground
Do stand but in a forced affection;
For they have grudged us contribution:
The enemy, marching along by them,
By them shall make a fuller number up,
Come on refresh'd, new-added, and encouraged;
From which advantage shall we cut him off,   210
If at Philippi we do face him there,
These people at our back.
    Cas.   Hear me, good brother.
    Bru. Under your pardon. You must note beside
That we have tried the utmost of our friends,
Our legions are brim-full, our cause is ripe:
The enemy increaseth every day;
We, at the height, are ready to decline.
There is a tide in the affairs of men
Which, taken at the flood, leads on to fortune;
Omitted, all the voyage of their life   220
Is bound in shallows and in miseries.
On such a full sea are we now afloat;
And we must take the current when it serves
Or lose our ventures.
    Cas.   Then, with your will, go on;
We'll along ourselves, and meet them at Philippi.
    Bru. The deep of night is crept upon our talk,
And nature must obey necessity;
Which we will niggard with a little rest.
There is no more to say?
    Cas.   No more. Good night:
Early to-morrow will we rise, and hence.   230
    Bru. Lucius! [*Enter* LUCIUS.] My gown.
    [*Exit* LUCIUS.] Farewell, good Messala:
Good night, Titinius. Noble, noble Cassius,
Good night, and good repose.
    Cas.   O my dear brother!
This was an ill beginning of the night:
Never come such division 'tween our souls!
Let it not, Brutus.
    Bru.   Everything is well.

Cas. Good night, my lord.
Bru.   Good night, good brother.
Tit. Mes. Good night, Lord Brutus.
Bru.   Farewell, every one.
                [*Exeunt all but* BRUTUS.

Re-enter LUCIUS, *with the gown.*

Give me the gown. Where is thy instrument?
Luc. Here in the tent.
Bru.   What, thou speak'st drowsily?   *240*
Poor knave, I blame thee not; thou art o'er-
watch'd.
Call Claudius and some other of my men;
I'll have them sleep on cushions in my tent.
Luc. Varro and Claudius!

Enter VARRO *and* CLAUDIUS.

Var. Calls my lord?
Bru. I pray you, sirs, lie in my tent and sleep;
It may be I shall raise you by and by
On business to my brother Cassius.
Var. So please you, we will stand and watch
    your pleasure.
Bru. I will not have it so: lie down, good
    sirs;   *250*
It may be I shall otherwise bethink me.
Look, Lucius, here's the book I sought for so;
I put it in the pocket of my gown.

    VARRO *and* CLAUDIUS *lie down.*

Luc. I was sure your lordship did not give it me.
Bru. Bear with me, good boy, I am much for-
getful.
Canst thou hold up thy heavy eyes awhile,
And touch thy instrument a strain or two?
Luc. Ay, my lord, an't please you.
Bru.   It does, my boy:
I trouble thee too much, but thou art willing.
Luc. It is my duty, sir.   *260*
Bru. I should not urge thy duty past thy might;
I know young bloods look for a time of rest.
Luc. I have slept, my lord, already.
Bru. It was well done; and thou shalt sleep
again;
I will not hold thee long: if I do live,
I will be good to thee.
    Music, and a song.
This is a sleepy tune. O murderous slumber,
Lay's thou thy leaden mace upon my boy,
That plays thee music? Gentle knave, good
    night;   *269*
I will not do thee so much wrong to wake thee:
If thou dost nod, thou break'st thy instrument;
I'll take it from thee; and, good boy, good night.
Let me see, let me see; is not the leaf turn'd
down
Where I left reading? Here it is, I think.

Enter the GHOST *of* CÆSAR.

How ill this taper burns! Ha! who comes here?
I think it is the weakness of mine eyes
That shapes this monstrous apparition.
It comes upon me. Art thou anything?
Art thou some god, some angel, or some devil,
That makest my blood cold and my hair to stare?
Speak to me what thou art.   *281*
Ghost. Thy evil spirit, Brutus.
Bru. Why comest thou?
Ghost. To tell thee thou shalt see me at Philippi.
Bru. Well; then I shall see thee again?
Ghost. Ay, at Philippi.
Bru. Why, I will see thee at Philippi, then.
                            [*Exit* GHOST.
Now I have taken heart thou vanishest:
Ill spirit, I would hold more talk with thee.
Boy, Lucius! Varro! Claudius! Sirs, awake!
Claudius!   *291*
Luc. The strings, my lord, are false.
Bru. He thinks he still is at his instrument.
Lucius, awake!
Luc. My lord?
Bru. Didst thou dream, Lucius, that thou so
criedst out?
Luc. My lord, I do not know that I did cry.
Bru. Yes, that thou didst: didst thou see any
thing?
Luc. Nothing, my lord.
Bru. Sleep again, Lucius. Sirrah Claudius!
[*To* VARRO] Fellow thou, awake!   *301*
Var. My lord?
Clau. My lord?
Bru. Why did you so cry out, sirs, in your
sleep?
Var. and Clau. Did we, my lord?
Bru.   Ay: saw you anything?
Var. No, my lord, I saw nothing.
Clau.   Nor I, my lord.
Bru. Go and commend me to my brother Cas-
sius;
Bid him set on his powers betimes before,
And we will follow.
Var. and Clau.   It shall be done, my lord. *309*
                            [*Exeunt.*

ACT V

SCENE I. *The plains of Philippi*
Enter OCTAVIUS, ANTONY, *and their* ARMY.

Oct. Now, Antony, our hopes are answered:
You said the enemy would not come down,
But keep the hills and upper regions:
It proves not so: their battles are at hand;
They mean to warn us at Philippi here,

Answering before we do demand of them.

Ant. Tut, I am in their bosoms, and I know
Wherefore they do it: they could be content
To visit other places; and come down
With fearful bravery, thinking by this face　　　*10*
To fasten in our thoughts that they have courage;
But 'tis not so.

Enter a MESSENGER.

Mess.　　　　Prepare you, generals:
The enemy comes on in gallant show;
Their bloody sign of battle is hung out,
And something to be done immediately.

Ant. Octavius, lead your battle softly on,
Upon the left hand of the even field.

Oct. Upon the right hand I; keep thou the left.

Ant. Why do you cross me in this exigent?

Oct. I do not cross you; but I will do so.　　　*20*
March.

Drum. Enter BRUTUS, CASSIUS, *and their Army;*
LUCILIUS, TITINIUS, MESSALA, *and others.*

Bru. They stand, and would have parley.

Cas. Stand fast, Titinius: we must out and talk.

Oct. Mark Antony, shall we give sign of battle?

Ant. No, Cæsar, we will answer on their
charge.
Make forth; the generals would have some words.

Oct. Stir not until the signal.

Bru. Words before blows: is it so, countrymen?

Oct. Not that we love words better, as you do.

Bru. Good words are better than bad strokes,
Octavius.

Ant. In your bad strokes, Brutus, you give
good words:　　　　　　　　　　　　　*30*
Witness the hole you made in Cæsar's heart,
Crying, "Long live! hail, Cæsar!"

Cas.　　　　　　　　　　　　Antony,
The posture of your blows are yet unknown;
But for your words, they rob the Hybla bees,
And leave them honeyless.

Ant.　　　　　　　Not stingless too.

Bru. O, yes, and soundless too;
For you have stol'n their buzzing, Antony,
And very wisely threat before you sting.

Ant. Villains, you did not so, when your vile
daggers
Hack'd one another in the sides of Cæsar:　　*40*
You show'd your teeth like apes, and fawn'd like
hounds,
And bow'd like bondmen, kissing Cæsar's feet;
Whilst damned Casca, like a cur, behind
Struck Cæsar on the neck. O you flatterers!

Cas. Flatterers! Now, Brutus, thank yourself:
This tongue had not offended so to-day,
If Cassius might have ruled.

Oct. Come, come, the cause: if arguing make us
sweat,
The proof of it will turn to redder drops.
Look;　　　　　　　　　　　　　　　*50*
I draw a sword against conspirators;
When think you that the sword goes up again?
Never, till Cæsar's three and thirty wounds
Be well avenged; or till another Cæsar
Have added slaughter to the sword of traitors.

Bru. Cæsar, thou canst not die by traitors'
hands,
Unless thou bring'st them with thee.

Oct.　　　　　　　　　　　　So I hope;
I was not born to die on Brutus' sword.

Bru. O, if thou wert the noblest of thy strain,
Young man, thou couldst not die more honourable.　　　　　　　　　　　　　　　*60*

Cas. A peevish school boy, worthless of such
honour,
Join'd with a masker and a reveller!

Ant. Old Cassius still!

Oct.　　　　　　　Come, Antony, away!
Defiance, traitors, hurl we in your teeth:
If you dare fight to-day, come to the field;
If not, when you have stomachs.

[Exeunt OCTAVIUS, ANTONY, *and their army.*

Cas. Why, now, blow wind, swell billow, and
swim bark!
The storm is up, and all is on the hazard.

Bru. Ho, Lucilius! hark, a word with you.

Lucil.　　　　　　　*[Standing forth]* My Lord?
BRUTUS *and* LUCILIUS *converse apart.*

Cas. Messala!

Mes. [Standing forth] What says my general?

Cas. Messala,　　　　　　　　　　　*71*
This is my birthday; as this very day
Was Cassius born. Give me thy hand, Messala:
Be thou my witness that against my will,
As Pompey was, am I compell'd to set
Upon one battle all our liberties.
You know that I held Epicurus strong
And his opinion: now I change my mind,
And partly credit things that do presage.
Coming from Sardis, on our former ensign　　*80*
Two mighty eagles fell, and there they perch'd,
Gorging and feeding from our soldiers' hands
Who to Philippi here consorted us:
This morning are they fled away and gone;
And in their steads do ravens, crows, and kites,
Fly o'er our heads and downward look on us,
As we were sickly prey: their shadows seem
A canopy most fatal, under which
Our army lies, ready to give up the ghost.

Mes. Believe not so.

Cas.　　　　　　　I but believe it partly;　　*90*
For I am fresh of spirit and resolved

To meet all perils very constantly.

Bru. Even so, Lucilius.

Cas.   Now, most noble Brutus,
The gods to-day stand friendly, that we may,
Lovers in peace, lead on our days to age!
But since the affairs of men rest still incertain,
Let's reason with the worst that may befall.
If we do lose this battle, then is this
The very last time we shall speak together:
What are you then determined to do?   *100*

Bru. Even by the rule of that philosophy
By which I did blame Cato for the death
Which he did give himself, I know not how,
But I do find it cowardly and vile,
For fear of what might fall, so to prevent
The time of life: arming myself with patience
To stay the providence of some high powers
That govern us below.

Cas.   Then, if we lose this battle,
You are contented to be led in triumph
Thorough the streets of Rome?   *110*

Bru. No, Cassius, no: think not, thou noble
      Roman,
That ever Brutus will go bound to Rome;
He bears too great a mind. But this same day
Must end that work the ides of March begun;
And whether we shall meet again I know not.
Therefore our everlasting farewell take:
For ever, and for ever, farewell, Cassius!
If we do meet again, why, we shall smile;
If not, why then, this parting was well made.

Cas. For ever, and for ever, farewell, Brutus!
If we do meet again, we'll smile indeed;   *121*
If not, 'tis true this parting was well made.

Bru. Why, then, lead on. O, that a man might
      know
The end of this day's business ere it come!
But it sufficeth that the day will end,
And then the end is known. Come, ho! away!
                                           [*Exeunt.*

SCENE II. *The same: the field of battle*
      Alarum. Enter BRUTUS *and* MESSALA.

Bru. Ride, ride, Messala, ride, and give these
      bills
Unto the legions on the other side. [*Loud alarum.*]
Let them set on at once; for I perceive
But cold demeanour in Octavius' wing,
And sudden push gives them the overthrow.
Ride, ride, Messala: let them all come down.
                                           [*Exeunt.*

SCENE III. *Another part of the field*
      Alarums. Enter CASSIUS *and* TITINIUS.

Cas. O, look, Titinius, look, the villains fly!
Myself have to mine own turn'd enemy:

This ensign here of mine was turning back;
I slew the coward, and did take it from him.

Tit. O Cassius, Brutus gave the word too early:
Who, having some advantage on Octavius,
Took it too eagerly: his soldiers fell to spoil,
Whilst we by Antony are all enclosed.

      Enter PINDARUS.

Pin. Fly further off, my lord, fly further off;
Mark Antony is in your tents, my lord: *10*
Fly, therefore, noble Cassius, fly far off.

Cas. This hill is far enough. Look, look, Titin-
      ius;
Are those my tents where I perceive the fire?

Tit. They are, my lord.

Cas.   Titinius, if thou lovest me,
Mount thou my horse, and hide thy spurs in him
Till he have brought thee up to yonder troops
And here again; that I may rest assured
Whether yond troops are friend or enemy

Tit. I will be here again, even with a thought.
                                           [*Exit.*

Cas. Go, Pindarus, get higher on that hill;   *20*
My sight was ever thick; regard Titinius,
And tell me what thou notest about the field.
      PINDARUS *ascends the hill.*
This day I breathed first: time is come round,
And where I did begin, there shall I end;
My life is run his compass. Sirrah, what news?

Pin. [*Above*] O my lord!

Cas. What news?

Pin. [*Above*] Titinius is enclosed round about
With horsemen, that make to him on the spur;
Yet he spurs on. Now they are almost on him.
Now, Titinius! Now some light. O, he lights
      too.   *31*
He's ta'en. [*Shout.*] And, hark! they shout for
      joy.

Cas. Come down, behold no more.
O, coward that I am, to live so long,
To see my best friend ta'en before my face!

      PINDARUS *descends.*

Come hither, sirrah:
In Parthia did I take thee prisoner;
And then I swore thee, saving of thy life,
That whatsoever I did bid thee do,
Thou shouldst attempt it. Come now, keep thine
      oath;   *40*
Now be a freeman: and with this good sword,
That ran through Cæsar's bowels, search this
      bosom.
Stand not to answer: here, take thou the hilts;
And, when my face is cover'd, as 'tis now,
Guide thou the sword. [PINDARUS *stabs him.*]
Cæsar, thou art revenged,

Even with the sword that kill'd thee.   [*Dies.*
 Pin. So, I am free; yet would not so have been,
Durst I have done my will. O Cassius,
Far from this country Pindarus shall run,
Where never Roman shall take note of him.   *50*
                                          [*Exit.*

Re-enter TITINIUS *with* MESSALA.

 Mes. It is but change, Titinius; for Octavius
Is overthrown by noble Brutus' power,
As Cassius' legions are by Antony.
 Tit. These tidings will well comfort Cassius.
 Mes. Where did you leave him?
 Tit.   All disconsolate,
With Pindarus his bondman, on this hill.
 Mes. Is not that he that lies upon the ground?
 Tit. He lies not like the living. O my heart!
 Mes. Is not that he?
 Tit.   No, this was he, Messala,
But Cassius is no more. O setting sun,   *60*
As in thy red rays thou dost sink to night,
So in his red blood Cassius' day is set;
The sun of Rome is set! Our day is gone;
Clouds, dews, and dangers come; our deeds are
  done!
Mistrust of my success hath done this deed.
 Mes. Mistrust of good success hath done this
  deed.
O hateful error, melancholy's child,
Why dost thou show to the apt thoughts of men
The things that are not? O error, soon con-
  ceived,
Thou never comest unto a happy birth,   *70*
But kill'st the mother than engender'd thee!
 Tit. What, Pindarus! where art thou, Pin-
  darus?
 Mes. Seek him, Titinius, whilst I go to meet
The noble Brutus, thrusting this report
Into his ears; I may say, thrusting it;
For piercing steel and darts envenomed
Shall be as welcome to the ears of Brutus
As tidings of this sight.
 Tit.   Hie you, Messala,
And I will seek for Pindarus the while.
                              [*Exit* MESSALA.
Why didst thou send me forth, brave Cassius? *80*
Did I not meet thy friends? and did not they
Put on my brows this wreath of victory,
And bid me give it thee? Didst thou not hear
  their shouts?
Alas, thou hast misconstrued everything!
But, hold thee, take this garland on thy brow;
Thy Brutus bid me give it thee, and I
Will do his bidding. Brutus, come apace,
And see how I regarded Caius Cassius.
By your leave, gods: this a Roman's part: *89*

Come, Cassius' sword, and find Titinius' heart.
                              [*Kills himself.*

Alarum. Re-enter MESSALA, *with* BRUTUS, YOUNG
  CATO, STRATO, VOLUMNIUS, *and* LUCILIUS.

 Bru. Where, where, Messala, doth his body
  lie?
 Mes. Lo, yonder, and Titinius mourning it.
 Bru. Titinius' face is upward.
 Cato.   He is slain.
 Bru. O Julius Cæsar, thou art mighty yet!
Thy spirit walks abroad and turns our swords
In our own proper entrails. [*Low alarums.*]
 Cato.   Brave Titinius!
Look, whether he have not crown'd dead Cas-
  sius!
 Bru. Are yet two Romans living such as these?
The last of all the Romans, fare thee well!
It is impossible that ever Rome   *100*
Should breed thy fellow. Friends, I owe more
  tears
To this dead man than you shall see me pay.
I shall find time, Cassius, I shall find time.
Come, therefore, and to Thasos send his body:
His funerals shall not be in our camp,
Lest it discomfort us. Lucilius, come;
And come, young Cato; let us to the field.
Labeo and Flavius, set our battles on:
'Tis three o'clock; and, Romans, yet ere night
We shall try fortune in a second fight.   [*Exeunt.*

SCENE IV. *Another part of the field*

Alarum. Enter fighting, SOLDIERS *of both armies;*
  then BRUTUS, YOUNG CATO, LUCILIUS, *and others.*

 Bru. Yet, countrymen, O, yet hold up your
  heads!
 Cato. What bastard doth not? Who will go
  with me?
I will proclaim my name about the field:
I am the son of Marcus Cato, ho!
A foe to tyrants and my country's friend;
I am the son of Marcus Cato, ho!
 Bru. And I am Brutus, Marcus Brutus, I;
Brutus, my country's friend; know me for
  Brutus!   [*Exit.*
 Lucil. O young and noble Cato, art thou down?
Why, now thou diest as bravely as Titinius;   *10*
And mayst be honour'd, being Cato's son.
 1st Sold. Yield, or thou diest.
 Lucil.   Only I yield to die:
There is so much that thou wilt kill me straight;
 Offering money.
Kill Brutus, and be honour'd in his death.
 1st Sold. We must not. A noble prisoner!
 2nd Sold. Room, ho! Tell Antony, Brutus is
  ta'en.

1st Sold. I'll tell the news. Here comes the
general.

Enter ANTONY.

Brutus is ta'en, Brutus is ta'en, my lord.
   Ant. Where is he?
   Lucil. Safe, Antony; Brutus is safe enough:
I dare assure thee that no enemy   21
Shall ever take alive the noble Brutus:
The gods defend him from so great a shame!
When you do find him, or alive or dead,
He will be found like Brutus, like himself.
   Ant. This is not Brutus, friend; but, I assure
you,
A prize no less in worth: keep this man safe;
Give him all kindness: I had rather have
Such men my friends than enemies. Go on,
And see whether Brutus be alive or dead;   30
And bring us word unto Octavius' tent
How everything is chanced.   [*Exeunt.*

SCENE V. *Another part of the field.*

Enter BRUTUS, DARDANIUS, CLITUS, STRATO, *and*
VOLUMNIUS.

   Bru. Come, poor remains of friends, rest on
this rock.
   Cli. Statilius show'd the torch-light, but, my
lord,
He came not back: he is or ta'en or slain.
   Bru. Sit thee down, Clitus: slaying is the word;
It is a deed in fashion. Hark thee, Clitus.
   Whispers.
   Cli. What, I, my lord? No, not for all the world.
   Bru. Peace then! no words.
   Cli.   I'll rather kill myself.
   Bru. Hark thee, Dardanius. [*Whispers.*]
   Dar.   Shall I do such a deed?
   Cli. O Dardanius!
   Dar. O Clitus!   10
   Cli. What ill request did Brutus make to thee?
   Dar. To kill him, Clitus. Look, he meditates.
   Cli. Now is that noble vessel full of grief,
That it runs over even at his eyes.
   Bru. Come hither, good Volumnius; list a
word.
   Vol. What says my lord?
   Bru.   Why, this, Volumnius:
The ghost of Cæsar hath appear'd to me
Two several times by night; at Sardis once,
And, this last night, here in Philippi fields:
I know my hour is come.
   Vol.   Not so, my lord.   20
   Bru. Nay, I am sure it is. Volumnius.
Thou seest the world, Volumnius, how it goes;
Our enemies have beat us to the pit:
   Low alarums.

It is more worthy to leap in ourselves
Than tarry till they push us. Good Volumnius,
Thou know'st that we two went to school to-
gether:
Even for that our love of old, I prithee,
Hold thou my sword-hilts, whilst I run on it.
   Vol. That's not an office for a friend, my lord.
[*Alarum still.*]
   Cli. Fly, fly, my lord; there is no tarrying
here.   30
   Bru. Farewell to you; and you; and you,
Volumnius.
Strato, thou hast been all this while asleep;
Farewell to thee too, Strato. Countrymen,
My heart doth joy that yet in all my life
I found no man but he was true to me.
I shall have glory by this losing day
More than Octavius and Mark Antony
By this vile conquest shall attain unto.
So fare you well at once; for Brutus' tongue
Hath almost ended his life's history: 40
Night hangs upon mine eyes; my bones would
rest,
That have but labour'd to attain this hour.
   Alarum. Cry within, "Fly, fly, fly!"
   Cli. Fly, my lord, fly.
   Bru.   Hence, I will follow.
[*Exeunt* CLITUS, DARDANIUS, *and* VOLUMNIUS.
I prithee, Strato, stay thou by thy lord:
Thou art a fellow of a good respect;
Thy life hath had some smatch of honour in it: ·
Hold then my sword, and turn away thy face,
While I do run upon it. Wilt thou, Strato?
   Stra. Give me your hand first. Fare you well,
my lord.
   Bru. Farewell, good Strato. [*Runs on his sword.*]
Cæsar, now be still: 50
I kill'd not thee with half so good a will. [*Dies.*

Alarum. Retreat. Enter OCTAVIUS, ANTONY, MES-
SALA, LUCILIUS, *and the army.*

   Oct. What man is that?
   Mes. My master's man. Strato, where is thy
master?
   Stra. Free from the bondage you are in, Messala:
The conquerors can but make a fire of him;
For Brutus only overcame himself,
And no man else hath honour by his death.
   Lucil. So Brutus should be found. I thank thee,
Brutus,
That thou has proved Lucilius' saying true.
   Oct. All that served Brutus, I will entertain
them.   60
Fellow, wilt thou bestow thy time with me?
   Stra. Ay, if Messala will prefer me to you.
   Oct. Do so, good Messala.

Mes. How died my master, Strato?

Stra. I held the sword, and he did run on it.

Mes. Octavius, then take him to follow thee,
That did the latest service to my master.

Ant. This was the noblest Roman of them all:
All the conspirators save only he
Did that they did in envy of great Cæsar;   70
He only, in a general honest thought
And common good to all, made one of them.

His life was gentle, and the elements
So mix'd in him that Nature might stand up
And say to all the world, "This was a man!"

Oct. According to his virtue let us use him,
With all respect and rites of burial.
Within my tent his bones to-night shall lie,
Most like a soldier, order'd honourably.
So call the field to rest; and let's away   80
To part the glories of this happy day.   [*Exeunt.*

❧ AS YOU LIKE IT

DRAMATIS PERSONÆ

DUKE SENIOR, *living in banishment*
FREDERICK, *his brother, and usurper of his dominions*
AMIENS | *lords attending on the banished Duke*
JAQUES |
LE BEAU, *a courtier attending upon Frederick*
CHARLES, *wrestler to Frederick*
OLIVER |
JAQUES | *sons of Sir Rowland de Boys*
ORLANDO |
ADAM | *servants to Oliver*
DENNIS |
TOUCHSTONE, *a clown*
SIR OLIVER MARTEXT, *a vicar*
CORIN | *shepherds*
SILVIUS |
WILLIAM, *a country fellow, in love with Audrey*

THREE LORDS, *attending on the banished Duke*
TWO LORDS, *attending on Frederick*
TWO PAGES, *attending on the banished Duke*
HYMEN

A FORESTER
ROSALIND, *daughter to the banished Duke*
CELIA, *daughter to Frederick*
PHEBE, *a shepherdess*
AUDREY, *a country wench*

NON-SPEAKING: *Lords, Foresters, and Attendants*

SCENE: *Oliver's house, Duke Frederick's court, and the Forest of Arden*

ACT I

SCENE I. *Orchard of Oliver's house*

Enter ORLANDO and ADAM.

Orl. As I remember, Adam, it was upon this fashion; bequeathed me by will but poor a thousand crowns, and, as thou sayest, charged my brother, on his blessing, to breed me well: and there begins my sadness. My brother Jaques he keeps at school, and report speaks goldenly of his profit: for my part, he keeps me rustically at home, or, to speak more properly, stays me here at home unkept; for call you that keeping for a gentleman of my birth, that differs not from the stalling of an ox? His horses are bred better; for, besides that they are fair with their feeding, they are taught their manage, and to that end riders dearly hired: but I, his brother, gain nothing under him but growth; for the which his animals on his dunghills are as much bound to him as I. Besides this nothing that he so plentifully gives me, the something that nature gave me his countenance seems to take from me: he lets me feed with his hinds, bars me the place of a brother, and, as much as in him lies, mines my gentility with my education. This is it, Adam, that grieves me; and the spirit of my father, which I think is within me, begins to mutiny against this servitude: I will no longer endure it, though yet I know no wise remedy how to avoid it.

Adam. Yonder comes my master, your brother.

Orl. Go apart, Adam, and thou shalt hear how he will shake me up. 30

Enter OLIVER.

Oli. Now, sir! what make you here?
Orl. Nothing: I am not taught to make any thing.
Oli. What mar you then, sir?
Orl. Marry, sir, I am helping you to mar that which God made, a poor unworthy brother of yours, with idleness.
Oli. Marry, sir, be better employed, and be naught awhile. 39
Orl. Shall I keep your hogs and eat husks with them? What prodigal portion have I spent, that I should come to such penury?
Oli. Know you where you are, sir?
Orl. O, sir, very well: here in your orchard.
Oli. Know you before whom, sir?
Orl. Ay, better than him I am before knows me. I know you are my eldest brother; and, in the gentle condition of blood, you should so know me. The courtesy of nations allows you my better, in that you are the first-born; but the same tradition takes not away my blood, were there twenty brothers betwixt us: I have as much of my father in me as you; albeit, I confess, your coming before me is nearer to his reverence.
Oli. What, boy!
Orl. Come, come, elder brother, you are too young in this.
Oli. Wilt thou lay hands on me, villain?
Orl. I am no villain; I am the youngest son

of Sir Rowland de Boys; he was my father, and
he is thrice a villain that says such a father begot
villains. Wert thou not my brother, I would not
take this hand from thy throat till this other had
pulled out thy tongue for saying so: thou hast
railed on thyself.

Adam. Sweet masters, be patient: for your
father's remembrance, be at accord.

Oli. Let me go, I say.

Orl. I will not, till I please: you shall hear me.
My father charged you in his will to give me
good education: you have trained me like a
peasant, obscuring and hiding from me all gentleman-like qualities. The spirit of my father
grows strong in me, and I will no longer endure
it: therefore allow me such exercises as may become a gentleman, or give me the poor allottery
my father left me by testament; with that I will
go buy my fortunes.

Oli. And what wilt thou do? beg, when that is
spent? Well, sir, get you in: I will not long
be troubled with you; you shall have some part
of your will: I pray you, leave me.

Orl. I will no further offend you than becomes
me for my good.

Oli. Get you with him, you old dog.

Adam. Is "old dog" my reward? Most true,
I have lost my teeth in your service. God be
with my old master! he would not have spoke
such a word. [*Exeunt* ORLANDO *and* ADAM.

Oli. Is it even so? begin you to grow upon
me? I will physic your rankness, and yet give no
thousand crowns neither. Holla, Dennis!

Enter DENNIS.

Den. Calls your worship?

Oli. Was not Charles, the Duke's wrestler,
here to speak with me?

Den. So please you, he is here at the door and
importunes access to you.

Oli. Call him in. [*Exit* DENNIS.] 'Twill be a
good way; and to-morrow the wrestling is.

Enter CHARLES.

Cha. Good morrow to your worship. *100*

Oli Good Monsieur Charles, what's the new
news at the new court?

Cha. There's no news at the court, sir, but
the old news: that is, the old Duke is banished
by his younger brother the new Duke; and three
or four loving lords have put themselves into
voluntary exile with him, whose lands and revenues enrich the new Duke; therefore he gives
them good leave to wander.

Oli. Can you tell if Rosalind, the Duke's
daughter, be banished with her father? *111*

Cha. O, no; for the Duke's daughter, her
cousin, so loves her, being ever from their cradles
bred together, that she would have followed her
exile, or have died to stay behind her. She is at
the court, and no less beloved of her uncle than
his own daughter; and never two ladies loved as
they do.

Oli. Where will the old Duke live?

Cha. They say he is already in the forest of
Arden, and a many merry men with him; and
there they live like the old Robin Hood of England: they say many young gentlemen flock to
him every day, and fleet the time carelessly as
they did in the golden world.

Oli. What, you wrestle to-morrow before the
new Duke?

Cha. Marry, do I, sir; and I came to acquaint
you with a matter. I am given, sir, secretly to
understand that your younger brother Orlando
hath a disposition to come in disguised against
me to try a fall. To-morrow, sir, I wrestle
for my credit; and he that escapes me without
some broken limb shall acquit him well. Your
brother is but young and tender; and, for your
love, I would be loath to foil him, as I must, for
my own honour, if he come in: therefore, out of
my love to you, I came hither to acquaint you
withal, that either you might stay him from his
intendment or brook such disgrace well as he
shall run into, in that it is a thing of his own
search and altogether against my will.

Oli. Charles, I thank thee for thy love to me,
which thou shalt find I will most kindly requite.
I had myself notice of my brother's purpose
herein and have by underhand means laboured
to dissuade him from it, but he is resolute. I'll
tell thee, Charles: it is the stubbornest young
fellow of France, full of ambition, an envious
emulator of every man's good parts, a secret and
villainous contriver against me his natural
brother; therefore use thy discretion; I had as lief
thou didst break his neck as his finger. And thou
wert best look to't; for if thou dost him any
slight disgrace or if he do not mightily grace
himself on thee, he will practise against thee by
poison, entrap thee by some treacherous device,
and never leave thee till he hath ta'en thy life by
some indirect means or other; for, I assure thee,
and almost with tears I speak it, there is not one
so young and so villainous this day living. I
speak but brotherly of him; but should I anatomize him to thee as he is, I must blush and
weep, and thou must look pale and wonder.

Cha. I am heartily glad I came hither to you.
If he come to-morrow, I'll give him his payment:
if ever he go alone again, I'll never wrestle for

prize more: and so God keep your worship!

Oli. Farewell, good Charles. [*Exit* CHARLES.] Now will I stir this gamester: I hope I shall see an end of him; for my soul, yet I know not why, hates nothing more than he. Yet he's gentle, never schooled, and yet learned, full of noble device, of all sorts enchantingly beloved, and indeed so much in the heart of the world, and especially of my own people, who best know him, that I am altogether misprised: but it shall not be so long; this wrestler shall clear all: nothing remains but that I kindle the boy thither; which now I'll go about.   [*Exit.*   *180*

SCENE II. *Lawn before the Duke's palace*

Enter CELIA *and* ROSALIND.

Cel. I pray thee, Rosalind, sweet my coz, be merry.

Ros. Dear Celia, I show more mirth than I am mistress of; and would you yet I were merrier? Unless you could teach me to forget a banished father, you must not learn me how to remember any extraordinary pleasure.

Cel. Herein I see thou lovest me not with the full weight that I love thee. If my uncle, thy banished father, had banished thy uncle, the Duke my father, so thou hadst been still with me, I could have taught my love to take thy father for mine: so wouldst thou, if the truth of thy love to me were so righteously tempered as mine is to thee.

Ros. Well, I will forget the condition of my estate, to rejoice in yours.

Cel. You know my father hath no child but I, nor none is like to have: and, truly, when he dies, thou shalt be his heir, for what he hath taken away from thy father perforce, I will render thee again in affection; by mine honour, I will; and when I break that oath, let me turn monster: therefore, my sweet Rose, my dear Rose, be merry.

Ros. From henceforth I will, coz, and devise sports. Let me see; what think you of falling in love?

Cel. Marry, I prithee, do, to make sport withal: but love no man in good earnest; nor no further in sport neither than with safety of a pure blush thou mayst in honour come off again.

Ros. What shall be our sport, then?

Cel. Let us sit and mock the good housewife Fortune from her wheel, that her gifts may henceforth be bestowed equally.

Ros. I would we could do so, for her benefits are mightily misplaced, and the bountiful blind woman doth most mistake in her gifts to women.

Cel. 'Tis true; for those that she makes fair she scarce makes honest, and those that she makes honest she makes very ill-favouredly.

Ros. Nay, now thou goest from Fortune's office to Nature's: Fortune reigns in gifts of the world, not in the lineaments of Nature.

Enter TOUCHSTONE.

Cel. No? when Nature hath made a fair creature, may she not by Fortune fall into the fire? Though Nature hath given us wit to flout at Fortune, hath not Fortune sent in this fool to cut off the argument?   *50*

Ros. Indeed, there is Fortune too hard for Nature, when Fortune makes Nature's natural the cutter-off of Nature's wit.

Cel. Peradventure this is not Fortune's work neither, but Nature's; who perceiveth our natural wits too dull to reason of such goddesses and hath sent this natural for our whetstone; for always the dulness of the fool is the whetstone of the wits. How now, wit! whither wander you?

Touch. Mistress, you must come away to your father.   *61*

Cel. Were you made the messenger?

Touch. No, by mine honour, but I was bid to come for you.

Ros. Where learned you that oath, fool?

Touch. Of a certain knight that swore by his honour they were good pancakes and swore by his honour the mustard was naught: now I'll stand to it, the pancakes were naught and the mustard was good, and yet was not the knight forsworn.   *71*

Cel. How prove you that, in the great heap of your knowledge?

Ros. Ay, marry, now unmuzzle your wisdom.

Touch. Stand you both forth now: stroke your chins, and swear by your beards that I am a knave.

Cel. By our beards, if we had them, thou art. *79*

Touch. By my knavery, if I had it, then I were; but if you swear by that that is not, you are not forsworn: no more was this knight, swearing by his honour, for he never had any; or if he had, he had sworn it away before ever he saw those pancakes or that mustard.

Cel. Prithee, who is't that thou meanest?

Touch. One that old Frederick, your father, loves.

Cel. My father's love is enough to honour him: enough! speak no more of him; you'll be whipped for taxation one of these days.   *91*

Touch. The more pity, that fools may not speak wisely what wise men do foolishly.

Cel. By my troth, thou sayest true; for since the little wit that fools have was silenced, the little foolery that wise men have makes a great show. Here comes Monsieur Le Beau.

Ros. With his mouth full of news.

Cel. Which he will put on us, as pigeons feed their young.   *100*

Ros. Then shall we be news-crammed.

Cel. All the better; we shall be the more marketable.

Enter LE BEAU.

Bon jour, Monsieur Le Beau: what's the news?

Le Beau. Fair princess, you have lost much good sport.

Cel. Sport! of what colour?

Le Beau. What colour, madam! how shall I answer you?

Ros. As wit and fortune will.   *110*

Touch. Or as the Destinies decree.

Cel. Well said: that was laid on with a trowel.

Touch. Nay, if I keep not my rank—

Ros. Thou losest thy old smell.

Le Beau. You amaze me, ladies: I would have told you of good wrestling, which you have lost the sight of.

Ros. Yet tell us the manner of the wrestling.

Le Beau. I will tell you the beginning; and, if it please your ladyships, you may see the end; for the best is yet to do; and here, where you are, they are coming to perform it.

Cel. Well, the beginning, that is dead and buried.

Le Beau. There comes an old man and his three sons—

Cel. I could match this beginning with an old tale.

Le Beau. Three proper young men, of excellent growth and presence.   *130*

Ros. With bills on their necks, "Be it known unto all men by these presents."

Le Beau. The eldest of the three wrestled with Charles, the Duke's wrestler; which Charles in a moment threw him and broke three of his ribs, that there is little hope of life in him: so he served the second, and so the third. Yonder they lie; the poor old man, their father, making such pitiful dole over them that all the beholders take his part with weeping.   *140*

Ros. Alas!

Touch. But what is the sport, monsieur, that the ladies have lost?

Le Beau. Why, this that I speak of.

Touch. Thus men may grow wiser every day: it is the first time that ever I heard breaking of ribs was sport for ladies.

Cel. Or I, I promise thee.

Ros. But is there any else longs to see this broken music in his sides? is there yet another dotes upon rib-breaking? Shall we see this wrestling, cousin?

Le Beau. You must, if you stay here; for here is the place appointed for the wrestling, and they are ready to perform it.

Cel. Yonder, sure, they are coming: let us now stay and see it.

Flourish. Enter DUKE FREDERICK, *Lords,* ORLANDO, CHARLES, *and Attendants.*

Duke F. Come on: since the youth will not be entreated, his own peril on his forwardness.

Ros. Is yonder the man?   *160*

Le Beau. Even he, madam.

Cel. Alas, he is too young! yet he looks successfully.

Duke F. How now, daughter and cousin! are you crept hither to see the wrestling?

Ros. Ay, my liege, so please you give us leave.

Duke F. You will take little delight in it, I can tell you; there is such odds in the man. In pity of the challenger's youth I would fain dissuade him, but he will not be entreated. Speak to him, ladies; see if you can move him.

Cel. Call him hither, good Monsieur Le Beau.

Duke F. Do so: I'll not be by.

Le Beau. Monsieur the challenger, the princesses call for you.

Orl. I attend them with all respect and duty.

Ros. Young man, have you challenged Charles the wrestler?   *179*

Orl. No, fair princess; he is the general challenger: I come but in, as others do, to try with him the strength of my youth.

Cel. Young gentleman, your spirits are too bold for your years. You have seen cruel proof of this man's strength: if you saw yourself with your eyes or knew yourself with your judgement, the fear of your adventure would counsel you to a more equal enterprise. We pray you, for your own sake, to embrace your own safety and give over this attempt.   *190*

Ros. Do, young sir; your reputation shall not therefore be misprised: we will make it our suit to the Duke that the wrestling might not go forward.

Orl. I beseech you, punish me not with your hard thoughts; wherein I confess me much guilty, to deny so fair and excellent ladies any thing. But let your fair eyes and gentle wishes go with me to my trial: wherein if I be foiled, there is but one shamed that was never gracious; if killed, but one dead that is willing to be so: I shall do my friends no wrong, for I have none to lament me, the world no injury, for in it I have nothing;

only in the world I fill up a place, which may be
better supplied when I have made it empty.

Ros. The little strength that I have, I would
it were with you.

Cel. And mine, to eke out hers.

Ros. Fare you well: pray heaven I be deceived in you!   *210*

Cel. Your heart's desires be with you!

Cha. Come, where is this young gallant that is
so desirous to lie with his mother earth?

Orl. Ready, sir; but his will hath in it a more
modest working.

Duke F. You shall try but one fall.

Cha. No, I warrant your Grace, you shall not
entreat him to a second, that have so mightily
persuaded him from a first.   *219*

Orl. An you mean to mock me after, you should
not have mocked me before: but come your ways.

Ros. Now Hercules be thy speed, young man!

Cel. I would I were invisible, to catch the
strong fellow by the leg.

     They wrestle.

Ros. O excellent young man!

Cel. If I had a thunderbolt in mine eye, I can
tell who should down.

Shout. CHARLES *is thrown.*

Duke F. No more, no more.

Orl. Yes, I beseech your Grace: I am not yet
well breathed.   *230*

Duke F. How dost thou, Charles?

Le Beau. He cannot speak, my lord.

Duke F. Bear him away. What is thy name,
young man?

Orl. Orlando, my liege; the youngest son of
Sir Rowland de Boys.

Duke F. I would thou hadst been son to some
man else:
The world esteem'd thy father honourable,
But I did find him still mine enemy:
Thou shouldst have better pleased me with this
deed
Hadst thou descended from another house.   *240*
But fare thee well; thou art a gallant youth:
I would thou hadst told me of another father.

     [*Exeunt* DUKE FREDERICK, *train, and* LE BEAU.

Cel. Were I my father, coz, would I do this?

Orl. I am more proud to be Sir Rowland's son,
His youngest son; and would not change that
calling,
To be adopted heir to Frederick.

Ros. My father loved Sir Rowland as his soul,
And all the world was of my father's mind:
Had I before known this young man his son,
I should have given him tears unto entreaties, *250*
Ere he should thus have ventured.

Cel.   Gentle cousin,

Let us go thank him and encourage him:
My father's rough and envious disposition
Sticks me at heart. Sir, you have well deserved:
If you do keep your promises in love
But justly, as you have exceeded all promise,
Your mistress shall be happy.

Ros.   Gentleman,
     Giving him a chain from her neck.
Wear this for me, one out of suits with fortune,
That could give more, but that her hand lacks
     means.
Shall we go, coz?

Cel.   Ay. Fare you well, fair gentleman.

Orl. Can I not say, I thank you? My better
     parts   *261*
Are all thrown down, and that which here stands
     up
Is but a quintain, a mere lifeless block.

Ros. He calls us back: my pride fell with my
     fortunes;
I'll ask him what he would. Did you call, sir?
Sir, you have wrestled well and overthrown
More than your enemies.

Cel.   Will you go, coz?

Ros. Have with you. Fare you well.

     [*Exeunt* ROSALIND *and* CELIA.

Orl. What passion hangs these weights upon
     my tongue?
I cannot speak to her, yet she urged conference.
O poor Orlando, thou art overthrown!   *271*
Or Charles or something weaker masters thee.

         Re-enter LE BEAU.

Le Beau. Good sir, I do in friendship counsel you
To leave this place. Albeit you have deserved
High commendation, true applause, and love,
Yet such is now the Duke's condition
That he misconstrues all that you have done.
The Duke is humorous: what he is, indeed,
More suits you to conceive than I to speak of.

Orl. I thank you, sir: and, pray you, tell me
     this;   *280*
Which of the two was daughter of the Duke
That here was at the wrestling?

Le Beau. Neither his daughter, if we judge by
     manners;
But yet indeed the lesser is his daughter:
The other is daughter to the banish'd Duke,
And here detain'd by her usurping uncle
To keep his daughter company; whose loves
Are dearer than the natural bond of sisters.
But I can tell you that of late this Duke
Hath ta'en displeasure 'gainst his gentle niece,
Grounded upon no other argument   *291*
But that the people praise her for her virtues
And pity her for her good father's sake;

And, on my life, his malice 'gainst the lady
Will suddenly break forth. Sir, fare you well:
Hereafter, in a better world than this,
I shall desire more love and knowledge of you.

Orl. I rest much bounden to you: fare you
well.   [*Exit* LE BEAU.
Thus must I from the smoke into the smother;
From tyrant Duke unto a tyrant brother: *300*
But heavenly Rosalind!   [*Exit.*

SCENE III. *A room in the palace*

Enter CELIA *and* ROSALIND.

Cel. Why, cousin! why, Rosalind! Cupid have
mercy! not a word?

Ros. Not one to throw at a dog.

Cel. No, thy words are too precious to be
cast away upon curs; throw some of them at me;
come, lame me with reasons.

Ros. Then there were two cousins laid up;
when the one should be lamed with reasons and
the other mad without any.

Cel. But is all this for your father?   *10*

Ros. No, some of it is for my child's father.
O, how full of briers is this working-day
world!

Cel. They are but burs, cousin, thrown upon
thee in holiday foolery: if we walk not in the
trodden paths, our very petticoats will catch
them.

Ros. I could shake them off my coat: these
burs are in my heart.

Cel. Hem them away.

Ros. I would try, if I could cry "hem" and
have him.   *20*

Cel. Come, come, wrestle with thy affections.

Ros. O, they take the part of a better wrestler
than myself!

Cel. O, a good wish upon you! you will try
in time, in despite of a fall. But, turning these
jests out of service, let us talk in good earnest: is
it possible, on such a sudden, you should fall into
so strong a liking with old Sir Rowland's youngest son?

Ros. The Duke my father loved his father
dearly.   *31*

Cel. Doth it therefore ensue that you should
love his son dearly? By this kind of chase, I
should hate him, for my father hated his father
dearly; yet I hate not Orlando.

Ros. No, faith, hate him not, for my sake.

Cel. Why should I not? doth he not deserve
well?

Ros. Let me love him for that, and do you love
him because I do. Look, here comes the Duke. *41*

Cel. With his eyes full of anger.

Enter DUKE FREDERICK, *with Lords.*

Duke F. Mistress, dispatch you with your
safest haste
And get you from our court.

Ros.   Me, uncle?

Duke F.   You, cousin:
Within these ten days if that thou be'st found
So near our public court as twenty miles,
Thou diest for it.

Ros.   I do beseech your Grace,
Let me the knowledge of my fault bear with me:
If with myself I hold intelligence
Or have acquaintance with mine own desires,   *50*
If that I do not dream or be not frantic—
As I do trust I am not—then, dear uncle,
Never so much as in a thought unborn
Did I offend your Highness.

Duke F.   Thus do all traitors:
If their purgation did consist in words,
They are as innocent as grace itself:
Let it suffice thee that I trust thee not.

Ros. Yet your mistrust cannot make me a
traitor:
Tell me whereon the likelihood depends.

Duke F. Thou art thy father's daughter; there's
enough.   *60*

Ros. So was I when your Highness took his
dukedom;
So was I when your Highness banish'd him:
Treason is not inherited, my lord;
Or, if we did derive it from our friends,
What's that to me? my father was no traitor:
Then, good my liege, mistake me not so much
To think my poverty is treacherous.

Cel. Dear sovereign, hear me speak.

Duke F. Ay, Celia we stay'd her for your sake,
Else had she with her father ranged along.   *70*

Cel. I did not then entreat to have her stay;
It was your pleasure and your own remorse:
I was too young that time to value her;
But now I know her: if she be a traitor,
Why so am I; we still have slept together,
Rose at an instant, learn'd, play'd, eat together,
And wheresoe'er we went, like Juno's swans,
Still we went coupled and inseparable.

Duke F. She is too subtle for thee; and her
smoothness,
Her very silence, and her patience   *80*
Speak to the people, and they pity her.
Thou art a fool: she robs thee of thy name;
And thou wilt show more bright and seem more
virtuous
When she is gone. Then open not thy lips:
Firm and irrevocable is my doom
Which I have pass'd upon her; she is banish'd.

Cel. Pronounce that sentence then on me, my
   liege:
I cannot live out of her company.
Duke F. You are a fool. You, niece, provide
   yourself:
If you outstay the time, upon mine honour,   *90*
And in the greatness of my word, you die.
        [*Exeunt* DUKE FREDERICK *and Lords.*
Cel. O my poor Rosalind, whither wilt thou go?
Wilt thou change fathers? I will give thee mine.
I charge thee, be not thou more grieved than I am.
Ros. I have more cause.
Cel.   Thou hast not, cousin;
Prithee, be cheerful: know'st thou not, the Duke
Hath banish'd me, his daughter?
Ros.   That he hath not.
Cel. No, hath not? Rosalind lacks then the love
Which teacheth thee that thou and I am one:
Shall we be sunder'd? shall we part, sweet girl?
No: let my father seek another heir.   *101*
Therefore devise with me how we may fly,
Whither to go, and what to bear with us;
And do not seek to take your change upon you,
To bear your griefs yourself and leave me out;
For, by this heaven, now at our sorrows pale,
Say what thou canst, I'll go along with thee.
Ros. Why, whither shall we go?
Cel. To seek my uncle in the forest of Arden.
Ros. Alas, what danger will it be to us,   *110*
Maids as we are, to travel forth so far!
Beauty provoketh thieves sooner than gold.
  Cel. I'll put myself in poor and mean attire
And with a kind of umber smirch my face;
The like do you: so shall we pass along
And never stir assailants.
Ros.   Were it not better,
Because that I am more than common tall,
That I did suit me all points like a man?
A gallant curtle-axe upon my thigh,   *119*
A boar-spear in my hand; and—in my heart
Lie there what hidden woman's fear there will—
We'll have a swashing and a martial outside,
As many other mannish cowards have
That do outface it with their semblances.
  Cel. What shall I call thee when thou art a man?
  Ros. I'll have no worse a name than Jove's own
   page;
And therefore look you call me Ganymede.
But what will you be call'd?
  Cel. Something that hath a reference to my state;
No longer Celia, but Aliena.   *130*
  Ros. But, cousin, what if we assay'd to steal
The clownish fool out of your father's court?
Would he not be a comfort to our travel?
  Cel. He'll go along o'er the wide world with me;
Leave me alone to woo him. Let's away,

And get our jewels and our wealth together,
Devise the fittest time and safest way
To hide us from pursuit that will be made
After my flight. Now go we in content
To liberty and not to banishment. [*Exeunt.*   *140*

ACT II

SCENE I. *The forest of Arden*

Enter DUKE SENIOR, AMIENS, *and two or three*
LORDS, *like foresters.*

  Duke S. Now, my co-mates and brothers in
   exile,
Hath not old custom made this life more sweet
Than that of painted pomp? Are not these woods
More free from peril than the envious court?
Here feel we but the penalty of Adam,
The seasons' difference, as the icy fang
And churlish chiding of the winter's wind,
Which, when it bites and blows upon my body
Even till I shrink with cold, I smile and say
"This is no flattery: these are counsellors   *10*
That feelingly persuade me what I am."
Sweet are the uses of adversity,
Which, like the toad, ugly and venomous,
Wears yet a precious jewel in his head;
And this our life exempt from public haunt
Finds tongues in trees, books in the running
   brooks,
Sermons in stones, and good in everything.
I would not change it.
  Ami.   Happy is your Grace,
That can translate the stubbornness of fortune
Into so quiet and so sweet a style.   *20*
  Duke S. Come, shall we go and kill us venison?
And yet it irks me the poor dappled fools,
Being native burghers of this desert city,
Should in their own confines with forked heads
Have their round haunches gored.
  1st Lord.   Indeed, my lord,
The melancholy Jaques grieves at that,
And, in that kind, swears you do more usurp
Than doth your brother that hath banish'd you.
To-day my Lord of Amiens and myself
Did steal behind him as he lay along   *30*
Under an oak whose antique root peeps out
Upon the brook that brawls along this wood:
To the which place a poor sequester'd stag,
That from the hunter's aim had ta'en a hurt,
Did come to languish, and indeed, my lord,
The wretched animal heaved forth such groans
That their discharge did stretch his leathern coat
Almost to bursting, and the big round tears
Coursed one another down his innocent nose
Is piteous chase; and thus the hairy fool,   *40*
Much marked of the melancholy Jaques,

Stood on the extremest verge of the swift brook,
Augmenting it with tears.
   Duke S.   But what said Jaques?
Did he not moralize this spectacle?
   1st Lord. O, yes, into a thousand similes.
First, for his weeping into the needless stream;
"Poor deer," quoth he "thou makest a testament
As worldlings do, giving thy sum of more
To that which had too much": then, being there
   alone,
Left and abandon'd of his velvet friends,   50
"'Tis right," quoth he; "thus misery doth part
The flux of company": anon a careless herd,
Full of the pasture, jumps along by him
And never stays to greet him; "Ay," quoth
   Jaques,
"Sweep on, you fat and greasy citizens;
'Tis just the fashion: wherefore do you look
Upon that poor and broken bankrupt there?"
Thus most invectively he pierceth through
The body of the country, city, court,
Yea, and of this our life, swearing that we   60
Are mere usurpers, tyrants, and what's worse,
To fright the animals and to kill them up
In their assign'd and native dwelling-place.
   Duke S. And did you leave him in this con-
templation?
   2nd Lord. We did, my lord, weeping and com-
menting
Upon the sobbing deer.
   Duke S.   Show me the place:
I love to cope him in these sullen fits,
For then he's full of matter.
   1st Lord. I'll bring you to him straight.
                        [Exeunt.

Scene ii. *A room in the palace*

Enter DUKE FREDERICK, *with* LORDS.

   Duke F. Can it be possible that no man saw
them?
It cannot be: some villains of my court
Are of consent and sufferance in this.
   1st Lord. I cannot hear of any that did see her.
The ladies, her attendants of her chamber,
Saw her a-bed, and in the morning early
They found the bed untreasured of their mistress.
   2nd Lord. My lord, the roynish clown, at
whom so oft
Your Grace was wont to laugh, is also missing.
Hisperia, the princess' gentlewoman,   10
Confesses that she secretly o'erheard
Your daughter and her cousin much commend
The parts and graces of the wrestler
That did but lately foil the sinewy Charles;
And she believes, wherever they are gone,
That youth is surely in their company.

   Duke F. Send to his brother; fetch that gallant
hither;
If he be absent, bring his brother to me;
I'll make him find him: do this suddenly,
And let not search and inquisition quail   20
To bring again these foolish runaways.   *[Exeunt.*

Scene iii. *Before Oliver's house*

Enter ORLANDO *and* ADAM, *meeting.*

   Orl. Who's there?
   Adam. What, my young master? O my gentle
master!
O my sweet master! O you memory
Of old Sir Rowland! why, what make you here?
Why are you virtuous? why do people love you?
And wherefore are you gentle, strong and valiant?
Why would you be so fond to overcome
The bonny priser of the humorous Duke?
Your praise is come too swiftly home before you.
Know you not, master, to some kind of men   10
Their graces serve them but as enemies?
No more do yours: your virtues, gentle master,
Are sanctified and holy traitors to you.
O, what a world is this, when what is comely
Envenoms him that bears it!
   Orl. Why, what's the matter?
   Adam.   O unhappy youth!
Come not within these doors; within this roof
The enemy of all your graces lives:
Your brother—no, no brother; yet the son—
Yet not the son, I will not call him son   20
Of him I was about to call his father—
Hath heard your praises, and this night he means
To burn the lodging where you use to lie
And you within it: if he fail of that,
He will have other means to cut you off.
I overheard him and his practices.
This is no place; this house is but a butchery:
Abhor it, fear it, do not enter it.
   Orl. Why, whither, Adam, wouldst thou have
me go?
   Adam. No matter whither, so you come not
here.   30
   Orl. What, wouldst thou have me go and beg
my food?
Or with a base and boisterous sword enforce
A thievish living on the common road?
This I must do, or know not what to do:
Yet this I will not do, do how I can;
I rather will subject me to the malice
Of a diverted blood and bloody brother.
   Adam. But do not so. I have five hundred
crowns,
The thrifty hire I saved under your father,
Which I did store to be my foster-nurse   40
When service should in my old limbs lie lame

And unregarded age in corners thrown:
Take that, and He that doth the ravens feed,
Yea, providently caters for the sparrow,
Be comfort to my age! Here is the gold;
All this I give you. Let me be your servant:
Though I look old, yet I am strong and lusty;
For in my youth I never did apply
Hot and rebellious liquors in my blood,
Nor did not with unbashful forehead woo   50
The means of weakness and debility;
Therefore my age is as a lusty winter,
Frosty, but kindly: let me go with you;
I'll do the service of a younger man
In all your business and necessities.

Orl. O good old man, how well in thee appears
The constant service of the antique world,
When service sweat for duty, not for meed!
Thou art not for the fashion of these times,
Where none will sweat but for promotion,   60
And having that, do choke their service up
Even with the having: it is not so with thee.
But, poor old man, thou prunest a rotten tree,
That cannot so much as a blossom yield
In lieu of all thy pains and husbandry.
But come thy ways; we'll go along together,
And ere we have thy youthful wages spent,
We'll light upon some settled low content.

Adam. Master, go on, and I will follow thee
To the last gasp, with truth and loyalty.   70
From seventeen years till now almost fourscore
Here lived I, but now live here no more.
At seventeen years many their fortunes seek;
But at fourscore it is too late a week:
Yet fortune cannot recompense me better
Than to die well and not my master's debtor.
                                              [*Exeunt.*

Scene iv. *The Forest of Arden*

Enter ROSALIND *for Ganymede,* CELIA *for Aliena, and* TOUCHSTONE.

Ros. O Jupiter, how weary are my spirits!

Touch. I care not for my spirits, if my legs were not weary.

Ros. I could find in my heart to disgrace my man's apparel and to cry like a woman; but I must comfort the weaker vessel, as doublet and hose ought to show itself courageous to petticoat: therefore courage, good Aliena!

Cel. I pray you, bear with me; I cannot go no further.   10

Touch. For my part, I had rather bear with you than bear you; yet I should bear no cross if I did bear you, for I think you have no money in your purse.

Ros. Well, this is the forest of Arden.

Touch. Ay, now am I in Arden; the more fool

I; when I was at home, I was in a better place: but travellers must be content.

Ros. Ay, be so, good Touchstone.

Enter CORIN *and* SILVIUS.

Look you, who comes here; a young man and an old in solemn talk.   21

Cor. That is the way to make her scorn you still.

Sil. O Corin, that thou knew'st how I do love her!

Cor. I partly guess; for I have loved ere now.

Sil. No, Corin, being old, thou canst not guess,
Though in thy youth thou wast as true a lover
As ever sigh'd upon a midnight pillow:
But if thy love were ever like to mine—
As sure I think did never man love so—
How many actions most ridiculous   30
Hast thou been drawn to by thy fantasy?

Cor. Into a thousand that I have forgotten.

Sil. O, thou didst then ne'er love so heartily!
If thou remember'st not the slightest folly
That ever love did make thee run into,
Thou hast not loved:
Or if thou hast not sat as I do now,
Wearying thy hearer in thy mistress' praise,
Thou hast not loved:
Or if thou hast not broke from company   40
Abruptly, as my passion now makes me,
Thou hast not loved.
O Phebe, Phebe, Phebe!   [*Exit.*

Ros. Alas, poor shepherd! searching of thy wound,
I have by hard adventure found mine own.

Touch. And I mine. I remember, when I was in love I broke my sword upon a stone and bid him take that for coming a-night to Jane Smile; and I remember the kissing of her batlet and the cow's dugs that her pretty chopt hands had milked; and I remember the wooing of a peascod instead of her, from whom I took two cods and, giving her them again, said with weeping tears, "Wear these for my sake." We that are true lovers run into strange capers; but as all is mortal in nature, so is all nature in love mortal in folly.

Ros. Thou speakest wiser than thou art ware of.

Touch. Nay, I shall ne'er be ware of mine own wit till I break my shins against it.   60

Ros. Jove, Jove! this shepherd's passion
Is much upon my fashion.

Touch. And mine; but it grows something stale with me.

Cel. I pray you, one of you question yond man
If he for gold will give us any food:
I faint almost to death.

Touch.   Holla, you clown!

Ros. **Peace,** fool: he's not thy kinsman.

Cor.   Who calls?

Touch. Your betters, sir.

Cor.   Else are they very wretched.

Ros. Peace, I say. Good even to you, friend.

Cor. And to you, gentle sir, and to you all.

Ros. I prithee, shepherd, if that love or gold
Can in this desert place buy entertainment,
Bring us where we may rest ourselves and feed:
Here's a young maid with travel much oppress'd
And faints for succour.

Cor.   Fair sir, I pity her
And wish, for her sake more than for mine own,
My fortunes were more able to relieve her;
But I am shepherd to another man
And do not shear the fleeces that I graze:
My master is of churlish disposition   80
And little recks to find the way to heaven
By doing deeds of hospitality:
Besides, his cote, his flocks, and bounds of feed
Are now on sale, and at our sheepcote now,
By reason of his absence, there is nothing
That you will feed on; but what is, come see,
And in my voice most welcome shall you be.

Ros. What is he that shall buy his flock and
     pasture?

Cor. That young swain that you saw here but
     erewhile,
That little cares for buying any thing.   90

Ros. I pray thee, if it stand with honesty,
Buy thou the cottage, pasture, and the flock,
And thou shalt have to pay for it of us.

Cel. And we will mend thy wages. I like this
     place,
And willingly could waste my time in it.

Cor. Assuredly the thing is to be sold:
Go with me: if you like upon report
The soil, the profit, and this kind of life,
I will your very faithful feeder be
And buy it with your gold right suddenly.   100
                              [*Exeunt.*

Scene v. *The forest*

Enter AMIENS, JAQUES, *and others.*
SONG

Ami.   Under the greenwood tree
          Who loves to lie with me,
          And turn his merry note
          Unto the sweet bird's throat,
     Come hither, come hither, come hither:
          Here shall he see
          No enemy
     But winter and rough weather.

Jaq. More, more, I prithee, more.

Ami. It will make you melancholy, Monsieur
Jaques.   11

Jaq. I thank it. More, I prithee, more. I can
suck melancholy out of a song, as a weasel sucks
eggs. More, I prithee, more.

Ami. My voice is ragged: I know I cannot
please you.

Jaq. I do not desire you to please me; I do
desire you to sing. Come, more; another stanzo:
call you 'em stanzos?

Ami. What you will, Monsieur Jaques.   20

Jaq. Nay, I care not for their names; they owe
me nothing. Will you sing?

Ami. More at your request than to please
myself.

Jaq. Well then, if ever I thank any man, I'll
thank you; but that they call compliment is like
the encounter of two dog-apes, and when a man
thanks me heartily, methinks I have given him a
penny and he renders me the beggarly thanks.
Come, sing; and you that will not, hold your
tongues.

Ami. Well, I'll end the song. Sirs, cover the
while; the Duke will drink under this tree. He
hath been all this day to look you.

Jaq. And I have been all this day to avoid him.
He is too disputable for my company; I think of
as many matters as he, but I give heaven thanks
and make no boast of them. Come, warble, come.

SONG

[*All together here.*]
          Who doth ambition shun
          And loves to live i' the sun,   41
          Seeking the food he eats
          And pleased with what he gets,
     Come hither, come hither, come hither:
          Here shall he see
          No enemy
     But winter and rough weather.

Jaq. I'll give you a verse to this note that I made
yesterday in despite of my invention.

Ami. And I'll sing it.   50

Jaq. Thus it goes:

          If it do come to pass
          That any man turn ass,
          Leaving his wealth and ease,
          A stubborn will to please,
     Ducdame, ducdame, ducdame:
          Here shall he see
          Gross fools as he,
          An if he will come to me.

Ami. What's that "ducdame"?   60

Jaq. 'Tis a Greek invocation, to call fools into a circle. I'll go sleep, if I can; If I cannot, I'll rail against all the first-born of Egypt.

Ami. And I'll go seek the Duke: his banquet is prepared.   *[Exeunt Severally.*

SCENE VI. *The forest*

Enter ORLANDO AND ADAM.

Adam. Dear master, I can go no further: O, I die for food! Here lie I down, and measure out my grave. Farewell, kind master.

Orl. Why, how now, Adam! no greater heart in thee? Live a little; comfort a little; cheer thyself a little. If this uncouth forest yield any thing savage, I will either be food for it or bring it for food to thee. Thy conceit is nearer death than thy powers. For my sake be comfortable; hold death awhile at the arms' end: I will here be with thee presently; and if I bring thee not something to eat, I will give thee leave to die: but if thou diest before I come, thou art a mocker of my labour. Well said! thou lookest cheerly, and I'll be with thee quickly. Yet thou liest in the bleak air: come, I will bear thee to some shelter; and thou shalt not die for lack of a dinner, if there live any thing in this desert. Cheerly, good Adam!   *[Exeunt.*

SCENE VII. *The forest*

A table set out. Enter DUKE SENIOR, AMIENS, *and* LORDS *like outlaws.*

Duke S. I think he be transform'd into a beast; For I can no where find him like a man.

1st Lord. My lord, he is but even now gone hence:
Here was he merry, hearing of a song.

Duke S. If he, compact of jars, grow musical, We shall have shortly discord in the spheres. Go, seek him: tell him I would speak with him.

Enter JAQUES.

1st Lord. He saves my labour by his own approach.

Duke S. Why, how now, monsieur! what a life is this,
That your poor friends must woo your company?
What, you look merrily!   *11*

Jaq. A fool, a fool! I met a fool i' the forest,
A motley fool; a miserable world!
As I do live by food, I met a fool;
Who laid him down and bask'd him in the sun,
And rail'd on Lady Fortune in good terms,
In good set terms and yet a motley fool.
"Good morrow, fool," quoth I. "No, sir," quoth he,

"Call me not fool till heaven hath sent me fortune":
And then he drew a dial from his poke,   *20*
And, looking on it with lack-lustre eye,
Says very wisely, "It is ten o'clock:
Thus we may see," quoth he, "how the world wags:
'Tis but an hour ago since it was nine,
And after one hour more 'twill be eleven;
And so, from hour to hour, we ripe and ripe,
And then, from hour to hour, we rot and rot;
And thereby hangs a tale." When I did hear
The motley fool thus moral on the time,
My lungs began to crow like chanticleer,   *30*
That fools should be so deep-contemplative,
And I did laugh sans intermission
An hour by his dial. O noble fool!
A worthy fool! Motley's the only wear.

Duke S. What fool is this?

Jaq. O worthy fool! One that hath been a courtier,
And says, if ladies be but young and fair,
They have the gift to know it: and in his brain,
Which is as dry as the remainder biscuit
After a voyage, he hath strange places cramm'd
With observation, the which he vents   *41*
In mangled forms. O that I were a fool!
I am ambitious for a motley coat.

Duke S. Thou shalt have one.

Jaq.   It is my only suit;
Provided that you weed your better judgments
Of all opinion that grows rank in them
That I am wise. I must have liberty
Withal, as large a charter as the wind,
To blow on whom I please; for so fools have;
And they that are most galled with my folly,   *50*
They most must laugh. And why, sir, must they so?
The "why" is plain as way to parish church:
He that a fool doth very wisely hit
Doth very foolishly, although he smart,
Not to seem senseless of the bob: if not,
The wise man's folly is anatomized
Even by the squandering glances of the fool.
Invest me in my motley; give me leave
To speak my mind, and I will through and through
Cleanse the foul body of the infected world,   *60*
If they will patiently receive my medicine.

Duke S. Fie on thee! I can tell what thou wouldst do.

Jaq. What, for a counter, would I do but good?

Duke S. Most mischievous foul sin, in chiding sin:
For thou thyself hast been a libertine,
As sensual as the brutish sting itself;

And all the embossed sores and headed evils
That thou with license of free foot hast caught,
Wouldst thou disgorge into the general world.
  Jaq. Why, who cries out on pride   70
That can therein tax any private party?
Doth it not flow as hugely as the sea,
Till that the weary very means do ebb?
What woman in the city do I name,
When that I say the city-woman bears
The cost of princes on unworthy shoulders?
Who can come in and say that I mean her,
When such a one as she such is her neighbour?
Or what is he of basest function
That says his bravery is not on my cost,   80
Thinking that I mean him, but therein suits
His folly to the mettle of my speech?
There then; how then? what then? Let me see
    wherein
My tongue hath wrong'd him: if it do him right,
Then he hath wrong'd himself; if he be free,
Why then my taxing like a wild-goose flies,
Unclaim'd of any man. But who comes here?

    Enter ORLANDO, *with his sword drawn.*

  Orl. Forbear, and eat no more.
  Jaq.   Why, I have eat none yet.
  Orl. Nor shalt not, till necessity be served.
  Jaq. Of what kind should this cock come of?
  Duke S. Art thou thus bolden'd, man, by thy
    distress,   91
Or else a rude despiser of good manners,
That in civility thou seem'st so empty?
  Orl. You touch'd my vein at first: the thorny
    point
Of bare distress hath ta'en from me the show
Of smooth civility: yet am I inland bred
And know some nurture. But forbear, I say:
He dies that touches any of this fruit
Till I and my affairs are answered.
  Jaq. An you will not be answered with reason,
I must die.   101
  Duke S. What would you have? Your gentleness
    shall force
More than your force move us to gentleness.
  Orl. I almost die for food; and let me have it.
  Duke S. Sit down and feed, and welcome to our
    table.
  Orl. Speak you so gently? Pardon me, I pray
    you:
I thought that all things had been savage here;
And therefore put I on the countenance
Of stern commandment. But whate'er you are
That in this desert inaccessible,   110
Under the shade of melancholy boughs,
Lose and neglect the creeping hours of time;
If ever you have look'd on better days,

If ever been where bells have knoll'd to church,
If ever sat at any good man's feast,
If ever from your eyelids wiped a tear
And know what 'tis to pity and be pitied,
Let gentleness my strong enforcement be:
In the which hope I blush, and hide my sword.
  Duke S. True is it that we have seen better
    days,   120
And have with holy bell been knoll'd to church
And sat at good men's feasts, and wiped our eyes
Of drops that sacred pity hath engender'd:
And therefore sit you down in gentleness
And take upon command what help we have
That to your wanting may be minister'd.
  Orl. Then but forbear your food a little while,
Whiles, like a doe, I go to find my fawn
And give it food. There is an old poor man,
Who after me hath many a weary step   130
Limp'd in pure love: till he be first sufficed,
Oppress'd with two week evils, age and hunger,
I will not touch a bit.
  Duke S.   Go find him out,
And we will nothing waste till you return.
  Orl. I thank ye; and be blest for your good com-
    fort!   [*Exit.*
  Duke S. Thou seest we are not all alone un-
    happy:
This wide and universal theatre
Presents more woeful pageants than the scene
Wherein we play in.
  Jaq.   All the world's a stage,
And all the men and women merely players: *140*
They have their exits and their entrances;
And one man in his time plays many parts,
His acts being seven ages. At first the infant,
Mewling and puking in the nurse's arms.
And then the whining school-boy, with his satchel
And shining morning face, creeping like snail
Unwillingly to school. And then the lover,
Sighing like furnace, with a woeful ballad
Made to his mistress' eyebrow. Then a soldier,
Full of strange oaths and bearded like the pard,
Jealous in honour, sudden and quick in quarrel,
Seeking the bubble reputation
Even in the cannon's mouth. And then the justice,
In fair round belly with good capon lined,
With eyes severe and beard of formal cut,
Full of wise saws and modern instances;
And so he plays his part. The sixth age shifts
Into the lean and slipper'd pantaloon,
With spectacles on nose and pouch on side, *159*
His youthful hose, well saved, a world too wide
For his shrunk shank; and his big manly voice,
Turning again toward childish treble, pipes
And whistles in his sound. Last scene of all,
That ends this strange eventful history,

Is second childishness and mere oblivion,
Sans teeth, sans eyes, sans taste, sans everything.

Re-enter ORLANDO, *with* ADAM.

Duke S. Welcome. Set down your venerable
burden
And let him feed.
  Orl. I thank you most for him.
  Adam.   So had you need:
I scarce can speak to thank you for myself.   *170*
  Duke S. Welcome; fall to: I will not trouble you
As yet, to question you about your fortunes.
Give us some music; and, good cousin, sing.

                    SONG

Ami. Blow, blow, thou winter wind,
          Thou art not so unkind
              As man's ingratitude;
          Thy tooth is not so keen,
          Because thou art not seen,
              Although thy breath be rude.   *179*
Heigh-ho! sing, heigh-ho! unto the green holly:
Most friendship is feigning, most loving mere
  folly:
          Then, heigh-ho, the holly!
          This life is most jolly.

          Freeze, freeze, thou bitter sky,
          That dost not bite so nigh
              As benefits forgot:
          Though thou the waters warp,
          Thy sting is not so sharp
              As friend remember'd not.
Heigh-ho! sing, &c.   *190*
  Duke S. If that you were the good Sir Row-
    land's son,
As you have whisper'd faithfully you were,
And as mine eye doth his effigies witness
Most truly limn'd and living in your face,
Be truly welcome hither: I am the Duke
That loved your father: the residue of your for-
  tune,
Go to my cave and tell me. Good old man,
Thou art right welcome as thy master is.
Support him by the arm. Give me your hand,
And let me all your fortunes understand. [*Exeunt.*

ACT III

SCENE I. *A room in the palace*

Enter DUKE FREDERICK, LORDS, *and* OLIVER.

Duke F. Not see him since? Sir, sir, that cannot
  be:
But were I not the better part made mercy,
I should not seek an absent argument
Of my revenge, thou present. But look to it:

Find out thy brother, wheresoe'er he is;
Seek him with candle; bring him dead or living
Within this twelvemonth, or turn thou no more
To seek a living in our territory.
Thy lands and all things that thou dost call thine
Worth seizure do we seize into our hands,   *10*
Till thou canst quit thee by thy brother's mouth
Of what we think against thee.
  Oli. O that your Highness knew my heart in
    this!
I never loved my brother in my life.
  Duke F. More villain thou. Well, push him out
    of doors;
And let my officers of such a nature
Make an extent upon his house and lands:
Do this expediently and turn him going. [*Exeunt.*

SCENE II. *The forest*

Enter ORLANDO, *with a paper.*

Orl. Hang there, my verse, in witness of my
  love:
      And thou, thrice-crowned queen of night,
        survey
With thy chaste eye, from thy pale sphere above,
      Thy huntress' name that my full life doth
        sway.
O Rosalind! these trees shall be my books
      And in their barks my thoughts I'll character;
That every eye which in this forest looks
      Shall see thy virtue witness'd every where.
Run, run, Orlando; carve on every tree   *9*
The fair, the chaste, and unexpressive she. [*Exit.*

Enter CORIN *and* TOUCHSTONE.

Cor. And how like you this shepherd's life,
Master Touchstone?
  Touch. Truly, shepherd, in respect of itself,
it is a good life; but in respect that it is a shepherd's life, it is naught. In respect that it is
solitary, I like it very well; but in respect that it
is private, it is a very vile life. Now, in respect
it is in the fields, it pleaseth me well; but in
respect it is not in the court, it is tedious. As it
is a spare life, look you, it fits my humour well;
but as there is no more plenty in it, it goes much
against my stomach. Hast any philosophy in
thee, shepherd?
  Cor. No more but that I know the more one
sickens the worse at ease he is; and that he that
wants money, means, and content is without
three good friends; that the property of rain is to
wet and fire to burn; that good pasture makes fat
sheep, and that a great cause of the night is lack
of the sun; that he that hath learned no wit by
nature nor art may complain of good breeding or
comes of a very dull kindred.

Touch Such a one is a natural philosopher. Wast ever in court, shepherd?

Cor. No, truly.

Touch. Then thou art damned.

Cor. Nay, I hope.

Touch. Truly, thou art damned, like an ill-roasted egg all on one side. 39

Cor. For not being at court? Your reason.

Touch. Why, if thou never wast at court, thou never sawest good manners; if thou never sawest good manners, then thy manners must be wicked; and wickedness is sin, and sin is damnation. Thou art in a parlous state, shepherd.

Cor. Not a whit, Touchstone: those that are good manners at the court are as ridiculous in the country as the behaviour of the country is most mockable at the court. You told me you salute not at the court, but you kiss your hands: that courtesy would be uncleanly, if courtiers were shepherds.

Touch. Instance, briefly; come, instance.

Cor. Why, we are still handling our ewes, and their fells, you know, are greasy.

Touch. Why, do not your courtier's hands sweat? and is not the grease of a mutton as wholesome as the sweat of a man? Shallow, shallow. A better instance, I say; come.

Cor. Besides, our hands are hard. 60

Touch. Your lips will feel them the sooner. Shallow again. A more sounder instance, come.

Cor. And they are often tarred over with the surgery of our sheep; and would you have us kiss tar? The courtier's hands are perfumed with civet.

Touch. Most shallow man! thou worms-meat, in respect of a good piece of flesh indeed! Learn of the wise, and perpend: civet is of a baser birth than tar, the very uncleanly flux of a cat. Mend the instance, shepherd. 71

Cor. You have too courtly a wit for me: I'll rest.

Touch. Wilt thou rest damned? God help thee, shallow man! God make incision in thee! thou art raw.

Cor. Sir, I am a true labourer: I earn that I eat, get that I wear, owe no man hate, envy no man's happiness, glad of other men's good, content with my harm, and the greatest of my pride is to see my ewes graze and my lambs suck.

Touch. That is another simple sin in you, to bring the ewes and the rams together and to offer to get your living by the copulation of cattle; to be bawd to a bell-wether, and to betray a she-lamb of a twelvemonth to a crooked-pated, old, cuckoldy ram, out of all reasonable match. If thou beest not damned for this, the devil him-self will have no shepherds; I cannot see else how thou shouldst 'scape. 90

Cor. Here comes young Master Ganymede, my new mistress's brother.

Enter ROSALIND, *with a paper, reading.*

Ros. "From the east to western Ind,
  No jewel is like Rosalind.
  Her worth, being mounted on the wind,
  Through all the world bears Rosalind.
  All the pictures fairest lined
  Are but black to Rosalind.
  Let no fair be kept in mind
  But the fair of Rosalind." 100

Touch. I'll rhyme you so eight years together, dinners and suppers and sleeping-hours excepted: it is the right butter-women's rank to market.

Ros. Out fool!

Touch. For a taste:
  If a hart do lack a hind,
  Let him seek out Rosalind.
  If the cat will after kind,
  So be sure will Rosalind. 110
  Winter garments must be lined,
  So must slender Rosalind.
  They that reap must sheaf and bind;
  Then to cart with Rosalind.
  Sweetest nut hath sourest rind,
  Such a nut is Rosalind.
  He that sweetest rose will find
  Must find love's prick and Rosalind.
This is the very false gallop of verses: why do you infect yourself with them? 120

Ros. Peace, you dull fool! I found them on a tree.

Touch. Truly, the tree yields bad fruit.

Ros. I'll graff it with you, and then I shall graff it with a medlar: then it will be the earliest fruit i' the country; for you'll be rotten ere you be half ripe, and that's the right virtue of the medlar.

Touch. You have said; but whether wisely or no, let the forest judge. 130

Enter CELIA, *with a writing.*

Ros. Peace!
Here comes my sister, reading: stand aside.

Cel. [*Reads*]
  "Why should this a desert be?
    For it is unpeopled? No:
  Tongues I'll hang on every tree,
    That shall civil sayings show:
  Some, how brief the life of man
    Runs his erring pilgrimage,
  That the stretching of a span
    Buckles in his sum of age; 140

Some, of violated vows
'Twixt the souls of friend and friend:
But upon the fairest boughs,
Or at every sentence end,
Will I Rosalind write,
Teaching all that read to know
The quintessence of every sprite
Heaven would in little show.
Therefore Heaven Nature charged
That one body should be fill'd *150*
With all graces wide-enlarged:
Nature presently distill'd
Helen's cheek, but not her heart,
Cleopatra's majesty,
Atalanta's better part,
Sad Lucretia's modesty.
Thus Rosalind of many parts
By heavenly synod was devised,
Of many faces, eyes, and hearts,
To have the touches dearest prized. *160*
Heaven would that she these gifts should
have,
And I to live and die her slave."

Ros. O most gentle pulpiter! what tedious homily of love have you wearied your parishioners withal, and never cried "Have patience, good people"!

Cel. How now! back, friends! Shepherd, go off a little. Go with him, sirrah.

Touch. Come, shepherd, let us make an honourable retreat; though not with bag and baggage, yet with scrip and scrippage. *171*
[*Exeunt* CORIN *and* TOUCHSTONE.

Cel. Didst thou hear these verses?

Ros. O, yes, I heard them all, and more too; for some of them had in them more feet than the verses would bear.

Cel. That's no matter: the feet might bear the verses.

Ros. Ay, but the feet were lame and could not bear themselves without the verse and therefore stood lamely in the verse. *180*

Cel. But didst thou hear without wondering how thy name should be hanged and carved upon these trees?

Ros. I was seven of the nine days out of the wonder before you came; for look here what I found on a palm-tree. I was never so berhymed since Pythagoras' time, that I was an Irish rat, which I can hardly remember.

Cel. Trow you who hath done this?

Ros. Is it a man? *190*

Cel. And a chain, that you once wore, about his neck. Change you colour?

Ros. I prithee, who?

Cel. O Lord, Lord! it is a hard matter for friends to meet; but mountains may be removed with earthquakes and so encounter.

Ros. Nay, but who is it?

Cel. Is it possible?

Ros. Nay, I prithee now with most petitionary vehemence, tell me who it is. *200*

Cel. O wonderful, wonderful, and most wonderful wonderful! and yet again wonderful, and after that, out of all hooping!

Ros. Good my complexion! dost thou think, though I am caparisoned like a man, I have a doublet and hose in my disposition? One inch of delay more is a South-sea of discovery; I prithee, tell me who is it quickly, and speak apace. I would thou couldst stammer, that thou mightst pour this concealed man out of thy mouth, as wine comes out of a narrow-mouthed bottle, either too much at once, or none at all. I prithee, take the cork out of thy mouth that I may drink thy tidings.

Cel. So you may put a man in your belly.

Ros. Is he of God's making? What manner of man? Is his head worth a hat, or his chin worth a beard?

Cel. Nay, he hath but a little beard. *219*

Ros. Why, God will send more, if the man will be thankful: let me stay the growth of his beard, if thou delay me not the knowledge of his chin.

Cel. It is young Orlando, that tripped up the wrestler's heels and your heart both in an instant.

Ros. Nay, but the devil take mocking: speak, sad brow and true maid.

Cel. I' faith, coz, 'tis he.

Ros. Orlando?

Cel. Orlando. *230*

Ros. Alas the day! what shall I do with my doublet and hose? What did he when thou sawest him? What said he? How looked he? Wherein went he? What makes he here? Did he ask for me? Where remains he? How parted he with thee? and when shalt thou see him again? Answer me in one word.

Cel. You must borrow me Gargantua's mouth first: 'tis a word too great for any mouth of this age's size. To say ay and no to these particulars is more than to answer in a catechism. *241*

Ros. But doth he know that I am in this forest and in man's apparel? Looks he as freshly as he did the day he wrestled?

Cel. It is easy to count atomies as to resolve the propositions of a lover; but take a taste of my finding him, and relish it with good observance. I found him under a tree, like a dropped acorn.

Ros. It may well be called Jove's tree, when it drops forth such fruit. 250

Cel. Give me audience, good madam.

Ros. Proceed.

Cel. There lay he, stretched along, like a wounded knight.

Ros. Though it be pity to see such a sight, it well becomes the ground.

Cel. Cry "holla" to thy tongue, I prithee; it curvets unseasonably. He was furnished like a hunter. 259

Ros. O, ominous! he comes to kill my heart.

Cel. I would sing my song without a burden: thou bringest me out of tune.

Ros. Do you not know I am a woman? when I think, I must speak. Sweet, say on.

Cel. You bring me out. Soft! comes he not here?

Enter ORLANDO *and* JAQUES.

Ros. 'Tis he: slink by, and note him.

Jaq. I thank you for your company; but, good faith, I had as lief have been myself alone. 270

Orl. And so had I; but yet, for fashion sake, I thank you too for your society.

Jaq. God be wi' you: let's meet as little as we can.

Orl. I do desire we may be better strangers.

Jaq. I pray you, mar no more trees with writing love-songs in their barks.

Orl. I pray you, mar no moe of my verses with reading them ill-favouredly.

Jaq. Rosalind is your love's name? 280

Orl. Yes, just.

Jaq. I do not like her name.

Orl. There was no thought of pleasing you when she was christened.

Jaq. What stature is she of?

Orl. Just as high as my heart.

Jaq. You are full of pretty answers. Have you not been acquainted with goldsmiths' wives, and conned them out of rings? 289

Orl. Not so; but I answer you right painted cloth, from whence you have studied your questions.

Jaq. You have a nimble wit: I think 'twas made of Atalanta's heels. Will you sit down with me? and we two will rail against our mistress the world and all our misery.

Orl. I will chide no breather in the world but myself, against whom I know most faults.

Jaq. The worst fault you have is to be in love. 300

Orl. 'Tis a fault I will not change for your best virtue. I am weary of you.

Jaq. By my troth, I was seeking for a fool when I found you.

Orl. He is drowned in the brook: look but in, and you shall see him.

Jaq. There I shall see mine own figure.

Orl. Which I take to be either a fool or a cipher.

Jaq. I'll tarry no longer with you: farewell, good Signior Love. 310

Orl. I am glad of your departure: adieu, good Monsieur Melancholy. [*Exit* JAQUES.

Ros. [*Aside to* CELIA] I will speak to him like a saucy lackey and under that habit play the knave with him. Do you hear, forester?

Orl. Very well: what would you?

Ros. I pray you, what is't o'clock?

Orl. You should ask me what time o'day: there's no clock in the forest. 319

Ros. Then there is no true lover in the forest; else sighing every minute and groaning every hour would detect the lazy foot of Time as well as a clock.

Orl. And why not the swift foot of Time? had not that been as proper?

Ros. By no means, sir: Time travels in divers paces with divers persons. I'll tell you who Time ambles withal, who Time trots withal, who Time gallops withal, and who he stands still withal.

Orl. I prithee, who doth he trot withal? 330

Ros. Marry, he trots hard with a young maid between the contract of her marriage and the day it is solemnized: if the interim be but a se'nnight, Time's pace is so hard that it seems the length of seven year.

Orl. Who ambles Time withal?

Ros. With a priest that lacks Latin and a rich man that hath not the gout, for the one sleeps easily because he cannot study and the other lives merrily because he feels no pain, the one lacking the burden of lean and wasteful learning, the other knowing no burden of heavy tedious penury; these Time ambles withal.

Orl. Who doth he gallop withal?

Ros. With a thief to the gallows, for though he go as softly as foot can fall, he thinks himself too soon there.

Orl. Who stays it still withal?

Ros. With lawyers in the vacation; for they sleep between term and term and then they perceive not how Time moves. 351

Orl. Where dwell you, pretty youth?

Ros. With this shepherdess, my sister; here in the skirts of the forest, like fringe upon a petticoat.

Orl. Are you native of this place?

Ros. As the cony that you see dwell where she is kindled.

Orl. Your accent is something finer than you could purchase in so removed a dwelling.   *360*

Ros. I have been told so of many: but indeed an old religious uncle of mine taught me to speak, who was in his youth an inland man; one that knew courtship too well, for there he fell in love. I have heard him read many lectures against it, and I thank God I am not a woman, to be touched with so many giddy offences as he hath generally taxed their whole sex withal.

Orl. Can you remember any of the principal evils that he laid to the charge of women?   *370*

Ros. There were none principal; they were all like one another as half-pence are, every one fault seeming monstrous till his fellow-fault came to match it.

Orl. I prithee, recount some of them.

Ros. No, I will not cast away my physic but on those that are sick. There is a man haunts the forest, that abuses our young plants with carving "Rosalind" on their barks; hangs odes upon hawthorns and elegies on brambles, all, forsooth, deifying the name of Rosalind: if I could meet that fancy-monger, I would give him some good counsel, for he seems to have the quotidian of love upon him.

Orl. I am he that is so love-shaked: I pray you, tell me your remedy.

Ros. There is none of my uncle's marks upon you: he taught me how to know a man in love; in which cage of rushes I am sure you are not prisoner.   *390*

Orl. What were his marks?

Ros. A lean cheek, which you have not, a blue eye and sunken, which you have not, an unquestionable spirit, which you have not, a beard neglected, which you have not; but I pardon you for that, for simply your having in beard is a younger brother's revenue: then your hose should be ungartered, your bonnet unbanded, your sleeve unbuttoned, your shoe untied, and everything about you demonstrating a careless desolation; but you are no such man; you are rather point-device in your accoutrements as loving yourself than seeming the lover of any other.

Orl. Fair youth, I would I could make thee believe I love.

Ros. Me believe it! you may as soon make her that you love believe it; which, I warrant, she is apter to do than to confess she does: that is one of the points in the which women still give the lie to their consciences. But, in good sooth, are you he that hangs the verses on the trees, wherein Rosalind is so admired?

Orl. I swear to thee, youth, by the white hand of Rosalind, I am that he, that unfortunate he.

Ros. But are you so much in love as your rhymes speak?

Orl. Neither rhyme nor reason can express how much.   *419*

Ros. Love is merely a madness, and, I tell you, deserves as well a dark house and a whip as madmen do: and the reason why they are not so punished and cured is that the lunacy is so ordinary that the whippers are in love too. Yet I profess curing it by counsel.

Orl. Did you ever cure any so?

Ros. Yes, one, and in this manner. He was to imagine me his love, his mistress; and I set him every day to woo me: at which time would I, being but a moonish youth, grieve, be effeminate, changeable, longing and liking, proud, fantastical, apish, shallow, inconstant, full of tears, full of smiles, for every passion something and for no passion truly anything, as boys and women are for the most part cattle of this colour; would now like him, now loathe him; then entertain him, then forswear him; now weep for him, then spit at him; that I drave my suitor from his mad humour of love to a living humour of madness; which was, to forswear the full stream of the world and to live in a nook merely monastic. And thus I cured him; and this way will I take upon me to wash your liver as clean as a sound sheep's heart, that there shall not be one spot of love in't.

Orl. I would not be cured, youth.

Ros. I would cure you, if you would but call me Rosalind and come every day to my cote and woo me.

Orl. Now, by the faith of my love, I will: tell me where it is.   *450*

Ros. Go with me to it and I'll show it you: and by the way you shall tell me where in the forest you live. Will you go?

Orl. With all my heart, good youth.

Ros. Nay, you must call me Rosalind. Come, sister, will you go?   [*Exeunt.*

SCENE III. *The forest*

Enter TOUCHSTONE *and* AUDREY; JAQUES
behind.

Touch. Come apace, good Audrey: I will fetch up your goats, Audrey. And how, Audrey? am I the man yet? doth my simple feature content you?

Aud. Your features! Lord warrant us! what features?

Touch. I am here with thee and thy goats, as the most capricious poet, honest Ovid, was among the Goths.

Jaq. [*Aside*] O knowledge ill-inhabited, worse
than Jove in a thatched house!   *11*

Touch. When a man's verses cannot be understood, nor a man's good wit seconded with the
forward child Understanding, it strikes a man
more dead than a great reckoning in a little room.
Truly, I would the gods had made thee poetical.

Aud. I do not know what "poetical" is: is it
honest in deed and word? is it a true thing?

Touch. No, truly; for the truest poetry is the
most feigning; and lovers are given to poetry,
and what they swear in poetry may be said as
lovers they do feign.

Aud. Do you wish that the gods had made
me poetical?

Touch. I do, truly; for thou swearest to me
thou art honest: now, if thou wert a poet, I
might have some hope thou didst feign.

Aud. Would you not have me honest?

Touch. No, truly, unless thou wert hard-
favoured; for honesty coupled to beauty is to
have honey a sauce to sugar.   *31*

Jaq. [*Aside*] A material fool!

Aud. Well, I am not fair; and therefore I
pray the gods make me honest.

Touch. Truly, and to cast away honesty upon
a foul slut were to put good meat into an unclean
dish.

Aud. I am not a slut, though I thank the gods
I am foul.   *39*

Touch. Well, praised be the gods for thy foulness! sluttishness may come hereafter. But be
it as it may be, I will marry thee, and to that end
I have been with Sir Oliver Martext, the vicar of
the next village, who hath promised to meet me
in this place of the forest and to couple us.

Jaq. [*Aside*] I would fain see this meeting.

Aud. Well, the gods give us joy!

Touch. Amen. A man may, if he were of a
fearful heart, stagger in this attempt; for here
we have no temple but the wood, no assembly
but horn-beasts. But what though? Courage!
As horns are odious, they are necessary. It is
said, "many a man knows no end of his goods":
right; many a man has good horns, and knows
no end of them. Well, that is the dowry of his
wife; 'tis none of his own getting. Horns? Even
so. Poor men alone? No, no; the noblest deer
hath them as huge as the rascal. Is the single
man therefore blessed? No: as a walled town is
more worthier than a village, so is the forehead
of a married man more honourable than the bare
brow of a bachelor; and by how much defence
is better than no skill, by so much is a horn
more precious than to want. Here comes Sir
Oliver.

Enter SIR OLIVER MARTEXT.

Sir Oliver Martext, you are well met: will you
dispatch us here under this tree, or shall we go
with you to your chapel?

Sir Oli. Is there none here to give the woman?

Touch. I will not take her on gift of any man.

Sir Oli. Truly, she must be given, or the marriage is not lawful.   *71*

Jaq. [*Advancing*] Proceed, proceed: I'll give
her.

Touch. Good even, good Master What-ye-
call't: how do you, sir? You are very well met:
God 'ild you for your last company: I am very
glad to see you: even a toy in hand here, sir:
nay, pray be covered.

Jaq. Will you be married, motley?   *79*

Touch. As the ox hath his bow, sir, the horse
his curb, and the falcon her bells, so man hath
his desires; and as pigeons bill, so wedlock would
be nibbling.

Jaq. And will you, being a man of your breeding, be married under a bush like a beggar?
Get you to church, and have a good priest that
can tell you what marriage is: this fellow will
but join you together as they join wainscot; then
one of you will prove a shrunk panel and, like
green timber, warp, warp.   *90*

Touch. [*Aside*] I am not in the mind but I were
better to be married of him than of another: for
he is not like to marry me well; and not being
well married, it will be a good excuse for me
hereafter to leave my wife.

Jaq. Go thou with me, and let me counsel thee.

Touch. Come, sweet Audrey:
We must be married, or we must live in bawdry.
Farewell, good Master Oliver: not—   *100*
        O sweet Oliver,
        O brave Oliver,
        Leave me not behind thee:
but—
        Wind away,
        Begone, I say,
        I will not to wedding with thee.
            [*Exeunt* JAQUES, TOUCHSTONE *and* AUDREY.

Sir Oli. 'Tis no matter: ne'er a fantastical knave
of them all shall flout me out of my calling.
                                           [*Exit. 109*

SCENE IV. *The forest*

Enter ROSALIND *and* CELIA.

Ros. Never talk to me; I will weep.

Cel. Do, I prithee; but yet have the grace to
consider that tears do not become a man.

Ros. But have I not cause to weep?

Cel. As good cause as one would desire; therefore weep.

Ros. His very hair is of the dissembling colour.

Cel. Something browner than Judas': marry, his kisses are Judas' own children. 10

Ros. I' faith, his hair is of a good colour.

Cel. An excellent colour: your chestnut was ever the only colour.

Ros. And his kissing is as full of sanctity as the touch of holy bread.

Cel. He hath bought a pair of cast lips of Diana: a nun of winter's sisterhood kisses not more religiously; the very ice of chastity is in them.

Ros. But why did he swear he would come this morning, and comes not? 21

Cel. Nay, certainly, there is no truth in him.

Ros. Do you think so?

Cel. Yes; I think he is not a pick-purse nor a horse-stealer, but for his verity in love, I do think him as concave as a covered goblet or a worm-eaten nut.

Ros. Not true in love?

Cel. Yes, when he is in; but I think he is not in. 30

Ros. You have heard him swear downright he was.

Cel. "Was" is not "is"; besides, the oath of a lover is no stronger than the word of a tapster; they are both the confirmer of false reckonings. He attends here in the forest on the Duke your father.

Ros. I met the Duke yesterday and had much question with him: he asked me of what parentage I was; I told him, of as good as he; so he laughed and let me go. But what talk we of fathers, when there is such a man as Orlando?

Cel. O, that's a brave man! he writes brave verses, speaks brave words, swears brave oaths, and breaks them bravely, quite traverse, athwart the heart of his lover; as a puisny tilter, that spurs his horse but on one side, breaks his staff like a noble goose: but all's brave that youth mounts and folly guides. Who comes here?

Enter CORIN.

Cor. Mistress and master, you have oft inquired 50
After the shepherd that complain'd of love,
Who you saw sitting by me on the turf,
Praising the proud disdainful shepherdess
That was his mistress.

Cel. Well, and what of him?

Cor. If you will see a pageant truly play'd,
Between the pale complexion of true love
And the red glow of scorn and proud disdain,
Go hence a little and I shall conduct you,

If you will mark it.

Ros. O, come, let us remove:
The sight of lovers feedeth those in love. 60
Bring us to this sight, and you shall say
I'll prove a busy actor in their play. [*Exeunt.*

SCENE V. *Another part of the forest*

Enter SILVIUS *and* PHEBE.

Sil. Sweet Phebe, do not scorn me; do not, Phebe;
Say that you love me not, but say not so
In bitterness. The common executioner,
Whose heart the accustom'd sight of death makes hard,
Falls not the axe upon the humbled neck
But first begs pardon: will you sterner be
Than he that dies and lives by bloody drops?

Enter ROSALIND, CELIA, *and* CORIN, *behind.*

Phe. I would not be thy executioner:
I fly thee, for I would not injure thee.
Thou tell'st me there is murder in mine eye: 10
'Tis pretty, sure, and very probable,
That eyes, that are the frail'st and softest things,
Who shut their coward gates on atomies,
Should be call'd tyrants, butchers, murderers!
Now I do frown on thee with all my heart;
And if mine eyes can wound, now let them kill thee:
Now counterfeit to swoon; why now fall down;
Or if thou canst not, O, for shame, for shame,
Lie not, to say mine eyes are murderers!
Now show the wound mine eye hath made in thee: 20
Scratch thee but with a pin, and there remains
Some scar of it; lean but upon a rush,
The cicatrice and capable impressure
Thy palm some moment keeps; but now mine eyes,
Which I have darted at thee, hurt thee not,
Nor, I am sure, there is no force in eyes
That can do hurt.

Sil. O dear Phebe,
If ever—as that ever may be near—
You meet in some fresh cheek the power of fancy,
Then shall you know the wounds invisible 30
That love's keen arrows make.

Phe. But till that time
Come not thou near me: and when that time comes,
Afflict me with thy mocks, pity me not;
As till that time I shall not pity thee.

Ros. And why, I pray you? Who might be your mother,

That you insult, exult, and all at once,
Over the wretched? What though you have no
    beauty—
As, by my faith, I see no more in you
Than without candle may go dark to bed—
Must you be therefore proud and pitiless?   *40*
Why, what means this? Why do you look on me?
I see no more in you than in the ordinary
Of nature's sale-work. 'Od's my little life,
I think she means to tangle my eyes too!
No, faith, proud mistress, hope not after it:
'Tis not your inky brows, your black silk hair,
Your bugle eyeballs, nor your cheek of cream,
That can entame my spirits to your worship.
You foolish shepherd, wherefore do you follow
    her,
Like foggy south puffing with wind and rain? *50*
You are a thousand times a properer man
Than she a woman: 'tis such fools as you
That makes the world full of ill-favour'd chil-
    dren:
'Tis not her glass, but you, that flatters her;
And out of you she sees herself more proper
Than any of her lineaments can show her.
But, mistress, know yourself: down on your
    knees,
And thank heaven, fasting, for a good man's love:
For I must tell you friendly in your ear,
Sell when you can: you are not for all markets:
Cry the man mercy; love him; take his offer: *61*
Foul is most foul, being foul to be a scoffer.
So take her to thee, shepherd: fare you well.
    Phe. Sweet youth, I pray you, chide a year
    together:
I had rather hear you chide than this man woo.
    Ros. He's fallen in love with your foulness and
she'll fall in love with my anger. If it be so, as
fast as she answers thee with frowning looks, I'll
sauce her with bitter words. Why look you so
upon me?   *70*
    Phe. For no ill will I bear you.
    Ros. I pray you, do not fall in love with me,
For I am falser than vows made in wine:
Besides, I like you not. If you will know my
    house,
'Tis at the tuft of olives here hard by.
Will you go, sister? Shepherd, ply her hard.
Come, sister. Shepherdess, look on him better,
And be not proud: though all the world could see,
None could be so abused in sight as he.
Come, to our flock.   *80*
        [*Exeunt* ROSALIND, CELIA *and* CORIN.
    Phe. Dead shepherd, now I find thy saw of
    might,
"Who ever loved that loved not at first sight?"
    Sil. Sweet Phebe—

    Phe.   Ha, what say'st thou, Silvius?
    Sil. Sweet Phebe, pity me.
    Phe. Why, I am sorry for thee, gentle Silvius.
    Sil. Wherever sorrow is, relief would be:
If you do sorrow at my grief in love,
By giving love your sorrow and my grief
Were both extermined.
    Phe. Thou hast my love: is not that neighbour-
    ly?   *90*
    Sil. I would have you.
    Phe.   Why, that were covetousness.
Silvius, the time was that I hated thee,
And yet it is not that I bear thee love;
But since that thou canst talk of love so well,
Thy company, which erst was irksome to me,
I will endure, and I'll employ thee too:
But do not look for further recompense
Than thine own gladness that thou art employ'd.
    Sil. So holy and so perfect is my love,
And I in such a poverty of grace,   *100*
That I shall think it a most plenteous crop
To glean the broken ears after the man
That the main harvest reaps: loose now and then
A scatter'd smile, and that I'll live upon.
    Phe. Know'st thou the youth that spoke to me
    erewhile?
    Sil. Not very well, but I have met him oft;
And he hath bought the cottage and the bounds
That the old carlot once was master of.
    Phe. Think not I love him, though I ask for
    him;
'Tis but a peevish boy; yet he talks well;   *110*
But what care I for words? yet words do well
When he that speaks them pleases those that
    hear.
It is a pretty youth: not very pretty:
But, sure, he's proud, and yet his pride becomes
    him:
He'll make a proper man: the best thing in him
Is his complexion; and faster than his tongue
Did make offence his eye did heal it up.
He is not very tall; yet for his years he's tall:
His leg is but so so; and yet 'tis well:
There was a pretty redness in his lip,   *120*
A little riper and more lusty red
Than that mix'd in his cheek; 'twas just the
    difference
Betwixt the constant red and mingled damask.
There be some women, Silvius, had they mark'd
    him
In parcels as I did, would have gone near
To fall in love with him; but, for my part,
I love him not nor hate him not; and yet
I have more cause to hate him than to love him:
For what had he to do to chide at me?
He said mine eyes were black and my hair black;

And, now I am remember'd, scorn'd at me: *131*
I marvel why I answer'd not again:
But that's all one; omittance is no quittance.
I'll write to him a very taunting letter,
And thou shalt bear it: wilt thou, Silvius?
  Sil. Phebe, with all my heart.
  Phe.   I'll write it straight;
The matter's in my head and in my heart:
I will be bitter with him and passing short.
Go with me, Silvius.   [*Exeunt.*

ACT IV

SCENE I. *The forest*

Enter ROSALIND, CELIA, *and* JAQUES.

Jaq. I prithee, pretty youth, let me be better
acquainted with thee.
  Ros. They say you are a melancholy fellow.
  Jaq. I am so; I do love it better than laughing.
  Ros. Those that are in extremity of either are
abominable fellows and betray themselves to
every modern censure worse than drunkards.
  Jaq. Why, 'tis good to be sad and say nothing.
  Ros. Why then, 'tis good to be a post.   *9*
  Jaq. I have neither the scholar's melancholy,
which is emulation, nor the musician's, which is
fantastical, nor the courtier's, which is proud,
nor the soldier's, which is ambitious, nor the
lawyer's, which is politic, nor the lady's, which
is nice, nor the lover's, which is all these: but it is
a melancholy of mine own, compounded of many
simples, extracted from many objects, and indeed
the sundry contemplation of my travels, in which
my often rumination wraps me in a most humorous sadness.   *20*
  Ros. A traveller! By my faith, you have great
reason to be sad: I fear you have sold your own
lands to see other men's; then, to have seen much
and to have nothing, is to have rich eyes and
poor hands.
  Jaq. Yes, I have gained my experience.
  Ros. And your experience makes you sad: I had
rather have a fool to make me merry than experience to make me sad; and to travel for it too!

Enter ORLANDO.

Orl. Good day and happiness, dear Rosalind!
  Jaq. Nay, then, God be wi' you, an you talk in
blank verse.   [*Exit.*
  Ros. Farewell, Monsieur Traveller: look you
lisp and wear strange suits, disable all the benefits of your own country, be out of love with
your nativity, and almost chide God for making
you that countenance you are, or I will scarce
think you have swam in a gondola. Why, how
now, Orlando! where have you been all this

while? You a lover! An you serve me such another trick, never come in my sight more.   *41*
  Orl. My fair Rosalind, I come within an hour of
my promise.
  Ros. Break an hour's promise in love! He that
will divide a minute into a thousand parts and
break but a part of the thousandth part of a
minute in the affairs of love, it may be said of
him that Cupid hath clapped him o' the shoulder,
but I'll warrant him heart-whole.
  Orl. Pardon me, dear Rosalind.   *50*
  Ros. Nay, an you be so tardy, come no more in
my sight: I had as lief be wooed of a snail.
  Orl. Of a snail?
  Ros. Ay, of a snail; for though he comes slowly,
he carries his house on his head; a better jointure,
I think, than you make a woman: besides, he
brings his destiny with him.
  Orl. What's that?
  Ros. Why, horns, which such as you are fain to
be beholding to your wives for: but he comes
armed in his fortune and prevents the slander of
his wife.
  Orl. Virtue is no horn-maker; and my Rosalind
is virtuous.
  Ros. And I am your Rosalind.
  Cel. It pleases him to call you so; but he hath
a Rosalind of a better leer than you.
  Ros. Come, woo me, woo me, for now I am in a
holiday humour and like enough to consent.
What would you say to me now, an I were your
very very Rosalind?   *71*
  Orl. I would kiss before I spoke.
  Ros. Nay, you were better speak first, and
when you were gravelled for lack of matter, you
might take occasion to kiss. Very good orators,
when they are out, they will spit; and for lovers
lacking—God warn us!—matter, the cleanliest
shift is to kiss.
  Orl. How if the kiss be denied?
  Ros. Then she puts you to entreaty, and there
begins new matter.   *81*
  Orl. Who could be out, being before his beloved mistress?
  Ros. Marry, that should you, if I were your
mistress, or I should think my honesty ranker
than my wit.
  Orl. What, of my suit?
  Ros. Not out of your apparel, and yet out of
your suit. Am not I your Rosalind?
  Orl. I take some joy to say you are, because I
would be talking of her.   *91*
  Ros. Well in her person I say I will not have
you.
  Orl. Then in mine own person I die.
  Ros. No, faith, die by attorney. The poor world

is almost six thousand years old, and in all this time there was not any man died in his own person, *videlicet*, in a love-cause. Troilus had his brains dashed out with a Grecian club; yet he did what he could to die before, and he is one of the patterns of love. Leander, he would have lived many a fair year, though Hero had turned nun, if it had not been for a hot midsummer night; for, good youth, he went but forth to wash him in the Hellespont and being taken with the cramp was drowned: and the foolish chroniclers of that age found it was "Hero of Sestos." But these are all lies: men have died from time to time and worms have eaten them, but not for love.

Orl. I would not have my right Rosalind of this mind, for, I protest, her frown might kill me.

Ros. By this hand, it will not kill a fly. But come, now I will be your Rosalind in a more coming-on disposition, and ask me what you will, I will grant it.

Orl. Then love me, Rosalind.

Ros. Yes, faith, will I, Fridays and Saturdays and all.

Orl. And wilt thou have me?

Ros. Ay, and twenty such.

Orl. What sayest thou?   120

Ros. Are you not good?

Orl. I hope so.

Ros. Why then, can one desire too much of a good thing? Come, sister, you shall be the priest and marry us. Give me your hand, Orlando. What do you say, sister?

Orl. Pray thee, marry us.

Cel. I cannot say the words.

Ros. You must begin, "Will you, Orlando—"

Cel. Go to. Will you, Orlando, have to wife this Rosalind?   131

Orl. I will.

Ros. Ay, but when?

Orl. Why now; as fast as she can marry us.

Ros. Then you must say, "I take thee, Rosalind, for wife."

Orl. I take thee, Rosalind, for wife.

Ros. I might ask you for your commission; but I do take thee, Orlando, for my husband: there's a girl goes before the priest; and certainly a woman's thought runs before her actions.   141

Orl. So do all thoughts; they are winged.

Ros. Now tell me how long you would have her after you have possessed her.

Orl. For ever and a day.

Ros. Say "a day," without the "ever." No, no, Orlando; men are April when they woo, December when they wed: maids are May when they are maids, but the sky changes when they are wives. I will be more jealous of thee than a Barbary cock-pigeon over his hen, more clamorous than a parrot against rain, more new-fangled than an ape, more giddy in my desires than a monkey: I will weep for nothing, like Diana in the fountain, and I will do that when you are disposed to be merry; I will laugh like a hyen, and that when thou art inclined to sleep.

Orl. But will my Rosalind do so?

Ros. By my life, she will do as I do.

Orl. O, but she is wise.   160

Ros. Or else she could not have the wit to do this: the wiser, the waywarder: make the doors upon a woman's wit and it will out at the casement; shut that and 'twill out at the key-hole; stop that, 'twill fly with the smoke out at the chimney.

Orl. A man that had a wife with such a wit, he might say, "Wit, whither wilt?"

Ros. Nay, you might keep that check for it till you met your wife's wit going to your neighbour's bed.   171

Orl. And what wit could wit have to excuse that?

Ros. Marry, to say she came to seek you there. You shall never take her without her answer, unless you take her without her tongue. O, that woman that cannot make her fault her husband's occasion, let her never nurse her child herself, for she will breed it like a fool!

Orl. For these two hours, Rosalind, I will leave thee.   181

Ros. Alas! dear love, I cannot lack thee two hours.

Orl. I must attend the Duke at dinner: by two o'clock I will be with thee again.

Ros. Ay, go your ways, go your ways; I knew what you would prove: my friends told me as much, and I thought no less: that flattering tongue of yours won me: 'tis but one cast away, and so, come, death! Two o'clock is your hour?

Orl. Ay, sweet Rosalind.   191

Ros. By my troth, and in good earnest, and so God mend me, and by all pretty oaths that are not dangerous, if you break one jot of your promise or come one minute behind your hour, I will think you the most pathetical break-promise and the most hollow lover and the most unworthy of her you call Rosalind that may be chosen out of the gross band of the unfaithful: therefore beware my censure and keep your promise.   200

Orl. With no less religion than if thou wert indeed my Rosalind: so adieu.

Ros. Well, Time is the old justice that examines all such offenders, and let Time try: adieu.

[*Exit* ORLANDO.

Cel. You have simply misused our sex in your love-prate: we must have your doublet and hose plucked over your head, and show the world what the bird hath done to her own nest.

Ros. O coz, coz, coz, my pretty little coz, that thou didst know how many fathom deep I am in love! But it cannot be sounded: my affection hath an unknown bottom, like the bay of Portugal.

Cel. Or rather, bottomless, that as fast as you pour affection in, it runs out.

Ros. No, that same wicked bastard of Venus that was begot of thought, conceived of spleen, and born of madness, that blind rascally boy that abuses every one's eyes because his own are out, let him be judge how deep I am in love. I'll tell thee, Aliena, I cannot be out of the sight of Orlando: I'll go find a shadow and sigh till he come.

Cel. And I'll sleep.   *[Exeunt.*

SCENE II. *The forest*

Enter JAQUES, LORDS, *and Foresters.*

Jaq. Which is he that killed the deer?

1st Lord. Sir, it was I.

Jaq. Let's present him to the Duke, like a Roman conqueror; and it would do well to set the deer's horns upon his head, for a branch of victory. Have you no song, forester, for this purpose?

1st For. Yes, sir.

Jaq. Sing it: 'tis no matter how it be in tune, so it make noise enough.   *10*

SONG

1st For. What shall he have that kill'd the
       deer?
       His leather skin and horns to wear.
       Then sing him home;
The rest shall bear this burden.
       Take thou no scorn to wear the horn;
       It was a crest ere thou wast born:
          Thy father's father wore it,
          And thy father bore it:
       The horn, the horn, the lusty horn
       Is not a thing to laugh to scorn.   *[Exeunt.*

SCENE III. *The forest*

Enter ROSALIND *and* CELIA.

Ros. How say you now? Is it not past two o'clock? and here much Orlando!

Cel. I warrant you, with pure love and troubled brain, he hath ta'en his bow and arrows and is gone forth to sleep. Look, who comes here.

Enter SILVIUS.

Sil. My errand is to you, fair youth;
My gentle Phebe bid me give you this:
I know not the contents; but, as I guess
By the stern brow and waspish action
Which she did use as she was writing of it,   *10*
It bears an angry tenour: pardon me;
I am but as a guiltless messenger.

Ros. Patience herself would startle at this letter
And play the swaggerer; bear this, bear all:
She says I am not fair, that I lack manners;
She calls me proud, and that she could not love
       me,
Were man as rare as phœnix. 'Od's my will!
Her love is not the hare that I do hunt:
Why writes she so to me? Well, shepherd, well,
This is a letter of your own device.   *20*

Sil. No, I protest, I know not the contents:
Phebe did write it.

Ros.   Come, come, you are a fool
And turn'd into the extremity of love.
I saw her hand: she has a leathern hand,
A freestone-colour'd hand; I verily did think
That her old gloves were on, but 'twas her hands:
She has a huswife's hand; but that's no matter:
I say she never did invent this letter;
This is a man's invention and his hand.

Sil. Sure, it is hers.   *30*

Ros. Why, 'tis a boisterous and a cruel style,
A style for challengers; why, she defies me,
Like Turk to Christian: women's gentle brain
Could not drop forth such giant-rude invention,
Such Ethiope words, blacker in their effect
Than in their countenance. Will you hear the
       letter?

Sil. So please you, for I never heard it yet;
Yet heard too much of Phebe's cruelty.

Ros. She Phebes me: mark how the tyrant
       writes. *[Reads.]*
   "Art thou god to shepherd turn'd,   *40*
       That a maiden's heart hath burn'd?"
Can a woman rail thus?

Sil. Call you this railing?

Ros. *[Reads]*
   "Why, thy godhead laid apart,
       Warr'st thou with a woman's heart?"
Did you ever hear such railing?
   "Whiles the eye of man did woo me,
       That could do no vengeance to me."
Meaning me a beast.
   "If the scorn of your bright eyne   *50*
       Have power to raise such love in mine,
       Alack, in me what strange effect
       Would they work in mild aspect!
       Whiles you chid me, I did love;

How then might your prayers move!
He that brings this love to thee
Little knows this love in me:
And by him seal up thy mind;
Whether that thy youth and kind
Will the faithful offer take   60
Of me and all that I can make;
Or else by him my love deny,
And then I'll study how to die."

Sil. Call you this chiding?

Cel. Alas, poor shepherd!

Ros. Do you pity him? no, he deserves no pity.
Wilt thou love such a woman? What, to make
thee an instrument and play false strains upon
thee! not to be endured! Well, go your way to
her, for I see love hath made thee a tame snake,
and say this to her: that if she love me, I charge
her to love thee; if she will not, I will never have
her unless thou entreat for her. If you be a true
lover, hence, and not a word; for here comes
more company.   [*Exit* SILVIUS.

Enter OLIVER.

Oli. Good morrow, fair ones: pray you, if you
know,
Where in the purlieus of this forest stands
A sheep-cote fenced about with olive trees?

Cel. West of this place, down in the neighbour
bottom:
The rank of osiers by the murmuring stream   80
Left on your right hand brings you to the place.
But at this hour the house doth keep itself;
There's none within.

Oli. If that an eye may profit by a tongue,
Then should I know you by description;
Such garments and such years: "The boy is fair,
Of female favour, and bestows himself
Like a ripe sister: the woman low
And browner than her brother." Are not you
The owner of the house I did enquire for?   90

Cel. It is no boast, being ask'd, to say we are.

Oli. Orlando doth commend him to you both,
And to that youth he calls his Rosalind
He sends this bloody napkin. Are you he?

Ros. I am: what must we understand by this?

Oli. Some of my shame; if you will know of me
What man I am, and how, and why, and where
This handkercher was stain'd.

Cel.   I pray you, tell it.

Oli. When last the young Orlando parted from
you
He left a promise to return again   100
Within an hour, and pacing through the forest,
Chewing the food of sweet and bitter fancy,
Lo, what befel! he threw his eye aside,
And mark what object did present itself:

Under an oak, whose boughs were moss'd with
age
And high top bald with dry antiquity,
A wretched ragged man, o'ergrown with hair,
Lay sleeping on his back: about his neck
A green and gilded snake had wreathed itself,
Who with her head nimble in threats approach'd
The opening of his mouth; but suddenly,   111
Seeing Orlando, it unlink'd itself,
And with indented glides did slip away
Into a bush: under which bush's shade
A lioness, with udders all drawn dry,
Lay couching, head on ground, with catlike
watch,
When that the sleeping man should stir; for 'tis
The royal disposition of that beast
To prey on nothing that doth seem as dead:
This seen, Orlando did approach the man   120
And found it was his brother, his elder brother.

Cel. O, I have heard him speak of that same
brother;
And he did render him the most unnatural
That lived amongst men.

Oli.   And well he might so do,
For well I know he was unnatural.

Ros. But, to Orlando: did he leave him there,
Food to the suck'd and hungry lioness?

Oli. Twice did he turn his back and purposed
so;
But kindness, nobler ever than revenge,
And nature, stronger than his just occasion,   130
Made him give battle to the lioness,
Who quickly fell before him: in which hurtling
From miserable slumber I awaked.

Cel. Are you his brother?

Ros.   Was't you he rescued?

Cel. Was't you that did so oft contrive to kill
him?

Oli. 'Twas I; but 'tis not I: I do not shame
To tell you what I was, since my conversion
So sweetly tastes, being the thing I am.

Ros. But, for the bloody napkin?

Oli.   By and by.
When from the first to last betwixt us two   140
Tears our recountments had most kindly
bathed,
As how I came into that desert place:
In brief, he led me to the gentle Duke,
Who gave me fresh array and entertainment,
Committing me unto my brother's love;
Who led me instantly unto his cave,
There stripp'd himself, and here upon his arm
The lioness had torn some flesh away,
Which all this while had bled; and now he
fainted
And cried, in fainting, upon Rosalind.   150

Brief, I recover'd him, bound up his wound;
And, after some small space, being strong at
   heart,
He sent me hither, stranger as I am,
To tell this story, that you might excuse
His broken promise, and to give this napkin
Dyed in his blood unto the shepherd youth
That he in sport doth call his Rosalind.

                              [ROSALIND *swoons*.

Cel. Why, how now, Ganymede! sweet Ganymede!

Oli. Many will swoon when they do look on blood.

Cel. There is more in it. Cousin Ganymede!

Oli. Look, he recovers.   161

Ros. I would I were at home.

Cel.   We'll lead you thither.
I pray you, will you take him by the arm?

Oli. Be of good cheer, youth: you a man! you lack a man's heart.

Ros. I do so, I confess it. Ah, sirrah, a body would think this was well counterfeited! I pray you, tell your brother how well I counterfeited. Heigh-ho!   169

Oli. This was not counterfeit: there is too great testimony in your complexion that it was a passion of earnest.

Ros. Counterfeit, I assure you.

Oli. Well then, take a good heart and counterfeit to be a man.

Ros. So I do: but, i'faith, I should have been a woman by right.

Cel. Come, you look paler and paler: pray you, draw homewards. Good sir, go with us.

Oli. That will I, for I must bear answer back How you excuse my brother, Rosalind.   181

Ros. I shall devise something: but, I pray you, commend my counterfeiting to him. Will you go?   [*Exeunt.*

ACT V

SCENE I. *The forest*

Enter TOUCHSTONE *and* AUDREY.

Touch. We shall find a time, Audrey; patience, gentle Audrey.

Aud. Faith, the priest was good enough, for all the old gentleman's saying.

Touch. A most wicked Sir Oliver, Audrey, a most vile Martext. But, Audrey, there is a youth here in the forest lays claim to you.

Aud. Ay, I know who 'tis; he hath no interest in me in the world: here comes the man you mean.   10

Touch. It is meat and drink to me to see a clown: by my troth, we that have good wits have much to answer for; we shall be flouting; we cannot hold.

                Enter WILLIAM.

Will. Good even, Audrey.

Aud. God ye good even, William.

Will. And good even to you, sir.

Touch. Good even, gentle friend. Cover thy head, cover thy head; nay, prithee, be covered. How old are you, friend?   20

Will. Five and twenty, sir.

Touch. A ripe age. Is thy name William?

Will. William, sir.

Touch. A fair name. Wast born i' the forest here?

Will. Ay, sir, I thank God.

Touch. "Thank God"; a good answer. Art rich?

Will. Faith, sir, so so.

Touch. "So so" is good, very good, very excellent good; and yet it is not; it is but so so. Art thou wise?   31

Will. Ay, sir, I have a pretty wit.

Touch. Why, thou sayest well. I do now remember a saying, "The fool doth think he is wise, but the wise man knows himself to be a fool." The heathen philosopher, when he had a desire to eat a grape, would open his lips when he put it into his mouth; meaning thereby that grapes were made to eat and lips to open. You do love this maid?   40

Will. I do, sir.

Touch. Give me your hand. Art thou learned?

Will. No, sir.

Touch. Then learn this of me: to have, is to have; for it is a figure in rhetoric that drink, being poured out of a cup into a glass, by filling the one doth empty the other; for all your writers do consent that *ipse* is he: now, you are not *ipse*, for I am he.

Will. Which he, sir?   50

Touch. He, sir, that must marry this woman. Therefore, you clown, abandon—which is in the vulgar leave—the society—which in the boorish is company—of this female—which in the common is woman; which together is, abandon the society of this female, or, clown, thou perishest; or, to thy better understanding, diest; or, to wit, I kill thee, make thee away, translate thy life into death, thy liberty into bondage: I will deal in poison with thee, or in bastinado, or in steel; I will bandy with thee in faction; I will o'er-run thee with policy; I will kill thee a hundred and fifty ways: therefore tremble, and depart.

Aud. Do, good William.

Will. God rest you merry, sir.   [*Exit.*

Enter CORIN.

Cor. Our master and mistress seeks you; come, away, away!

Touch. Trip, Audrey! trip, Audrey! I attend, I attend.   [*Exeunt.*

SCENE II. *The forest*

Enter ORLANDO *and* OLIVER.

Orl. Is't possible that on so little acquaintance you should like her? that but seeing you should love her? and loving woo? and, wooing, she should grant? and will you persever to enjoy her?

Oli. Neither call the giddiness of it in question, the poverty of her, the small acquaintance, my sudden wooing, nor her sudden consenting; but say with me, I love Aliena; say with her that she loves me; consent with both that we may enjoy each other: it shall be to your good; for my father's house and all the revenue that was old Sir Rowland's will I estate upon you, and here live and die a shepherd.

Orl. You have my consent. Let your wedding be to-morrow: thither will I invite the Duke and all's contented followers. Go you and prepare Aliena; for look you, here comes my Rosalind.

Enter ROSALIND.

Ros. God save you, brother.   20

Oli. And you, fair sister.   [*Exit.*

Ros. O, my dear Orlando, how it grieves me to see thee wear thy heart in a scarf!

Orl. It is my arm.

Ros. I thought thy heart had been wounded with the claws of a lion.

Orl. Wounded it is, but with the eyes of a lady.

Ros. Did your brother tell you how I counterfeited to swoon when he showed me your handkercher?   30

Orl. Ay, and greater wonders than that.

Ros. O, I know where you are: nay, 'tis true: there was never any thing so sudden but the fight of two rams and Cæsar's thrasonical brag of "I came, saw, and overcame"; for your brother and my sister no sooner met but they looked, no sooner looked but they loved, no sooner loved but they sighed, no sooner sighed but they asked one another the reason, no sooner knew the reason but they sought the remedy; and in these degrees have they made a pair of stairs to marriage which they will climb incontinent, or else be incontinent before marriage: they are in the very wrath of love and they will together; clubs cannot part them.

Orl. They shall be married to-morrow, and I will bid the Duke to the nuptial. But, O, how bitter a thing it is to look into happiness through another man's eyes! By so much the more shall I to-morrow be at the height of heart-heaviness, by how much I shall think my brother happy in having what he wishes for.

Ros. Why then, to-morrow I cannot serve your turn for Rosalind?

Orl. I can live no longer by thinking.

Ros. I will weary you then no longer with idle talking. Know of me, then, for now I speak to some purpose, that I know you are a gentleman of good conceit: I speak not this that you should bear a good opinion of my knowledge, insomuch I say I know you are; neither do I labour for a greater esteem than may in some little measure draw a belief from you, to do yourself good and not to grace me. Believe then, if you please, that I can do strange things: I have, since I was three year old, conversed with a magician, most profound in his art and yet not damnable. If you do love Rosalind so near the heart as your gesture cries it out, when your brother marries Aliena, shall you marry her: I know into what straits of fortune she is driven; and it is not impossible to me, if it appear not inconvenient to you, to set her before your eyes to-morrow, human as she is, and without any danger.

Orl. Speakest thou in sober meanings?

Ros. By my life, I do; which I tender dearly, though I say I am a magician. Therefore, put you in your best array; bid your friends; for if you will be married to-morrow, you shall, and to Rosalind, if you will.   81

Enter SILVIUS *and* PHEBE.

Look, here comes a lover of mine and a lover of hers.

Phe. Youth, you have done me much ungentleness,
To show the letter that I writ to you.

Ros. I care not if I have: it is my study
To seem despiteful and ungentle to you:
You are there followed by a faithful shepherd;
Look upon him, love him; he worships you.

Phe. Good shepherd, tell this youth what 'tis to love.

Sil. It is to be all made of sighs and tears;
And so am I for Phebe.   91

Phe. And I for Ganymede.

Orl. And I for Rosalind.

Ros. And I for no woman.

Sil. It is to be all made of faith and service;
And so am I for Phebe.

Phe. And I for Ganymede.

Orl. And I for Rosalind.

Ros. And I for no woman.

Sil. It is to be all made of fantasy,   *100*
All made of passion, and all made of wishes,
All adoration, duty, and observance,
All humbleness, all patience, and impatience,
All purity, all trial, all observance;
And so am I for Phebe.

Phe. And so am I for Ganymede.

Orl. And so am I for Rosalind.

Ros. And so am I for no woman.

Phe. If this be so, why blame you me to love
you?   *110*

Sil. If this be so, why blame you me to love
you?

Orl. If this be so, why blame you me to love
you?

Ros. Who do you speak to, "Why blame you
me to love you?"

Orl. To her that is not here, nor doth not hear.

Ros. Pray you, no more of this; 'tis like the
howling of Irish wolves against the moon. [*To*
SILVIUS] I will help you, if I can: [*To* PHEBE] I
would love you, if I could. To-morrow meet me
all together. [*To* PHEBE] I will marry you, if ever
I marry woman, and I'll be married to-morrow:
[*To* ORLANDO] I will satisfy you, if ever I satisfied man, and you shall be married to-morrow:
[*To* SILVIUS] I will content you, if what pleases
you contents you, and you shall be married to-
morrow. [*To* ORLANDO] As you love Rosalind,
meet: [*To* SILVIUS] as you love Phebe, meet: and
as I love no woman, I'll meet. So fare you well:
I have left you commands.   *131*

Sil. I'll not fail, if I live.

Phe. Nor I.

Orl. Nor I.   [*Exeunt.*

SCENE III. *The forest*

Enter TOUCHSTONE *and* AUDREY.

Touch. To-morrow is the joyful day, Audrey;
to-morrow will we be married.

Aud. I do desire it with all my heart; and I
hope it is no dishonest desire to desire to be a
woman of the world. Here come two of the
banished Duke's pages.

Enter TWO PAGES.

1st Page. Well met, honest gentleman.

Touch. By my troth, well met. Come, sit, sit,
and a song.   9

2nd Page. We are for you: sit i' the middle.

1st Page. Shall we clap into't roundly, without
hawking or spitting or saying we are hoarse,
which are the only prologues to a bad voice?

2nd Page. I' faith, i' faith; and both in a tune, like
two gipsies on a horse.

SONG

It was a lover and his lass,
    With a hey, and a ho, and a hey nonino,
That o'er the green corn-field did pass
    In the spring time, the only pretty ring time,
When birds do sing, hey ding a ding, ding: *21*
Sweet lovers love the spring.

Between the acres of the rye,
    With a hey, and a ho, and a hey nonino,
These pretty country folks would lie,
    In spring time, &c.

This carol they began that hour,
    With a hey, and a ho, and a hey nonino,
How that a life was but a flower
    In spring time, &c.   *30*

And therefore take the present time,
    With a hey, and a ho, and a hey nonino;
For love is crowned with the prime
    In spring time, &c.

Touch. Truly, young gentlemen, though there
was no great matter in the ditty, yet the note was
very untuneable.

1st Page. You are deceived, sir: we kept time,
we lost not our time.   *39*

Touch. By my troth, yes; I count it but time
lost to hear such a foolish song. God be wi' you;
and God mend your voices! Come, Audrey.

                                              [*Exeunt.*

SCENE IV. *The forest*

Enter DUKE SENIOR, AMIENS, JAQUES, ORLANDO,
            OLIVER, *and* CELIA.

Duke S. Dost thou believe, Orlando, that the
    boy
Can do all this that he hath promised?

Orl. I sometimes do believe, and sometimes do
    not;
As those that fear they hope, and know they fear.

Enter ROSALIND, SILVIUS, *and* PHEBE.

Ros. Patience once more, whiles our compact is
    urged:
You say, if I bring in your Rosalind,
You will bestow her on Orlando here?

Duke S. That would I, had I kingdoms to give
    with her.

Ros. And you say, you will have her, when I
    bring her?

Orl. That would I, were I of all kingdoms
    king.   *10*

Ros. You say, you'll marry me, if I be willing?

Phe. That will I, should I die the hour after.

Ros. But if you do refuse to marry me,
You'll give yourself to this most faithful shep-
herd?
Phe. So is the bargain.
Ros. You say, that you'll have Phebe, if she
will?
Sil. Though to have her and death were both
one thing.
Ros. I have promised to make all this matter
even.
Keep you your word, O Duke, to give your
daughter;
You yours, Orlando, to receive his daughter: 20
Keep your word, Phebe, that you'll marry
me,
Or else, refusing me, to wed this shepherd:
Keep your word, Silvius, that you'll marry
her,
If she refuse me: and from hence I go,
To make these doubts all even.
                    [*Exeunt* ROSALIND *and* CELIA.
Duke S. I do remember in this shepherd boy
Some lively touches of my daughter's favour.
Orl. My lord, the first time that I ever saw
him
Methought he was a brother to your daughter:
But, my good lord, this boy is forest-born,   30
And hath been tutor'd in the rudiments
Of many desperate studies by his uncle,
Whom he reports to be a great magician,
Obscured in the circle of this forest.

Enter TOUCHSTONE *and* AUDREY.

Jaq. There is, sure, another flood toward, and
these couples are coming to the ark. Here comes
a pair of very strange beasts, which in all tongues
are called fools.
Touch. Salutation and greeting to you all!
Jaq. Good my lord, bid him welcome: this is
the motley-minded gentleman that I have so often
met in the forest: he hath been a courtier, he
swears.
Touch. If any man doubt that, let him put me to
my purgation. I have trod a measure; I have
flattered a lady; I have been politic with my
friend, smooth with mine enemy; I have undone
three tailors; I have had four quarrels, and like
to have fought one.
Jaq. And how was that ta'en up?   50
Touch. Faith, we met, and found the quarrel
was upon the seventh cause.
Jaq. How seventh cause? Good my lord, like
this fellow.
Duke S. I like him very well.
Touch. God 'ild you, sir; I desire you of the
like. I press in here, sir, amongst the rest of

the country copulatives, to swear and to forswear; according as marriage binds and blood
breaks: a poor virgin, sir, an ill-favoured thing,
sir, but mine own; a poor humour of mine, sir, to
take that that no man else will: rich honesty
dwells like a miser, sir, in a poor house; as your
pearl in your foul oyster.
Duke S. By my faith, he is very swift and sententious.
Touch. According to the fool's bolt, sir, and
such dulcet diseases.
Jaq. But, for the seventh cause; how did you
find the quarrel on the seventh cause?   70
Touch. Upon a lie seven times removed—bear
your body more seeming, Audrey—as thus, sir.
I did dislike the cut of a certain courtier's beard:
he sent me word, if I said his beard was not cut
well, he was in the mind it was: this is called the
Retort Courteous. If I sent him word again "it
was not well cut," he would send me word, he
cut it to please himself: this is called the Quip
Modest. If again "it was not well cut," he disabled my judgement: this is called the Reply
Churlish. If again "it was not well cut," he
would answer, I spake not true: this is called the
Reproof Valiant. If again "it was not well cut,"
he would say, I lied: this is called the Countercheck Quarrelsome: and so to the Lie Circum-
stantial and the Lie Direct.
Jaq. And how oft did you say his beard was not
well cut?
Touch. I durst go no further than the Lie Cir-
cumstantial, nor he durst not give me the Lie
Direct; and so we measured swords and parted.
Jaq. Can you nominate in order now the degrees
of the lie?
Touch. O sir, we quarrel in print, by the book;
as you have books for good manners: I will name
you the degrees. The first, the Retort Courteous;
the second, the Quip Modest; the third, the Reply Churlish; the fourth, the Reproof Valiant;
the fifth, the Countercheck Quarrelsome; the
sixth, the Lie with Circumstance; the seventh,
the Lie Direct. All these you may avoid but the
Lie Direct; and you may avoid that too, with an
If. I knew when seven justices could not take up
a quarrel, but when the parties were met themselves, one of them thought but of an If, as, "If
you said so, then I said so"; and they shook
hands and swore brothers. Your If is the only
peace-maker; much virtue in If.
Jaq. Is not this a rare fellow, my lord? he's as
good as anything and yet a fool.   110
Duke S. He uses his folly like a stalking-horse
and under the presentation of that he shoots his
wit.

Enter HYMEN, ROSALIND, *and* CELIA. *Still Music.*

Hym. Then is there mirth in heaven,
  When earthly things made even
   Atone together.
 Good Duke, receive thy daughter:
 Hymen from heaven brought her,
  Yea, brought her hither,
 That thou mightst join her hand with his
 Whose heart within his bosom is. *121*

Ros. [*To* DUKE] To you I give myself, for I am
 yours.
[*To* ORLANDO] To you I give myself, for I am
 yours.

Duke S. If there be truth in sight, you are my
 daughter.

Orl. If there be truth in sight, you are my Rosalind.

Phe. If sight and shape be true,
Why then, my love adieu!

Ros. I'll have no father, if you be not he:
I'll have no husband, if you be not he:
Nor ne'er wed woman, if you be not she. *130*

Hym. Peace, ho! I bar confusion:
 'Tis I must make conclusion
  Of these most strange events.
 Here's eight that must take hands
 To join in Hymen's bands,
  If truth holds true contents.
  You and you no cross shall part:
  You and you are heart in heart:
  You to his love must accord,
  Or have a woman to your lord: *140*
 You and you are sure together,
 As the winter to foul weather.
 Whiles a wedlock-hymn we sing,
 Feed yourselves with questioning;
 That reason wonder may diminish,
 How thus we met, and these things finish.

Song

Wedding is great Juno's crown:
 O blessed bond of board and bed!
'Tis Hymen peoples every town;
 High wedlock then be honoured: *150*
Honour, high honour, and renown,
To Hymen, god of every town!

Duke S. O my dear niece, welcome thou art to me!
Even daughter, welcome, in no less degree.

Phe. I will not eat my word, now thou art mine;
Thy faith my fancy to thee doth combine.

Enter JAQUES DE BOYS.

Jaq. de B. Let me have audience for a word or
 two.
I am the second son of old Sir Rowland,

That bring these tidings to this fair assembly.
Duke Frederick, hearing how that every day *160*
Men of great worth resorted to this forest,
Address'd a mighty power; which were on
 foot,
In his own conduct, purposely to take
His brother here and put him to the sword:
And to the skirts of this wild wood he came;
Where meeting with an old religious man,
After some question with him, was converted
Both from his enterprise and from the world,
His crown bequeathing to his banish'd brother,
And all their lands restored to them again *170*
That were with him exiled. This to be true,
I do engage my life.

Duke S.   Welcome, young man;
Thou offer'st fairly to thy brothers' wedding:
To one his lands withheld, and to the other
A land itself at large, a potent dukedom.
First, in this forest let us do those ends
That here were well begun and well begot:
And after, every of this happy number
That have endured shrewd days and nights with
 us
Shall share the good of our returned fortune, *180*
According to the measure of their states.
Meantime, forget this new-fall'n dignity
And fall into our rustic revelry.
Play, music! And you, brides and bridegrooms all,
With measure heap'd in joy, to the measures fall.

Jaq. Sir, by your patience. If I heard you
 rightly,
The Duke hath put on a religious life
And thrown into neglect the pompous court?

Jaq de B. He hath.

Jaq. To him will I; out of these convertites
There is much matter to be heard and learn'd. *191*
[*To* DUKE] You to your former honour I be-
 queath;
Your patience and your virtue well deserves it:
[*To* ORLANDO] You to a love that your true faith
 doth merit:
[*To* OLIVER] You to your land and love and great
 allies:
[*To* SILVIUS] You to a long and well-deserved
 bed:
[*To* TOUCHSTONE] And you to wrangling; for
 thy loving voyage
Is but for two months victuall'd. So, to your
 pleasures:
I am for other than for dancing measures.

Duke S. Stay, Jaques, stay. *200*

Jaq. To see no pastime: what you would have
I'll stay to know at your abandon'd cave. [*Exit.*

Duke S. Proceed, proceed; we will begin these
 rites,

As we do trust they'll end, in true delights,
    A dance.

EPILOGUE

Ros. It is not the fashion to see the lady the epilogue; but it is no more unhandsome than to see the lord the prologue. If it be true that good wine needs no bush, 'tis true that a good play needs no epilogue; yet to good wine they do use good bushes, and good plays prove the better by the help of good epilogues. What a case am I in then, that am neither a good epilogue nor cannot insinuate with you in the behalf of a good play! I am not furnished like a beggar, therefore to beg will not become me: my way is to conjure you; and I'll begin with the women. I charge you, O women, for the love you bear to men, to like as much of this play as please you: and I charge you, O men, for the love you bear to women—as I perceive by your simpering, none of you hates them—that between you and the women the play may please. If I were a woman I would kiss as many of you as had beards that pleased me, complexions that liked me and breaths that I defied not: and, I am sure, as many as have good beards or good faces or sweet breaths will, for my kind offer, when I make curtsy, bid me farewell.   [*Exeunt.*